# MANAGEMENT

**Chuck Williams**
Texas Christian University

**THOMSON**

**SOUTH-WESTERN**

## Management, 2e
by Chuck Williams

**Vice President/Team Director:**
Mike Roche

**Sr. Acquisitions Editor:**
John Szilagyi

**Developmental Editor:**
Jamie Gleich Bryant

**Marketing Manager:**
Rob Bloom

**Production Editor:**
Kelly Keeler

**Manufacturing Coordinator:**
Rhonda Utley

**Compositor:**
Pre-Press Company, Inc.

**Printer:**
Quebecor World, US Bypass 60,
Versailles, KY 40384-0002

**Design Project Manager:**
Mike Stratton

**Internal Designer:**
Mike Stratton

**Photography Manager:**
Deanna Ettinger

**Photo Researcher:**
Charlotte Goldman

For more information
contact South-Western,
5191 Natorp Boulevard,
Mason, Ohio 45040.
Or you can visit our Internet site at:
http://www.swcollege.com

Library of Congress Cataloging-in-Publication Data

Williams, Chuck, 1959–
   Management / Chuck Williams.—2nd ed.
     p. cm.
   Includes bibliographical references and index.
   ISBN 0-324-11792–2
   Softcover Version ISBN 0-324-11794–9
   1. Management.  I. Title.

HD31 .W5167 2003
658—dc21                     2002019159

Printed in the United States of America
1 2 3 4 5 05 04 03 02

To Jenny, Ben, Rebecca, and Zack

The book is done. Let's play.

# BRIEF CONTENTS

v

vi

ix

## Chapter Fourteen — *Managing Human Resource Systems*

XV

# Preface

If you walk down the aisle of the business section in your local bookstore (or surf the "Business" page at Amazon.com), you'll find hundreds of books that explain precisely what companies need to do to be successful. Unfortunately, these books tend to be faddish, changing every few years. Lately, the best-selling business books have emphasized technology, leadership, and dealing with change, whereas ten years ago the hot topics were reengineering, going global, mergers, and management buyouts.

One thing that hasn't changed, though, and never will, is the importance of good management. **Management** is getting work done through others. Organizations can't succeed for long without it. Well-managed companies are competitive because their work forces are smarter, better trained, more motivated, and more committed. Furthermore, good management leads to satisfied employees who, in turn, provide better service to customers. Because employees tend to treat customers the same way that their managers treat them, good management can improve customer satisfaction. Finally, companies that practice good management consistently have greater revenues and profits than companies that don't.

In writing *Management 1e*, my goal was to write a textbook that students would enjoy, that students would refer to for practical, theory-driven advice, and that encouraged students to put theory-driven knowledge into practice for themselves. For the Second Edition, my goal was to update the content to reflect the changing face of management and to keep the text relevant, fresh, and interesting for the student. In short, the ideas and concepts you'll learn about in this book can improve the performance of the organization and department where you work, can even help you solve job-related problems, and can improve your own job performance, even if you're not a manager.

So welcome to *Management 2e*! Please take a few minutes to read the preface and familiarize yourself with the approach (combining theory with specific stories and examples), features, pedagogy, and end-of-chapter assignments in *Management*. This is time well spent. After all, besides your instructor, this book will be your primary learning tool.

## Combining Theory with Specific, Up-to-Date Stories and Examples

Say "theory" to college students and they assume that you're talking about complex, arcane ideas and terms that have nothing to do with the "real world," but which need to be memorized for a test and then forgotten (at least until the final exam). However, students needn't be wary of theoretical ideas and concepts. Theories are simply good ideas. And good theories are simply good ideas that have been tested through rigorous scientific study and analysis.

Where textbooks go wrong is that they stop at theory and read like dictionaries. Or, they focus on theoretical issues related to research rather than practice. However, good management theories (i.e., good ideas) needn't be complex and arcane. In fact, the late Rensis Likert, of the University of Michigan, once said that there is nothing as practical as a good theory.

So, to make sure that you're exposed to good ideas (i.e., good theories), that you can refer to for practical, theory-driven advice, and which encourage you to put theory-driven knowledge into practice for yourselves, each chapter in this book contains 50 to 60 specific stories and examples that illustrate how managers are using management ideas in their organizations. Let's use an example from Chapter 8 on Global Management to show you what I mean. One of the key issues in Global Management is successfully preparing employees for international assignments. In fact, the difficulty of adjusting to language, cultural, and social differences in another country is the primary reason that so many businesspersons fail in international assignments. Consequently, you'll read this passage in Chapter 8.

> For example, it is estimated that 10 percent to 45 percent of American expatriates sent abroad by their companies will return to the United States before they have successfully completed their international assignments. Of those who do complete their international assignments, as many as 30 percent to 50 percent are judged by their companies to be no better than marginally effective.

In other words, this is fairly standard, research-based information. You'll find it in most textbooks. Is it important for students to know this information? You bet! Is it likely that students will find this and the thousands of other pieces of theory and research-based facts throughout the book particularly compelling or interesting (and thus easier to learn)? Ah, there's the problem. However, what if we combined theory and research with specific, "real world" stories and examples that illustrated good or poor use of those theories? For instance, the passage shown below is also in Chapter 8, where it immediately follows the research-based information about the difficulty of adjusting to foreign cultures.

> *In his book* Blunders in International Business*, David Ricks tells the story of an American couple in Asia. After a walk with their dog, the Americans had dinner at a local restaurant. Since the waiters and waitresses did not speak English, they ordered by pointing to items on the menu. Because their dog was hungry, they pointed to the dog and to the kitchen. The waiter had trouble understanding, but finally took the dog to the kitchen. The American couple assumed that this meant the dog could not be fed in the dining room, but was going to be fed in the kitchen. Unfortunately, to the couple's dismay, the waiter and the chef returned later to proudly show them how well they had cooked the poodle.*

After reading this passage, students have a vivid understanding about what can go wrong if people don't receive cultural and language training before traveling or moving to another country. Why does this help students learn? Because the first passage cites theory and research on the effectiveness of cross-cultural training and the second brings the theory and research alive by indicating what can go wrong if you don't get that cross-cultural training.

Moreover, the stories and examples you'll read in each chapter are relevant and up-to-date. You'll read how and why Ted Waitt, founder of Gateway Computers (No doubt you've seen him on TV in those great commercials with the talking Gateway cow!) hired an experienced manager from AT&T to be Gateway's new CEO, only to have to fire him and then return as CEO, all within 18 months. You'll read about the strategic problems facing Kodak because of the increasing popularity of digital photography (Who needs film anymore – let alone film processing products?). You'll read how after five years of diversifying its business away from chip making, Intel has gone back to basics by refocusing on its core business of making integrated computer chips. As a result, Intel sold off its interactive media-services division, closed iCat, a business that managed Web sites for small businesses, and shut down a business that streamed video and audio content for other companies. CEO Craig Barrett admits that Intel had "screwed up" by focusing too much on these other businesses. But, by refocusing on integrated computer chips, Barrett said, "We're prioritizing our investments – you allocate your resources into the areas of highest return. The core competency has always been integrated circuits." And you'll read how Kellogg's, the cereal company, which isn't known for being particularly innovative, is using multifunctional design teams of comprised of market researchers, food technologists, engineers, and cooks to develop new cereals and breakfast foods. On average, each chapter has 25 to 30 brand new stories or examples to help you understand how management concepts and theories are being used in the business world.

In short, both research and theory *and* stories and examples are important for effective learning. Therefore, this book contains thousands of specific examples and stories to make management theories and ideas more interesting. So, to get more out of this book, read and understand the theories and theoretical ideas. Then read the stories or examples to learn how those ideas should or should not be used in practice. You'll find that both are current and up-to-date.

## So What's New?

If you are already familiar with the First Edition's approach of reinforcing research and theory with stories and examples you may be asking yourself, "So what's new?" The answer is quite a bit. To keep pace with the evolution of management, the First Edition underwent a rigorous review process that identified areas where I could strengthen and refine the text. For example, the Second Edition includes 54 more figures, tables, and diagrams throughout the text in order to better illustrate the material. This will make it easier for students to visualize and learn management concepts.

In addition to the 25 to 30 new examples and stories in each chapter, many content areas have been revised or expanded. For example, Chapter 5 (Managing Information) has been thoroughly revised. Technical discussions about data storage have been replaced with a section on how to protect data networks. In Chapter 6 (Decision Making), the section on individual decision making now has material on decision software and how to avoid sticking with a decision once you know it's the wrong one (i.e., de-escalation of commitment), and I have added a discussion of the stepladder technique to the section on group decision making. During the review process, reviewers cited financial control as a topic that could use more support, so I have expanded the discussion of economic value added in Chapter 7 (Control). This new material is supported by an exhibit that describes the basic accounting tools for controlling financial performance. Another exhibit explains common financial ratios, and another outlines common types of budgets. Political risk is an increasingly hot topic for companies that want to expand operations globally, so Chapter 8 has an updated section on evaluating the political risk factors operating in various countries. In this Second Edition, Chapter 10 has an expanded discussion on various approaches to managing innovation, and Chapter 12 has new information on female managers at Fortune 500 companies and on diversity paradigms and principals. Chapter 14 has added a section on Internet training and e-learning, a section on stock options, tips for reducing the chances of wrongful discharge suits, and guidelines for conducting layoffs and supporting lay-off survivors. Chapter 15 gives more space to the discussion of managing service operations and inventory turns. Numerous new exhibits in Chapter 16 help distill the main ideas for using each motivational theory, plus a new section in Chapter 17 reviews the issue of outcomes of path-goal theory. And Chapter 18 includes a thoroughly revised section on multi-cultural communication, tips on dealing with Internet gripe sites, and new sections on Employee Assistance Programs (EAPs) and organizational silence.

The features in each chapter have been updated as well. All of the *What Would You Do?* and *What Would You Do-II?* cases in each chapter are completely new. You'll read about companies like Airbus, Dell, BP Amoco, Regal Cinemas, and Sandler O'Neill. I have kept the best *Been There, Done That* interviews from the First Edition and have added new interviews with CEOs of companies like Starbucks, McDonald's, and the Body Shop. Likewise, I have kept only the best *Personal Productivity Tips* and added new ones in each chapter to help you be a more effective manager. And a new video feature called *CNN Headline News* now appears in every chapter. You'll read (and watch videos) about human rights initiatives at Nike, portfolio strategy changes at Disney, control problems at the IRS (i.e., fewer audits, reduction in back taxes, and fewer property seizures), and team training for businesspeople offered by NASA, to name a few.

So what is new in *Management 2e*? Quite a bit.

## Book Features

A tremendous amount of time and thought went into planning this textbook. I reviewed over 25 top selling textbooks in Management, Marketing, Finance, Statistics, and Economics. I asked more than 200 students and dozens of professors what they specifically liked and disliked about their textbooks. And, I pulled some of my favorite books (many of which were not about business) from my bookshelf to figure out what made them great books. Only then did I create the plan and organization for *Management 1e*. The Second Edition retains the popular features of the first edition and adds some new ones. So take a few minutes now to familiarize yourself with its features. Doing so will help you get more out of the book and your management class.

✗ **Blast from the Past** – Nearly every management textbook contains the standard "history of management" chapter. However, after discussions with dozens of management professors, I learned that most of them struggled to teach it and that their students rarely saw its relevance. As a result, most of them no longer teach the history of management. So rather than write a chapter that professors wouldn't teach and that students wouldn't read, I decided instead to include a *Blast from the Past* historical feature in most of the chapters. The advantage of this approach is that students are exposed to management history in small bites, which is easier to consume than all at once. Also, since students come across the *Blast from the Past* in the normal course of reading a chapter, it's easier for them to see the link between historical management ideas and what they're studying today. The result, I hope, is that students will appreciate how yesterday's thinkers and pioneers paved the way for today's management theories and practice.

✗ **Been There, Done That** – My twin brother, who is a critical-care neurologist, likes to tease me by saying, "Those who can, do. Those who can't, teach." While I can't print my typical response here (ah, sibling rivalry), I do have to admit that he's partially right. We give special credibility to "experts" who can "walk their talk." For instance, in the last few years, I've had the opportunity to teach in Europe during the summer. Of course, I've also taken the opportunity to travel. But, if you know anything about Europe, you know that there are just too many countries, too many places to see, and not enough time or money to see them all. However, my wife and I started using travel guides written by Rick Steves, who hosts a PBS TV show called

*Travels in Europe.* Steves' books provide daily itineraries for travel sights that include specific advice on where to eat, where to stay, and what to do. My wife and I followed these plans and had a wonderful time in Europe for about half the price that most Americans pay. Why were we willing to trust his advice? His words explain it best. "I've spent twenty years exploring Europe through the back door. This book, which has evolved over twelve editions, is my report to you after a virtual lifetime in the travelers' school of hard knocks. Experience is a great teacher. These are my notes, taken in the hope that you'll learn from my mistakes rather than your own and have the best possible trip." In other words, Rick Steves has visited every bed and breakfast, every restaurant, and every castle in his books. He figured out what worked for him, and shared that advice with others.

Most management problems work the same way. There's no point in starting from scratch when someone else has already faced the problem before. Who could be better to talk to about a problem than someone who has already "been there and done that?" So, if you want to learn about management from people who have faced and solved management problems firsthand, read the *Been There, Done That* interviews with experienced managers that you'll find in almost every chapter.

✗ **Personal Productivity Tips** – *PC Magazine* publishes a "road warrior's" guide to traveling with a laptop computer and doing business on the road. This guide discusses the importance of backup batteries, the necessity of toolkits for taking apart phone jacks in motel rooms (to rig a connection to your laptop modem at 3 A.M. so you can download that last killer slide for the 8 A.M. presentation), and many other things you'd never think of that could prevent computer-related disasters when you travel. Readers love the road warrior's guide because it's so helpful and useful. By contrast, most students believe that management theory is too abstract to be of any use to them. Therefore, to help students make the leap from management theory to management practice, you'll find three to four *Personal Productivity Tips* in each chapter. Located in the margins, *Personal Productivity Tips* are designed to give quick, useful, practical management advice that can make an immediate difference. So if you want to learn how to get a passport, how to encrypt computer files and email (so that confidential company information remains confidential), how to use conflict to solve problems, how to create an electronic resume (and we don't mean using a word processor), or how to ask for a raise or more, read the *Personal Productivity Tips* in the margins of each chapter.

✗ **What Really Works?** – Some studies show that two drinks a day increases life expectancy by decreasing your chances of having a heart attack. Yet other studies show that two drinks a day will shorten your life expectancy. For years, we've "buttered" our morning toast with margarine instead of butter because it was supposed to be better for our health. However, new studies now show that the trans-fatty acids in margarine may be just as bad for our arteries as butter. Confusing scientific results like these frustrate ordinary people who want to "eat right" and "live right." It also makes many people question just how useful most scientific research really is.

Managers also have trouble figuring out what works, based on the scientific research published in journals like the *Academy of Management Journal*, the *Academy of Management Review*, the *Strategic Management Journal*, the *Journal of Applied Psychology*, and *Administrative Science Quarterly*. It's common for *The Wall Street Journal* to quote a management research article from one of these journals that says that total quality management is the best thing since sliced bread (without butter or margarine). Then, just six months later, *The Wall Street Journal* will quote a different article from the same journal that says that total quality management doesn't work. If management professors and researchers have trouble deciding what works and what doesn't, how can practicing managers know?

Thankfully, a research tool called meta-analysis, which is a study of studies, is helping management scholars understand how well their research supports management theories. Fortunately, meta-analysis is also useful for practicing managers, because it shows what works and the conditions under which management techniques may work better or worse in the "real world." Meta-analysis is based on the simple idea that if one study shows that a management technique doesn't work and another study shows that it does, an average of those results is probably the best estimate of how well that management practice works (or doesn't work). Fortunately, you don't need a Ph.D. to understand the statistics reported in a meta-analysis. In fact, one primary advantage of meta-analysis over traditional significance tests is that you can convert meta-analysis statistics into intuitive numbers that anyone can easily understand. Indeed, each meta-analysis reported in the *What Really Works?* sections of this textbook is accompanied by an easy-to-understand statistic called the probability of success. As its name suggests, the probability of success uses a bar graph and a percentage (zero percent to 100 percent) to indicate the likelihood that a management technique will actually work.

Of course, no idea or technique works every time and in every circumstance. However, in today's competitive, fast-changing, global marketplace, few managers can afford to overlook proven management strategies like those discussed in *What Really Works?* feature of this book.

✗ **CNN Headline News – New in this edition,** It's clear that business is a popular topic in the news. Indeed, publications like *The Wall Street Journal, Business Week, The Financial Times,* and *Fortune* magazine are dedicated to reporting exclusively on business and financial topics. Other than politics, business news is probably one of the most regularly reported topics in broadcast and print media! A new feature titled *CNN Headline News* brings this aspect of current business events into the text by linking two- to four-minute video clips from CNN business and financial programming to chapter concepts. Each CNN feature concludes with questions and exercises that help you make the leap from theory to practice. For example, in Chapter 7 (Control), you will read about management control as it relates to the IRS. After lengthy congressional hearings in which taxpayers testified to abuses of power by the IRS, the much-despised agency shifted from a control function (making sure people paid taxes – and penalties if they didn't) to a customer service function (helping taxpayers navigate the complex tax codes). The CNN feature article on the IRS discusses this shift and concludes by asking you first to determine the level of control needed at the present-day IRS and then to create a balanced scorecard for the federal agency. These exercises extend your understanding of concepts of management control by asking you to apply them to real-world situations that companies face each day.

    *CNN Headline News* features also give students the opportunity to review the case more fully using InfoTrac, a research database maintained by the Gale Research Group. Research articles from InfoTrac are used in every case, and article numbers are listed in the citations so that students can easily locate the materials used to write the case. By reviewing the articles used to write the feature, students will get a deeper understanding of the issues and events presented.

## Pedagogy

    Pedagogical features are meant to reinforce learning, but they don't have to be boring. Accordingly, the teaching tools used in *Management* will help students learn and hold their interest, too.

✗ **Chapter Outline and Numbering System, Learning Objectives, and Section Reviews** – Because of their busy schedules, very few students have the opportunity to read a chapter from beginning to end in one sitting. Typically, it takes students anywhere from two to five study sessions to completely read a chapter. Accordingly, at the beginning of each chapter, you'll find a detailed chapter outline in which each major part in the chapter is broken out into numbered sections and subsections. For example, the outline for the first part of Chapter 3, on Ethics and Social Responsibility, looks like this:

> *What Would You Do?*
> *Basics of Control*
>     *1. The Control Process*
>         *1.1 Standards*
>         *1.2 Comparison to Standards*
>         *1.3 Corrective Action*
>         *1.4 Dynamic, Cybernetic Process*

    The numbered information contained in the chapter outline is then repeated in the chapter as learning objectives (at the beginning of major parts of the chapter) and as numbered headings and subheadings (throughout the chapter) to help students remember precisely where they are in terms of the chapter outline. Finally, instead of a big summary at the end of the chapter, students will find detailed reviews at the end of each section.

    Together, the chapter outline, numbering system, learning objectives, section headings (which mark the beginning of a section), and section reviews (which mark the end of a section) allow students to break the chapter into smaller, self-contained sections that can be read in their entirety over multiple study sessions. Furthermore, the numbered headings and outline should make it easier for instructors and students to know what is being assigned or discussed in class ("In section 3.1 of chapter 3....").

✗ All new **What Would You Do?** And **What Really Happened?** – At the beginning of each chapter, there is an opening case called *What Would You Do?* in which a manager faces an interesting problem or situation that is tied to the information presented in the chapter. Three to five specific teaser questions are usually posed at the end of the case, along with the general question, "If you were this manager, what would you do?" Then at the end of each chapter, students find out the answers to these questions in a follow-up to the opening case called *What Really Happened?* Unlike most textbooks in which the follow-up to the opening case is typically very short, or is simply a technique for presenting more review questions, each *What Really Happened?* is typically a page or longer, answers each of the questions posed in the opening case, and provides enough information for students to understand how things turned out, what the company did and why they did it, and whether it worked. Finally, each *What Really Happened?* shows how companies combined various ideas from the chapter to try to solve specific business problems. All the *What Would You Do?* and *What Really Happened?* cases are brand new for this edition, and in addition to those mentioned above, you'll read about companies like Airbus, EasyJet, Dell, Wal-Mart, Kimberly-Clark, Medtronic, and Mutuals.com.

✗ **Key Terms** – Key terms appear in boldface in the text, with definitions in the margins to make it easy for students to check their understanding. A complete alphabetical list of key terms appears at the end of each chapter as a study checklist, with page citations for easy reference.

## End of Chapter Assignments

In most textbooks, there are only two or three end-of-chapter assignments. By contrast, at the end of each chapter in *Management*, there are four assignments from which to choose (But if you count the *CNN Headline News* feature mentioned above, it's really five assignments). This gives instructors more choice in selecting just the right assignment for their classes. It also gives students a greater variety of activities, making it less likely that they'll repeat the same kind of assignment chapter after chapter.

✗ **What Would You Do–II?** – Similar to the case which opens the chapter, *What Would You Do–II?* is a case in which a manager faces an interesting problem or situation that is tied to the information presented in the chapter. Students are expected to analyze the case and suggest solutions. Read about dilemmas facing Levi Strauss, Clear Channel Radio, Lego's, Coke, and Borders, among others.

✗ **Management Decisions** – There are two *Management Decisions* in each chapter. Typically, these are somewhat shorter, more focused assignments in which students must decide what to do and then answer several questions to explain their choices. For example, students must decide which of two employees deserves a promotion, what the company policy should be on personal use of email, whether flexible work schedules are family friendly or discriminatory toward workers who don't have children at home, and more. Some *Management Decision* features includes Internet references and locations so that students can gather additional information before deciding what to do.

✗ **Develop Your Managerial Potential** – *Develop Your Managerial Potential* assignments have one purpose: To help students develop their present and future capabilities as managers. What students learn through these assignments is not traditional "book-learning" based on memorization and regurgitation, but practical knowledge and skills that help managers perform their jobs better. Assignments include interviewing managers, dealing with the press, visiting a charity or nonprofit, learning from failure, working in someone else's shoes, 360-degree feedback, and more.

### What Would You Do–II

**Lego**

As you look over your calendar, your hands automatically begin to rub your temples. The annual Toy Fair is right around the corner, and newspapers and magazines around the world are publishing their lists of the most successful toys of last year and their predictions of what will be hot next year. Unfortunately, you pretty much know that none of your company's products will be on any of them. Founded nearly 70 years ago by your grandfather, Lego has a long history in the toy industry, but it can't seem to keep up with today's kids' (or even ~~~~~~~~~ kids') thirst for so-called interactive toys. Techn~~~~~~~~~ are interactive, but nowadays that means batter~~~~~~~~~ software-driven, and done-for-you rather than ~~~~~~~~~

the fact tha~~~~
twentieth-c~~~~
ues, howeve~~~~
Your comp~~~~
in the last s~~~~
ferent. And~~~~
signal a dep~~~~
have pages~~~~
set "right."~~~~

### Develop Your Managerial Potential

**An Individual SWOT Analysis**

In order to maintain and sustain a competitive advantage, companies continue to analyze their overall strategy in light of their current situation. In doing so, a SWOT analysis is often used. The SWOT analysis focuses on the strengths and weaknesses evident in the firm's internal environment and the opportunities and threats present in the firm's external environment. One way to gain experience in conducting a SWOT analysis is to perform one on yourself—in other words, conduct a personal SWOT analysis.

Assume you have just completed your college education and are ready to apply for a job as a manager of a small to medium-sized facility. Perform a personal SWOT analysis to determine

them~~~~
in ma~~~~
know~~~~
ful m~~~~
neede~~~~
Once~~~~
come~~~~
tions~~~~
to inc~~~~
O~~~~
ment~~~~
point~~~~
sonal~~~~

### Management Decisions

**Hack Attack**

As you clear off your desk, getting ready to leave for the night, the phone rings. The voice on the other end of the line is Sue, your company's network administrator. She informs you that a hacker has just broken into the company's e-commerce site. One of the databases entered by the intruder contains personal customer data, including names, addresses, and credit card information. You immediately ask questions, attempting to determine the potential damage caused by this attack. According to Sue, approximately 3.3 million customer files, both past and present, could have been compromised. Upon noticing the intrusion, Sue immediately closed down the network and ordered her staff to get on the phone with the software company's technical support to

on any giver~~~~
tempt on Eg~~~~
only get in,~~~~
rently, Eggh~~~~
turn to wher~~~~
gin to race t~~~~
customers, s~~~~
minish custo~~~~
you notify t~~~~
would-be ha~~~~
think to you~~~~
"We're open~~~~

**✗ Study Tip – New to this edition** Knowing how to study effectively is not an innate talent. So in this edition of *Management*, I have added a study tip to each chapter. Eighteen different tips give students many options for reviewing key concepts and mastering chapter content. Students are challenged to write their own tests and exchange them in a study group, recreate chapter exhibits by using the worksheets on the Williams Web site, explain the chapter concepts to a friend who is not in the class, cut up the text glossary to make a quiz-bowl game, and much more.

## Instructor Supplements

**✗ Comprehensive Instructor's Manual** (ISBN 0324-11798-1) – **Thoroughly revised in this edition** The Instructor's Manual to accompany the Second Edition has been completely redone to help instructors in every type of class. In addition to the chapter outlines, additional activities, and solutions you expect, the new manual includes one pedagogy grid and three lesson plans per chapter.

Each chapter of the Instructor's Manual opens with a pedagogy grid that details all of the pedagogy in the chapter and the companies and teaching points presented. By giving you all the options you have in the chapter and the chapter content addressed by each option, you will be able to decide what you want to emphasize and assign your students. Following the pedagogy grid is a series of three lesson plans: a lecture lesson plan, a group-work lesson plan for professors who have smaller sections and/or more time during the semester; and a video lesson plan, including pre-viewing, viewing, and post-viewing activities. The purpose of the video-only lesson plan is to illustrate how to teach using video without "losing time."

Each type of lesson plan includes pre-class preparation for professor and for students; how to organize the content for the chapter during the class period; a list of possible assignments; and more. Suggestions on how to divide the lesson plan for classes meeting two times a week, as well as for classes meeting three times a week, are also part of each plan.

A detailed chapter outline (lecture notes) is still part of the Instructor's Manual. The lecture notes include additional examples, teaching notes for key concepts and for feature boxes, and prompts for where to show the video. Solutions for chapter features are included, plus 10 discussion questions per chapter, and five group activities per chapter and five new Internet activities per chapter.

In addition to all of these teaching tools, an appendix titled, "Teaching Your First Management Course," can be found at the end of the Instructor's Manual. This appendix is designed specifically to meet the needs and concerns of the first-time instructor.

**✗ Test Bank** (ISBN 0-324-11799-X) –The Test Bank for the Second Edition of *Management* builds on the solid foundation of the First Edition. Each chapter contains at least 150 questions from which to choose: 65 true-false, 70 multiple-choice, 10 short-answer, and five critical-thinking questions. Thorough solutions are provided for each question, including difficulty ratings and page references where solutions appear in the text. A correlation table at the beginning of each test bank chapter makes it easy for instructors to select the appropriate mix of questions for their students.

A computerized version of the text bank is available on your Instructor Resource CD-ROM and by special request. ExamView (ISBN 0324-11850-3) allows to you create, edit, store, print, and otherwise customize your quizzes, tests, and exams. The system is menu-driven making it quick and easy to use.

**✗ Turner Learning CNN Video** (ISBN 0-324-11791-4) – **New to this edition** Nothing helps students master management concepts like seeing them put into practice in the real world. New video examples from CNN's extensive news-footage library have been selected to go with each chapter. The 21 clips are the basis for the *CNN Headline News* cases and questions. Clips are short, so you can view and review them easily and quickly.

**✗ PowerPoint Slides** (ISBN 0-324-11790-6) – A rich set of PowerPoint slides, *with teaching notes*, will make class preparations easy and interesting. The approximately 30 to 50 slides per chapter cover all key concepts, terms, features, cases, and even some exhibits from the text. Animations and transitions add movement to many of the slides, allowing instructors to show one point at a time and adding a dynamic feel that will hold student interest throughout the presentation. Ample teaching notes offer additional insights and examples plus important points to cover in lectures.

**✗ Acetate Transparencies** (ISBN 0-324-11851-1) – For adopters without access to PowerPoint, a set of over 100 transparencies is available upon request. These transparencies can supplement lectures by displaying the key concepts and illustrations from the text.

✗ **Instructor Resource CD-ROM (IRCD)** (ISBN 0-324-16593-5) – For your convenience, the Instructor Manual, Test Bank, ExamView Software, and PowerPoint presentation are available on a single CD-ROM, the IRCD.

✗ **Web Tutor™** (ISBN 0-324-15059-8 for WebCT, ISBN 0-324-15060-1 for Blackboard) – Online learning is growing at a rapid pace. Whether you are looking to offer courses at a distance or to offer a web-enhanced classroom, South-Western/Thomson Learning offers you a solution with WebTutor™. WebTutor™ provides instructors with text-specific content that interacts with the two leading systems of higher education course management – WebCT and Blackboard.

     WebTutor™ is a turnkey solution for instructors who want to begin using technology like Blackboard or WebCT but who do not have web-ready content available, or who do not want to be burdened with developing their own content. WebTutor uses the Internet to turn everyone in your class into a front-row student. WebTutor offers interactive study guide features such as quizzes, concept reviews, flashcards, discussion forums, additional video clips, and more. Instructor tools are also provided to facilitate communication between students and faculty.

✗ **Williams Web site (http://williams.swcollege.com)** – The Williams Web site contains a wealth of resources for both instructors and students. Here is what's available only for professors at the Instructor Resource page of the Williams Web site:

  ✱ A features archive gives you access to the *What Would You Do?* and *What Really Happened?* from the First Edition. You will also find edited *Been There, Done That* features, *What Would You Do-II?* and *What Really Happened-II?* features, plus *Management Decisions* and *Developing Your Managerial Potential* exercises that didn't make it into the Second Edition.

  ✱ The full PowerPoint presentation with teaching notes.

  ✱ A sample Test Bank chapter will give you an idea of what to expect from the full supplement. Chapter 1 is the basis of the sample, which shows you a few questions of each type with solutions and rationales.

  ✱ Files for the full Instructor's Manual are also available online. If you don't have your materials on hand, you can download the chapters you need and customize them to suit your lesson plan.

  ✱ An additional *What Would You Do?* generally on e-commerce issues facing companies, or special management concerns for e-commerce companies. The accompanying *What Really Happened?* is also online, with access restricted to professors.

  ✱ Solutions for student Internet activities, both basic and advanced, with teaching tips.

  ✱ Abstracts of two current management articles with links.

  ✱ Lists of additional resources and links to relevant sites when possible.

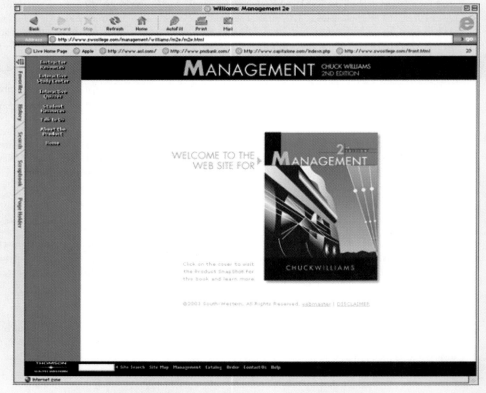

Here is what's available for students at the Williams Web site:
* A 10-question quiz for each chapter
* Worksheets based on the illustrations from the text have been created so that students can test and check their understanding of the key points in each chapter.
* Links to all the URLs from the book
* Glossary from the text
* One basic and one advanced Internet activity per chapter
* A supplemental *What Would You Do?* relating to e-commerce and dot com companies
* Links to basic study aids on the Internet
* Links to information relevant to the chapter content but not necessarily in text

## Student Supplements

✗ **Study Guide** (ISBN 0-324-11796-5) – The Study Guide is designed to help students review the text's key concepts and prepare for tests. Each study guide chapter begins with questions that will help students approach the text's *What Would You Do?* opening case. A chapter outline, containing the learning objectives, key term definitions, and major points in the chapter, serves as a useful review tool. After reading the chapter and reviewing the outline, students can test their understanding with multiple-choice, true-false, short-answer, agree-disagree, and critical-thinking questions similar to those they might see on the tests. Solutions with text page references appear at the end of each study guide chapter.

✗ **Williams Xtra!** (ISBN 0324-11789-2) – **New to this edition** Packaged free with every new copy of *Management 2e*, the Williams Xtra! CD-ROM provides access to a robust set of additional online learning tools. New and exciting content and review opportunities include:
* 11 supplemental CNN video clips with cases, questions, and solutions. These clips are completely different than the ones the students will see in class and help students solidify their knowledge.
* 25 to 30 interactive quiz questions for each chapter.
* *Experiencing Management*, an experiential learning tool.
* Links to InfoTrac College Edition (http://www.infotrac-college.com) to help students with research and allow them to consult the articles used to create the *CNN Headline News* features.
* Complete business and management glossaries.
* "Ask Chuck" video clips, in which the author responds to Frequently Asked Questions in each chapter.

The CD-ROM requires Internet Explorer or Netscape Navigator 3.0 or higher.

✗ **InfoTrac** (ISBN 0-324-11789-2) – **New to this edition** Packaged free with every new copy of *Management 2e* is a password for the InfoTrac database by Gale Research. InfoTrac enables students to connect with the real world of management through academic journals, business and popular magazines and newspapers, and a vast array of government publications. InfoTrac was used in creating the *CNN Headline News* feature in each chapter. Article numbers are given in the source lines so that students can easily consult the research materials. InfoTrac can also be a valuable tool for working through the *What Would You Do-II?* at the end of each chapter.

✗ **Wall Street Journal Edition** – Bring the most up-to-date, real-world events into your classroom through *The Wall Street Journal*. *The Wall Street Journal* is synonymous with the latest word on business, and *Management, 2nd edition* makes it easy for students to apply management concepts to this authoritative publication through a special subscription offer. For a nominal additional cost, *Management, 2nd edition* can be packaged with a card entitling students to a 15-week subscription to both the print and interactive versions of *The Wall Street Journal*. Contact your South-Western/Thomson Learning sales representative for package pricing and ordering information.

**THE WALL STREET JOURNAL.**

## Acknowledgements

Let's face it, writing a textbook is a long and lonely process. It's surely the most difficult (and rewarding) project I've ever tackled. And, as I sat in front of my computer with a rough outline on the left side of my desk, a two-foot stack of journal articles on the floor, and a blank screen in front of me, it was easy at times to feel isolated. But, as I found out, a book like this doesn't get done without the help of many other talented people.

First, I'd like to thank the outstanding team of supplement authors: Jennifer Dose (Messiah University), who wrote the fantastic Study Guide; Susan Peterson (Scottsdale Community College), who completely revised and created the many new features in the Instructor's Manual; David Leuser (Plymouth State College), for the outstanding test bank; Dennis Middlemist (Colorado State University), for the superb PowerPoint slides; and Nancy H. Leonard (Lewis Clark State College), who developed the robust Web content for this book. I'd also like to give special thanks to Russell Hardy of the University of New Mexico for providing the new end-of-chapter pedagogy for this edition. It's difficult to write using someone else's style, but Russell achieved this in the great exercises he created.

I'd also like to thank the world-class team at South-Western/Thomson Learning for the outstanding support (and patience) they provided while I wrote this book; John Szilagyi, who heads the Management group at South-Western, was calm, collected, and continuously positive through the major ups and downs of this project; Rob Bloom, who was in charge of marketing the book, did an outstanding job of developing marketing themes and approaches; and Kelly Keeler, who managed the production process, was consistently upbeat and positive with me when I deserved otherwise. Authors are prone to complain about their publishers. But that hasn't been my experience at all. Pure and simple, everyone at South-Western has been great to work with throughout the entire project. Special thanks go to Jamie Gleich Bryant, of Bryant Editorial Development, who was my developmental editor and with whom I had the most contact while writing the book. Jamie worked with reviewers, edited the manuscript, managed the development of supplements, provided superb feedback and guidance at every stage of the book, and nudged and prodded me to write faster, make improvements, and maintain the high quality standards that were set when I began writing. Jamie's enthusiasm, professionalism, commitment, and attention to detail made me a better writer, made this a better book, and made me appreciate my good fortune to work with such an outstanding talent. Thanks, Jamie, and here's to many more editions.

I'd like to thank an outstanding set of reviewers whose diligent and thoughtful comments helped shape the First Edition and whose rigorous feedback improved the Second Edition.

Ali Abu-Rahma
*United States International University*

William Acar
*Kent State University*

David C. Adams
*Manhattanville College*

Bruce R. Barringer
*University of Central Florida*

Gayle Baugh
*University of West Florida*

Katharine A. Bohley
*University of Indianapolis*

Michael Boyd
*Owensboro Community College*

Diane P. Caggiano
*Fitchburg State College*

Nicolette DeVille Christensen
*Guilford College*

Kathy Daruty
*Pierce College*

Jennifer Dose
*Messiah University*

Kimborough Ferrell
*Spring Hill College*

Charles R. Franz
*University of Missouri-Columbia*

Anu A. Gokhale
*Illinois State University*

Barry Allen Gold
*Pace University*

Russell F. Hardy
*New Mexico State University*

David Hennessey
*Mount Mercy College*

Jim Jawahar
*Illinois State University*

Paul N. Keaton
*University of Wisconsin-La Crosse*

Ellen Ernst Kossek
*Michigan State University*

Donald R. Leavitt
*Western Baptist College*

Jerrold Leong
*Oklahoma State University*

Linda Livingstone
*Baylor University*

Thomas B. Loughman
*Columbus State University*

George Marron
*Arizona State University*

Lynda Martin
*Oklahoma State University*

Robert McGowan
*University of Denver*

Sherry Moss
*Florida International University*

Stephanie Newport
*Austin Peay State University*

James S. O'Rourke, IV
*University of Notre Dame*

Rhonda S. Palladi
*Georgia State University*

David M. Porter, Jr.
*UCLA*

Amit Shah
*Frostburg State University*

Thomas Shaughnessy
*Illinois Central College*

James Smas
*Kent State University*

James O. Smith
*East Carolina University*

Gregory K. Stephens
*Texas Christian University*

Joseph Tagliaferre
*Pennsylvania State University*

Jennie Carter Thomas
*Belmont University*

James Thornton
*Champlain College*

Mary Jo Vaughan
*Mercer University*

Finally, my family deserves the greatest thanks of all for their love, patience, and support. Writing a textbook is an enormous project with incredible stresses and pressures on authors as well as their loved ones. However, throughout this project, my wife, Jenny, was unwavering in her support of my writing. She listened patiently, encouraged me when I was discouraged, read and commented on most of what I wrote, gave me the time to write, and took wonderful care of me and our children during this long process. My children, Benjamin, Rebecca, and Zack, also deserve special thanks for their patience and for understanding why Dad was locked away at the computer for all of this time. While writing this book has been the most rewarding professional experience of my career, it pleases me no end that my family is as excited as I am that it's done. So, to Jenny, Benjamin, Rebecca, and Zack. The book is done. Let's play.

## Meet the Author

### Chuck Williams
Texas Christian University

Chuck Williams is an Associate Professor of Management and Associate Dean at the M.J. Neeley School of Business at Texas Christian University. He received his B.A. in Psychology from Valparaiso University, and specialized in the areas of Organizational Behavior, Human Resources, and Strategic Management while earning his M.B.A and Ph.D. in Business Administration from Michigan State University. Previously, he taught at Michigan State University and was on the Faculty of Oklahoma State University.

His research interests include employee recruitment and turnover, performance appraisal, and employee training and goal-setting. Chuck has published research in the *Journal of Applied Psychology*, the *Academy of Management Journal, Human Resource Management Review, Personnel Psychology*, and the *Organizational Research Methods Journal*. He was a member of the *Journal of Management*'s Editorial Board, and serves as a reviewer for numerous other academic journals. He was also the webmaster for the Research Methods Division of the Academy of Management (http://www.aom.pace.edu/rmd). Chuck is also a co-recipient of the Society for Human Resource Management's Yoder-Heneman Research Award.

Chuck has consulted for a number of organizations, General Motors, IBM, JCPenney, Tandy Corporation, Trism Trucking, Central Bank and Trust, StuartBacon, the City of Fort Worth, the American Cancer Society, and others. He has taught in executive development programs at Oklahoma State University, The University of Oklahoma, and Texas Christian University.

Chuck teaches a number of different courses, but has been privileged to teach his favorite course, Introduction to Management, for nearly 20 years. His teaching philosophy is based on four principles: (1) courses should be engaging and interesting; (2) there's nothing as practical as a good theory; (3) students learn by doing; and (4) students learn when they are challenged. The undergraduate students at TCU's Neeley School of Business named him instructor of the year. He has also been a recipient of TCU's Dean's Teaching Award.

# 1

## Introduction to Management

**CHAPTER** 1

# one

# Management

## What Would You Do?

**Headquarters, NextJump, Inc., New York, New York.** Charlie Kim started his new company, NextJump, after an exhausting two years at Morgan Stanley, a New York investment bank, where he worked 80-hour weeks. Kim figured that most people left Morgan Stanley for jobs at companies that allowed them to have personal lives. "People were working until 1 A.M., drinking coffee, eating junk," he says, "and they were miserable." Kim committed to run NextJump in a fair way for employees. He backed up his commitment by not allowing employees to work late nights or weekends. He said, "I don't want anyone to be drained or exhausted." And unlike many tech startups, beds, cots, and futons weren't permitted. Said Kim, "If you need to sleep, you should go home." Alice Park, NextJump's director of product development, said getting kicked out of the office by the boss was "a little strange to me at first. I had come from an investment bank, where it seemed normal to work until 9 or 10 at night. But people here have a different style of working."

Kim also figured that work would be more fun if everybody knew each other, so within a year, he brought in three of his friends as partners. This partnership worked so well that NextJump continued its policy of hiring friends. As NextJump grew from 30 to 105 employees in just three months, its employees ended up working with their college roommates, their prom dates, and their brothers and sisters. The company even displayed a diagram of a "family tree," which showed how everyone in the company was connected to everyone else. As a finishing touch to making NextJump a great place to work, Kim bought gym memberships for everyone (and then encouraged them to work out whenever they wanted) and hired a masseuse to give massages on company time.

For a while, NextJump was a good company and an even better place to work. But problems soon emerged. Key people often missed important meetings because they were at the gym. Furthermore, even when everyone could attend, staff meetings became turbulent, too large, and disorganized. Meetings had been well run when the company was small, but now they turned into arguments about key company decisions, such as determining which products to sell, or whether the company should offer print products in addition to those it sold online. These problems were compounded when employees openly questioned the decisions of management and anyone else outside their small circle of friends. Peter Rommeny, NextJump's former HR director, said, "You have a group of five, six, ten people—all best friends who went to school together. If one gets disillusioned, it affects the rest of the people in that group. . . . You kind of have to walk on eggshells to provide disciplinary conversation or feedback. Whatever you say to one person will get out to everyone else in the group."

After several months of continuous griping and out-of-control meetings, a frustrated Charlie Kim fired a dozen employees who he felt were at the root of the problems. He said, "We were spending too much time managing negative people." But because of the tight friendships in the company, most of which had existed before people were hired, another half-dozen people immediately quit. Morale and company performance plummeted. Instead of making things better, the firings made them much worse. Kim lost sleep and became depressed.

Slowly he came to the realization that he, too, needed to change for the company to succeed, that what had worked when the company had just 10 employees was not going to work when it had 130. After some encouragement from friends, advisors, and investors, he began to consider the following issues: *What are my primary responsibilities as a top manager? Does that include keeping workers happy and comfortable? Making the* transition from employee to manager has been one of the most stressful in my life. Are my experiences unique? What mistakes do managers typically make? Finally, what does it takes to be a manager and have I

got that? **If you were the CEO of Next-Jump, what would you do?**

**Sources:** P. Kruger, "Stop the Insanity! A New Generation of Dotcom Entrepreneurs Are Creating Companies that Work—Without Expecting People to Spend Every Waking Moment at

Work. Here's How to Build a Saner Startup," *Fast Company*, 1 July 2000, 240. R. Silverman, "For Charlie Kim, Company of Friends Proves a Lonely Place—A Dot-Com Founder Brought In Buddies and Colleagues; All Was Fine—on the Way Up," *The Wall Street Journal*, 1 February 2001, A1.

*[handwritten margin notes: mgmt / Def. / functions / Kinds of mgr / Do / Expectations / mistakes / Good mgr = comp. adv / transition / efficient effective]*

The issues facing Charlie Kim and NextJump are fundamental to any organization: What is management, and what do managers do? Good management is basic to starting a business, growing a business, and maintaining a business once it has achieved some measure of success.

This chapter begins by defining management and discussing the functions of management. Next, we look at what managers do by examining the four kinds of managers and reviewing the various roles that managers play. Third, we investigate what it takes to be a manager by reviewing management skills, what companies look for in their managers, the most serious mistakes managers make, and what it is like to make the tough transition from being a worker to being a manager. We finish this chapter by examining the competitive advantage that companies gain from good management. In other words, we end the chapter by learning how to establish a competitive advantage through people.

## What Is Management?

Have you ever noticed the difference between good and bad auto repair shops? Differences usually start with the service manager who greets you when you bring in your car. Understanding that most people don't know much about cars, good service managers ask dozens of detailed questions about the car's problems, what it does, the noises it makes, and the circumstances under which the problems occur. When DaimlerChrysler wanted to make sure that all of its Chrysler dealerships had good service managers, it hired a management consulting firm to create the *ServiceAnalyzer*, a computer-based tool that helps service managers at all Chrysler dealerships intuitively walk customers through a series of questions that fully describe the car's problem and when it occurs. Daimler-Chrysler used the *ServiceAnalyzer* to solve problems and improve customer satisfaction. But what DaimlerChrysler was paying for when the *ServiceAnalyzer* was created was good management advice.[1] Of course, DaimlerChrysler isn't the only organization in search of good management ideas. Nearly all companies are. In fact, it's estimated that companies paid management consultants over $138 billion for management advice last year.[2] Clearly, companies are looking for help with basic management issues, like how to make things happen, how to beat the competition, how to manage large-scale projects and processes, and how to effectively lead people. This textbook will help you understand some of the basic issues that management consultants help companies resolve (and unlike DaimlerChrysler, this won't cost millions of dollars).[3]

*[handwritten margin notes: make things happen / beat competition / mg proj. & processes / lead]*

*After reading these next two sections, you should be able to*
1. *describe what management is.*
2. *explain the four functions of management.*

### 1. Management Is . . .

Many of today's managers got their start welding on the factory floor, clearing dishes off tables, helping customers fit a suit, or wiping up a spill in aisle 3. Similarly, lots of you will start at the bottom and work your way up. There's no better way to get to know

*[page number in margin: 4]*

### Do You Know How Efficient Your Business Is?

Many managers fail to keep track of one of the most important outcomes in business: efficiency. Summit Polymers initially paid $280,000 for robots to paint and dry the dashboard vents in Toyota cars. When Toyota showed Summit how to do the same thing with $150 paint guns and much cheaper high-intensity lights, efficiency soared as Summit produced more with much less. Merck, a pharmaceutical company, improved efficiency by knocking five weeks off the time it takes to launch new products. If you want to improve how well your company is performing, keep close track of efficiency and productivity.

**Source:** G. Harris, "The Cure: with Big Drugs Dying, Merck Didn't Merge—It Found New Ones—Some Inspired Research, Aided by a Bit of Luck, Saves Company's Independence—The Path to a Novel Painkiller," *The Wall Street Journal*, 1 January 2001, A1. N. Shirouzu, "Gadget Inspector: Why Toyota Wins such High Marks on Quality Surveys—Hajime Oba is a Key Coach as Japanese Auto Maker Steps up U.S. Production—Striving to Reach Heijunka," *The Wall Street Journal*, 15 March 2001, A1.

**management**
getting work done through others

**efficiency**
getting work done with minimum of effort, expense, or waste

**effectiveness**
accomplishing tasks that help fulfill organizational objectives

**planning**
determining organizational goals and a means for achieving them

**organizing**
deciding where decisions will be made, who will do what jobs and tasks, who will work for whom

**leading**
inspiring and motivating workers to work hard to achieve organizational goals

**controlling**
monitoring progress toward goal achievement and taking corrective action when needed

your competition, your customers, and your business. But whether you begin your career at the entry level or as a supervisor, your job is not to do the work, but to help others do their work. **Management** is getting work done through others. Pat Carrigan, a former elementary school principal who became a manager at a General Motor's car parts plant, said, "I've never made a part in my life, and I don't really have any plans to make one. That's not my job. My job is to create an environment where people who do make them can make them right, can make them right the first time, can make them at a competitive cost, and can do so with some sense of responsibility and pride in what they're doing. I don't have to know how to make a part to do any of those things."[4]

Pat Carrigan's description of managerial responsibilities indicates that managers also have to be concerned with efficiency and effectiveness in the work process. **Efficiency** is getting work done with a minimum of effort, expense, or waste. For example, at Springfield Remanufacturing Company (SRC), the machines are shut off for a half an hour each week so that the 800 employees can break into small groups to study the company's weekly financial statements. With full information about the costs of labor, electricity, and raw materials, everyone at SRC can help increase efficiency by doing more with less cost and waste. For example, the workers learned that each sale of a rebuilt No. 466 crankshaft contributes $17.60 an hour toward paying overhead expenses. When they are able to rebuild these crankshafts quickly and efficiently, the additional inventory of finished crankshafts can generate as much as $170 a day that can be used to pay overhead costs, such as utility expenses or the salaries of scheduling and purchasing personnel. Countless small, efficiency-minded choices like this have helped SRC become one of the most profitable companies in its industry.

By itself, efficiency is not enough to ensure success. Managers must also strive for **effectiveness**, which is accomplishing tasks that help fulfill organizational objectives, such as customer service and satisfaction. For instance, if you've ever walked into a Home Depot, the warehouse-sized hardware stores, you've probably had trouble getting someone to help you. So has Dian Diemler, a loyal but frustrated Home Depot customer. She said, "I've followed employees around the store while they help other people in order to wait my turn."[5] To solve this problem, Home Depot has started a program called Service Performance Improvement (SPI) that prevents employees from running forklifts and stocking shelves between 8 A.M. and 8 P.M. Store manager Steve Moody also encourages his employees to wait in the "neutral zone" at the front of the store (between the cash registers and the store shelves) and to be aggressive in asking customers if they need help. The goal is to encourage orange-clad Home Depot employees to be efficient (by restocking shelves) and effective (by first helping customers).[6]

## Review 1
### Management Is . . .

Good management is working through others to accomplish tasks that help fulfill organizational objectives as efficiently as possible.

## 2. Management Functions

Traditionally, a manager's job has been described according to the classical functions of management: planning, organizing, leading, and controlling. **Planning** is determining organizational goals and a means for achieving them. **Organizing** is deciding where decisions will be made, who will do what jobs and tasks, and who will work for whom in the company. **Leading** is inspiring and motivating workers to work hard to achieve organizational goals. **Controlling** is monitoring progress toward goal achievement and taking corrective action when progress isn't being made.

# WhatReallyWorks

## Meta-Analysis

**Some studies show that having two drinks a day increases life expectancy by decreasing your chances of having a heart attack. Yet other studies show that having two drinks a day shortens life expectancy. For years, we've "buttered" our morning toast with margarine instead of butter because it was supposed to be better for our health. However, new**

studies now show that the trans-fatty acids in margarine may be just as bad for our arteries as butter. Confusing scientific results like these frustrate ordinary people who want to "eat right" and "live right." They also make many people question just how useful most scientific research really is.

Managers also have trouble figuring out what works, based on the scientific research published in journals like the *Academy of Management Journal*, the *Academy of Management Review*, the *Strategic Management Journal*, the *Journal of Applied Psychology*, and *Administrative Science Quarterly*. It's common for *The Wall Street Journal* to quote a management research article from one of these journals that says that total quality management is the best thing since sliced bread (without butter or margarine). Then, just six months later, *The Wall Street Journal* will quote a different article from the same journal that says that total quality management doesn't work. If management professors and researchers have trouble deciding what works and what doesn't, how can practicing managers know?

Thankfully, a research tool called **meta-analysis**, which is a study of studies, is helping management scholars understand how well their research supports management theories. Meta-analysis is also useful for practicing managers because it shows what works and the conditions under which management techniques may work better or worse in the "real world." Meta-analysis is based on the simple idea that if one study shows that a management technique doesn't work and another study shows that it does, an average of those results is probably the best estimate of how well that management practice works (or doesn't work). For example, medical researchers Richard Peto and Rory Collins averaged all of the different results from several hundred studies investigating the relationship between aspirin and heart attacks. Their analysis, based on more than 120,000 patients from numerous studies, showed that aspirin lowered the incidence of heart attacks by an average of 4 percent. Prior to this study, doctors prescribed aspirin as a preventive measure for only 38 percent of heart attack victims. Today, because of the meta-analysis results, doctors prescribe aspirin for 72 percent of heart attack victims.

Fortunately, you don't need a Ph.D. to understand the statistics reported in a meta-analysis. In fact, one primary advantage of meta-analysis over traditional significance tests is that you can convert meta-analysis statistics into intuitive numbers that anyone can easily understand.

Each meta-analysis reported in the "What Really Works?" section of this textbook is accompanied by an easy-to-understand statistic called the *probability of success*. As its name suggests, the *probability of success* shows how often a management technique will work.

For example, meta-analyses suggest that the best predictor of a job applicant's on-the-job performance is a test of general mental ability. In other words, smarter people tend to be better workers. The average correlation (one of those often-misunderstood statistics) between scores on general mental ability tests and job performance is .60. However, very few people understand what a correlation of .60 means. What most managers want to know is how often they will hire the right person if they choose job applicants based on general mental ability test scores. Likewise, they want to know how much of a difference a cognitive ability test makes when hiring new workers. The probability of success may be high, but if the difference isn't really that large, is it really worth a manager's time to have job applicants take a general mental ability test?

Well, our user-friendly statistics indicate that it's wise to have job applicants take a general mental ability test. In fact, the probability of success, shown in graphical form below, is 76 percent. This means that an employee hired on the basis of a good score on a general mental ability test stands a 76 percent chance of being a better performer than someone picked at random from the pool of all job applicants. So, chances are, you're going to be right much more often than wrong if you use a general mental ability test to make hiring decisions.

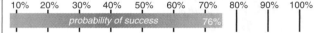

### General Mental Ability

In summary, each "What Really Works?" section in this textbook is based on meta-analysis research, which provides the best scientific evidence that management professors and researchers have about what works and what doesn't work in management. An easy-to-understand index known as the "probability of success" will be used to indicate how well a management idea or strategy is likely to work in the workplace. Of course, no idea or technique works every time and in every circumstance. However, the management ideas and strategies discussed in the "What Really Works?" sections of this textbook can usually make a meaningful difference where you work. In today's competitive, fast-changing, global marketplace, few managers can afford to overlook proven management strategies like the ones discussed in "What Really Works?"

**Sources:** R.J. Grisson, "Probability of the Superior Outcome of One Treatment over Another," *Journal of Applied Psychology* 79 (1994): 314-316. J.E. Hunter & F.L. Schmidt, *Methods of Meta-analysis: Correcting Error and Bias in Research Findings* (Beverly Hills, CA: Sage, 1990).

6

**meta-analysis**
a study of studies, a statistical approach that provides the best scientific estimate of how well management theories and practices work

Studies indicate that managers who perform these management functions well are better managers. The more time that chief executive officers (CEOs) spend planning, the more profitable their companies are.[7] Over a 25-year period, AT&T found that employees with better planning and decision-making skills were more likely to be promoted into management jobs, to be successful as managers, and to be promoted into upper levels of management.[8]

The evidence is clear. Managers serve their companies well when they plan, organize, lead, and control. However, companies with familiar names like AT&T, Dell Computers, General Motors, and J.C. Penney's are facing tremendous changes and are asking—if not demanding—that managers change the way they perform these functions. According to *Fortune* magazine, these changes are embodied in the difference between "old" management and "new" management. Old-style managers think of themselves as the "manager" or the "boss." New-style managers think of themselves as sponsors, team leaders, or internal consultants. Old-style managers follow the chain of command (reporting to the boss, who reports to the next boss at a higher managerial level, etc.), while new-style managers work with anyone who can help them accomplish their goals. Old-style managers make decisions by themselves. New-style managers ask others to participate in decisions. Old-style managers keep proprietary company information confidential. New-style managers share that information with others. Old-style managers demand long hours. New-style managers demand results.[9]

Such changes don't make the classical managerial functions obsolete. Indeed, managers are still responsible for performing the functions of management. For example, consider this description of a new-style manager and the people she works with (not the people who work for her, which is "old" management). The managerial functions represented by each action have been inserted in brackets.

> Three years ago Ransom asked her workers at a 100-person plant in Fairfield, California, to redesign the plant's operations [*planning and organizing*]. As she watched, intervening only to answer the occasional question [*controlling*], a team of hourly workers established training programs, set work rules for absenteeism [*controlling*], and reorganized the once-traditional factory into five customer-focused business units [*organizing and leading*]. As the workers took over managerial work [*decision making, organizing, and leading*], Ransom used her increasing free time to attend to the needs of customers and suppliers [*planning and controlling*].[10]

As indicated within the brackets, Ransom and the members of her work group still perform the classical management functions. They just do them differently than old-style managers.

To reconcile the "new" with the "old," this textbook is organized around these four management functions (see Exhibit 1.1), which have evolved out of the traditional functions:

- making things happen
- meeting the competition
- organizing people, projects, and processes
- leading

Note that these functions do not *replace* the classical functions of management; they *build* on them. For example, two of the four chapters under "Part 2: Making Things Happen" are classical management functions (planning and controlling). Furthermore, two of the four classical functions of management, organizing and leading, remain as part of the "new" management functions. Finally, a brand new management function, meeting the competition, has been added to reflect the importance of adapting and innovating to remain competitive in today's ever-changing and increasingly global marketplace.

EXHIBIT 1.1

## MANAGEMENT FUNCTIONS AND ORGANIZATION OF THE TEXTBOOK

**Planning**
**Controlling**

### Part One: Introduction to Management

Chapter  1, Management
Chapter  2, Organizational Environments and Cultures
Chapter  3, Ethics and Social Responsibility

### Part Two: Making Things Happen

Chapter  4, Planning
Chapter  5, Managing Information
Chapter  6, Decision Making
Chapter  7, Control

### Part Three: Meeting the Competition

Chapter  8, Global Management
Chapter  9, Organizational Strategy
Chapter 10, Innovation and Change
Chapter 11, Designing Adaptive Organizations

**Organizing**

### Part Four: Organizing People, Projects, and Processes

Chapter 12, Managing Individuals and a Diverse Work Force
Chapter 13, Managing Teams
Chapter 14, Managing Human Resource Systems
Chapter 15, Managing Service and Manufacturing Operations

### Part Five: Leading

**Leading**

Chapter 16, Motivation
Chapter 17, Leadership
Chapter 18, Managing Communication

Throughout this text, the major sections within a chapter will be numbered using a single digit: 1, 2, 3, etc. The subsections will be consecutively numbered, beginning with the major section number. For example, "2.1" marks the first subsection under the second major section. This numbering system should help you easily see the relationships among topics and follow the topic sequence. It will also help your instructor refer to specific topics during class discussion.

*Now let's take a close look at each of the management functions: **2.1** Making Things Happen; **2.2** Meeting the Competition; **2.3** Organizing People, Projects, and Processes; and **2.4** Leading.*

### 2.1 Making Things Happen

For most of its existence, Gateway Computers had been a small, informally run organization. Rock music was played on the factory floor, and, reflecting its South Dakota roots, the company put its now-famous cow spots on the side of Gateway shipping boxes. But, struggling under tremendous growth, Gateway founder Ted Waitt hired Jeff Weitzen from AT&T to be Gateway's new CEO. At first, with Waitt remaining CEO

8

and Weitzen apprenticing to replace him, Gateway thrived; sales increased by 37 percent, net income tripled, and the stock price quadrupled. However, after Waitt became chairman of the board and distanced himself from Gateway's day-to-day activities, the new CEO Weitzen began implementing changes and policies that he thought would lead to even more improvement. While some things worked, many backfired in spectacular ways. For example, rather than relying on the management team that had built Gateway's success over two decades, Weizten replaced them with high-level managers from AT&T, GE, Nike, and PepsiCo. Meetings and conference calls, intended to improve communication and decision making, proliferated and prevented people from doing their work. A long-standing employee said, "The week [before] I left Gateway, I was on conference calls for 26 hours." Decision making slowed to a crawl. Mike Hammond, Gateway's first employee, said, "You'd schedule an appointment, do some PowerPoints, do your presentation—if the meeting didn't get rescheduled—and you'd get asked a bunch of questions, and then you gotta come back with the answers." Policies, intended to standardize operating procedures, angered employees and harmed customer satisfaction. For example, any customer service representatives who spent more than 13 minutes on the phone with a customer lost their monthly bonus. As a result, service reps did almost anything, such as lying, or pretending the phone connection was bad, to get customers off the line.[11]

In his zeal to "professionalize" Gateway's management practices, new Gateway CEO Jeff Weitzen forgot that the most important management function is making things happen. To "make things happen," you must determine what you want to accomplish, plan how to achieve these goals, gather and manage the information needed to make good decisions, and control performance, so that you can take corrective action if performance falls short. In his estimation, company founder Ted Waitt took corrective action when he and Gateway's board of directors fired Weitzen for his failure to make things happen at

When Ted Waitt, pictured here, relinquished day-to-day control of Gateway, the new management team's policies and procedures actually angered employees and harmed customer satisfaction. Waitt ultimately reclaimed control of the company and reinstated the old management team.

© LAYNE KENNEDY/CORBIS

Gateway. After Gateway's board reinstalled Waitt as CEO, his first step was to hire back the management team that had overseen Gateway's phenomenal growth. In Chapters 4-7, you will learn more about how to make things happen.

## 2.2 Meeting the Competition

Palm, Inc., maker of the Palm Pilot, an electronic personal planner, was not in business 10 years ago. At that time, most businesspeople used paper-based planners such as Day Timers and Filofax. Today, however, 13 million people—and many more by the time you read this—use Palm Pilots to manage their calendars, contacts, and daily to-do lists. In fact, it took less than 18 months for Palm, Inc. to sell its first 1 million Palm Pilots. And when Palm, Inc. went public by selling shares of stock, expectations of its success were so strong that the company raised $53.4 billion in just two days!

However, one year after going public, Palm's future wasn't as rosy. The company founders left to start a business that sells the Visor, another electronic personal planner (with expansion slots for an MP3 player, a digital camera, and a cell phone) that has reduced Palm's market share from 83 percent of the market to just 63 percent. Furthermore, Microsoft, which budgets $300 million a year for research and development for handheld electronic personal planners, has revised the software and functionality for PocketPCs sold by Compaq, Casio, and Hewlett Packard and is intent on improving on its 8 percent market share. Palm's stranglehold on the Palm PC market evaporated so quickly that *Fortune* magazine concluded, "It's ironic that a company known for helping people plan and schedule could be so ham-handed in managing its own affairs, but such is the case with Palm."[12]

Palm's situation is not unique. With free trade agreements that promote international competition, shorter product development cycles, and barriers to entry falling in most industries, market followers will continue to topple market leaders as companies are exposed to more competition than ever in the next decade. Companies, such as Palm, Inc., that want to remain market leaders must consider the threat from international competitors, have a well-thought-out competitive strategy, be able to embrace change and foster new product and service ideas, and structure their organizations to quickly adapt to changing customers and competitors. Thus, "meeting the competition" is a critical management function in today's business world. In Chapters 8-11, you will learn some management skills for meeting the competition.

## 2.3 Organizing People, Projects, and Processes

When the toy company Mattel paid $3.8 billion for The Learning Company, which develops and markets games and educational software, it thought it was investing in the future of the toy industry. Because of the Learning Company's range of products, from role-playing games like *Myst*, to fun, investigative, and educational games like *Carmen San Diego*, Mattel expected The Learning Company to grow and return above-average profits for years to come. Yet, just three years after the purchase, The Learning Company was in such disarray, losing $1 million a day, that it cost Mattel CEO Jill Barad her job. Vance Diggins, one of the managers brought in to clean up the mess after Mattel sold the company, said, "It was like we were fighting a brushfire that couldn't be contained."[13] Besides out-of-control spending, one of the key problems was that the company was organized as seven different, autonomous work units that didn't share resources or even talk to each other. Said one manager, "We knew things were bad when we organized an executive staff meeting, and three of the unit's general managers had never met one another. And they had been working in the same complex."[14]

However, after establishing tight spending controls, reorganizing the seven units into three to promote resource sharing and to get managers to work together, The Learning Company is again turning a profit. Unfortunately, Mattel found out that even technology companies can't run well without considering basic people issues and work processes (how the work gets done). Therefore, our next management function is "organizing people, projects, and processes." You will learn about this management function in Chapters 12-15.

### 2.4 Leading

In these litigious times, managers are sued for sexual harassment, wrongful discharge, and discrimination. They are shot at, lampooned in the funny pages (*Dilbert* cartoons adorn cubicle and office walls in businesses all over the world), and, in general, not accorded the respect they once had. In periods of corporate layoffs, managers are often feared and disliked.

How is it, then, amidst general corporate distrust, that before her death Mary Kay Ash, founder of Mary Kay cosmetics, and Herb Kelleher, founder, former CEO, and now chairman of Southwest Airlines, were not only respected, but loved by the people they led?[15] Gloria Mayfield, a former IBMer and a graduate of Harvard's MBA program, said, "I didn't see much recognition at IBM. At Mary Kay, if you do well, you know *for a fact* you'll get recognition. It's not influenced by politics." Mayfield continued, "Mary Kay calls you her daughter and looks you dead in the eye. She makes you feel you can do anything. She's sincerely concerned about your welfare."[16]

At Southwest Airlines, pilots pitch in at the boarding gate, ticket agents help with the luggage, and employees in general do whatever needs to be done to keep customers happy. These positive attitudes help Southwest achieve the highest productivity in the industry, flying two-to-three times as many passengers per employee as its competitors at a cost that is 25 percent to 40 percent cheaper.[17] Kelleher, a notorious jokester and storyteller, drew exceptional effort from his troops by putting people first and by making work fun. When he finished negotiating a new contract with Southwest's flight attendants, he celebrated by leading the cafeteria crowd of Southwest workers in cheers. He dressed up as Elvis, the Easter Bunny, and a boxer, complete with gloves and a silk robe, all to shape Southwest's corporate culture and win the hearts of his loyal work force.[18]

No one who has worked for an ordinary manager would ever deny the positive effects that inspirational leaders, such as Mary Kay and Herb Kelleher, bring to their companies. Thus, our last management function is "leading," which you will learn about in Chapters 16-18.

For nearly 40 years, Mary Kay Ash was the leader of her own cosmetics empire. She mesmerized and inspired an army of women to sell Mary Kay products door-to-door. Her charismatic and inspirational leadership was one of the many reasons she was a good manager.

© FRITZ HOFFMANN/THE IMAGE WORKS

MARY KAY

Managerial jobs have traditionally been described according to the classical functions of management: planning, organizing, leading, and controlling. Although managers still perform these managerial functions, companies and the managers who run them have undergone tremendous changes in the last decade. Accordingly, this text incorporates the classical functions of management into broader, updated management functions: making things happen; meeting the competition; organizing people, projects, and processes; and leading.

## What Do Managers Do?

Not all managerial jobs are the same. The demands and requirements placed on the chief executive officer of General Motors are significantly different from those placed on the manager of your local Wendy's restaurant.

*After reading these next two sections, you should be able to*
*3.   describe different kinds of managers.*
*4.   explain the major roles and subroles that managers perform in their jobs.*

### 3. Kinds of Managers

*As shown in Exhibit 1.2, there are four kinds of managers, each with different jobs and responsibilities: 3.1 Top Managers, 3.2 Middle Managers, 3.3 First-Line Managers, and 3.4 Team Leaders.*

#### 3.1 Top Managers

**top managers**
executives responsible for the overall direction of the organization

**Top managers** hold positions like chief executive officer (CEO) or chief operating officer (COO) and are responsible for the overall direction of the organization. Top managers have the following responsibilities.[19] First, they are responsible for creating a context for change. In fact, the CEOs of Gillette, Lucent Technologies, Mattel, Xerox, Campbell Soup, and Aetna were all fired within a year's time precisely because they had not moved fast enough to bring about significant changes in their companies.[20] Creating a context for change also includes forming a long-range vision or mission for their companies. As one CEO said, "The CEO has to think about the future more than anyone."

Second, much more than used to be the case, top managers are responsible for developing employees' commitment to and ownership in the company's performance. Stories abound at Southwest Airlines about Herb Kelleher's willingness to listen to his employees. One such story has Kelleher out until four in the morning drinking in a bar with a Southwest mechanic. The point of the story is that Kelleher, supposedly the most important person in the company, was listening to the mechanic, supposedly one of the least important persons in the company, so he (Kelleher) could fix whatever was wrong.[21]

Third, top managers are responsible for creating a positive organizational culture through language and action. Top managers impart company values, strategies, and lessons through what they do and say to others, both inside and outside the company. One CEO said, "I write memos to the board and our operating committee. I'm sure they get the impression I dash them off, but usually they've been drafted ten or twenty times. The bigger you get, the more your ability to communicate becomes important. So what I write, I write very carefully. I labor over it."[22] Philip Condit, Boeing's CEO, recognizes this responsibility by emphasizing three simple messages every time he speaks to Boeing managers and employees: "run healthy core businesses, leverage strengths into new products, and open new frontiers. Says Condit, "I try to [use] exactly the same words every

*"Kelleher listens to mechanic"*

*tal*

*△ ∀*

EXHIBIT 1.2

## JOBS AND RESPONSIBILITIES OF FOUR KINDS OF MANAGERS

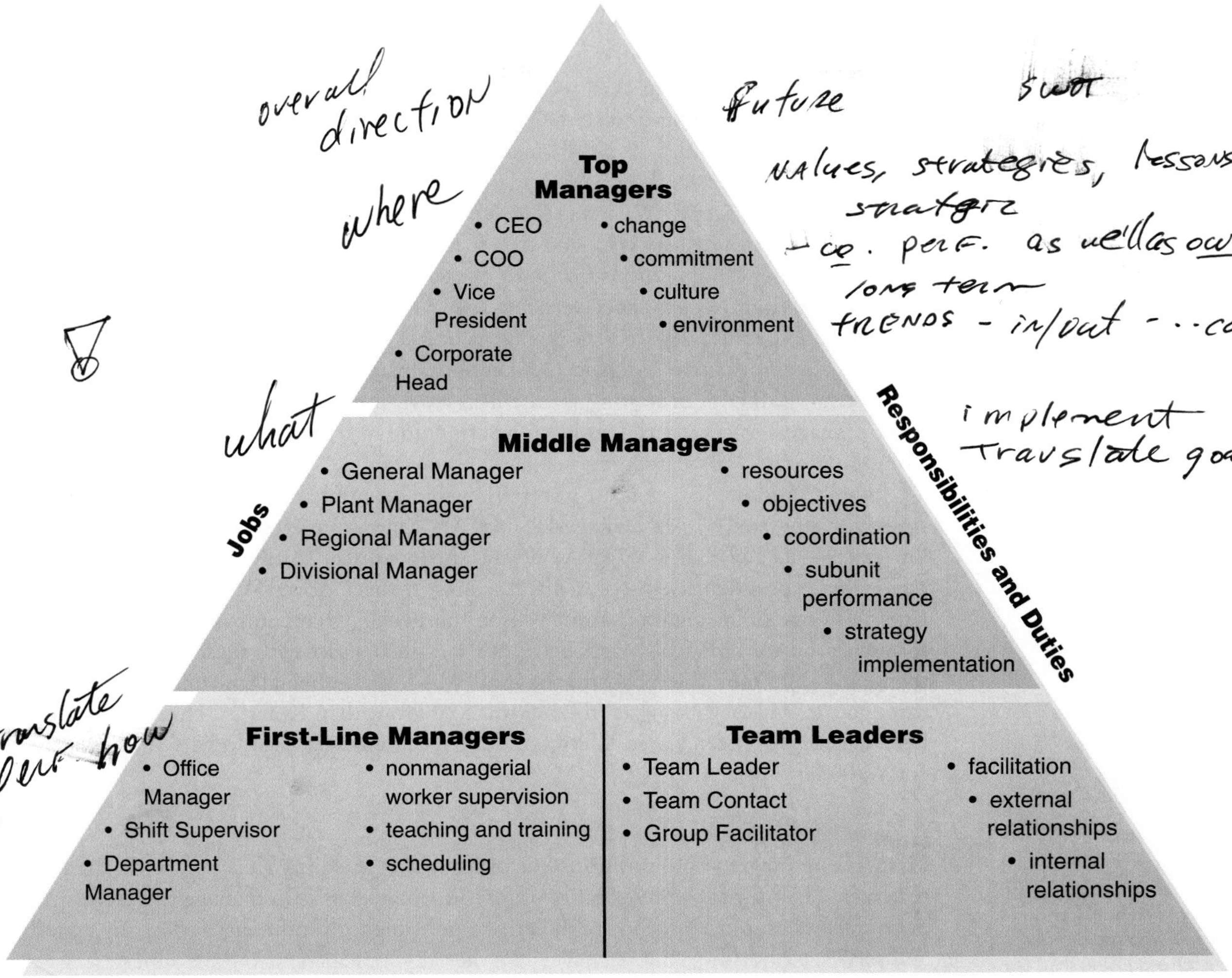

*Handwritten annotations: overall direction / where / future / swot / values, strategies, lessons, & Ex- / strategic / + co. perf. as well as own perf. / long term / trends - in/out ...coming. / implement / translate goals - / what / Jobs / translate perf how / Responsibilities and Duties*

**Top Managers**
- CEO
- COO
- Vice President
- Corporate Head

- change
- commitment
- culture
- environment

**Middle Managers**
- General Manager
- Plant Manager
- Regional Manager
- Divisional Manager

- resources
- objectives
- coordination
- subunit performance
- strategy implementation

**First-Line Managers**
- Office Manager
- Shift Supervisor
- Department Manager

- nonmanagerial worker supervision
- teaching and training
- scheduling

**Team Leaders**
- Team Leader
- Team Contact
- Group Facilitator

- facilitation
- external relationships
- internal relationships

13

*Handwritten: Sittions → excourses / 9-11*

time so that you don't produce a lot of, 'Last time you said this, this time you said that.' You've got to say the same thing over and over and over."[23]

Finally, top managers are responsible for monitoring their business environments. This means that top managers must closely monitor customer needs, competitors' moves, and long-term business, economic, and social trends. Rick Wagoner, president and CEO of General Motors, reads six daily newspapers, monitors his Internet connections and news sources all day, and skims a variety of magazines from all over the world. Says Wagoner, "You've gotta know what the hell is going on in your business. If you've got a problem in China, you've gotta get into it and make sure that it's getting fixed. You've got to be on top of your business enough to know where are the problems, where are the opportunities."[24]

**middle managers**
managers responsible for setting objectives consistent with top management's goals, and planning and implementing subunit strategies for achieving these objectives

### 3.2 Middle Managers

**Middle managers** hold positions like plant manager, regional manager, or divisional manager. They are responsible for setting objectives consistent with top management's goals and planning and implementing subunit strategies for achieving these objectives.

One specific middle management responsibility is to plan and allocate resources to meet objectives. Another major responsibility is to coordinate and link groups, departments, and divisions within a company. Rather than calling the shots from company headquarters, each Monday morning in Bentonville, Arkansas, all of Wal-Mart's regional vice presidents, accompanied by merchandise buyers and personnel managers, board 15 company planes as they fly out to spend the next four days visiting the stores in each sales territory. The regional vice presidents then reconvene in Bentonville on Fridays and on Saturday mornings to share ideas and solve the problems they identified on their weekly trips.[25]

A third responsibility of middle management is to monitor and manage the performance of the subunits and individual managers who report to them. For example, one of the first things that Andy Wilson, a Wal-Mart regional vice president, will do when he visits a store in his territory is to find the store manager and then make a walking inspection of the store. On one inspection tour of a new store in his territory, Wilson was disappointed to find that products were not displayed according to headquarters' plans. Furthermore, because department managers had been slow to reorder products, many shelves were empty because replacement supplies had not yet arrived from the Wal-Mart warehouses. Rather than waiting for the next truck shipment, Wilson told the department managers to correct the problem by arranging to transfer out-of-stock products from the nearest Wal-Mart store.[26]

Finally, middle managers are also responsible for implementing the changes or strategies generated by top managers. Since Wal-Mart competes by selling products at low prices—its advertising slogan is "always the low price," Andy Wilson and the other regional vice presidents visit competitors' stores to check prices. At a Kmart that competes with one of his region's stores, Wilson found signs that compared the Kmart price for each product with Wal-Mart's price. Wilson filled a cart with these items, purchased them, and then took them back to the local Wal-Mart. When all the items were run through the Wal-Mart scanner, the bill was $20 lower than Kmart.[27] However, if the Kmart prices had been lower, Wilson and the local managers would have immediately cut Wal-Mart's prices.

### 3.3 First-Line Managers

**First-line managers** hold positions like office manager, shift supervisor, or department manager. The primary responsibility of first-line managers is to manage the performance of entry-level employees, who are directly responsible for producing a company's goods and services. Thus, first-line managers are the only managers who don't supervise other managers. For example, DialAmerica Marketing is a large telemarketing company, one of those firms whose sales representatives always seem to call you at home during dinner or your favorite TV show. Working as a telemarketing representative can be a high-stress, thankless job. However, each shift supervisor's job is to encourage, monitor, and reward the performance of his or her telemarketing representatives. For example, during the evening shift, which is "prime time" because more Americans can be reached by phone then than at any other time of the day, shift supervisors listen in on telemarketing representatives' calls to customers. They also track each representative's sales on a blackboard and provide lots of encouragement and praise for achieving goals.[28]

First-line managers also teach entry-level employees how to do their jobs. Because telemarketing work is so stressful, most workers quit after three or four months on the job. In fact, any stay over three months is considered long-term employment. Because employee turnover is so high, DialAmerica's supervisors are constantly training new employees. This is one of the reasons that supervisors listen in on telemarketing representatives' phone calls: to observe their performance so that they can teach them how to make sales. For example, after listening in on one representative's calls, a supervisor called the representative in to encourage her not to rush through the prepared script that must be read to each customer.[29]

First-line managers also make detailed schedules and operating plans based on middle management's intermediate range plans. In fact, contrary to the long-term plans of top managers (three-to-five years out) and the intermediate plans of middle managers (six-to-eighteen months out), first-line managers engage in plans and actions that typically produce results within two weeks.[30] For example, consider the job of nurse supervisor in charge of admissions in a nursing home. Each time someone new is admitted to the nursing home, this first-line supervisor must make sure that the admissions clerks and bookkeepers process the insurance and government papers, the dietary staff and rehabilitation workers put together a complete care plan, the social worker has obtained a complete medical and family history, and housekeeping has prepared and cleaned the new admission's room. Each of these activities must be performed no more than a week after being scheduled.[31]

### 3.4 Team Leaders

The fourth kind of manager is a team leader. This relatively new kind of management job developed as companies shifted to self-managing teams, which, by definition, have no formal supervisor. In traditional management hierarchies, first-line managers are responsible for the performance of nonmanagerial employees and have the authority to hire and fire workers, make job assignments, and control resources. By contrast, team leaders have a much different role, because teams in this new structure now perform nearly all of the functions performed by first-line managers under traditional hierarchies. Instead of directing individuals' work, **team leaders** facilitate team activities toward goal accomplishment. For example, Hewlett-Packard advertises its team leader positions with an ad that says, "Job seeker must enjoy coaching, working with people, and bringing about improvement through hands-off guidance and leadership."[32] Team leaders who fail to understand this key difference often struggle in their roles. A team leader at Texas Instruments said, "I didn't buy into teams, partly because there was no clear plan on what I was supposed to do. . . . I never let the operators [team members] do any scheduling or any ordering of parts because that was mine. I figured as long as I had that, I had a job."[33]

Team leaders fulfill the following responsibilities.[34] First, team leaders are responsible for facilitating team performance. This doesn't mean team leaders are responsible for team performance. They aren't. The team is. Team leaders help their teams plan and schedule work, learn to solve problems, and work effectively with each other. Eric Doremus, a team leader whose team helped develop the B-2 bomber, said, "My most important task was not trying to figure out everybody's job. It was to help this team feel as if they owned the project by getting them whatever information, financial or otherwise, they needed. I knew that if we could all charge up the hill together, we would be successful."[35]

Second, team leaders are responsible for managing external relationships. Team leaders act as the bridge or liaison between their teams and other teams, departments, and divisions in a company. For example, if a member of Team A complains about the quality of Team B's work, Team B's leader is responsible for solving the problem by initiating a meeting with Team A's leader. Together, these team leaders are responsible for getting members of both teams to work together to solve the problem. If it's done right, the problem is solved without involving company management or blaming members of the other team.[36]

Third, team leaders are responsible for internal team relationships. Getting along with others is much more important in team structures, because team members can't get work done without the help of their teammates. And when conflicts arise on a six-, seven-, or eight-person team, the entire team suffers. So it is critical for team leaders to know how to help team members resolve conflicts. For example, at XEL Communications Corporation, the standard procedure is for a team leader to take the fighting team members to a conference room. The team leader attempts to mediate the disagreement, hearing each side, and encouraging the team members to agree to a practical solution.[37] Hewlett-Packard says that in extreme cases, team leaders can dissolve the team and reassign all team members to different teams.[38] Such instances, however, are rare. You will learn more about teams in Chapter 13.

**team leaders**
managers responsible for facilitating team activities toward goal accomplishment

There are four different kinds of managers. Top managers are responsible for creating a context for change, developing attitudes of commitment and ownership, creating a positive organizational culture through words and actions, and monitoring their company's business environments. Middle managers are responsible for planning and allocating resources, coordinating and linking groups and departments, monitoring and managing the performance of subunits and managers, and implementing the changes or strategies generated by top managers. First-line managers are responsible for managing the performance of nonmanagerial employees, teaching direct reports how to do their jobs, and making detailed schedules and operating plans based on middle management's intermediate-range plans. Team leaders are responsible for facilitating team performance, managing external relationships, and facilitating internal team relationships.

## 4. Managerial Roles

So far, we have described managerial work by focusing on the functions of management (making things happen; meeting the competition; organizing people, projects, and processes; and leading), and by examining the four kinds of managerial jobs (top managers, middle managers, first-line managers, and team leaders). Although these are valid and accurate ways of categorizing managerial work, if you follow managers around as they perform their jobs, you would probably not use the terms "planning," "organizing," "leading," and "controlling" to describe what they do.

In fact, that's exactly the same conclusion that management researcher Henry Mintzberg came to when he followed five American CEOs around. Mintzberg spent a week "shadowing" each CEO and analyzing their mail, who they talked to, and what they did.

*Mintzberg concluded that managers fulfill three major roles while performing their jobs:* [39]
1. *interpersonal roles*
2. *informational roles*
3. *decisional roles*

*In other words, managers talk to people, gather and give information, and make decisions. Furthermore, as shown in Exhibit 1.3, these three major roles can be subdivided into ten subroles. Let's examine each major role—4.1 interpersonal, 4.2 informational, and 4.3 decisional roles—and their ten subroles.*

### 4.1 Interpersonal Roles

More than anything else, management jobs are people-intensive. Estimates vary with the level of management, but most managers spend between two-thirds and four-fifths of their time in face-to-face communication with others.[40] If you're a loner, or if you consider dealing with people a "pain," then you may not be cut out for management work. In fulfilling the interpersonal role of management, managers perform three interpersonal subroles: figurehead, leader, and liaison.

In the **figurehead role**, managers perform ceremonial duties, like greeting company visitors, making opening remarks when a new facility opens, or representing the company at a community luncheon to support local charities. Each time that Coca-Cola opens a new bottling plant somewhere around the world, Coke's CEO flies in on the Coke corporate jet for an opening celebration. For example, in Poland, Coke's CEO and Polish government officials christened Coke's new Warsaw bottling plant by drinking the first Coca-Colas produced by Polish workers. The Cokes were tied together with long red ribbons to symbolize cooperation between Coke and the Polish people.[41]

In the **leader role**, managers motivate and encourage workers to accomplish organizational objectives. At Chiat/Day, one of the world's leading advertising companies, managers found a mannequin arm and decided to turn it into a fun company award.

**figurehead role**
the interpersonal role managers play when they perform ceremonial duties

**leader role**
the interpersonal role managers play when they motivate and encourage workers to accomplish organizational objectives

EXHIBIT 1.3

MINTZBERGS'S MANAGERIAL ROLES AND SUBROLES

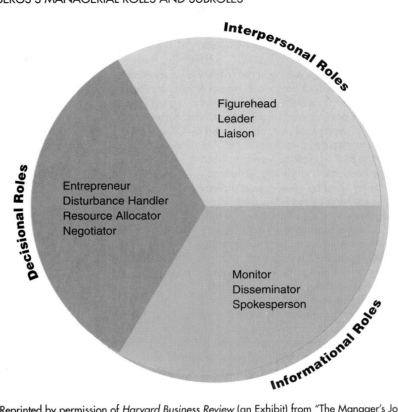

Every month, one employee in Chiat/Day's New York office receives the "Right Arm Award" for outstanding performance, like pulling an all-nighter to meet a client's deadline. Right Arm Award winners also receive a gift certificate good for dinner for two at a restaurant of their choice. Says Chiat/Day's CEO, "We always have fun with it. It's something that everyone looks forward to."[42] The point? To motivate Chiat/Day's workers through frequent praise and recognition.

In the **liaison role**, managers deal with people outside their units. Studies consistently indicate that managers spend as much time with "outsiders" as they do with their own subordinates and their own bosses. In addition to his normal duties, Rajesh Hukku, chairman of j-Flex Solutions, a maker of financial-services software, regularly goes on sales calls, helps close sales deals, and markets his product to potential customers at industry conventions and forums.[43] Likewise, Dennis Kozlowski, CEO of Tyco, began a typical 16-hour day by having breakfast with investment bankers, flying to New Jersey to meet with the employees of a company that Tyco just purchased, and then driving into New York to have dinner with the CEO of one of Tyco's suppliers. The next morning, after five hours of sleep, he began with an extended phone call to European-based staffers, and then completed more meetings with investors and employees.[44]

### 4.2 Informational Roles

While managers spend most of their time in face-to-face contact with others, most of that time is spent obtaining and sharing information. Indeed, Mintzberg found that the

**liaison role**
the interpersonal role managers play when they deal with people outside their units

# "headline news"

## Forget Road Rage: It's Desk Rage You Have to Worry About

Forget road rage. It's desk rage you really have to worry about. Although the Occupational Safety and Health Administration reports declining workplace deaths, homicide is the second leading cause of fatal occupational injury in the United States. In 1999, of the 631 workplace murders reported by OSHA, 68 of them were committed by coworkers. In 1997, coworkers committed 61 of the 812 workplace homicides. So as workplace homicide is declining, incidence of workers being killed by colleagues is increasing. Your risk of dying on the job is declining, but it is more likely that if you do, it will be the person in the next cubicle who is responsible.

But it's not just murder that is of concern. Aggression, stalking, threats, harassment, shouting, and bullying are all forms of violence that can be chronicled in today's workplace. Lately, bullying is getting quite a bit of media attention, particularly in publications like *HR Management* and *Risk Management*. Ironically, amidst corporate America's "people management skills" culture, bullying is on the rise. While companies are trumpeting their people as their greatest asset and are emphasizing good people management, thousands of employees are going to work every day with an overwhelming feeling of dread.

When labor shortages crimp the talent pool for workers and managers alike, people who are successful at a particular aspect of their job are often quickly promoted to a managerial position—whether or not they have management skills. The initial stages in the transition to management can be especially harsh. Faced with the sudden responsibility for a team or department, along with a new accountability to top management, new and inexperienced managers may resort to bullying as a management style. Alison Campbell, founder of a helpline for bullying victims, faults technology. "Rather than managers sitting down with colleagues and discussing issues," she said, "they do everything via email. Managers need to be retrained in people skills."

Because bullying is so covert, it is difficult to identify. Often the bully is the supervisor, and the taboo against going over someone's head is so entrenched that bullied workers are reluctant to speak up. If a company lacks an anti-bullying policy, workers tend to just leave their jobs, one way or another. Max Mason, an IT worker with City Bank, shot himself while receiving psychiatric care related to an attempted overdose brought on by work trauma.

Perpetual nitpicking may not seem a likely candidate for inclusion in a violence prevention program, but increasingly companies are drafting anti-bullying policies, not only to protect their workers, but also their managers. As well they should. A new video game titled Red Faction features miners on Mars who rebel against and kill their supervisors. By all accounts, it's gaining popularity.

1. Describe a corporate environment where you think bullying would thrive. Where would it wither on the vine?

2. What do you think are the key elements in creating a violence prevention program or an anti-bullying policy? Would a simple policy stating that "all employees are required to treat each other with respect" suffice? What would be the pitfalls of such a succinct policy? The advantages?

3. Have you ever been the victim of workplace bullying? Have you ever found yourself bullying a colleague in an attempt to get an important or time-sensitive project completed? When?

**Sources:** John T. Adams III, "Workplace Deaths Decline, Co-Worker Homicides Rise," *HR Magazine*, February 2001, p. 12. Helen Beckett, "The Violence of Silence," *Computer Weekly*, 4 November 1999, p. 49. Isabel Choat, "Beware the Bully," *Computer Weekly*, 21 October 1999, p. 66. Jane McDonald, "Murder at Work," *Risk Management*, March 2001, p 7. Carlos Tejada, "Work Week: The Checkoff," *The Wall Street Journal*, 17 July 2001, wsj.com. http://www.bullybusters.org; http://www.osha.gov; http://www.redfaction.com

---

managers in his study spent 40 percent of their time giving and getting information from others. In this regard, management can be viewed as processing information, gathering information by scanning the business environment and listening to others in face-to-face conversations, and then sharing that information with people inside and outside the company. Mintzberg described three informational subroles: monitor, disseminator, and spokesperson.

In the **monitor role**, managers scan their environment for information, actively contact others for information, and, because of their personal contacts, receive a great deal of unsolicited information. Besides receiving firsthand information, managers monitor their environment by reading local newspapers and *The Wall Street Journal* to keep track of customers, competitors, and technological changes that may affect their busi-

**monitor role**
the informational role managers play when they scan their environment for information

nesses. However, managers can now take advantage of electronic monitoring and distribution services that track the news wires (Associated Press, Reuters, etc.) for stories related to their businesses. These services literally deliver customized electronic newspapers to managers, including only the stories on topics the managers specify. One such company is Business Wire. Business Wire (**www.businesswire.com**) offers services like IndustryTrak, which monitors and distributes daily news headlines from 23 major industries; CompetitorTrak, which keeps round-the-clock track of new stories in categories chosen by each subscriber; and BW News Clips, a joint venture with DataTimes, that provides electronic news clips from more than 500 U.S. and foreign sources.[45]

Because of their numerous personal contacts and because of the access they have to subordinates, managers are often hubs for distribution of critical information. In the **disseminator role**, managers share the information they have collected with their subordinates and others in the company. Although there will never be a complete substitute for face-to-face dissemination of information, the primary methods of communication in large companies like Boeing and Cisco Systems are email and voice mail. Phil Condit, Boeing's CEO, sends email to 160,000 Boeing employees, sharing information with them and asking for feedback. John Chambers, Cisco's CEO, says that 90 percent of his communication with employees is through email and voice mail. Says Chambers, "If you don't have the ability to interface with customers, employees, and suppliers, you can't manage your business."[46]

In contrast to the disseminator role, in which managers distribute information to employees inside the company, in the **spokesperson role**, managers share information with people outside their departments and companies. One of the most common ways in which CEOs serve as spokespeople for their companies is at annual meetings with company shareholders or the board of directors. For example, at a recent Sears annual shareholder meeting, CEO Alan Lacy told investors that Sears would try to increase sales through specialty store formats, such as a 55,000 square foot hardware store (based on Sears tools, which come with a lifetime warranty); the *Great Indoors*, which sells furniture and home decorating ideas; and *Brand Central*, which will basically be electronics and appliance centers.[47] Likewise, at a Nortel Networks annual shareholder meeting, CEO John Roth announced that with his pending retirement, the company would be looking for a new CEO. Furthermore, because of the current Chief Operating Officer's medical problems, the company would also be hiring a new COO as well.[48]

## 4.3 Decisional Roles

While managers spend most of their time in face-to-face contact with others, obtaining and sharing information, that time, according to Mintzberg, is not an end in itself. The time spent talking to and obtaining and sharing information with people inside and outside of the company is useful to managers because it helps them make good decisions. According to Mintzberg, managers engage in four decisional subroles: entrepreneur, disturbance handler, resource allocator, and negotiator.

In the **entrepreneur role**, managers adapt themselves, their subordinates, and their units to incremental change. At Bic, manufacturer of disposable pens, razors, and cigarette lighters, each Friday at 2:15 P.M. workers leave their jobs on the manufacturing line to meet in a conference room. Then, one by one, ideas are pulled from the employee suggestion box, read aloud, discussed, and then voted on. Suggestions range from solutions that prevent machines from spraying oil on the floor to having the huge company trash bins emptied just once a week—because they weren't even half full when emptied twice a week. Once an idea is approved, it's handed down the table to the appropriate supervisor who then has 10 days to put the idea into place. Step by step, Bic's employee ideas improve morale, boost company productivity, and reinforce the idea that change is welcome and expected. Indeed, in one year at one Bic plant, 577 out of 684 hourly employees submitted 2,999 suggestions, of which 2,368 were actually used.[49]

**disseminator role**
the informational role managers play when they share information with others in their departments or companies

**spokesperson role**
the informational role managers play when they share information with people outside their departments or companies

**entrepreneur role**
the decisional role managers play when they adapt themselves, their subordinates, and their units to incremental change

**disturbance handler role**
the decisional role managers play when they respond to severe problems that demand immediate action

By contrast, in the **disturbance handler role**, managers respond to pressures and problems so severe that they demand immediate attention and action. Managers often play the role of disturbance handler when the company board hires a new CEO, charged with turning around a failing company. When *Reader's Digest*'s net income fell from $264 million to $80.6 million in one year, and when circulation dropped to a three-decade low of 12.5 million readers (down from 18 million), new CEO Thomas Ryder laid off 17 percent of employees, cut retirement benefits, and sold off a $100 million art collection accumulated by company founders and displayed at company headquarters. Because company staffers took nearly a year to develop new mail campaigns, which are used to increase subscriptions and sell other *Reader's Digest* products, Ryder hired outside firms to do the same job. Today, new mail campaigns are developed in 13 weeks.[50] Furthermore, revenues and net income have begun to rise. Likewise, Peter Bonfield, CEO of British Telecom (BT), the leading provider of traditional and wireless phone services in Britain, announced that BT will spin off its cell phone division, BT Wireless, to shareholders. BT hopes to raise nearly $9 billion from this move, which it will use to reduce the company's rather large and expensive $30 billion of debt by nearly one-third.[51] In both instances, the CEOs of *Reader's Digest* and British Telecom served as disturbance handlers, trimming work forces, cutting costs, and moving quickly to turn around their companies.

**resource allocator role**
the decisional role managers play when they decide who gets what resources

In the **resource allocator role**, managers decide who will get what resources and how many resources they get. When Scott Paper reported a loss of $300 million, its new CEO used a four-step plan to quickly and dramatically change the allocation of resources: Step one, determine what business you're in. Scott Paper was already the largest paper tissue company in the world. Step two, keep those resources and sell off the other assets, like a coated-paper business and a power plant. Step three, make one-time major cuts. The first week on the job, he fired 9 of the 11 top managers at the company. He

The Bic Employee Suggestion Program is an example of how managers can implement incremental change. While fostering employee creativity in problem solving, the Bic's employee suggestion program also reinforces the idea that change is welcome and expected.

20

© COURTESY BIC CORPORATION

then sold the corporate headquarters, 750,000 square feet on 55 rolling acres, which he replaced with a 30,000 square foot building, less than 5 percent of the size of the former headquarters. Of the headquarters staff, the CEO laid off 71 percent, reducing the overall headcount 20 percent. Finally, step four, invest your resources in the right business strategy. While the overall headcount shrank by 20 percent, hiring in marketing grew because the CEO had determined that Scott had great products but lousy marketing of those products. So Scott Paper put its resources into developing a strong marketing strategy. Within a year, Scott emerged as a very different company, with a very different allocation of resources and record profits.[52]

In the **negotiator role**, managers negotiate schedules, projects, goals, outcomes, resources, and employee raises. For Michael O'Leary, CEO of Dublin-based Ryanair, Europe's low-cost airline with fares sometimes as much as 80 percent lower than established airlines, negotiation is a key part of his strategy. In part, Ryanair achieves costs 30 percent below average and has 40 percent higher productivity, because it flies to secondary airports near, but not in, major cities. Because these airports, such as Beauvais just outside of Paris, are eager for business, Ryanair can negotiate airport fees as low as $1.50 per passenger, compared to $15 to $22 per passenger at Europe's major airports, like London Heathrow or Paris's Charles DeGaulle. Lower costs like these allow Ryanair to break even when its planes are half full, compared to major carriers, such as British Airways, which must fly its planes at 77 percent full to break even.[53] And with 30 more secondary airports bidding for its business, Ryanair is in the driver's seat to keep airport fees, and its costs and prices, low for years to come. Negotiating, as you can see, is a key to success and a basic part of managerial work.

### Review 4
#### Managerial Roles

Managers perform interpersonal, informational, and decisional roles in their jobs. In fulfilling the interpersonal role, managers act as figureheads by performing ceremonial duties, as leaders by motivating and encouraging workers, and as liaisons by dealing with people outside their units. In performing their informational role, managers act as monitors by scanning their environment for information, as disseminators by sharing information with others in the company, and as spokespeople by sharing information with people outside their departments or companies. In fulfilling decisional roles, managers act as entrepreneurs by adapting their units to incremental change, as disturbance handlers by responding to larger problems that demand immediate action, as resource allocators by deciding resource recipients and amounts, and as negotiators by bargaining with others about schedules, projects, goals, outcomes, and resources.

## What Does It Take to Be a Manager?

I didn't have the slightest idea what my job was. I walked in giggling and laughing because I had been promoted and had no idea what principles or style to be guided by. After the first day, I felt like I had run into a brick wall. (Sales Representative #1)

Suddenly, I found myself saying, boy, I can't be responsible for getting all that revenue. I don't have the time. Suddenly you've got to go from [taking care of] yourself and say now I'm the manager, and what does a manager do? It takes a while thinking about it for it to really hit you . . . a manager gets things done through other people. That's a very, very hard transition to make.[54] (Sales Representative #2).

The above statements were made by two star sales representatives, who, on the basis of their superior performance, were promoted to the position of sales manager. Their comments clearly indicate that at first they did not feel confident about their ability to do their jobs as managers. Like most new managers, these sales managers were suddenly faced with the realization that the knowledge, skills, and abilities that led to success early in their careers (and which were probably responsible for their promotion into the ranks of management) would not necessarily help them succeed as managers. As sales representatives, they were only responsible for managing their own performance. But as sales managers, they were now directly responsible for supervising all of the sales representatives in their sales territories. Furthermore, they were now held directly accountable for whether those sales representatives achieved their sales goals.

If performance in nonmanagerial jobs doesn't necessarily prepare you for a managerial job, then what does it take to be a manager?

*After reading these next three sections, you should be able to*
5. *explain what companies look for in managers.*
6. *discuss the top mistakes that managers make in their jobs.*
7. *describe the transition that employees go through when they are promoted to management.*

## 5. What Companies Look for in Managers

Broadly speaking, when companies look for employees who would be good managers, they look for individuals who have technical skills, human skills, conceptual skills, and the motivation to manage.[55] Exhibit 1.4 shows the relative importance of these four skills to the jobs of team leaders, first-line managers, middle managers, and top managers.

**Technical skills** are the ability to apply the specialized procedures, techniques, and knowledge required to get the job done. For the sales managers described above, technical skills are the ability to find new sales prospects, develop accurate sales pitches based

**technical skills**
the ability to apply the specialized procedures, techniques, and knowledge required to get the job done

---

EXHIBIT 1.4

RELATIVE IMPORTANCE OF MANAGERIAL SKILLS TO DIFFERENT MANAGERIAL JOBS

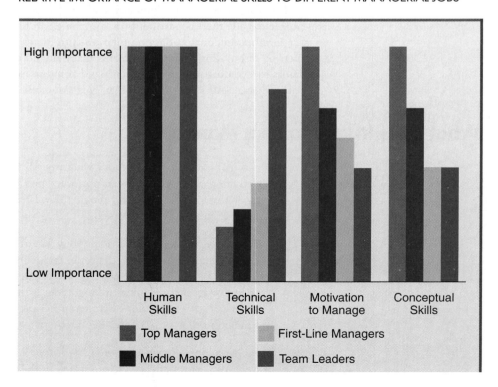

**Have You Trained Your Replacement?**

Fred Smith, CEO and founder of Federal Express, had heart bypass surgery. What made Smith's illness especially newsworthy was that FedEx had not designated a successor. If Smith had died, FedEx would have temporarily been without a CEO. But training a replacement isn't just an issue for top managers. According to Eugene Jennings, Professor Emeritus at Michigan State University, managers who haven't trained replacements will find it much harder to get promoted. So, if you want to increase your chances of getting that next promotion, begin training your replacement today.

**Source:** R. Brooks, "Companies: FedEx's CEO Undergoes Surgery for a Heart Bypass—A Vital Leader Is Expected to Resume His Duties Soon," *The Wall Street Journal*, 27 November 2000, 4.

**human skill**
the ability to work well with others

**conceptual skill**
the ability to see the organization as a whole, how the different parts affect each other, and how the company fits into or is affected by its environment

**motivation to manage**
an assessment of how enthusiastic employees are about managing the work of others

on customer needs, and close the sale. For a nurse supervisor, technical skills include being able to insert an IV or operate a "crash cart" if a patient goes into cardiac arrest.

Technical skills are most important for lower-level managers and team leaders because they supervise the workers who produce products or serve customers. Team leaders and first-line managers need technical knowledge and skills to train new employees and help employees solve problems. Technical knowledge and skills are also needed to troubleshoot problems that employees can't handle. Technical skills become less important as managers rise through the managerial ranks, but they are still important. Indeed, Bill Gates, founder and Chairman of Microsoft Corporation, which produces DOS and Windows, spends roughly 40 percent of his time dealing with the technical issues related to development of Microsoft software products.[56]

**Human skill** is the ability to work well with others. Managers with people skills work effectively within groups, encourage others to express their thoughts and feelings, are sensitive to others needs and viewpoints, and are good listeners and communicators. Human skills are equally important at all levels of management, from first-line supervisors to CEOs. However, because lower-level managers spend much of their time solving technical problems, upper-level managers may actually spend more time dealing directly with people. On average, first-line managers spend 57 percent of their time with people, middle managers spend 63 percent of their time directly with people, and top managers spend as much as 78 percent of their time dealing with people.[57]

**Conceptual skill** is the ability to see the organization as whole, how the different parts of the company affect each other, and how the company fits into or is affected by its external environment, such as the local community, social and economic forces, customers, and competition. Good managers have to be able to recognize, understand, and reconcile multiple complex problems and perspectives. In other words, managers have to be smart! In fact, intelligence makes so much difference for managerial performance that managers with above-average intelligence typically outperform managers of average intelligence by approximately 48 percent.[58] Clearly, companies need to be careful to promote smart workers into management. Conceptual skill increases in importance as managers rise through the management hierarchy.

However, there is much more to good management than intelligence. For example, making the department genius a manager can be disastrous if that genius lacks technical skills, human skills, or one other factor known as the motivation to manage. **Motivation to manage** is an assessment of how motivated employees are to interact with superiors, participate in competitive situations, behave assertively toward others, tell others what to do, reward good behavior and punish poor behavior, perform actions that are highly visible to others, and handle and organize administrative tasks. Managers typically have a stronger motivation to manage than their subordinates, and managers at higher levels usually have stronger motivation to manage than managers at lower levels. Furthermore, managers with stronger motivation to manage are promoted faster, are rated by their employees as better managers, and earn more money than managers with a weak motivation to manage.[59]

## Review 5
### What Companies Look for in Managers

Companies do not want one-dimensional managers. They want managers with a balance of skills. They want managers who know their stuff (technical skills), are equally comfortable working with blue-collar and white-collar employees (human skills), are able to assess the complexities of today's competitive marketplace and position their companies for success (conceptual skills), and want to assume positions of leadership and power (motivation to manage). Technical skills are most important for lower-level managers, human skills are equally important at all levels of management, and conceptual skills and motivation to manage increase in importance as managers rise through the managerial ranks.

## 6. Mistakes Managers Make

Another way to understand what it takes to be a manager is to look at the mistakes managers make. In other words, we can learn just as much from what managers shouldn't do as we can from what they should do. Exhibit 1.5 lists the top ten mistakes managers make.

Several studies of U.S. and British managers have compared "arrivers," or managers who made it all the way to the top of their companies, to "derailers," managers who were successful early in their careers but were knocked off the fast track by the time they reached middle to upper levels of management.[60] The first result they found was that there were few differences between arrivers and derailers. For the most part, both groups were talented and both groups had weaknesses. But what distinguished derailers from arrivers was that derailers possessed two or more "fatal flaws" with respect to the way that they managed people! By contrast, arrivers, who were by no means perfect, usually had no more than one fatal flaw, or they had found ways to minimize the effects of their flaws on the people with whom they work.

The number one mistake made by derailers was that they were insensitive to others by virtue of their abrasive, intimidating, and bullying management style. The authors of one study cited the manager who walked into his subordinate's office and interrupted a meeting by saying, "I need to see you." When the subordinate tried to explain that he wasn't available because he was in the middle of a meeting, the manager barked, "I don't give a damn. I said I wanted to see you now."[61] Not surprisingly, only 25 percent of derailers were rated by others as being good with people, compared to 75 percent of arrivers.

An intimidating management style may also have been partly responsible for Kmart's firing its former CEO, Joseph Antonini. According to *Forbes* magazine, Antonini publicly berated his senior corporate executives in front of Kmart store personnel, regularly using words like "stupid," "jerk," and "inept." He also told them they weren't worth the salary they were paid.[62] Even the U.S. Army recognizes the seriousness of managers being insensitive to others. For example, officers who have been promoted to the rank of gen-

24

EXHIBIT 1.5

### TOP TEN MISTAKES THAT MANAGERS MAKE

1. Insensitive to others: abrasive, intimidating, bullying style.
2. Cold, aloof, arrogant.
3. Betrayal of trust.
4. Overly ambitious: thinking of next job, playing politics.
5. Specific performance problems with the business.
6. Overmanaging: unable to delegate or build a team.
7. Unable to staff effectively.
8. Unable to think strategically.
9. Unable to adapt to boss with different style.
10. Overdependent on advocate or mentor.

**Source:** M.W. McCall, Jr. & M.M. Lombardo, "What Makes a Top Executive?" *Psychology Today,* February 1983, 26-31.

Not being able to build a team is a fatal management mistake. At Levi-Strauss, managers on the diversity council, pictured here, work as a team to ensure the company has a diverse employee base. Levi's diversity managers take care to build strong teams and avoid making a fatal management mistake.

eral are officially sent to the Brigadier General Training Conference. Informally, however, the Army calls this "charm school." The basic goal of this training is simple: to encourage new generals to get in touch with and lose their "inner jerk." Says Lt. Col. Howard Olsen, who runs the training, "Each and every one of you has something that makes you a jerk. Some of you have more than one. I know. I've talked to you."[63]

The second mistake was that derailers were often cold, aloof, or arrogant. While this sounds like insensitivity to others, this has more to do with derailed managers being so smart, so expert in their areas of knowledge, that they treated others with contempt because they weren't experts, too. For example, the Ameritech phone company called in an industrial psychologist to counsel its vice president of human resources because she had "been blamed for ruffling too many feathers at the regional telephone company."[64] Interviews with the vice president's coworkers and subordinates revealed that everyone thought she was brilliant, that she was "smarter and faster than other people," that she "generates a lot of ideas," and that she "loves to deal with complex issues." Unfortunately, these smarts were accompanied by a cold, aloof, and arrogant management style. The people she worked with complained that she did "too much too fast," that she treats co-workers with "disdain," that she "impairs teamwork," that she "doesn't always show her warm side," and that she has "burned too many bridges."

The third and fourth mistakes made by derailers, betraying a trust and being overly ambitious, indicate a lack of concern for coworkers and subordinates. Betraying a trust doesn't mean being dishonest. Instead, it means making others look bad by not doing what you said you would do when you said you would do it. That mistake, in itself, is not fatal, because managers and their workers aren't machines. Tasks go undone in every company every single business day. There's always too much to do and not enough time, people, money, or resources to do it. The fatal betrayal of trust is failing to inform others when things would not be done on time. This failure to admit mistakes, to quickly inform others of the mistakes, to take responsibility for the mistakes, and then to fix the mistakes without blaming others clearly distinguished the behavior of derailers from arrivers.

The fourth mistake, mentioned above, was being overly political and ambitious. Managers who always have their eye on their next job rarely do more than establish superficial relationships with peers and coworkers. In their haste to gain credit for successes that would be noticed by upper management, they make the fatal mistake of treating people like they don't matter.

The fatal mistakes of being unable to delegate, to build a team, and to staff effectively indicate that many derailed managers were unable to make the most basic transition to managerial work: to quit being hands-on doers and get work done through others. Two things go wrong when managers make these mistakes. First, when managers meddle in decisions that their subordinates should be making, when they can't quit being doers, they alienate the people who work for them. Second, because they are trying to do their subordinates' jobs in addition to their own, managers who fail to delegate to their workers will not have enough time to do much of anything well. For example, before becoming president of Harvard University, Neil Rudenstine's management style had always been to take on more and more work himself. So when he became a university president and the demands placed on him increased, he responded by working even longer hours, usually 12 to 14 hours a day. For example, on the day before Thanksgiving, normally a quiet day on college campuses as students travel home to be with their families, Dr. Rudenstine began his day with an 8 A.M. meeting with several deans, had lunch with visiting Russian dignitaries, attended a faculty meeting, and finished his day with a dormitory dinner and reception for students. He got home at 8:30 P.M., more than 12 hours after the start of his day. While it is the norm for university presidents to put in long hours, Dr. Rudenstine made it even tougher on himself by failing to delegate work to his associates. Figuring out how to solve the shortage of parking spaces on campus or arranging to have contractors fix leaky roofs are not good uses of a university president's time. Indeed, the combination of long hours and his inability to delegate led to mental and physical exhaustion and a physician-mandated leave of absence from his job as Harvard University president.[65]

### Review 6
### Mistakes Managers Make

Another way to understand what it takes to be a manager is to look at the top mistakes managers make. Five of the most important mistakes made by managers are being abrasive and intimidating; being cold, aloof, or arrogant; betraying trust; being overly ambitious; and failing to build a team and then delegate to that team.

## 7. The Transition to Management: The First Year

In her book *Becoming a Manager: Master of a New Identity*, Harvard Business School professor Linda Hill followed the development of 19 people in their first year as managers. Two overall themes emerged from Dr. Hill's study. First, becoming a manager produced a profound psychological transition that changed the way these managers viewed themselves and others. Second, the only way to really learn how to manage was to be a manager. As shown in Exhibit 1.6, a good way to appreciate the magnitude of the changes these managers experienced is to describe their thoughts, expectations, and realities as they evolved over the course of their first year in management.

Initially, the managers in Hill's study believed that their job was to exercise formal authority and to manage tasks—basically being the boss, telling others what to do, making decisions, and getting things done. One manager said, "Being the manager means running my own office, using my ideas and thoughts." Another said, "It's [the office] my baby. It's my job to make sure it works." In fact, most of the new managers were attracted to management positions because they wanted to be "in charge." Surprisingly, the new managers did not believe that their job was to manage people. The only two aspects of people management mentioned by the new managers were hiring and firing.

After six months, most of the new managers had come to the conclusion that their initial expectations about managerial work were wrong. Management wasn't being "the boss." It wasn't just about making decisions and telling others what to do. The first surprise to the new managers was the fast pace and heavy workload involved in being a manager. One manager stated, "This job is much harder than you think. It is 40 to 50

**Find Someone To Talk To**

Management is inherently stressful, and managers need to be able to talk to someone about those stresses. Because of their positions and power, many managers find it difficult to confide in company insiders. Consequently, managers are likely to form close, long-lasting relationships with consultants. Likewise, by becoming members of organizations such as the Young President's Organization or The Executive Committee, top managers get honest, unbiased advice by regularly meeting with 12 to 16 top managers (from other companies and industries) where they live. When you become the boss (or if you already are), find someone to talk to about your job. It helps.

**Source:** M. Lefko, "It's Lonely at the Top—Who Do You Turn To? (Chief Executive Officers, Management Techniques and Analysis)," *Los Angeles Business Journal*, 28 May 2001, 48.

percent more work than being a producer! Who would have ever guessed?" The pace of managerial work was startling, too. Another manager said, "You have eight or nine people looking for your time . . . coming into and out of your office all day long." A somewhat frustrated manager declared that management was "a job that never ended," "a job you couldn't get your hands around."

Informal descriptions like this are consistent with studies that indicate that the average first-line manager spends no more than two minutes on a task before being interrupted by a request from a subordinate, a phone call, or an email. The pace is somewhat less hurried for top managers, who spend an average of approximately nine minutes on a task before having to switch to another. In practice, this means that supervisors may perform 30 different tasks per hour, while top managers perform seven different task per hour, with each task typically different from the one that preceded it. A manager described this frenetic level of activity by saying, "The only time you are in control is when you shut your door, and then I feel I am not doing the job I'm supposed to be doing, which is being with the people."

The other major surprise after six months on the job was that the managers' expectations about what they should do as managers were very different from their subordinates' expectations. Initially, the managers defined their jobs as helping their subordinates perform their jobs well. For the managers, who still defined themselves as doers rather than managers, assisting their subordinates meant going out on sales calls or handling customer complaints. One manager said, "I like going out with the rep, who may need me to lend him my credibility as manager. I like the challenge, the joy in closing. I go out with the reps and we make the call and talk about the customer; it's fun." But when the managers "assisted" in this way, their subordinates were resentful and viewed their help as interference. What the subordinates wanted in the way of assistance was for their managers to solve problems that they couldn't solve. Once the managers realized this contradiction, they embraced their role as problem-solver and troubleshooter. Thus, they could help without interfering with their subordinates' jobs.

After a year on the job, most of the managers no longer thought of themselves as doers, but managers. In making the transition, they finally realized that people management was the most important part of their jobs. One manager summarized the lesson that had taken him a year to learn by saying, "As many demands as managers have on their time, I think their primary responsibility is people development. Not production,

---

**EXHIBIT 1.6**

THE TRANSITION TO MANAGEMENT: INITIAL EXPECTATIONS, AFTER SIX MONTHS, AND AFTER A YEAR

| MANAGERS' INITIAL EXPECTATIONS | AFTER SIX MONTHS AS A MANAGER | AFTER A YEAR AS A MANAGER |
|---|---|---|
| • Be the boss | • Initial expectations were wrong | • No longer "doers" |
| • Formal authority | • Fast pace | • Communication, listening, & positive reinforcement |
| • Manage tasks | • Heavy workload | • Job is people development |
| • Job is not managing people | • Job is to be problem-solver and troubleshooter for subordinates | |

**Source:** L.A. Hill, *Becoming a Manager: Mastery of a New Identity* (Boston, MA: Harvard Business School Press, 1992).

# BeenThereDoneThat

## Travis Reynolds, A Brand New Manager

**Travis Reynolds, 24, is a first-level manager for a financial services company offering insurance, 401Ks, retirement planning, and mutual funds to its customers. Travis has been a manager for nine months.**

**Q:** What responsibilities do you have in your job?

**A:** My job is supervision, training, and running the office (expenses and personnel). I'm also in charge of how the office and sales associates use technology. I recruit new sales associates and spend a lot of time with them while they're still learning the job. I help them with their daily activities, such as seeing potential customers, preparing for sales calls, calling for appointments, and doing insurance and financial applications correctly. I assist them whenever they need help, explaining new products and sometimes going out on sales calls with them.

**Q:** What was your first month as a manager like?

**A:** (He laughs.) High stress! I set very high expectations for myself. Being a numbers-oriented person (Travis has a degree in Finance), I was very frustrated. I was looking at and trying to make decisions by the numbers, and that doesn't work well when you're dealing with people.

**Q:** In retrospect, do you know now what you were doing wrong?

**A:** I didn't look at individual situations. I have a great manager who empowers me, but I wasn't empowering the associates who work for me. I came down on them like a steel hammer because they weren't meeting their numbers. I was very autocratic. There was a lot of conflict between the associates and me the first couple of months because of my management style. In fact, it was so bad that on my first day, during the morning sales meeting, one of the associates got up and left because he was so upset with the tough way in which I was running the meeting. It took me a long time to mend fences.

**Q:** Did you ever think about quitting?

**A:** No. I eventually learned a new system of managing. My senior managers advised me on ways to empower rather than being autocratic. They taught me how to be more people-oriented without losing track of the results and numbers that my department has to produce. You don't have to give up one for the other.

**Q:** What prompted you to change?

**A:** (He laughs again.) Well, that associate leaving my first meeting was a sign, wasn't it? It didn't happen immediately, though. It was still pretty rough around the office for several more months. In terms of dealing with people, I guess I had to learn the hard way. New associates were literally running away from me. The group would disburse when I came into the break room for some coffee. But even more serious than that, I noticed that they weren't coming to me for help. And you can't identify and solve problems unless your people bring them to you.

**Q:** Any idea why you were so tough on them and yourself at first?

**A:** I was trying to establish a difference between myself and the previous manager, who was very positive with the associates. As soon as I got the title, I felt like I had to prove my worth. Sales people are entrepreneurial. They come into this line of work to be their own boss. So when I played the role of the tough, controlling supervisor, I contradicted everything that attracted them to the job and our company. It's funny. I still have an email from one of my bosses that said "Now that you've been promoted, don't get a big head." I still reread that occasionally to remind myself that the agents are my customers. I realize now that my job is to help them make sales.

**Q:** Would you recommend a management job to others?

**A:** Yes. I love it! I like interacting with people. I like watching them be successful. I can't take credit for it, but I like to see them be successful, especially when they turn it around. For example, I had an agent in my office two days ago who was making the very basic mistake of not setting up enough appointments. It was an issue of time management. In this job, we say that you have to dial 40 times to reach 15 prospects to set up 6 appointments. So I coached him on time management and phone-calling skills. The next day, he made 52 calls, reached 18 prospects, and set up appointments with 9. That made me extremely happy. It was a baby step, but it was important. Going from one appointment a day to nine is a huge difference.

but people development." Another indication of how much their views had changed was that most of the managers now regretted the rather heavy-handed approach they had used in their early attempts to manage their subordinates. "I wasn't good at managing . . . , so I was bossy like a first-grade teacher." "Now I see that I started out as a drill sergeant. I was inflexible, just a lot of how-to's." By the end of the year, most of the managers had abandoned their authoritarian approach for one based on communication, listening, and positive reinforcement. One manager explained, "Last night at five I handed out an award in the board-room just to the individual. It was the first time in his career that he had done [earned] $100,000, and I gave him a piece of glass [a small award] and said I'd heard a rumor that somebody here just crossed over $100,000 and I said congratulations, shook his hand, and walked away. It was not public in the sense that I gathered everybody around. But I knew and he did too."

Finally, after beginning their year as managers in frustration, the managers came to feel comfortable with their subordinates, with the demands of their jobs, and with their emerging managerial styles. While being managers had made them acutely aware of their limitations and their need to develop as people, it also provided them with an unexpected reward of the thrill of coaching and developing the people who worked for them. One manager said, "It gives me the best feeling to see somebody do something well after I have helped them. I get excited." Another stated, "I realize now that when I accepted the position of branch manager that it is truly an exciting vocation. It is truly awesome, even at this level; it can be terribly challenging and terribly exciting."

### Review 7
### The Transition to Management: The First Year

Managers often begin their jobs by using more formal authority and less people management. However, most managers find that being a manager has little to do with "bossing" their subordinates. After six months on the job, the managers were surprised at the fast pace, the heavy workload, and that "helping" their subordinates was viewed as interference. After a year on the job, most of the managers no longer thought of themselves as doers, but managers who get things done through others. And, because they finally realized that people management was the most important part of their job, most of them had abandoned their authoritarian approach for one based on communication, listening, and positive reinforcement.

## Why Management Matters

If you walk down the aisle of the business section in your local bookstore, you'll find hundreds of books that explain precisely what companies need to do to be successful. Unfortunately, business books tend to be faddish, changing every few years. Lately, the best-selling business books have emphasized technology, reengineering, and going global, whereas 10 years ago the hot topics were joint ventures, mergers, and management buyouts. One thing that hasn't changed, though, is the importance of good people and good management: Companies can't succeed for long without them.

*After reading this section, you should be able to*

8. *explain how and why companies can create competitive advantage through people.*

## 8. Competitive Advantage Through People

Let's pretend that it's 20 years ago and you just inherited $5,000. However, you can't spend the money. The will stipulates that you have to invest the money in the stock market and that you can't touch the stocks, win or lose, for 20 years. After that time, you can cash in your stocks and do what you want. If you had been really smart, or really lucky, you would have taken your $5,000, split it up, and invested $1000 in five companies: Plenum Publishing, Circuit City, Tyson Foods, Wal-Mart, and Southwest Airlines. If you had done that, your $1,000 investments would have grown to $156,890; $164,100; $181,180; $198,070; and $217,750; respectively, after 20 years. Your initial $5,000 investment would be worth a total of $917,990.00, for a spectacular return on investment of 18,359.80 percent.[66] In fact, no other combination of companies could produce as large a return, because these companies were the five top-performing companies in American business over the last two decades.

Naturally, you might wonder how these companies achieved their phenomenal success. Did they invent a new technology in a fast-growth business, did they have few competitors, or were they just lucky? Well, none is a high-technology company. Plenum is an old-fashioned book publisher. Circuit City sounds high-tech, but is just a retailer that happens to sell electronics and computers. Tyson Foods raises and sells chickens. Wal-Mart is a discount retail chain. And Southwest Airlines is a no-frills, low-cost airline. Also, each of these companies achieved their success in highly competitive industries, which, by definition, are supposed to lower company profits, because companies have to either lower prices (and thus profits) or invest huge amounts of money in product innovation just to keep the customers they have.[67] So each of these companies should have found it enormously difficult to make above-average profits. Nonetheless, they did. Why? Because they effectively managed their people.

In his books, *Competitive Advantage Through People* and *The Human Equation: Building Profits by Putting People First*, Stanford University business professor Jeffrey Pfeffer contends that what separated these companies from their competitors and made them top performers was the way they treated their work forces, in other words, management.[68] Managers in these companies used ideas like employment security, selective hiring, self-managed teams and decentralization, high pay contingent on company performance, extensive training, reduced status distinctions (between managers and employees), and extensive sharing of financial information to achieve financial performance that, on average, was 40 percent higher than other companies. These ideas, which are explained in detail in Exhibit 1.7, help organizations develop work forces that are smarter, better trained, more motivated, and more committed than their competitors' work forces. And, as indicated by the phenomenal growth and return on investment

---

| EXHIBIT 1.7 | |
|---|---|
| | COMPETITIVE ADVANTAGE THROUGH PEOPLE: MANAGEMENT PRACTICES |

1. **Employment Security**—Employment security is the ultimate form of commitment that companies can make to their workers. Employees can innovate and increase company productivity without fearing the loss of their jobs.

2. **Selective Hiring**—If employees are the basis for a company's competitive advantage, and those employees have employment security, then the company needs to aggressively recruit and selectively screen applicants in order to hire the most talented employees available.

3. **Self-Managed Teams and Decentralization**—Self-managed teams are responsible for their own hiring, purchasing, job assignments, and production. Self-managed teams can often produce enormous increases in productivity through increased employee commitment and creativity. Decentralization allows employees who are closest to (and most knowledgeable about) problems, production, and customers to make timely decisions. Decentralization increases employee satisfaction and commitment.

4. **High Wages Contingent on Organizational Performance**—High wages are needed to attract and retain talented workers and to indicate that the organization values its workers. Employees, like company founders, shareholders, and managers, need to share in the financial rewards when the company is successful. Why? Because employees who have a financial stake in their companies are more likely to take a long-run view of the business and think like business owners.

5. **Training and Skill Development**—Like a high-tech company that spends millions of dollars to upgrade computers or research and development labs, a company whose competitive advantage is based on its people must invest in the training and skill development of its people.

6. **Reduction of Status Differences**—These are fancy words that indicate that the company treats everyone, no matter what their job, as equals. There are no reserved parking spaces. Everyone eats in the same cafeteria and has similar benefits. The result: Much improved communication as employees focus on problems and solutions rather than how they are less valued than managers.

7. **Sharing Information**—If employees are to make decisions that are good for the long-run health and success of the company, they need to be given information about costs, finances, productivity, development times, and strategies that were previously known only by company managers.

---

**Source:** J. Pfeffer, *The Human Equation: Building Profits by Putting People First* (Boston, MA: Harvard Business School Press, 1996).

earned by these companies, smarter, better trained, and more committed work forces provide superior products and service to customers, who keep buying and who, by telling others about their positive experiences, bring in new customers.

Pfeffer also argues that companies that invest in their people will create long-lasting competitive advantages that are difficult for other companies to duplicate. Indeed, studies clearly demonstrate that sound management practices can produce substantial advantages in three critical areas of organizational performance: sales revenues, profits, and customer satisfaction. For example, a study of nearly 1,000 U.S. firms indicated that companies that use *just some* of the ideas shown in Exhibit 1.7 had $27,044 more sales per employee and $3,814 more profit per employee than companies that didn't.[69] For a 100-person company, these differences amount to $2.7 million more in sales and nearly $400,000 more in annual profit! For a 1,000-person company, the difference grows to $27 million more in sales and $4 million more in annual profit!

Another study found that poorly performing companies that adopted management techniques as simple as setting expectations (setting goals, results, and schedules) coaching (informal, ongoing discussions between managers and subordinates about what is being done well and what could be done better), reviewing (annual, formal discussion about results), and rewarding (adjusting salaries and bonuses based on employee performance and results) were able to improve average return on investment from 5.1 percent to 19.7 percent and increase sales by $94,000 per employee![70] So, in addition to significantly improving the profitability of healthy companies, sound management practices can turn around failing companies.

Research also indicates that managers have an important effect on customer satisfaction. However, many people find this surprising. They don't understand how managers, who are largely responsible for what goes on inside the company, can affect what goes on outside the company. They wonder how managers, who often interact with customers under negative conditions (when customers are angry or dissatisfied), can actually improve customer satisfaction. It turns out that managers influence customer satisfaction through employee satisfaction. When employees are satisfied with their jobs, their bosses, and the companies they work for, they provide much better service to customers.[71] In turn, customers are more satisfied, too.

## Review 8
### Competitive Advantage through People

Why does management matter? Well-managed companies are competitive because their work forces are smarter, better trained, more motivated, and more committed. Furthermore, companies that practice good management consistently have greater revenues and profits than companies that don't. Finally, good management matters because good management leads to satisfied employees who, in turn, provide better service to customers. Because employees tend to treat customers the same way that their managers treat them, good management can improve customer satisfaction.

## What Really Happened?

In the opening case, you learned that NextJump founder Charlie Kim was having trouble with the basic issues discussed in this chapter. What is management? What do managers do? And, what does it take to be a manager? Find out what really happened as Charlie Kim and NextJump addressed these issues and tried to turn the company around.

### What are my primary responsibilities as a top manager? Does that include keeping workers happy and comfortable?

In good times or bad, top managers are responsible for the overall direction and performance of their companies. Indeed, Charlie Kim was the person who raised funding from investors to grow NextJump from 30 to 105 employees so it could expand into New York, Boston, San Francisco, and Washington. Likewise, when things began to go wrong at NextJump, Charlie Kim was responsible for finding a way to set them right (see below). Are top managers also responsible for keeping workers happy and comfortable? Without a doubt, they are. More specifically, top managers are responsible for developing attitudes of commitment and ownership and for creating a positive organizational culture through words and actions. Charlie Kim felt that he was meeting this responsibility by hiring friends and encouraging employees to leave the office by 6:30 P.M. so that they could spend time with their families. However, top managers are also responsible for encouraging managers and employees to quickly recognize and embrace the need for change. Unfortunately, as we learned, under Charlie's leadership, NextJump's employees were more concerned about griping and getting to the gym during business hours.

### Making the transition from employee to manager has been one of the most stressful in my life. Are my experiences unique? What mistakes do managers typically make?

Another way to understand what it takes to be a manager is to look at the mistakes managers make. In other words, we can learn just as much from what managers shouldn't do as we can from what they should. Five of the most important mistakes made by managers are being abrasive and intimidating; being cold, aloof, or arrogant; betraying trust; being overly ambitious; and failing to build a team and then delegate to that team. While no one would describe Charlie Kim as abrasive or intimidating, he became increasingly separated (i.e., cold and aloof) from the people who worked for him. As one employee stated, "I had to ride up in the elevator with Charlie the other day. It was so awkward. We had nothing to say to each other." And, while this wasn't his intention, Charlie betrayed his workers' trust by unexpectedly firing 12 employees (roughly 10 percent of the company) in one afternoon. This single act was also contrary to his personal beliefs and reasons for starting the company, to create a fair and reasonable work place that permitted employees to succeed on the job and at home. This doesn't mean that managers should never fire employees. But it does mean that managers need to consider how their actions will affect the organization's employees. Remember, good management leads to satisfied employees who, in turn, provide better service to customers. Because employees tend to treat customers the same way that their managers treat them, good management can improve customer satisfaction. Conversely, when managers proclaim one thing (a worker friendly workplace) and then do another (unexpectedly fire 10 percent of their work force in one afternoon), they can expect unhappy employees whose dissatisfaction will, in turn, negatively affect how employees do their jobs and how the company performs. Not surprisingly, Charlie's decision to fire 12 workers at once prevented him from forming a successful team, which is the fifth mistake that managers make.

### Finally, what does it takes to be a manager and have I got that?

Companies want managers with a balance of skills. They want managers who know their stuff (technical skills), are equally comfortable working with all kinds of people (human skills), are able to position their companies for success in today's competitive marketplaces (conceptual skills), and want to take charge (motivation to manage). In retrospect, Charlie Kim had the technical skills and conceptual skills to form NextJump, to help it create its first products, and to convince investors to put millions of dollars into the company. However, by his own admission, he was reluctant to take charge and lacked the people skills needed to run the company. Therefore, he hired 58-year old Richard Pregiato to replace himself as CEO. While Pregiato had no technical experience himself (but, as a CEO, this didn't matter, because technical skills become less important at higher levels), he did have what NextJump needed in a CEO, 30 years of management experience in banking and technology companies. What were Pregiato's first impressions? He said, "It was very clear: the place needed a plan. There were people who needed a large degree of management, a large degree of guidance." And, "Charlie really needed a buddy at that time." Pregiato's solutions were straight out of Management 101. First, have each manager write detailed plans for their units, with clear goals and specific measures to track their progress. Second, add middle managers to coordinate and link different parts of the company and implement the changes or strategies generated by top management. Griping and out-of-control meetings were soon a thing of the past. Third, build a relationship with Charlie Kim. Kim and Pregiato drove together to frequent meetings between New York and Boston, and even began working out together (after work). Said Kim, "He's in his grandpa shorts lifting his little weights. We're talking the whole time." Fourth, employees were no longer allowed to work out or receive massages on company time. In short, by recognizing his own limitations, firing himself, and then hiring Pregiato as CEO, Charlie Kim ultimately came to recognize what it takes to be a manager.

**Sources:** P. Kruger, "Stop the Insanity! A New Generation of Dotcom Entrepreneurs are Creat-ing Companies that Work—Without Expecting People to Spend Every Waking Moment at Work. Here's How to Build a Saner Startup," *Fast Company*, 1 July 2000, 240. R. Silverman, "For Charlie Kim, Company of Friends Proves a Lonely Place—A Dot-Com Founder Brought In Buddies and Colleagues; All Was Fine—on the Way Up," *The Wall Street Journal*, 1 February 2001, A1.

K

conce
contro
dissem
disturb
effectiv
efficien
entrepr
figureh
first-lin

negotiator role *(21)*
organizing *(5)*
planning *(5)*
resource allocator role *(20)*
spokesperson role *(19)*
team leaders *(15)*
technical skills *(22)*
top managers *(12)*

W

**Promoti**
What a j
vacation
It seems
adise, yo
what you
the tempt
signal to y
been emp
was recent
cause of h
ment. Bef
that he co

Unfort
Joe appear
expresses h
to discuss t
subordinate
tary claims that Joe was a mini "Hitler" while you were gone. During your absence, several impromptu decisions had to be made and from Joe's comments, he seems to have handled them accordingly. As you listen, you tell yourself that you probably

o the same conclusions, but, then, you are
have encountered similar decisions
ty-six years as a manager with the firm.
briefing you, you do your best to reassure
well during your absence; however, he is
ith the decisions that he made. In fact, as
nore information, he tells you that he
n charge again. He wonders if you made
n the promotion and asks you to recon-
ur assistant. Even though it has been
s promotion, you still haven't hired a full-
e him. Joe informs you that he would be
mer job and encourages you to name a
e assistant manager position. What can
ety? How can you help him understand
ear and work to overcome it? **If you**
t would you do?**

**Source:** A. Fisher, "From Stud to Dud—In Just One Promotion," *Fortune*, 2 April 2000.

MEMO // VCR
Feb //

5800 CAMP BOWIE
SUITE M
FORT WORTH, TX 76107
(817) 738-6531 PHONE
(817) 738-6045 FAX

**QuikPrinT** sm
QUALITY PRINTING & COPYING

## Management Decisions

### "Can I have tomorrow night off?"

It's 4:00 P.M. as you begin your last inspection of the production area. Only two hours until you go home, eat your dinner, relax, and spend some much-needed time with your family. As you finish your rounds, you notice an employee is sitting in your office. As you get closer, you see that it is Frank, an operator on the evening shift. Frank greets you as you walk in your office and the two of you make small talk about the previous night's production run. Frank informs you that his son's Little-League baseball team has made it to the playoffs for the state championship and he wants to take tomorrow night off to watch this important game. As you listen, you remember attending your own son's games and know how important this game is to both Frank and his son, after all, this opportunity may never occur again. However, as a just-in-time supplier to a local manufacturing facility, you also know that tomorrow's production run has to be completed. The best person to take Frank's position is Bobby, who is on vacation for the next five days. In Bobby's absence, three of your operators are helping out by alternating a double shift. Allowing Frank to take off without a replacement would seriously hamper the other four evening shift operators and would jeopardize the entire night's production cycle. As a first-line supervisor, making decisions such as this is your least favorite aspect of the job. On one hand you empathize with Frank and want to be flexible to his needs, yet on the other, you have to uphold your duty to fulfill the nightly production quota.

#### Questions

1. Would you let Frank have the night off? Why or Why not?
2. As a manager in this situation, what other options might you consider before making your decision?

**Source:** Sue Shellenbarger, "Work & Family: Push for Flexibility Puts Special Pressure On Factory Managers," *The Wall Street Journal,* 9 May, 2001.

## Management Decisions

### Eeny Meeny Miny Mo . . .

You are the regional director of research and development for a mid-sized chemical company. This morning, two project directors called to schedule appointments to see you concerning a memo your office released yesterday informing all staff members of budget cuts for the new fiscal year. Because of factors beyond the company's control—a slowing economy, declining sales, lowered earnings projections, and so forth, company officials have mandated an across-the-board cost reduction of 15 percent in all departments. Unfortunately, this reduction will affect your department the most since research and development costs have averaged 23 percent of the company's total expenditures over the last five years. Despite the fact that every dollar invested in chemical research today will yield two dollars of operating income over six years, only one of the two lead projects your department is working on will be fully-funded under the new budget. Both project directors will be campaigning for their specific project, and it will be your decision to choose which one receives full funding and which one does not. As you check your daily calendar for possible meeting times, you recall that both projects are equally viable and are expected to require approximately the same amount of money and resources. In meeting with each project director individually, however, you will need to gather specific information in order to make an unbiased, informed decision.

#### Questions

1. Assuming the role of disseminator, write the script for the part of the meeting that you tell your project directors you can only fund one project.
2. Assuming the role of resource allocator, what questions will you likely ask to help you make your decision?

**Source:** N. Gross, "Measuring the Muscle of R&D Spending," *Business Week,* 11 June 2001.

# Develop Your Managerial Potential

### Interview Two Managers

Welcome to the first "Develop Your Managerial Potential" activity! These assignments have one purpose: To help you develop your present and future capabilities as a manager. What you will be learning through these assignments is not traditional "book-learning" based on memorization and regurgitation, but practical knowledge and skills that help managers perform their jobs better. Lessons from some of the assignments—for example, goal setting—can be used for immediate benefit. Other lessons will obviously take time to accomplish, but you can still benefit now by making specific plans for future improvement.

### Step 1: Interview Two Practicing Managers

In her book *Becoming a Manager: Master of a New Identity*, Harvard Business School professor Linda Hill conducted extensive interviews with 19 people in their first year as managers. To learn firsthand what it's like to be a manager, interview two managers that you know, asking them some of the same questions, shown below, that Professor Hill asked her managers. Be sure to interview managers with different levels of experience. Interview one person with at least five years' experience as a manager and then interview another person with no more than two years' experience as a manager. Ask the managers these questions:

1. Briefly describe your current position and responsibilities.
2. What do your subordinates expect from you on the job?
3. What are the major stresses and challenges you face on job?
4. What, if anything, do you dislike about the job?
5. What do you like best about your job?
6. What are the critical differences between average managers and top-performing managers?
7. Think about the skills and knowledge that you need to be effective in your job. What are they and how did you acquire them?
8. What have been your biggest mistakes thus far? Could you have avoided them? If so, how?

### Step 2: Prepare to Discuss Your Findings

Prepare to discuss your findings in class or write a report (if assigned by your instructor). What conclusions can you draw from your interview data?

**Source:** L.A. Hill, *Becoming a Manager: Mastery of a New Identity* (Boston, MA: Harvard Business School Press, 1992).

# Study Tip

Use your textbook more like a notebook and less like a reference book. The margins are a great place for writing questions on content you don't understand, highlighting important concepts, and adding examples to help you remember the material. Writing in your book makes it a more comprehensive resource for management and a better study tool.

**CHAPTER**  2

# Organizational Environments & Cultures

## What Would You Do?

**Luton Airport, North of London, England.** Starting your own airline seems like a great idea. British billionaire Richard Branson built Virgin Atlantic Airways from nothing into a great success in less than a decade. You think to yourself, "He looks like he's having fun. Why not?" Then, on a trip to Boeing, the U.S. passenger jet manufacturer, someone suggests that you look at Southwest Airlines, which runs the lowest cost, yet most profitable airline in U.S. history. After taking a Southwest flight, you know that their business model (use only one plane, the 737, to simplify maintenance and pilot and flight attendant training and certification; ensure quick turnarounds at the gate to keep planes full and in the air; take most of your reservations on the Internet to reduce costs; fly out of smaller, underused airports with much lower landing fees; maintain a fun culture that treats employees and customers right) will work in Europe. The dominant airlines, including British Airways, Lufthansa, Air France, and others, are heavily subsidized by their governments, face little competition, and are inefficient. You know that you will be able to undercut their prices and still make a significant profit!

So you start EasyJet by leasing two Boeing 737s that fly from Glasgow and Edinburgh in Scotland to London's Luton airport, the smallest of London's four airports and 32 miles (roughly 50 minutes) north of central London. With prices half that of the major carriers, customers race to fly your planes. Within three years, EasyJet is flying 28 routes to 18 different cities. However, you aren't the only one with this great idea. Dublin-based RyanAir; Portugal's PGA; U.K.-based British Midland, Debonair, and AirOne; and Richard Branson's Virgin Express are also trying to establish themselves as low-cost airlines in Europe.

The biggest threat, though, now comes from the largest airline in Europe, British Airways (BA). BA became a direct competitor by starting its own low-cost airline, Go, based out of London's Stansted airport. But it just wasn't BA, with its huge financial resources, entering the game, it was they way they did it. BA's CEO invited you to tea, ostensibly to discuss the possibility of investing in your company. You were flattered, opened up your books to show them the numbers, and let BA closely examine every single part of the company. But it was just a trick. BA didn't want to invest in EasyJet. It wanted to put you out of business. And with Go's initial success, £40 million ($60 million) in revenue and 700,000 passengers in its first year alone, you should be worried. Go's managing director said, "I underestimated the huge potential."

With start-up costs, intense competition, and rising fuel prices, you lose £5 million (about $7.5 million) the first year. As if this weren't enough, London's Luton airport, which is owned and run for profit by Barclays Bank, tries to raise its landing fees from £1.80 ($2.70) to £7.50 ($11.25) per passenger. With 65 percent of your passengers flying through Luton airport, this increased cost will make it much more difficult to make a profit and keep prices low. And, at this point, you haven't been able to convince the Civil Aviation Authority to regulate these charges (airports are privatized and deregulated in Britain). The best you can do is dig in your heals and stall. You told the newspapers, "We were not willing to be dragged into negotiations with a gun against our heads, which is what Barclays was hoping for."

So the question is "Will you make it?" The odds are stacked against you. In the United States, 130 airlines have gone out of business in the last 25 years, most of them new start-ups like EasyJet. The same forces that brought them down could bring EasyJet down too. You know that Southwest Airline's low-cost model worked in the United States, but can it work in Europe when so many other air carriers are following the same model? So what do you do about the competition? Also, is there anything you can do to influence the cost of landing fees at Luton airport? If EasyJet continues to grow, dealing with airport authorities will become increasingly important. For example, Swissair used its political and financial leverage to try to prevent you from flying between Geneva, Switzerland, and Barcelona, Spain. So how do you deal with potentially uncontrollable industry regulators and gatekeepers? Finally, how do you make sense of all this? Your initial business plan was sound and recognized the fantastic opportunities for low-cost airlines in Europe. But now those opportunities seem to be overwhelmed by a growing number of threats.

**If you were the founder and CEO of EasyJet airlines, what would you do?**

**Sources:** D. Appell, "The EasyEmpire Strikes Back: Throwing Down the Gauntlet to Europe's Old-Guard Airlines, the Young Greek Entrepreneur Who Birthed Easyjet Airlines and Easyrentacar Has Been Shaking Up the Continent's Budget Travel Market," *Arthur Frommer's Budget Travel.* [Online] Available http://www. msnbc.com/news/587392.asp?0dm=C29JL, 22 June 2001. M. Harrison, "Easythis, Easythat, Easyfloat: At Least, That's How Stelios Haji-Ioannou (That's Stelios to You) Would Like to See the Stock Market Debut of EasyJet, the Cut-Price Airline He Has Shouldered into the Big Time. But Will It Be that Simple?" *The Independent—London,* 11 October 2000, 1B. K. Kemp, "Airlines Net Sky-High Results," *The Sunday Herald,* 11 June 1999, 16. Wysocki, Jr., "The Challengers—Headwinds: The Odds Are Against Starting an Airline—And Still They Try—With Tenacity and Little Else, These Two Men Took on Majors' Entrenched System— Getting Past `The Sniff Test'," *The Wall Street Journal,* 16 April 2001, A1.

Starting a new airline is incredibly difficult. Wherever you look, you see changes and forces beyond your control that threaten your ability to make your new business a success. This chapter examines the internal and external forces that affect companies. We begin by explaining how the changes in external organizational environments affect companies. Next, we examine the two kinds of external organizational environments: the general environment that affects all organizations and the specific environment unique to each company. Then, we learn how managers make sense of their changing general and specific environments. The chapter finishes with a discussion of internal organizational environments by focusing on organizational culture.

## External Environments

**external environments**
all events outside a company that have the potential to influence or affect it

**External environments** are the forces and events outside a company that have the potential to influence or affect it. For instance, despite consumer objections, the German government actually ordered Wal-Mart's German stores (i.e., Wertkauf-Mann) to do something it wouldn't normally do: raise prices. Claudia Haemel, who lives in Frankfurt and was surprised by this, said, "I have nothing against these [lower] prices if it makes basic foods cheaper for the consumer." She also said that large grocery store chains, like the Tengelmann Group, that Wal-Mart competes with in Germany, "are big enough. They should protect themselves." So, if consumers didn't object, why did the German government insist that Wal-Mart raise its prices? The sole reason is that it is against German law to sell products below cost. This law is supposed to prevent larger companies like Wal-Mart from taking advantage of smaller companies that would be unable to match below-cost prices.[1] While Wal-Mart managers probably anticipated that the German government would regulate its store hours (Germany's Ladenschlußgesetz, or store closing laws, dictate that stores can only be open till 8:00 P.M. on weekdays and 4:00 P.M. on Saturdays. Stores are closed on Sundays.), it probably didn't expect that it would influence its ability to set prices. Thus, even the largest companies in the world, like Wal-Mart, are influenced by events in their external environments.

*After reading the next four sections, you should be able to*
1. *discuss how changing environments affect organizations.*
2. *describe the four components of the general environment.*
3. *explain the five components of the specific environment.*
4. *describe the process that companies use to make sense of their changing environments.*

# 1. Changing Environments

*Let's examine the three basic characteristics of changing external environments: 1.1 environmental change, 1.2 environmental complexity, 1.3 environmental munificence, and 1.4 the uncertainty that environmental change, complexity, and munificence can create for organizational managers.*

## 1.1 Environmental Change

**environmental change**
the rate at which a company's general and specific environments change

**stable environment**
environment in which the rate of change is slow

**Environmental change** is the rate at which a company's general and specific environments change. In **stable environments**, the rate of environmental change is slow. For instance, the liquor industry has not changed much since Prohibition was repealed in 1933. Most states use a "three-tier" system to control the sale and distribution of alcohol.[2] Breweries, wineries, and distilleries sell their products to wholesale distributors who, in turn, sell to liquor retailers who then sell to the public. Even the Internet hasn't brought much change to the industry. Wine e-tailers, such as Wineshopper.com and Wine.com (which merged and were then purchased by eVineyard.com), have spent over $200 million to promote Internet sales of wine, only to barely dent traditional retail sales. Progress is slow because only 30 states allow direct shipments of wine to people in other states. Furthermore, this is unlikely to change, as 40 bills supporting Internet sales and distribution of wine were proposed in state legislatures last year, but only one passed.[3] eVineyard hopes to get around these issues by simply obtaining retail licenses in the states it serves (27 at the moment). Then, when an order for wine comes in via its Web site, it can pass that order to a wholesaler who ships the wine to the customer for eVineyard. But even this approach is built on the "three-tier" system that has been in place for nearly 70 years.[4] So, in reality, little has changed.

**dynamic environment**
environment in which the rate of change is fast

In **dynamic environments**, however, the rate of environmental change is fast. EA Sports is a company that competes in one of the most dynamic external environments—video games. Its best-selling products are sports games, like Madden NFL (football), NBA Live (basketball), NHL Hockey, Tiger Woods PGA Tour (golf), and FIFA Soccer. EA Sports' business environment is dynamic because gaming technology changes so quickly. EA Sports produced its first product for the Atari 800, one of the earliest computers designed to play computer games. However, the more powerful Commodore 64 replaced the Atari 800, which was then replaced by the Commodore Amiga, followed by the 8-bit Nintendo, the 16-bit Sega Genesis, the 32-bit and 64-bit Segas, Nintendos, Sony PlayStations, desktop computers, and now the Sony PlayStation2, the Nintendo Gamecube, and Microsoft's Xbox. With game development costs running around $1 million, if EA guesses wrong and develops games for computers that will soon become obsolete, it could join the dozens of game companies that have already closed their doors.[5]

**punctuated equilibrium theory**
theory that holds that companies go through long, simple periods of stability (equilibrium), followed by short periods of dynamic, fundamental change (revolution), and ending with a return to stability (new equilibrium)

While it seems that companies would either be in stable external environments *or* dynamic external environments, recent research suggests that companies often experience both stable and dynamic external environments. According to **punctuated equilibrium theory**, companies go through long, simple periods of stability (equilibrium), followed by short, complex periods of dynamic, fundamental change (revolutionary periods), finishing with a return to stability (new equilibrium).[6]

As shown in Exhibit 2.1, one example of punctuated equilibrium is the U.S. airline industry. Twice in the last 25 years, the U.S. airline industry has experienced revolutionary periods. The first, from mid-1979 to mid-1982, occurred immediately after airline deregulation in 1978. Prior to deregulation, the federal government controlled where airlines could fly, when they could fly, and the number of flights they could have on a particular route. After deregulation, these choices were left to the airlines. The large financial losses during this period clearly indicate that the airlines had trouble adjusting to the intense competition that occurred after deregulation. However, by mid-1982, profits returned to the industry and held steady until mid-1989. Then, after experiencing record growth and profits, U.S. airlines lost billions of dollars between 1989 and 1993

EXHIBIT 2.1

PUNCTUATED EQUILIBRIUM: U.S. AIRLINE PROFITS FROM 1976 TO 1999

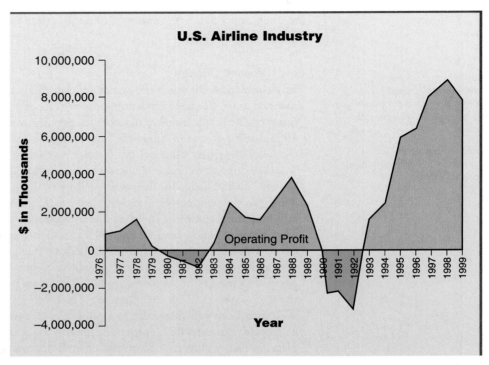

**Source:** "Earnings Summary, 1938-1999,: U.S. Scheduled Airlines," Air Transport Association, [Online] Available http://www.air-transport.org/public/industry/display1.asp?id=11, 16 June 2001.

as the industry went through dramatic changes. Key expenses, like jet fuel and employee salaries, which had held steady for years, suddenly increased. Furthermore, revenues, which had grown steadily year after year, suddenly dropped because of dramatic changes in the airlines' customer base. Business travelers, who typically pay full-priced fares, comprised more than half of all passengers during the 1980s. But now the largest customer base is leisure travelers who, in contrast to business travelers, want the cheapest flights they can get.[7] With expenses suddenly up and revenues suddenly down, the airlines responded to these changes in their business environment by laying off 5 to 10 percent of all workers, canceling orders for new planes, and getting rid of routes that were not profitable. Starting in 1993 and lasting till 1998, these changes helped profits return even stronger. The industry began to stabilize, if not flourish, just as punctuated equilibrium theory predicts.[8]

And while it's not reflected in Exhibit 2.1 (the data weren't available when I wrote this), the terrorist attack of September 11, 2001, in which two planes were flown into the World Trade Center towers in New York City, one plane was flown into the Pentagon in Washington, D.C., and one plane was crashed in Pennsylvania, clearly began another period of revolutionary change for the airline industry. The immediate effect was a 20 percent drop in scheduled flights, a 40 percent drop in passengers, and losses so large (billions of dollars) that the U.S. government approved a $15 billion bailout to keep airlines in business. Large changes in airport security also affected airports, the airlines themselves, and airline customers. We can only hope that by the time you read this the airline industry has moved through this revolutionary period of change back to a more stable period of equilibrium.

## 1.2 Environmental Complexity

**environmental complexity**
the number of external factors in the environment that affect organizations

**simple environment**
an environment with few environmental factors

**complex environment**
an environment with many environmental factors

**Environmental complexity** is the number of external factors in the environment that affect organizations. **Simple environments** have few environmental factors, whereas **complex environments** have many environmental factors. For example, the baking industry exists within a relatively simple external environment. Except for more efficient ovens (i.e., technology), bread is baked, wrapped, and delivered fresh to stores each day much as it always has been. Likewise, although some new breads have become popular, the white and wheat breads that customers bought 20 years ago are still today's best sellers. Baking bread is a highly competitive, but simple business environment that has experienced few changes.

By contrast, in recent years, cereal companies like Kellogg's, the maker of popular cereals, find themselves in a more complex environment in which three significant changes have occurred. The first significant change has been more competition. Twenty years ago, Kellogg's competed against just a few cereal companies, like General Mills and Post. Today, Kellogg's competes against those companies, plus a dozen more private-label store brands (IGA, Good Value, etc.).

The second significant change in the cereal industry has been significant price cuts. For years, Kellogg's made gross profits of 50 percent on a box of cereal. In other words, it only cost Kellogg's $2.50 to make a $5 box of cereal. Yet, with profits that high, private-label store brands could still make a profit of $1 per box by slashing the price to $3.50 per box of cereal.

The third significant change has been the entrance of Wal-Mart into the grocery business. Wal-Mart, much more than other national grocery chains, relies on cheaper private-label store brands, like its own Sam's Choice soft drinks and Old Roy dog food. Consumers like these products because they cost substantially less than brand-name products. However, Wal-Mart prefers private-label store brands because, even with their lower prices, the store makes a higher profit on these brands. So when Wal-Mart aggressively expanded into the grocery business in the last few years, Kellogg's saw its market share drop even more as Wal-Mart pushed cheaper, private-label cereals. Together, these three changes have made Kellogg's external environment much more complex than it used to be.[9]

## 1.3 Environmental Munificence

**environmental munificence**
degree to which an organization's external environment has an abundance or scarcity of critical organizational resources

The third characteristic of external environments is environmental munificence. **Environmental munificence** is the degree to which an organization's external environment has an abundance or scarcity of critical organizational resources.

For many companies over the last few years, qualified employees were scarce. While companies continued to lay off workers in particular industries or regions, good job applicants were difficult to find. The reason was simple: Demand for job applicants exceeded the supply. In fact, the number of job openings at companies was five times greater than the number of layoffs.[10] Consequently, employers had to work harder than ever before to find and attract skilled employees, especially in technological and professional jobs.

As a result, Cisco Systems started a "Friends" program to help recruit more engineers. When potential job applicants visited Cisco's Internet home page to read about job openings, they could electronically submit their resumes on the "Friends" page (**http://www.cisco.com/jobs/friends/**). An email would then automatically be forwarded to a Cisco employee who had volunteered to be a "Friend." That "Friend" would call the job applicant within 24 hours. The program, which has been an overwhelming success, helped Cisco solve the problem of job applicant scarcity.[11]

However, as I have written this chapter, the economy and the job market have cooled considerably. With the first layoffs in its history (5,000 out of 44,000 workers), Cisco's Friends program is temporarily on hold.[12] Yet, Cisco's bad news is good news

EXHIBIT 2.2

ENVIRONMENTAL CHANGE, COMPLEXITY & MUNIFICENCE

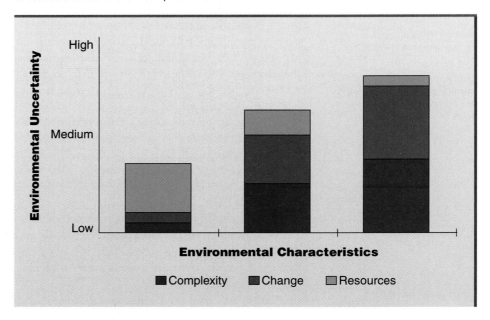

for companies that have recently had difficulty attracting qualified workers. Layoffs at dotcoms and technical companies (Nortel Networks has laid off 20,000 employees), along with widespread hiring freezes in other industries, have made it much easier to find and hire qualified employees, who are no longer quite as scarce as they were just a few years ago.[13]

### 1.4 Uncertainty

Exhibit 2.2 shows that environmental change, complexity, and resources (i.e., munificence) affect environmental **uncertainty**, which is how well managers can understand or predict the external changes and trends affecting their businesses. Starting at the left side of the figure, environmental uncertainty is lowest when there is little complexity and change and when resources are plentiful. In these environments, managers feel confident that they can understand and predict the external forces that affect their business. By contrast, the right side of the figure indicates that environmental uncertainty is highest when there is much complexity and change and when resources are scarce. In these environments, managers may not be at all confident that they can understand and predict the external forces affecting their businesses.

### Review 1
### Changing Environments

Environmental change, complexity, and munificence are the basic components of external environments. Environmental change is the rate at which conditions or events affecting a business change. Environmental complexity is the number of external factors in an external environment. Environmental munificence is the scarcity or abundance of resources available in the external environment. The greater the rate of environmental change and environmental complexity and the lower the environmental munificence, the less confident managers are that they can understand and predict the trends affecting their businesses. According to punctuated equilibrium theory, companies experience periods of stability followed by short periods of dynamic, fundamental change, followed by a return to periods of stability.

**uncertainty**
extent to which managers can understand or predict which environmental changes and trends will affect their businesses

42

*EXHIBIT 2.3*

GENERAL AND SPECIFIC ENVIRONMENTS

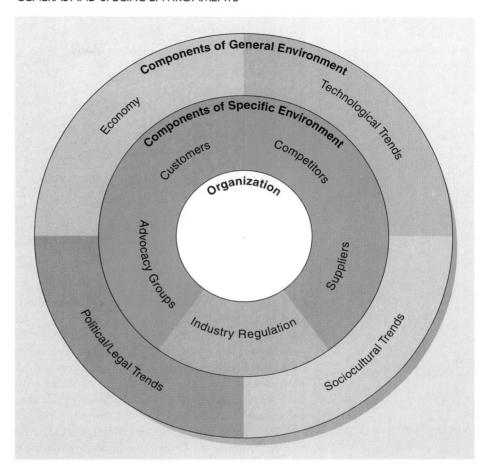

## 2. General Environment

**general environment**
the economic, technological, sociocultural, and political trends that indirectly affect all organizations

**specific environment**
the customers, competitors, suppliers, industry regulations, and advocacy groups that are unique to an industry and that directly affect how a company does business

Exhibit 2.3 shows the two kinds of external environments that influence organizations: the general environment and the specific environment. The **general environment** consists of the economy and the technological, sociocultural, and political/legal trends that indirectly affect all organizations. Changes in any sector of the general environment eventually affect most organizations. For example, most businesses benefit when the Federal Reserve lowers its prime lending rate, because then banks and credit card companies will often lower the interest rates they charge for loans. Consumers, who can then borrow money more cheaply, will borrow more money to buy homes, cars, refrigerators, and large-screen TVs. By contrast, each organization has a **specific environment** that is unique to that firm's industry and directly affects the way it conducts day-to-day business. The specific environment, which will be discussed in detail in Section 3 of this chapter, includes customers, competitors, suppliers, industry regulation, and advocacy groups.

*Let's take a closer look at the four components of the general environment: 2.1 the economy, and the 2.2 technological, 2.3 sociocultural, and 2.4 political/legal trends that indirectly affect all organizations.*

43

The economy in general, and the stock markets in particular, are extremely important components of a firm's external environment. When a firm's stock dips, the firm has less money to invest in its growth. It is more difficult to leverage a lower-value company to raise capital.

AP PHOTO/ED BAILEY

### 2.1 Economy

The current state of a country's economy affects most organizations operating in it. A growing economy means that, in general, more people are working and therefore have relatively more money to spend. More products are being bought and sold than in a static or shrinking economy. While a growing economy doesn't mean that sales of an individual firm are necessarily growing, it does provide an environment favorable to business growth. On the other hand, a shrinking economy means that consumers have less money to spend. Also, relatively fewer products are being bought and sold. Thus, a shrinking economy makes growth for individual businesses more difficult.

For example, as I write this chapter, the U.S. economy is in the second year of an economic slowdown. Growth is still positive, but it's much slower (1 to 2 percent) than previously. Still, things could be worse. With interest rates low, it costs companies little to borrow money and there's little upward pressure on business costs (i.e., low inflation). Unemployment rates are at historically low levels, but are rising, thanks to frequent layoffs stemming from company losses. In fact, the Conference Board's Help Wanted Advertising Index, which measures the number of advertised job openings, is at its lowest level in a decade.[14] As mentioned earlier in the chapter, this corresponds with large numbers of corporate layoffs. By contrast, Japan's economy is in much worse shape as it rolls into its tenth straight year of economic recession. A *Fortune* magazine article summed up Japan's economy like this: "The yen in turn is weakening, unemployment has hit postwar highs, and the stock market is in free fall. Think the Nasdaq's recent blow off [a 50 percent drop in value] is bad? Japan's main index hit a 16-year low on March 12, and most analysts are still screaming 'Sell!' There are fewer banks today than there were a decade ago, but they're still in trouble—and the trouble is only intensifying as the economy continues to slide."[15] In short, for close to a decade, Japanese businesses have operated in an unhealthy, shrinking economy.

Of course, by the time you read this, the Japanese economy could be growing and the U.S. economy could be shrinking into a recession (negative growth). Because the economy influences basic business decisions, like whether to hire more employees, expand production, or take out loans to purchase equipment, managers scan their economic environments for signs of change. Unfortunately, the economic statistics that managers rely on when making these decisions are notoriously poor predictors of *future* economic activity. A manager who decides to hire 10 more employees because economic data suggest future growth could very well have to lay off those newly hired

# "headline news"

## Economic Policy's Rock Star: Alan Greenspan

Perhaps the most predictable feature of business reporting is Alan Greenspan. As Greenspan makes his quarterly pilgrimage toward the congressional building, reporters speculate on the content of his announcement based on his tie. Deciphering his speeches is like playing the cryptoquip in the newspaper, equally enigmatic if not as fun. Greenspan-watching has become an increasingly popular national sport.

The chief of American monetary policy is an economic icon. The seven-person Federal Reserve Board (Fed) is in control of the U.S. money supply, and Greenspan is its Chairman. Normally, the Fed can create economic recession or strengthen economic expansion by increasing or decreasing the growth rate of the money supply. The Fed does this by setting the interest rates that banks and financial institutions pay to the U.S. Treasury for dollars. Higher interest rates reduce the supply and curb inflation. Lower interest rates have the opposite effect, with the added bonus of lower unemployment and greater GDP growth. Greenspan is at the helm of the U.S. economy, which has performed brilliantly over the last decade.

Greenspan is also surrounded by great controversy. Fearing rising inflation, he hiked short-term interest rates six times in the final 18 months of President Clinton's term before realizing that he had created a liquidity crunch. This caused rumors of an economic slowdown and predictions of eventual recession. By March 2001, some of America's most successful companies had announced monumental cutbacks: DaimlerChrysler, 26,000; Procter & Gamble, 17,000; Lucent, 10,000; General Motors, 15,000. Consumer confidence started to slip, and consumer spending teetered on the edge of decline.

Greenspan critics charge he was too fearful of the tight labor market in the United States—something most workers like because it means increased pay and more job opportunities. Tight labor, however, increases labor costs, costs that ultimately increase the cost of goods sold and the final price of goods and services to the consumer, resulting in inflation.

Despite regularly gloomy reporting, there is not a universally bad feeling about the economy. Murray Weidenbaum, former economic advisor to President Reagan, reminds us that today's companies are required to announce impending layoffs. There are no penalties for overestimating how many people you will let go, but there are significant ones for underestimating the numbers. It is in a company's best interest to pad the figure. Other economists suggest some post-boom perspective. As unemployment inches higher, reaching 5 percent by the end of

2001, University of Baltimore economist Richard Clinch remarks, "In 1995, that would have seemed great, wouldn't it?"

Corporate America's woes cannot be blamed entirely on the Fed's monetary policy. Poor management decisions made during the economic expansion are coming home to roost. Cisco built far more inventory than it could possibly sell, and Lucent enacted a wacky pricing policy whereby it underwrote customer purchases, basically giving away its revenue-generating product for free. General Motors (GM) and Procter & Gamble (P&G) suffered from poor product decisions—GM with poor products and P&G subsidizing poor-performing products with the company's star brands.

And make no mistake. As American corporations increasingly rely on the financial arms of their companies to provide profits, Greenspan's wingspan has greater reach. Ford, General Electric, GM, Sears Roebuck, and many others have their own financing companies that generate finance-related income. In fact, GM and Ford are starting to look more like they're in the finance business than the automotive business. Ford Motor Credit chips in a full 70 percent of Ford's profits, while GMAC is responsible for a similar amount of its parent's profits. Migrating to the financial industry signals that Detroit has much more to worry about than economic cycles. And that's something Greenspan can't fix.

1. Can sound management practices mitigate the influence of the Federal Reserve and interest rate changes? Explain.
2. What do you think will be the ultimate end for companies, like Ford and GM, who increasingly rely on their financial-services arms to provide corporate profitability?
3. How do changes in interest rates affect you as a student, now and as you approach graduation?

**Sources:** Andrew Bary, "Money from Nothing," *Barron's Online*, 23 July 2001, WSJ Interactive, http://www.interactive.wsj.com. M. A. Espinosa-Vega, "How Powerful Is Monetary Policy in the Long Run?" *Economic Review*, July 1998 (88:3), 12. T. W. Maier, "Prophets and Losses," *Insight on the News*, 12 March 2001, 10. J. Malvaux, "Economic Slowdown Bad News for Student Debtors," *Black Issues in Higher Education*, 15 March 2001, 46. S. Taub, "SEC Investigates Lucent's Accounting Practices," *CFO*, 9 February 2001, http://www.cfo.com. C. M. Zoakos, "The Fed's Folly," *International Economy*, March 2001 (15:2), 21.

45

### Computer Skills and Lifetime Earnings

People with basic computer skills earn 15 percent to 30 percent higher lifetime incomes than those without them. Computers are becoming an integral part of all kinds of work. What should you do to learn about computers? Subscribe to *PC Magazine*, *PC World*, or *Mac World*. Buy a book about Microsoft Office and then take tests to be Microsoft Office User certified (see **http://www.microsoft.com/traincert/mcp/mous/default.asp**) in Word, Excel, PowerPoint, or Access. Take more than the required computer classes for your degree. Unless you want less job security and earning power, start learning more about computers today.

**Source:** J. Hearn & D. Lewis, "Keyboarding Course Work and Employment, Earnings, and Educational Attainment," *Journal of Education for Business* 68 (1993): 147. C. Meares & J. Sargent, Jr., "The Digital Work Force: Building Infotech Skills at the Speed of Innovation," *U.S. Department of Commerce, Technology Administration, Office of Technology Policy.* [Online] Available http://www.ta.doc.gov/reports/itsw/Digital.pdf, 23 June 2001.

**business confidence indices**
indices that show managers' level of confidence about future business growth

**technology**
knowledge, tools, and techniques used to transform input into output

workers when the economic growth does not occur. In fact, a famous economic study found that at the beginning of a business quarter (a period of only three months), even the most accurate economic forecasters could not accurately predict whether economic activity would grow or shrink in that same quarter![16]

Because economic statistics are such poor predictors, some managers try to predict future economic activity by keeping track of business confidence. **Business confidence indices** show how confident actual managers are about future business growth. For example, the Cahners Business Confidence Index is a monthly telephone survey of 400 senior business executives in the electronics, computer, construction, consumer goods, and manufacturing industries. Another widely cited measure is the U.S. Chamber of Commerce Business Confidence Index, which asks 7,000 small business owners to express their optimism (or pessimism) about future business sales and prospects. Managers often prefer business confidence indices to economic statistics, because they know that the level of confidence reported by real managers affects their business decisions. In other words, it's reasonable to expect managers to make decisions today that are in line with their expectations concerning the economy's future. So if Cahner's Business Confidence Index suddenly drops, managers would think hard about hiring new employees, or might stop plans to increase production for fear of being stuck with unsold inventory should the economy slow dramatically in the future.

### 2.2 Technological Component

**Technology** is the knowledge, tools, and techniques used to transform input (raw materials, information, etc.) into output (products and services). For example, the knowledge of authors, editors, and artists (technology) and the use of equipment like computers and printing presses (also technology) transformed paper, ink, and glue (raw material inputs) into this book (the finished product). In the case of a service company such as an airline, the technology would consist of equipment, like airplanes, repair tools, and computers, and the knowledge of mechanics, ticketers, and flight crews. The output would be the service of transporting people from one place to another.

Changes in technology can help companies provide better products or produce their products more efficiently. For example, advances in surgical techniques and imaging equipment have made open-heart surgery much faster and safer in recent years. While technological changes can benefit a business, they can also threaten it. For example, CD-ROM technology has allowed publishers of traditional print material, like books and encyclopedias, to cheaply add videos, sound, and animation to their products. Since the arrival of CD-ROM encyclopedias, sales of the paper version of Encyclopedia Britannica are down by 50 percent. Rather than pay $1,250 for Britannica's 32-volume edition, consumers can buy it for $70 in CD-ROM format or use it for *free* on the Internet at **http://www.britannica.com**![17] However, Internet advertising revenues, which Britannica.com uses to fund its Web operation, are not enough to allow the company to earn a profit. As a result, it has had to lay off 150 of its 300 employees.[18] Companies must embrace new technology and find effective ways to use it to improve products and services or decrease costs. If they don't, they will lose out to competitors who do. Chapter 10, on Organizational Change and Innovation, provides a more in-depth discussion of how technology affects a company's competitive advantage.

### 2.3 Sociocultural Component

The sociocultural component of the general environment refers to the demographic characteristics and general behavior, attitudes, and beliefs of people in a particular society. Sociocultural changes and trends influence organizations in two important ways.

46

EXHIBIT 2.4

DEMOGRAPHICS: PERCENTAGE OF MARRIED WOMEN WITH CHILDREN WHO WORK

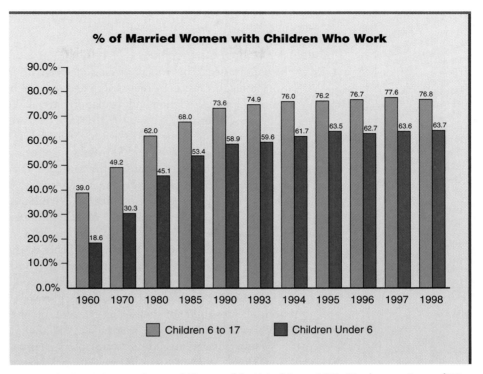

**Source:** U.S. Census Bureau, *Statistical Abstract of the United States,1999.* "Employment Status of Women by Marital Status and Presence and Age of Children: 1960 to 1998," Table No. 631 (Washington, D.C.: U.S. Government Printing Office, 1999).

First, changing demographic characteristics, such as the number of people with particular skills or the growth or decline in particular population segments (single or married; old or young; men or women; Caucasians, Hispanics, Blacks, or Asians; etc.) affects how companies run their businesses. For example, Exhibit 2.4 shows that married women with children are much more likely to work today than four decades ago. In 1960, only 18.6 percent of women with children under 6 years old and 39 percent of women with children between the ages of 6 and 17 worked. In 1998, those percentages had risen to 63.7 percent and 76.8 percent, respectively. Today, with traffic congestion creating longer commutes and with both parents working longer hours, employees are much more likely to value products and services that allow them to recapture free time with their families. Priscilla La Barbera, a marketing professor at New York University, believes that there's been a "societal shift" in the way people view their free time. She said, "People are beginning to realize that their time has real value."[19] Companies such as 3Com in Santa Clara, California, help their employees by providing a service that lets them drop off and pick up their dry cleaning at their desks. Likewise, they can visit the dentist by walking to the parking lot, where the dentist's office is set up in a van. Circles, an organization that provides employee concierge services for 50 companies, helps employees create more free time by planning their vacations or running their errands.[20]

Second, sociocultural changes in behavior, attitudes, and beliefs also affect the demand for a business's products and services. Furthermore, today's harried worker/parent can hire babyproofing agencies (to baby proof their homes), emergency babysitting services, bill payers, birthday party planners, kiddie taxi services, personal assistants, and personal chefs.[21] All of these services are a direct result of the need for free time, which is a result of the sociocultural changes associated with a much higher percentage of women in the work place.

### 2.4 Political/Legal Component

The political/legal component of the general environment includes the legislation, regulation, and court decisions that govern and regulate business behavior. Throughout the last decade, new legislation and regulation have placed additional responsibilities on companies. Unfortunately, many managers are unaware of these new responsibilities. For example, according to the 1991 Civil Rights Act (**http://www.eeoc.gov/laws/cra91.html**), if an employee is sexually harassed by anyone at work (a supervisor, a coworker, or even a customer), the company—not just the harasser—is potentially liable for damages, attorneys' fees, and back pay.[22] Under the Family and Medical Leave Act (**http://www.dol. gov/dol/esa/public/regs/compliance/whd/whdfs28.htm**), employees who have been on the job one year are guaranteed 12 weeks of unpaid leave a year to tend to their own illnesses or to their elderly parents, a newborn baby, or a newly adopted child. Employees are guaranteed the same job, pay, and benefits when they return to work.[23] Because of the 1990 Clean Air Act (**http://www.epa.gov/oar/oaqps/peg_caa/pegcaain.html**), companies located in regions with high levels of polluted air must reduce the number of employees who drive to work each day by approximately 25 percent. Companies are exploring the possibility of sponsoring car pools or renting buses and vans, because the fines for noncompliance can be as high as $25,000 per day![24]

Many managers are also unaware of the potential legal risks associated with traditional managerial decisions like recruiting, hiring, and firing employees. Indeed, it is increasingly common for businesses and managers to be sued for negligent hiring and supervision, defamation, invasion of privacy, emotional distress, fraud, and misrepresentation during employee recruitment.[25] Likewise, there were few wrongful termination cases (i.e., unfairly firing employees) 25 years ago, but today, there are more than 24,000 such cases a year in the U.S. court system.[26] In fact, wrongful termination lawsuits have increased by 77 percent and now account for 13 percent of all lawsuits against companies.[27] One in four employers are eventually sued for wrongful termination. Employers lose 70 percent of these cases, and a typical settlement payment to former employees will cost an average of $500,000 or more.[28]

Another area in which companies face potential legal risks these days is from customer-initiated lawsuits. For example, under product liability law, manufacturers can be liable for products made decades ago. Also, the law, as it is now written, does not consider whether manufactured products have been properly maintained and used. In one product liability case, a customer changed the product, did not follow the manufacturer's written instructions, and violated the manufacturer's warnings that were clearly marked on the product and in the instruction manual. Yet, despite the customer's negligence, the company was forced to recall the product (at tremendous expense) and pay damages of $6 million.[29] Why? Because product liability only requires plaintiffs to demonstrate that they were damaged by the manufacturer's product. In turn, under the concept of "strict liability," the burden of proof is shifted to the company, which must now prove that the product was safe.[30] So, once damages have been shown, the company is assumed guilty until it proves its innocence.

Not everyone agrees that companies face severe legal risks. Indeed, many believe that the government should do more to regulate and restrict business behavior and that it should be easier for average citizens to sue dishonest or negligent corporations. From a managerial perspective, the best medicine against legal risk is prevention. As a manager, it is your responsibility to educate yourself about the laws, regulations, and potential lawsuits that could affect your business. Failure to do so may put you and your company at risk of sizable penalties, fines, or legal charges.

### Review 2
#### General Environment

The general environment consists of economic, technological, sociocultural, and political/legal events and trends that affect all organizations. Because the economy influences basic business decisions, managers often use economic statistics and business confidence indices to predict future economic activity. Changes in technology, which is used to transform input into output, can be a benefit or a threat to a business. Sociocultural trends, like changing demographic characteristics, affect how companies run their businesses. Similarly, sociocultural changes in behavior, attitudes, and beliefs affect the demand for a business's products and services. Court decisions and revised federal and state laws have placed much larger political/legal responsibilities on companies. The best way to manage legal responsibilities is to educate managers and employees about laws and regulations and potential lawsuits that could affect a business.

## 3. Specific Environment

In contrast to general environments that indirectly influence organizations, changes in an organization's specific environment directly affect the way a company conducts its business. If customers decide to use another product, or a competitor cuts prices 10 percent, or a supplier can't deliver raw materials, or federal regulators specify that industry pollutants must be reduced, or environmental groups accuse your company of selling unsafe products, the impact on your business is immediate.

*Let's examine how the 3.1 customer, 3.2 competitor, 3.3 supplier, 3.4 industry regulation, and 3.5 advocacy group components of the specific environment affect businesses.*

### 3.1 Customer Component

Customers purchase products and services. Companies cannot exist without customer support. Therefore, monitoring customers' changing wants and needs is critical to business success. For example, over the last 25 years, the size of the average house has increased from 1,140 square feet to more than 2,225 square feet. Ironically, though, that larger house sits on a lot one-third to one-half smaller than before.[31] Why? Because today's homeowner's would rather be enjoying themselves in their larger, nicer homes than taking care of their yards. Contractors, such as D.R. Horton, one of the nation's largest and most successful homebuilders with 91 straight quarters of revenue growth, have thrived by paying attention to these changes. In contrast to most builders who discourage home buyers from making changes to standard architectural plans, Horton's customization strategy means that the company says "yes" to giving home buyers exactly what they want.[32] Another changing want and need is "24/7/365," meaning business availability 24 hours a day, 7 days a week, 365 days per year. In short, customers expect to be able to do business around the clock. This is why companies such as Wal-Mart, which restocks its shelves from 10 P.M. to 8:00 A.M., now keep their doors open 24 hours a day. Finally, after a decade of surging growth and personal spending (i.e., acquisition of too much "stuff"), people now value experiences more than things. So, the next time customers are looking to spend their money, they may choose a unique experience (such as travel, riding in a World War II tank, or a massage) rather than buying a unique thing.[33]

There are two basic strategies for monitoring customers: reactive and proactive. *Reactive customer monitoring* is identifying and addressing customer trends and problems after they occur. One reactive strategy is to identify customer concerns by listening closely to customer complaints. Not only does listening to complaints help identify problems, but the way in which companies respond to complaints indicates how closely they are attending to customer concerns. For example, companies that respond quickly to customer letters of complaint are viewed much more favorably than companies that are slow to respond or never respond. In particular, studies have shown that when a company's follow-up letter thanks customers for writing, offers a sincere, specific response to the customer's complaint (i.e., not a form letter, but an explanation of how the problem will be handled), and contains a small gift, coupons, or a refund to make up for the problem, customers will be much more likely to purchase products or services again from that company.[34] By contrast, companies that don't respond promptly to customer complaints are likely to find customer rants and tirades posted publicly on places like **http://www.planetfeedback.com** and **http://www.ecomplaints.com**. Customers hope that complaints posted on these sites will force someone to address their problems. For example, the day after Lena West posted a complaint against Budget Rent-a-Car on eComplaints.com, she received an email containing an apology and a promise to solve her problem.[35]

*Proactive monitoring* of customers means trying to sense events, trends, and problems before they occur (or before customers complain). For example, Cotton Incorporated, the trade group that encourages consumers to purchase cotton clothing ("The look, the feel of cotton. . ."), publishes a quarterly newsletter called *Lifestyle Monitor* that reports the results of ongoing research. According to Cotton Inc.'s president and CEO, the research is an "early radar detection system" for changes in consumer attitudes and behavior regarding clothing, appearance, fashion, home furnishings, and other topics.[36] To illustrate, this research indicates that blue jeans continue to be as popular as ever. Eighty-five percent of respondents disagreed with a statement saying, "Jeans are in my past, not in my future." Consistent with this statement, the average woman owns seven pairs of jeans, and there's an 81 percent chance that her next pair of jeans will be some shade of blue.[37] Furthermore, when women were asked whether "A good-looking man looks most sexy in denim jeans and a casual shirt, or a jacket and tie or slacks and a nice sweater?", 53 percent said denim jeans, 25 percent said slacks and a sweater, and 20 percent said a jacket and tie.[38]

### 3.2 Competitor Component

**competitors**
companies in the same industry that sell similar products or services to customers

**Competitors** are companies in the same industry that sell similar products or services to customers. GM, Ford, and DaimlerChrysler all compete for automobile customers. NBC, ABC, CBS, and Fox compete for TV viewers' attention. And McDonald's, Burger King, and Wendy's compete for fast-food customers' dollars. Often, the difference between business success and failure comes down to whether your company is doing a better job of satisfying customer wants and needs than the competition. Consequently, companies need to keep close track of what their competitors are doing. To do this, managers perform what's called a **competitive analysis**, which is deciding who your competitors are, anticipating competitors' moves, and determining competitors' strengths and weaknesses.

**competitive analysis**
a process for monitoring competitors that involves identifying competitors, anticipating their moves, and determining their strengths and weaknesses

Surprisingly, because they tend to focus on only two or three well-known competitors with similar goals and resources, managers often do a poor job of identifying potential competitors.[39] For example, Coke and Pepsi undoubtedly spend more time keeping track of each other than they do Dr. Pepper or Snapple. Likewise, Xerox, which touts itself as "the document company," meaning copiers, printers, fax machines, and scanners, focused on doing battle with its largest competitors in the copying business, Canon and Ricoh. By doing so, it ignored Hewlett-Packard and its inkjet printers and lost billions in sales in the process in the small office, home office (SOHO) market. In fact, inkjet printers exploded so much in popularity over the last 10 years, that HP's highly profitable printer division is now larger than *all* of Xerox.[40]

## PersonalProductivityTip

**Improve Your Competitive IQ**

Ninety percent of organizations do a poor job gathering information about competitors. However, by using publicly available information, you can improve your competitive IQ. You can get information from government documents, public speeches, published writings, press releases, court transcripts, industry seminars, trade shows, and U.S. embassies (which write detailed studies for each country). One example is the Foreign Broadcast Information Service, published by the U.S. State Department, which contains translations of worldwide radio and TV broadcasts. However, competitive intelligence is not spying, which is illegal. For more information, see the Society of Competitive Intelligence Professionals (**http://www.scip.org**) and the U.S. Economic Espionage Act of 1996 (**http://www.nacic.gov/pubs/eea_96.htm**).

**Source:** N. King, Jr., & J. Bravin, "Call It Mission Impossible Inc.—Corporate-Spying Firms Thrive," *The Wall Street Journal*, 3 July 2000, B1.

The second mistake managers make when analyzing the competition is to underestimate potential competitors' capabilities. When this happens, managers don't take the steps they should to continue to improve their products or services. The result can be significant decreases in both market share and profits. For example, with software products like Cool Talk, Internet Phone, and Web Phone, it is possible to make very inexpensive long-distance phone calls on the Internet. To use Internet Phone, you need an Internet service provider (typically $12 to $20 a month); a computer with a sound card, speakers, and a microphone; and phone software, which costs anywhere from $20 to $50. The sound quality using Internet Phone is only as good as AM radio, but with people used to poor quality sound on their cell phones, poor sound quality doesn't deter people from making Internet calls anymore.[41] Today, Internet Phone use is still small, constituting just 3 percent of all international calls. However, in Japan, more than 12 percent of international calls are made over the Internet and use is even greater in China.[42] By 2004, the International Telecommunication Union, which sets standards for the telecommunication industry, estimates that 40 percent of all international telephone calls will be made over the Internet because of much lower prices. For instance, international long distance, for which traditional phone companies charge anywhere from 15 cents to more than a $1 a minute, only costs 3 to 8 cents a minute using the Internet.[43] Yet, when a phone company manager was asked whether he was worried about the likes of Internet Phone, his response was "Some people will use it. But it won't really affect our business."[44]

### 3.3 Supplier Component

**suppliers**
companies that provide material, human, financial, and informational resources to other companies

**Suppliers** are companies that provide material, human, financial, and informational resources to other companies. U.S. Steel buys iron ore from suppliers to make steel products. When IBM sells a mainframe computer, it also provides support staff, engineers, and other technical consultants to the company that bought the computer. If you're shopping for desks, chairs, and office supplies, chances are Office Depot will be glad to help your business open a revolving charge account to pay for your purchases. Or when a clothing manufacturing firm has spent $100,000 to purchase new

Traditional long distance companies are increasingly pressured by Internet telephony. At the Easy Everything Internet Café in New York City, each of the hundreds of computer terminals have a telephone handset where users can make inexpensive Internet long distance calls.

COURTESY EASYEVERYTHING INTERNET CAFE, NEW YORK CITY

high-pressure "water drills" to be used to cut shirt and pants patterns to precise sizes, the water drill manufacturer will, as part of the purchase, agree to train workers on how to use the machinery.

A key factor influencing the relationship between companies and their suppliers is how dependent they are on each other.[45] **Supplier dependence** is the degree to which a company relies on a supplier because of the importance of the supplier's product to the company and the difficulty of finding other sources of that product. Supplier dependence is very strong in the diamond business, given that DeBeers Consolidated Mines provides 65 percent of the wholesale diamonds in the world. Because DeBeers typically offers better diamonds at cheaper prices, it has dominated the diamond industry for more than a century, controlling the supply, price, and quality of the best diamonds on the market. One example of this degree of control is that DeBeers' 125 customers, or "sightholders," as they're known in the industry, are summoned to DeBeers' London office 10 times a year and are given a shoebox of diamonds that they have to buy. If they refuse, they lose the opportunity to purchase any more diamonds. DeBeers dominance of its suppliers continues today as it considers selling diamonds under the DeBeers brand name, putting it in direct competition with each of its 125 sightholders. There is little the sightholders can do. Said one, "Imagine if the Ford car company said, 'I'm going to make a bad car this year, and you have to buy it or I'll never sell you a car again.' "[46]

**Buyer dependence** is the degree to which a supplier relies on a buyer because of the importance of that buyer to the supplier and the difficulty of selling its products to other buyers. For example, because it believed that the clothes sold in its stores were too expensive, Wal-Mart's Canadian division sent letters to its clothing suppliers, demanding a "retroactive, nonnegotiable price rollback of between 4 and 10 percent." So if Wal-Mart had purchased $100,000 of goods from a supplier in the last six months, it expected to receive a refund from the supplier totaling between $4,000 and $10,000. The suppliers were furious, but had little choice since Wal-Mart was one of their largest customers. The suppliers claimed that Wal-Mart told them that if they did not pay the 4 to 10 percent "mark down allowance," their orders would be canceled and Wal-Mart would end their business relationship.[47]

As Wal-Mart's demand indicates, greater buyer or seller dependence can lead to **opportunistic behavior,** in which one party benefits at the expense of the other. For example, because there are hundreds of small clothing manufacturers but few department stores to buy those clothes, department stores often demand that clothing suppliers follow strict guidelines. And if they fail to follow those guidelines, the suppliers are punished. Ames Department Stores penalizes its suppliers $300 for incorrect labels, $500 for the wrong packing materials, and 5 percent of the total cost of an order if the shipment arrives late or early![48]

Opportunistic behavior between buyers and suppliers will never be completely eliminated. However, many companies believe that both buyers and suppliers can benefit by improving the buyer-supplier relationship.[49] When Sears was choosing a food and guest services supplier for its headquarters in the massive Sears Tower—one of the tallest buildings in the world—18 different suppliers wanted its business. John Hulka, who is Sears' group manager for conference, travel, and food services, chose Aramark Corporation to be its supplier for one very important reason. Aramark, unlike the others, was willing to have an on-site manager to provide consistent service and to manage the buyer (Sears) and seller (Aramark) relationship. Indeed, most mornings about 7 A.M., Hulka meets with Nancy Naatz, the Aramark manager in charge of providing food and food services for Sears' employee food court, executive dining room, and for special events. James McManus, Aramark's president of business services said that managers like Naatz "have the flexibility to do whatever is necessary to keep the customer and clients happy. If they aren't happy, there are huge implications for us."[50] In contrast to opportunistic

**supplier dependence**
degree to which a company relies on a supplier because of the importance of the supplier's product to the company and the difficulty of finding other sources of that product

**buyer dependence**
degree to which a supplier relies on a buyer because of the importance of that buyer to the supplier and the difficulty of selling its products to other buyers

**opportunistic behavior**
transaction in which one party in the relationship benefits at the expense of the other

behavior, buyer-supplier transactions like Sears' and Aramark's is built on **relationship behavior,** which focuses on establishing a mutually beneficial, long-term relationship between buyers and suppliers.[51]

### 3.4 Industry Regulation Component

In contrast to the political/legal component of the general environment that affects all businesses, the **industry regulation** component consists of regulations and rules that govern the business practices and procedures of specific industries, businesses, and professions. For example, if you buy two apple pies from a neighbor who makes a little extra money selling homemade baked goods, your neighbor could be fined. In most states, it is illegal to sell food from your home. State regulations typically require a business license plus a state certificate of inspection that indicates that the food is stored properly; insects have not infested the premises; ovens are state approved; electrical wiring, lighting, and smoke detectors are up to code; and so on.[52] Likewise, only the car industry is subject to CAFE regulations. CAFE stands for the Corporate Average Fuel Economy regulations that require American auto manufacturers to sell cars that average 27.5 miles per gallon.[53]

Regulatory agencies affect businesses by creating and enforcing rules and regulations to protect consumers, workers, or society as a whole. For example, after seven years of planning, the Department of Health and Human Services issued rules and regulations regarding the quality of care to be provided in 17,000 nursing homes across the United States. The law not only spells out standards concerning health, safety, nutrition, and cleanliness, but it also authorizes fines for nursing homes that fail to meet these standards. Punishments for minor violations begin at $50 but can go as high as $10,000 a day for serious violations. Furthermore, anyone who lets a nursing home know when the government will be making its surprise annual inspection can be fined $2,000.[54]

There are nearly 100 federal government agencies and regulatory commissions that can affect nearly any kind of business. Exhibit 2.5 lists some of the most influential federal agencies and commissions, as well as their responsibilities and their Web sites.

Overall, the number of federal regulations has nearly tripled in the last 25 years. However, businesses are not just subject to federal regulations. They must also meet state, county, and city regulations, too. Surveys indicate that managers rank government regulation as one of the most demanding and frustrating parts of their jobs.[55]

### 3.5 Advocacy Groups

**Advocacy groups** are groups of concerned citizens who band together to try to influence the business practices of specific industries, businesses, and professions. The members of a group generally share the same point of view on a particular issue. For example, environmental advocacy groups might try to get manufacturers to reduce smokestack pollution emissions. Unlike the industry regulation component of the specific environment, advocacy groups cannot force organizations to change their practices. However, they can use a number of techniques to try to influence companies: public communications, media advocacy, and product boycotts.

The **public communications** approach relies on *voluntary* participation by the news media and the advertising industry to send out an advocacy group's message. For example, public service announcements for *World No Tobacco Day*, which is sponsored by the Campaign for Tobacco-Free Kids, the American Cancer Society, and the American Heart Association, among others, are played on radio and television stations on May 31 each year. These public service announcements use well-known athletes, such as Olympic gold medallist Tara Lipinski to warn against the effects of tobacco products and second-hand smoke. Lipinski, whose grandfather died from emphysema, said, "I've seen the negative effects of tobacco use firsthand, and I know how devastating

EXHIBIT 2.5

FEDERAL REGULATORY AGENCIES AND COMMISSIONS

| FEDERAL AGENCY | REGULATORY RESPONSIBILITIES |
| --- | --- |
| Consumer Product Safety Commission<br>http://www.cpsc.gov/ | Reduce risk of injuries and deaths associated with consumer products, set product safety standards, enforce product recalls, and provide consumer education |
| Environmental Protection Agency<br>http://www.epa.gov/ | Reduce and control pollution through research, monitoring, standard setting, and enforcement activities |
| Equal Employment Opportunity Commission<br>http://www.eeoc.gov/ | Promote fair hiring and promotion practices |
| Federal Communications Commission<br>http://www.fcc.gov/ | Regulate interstate and international communications by radio, television, wire, satellite, and cable |
| Federal Reserve System<br>http://www.federalreserve.gov/ | As the nation's central bank, control interest rates and money supply, and monitor the U.S. banking system to produce a growing economy with stable prices |
| Federal Trade Commission<br>http://www.ftc.gov/ | Restrict unfair methods of business competition and misleading advertising, and enforce consumer protection laws |
| Food and Drug Administration<br>http://www.fda.gov/ | Protect the nation's health by making sure food, drugs, and cosmetics are safe |
| National Labor Relations Board<br>http://www.nlrb.gov/ | Monitor union elections and stop companies from engaging in unfair labor practices |
| Occupational Safety & Health Administration<br>http://www.osha.gov/ | Save lives, prevent injuries, and protect the health of workers |
| Securities and Exchange Commission<br>http://www.sec.gov/ | Protect investors in the bond and stock markets, guarantee access to information on publicly traded securities, and regulate firms that sell securities or give investment advice |

they can be. That's why it's so important to me to let people know that it's never too late to quit, especially when you run the risk of exposing those around you to second-hand smoke." Matthew L. Myers, President of the Campaign for Tobacco-Free Kids, said, "Research tells us that the average smoker tries to quit seven times before quitting for good. Any attempt to give up tobacco is a positive step towards becoming tobacco-free." Therefore, to encourage smokers to keep trying to quit, the different athletes used in the ads explain that even when they fell short of their goals, they kept trying until they succeeded.[56]

In contrast to the public communications approach, media advocacy is a much more aggressive form of advocacy. A **media advocacy** approach typically involves framing issues as public issues (i.e., affecting everyone); exposing questionable, exploitative, or unethical practices; and forcing media coverage by buying media time or creating controversy that is likely to receive extensive news coverage. PETA, People for the Ethical Treatment of Animals, which has offices in Virginia, England, Italy, and Germany, uses controversial publicity stunts and advertisements to try to change the behavior of large organizations, fashion designers, medical researchers, and anyone else it believes is hurting or mistreating animals. PETA's cofounder and president Ingrid Newkirk says, "People now know that if they do something ghastly to an animal, they can't necessarily get away with it. When we started, nobody knew what animal rights meant. . . . Now, it's an issue." PETA protestors have stripped naked in front of the White House in front of a banner saying, "I'd rather go naked than wear fur." From PETA's perspective, any

**media advocacy**
an advocacy group tactic of framing issues as public issues, exposing questionable, exploitative, or unethical practices, and forcing media coverage by buying media time or creating controversy that is likely to receive extensive news coverage

**product boycott**
an advocacy group tactic of protesting a company's actions by convincing consumers not to purchase its product or service

animal-based product is bad. So, to discourage college students from consuming milk, it made fun of the well-known "Got milk?" ads by covering college campuses with ads saying, "Got beer?" which suggested that beer was more nutritious than milk. It pulled the ads after Mothers Against Drunk Driving protested. Rick McCarty, director of issues management at the National Cattlemen's Beef Association, a frequent target of PETA's protestors, said, "PETA thinks there is no such thing as bad media coverage. And they're very unrepentant about it."[57]

A **product boycott** is a tactic in which an advocacy group actively tries to convince consumers not to purchase a company's product or service. Ecopledge.com is an advocacy group that has signed up 150,000 college students online, all of whom have agreed to boycott organizations that don't respond to their demands. Ecopledge.com, which gives each company one year to make changes and then calls for a boycott, has had success getting General Motors and Ford Motor to leave the Global Climate Coalition, which is against adopting the Kyoto (Japan) agreement on measures to end global warming. It also convinced Coca-Cola to use more recycled plastic in its bottles. It is now targeting Staples, an office supply chain, for selling products made of old-growth wood fibers; Dell computer, which it wants to hold responsible for recycling its customers' computers when they are no longer useful; and Sprint, the telecommunications company, for not printing its phone bills on recycled paper.[58]

## Review 3
### Specific Environment

The specific environment is made up of five components: customers, competitors, suppliers, industry regulators, and advocacy groups. Companies can monitor customers' needs by identifying customer problems after they occur or by anticipating problems before they occur. However, because they tend to focus on well-known competitors, managers often underestimate their competition or do a poor job of identifying future competitors. Since suppliers and buyers are very dependent on each other, that dependence sometimes leads to opportunistic behavior, in which one benefits at the expense of the other. Regulatory agencies affect businesses by creating rules and then enforcing them. Overall, the level of industry regulation has nearly tripled in the last 25 years. Advocacy groups cannot regulate organization practices. However, through public communications, media advocacy, and product boycotts, they try to convince companies to change their practices.

## 4. Making Sense of Changing Environments

*In Chapter 1, you learned that managers are responsible for making sense of their business environments. However, our just-completed discussions of the general and specific environments indicate that making sense of business environments is not an easy task. Because external environments can be dynamic, confusing, and complex, managers use a three-step process to make sense of the changes in their external environments: 4.1 environmental scanning, 4.2 interpreting environmental factors, and 4.3 acting on threats and opportunities.*

### 4.1 Environmental Scanning

**environmental scanning**
searching the environment for important events or issues that might affect an organization

**Environmental scanning** is searching the environment for important events or issues that might affect an organization. Managers scan the environment to stay up-to-date on important factors in their industry. For example, a survey conducted by the International Hotel Association indicated that technology and prices were the most important trends being tracked and scanned by international hotel chain executives. In particular, they were looking for any information about the rates that competitors were charging for hotel rooms in particular international markets or on how to install and use global reservation systems.[59]

Managers also scan their environments to reduce uncertainty. When California began rolling blackouts to ration its limited production of electricity, businesses began looking for novel ways to shield themselves from having electricity unexpectedly turned off. Evans Keller, who raises one million turkeys on his farm in arid central California, purchased eight small generators that he can hook up to tractors to run fans and water misters to keep his turkeys cool in the event that the state turns off power in his area. Keller, whose appeal to Pacific Gas and Electric to be exempted from the blackouts was denied, said, "Believe me, we're not proud. We'll do what we have to do to protect our investment."[60]

Organizational strategies also affect environmental scanning. In other words, managers pay close attention to trends and events that are directly related to their company's ability to compete in the marketplace.[61] And by keeping their eyes and ears open, managers sometimes come across important information by accident. For example, Gary Costley, an employee of Kellogg's, was pulling into the parking lot at work when he noticed a crane on the loading dock of the General Foods' Post cereal plant across the street. He could see that the crane was unloading a special machine made by a German company for manufacturing cereal. This caught his attention, because Kellogg's was having trouble getting a similar machine from a French manufacturer to work. So he went to a store, purchased a camera and film, and stood across the street taking pictures. A Post employee yelled, "Hey, you can't do that." Costley responded, "I'm standing on a public street taking photos. You shouldn't unload your machines in plain sight." The pictures helped convince Kellogg's management to buy the German machines and to not spend any more time or money to make the French machines work.[62]

Finally, environmental scanning is important because it contributes to organizational performance. Environmental scanning helps managers detect environmental changes and problems before they become organizational crises.[63] Furthermore, companies whose CEOs do more environmental scanning have higher profits.[64] CEOs in better-performing firms scan their firm's environments more frequently and scan more key factors in their environments in more depth and detail than do CEOs in poorer performing firms.[65]

### 4.2 Interpreting Environmental Factors

After scanning, managers determine what environmental events and issues mean to the organization. Typically, managers either view environmental events and issues as threats or opportunities. When managers interpret environmental events as threats, they take steps to protect the company from further harm. For example, in France, the neighborhood boulangerie, boucherie, fromagerie, patisserie, and poissonnerie (bakery, butcher, cheese, pastry, and fish shops) have begun to go out of business in large numbers. Their existence is now threatened by Carrefour, a grocery chain that runs huge hypermarkets that are sometimes as large as three football fields. French shoppers load up on cartloads of groceries once a week at the Carrefour to save scarce time and money. One of the best buys is France's traditional loaf of bread, the baguette, which sells for about $1 at small bakeries but goes for 40 cents at the hypermarket. So with their businesses in decline, neighborhood boulangerie, boucherie, fromagerie, patisserie, and poissonnerie have turned to the French government for help, asking it to enact laws limiting construction of new hypermarkets. They're also asking the French government to prevent hypermarkets from selling products below cost, a practice that hypermarkets say they don't use.[66]

By contrast, when managers interpret environmental events as opportunities, they will consider strategic alternatives for taking advantage of those events to improve company performance. Seeing opportunities at opposite ends of the food industry, London-based Unilever paid $2.3 billion for Slim Fast, the maker of nutritional supplements, powders, and bars that help people lose weight, and $326 million for Ben & Jerry's, known for its premium ice cream (Cherry Garcia) and emphasis on social responsibility. When asked why Unilever bought these very different companies, Andrew Lazar, an investment analyst said, "People are flocking to opposite ends of the food spectrum. Clearly, Unilever's acquisitions . . . hit at both sides." However, Unilever also sees an opportunity to expand global sales of both brands. Only 6 percent of Slim Fast's sales are outside of North America, and Unilever hopes to use its worldwide distribution and sales network to dramatically increase that number. Likewise, the purchase of Ben and Jerry's gives Unilever, the world's largest distributor of ice cream, a so-called super premium brand of its own to compete against Häagen-Dazs, the best-selling premium ice cream in the world.[67]

### 4.3 Acting on Threats and Opportunities

After scanning for information on environmental events and issues, and interpreting them as threats or opportunities, managers have to decide how to respond to these environmental factors. However, deciding what to do under conditions of uncertainty is difficult. Managers are never completely confident that they have all the information they need or that they correctly understand the information they have.

Because it is impossible to comprehend all the factors and changes, managers rely on simplified models of external environments called "cognitive maps." **Cognitive maps** summarize the perceived relationships between environmental factors and possible organizational actions. For example, the cognitive map shown in Exhibit 2.6 represents a

**cognitive maps**
graphic depictions of how managers believe environmental factors relate to possible organizational actions

---

EXHIBIT 2.6

COGNITIVE MAPS

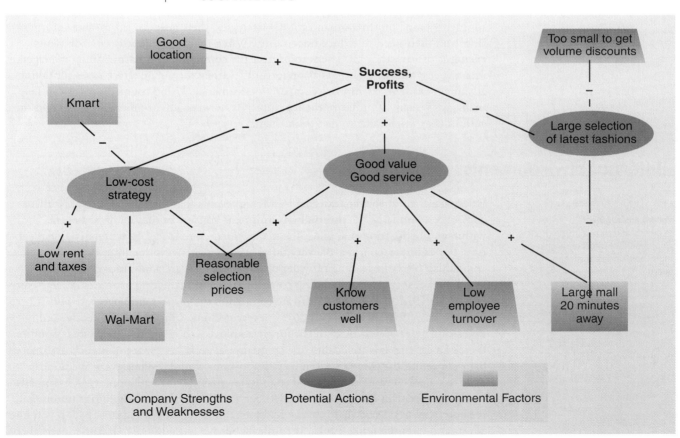

small clothing store owner's interpretation of her business environment. The map shows three kinds of variables. The first, shown as rectangles, are environmental factors, such as a Wal-Mart or a large mall 20 minutes away. The second, shown in ovals, are potential actions that the store owner might take, such as a low-cost strategy; a good value, good service strategy; or a large selection of the latest fashions strategy. The third, shown as trapezoids, are company strengths, such as low employee turnover, and weaknesses, such as small size.

The arrows on the map indicate whether the manager believes there is a positive or negative relationship between variables. For example, the manager believes that a low-cost strategy wouldn't work, because Wal-Mart and Kmart are nearby. Offering a large selection of the latest fashions would not work either—not with the small size of the store and that large nearby mall. However, this manager believes that a good value, good service strategy would lead to success and profits, because of low employee turnover, a good knowledge of customers, a reasonable selection of clothes at reasonable prices, and a good location.

In the end, managers must complete all three steps—environmental scanning, interpreting environmental factors, and acting on threats and opportunities—to make sense of changing external environments. Environmental scanning helps managers more accurately interpret their environments and take actions that improve company performance. Through scanning, managers keep tabs on what competitors are doing, identify market trends, and stay alert to current events that affect their company's operations. Armed with the environmental information they have gathered, managers can then minimize the impact of threats and turn opportunities into increased profits.

### Review 4
#### Making Sense of Changing Environments

Managers use a three-step process to make sense of external environments: environmental scanning, interpreting information, and acting on it. Managers scan their environments based on their organizational strategies, their need for up-to-date information, and their need to reduce uncertainty. When managers identify environmental events as threats, they take steps to protect the company from harm. When managers identify environmental events as opportunities, they formulate alternatives for taking advantage of them to improve company performance. Using cognitive maps can help managers visually summarize the relationships between environmental factors and the actions they might take to deal with them.

## Internal Environments

**internal environment**
the events and trends inside an organization that affect management, employees, and organizational culture

External environments are external trends and events that have the potential to affect companies. Similarly, the **internal environment** consists of the trends and events within an organization that affect the management, employees, and organizational culture. For example, consider the very different internal environments at two software companies: SAS, the leading provider of statistical software, and Trilogy Software, which makes software for handling complex sales and marketing processes at large companies like IBM. Unlike most software companies that expect employees to work 12- to 14-hour days, SAS offices close at 6 P.M. every evening. Employees also receive unlimited sick days each year. And to encourage employees to spend time with their families, there's an on-site daycare facility, the company cafeteria has plenty of highchairs and baby seats, and the company even has a seven-hour workday. Plus, every Wednesday, M&M chocolate candies, plain and peanut, are passed out to all employees, eventually totalling more than 22.5 tons of M&Ms per year. David Russo, who heads up Human Resources for SAS, said that founder and CEO Jim Goodnight's idea is that "if you hire adults and treat them like adults, then they'll behave like adults." [68] If SAS's internal environment is designed for "adults," it's fair to say that Trilogy Software's internal envi-

Internal environments are important because they affect how people think, feel, and act while on the job. At SAS, the cafeteria pianist is just one of the perks employees enjoy. Because of such a positive and balanced corporate culture, SAS has extremely low attrition and is regularly hailed as one of the best corporations in America to work for.

COURTESY OF SAS INSTITUTE

ronment is designed to be like a college campus. In fact, each new hire spends three months in "Trilogy University" (TU), a boot camp that teaches them about the software industry. At TU they are actually expected to create new products or improve existing ones. And, unlike SAS, Trilogy is open for business at all hours. In fact, TU's posted business hours are 8 A.M. to midnight, Monday through Saturday, and noon to 8 P.M. on Sunday. Indeed, at 10 P.M. one night, founder Joe Liemandt plays the role of Alex Trebek in a *Jeopardy*-like game in which a group of new hires at TU are quizzed on Trilogy's various products, customers, and employees.[69]

Internal environments are important because they affect what people think, feel, and do at work. Given SAS's internal environment, it shouldn't surprise you to know that almost no one quits. In a typical software company the same size as SAS, 1,000 people would quit each year. At SAS, only 130 leave each year.[70] Likewise, given Trilogy's internal environment, it's the rule and not the exception to quickly give employees, even brand new ones, as much responsibility as they can handle. Jeff Daniels, Trilogy's lead recruiter, said, "You don't have to sit around here earning tenure before you can see a customer. One of our TUers, a guy from Harvard, is already working on accounts in France. I go out and tell my recruits, 'A kid your age was here for a month and a half, and now he's in Paris. That's Trilogy.' I don't go around saying this is the place for everyone. It's not. But it's definitely an environment where people who are passionate about what they do can thrive." Comments such as these reflect the key component in internal environments, organization culture.[71] More specifically, **organizational culture** is the set of key values, beliefs, and attitudes shared by organizational members.

**organizational culture**
the values, beliefs, and attitudes shared by organizational members

*After reading the next section, you should be able to*
*5. explain how organizational cultures are created and how they can help companies be successful.*

## 5. Organizational Cultures: Creation, Success, and Change

*Let's take a closer look at 5.1 how organizational cultures are created and maintained, 5.2 the characteristics of successful organizational cultures, and 5.3 how companies can accomplish the difficult task of changing organizational cultures.*

# BlastFromThePast

## Capturing Corporate Culture by Writing Corporate History

Typically, the "Blast from the Past" features in this book will teach you something about the history of management ideas presented in a chapter. This time, however, instead of learning about the history of internal and external organizational environments, you will learn how companies are capturing their corporate cultures by writing their

corporate histories. Three basic questions are relevant to the issue of cultures and corporate history: Why? How? and How much?

Why should a company capture its corporate culture by writing its corporate history? When it comes to corporate culture, history matters, because it helps employees and managers understand the key people, events, and changes that shaped a company. For example, McDonald's helps preserve its history and culture each year as it celebrates founder Ray Kroc's birthday by having McDonald's executives spend the day working in its restaurants. According to Kroc, this is to remind McDonald's managers that "if it's below [their] dignity to mop floors, clean toilets, and roll up [their] sleeves, then [they] are not going to succeed: [Their] attitude is wrong." McDonald's even created an exhibit called "Talk to Ray," in which, thanks to messages videotaped before his death, anyone can "ask" Ray questions about McDonald's values and history.

How does a company capture its history? According to Willa Baum, who directs the Regional Oral History Office at the University of California, Berkeley, "You start with who's alive and has a good memory, and then expand out. You want to have people who represent the workers and can talk about the progression and changes in the organization from their perspective." For example, Clarence Leis, who was the second manager of the very first Wal-Mart store, tells this story about Wal-Mart founder Sam Walton and how Wal-Mart developed its strategy of everyday low prices:

Rogers [the store in Rogers, Arkansas] had been open about a year, and everything was just piled up on tables, with no rhyme or reason whatsoever. Sam [Walton] asked me to kind of group the stuff by category or department, and that's when we began our department system. The thing I remember most, though, was the way we priced goods. Merchandise would come in and we would just lay it down on the floor and get out the invoice. Sam wouldn't let us hedge on a price at

all. Say the list price was $1.98, but we had only paid 50 cents. Initially, I would say, "Well, it's originally $1.98, so why don't we sell it for $1.25?" And he'd say, "No. We paid 50 cents for it. Mark it up 30 percent, and that's it. No matter what you pay for it, if we get a great deal, pass it on to the customer." And of course that's what we did.

What does it cost to capture a company's history? It depends on what kind and how extensive a history a company wants. Oral histories, in which videotaped interviews are recorded and edited together, much like a movie, can be expensive. For midsized companies, the cost of an oral history can run between $20,000 and $30,000. A rough estimate is approximately $1,000 an hour of filmed interviews. This includes the cost of interviewing, transcribing, editing, and indexing for research purposes. Written histories can also be expensive. A British firm Royal Insurance spent roughly half a million dollars for 50,000 copies of a full-color, 240-page book to celebrate its 150th year in business.

Many companies consider the money well spent. Hamish MacGibbon, director of publisher James & James, which has published over 40 company histories, said, "It [a company history] is a way of engaging people in what the company is about and getting across certain messages. It says, 'This is why we're good at what we're doing, why we're a good company to trade with, invest in or work for, or why we're doing a good job for the community.' In short, it gets people involved in the culture of a company."

**Sources:** K.D. Conti, "Oral Histories: The Most Overlooked Public Relations Tool," *Communication World*, June-July 1995, 52-54. N. Hassell, "Trading on the Past," *Management Today*, March 1996, 81-82. M.A. Salva-Ramirez, "McDonald's: A Prime Example of Corporate Culture," *Public Relations Quarterly*, Winter 1995, 30-32. S. Walton & J. Huey, *Sam Walton: Made in America* (New York: Doubleday, 1992).

## 5.1 Creation and Maintenance of Organizational Cultures

A primary source of organizational culture is the company founder. Founders like Thomas J. Watson (IBM), Sam Walton (Wal-Mart), Bill Gates (Microsoft), or Frederick Maytag (Maytag) create organizations in their own images that they imprint with their beliefs, attitudes, and values. For example, Thomas J. Watson, Sr. proclaimed that IBM's three basic beliefs were the pursuit of excellence, customer service, and showing "respect for the individual," meaning company employees. Microsoft employees share founder Bill Gates' intensity for staying ahead of software competitors. Says a Microsoft vice president, "No matter how good your product, you are only 18 months away from failure."[72]

**Struggling with the Culture? Count on Informal Encounters**

New employees can have trouble fitting into a new organizational culture. When that happens, the best thing to do is to talk to experienced coworkers in informal encounters, like in the hall, on the staircase, at lunch, or after work over a beer. Authors Don Cohen and Laurence Prusak say, "Telling and listening to stories, chatting, sharing a little gossip, are the main ways that people in organizations come to trust and understand one another." In informal, face-to-face encounters, people will tell you how things really work (i.e., the culture). So, if you're new and feeling lost, bump into someone in the hallway.

**Source:** D. Cohen & L. Prusak, *In Good Company: How Social Capital Makes Organizations Work.* (Boston, MA: Harvard Business School Press, 2001).

**organizational stories**
stories told by organizational members to make sense of organizational events and changes and to emphasize culturally consistent assumptions, decisions, and actions

**organizational heroes**
people celebrated for their qualities and achievements within an organization

While company founders are instrumental in the creation of organizational cultures, founders retire, die, or choose to leave their companies. So when the founders are gone, how are the founders' values, attitudes, and beliefs sustained in the organizational culture? Answer: stories and heroes.

Organizational members tell **organizational stories** to make sense of organizational events and changes, and to emphasize culturally consistent assumptions, decisions, and actions.[73] At Wal-Mart, stories abound about founder Sam Walton's thriftiness as he strove to make Wal-Mart the low cost retailer that it is today.

> In those days, we would go on buying trips with Sam, and we'd all stay, as much as we could, in one room or two. I remember one time in Chicago when we stayed eight of us to a room. And the room wasn't very big to begin with. You might say we were on a pretty restricted budget. (Gary Reinboth, one of Wal-Mart's first store managers.)[74]

Today, Sam Walton's thriftiness still permeates Wal-Mart. Everyone, including top executives and the CEO, flies coach rather than business or first class. When traveling on business, it's still the norm to share rooms (though two to a room and not eight!) at inexpensive hotels like Motel 6 and Super 8 instead of more expensive Holiday Inns. Likewise, on business travel, Wal-Mart will only reimburse up to $15 per meal, which is half to one-third the reimbursement rate at similar-sized companies (remember, Wal-Mart is one of the largest companies in the world). And, at one of its annual meetings, new CEO Lee Scott reinforced Sam Walton's beliefs by exhorting Wal-Mart employees to bring back and use the free pencils and pens from their travels. Most people in the audience didn't think he was kidding.[75]

A second way in which organizational culture is sustained is by recognizing and celebrating heroes. By definition, **organizational heroes** are organizational people admired for their qualities and achievements within the organization. The company motto of USAA, the United Services Automobile Association, which provides insurance to people in the U.S. Army, Navy, Air Force, Marines, and Coast Guard, is "We know what it means to serve." Mrs. Lawless, an elderly widow of a military officer, called Stephanie Valadez, a USAA customer service representative, during an ice storm. She called for help because her home was without heat and she couldn't get out to get the medicine that she needed. She told Stephanie, "My husband told me that if I ever had a problem and didn't know where else to turn, I should call USAA. He said you would take care of me." Stephanie immediately called the Red Cross, who in turn helped with the heat in her home and her medicine. She also stayed on the line for an extended time to comfort Mrs. Lawless. Ironically, though, she did this despite the fact that her computer screen indicated that Mrs. Lawless's insurance policy had long since lapsed. Kent Williams of USAA said, "I suspect that most other companies would have hung up on Mrs. Lawless. But hanging up isn't part of our mind-set. That's what we mean when we say that customer service is a relationship, not a transaction."[76]

### 5.2 Successful Organizational Cultures

Preliminary research shows that organizational culture is related to organizational success. As shown in Exhibit 2.7, cultures based on adaptability, involvement, a clear mission, and consistency can help companies achieve higher sales growth, return on assets, profits, quality, and employee satisfaction.[77]

*Adaptability* is the ability to notice and respond to changes in the organization's environment. Cultures need to reinforce important values and behaviors, but they become

EXHIBIT 2.7

SUCCESSFUL ORGANIZATIONAL CULTURES

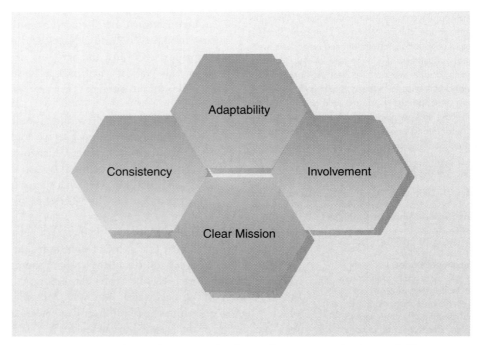

**Source:** D.R. Denison & A.K. Mishra, "Toward a Theory of Organizational Culture and Effectiveness," *Organization Science* 6 (1995): 204-223.

dysfunctional if they prevent change. At Trilogy Software, one of the key beliefs and values is that the company is "built to last." This means that "We are building a living and learning organization, not a monument; we show flexibility, innovation, and a willingness to adapt. In everything we do, we look past the boundaries of our teams, our short-term goals, and ourselves. Our work is never finished, because Trilogy is never finished." Trilogy's other key beliefs, integrity, customer success, great people, and great technology, are shown in Exhibit 2.8.

In cultures that promote higher levels of *employee involvement* in decision making, employees feel a greater sense of ownership and responsibility. For instance, some people question whether SAS's fantastic benefits create a sense of entitlement, rather than a sense of ownership and responsibility. David Russo, who heads human resources for SAS, said, "To some people, this looks like the Good Ship Lollipop, floating down a stream. It's not. It's part of a soundly designed strategy." And that strategy is to take away anything that gets in the way of people doing their work. Need to work out to maintain your health? SAS has a 36,000 square foot gym for aerobics, basketball, yoga, weight lifting, and exercise machines. They'll even wash and dry your sweaty work out clothes. Worried about your aging father in Chicago? Call the elder-care coordinator who will make calls to check on delivery of medicine or the availability and quality of assisted care facilities. Need allergy shots or a prescription refill? Both can be handled at work. At SAS, this strategy works. Said employee Kathy Passarella, "You're given the freedom, the flexibility, and the resources to do your job. Because you're treated well, you treat the company well. When you walk down the halls here, it's rare that you hear people talking about anything but work."[78]

A **company's vision** is its purpose or reason for existing. In organizational cultures in which there is a clear organizational vision, the organization's strategic purpose and di-

**company vision**
a company's purpose or reason for existing

**EXHIBIT 2.8**

### TRILOGY SOFTWARE'S CULTURAL BELIEFS AND VALUES

As Trilogy has grown from a start-up to one of the most successful companies in e-commerce, our organization has adopted a set of values that guides us in everything we do.

**Integrity.** Integrity defines how we act, both as individuals and as a company. Put simply: We do what we say. We follow through on our commitments to our employees, our customers, and the community. We are honest and truthful when we make promises, and relentless with their delivery. Our integrity is reflected in our respect for others. We realize that we are part of something bigger than we are, and that our actions represent the entire organization. Integrity for us is not a value of expedience. We live it, always.

**Customer success.** Trilogy is building a customer-centric company. Our purpose is to deliver the high-value technology solutions that help our customers achieve their business goals. We form long lasting partnerships with customers through repeated successful delivery. We have a strong commitment to the success of our customers. We know our customers, and our daily goals are aligned behind making them successful.

**Great people.** Trilogy's business is driven by innovation and built on intellectual property. Our people are the backbone of our business. To build a great business and a great company, we need great people. Great people have a deep domain expertise and a broad business perspective. They constantly stretch themselves and grow their knowledge. Great people are results driven and they prioritize for impact. They get the job done. Great people are also leaders; they are an example for others, they energize their teams, they create a great vision, and they act with values. What is the best thing about Trilogy? It's the people.

**Built to last.** We are building Trilogy into one of the great, admired, and lasting companies of the next century. Trilogy is more than the people, more than our current products or customers—Trilogy is an institution that will outlast all of us. We make choices with this in mind, choosing initiatives that provide sustainable growth, choosing people for their potential as much as for their current capability. We are building a living and learning organization, not a monument; we show flexibility, innovation, and a willingness to adapt. In everything we do, we look past the boundaries of our teams, our short-term goals, and ourselves. Our work is never finished, because Trilogy is never finished.

**Great technology.** Trilogy's leverage in the marketplace comes from our ability to solve valuable business problems for our customers with sophisticated technology. Great technology is the key: it delivers the value we promise, and allows us to make big promises. Great technology is used and relied upon by customers because it works. It becomes the gold standard solution and is widely adopted in an industry. At Trilogy, we constantly expand our technical expertise, translating it into software so that we can continue to win competitive battles on the strength of our technology. We have a passion for technology. It's the way we express ourselves.

**Source**: "Trilogy Values: The Beliefs that Guide our Organization," Trilogy Software. [Online] Available http://www.trilogy.com/sections/about_us/our_values.cfm, 21 June 2001.

rection are apparent to everyone in the company. And when managers are uncertain about their business environments, the vision helps guide the discussions, decisions, and behavior of the people in the company. At F.H. Faulding & Company, an Australian-based provider of healthcare products and services doing business in 70 countries, the vision is "delivering innovative and valued solutions in healthcare."[79] This vision reinforces Faulding's mission by letting employees know why the company is in business (to deliver healthcare solutions) and the values that really matter (innovative and valued solutions). To give its employees even more guidance, Faulding has clearly defined each of the key words in the vision statement. For example, "delivering" is defined to mean targeting quality drugs, products, and services to the right place at the right time while concentrating on a global perspective. Likewise, "solutions" is defined as being focused, timely, and profitable by making useful quality products and services that satisfy customers' and partners' needs. Specific vision statements strengthen organizational cultures by letting everyone know why the company is in business, what really matters (i.e., values), and how those values can be used to guide daily actions and behaviors.[80] Commenting on the value of the vision statement for Faulding, Donna Martin, the senior vice president of human resources said, "A vision has to be more than a set of target revenue or profit numbers to meet. It has to be elevating, inspiring, with a strong emphasis

# BeenThereDoneThat

**Howard Schulz is the founder, chairperson, and CEO of Starbucks Coffee. In this interview he talks about his beliefs and Starbuck's corporate culture.**

**Q:** Why do you believe in "sharing success"?

**A:** Success is best when it is shared. If you want to create an enduring enterprise today, you need to see that the most significant component—the people who build the company—are part of the fabric of the enterprise. Success has to be shared so nobody is left behind.

**Q:** How have you shared success at Starbucks?

**A:** In the late '80s, we recognized that building a company like Starbucks would be a very difficult endeavor. We envisioned a national retail company, not franchise-based but company-owned stores, that was highly dependent on people, specifically part-time workers. And so we created a unique benefits program that provided equity in the form of stock options and comprehensive health care to part-time workers. I believe we were the first, and still today one of the few, companies to provide those benefits to part-time people. We also shared our governing values and guiding principles. We tried to make sure that the foundation on which we were building the company was linked to everyone in the organization, not just to a few select people at the top. That has given us the ability not only to attract world-class people at all levels of the company, but also to retain them and to retain our values as we have grown from 11 stores and 100 employees in 1987 to 2,400 stores and 40,000 employees today.

**Q:** How do you manage people?

**A:** In today's business environment, people often bring a degree of cynicism with them when they enter a company. People are less believing in the gospel of a company and the promises of management than they were 20 years ago. And yet to build respect and confidence with your customers, you must build respect and confidence with your people first. We have tried to create a grassroots component inside our business in which people have access to how decisions are made, why decisions are made, and then, if they feel free, as I think they do in our environment, to both criticize and compliment and to discuss their feelings about how we are running our business. Every quarter, we stand in front of all of our people in an open forum everywhere we do business to discuss the last quarter's results. We also discuss openly our plans, decisions, strategies, and concerns. We've been doing this now for almost 10 years. So, built into our culture is the sense that people can say what they feel, and what they feel is important for me to hear. There's no retribution. What comes out of that is a tremendous trust. We're a better company because our people participate in the decisions and feel a sense of belonging as part of the decision-making process.

**Q:** How do you manage to create a culture of meaning and loyalty around coffee? I mean, some people think it takes some great cause, but you've done it with coffee,

**A:** I think that every business has to stand for something, and people have to understand what the cause is. People want to feel that they are part of something that is bigger than themselves. So, in a sense, our business is not about coffee; obviously coffee is at the center of what we do, but it's about the experience we create in our stores and in our company. Coffee has been at the center of conversation for hundreds of years, and it's a conduit to what we do. We bring a passionate commitment to the quality of the coffee and to the kind of company that we're trying to build. We want to be proud of the equity in our name. We want to share what we do with our friends and family and have people feel a sense of pride about working for a company that evokes a sense of emotion and pride that is bigger than the job they are doing.

**Q:** What kind of experience do you want people to have when they stop at Starbucks for coffee?

**A:** I think the experience is somewhat different for every person, but we are trying to create a "third place" for our customers. Never before have people been so busy, harried, and stressed as they are today. A "third place" is a place between home and work where people can come to get their own personal time out, their respite, meet with friends, have a sense of gathering. In a sense, Starbucks has become an extension of people's front porch. There's a level of trust in what we stand for, a sense of reliability, and this has transformed itself into Starbucks being the most frequented retail store in America. Our average customer comes in 18 times a month, and over 10 million customers a week come into our stores.

**Q:** Is that what you mean when you talk about the "true source of competitive advantage"? It's transforming coffee from a commodity into a memorable and meaningful experience?

**A:** That's exactly what I mean. We've never viewed coffee as a commodity. And we've never viewed our people as commodities. I think the foundation of our success is the passionate commitment we have to the quality of coffee that we buy and roast, and making sure that the people in our company are not simply a line item. We view our people as business partners. My primary role or responsibility is to make absolutely sure that the culture of our company is compatible with the kind of people that we want to attract and retain. My job is to create a sense of belonging and build a sense of trust and confidence in what this company stands for with our employees and customers. The reason that our customers come back is the quality of the coffee and the quality of the experience. And the experience comes to life because of our people. We can't expect our customers to have trust in what we do if the people who represent us don't trust the company.

**Q:** What are some of the things you do personally to tend to your people?

**A:** I spend a significant portion of my time in trying to touch as many people as I possibly can during the work week. That means visiting lots of stores, walking the halls of our company, communicating via email, communicating in every way possible. I want our people to know how much they are appreciated and to know why the contribution they make every day is so valuable. There is no replacement for being in front of people face-to-face, eyeball-to-eyeball, and communicating the values of our company. I honestly feel that we are in the "people business." Yes, we will likely do about $1.7 billion this year, but when you consider that the average sale in Starbucks stores everyday is $3.60, you begin to see how many customers we deal with. If our people are not excited, enthused, and passionate about what we're doing, we've got a real problem.

**Q:** Will you stay with coffee or get into theme parks? What is your future?

**A:** I think every company must stick to its knitting, understand its core competency, know what the value proposition is for the

customer, and do everything possible to get close to the customer. So you won't see us getting far afield from what we do now.

The future is leveraging our core competency. We are still in the infant stages of growing our retail business. We open up two new stores every business day. And yet with only 2,400 stores, we're less than 50 percent of the way to our goal in the United States alone. This is a very large market. We only have five percent market share of coffee consumption in America. So, we're still growing our core retail business. And we're looking at ways to build complimentary channels of distribution.

**Source:** "Interview with Howard Schultz: Sharing Success," *Executive Excellence*, November 1999, 16. Used with permission

---

**consistent organizational cultures** when a company actively defines and teaches organizational values, beliefs, and attitudes

on the future. A vision has to be a compelling and crystal-clear statement about where the organization is heading."[81]

Finally, in **consistent organizational cultures**, the company actively defines and teaches organizational values, beliefs, and attitudes. Consistent organizational cultures are also called strong cultures, because the core beliefs are widely shared and strongly held. The culture aboard nuclear submarines is an example of a highly consistent, extremely strong organizational culture. Because they are driven by nuclear power, the threat of a nuclear accident is real (though no accident has ever occurred on a U.S. nuclear submarine). Accordingly, two of the key cultural values are prevention and containment, that is, preventing and containing system failures that could lead to a nuclear spill or accident. Consequently, crewmembers spend three hours a day learning and practicing jobs outside of their responsibility. In theory, any crewmember should know what to do in almost any situation to prevent a small problem from becoming a crisis. Another important cultural value is quiet. Unlike ships that engage in direct battles, submarines hide, trying to avoid detection. Since a sound can easily be heard hundreds of miles away, the dropping of a tool or slamming of a door can easily give away the submarine's position. Thus, every procedure, rule, and practice is designed to be done quietly.[82]

### 5.3 Changing Organizational Cultures

Organizational cultures exist on three levels.[83] First, on the surface level, are the reflections of an organization's culture that can be seen, heard, or observed, such as symbolic artifacts (i.e., dress codes, office layouts, etc.) and workers' and managers' behaviors. Next, just below the surface, are the values and beliefs expressed by people in the company. You can't see these, but by listening carefully to what people say and how decisions are made or explained, those values and beliefs become clear. Finally, unconsciously held assumptions and beliefs are buried deep below the surface. These are the unwritten views and rules that so are strongly held and so widely shared that they are rarely discussed or even thought about unless someone attempts to change them or unknowingly violates them. For example, about five years ago, when IBM's new CEO Louis Gerstner was frustrated with his ability to change IBM's culture, he decreed that the core IBM beliefs set forth by founder Thomas J. Watson, Sr. (excellence, customer satisfaction, and respect for the individual) be replaced with the eight new principles. Instead of responding to his attempts to improve the company, many IBMers were shocked because Thomas J. Watson, Jr., who succeeded his father as IBM's CEO, once

65

stated that IBM's success was dependent on its ability to change everything "except those basic beliefs." [84]

So when it comes to changing cultures, it can be very difficult to change unconscious assumptions and beliefs held deep below the surface. Instead, managers should focus on the parts of the organizational culture they can control, including observable surface-level items, such as worker behaviors; symbolic artifacts; and expressed values and beliefs, which can be influenced through employee selection. Let's learn how these can be used to change organizational cultures.

One way of changing a corporate culture is to use behavioral addition or behavioral substitution to establish new patterns of behavior among managers and employees. [85] **Behavioral addition** is the process of having managers and employees perform a new behavior, while **behavioral substitution** is having managers and employees perform a new behavior in place of another behavior. The key in both instances is to choose behaviors that are central to and symbolic of the "old" culture you're changing and the "new" culture that you want to create. One of the key behavioral changes at Continental airlines in the last decade is that the airline has gone from last to first in terms of on-time arrivals. Under the "late-arrival culture," a flight attendant would be more worried about leaving the gate with the right number of meals on the plane than leaving on time. According to CEO Gordon Bethune, a flight attendant would say, "Tough luck, buddy [to the flight caterer], I don't care. I am not going without the 20 meals. That's your problem." Then the caterer would have to get the missing meals and the flight would be 20 minutes late. However, once Continental started rewarding its flight attendants and other employees for on-time arrivals and departures, behavior began to change (see Chapter 10 for a more detailed explanation of this change process). According to Bethune, now, under the "on-time arrival culture," the flight attendant would look at the caterer who didn't provide enough meals for the flight and say, "Hey, don't you do this to me again." She would then close the plane's door and leave the gate on time by "finding some investment bankers in the back who will trade food for booze." According to Bethune, "That's how she gets paid. That's how behavior changes: We become collective winners and give things customers' value." [86]

Another way in which managers can begin to change corporate culture is to change the **visible artifacts** of their old culture, such as the office design and layout, company dress code, and recipients (or nonrecipients) of company benefits and perks like stock options, personal parking spaces, or the private company dining room. Besides changing who was responsible for oil drilling decisions at UPR, Jack Messman also implemented a "smart casual" dress code for every day of the week. And on Fridays, even blue jeans were acceptable, as long as employees were not scheduled to visit with customers. Messman also moved the company headquarters, because the current headquarters, with its wood-paneled walls and plush carpeting, was no longer consistent with the new, informal culture. Another company making sizable changes in visible corporate artifacts is Yellow Freight, a trucking company. The courtyard fountains, once a prominent sign of company success, are now viewed as a needless expense and have been turned off. Expensive paintings, once displayed in the headquarters lobby, have been replaced by pictures of trucks and freight terminals. The executive dining room, once reserved for senior managers, has been converted to a conference room that anyone can use for special occasions. [87]

Cultures can also be changed by hiring and selecting people with values and beliefs consistent with the company's desired culture. *Selection* is the process of gathering information about job applicants to decide who should be offered a job. As discussed in Chapter 14 on Human Resources, most selection instruments measure whether job applicants have the knowledge, skills, and abilities needed to succeed in their jobs. However, companies are increasingly testing job applicants for their fit with

---

**behavioral addition**

the process of having managers and employees perform new behaviors that are central to and symbolic of the new organizational culture that a company wants to create

**behavioral substitution**

the process of having managers and employees perform new behaviors central to the "new" organizational culture in place of behaviors that were central to the "old" organizational culture

**visible artifacts**

visible signs of an organization's culture, such as the office design and layout, company dress code, and company benefits and perks, like stock options, personal parking spaces, or the private company dining room

66

the company's desired culture (i.e., values and beliefs). Management consultant Ram Charan says, "A poor job match is not only harmful to the individual but also to the company."[88] At Bristol-Myers, people who didn't fit the culture tended to leave. Ben Dowell, who runs Bristol-Myers' Center for Leadership Development, said "What came through was, those who left were uncomfortable in our culture or violated some core area of our value system."[89] The first step to successfully hiring people who have values consistent with the desired culture is to define and describe that culture. Bristol-Myers hired an organizational psychologist who spent four months interviewing senior managers. He concluded that Bristol-Myers' culture was team-driven and focused on research and development, which meant that it valued self-motivated, intellectually curious people.

The second step is to insure applicant fit with the culture by using selection tests, instruments, and exercises to measure these values and beliefs in job applicants. (See Chapter 14 for a complete review of applicant and managerial selection.) At Southwest Airlines, humor and a good attitude are two of the most important requirements in its new hires. Chairman and former CEO Herb Kelleher said, "What's important is that a customer should get off the airplane feeling: 'I didn't just get from A to B. I had one of the most pleasant experiences I ever had and I'll be back for that reason.'"[90] For instance, on a flight from Houston to Dallas, a flight attendant addresses passengers over the speaker system, saying, "Could y'all lean in a little toward the center aisle, please?" Met with confused looks from passengers, she continues, "Just a bit, please. That's it. No, the other way, sir. Thanks. You see, the pilot has to pull out of this space here, and he needs to be able to check the rearview mirrors." Then Marilyn and her fellow flight attendants rap the flight safety instructions, "Federal regulations say you must comply/If you don't, you can kiss your seatmate goodbye! Chhh—ch-ch-chhh—ch-ch." Corny, yes, but exactly what Southwest and its customers want, and they get it by hiring people consistent with their hard-working, fun-loving culture. Says Kelleher, "We draft great attitudes. If you don't have a good attitude, we don't want you, no matter how skilled you are. We can change skill level through training. We can't change attitude."[91]

Corporate cultures are very difficult to change. Consequently, there is no guarantee that any one approach, changing visible cultural artifacts or behavioral substitution or hiring people with values consistent with a company's desired culture, will change a company's organizational culture. However, the best results are obtained by combining these methods. Together, these are some of the best tools that managers have for changing culture, because they send the clear message to managers and employees that "the accepted way of doing things" has changed.

67

## Review 5

### Organizational Cultures: Creation, Success, and Change

Organizational culture is the set of key values, beliefs, and attitudes shared by organizational members. Organizational cultures are often created by company founders and then sustained through the telling of organizational stories and the celebration of organizational heroes. Adaptable cultures that promote employee involvement, that make clear the organization's strategic purpose and direction, and that actively define and teach organizational values and beliefs can help companies achieve higher sales growth, return on assets, profits, quality, and employee satisfaction. Organizational cultures exist on three levels: the surface level, where cultural artifacts and behaviors can be observed; just below the surface, where values and beliefs are expressed; and deep below the surface, where unconsciously held assumptions and beliefs exist. Managers can begin to change company cultures by focusing on the top two levels and by using behavioral substitution and behavioral addition, changing visible artifacts, and selecting job applicants with values and beliefs consistent with the desired company culture.

## What Really Happened?

Many people believe that managers have total control over their organizations. If management wants something done, it happens. Yet, as you learned in the case of EasyJet, managers cannot control all external factors. However, a lack of control isn't necessarily a bad thing. Companies can succeed by scanning their business environments for events and trends, interpreting what those changes mean, and then acting to adapt to those changes. Read the following to find out what really happened to EasyJet as it tried to make sense of the changes in its external environment.

**So the question is "Will you make it?" The odds are stacked against you. In the United States, 130 airlines have gone out of business in the last 25 years, most of them new start-ups like EasyJet. The same forces that brought them down could bring EasyJet down too.**

Many people mistakenly believe that the answer to the question "Will your company make it?" is a function of whether a company has sufficient funds, strong management capability, and a sound strategy. While clearly important, you can't answer this question without taking a look at external environments, meaning the forces and events outside a company that have the potential to influence or affect it. Organizations are influenced by two kinds of external environments: the general environment, which consists of economic, technological, sociocultural, and political/legal events and trends, and the specific environment, which consists of customers, competitors, suppliers, industry regulators, and advocacy groups.

At this point in its young life, EasyJet faces challenges in the economic, supplier, competitor, and industry components of its environment (the latter two are discussed below). EasyJet faces a slowing economy with rising jet prices. However, unlike most airlines, it has not used financial hedging to protect itself from suddenly rising prices (hedging is a method of shielding companies from the risk associated with changing prices). Increasing fuel prices will make it much more difficult to keep prices low. In terms of suppliers, EasyJet decided early on to not use travel agents to book tickets. In fact, some of its first ads said, "Cut out travel agents. Book direct." When EasyJet first flew from London to Athens, travel agents took the company to court to force it to sell tickets through them. Founder Stelios Haji-Ioannou, who is originally from Greece, then put out another ad that promised a free ticket to anyone who came to court to support EasyJet. Nearly 1,000 people showed up for the free tickets, including some travel agents! Today, as from the start, EasyJet books all of its tickets to reduce costs and avoid paying commissions to travel agents. In fact, nearly 90 percent of its tickets are purchased via its **http://www.easyjet.com** Web site. Travel agents don't make a dime in commissions and EasyJet keeps its prices low. Says Stelios with a smile, "We have a very simple relationship with travel agents. We hate them and they hate us."

**You know that Southwest Airline's low-cost model worked in the United States, but can it work in Europe when so many other air carriers are following the same model? So what do you do about the competition?**

In the United States, Southwest Airlines is the only major, low-cost airline that flies coast to coast (there are five regional low-cost airlines). However, in Europe, EasyJet faces competition from Dublin-based RyanAir; Portugal's PGA; U.K.-based British Midland, Debonair, and AirOne airlines; and Richard Branson's Virgin Express. One of the first things that EasyJet or any other company needs to do is conduct a competitive analysis. That is, decide who their competitors are, anticipate their moves, and then determine their strengths and weaknesses. Surprisingly, because they tend to focus on only two or three well-known competitors with similar goals and resources, managers often do a poor job of identifying potential competitors. Managers also need to be sure to not underestimate competitors' capabilities. When this happens, managers don't take the steps they should to continue to improve their products or services. The result can be significant decreases in both market share and profits. Fortunately, neither of these mistakes has been made at EasyJet.

More than any of its competitors, EasyJet has used technology to keep prices low. By only offering online promotions, by discounting purchases made on the Web, and by charging extra for phone bookings, more than 90 percent of its customers, the highest rate in the industry, book tickets on the Web. And, if it can get 100 percent of its customers to buy online, it will save nearly 30 percent per ticket compared to its competitors. Moreover, as EasyJet expands throughout Europe, it translates its Web site into new languages for each new market. That's much cheaper than having to hire another set of staffers who are fluent in new languages.

And while the computer system is highly complex to allow EasyJet to fill as many seats as possible, its ticketing rules are extremely simple. The earlier you purchase, the cheaper your ticket. And, because of its price promise, EasyJet won't undercut customers who buy early by selling empty seats for cheap on the day of departure. Still, with its low cost and yield management software, it flies its jets 84 percent full, much higher than the industry average of 70 percent.

So can EasyJet beat or meet the competition? Thus far, the answer is yes. When British Airway's low-cost airline, Go, was started three years ago, Stelios got even by getting tickets for Go's inaugural flight. He and his management team showed up in EasyJet's trademark color orange to hand out coupons promising free flights. Journalists on hand ignored Go's CEO and interviewed Stelios. Go still exists, but

BA sold it because of huge losses. Moreover, Stelios has outlasted Bob Ayling, the BA CEO who tricked him into believing that BA wanted to invest in EasyJet. Said Stelios, "If you'd asked anyone at the time if I would survive longer than the boss of the World's Favourite Airline [British Airlines' motto], they would have laughed at you. Outlasting a BA chief executive shows that I've got staying power."

**Also, is there anything you can do to influence the cost of landing fees at Luton airport? If EasyJet continues to grow, dealing with airport authorities will become increasingly important. For example, Swissair used its political and financial leverage to try to prevent you from flying between Geneva, Switzerland, and Barcelona, Spain. So how do you deal with potentially uncontrollable industry regulators and gatekeepers?**

The industry regulation component of the specific environment consists of regulations and rules that govern the business practices and procedures of particular industries, businesses, and professions. Regulatory agencies affect businesses by creating and enforcing rules and regulations that are supposed to protect consumers, workers, or society as a whole. However, surveys indicate that managers rank industry regulation as one of the most demanding and frustrating parts of their jobs. This is certainly true for Stelios and EasyJet. In fact, Stelios is so frustrated with Barclays Bank, Luton Airport's owner, for tripling landing fees that he cut his Barclays credit card in half on television and is threatening to reduce the number of EasyJet flights out of the airport. He said, "It would not be realistic to try to uproot the company from Luton, but what we are trying to do is make it more immune by growing our operations out of Liverpool and Geneva and by establishing a base at Amsterdam." He went on to say, "Don't discount the possibility of us developing a third UK hub—it could be Cardiff or Newcastle or Glasgow. Next time there is a Barclays-style problem, we want to make sure it af-

fects as small a part of the business as possible."

**Finally, how do you make sense of all this? Your initial business plan was sound and recognized the fantastic opportunities for low-cost airlines in Europe. But now those opportunities seem to be overwhelmed by a growing number of threats.**

Managers use a three-step process to make sense of external environments. First, they scan their environments based on their organizational strategies, their need for up-to-date information, or their need to reduce uncertainty. Second, when they identify environmental events as threats, they take steps to protect their companies from harm. And third, when they identify environmental events as opportunities, they formulate strategies to improve company performance.

Stelios realized that the same principles used to start and run EasyJet could also be used in other industries. For instance, Stelios and his management team observed that the Internet cafés in the cities to which EasyJet flew were very expensive, run by nerds, and quickly failing. With more tourists traveling and nearly all business people needing access to email wherever they are, they figured they had another made-to-order business. The result? EasyEverything Internet Cafés, seating anywhere from 200 to 800 people, are open 24 hours a day in 24 cities in 10 countries. Users pay a dollar, a pound, 10 francs, or 200 pesetas to buy anywhere from 20 minutes to 4 hours of high-speed Internet access. You get more minutes for your money when demand is low, meaning the café is empty, and fewer minutes when it is bustling with customer activity. Customers get high-speed access, flat screen monitors, Web cams, and access to cheap Internet phone calls. With 2.2 million customers and $4.5 million a month in revenues, business is booming. In fact, 18 percent of revenues comes from ads displayed on computer monitors. Critics claimed the cafés would fail outside

Europe, but after six months, the monster EasyEverything in New York—it seats 800 people—is profitable. Additional stores are planned for San Francisco, Miami, Boston, and New York.

Likewise, Stelios has now started EasyRentacar in 14 locations. Like EasyJet and EasyEverything Internet Cafés, prices can be as much as two-thirds less than competitors provided you reserve early. For instance, prices start at about $14 a day and top out at $56 if you rent the last car in the lot, a price that is still cheaper than competitors. Stelios says, "There is no reason why hiring a car should be so expensive. By offering just one model [the Mercedes A-Class] and trading only on the Internet, we can bring down costs."

Maurice Kelly, the chief executive who runs the EasyEverything Cafés, says, "He [Stelios] looks at old industries and smashes them to pieces. Why do car rentals have to offer lots of models? Why do airlines have to issue tickets?" Say Stelios, "What I want to achieve is to have a family of companies linked by a common brand but each developing its own identity."

**Sources:** D. Appell, "The EasyEmpire Strikes Back: Throwing Down the Gauntlet to Europe's Old-Guard Airlines, the Young Greek Entrepreneur Who Birthed Easyjet Airlines and Easyrentacar Has Been Shaking Up the Continent's Budget Travel Market," *Arthur Frommer's Budget Travel.* [Online] Available, http://stocks.msnbc.com/news/587392.asp, 22 June 2001. M. Fletcher, "High Flyer on Easy Street: King of Cut-Price Air Travel Takes off to Conquer New Online Territory," *Mail on Sunday,* 26 March 2000, 16. M. Harrison, "Easythis, Easythat, Easyfloat: At Least, That's How Stelios Haji-Ioannou (That's Stelios to You) Would Like to See the Stock Market Debut of Easyjet, the Cut-Price Airline He Has Shouldered into the Big Time. But Will It Be That Simple?" *The Independent—London,* 11 October 2000, 1B. K. Kemp, "Airlines Net Sky-High Results," *The Sunday Herald,* 11 June 1999, 16. R. Morais, "Proving Papa Wrong," *Forbes,* 9 July 2001. Wysocki, Jr., "The Challengers—Headwinds: The Odds Are Against Starting an Airline—And Still They Try—With Tenacity and Little Else, These Two Men Took on Majors' Entrenched System—Getting Past 'The Sniff Test'," *The Wall Street Journal,* 16 April 2001, A1.

## Key Terms

| | | |
|---|---|---|
| advocacy groups *(53)* | environmental complexity *(41)* | public communications *(53)* |
| behavioral addition *(66)* | environmental munificence *(41)* | punctuated equilibrium theory *(39)* |
| behavioral substitution *(66)* | environmental scanning *(55)* | relationship behavior *(53)* |
| business confidence indices *(46)* | external environments *(38)* | simple environment *(41)* |
| buyer dependence *(52)* | general environment *(43)* | specific environment *(43)* |
| cognitive maps *(57)* | industry regulation *(53)* | stable environment *(39)* |
| company vision *(62)* | internal environment *(58)* | supplier dependence *(52)* |
| competitive analysis *(50)* | media advocacy *(54)* | suppliers *(51)* |
| competitors *(50)* | opportunistic behavior *(52)* | technology *(46)* |
| complex environment *(41)* | organizational culture *(59)* | uncertainty *(42)* |
| consistent organizational cultures *(65)* | organizational heroes *(61)* | visible artifacts *(66)* |
| dynamic environment *(39)* | organizational stories *(61)* | |
| environmental change *(39)* | product boycott *(55)* | |

## What Would You Do-II

### Ford versus Firestone

It is 8:30 A.M. Monday morning. You have just received a phone call informing you that another Ford Explorer has been involved in a fatal roll-over accident. Two of the passengers were killed and the other two are seriously injured. Original equipment Firestone tires are suspected to be the cause of the accident. A police officer on the scene states that the tread of the left rear tire tore off "like a banana peel," which caused the vehicle to lose control and roll over four to five times before coming to a stop.

As President and CEO of Ford Motor Company, you have known about problems with Firestone tires on Ford Explorers in the Middle East and in South America since late 1998, however, only recently have problems begun to appear in the United States. To date, there have been 88 deaths and over 1,400 accidents connected to Ford Explorers equipped with Firestone tires. Additionally, since 1992, more than 100 suits have been filed by injured motorists or their families against Ford and Firestone. Many questions remain to be answered. Are the Firestone tires defective and are they dangerous? Are the problems related to owner abuse or misuse? Does the Explorer have an inherent design flaw that makes it more susceptible to a loss of control or rollover? It may take weeks or months to dig through the data needed to answer these questions; however, after this morning's phone call, you know that a decision must be made. Ford Motor Company must push Firestone to recall the affected tires.

Your staff has prepared the associated cost and logistic problems connected with such a recall. A recall of this magnitude will involve over 6.5 million tires initially and possibly up to 13 million long-term. Completing the recall could take up to 18 months to complete and will undoubtedly affect the year-end earnings for the company. Additionally, up to three assembly plants will have to be idled for up to one month so that stockpiled tires can be shipped to aid in recall efforts. Early cost figures for shutting down the three plants for one month have been estimated at $100 million, which doesn't include the cost of temporary unemployment for the laid-off workers or the costs associated with the loss of productivity and decreased sales.

To further compound the problem, Bridgestone, the parent company of Firestone, alleges that Ford Motor Company advised Explorer owners to lower inflation pressures (from 30 psi to 26 psi) in order to reduce the possibility of rollover and to improve ride characteristics. This decrease in pressure, according to Bridgestone officials, increased the probability of excessive heat damage and subsequent tread separation within the tires. Engineers with Ford have refuted the claim saying that other brands of tires used on Ford Explorers have exhibited no damage when operated at the lower pressure. The problem, at this point, is not to determine who is at fault, but to determine how this problem can be resolved in a manner that will maintain the level of consumer confidence and trust that Ford Motor Company has developed with the American public over the years. An additional constraint in this issue is the potential of damaging the close-knit relationship that Ford has developed with Firestone for over 95 years. To complicate matters further, Martha Firestone Ford, the mother of William Clay Ford, Ford's current Chairman, is a Firestone heiress. Her father was a chief executive with Firestone in its infancy. Therefore, more than just a name is at stake. How are you going to ensure that the American public maintains its level of trust and respect for your company as you initiate a recall to replace all of the 13 million potentially defective tires installed on your company's vehicles? What, if anything, could you do to satisfy both your customers and maintain your relationship with Firestone, one of your long-term suppliers? **If you were the President and CEO of Ford Motor Company, what would you do?**

**Sources:** J. Greenwald, "Firestone's Tire Crisis," *Time,* 21 August 2000, 64-65. M. Lavelle, "Where the Rubber Meets the Road," *U.S. News & World Report,* 4 September 2000, 43. A. Taylor, "Jac Nasser's Biggest Test," *Fortune,* 18 September 2000, 123-128. D. Eisenberg, "Is This Vehicle Safe?," *Time,* 2 October 2000, 59. T. Aeppel, "Ford Intends to Replace Millions of Tires," *The Wall Street Journal,* 23 May 2001. B.

Garfield, "Nasser Spot Lacks Star Quality, But Gets Tire Message Across," *Advertising Age*, 28 August 2000. J. Nasser, "A Letter from Ford CEO Nasser To Bridgestone/Firestone CEO Lampe," *Wall Street Journal*, 23 May 2001. J. Lampe, "Letter from Firestone to Ford, Ending Business Relationship," *The Wall Street Journal*, 21 May 2001. M. Geyelin, "Firestone Quits as Tire Supplier to Ford," *Wall Street Journal*, 22 May 2001. B. Clark, "Ford vs. Firestone," *Newsweek*, 18 September 2000.

## Management Decisions

### Culture Shock

As a vice president of a medium-sized communications technology company located on the West Coast, you have been involved in several acquisitions of smaller firms over the last few years, each having resulted in increased growth and profitability for your firm. Recently, your company has been discussing plans to acquire a small, relatively new, computer-networking services company located on the East Coast. Your firm is interested in this acquisition because it has the skills, equipment, and knowledge desperately needed but currently lacking in your firm. Additionally, the majority of your current clients are located in and around the Silicon Valley.

The firm being considered has a solid reputation and a growing number of customers located on the East Coast. If this acquisition occurs, it will serve to broaden the services currently provided by your firm, increase your firm's presence nationwide, and strengthen your firm's core competencies by alleviating the need to outsource certain activities. Investment capital has already been garnered to facilitate the acquisition.

Tomorrow morning, you and several other top executives will decide whether to go forward with the proposed acquisition. Unfortunately, one item makes you uncomfortable with this plan. In comparing the two companies, you have found that your firm's corporate culture differs dramatically from that of the firm being considered. Although some of your colleagues denounce this as being an insignificant problem and one that can be easily solved, you consider it to be one of high importance.

Your firm is larger and more bureaucratic, is formal in structure, and utilizes centralized decision-making techniques. Typically before key decisions are made, an extensive amount of time is spent involving group discussions and developing consensus before any action is taken. Additionally, there is a clear chain of command within your firm, and individuals have distinct job descriptions and duties. On the other hand, the proposed company's structure and culture appears to be very informal. The organizational hierarchy is relatively flat, with key decisions being made at all levels. Employees have no clear responsibilities or duties and are empowered to "take the ball and run with it." The firm's founder claims that it is their unique culture that has resulted in the firm's rapid growth in market share, profitability, and innovativeness.

Your main fear regarding the proposed acquisition is that the new company's culture will be too different to effectively mesh the two companies together. Further, it is your belief that the employees of the new company will feel trapped and constrained by your firm's formalized structure. As you look over the acquisition proposal, the projections and possibilities are certainly appealing. If the acquisition becomes a success, your firm could stand to become the largest, most-powerful communications firm in the industry. Tomorrow morning, you and four others will vote to move forward or abandon the proposed acquisition.

### Questions

1. How will you vote and why?
2. If you vote to pursue the acquisition, what changes might you recommend to ensure that the acquisition and subsequent transition succeeds?
3. If you vote to abandon the acquisition, what changes might you propose that (if accepted by the group) would change your mind regarding pursuing the acquisition?

**Source:** M. Roger, "How Culture Affects Mergers and Acquisitions," *Industrial Management*, September 2000.

71

## Management Decisions

### The Lights Are Off, But Somebody Is Home

As you look out your office window over Santa Clara, everything looks like business as usual, but that couldn't be farther from the truth. California is in the fourth month of its severe energy crisis and rolling blackouts, and the high-demand summer season is still months away.

Research and manufacturing at Intel have been steady and you haven't been hit by the rolling power blackouts. Business has been good, and there are rumors of another expansion circulating. But the past four months have been brutal. The threat of random power outages has made you very anxious. If the electricity fluctuates for even a fraction of a second, Intel loses millions of dollars because chips being made can be ruined. Although you're doing your part by keeping your office lights off during daytime hours, you still wonder how long before you lose at electricity roulette.

On the corner of your desk, you see an attractive brochure of the Smokey Mountains that must have just arrived in the morning mail. It looks like a vacation promo. It is from the State of Tennessee, but not from the tourist board—from the Department of Economic and Community Development. The title reads, "The Lights Are Always on in Tennessee," and there's a flashlight attached. Inside you read a convincing marketing piece about relocating business to the Volunteer State. Perhaps Tennessee would be a good place to expand.

Really, you're unsure about pitching expanding so far away to the board. In fact, you're one of those 57 percent of Californians who do not believe there is an actual power shortage. Still, the idea bears consideration.

Use the Internet sites listed below to research the energy situation and costs in both California and Tennessee. Issues you will want to consider relative to the energy situation include the political environment, the regulatory situation, the available power supply now and any plans for expansion, cost of energy, stability of energy supply, etc. In addition, you will also need to take into account the cost of relocation, labor supply in both states, the impact of moving on your distribution system, etc.

**Additional Internet Resources**
http://www.energy.gov/business/index.html    This is the United States Department of Energy Web site. The energy reduction link can help identify areas where businesses can reduce energy consumption.
http://www.energy.ca.gov/    Find out about California's energy situation by visiting the Web site for the Energy Commission. Statistics, information on rebates, as well as the details of the peak load reduction program are all given.
http://www.state.tn.us/ecd/ and http://www.state.tn.us/ecd/energy_info.htm    These sites are part of the State of Tennessee Department of Economic and Community Development. As such, they provide information on energy issues in Tennessee and on relocation issues.

http://www.infotrac-college.com    Use your password to gain access to numerous articles about California's energy situation. Be specific in your keyword search so that you are not overwhelmed by too much information.

**Questions**
1. As a manager, you will nearly always have a situation where the grass seems greener on the other side. The trick is to determine whether it really is and then decide what you need to do. A critical first step is understanding the environment your business is operating in. Write a two-page assessment of the external environment, as it relates to energy issues, in California and in Tennessee (one page for each state).
2. Based on the information you outline in your assessment, decide whether to continue with expansion projects in California or to move to Tennessee. What were the most important criteria in your decision? Why?
3. Using your campus library's research databases, look up articles dating from January 2001 to see what Intel's CEO really decided. Compare his decision with yours. What are the differences?

**Sources:** "California's No-Brainer," *The Wall Street Journal*, 5 March 2001, A22. A. Cardwell, "Move East, Young Company—Small Town USA Uses California's Power Crisis to Woo High-Tech Business Away from the West Coast," *Ziff Davis Smart Business for the New Economy*, 1 August 2001, 28. "Power Crisis Is Likely to Short-Circuit Intel Expansion in California Technology," *Los Angeles Times*, 9 January 2001, C-11. "Power Decisions," *Electronic News*, 15 January 2001, 4.

## Develop Your Managerial Potential

### Dealing with the Press
In this age of 24-hour cable news channels, tabloid news shows, and aggressive local and national news reporters intent on exposing corporate wrong-doing, one of the most important skills for a manager to learn is how to deal effectively with the press. Test your ability to deal effectively with the press by putting yourself in the following situations. To make the situation more realistic, read each scenario and then give yourself two minutes to write a response to each question.

### Fatty Restaurant Food Contributes to Heart Attacks
Today, in the nation's capital, a public-interest group held a press conference to release the results of a study that found that the food sold in most Chinese restaurants is high in fat. The group claims that the most popular Chinese dishes, like orange chicken, pork fried rice, and Hunan beef, contain nearly as much fat as the food you get from fast-food chains like McDonald's, Wendy's, and Burger King. (Much of it is fried or is covered with heavy sauces.) Furthermore, the group says that customers who hope to keep their cholesterol and blood pressure low by eating Chinese food are just fooling themselves.

A TV reporter from Channel 5 called your Szechuan-style Chinese restaurant "Szechuan" to get your response to this study. When she and the camera crew arrived, she asked you the following questions. (To simulate these conditions, give yourself only two minutes to write a response to each question.)

1. "A new study released today claims that food sold in Chinese restaurants is on average nearly as fattening as that sold at fast-food restaurants. How healthy is the food that you serve at Szechuan's?"
2. "Get the camera in close here [camera closes in to get the shot] because I want the audience at home to see that you don't provide any information on your menu about calories, calories from fat, or cholesterol. Without this information [camera pulls back to get a picture of you and the reporter], how can your customers know that the food that you serve is healthy for them?"
3. "These new studies were based on lunches and dinners sampled from Chinese restaurants across the nation. A local company, Huntington Labs, has agreed to test foods from local restaurants so that we can provide accurate information to our viewers. Would you agree to let us sample the main

dishes in your restaurant to test the level of calories, calories from fat, and cholesterol? Furthermore, can we take the cameras into your restaurant, so that we can get your customers' reactions to these studies?"

**Hotel Customer Dies in Strange Accident**

"Beep." You look at your watch. It's 4 A.M. This has been the longest night of your life. You've worked for the Hamada Jackson hotel for about a year as the late-night manager. The pay is OK, but the best part is that it's safe, really quiet, and you can study. Your college grades have gotten much better since you started, and it looks like you'll be able to make it into graduate school. But you didn't get any studying done tonight. Channel 8's news crew just left. They were monitoring the police scanner around 1:15 A.M., right after you called 911 in a panic. One of your responsibilities is to take a quick walk through the hallways a couple of times a night just to make sure everything is OK. When you made your 1 A.M. check, everything was quiet until you hit the last hallway on the west side of the hotel. As you came around the corner, you almost stepped on her. Somehow, in a freak accident, a young woman who, according to your records, had checked into the hotel at about 10:30 P.M., an hour before you came on duty, was dead on the floor. She was still soaking wet from the rain that had started that afternoon. You learned later that she had been electrocuted when she put her card-key in the lock of her metal door.

Much to your dismay, the Channel 8 news crew arrived 10 minutes after the cops and the emergency medical team. After videotaping the scene and the crews loading the body into the ambulance, they turned their attention, lights, and camera on you. (To simulate these conditions, give yourself only two minutes to write a response to each question.)

1. "Can you tell us what happened? The emergency medical team told us that the burns on her hands and the smell of smoke led them to believe that she was electrocuted in your hotel hallway. Can you tell us what happened and how someone could be electrocuted in this way?"
2. "What was the victim's name? How old was she? Where is she from? Do you know what she was doing while staying at the hotel?"
3. "The emergency medical team estimated the time of death to be between 10:30 and 11:00 P.M., which means that the body has been in the hallway for several hours. Does your hotel have a security force? Why wasn't somebody making periodic checks of the premises to make sure everything was safe? Also, does anybody on the staff have any medical training to deal with emergencies like choking, heart attacks, or things like this?"

**Sources:** P. Flanagan, "Ten Public Relations Pitfalls," *Management Review*, October 1995, 45-48. D. Gellene, "Sears Drops Car Repair Incentives: The Company Says 'Mistakes Have Been Made' in Its Aggressive Commission Program," *Los Angeles Times*, 23 June 1992, 1. P. Hertneky, "Mastering the Media: Press Handling for Restaurant Managers" *Restaurant Hospitality*, June 1995, 59-69. B. Horowitz, "Intel Needs Damage Control," *USA Today*, 13 December 1994. L. Koss-Feder, "Crisis Brings Media Scrutiny," *Hotel & Motel Management*, 14 August 1995, 5. "How to Get Your CEO in Print or in Front of TV Cameras in the Right Light," *PR News*, 21 April 1997.

## Study Tip

Create your own diagram of the business environment and compare it to the example in the chapter. Read a selection of business press articles and list the factors at play in each of the articles you read. Visit the *Management* Web site at **http://williams.swcollege.com** and use your Xtra! CD-ROM for a wealth of review and mastery activities.

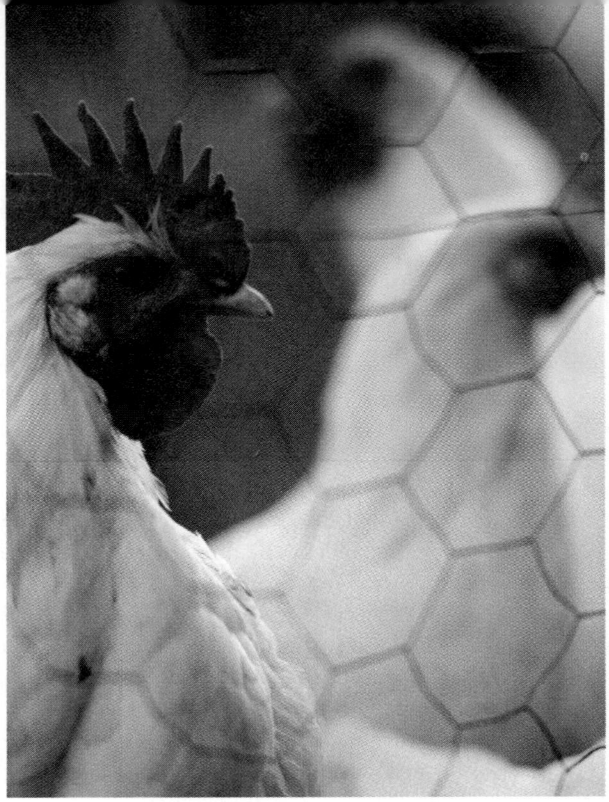

CHAPTER 3

outline

# three

# Ethics and Social Responsibility

## What Would You Do?

**McDonald's Plaza, Oak Brook, IL.** "Welcome to McDonald's. May I take your order, please?" "Yes, I'd like an Egg McMuffin, hash browns, a small orange juice, and a large coffee." More than five million times a day, someone in the United States orders an Egg McMuffin at a McDonald's. In fact, McDonald's 13,000 U.S. restaurants buy 2.5 percent of the 75 billion eggs produced each year in the United States.

Customers go to McDonald's for its quick service and good prices. But that doesn't matter to PETA, People for the Ethical Treatment of Animals, a Virginia-based advocacy group run by vegetarian activists who only care about advancing the rights of animals worldwide. For the last few years, PETA has been running a "McCruelty to Go" publicity campaign against McDonald's. Through 400 demonstrations in 23 countries, numerous magazine and billboard ads, and its **http:// www.mccruelty.com** Web site, PETA has pressured McDonald's to require the farmers from whom it gets its food products to treat animals more "humanely." PETA wants McDonald's to buy eggs only from suppliers that don't debeak hens (cutting off a chicken's beak reduces damage from chicken fighting), that give egg-laying hens 72 square inches of living space (most egg-laying hens are in small cages no larger than half a piece of paper, which, according to PETA, prevent them from standing up, stretching their legs and wings, or moving around), and that don't withhold food to increase molting and thus egg production (forced molting, meaning the shedding of feathers, is a process in which birds are rested from egg production and food is temporarily withheld. This restores hens' ability to lay eggs).

Of course, not everyone agrees with PETA's views and recommendations. Egg farmers say that they go to great lengths to treat their hens well and keep them in good health. Jerry Armstrong, who has an egg ranch with one million hens, said, "We're always concerned with our birds' welfare. If they're not happy and contented, they won't lay eggs and we're out of the egg business." The egg industry says that hens are kept in cages to decrease costs, which matters to consumers, but also to improve sanitation and bird health. If McDonald's adopts PETA's recommendations to double the size of hen's cages, the cost of a dozen eggs could increase by 15 or 20 cents. And with too many egg producers in an overly crowded market, increased costs of any kind, but especially those that would require producers to double the size of their production facilities, could lead to huge costs and losses. Jerry Armstrong claims, "These rules would put me out of business."

What is the ethical thing to do in this situation? Should McDonald's give in to PETA's demands, or should it ignore them? Given that protests are not a new thing for McDonald's, how does it decide how serious an issue this is and the lengths to which it should go to address these issues, if any? If McDonald's seriously considers PETA's demands, how does it decide whose interests take precedence? Is it more socially responsible to require its egg suppliers to change their practices if changing them leads to financial losses and puts some suppliers out of business? Which comes first, the chickens or the egg producers? No matter what McDonald's decides, someone or some group will be very unhappy.

**If you were making this decision for McDonald's, what would you do?**

**Sources:** "Egg Production Information," American Egg Board. [Online] Available http://www.aeb.org/eii/production.html, 29 June 2001. D. Campbell, "Chicken Run: McDonald's Takes a Cue from the Hit Film and Demands Better Conditions for Hens Used to Supply Eggs for Its McMuffins," *The Guardian*, 8 September 2000. T. Perry, "Egg Producers Are McMiffed: Industry Balks at McDonald's Tough Rules on Hen Treatment," *Los Angeles Times*, 7 September 2000, C1. D. Wetzel, "McDonalds to Require Its Egg Suppliers to Improve Conditions for Hens," *Chicago Tribune*, 24 August 2001.

McDonald's chicken-egg producer dilemma is an example of the tough decisions that managers face about ethics and social responsibility. Unfortunately, one of the "real world" aspects of these decisions is that no matter what you decide, someone or some group will be unhappy with the decision. Managers don't have the luxury of choosing theoretically-optimal, win-win solutions that are obviously correct to everyone involved. In practice, solutions to ethics and social responsibility problems aren't optimal. Often, they are "make-do" or "do the least harm" kinds of solutions. Clear rights and wrongs rarely reveal themselves to managers charged with "doing the right thing." The business world is much messier than that.

We begin this chapter by examining ethical behavior in the workplace and how the 1991 U.S. Sentencing Guidelines now make ethical behavior much more important for businesses. Second, we examine the influences on ethical decision making and review practical steps that managers can take to improve ethical decision making. We finish by reviewing to whom organizations are socially responsible, what organizations are socially responsible for, how they can respond to societal expectations for social responsibility, and whether social responsibility hurts or helps an organization's economic performance.

# What Is Ethical and Unethical Workplace Behavior?

**ethics**
the set of moral principles or values that defines right and wrong for a person or group

**Ethics** is the set of moral principles or values that defines right and wrong for a person or group. Unfortunately, several studies have produced distressing results about the state of ethics in today's business world. In a nationwide survey of 2,300 workers, 75 percent indicated that they had seen unethical behavior at work, such as deceptive sales practices, unsafe working conditions, environmental breaches, and mishandling of confidential or proprietary information within the last year.[1] A similar survey of 2,293 workers across 48 states found that less than half (47 percent) felt that the senior leaders in their companies were ethical.[2] Furthermore, 60 percent of workers felt substantially pressured to commit unethical or illegal acts at work. Only 6 percent reported feeling little pressure to commit such acts.[3] Finally, in a study of 1,324 randomly selected workers, managers, and executives across multiple industries, 48 percent of respondents admitted to committing an unethical or illegal act in the past year! These acts included cheating on an expense account, discriminating against coworkers, forging signatures, paying or accepting kickbacks, and "looking the other way" when environmental laws were broken.[4] Winn Swenson, director for integrity management services at KPMG, said, "Corporations need to recognize that the problem is out there."[5]

However, these studies also contained good news. When people are convinced that they work in an ethical work environment, they are six times more likely to stay with that company than if they believe that they work in an unethical environment.[6] In short, a lot of work needs to be done to make workplaces more ethical, but, and this is very important, managers and employees want this to happen.

*After reading the next three sections, you should be able to*
*1. discuss how the nature of a management job creates the possibility for ethical abuses.*
*2. identify common kinds of workplace deviance.*
*3. describe the 1991 U.S. Sentencing Commission Guidelines and how its recommendations now make ethical behavior much more important for businesses.*

## 1. Ethics and the Nature of Management Jobs

**ethical behavior**
behavior that conforms to a society's accepted principles of right and wrong

**Ethical behavior** follows accepted principles of right and wrong. For example, the Malden Mills manufacturing plant burned to the ground just before Christmas. Instead of closing the plant, laying off workers, and then taking a large insurance settlement of $300 million, owner Aaron Feuerstein promised his 3,000 workers that they would still have jobs. As the plant was being rebuilt, Feuerstein met his weekly payroll of $1.5 mil-

**Build Up Your "Forget You Fund"**

Mike Royko, a columnist for the *Chicago Tribune*, boiled business ethics down to two key ingredients. The first is your conscience. Royko says that if your parents didn't do their job, you won't have one. Ingredient number two is to get a "Forget You Fund" (FUF). Basically, an FUF is three- to six-months' worth of paychecks in the bank. When your boss asks you do something that you cannot in good conscience do, quit! Royko said that an FUF takes the control that your boss and the company have over you and replaces it with your freedom to do what you think is right.

lion and covered the medical expenses of 33 injured workers. Despite the insurance settlement, the company had to borrow significant funds to rebuild the factory. Still, Feuerstein felt he did the "right thing." Feuerstein said, "It's the right thing to do because I think a business, yes, must maximize the profitability to the shareholder, but it means something more than that. There's a right way to treat employees, to treat them with respect, not as a pair of hands, and to give them the loyalty and trust that they expect and to treat them as human beings."[7]

By contrast, unethical management behavior occurs when managers personally violate accepted principles of right and wrong. The authority and power inherent in some management positions can tempt managers to engage in unethical practices. Since managers often control company resources, there is a risk that some managers will cross over the line from legitimate use of company resources to personal use of those resources.

For example, treating a client to dinner is a common and legitimate business practice in many companies. But what about treating a client to a ski trip? Taking the company jet to attend a business meeting in San Diego is legitimate. But how about using the jet to come home to Chicago by way of Honolulu? Human resources can be misused as well. For example, unless it's in an employee's job description, using an employee to do personal chores, like picking up the manager's dry cleaning, is unethical behavior.

Handling information is another area in which managers must be careful to behave ethically. Information is a key part of management work. Managers collect it, analyze it, act on it, and disseminate it. However, they are also expected to deal in truthful information and, when necessary, to keep confidential information confidential. Leaking company secrets to competitors, "doctoring" the numbers, wrongfully withholding information, or lying are some possible misuses of the information entrusted to managers. For example, in Hong Kong, "Ba dan" literally means white sheet. At Bausch & Lomb's Hong King division, managers used the term "Ba dan" to refer to the fake sales numbers they sent to company headquarters each month. To maintain its status as Bausch & Lomb's top international division, Hong Kong managers would fake the sales numbers for its Southeast Asian customers. Then, to make the fake numbers look like real sales, it would ship its product (glasses and contact lenses) to a phony customer warehouse.[8] Bausch & Lomb used company auditors plus its internal security department, which was run by ex-Secret Service agents and police officers, to set up "sting" operations to catch the employees who were running the "Ba dan" scam in Hong Kong.

A third area in which managers must be careful to engage in ethical behavior is the way in which they influence the behavior of others, especially those they supervise. Managerial work gives managers significant power to influence others. If managers tell employees to perform unethical acts (or face punishment), such as "faking the numbers to get results," then they are abusing their managerial power. This is sometimes called the "move it or lose it" syndrome. "Move it or lose it" managers tell employees, "Do it. You're paid to do it. If you can't do it, we'll find somebody who can."[9]

Not all unethical managerial influence is intentional, however. Sometimes managers unintentionally influence employees to act unethically by creating policies that inadvertently reward employees for unethical acts. Cisco Systems, the company that makes the switches and routers that run the Internet, had a policy that permitted its managers and employees to invest in Cisco suppliers. For example, Deborah Traficante and her Cisco sales team sold $16 million of networking equipment to MegsINet, a small Internet service provider. She also helped MegsINet get a loan from Cisco's financing division to pay for the purchase. But, in addition to the standard sales commission that she earned from Cisco, MegsINet arranged for her to pay 56 cents a share for 85,714 shares of MegsINet stock. When another company purchased MegsINet ten months later, she made $200,000 on the transaction. At most companies, employees are not allowed to invest in or profit in any way from their suppliers or customers. A spokesperson for

77

Hewlett-Packard said, "It might cause the appearance, if not the actuality, of divided loyalty." Charles Elson, director of the Corporate Governance Center at the University of Delaware, said, "Any time that someone is potentially on both sides of a transaction, it's a problem." Cisco has now changed its conflict-of-interest policy to prevent this from happening again.[10]

Setting goals is another way that managers influence the behavior of their employees. If managers set unrealistic goals, the pressure to perform and to achieve these goals can influence employees to engage in unethical business behaviors. For example, at Bausch & Lomb, there was tremendous pressure to achieve double-digit increases in revenues each year. Said a former company president, "Once you signed up for your target number, you were expected to reach it," no excuses accepted. The pressure to make numbers was so great that Bausch & Lomb told its customers that they could buy Bausch & Lomb's best-selling glasses and contact lenses only if they also bought slow-selling products that they didn't want. Furthermore, when competitors came out with disposal contact lenses, Bausch & Lomb simply took the regular contact lenses it had sold for 15 years and fraudulently repackaged them to consumers as the advanced, disposable contacts.[11] The company later settled a class-action lawsuit in which it agreed to pay $68 million to consumers who thought they were buying the better, newer contacts.[12] As a result of all of these problems, Bausch & Lomb has changed its compensation and reward systems to reward managers and employees for long-term rather than short-term performance.

## Review 1
### Ethics and the Nature of Management Jobs

Ethics is the set of moral principles or values that define right and wrong. Ethical behavior occurs when managers follow those principles and values. Because they set the standard for others in the workplace, managers can model ethical behavior by using resources for company and not personal business. Furthermore, managers can encourage ethical behavior by handling information in a confidential and honest fashion, by not using their authority to influence others to engage in unethical behavior, by not creating policies that unintentionally reward employees for unethical behavior, and by setting reasonable rather than unreasonable goals.

## 2. Workplace Deviance

Depending on which study you look at, one-third to three-quarters of all employees admit that they have stolen from their employers or committed computer fraud, embezzled funds, vandalized company property, sabotaged company projects, or been "sick" from work when they really weren't sick. Experts estimate that unethical behaviors like these, which researchers call "workplace deviance," may cost companies as much as $400 billion a year.[13]

More specifically, **workplace deviance** is unethical behavior that violates organizational norms about right and wrong. Exhibit 3.1 shows that workplace deviance can be categorized by how deviant the behavior is, from minor to serious, and by the target of the deviant behavior, either the organization or particular people in the workplace.[14] One kind of workplace deviance, called **production deviance**, hurts the quality and quantity of work produced. Examples include leaving early, taking excessively long work breaks, purposively working slower, or intentionally wasting resources.

**Property deviance** is unethical behavior aimed at company property. Examples include sabotaging, stealing, or damaging equipment or products, or overcharging for services and then pocketing the difference. While it's certainly scary to think about, Boeing, the passenger jet manufacturer, has had instances of product sabotage. In a number of instances during routine product testing, the manufacturer has found wires cut in its 737 jets. Each 737 has 36,000 miles of wiring. No one has ever been caught for cutting the wires. A spokesperson for EasyJet, a London-based airline, recently said, "This incident

**workplace deviance**
unethical behavior that violates organizational norms about right and wrong

**production deviance**
unethical behavior that hurts the quality and quantity of work produced

**property deviance**
unethical behavior aimed at the organization's property

78

EXHIBIT 3.1

TYPES OF WORKPLACE DEVIANCE

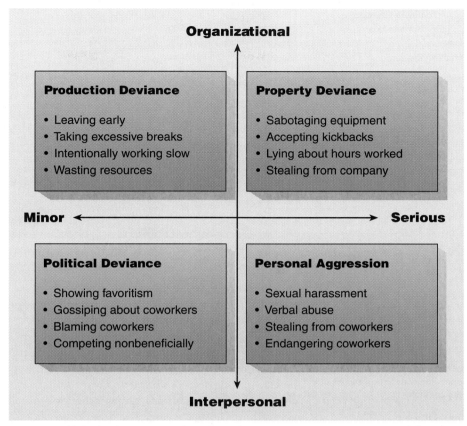

**Source:** Republished with permission of Academy of Management, PO Box 3020, Briar Cliff Manor, NY, 10510-8020. "A Typology of Deviant Workplace Behaviors," (Figure), S.L. Robinson & R.J. Bennett. *Academy of Management Journal*, 1995, Vol. 38. Reproduced by permission of the publisher via Copyright Clearance Center, Inc.

is very disturbing, and we are demanding a full investigation into how it could have happened. We need a guarantee from Boeing that these planes are 100 percent free of any further problems. Like all airlines, we rely on the manufacturer delivering a safe product."[15] Sometimes, however, property deviance occurs with company property, rather than company products. An employee planted a software bomb in the centralized file server that contained Omega Engineering's key programs and data. The code destroyed the programs and data that ran the machines in the company's manufacturing plant. The company lost $10 million as a result, including $2 million in reprogramming costs. Eighty employees had to be laid off because of lost business resulting from the incident.[16]

**shrinkage**
employee theft of company merchandise

Another common form of property deviance called **shrinkage** is the theft of company merchandise by employees. Shrinkage costs traditional U.S. retailers more than $29 billion a year! However, shrinkage costs e-tailers, retail companies that sell on the Internet, approximately $1 billion a year. For example, Kozmo.com installed a digital surveillance system at its distribution center in Memphis, Tennessee. The system showed employees stuffing CDs and DVDs under their clothes. Don McVicker, vice president of loss prevention at Kozmo, said, "We have zero tolerance for theft. This security system makes preventing losses so much easier and more effective." Kim Warne, from Sensormatic, which sells electronic security equipment to retailers, said, "Some of these dot-com companies were so focused on getting their money in place, they didn't think about security. Now the ones that are left are

Although violence in the United States is on the decline, workplace violence is not. Police are pictured standing guard outside the Navistar Engine plant near Chicago, where a man shot and killed five coworkers and injured four others before turning the gun on himself.

AP PHOTO/CHARELS BENNETT

**political deviance**
using one's influence to harm others in the company

**personal aggression**
hostile or aggressive behavior toward others

getting to a point where they have to watch every dime, and they are focusing on security more and more." On average, a dishonest employee will work for a company for nine months and steal $1,023 worth of goods or services.[17]

While workplace and production deviance harm companies, political deviance and personal aggression are unethical behaviors that hurt particular people within companies. **Political deviance** is using one's influence to harm others in the company. Examples include making decisions based on favoritism rather than performance, spreading rumors about coworkers, or falsely blaming others for mistakes they didn't make. **Personal aggression** is hostile or aggressive behavior toward others. Examples include sexual harassment, verbal abuse, stealing from coworkers, or personally threatening coworkers. One of the fastest growing kinds of personal aggression is workplace violence. A former Navistar employee forced his way into a Chicago factory and killed four people after firing 30 shots from an AK-47. The day after Christmas, an employee of Edgewater Technology walked into the accounting department and shot seven people dead. And then in the worst mass murder in Hawaii's history, a frustrated copier repairman killed seven people outside a parts warehouse in Honolulu.[18] More than 2 million Americans are victims of workplace violence each year. Like the cases described above, somewhere between 650 and 1,000 people are killed at work each year.[19] While many victims are police officers, security guards, or taxi drivers, store owners and company managers are most often killed.[20] For more information on workplace violence, see the Occupational Safety & Health Administration Web site, **http://www.cdc.gov/niosh/violfs.html**.

### Review 2
### Workplace Deviance
Workplace deviance is behavior that violates important organizational norms about right and wrong and harms the organization or its workers. Production deviance and property deviance harm the company, whereas political deviance and personal aggression harm individuals within the company.

## 3. U.S. Sentencing Commission Guidelines

A male supervisor is sexually harassing female coworkers. A sales representative offers a $10,000 kickback to persuade an indecisive customer to do business with his company. A company president secretly meets with her biggest competitor's CEO, and both agree not to compete in markets where the other has already established customers. Each of these behaviors is clearly unethical (and, in these cases, illegal, too). Historically, if management was unaware of such activities, the company could not be held responsible for an employee's unethical acts. However, under the 1991 U.S. Sentencing Commission Guidelines, companies can be prosecuted and *punished even if management didn't know about the unethical behavior.* Moreover, penalties can be substantial, with maximum fines approaching $300 million![21]

*Let's examine 3.1 to whom the guidelines apply and what they cover and 3.2 how, according to the guidelines, an organization can be punished for the unethical behavior of its managers and employees.*

### 3.1 Who, What, and Why?

Nearly all businesses, nonprofits, partnerships, labor unions, unincorporated organizations and associations, incorporated organizations, and even pension funds, trusts, and joint stock companies are covered by the guidelines. If your organization can be characterized as a business (remember, nonprofits count too), then it is subject to the guidelines.[22]

The guidelines cover federal laws, such as invasion of privacy, price fixing, fraud, customs violations, antitrust violations, civil rights violations, theft, money laundering, conflict of interest, embezzlement, dealing in stolen goods, copyright infringements, extortion, and more. However, it's not enough to stay "within the law." The purpose of the guidelines is not just to punish companies *after* they or their employees break the law. The purpose is to encourage companies to take proactive steps that will discourage or prevent white-collar crime *before* it happens. The guidelines also give companies an incentive to cooperate with and disclose illegal activities to federal authorities.[23]

### 3.2 Determining the Punishment

The guidelines impose smaller fines on companies that take proactive steps to encourage ethical behavior or voluntarily disclose illegal activities to federal authorities. Essentially, the law uses a "carrot-and-stick" approach. The stick is the threat of heavy fines that can total millions of dollars. The carrot is greatly reduced fines, but only if the company has started an effective compliance program (discussed below) to encourage ethical behavior *before* the illegal activity occurs.[24] Understanding how a company's punishment is determined can help you understand the importance of establishing a compliance program.

The first step is computing the base fine by determining what level offense has occurred. The level of the offense (i.e., the seriousness of the problem) is figured by examining the kind of crime, the loss incurred by the victims, and how much planning went into the crime. For example, committing simple fraud is a level 6 offense (there are 38 levels in all). But if the victims of that fraud lost more than $5 million, that level 6 offense becomes a level 22 offense. Moreover, anything beyond minimal planning to commit the fraud results in an increase of two levels to a level 24 offense. How much of a difference would this make to the company? Crimes at or below level 6 incur a base fine of $5,000, whereas the base fine for level 24 is $2.1 million. So the difference is $2.095 million! The base fine for level 38, the top-level offense, is an astounding $72.5 million!

After assessing a base fine, the judge computes a culpability score, which is a way of assigning blame to the company. Higher culpability scores suggest greater corporate responsibility in conducting, encouraging, or sanctioning illegal or unethical activity. The culpability score is a number ranging from a minimum of 0.05 to a maximum of 4.0. A company that already has a compliance program and voluntarily reports the offense to authorities will incur a culpability score of 0.05. By contrast, a company in which management secretly plans, approves, and participates in illegal or unethical activity will receive the maximum score of 4.0.

The culpability score is critical, because the total fine is computed by multiplying the base fine by the culpability score. Going back to our level 24 fraud offense, a company with a compliance program that turns itself in will only be fined $105,000 ($2,100,000 × 0.05). However, a company that secretly plans, approves, and participates in illegal activity will be fined $8.4 million ($2,100,000 × 4.0)! The difference is even

EXHIBIT 3.2

COMPLIANCE PROGRAM STEPS FOR THE 1991 U.S. SENTENCING GUIDELINES

1. Establish standards and procedures to meet the company's business needs.
2. Put upper-level managers in charge of the compliance program.
3. Don't delegate decision-making authority to employees who are likely to act illegally or unethically.
4. Use auditing, monitoring, and other methods to encourage employees to report violations.
5. Use company publications and training to inform employees about the company's compliance standards and procedures.
6. Enforce compliance standards by fairly and consistently disciplining violators.
7. After violations occur, find appropriate ways to improve the compliance program.

**Source:** D.R. Dalton, M.B. Metzger, & J.W. Hill, "The 'New' U.S. Sentencing Commission Guidelines: A Wake-up Call for Corporate America," *Academy of Management Executive* 8 (1994): 7-16.

more astronomical for level 38 offenses. The "good guys" are only fined $3.635 million, whereas the "bad guys" are fined a whopping $290 million! These differences clearly show the importance of having a compliance program in place.

Fortunately, for those who want to avoid paying these stiff fines, the 1991 U.S. Sentencing Guidelines are clear on the seven necessary components of an effective compliance program.[25] Exhibit 3.2 lists those components. Caremark International, a managed-care service provider in Delaware pleaded guilty to criminal charges regarding its physician contracts and improper patient referrals. When it was sued by shareholders for negligence and poor management, the Delaware courts dismissed the case, ruling that its ethics compliance program, built on the components described in Exhibit 3.2, was a "good-faith attempt" to monitor employees and that the company did not knowingly allow illegal and unethical behavior to occur. The Delaware court went on to rule that a compliance program based on the U.S. Sentencing Guidelines was enough to shield the company from liability.[26]

For more information, see "An Overview of the Organizational Sentencing Guidelines" at **http://www.ussc.gov/training/corpover.PDF** and "Organization Sentencing Guidelines: Questions and Answers" at **http://www.ussc.gov/training/corpq&a.pdf**.

### Review 3
#### U.S. Sentencing Commission Guidelines
Under the 1991 U.S. Sentencing Commission Guidelines, companies can be prosecuted and fined up to $300 million for employees' illegal actions. Fines are computed by multiplying the base fine by a culpability score, which ranges from 0.05 to 4.0. Companies that establish compliance programs to encourage ethical behavior can reduce their culpability scores and their fines. Companies without compliance programs can pay fines four times larger than companies with established compliance programs. Compliance programs must establish standards and procedures, be run by top managers, encourage hiring and promotion of honest and ethical people, encourage employees to report violations, educate employees about compliance, punish violators, and find ways to improve the program after violations occur.

## How Do You Make Ethical Decisions?

On a cold morning in the midst of a winter storm, schools were closed and most people had decided to stay home from work. However, Richard Addessi had already showered, shaved, and dressed for the office. Addessi, whose father worked at IBM for 36 years, was just four months short of his 30-year anniversary with the company. Addessi kissed his wife Joan goodbye, but before he could get to his car, he fell dead on the garage floor of a sudden heart attack. Having begun work at IBM at the age of 18, he was just 48 years old.[27]

You're the vice president in charge of benefits at IBM. Given that he was four months short of full retirement, do you award full retirement benefits to Mr. Addessi's wife and daughters? If the answer is yes, they will receive his full retirement benefits of $1,800 a month and free lifetime medical coverage. If you say no, Mrs. Addessi and her daughters will only receive $340 a month. They will also have to pay $473 a month just to continue their current medical coverage. As the VP in charge of benefits at IBM, what would be the ethical thing to do?

*After reading the next two sections, you should be able to*
*4. describe what influences ethical decision making.*
*5. explain what practical steps managers can take to improve ethical decision making.*

## 4. Influences on Ethical Decision Making

So, what did IBM decide to do? Since Richard Addessi was four months short of 30 years with the company, IBM officials felt they had no choice but to give Joan Addessi and her two daughters the smaller, partial retirement benefits. Do you think that IBM's decision was ethical? Probably many of you don't. You wonder how the company could be so heartless as to not give Richard Addessi's family the full benefits to which you believe they were entitled. Yet others might argue that IBM did the ethical thing by strictly following the rules laid out in its pension benefit plan. After all, being fair means applying the rules to everyone. While some ethical issues are easily solved, for many there are no clearly right or wrong answers.

*The ethical answers that managers choose depend on 4.1 the ethical intensity of the decision, 4.2 the moral development of the manager, and 4.3 the ethical principles used to solve the problem.*

### 4.1 Ethical Intensity of the Decision

Managers don't treat all ethical decisions the same. The manager who has to decide whether to deny or extend full benefits to Joan Addessi and her family is going to treat that decision much more seriously than the manager who has to deal with an assistant who has been taking computer diskettes home for personal use. The difference between these decisions is one of **ethical intensity**, which is how concerned people are about an ethical issue. When addressing issues of high ethical intensity, managers are more aware of the impact their decisions have on others. They are more likely to view the decision as an ethical or moral decision rather than an economic decision. They are also more likely to worry about doing the "right thing."

Ethical intensity depends on six factors: [28]

- magnitude of consequences
- social consensus
- probability of effect
- temporal immediacy
- proximity of effect
- concentration of effect.

**Magnitude of consequences** is the total harm or benefit derived from an ethical decision. The more people who are harmed or the greater the harm to those people, the larger the consequences. **Social consensus** is agreement on whether behavior is bad or good. For example, other than the act of self-defense, most people agree that killing is wrong. However, people strongly disagree about whether abortions or the death penalty are wrong. **Probability of effect** is the chance that something will happen and then

**ethical intensity**
the degree of concern people have about an ethical issue

**magnitude of consequences**
the total harm or benefit derived from an ethical decision

**social consensus**
agreement on whether behavior is bad or good

**probability of effect**
the chance that something will happen and then harm others

83

result in harm to others. For example, the probability of effect is strong for cigarettes. We know that cigarette smoking strongly increases the chances of heart attack, cancer, and emphysema. We also know that the nicotine in cigarettes is addictive, and that once you start, it's hard to stop. Consequently, smokers are very likely to contract one of these diseases.

**Temporal immediacy** is the time between an act and the consequences the act produces. Temporal immediacy is stronger if a manager has to lay off workers next week as opposed to three months from now. **Proximity of effect** is the social, psychological, cultural, or physical distance of a decision maker to those affected by his or her decisions. In the previous example, proximity of effect would be greater for the manager who works with employees who are to be laid off than it would be for a manager who works where no layoffs are occurring. Finally, whereas the magnitude of consequences is the total effect across all people, **concentration of effect** is how much an act affects the average person. Cheating 10 investors out of $10,000 apiece is a greater concentration of effect than cheating 100 investors out of $1,000 apiece.

Many people will likely feel IBM was wrong to deny full benefits to Joan Addessi. Why? Because IBM's decision met five of the six characteristics of ethical intensity. The difference in benefits ($23,000 per year) is likely to have serious consequences on the family. The decision is certain to affect them. It will affect them immediately. We can closely identify with Joan Addessi and her daughters (as opposed to IBM's faceless, nameless corporate identity). And the decision will have a concentrated effect on the family in terms of their monthly benefits ($1,800 and free medical coverage if you award full benefits versus $340 a month and medical care that costs $473 per month if you don't).

The exception, as we will discuss below, is social consensus. Not everyone will agree that IBM's decision was unethical. The judgment also depends on your level of moral development and which ethical principles you use to decide.

### 4.2 Moral Development

A friend of yours has given you the latest version of Microsoft Word. She stuffed the computer disks in your backpack with a note saying that you should install it on your computer and get it back to her in a couple of days. You're tempted. You have papers to write, notes to take, presentations to plan. Besides, all of your friends have the same version of Microsoft Word. They didn't pay for it either. Copying the software to your hard drive without buying your own copy clearly violates copyright laws. But no one would find out. Even if they do, Microsoft isn't going to come after you. Microsoft goes after the big fish, companies that illegally copy and distribute software to their workers. Your computer has booted up, and you've got your mouse in one hand and the installation disk in the other. What are you going to do?[29]

In part, according to Lawrence Kohlberg, the decision will be based on your level of moral development. Kohlberg identified three phases of moral development, with two stages in each phase (see Exhibit 3.3).[30] At the **preconventional level of moral development,** people decide based on selfish reasons. For example, if you were in Stage 1, the punishment and obedience stage, your primary concern would be to avoid trouble. So, you wouldn't copy the software. Yet, in Stage 2, the instrumental exchange stage, you make decisions that advance your wants and needs. So, you copy the software.

People at the **conventional level of moral development** make decisions that conform to societal expectations. In Stage 3, the good boy—nice girl stage, you normally do what the other "good boys" and "nice girls" are doing. If everyone else is illegally copying software, you will, too. In the law and order stage, Stage 4, you do whatever the law permits, so you wouldn't copy the software.

People at the **postconventional level of moral development** always use internalized ethical principles to solve ethical dilemmas. In Stage 5, the social contract stage, you would refuse to copy the software because, as a whole, society is better off when the rights of others—in this case, the rights of software authors and manufacturers—are

---

**temporal immediacy**
the time between an act and the consequences the act produces

**proximity of effect**
the social, psychological, cultural, or physical distance between a decision maker and those affected by his or her decisions

**concentration of effect**
the total harm or benefit that an act produces on the average person

**preconventional level of moral development**
first level of moral development in which people make decisions based on selfish reasons

**conventional level of moral development**
second level of moral development in which people make decisions that conform to societal expectations

**postconventional level of moral development**
third level of moral development in which people make decisions based on internalized principles

## PersonalProductivityTip

### Could You Tell Your Parents or the Public?

Besides the sleep test, managers also judge the ethics of what they're doing by trying to anticipate how others would view their actions. One manager said, "Ummm . . . This is going to sound trite. But if you can comfortably tell your parents, I think you are probably doing the right thing." Or, "Can you tell your grandfather about it and be proud?" Practicing managers were also aware of the importance of how their choices were viewed by the general public. Said one manager, "If you wouldn't share it with '60 Minutes' news cameras, don't do it."

**Sources:** J.L. Badaracco, Jr. & A.P. Webb, "Business Ethics: A View from the Trenches," *California Management Review* 37 (1995): 8-28.

not violated. In Stage 6, the universal principle stage, you might or might not copy the software, depending on your principles of right and wrong. Moreover, you will stick to your principles even if your decision conflicts with the law (Stage 4) or what others believe is best for society (Stage 5). For example, someone with socialist or communist beliefs would probably choose to copy the software, because they view goods and services as owned by society rather than by individuals and corporations. (For information about the do's, don'ts, and legal issues concerning software piracy, see the Software & Information Industry Association Web site at **http://www.siia.net/piracy/default.asp**.)

Kohlberg originally predicted that people would progress sequentially from earlier stages to later stages. We now know that one's level of moral maturity can change, depending on individual and situational factors. As people age, become more educated, or deal with dilemmas high in ethical intensity, they are more likely to make ethical decisions using a higher level of moral maturity.

### *4.3 Principles of Ethical Decision Making*

Besides an issue's ethical intensity and a manager's level of moral maturity, the particular ethical principles that managers use will also affect how they solve ethical dilemmas. Unfortunately, there is no one "ideal principle" by which to make ethical business decisions.

According to Professor Larue Hosmer, a number of different ethical principles can be used to make business decisions: long-term self-interest, personal virtue, religious injunctions, government requirements, utilitarian benefits, individual rights, and distributive justice.[31] What these ethical principles have in common is that they encourage managers and employees to take others' interests into account when making ethical decisions. At the same time, however, these principles can lead to very different ethical actions. This is illustrated by using these principles to decide whether to award full benefits to Joan Addessi and her children.

**principle of long-term self-interest** ethical principle that holds that you should never take any action that is not in your or your organization's long-term self-interest

According to the **principle of long-term self-interest**, you should never take any action that is not in your or your organization's long-term self-interest. While it sounds as if the principle of self-interest promotes selfishness, it doesn't. What we do to maximize our long-term interests (save more, spend less, exercise every day, watch what we eat) is often very different from what we do to maximize short-term interests (max out our credit cards, be a couch potato, eat whatever we want). At any single time, IBM has nearly 1,000 employees who are just months away from retirement. Thus, because of the

*EXHIBIT 3.3*

KOHLBERG'S STAGES OF MORAL DEVELOPMENT

Preconventional Level
- Stage 1: Punishment and Obedience
- Stage 2: Instrumental Exchange

Conventional Level
- Stage 3: Good Boy—Nice Girl
- Stage 4: Law and Order

Post Conventional Level
- Stage 5: Legal Contract
- Stage 6: Universal Principle

**Source:** W. Davidson III & D. Worrell, "Influencing Managers to Change Unpopular Corporate Behavior Through Boycotts and Divestitures," *Business & Society* 34 (1995): 171-196.

**The "Sleep Test"**

Professors use fancy words like "utilitarian benefits" to describe ethical decision making. However, practicing managers refer to something much simpler, the "sleep test." "If I do this, can I sleep at night?" "Can I look at myself in the mirror in the morning?" The bottom line is what you're comfortable with. "I want . . . to be able to both meet my house payments and have some dignity left." In short, if you're asked to do something that just "feels" wrong, sleep on it. If it still feels wrong in the morning, don't do it.

**Sources:** J.L. Badaracco, Jr. & A.P. Webb, "Business Ethics: A View from the Trenches," *California Management Review* 37 (1995): 8-28.

---

**principle of personal virtue**
ethical principle that holds that you should never do anything that is not honest, open, and truthful, and which you would not be glad to see reported in the newspapers or on TV

**principle of religious injunctions**
ethical principle that holds that you should never take any action that is not kind and that does not build a sense of community

**principle of government requirements**
ethical principle that holds that you should never take any action that violates the law, for the law represents the minimal moral standard

**principle of utilitarian benefits**
ethical principle that holds that you should never take any action that does not result in greater good for society

**principle of individual rights**
ethical principle that holds that you should never take any action that infringes on others' agreed-upon rights

**principle of distributive justice**
ethical principle that holds that you should never take any action that harms the least among us: the poor, the uneducated, the unemployed

---

costs involved, it serves IBM's long-term interest to pay full benefits only after employees have put in their 30 years.

The **principle of personal virtue** holds that you should never do anything that is not honest, open, and truthful, and which you would not be glad to see reported in the newspapers or on TV. Using the principle of personal virtue, IBM should have quietly awarded Joan Addessi her husband's full benefits. Had it done so, it could have avoided the publication of an embarrassing *Wall Street Journal* article on this topic.

The **principle of religious injunctions** holds that you should never take an action that is unkind or that harms a sense of community, such as the positive feelings that come from working together to accomplish a commonly accepted goal. Using the principle of religious injunctions, IBM would have been concerned foremost with compassion and kindness. Thus, it would have awarded full benefits to Joan Addessi.

According to the **principle of government requirements**, the law represents the minimal moral standards of society, so you should never take any action that violates the law. Using the principle of government requirements, IBM would deny full benefits to Joan Addessi because her husband did not work for the company for 30 years. Indeed, an IBM spokesperson stated that making exceptions would violate the federal Employee Retirement Income Security Act of 1974.

The **principle of utilitarian benefits** states that you should never take any action that does not result in greater good for society. In short, you should do whatever creates the greatest good for the greatest number. At first, this principle suggests that IBM should award full benefits to Joan Addessi. However, if IBM did this with any regularity, the costs would be enormous, profits would shrink, and IBM's stock price would drop, harming countless shareholders, many of whom rely on IBM stock dividends for retirement income. So, in this case, the principle does not lead to a clear choice.

The **principle of individual rights** holds that you should never take any action that infringes on others' agreed-upon rights. Using the principle of individual rights, IBM would deny Joan Addessi full benefits. If it carefully followed the rules specified in its pension plan, and if it permitted Mrs. Addessi due process, meaning the right to appeal the decision, then IBM would not be violating Mrs. Addessi's rights. In fact, it could be argued that providing full benefits to Mrs. Addessi would violate the rights of employees who had to wait 30 years to receive full benefits.

Finally, the **principle of distributive justice** is that you should never take any action that harms the least among us in some way. This principle is designed to protect the poor, the uneducated, and the unemployed. While Joan Addessi could probably find a job, after 20 years as a stay-at-home mom, it's unlikely that she could easily find one that would support herself and her daughters in the manner to which they are accustomed. Using the principle of distributive justice, IBM would award her full benefits.

As stated at the beginning of this chapter, one of the "real world" aspects of ethical decisions is that no matter *what* you decide, someone or some group will be unhappy with the decision. This corollary is also true: No matter *how* you decide, someone or some group will be unhappy. Consequently, although all of these different ethical principles encourage managers to balance others' needs against their own, they can also lead to very different ethical actions. So, even when managers strive to be ethical, there are often no clear answers when it comes to doing "the" right thing.

## Review 4
### Influences on Ethical Decision Making

Three factors influence ethical decisions: the ethical intensity of the decision, the moral development of the manager, and the ethical principles used to solve the problem. Ethical intensity is strong when decisions have large, certain, immediate consequences, and when we are physically or psychologically close to those affected by the decision. There are three phases of moral maturity and two steps within each phase. At the preconven-

86

tional level, decisions are made for selfish reasons. At the conventional level, decisions conform to societal expectations. At the postconventional level, internalized principles are used to make ethical decisions. Finally, managers can use a number of different principles when making ethical decisions: self-interest, personal virtue, religious injunctions, government requirements, utilitarian benefits, individual rights, and distributive justice.

## 5. Practical Steps to Ethical Decision Making

*Managers can encourage more ethical decision making in their organizations by 5.1 carefully selecting and hiring new employees, 5.2 establishing a specific code of ethics, 5.3 training employees how to make ethical decisions, and 5.4 creating an ethical climate.*

### 5.1 Selecting and Hiring Ethical Employees

If you found a wallet containing $50, would you return it with the money? *Reader's Digest* magazine examined this question by leaving 120 wallets in an unscientifically selected sample of three big cities, three large suburban areas, and three small towns.[32] Each wallet contained $50, a name, a local address, family pictures, notes, and coupons—in other words, what you'd find in most wallets. Overall, 67 percent of the wallets were returned with the $50. The wallets were more likely to be returned by women (72 percent) than by men (62 percent), and were more likely to be returned in small towns (80 percent) than in major cities (70 percent), suburbs (60 percent), or medium cities (57 percent). In a similar study in New York City, 100 wallets containing $2 and various personal artifacts were left around town, but only 34 percent were returned. This time, women were twice as likely to return the wallets as men.[33] Finally, in Chicago, wallets, purses, a personal stereo, and a cell phone were left in public places. Twenty-four (45 percent) people kept the objects, 14 (26 percent) returned them, and 15 (28 percent) walked right by them, doing nothing at all. Mikal Clay, who conducted the study, said, "One guy came off a casino boat—he must have lost, because when he saw the purse he whooped and grabbed it. But when he found there wasn't much inside, he threw it into the river in frustration."[34]

**overt integrity test**
written test that estimates employee honesty by directly asking job applicants what they think or feel about theft or about punishment of unethical behaviors

As an employer, you can increase your chances of hiring the honest person who returns the wallet with the money if you give job applicants integrity tests. **Overt integrity tests** estimate employee honesty by directly asking job applicants what they think or feel about theft or about punishment of unethical behaviors.[35] For example, an employer might ask an applicant, "Do you think you would ever consider buying something from somebody if you knew the person had stolen the item?" or "Don't most people steal from their companies?" Surprisingly, because they believe that the world is basically dishonest and that dishonest behavior is normal, unethical people will usually answer yes to such questions.[36]

**personality-based integrity test**
written test that indirectly estimates employee honesty by measuring psychological traits, such as dependability and conscientiousness

**Personality-based integrity tests** indirectly estimate employee honesty by measuring psychological traits such as dependability and conscientiousness. For example, prison inmates serving time for white-collar crimes (counterfeiting, embezzlement, and fraud) scored much lower than a comparison group of middle-level managers on scales measuring reliability, dependability, honesty, conscientiousness, and abiding by rules.[37] These results show that companies can selectively hire and promote people who will be more ethical.[38] For more on integrity testing, see the "What Really Works?" feature in this chapter.

### 5.2 Codes of Ethics

As shown in Exhibit 3.4, James Cash Penney, founder of the JCPenney Company, established one of the first modern codes of business conduct in 1913. Indeed, the last statement in the code encouraged Penney's employees to test their actions by asking, "Does it square with what is right and just?"

Today, nine out of ten large corporations have an ethics code in place. However, two things must happen if those codes are to encourage ethical decision making and behavior.[39]

# WhatReallyWorks

## Integrity Tests

Under the 1991 U.S. Sentencing Commission Guidelines, unethical employee behavior can lead to multimillion dollar fines for corporations. Moreover, workplace deviance, like stealing, fraud, and vandalism, can cost companies an estimated $200 billion a year. One way to reduce workplace deviance and the chance of a large fine for

unethical employee behavior is to use overt and personality-based integrity tests to screen job applicants.

One hundred eighty-one studies, with a combined total of 576,460 study participants, have examined how well integrity tests predict job performance and various kinds of workplace deviance. Not only do these studies show that integrity tests can help companies reduce workplace deviance, but they have the added bonus of helping companies hire workers who are better performers in their jobs.

### Workplace Deviance (Counterproductive Behaviors)

Compared to job applicants who score poorly, there is an 82 percent chance that job applicants who score well on overt integrity tests will participate in less illegal activity, unethical behavior, drug abuse, or workplace violence.

**Overt Integrity Tests & Workplace Deviance**

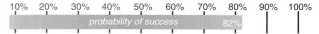

Personality-based integrity tests also accurately predict who will engage in workplace deviance. Compared to job applicants who score poorly, there is a 68 percent chance that job applicants who score well on personality-based integrity tests will participate in less illegal activity, unethical behavior, excessive absences, drug abuse, or workplace violence.

**Personality-Based Integrity Tests & Workplace Deviance**

### Job Performance

Integrity tests not only reduce unethical behavior and workplace deviance, but they also help companies hire better performers. Compared to employees who score poorly, there is a 69 percent

chance that employees who score well on overt integrity tests will be better performers.

**Overt Integrity Tests & Job Performance**

The figures are nearly identical for personality-based integrity tests. Compared to those who score poorly, there is a 70 percent chance that employees who score well on personality-based integrity tests will be better at their jobs.

**Personality-Based Integrity Tests & Job Performance**

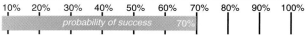

### Theft

While integrity tests can help companies decrease most kinds of workplace deviance and increase employees' job performance, they have a smaller effect on a specific kind of workplace deviance: theft. Compared to employees that score poorly, there is a 57 percent chance that employees who score well on overt integrity tests will be less likely to steal. No theft data were available to assess personality-based integrity tests.

**Overt Integrity Tests & Theft**

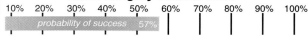

**Source:** D.S. Ones, C. Viswesvaran, & F.L. Schmidt, "Comprehensive Meta-Analysis of Integrity Test Validities: Findings and Implications for Personnel Selection and Theories of Job Performance," *Journal of Applied Psychology* 78 (1993): 679-703.

First, companies must communicate the codes to others both within and outside the company. An excellent example of a well-communicated code of ethics can be found at Nortel Networks' Internet site at **http://www.nortelnetworks.com/corporate/community/ ethics/index.html**. With the click of a computer mouse, anyone inside or outside the company can obtain detailed information about the company's core values, specific ethical business practices, and much more.

Second, in addition to general guidelines and ethics codes like "do unto others as you would have others do unto you," management must also develop practical ethical

EXHIBIT 3.4

JCPENNEY 1913 CODE OF CONDUCT

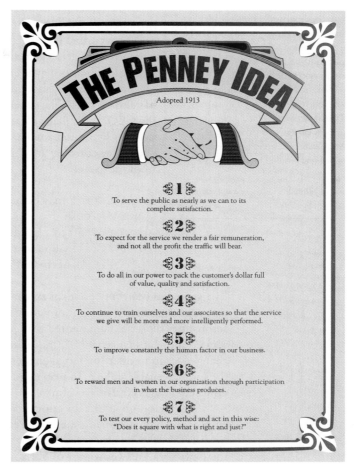

THE PENNEY IDEA

Adopted 1913

**1**
To serve the public as nearly as we can to its complete satisfaction.

**2**
To expect for the service we render a fair remuneration, and not all the profit the traffic will bear.

**3**
To do all in our power to pack the customer's dollar full of value, quality and satisfaction.

**4**
To continue to train ourselves and our associates so that the service we give will be more and more intelligently performed.

**5**
To improve constantly the human factor in our business.

**6**
To reward men and women in our organization through participation in what the business produces.

**7**
To test our every policy, method and act in this wise: "Does it square with what is right and just?"

**Source:** JCPenney. [Online] Available http://www.jcpenney.net/company/history/history.htm, 6 October 2001.

standards and procedures specific to the company's line of business. Visitors to Nortel's Internet site can instantly access references to 36 specific ethics codes, ranging from bribes and kickbacks to expense vouchers and illegal copying of software. For example, most business people believe that it is wrong to take bribes or other gifts from a company that wants your business. Therefore, one of Nortel Network's ethical guidelines is "Under no circumstances is it acceptable to offer, give, solicit, or receive any form of bribe, kickback, or inducement. This principle applies to Nortel Networks transactions everywhere in the world, even where the practice is widely considered 'a way of doing business.' Under some statutes (such as the U.S. Foreign Corrupt Practices Act), there are criminal actions that can lead to prosecution."[40] And just to be sure there's no confusion over what constitutes, say, a gift, Nortel Network's guidelines are even more specific, stating, "Nortel Networks employees must not accept gifts and gratuities from suppliers or potential suppliers, except for promotional items of limited value (such as inexpensive pens, mugs, and calendars that bear the company's name)."[41]

Specific codes of ethics such as these make it much easier for employees to decide what they should do when they want to do the "right thing."

**Consider Ethics from the Start**

Many jobs begin with a short honeymoon period in which you're excited and still relatively idealistic. This is a good time to write down your thoughts about the ethical aspects of the job. Start positive. Describe your ethical aspirations (i.e., satisfied customers) and what you will do to accomplish them (i.e., be completely honest). Then, go negative. Describe parts of the job in which you fear that your ethics may be compromised. Then describe unethical behaviors that people may perform on the job (so you can avoid them). Review these lists occasionally to determine if your ethics are what you wanted them to be.

**Source**: D. M. Porter, Jr., The Anderson School, University of California, Los Angeles, from his review of this chapter, 22 January 1997.

## 5.3 Ethics Training

The first objective of ethics training is to develop employee awareness about ethics.[42] This means helping employees recognize what issues are ethical issues and then avoid the rationalization of unethical behavior: "This isn't really illegal or immoral," or "No one will ever find out." Two companies have created board games to improve awareness about ethical issues.[43] Citicorp Bank has a game called "The Work Ethic," in which players win or lose points depending on their answers to legal, regulatory, policy-related, and judgmental questions. Defense contractor Lockheed Martin has also created "The Ethics Challenge," which every employee, including the CEO, must play at least once a year. To play the board game, Lockheed workers sit around a table, roll dice, and then move their tokens ahead when they correctly answer ethics questions. Here's a sample question from the game:

> A kickback may be in the form of:
> A. Cash
> B. Gift to a family member
> C. Donation to a charity at your request
> D. All of these (the correct answer)

The game has been very popular, except for one year in which it was revised to not indicate which answers were right or wrong. Brian Sears, an ethics officer for Lockheed's aeronautics division, commented that engineers, who are used to "correct answers" wanted more guidance. Said Sears, "They had a hard time with it," so the game was changed again to offer "preferred answers."[44] Boeing's "Ethics Challenge" game, which is similar, is available online. To play it, go to **http://active.boeing.com/companyoffices/ethicschallenge/cfm/initial.cfm**.

The second objective for ethics training programs is to achieve credibility with employees. Not surprisingly, employees can be highly suspicious of management's reasons for offering ethics training. At NYNEX, the regional telephone company for the New York area (now part of Verizon Communications), employees initially assumed that management instituted the program to get employees to "rat" on each other. So they labeled the program, "1-800-SNITCH."[45] One of the ways in which companies mistakenly hurt the credibility of their ethics programs is by having outside instructors and consultants conduct the classes.[46] Employees often complain that outside instructors and consultants are teaching theory that has nothing to do with their jobs and the "real world." This is why Boeing has a vice president of ethics who employs 55 people to teach Boeing's 194,000 employees the difference between right and wrong in the aerospace industry.[47] Ethics training becomes even more credible when top management teaches the initial ethics training classes to their subordinates, who in turn teach it to theirs. In time, most managers will have taken and taught the ethics class, thereby pushing ethics training and principles throughout the entire company.[48]

The third objective of ethics training is to teach employees a practical model of ethical decision making. A basic model should help them think about the consequences their choices will have on others and consider how they will choose between different solutions. Exhibit 3.5 presents a basic model of ethical decision making.

## 5.4 Ethical Climate

In study after study in which researchers have asked, "What is the most important influence on your ethical behavior at work?", the answer comes back, "My manager." The first step in establishing an ethical climate is for managers to act ethically themselves. Managers who decline to accept lavish gifts from company suppliers; who only use the company phone, fax, and copier for business and not personal use; or who

EXHIBIT 3.5

### A BASIC MODEL OF ETHICAL DECISION MAKING

1. **Identify the problem.** What makes it an ethical problem? Think in terms of rights, obligations, fairness, relationships, and integrity. How would you define the problem if you stood on the other side of the fence?

2. **Identify the constituents.** Who has been hurt? Who could be hurt? Who could be helped? Are they willing players, or are they victims? Can you negotiate with them?

3. **Diagnose the situation.** How did it happen in the first place? What could have prevented it? Is it going to get worse or better? Can the damage now be undone?

4. **Analyze your options.** Imagine the range of possibilities. Limit yourself to the two or three most manageable. What are the likely outcomes of each? What are the likely costs? Look to the company mission statement or code of ethics for guidance.

5. **Make your choice.** What is your intention in making this decision? How does it compare with the probable results? Can you discuss the problem with the affected parties before you act? Could you disclose without qualm your decision to your boss, the CEO, the board of directors, your family, or society as a whole?

6. **Act.** Do what you have to do. Don't be afraid to admit errors. Be as bold in confronting a problem as you were in causing it.

Source: L.A. Berger, "Train All Employees to Solve Ethical Dilemmas," *Best's Review—Life-Health Insurance Edition* 95 (1995): 70-80.

keep their promises to employees, suppliers, and customers encourage others to believe that ethical behavior is normal and acceptable.

A second step in establishing an ethical climate is for top management to be active in the company ethics program. For example, Thomas Russo heads the corporate advisory division in charge of ethical behavior at Lehman Brothers, a Wall Street investment firm. Russo is not just a middle-level manager reporting to upper management. As a top-level managing director, he runs the firm's general counsel (legal), credit, and corporate audit departments. He says, "Just three or four years ago, [Wall Street] wouldn't have put the emphasis on preventive steps. We are putting an [ethics] system into place to prevent problems."[49]

A third step is to put in place a reporting system that encourages managers and employees to report potential ethics violations. **Whistleblowing**, that is, reporting others' ethics violations, is a difficult step for most people to take. Potential whistleblowers often fear that they will be punished rather than the ethics violators.[50] Managers who have been interviewed about whistleblowing have said, "In every organization, someone's been screwed for standing up." "If anything, I figured that by taking a strong stand I might get myself in trouble. People might look at me as a 'goody two shoes.' Someone might try to force me out." This is exactly what happened to Sandy Baratta, who used to be a vice president at Oracle, which makes database software used by most large companies. Baratta was fired, she alleges, for complaining about Oracle's treatment of women and unethical business practices. Under the State of California's whistleblower protection laws, a California jury awarded her $2.6 million in damages. Oracle is appealing the ruling.[51] Today, however, many federal and state laws protect the rights of whistleblowers (see **http://www.whistleblowers.org** for more information). In addition, some companies, like Northrup Grumman, a defense contractor, have made it easier to report possible violations by establishing anonymous, toll-free corporate ethics hot lines. Nortel Networks even publicizes which of its ethics hot lines don't have caller ID (so that they cannot identify the caller's phone number). However, the factor that does the most to discourage whistleblowers from reporting problems is lack of company action on their complaints.[52]

Thus, the final step in developing an ethical climate is for management to fairly and consistently punish those who violate the company's code of ethics. At Allied Security, which provides security guards to corporations, one of its guards reported a fire at a building he was guarding. He reduced the damage by quickly calling the local fire

**whistleblowing**
reporting others' ethics violations to management or legal authorities

91

department. But when Allied's investigators conducted a routine investigation, they discovered that the guard, who had become a local hero for preventing the fire from spreading, had set the fire himself. Allied filed criminal arson charges against the employee and then reimbursed its customer for $50,000 in property damage.[53]

### Review 5
#### Practical Steps to Ethical Decision Making
Employers can increase the chances of hiring more ethical employees by administering overt integrity tests and personality-based integrity tests to all job applicants. Most large companies now have corporate codes of ethics. But for those codes to affect ethical decision making, they must be known both inside and outside the organization. In addition to offering general rules, ethics codes must also offer specific, practical advice. Ethics training seeks to make employees aware of ethical issues, to make ethics a serious, credible factor in organizational decisions, and to teach employees a practical model of ethical decision making. The most important factors in creating an ethical business climate are the personal examples set by company managers, involvement of management in the company ethics program, a reporting system that encourages whistleblowers to report potential ethics violations, and fair but consistent punishment of violators.

## What Is Social Responsibility?

**social responsibility**
a business's obligation to pursue policies, make decisions, and take actions that benefit society

**Social responsibility** is a business's obligation to pursue policies, make decisions, and take actions that benefit society.[54] Unfortunately, because there are strong disagreements over to whom and for what in society organizations are responsible, it can be difficult for managers to know what is or will be perceived as socially responsible corporate behavior. For example, Gillette Corporation's use of rats and rabbits for product testing continues to draw protests from PETA (People for the Ethical Treatment of Animals, **http://www. peta-online.org**) and from elementary school teachers who encourage their students to write directly to Gillette. In one such letter, a 13-year-old wrote, "Would you like it if someone put acids in your eyes and shoved cleaning materials down your throat?" In response to complaints, Gillette now spends about a million dollars a year on alternatives to animal testing. However, Gillette argues that eliminating animal testing altogether would be socially irresponsible, because it is critical to producing a safe product for its customers. Furthermore, if a product liability lawsuit were to be filed against the company, its best legal defense would be the scientific testing it performs on rats and rabbits.[55] By contrast, The Body Shop, a British-based retailer of skin and hair products, is squarely against any kind of product testing involving animals. The company's Web site states, "We consider such tests to be morally and scientifically indefensible. We use our purchasing power to try to stop cosmetics ingredient suppliers' animal testing. We also support and use alternative tests, inform the public and, most importantly, campaign to ban cosmetics tests on animals."[56]

*After reading the next four sections, you should be able to explain*
*6. to whom organizations are socially responsible.*
*7. for what organizations are socially responsible.*
*8. how organizations can choose to respond to societal demands for social responsibility.*
*9. whether social responsibility hurts or helps an organization's economic performance.*

**shareholder model**
view of social responsibility which holds that an organization's overriding goal should be profit maximization for the benefit of shareholders

## 6. To Whom Are Organizations Socially Responsible?

There are two perspectives on to whom organizations are socially responsible: the shareholder model and the stakeholder model. According to Nobel prize-winning economist Milton Friedman, the only social responsibility that organizations have is to satisfy their owners, that is, company shareholders. This view—called the **shareholder model**—

holds that the only social responsibility that businesses have is to maximize profits. By maximizing profit, the firm maximizes shareholder wealth and satisfaction. More specifically, as profits rise, the company stock owned by company shareholders generally increases in value. For example, over the last decade, EMC, a manufacturer of computer hard drives and storage devices, has given its shareholders an average annual return of 82 percent, by far the highest among Fortune 500 companies.[57] If you invested $1,000 in EMC ten years ago, that money would now be worth $398,762.00![58] (This figure does not include stock splits. When stock prices get high, companies split the stock. For example, if a stock costs $200, and the company splits the stock, one $200 share of stock now becomes two shares of stock, each worth $100.)

Friedman argues that it is socially irresponsible for companies to divert their time, money, and attention from maximizing profits to social causes and charitable organizations. The first problem he sees is that organizations cannot act effectively as moral agents for all company shareholders. While shareholders are likely to agree on investment issues concerning a company, it's highly unlikely that they possess common views on what social causes a company should or should not support. For example, corporate donations to the Boy Scouts dropped significantly after the U.S. Supreme Court ruled 5-4 that the Boy Scouts do not have to accept homosexual troop leaders. Chase Manhattan Bank, Levi-Strauss & Co., Textron, and Wells Fargo have all stopped donating to the Boy Scouts. Tom Unger of Wells Fargo said, "The Boy Scouts are as American as apple pie, but this was an easy decision to make. We really have to, as a company, return to what our core vision and values are, and that's to not discriminate." Yet, while corporate donations are down, overall donations to the Boy Scouts have risen. [59] Rather than act as moral agents, Friedman argues that companies should maximize profits for shareholders. Shareholders can then use their time and increased wealth to contribute to the social causes, charities, or institutions they want, rather than those that companies want.

The second major problem, according to Friedman, is that the time, money, and attention diverted to social causes undermine market efficiency.[60] In competitive markets, companies compete for raw materials, talented workers, customers, and investment funds. Spending money on social causes means there is less money to purchase quality materials or to hire talented workers who can produce a valuable product at a good price. If customers find the product less desirable, sales and profits will fall. If profits fall, stock prices will decrease and the company will have difficulty attracting investment funds that could be used to fund long-term growth. In the end, Friedman argues, diverting the firm's money, time, and resources to social causes hurts customers, suppliers, employees, and shareholders.

By contrast, under the **stakeholder model**, management's most important responsibility is long-term survival (not just maximizing profits), which is achieved by satisfying the interests of multiple corporate stakeholders (not just shareholders). **Stakeholders** are persons or groups with a legitimate interest in a company. [61] Since stakeholders are interested in and affected by the organization's actions, they have a "stake" in what those actions are. Consequently, stakeholder groups may try to influence the firm to act in their own interests. Exhibit 3.6 shows the various stakeholder groups that the organization must satisfy to assure long-term survival.

Being responsible to multiple stakeholders raises two basic questions. First, how does a company identify organizational stakeholders? Second, how does a company balance the needs of different stakeholders? Distinguishing between primary and secondary stakeholders can answer these questions.[62]

Some stakeholders are more important to the firm's survival than others. **Primary stakeholders** are groups, such as shareholders, employees, customers, suppliers, governments, and local communities, on which the organization depends for long-term survival. So when managers are struggling to balance the needs of different stakeholders, the stakeholder model suggests that the needs of primary stakeholders take precedence over the needs of secondary stakeholders. However, contrary to the shareholder model, no primary stakeholder group is more or less important than another, since all are critical

**stakeholder model**
theory of corporate responsibility which holds that management's most important responsibility, long-term survival, is achieved by satisfying the interests of multiple corporate stakeholders

**stakeholders**
persons or groups with a "stake" or legitimate interest in a company's actions

**primary stakeholder**
any group on which an organization relies for its long-term survival

EXHIBIT 3.6

STAKEHOLDER MODEL OF CORPORATE SOCIAL RESPONSIBILITY

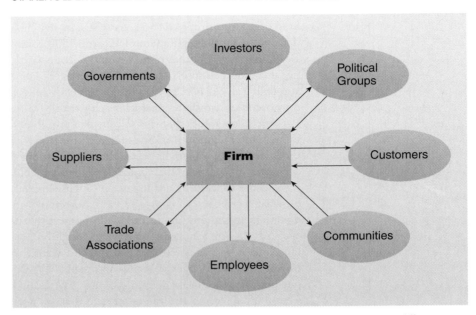

**Source:** Republished with permission of Academy of Management, PO Box 3020, Briar Cliff Manor, NY, 10510-8020. "The Stakeholder Theory of the Corporation: Concepts, Evidence and Implications" (Figure), T. Donaldson & L.E. Preston, *Academy of Management Review*. 1995, Vol. 20. Reproduced by permission of the publisher via Copyright Clearance Center, Inc.

to the firm's success and survival. So managers must try to satisfy the needs of all primary stakeholders. Exhibit 3.7 displays a list of issues that organizations will probably have to address to keep their primary stakeholders satisfied.

Addressing the concerns of primary stakeholders is important, because if a stakeholder group becomes dissatisfied and terminates its relationship with the company, the company could be seriously harmed or go out of business. For example, when Ameri-Serve Food Distribution, the company that supplies chicken, beef, pickles, and giveaway toys to Burger King Restaurants, experienced financial troubles, it fell behind on payments to its major suppliers. Richard Cogdill of Pilgrim's Pride, which supplied chicken to AmeriServe (which then supplied it to Burger King), said, "AmeriServe was very bad" about making payments. Therefore, Pilgrim's Pride and other suppliers notified Ameri-Serve that they would not ship any more of their products to AmeriServe distribution centers unless paid in cash before or at the time of delivery. The danger for AmeriServe was that this problem could spread to other stakeholder groups, such as Burger King, its key customer. This is just what happened. In July, with its restaurants running low on supplies, Burger King warned AmeriServe that if things didn't improve, it could lose Burger King's business. By September, there was no improvement. In November, Burger King sent a letter to all Burger King restaurants indicating that AmeriServe had been terminated as a Burger King supplier. In the end, AmeriServe filed for chapter 11 bankruptcy protection because it owed $2 billion in claims to suppliers and other creditors, but only had $300 million in assets to pay toward what it owed.[63]

**Secondary stakeholders,** such as the media and special interest groups, can influence or be influenced by the company. Yet in contrast to primary stakeholders, they do not engage in regular transactions with the company and are not critical to its long-term survival. Consequently, meeting the needs of primary stakeholders is usually more

**secondary stakeholder**
any group that can influence or be influenced by the company and can affect public perceptions about its socially responsible behavior

EXHIBIT 3.7

## ISSUES IMPORTANT TO PRIMARY STAKEHOLDERS

### COMPANY

Company history, industry background, organization structure, economic performance, competitive environment, mission or purpose, corporate codes, stakeholder and social issues management systems.

### EMPLOYEES

Benefits, compensation and rewards, training and development, career planning, employee assistance programs, health promotion, absenteeism and turnover, leaves of absence, relationships with unions, dismissal and appeal, termination, layoffs, retirement and termination counseling, employment equity and discrimination, women in management and on the board, day care and family accommodation, employee communication, occupational health and safety, and part-time, temporary, or contract employees.

### SHAREHOLDERS

Shareholder communications and complaints, shareholder advocacy, shareholder rights, and other shareholder issues.

### CUSTOMERS

Customer communications, product safety, customer complaints, special customer services, and other customer issues.

### SUPPLIERS

Relative power, general policy, and other supplier issues.

### PUBLIC STAKEHOLDERS

Public health, safety, and protection, conservation of energy and materials, environmental assessment of capital projects, other environmental issues, public policy involvement, community relations, social investment and donations.

**Source:** M.B.E. Clarkson, "A Stakeholder Framework for Analyzing and Evaluating Corporate Social Performance," *Academy of Management Review* 20 (1995): 92-117.

Environmentalists from Rainforest Relief and Wetlands Rainforest Action Group hold up a banner outside a New Jersey Home Depot store. Protestors convinced the company to quit selling wood and wood products from threatened old-growth forests.

© AP PHOTO/MIKE DERER

# BeenThereDoneThat

Anita Roddick, founder and cochair of The Body Shop International PLC

Anita Roddick and her business The Body Shop, which sells natural hair and skin products in stores around the world, have been addressing issues of corporate social responsibility for 25 years. In this interview, she shares her progressive ideas and critical thoughts on this issue.

**Q:** In *Business as Unusual,* you write, "Leaders in world business are the first true global citizens. As businesspeople, we have worldwide capability and responsibility." Is business shirking that responsibility?

**A:** Business is the fault of so many problems now. Not small-scale businesses—they're the whole underbelly of American and English and other countries' economic well-being. The real criminal behavior is in the large, multinational corporations.

A business should, of course, make profits, or it can't survive—that's like breathing. But if you concentrate your entire life on profits, it makes for a pretty bloody pathetic existence. I think socially responsible companies have shown that you can make a profit, that there's no invisible divide between culture values and workplace values. You can keep your company breathlessly alive. You can be more about public good than private greed.

**Q:** What should business be asked to change?

**A:** Number one, businesses should be audited socially and environmentally—as stringently as they are audited financially—before they're allowed to get onto a stock market.

I think that there has to be real new barometers of measurement of cost—you know, what does it cost to clean up your environmental messes? In terms of your social or environmental auditing, you have to be transparent in your business behavior to all of your stakeholders, not just your financial investors. And I think businesses shouldn't whine endlessly about wanting to get fewer restrictions. We should be penalized if we mess up and if we act in an appalling way.

And if goods are made with slave labor or child labor or sweatshop labor, they should be taxed—have a social penalty put on them. That would help level the playing field for those workers in this country and in Europe who have lost their jobs because companies have been pitting worker against worker.

Finally, there should be a code of conduct that should be legal, should have teeth to it, and should probably be audited and checked. Not so much by government, because governments are now in the pockets of business, but possibly by the United Nations. There should be penalties. And I think nongovernmental organizations should have a huge play in this.

**Q:** In your new book, you ask the rhetorical questions, "What on Earth is a skin and hair care company doing getting involved in political activism anyway? Why don't we just shut up and stick to selling shampoo and soap?" I had a different question: Why aren't you heading an NGO [Non-Governmental Organization] rather than running a skin and hair care company? After all, as you write, "No one needs anything we sell."

**A:** I think it's because The Body Shop is acting like an NGO as well, and so we're getting the best of both worlds. Also, the voice I have is solely because I'm on a business panel. If I was an erudite, smart activist that had an NGO behind her, I would not get a quarter, a nanopercentage of the press I do when I stand up against the WTO [World Trade Organization]. I do things in a way that is contrary, and the media loves controversy and confrontation.

I stand on the company to trumpet these issues and the criminal behavior of business in many cases. For instance, I've just been in the center of an enormous storm in England simply because I stood up and said something that I've been repeating for 20 years, which is that to claim that a wrinkle cream that is "anti-aging" is disingenuous, and that it's God's gentle way of defining the stupid from the smart. So this huge industry—which makes an enormous amount of money on one issue, on one phony medical condition—has suddenly realized that the power that I've got to challenge that is very frightening. And it's only because I'm in business and it's only because I'm in the beauty industry that I can say all this.

**Q:** Do you feel as though you and the social-responsibility movement are having an impact on the Fortune 500?

**A:** I don't think the movement has made a hoot within the big corporations, except for words—they've corralled all the words of social responsibility for their advertisements. And there's this bloody stupid initiative in the United Nations, Global Compact, where big, rapacious companies [make a contribution] and they can wear the United Nations logo.

But I don't think in terms of penalties the movement has gotten through yet. You still won't be penalized for screwing up.

**Q:** Outside of penalties, how do you get hard-nosed corporate types to pay attention to "the soft side of business"?

**A:** Trying to show them the fruits of their behavior would be one way. For example, if I could—and I've never been able to do this—get a group of Shell officials to show them what their behavior has done in Ogoniland, Nigeria, they would say, "We'll never do this again." People are basically good, you know.

And dialoguing is really essential. You sit with your battlefield enemies—say, the Ogoni people versus the Shell officials—and keep open the channels of dialogue. This is where third-party groups like myself or the NGOs can help: We can come in and position that dialogue.

And the change is going to happen anyway, because one of the most important things that I've seen in the last 10 years is the role of corporate reputation. They talk about brand equity, and equity usually equates with financial worth. So reputation is really important, and I think changes are going to be forced on the companies by this group of vigilante consumers—the activists, the social dissenters, the fair traders . . .

all of those people who collectively, through the Internet, have an enormously powerful voice.

**Q:** So legislation isn't the answer?

**A:** Oh, no. Unless you're in Scandinavia, change is going to come by popular protest. Look at the genetically modified food scandal in England. Monsanto came in with huge financial support from the British government, and then we had the entire movement organized by The Ecologist magazine, by Greenpeace, by Friends of the Earth. This is what worked in England. We got the tabloids and the broadsheet press on our side of the cause, and the government was just scratching their bloody heads and thinking, "What in hell hit us?" Poor Monsanto fled. So it's got to be a movement, a people-power movement.

**Q:** But most people are skeptical of the whole idea of a company that's in business to do good. How do you overcome the cynicism of people who assume that your motives are financial rather than altruistic?

**A:** You can't. You tell them what you're doing, and they can check it out. They do it, or they don't.

**Q:** Why do you think so many businesspeople and observers gloat when progressive companies such as The Body Shop fall prey to everyday business troubles?

**A:** I don't know the human psyche at all. Maybe there's just no generosity of spirit. Maybe it's because we stick our heads out, and people love conformity and homogeneity.

There is a conspiracy in the media about this. They will not talk about the social-responsibility movement, and any-time they want to talk about it, they want to shove you onto the religious program, because it's dealing with spiritual development, and they think it's fluffy. They call it soft, when in fact it's the hardest thing in the world to run a socially responsible company.

**Q:** I can tell—in *Business as Unusual,* you tell one story after another about dealing with professional consultants and executives who don't care about preserving The Body Shop's values.

**A:** The hardest thing for me is the marketing people, because they focus on us as a brand and our customers as consumers. We've never called it a brand; we call it The Body Shop. In 20 years, we've never, ever, ever called a customer a consumer. Customers aren't there to consume. They're there to live, love, die, get married, have friendships—they're not put on this planet to bloody consume.

**Q:** After all these years, do you still feel as great a need to work toward social change?

**A:** If I don't do this type of stuff, it's like a death to me. Right now, I'm looking at the southern California sky, I'm buying a new pair of shoes, I've got people coming over for dinner. It's wonderful. But it's a death unless there's a purpose for what I'm doing. Somehow or another, I managed by total accident—an amazing accident—to trip over an idea of creating wealth and position and empowerment and resources for a lot of people. And bugger me, I'm bloody going to use it for public good. (Copyright Conference Board, Inc. Jan 2001)

**Source:** M. Budman, "Questioning Authority," *Across the Board* 38 no. 1 (2001): 15-16.

important than meeting the needs of secondary stakeholders. While not critical to long-term survival, secondary stakeholders are still important, because they can affect public perceptions and opinions about socially responsible behavior. For instance, because of a protest campaign by environmental groups, Centex and Kaufman & Broad, two of the largest homebuilders in the United States agreed to quit buying lumber products from "old-growth" trees in endangered forests. Both companies quickly agreed to the demand after seeing the hundreds of protests at Home Depot hardware stores (which also convinced Home Depot to stop buying old-growth wood). A spokesperson for Centex said, "The action was in part motivated by the environmentalists, but also the company's own regard for the environment." Kaufman & Broad's CEO put a more positive spin on the move, saying, "The world's old-growth forests are indeed threatened. This is ultimately a threat to all of us."[64]

So to whom are organizations socially responsible? Many, especially economists and financial analysts, continue to argue that organizations are only responsible to shareholders. However, since the Depression, when General Electric identified shareholders, employees, customers, and the general public as its stakeholders; since 1947, when Johnson & Johnson listed customers, employees, managers, and shareholders as its stakeholders; and since 1950, when Sears Roebuck announced that its most important stakeholders were "customers, employees, community, and stockholders," top managers have increasingly come to believe that they and their companies must be socially responsible to their stakeholders.[65] Surveys show that as many as 80 percent of top-level managers believe that it is unethical to focus just on shareholders. Similarly, 29 states have changed their laws to allow company boards of directors to consider the needs of employees, creditors, suppliers, customers, and local communities, besides those of shareholders.[66] So while there is not complete agreement, a majority of opinionmakers would argue that companies must be socially responsible to their stakeholders.

### Review 6
### To Whom Are Organizations Socially Responsible?
Social responsibility is a business's obligation to benefit society. To whom are organizations socially responsible? According to the shareholder model, the only social responsibility that organizations have is to maximize shareholder wealth by maximizing company profits. According to the stakeholder model, companies must satisfy the needs and interests of multiple corporate stakeholders, not just shareholders. However, the needs of primary stakeholders, on which the organization relies for its existence, take precedence over those of secondary stakeholders.

## 7. For What Are Organizations Socially Responsible?

If organizations are to be socially responsible to stakeholders, for what are they to be socially responsible? As illustrated in Exhibit 3.8, companies can best benefit their stakeholders by fulfilling their economic, legal, ethical, and discretionary responsibilities.[67] Exhibit 3.8 indicates that economic and legal responsibilities play a larger part in a company's social responsibility than do ethical and discretionary responsibilities. However, the relative importance of economic, legal, ethical, and discretionary responsibilities depends on the expectations that society has toward corporate social responsibility at a particular point in time.[68] A century ago, society expected businesses to meet their economic and legal responsibilities and little else. Today, however, when society judges whether businesses are socially responsible, ethical and discretionary responsibilities are considerably more important than they used to be.

Historically, **economic responsibility**, making a profit by producing a product or service valued by society, has been a business's most basic social responsibility. Organizations that don't meet their financial and economic expectations come under tremendous pressure. For example, company boards are very, very quick these days to fire CEOs. Typically, all it takes is two or three bad quarters in a row. Thomas Neff, who heads the executive recruiting firm Spencer Stuart said, "It used to be a couple of years [and not

**economic responsibility**
the expectation that a company will make a profit by producing a valued product or service

### EXHIBIT 3.8

SOCIAL RESPONSIBILITIES

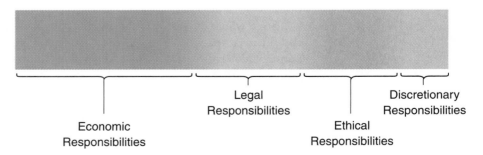

**Total Social Responsibilities**

Economic Responsibilities

Legal Responsibilities

Ethical Responsibilities

Discretionary Responsibilities

**Source:** Republished with permission of Academy of Management, PO Box 3020, Briar Cliff Manor, NY, 10510-8020. "A Three-Dimensional Conceptual Model of Corporate Performance." (Figure 3.3) A. B. Carroll, *Academy of Management Review*, 1979, Vol. 4. Reproduced by permission of the publisher via Copyright Clearance Center, Inc.

2 or 3 quarters]. It has changed dramatically in the last year." William Rollnick, who became acting chairman of Mattel after the company fired CEO Jill Barad, said, "There's zero forgiveness. You screw up and you're dead." Indeed, 38 of the largest 200 firms in the United States have gotten rid of the CEOs in the last two years.[69]

**legal responsibility**
the expectation that a company will obey society's laws and regulations

**Legal responsibility** is the expectation that companies will obey a society's laws and regulations as they try to meet their economic responsibilities. For example, under the 1990 Clean Air Act, the smell of fresh baked bread is now illegal. Actually, it's not the smell that is illegal, but the ethanol that is emitted when baking bread.[70] Ethanol itself is nontoxic; however, it contributes to pollution, because it promotes the formation of the harmful atmospheric compound ozone. Consequently, to meet the law, large bakery plants may have to spend millions to purchase catalytic oxidizers that remove ethanol emissions.[71]

**ethical responsibility**
the expectation that a company will not violate accepted principles of right and wrong when conducting its business

**Ethical responsibility** is society's expectation that organizations will not violate accepted principles of right and wrong when conducting their business. Because different stakeholders may disagree about what is or is not ethical, meeting ethical responsibilities is more difficult than meeting economic or legal responsibilities. For example, several years ago a jury awarded an 81-year-old woman $2.9 million in punitive damages to compensate for the third-degree burns she suffered after spilling coffee in her lap while going through a McDonald's drive-through window.[72] Most Americans thought the verdict was ludicrous, that it was just another example of a money-hungry jury out to pick the pockets of a big company. Was it illegal for McDonald's to serve coffee at 180 degrees, which, on average, is 20 degrees hotter than other restaurants? No. But after receiving nearly 700 customer complaints about coffee burns, was it right for McDonald's to continue serving coffee at 180 degrees? After receiving 700 complaints, was it right for McDonald's not to warn customers about the danger of second- or third-degree burns (which can require skin-graft surgery)? McDonald's now has warning signs about hot beverages posted on its drive-through windows, and it has lowered the temperature of the hot drinks it sells.[73]

**discretionary responsibilities**
the expectation that a company will voluntarily serve a social role beyond its economic, legal, and ethical responsibilities

**Discretionary responsibilities** pertain to the social roles that businesses play in society beyond their economic, legal, and ethical responsibilities. For example, American Express and its cardholders teamed up with the charitable organization Share Our Strength to fight hunger in America. Every time someone used an American Express Card to make a purchase, American Express donated three cents to Share Our Strength.[74] While three cents doesn't seem like much, the hundreds of thousands of daily American Express transactions produced $21 million in contributions in three years. While American Express has discontinued this program (though it still supports Share Our Strength), dozens of other companies now support the fight against hunger at the Hunger Site, **http://www. thehungersite.com**. Each time someone clicks on the "donate free food" button, sponsors of The Hunger Site donate money to pay for food to be sent to Bosnia, Indonesia, Mozambique, or wherever people suffer from hunger. Thanks to the corporate sponsors and 101 million visitors, almost 200 million cups of food have been distributed thus far.[75] Discretionary responsibilities such as these are voluntary. Companies will not be considered unethical if they don't perform them. However, today, corporate stakeholders expect companies to do much more than in the past to meet their discretionary responsibilities.

## Review 7
### For What Are Organizations Socially Responsible?
Companies can best benefit their stakeholders by fulfilling their economic, legal, ethical, and discretionary responsibilities. Being profitable, or meeting one's economic responsibility, is a business's most basic social responsibility. Legal responsibility consists of following a society's laws and regulations. Ethical responsibility means not violating accepted principles of right and wrong when doing business. Discretionary responsibilities are social responsibilities beyond basic economic, legal, and ethical responsibilities.

99

**social responsiveness**
the strategy chosen by a company to respond to stakeholders' economic, legal, ethical, or discretionary expectations concerning social responsibility

**reactive strategy**
a social responsiveness strategy in which a company chooses to do less than society expects

**defensive strategy**
a social responsiveness strategy in which a company chooses to admit responsibility for a problem but do the least required to meet societal expectations

**Social responsiveness** is the strategy chosen by a company to respond to stakeholders' economic, legal, ethical, or discretionary expectations concerning social responsibility. A social responsibility problem exists whenever company actions do not meet stakeholder expectations. One model of social responsiveness, shown in Exhibit 3.9, identifies four strategies for responding to social responsibility problems: reactive, defensive, accommodative, and proactive. These strategies differ in the extent to which the company is willing to act to meet or exceed society's expectations.

A company using a **reactive strategy** will do less than society expects. It may deny responsibility for a problem or fight any suggestions that the company should solve a problem. For example, *Consumer Reports* magazine published a report showing that the Suzuki Samurai would tip over when drivers changed lanes or went around corners at normal speeds. The Samurai, a four-wheel-drive vehicle, was easy to tip over because it was a lightweight vehicle with a high center of gravity and a narrow wheelbase. Rather than admit this safety problem, Suzuki Corporation immediately embarked on a multi-million dollar television advertising campaign to dispute *Consumer Reports'* findings.[76]

By contrast, a company using a **defensive strategy** would admit responsibility for a problem, but would do the least required to meet societal expectations. When the sudden and unpredictable tread separation problems associated with Firestone ATX tires first became public knowledge, Firestone's response was to deny that there were problems (a reactive strategy). However seven months later, when public fury over the problem grew intense, Firestone recalled 6.5 million of the 15-inch, ATX tires. However, Firestone angered U.S. lawmakers by refusing to recall all the tires recommended by the National Highway Traffic Safety Administration (a defensive strategy).[77] Firestone also frustrated and angered consumers at that time by proposing a "phased rollout," in which it would first replace tires in southern and western states—where higher temperatures seemed to be related to the problems. Steven Fink, president of Lexicon Communications, a crisis management consulting firm, criticized Firestone's response: "After they announced the recall, they were not prepared to deal with it. They were telling consumers they will have to wait up to a year to get tires."[78] In fact, Firestone's crisis management firm was so frustrated with the company's refusal to admit the problem and quickly act

*EXHIBIT 3.9*

SOCIAL RESPONSIVENESS

| Reactive | Defensive | Accommodative | Proactive |
|----------|-----------|---------------|-----------|
| Fight all the way | Do only what is required | Be progressive | Lead the industry |

| Withdrawal | Public Relations Approach | Legal Approach | Bargaining | Problem Solving |

DO NOTHING ← → DO MUCH

**Source:** Republished with permission of Academy of Management, PO Box 3020, Briar Cliff Manor, NY, 10510-8020. "A Three-Dimensional Conceptual Model of Corporate Performance." (Figure 3.3) A. B. Carroll, *Academy of Management Review,* 1979, Vol. 4. Reproduced by permission of the publisher via Copyright Clearance Center, Inc.

# BlastFromThePast

## 100 Years of Corporate Philanthropy

Corporate philanthropy has changed tremendously in the last century. For example, in the 1800s, under the doctrine of *ultra vires* (behavior beyond the incidental powers of the firm), it was illegal for companies to make charitable contributions. By law, corporate funds could only be spent for "business-related" purposes. One of the first legal tests of

*ultra vires* was the 1881 Old Colony Railroad case, in which the company financially supported a "world peace jubilee and international music festival." The court ruled that contributing money to the music festival had damaged stockholders, because the festival was not business-related.

Fifteen years later, in 1896, courts broadened the definition of what was considered business-related. In Steinway v. Steinway & Sons et al. (1896), the court ruled that it was appropriate for the Steinway company to use its funds to build homes, churches, and schools for its employees. Though these acts clearly benefited local neighborhoods and towns, they were viewed as business-related, because they also benefited Steinway's employees. So by the late 1800s, providing social benefits to employees had become an acceptable and legal form of corporate philanthropy.

The next significant change occurred in 1917 during World War I. The Red Cross, with the support of President Woodrow Wilson, began its "Red Cross dividend" program, which used a creative work-around to avoid legal restrictions on corporate giving. Needing to raise $100 million to meet wartime needs, the Red Cross mailed a standard form letter, encouraging corporations to declare a special earnings dividend that would be paid directly to the Red Cross rather than to corporate shareholders. Interested companies then asked shareholders to vote on the special dividend. Freed from the legal restrictions that had previously prevented this kind of corporate giving, shareholders from more than 1,100 companies raised nearly $20 million by voting to declare Red Cross dividends. Contrary to negative public perceptions of businesses at the time, this indicated that companies and their shareholders were willing to make charitable contributions.

The next major change occurred from 1936 to 1945 as corporate giving increased by a factor of nine to $270 million a year (the equivalent of billions in today's dollars). Unlike the Red Cross dividend, most of these contributions were encouraged by the excess profits tax that, after a particular level, taxed 90 cents out of each extra dollar of profit. However, companies could avoid the excess profits tax by making donations to their local communities. While most companies gave because it was in their financial interest to do so, it's important to know that corporate giving dropped by only 19 percent the year that Congress repealed the excess profits tax, and by only 11 percent two years following repeal. In other words, by the early 1950s, corporate philanthropy had become the right thing to do, even if companies did not receive a direct financial benefit.

In the late 1940s and early 1950s, another significant change in corporate philanthropy took place. The American Bar Association Committee on Business Corporations suggested that states change the basic legal definition of a corporation so that companies could make donations without having to demonstrate a business-related purpose. Within six years, 27 states had adopted the ABA recommendation to encourage corporate giving. Remaining states adopted the change after a 1953 U.S. Supreme Court ruling. The Supreme Court let stand a lower court's ruling that it was legal for A.P. Smith Manufacturing, a New Jersey company, to donate $1,500 to Princeton University, despite any obvious financial benefit to the company.

Today, with corporate giving and philanthropy legal for more than 50 years, U.S. companies donate approximately $6 billion a year to communities, causes, and charities.

**Sources:** L. Light & P. Eng, "Charity Cases: When Charity Doesn't Begin at Home," *Business Week*, 27 November 1995. M. Sharfman, "Changing Institutional Rules: The Evolution of Corporate Philanthropy: 1883-1953," *Business and Society* 33, no. 34 (December 1994): 236.

---

to restore consumer confidence (by immediately apologizing and quickly recalling and replacing all tires) that it quit.[79]

**accommodative strategy**
a social responsiveness strategy in which a company chooses to accept responsibility for a problem and to do all that society expects to solve that problem

A company using an **accommodative strategy** would accept responsibility for a problem and take a progressive approach by doing all that was expected to solve the problem. In contrast to Suzuki, Nissan Motors took an accommodative strategy when it voluntarily recalled 33,000 minivans that were prone to catch fire when the engine's fan belt broke. Nissan spent $45 million to fix the vans, installing a brand new heavy-duty cooling system with warning lights in each vehicle. However, it also reimbursed customers for 900 vans that were beyond repair. Then it destroyed the 900 vans so that they could not be resold to unsuspecting used-car buyers. To maintain customers' goodwill, Nissan also made other major repairs on the vans, such as air conditioning or transmission repairs, for free.[80]

**proactive strategy**
a social responsiveness strategy in which a company anticipates responsibility for a problem before it occurs and would do more than society expects to address the problem

Finally, a company using a **proactive strategy** would anticipate responsibility for a problem before it occurred, do more than expected to address the problem, and lead the industry in its approach. For example, McDonald's began its McRecycle USA program to increase its use of recycled materials in McDonald's restaurants. Of course, there's nothing proactive or leading edge about a company recycling program. Lots of companies have them. However, McDonald's discovered that it simply could not buy the recycled materials it needed. There just weren't enough recycled materials available at the time. McDonald's innovative solution was to take out full-page advertisements in newspapers around the country. These advertisements let recycling companies know that it was committed to spending $100 million a year to buy recycled products for its restaurants! In the advertisement, McDonald's listed a toll-free 800 phone number that potential suppliers could call to find out what materials the company needed. The ads were a phenomenal success. McDonald's now spends more than $250 million a year on recycled products in its playgrounds, floor and ceiling tiles, and paper products.[81]

### Review 8
#### Responses to Demands for Social Responsibility

Social responsiveness is a company response to stakeholders' demands for socially responsible behavior. There are four social responsiveness strategies. When a company uses a reactive strategy, it denies responsibility for a problem. When it uses a defensive strategy, it takes responsibility for a problem, but does the minimum required to solve it. When a company uses an accommodative strategy, it accepts responsibility for problems and does all that society expects to solve them. Finally, when a company uses a proactive strategy, it does much more than expected to solve social responsibility problems.

## 9. Social Responsibility and Economic Performance

One question that managers often ask is, "Does it pay to be socially responsible?" While this is an understandable question, asking whether social responsibility pays is a bit like asking if giving to your favorite charity will help you get a better-paying job. The obvious answer is no. There is not an inherent relationship between social responsibility and economic performance.[82] However, this doesn't stop supporters of corporate social responsibility from claiming a positive relationship. For example, one study shows that the Domini 400 Social Index, which is a stock fund consisting of 400 socially responsible companies, has out-performed the Standard and Poor's 500 (an index of 500 stocks representative of the entire economy) by nearly 5 percent. On the other hand, critics have plenty of facts to support their claim that social responsibility hurts economic performance. For example, another study of 42 socially responsible mutual funds found that the socially responsible companies under-performed the Standard and Poor's 500 by 8 percent.[83]

When it comes to social responsibility and economic performance, the first reality is that being socially responsible can sometimes cost a company significantly. During the 1980s, American multinational corporations were under intense public pressure to withdraw their operations from South Africa. Political activists argued that if businesses withdrew from South Africa, the white-controlled government would be hurt economically. Thus, it would be more difficult for it to maintain its system of apartheid against black South Africans. Many companies chose to pull their businesses out of South Africa. Yet when they did, they paid a steep price, selling corporate land, buildings, and equipment at a fraction of their value. Furthermore, within days of announcing that they were leaving South Africa, their company stock price dropped an average of 5.5 percent.[84] Here, socially responsible behavior not only harmed companies financially, but also harmed company shareholders financially. Nonetheless, hundreds of top managers still felt it was the right thing to do.

Likewise, under pressure from the federal government, from cities that were threatening lawsuits, and from anti-gun protestors, the gun manufacturer Smith & Wesson announced that it would put safety locks on its guns and develop smart gun technology that only allows guns to fire for their owners. It did so knowing that this move could

# "headline news"

## Is Nike Still Sweating Over Worker Rights?

After a decade of apathy, college students are rallying around a new cause—workers' rights. Over eighty U.S. colleges and universities have joined the Worker Rights Consortium (WRC), a group that is dedicated to improving working conditions in overseas factories run by multinational corporations. More than 150 have joined the Fair Labor Association (FLA), a group with a similar mission. Students at member colleges and universities are boycotting companies that have documented cases of worker exploitation, particularly those that have licensing agreements with their respective schools. Students are hoping to pressure administrators into canceling agreements with the companies who provide logo apparel to the athletic department and the campus bookstore.

Over the last decade, working conditions of offshore workers have become an increasingly popular social issue in the United States, and Kathy Lee Gifford hasn't been the only target. The Gap, Liz Claiborne, Wal-Mart, Nike, McDonald's, and even socially-responsible Starbucks have all found themselves under attack from various activist groups.

Nike has been particularly hard-hit by the critics. It has been lambasted by the FLA, the WRC, the Global Exchange, and numerous others for what they consider unfair labor practices in Nike's overseas factories. In 1998, Michael Moore, the producer of *Roger and Me,* even did a piece on Phil Knight, cofounder of Nike. The coverage was extremely unflattering, and Knight fought back by posting outtakes of the filming on Nike's Web site. Clips revealed the duplicity of Moore, who was caught on tape saying, "I honestly think you're the good guy." Unfortunately, the damage had already been done.

Later that same year, Knight gave a landmark speech that recognized Nike's past transgressions and outlined a sweeping plan to improve working conditions throughout its manufacturing supply chain. His plan was much hailed by the audience and the activists it was meant to appease. Even members of the Global Exchange applauded Nike's proactive stance.

Scarcely a year later, however, the Global Exchange criticized Nike for not following through fast enough. But Nike spokespeople are holding fast. The progress toward meeting planned goals is updated regularly on Nike's Web site (http://www.nikebiz.com). Nike management is also vocal about the changes it has made, such as increasing wages more than 100 percent for entry-level shoe workers, increasing the minimum working age to eighteen, publicly posting reports and audits of its factories, increasing monitoring staff, and joining the Global Alliance for Workers and Communities.

All of this, however, wasn't enough for some students, who continue to fuel high-profile protests despite their relatively small numbers. The most scathing boycott came from the University of Oregon, Knight's alma mater, in spring of 2000. When a mere 7.5 percent of the student body elected to join the WRC (in a referendum with only 10 percent voter turnout) and the administration approved, Knight withdrew a $30 million donation earmarked for improvements to U of O's stadium. Many students contended that this constituted retaliation. Knight, however, saw it differently: "The university inserted itself into the new global economy where I make my living. And it inserted itself on the wrong side, fumbling a teaching moment."

According to the Christian Science Monitor, over half of U.S. imports—valued at over $750 billion—come from developing countries in Asia, Latin America, and the former Soviet Union. This means that the worker rights debate is far from over. But when the tag in your sweatshirt says "Made in Indonesia," does that necessarily mean that it was made by a twelve-year old, working a 14-hour shift with one bathroom break, all for 11 cents an hour? How will you tell?

1. Should a worker in Knoxville be paid the same as someone doing the same job in New York City? What obligation does a company have to consider the cost of living in a certain area when determining the wages it pays?
2. And if a worker is willing to work for the wages paid, is there an obligation on the part of the company to raise them? In other words, if the worker is pleased with her wages, is there a problem?
3. How willing are you as a consumer to pay more for goods to enable the increased wages of overseas workers or to support higher-wage-earning American workers?
4. Should college benefactors support institutions that oppose their values, beliefs, and sometimes, livelihoods, as in the case of Knight and the University of Oregon? Explain.

**Sources:** B. Herzog, "Reports Disagree on Labor Rights at Nike Factories," *The Oregonian* (Portland, Ore.), 16 May 2001, no page citation. C. Kernhagen, "Sweatshop Blues: Companies Love Misery," *Dollars and Sense,* March–April 1999, 18. P. Knight, "Global Manufacturing: The Nike Story Is Just Good Business," *Vital Speeches,* 1 August 1998 (64), 637. M. Loftus, "A Swoosh Under Siege," *U.S. News & World Report,* 12 April 1999, 40. V. O. Manager, "Letters to the Editor: Nike Is Improving Worker Conditions," *The Wall Street Journal,* 8 June 2001, A15. D. L. Marcus, "The Other Shoe Drops," *U.S. News & World Report,* 15 May 1999, 43. "Reality Check," *Time,* 27 April 1998, 22. "Rights Group Says Nike Isn't Fulfilling Promises to Reform Sweatshops," *The Wall Street Journal,* 16 May 2001, http://www.wsjinteractive.com. M. Rust, "Campus in a Sweat," *Insight on the News,* 26 June 2000, 10. M. Selinger, "Did Nike Say to 'Just Do It'—Brutally?" *Insight on the News,* 28 December 1998, 40. T. Vickery, "Who's Watching the Shop Floor?" *Christian Science Monitor,* 30 April 2001, 11. http://www.fairlabor.org; http://www.nikebiz.com/labor/index.shtml; http://www.workersrights.org/.

103

anger its key stakeholder, the gun owners that bought its products. Indeed, gun owners and the National Rifle Association boycotted Smith & Wesson and its products because of their firm belief against government regulation and for the second amendment (the right to bear arms). The former CEO Ed Shultz, who was responsible for this decision, said, "There wasn't any question there was going to be a hit. The question was how big the hit would be and for how long." The hit was immediate as sales dropped enough to force layoffs of 125 of the 725 employees at its Springfield, Missouri, plant. So, why make this decision if you know it's going to hurt your company financially? Ed Shultz said, "I couldn't answer the question 'Was I doing everything I knew how to do to prevent accidents?' Would I put locks on our guns if it might save one child? The answer was yes." Harvard law professor Joseph Singer said, "Shultz may have done something that was in the best long-term interests of the company—making it seem like a corporate citizen and just doing the right thing—but since the law doesn't require others to do it, in the short run it may have hurt the company."[85]

The second reality of social responsibility and economic performance is that sometimes it does pay to be socially responsible. The mission of Worldwise (**http://www.worldwise.com**), which sells environmentally friendly consumer products, is "to make environmentally responsible products that work as well or better, look as good or finer, and cost the same or less as the competition." For example, its pet water bowls are made out of 125 recycled bottle caps. Likewise, its ecoplanter, which looks a like heavy, terra-cotta planter, is light, cheap, and made from 100 percent recycled plastic. In short, Worldwise doesn't think you should have to pay more to buy or use environmentally friendly products. In fact, its products are priced competitively enough to be sold in Wal-Mart, Target, and Home Depot. CEO Aaron Lamstein said, "Part of our concept is that we must have an incredibly focused mission that includes equally environmental and social issues and economic issues—that is, making sure that we have a really solid, healthy, financially secure business. You can't put one in front of the other. You can't be successful if you can't do both." The company, only 11 years old, has been profitable each of the last six years.[86]

The third reality of social responsibility and economic performance is that while socially responsible behavior may be "the right thing to do," it does not guarantee profitability. Socially responsible companies experience the same ups and downs in economic performance that traditional businesses do. A good example is Ben & Jerry's Homemade Ice Cream. Ben & Jerry's started in 1978 when founders Ben Cohen and Jerry Greenfield mailed away for a $5 course on how to make ice cream. Ben & Jerry's is as well known for its reputation as a socially responsible company as it is for its super premium ice cream. Ben & Jerry's donates 7.5 percent of its pretax profits to social causes supporting AIDS patients, the homeless, and the environment.[87] Moreover, customers buy Ben & Jerry's ice cream because it tastes great *and* because they want to support a socially responsible company. As Ben Cohen says, "We see ourselves as somewhat of a social service agency and somewhat of an ice cream company."[88] But, and this is a big but, despite its outstanding reputation as a socially responsible company, Ben & Jerry's has consistently had financial troubles since going public (selling shares of stock to the public) a decade ago. In fact, its financial problems became so severe that Ben and Jerry sold the company to British-based Unilever. Being socially responsible may be the "right thing to do," but it doesn't guarantee business success.

However, while Ben & Jerry's struggled, Seattle-based Starbucks Coffee, which markets itself as a socially responsible company, grew from 11 to more than 4,100 gourmet coffee shops worldwide. Starbucks pays its coffee shop workers much more than minimum wage, provides full health insurance coverage to anyone who works at least 20 hours a week, and gives employees with six or more months at the company the chance to participate in its stock options program. Besides taking good care of its employees, Starbucks also makes an annual six-figure charitable contribution to CARE, an interna-

Boston Mayor Thomas M. Menino reads to Boston area elementary children at the kickoff of the back-to-school All Books for Children Book Drive, sponsored by Star-bucks. The Seattle-based coffee company is renowned not only for its financial success, but also for its widespread corporate philanthropy.

AP PHOTO/WILLIAM PLOWMAN

tional relief agency, for feeding, clothing, and educating the poor in the coffee-growing regions where it gets its coffee beans.[89] Likewise, workers from its 4,100 stores world-wide are paid to volunteer in community service programs, such as Earth Day clean-ups, regional AIDS walks, and local literacy organizations. For example, Starbucks workers in the 19 New Zealand stores donate about 100 hours of volunteer work each week. Aasha Murthy, Starbucks' general manager in New Zealand, said, "Any company can write out a check to a worthy cause, send it off, and think nothing more of it, but that isn't what Starbucks is about. We've got an enormous amount of talent, energy, and passion in our business and that comes from our staff. So we decided to donate their skills. We want Starbucks New Zealand to be a successful organization, not just a profitable one, and there's more than one dimension to success. We want to reach out to the community we're part of."[90]

In the end, if company management chooses a proactive or accommodative strategy toward social responsibility (rather than a defensive or reactive strategy), it should do so because it wants to benefit society and its corporate stakeholders, not because it expects a better financial return.

## Review 9
### Social Responsibility and Economic Performance
Does it pay to be socially responsible? Sometimes it costs, and sometimes it pays. Overall, there is no clear relationship between social responsibility and economic performance. Consequently, managers should not expect an economic return from socially responsible corporate activities. If your company chooses to practice a proactive or accommodative social responsibility strategy, it should do so to better society and not to improve its financial performance.

## What Really Happened?

Contrary to popular belief, a clear choice between right and wrong rarely reveals itself to managers charged with "doing the right thing." The business world is much messier than that. Plus, in practice, solutions to ethics and social responsibility problems aren't optimal. Often, they are "make do" or "do the least harm" kinds of solutions. Let's find out what really happened at McDonald's as it struggled with the real-world tradeoffs between PETA's demands that its egg suppliers treat animals humanely and the business demands associated with supplying those eggs.

### What is the ethical thing to do in this situation?

Ethical behavior follows accepted standards of right and wrong. However, it's difficult to judge what's ethical in this instance, because at this point there are no accepted ethical standards when it comes to the egg industry. Industry standards are different in the United States, Canada, and Europe. For example, caging hens is illegal in the United Kingdom and several European Countries, but is accepted practice in the United States. And while PETA maintains that being kept in small cages mistreats egg-laying hens, the egg industry believes that using small cages is economical, prevents the spread of disease, maintains sanitation, and, when combined with an automatic feeding system, provides the ability to deliver a balanced diet of proteins, fats, carbohydrates, vitamins, and minerals.

### Should McDonald's give in to PETA's demands or should it ignore them? Given that protests are not a new thing for McDonald's, how does it decide how serious an issue this is and the lengths to which it should go to address these issues, if any?

How serious are PETA's demands and how seriously should McDonald's take them? Ethical intensity is how concerned or how serious people are about an ethical issue. When addressing issues of high ethical intensity, managers are more aware of the impact their decisions have on others. They are more likely to view the decision as an ethical or moral decision rather than an economic decision. They are also more likely to worry about doing the "right thing." Ethical intensity is strong when decisions have large, certain, immediate consequences, and when we are physically or psychologically close to those affected by the decision.

In the last few years, McDonald's has enlisted the help of a team of university and professional experts to form the McDonald's Animal Advisory Council. The council's role is to provide McDonald's with information, advice, and expertise and to make recommendations to McDonald's and its suppliers regarding animal welfare problems and progress. Because of its work with this council, McDonald's upper management viewed the treatment of hens as an "ethically intense" issue rather than an economic decision.

Furthermore, McDonald's developed a set of Animal Welfare Guiding Principles for itself and its suppliers to follow. Those principles were to provide customers with safe food (safety), to treat animals with care and respect (quality assurance), to make sure that animals are free from cruelty, abuse, and neglect (animal treatment), to work with suppliers to monitor and improve animal welfare practices (partnership), to lead the industry by working with scientific experts and suppliers to improve animal welfare practice (leadership), to measure how its corporate purchasing leads to improved animal welfare (performance measurement), and to communicate its animal welfare programs, plans, and progress (communication).

So what did McDonald's decide? Because of its Animal Welfare council and guidelines, McDonald's decided that it would no longer purchase eggs from suppliers that debeaked chickens, kept them in overly small cages, and withheld food to increase molting and thus egg production. Bob Langert, who heads up animal welfare and environmental programs for McDonald's, said, "We think we're moving the needle on an important issue. When it comes to social responsibility, McDonald's plans to be a leader."

### If McDonald's seriously considers PETA's demands, how does it decide whose interests take precedence?

There are two views on this issue. The shareholder model says that McDonald's should only concern itself with what its shareholders think of animal welfare programs. And if McDonald's can convince its shareholders that the costs are low and the benefits are high, then the shareholders would probably approve, because it will help the company be more profitable. By contrast, the stakeholder model says that companies must satisfy the needs and interests of multiple corporate stakeholders. The problem for McDonald's is that as the world's largest restaurant, it has to try to balance the needs of many different stakeholder groups.

So if McDonald's is supposed to satisfy the needs of multiple stakeholders, and the stakeholders disagree, how does it decide whose wishes take precedence? The stakeholder model argues that the needs of primary stakeholders (customers, employees, suppliers, shareholders, etc.) on which the organization relies for its existence take precedence over those of secondary stakeholders (the press, advocacy groups). But what if primary stakeholders disagree?

In this case, McDonald's was lucky enough to be reconsidering its views on animal welfare and treatment at exactly the same time that the United Egg Producer's Animal Welfare Committee was addressing the same issues. Committee chair and Professor Jeff Armstrong of Purdue University said, "When McDonald's went looking for a way to address their concerns about laying operations, they were excited to find that the United Egg Producers had what they needed." The key, according to Bob Krouse, a member of that committee and CEO of Midwest

Poultry Services, was that, "Egg producers knew they needed to have a production based on science, not just experience or common practices." Armstrong said, "The guidelines are based on the best available science. That means we validated certain practices and counseled against others based on objective studies and not just emotion or status quo." The UEP guidelines, which are near completion, increased cage sizes from 67 to 82 square inches, more than the 72 inches recommended by McDonald's. However, contrary to McDonald's, the UEP permits forced molting under specific conditions, something that McDonald's does not permit.

**Is it more socially responsible to require its egg suppliers to change their practices if changing them leads to financial losses and puts some of them out of business? Which comes first, the chickens or the egg producers?**

Social responsibility is a business's obligation to pursue policies, make decisions, and take actions that benefit society. Unfortunately, there is little agreement on what does or does not benefit society. Being profitable, or meeting one's economic responsibility, is a business's most basic social respon-

sibility. However, companies also have legal (comply with the law), ethical (do the right thing), and discretionary (do more than what's expected) responsibilities to fulfill.

Again, this means that corporate efforts to behave in a socially responsible manner often require tradeoffs. In this instance, McDonald's felt that the negative fallout to its business from not pushing animal welfare practices would be greater than the increased costs of requiring its suppliers to decrease the number of hens per cage. In short, somebody has to pay for corporate responsibility. Armstrong said, "Producers' margins are slim. Ultimately, farmers can incorporate practices that are more animal friendly—but somebody needs to pay for them." The key question for egg producers is will McDonald's back up its commitment to animal welfare practices by paying them an additional 15 to 25 cents per dozen to cover the increased costs of following its animal welfare practices (larger cages, no forced molting, and no debeaking)? Tom Miner, a food consultant, believes that McDonald's will cover those costs. He said, "They have the best kind of relationship with the farmers and it's a major advantage in the market. Setting

a good example at home [in the United States] will help McDonald's establish sound supply chains with farmers in new markets abroad." McDonald's spokesperson Walt Riker said, "We are doing this because we feel the social responsibility to enhance animal welfare. As to the costs, we don't have the details yet and will work on this with our suppliers."

**Sources:** "Eggs Over Easy Thanks to Egg Producers, " *Ag Answers.* [Online] Available http://www.agriculture.purdue.edu/aganswers/2000/8-29%20_Eggs_Over_Easy.html, 29 June 2001. "Egg Production Information," American Egg Board. [Online] Available, http:// www.aeb.org/eii/production.html, 29 June 2001. "McDonald's Animal Welfare Council," *McDonald's.* [Online] Available, http:// www.mcdonalds.com/countries/usa/community/welfare/index.html, 29 June 2001. "McDonald's Animal Welfare Guiding Principles," *McDonald's.* [Online] Available http://www.mcdonalds.com/corporate/social/animalwelfare/index.html, 29 June 2001. D. Campbell, "Chicken Run: McDonald's Takes a Cue from the Hit Film and Demands Better Conditions for Hens Used to Supply Eggs for Its Mcmuffins," *The Guardian*, 8 September 2000. T. Perry, "Egg Producers Are McMiffed Industry Balks at McDonald's Tough Rules on Hen Treatment," *Los Angeles Times*, 7 September 2000, C1. D. Wetzel, "McDonalds to Require Its Egg Suppliers to Improve Conditions for Hens," *Chicago Tribune*, 24 August 2001.

107

## Key Terms

## Payday Lending—Robbing Peter to Pay Paul

It feels good to stretch your legs. You've just completed a morning meeting with several executives from ACE Cash Express, the largest chain in the payday lending industry, based in Irving, Texas. ACE is interested in forming a partnership with Goleta National Bank, a locally owned and operated, federally chartered bank, of which you happen to be president. ACE has just discussed with you their plans to expand their check-cashing business to several states that currently prohibit "payday" loans. Payday loans are small, short-term loans, usually ranging between $100 and $500 and lasting five to 15 days, or until the next payday. In order to qualify, customers typically provide a driver's license, proof of employment, and evidence of a current bank account. Most payday loans require the customer to write a post-dated check for the amount of the loan plus a fee. Fees range anywhere from $15 to $30 per $100 loan, which calculates to an annual percentage rate (APR) of between 391 percent and 521 percent for a 14-day loan. At the date of maturity, customers can choose to pay off the loan with cash, receiving their original check back; allow the firm to process the check; allow the firm to electronically withdraw funds from their account; or extend the loan for another two-week period.

ACE is interested in a joint venture with your bank because, as a federally chartered bank, this partnership will allow them to circumvent state usury laws, which currently impose interest rate caps on small loans. Usury laws are laws designed to protect consumers by limiting annual interest rates on small loans to a maximum of 36 percent in most states. In the states that do not allow "payday" loans, ACE would be merely acting as an intermediary. They wouldn't actually loan the money, your bank would. As a national bank, your federal charter allows you to export your financial services to other states, thus bypassing state usury laws.

You've read that the payday lending industry can be quite lucrative (ACE's net income has grown annually at 36 percent),

and you are always looking for ways to improve your bank's bottom line. During the meeting, the representatives from ACE shared some statistics from a recent annual report on the payday lending industry in Colorado. In a recent year, 188 lenders in that state provided approximately 375,000 payday loans for a total of $43,000,000. The average APR was 486 percent and the average term of the loan was 17 days. The inherent risk associated with this deal will be minimal since ACE will assume the responsibility of collections on all of the loans your bank provides. Unfortunately, you've also read that these loans tend to prey upon low-income, less formally educated people. Typically, consumers only resort to these types of loans because they have exhausted all other forms of credit. Payday lending creates a situation in which the customer is borrowing money on next week's paycheck to pay today's bills. It creates a cycle that cannot be broken and can eventually ruin a person's credit history. In fact, just yesterday, you read in the local paper about a lady who borrowed $250 on a payday loan. After rolling it over for 26 weeks, she had paid a total of $640 in fees without having touched the principal. As a result of complaints, many states are attempting to close up the loopholes that allow payday lenders to charge such high interest rates. In spite of the negative consequences, it is very profitable and completely legal. Besides, if you don't take ACE's offer, they will surely find someone who will. It might even be your closest competitor. How are you going to make this decision? No matter what you do, you'll probably step on toes. Whose toes are most important? **If you were the president of Goleta National Bank, would you enter into the agreement with ACE Cash Express?**

**Sources:** P. Beckett, "Exploiting a Loophole, Banks Skirt State Laws on High Interest Rates," *The Wall Street Journal*, 25 May 2001. J.A. Fox, "Safe Harbor for Usury: Recent Developments in Payday Lending," *Advancing the Consumer Interest*, Spring/Summer 2000. J.A. Fox, "The Growth of Legal Loan Sharking: A Report on the Payday Loan Industry," *Consumer Federation of America*, November 1998.

# Management Decisions

## To Lie or to Tell the Truth?

Ethical dilemmas in the workplace occur often. Some are completely obvious, while others are subtle. Suppose you are the purchasing agent for a large corporation. A supplier has approached you regarding a recently submitted bid and has stated that if you choose his company as the winning bidder, he will provide you and your spouse with round-trip airfare tickets to Hawaii. His company's bid is 25 percent higher than the lowest bid. Accepting his offer would clearly be an unethical response, since it provides you, the purchasing agent, with a gain (airline

tickets for you and your spouse) and costs your company money by accepting the proposal from the supplier with the highest price. Additionally, since your company has a policy forbidding cash, gifts, and other entitlements from suppliers and vendors, you would most likely lose your job if anyone found out. Therefore, the only ethical choice is to refuse the supplier's offer and award the contract to the vendor with the best product and the best price.

Now look at a scenario that is less obvious. Assume that you have recently been hired as an entry-level manager for a small marketing agency and your supervisor, Ms. Johnson, tells you that she is running behind on an advertising proposal for a client. Ms. Johnson states that the client will be dropping in this afternoon to discuss the proposal. She has asked that you intercept the client and tell him that she was called out of town for an emergency business meeting and to inform him that she will contact him when she returns from her trip. Delaying the client will buy Ms. Johnson the necessary time to finalize the client's proposal and allow her to appear more professional when she presents the proposal to him. In this dilemma, the gain is more time for Ms. Johnson to complete her assignment and the cost is that the client is delayed and deceived. There appears to be no personal gain for you.

**Questions**
1. Describe what you would do in the preceding scenario: accept the order from Ms. Johnson or refuse to cover for her?
2. Suppose a colleague tells you that your predecessor was fired for refusing to accommodate Ms. Johnson and her continual demands for unethical behavior/unethical responses. Would that change your decision for question 1? Why or why not?
3. If you had to choose a principle of ethical decision making to support your decision to this scenario, which principle would you choose and why?

## Management Decisions

### Do You Feel the Pressure?
As the CEO of Burger King, a unit of the Britain-based Diageo PLC, you strive to stay abreast of changes in the fast-food industry. One of the changes that has kept your interest in the past few months is the advocacy group PETA (People for the Ethical Treatment of Animals) and their campaign against rival McDonald's Corp. PETA recently imposed a one-year moratorium on their "McCruelty" campaign (which involved over 400 demonstrations in 23 countries) as McDonald's vowed to take steps toward preventing animal cruelty practiced by the suppliers of their products. In the tentative agreement between McDonald's and PETA, McDonald's has agreed to begin enforcement of several animal-friendly guidelines. McDonald's will now implement surprise inspections and audits of supplying slaughterhouses to determine if they are following proper guidelines for the humane treatment of animals. Those slaughterhouses that are found to be not in compliance with the established guidelines will be suspended as suppliers to the fast-food giant. To reduce the possibility of improperly handling poultry, McDonald's will provide financial incentives to chicken farmers who supply chickens without broken bones. McDonald's will also announce to its egg suppliers that it will no longer purchase eggs from those who raise egg-laying hens in cages smaller than 72 square inches of space per bird. And McDonald's has agreed to purchase chickens and eggs only from suppliers who promise not to debeak their birds. As the second largest fast-food chain behind McDonald's, you are certain that these changes will have some spill-over effect on your restaurant, the only question is to what extent and when.

A few days later, you get your answer. This morning, a courier delivered a letter from PETA announcing a potential campaign against your organization, code named "Murder King." In the letter, PETA describes the proposal set forth by the McDonald's Corp. and urges Burger King to meet or exceed these guidelines. The letter implores you to visit the Web site **http://www.murderking.com**, where you find your name, address, and telephone number listed as the contact person for Burger King. The Web site further advises PETA members to contact you and recommend that you adopt the new guidelines.

It doesn't stop there. The Web site lists plans for demonstrations by PETA organizers at 800 Burger King restaurants worldwide, the implementation of provocative ad campaigns, and the use of Hollywood celebrities, including Richard Pryor, Alec Baldwin, and James Cromwell, to denounce your products. Video clips available on the Web site show inhumane activities being conducted at slaughterhouses which currently supply cattle and swine for your restaurants. Suddenly, you realize that something must be done. Your industry is competitive enough. The last thing you need to deal with is an angry mob protesting your products in front of your restaurants, especially when your biggest competitor is basking in the glow of its recent success.

**Questions**
1. Will you conform to PETA's wishes to adopt tougher policies against animal cruelty? Why or why not?
2. What kind of social responsibility strategy will you choose to implement in response to PETA's threatened "Murder King" campaign?

**Sources:** R. Gibson, "Burger King to Embrace Animal-Treatment Standards," *The Wall Street Journal*, 28 June 2001 http:// interactive. wsj.com. R. Gibson, "PETA Targets Wendy's Intl. in Animal-Rights Campaign," *The Wall Street Journal*, 2 July 2001 http://interactive.wsj.com. B. Friedrich, "PETA Halts 'Murder King' Protests," PETA Web site http://www.peta.org, 28 June 2001. "Peta Imposes One-Year Moratorium on McDonald's Campaign," PETA Web site http://www.peta.org.

# Develop Your Managerial Potential

**"It is only the farmer who faithfully plants seeds in the Spring, who reaps a harvest in the Autumn."**
**—B.C. Forbes, Founder of *Forbes* Magazine**

The purpose of these assignments is to develop your present and future capabilities as a manager. Since stakeholders increasingly expect companies to do more to fulfill their discretionary responsibilities, chances are you and your company will be expected to support your community in some significant way. To begin learning about community needs and corporate social responsibility, you are assigned to visit a local charity or nonprofit organization of your choosing, perhaps a hospital, the Red Cross, Goodwill, Planned Parenthood, a soup kitchen, or a homeless shelter. Talk to the people who work or volunteer there. Gather the information you need to answer the following questions.

**Questions**

1. What is the organization's mission?
2. Who does the organization serve and how does it serve them?
3. What percentage of the organization's donations is used for administrative purposes? What percentage is used to directly benefit those served by the organization? What is the ratio of volunteers to paid workers?
4. What job or task does the "typical" volunteer perform for the organization? How much time per week does the typical volunteer give to the organization? For what jobs do they need more volunteers?
5. How does the business community support the organization?
6. Why are you interested in the activities of this organization?

# Study Tip

Every chapter in this book contains diagrams and tables to illustrate the text material. Your Xtra! CD-ROM contains worksheets made from these exhibits to help you review. Download them, fill them in, and then check your work by comparing your worksheet to the original exhibit in the chapter.

110

# 2
PART

# Making Things Happen

# CHAPTER 4

*outline*

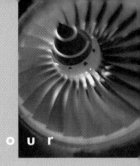

# four

# Planning

## What Would You Do?

**Airbus Headquarters, Toulouse, France.** When most people think of jet travel, they think of Boeing, the Seattle-based (soon to be Chicago-based) jet manufacturer famous for its 737, the workhorse of the skies, and its 747 "jumbo jet," the largest passenger jet in the world with its unmistakable profile. Indeed, 82 percent of the passenger jets in use are Boeing jets.

Fewer, though, know about Airbus, the European manufacturer, founded more than 25 years ago as a government-supported (i.e., funded) consortium of four companies, British Aerospace, DaimlerChrysler Aerospace, France's Aerospatiale, and Spain's Casa. The goal when starting Airbus was simple: Win business away from Boeing, the market leader. Airbus's management declared that, "Because no single European manu-facturer had the resources to overcome the U.S. giants, it was clear that they would have to cooperate to beat a com-mon rival." From the start, the Airbus consortium has received at least $10 bil-lion in European government subsidies. And it's never made a profit. Critics claim that the partners (and their govern-ments) have been more interested in cre-ating jobs than anything else.

Progress has been slow. It took more than seven years before one of the major

U.S. airlines purchased an Airbus jet. Robert Kugel, an investment analyst who follows the aerospace industry, said, "U.S. carriers wouldn't touch European airliners with a ten-foot pole. They had a reputation for poor quality and mainte-nance." Investing in passenger jets is different from most other business deci-sions. The jets directly affect the produc-tivity and training of ground crews, pi-lots, and flight attendants, as well as the comfort and convenience of passengers. Moreover, buying a passenger jet is a long-term commitment. It depends on trust, which explains why U.S. airlines were so slow to purchase Airbus's first products. Boeing certainly recognizes this aspect of the industry. One of its top managers said, "Buying an airplane is like getting married, it is a question of whom do you want to deal with for the next 15 to 25 years?"

However, some progress has been made. For example, the A320, which seats 150 people and is seven inches wider (an extra inch per seat), has been a spectacular success, eating into the sales of Boeing's workhorse 737. Richard Aboulafia, director of an aviation re-search group, said, "That inch makes a difference, because North American rear ends aren't getting any smaller." The A320 is also cheaper to buy and much cheaper to maintain. Consequently, thanks primarily to the A320, Airbus

makes and sells 19 percent of all new passenger jets.

So the question remains, how can Air-bus take more business away from Boe-ing? You decide to write an "Airbus Mas-ter Plan." But how do you make a plan that works? Products change so quickly that you can't afford to lock yourself into an inflexible plan that will be obsolete within a few years. Finally, if the plan is going to work, it has to be something that all managers in the company, from top to bottom, can believe in and make happen. So what will the plan have to look like to accomplish that?

**If you were the president of Airbus, what would you do?**

**Sources:** M. Brelis, "Duel at 30,000 Feet with Intense Marketing, Innovations—And a Dollop of Ill Will—Boeing and Airbus Fight to Rule Skies," *The Boston Globe*, 18 June 2000, F1. G. Edmonson, J. Rae-Dupree, & K. Capell, "Overhauling Airbus. (Airbus Is Expected to Provide Increasing Competition for Boeing)," *Business Week*, 2 August 1999, 14. D. Lynch, "Airbus Comes of Age with A-380 Super-Jumbo Jet Challenges Boeing's Last Monopoly," *USA Today*, 21 June 2001, B1. D. O'Connell, "New-Look Boeing Gets Ready to Spread Its Wings," *The Scotsman*, 12 February 2001, 5. A. Taylor, III, "Blue Skies for Airbus: Lately It's Been Nothing But. Orders Have Taken Off, And Archrival Boeing Has Run into Head-winds. Now Airbus Wants to Build a Super-jumbo to Carry 30 Percent More People Than a 747," *Fortune*, 2 August 1999, 102. G. Thomas, "Airbus, Boeing & Commonality," *Air Transport World*, 1 April 2001, 26.

As Airbus's troubles show, creating and executing a plan is one of the most important tasks a manager has. This chapter begins by examining the costs and benefits of planning. Next, you will learn how to make a plan that works. Then, you will look at the different kinds of plans that are used from the top to the bottom in most companies. Finally, you will investigate the different kinds of special-purpose plans that managers use today.

## Planning

**planning**
choosing a goal and developing a strategy to achieve that goal

**Planning** is choosing a goal and developing a method or strategy to achieve that goal. In 2000, Carlos Ghosn (rhymes with stone), Nissan's president and Chief Operating Officer stood in front of television cameras and told the world that Nissan was in "bad shape." However, he also announced that Nissan's goal was to be profitable within two years by following the details laid out in Nissan's new Revival Plan. The plan had taken six months to develop. Ghosn said, "I didn't have a plan in mind. I knew Nissan by the figures. I have seen many horrible situations, but if you limit yourself to the figures it's a very artificial analysis." So he put together 12 managerial teams to determine how to fix Nissan's purchasing costs, marketing strategy, excessive debt, and boring products. In terms of costs, since Nissan purchases 60 percent of the parts and services used to assemble its cars, Ghosn went to suppliers with this message: Costs must be cut by 20 percent over the next three years. Similarly, five factories were being closed and 21,000 workers were being laid off. In terms of marketing strategy and boring products, Nissan's plan was to bring 15 new cars or trucks to market in three years time. Nissan's new design director, Shiro Nakamura, who was brought in to spiff up Nissan's product line, said, "We have an incredible number of projects we are doing in a very short time. I've never experienced this kind of tough schedule." Thus far, the plan is well ahead of schedule. Nissan was profitable just over a year into the plan, with the best profit and revenue growth the company had seen in over a decade. And while its turnaround thus far is encouraging, Ghosn still says, "What we have done today is only 5 percent. We [still] have 95 percent [of the plan] to do."[1]

*After reading these next two sections, you should be able to*
*1. discuss the costs and benefits of planning.*
*2. describe how to make a plan that works.*

## 1. Costs and Benefits of Planning

Are you one of those naturally organized people who always makes a daily to-do list, who always writes everything down so you won't forget, and who never misses a deadline because you keep track of everything with your handy time-management notebook or your Palm PC? Or are you one of those flexible, creative, go-with-the-flow people who dislike planning and organizing because it restricts your freedom, energy, and performance? Some people are natural planners. They love it and can only see the benefits of planning. However, others dislike planning and can only see its disadvantages. It turns out that both views are correct.

*Planning has advantages and disadvantages. Let's learn about 1.1 the benefits and 1.2 the pitfalls of planning.*

### 1.1 Benefits of Planning
Planning has several important benefits: intensified effort, persistence, direction, and creation of task strategies.[2] First, managers and employees put forth greater effort when following a plan. Take two workers. Instruct one to "do his or her best" to increase production, and instruct the other to achieve a 2 percent increase in production each month. Research shows that the one with the specific plan will work harder.[3] Tiger

**"Fail Forward" to Learn from Failure**

Failing forward means learning something when you fail. To fail forward, experiment by trying several different things. You'll learn what works and what doesn't. When things fail, gather a group with different backgrounds to analyze what went wrong. Identify the failure as soon as possible. This gives you more time to analyze the problem and figure out how to fix it. Don't blame anyone. Be glad that someone brought the failure to your attention. Thomas Edison failed 10,000 times before inventing light bulb filaments. Abraham Lincoln lost 12 times before finally being elected to office. You can fail forward by learning from your failures, too.

**Source:** Harvard Management Update, "Learn by 'Failing Forward,'" *The Globe and Mail,* 31 October 2000, B17.

Woods may be the most dominant young athlete in the history of sports, winning 40 percent (20 of 50) of the tournaments he's entered. Most of the other top pro golfers would be happy to win three or four tournaments over the same period. While Tiger is clearly talented, what sets him apart from the other top golfers in the world is his work ethic. Martina Navratilova, who won a record 167 tennis tournaments, including nine Wimbledon singles titles, said, "At this level, talent is a given. But Tiger works harder than anyone out there, and that's why he's kicking butt." Tiger is often the first player on the practice tee in the morning and the last off of it at night, even during tournaments when he's trying to sharpen a particular part of his golf game. According to Joe Montana, former San Francisco 49er and winner of four Super Bowls, hard work matters even for elite athletes because, "No matter who you are, no matter how good an athlete you are, we're creatures of habit. The better your habits are, the better they'll be in pressure situations."[4]

Second, planning leads to persistence, that is, working hard for long periods. In fact, planning encourages persistence even when there may be little chance of short-term success.[5] Mary Kay Ash overcame numerous professional and personal obstacles before founding Mary Kay Cosmetics. For example, after 11 years as head of sales for a company (which she won't name), she was replaced by her assistant, a man whom she had spent the previous nine months training. Then, despite her proven track record and years of experience, the company paid him twice what they had been paying her. Frustrated, she quit to start her own company, only to have her 45-year-old husband suddenly die of a heart attack a month prior to the company's startup. Today, because of her persistence and hard work, Mary Kay Cosmetics has 750,000 sales representatives worldwide and is the leading cosmetics company in the United States, with over $2.5 billion in annual sales.[6] McDonald's founder Ray Kroc, who was a keen believer in the power of persistence, had this quote from President Calvin Coolidge hung in all of his executives' offices: "Nothing in the world can take the place of persistence. Talent will not; nothing is more common than unsuccessful men with talent. Genius will not; unrewarded genius is almost a proverb. Education will not; the world is full of educated derelicts. Persistence and determination alone are omnipotent."

The third benefit of planning is direction. Plans encourage managers and employees to direct their persistent efforts *toward* activities that help accomplish their goals and *away* from activities that don't. For example, a large insurance company wanted to improve the way its managers gave employees performance evaluation feedback. To help managers improve, company trainers taught them 43 effective performance feedback behaviors. Examples included, "I will give my subordinate a clear understanding of the results I expect him or her to achieve," or "During the performance appraisal interview, I will be very supportive, stressing good points before discussing needed improvement." However, during training, managers were instructed to choose just 12 behaviors (out of the 43) on which they wanted to make the most improvement. When subordinates rated their managers on the 43 effective feedback behaviors, it became clear that no matter which 12 behaviors different managers chose, they only improved on the 12 behaviors for which they had set improvement goals. Plans direct behavior toward activities that lead to goal accomplishment and away from those that don't.

The fourth benefit of planning is that it encourages the development of task strategies. After selecting a goal, it's natural to ask, "How can it be achieved?" For example, after several years of losses, Delta Airlines wanted to reduce its costs from 9.76 cents per seat-mile to 7.5 cents per seat-mile, or nearly $2 billion per year. After announcing this goal, Delta's CEO asked his top managers and the pilots' and attendants' unions for their ideas, stating, "We've set a cost-reduction goal, and everything . . . is open for negotiation."[7] What were their suggestions? Cut 10,000 jobs, but when possible, encourage voluntary leaving through financial severance or buyout packages. Another suggestion was to

115

end Delta's prized decade-long marketing relationship with Walt Disney World in Florida. Delta was paying Disney $2 million a year to sponsor its Tomorrowland attraction at Disney World and to be known as the "Official Airline of Walt Disney World." Managers and employees also suggested that Delta could offset its costs per mile by growing its cargo business. Since Delta planes used only 40 percent of the cargo space available in the belly of each passenger jet, the company could increase revenue and decrease costs by selling that freight capacity to companies that might otherwise use United Parcel Service or Federal Express to ship goods.[8] As this example shows, planning not only encourages people to work hard for extended periods and to engage in behaviors directly related to goal accomplishment, but it also encourages them to think of better ways to do their jobs.

Finally, perhaps the most compelling benefit of planning is that it has been proven to work for both companies and individuals. On average, companies with plans have larger profits and grow much faster than companies that don't.[9] The same holds true for individual managers and employees. There is no better way to improve the performance of the people who work in a company than to have them set goals and develop strategies for achieving those goals. For more on the benefits of planning, see the "What Really Works?" feature in this chapter.

### 1.2 Planning Pitfalls

Despite the significant benefits associated with planning, planning is not a cure-all. Plans won't fix all organizational problems. In fact, many management authors and consultants believe that planning can harm companies in several ways.[10]

The first pitfall of planning is that it can impede change and prevent or slow needed adaptation. Sometimes companies become so committed to achieving the goals set forth in their plans or they become so intent on following the strategies and tactics spelled out in them, that they fail to see that their plans aren't working or that their goals need to change. Ironically, as Aetna became the largest healthcare company in the United States, providing medical coverage to 1 in 10 Americans, it also became the most disliked healthcare provider. Hospitals and doctors complained that the company was slow to pay and required them to follow needless regulations. Dr. Williams Hardcastle says that his office manager "spends most of her time on hold," seeking surgical precertifications from Aetna. However, despite spending $32 million a year for precertification, Aetna almost never denies approval for medical treatment. Aetna's "hard-ball" approach to medical coverage was supposed to hold down costs and increase profits, but it didn't turn out that way. Aetna is half as profitable as its competitors. Indeed, Aetna's new CEO Dr. John Rowe, who was brought in because the former CEO was unable to understand why Aetna's plans weren't working, admits that "Aetna is like a patient with a lot of problems."[11]

The second pitfall of planning is that it can create a false sense of certainty. Planners sometimes feel that they know exactly what the future holds for their competitors, their suppliers, and their companies. However, all plans are based on assumptions. "The price of gasoline will increase by 4 percent per year." "Exports will continue to rise." For plans to work, the assumptions on which they are based must hold true. If the assumptions turn out to be false, then plans based on them are likely to fail. For example, as cell phones became cheaper and more reliable, Nokia, a Finland-based manufacturer of cell phones, experienced tremendous growth in its business. So when sales suddenly dropped by 25 percent, Nokia was caught off guard. Officially, company management blamed "logistical hiccups." However, *The Wall Street Journal* concluded that, "Nokia didn't see it coming and didn't know how to handle it [the drop in sales]."[12] Because Nokia assumed that its cellular phone sales would continue to grow, it bought parts at high prices and did a poor job of controlling its costs. When the assumption (i.e., continued growth) underlying its production plans turned out to be false, the result was a 30 percent decline in operating profits. Jorma Ollila, Nokia's CEO, said the problems were "driven by economic uncertainty, the ongoing technology transition, and less aggressive marketing by the operators [companies that sell mobile phone services]."[13]

# BlastFromThePast

## Pericles of Athens, c. 495–429 B.C., Founder of Planning?

Three key components of modern-day planning—vision, nondetachment, and flexibility—may have originated with Pericles of Athens, who led Greece until his death in 429 B.C. Pericles was elected general, or strategos, in 458 B.C. Unlike modern leaders who routinely serve two-, four-, or six-year terms, Pericles faced yearly elections. Nonetheless,

he was elected to the position of strategos for 30 years. Generals in Pericles' time were not just military strategists and leaders. Like today's presidents and prime ministers, they were also responsible for managing foreign affairs and governing domestic affairs.

According to Pericles, a leader's primary responsibility was to have a vision and then share it effectively with others. In a speech to the people of Athens, obviously made during an election, Pericles described himself as "one who has at least as much ability as anyone else to see what ought to be done and explain what he sees." He went on to say that "a man who has the knowledge but lacks the power clearly to express it is no better off than if he never had any ideas at all." In a time of monarchies and tyrannical rulers, Pericles' unique vision for Athens was democratic. Laws were made by the assembly, executed by the Council of 500, and applied in courts of law to citizens who broke them. Pericles' democratic vision was evident in his view of war. Most leaders of his day had little regard for the lives of troops, viewing them, like horses and carriages, as expendable resources to be used to obtain the objectives of war. By contrast, "his chief maxim of war was, never to venture a battle unless he was almost certain of victory, and not to lavish the blood of the citizens. He used to say frequently, that were it in his power, they should be immortal; that when trees were felled, they shoot to life again in a little time, but when men once die, they are lost forever."

Perhaps better than modern company planners, the Athenians understood that planners could not be effective unless they were close to the events they were planning. Consequently, Athe-

nians expected candidates for the position of strategos to have demonstrated their capabilities as warriors in individual combat and as military leaders. Furthermore, strategos were expected to guide their troops from the front line where they could observe the battle, adapt plans, and, if necessary, demonstrate leadership by fighting alongside troops. Athenians understood that plans are not abstract theories, but guidelines for action. Planners detached from the events for which they are planning will, on average, be poor planners.

Finally, while Pericles may have been the founder of planning, he understood that plans were a means to an end and that good planning required the flexibility to abandon a plan should circumstance require doing so. Pericles is known for the statement "opportunity waits for no man." He realized that circumstances could change and that unanticipated events could render plans useless. Thus, he placed as much importance on adapting plans as on creating them. Pericles maintained, "There is often no more logic in the course of events than there is in the plans of men; this is why we blame our luck when things happen in ways that we did not expect."

**Sources:** S. Cummings, "Pericles of Athens—Drawing from the Essence of Strategic Leadership," *Business Horizons* 38, no. 6 (1995): 22. "Pericles," *Compton's Encyclopedia*, 1 January 1994. C. Rollin, "Rollin's Ancient History: History of the Persians and Grecians," Sections XII–XIV and VIII–XI, *History of the World*, 1 January 1992. "Works of Thucydides," Books 1 and 2, *Monarch Notes*, 1 January 1963.

The third pitfall of planning is the detachment of planners. In theory, strategic planners and top-level managers are supposed to focus on the big picture and not concern themselves with the details of implementation, that is, carrying out the plan. According to management professor Henry Mintzberg, detachment leads planners to plan for things they don't understand.[14] Plans are not meant to be abstract theories. They are meant to be guidelines for action. Consequently, planners need to be familiar with the daily details of their businesses if they are to produce plans that can work.

For example, if you doubt that the "details" are important to good execution of a plan, imagine that you're about to have coronary bypass surgery to replace four clogged arteries. Rather than having an experienced cardiologist perform your surgery, you're going under the knife of a first-year medical intern. The intern is a fully qualified M.D. who clearly understands the theory and the plan behind bypass surgery, but has never performed such an operation. As you lie on the operating table, who is the last person you'd like to see as the anesthesia kicks in, the first-year intern who knows the plan but has never done a bypass, or the experienced cardiologist who has followed the plan hundreds of times? Planning works better when the people developing the plan are not detached from the process of executing the plan.

Planning is choosing a goal and developing a method to achieve that goal. Planning is one of the best ways to improve organizational and individual performance. It encourages people to work harder (intensified effort), to work hard for extended periods (persistence), to engage in behaviors directly related to goal accomplishment (directed behavior), and to think of better ways to do their jobs (task strategies). But most important, companies that plan have larger profits and faster growth than companies that don't plan. However, planning also has three potential pitfalls. Companies that are overly committed to their plans may be slow to adapt to changes in their environment. Planning is based on assumptions about the future, and when those assumptions are wrong, plans are likely to fail. Finally, planning can fail when planners are detached from the implementation of plans.

## 2. How to Make a Plan that Works

Planning is a double-edged sword. If done right, planning brings about tremendous increases in individual and organizational performance. At Pixar Animation Studios, the plan is to produce one movie a year. Pixar, which makes digitally animated movies, only produced three movies, *Toy Story*, *A Bug's Life*, and *Toy Story 2*, in five years. So while making one movie a year is nothing for traditional movie studies, making a movie a year has been a significant, long-term goal for Pixar. To achieve this goal, Pixar has implemented a plan to hire more people (550 people now work at Pixar, up from 400), add new divisions to develop new movies (story creation) and to manage movie development (shot by shot), increase its computer capabilities (with a several hundredfold increase in computer power and storage), and a move into a new headquarters which fosters collaboration and creativity (compared to the four different locations in which people previously worked). The plan in place includes four new movies: *Monsters, Inc.* (released in summer 2001), *Finding Nemo*, and two that haven't been announced yet, by 2005. However, if planning is done wrong, it can have just the opposite effect and harm individual and organizational performance. Pixar's first three films, *Toy Story*, *A Bug's Life*, and *Toy Story 2*, were critical and box office successes. The risk from Pixar's plan is that increasing the frequency of its films may lead to poorer quality. Paul Dergarabedian, president of a box-office tracking company, said, "The more movies you have, the greater the chance you'll falter once in awhile." Indeed, CEO Steve Jobs said

No stranger to Hollywood success, Pixar is planning to increase its output to one movie each year. With all the work that goes into a single computer-animated feature, this is a significant long-term goal for Pixar. A detailed plan is in place to help the studio achieve it.

© MARK RICHARDS/PHOTOEDIT

**S.M.A.R.T. goals**
goals that are specific, measurable, attainable, realistic, and timely

that while Pixar's "priority is still to make films that are really great, not every one of our films will succeed."[15]

*In this section, you will learn how to make a plan that works. As depicted in Exhibit 4.1, planning consists of 2.1 setting goals, 2.2 developing commitment to the goals, 2.3 developing effective action plans, 2.4 tracking progress toward goal achievement, and 2.5 maintaining flexibility in planning.*

### 2.1 Setting Goals

Since planning is choosing a goal and developing a method or strategy to achieve that goal, the first step in planning is to set goals. To direct behavior and increase effort, goals need to be specific and challenging.[16] For example, deciding to "increase sales this year" won't direct and energize workers as much as deciding to "increase North American sales by 4 percent in the next six months." Likewise, choosing to "drop a few pounds" won't motivate you as much as choosing to "lose 15 pounds." Specific, challenging goals provide a target for which to aim and a standard against which to measure success.

One way of writing effective goals for yourself, your job, or your company is to use the S.M.A.R.T. guidelines. **S.M.A.R.T. goals** are Specific, Measurable, Attainable, Realistic, and Timely.[17] Let's see how a heating, ventilation, and air conditioning (HVAC) company might use S.M.A.R.T. goals in its business.

The HVAC business is cyclical. It's extremely busy at the beginning of summer, when homeowners find that their air conditioning isn't working, and at the beginning of winter, when furnaces and heat pumps need repair. During these times, most HVAC companies have more business than they can handle. But at other times of year, business can be very slow. So a *specific* goal would be to increase sales by 50 percent during the fall and spring, when business is slower. This goal could be *measured* by keeping track of the number of annual maintenance contracts sold to customers. This goal of increasing sales during the off seasons is *attainable*, because maintenance contracts typically include spring tune-ups (air-conditioning systems) and fall tune-ups (furnace or heating systems). Moreover, a 50 percent increase in sales during the slow seasons is *realistic*. Since customers want their furnaces and air conditioners to work the first time it gets cold (or hot) each year, they are likely to buy service contracts that ensure their equipment is in working order. Tune-up work can then be scheduled during the slow seasons, increasing sales at those times. Finally, this goal can be made *timely* by asking the staff to push sales of maintenance contracts before Labor Day, the traditional end of summer, when people

119

---

**EXHIBIT 4.1**

### HOW TO MAKE A PLAN THAT WORKS

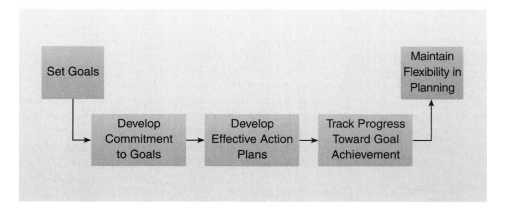

**Are You an Owl or an Early Bird?**

What time do you wake up on Saturday morning? Are you up and out of bed by 7:00 A.M., or are you up just in time to make it to the table for lunch? The term *morningness* describes a preference for morning activities. Studies show that morningness affects performance. Students with morning orientations get much better grades in 8:00 A.M. classes than do students with evening orientations (3.27 versus 2.78). So, to do a better job of achieving your goals, plan to do your most challenging work when you're at your peak energy levels and your routine work when your energy is low.

**Sources**: J.P. Guthrie, R.A. Ash, and V. Bendapudi, "Additional Evidence for a Measure of Morning," *Journal of Applied Psychology* 80 (1995): 186-190.

**goal commitment**
the determination to achieve a goal

start thinking about the cold days ahead, and in March, when winter-weary people start longing for hot days in air-conditioned comfort. The result would be more work during the slow fall and spring seasons.

### 2.2 Developing Commitment to Goals

Just because a company sets a goal doesn't mean that people will try to accomplish it. If workers don't care about a goal, then the goal won't encourage them to work harder or smarter. Thus, the second step in planning is to develop commitment to goals.

**Goal commitment** is the determination to achieve a goal. Commitment to achieve a goal is not automatic. Managers and workers must choose to commit themselves to a goal. For example, Professor Edwin Locke, the foremost expert on how, why, and when goals work, told a story about an overweight friend. After not seeing him for years, Locke ran into his friend, who had finally lost 75 pounds. Because of the change, he nearly walked by without recognizing him. Locke said, "So I asked him how he did it, knowing how hard it was for most people to lose so much weight." His friend responded, "Actually, it was quite simple. I simply decided that I *really wanted* to do it."[18] Said in another way, goal commitment is really wanting to achieve a goal.

So how can managers bring about goal commitment? The most popular approach is to set goals participatively. Rather than assigning goals to workers ("Johnson, you've got 'til Tuesday of next week to redesign the flex capacitor so it gives us 10 percent more output"), managers and employees choose goals together. The goals are more likely to be realistic and attainable if employees participate in setting them. Also, people are more likely to strive for a goal they feel they have a reasonable chance of attaining. For example, would you be more likely to stick to an exercise program that required one-half hour per day or one that required three hours per day?

Another technique for gaining commitment to a goal is to make the goal public. For example, college students who publicly communicated their semester grade goals ("This semester, I'm shooting for a 3.5") to significant others (usually a parent or sibling) were much more committed to achieving their grades. More importantly, students who told others about their goals earned grades that were nearly a half-grade higher than students who did not tell others about their grade goals.[19] So, one way to increase commitment to goals is to "go public" by having individuals or work units tell others about their goals. For example, work units could post their goals on a bulletin board for all to see.

Another way to increase goal commitment is to obtain top management's support. Top management can show support for a plan or program by providing funds, speaking publicly about the plan, or participating in the plan itself. When General Electric (GE) announced its new "six sigma" program in which it planned to improve quality by reducing the number of product or service errors to just 3.4 defects or errors per million, top management put an incredible amount of support behind the program. Every employee went through two weeks of intense training in statistical process control. At the end of training, they were expected to demonstrate what they had learned by completing two on-the-job projects that would increase quality or decrease costs. Statistical tools, formulas, guidelines, readings, and employee discussions were made available on the GE Intranet to support six sigma efforts. Furthermore, 4,500 six sigma project leaders, known internally at GE as "black belts" because of their advanced six sigma training, experience, and expertise, worked full-time throughout the company, managing various improvement projects. Finally, GE shared feedback on six sigma progress by tracking and measuring the results of six sigma projects worldwide. The results thus far indicate an internal savings of more than $2 billion a year. None of this would have happened without complete support from GE's top management, which invested $500 million and four years time to make the program a success and to institutionalize it in GE's culture.[20]

## 2.3 Developing Effective Action Plans

**action plan**
the specific steps, people, and resources needed to accomplish a goal

The third step in planning is to develop effective action plans. An **action plan** lists the specific steps, people, resources, and time period for accomplishing a goal. For example, USAir, an east coast-based airline, announced a "Management Action Program" to significantly reduce costs and increase revenues. This program (i.e., plan) had three steps:

1. Cut all unprofitable routes.
2. Use technology to cut costs and increase efficiency.
3. Outsource any task that can be done better and cheaper by someone else.

In step one, the company cut flights to money-losing destinations, such as Austin, Texas, San Antonio, Texas, Cincinnati, Ohio, and Albuquerque, New Mexico. Today, USAir flies only 90 percent of the routes it once did. But, the routes it flies *are* profitable. Peter Haak, USAir's assistant vice president for schedules, said, "So we took seats out of the air, but we grew the revenue—a $211 million change in one quarter. That's really news." In step two, USAir installed an expensive computer-run, yield-management system called "Excalibur" to monitor how its prices compared to its competitors' prices. Excalibur helps USAir determine when to cut prices to stay competitive. Consequently, despite cutting prices, revenues are actually increasing, because USAir's jets now fly with fewer empty seats than previously. In step three, outsourcing, USAir is saving money by having outside companies handle cargo ($15 million saved), purchasing ($92 million saved), and crew scheduling ($40 million saved).[21] The only thing missing from USAir's plan was a specific goal and time period for accomplishing its cost savings. For example, Delta's CEO gave the company three years to reduce its costs from 9.76 to 7.5 cents per seat-mile.[22]

## 2.4 Tracking Progress

**proximal goals**
short-term goals or subgoals

**distal goals**
long-term or primary goals

The fourth step in planning is to track progress toward goal achievement. There are two accepted methods of tracking progress. The first is to set proximal goals and distal goals. **Proximal goals** are short-term goals or subgoals, whereas **distal goals** are long-term or primary goals.[23] The idea behind setting proximal goals is that they may be more motivating and rewarding than waiting to achieve far-off distal goals. When profits dropped 48 percent at Office Depot, new CEO Bruce Nelson put new plans into place. In the short-term, his goal was to clean up the company's balance sheet by increasing cash flows and reducing debt. This was accomplished by closing 70 poorly performing stores, reducing the number of items carried in each store, hiring "mystery shoppers" to pose as guests to measure customer service, and then adding new signs and lighting to make things easier to find. However, Nelson has three different goals for Office Depot in the long-term. First, put most of the company's money into international growth, where it thinks it can make the largest return. Second, partner with Microsoft to put new "Business Solution Centers" into each store to advise small business owners how to incorporate technology into their companies. Third, redo the store format, which is based on a typical department store layout, to a circular design with lower shelves to make it easier for customers to find and use products. Nelson said, "Right now customers can't tell the difference between Office Depot, Office Max, and Staples. I want to change the in-store experience so that the customer will remember their experience at Office Depot."[24]

The second method of tracking progress is to gather and provide performance feedback. Regular, frequent performance feedback allows workers and managers to track their progress toward goal achievement and make adjustments in effort, direction, and strategies.[25] For example, Exhibit 4.2 shows the result of providing feedback on safety behavior to the makeup and wrapping workers in a large bakery company. The company had a worker safety record that was two-and-a-half times worse than the industry average. During the baseline period, workers in the wrapping department, who measure and mix ingredients, roll the bread dough, and place it into baking pans, performed their

121

EXHIBIT 4.2

EFFECTS OF GOAL-SETTING, TRAINING, AND FEEDBACK ON SAFE BEHAVIOR IN A
BREAD FACTORY

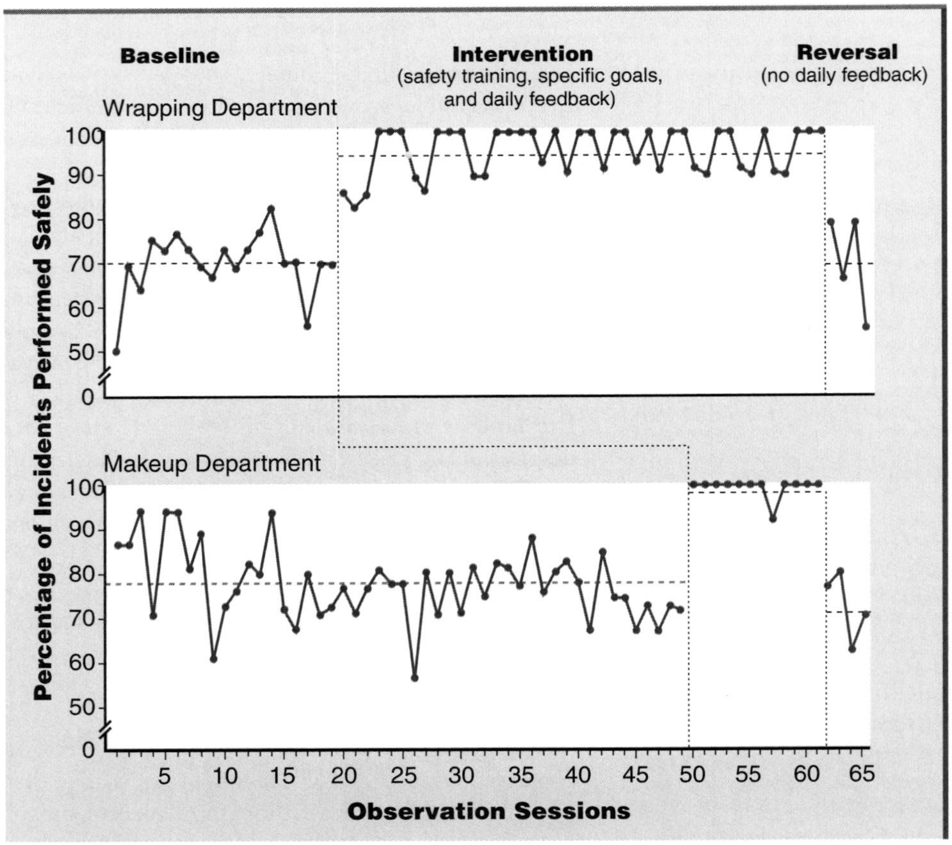

**Source:** Reprinted with permission of Journal of Applied Psychology. "A Behavioral Approach to Occupational Safety: Pinpointing and Reinforcing Safe Performance in a Food Manufacturing Plant." Komaki, J., Barwick, K.D., & Scott, L.R., *Journal of Applied Psychology*, 1978, V63. Reproduced with permission of the publisher.

jobs safely about 70 percent of the time. The baseline safety record for workers in the makeup department, who bag and seal baked bread and assemble, pack, and tape cardboard cartons for shipping, was a bit better at 78 percent.

Yet, after the company gave workers 30 minutes of safety training, set a goal of 90 percent safe behavior, and then provided daily feedback (such as a chart similar to Exhibit 4.2), performance improved dramatically. During the intervention period, the percentage of safely performed behaviors rose to an average of 95.8 percent for wrapping workers and 99.3 percent for workers in the makeup department, and never fell below 83 percent. Thus, the combination of training, a challenging goal, and feedback led to a dramatic increase in performance.

However, the importance of feedback alone can be seen in the reversal stage, when the company quit posting daily feedback on safe behavior. Without daily feedback, the percentage of safely performed behavior returned to baseline levels, 70.8 percent for the wrapping department and 72.3 percent for the makeup department. For planning to be effective, workers need a specific, challenging goal and regular feedback to track their progress.

# "headline news"

## Apple Selling Computers from Its Own Shopping Cart

If there's a CEO that has nine lives, then it's Steve Jobs. Despite building a cult-like following of users, Jobs and his company, Apple Computer, have been no strangers to adversity over the years. At each bad turn, Jobs has been able to pull a rabbit out of his hat, like the iMac in 1998, to bring the company back to life. In December 2000, when the company posted its first loss in three years, Jobs was holding another trump card—Apple stores.

Even though Apple's 5 percent share of the PC market is larger than the share that either Mercedes-Benz or BMW have of the automotive market, it's not enough to make the Mac a ubiquitous product, let alone to put it on the map with the likes of Dell. Jobs even acknowledges that most people "don't even consider Apple" when purchasing a computer.

In May 2001, Jobs publicly announced a plan to open twenty-five retail stores across the United States by the end of the year, with an unspecified number of stores planned for 2002. After the press release, it was as if someone had opened the floodgate. Apple quickly opened a half dozen of the twenty-five promised stores. The starkly decorated Apple stores are outfitted with computers, on which consumers can test all of the Mac's best and most cutting-edge features, and then purchase one configured just for them. "The Apple stores offer an amazing new way to buy a computer," said Jobs. "Customers can now learn and experience the things they can actually do with a computer, like make movies, burn custom music CDs, and publish their digital photos on a personal Web site."

Despite Jobs' claims, Apple stores really don't offer an amazing new way to buy a computer, just a new way to buy a Mac. The plan to open retail stores was two years in the making and was clearly modeled after Gateway. Generally, the plan for the stores was well received by analysts who cited Apple's weak distribution strategy as a primary concern in the company's future health. In order to ensure the stores were successful, Apple created a prototype store in a warehouse on its main campus in Cupertino, California. Apple then recruited personnel who could help it make the transition from consumer products manufacturer to retailer. It lured key people away from retailing heavyweights Target, Corp.; Gap, Inc.; and Bloomingdales.

The first two retail stores, opened in Tyson's Corner, Virginia, and Glendale, California, booked nearly $600,000 in sales, saw 7,700 visitors on their first two-day weekend, and got great press. With each new store opening, consumers wait in long lines to get in and see what the buzz is about. The opening in Plano, Texas, also coincided with the grand opening of the mall where the Apple store is located. People started lining up outside the entry at 5:30 am, where the crowds seemed to be coming out for the mall opening. Really everyone was just waiting to get into the Apple store.

Easy initial success, however, may belie future difficulties. Apple risks alienating its resellers, like Circuit City and Best Buy, by selling against them head-to-head. It also needs to tread lightly and learn from Gateway's mistakes, specifically opening too many outlets too quickly. If Apple can manage this delicate balancing act in a time when demand for computers is waning, it may just double its market share. That's another 25 million customers, or rather, devotees.

1. Track Apple's progress toward its store goal of increased market share. Are the stores achieving the goals they were conceived to reach?
2. Given the state of the PC industry and the external business environment, evaluate Apple's plan for increasing market share. Was it the best plan to implement, or can you conceive of another plan that may have been more successful?

Sources: H. Bethany, "Apple's Challenge: Retail Balancing Act," *eWeek*, 11 June 2001, 67. J. Dalrymple, "Apple Store Opens to Big Crowd in Texas," *MacCentral Online*, 3 August 2001, http://maccentral.macworld.com/news/0108/03.applestoretexas.shtml. D. Hawaleshka, "Apple's Core Strategy," *Maclean's*, 22 January 2001, 27. M. Martinez, "Go Ahead and Squeeze the Fruit," *Kiplinger's Personal Finance Magazine*, August 2001 (55:8), 28. C. Null, "Apple's Own Fruit Stand," *Ziff Davis Smart Business for the New Economy*, 1 September 2001, 34. R. Strohmeyer, "Reinventing Macintosh," *Ziff Davis Smart Business for the New Economy*, 1 April 2001, 52. P. Wing Tam and G. McWilliams, "Apple Is Mulling Own Store Chain to Expand Sales," *The Wall Street Journal*, 29 September 2001, B1. P. Tam, "Apple to Open 25 Retail Stores this Year in a Bid to Reach Out to New Customers," *The Wall Street Journal*, 16 May 2001, B8. http://www.apple.com/retail/.

### 2.5 Maintaining Flexibility

Because action plans are sometimes poorly conceived and goals sometimes turn out to not be achievable, the last step in developing an effective plan is to maintain flexibility. Claren Wooten and his partner started Metamorphosis Studios to build custom Web sites for companies. However, most of their customers got sticker shock and walked away because they couldn't believe that it would cost $3,000 to $6,000 to produce a Web site (more like $25,000 to $50,000 today). They wanted a sophisticated Web site, but not at that price. So rather than continue to struggle as a custom maker and designer of Web sites, Metamorphosis Studios morphed into an online store that allowed small businesses to buy predesigned, customizable Web sites. Wooten said that this "enabled us to reduce our price to only a couple of hundred dollars without sacrificing quality. No one had really taken that approach before—and we would never have thought to take it had we not listened to our small-business customers."[26] Today, Metamorphosis Studios has become Network Solutions, **http://www.networksolutions.com**, a one-stop Internet solution for building your own Web site, sending out personalized email (for marketing), purchasing the domain name (i.e., mycompany.com) you want, and many other services at reasonable prices for small businesses. So when plans fail, it is far better to scrap the plan and start over than it is to ride the failing plan into the ground.

An even more desirable strategy is to build flexibility into planning from the start. One method of maintaining flexibility while planning is to adopt an options-based approach.[27] The goal of **options-based planning** is to keep options open by making small, simultaneous investments in many options or plans. Then when one or a few of these plans emerge as likely winners, you invest even more in these plans while discontinuing or reducing investment in the others. In part, options-based planning is the opposite of traditional planning. For example, the purpose of an action plan is to commit people and resources to a particular course of action. However, the purpose of options-based planning is to leave those commitments open. Holding options open gives you choices, and choices give you flexibility. Options-based planning is especially useful when uncertainty is high and you don't know how things will change or what will work in the future. Because uncertainty runs very strong in high tech industries, it makes sense to take an options-based planning approach to invest in many different companies and many different technologies. In the last few years, Intel has done just that, investing $8.2 billion in 350 new technology companies. Leslie Vadasz, who makes these investments for Intel, knows that some will fail, some will succeed, and if he's lucky, a few will be "megawinners," such as Red Hat Software, the leading Linux software company, and Broadcast.com, for which Yahoo! paid $5 billion. Some of Intel's options-based planning is strictly for investment purposes, that is, to increase its financial return. However, many of its options investments are in companies whose technologies can strengthen Intel's core business, computer chips. For example, Intel invested in Primarion because its technology reduces electrical interference in computer chips which occurs when the wires in the chip are closer together. This happens when more integrated circuits are packed into chips to make them faster. If Primarion's technology pays off, Intel's chips should be able to run even faster, giving it a competitive advantage. Said Vadasz, "You judge your return on how you met your strategic goals, and count the money later."[28]

Another method of maintaining flexibility while planning is to take a learning-based approach. In contrast to traditional planning, which assumes that initial action plans are correct and will lead to success, **learning-based planning** assumes that action plans need to be continually tested, changed, and improved as companies learn better ways of achieving goals.[29] Because the purpose is constant improvement, learning-based planning not only encourages flexibility in action plans, but it also encourages frequent reassessment and revision of organizational goals.

For example, Knight-Ridder Corporation, which owns the second-largest newspaper chain in the United States, created project "25/43" to reverse the sharp decline in newspaper readership among people between the ages of 25 and 43. In contrast to traditional newspapers, where editors and reporters drive the newspaper's content and design, the first step in Knight-Ridder's learning-based planning was to ask readers what they wanted in their newspaper. The second step was to test those ideas and keep the ones that readers liked. Suggested changes included columns on environmental tips, shopping, parenting, high-tech, and fitness. Readers also insisted on shorter articles, the use

**options-based planning**
maintaining planning flexibility by making small, simultaneous investments in many alternative plans

**learning-based planning**
learning better ways of achieving goals by continually testing, changing, and improving plans and strategies

of color, and better layouts and indexes, which made it easier to find what they were looking for. As the third and final step, which is the key to learning-based planning, Knight-Ridder now regularly questions, experiments, and tests the changes it makes. Knight-Ridder's vice president of news said,

> Routinely now, our papers go to focus groups when they are going to try something new. Many of our editors have established a 25/43 goal, which means they conduct research, involve task forces from their newsrooms and other departments, assess the strengths and weaknesses of their papers, propose changes, and test some of these changes in the marketplace. It sounds so simple, but it is not the way the newspaper business tended to operate.[30]

### Review 2
#### How to Make a Plan that Works

There are five steps to making a plan that works: (1) Set S.M.A.R.T. goals—goals that are Specific, Measurable, Attainable, Realistic, and Timely. (2) Develop commitment to the goal from the people who contribute to goal achievement. Managers can increase workers' goal commitment by encouraging worker participation in goal setting, making goals public, and getting top management to show their support for workers' goals. (3) Develop action plans for goal accomplishment. (4) Track progress toward goal achievement by setting both proximal and distal goals and by providing workers regular performance feedback. (5) Maintain flexibility. Keeping options open through options-based planning and seeking continuous improvement through learning-based planning help organizations maintain flexibility as they plan.

## Kinds of Plans

Chances are, you may have heard of Waste Management International, the largest garbage and recycling company in the United States. But you're probably not familiar with United Waste Systems, a small garbage company only 3.6 percent the size of Waste Management. Yet, despite its smaller size, United Waste makes more profit per dollar of revenue than does Waste Management (a 24 percent operating margin versus 18 percent for Waste Management).[31]

What makes United Waste Systems more profitable than Waste Management? It has instituted successful planning processes at each level of the company. Beginning at the top, the company has a clear mission. Says CEO Bradley Jacobs, "We are not in medical waste. We are not in hazardous waste. We are not in incineration." What the company is in are rural areas, where, unlike giant Waste Management, it has little competition in the trash-pickup business. But once the trash is picked up, it's got to be delivered to a dump. Since competitors pay cities upwards of $45 per ton to empty their garbage trucks at municipally owned dumps, United's middle managers are in charge of a plan to find, buy, and run company-owned dump sites. Why? Because this lowers United's dumping costs to just $29 a ton. Finally, at lower levels, company managers and employees focus on plans to lower costs and increase productivity. For example, in Belchertown, Massachusetts, United has a one-truck, two-person crew pick up trash for the entire town on Wednesdays, Thursdays, and Fridays. The same route used to be covered by two trucks and two crews from another waste hauler.

*After reading the next two sections, you should be able to*
3. *discuss how companies can use plans at all management levels, from top to bottom.*
4. *describe the different kinds of special-purpose plans that companies use to plan for change, contingencies, and product development.*

# 3. Planning from Top to Bottom

*Planning works best when the goals and action plans at the bottom and middle of the organization support the goals and action plans at the top of the organization. In other words, planning works best when everybody pulls in the same direction. Exhibit 4.3 illustrates this planning continuity, beginning at the top with a clear definition of the company vision and ending at the bottom with the execution of operational plans. Let's see how 3.1 top managers create the organizational vision and mission, 3.2 middle managers develop tactical plans and use management by objectives to motivate employee*

EXHIBIT 4.3

PLANNING FROM TOP TO BOTTOM

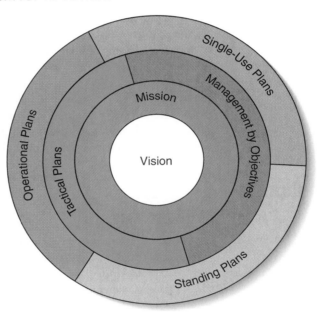

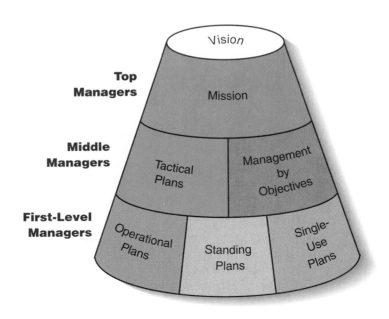

*efforts toward the overall vision and mission, and 3.3 first-level managers use operational, single-use, and standing plans to implement the tactical plans.*

### 3.1 Starting at the Top

As shown in Exhibit 4.4, top management is responsible for developing long-term **strategic plans** that make clear how the company will serve customers and position itself against competitors in the next two to five years. (The strategic planning and management process is reviewed in its entirety in Chapter 9.) Strategic planning begins with the creation of an organizational vision and an organizational mission.

A **vision** is a statement of a company's purpose or reason for existing.[32] Vision statements should be brief—no more than two sentences. They should also be enduring, inspirational, clear, and consistent with widely shared company beliefs and values. For example, Exhibit 4.5 shows the vision statement of Merck Corporation, a leading pharmaceutical firm. Merck's vision is enduring. It doesn't change if Merck uses natural or synthetic chemical compounds or if its researchers use high-tech gene-splicing or low-tech petri dishes. The vision of "innovations and solutions that improve the quality of life," "meaningful work," and "superior rate of return" stays the same. Plus, the vision is clear, inspirational, and consistent with the Merck company values, shown in Exhibit 4.5. Other examples of organizational visions are Walt Disney Corporation's "to make people happy" and Schlage Lock Company's "to make the world more secure."[33]

The **mission**, which flows from the vision, is a more specific goal that unifies company-wide efforts, stretches and challenges the organization, and possesses a finish line and a timeframe. For example, in 1961, President John F. Kennedy established an organizational mission for NASA with this simple statement: "Achieving the goal, before this decade is out, of landing a man on the moon and returning him safely to earth."[34] NASA achieved this goal on 20 July 1969, when astronaut Neil Armstrong walked on the moon. Once a mission has been accomplished, a new one should be chosen. Again, however, the new mission must grow out of the organization's vision, which does not change over time. For example, NASA's vision statement is "As explorers, pioneers, and

**strategic plans**
overall company plans that clarify how the company will serve customers and position itself against competitors over the next two to five years

**vision**
inspirational statement of an organization's enduring purpose

**mission**
statement of a company's overall goal that unifies company-wide efforts toward its vision, stretches and challenges the organization, and possesses a finish line and a time-frame

---

**EXHIBIT 4.4**

TIMELINES FOR STRATEGIC, TACTICAL, AND OPERATIONAL PLANS

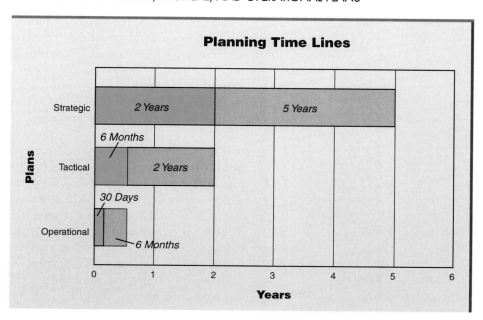

**Planning Time Lines**

Plans — Strategic: 2 Years, 5 Years; Tactical: 6 Months, 2 Years; Operational: 30 Days, 6 Months

Years: 0 1 2 3 4 5 6

| EXHIBIT 4.5 | |
| --- | --- |
| | MERCK CORPORATION'S VISION AND VALUES |

### MERCK'S VISION

To provide society with superior products and services—innovations and solutions that improve the quality of life and satisfy customer needs—to provide employees with meaningful work and advancement opportunities and investors with a superior rate of return.

### MERCK'S VALUES

1. Our business is preserving and improving human life. All of our actions must be measured by our success in achieving this goal. We value above all our ability to serve everyone who can benefit from the appropriate use of our products and services, thereby providing lasting consumer satisfaction.

2. We are committed to the highest standards of ethics and integrity. We are responsible to our customers, to Merck employees and their families, to the environments we inhabit, and to the societies we serve worldwide. In discharging our responsibilities, we do not take professional or ethical shortcuts. Our interactions with all segments of society must reflect the high standards we profess.

3. We are dedicated to the highest level of scientific excellence and commit our research to improving human and animal health and the quality of life. We strive to identify the most critical needs of consumers and customers, we devote our resources to meeting those needs.

4. We expect profits, but only from work that satisfies customer needs and benefits humanity. Our ability to meet our responsibilities depends on maintaining a financial position that invites investment in leading-edge research and that makes possible effective delivery of research results.

5. We recognize that the ability to excel—to most competitively meet society's and customers' needs—depends on the integrity, knowledge, imagination, skill, diversity and teamwork of employees, and we value these qualities most highly. To this end, we strive to create an environment of mutual respect, encouragement and teamwork—a working environment that rewards commitment and performance and is responsive to the needs of employees and their families.

**Sources**: J.C. Collins & J.I. Porras, "Organizational Vision and Visionary Organizations," *California Management Review*, Fall 1991, 30-52. "The Merck Corporate Philosophy," [Online] Available http://www.merck.com/overview/philosophy.html, 3 July 2001. Copyright © 1995-2001 Merck & Co., Inc., Whitehouse Station, NJ, USA. All rights reserved.

innovators, we boldly expand frontiers in air and space to inspire and serve America, and to benefit the quality of life on earth."

Companies can set missions in four ways.[35] One is **targeting**, setting a clear, specific target and "aiming" for it. For example, Medtronic, one of the world's leading medical technology companies, provides products and solutions for people with chronic disease. Medtronic's mission is "To contribute to human welfare by the development of biomedical devices that restore health, relieve pain, and extend life." Medtronic makes sure all of its employees aim for this mission through its regularly held medallion ceremonies, where all new hires are awarded a medallion with a "rising man" on it who represents the company mission, and are asked by the CEO to "Put this medallion at your workplace and remember why you're here: not just to make money for yourself or the company, but to help restore people to full life and health."[36] Medtronic CEO and Chairman William George describes a medallion ceremony that occurred in Switzerland:

> After the ceremony, the European team arranged for four patients and their physicians to tell their stories. One of them was a big Swiss farmer suffering from the tremors of Parkinson's disease. His physician asked him to demonstrate how he had lost his tremor. Then he asked him to shut the device off and immediately the tremors returned. As he turned the device back on, the tremors stopped immediately and a loud gasp went up from the employees in the audience. In that instant our 150 new Swiss employees "got it": they knew why the quality of their pacemakers, defibrillators, and stimulators had to be perfect and what they were working for.[37]

**targeting**
mission stated as a clear, specific company goal

A second type of mission is the **common-enemy mission**, in which the company vows to defeat one of its corporate rivals. Pepsi's aspirations of beating Coke, Burger King's desire to defeat McDonald's, or Avis's hopes ("We're number two. We try harder.") to catch Hertz Rental Cars are all examples of common-enemy missions. At one point, when Honda was only making motorcycles, its mission was "We will crush, squash, and slaughter Yamaha." A third type of mission is the **role-model mission**. Here, rather than focusing on defeating specific competitors, as in the common-enemy mission, the company emulates the characteristics and practices of a successful company. For example, the CEO of Giro Sports Design vowed "to be to the cycling industry what Nike is to athletic shoes."[38] A fourth type of mission is the **internal-transformation mission**, in which the company aims to achieve dramatic changes to remain competitive in its markets. For example, at the beginning of the chapter, you learned about Carlos Ghosn, Nissan's president and chief operating officer. Ghosn announced that Nissan was in "bad shape" but that by following the Nissan Revival Plan to cut costs and make its products exciting, Nissan would be profitable again within two years. Nissan's transformation was very fast, as it returned to profitability just over a year into the plan with the best profit and revenue growth the company had seen in over a decade.[39]

Before leaving this section, you should know that there is disagreement among academics and business people regarding the differences between organizational visions and missions. Some say that a vision is a statement of a company's purpose or reason for existing, while others would say that's a mission statement. The bottom line is that developing a statement of purpose and then linking long-term and short-term goals to that statement is critical to success. Studies consistently show that companies with more comprehensive vision/mission statements do better financially than those with ambiguous visions/missions or none at all.[40]

## 3.2 Bending in the Middle

Middle management is responsible for developing and carrying out tactical plans to accomplish the organization's mission. **Tactical plans** specify how a company will use resources, budgets, and people to accomplish specific goals within its mission. Whereas strategic plans and objectives are used to focus company efforts over the next two to five years, tactical plans and objectives are used to direct behavior, efforts, and attention over the next six months to two years. For example, after three years of losses, Disneyland Paris managed to earn a profit in its fourth year of operation by making specific changes in its tactical plans that were not helping the company accomplish its mission "to make people happy." Management redesigned special package deals (for tickets, hotel, and food), because it realized that most families only wanted to spend two or three days at the park instead of five days or longer, which was the original tactical plan. Likewise, to increase attendance, Disney cut admission prices by 20 percent and hotel and food prices by 10 percent. Finally, management realized that it had miscalculated by "Europeanizing" park rides and shows. It turned out that European visitors wanted an "American experience." So instead of sit-down restaurants with waiters and servers, the emphasis is now on fast food and self-service. Rather than fine food and fine wines, restaurants serve hamburgers, brownies, stuffed potatoes, and carbonated beverages in disposable paper cups.[41] Today, Disneyland Paris is the number one tourist destination in Europe.[42]

Management by objectives (see the feature "What Really Works? Management by Objectives") is a management technique often used to develop and carry out tactical plans. **Management by objectives**, or MBO, is a four-step process in which managers and their employees (1) discuss possible goals, (2) participatively select goals that are challenging, attainable, and consistent with the company's overall goals, (3) jointly develop tactical plans that lead to accomplishment of tactical goals and objectives, and (4) meet regularly to review progress toward accomplishment of those goals. Lee Iacocca, the former CEO who brought Chrysler Corporation back from the verge of bankruptcy, credits MBO (though he called it a "quarterly review system") for his 30

After changing its original tactical plan, Disneyland Paris has become one of the most popular destinations in Europe. In fact, the park welcomed its 100,000,000th visitor in January 2001, less than 10 years after it opened its gates.

years of extraordinary success as a manager. Iacocca said, "Over the years, I've regularly asked my key people—and I've had them ask *their* key people, and so on down the line—a few basic questions: 'What are your objectives for the next ninety days? What are your plans, your priorities, your hopes? And how do you intend to go about achieving them?'"[43]

When done right, MBO is an extremely effective method of tactical planning. However, MBO is not without disadvantages.[44] Some MBO programs involve excessive paperwork, requiring managers to file annual statements of plans and objectives, plus quarterly or semiannual written reviews assessing goal progress. However, electronic and Web-based management systems and software, such as WebMBO **http://www.webmbo. com**), which automates the MBO process, are making it easier for managers and employees to set goals, link them to the organization's strategic direction, and continuously track and evaluate their progress.[45] Another difficulty is that managers are frequently reluctant to give employees feedback about their performance. A third disadvantage is that managers and employees sometimes have difficulty agreeing on goals. And when employees are forced to accept goals that they don't want, goal commitment and employee effort suffer. Last, because MBO focuses on quantitative, easily measured goals, employees may neglect important unmeasured parts of their jobs. In other words, if your job performance is judged only by whether you reduce costs by 3 percent or raise revenues by 5 percent, then you are unlikely to give high priority to the unmeasured, but still important parts of your job, like mentoring new employees or sharing new knowledge and skills with coworkers.

### 3.3 Finishing at the Bottom

Lower-level managers are responsible for developing and carrying out **operational plans**, which are the day-to-day plans for producing or delivering the organization's products and services. Operational plans direct the behavior, efforts, and priorities of operative

**operational plans**
day-to-day plans, developed and implemented by lower-level managers, for producing or delivering the organization's products and services over a 30-day to 6-month period

# WhatReallyWorks

## Management by Objectives

For years, both managers and management researchers have wondered how much of a difference planning made in terms of organizational performance, or whether it really made any difference at all. While proponents argued that planning encouraged workers to work hard, to persist in their efforts, to engage in behaviors directly related to goal accomplishment, and to develop better strategies for achieving goals, opponents argued that planning impeded organizational change and adaptation, created the illusion of managerial control, and artificially separated thinkers and doers.

Now, however, the results from 70 different organizations strongly support the effectiveness of management by objectives (i.e., short-term planning).

### Management by Objectives (MBO)

Management by objectives is a process in which managers and subordinates at all levels in a company sit down together to jointly set goals, to share information and discuss strategies that could lead to goal achievement, and to regularly meet to review progress toward accomplishing those goals. Thus, MBO is based on goals, participation, and feedback. On average, companies that effectively use MBO will out produce those that don't use MBO by an incredible 44.6 percent! And in companies where top management is committed to MBO, that is, where objective setting begins at the top, the average increase in performance is an even more astounding 56.5 percent. By contrast, when top management does not participate in or support MBO, the average increase in productivity drops to 6.1 percent. In all, though, there is a 97 percent chance that companies that use MBO will outperform those that don't! Thus, MBO can make a very big difference to the companies that use it.

**MBO**

| 10% | 20% | 30% | 40% | 50% | 60% | 70% | 80% | 90% | 100% |

*probability of success*          97%

**Sources:** R. Rodgers & J.E. Hunter, "Impact of Management by Objectives on Organizational Productivity," *Journal of Applied Psychology* 76 (1991): 322-336.

---

employees for periods ranging from 30 days to six months. There are three kinds of operational plans: single-use plans, standing plans, and budgets.

**single-use plans**
plans that cover unique, one-time-only events

**Single-use plans** deal with unique, one-time-only events. For example, Bank One announced that it would fold Internet bank WingspanBank.com, which it had started three years ago, into its existing online services for Bank One customers, **http://www.bankone.com**. With separate marketing budgets, staffs, and computer systems, combining both sites "eliminates the substantial expense of supporting another brand," said the company. It should take less than six months to move Wingspan's 225,000 customer accounts to Bankone.com, which has over 700,000 accounts. No layoffs will occur at WingspanBank.com as a result of the one-time move.[46]

**standing plans**
plans used repeatedly to handle frequently recurring events

Unlike single-use plans that are created, carried out, and then never used again, **standing plans** save managers time, because they are created once and then used repeatedly to handle frequently recurring events. If you encounter a problem that you've seen before, someone in your company has probably written a standing plan that explains how to address it. There are three kinds of standing plans: policies, procedures, and rules and regulations.

**policy**
standing plan that indicates the general course of action that should be taken in response to a particular event or situation

**Policies** indicate the general course of action that company managers should take in response to a particular event or situation. A well-written policy will also specify why the policy exists and what outcome the policy is intended to produce. For example, over the years construction company Fisher Development has done nearly $3 billion of work for The Gap, building every Gap, Gap Kids, Baby Gap, Banana Republic, and Old Navy store in the United States. Plus, it has retrofitted over 10,000 Gap stores. In fact, the relationship between The Gap and Fisher Development was so close that other builders simply quit trying to get The Gap's business. Barry Shames, CEO of Shames Construction, said, "There's no sense beating your head against the wall." It's estimated that Fisher Development earned $242 million in profit while completing these jobs. However, thanks to a new policy, The Gap will now bid out all construction work for new

131

stores or for redoing existing stores. Indeed, Shames and 15 other general contractors, not including Fisher Development, were invited to bid on construction projects. Shames Construction is now redoing the interior of a Banana Republic and an Old Navy. The reason for the change in policy is simply to reduce costs. A Gap spokesperson said, "It just makes good business sense to have more than one general contractor."[47]

**procedure**
standing plan that indicates the specific steps that should be taken in response to a particular event

**Procedures** are more specific than policies, because they indicate the series of steps that should be taken in response to a particular event. One area in which companies can improve procedures is in the area of travel and reimbursement. At Heidrick & Struggles, an executive recruiting firm, 200 partners in 17 locations were using 35 different travel agents to make travel reservations. President David Anderson said, "Every one of our offices made its own travel arrangements. We had no knowledge or control."[48] Consequently, Heidrick & Struggles changed its travel booking procedures, replacing the 35 travel agencies with American Express Travel Services, which not only provides American Express Cards dedicated for business travel expenses, but also allows Heidrick & Struggles workers to make much cheaper hotel, car, and airline reservations by calling American Express or by going to the centralized online travel reservation site that American Express set up for the company. The key, however, to making these procedures work is to get employees to follow them. An airline manager who works with corporate travel programs said, "Yes, employees go around the programs, and it drives travel managers crazy." Consequently, at many companies with such programs, employees who don't follow the new procedures receive smaller refunds for travel expenses. [49]

**rules and regulations**
standing plans that describe how a particular action should be performed, or what must happen or not happen in response to a particular event

**Rules and regulations** are even more specific than procedures, because they specify what must happen or not happen. They describe precisely how a particular action should be performed. For instance, rules and regulations forbid many managers from writing job reference letters for employees who have worked at their firms. Companies insist on such rules because a negative reference letter may prompt a former employee to sue for defamation of character.[50]

Another area in which companies are struggling to create effective rules and regulations is the Internet. For example, several years ago, a study by Nielsen Media Research found that of the 54 million "hits" to Penthouse Magazine's Web site during a two-month period, the most came from workers at IBM, Apple, Hewlett-Packard, and AT&T.[51] As a result of behaviors like these, more than 75 percent of major U.S. companies now block or monitor workers' Web use, while 38 percent review employees' email. Tim Carney, founder of a network security firm, said, "If you're going to supply a company car, you can dictate they won't drag-race it. The same thing holds with Internet access."[52] The New York Times fired 22 employees for inappropriate use of email, Xerox fired 40 people, and Dow Chemical fired 50 and disciplined 200 others for emailing and accessing pornographic material at work. In fact, one out of four companies has fired someone for inappropriate workplace use of the Internet. Why do companies need to take these steps? Because, says Roland Cloutier, at Brac Solutions, a network security firm, "You have Joe Schmoe going to some porno dot-com site while a female counterpart walks behind him, and it's a potential lawsuit."[53]

**budgeting**
quantitative planning through which managers decide how to allocate available money to best accomplish company goals

Budgets are the third kind of operational plan. **Budgeting** is quantitative planning, because it forces managers to decide how to allocate available money to best accomplish company goals. According to Jan King, author of *Business Plans to Game Plans*, "Money sends a clear message about your priorities. Budgets act as a language for communicating your goals to others." For example, Exhibit 4.6 shows the operating budget for the General Fund of Austin, Texas. With nearly half this budget dedicated to public safety (48 percent), it's clear that keeping the city safe is the Austin city government's most important task. Budgeting is a critical management task, one that most managers could do better. For more detailed information about budgeting, see *Essential Managers: Managing Budgets* by Stephen Brookson, or *Budgeting Basics & Beyond: A Complete Step-By-Step Guide for Nonfinancial Managers* by Jae K. Shim and Joel G. Siegel. Both books are written for budget beginners.

EXHIBIT 4.6

AUSTIN, TEXAS, BUDGET FOR GENERAL FUND USE

**Austin, Texas, Budget For General Fund Use**

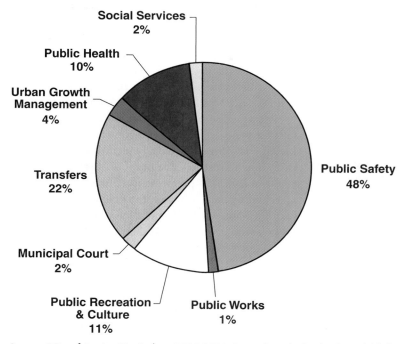

**Source**: "City of Austin, City Budget: 2000-2001 General Fund," [Online] Available http://www.ci.austin. tx.us/budget/00-01/approved/general_fund.pdf, 1 July 2001.

## Review 3
### Planning from Top to Bottom

Proper planning requires that the goals at the bottom and middle of the organization support the objectives at the top of the organization. Top management develops strategic plans that indicate how a company will serve customers and position itself against competitors over a two- to five-year period. Strategic planning starts with the creation of an organizational vision and mission. There are four kinds of organization missions: targeting, common enemy, role model, and internal transformation. Middle managers use techniques like management by objectives to develop tactical plans that direct behavior, efforts, and priorities over the next six months to two years. Finally, lower-level managers develop operational plans that guide daily activities in producing or delivering an organization's products and services. Operational plans typically span periods ranging from 30 days to six months. There are three kinds of operational plans: single-use plans, standing plans (policies, procedures, and rules and regulations), and budgets.

## 4. Special-Purpose Plans

You wouldn't use a hammer to flip your pancakes. You wouldn't hire a Ph.D. in archeology to install a new hard drive in your computer. And you wouldn't light an acetylene torch to make popcorn. Everyone knows that a big part of getting a job done right is to hire people who know what they're doing. Or, if you're brave enough to try to fix something on your own, the secret to getting something done right is to use the right tools.

*Plans are like tools and technicians. If you use the wrong one, your plan will fail. But if you use them for what they were intended, they'll serve you well. Let's examine how companies use special-purpose plans to plan for 4.1 change, 4.2 contingencies, and 4.3 product development. Make sure all the special-purpose plans reviewed in this section end up in your planning toolbox.*

### 4.1 Planning for Change

People are creatures of habit. It's extremely difficult to get them to change. Therefore, managers and employees are more comfortable trying to achieve small incremental improvements than overhauling the way they do business. They know that if they work a little harder, plan a bit smarter, and don't catch any unlucky breaks, they should be able to hit 3 percent, 4 percent, or 5 percent improvement goals year after year.

However, sometimes doing more of the same won't improve business performance sufficiently to achieve the company's mission. When this is the case, companies use stretch goals. **Stretch goals**, by definition, are extremely ambitious goals that you don't know how to reach.[54] The purpose of stretch goals is to achieve extraordinary improvements in company performance. Stretch goals are so demanding that they force managers and workers to throw away old comfortable solutions and adopt radical, never-used solutions. Steve Kerr, former dean of the University of Southern California's Business School, who is now Morgan Stanley's "Chief Learning Officer," illustrates the idea of stretch goals with this story:

> You give a team an orange and say that each person must handle the orange—you can throw it to each other, do anything you want—but the orange has to end up in the hands of the person who started it. The group throws the orange back and forth, and you time it. The first time we did it, it took nine seconds. When asked to improve, they stood a little closer, threw it a little faster, and got it down to seven seconds. Then we said, "Many groups do this in less than a second, and it's possible to do it in less than half a second." In the third trial, the team did it in less than a second, by simply stacking up their hands. The guy with the orange dropped it, it went swoosh through everybody's hands, and he caught it at the bottom—that was it. It was a neat example of the power of a stretch goal.[55]

Since the first reaction to most stretch goals is "You've got to be kidding," Kerr recommends setting "achievable" stretch goals. However, knowing what is too easy (and thus not a stretch goal) and what is too difficult (and thus not achievable) is difficult. One way companies choose a stretch goal of just the right difficulty is by benchmarking. **Benchmarking** is the process of identifying outstanding practices, processes, and standards in other companies and adapting them to your company.[56] For example, one of the biggest hassles associated with most hospital stays is the amount of paperwork and time it takes to complete the admissions process. If you were a hospital administrator, who would you benchmark to learn how to streamline your slow, cumbersome admissions process? What business or company would know how to handle admissions-like situations and paperwork faster than your hospital? Well, many hospitals actually benchmark their admissions processes against Marriott Hotels. Think about it. Both admit people to rooms, typically for no more than a couple of nights, but longer if necessary. Both collect basic information, such as your name, address, phone number, and how payment will be made (a credit card for the hotel and a medical insurance card for the hospital). And both try to determine your preferences upon admission (smoking or nonsmoking room, the kind of room you desire, food preferences, etc.). The processes are nearly identical. Consequently, benchmarking helps employees realize that they can achieve extraordinary levels of performance; after all, it's being done at another company—in this case, Marriott.

**stretch goals**
extremely ambitious goals that, initially, employees don't know how to accomplish

**benchmarking**
the process of identifying outstanding practices, processes, and standards in other companies and adapting them to your company

# BeenThereDoneThat

## Steve Kerr Discusses Stretch Goals at GE

Steve Kerr, now at Morgan Stanley, was the "chief learning officer" of General Electric. Before coming to GE, he was a management professor and the dean of the University of Southern California's business school. In this interview from *Fortune Magazine*, he discusses the right and wrong ways of using stretch goals.

**Q:** GE has been touting stretch targets for years, yet you say they can be destructive. What gives?

**A:** Most organizations don't have a clue about how to manage stretch goals. It's popular today for companies to ask their people to double sales or increase speed to market threefold. But then they don't provide their people with the knowledge, tools, and means to meet such ambitious goals. We all agree that generally you get more output by committing more input, but now corporate America seems to be trying to get more output just by demanding more output. Ask them to explain the incongruity, and they say, "We're smarter now. We're not going to give you more people, or money, or physical space; we're not going to give you more of any resource, so your solution is going to have to be to work smarter, get out of the box, and be creative."

**Q:** So what happens?

**A:** To meet stretch targets, people use the only resource that's not constrained, which is their personal time. I think that's immoral. People are under tremendous stress. And that's what I'm seeing all around this country; people working evenings, working Saturdays, working Sundays to achieve these stretch targets. Americans, in fact, now work longer days with fewer vacations than people in almost any other developed country. Therefore, we have a moral obligation to try to give people the tools to meet tough goals. I think it's totally wrong if you don't give employees the tools to succeed, then punish them when they fail.

**Q:** Why bother with stretch targets in the first place if they're going to harm workers?

**A:** Well, if done right, a stretch target, which basically is an extremely ambitious goal, gets your people to perform in ways they never imagined possible. It's a goal that, by definition, you don't know how to reach. You might, for instance, ask people to cut costs by half or reduce product-development time from years to months. Stretch targets are an artificial stimulant for finding ways to work more efficiently. They force you to think "out of the box."

**Q.** What's the right approach?

**A.** No. 1, don't set goals that stress people crazily. No. 2, if you do set goals that stretch them or stress them crazily, don't punish failure. No. 3, if you're going to ask them to do what they have never done, give them whatever tools and help you can.

**Q:** But you can't really just pull a goal out of thin air.

**A:** No, of course not. You've got to find a middle ground. If you set easy goals, people may meet them but probably won't exceed them by very much. If you set extremely hard goals, people lose faith in them.

Also, in this interdependent world of ours, you have to realize that when you set a stretch goal, it has implications for somebody else. Say I set a stretch goal for sales. You have been selling 10 widgets a day, and now I want you to double it to 20. But you can't sell those extra widgets if manufactur-

ing doesn't make them. So once we set that stretch goal, how many widgets should manufacturing build? If you don't make your numbers, you end up with that dreaded thing called inventory. It's hard not to get grouchy when manufacturing builds stuff that doesn't sell. That's a tough thing not to punish.

**Q:** What's the solution?

**A:** In this example, manufacturing and sales are going to have to communicate much more closely and adjust output as the year goes on.

**Q:** Should everyone be given the same stretch goals?

**A:** No, not at all. The danger is that you can end up hurting your best people. A golden rule of every work system is, "Don't hurt the high performers." The folks in your best-performing business units may already be stretching themselves to the limit.

**Q:** What repercussions are there?

**A:** One issue is self-punishment. If you're truly setting stretch goals, by definition you can't have a high degree of success. For individuals who are high achievers, it's not their style to miss goals. So you end up making people who are winners feel as if they're losers.

**Q:** How do you know stretch goals are working?

**A:** You measure progress in three ways. One, you compare what you're doing now with your own past performance; two, you look for meaningful progress toward the stretch goal; and three, you benchmark competitors and see if you're doing at least as well as they are.

**Q:** And if it does work, what does the employee get out of it?

**A:** Money, for one thing. In a typical gain-sharing arrangement, you might split the incremental gain or savings sixty-forty or fifty-fifty. Say, if the people at a factory save $300,000, they get $150,000 and the company $150,000. Then there are the nonfinancial rewards. These may include increased job security and personal satisfaction.

**Q:** What are the most important things for managers to remember about stretch goals?

**A:** I think you absolutely have to honor the don't-punish-failure concept; stretch targets become a disaster without that. Also, you have to provide the right tools. Finally, you have to understand that stretch goals cannot be targets that you absolutely have to reach. Because if you absolutely need the results, let's face it, you're going to have to punish failure to reach it. On the other hand, there should never be excuses for failure to reach real goals like quarterly earnings or sales targets. Stretch goals are supplemental to those basic goals. All these points may not be rocket science, but you would be surprised how often managers violate them.

**Source:** S. Sherman, "Stretch Goals: The Dark Side of Asking for Miracles," *Fortune,* 13 November 1995. Reprinted with permission from publisher.

135

Based on General Electric's experience, Kerr strongly recommends that companies not punish managers and workers when they fail to achieve stretch goals. Since the purpose of stretch goals is to achieve extraordinary improvements in performance, it is a mistake for companies to measure progress by assessing whether new levels of performance meet or fall short of the stretch goal. For example, Kerr would likely argue that it was wrong for DaimlerChrysler's board of directors to cut top management's annual bonuses by 18 percent because DaimlerChrysler failed to achieve stretch goals for improvements in car quality. Because of the inherent difficulty of stretch goals, companies need to assess progress by comparing new levels of performance to old levels. For example, though DaimlerChrysler's board punished top management by reducing its annual bonus, the punishment wasn't because quality didn't improve. DaimlerChrysler spokesperson Steve Harris said, "We just didn't reach the tough stretch goals we set," noting that DaimlerChrysler had made double-digit percentage improvements in quality in the last year.[57] What do you think? Did DaimlerChrysler managers fail because they didn't achieve their stretch goal? Or did they succeed because they achieved double-digit improvements in quality?

### 4.2 Planning for Contingencies

When senior managers from Duke Energy Corp., an electric utility company, met for a two-day meeting, their job was to confront three different scenarios about the future that might affect their business. In the first scenario, called the "economic treadmill," they assumed that U.S. economic growth would slow to just 1 percent a year. In this scenario, energy prices would drop, making it difficult for Duke to pay the significant debt it had accumulated in the last few years to build new electric plants. In the "market.com" scenario, the Internet would lead to fully deregulated market trading of electricity and gas, giving industrial and home buyers an advantage over energy producers and sellers. Finally, the "flawed competition" scenario assumes that deregulation will be uneven and inconsistent from state to state, producing volatile swings in energy demand, supply, and prices. Why is Duke considering these different planning scenarios? Because with $9 billion in debt to pay off, even small changes in growth, energy costs, or deregulation could affect the profitability of the company by tens of millions of dollars.[58]

**scenario planning**
the process of developing plans to deal with several possible future events and trends that might affect the business

**Scenario planning** is the process of developing plans to deal with events and trends that might affect a business in the future. It helps managers answer "what if" questions and prepare responses should those "what if" scenarios actually occur. You probably do scenario planning often in your own life. Your plans could go something like this: "If I get the scholarship I applied for, I won't work this term. If I don't get it, I'll apply to work in the library."

Scenario planning was first used extensively in World War II when teams of U.S. and British military strategists created scenarios by assuming the role of enemy battle planners. Their job was to devise alternative strategies that enemy forces might use to attack Allied troops and to figure out the best way to defend against each strategy.[59] By anticipating possible enemy strategies and planning actions to counter each one, Allied commanders could be ready no matter which strategy the enemy actually employed.

Scenario planning can be broken down into these steps:[60]

1. *Define the scope of the scenario.* The scope might include a time frame, assumptions about the product, and a geographic area in which the scenario is to take place. For example, a hospital might create a scenario like this:

   > Ten years from now, most hospital care (the product) will be short-term or outpatient treatment, and rather than just treating local community residents, our hospital will serve a wider geographic area, as doctors use the Internet and teleconferencing to offer medical analysis and treatment to patients who currently live too far away to be treated by hospital staff.

2. *Identify the major stakeholders (customers, suppliers, competitors, government, etc.) and the roles you expect them to play in the scenario.* Today, health maintenance organizations, HMOs, are one of the leading suppliers of health care. HMOs have brought down the cost of medical care by only allowing patients to be treated by doctors who participate in the HMO and then by closely controlling the amount of money paid to those doctors. However, if the Internet and teleconferencing make it easier and economical for patients to receive medical advice and treatment from doctors and hospitals in other cities, then HMOs may have to allow patients to regularly receive treatment from doctors outside of their local HMOs.

3. *Identify basic political, economic, societal, technological, competitive, and legal trends that you expect to occur in the scenario. Explain how and why each trend will occur and what effects it will have.* For example, in the scenario described in Step 1, use of the Internet and teleconferencing technology means that local hospitals will compete with each other and with distant hospitals and clinics. So a hospital in Indianapolis, Indiana, might find itself and its doctors competing with the renowned Mayo Clinic in Rochester, Minnesota. This might mean that local hospitals have to cut prices or develop particular specialties in order to attract patients.

4. *Identify key uncertainties and the likely outcomes associated with them.* One of the key uncertainties is how hospitals will change if they primarily provide short-term and outpatient care. Will they become much smaller? If so, will they need fewer doctors, nurses, and staffers? Will this make it easier or more difficult for hospitals to be profitable? Another set of uncertainties would be the legal questions surrounding "distant" care. Traditionally, medical care requires doctors to have face-to-face visits with their patients. However, with technology allowing doctors to recommend treatment without traditional face-to-face visits, would patients be more likely to sue if something went wrong? Would hospitals and doctors then deal with the threat of lawsuits by requiring patients to sign waivers in order to gain access to "distant" care?

5. *Using Steps 1 through 4, put together your initial scenarios.* A common technique is to write scenarios that use different combinations of key uncertainties. Another is to create best-case and worst-case scenarios. A best-case scenario in this instance would be one in which your hospital wants to take the lead in using technology to provide "distant" care to patients. A worst-case scenario would be if your hospital was losing patients and revenues to another hospital that was aggressively using technology to provide "distant" care.

6. *Check for consistency and plausibility of facts and assumptions in each scenario.* The key here is to make sure that the scenario holds together as a whole. There shouldn't be any obviously inconsistent facts. For example, if the scenario states that the use of "distant" care will increase, it wouldn't make sense to also write that hospitals would be spending less money on technology when, in fact, they'd probably be spending much more. Before being used, each scenario should be read and checked by a number of people within an organization and industry.

7. *Write the final scenarios and conduct a series of planning sessions for management teams to develop contingency plans for each scenario.* For example, Exhibit 4.7 describes two scenarios developed and used by American Transitional Care, a company that offers low-cost, short-term hospitalization for patients in need of acute medical care.

8. *Develop measures or signposts for each scenario that allow managers to know when the events predicted in this scenario are occurring.* Once scenarios have been created, signposts or measures serve as triggers to let managers know when their business environments have changed (i.e., various scenarios) and when they should implement action plans to address those changes. For example, at Solutia, a chemical company, managers put together four different short-term outcomes for each scenario, with each set of outcomes containing short-term signposts that allow the company to

EXHIBIT 4.7

## SCENARIOS CREATED BY AMERICAN TRANSITIONAL CARE

American Transitional Care offers low-cost hospital care for patients in need of acute medical treatment. It created the following scenarios as part of its scenario planning process.

### SCENARIO 1—THE REGULATORS RETURN

This scenario assumes strong economic growth and increased regulation of health care. Fearful of spiraling medical costs, government planners put regulatory controls into effect for all medical treatment. Nonmedical decision makers, such as employers, HMOs, insurance companies, and government agencies, whose primary concern is cost-containment, have much more say and influence on the kind, quality, and duration of health care. Medical providers who exceed the cost of treatments deemed acceptable by these groups are not reimbursed for their costs. Physician incomes begin to shrink. Older, more experienced physicians, frustrated by the changes, begin to retire in their early fifties. Consequently, physicians become less and less involved in most patients' medical decisions and treatment.

### SCENARIO 2—THE ENGINE SLOWS

This scenario assumes slower economic growth. Because tax revenues have declined, the federal government places strong controls on what it is willing to pay for federal health care plans. With more employees out of work and the cost of medical insurance rising, fewer people are covered by insurance plans. Accordingly, hospitals cut costs by consolidating and closing low-use departments and facilities. As the recession worsens, the federal government cuts federal health subsidies. Hospitals come under more cost pressures as improved drug treatments, less invasive surgical procedures, and coverage offered by insurance companies combine to reduce the number of people who need hospital-based treatment and the duration of hospital stays. Thus, faced by an increasing number of empty beds and more patients who can't pay for the beds that are occupied, hospitals are generally unprofitable. In many communities, local hospitals have to be closed to stem the loss of funds.

**Source:** R.D. Zentner & B.D. Gelb, "Scenarios: A Planning Tool for Health Care Organizations," *Hospital & Health Services Administration* 36 (1991): 211.

abandon or embrace different scenarios or strategies in days. These signposts proved effective when Solutia was deciding whether to resell another company's chemical, one used in computer chip production. At first, said Mitch Pulwer, Solutia's chief scenario strategist, "We thought that because of our expertise, we'd have a wonderful new business opportunity here." But when one of the key signposts, prices for chip memory, dropped significantly, Solutia decided against the project within days.[61]

### 4.3 Planning for Product Development

Drip, drip, drip. Time to replace that leaky faucet? Just a few years ago, your only choice would have been chrome, not pretty, but functional. However, that changed when Moen, which manufactures plumbing fixtures, decided it was in the home decorating business, selling "jewelry for the bathroom and the kitchen." President Jeff Svoboda calls this Moen's "9 to 5" strategy, meaning that if customers had a choice of new styles, they would buy a new Moen faucet every five years instead of every nine years. The only problem was that Moen averaged only one new product line per year. Today, though, Moen's 50 design engineers work on three to 15 new faucet product lines per year. The speed-up was accomplished by using "ProjectNet," an online collaboration site where Moen's designers share product plans and designs with suppliers all over the world. When a supplier makes changes, those changes are then saved in a master Web file for later use, cutting development time by one-third. Likewise, Moen has used its Web site to even allow customers to design and customize their kitchens, bathrooms, and faucets. So with more products being developed at a faster pace, Moen's sales are up dramatically in the last few years, moving it from third in the industry to a tie for first.[62]

Moen's ambitious "9 to 5" strategy has resulted in faster product development cycles. This is important in the current home improvement boom, where form is as important—if not more important—than function.

**aggregate product plans**
plans developed to manage and monitor all new products in development at any one time

139

Product development is an increasingly important competitive tool. Like Moen, companies that are the first to market with new products or newly redesigned products that customers want can quickly increase market share, earn higher profits, and stay ahead of competitors who are forced to play catch-up.

The first step in effective product-development planning is to create an aggregate project plan.[63] Because very few companies can survive by relying on just one product, companies develop **aggregate product plans** to manage and monitor all new products in development at any one time. Aggregate product plans should indicate the resources (funds, equipment, facilities, materials, and employees) being used for each product and that product's place within the company's mission and strategic plan.

More than anything else, aggregate product plans help companies avoid the classic mistake of having too many products in development at any one time. For example, in one subsidiary of an American firm, a product-development staff of 40 people was responsible for almost 140 projects. Not surprisingly, the subsidiary's managing director complained that "Nothing is getting done as well as we would like." And when asked if all 140 projects were equally important to the company, he replied, "We have no method of weighing the merits of one against another."[64] By contrast, after creating an aggregate product plan, a large manufacturer of scientific instruments and laboratory equipment reduced the number of products it planned to develop by nearly two thirds. After topping out at a high of 30 products, it now has a much more manageable group of 11 products, all of which are consistent with the company's long-term strategic goals.

Besides keeping the overall set of products in balance and limited to a reasonable number, the second step is effective management of the product-development process itself. Four factors lead to a better, faster product-development process: cross-functional teams, internal and external communication, overlapping development phases, and frequent testing of product prototypes.[65]

*Cross-functional teams*, which are made up of individuals from different functional backgrounds (e.g., manufacturing, engineering, marketing), make better product-development decisions. The diversity of functional backgrounds means that cross-functional teams have a greater amount and variety of information, knowledge, and experience available as they develop new products. At food manufacturer Sara Lee, cross-functional teams test and bring new food products to market. Paul Bernthal, senior vice president of Research and Development, said, "One of our core competencies is the diverse background of our R&D group. Our staff has backgrounds in culinary arts, food science, meat science, grain science, animal science, package engineering, and chemical engineering, with varying degrees, including B.S., M.S., M.B.A. and Ph.D." He continued, "As a development company, cross-functional teams help bring us to market more quickly. And with all of us under one roof, there is a greater understanding of each group's functions."[66] According to Sandy Glatter, director of Bakery Research and Development, when Sara Lee was testing its new microwave calzone products (a calzone is pizza dough with meat, cheeses, or veggies baked in the middle), "We utilized our meat products group and combined their expertise with the bakery side to enter a category that we were not competing in—hand-held sandwiches." Then, "We leveraged our refrigerated folks to help determine the types of meats that should go inside and truly differentiate our product, making Calzone Creations live up to the Sara Lee name."[67]

Frequent *internal and external communication* is the second critical factor in the product-development process. Like cross-functional teams, frequent internal communication between product-development team members increases the amount of relevant information used to make decisions. It also builds group cohesion and reduces mistakes and misunderstandings that are commonplace in the product-development process. External communication with outsiders, such as customers and suppliers, broadens development team members' perspectives by helping them see their product and its uses through others' eyes. While communication with outsiders is typically beneficial, development teams may want to give more weight to what customers and suppliers do with new products (during product testing) than what they say they will do. For example, surveys and focus groups of fast-food restaurant customers usually result in the same conclusion: customers say they want healthier, low-fat food on the menu. However, Taco Bell's border lights, McDonald's McLean, Kentucky Fried Chicken's skinless chicken, and Pizza Hut's low-cal pizza all flopped and have been removed from restaurant menus. Not surprisingly, a National Restaurant Association study found a large difference between what people say they will eat (fruit, vegetables, etc.) and what they really eat (cheeseburgers and french fries).[68]

*Overlapping development phases* is the third critical factor when planning the product-development process. In contrast to a sequential design process, where each step (product plans and specs, product testing, product roll-out) must be completed before beginning the next step, overlapping development means multiple product-development steps and phases are started and completed at the same time. Exhibit 4.8 shows the development time line used by Silicon Graphics Incorporated (SGI) to develop one of its new "supercomputer" computer servers. The white rectangles indicate traditional planning processes. Here, SGI created the block diagram (the general plan) and the system specifications (the details behind the plan) that it wanted in its new computer. Notice, however, that product testing, indicated by the gray (computer software simulations) and black rectangles (prototype hardware testing), began long before SGI had completed its plans and detailed product specifications. The primary advan-

EXHIBIT 4.8

SILICON GRAPHICS: OVERLAPPING PRODUCT-DEVELOPMENT PHASES FOR A NEW "SUPERCOMPUTER" SERVER

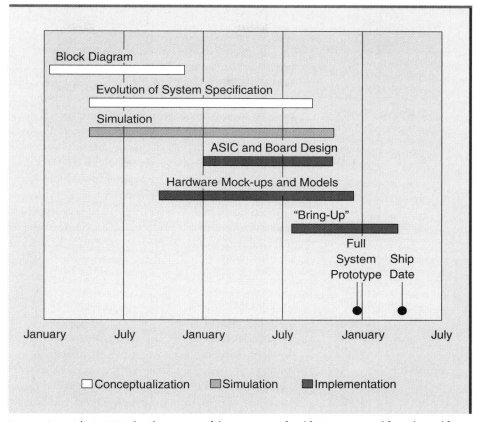

**Source:** Copyright © 1995, by The Regents of the University of California. Reprinted from the *California Management Review*, Vol 38, No 1. By permission of the Regents.

tage of overlapping development is that it speeds up product development and makes the entire process much more flexible. In fact, SGI began software simulation testing just four months after product development began. And by having customers participate in product testing at an early stage, SGI had the flexibility to incorporate their feedback (and any last-minute changes in computer technology—which always occur at a rapid pace).[69]

The last critical component in the product-development process is *frequent testing of product prototypes*. A **product prototype** is a full-scale, working model that is being tested for design, function, and reliability. A good product plan or blueprint is essential. Very few new products succeed without them. But planning is no substitute for the hands-on learning that comes from frequent testing of product prototypes. At Lear Corporation, which designs and makes automotive interiors for companies like General Motors, designers, engineers, and sculptors used to make initial design prototypes with 3D clay models of seats and doors. These days, however, with advanced CAD (computer aided design) software, prototyping is as much "virtual" as it is "hands-on." In fact, Lear has constructed a special "reality center" with a screen stretching 20 feet wide and 8 feet tall to view computerized prototypes. As the lights come down and the

**product prototype**
a full-scale, working model of a final product that is being tested for design, function, and reliability

computerized 3D design is projected onto the screen, it feels as if you're actually sitting in a new car. Glance to the right and you view the center console and controls. Turn to your right and view the passenger seat. Make the computer "glance" over your "right shoulder" and you can see what the back seat looks like, too.[70] Normally, it takes Lear three years to completely design the interior of a new car, but with its CAD-based virtual reality prototypes, it has been able to cut that development time in half.

Prototype testing works best as a "hands-on" process. It begins by testing a prototype, making changes in the product based on what you learned, testing the new version of the prototype, and then making changes again, and so on. While Lear now makes many of these tests and changes on computers, it realized that there are limitations to completely relying on computer-based design prototypes. Leather seats have to be sat on. Real people need to try the steering wheel and controls for functionality and logic. Steven Allen, who designed interiors at Lear, said, "Our goal is always to get to market faster. But you've got to be able to put a qualified rear end in the seat. If you don't understand sculpture in the real world, you can't sculpt on a computer." So Lear always makes at least one physical product prototype of everything it develops in its design center. In fact, to make its virtual prototypes more realistic, Lear builds "mistakes" into its computer models, such as leather textures with folds in the leather that mimic real seats. Steve Allen said, "My goal is to destroy the difference between what's real and what's perceived," says Allen. "I don't want any doubt that you're looking at a product, not a concept."[71]

## Review 4
### Special-Purpose Plans
Companies use special-purpose plans to deal with change, contingencies, and product development. Stretch goals are used to encourage workers to discover creative ways of doing their work. Benchmarking can be used to set challenging, achievable stretch goals. Managers and workers should not be punished for failing to achieve stretch goals. Scenario planning helps managers anticipate and prepare for future contingency factors that could influence their businesses. The steps of scenario planning are (1) define the scenario scope, (2) identify the major stakeholders, (3) identify trends, (4) identify key uncertainties, (5) create initial scenarios, (6) check for consistency and plausibility, (7) develop contingency plans for each scenario, and (8) develop measures or signposts that serve as triggers to let managers know when their business environments have changed. Aggregate product plans help companies manage all products in development at any one time and avoid developing too many low-priority products. Product-development processes can be accelerated by planning to use cross-functional teams, promoting internal and external communication, using overlapping development phases, and frequently testing product prototypes.

## What Really Happened?

Trying to overtake a market-dominating company like Boeing Aerospace is tough to do, especially when it holds 82 percent of the market! However, it's possible to compete against the best companies in the world if you have a sound, flexible plan that everyone in the company adheres to. Let's find out what really happened at Airbus as it tried to catch up to Boeing in the passenger jet business.

### You decide to write an "Airbus Master Plan." But how can you make a plan that works?

Planning is one of the best ways to improve organizational and individual performance. It encourages people to work harder (intensified effort), to work hard for extended periods (persistence), to engage in behaviors directly related to goal accomplishment (directed behavior), and to think of better ways to do their jobs (task strategies). But most important, companies that plan have larger profits and faster growth than companies that don't plan.

For Airbus to have a successful plan, it needed to set specific goals, develop commitment to goals, develop action plans, track progress, and maintain flexibility. Airbus's foremost goal was to grow, to take business away from Boeing. However, this was not growth for growth's sake. Growth was key for Airbus because of economies of scale. It can cost as much as $15 billion to design and introduce a new jetliner. The more orders received for that jet, the easier it is to spread its costs. In fact, jet costs drop 20 percent every time jet production doubles. Another of Airbus's key goals was to build planes that were easier and cheaper to maintain than Boeing's planes. When an airline buys a passenger jet, it will be using that jet for another 20 to 25 years. Consequently, the cost of maintaining that jet is just as important as the jet's initial cost. Airbus claims that over the life of a plane, its maintenance costs can be 10 to 15 percent less than Boeing's. And given its quickly rising sales, it seems to be delivering those reduced costs. Frederick Brace, the vice president of finance for United Airlines, said, "Once you get an Airbus in your fleet, you tend to want more of them. They make a good plane that is very economical to operate."

### Products change so quickly that you can't afford to lock yourself into an inflexible plan that will be obsolete within a few years.

Options-based planning, in which the goal is to "keep your options open," is one way that companies are building flexibility into their planning processes. The options-based approach is to make small investments in many options or plans. When it becomes clear which option or plan is likely to work, you "strike" that option by making a much larger investment in it. One of the ways in which Airbus built flexibility into its planning process was by deciding to build and offer a full range of planes, from the 107-seat A318, to the 380-seat A340, to the newly proposed A380, which would compete with Boeing's 747 and carry up to 555 passengers. Strictly speaking, this wasn't options-based planning because of the large development costs associated with new planes. On the other hand, it was options-based planning because offering a range of planes (with the proposed A380, Airbus builds 15 different planes) made it much easier for Airbus to shift its resources behind the planes that customers wanted. However, Airbus took the idea of flexibility and options-based planning even further by designing a single cockpit for all of its planes. Ron Aramini, senior vice president at America West said, "It's a tremendous advantage to the airline to use the same crew member on several planes." In fact, because the cockpits are similar, it takes only 8 days of retraining to move a pilot from Airbus's single-aisle A320 to its double-aisle, wide body A330. By contrast, it takes nearly twice as long to retrain a pilot who moves from a Boeing 737 to a 747. Jim Eckes of Indoswiss Aviation in Hong Kong said, "It's not just pricing. The common cockpit strategy is a winner; they have caught Boeing napping on that issue." Consequently, no matter which Airbus jet the airlines used, their pilots would quickly adapt to be able to fly them.

### Finally, if the plan is going to work, it has to be something that all managers in the company, from top to bottom, can believe in and make happen. So what will the plan have to look like to accomplish that?

Airbus needed to develop strategic plans that made clear how the company would serve customers and that would position itself against competitors. In terms of serving customers, or the passengers who fly on its jets, Airbus has focused on ergonomics and comfort. Airbus's first top-selling plane, the Airbus A320, was seven inches wider, giving passengers an extra inch per seat. So Airbus continued this practice on most of its other jets. Stephen Wolf, chairman of U.S. Airways, which has ordered 430 Airbus jets in the last five years, said, "Airbus aircraft offer greater flexibility for wider seats, more overhead bin space, and more aisle space—all important in a consumer-conscious business." Airbus's management summarized its views on passenger comfort in this way: "The aim of Airbus is to maximize operators' revenues. But as passenger expectations rise with respect to improvements in comfort and service, . . . we design our aircraft with passenger comfort in mind. In our view, ergonomics are as important as aeronautics."

In terms of positioning itself against competitors, Airbus has gone the route of innovation, hoping that new features, functionality, and lower costs would result. One of Airbus's first breakthroughs was the first computerized flight-control system. While most systems are mechanical in nature, Airbus' computer-based system was lighter, cheaper, and more reliable. And by combining this computerized system with the use of carbon fiber composites in the structural body of its planes, Airbus has been able to significantly reduce flying weight and costs. With these advances, companies that used to buy from Boeing are now buying from Airbus. JetBlue is a new low-cost airline in New York City that is modeled after Southwest Airlines. Its CEO David Neeleman said, "We had an all-Boeing team . . . but when it came down to it, the A320 was superior. Our business plan was to use 737s, but every airline that we talked to that was operating the two side-by-side all basically said they would not consider buying another 737."

So how well have Airbus's plans been working? Spectacularly well. Only five years ago, Airbus was selling just 19 percent of all new planes. Today, however, depending on which numbers are used, it has now pulled even or surpassed Boeing in terms of new passenger jet sales. That's a remarkable turnaround in such a short time. Rainer Hertrich, CEO of European Aeronautic Defense and Space, which owns 80 percent of Airbus, said, "Some years ago, we were not taken as serious competition by Boeing. Now they are acknowledging we are on an equal, level playing field." However, Airbus is still not profitable. But even there it has made progress. Airbus is no longer part of a four-company/four-government consortium. By the time you read this, Airbus will probably be a public company, with publicly traded stock, just like Boeing. Removing politics from the mix has allowed Airbus to become even more efficient. It now has a centralized purchasing system, as well as a centralized accounting system that lets it know the precise costs and profits of each of its planes. And with a new focus on the bottom line, Airbus has reduced the number of workers from 43,000 to 37,000 employees, thus increasing sales per worker from $213,000 to $358,000. Airbus's CEO now says, "Our challenge and our reward is shareholder value. This management is very focused on profitability."

**Sources:** M. Brelis, "Duel at 30,000 Feet with Intense Marketing, Innovations—And a Dollop of Ill Will—Boeing and Airbus Fight to Rule Skies," *The Boston Globe*, 18 June 2000, F1. G. Edmonson, J. Rae-Dupree, & K. Capell, "Overhauling Airbus. (Airbus Is Expected to Provide Increasing Competition for Boeing)," *Business Week*, 2 August, 1999, 14. D. Lynch, "Airbus Comes of Age with A-380 Super-Jumbo Jet Challenges Boeing's Last Monopoly," *USA Today*, 21 June 2001, B1. D. O'Connell, "New-Look Boeing Gets Ready to Spread Its Wings," *The Scotsman*, 12 February, 2001, 5. B. Taylor, III, "Blue Skies for Airbus: Lately It's Been Nothing But. Orders Have Taken Off, And Archrival Boeing Has Run into Headwinds. Now Airbus Wants to Build a Super-jumbo to Carry 30 Percent More People than a 747," *Fortune*, 2 August 1999, 102. G. Thomas, "Airbus, Boeing & Commonality," *Air Transport World*, 1 April 2001, 26.

## Key Terms

action plan *(121)*
aggregate product plans *(139)*
benchmarking *(134)*
budgeting *(132)*
common-enemy mission *(129)*
distal goals *(121)*
goal commitment *(120)*
internal-transformation mission *(129)*
learning-based planning *(124)*
management by objectives (MBO) *(129)*

mission *(127)*
operational plans *(130)*
options-based planning *(124)*
planning *(114)*
policy *(131)*
procedure *(132)*
product prototype *(141)*
proximal goals *(121)*
role-model mission *(129)*
rules and regulations *(132)*

S.M.A.R.T. goals *(119)*
scenario planning *(136)*
single-use plans *(131)*
standing plans *(131)*
strategic plans *(127)*
stretch goals *(134)*
tactical plans *(129)*
targeting *(128)*
vision *(127)*

**144**

## What Would You Do-II

### Tupperware, We're Still Here!

Mention the word "brand recognition" and people will immediately think about brand names such as Coca-Cola, McDonald's, and Tupperware. That's right, Tupperware, the name your mom believed in and trusted for years, still exists. Only a few consumers have trouble visualizing the "Super Crisp-It," the plastic device that magically keeps a head of lettuce grocery-fresh for weeks at a time.

However, many consumers today are unaware of where to go to buy Tupperware's products. For over 50 years, Tupperware products have been sold only through commissioned sales representatives. These sales representatives have been demonstrating Tupperware products in customers' homes through their famed Tupperware parties. At a typical party, the hostess invites many friends who delight in the preparation of a microwave-cooked meal and who are fascinated by the unique timesaving abilities provided by the Tupperware products. As an incentive for offering the use of her home, the hostess keeps many of the demonstrated items. In-home demonstrations and direct selling by product representatives have been the only avenues available for customers to purchase Tupperware products in the past.

Unfortunately, since a majority of women are working today, in addition to raising a family and maintaining a household, Tupperware parties are beginning to lose their edge nationwide. Most families cannot afford the precious time needed to offer or attend a Tupperware demonstration, even though many of the products can be demonstrated during one's lunch hour.

Increased competition has also begun to cut into Tupperware's ability to promote their products. Many manufacturers, such as Glad, Rubbermaid, and Sterilite, are producing food storage containers and utensils that compete directly with Tupperware's products. Additionally, these competing products are found in most local retail shops, further impacting Tupperware's sales. Direct selling has seen an increase in competition as well. Tupperware and others, such as Avon, Mary Kay, and Kirby, initially dominated the direct-selling market. Now many other products are sold in a similar format, including Pampered Chef and Home Interiors, who utilize a party format similar to Tupperware's.

In spite of increased competition and a resulting decrease in Tupperware demonstrations in America, Tupperware has flourished in other parts of the world. Currently, Tupperware products are available in over 100 countries, which provided $1.1 billion of revenue last year, an 8 percent increase over the previous fiscal year.

Despite the apparent success, as president of Tupperware, you believe that more can be done in the United States to improve sales and build product awareness. You need a plan to make your products more accessible to consumers and promote continued brand awareness. What kind of strategy will work? And what should your goals be? Afterall, you need a success. **If you were the president of Tupperware, what would you do?**

**Sources:** "Tupperware Corp.: Target Venture Paves Way for Products' Retail Debut," *The Wall Street Journal*, 18 July 2001 http://interactive.wsj.com. S. Kapellusch, "Mall Kiosks Raise Tupperware Image," *Arizona Republic*, 3 November 1999. Tupperware Web site, http://www.tupperware.com, Annual Report, 29 July 2001.

## Management Decisions

### What's Your Policy?

Ah, what's this, a post-it note from the boss attached to a couple of newspaper articles? The first story is about a McDonald's manager who used the company voice-mail system to record "intimate exchanges" with a coworker. For reasons that were not made clear in the article, McDonald's later played the tape for his wife. The manager sued, claiming that his voice-mail messages were private and protected because they could only be accessed by someone who possessed his voice-mail security password. McDonald's countered by claiming that since the voice-mail system was owned, run, and maintained by the company, nothing contained on the voice-mail system could be construed as personal or private.

The second news story is about Irene Wechselberg, a librarian at the University of California, Irvine. Irene works in the rare books department in the UC Library. Like most people, a large percentage of the emails that she sends and receives on her university email account are business-related. However, some are personal. When Irene went on medical leave, her supervisor asked for her email password so that the library staff could keep up with her responsibilities. (No doubt, Irene subscribed to several professional LISTSERV groups that kept up on issues related to rare books.) When she refused, calling the request an "invasion of privacy," the university redirected all of her email to her supervisor's computer. The campus is now in an uproar over this issue. The article quoted Daniel Tsang, a biographer and host of a campus radio show, as saying, "Just because the university owns the public buildings, does that mean the state has the right to install cameras in the bathroom?"

Oh, here's a second post-it note from the boss. "ASAP, write a policy that makes clear to all employees the appropriate and inappropriate uses of email. Without a clear policy, we're leaving ourselves exposed to problems, controversies, and potential lawsuits. Have a draft in my email account by 9:00 A.M. Monday."

### Questions

1. Before writing a rough draft of the email policy, specify, in writing, the purpose of the policy and its desired outcomes.
2. Write a rough draft of the new email policy for your company. Be as specific as possible about appropriate and inappropriate uses of email. Keep the policy short, no more than a page. Since it will be used to guide the actions of everyone in the company, make it easy to read and understand (no techno-speak).

**Sources:** M. Miller, "Should Email Be Private? UC, Employees Tangle over Rights of University to Access Computers of Staff on Leave," *Los Angeles Times*, 12 November 1995. D.H. Seifman & C.W. Trepanier, "Email and Voicemail Systems," *Employee Relations Law Journal*, 1 December 1995. D. Young, "Office Email: There's No Right of Privacy," *Chicago Tribune*, 8 April 1996.

## Management Decisions

### Cell Phone Dilemma

You've just finished reading an article in *The Wall Street Journal* discussing New York state's recent ban on cell phone usage while driving. You agree that talking on a cell phone while driving, along with other activities such as eating or searching for a radio station, is a distraction and can increase the probability of having an accident.

As you think about the implications the ban may have on individuals and companies, you begin to realize that most of your employees currently use cell phones on the job, many while driving. Suddenly, you find yourself subconsciously practicing scenario planning. Questions immediately pop into your head, such as would your company be held liable if an employee injures or kills someone while talking on a company-issued cell phone while driving? Should you develop a policy regarding safe cell phone use while driving? As a manufacturer, your company certainly has plenty of other safety policies in place, perhaps one concerning cell phones is needed. You decide to investigate the matter further before drafting a cell phone safety proposal.

In doing some basic research, you discover a case involving an investment broker who, while using a company-provided cell phone, ran a red light and killed the driver of a motorcycle. The family of the motorcycle rider sued the broker's employer, claiming that the employer encouraged the broker to use his cell phone after hours to maintain contact with clients. Although the investment-banking firm did not admit fault, it decided to avoid a jury trial by settling the suit for $500,000. Now you believe you have the ammunition needed to draft an operational plan about cell phone safety.

### Questions

1. Do you need a policy, a set of procedures, or rules and regulations? Or maybe all three?
2. As the manager in question, draft the appropriate operational plan(s) for this situation.

**Sources:** S. Shellenbarger, "Should Employers Set Limits on Cellphone Use in Vehicles?," *The Wall Street Journal*, 18 July 2001 B1. "Survey Shows About 3 Percent of Drivers Are Using Cellphones at Any Time," *The Wall Street Journal*, B1. 24 July 2001, http://www.wsj.com.

## Develop Your Managerial Potential

### What Do You Want To Be When You Grow Up?

What do you want to be when you grow up? Still not sure? Ask around. You're not alone. Chances are, your friends and relatives aren't certain either. Sure, they may have jobs and careers, but what you're likely to find out is that, professionally, many of them don't want to be where they are today. One reason this occurs is that people's interests change. Burnout is another reason that people change their minds about what they want to be when they grow up. For example, a former lawyer, Michael Stone, said, "I hated it." So he and a partner created a licensing agency that helps companies obtain licenses to sell products bearing the names and logos of corporations like Coca-Cola and Harley-Davidson. Another reason some people are unhappy with their current jobs or careers is that they were never in the right one to begin with. For example, lawyer Marsha Cohen said that it took the results of a personality test for her to realize why she disliked her jobs in large organizations. The reason? She was an introvert. Today, she runs her own small practice in international business and is much happier.

Getting the job and career you want is not easy. It takes time, effort, and persistence. Moreover, in today's ever-more-mobile society, it's common for people to have three to five fairly different career paths over the course of their working lives. No matter what you decide to be "when you grow up,"

your career-planning process will be easier (and more effective!) if you take the time to develop a personal career plan.

Write a personal career plan by answering the following questions. (*Hint:* Type it up. Treat this seriously. If you do it effectively, this plan could guide your career decisions for the next five to seven years.)

1. Describe your strengths and weaknesses. Don't just rely on your opinions of your abilities. Ask your parents, relatives, friends, and employers what they think, too. Encourage them to be honest and then be prepared to hear some things that you may not want to hear. Remember, though, this information can help you pick the right job or career.
2. Write an advertisement for the job you want to have five years from now. Be specific. Describe the company, title, responsibilities, required education, required experience, salary, and benefits that you desire. If you're not sure where to begin, model the advertisement for your ideal job after the employment ads appearing in the Sunday job listings.
3. Create a detailed plan to obtain this job. In the short-term, what classes do you need to take? Do you need to change your major? Do you need to get a business major or minor or maybe a minor in a foreign language? What kind of summer work experience will move you closer to getting the job

you want five years from now? What job do you need to get right out of college in order to get the work experience you need? At the very least, you should have a specific plan for each of the five years in your career plan. Don't worry too much about locking in your fourth- and fifth-year plans. Those are likely to change anyway. The value in planning is that it forces you to think about what you want and what steps you can take now to help achieve those goals.

4. Decide when you will monitor and evaluate the progress you're making with your plan. Career experts suggest that every six months is about right. How about your birthday and six months after your birthday? Others prefer January 1 and July 4, the beginning and middle of the calendar year. Whatever dates you choose, write them in your schedule. Furthermore, right now, before you forget, set five specific, challenging goals that you need to accomplish in the next six months in order to accomplish your career plans.

**Sources:** "20 Hot Job Tracks," *U.S. News & World Report*, 30 October 1995, 98-104. C. Boivie, "Planning for the Future . . . Your Future," *Journal of Systems Management* 44 (1993): 25-27. J. Connelly, "How to Choose Your Next Career," *Fortune*, 6 February 1995, 145-146. P. Sherrid, "A 12-Hour Test of My Personality," *U.S. News & World Report*, 31 October 1994, 109.

## Study Tip

Try to explain the key concepts of this chapter to a friend or family member who is not taking the class with you. This will help you identify areas where you need to review—and how much.

147

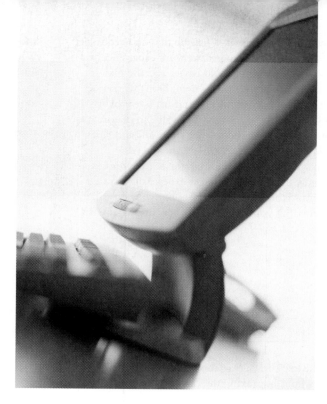

CHAPTER $5$

# Managing Information

## What Would You Do?

**Dell Computer Headquarters, Austin, Texas.** It's hard to imagine a more successful company than Dell Computers over the last 15 years. Started in Michael Dell's dorm room at the University of Texas at Austin in the mid-1980s, a $1,000 investment at Dell's inception would have been worth more than $100,000 after just six years. Over the last decade, Dell Computers has grown so fast and been so profitable that its stock price grew 29,600 percent. If you're having difficulty getting your head around a 29,600 percent increase, think of it this way: Dell's split-adjusted share price has grown from barely 23 cents per share to over $68 a share! In just the last three years alone, sales jumped from $3.4 to $12.3 billion per year (53 percent annual growth), while profits leapt from $140 to $944 million (89 percent annual growth). Furthermore, Dell's share of the PC market has doubled, and it continues to grow twice as fast as any of its competitors.

Dell achieved that growth by selling faster, more powerful, more expensive personal computers to more experienced buyers who were willing to pay a premium for a better personal computer. Dell's chief financial officer said, "Increasingly, we find that we don't need a discount. We are winning on quality and service." Likewise, catering to experienced buyers made sense for Dell because they needed less hand-holding and were thus less expensive to serve than new computer users.

However, the PC business has changed substantially in the last few years. As *Fortune* magazine described it, "Making PCs has been, is, and will continue to be a nasty business. It's a business in which competitors cut prices literally every week, where the product you make is obsolete just months after you make it, where customers choose between your boxes and essentially similar boxes made by a slew of rivals." If you're slow to sell a PC with a 16x speed CD-ROM because it's priced too high, you're certainly not going to be able to sell it when the technology races ahead two months later and your competitor sells the same PC with a 32x speed CD-ROM for 10 percent less than your machine. In other words, in the new PC business, computer components age quickly and can quickly lose their market value, if not their entire value in less than a year. With prices dropping below $1,000 a machine (most people can remember when the average price of a PC was $5,000!), and with those machines having basically the same components, will customers necessarily care any more about buying from Dell?

Thus, while Dell's initial strategy of "building a better box" worked great in the past, as prices on PCs drop like a rock, it's unlikely to work as well in the future. But this won't be the first time that Dell and his company have had to make major adjustments. Five years ago, when the company grew so fast it was spiraling out of control, Michael Dell brought in experienced top managers to manage the growth and the company's day-to-day operations, leaving him to focus on strategic issues and direction.

With PC prices dropping so quickly and technological advances moving so fast, the key is no longer just building a better PC, but quickly building a PC with the latest technological components at an aggressive price. However, doesn't that mean that Dell and its memory, hard drive, chip, and motherboard suppliers will have to work more closely (i.e., share more information) than they ever have before? How can that be done? And if Dell and its suppliers can figure out how to do that, won't that mean that its competitors can do the same thing? Why invest in an information system if it only gives you a temporary competitive advantage? If your competitors can buy the same inventory and customer tracking software that you have, you're only temporarily ahead of the game. Finally, in such a fast-moving, competitive environment, if information is the key, how is Dell to make sense of all of the information it generates from customers, uses within the company, and then shares with its suppliers? Having lots of data doesn't do you any good unless you know how to figure out what they mean. So what should Dell do with all that information once it gets its hands on it?

**If you were in charge at Dell Computers, what would you do?**

**Sources:** C. Lydgate, "Cutting Out the Middle Man," *Asian Business*, 1 May 1998, 12. G. McWilliams, "Dell's New Push: Cheaper Laptops Built to Order," *The Wall Street Journal*, 17 June 1999, B1. G. McWilliams, "Boss Talk: Dell to Detroit: Get into Gear Online! PC Whiz Advises Auto Makers Web Is Best Venue to Handle Suppliers, Serve Customers," *The Wall Street Journal*, 1 December 1999, B1.

G. McWilliams, "How Dell Fine Tunes Its PC Pricing to Gain Edge in a Slow Market: Working with Suppliers, It Quickly Passes Changes in Costs to Customers, Three Prices for One Product," *The Wall Street Journal*, 8 June 2001, A1. A. Serwer, L. Smith, & P. de Llosa, "Michael Dell Rocks: Actually, He's Plain Vanilla." *Fortune*, 11 May 1998, 58.

A generation ago, computer hardware and software had little to do with managing business information. Rather than storing information on hard drives, managers stored it in filing cabinets. Instead of uploading daily sales and inventory levels by satellite to corporate headquarters, they mailed hard-copy summaries to headquarters at the end of each month. Instead of word processing, there was the electric typewriter. Instead of spreadsheets, there were adding machines. Managers didn't communicate by email; they communicated by sticky notes. Phone messages weren't left on voice mail; assistants and coworkers wrote them down. Workers didn't use desktop or laptop computers as a daily tool to get work done; they scheduled limited access time to run batch jobs on the mainframe computer (and prayed that the batch job computer code they wrote would work—it often didn't).

Today, a generation later, computer hardware and software are an integral part of managing business information. In large part, this is due to something called **Moore's law**. Gordon Moore is one of the founders of Intel Corporation, which makes 80 percent of the integrated processors used in personal computers. In 1966, Moore predicted that every 18 months, the cost of computing would drop by 50 percent as computer-processing power doubled.[1] As shown in Exhibit 5.1, Moore was right. Every few years,

**Moore's law**
prediction that every 18 months, the cost of computing will drop by 50 percent as computer-processing power doubles

---

**EXHIBIT 5.1**

MOORE'S LAW

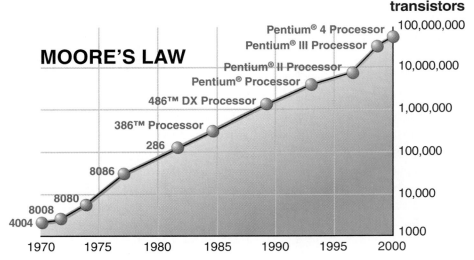

**Source:** "Moore's Law: Overviews," Intel Corporation. [Online] Available http://www.intel.com/research/silicon/mooreslaw.htm, 19 August 2001.

computer power, as measured by the number of transistors per computer chip, *has* more than doubled. Consequently, the computer sitting in your lap or your desk is not only smaller, but also much cheaper and more powerful than the large mainframe computers used by Fortune 500 companies in the early 1990s. In fact, if car manufacturers had achieved the same power increases and cost decreases attained by computer manufacturers, a fully outfitted Lexus or Mercedes sedan would cost less than $1,000!

We begin this chapter by explaining why information matters. In particular, you will learn the value of strategic information to companies, as well as the cost and characteristics of good information. Next, you will investigate the much more powerful (and cheaper!) information technologies that are changing the way companies use information. Finally, you will learn how companies capture, process, and protect information, how information is accessed and shared with those within and outside the company, and how knowledge and expertise (not just information or data) are shared, too.

## Why Information Matters

**raw data**
facts and figures

**information**
useful data that can influence peoples' choices and behavior

**Raw data** are facts and figures. For example, 11, $363, 128, and 6,100 are some data that I used the day I wrote this section of the chapter. However, facts and figures aren't particularly useful unless they have meaning. For example, you probably can't guess what these four pieces of raw data represent, can you? And if you can't, these data are useless. That's why researchers make the distinction between raw data and information. While raw data consists of facts and figures, **information** is useful data that can influence someone's choices and behavior. So what did those four pieces of data mean to me? Well, 11 stands for channel 11, the local CBS affiliate on which I watched part of the men's PGA golf tournament; $363 is how much it would cost me to rent a minivan for a week if I go skiing over spring break; 128 is for the 128 megabytes of memory that I want to add to my laptop computer (Prices are low right now; I'll probably buy it.); and 6,100 means that it's time to get the oil changed on my car.

*After reading the next two sections, you should be able to*
1. *explain the strategic importance of information.*
2. *describe the characteristics of useful information (i.e., its value and costs).*

### 1. Strategic Importance of Information

If you ask most top managers whether they thought real estate (i.e., office space, factory space, etc.) was critical to their businesses, most would say no. By contrast, Charles Woznick, president and CEO of Facility Information Systems (FIS), said "If you talk to somebody who manufactures automobiles, they can tell you what each of 40,000 parts costs down to the penny, and how many they will need to make cars this year."[2] However, according to Woznick, top managers should be paying attention to their real estate costs and gathering critical information to manage it. Using FIS's software, companies can determine how much vacant space they have, which workers are sitting at which desks, even if those desks are in New York, Hong Kong, or London, and whether they can move workers into the spaces they have or need to rent or build new space. Sprint, the telecommunications company, uses FIS to track 85,000 employees in its 23 million square feet of office space. Paul Savastano, director of information technology, said, "You can say I have this many workstations nationwide, how many are vacant, and where they are. If I can find 100 workstations in the appropriate city or combination of buildings, I can save the company several million dollars over the term of a new lease."[3]

*In today's hypercompetitive business environments, information, whether it's about real estate, product inventory, pricing, or costs, is as important as capital (i.e., money) for*

151

*business success. It takes money to get businesses started, but businesses can't survive and grow without the right information. Information has strategic importance for organizations, because it can be used 1.1 to obtain first-mover advantage and 1.2 to sustain a competitive advantage once it has been created.*

### 1.1 First-Mover Advantage

**First-mover advantage** is the strategic advantage that companies earn by being the first in an industry to use new information technology to substantially lower costs or to differentiate a product or service from competitors. For example, cable TV companies have taken an astounding (and surprising) lead over telephone companies in providing high-speed Internet access to peoples' homes. As I write this, 4.7 million homes have high-speed cable modems, compared to just 2.2 million that have high-speed digital subscriber lines from phone companies. Cable companies outflanked the phone companies by spending billions over the last three years to almost completely rewire their systems, replacing copper coaxial lines with 750 mHz digital lines that feed high-speed cable modems and digital TV cable channels alike (to compete with satellite TV, like Dish Network or DirectTV). By contrast, the phone companies, having run into unexpected technical difficulties and high expenses, are moving at a snail's pace in bringing high-speed DSL service to peoples' homes. Unlike cable companies, which are already able to provide high-speed Internet access in 99 percent of peoples' homes, the phone companies have refurbished their systems such that only 20 percent of households can now get DSL service. A senior engineer at one of the phone companies, discouraged by the problems and the slow progress, said, "All the capital in the world would not be enough to upgrade" the old phone systems to DSL.[4] Indeed, Stephen Burke, president of the cable TV division of Comcast, said, "We're beating DSL 80 percent of the time in our franchise areas. Getting a cable modem for a customer is like one's first kiss. You can never go back to things as they were."[5]

In all, first-mover advantages can be sizable. On average, first movers earn 30 percent market share, compared to 19 percent for companies that follow.[6] For example, banks that were early adopters of ATM technology were able to increase both market share and profits by 26 percent over nonadopters of ATM technology.[7] Likewise, over 70 percent of today's market leaders started as first movers.[8]

### 1.2 Sustaining a Competitive Advantage

Sustaining a competitive advantage through information technology is not easy to do. For example, smaller banks with fewer ATMs eventually caught up with larger banks by forming ATM networks like Plus and Cirrus. Because these networks allow ATM machines to process transactions on most bank cards (as long as you're willing to pay a small fee), it didn't matter whether a bank had two or 2,000 ATM machines. Furthermore, because new information technology always costs more when it is new, first-mover strategies are typically much more expensive than adopting technology after it has been established (and prices have fallen). This means that companies that establish first-mover advantage and then lose it can lose substantial amounts of money and market share. In many instances, this can put the company that had first-mover advantage out of business, such as failed Web companies like Pets.com and Webvan (a defunct Internet grocery store).[9]

According to the resource-based view of information technology shown in Exhibit 5.2, companies need to address three critical issues in order to sustain a competitive advantage through information technology. First, does the information technology create value for the firm by lowering costs or providing a better product or service? If an information technology doesn't add value, then investing in it would put a firm at a competitive disadvantage to companies that choose information technologies that do add value.

Second, is the information technology the same or different across competing firms? If all the firms have access to the same information technology and use it in the same way, then no firm has an advantage over another (i.e., competitive parity).

Third, is the firm's use of information technology difficult for another company to create or buy? If so, then a firm has established a sustainable competitive advantage over

EXHIBIT 5.2

USING INFORMATION TECHNOLOGY TO SUSTAIN A COMPETITIVE ADVANTAGE

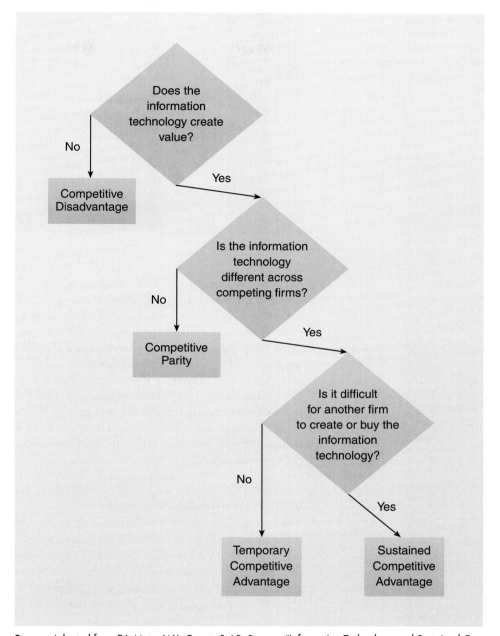

**Source:** Adapted from F.J. Mata, W.L. Fuerst, & J.B. Barney, "Information Technology and Sustained Competitive Advantage: A Resource-Based Analysis," *MIS Quarterly,* December 1995, 487-505.

153

competitors through information technology. If not, then the competitive advantage is just temporary, and competitors should eventually be able to duplicate the advantages the leading firm has gained from information technology. You'll learn more about sustainable competitive advantage and its sources in Chapter 9.

In short, the key to sustaining a competitive advantage is not faster computers, more memory, and larger hard drives. The key is using information technology to continuously improve and support the core functions of a business. For instance, Wal-Mart collects "market-basket data" every time someone goes through the register to better figure

Wal-Mart's information collection is second only to the Pentagon. Knowing what people are likely to purchase together helps the company place products throughout the store. Any parent who has purchased a toy whose batteries weren't included would appreciate having some placed in the toy aisle.

out what products customers are likely to purchase together. Because of these data, stored in the second largest database in the world (only the U.S. government's are larger), Wal-Mart knows that bananas are the most common item in shoppers' grocery carts. However, because these data indicated that people tend to buy bananas and cereal at the same time, it now places bananas near the cereal aisle, in addition to the fruits and vegetables aisle. Likewise, Kleenex can be found in the paper goods aisle, but also near cold medicine.[10] Measuring spoons are in the housewares aisle, but also next to the Crisco shortening. Every chance it gets, Wal-Mart digs further into this database to improve sales by making it easier for customers to find and buy what they want.

Companies like Wal-Mart that achieve first-mover advantage with information technology and then sustain it with continued investment create a moving target that competitors have difficulty hitting.

## Review 1
### Strategic Importance of Information
The first company to use new information technology to substantially lower costs or differentiate products or services often gains first-mover advantage, higher profits, and larger market share. However, creating a first-mover advantage can be difficult, expensive, and risky. According to the resource-based view of information technology, sustainable competitive advantage occurs when information technology adds value, is different across firms, and is difficult to create or acquire.

## 2. Characteristics and Costs of Useful Information

You work for Toyota Motor, the #4 automaker in the U.S. market, and you know that the company's goal is to have a higher share of the U.S. auto market than Daimler-Chrysler, which is #3. If you were trying to convince Chrysler or Dodge car owners to purchase a Toyota, wouldn't you like to know how old their cars are? People are much more likely to buy a new car when their car nears seven years old. Knowing this information could help you market Toyotas to Chrysler/Dodge car owners just as they were thinking about purchasing another one instead of just after they purchased a new one. Wouldn't you also like to know the repair record of their Chrysler or Dodge car and how much those repairs had cost them? This would allow you to send potential customers information comparing the average repair bills for Toyota cars they might buy to the actual repair bills they had been paying on their Chrysler or Dodge cars.

The answer to both questions is obviously "Yes!" Yes, you'd like to know how old people's Chrysler or Dodge cars are and what they pay for repairs for those cars. Information can influence peoples' choices and behavior, and you'd want to use this information to improve the chance that they would buy a Toyota instead of a Chrysler or Dodge. While this information would be fantastic to have, more than likely it would be difficult, expensive, or impossible to obtain. And if you somehow managed to get a hold of it, the data would probably be so out-of-date that it would be of little use.

*Information is useful when it is 2.1 accurate, 2.2 complete, 2.3 relevant, and 2.4 timely. However, there can be significant 2.5 acquisition, 2.6 processing, 2.7 storage, 2.8 retrieval, and 2.9 communication costs associated with useful information.*

### 2.1 Accurate Information

Information is useful when it is accurate. To be accurate, information must be reliable and valid. For instance, airline maintenance crews can't service and fix passenger jets unless they receive accurate information from plane crews or from the plane's own information system. In fact, at one time, the information systems on Boeing's 747 passenger jets indicated a large number of false problems—problems that didn't really exist.[11] If, for example, a member of the crew accidentally flipped a circuit breaker off, the 747's information system would indicate that the plane needed to be taken out of service to be fixed. However, simply resetting the circuit breaker switch would fix the problem. Since maintenance costs represent 20 percent of the cost of running an airline, inaccurate information can lead to expensive mistakes.

### 2.2 Complete Information

Information is useful when it is complete. To be complete, the amount of information must be sufficient to identify the problem and begin to identify potential solutions. Aircraft manufacturers recognized the importance of providing flight crews and maintenance personnel with more information about how their jets were running. Consequently, new-generation planes, like Boeing's 777, contain 600 computer sensors that airlines can use to fix problems and schedule maintenance. United Airlines feeds this information into a system called AMIS, Aircraft Maintenance Information System. In turn, ground crews use laptop computers to run diagnostic tests on information gleaned from AMIS, while flight crews use computer monitors to access hundreds of color graphs that continuously monitor and display the plane's performance.[12]

### 2.3 Relevant Information

Information is useful when it is relevant. Information is relevant when it pertains to the problem, so that decision makers can use it to define the problem and begin to identify potential solutions. The Federal Aviation Administration (FAA) classifies maintenance problems on planes into three categories.[13] Once a priority-one problem has been identified, it must be fixed after the plane lands or before it is allowed to take off. Anything that could lead to engine failure would be a priority-one problem. A priority-two problem does not require immediate action. The FAA allows planes with priority-two problems to take off, fly, and land for a specified time period. But the plane must be fixed within this timeframe, or the FAA will ground the plane. Priority-three problems are minor maintenance problems, like broken refrigerators or video monitors that airlines can fix at their own discretion. Since the new information systems, like United's AMIS system, provide information on all three kinds of problems, flight crews and maintenance crews are much more likely to have the relevant information they need to make good decisions.

### 2.4 Timely Information

Finally, information is useful when it is timely. To be timely, the information must be available when needed to define a problem or begin to identify possible solutions. If you've ever thought, "I wish I would've known that ahead of time," then you understand the importance of timely information and the opportunity cost of not having it. For the airlines, the information that can now be obtained on plane performance is not only more accurate, more complete, and more relevant, but also more timely. In fact, United Airline's maintenance crews track the performance and problems of their planes while they're en route to their destinations. For example, if you're 35,000 feet over the Pacific on the way back to San Francisco from your business trip to South Korea, United's West Coast ground crews are tracking the performance of your plane on their computer workstations. And because problems can be identified while planes are in the air, ground crews now have several hours to gather the tools, parts, and mechanical expertise needed to begin repairs as soon as the plane stops at the passenger gate. The timeliness of this information greatly increases the chances of keeping planes in service and on time.[14]

### 2.5 Acquisition Costs

**acquisition cost**
the cost of obtaining data that you don't have

**Acquisition cost** is the cost of obtaining data that you don't have. For example, Acxiom Inc. gathers and processes data for direct-mail marketing companies. If you've received an unsolicited, "preapproved" credit card application recently (and who hasn't?), chances are Acxiom helped the credit card company gather information about you. Where does Acxiom get that information? The first place it turns is to companies that sell consumer credit reports at a wholesale cost of $1 each. Acxiom also obtains information from retailers. Each time you use your credit card, retailers' checkout scanners gather information about your spending habits and product preferences. Many retailers sell this information to companies like Acxiom that use it for market research. So why pay for this information? Because acquiring it can help credit card companies do a better job of identifying who will mail back a signed credit card application and who will rip the credit card application in half and toss it in trash.[15]

### 2.6 Processing Costs

**processing cost**
the cost of turning raw data into usable information

**Processing cost** is the cost of turning raw data into usable information. As Max Gould, Aetna Life & Casualty's chief technology officer, said, "We have massive amounts of data. But whether we have massive amounts of information is another question."[16] Often, companies already have the data they want, but it's not in the form or combination that they need it to be in. When Prudential Insurance wanted to build a better customer database, it realized that it had good information on more than 10 million households, information that could help it do a better job of targeting its insurance, money market, and real estate services to those customers. However, the processing costs were enormous, because the raw data had to be processed from 15 different computer systems that stored the data in incompatible formats.

### 2.7 Storage Costs

**storage cost**
the cost of physically or electronically archiving information for later use and retrieval

**Storage cost** is the cost of physically or electronically archiving information for later use and retrieval. One of the reasons that credit card companies hire Acxiom to help them identify good customer prospects is that Acxiom maintains a database of the following information on about 195 million Americans: age, estimated income, home ownership, cars owned, occupation, children, number of credit cards, and so on. All of that information is stored in Acxiom's "data warehouse" outside of Little Rock, Arkansas. Acxiom uses 16 mainframes and 600,000 computer tapes to process and store all of that information. In all, Acxiom has 350 terabytes (a terabyte is the equivalent of 500 million pages of single-spaced text) of information in storage in its data warehouse. And it intends to store even more. Axciom's CEO said, "Our customers today are saying, 'Save everything, because we might find a use for this information a year from now.'"[17]

### 2.8 Retrieval Costs

**retrieval cost**
the cost of accessing already-stored and processed information

**Retrieval cost** is the cost of accessing already-stored and processed information. One of the most common misunderstandings about information is that it is easy and cheap to retrieve once the company has it. Not so. First, you have to find the information. Then, you've got to convince whoever has it to share it with you. Then the information has to be processed into a form that is useful for you. By the time you get the information you need, it may not be timely anymore.

For example, R.R. Donnelly & Sons is the largest printer of phone books in the world. Donnelly designed software that would make it easier to convert electronic information into the metal printing plates that are used to print each page of the phone book. When the software didn't work like it was supposed to, the printers who used the software to make the metal printing plates called the software designers to get the information they needed to fix the problem. An assistant then forwarded the request for information. However, it often took several weeks (sometimes months!) for the software designers to provide the information that fixed the problem.[18] Because phone book information is "perishable" (people move, numbers change, new numbers are added), the printers not only lost production time, but they also frequently had to start over in order to print the most up-to-date information in the phone book. In theory, retrieval should be quick and easy. In practice, it often isn't.

### 2.9 Communication Costs

**communication cost**
the cost of transmitting information from one place to another

**Communication cost** is the cost of transmitting information from one place to another. For example, the most important information that an electric utility company collects each month is the information from the electric meter attached to the side of your house. Traditionally, electric companies have employed meter readers to walk from house to house to gather information that would then be entered into company computers. However, meter readers are losing their jobs to radio networks that work by placing a small transceiver in your electric meter. Every five minutes, the transceiver uses radio waves to transmit data indicating how much electricity was used at your house. The data is transmitted to a nearby electric pole that holds a small computer. The small computer forwards the information to a somewhat larger computer within a quarter-mile range, which then sends the information to a base-station computer that is no more than nine miles away. The base-station computer completes the communication process by forwarding the information via phone lines or microwave towers to company headquarters. The cost: less than a $1 per month for each household.[19]

### Review 2
### Characteristics and Costs of Useful Information

Raw data are facts and figures. Raw data doesn't become information until it is in a form that can affect decisions and behavior. For information to be useful, it has to be reliable and valid (accurate), of sufficient quantity (complete), pertinent to the problems you're facing (relevant), and available when you need it (timely). Useful information does not come cheaply. The five costs of obtaining good information are the costs of acquiring, processing, storing, retrieving, and communicating information.

## Getting and Sharing Information

In 1907, Metropolitan Life Insurance built a huge office building in New York City for its brand new, state-of-the art information technology system. What was the system that represented such a breakthrough in information management? The advanced system was card files. That's right, the same card file systems that every library in America used before computers. Metropolitan Life's information "technology" consisted of 20,000 separate file drawers that sat in hundreds of file cabinets more than 15 feet tall. This filing system held 20 million insurance applications, 700,000 accounting books, and 500,000 death certificates. Metropolitan Life employed 61 workers who did nothing but sort, file, and climb ladders to pull files as needed.[20]

Less than a century later, the cost, inefficiency, and ineffectiveness of using this system that was previously state-of-the art would put a contemporary insurance company out of business within months. Today, if storms, fire, or accidents damage policyholders' property, insurance companies write checks on the spot to cover the losses. When policyholders buy a car, they call their insurance agent from the car dealership to activate their insurance before driving off in their new car. And now, insurance companies are marketing their products and services to customers directly from the Internet.

*Wow! From card files to Internet files in 95 years. The rate of change in information technology is spectacular. After reading the next two sections, you should be able to*
*3. explain the basics of capturing, processing, and protecting information.*
*4. describe how companies can share and access information and knowledge.*

## 3. Capturing, Processing, and Protecting Information

When you go to your local Rite Aid pharmacy to pick up a prescription, the pharmacist reviews an electronic file that shows all of the medications you're now taking. That same system automatically checks to make sure that your new prescription won't create adverse side effects by interacting with the other medications you take. When you pay for your prescription, Rite Aid's point-of-sale information system determines whether you've written any bad checks lately (to Rite Aid or other stores), records your payment, and then checks with the computer of the pharmaceutical company that makes your prescription drugs to see if it's time to reorder. Finally, Rite Aid protects your information to make sure that your data are readily available to only you, your physician, and your pharmacist.

*In this section, you will learn about the information technologies that companies like Rite Aid use to 3.1 capture, 3.2 process, and 3.3 protect information.*

### 3.1 Capturing Information

There are two basic methods of capturing information: manual and electronic. Manual capture of information is a labor-intensive process by which data are recorded and entered by hand into a data storage device. For example, when you applied for a driver's license, you probably recorded personal information about yourself by filling out a form. Then, after passing your driver's test, someone typed your handwritten information into the department of motor vehicles' computer database so that local and state police could access it from their patrol cars when they pulled you over for speeding. (Isn't information great?) The problem with manual capture of information is that it is slow, expensive, and often inaccurate.

Consequently, companies are relying more on electronic capture, in which data are electronically recorded and entered into electronic storage devices. For example, scientists are now using a software program called WinWedge 32 to capture research data electronically. By connecting their scientific instruments (scales, thermometers, etc.) directly to the computer, WinWedge 32 can automatically record the data from these instruments into a computer spreadsheet (like Lotus 1-2-3 or Microsoft Excel). Bill Moir, who researches for the U.S. Forest Service, said that the software allows him and other researchers to "dump data directly into the computer with no hand-entry errors and less time spent doing it."[21]

Bar codes and document scanners are the most common methods of electronically capturing data. **Bar codes** represent numerical data by varying the thickness and pattern of vertical bars. The primary advantage that bar codes offer is that the data they represent can be read and recorded in an instant with a hand-held or pen-type scanner. One pass of the scanner (okay, sometimes several) and "Beep!" The information has been captured. Bar codes were invented in 1952 and were first used to track parts inventory in factories in 1961. In 1967, railroad companies began using bar codes for tracking railroad cars. In 1973, the grocery business adopted the Universal Product Code, which required product manufacturers to place bar codes on their products or product labels.

**bar code**
a visual pattern that represents numerical data by varying the thickness and pattern of vertical bars

One of the most common tools that companies use to manage information is scanner technology. Bar codes are a standard feature at retailers, manufacturers, shippers, and numerous other types of businesses.

However, it took nearly two decades for bar code scanners to become standard equipment in most retail and grocery stores. Once adopted, bar codes cut checkout times in half, reduced data entry errors by 75 percent, and saved stores money because stockers didn't have to go through the labor-intensive process of placing a price tag on each item in the store.[22]

**electronic scanner**
an electronic device that converts printed text and pictures into digital images

Because they are inexpensive and easy to use, **electronic scanners**, which convert printed text and pictures into digital images, have become an increasingly popular method of electronically capturing data. However, text that has been digitized cannot be searched or edited like the regular text in your word processing software. Therefore, companies can use **optical character recognition** software to scan and convert original or digitized documents into ASCII text (American Standard Code for Information Interchange). ASCII text can be searched, read, and edited in standard word processing, email, desktop publishing, database management, and spreadsheet software.

**optical character recognition**
software to convert digitized documents into ASCII text (American Standard Code for Information Interchange) that can be searched, read, and edited by word processing and other kinds of software

Once data have been captured, they have to be stored before they are accessed and shared. Exhibit 5.3 describes the advantages and disadvantages of different kinds of data storage media.

### 3.2 Processing Information

**processing information**
transforming raw data into meaningful information

**Processing information** means transforming raw data into meaningful information that can be applied to business decision making. Evaluating sales data to determine the best and worst selling products, examining repair records to determine product reliability, or monitoring the cost of long-distance phone calls are all examples of processing raw data into meaningful information. And, with automated, electronic capture of data, increased processing power, and cheaper and more plentiful ways to store data, managers no longer worry about getting data. Instead, they scratch their heads about how to use the overwhelming amount of data that pours into their businesses every day. Furthermore, most managers know little about statistics and have neither the time nor the inclination to learn how to use them to analyze data.

**data mining**
the process of discovering unknown patterns and relationships in large amounts of data

One promising tool to help managers dig out from under the avalanche of data is data mining. **Data mining** is the process of discovering unknown patterns and relationships in large amounts of data.[23] Data mining works by using complex algorithms such as neural networks, rule induction, and decision trees. If you don't know what those are, that's okay. With data mining, you don't have to. Most managers only need to know that data mining looks for patterns that are already in the data but are too complex for them to spot on their own. For example, IBM has provided several National

EXHIBIT 5.3

ADVANTAGES AND DISADVANTAGES OF DIFFERENT KINDS OF DATA STORAGE DEVICES

| DATA STORAGE MEDIUM | ADVANTAGES | DISADVANTAGES |
|---|---|---|
| 1. Paper | • Most common form of data storage | • Expensive<br>• Takes tremendous space<br>• Manual search processes<br>• Only one person can access at a time |
| 2. Microfilm—picture of the data is stored on a small photographic slide | • Reel of microfilm can store hundreds of pages of data<br>• Inexpensive and cheaper than paper<br>• Requires little storage space<br>• Good for storing infrequently accessed data | • Only one person can access at a time<br>• Access only available where microfilm is stored<br>• Slow searches |
| 3. CDs—hold 650 megabytes of data | • Inexpensive<br>• Easy<br>• Nearly all computers have CD drives | • Need CD-burner to put data on CD<br>• Easily lost or misplaced |
| 4. DVDs—hold 4.7 gigabytes of data | • Becoming less expensive<br>• Easy<br>• DVD drives can read CDs | • Need special DVD-burner to put data on DVD<br>• Easily lost or misplaced<br>• Not all computers have DVD drives; CD drives cannot read DVDs |
| 5. Data Storage Tapes—magnetic tapes used to archive data for long-term storage | • Holds huge amounts of data<br>• Not much larger than floppy disks<br>• Portable, used to transport large files | • Requires special tape device for accessing and recording data<br>• Easily lost or misplaced |
| 6. Hard Drives—magnetic disks that read and write (store) data | • Primary storage for data used most often in performing jobs<br>• Fastest data retrieval<br>• Holds huge amounts of data<br>• Cheap storage | • Only one person can access at a time, unless drive is networked<br>• Access only available where drive is located, unless accessed via network or Internet<br>• Unreliability—drives can crash |
| 7. RAID—redundant array inexpensive disk system | • Uses a series of small disk drives together to act as a large disk drive (i.e., combining 10 20-gig hard drives to act as a 200-gig hard drive)<br>• More reliable since data are duplicated across small drives<br>• If one disk fails, backup data are immediately retrieved from another drive in the series<br>• Good for mission-critical data | • More expensive<br>• Typically must be networked to justify additional cost |

160

Basketball Association teams with data mining software called Advanced Scout. Advanced Scout allows basketball coaches to ask "What if?" questions like "What if I start a certain lineup or run certain plays?" "When should we go for more three-pointers?" and "Does this strategy lead to victory?" Dr. Inderpal Bhandari, a computer scientist at IBM, said, "The beauty of Advanced Scout is that it requires little computer training or data analysis background. It was written with the coach in mind."[24] Bob Salmi, assistant coach for the New York Knicks, said, "Using Advanced Scout is like having another coach on your team. There are patterns in all data. As coaches, we have ideas about why we win or lose, based on player performance and statistics. This technology allows us to get quick answers to questions and automatically identify patterns that may mean the difference between winning and losing. The ability to analyze data quickly and see previously unsuspected patterns in data can only help us make more intelligent decisions." Plus, Advanced Scout is easy to use. It asks users simple questions and makes suggestions that may help them find what they're looking for.

**data warehouse**
stores huge amounts of data that have been prepared for data mining analysis by being cleaned of errors and redundancy

**supervised data mining**
user tells the data mining software to look and test for specific patterns and relationships in a data set

**unsupervised data mining**
user simply tells the data mining software to uncover whatever patterns and relationships it can find in a data set

**association or affinity patterns**
when two or more database elements tend to occur together in a significant way

**sequence patterns**
when two or more database elements occur together in a significant pattern, but one of the elements precedes the other

**predictive patterns**
help identify database elements that are different

**data clusters**
when three or more database elements occur together (i.e., cluster) in a significant way

Data mining typically splits a data set in half, finds patterns in one half, and then tests the validity of those patterns by trying to find them again in the second half of the data set. The data typically come from a **data warehouse** that stores huge amounts of data that have been prepared for data mining analysis by being cleaned of errors and redundancy. For example, earlier in the chapter you read about Acxiom, which has 350 terabytes of information in storage at its data warehouse.

The data in a data warehouse can then be analyzed using two kinds of data mining. **Supervised data mining** usually begins with the user telling the data mining software to look and test for specific patterns and relationships in a data set. For instance, a grocery store manager might instruct the data mining software to determine if coupons placed in the Sunday paper increase or decrease profits. By contrast, with **unsupervised data mining**, the user simply tells the data mining software to uncover whatever patterns and relationships it can find in a data set. For example, Dr. John Nearhos is the general manager of the professional review division at Australia's Health Insurance Commission, which processes 300 million health insurance claims and makes $8 billion of payments each year. Dr. Nearhos gave IBM 10 data tapes with a total of three gigabytes of information and asked the company to use its data mining software to find anything that might help the commission cut costs. Three days later, the software had uncovered an illegal billing practice that was costing the commission millions of dollars that it shouldn't have to pay. Dr. Nearhos said, "I don't know if we would have ever made the connection on our own. I was able to make a call and put a stop to it that day. Data mining targets the problem areas for us and we can do the rest."[25]

Unsupervised data mining is particularly good at identifying association or affinity patterns, sequence patterns, and predictive patterns. It can also identify what data mining "techies" call data clusters.[26] **Association or affinity patterns** occur when two or more database elements tend to occur together in a significant way. Earlier in the chapter, you learned how Wal-Mart discovered that people tend to buy the following items at the same time: bananas and cereal, Kleenex and cold medicine, and Crisco and measuring spoons. These items are an example of an association or affinity pattern.

**Sequence patterns** occur when two or more database elements occur together in a significant pattern, but with one of the elements preceding the other. For example, by analyzing Web site registration and car purchasing behavior, a car company like Acura might find out that people who first register on the **http://www.acura.com** Web site are then more likely to purchase an Acura car. Or, a credit card company may find people who have been denied a request to raise their credit card limit may be more likely to change credit card companies in the next few months.

By contrast, predictive patterns are just the opposite of association or affinity patterns. While association or affinity patterns look for database elements that seem to go together, **predictive patterns** help identify database elements that are different. For example, mortgage companies can make more accurate lending decisions by studying a database that contains people who make their mortgage payments each month and those who don't, and then asking the data mining software to look for differences between the two. If reliable differences are found, those differences can then be used when approving or denying mortgage applications.

Data clusters are the last kind of pattern found by data mining. **Data clusters** occur when three or more database elements occur together (i.e., cluster) in a significant way. For example, after analyzing several years worth of repair and warranty claims, Ford might find that, compared to cars built in its Chicago plant, the cars it builds in Atlanta (first element) are more likely to have problems with overtightened fan belts (second element) that break (third element) and result in overheated engines (fourth element), ruined radiators (fifth element), and payments for tow trucks (sixth element), which are paid for by Ford's three-year, 36,000 mile warranty.

161

**protecting information**
the process of insuring that data are reliably and consistently retrievable in a usable format for authorized users, but no one else

Traditionally, data mining has been very expensive and very complex. Today, however, with services and analysis provided by companies such as Digimine.com, data mining is much more affordable and within reach of most companies' budgets. And, if it follows the path of most technology, it will become even easier and cheaper to use in the future.

### 3.3 Protecting Information

**Protecting information** is the process of insuring that data are reliably and consistently retrievable in a usable format for authorized users, but no one else. For instance, Drugstore.com is an online drugstore and health-aid retailer. When customers use Drugstore.com to purchase prescription medicine, they want to be confident that their medical and credit card information is available only to them, the pharmacists at Drugstore.com, and their doctors. In fact, Drugstore.com has an extensive privacy policy (see **http://www.drugstore.com/privacy.asp**) in which it assures its customers of the following:

We at drugstore.com recognize your right to confidentiality and are committed to protecting your privacy. We use the information that we collect on our site to provide you with a superior shopping experience. . . .

We protect your account information against unauthorized access or release. We will not give, sell, rent, or loan any identifiable personal information to any third party, unless you have authorized us to or we are legally required to do so. . . .

We will not release any prescription information in connection with any patient identification other than to the patient, the patient's authorized representative, or the prescribing or other authorized practitioner caring for the patient. At the direction of the patient, to the extent specifically authorized by law, we will release such information to other persons. . . .

When you place an order online or use the pharmacy, your personal information and credit card information are encrypted using SSL encryption technology before being sent over the Internet, making it virtually impossible for your information to be stolen or intercepted while being transferred to Drugstore.com. Your credit card information is always stored in encrypted form in a database that is away from our Web site database so it isn't connected to the Internet, and is therefore safe from hackers.

Companies like Drugstore.com find it necessary to protect information because of the numerous security threats to data and data security listed in Exhibit 5.4. From denial-of-service Web server attacks that can bring down some of the busiest and best-run sites on the Internet (i.e., Yahoo.com), to email viruses that spread quickly and result in data loss and business disruption, to keystroke monitoring in which every mouse and keystroke you make is unknowingly monitored, stored, and sent to unauthorized users, there are many ways for people inside and outside of companies to steal or destroy company data.

As shown in the right-hand column of Exhibit 5.4, there are numerous steps to properly securing data and data networks. Some of the most important are using firewalls, antivirus software for PCs and email servers, data encryption, and virtual private networks.[27]

If you have an Internet service provider, such as Microsoft Network (MSN) or America Online (AOL), any time you make a dial-up connection, there's literally nothing between your personal computer and the Internet. Data files and Web site information are downloaded directly to your PC. By contrast, **firewalls** are hardware or software devices that sit between the computers in an internal organizational network and

**firewall**
hardware or software device that sits between the computers in an internal organizational network and outside networks, such as the Internet

EXHIBIT 5.4

## SECURITY THREATS TO DATA AND DATA NETWORKS

| SECURITY PROBLEM | SOURCE | AFFECTS | SEVERITY | THE THREAT | THE SOLUTION |
|---|---|---|---|---|---|
| Denial-of-service Web server attacks and corporate network attacks | Internet hackers | All servers | High | Loss of data, disruption of service, and theft of service. | Implement firewall, password control, server-side review, threat monitoring, and bug fixes. |
| Unauthorized access to PCs | Local area network, Internet | All users, especially digital subscriber line and cable Internet users | High | Hackers take over PCs. Privacy can be invaded. Corporate users' systems are exposed to other machines on the network. | Close ports and firewall, disable file and print sharing, and use strong passwords. |
| Viruses, worms, Trojan horses | Email, downloaded and distributed software | All users | Moderate to high | Monitor activities and cause data loss, file deletion, and compromise security. | Use antivirus software and firewalls, and control Internet access. |
| Malicious scripts and applets | Rogue Web pages | All users | Mild, overestimated | Invade privacy, intercept passwords, and damage files or file system. | Disable browser script support, and use security and blocking software. |
| Email snooping | Hackers on your network and the Internet | All users | Moderate to high | People read your email from intermediate servers or packets, or they physically access your machine. | Encrypt message, ensure strong password protection, and limit physical access to machines. |
| Keystroke monitoring | Trojan horses, people with direct access to PCs | All users | High | Records everything typed at the keyboard and intercepts keystrokes before password masking or encryption occurs. | Use antivirus software to catch Trojan horses, control Internet access to transmission, and implement system monitoring and physical access control. |
| Referrers | Web sites you visit | Individual users | Mild | Send email notification of your web activity. | Use ad blockers and security packages. |
| Spam | Email | All users and corporations | Mild | Clogs email servers and inboxes with junk mail. HTML-based spam may be used for profiling and identifying users. | Filter known spam sources and senders, block Internet access by HTML messages. |
| Cookies | Web sites you visit | Individual users | Mild to moderate | Trace Web usage and permit the creation of personalized Web pages that track behavior and interest profiles. | Use cookie managers to control and edit cookies, and use ad blockers. |

**Source:** "Protect & Defend," B. Machrone, *PC* Magazine, 27 June 2000, 168-181.

163

outside networks, such as the Internet. Firewalls filter and check incoming and outgoing data. They prevent company insiders from accessing unauthorized sites or from sending confidential company information to people outside the company. Firewalls also prevent outsiders from identifying and gaining access to company computers and data. Indeed, if a firewall is working properly, the computers behind the company firewall literally cannot be seen or accessed by outsiders.

**virus**
a program or piece of code that attaches itself to other programs on your computer and can trigger anything from a harmless flashing message to the reformatting of your hard drive to the system-wide network shutdown

A **virus** is a program or piece of code that attaches itself to other programs on your computer and can trigger anything from a harmless flashing message to the reformatting of your hard drive to the system-wide network shutdown.[28] *Antivirus software for personal computers* scans email, downloaded files, and computer hard drives and memory to detect and stop computer viruses from doing damage. However, it is effective only to the extent that users of individual computers have and use up-to-date versions of antivirus software. With new viruses appearing all the time, users should update their antivirus software at least once a month. By contrast, *antivirus software for email servers* automatically scans email attachments, such as Microsoft Word documents, graphics, or text files, which contain viruses as they come across the company email server. The email server is simply a computer on which all email resides before being sent to everyone's personal computer. Think of email servers as airports and email as airplanes. Before heading off to their next destination, airplanes have to land at airports. Similarly, before being sent to individual users' personal computers, email has to first be sent to the company email server. At this point the antivirus software for email servers can scan for viruses and prevent infected files from being sent to others, even if individual personal computers lack antivirus software. So while antivirus software for personal computers prevents individual computers from being infected, antivirus software for email servers adds another layer of protection by preventing infected files from multiplying and being sent to others.

**data encryption**
transforms data into complex, scrambled digital codes that can only be unencrypted by authorized users who possess unique decryption keys

Another way of protecting information is to encrypt sensitive data. **Data encryption** transforms data into complex, scrambled digital codes that can only be unencrypted by authorized users who possess unique decryption keys. One method of data encryption is to use products such as *PGP Desktop Security* (**http://www.pgp.com**) to encrypt the files stored on personal computers. This is especially important with laptop computers, which are easily stolen. For example, the CEO of Qualcomm, a maker of chips and technologies used in mobile phones and wireless communication, had his laptop computer stolen after providing a presentation at a journalism conference. The stolen laptop contained megabytes of confidential corporate information, including several years of financial and strategic data.[29] And because of the increased likelihood of email snooping, in which people gain unauthorized access to email messages, it's also important to encrypt sensitive email messages and email file attachments. (See the Personal Productivity Tip about "Privacy Through Public Key Encryption" for an explanation about encoding email messages and attachments.)

The Internet works by cutting data into smaller packets that are numbered and reassembled in order after being transported from one location to another. Imagine a high-speed video of a finished, 1,000-piece jigsaw puzzle, with all the pieces numbered for easy assembly, which is quickly taken apart, moved from one place to another, and then quickly reassembled. The Internet does the same thing with software, text, data, or graphic files as it moves data files from one place to another. Unfortunately, since Internet data are not encrypted, "packet sniffer" software easily allows hackers to read everything you send or receive. For most of us, this is not a high-security risk. Hackers are not especially interested in what millions of ordinary people are doing on the Internet. However, there is a security risk for people away from their offices (i.e., sales people, business travelers, telecommuters who work at home, etc.) who interact with their company networks via the Internet. For them, packet sniffing can represent a substantial risk and an easy target for hackers. Previously, the only practical solution was to have employees dial-in to secure company phone lines for direct access to the company network. Of course, with international and long-distance phone calls, the costs quickly add up. However, **virtual private networks** (VPN) solve this problem by encrypting Internet data at both ends of the transmission process. Instead of making long-distance calls, employees dial an Internet Service Provider, such as MSN or AOL, that provides local service all over the world. Unlike typical Internet connections in which Internet data packets are unencrypted, the virtual private network encrypts the data sent by employees outside the company network, decrypts the data when they arrive within the

**virtual private network**
encrypts Internet data at both ends of the transmission process

# "headline news"

After following the instructions in what he thought was an innocuous email, Dell IT specialist Chuck Peterson walked into a room filled with 75 coworkers and some unfamiliar managers. Before he had finished panning the room, he knew what was about to happen. His fears were quickly confirmed when managers neatly followed a layoff script and told everyone in the room to turn in their ID badges on the way out. Peterson's job was gone in eight minutes.

As layoffs wash over corporate America, this scene is not isolated. And thanks to productivity gains realized through advanced technology, it is likely that these layoff victims have a computer on their desk and a voice-mail account for their phone. This raises the issue of sensitive trade data in new and troublesome ways.

Laid-off employees are often immediately locked out of their email and voice-mail accounts in the company's efforts to protect sensitive information from sabotage and theft. But attempts by laid-off employees to retrieve personal information stored on their work desktop computer are stymied as well. Vacation plans, personal address books, résumés, and any number of other nonbusiness-related data can be locked up, leaving laid-off employees fuming.

Information freeze-out leaves a bad taste in the mouths of those who have already swallowed a bitter firing, but companies contend that breaches of system security have risen during recent layoffs. Particularly threatening are IT employees who are laid off. Tom Noonan, chief executive of Internet Security Systems, one of the few companies that monitor networks for intruders, has seen more than just theft of trade secrets. Offenses include

Web page defacement and random changes to customer order data. As a result, companies are starting to create internal firewalls to protect select areas of their networks, such as the finance department or the CEO's office, from internal users.

Whether it is the employees or employers who are justified in this situation is hard to tell. What is clear is that companies need to communicate well before layoffs occur—preferably at the hiring stage—what information they consider theirs and what they consider as belonging to the employee. It may sound crass to learn the first day on the job what your rights are in the event of termination, but it will make sure there are no misconceptions in the end.

It goes without saying that handling layoffs is a delicate balancing act. Companies that get it right, however, will have more than a leg up on those that get it wrong when the economy improves.

1. *Which avenue do you think is the best all-around, the ramp (having one to two days to retrieve personal information) or the cliff (lockout immediately upon firing)? Balance the pros and cons to both employer and employee.*
2. *As a manager, how could you compassionately communicate a lockout situation to a recently fired employee?*

**Sources:** "Inside a Layoff: An Up-Close Look at How One Company Handles the Delicate Task of Downsizing," *Time*, 16 April 2001, 38. InfoTrac Article A73023904. Besty Morris, "White Collar Blues," *Fortune*, 23 July 2001, 99. InfoTrac Article A76474296. Riva Richmond, "Rising Layoffs Are a Boon to Internet Security Firms," *The Wall Street Journal*, 5 June 2001, B11.

165

company computer network, and does the same when data are sent back to the computer outside the network.

## Review 3
### Capturing, Processing, and Protecting Information

Electronic data capture (bar codes, scanners, optical character recognition, and devices that record data straight into structured data sets) is much faster, easier, and cheaper than manual data capture. Processing information means transforming raw data into meaningful information that can be applied to business decision making. Data mining helps managers with this transformation by discovering unknown patterns and relationships in data. Supervised data mining looks for patterns specified by managers, while unsupervised data mining looks for four general kinds of data patterns: association/affinity patterns, sequence patterns, predictive patterns, and data clusters. Protecting information insures that data are reliably and consistently retrievable in a usable format for authorized users, but no one else. Firewalls, antivirus software for PCs and email servers, data encryption, and virtual private networks are some of the best ways to protect information.

# 4. Accessing and Sharing Information and Knowledge

Imagine a situation in which the only way customers could contact your company would be to fax a company in Switzerland, which would then fax the customer faxes to you. A company would have to be crazy to do that, right? Well, that's exactly the situation that Ingersoll-Rand, a $5 billion manufacturing company, put itself in with its international customers. For example, Sermatec, which sells Ingersoll-Rand air compressors in Santiago, Chile, would fax its order for more air compressors to Ingersoll-Rand's international trading company in Switzerland, which would then fax the order to factories in North Carolina, Pennsylvania, and Tennessee. Sermatec's General Manager said, "It would take up to two weeks just to get confirmation that I'd placed an order." With no direct contact and no way to discover order status, distributors might as well have put a message in a bottle and dropped it in the ocean with the hope that Ingersoll-Rand would someday get the message and respond.

It didn't take long for Ingersoll-Rand's manager of global business systems to realize that "We had to make a change, and we had to make it quickly." So the company installed a $1.5 million system that lets customers make orders and check on pricing, inventory, and the status of previous orders from their own office computers. With instant access to this information, Sermatec increased its sales. Now when a customer calls about the price and availability of an Ingersoll-Rand part or product, Sermatec logs onto the system to provide an immediate answer. Moreover, Ingersoll-Rand has reduced product delivery times to distributors like Sermatec from well over a month to three days.[30]

*Today, information technologies are letting companies communicate, share, and provide data access to workers, managers, and customers in ways that were unthinkable just a few years ago. After reading this section, you should be able to explain how companies use information technology to improve 4.1 communication, 4.2 internal access and sharing of information, 4.3 external access and sharing of information, and 4.4 the sharing of knowledge and expertise.*

## 4.1 Communication

Email, voice messaging, and conferencing systems are changing how managers, workers, and customers communicate and work with each other. *Email*, the transmission of messages via computers, is the fastest growing form of communication in organizations. At 7 cents per message, email is the cheapest way to send a message and is substantially faster, usually appearing in the receiver's electronic mailbox within minutes, sometimes seconds.[31] Because of its similarity to regular mail (which devoted email users call "snail mail"), email is easy to learn and use.

Of course, the ease and simplicity of email create their own disadvantages: too much email! Patricia Baldwin, director of business simplification for Sun Microsystems, makers of Unix-based computers and the Java software language, gets more than 250 emails a day. Of those 250 messages, no more than 20 have any significant impact on her job.[32] Unfortunately, the volume of email that Patricia receives is not unique.

*Voice messaging,* or "voice mail," is a telephone answering system that records audio messages. Surveys indicate that 89 percent of respondents believe that voice messaging is critical to business communication, 78 percent believe that it improves productivity, and 58 percent would rather leave a message on a voice messaging system than with a receptionist.[33] Fred DeLuca, who runs Subway Sandwiches, said, "We started using voice mail about nine years ago. I like it because you don't have to have any special equipment— you see a phone, you make a call." Fred also likes voice mail because "voice messages have more texture—expression and emotion—than email or a memo does. Some people aren't readers; they're talkers, and you just can't capture them in writing the way you can in speech."[34]

**conferencing system**
communications system that lets two or more users in different locations see and talk to each other as if they were in the same room

**document conferencing**
communications system that allows two or more people in different locations to simultaneously view and make comments about a document

**application sharing**
communications system that allows two or more people in different locations to make changes in a document by sharing control of the software application running on one computer

Voice messaging systems are easy to use and cut costs because workers don't have to spend their time recording and forwarding messages. However, handling voice messages can take a considerable amount of time. Fred DeLuca said, "I get about 60 messages a day from employees and franchisees, and I listen to all of them. For my sanity, I set a time limit of 75 seconds, because people can be long-winded when they're excited. When I hear, 'You have 30 messages,' I know right away that I'll spend 60 minutes on voice mail. I take two minutes per message, listening and returning or forwarding."[35] By contrast, because people read six times faster than they can listen, 30 email messages can usually be handled in 10 to 15 minutes.[36] Plus, some companies have found that customers prefer to talk to "real" people, even if only to leave a message. Winguth, Dohahue & Co., an executive search firm in Los Altos, California, scrapped its $20,000 voice messaging system. Owner Ed Winguth said, "At first clients said it was terrific that we were in the 21st century. But soon customers started saying it was too cold and annoying. These were CEOs and VPs calling in. Our repeat customers really got annoyed."[37]

Unlike email and voice mail, which only permit users to leave messages, **conferencing systems** allow two or more users in different locations to see and talk to each other as if they were working side by side in the same room. There are three kinds of conferencing systems: document conferencing, application sharing, and video conferencing.[38] The key similarity across all three is that time and space don't matter when it comes to getting work done. No matter where people are, conferencing systems allow them to work together.

**Document conferencing**, also called "white boarding," allows two or more people to use computers to simultaneously view and make comments about a document. **Application sharing** takes document conferencing several steps further by allowing two or more people in different locations to actually make changes in a document by sharing control of the software application running on one computer. Here's how it works. A lawyer in Chicago and her client, a business person in San Francisco, are making the final changes on a contract for the business person's company. Step one: The lawyer and the business person talk on the phone while they work. Step two: Both use a second phone line or a company network to connect their computers as they talk. Step three: The lawyer opens the contract in word processing software and then starts the application sharing software. (Several companies make this software: Netscape's Conference, **http://www.netscape.com/** and Microsoft's NetMeeting, **http://www.microsoft.com/windows/netmeeting/**. Seconds later, the first page of the contract appears on the lawyer's computer in Chicago, and a few seconds after that, it appears on the business person's computer in San Francisco. Now both can make changes to the document. For example, the lawyer could change $5,000 to $50,000 on the first page while the business person is correcting a misspelling on page 20.[39] As the changes are being made, the computers communicate the changes over the phone line or network, so that both parties can work on identical versions of the file at all times.

There are numerous advantages to application sharing. Companies save an enormous amount of money and time by eliminating or reducing travel. Rather than holding a meeting to talk about proposed changes and then making them, the changes are made instantly. Therefore, there are no follow-up notes, emails, or faxes to make sure that agreed-on changes actually get made. Beyond the initial cost of the software, the only expense is for long-distance phone calls. Even that can be eliminated if both parties have fast enough systems to use the Internet to transmit their phone calls. Unlike videoconferencing, which is discussed next, document sharing runs well over standard phone lines. Thus, most companies and business people can use it now without having to invest funds for additional equipment.

167

**desktop videoconferencing**
communications system that allows two or more people in different locations to use video cameras and computer monitors to see and hear each other and share documents

**Desktop videoconferencing** allows two or more people in different locations to use video cameras and computer monitors to see and hear each other and to share documents. Unlike application sharing, desktop videoconferencing does not work well over regular phone lines. For adequate transmission of audio and video, participants need access to a high-speed network or high-speed connection to the Internet. All participants also need to place an audio microphone and a small inexpensive video camera on top of their personal computer. As shown in Exhibit 5.5, a participant in a desktop videoconference sees (and hears) live pictures of other participants. Also, like document sharing, participants can see the files they are sharing. While desktop videoconferencing is more expensive and harder to make work than application sharing, companies with high-speed networks should have few problems taking advantage of this technology.

### 4.2 Internal Access and Sharing

Two kinds of information technology are used by executives, managers, and workers inside the company to access and share information: executive information systems and intranets. An **executive information system (EIS)** uses internal and external sources of data to provide managers and executives the information they need to monitor and analyze organizational performance.[40] The goal of an EIS is to provide accurate, complete, relevant, and timely information to managers.

**executive information system (EIS)**
data processing system that uses internal and external data sources to provide the information needed to monitor and analyze organizational performance

For example, with the click of a mouse, senior and middle managers at United Cigar Stores can pull up graphs and charts of weekly and monthly sales on their computers to see if they're on target. If they're not, they can "drill down" for more information to help them figure out whether the problem is at the divisional, regional, or district level. The managers can look at charts and graphs of data for each of the company's 476 stores. Data can even be cross-referenced, looking at how, for example, various products (cigars, pipe tobacco, or cigarettes) sell in particular stores (hotel shops versus malls) or areas (Vancouver, Toronto, etc.).[41]

Since most managers are not computer experts, EISs must be easy to use and must provide information that managers want and need. Consequently, most EIS programs use touch screens, "point and click" commands, and easy-to-understand displays, such as color graphs, charts, and written summaries so that little learning or computer experience is required. In addition, basic commands such as *find, compare,* and *show* allow

| 168 | *EXHIBIT 5.5* |

DESKTOP VIDEOCONFERENCING

© R.W. JONES/CORBIS

# BlastFromThePast

## The History of Managing Information

The earliest recorded use of written information occurred nearly 60,000 years ago when Cro-Magnons, from whom modern humans descended, created and recorded a lunar calendar. The calendar consisted of 28 symbols carved into a reindeer antler and indicated when the waters would be high. The calendar was used to track

and kill deer, bison, and elk that would gather at river crossings.

For most of recorded history, information has been costly, difficult to obtain, and slow to spread. Because of the immense labor and time it took to hand-copy information, books, manuscripts, and written documents of any kind were rare and extremely expensive. Word of Joan of Arc's death in 1431 took 18 months to travel from France across Europe to Constantinople (now Istanbul, Turkey). Most people literally heard news and information from the town crier (Hear ye, Hear ye!) or from minstrel and acting groups who relayed information as they traveled from town to town. There were no newspapers. The average person could not read or write.

However, accurate, timely, relevant, and complete information has been important to businesses throughout history. Indeed, 99 percent of the stone tablets and animal-skin documents unearthed in our earliest cities were business and economic texts. Why? Because traders, crafts people, and local business people have always needed some way to keep track of trades, orders, and how much money (or gold, pigs, or chickens) was owed to whom. Consequently, businesses have pushed for and quickly adopted new information technologies that reduce the cost or increase the speed with which they can acquire, store, retrieve, or communicate information.

The first "technologies" to revolutionize the business use of information were paper and the printing press. In the 14th century, water-powered machines were created to pulverize rags into pulp to make paper. Paper prices, which were already cheaper than animal-skin parchments, quickly dropped by 400 percent. Less than a half-century later, Johannes Gutenberg invented the printing press, which greatly reduced the price and time needed to copy written information. For instance, in 1483 in Florence, Italy, a scribe would charge one florin (then, an Italian unit of money) to hand-copy one document page. By contrast, it would cost just three florins to have a printer set up and print 1,025 copies of the same document. Within 50 years of its invention, Gutenberg's printing press cut the cost of information by 1,000 percent!

What Gutenberg's printing press did for publishing, the manual typewriter did for daily communication. Before 1850, most business correspondence was written by hand and copied using the "letter press." With the ink still wet, the letter would be placed into a tissue paper "book." A hand press would then be used to squeeze the "book" and copy the still-wet ink onto tissue paper. By the 1870s, manual typewriters made it cheaper, easier, and faster to produce and copy business correspondence. Of course, in the 1980s, slightly more than a century later, typewriters were replaced by personal computers and word processing software for identical reasons.

The decreased cost and widespread use of printed information produced a growing need to organize and make sense of the explosion of information that overwhelmed the typical business. The cash register, invented in 1879, kept sales clerks honest by recording all sales transactions on a roll of paper securely locked inside the machine. But managers soon realized that its most important contribution was better management and control of their business. For example, department stores could track performance and sales by installing separate cash registers in the food, clothing, and hardware departments.

Time clocks, introduced in the 1890s, helped businesses keep track of worker hours and costs. Vertical file cabinets and the Woodruff file, invented in 1868, represented major advances in information storage and retrieval. Once sales orders or business correspondence were put in the proper file drawer, they could easily and quickly be found by anyone familiar with the system.

Finally, businesses have always looked for information technologies that would speed access to timely information. For instance, the Medici family, which opened banks throughout Europe in the early 1400s, used posting messengers to keep in contact with their more than 40 "branch" managers. The post messengers, who predate the U.S. Postal Service Pony Express by 400 years, could travel 90 miles per day, twice what average riders could cover, because the Medicis were willing to pay for the expense of providing them with fresh horses.

**Sources:** J. Burke, *The Day the Universe Changed* (Boston: Little, Brown & Company, 1985). S. Lubar, *Infoculture: The Smithsonian Book of Information Age Inventions* (Boston: Houghton, Mifflin, 1993). M. Rothschild, "Cro-Magnon's Secret Weapon," *Forbes ASAP: A Technology Supplement* 2 (13 September 1993): 19.

managers to easily and quickly get the information they need to make good decisions. Claim service managers at AIG, an insurance company, use their EIS, which they call their "dashboard," to see how well the company is running. With just a few mouse clicks, the EIS shows them costs, sales revenues, and other kinds of data displayed in color-coded charts and graphs. Managers can drill down to view data by region, state, time period, and kind of insurance coverage. Kevin Murray, CIO for AIG's claims service division, said, "From the perspective of an underwriter, adjuster, or upper-level executive, you can manipulate the information, juxtapose it, and change it any way you

**EXHIBIT 5.6**

CHARACTERISTICS OF BEST-SELLING EXECUTIVE INFORMATION SYSTEMS

### EASE OF USE

- **Few commands to learn.** Simply drag-and-drop or point-and-click to create charts and tables or get the information you need.
- **Important views saved.** Need to see weekly sales by store every Monday? Save that "view" of the data, and it will automatically be updated with new data every week.
- **3-D charts to display data.** Column, square, pie, ring, line, area, scatter, bar, cube, etc.
- **Geographic dimensions.** Different geographic areas are automatically color-coded for easy understanding.

### ANALYSIS OF INFORMATION

- **Sales tracking.** Track sales performance by product, region, account, and channel.
- **Easy-to-understand displays.** Information is displayed in tabular and graphical charts.
- **Time periods.** Data can be analyzed by current year, prior year, year to date, quarter to date, and month to date.

### IDENTIFICATION OF PROBLEMS AND EXCEPTIONS

- **Compare to standards.** Compares actual company performance (actual expenses versus planned expenses, or actual sales by sales quotas).
- **Trigger exceptions.** Allows users to set triggers (5 percent over budget, 3 percent under sales quota), which then highlights negative exceptions in red and positive exceptions in green.
- **Drill down.** Once exceptions have been identified, users can drill down for more information to determine why the exception is occurring.
- **Detect & alert newspaper.** When things go wrong, the EIS delivers a "newspaper" via email to alert managers to problems. The newspaper offers an intuitive interface for easily navigating and further analyzing the alert content.
- **Detect & alert robots.** Detect & alert robots keep an extra "eye" out for events and problems. Want to keep an eye out for news about one of your competitors? Use a news robot to track stories on Dow Jones News Retrieval. Robots can also be used to track stock quotes, internal databases, and email messages.

**Sources:** "Business Intelligence: Overview: Enterprise Services from Pilot Software," Accrue Software. [Online] Available http://www.pilotsw.com/Products/Accrue_Pilot_Suite/business_intelligence.html, 9 February 2002. Comshare home page. [Online] Available http://www.comshare.com/, February 2002.

**intranets**
private company networks that allow employees to easily access, share, and publish information using Internet software

**freeware**
computer software that is free to whoever wants it

**shareware**
computer software that you can try before you buy, but if you keep it beyond the trial period, usually 30 days, you must buy it

want. From a workflow perspective it saves time on both the business and IT end."[42] Exhibit 5.6 describes the capabilities of two of the best-selling products that companies use for EIS programs.

**Intranets** are private company networks that allow employees to easily access, share, and publish information using Internet software. Intranet Web sites are just like external Web sites, but the firewall separating the internal company network from the Internet only permits authorized internal access.[43] At Geffen Records, employees can pull up phone lists, schedules, news, and the release dates for new CDs. At Boeing, employees can access messages from top company leadership, information bulletins, and the doctor and hospital directory wherever they live. Boeing's Intranet also helps its engineers work together to design planes wherever they're located. At Turner Entertainment Group, employees can access information about CNN, the Cartoon Network, and the company newsletter; do company research; file expense reports; order supplies; and change their health insurance provider.[44]

Intranets are exploding in popularity. In 1995, the Business Research Group estimated that only 11 percent of midsize-to-large companies were using intranets.[45] Today, more than 80 percent have their own intranets.[46] The reasons for this phenomenal growth, as shown in Exhibit 5.7, are many. First, executive information systems can cost as much as several hundred thousand dollars to install for a small group of managers. In comparison, Intranets, which can be used by everyone in the company, are inexpensive. Much of the software required to set up an Intranet is either **freeware** (no cost) or **shareware** (try before you buy, usually less expensive than commercial software).

EXHIBIT 5.7

## WHY 80 PERCENT OF COMPANIES NOW USE INTRANETS

1. Intranets are inexpensive.
2. Intranets increase efficiencies and reduce costs.
3. Intranets are intuitive and easy to use (Web-based).
4. Intranets work across all computer systems and platforms (Web-based).
5. Intranets can be built on top of existing computer network.
6. Intranets work with software programs that easily convert electronic documents to HTML files for intranet use.

Second, intranets reduce costs, increase efficiencies, and save organizations money. General Electric expects to save $1.6 billion this year from using its intranet to purchase office supplies, handle reimbursement forms, and displace the millions of paper-based forms its 340,000 employees use each year.[47] With 1,000 internal Web sites and more than two million pages of information, Microsoft probably has one of the most advanced and used intranets in the world, with one third of its 30,000 employees using it every day. In fact, MSWeb, Microsoft's intranet, is so advanced, that nearly all company paperwork, forms, and paper documents have been moved onto it.[48]

Third, using Intranets is intuitive and easy. Point your cursor over a word or symbol that you're interested in. If the cursor turns from an arrow into a hand, indicating that the word or symbol is a link to further information, then click it. Presto! The information you want appears on the screen. That's all there is to it. As a result, companies are rushing to put as much information as they can on their Intranets. Indeed, a study of 323 companies in 10 different industries found that 23 percent of company intranets contained information on company benefits; 18 percent have information about savings plans, profit sharing, or company stock plans; 70 percent have information about jobs; 6 percent allow managers to conduct performance appraisals online; 24 percent are used for training; and 57 percent are used for corporate communications.[49]

Fourth, it doesn't matter if the people in marketing use the Macintosh operating system, the finance folks use Windows, and the information systems people use Unix systems—everyone can easily access information if it's available on the company intranet.[50] Intranets work across all kinds of computers and computer operating systems.

Fifth, if you already have a computer network in place, chances are your company already has the computer equipment and expertise to quickly and easily roll out an intranet.

Sixth, while it's not seamless, many software programs easily convert electronic documents from proprietary word processing (Word Perfect, Microsoft Word, etc.), spreadsheet (Lotus 1-2-3, Microsoft Excel), or graphics (Lotus Freelance or Microsoft PowerPoint) formats to the hypertext markup language (HTML) used to display text and graphics on the Internet and Intranets. Indeed, many HTML software editors are now as easy to use as word processors. So when employees have information that others in the company want access to, HTML editors make it easy to publish information on the company Intranet for all to see. Boeing's Intranet contains everything from corporate-policy material to maintenance manuals, and Boeing encourages its employees to publish any information that others might find useful.[51]

### 4.3 External Access and Sharing

Historically, companies have been unable or reluctant to let outside groups have access to corporate information. However, three information technologies—electronic data interchange, extranets, and the Internet—are making it easier to share company data with external groups like suppliers and customers. They're also the reducing costs, increasing

**electronic data interchange (EDI)**
the direct electronic transmission of purchase and ordering information from one company's computer system to another company's computer system

productivity, improving customer service, and speeding communications. As a result, managers are scrambling to find ways to use them in their own companies.

**Electronic data interchange,** or **EDI,** is the direct electronic transmission of purchase and ordering information from one company's computer system to another company's computer system. For example, when a Wal-Mart checkout clerk drags a CD across the checkout scanner, Wal-Mart's computerized inventory system automatically reorders another copy of that CD through the direct EDI connection that its computer has with the manufacturing and shipping computer at the company that published the CD, say Atlantic Records. No one at Wal-Mart or Atlantic Records fills out paperwork. No one makes phone calls. There are no delays to wait to find out whether Atlantic has the CD in stock. The transaction takes place instantly and automatically.

EDI saves companies money by eliminating step after step of manual information processing. One study found that EDI could save manufacturing companies $18 per transaction, retail companies $23 per transaction, and wholesalers $11 per transaction.[52] Of course, those are just averages. Some companies save more. R.J. Reynolds, which deals with more than 1,400 suppliers and tens of thousands of orders per year, said that EDI reduced the cost of orders from between $75 and $125 to just 93 cents![53] And when you consider that 70 percent of the data output from one company, like a purchase order, ends up as data input at another company, such as a sales invoice or shipping order, EDI also reduces data entry errors. Finally, EDI reduces order and delivery times. Hotel and motel chains like Marriott and Hilton have found that EDI has reduced the average time for food and beverage orders to their kitchens by half, from six days to three days.[54]

**extranet**
allows companies to exchange information and conduct transactions with outsiders by providing them direct, Web-based access to authorized parts of a company's intranet or information system

While EDI directly transmits information from one company's computer system to another's, an **extranet,** by contrast, allows companies to exchange information and conduct transactions with outsiders by providing them direct, Web-based access to authorized parts of a company's intranet or information system. Typically, user names and passwords are required to access an extranet.[55] For example, to make sure that its distribution trucks don't waste money by running half empty (or produce late deliveries to customers because it waited to ship until its trucks were full), General Mills uses an extranet to provide Web-based access to its trucking database to 20 other companies that ship their products over similar distribution routes. When other companies are ready to ship products, they log on to General Mills' trucking database, check the availability, and then enter the shipping load, place, and pickup time. Thus, by sharing shipping capacity on its trucks, General Mills' trucks run fully loaded all the time. In several test areas, General Mills saved 7 percent on shipping costs, or nearly $2 million in the first year. Cost savings will be even larger when the program is expanded company-wide.[56]

**Internet**
a global network of networks that allows users to send and retrieve data from anywhere in the world

Similar to the way in which extranets are used to handle transactions with suppliers and distributors, companies are reducing paperwork and manual information processing by using the Internet to electronically automate transactions with customers. The **Internet** is a global network of networks that allows users to send and retrieve data from anywhere in the world. Companies like Southwest Airlines (**http://www.iflyswa.com**), United Airlines (**http://www.ual.com**), and American Airlines (**http://www.aa.com**), as well as independent travel sites like Microsoft Expedia (**http://expedia.com**), have Internet sites where customers can purchase tickets without calling a ticket agent or the airline's toll-free number. However, most airlines have further automated the ticketing process by eliminating tickets altogether. Simply buy an e-ticket via the Internet and then show the airport ticket agent your driver's license or passport. The ticket agent then checks the database, confirms your e-ticket, issues you your boarding pass, and you're on your way. Together, Internet purchases and ticketless travel have the potential to fully automate the purchase of airline tickets. By eliminating the recording, printing, handling, and mailing costs of tickets and the commission that would have been paid to travel agents, the airlines save an estimated $25 to $35 per ticket.[57]

Transportation and logistics are one area where extranets can be very effective. General Mills uses its extranet to organize its distribution system and realizes great savings as a result.

© WALTER HODGES/GETTY IMAGES/STONE

In the long run, the goal is to link customer Internet sites with company intranets (or EDI) and extranets so that everyone—all the employees and managers within a company, and the suppliers and distributors outside the company—who is involved in providing a service or making a product for a customer is automatically notified when a purchase is made. For instance, Mexico-based Cemex SA, one of the largest cement companies in the world, uses electronic linkages between its customers (via the Internet), its cement plants and its main control room for cement production (via intranet or EDI), and its deliveries (via an extranet). David Bovet, a management consultant, said, "They are able to deliver ready-mix concrete to a construction site within a 20-minute window with 98 percent reliability. Cemex is differentiating itself in an industry that typically works with a three-hour commitment and 34 percent reliability."[58]

So, in the end, why should companies try to connect Internet sites for customers to company intranets, EDIs, and extranets? Because companies that use information technologies in these ways achieve increases in productivity 2.7 times larger than those that don't.[59] For more on the payoffs associated with connecting intranets, extranets, and the Internet, read the *Been There, Done That* interview with Mark Hoffman, CEO of Commerce One.

### 4.4 Sharing Knowledge and Expertise

At the beginning of the chapter, we distinguished between raw data, which consists of facts and figures, and information, which consists of useful data that influences someone's choices and behavior. One more important distinction needs to be made, namely, that data and information are not the same as knowledge. **Knowledge** is the understanding that one gains from information. Importantly, knowledge does not reside in information. Knowledge resides in people. That's why companies hire consultants or why family doctors refer patients to specialists. Unfortunately, it can be quite expensive to employ consultants, specialists, and experts. So companies have begun using two information technologies, decision-support systems and expert systems, to capture and share the knowledge of consultants, specialists, and experts with other managers and workers.

Unlike executive information systems that speed up and simplify the acquisition of information, **decision support systems (DSS)** help managers understand problems and

**knowledge**
the understanding that one gains from information

**decision support system (DSS)**
an information system that helps managers to understand specific kinds of problems and potential solutions and to analyze the impact of different decision options using "what if" scenarios

173

# BeenThereDoneThat

**Business-to-Business Information Exchanges: Why Their Time Has Come**

In this interview, Mark Hoffman, CEO of Commerce One, supplier of business-to-business information exchange software and services, describes the payoffs that companies can earn from creating a supply chain which connects their customers to the Internet, their suppliers and distributors to an extranet, and their managers and employees to an intranet.

**Q:** What are the ramifications of improving the supply chain?

**A:** Well, a lot of [supply chain management] is not very automated today. You know, purchase orders are still a paper process within a lot of companies. The conversion of bill of materials to purchase orders to automatic orders is really not that automated. EDI [electronic data interchange, a system connecting suppliers and buyers that predates the Internet] has added value, but only small parts [of the supply chain can be automated]. An example of this would be at GM. They send out orders over EDI, but it's only an outgoing signal; they don't get signals back via EDI. So all of that has to happen manually with paper and phones.

GM or Ford could save by just automating that process. And then when you look at longer term, basically the ability to shorten supply chain cycles, that's a ways away now. But as you do that, you start to get more reliability into the supply chain itself. Some of the estimates that have been made about being able to suck out excess inventory [within the auto industry supply chain] have been measured at $100 billion.

**Q:** Even before the Web, didn't U.S. companies make a lot of improvements in making their inventory systems more efficient?

**A:** Well, I think there are a lot of inefficiencies left. All the automation that went on in the '90s and the '80s involved people who were just trying to automate themselves within their own company. OK, now we've done a lot of that. And some of that is more efficient, quite frankly. But purchasing wasn't one of the areas they attacked in that efficiency. So we've got to get that purchasing more efficient. And you've got to get more efficiency in your inter-company communications, between divisions of your company, between your buyers/suppliers, between your partners.

**Q:** So what's different now that will make possible this extra savings?

**A:** The Internet is the lower-cost infrastructure that allows communication at a cheaper level than it's ever been before. Before the Internet, there wasn't any good vehicle that allowed universal communication. The Internet has now become that vehicle. So the infrastructure [costs are] lower. And [earlier on] there were no tools to help do [inter-company communications]. Now moving into the marketplace is a whole set of tools that allow collaboration and all these things to go on that they never had before.

**Q:** Do you think the industries like automobiles can save as much as you say they can?

**A:** I think so. I was on a panel with Phil Condit from Boeing, and he was just saying that one of the things they're looking at is the transaction cost of doing business. And so he's sensitized all of his managers to understand what the transaction cost is. He said if [he could] drive down the transaction cost, then [he could] lower his whole infrastructure cost by a huge amount. He said, "If you'd met one of my managers a year ago and asked what the transaction cost was, the guy would have said, 'What are you talking about?' Today the guy could probably tell you."

**Source:** L. Gomes, "E-Commerce (A Special Report): Case by Case, Words from a Believer: An Advocate of B-To-B Exchanges Explains Why He Thinks Their Time Will Come," *The Wall Street Journal*, 21 May 2001, R21.

potential solutions by acquiring and analyzing information with sophisticated models and tools.[60] Furthermore, unlike EIS programs that are broad in scope and permit managers to retrieve all kinds of information about a company, DSS programs are usually narrow in scope and targeted toward helping managers solve specific kinds of problems. DSS programs have been developed to help managers pick the shortest and most efficient routes for delivery trucks, to pick the best combination of stocks for investors, and to schedule the flow of inventory through complex manufacturing facilities.

It's important to understand that DSS programs don't replace managerial decision making; they improve it by furthering managers' and workers' understanding of the problems they face and the solutions that might work. For example, Apache Medical Systems (now owned by Cerner Corporation) makes a DSS for emergency room physicians.[61] Apache's DSS collects data on 17 different physiological signs, like blood pressure, respiratory rates, temperature, white blood counts, etc. Then, using a database containing the medical records of more than 400,000 people (with 100 diseases) who received treatment at more than 200 different emergency rooms, Apache's DSS gives a diagnosis and then rates the chances of a patient's survival using various treatment procedures. For a patient with heart problems, the Apache DSS would create a graph showing the likelihood (from zero to 100 percent) of surviving five more years, depending on whether the patient had coronary bypass surgery, an angioplasty, or drug treatment.

Apache's DSS also helps physicians analyze the impact of different decision options by using "What if?" scenarios. The ability to analyze "What if" scenarios is a key capability of all DSS systems. *What if* we continue with our current strategy, would that work? *What if* we tried something else? Apache's DSS helps physicians pose and answer "*What if* ?" questions by processing the latest information regarding a patient's health status three times a day and then printing out an unbiased, statistically-based estimate of whether a given treatment is working. For example, if a nurse receives two printouts, one in the morning, and then another in the afternoon, indicating that a patient's chances of survival have dropped from 75 percent to 55 percent, the nurse has a very good reason to contact the doctor to reconsider treatment options. Apache is not only helping doctors save lives, but it is also giving doctors the confidence to move patients out of intensive care earlier. With intensive care costs running about $2,500 a day, Apache helps the University of Michigan's Medical Center save $2.5 million a year in unnecessary treatments.[62]

**Expert systems** are created by capturing the specialized knowledge and decision rules used by experts and experienced decision makers. They permit nonexpert employees to draw on this expert knowledge base to make decisions. For example, when two companies draw up a contract, it usually takes at least two lawyers, one for each company. However, at Nynex, which is the phone company for New York City, company purchasing agents are drafting long-term, multimillion dollar contracts without using lawyers. Instead, they use an expert system designed and created by company lawyers to automate the creation of company contracts. Step 1: Choose from a menu of 20 types of contracts. Step 2: Answer 25 to 35 questions designed to fill out the contract details and to choose the right legal language and protection for the company. With the expert system, it takes an average of half an hour to complete and print a standard multimillion dollar contract. Without the expert system, the same contract took four hours of a purchasing manager's time, four hours of word processing, and two hours of an attorney's time. One of the managers who uses the expert system said, "I can just go bing, bam, boom, and it's done. My manager can feel confident that we've got all of the bases covered with each of the [legal] clauses."[63]

Most expert systems work by using a collection of "if-then" rules to sort through information and recommend a course of action. For example, let's say that you're using your American Express card to help your spouse celebrate a promotion. You buy dinner, and then some movie tickets. After the movie, you and your spouse stroll by a travel office that displays a Las Vegas poster in its window. Thirty minutes later, caught up in the moment, you find yourselves at the airport ticket counter trying to purchase last-minute tickets to Vegas. But there's just one problem. American Express didn't approve your purchase. In fact, the ticket counter agent is on the phone with an American Express customer service agent.

So what put a temporary halt to your weekend escape to Vegas? An expert system that American Express calls "Authorizer's Assistant." The first "if-then" rule that prevented your purchase was the rule "*if* a purchase is much larger than the cardholder's regular spending habits, *then* deny approval of the purchase." This rule is built into American Express's transaction-processing system that handles thousands of purchase requests per second. Now that the American Express customer service agent is on the line, he or she is prompted by the Authorizer's Assistant to ask the ticket counter agent to examine your identification. You hand over your driver's license and another credit card to prove you're you. Then the ticket agent asks for your address, phone number, social security number, and your mother's maiden name, and relays the information to American Express. Finally, your ticket purchase is approved. Why? Because you met the last series of "if-then" rules. *If* the purchaser can provide proof of identity and *if* the purchaser can provide personal information that isn't common knowledge, *then* approve the purchase.

## Review 4
### Accessing and Sharing Information and Knowledge

Email, voice messaging, and conferencing systems are changing how we communicate and work with each other. Email is cheap, fast, and easy to use. Though also easy to use, voice messages take more time to process than email. Application sharing and document and video conferencing let people in different locations work as if they were together in the same room. Executive information systems and Intranets facilitate internal sharing and access to company information. Electronic data interchange and the Internet allow external groups, like suppliers and customers, to easily access company information. Both decrease costs by reducing or eliminating data entry, data errors, and paperwork, and by speeding up communication. Organizations use decision support systems and expert systems to capture and share specialized knowledge with nonexpert employees.

## What Really Happened?

At the beginning of the chapter, you learned about the phenomenal success that Dell Computers achieved in the first decade and a half of its existence. In fact, *Fortune* magazine speculated that Dell might be the company of the decade. With its incredible early success, you might be surprised to learn that Dell has completely changed its strategy. On the other hand, it might not surprise you to know that Dell's completely different strategy revolves around the strategic use of information technology. Let's find out what really happened at Dell Computers as it used information technology to deal with the fierce competition and incredibly fast pace of the personal computer industry.

**With PC prices dropping so quickly and technological advances moving so fast, the key is no longer just building a better PC, but quickly building a PC with the latest technological components at an aggressive price. However, doesn't that mean that Dell and its memory, hard drive, chip, and motherboard suppliers will have to work more closely (i.e., share more information) than they**

**ever have before? How can that be done?**

Historically, companies have been unable or reluctant to let outside groups have access to corporate information. However, information technologies such as electronic data interchange, extranets, and the Internet are not only making it easier to share company data with external groups like suppliers and customers, they're also reducing costs, raising productivity, improving customer service, and speeding communications.

Indeed, Michael Dell says that, "One of the big changes that is brought about by information technology is that the cost of connections and linkages has gone down dramatically. So if you've got an operation that builds a component, the cost to communicate with that operation in an information sense, if it is done electronically, goes to zero. That means you can build a linkage between a components supplier and a manufacturer and make it very, very efficient." For example, Dell has direct information connections with its main suppliers of computer components (chips, hard drives, memory, etc.). It provides continuous

updates to those suppliers on its costs (for selling a PC to you and me), and in return receives continuous updates from its suppliers. Dell has even set up Internet portals (think of Yahoo.com) to enable suppliers to check on inventories, customer purchases, and so forth. In short, Dell took most of the information that it received from customers or generated internally and shared it with suppliers. Sharing all of this information is the equivalent of an early warning system that lets Dell and its suppliers know when prices are rising or falling, or what computer components are in or out of demand. The result is that Dell and its suppliers are closer to the PC market and its changes than any of its competitors.

**And if Dell and its suppliers can figure out how to do that, won't that mean that its competitors can do the same thing? Why invest in an information system if it only gives you a temporary competitive advantage? If your competitors can buy the same inventory and customer tracking software that you have, you're only temporarily ahead of the game.**

Why invest in an information system if it only gives you a temporary competitive advantage? Well, one reason to do so is to keep from falling behind your competition. But when most companies invest in information technology, they're hoping to create a first-mover advantage by being the first in an industry to use new information technology to substantially lower costs or to differentiate a product or service from competitors. However, creating a first-mover advantage can be difficult, expensive, and risky. Sometimes it fails. But it can succeed, if information technology adds value, is different across firms, and is difficult for other firms to create or acquire. Furthermore, faster computers, more memory, and larger hard drives are not the key to sustaining a competitive advantage that you created through information technology. The key is using information technology to continuously improve and support the core functions of a business. This is precisely what Dell Computers has done.

At Dell, because of the instantaneous, direct flow of information from customers (who buy PCs from the Dell Web site or its 1-800 phone line) to suppliers, Dell has no finished goods inventory. In other words, it doesn't have two-month-old hard drives sitting around its factories waiting to be installed in your newly ordered PC. In fact, the hard drive installed in a Dell PC is probably no more than a week old, and the hard drive manufacturer doesn't send it to Dell's factory until you order it. This ensures that Dell PCs have only the latest and newest technological components. And, since prices tend to fall as technologies mature, this also ensures that Dell pays the lowest costs for those components. In fact, because you pay for that PC before Dell orders its components and before Dell has to pay its suppliers, it literally has your cash for eight free days *before* booking the profit on your order. This also allows Dell to cut PC prices much faster than its competitors. A company spokesperson said, "Our flexibility allows us to be [priced] different even within a day." The results from this approach

have been nothing short of amazing. Dell's market share has grown from 6 percent of the PC market five years ago to 25 percent today. Competitors, such as Micron Electronics, which had been in the PC business for nearly two decades, find it difficult to compete. In fact, Micron has left the PC business altogether.

So why should companies seek first-mover advantage? Because, on average, first movers earn 30 percent market share compared to 19 percent for companies that follow. Moreover, over 70 percent of today's market leaders, like Dell Computers, started as first movers.

**Finally, in such a fast-moving, competitive environment, if information is the key, how is Dell to make sense of all of the information it generates from customers, uses within the company, and then shares with its suppliers? Having lots of data doesn't do you any good unless you know how to figure out what they mean. So what should Dell do with all that information once it gets its hands on it?**

Processing information means transforming raw data into meaningful information that can be applied to business decision making. Unfortunately, with automated, electronic capture of data, increased processing power, and cheaper and more plentiful ways to store data, managers have more data than they could ever imagine. The key is not getting data, but figuring out how to turn the overwhelming amount of data that pours into their businesses into meaningful information that can improve decision making. One promising tool to help managers dig out from under the avalanche of data is data mining. Data mining is the process of discovering unknown patterns and relationships in large amounts of data. Most managers need only to know that data mining looks for patterns that are already in the data but are too complex for them to spot on their own.

Most PC manufacturers have access to much of the same data that Dell

Computers does. Dell, however, uses and analyzes those data differently. Most PC makers determine computer prices by making sales estimates about how many PCs would sell in a particular quarter. Then, moving backward from the sales estimates, they determine sales prices and then what they're willing to pay for computer components like hard drives and memory chips. Factory production, in turn, is also based on those sales estimates. But woe to the company that gets the sales estimates wrong. Build too many computers and you're going to lose millions of dollars trying to sell older, more expensive, technologically out-of-date computers. By contrast, Dell doesn't estimate sales at all. Instead, because it relies on actual sales before ordering PC parts, and not sales estimates, it completely removes the possibility of getting sales estimates wrong. This allows Dell to carry almost no inventory in its factories, and thus almost no inventory costs. Over the last five years, Dell has used the information available from its "build-to-order" system to shrink inventory levels from 31 days of on-hand inventory down to just seven days of inventory. The result is that Dell's fixed overhead costs are just 11.5 cents per sales dollar, compared to 16 cents for Gateway, 21 cents for Compaq, and 22.5 cents for Hewlett-Packard.

**Sources:** C. Lydgate, "Cutting Out the Middle Man," *Asian Business*, 1 May 1998, 12. G. McWilliams, "Dell's New Push: Cheaper Laptops Built to Order," *The Wall Street Journal*, 17 June 1999, B1. G. McWilliams, "Boss Talk: Dell to Detroit: Get into Gear Online! PC Whiz Advises Auto Makers Web Is Best Venue to Handle Suppliers, Serve Customers," *The Wall Street Journal*, 1 December 1999, B1. G. McWilliams, "How Dell Fine Tunes Its PC Pricing to Gain Edge in a Slow Market: Working with Suppliers, It Quickly Passes Changes in Costs to Customers, Three Prices for One Product," *The Wall Street Journal*, 8 June 2001, A1. A. Serwer, L. Smith, & P. de Llosa, "Michael Dell Rocks: Actually, He's Plain Vanilla." *Fortune*, May 1998, 58.

177

## Key Terms

| | | |
|---|---|---|
| acquisition cost *(156)* | electronic scanner *(159)* | processing cost *(156)* |
| application sharing *(167)* | executive information system *(168)* | processing information *(159)* |
| association/affinity patterns *(161)* | expert systems *(175)* | protecting information *(162)* |
| bar code *(158)* | extranets *(172)* | raw data *(151)* |
| communication cost *(157)* | firewall *(162)* | retrieval cost *(156)* |
| conferencing system *(167)* | first-mover advantage *(152)* | sequence patterns *(161)* |
| data clusters *(161)* | freeware *(170)* | shareware *(170)* |
| data encryption *(164)* | information *(151)* | storage cost *(156)* |
| data mining *(159)* | Internet *(172)* | supervised data mining *(161)* |
| data warehouse *(161)* | intranets *(170)* | unsupervised data mining *(161)* |
| decision support system (DSS) *(173)* | knowledge *(173)* | virtual private network *(164)* |
| desktop videoconferencing *(168)* | Moore's law *(150)* | virus *(164)* |
| document conferencing *(167)* | optical character recognition *(159)* | |
| electronic data interchange (EDI) *(172)* | predictive patterns *(161)* | |

## What Would You Do-II

### Wegmans's Information Dilemma

As the president of Wegmans, a Rochester, New York-based grocer, acquiring and using information is nothing new to you and your firm. In order to gain and sustain a competitive advantage, you and your managers need to analyze sales, revenue, and cost data in a timely manner to make informed decisions. The problem is that by the time your IT staff receives the end-of-the-month data from each of the 76 stores, inputs the data into the more than 2,000 financial spreadsheet templates, and generates appropriate reports, the information is more than a week old. To complicate matters further, some of the data received from each of your stores cannot easily be compared to sister stores because each store utilizes stand-alone transactional processing systems. For example, each store has its own point-of-sale (POS) system (an infrared device that reads the bar code on the items sold in your stores) that feeds a database containing sales, cost, and inventory information. In addition to the POS system, each store also maintains separate databases containing consumer demographics, payroll, and order processing/distribution from the company's network of warehouses. When store managers finally receive their individual store reports, they are overly detailed and typically incomprehensible. In order to help interpret the reports, you currently have a team of 15 financial analysts on staff who assist managers in weeding through the mounds of data and help them extract relevant information to answer basic questions, such as "Why did produce sales for store #26 decrease by 3 percent last month?" Due to the problems mentioned above, store managers are constantly requesting more information that is timely, accurate, and relevant so that they can make better decisions regarding their individual stores. **As the president of Wegmans, what would you do to fulfill your store managers' requests?**

**Sources:** M. Nannery, "Wegmans Informed Decisions," *Chain Store Age*, May 2000. A. Benander, "Data Warehouse Administration and Management," *Information Systems Management*, Winter.

## Management Decisions

### Lease or Buy?

It has been over four years since your company last upgraded any of its computers or peripherals. Unfortunately, system outages and hardware malfunctions are beginning to disrupt worker performance. As the chief information officer (CIO) of a medium-sized accounting and consulting firm, maintaining an operational and efficient computer system is one of your main priorities. Over the last year, you have reported the need for newer computers and have presented several proposals toward upgrading the system in phases. Unfortunately, every time you broached the subject, the owner's response was "if it isn't broken, don't fix it." Now he is singing a different tune. Because of a recent system glitch, the company lost one of its biggest and oldest clients. As a result, the owner now agrees that the entire system needs to be upgraded immediately. In fact, just yesterday, he told you "to spare no expense, just buy it and have it up and running as soon as possible. We can't afford to lose another client because of our dilapidated information system."

You want to purchase machines from a name-brand, quality computer manufacturer. The previous machines, also produced by a well-known manufacturer, have only recently begun to exhibit hardware malfunctions. Therefore, due to advances in technology and improvements in quality, you reasonably expect that the new system will have a useful life of at least four years, possibly more. You have been on the phone all morning contacting vendors and requesting price quotes. All of the vendors you spoke to have similar purchase plans and most have lease arrangements. After analyzing the differences between leasing and purchasing, you have identified the advantages and disadvantages associated with each.

Although purchasing the computer system will result in a higher monthly payment compared to leasing, the units will belong to the company when paid off, a clear advantage. Additionally, the entire cost of purchasing and maintaining the computer system will be tax deductible, an element the owner will certainly approve of. The main disadvantage associated with purchasing the computer system includes having to pay for computer-related maintenance and repairs once the warranty period expires. An extended policy can be purchased to provide technical support and repairs after the warranty period; however, the monthly fee for this type of service is rather expensive. A second disadvantage associated with purchasing the computer system, one that you will soon face, is determining what to do with the old computer system. It was once common for many businesses to donate old computers to local school districts after an upgrade; however, due to recent technology initiatives within the local school system, most public schools in your area have better computers than your firm currently does. Therefore, disposing of the obsolete machines will be somewhat difficult.

The advantages of leasing a computer system include a smaller monthly payment; free 24-hour technical support and repair services; and the ability to upgrade to newer, faster machines when the lease period expires, approximately 24 months from now. Disposing of old computers is not a problem under the lease option since leased computers can be traded in on new computers when the lease expires. One of the biggest disadvantages of leasing a computer system is that it is very similar to renting. At the end of the lease period, you have two choices. Either pay a huge balloon payment and keep the two-year-old (outdated) computer system, or renew the lease and upgrade the system again. Given the owner's previous track record, you feel it will be difficult to convince the owner to upgrade the system again after only 24 months. You yourself doubt the need for replacing computers every two years since the majority of employees are currently using less than 20 percent of their computer's processing power at any given time. Additionally, after discussing the leasing option with several

accountants within the firm, one accountant informed you that certain computer leases, specifically operational leases, are not tax deductible and cannot be depreciated.

As you jot down the minimum system requirements on your legal pad, you ask yourself, should we buy or lease?

### Questions
1. Acting as the CIO mentioned above, which method would you recommend to the owner and why?
2. Go online to a well-known computer manufacturer such as Dell computers at **http://www.dell.com** or Gateway computers at **http://www.gateway.com** and compare their purchase/lease options. Reevaluate your recommendation. Did your decision change after viewing the two options? Why or why not?
3. Use the Internet Resources listed below to further your information-gathering. Once you have done all your research, review your decision again. Did it change after more extensive research? Why or why not?

### Additional Internet Resources
- Evaluate various machines by consulting several nonmarketing controlled (i.e., independent) sources of information. *Consumer Reports* (**http:www.consumerreports.com**) is an example. You may also wish to consult computer magazines like *PC World* (**http://www.pcworld.com**), *PC Magazine* (**http://www.pcmagazine.com**), and *Computer World* (**http://www.computerworld.com**). They regularly review hardware and software systems and may provide you with a more detailed analysis of the systems you are considering than you can find anywhere else.
- Consider checking shopping bots like **Gomez.com**, **MySimon.com**, and **cnet.com** and comparing features and prices. Other good price comparison tools are **PriceScan.com** and **Bizrate.com**. **Streetprices.com** is also a good resource for price shopping.
- If you're thinking of trying to get a deal, review auction sites. A popular site that specializes in electronics in **ubid.com**. Also try **http://www.pcbuyer.com** and **http://www.usauctions.com/compsub.htm**. PCCost (**http://www.pccost.com**) claims it sells computers and peripherals at cost, so check it out.
- And don't forget to check offers at retailers like Best Buy (**http://www.bestbuy.com**) and Circuit City (**http://www.circuitcity.com**). Even office supply retailers like Office Depot (**http://www.techdepot.com**) and Staples (**http://www.staples.com**) may have what you're looking for. At the very least, you will have something to compare your hot, Internet deal to!

## Management Decisions

### Hack Attack
As you clear off your desk, getting ready to leave for the night, the phone rings. The voice on the other end of the line is Sue,

your company's network administrator. She informs you that a hacker has just broken into the company's e-commerce site. One of the databases entered by the intruder contains personal customer data, including names, addresses, and credit card information. You immediately ask questions, attempting to determine the potential damage caused by this attack. According to Sue, approximately 3.3 million customer files, both past and present, could have been compromised. Upon noticing the intrusion, Sue immediately closed down the network and ordered her staff to get on the phone with the software company's technical support to begin repairing the breach. She informs you that she and her staff will do everything to repair the network and get it back online as soon as possible, but she asks about the information that might have been compromised. Should we tell someone? As the chief information officer (CIO) of Egghead.com, an Internet-based retailer, you assure her that you will notify the proper constituencies.

As you hang up the phone, you begin to calculate the different options of attempting to resolve this current problem. Attempted hacking is not new to your firm. Research shows that most well-known sites face up to five or six attempted intrusions on any given day. Unfortunately, this is the first successful attempt on Egghead.com's site. The fact that they were able to not only get in, but also enter a secure database is disturbing. Cur-

rently, Egghead.com has no policy and procedures manual to turn to when a network compromise has occurred. Questions begin to race through your mind. Do you risk notifying all of your customers, suppliers, and other stakeholders? Doing so might diminish customer confidence and result in decreased sales. Do you notify the press? Doing so would most likely advertise to would-be hackers that your site has serious security issues. You think to yourself, we might as well put up a billboard saying, "We're open, hack away."

## Questions

1. As the CIO of Egghead.com, would you alert all affected parties and inform them of the breach, or keep the information internal? What is the rationale behind your decision?
2. What policies and procedures could be implemented to keep this problem from recurring?

**Source:** M. Hicks, "Telling Customers the Bad News—When and How to Get the Word Out That Your Security's Been Breached," *eWeek*, 19 February 2001.

## Develop Your Managerial Potential

### Web Privacy Policy

With the advent of the Internet and its explosive growth, the need to protect an individual's privacy has increased dramatically in recent years. Many Internet Web sites require that personal information such as name, address, phone number(s), social security numbers, and credit card information be submitted before allowing a consumer to conduct any type of e-commerce transactions. Most Web-based companies have policies stating the extent to which this information will be used, the length of time the information will be kept, and what will happen to the information if the company folds. However, with the recent crash of many dotcoms, the industry has discovered that a significant portion of these policies are not worth the paper that they are printed on. For instance, Toysmart.com, a recent casualty of the dotcom bust, recently sought to gain approval from a bankruptcy court to auction off their database despite promising to never do so in their Web privacy policy. As more and more dotcoms fail, the opportunity to sell customer information, possibly the only tangible asset that an Internet-based firm owns, will most likely rise. One example of the detrimental effects of sensitive information being publicly released was recently observed when pharmaceutical company Eli Lilly accidentally released the email addresses of more than 600 people currently taking Prozac, a common antidepressant medication. In order to combat the problems caused by the release of sensitive and confidential information, privacy advocates are pushing for more stringent legislation to protect consumers and their personal information. In order to appease legislators and to promote self-regulation as opposed to government regulation, the Network Advertising Initiative (NAI) is proposing

several recommendations for Internet-based businesses to adopt in constructing or strengthening their privacy policies. These recommendations are as follows:

1. **The word "never" should be taken literally.** If a firm promises to never sell customer information, it should abide by its promise. Additionally, this promise should survive and remain true even if the firm's assets are parceled out as a result of bankruptcy hearings.
2. **Consumers should be given a choice.** If a firm decides to sell confidential customer information, customers should be given a choice before that information is released. Although this rule is currently being enforced through current legislation, the current privacy laws require the customer to "opt-out" if they wish their information not be released. This places the burden on the consumer to contact the retailer and inform them of their wish to keep their personal information private. Privacy advocates want the rule to be changed so that consumers must "opt-in," thereby placing the burden on retailers by requiring them to obtain the consumer's approval before information can be released.
3. **Companies should restrict the type of information disclosed.** Should a company sell information, they should limit the information disclosed to only names and addresses, typical of information found on most mailing lists. This would require companies to maintain separate databases, one for information that can be sold or disclosed, and the other, a secure database which contains more private information such as age, ethnicity, income, social security number, credit information, and so forth.

As a manager charged with constructing a privacy policy for your firm, you are instructed to visit a well-known company Web site and inspect its Web-privacy policy. As you read the policy, compare its policy with the information proposed above. What elements of its policy could be improved and what elements would you include in developing your own firm's Web-privacy policy? Using the information presented above and another firm's Web-privacy policy as a guide, draft a Web-privacy policy for your firm.

**Sources:** "Web Form Can Be Used By Consumers to Protect Privacy," *The Wall Street Journal*, 25 May 2001. P. Davidson, "Capitol Hill Support Brews for Internet Privacy Laws," *USA Today*, 12 July 2001. H. Green, "Your Right to Privacy: Going...Going...," *Business Week*, 23 April 2001.

## Study Tip

Imagine you are the professor, and make up your own test for Chapter 5. What are the main topics and key concepts that students should know? If you work with a study group, exchange practice tests. Work them individually then "grade" them collectively. This way you can discuss trouble spots and answer each other's questions.

# CHAPTER 6

# six

# Decision Making

## What Would You Do?

**London, England.** Eighty-nine cents in the United States for a gallon of gas? How could that be? Most people who pull up to the gas station for a fill-up are hoping for cheaper prices. But as head of research for British Petroleum Amoco (BP Amoco), you'd rather watch prices rise, which you certainly couldn't do with gas at 89 cents a gallon, down from $1.40 a gallon, and crude oil below $15 a barrel (down from $24 a barrel). Indeed, with gas and oil prices at their lowest level in 20 years, consumers are having a great time, driving as far and as long as they like, buying millions of tank-sized, gas-guzzling sport utility vehicles, and then pulling up to the gas pump to put 24 gallons of gas in one of those SUVs at a cost of $21.36 at 89 cents a gallon, not $33.60 at $1.40 a gallon, like they paid the year before.

While consumers love the low prices, you hate them. Because of the low prices, oil company profits have disappeared, causing oil company stock prices to drop by a third compared to the previous year. Following the stock drops were the inevitable employee layoffs to cut costs. And no matter what anybody says, laying people off is never "just business." Your top finance executive insisted that the layoffs were necessary to restore profits. Still, you took no joy in the cuts, as you

watched many long-time friends and associates leave the company. On top of that, company-wide budget cuts mean that you've got significantly less money in the oil exploration budget used to drill test wells and hopefully discover the next big reserve that will produce millions of barrels of crude oil for BP Amoco for years to come.

Ironically, these cuts come just as you were preparing to persuade top management to significantly increase its oil exploration budget for deepwater drilling. Most people know about land-based drilling, in which test wells are drilled 300 to 3,000 feet deep for oil, and offshore drilling, in which platform-based oil derricks sit in water less than 1,000 feet deep to drill 1,000 to 5,000 below the bottom of the sea floor in offshore locations like the Gulf of Mexico or the North Sea off the coast of Scotland. However, in deepwater drilling, oil companies either submerse an oil-drilling rig to the ocean floor or use a drill ship, the more popular option, to drill for oil in water as much as 10,000 feet deep. Drill ships use global positioning systems and sophisticated computer-controlled thrusters and propellers to monitor and maintain their precise location on the water surface above the drilling site, never floating more than two or three meters away from the desired drilling location, even in storms and rough waters.

The key difficulty is that deepwater drilling is incredibly expensive. The drill ships used in deep water drilling range in cost from $400 million to $1.2 billion, depending on their size, and can cost as much as $198,000 per day to lease. Furthermore, drilling a deepwater well typically costs $50 million, compared to about $1 million for an onshore well. Beyond that, near freezing temperatures can congeal oil, sand, and other materials into a clog as hard as a diamond that costs $200,000 a day to dig out. Yet, despite these costs, if you can uncover a major oil field, the numbers you've run seem to indicate that oil retrieved from deepwater drilling sites may cost from one-third to one-half less than the oil flowing from land-based oil wells. Of course, that's what you hope. You can never be sure until production begins.

Well, any way that you look at it, you're convinced that deepwater drilling is a good bet, but how can you demonstrate that to top management, especially considering the risks involved and the tough economic conditions? In part, it will depend on how risk averse top managers are. Are they willing to spend huge sums of money to potentially put BP Amoco in front of its competitors for years to come, or are they risk averse, wanting to sit back and see whether other oil companies have success with deepwater drilling first? Finally, it may come down to something as simple as how the problem is defined. Is the problem cutting costs to restore profitability, or is the problem investing company funds in smartly calculated risks that might pay off in huge increases in oil revenue? In the end, though, you don't want to just convince upper management to do what you want; you want to be right, too.

**If you were in charge of oil exploration for BP Amoco, what would you do?**

**Sources:** J. Biers, "Drilling's Leviathans Stumble To Sea: New Generation Rigs, Ships Born in Rough Waters," *Houston Chronicle,* 17 October 1999, Business 6. D. Fisher, "How Sir John Browne Turned BP Amoco into the Hottest Prospect in the Oil Patch," *Forbes,* 2 April 2001, 110. D. Ivanovich, "The New 2000 Millennium—World May Learn to Wean Itself from Oil: The Search for Crude Deepens, As Does the Concern over Its Future," *Houston Chronicle,* 24 October 1999, 1. S. Liesman & A. Sullivan, "Mystery Man: Exxon Mobil Merger Positions an Enigma at Oil Giant's Helm: Hardly a Household Name, Mr. Raymond Fostered a Revolution Quietly Playing Everyman at Valdez," *The Wall Street Journal,* 1 December 1999. Staff Reports, "Giant in the Gulf: BP Amoco's Massive Oil Drilling Platform Has Begun Pumping with 5 Wells in Gulf," *The New Orleans Times Picayune,* 3 December 1999, C1. K. Williams, "Transocean at Standoff on Drill Ship," *Houston Chronicle,* 10 June 2001, Business 2.

Even inexperienced managers know that decision making and problem solving are central parts of their jobs. Figure out what the problem is. Generate potential solutions. Pick the best solution. Make it work. Experienced managers, however, know how hard it really is to make good decisions and solve problems. One seasoned manager said: "I think the biggest surprises are the problems. Maybe I had never seen it before. Maybe I was protected by my management when I was in sales. Maybe I had delusions of grandeur, I don't know. I just know how disillusioning and frustrating it is to be hit with problems and conflicts all day and not be able to solve them very cleanly."[1] Undoubtedly, the manager in charge of oil exploration at BP Amoco feels the same frustration and uncertainty about deepwater drilling. Deepwater drilling holds fantastic potential which might, just might, pay off. However, deepwater drilling is incredibly expensive. And unlike its iffy payoffs, there's no uncertainty about its high costs. Any way you look at it, it's a tough decision for BP Amoco to make.

**decision making**
the process of choosing a solution from available alternatives

**rational decision making**
a systematic process of defining problems, evaluating alternatives, and choosing optimal solutions

**Decision making** is the process of choosing a solution from available alternatives.[2] We begin the chapter by reviewing **rational decision making**, a systematic process in which managers define problems, evaluate alternatives, and choose optimal solutions that provide maximum benefits to their organizations. We discuss the steps of rational decision making as well as its limitations. In the second part of the chapter, we look at how managers can improve their decisions. Here we discuss methods for improving rational decision making and how managers can use groups and group decision techniques to improve decisions.

## What Is Rational Decision Making?

Imagine that you've been away on business. On your first day back at the office, you sort through your phone messages and find this voice mail from the boss:

> You're a computer nut, aren't you? Whaddya call yourself, an Internet geek? Well, you know more about this stuff than anyone else in the office. Here's what I need from you. You've got three weeks to get it done. I want you to prepare a presentation and write a report that details the problems we've been having with our computers. It should also summarize our current and future computer needs. Talk to everyone. Find out what they need and want. Be sure to consider upgrade options. I don't want to spend a ton of money to improve our systems, only to have them be obsolete in two years. Finally, come up with at least five plans or options for getting

184

# BlastFromThePast

## Benjamin Franklin and Frederick W. Taylor

One of the earliest recorded instances of a rational approach to decision making in U.S. history can be found in Benjamin Franklin's "moral algebra," which he described as follows:

> My way is to divide half a sheet of paper by a line into two columns; writing over the one *Pro* and the other *Con*. Then, during three or four days' consideration, I put down under the different heads short hints of the different motives, that at different times occur to me, *for* or *against* the measure. When I have thus got them all together in one view, I endeavor to estimate their respective weights; and where I find two, one on each side, that seem equal, I strike them both out. If I find a reason *pro* equal to some two reasons *con*, I strike out the three. If I judge some two reasons *con*, equal to some three reasons *pro*, I strike out the five; and thus proceeding I find at length where the balance lies; and if, after a day or two of further consideration, nothing new that is of importance occurs on either side, I come to a determination accordingly.

However, the individual who had the greatest effect on how decisions are made in organizations is Frederick W. Taylor (1856–1915), the "Father of scientific management." Taylor once described scientific management as "seventy-five percent science and twenty-five percent common sense." Yet before Taylor, decision making in organizations could best be described as "seat-of-the-pants." Decisions were made haphazardly without any systematic study, thought, or collection of information. Prior to Taylor's time, most companies were very small, so few managers were needed. Most small companies were run by their owners or founders. For example, in 1849, Cyrus McCormick, founder of Chicago Harvester (predecessor of International Harvester), ran the largest factory in the United States. Amazingly, it employed just 123 workers. In 1870, the Pullman company, a manufacturer of railroad sleeping cars, was the largest, with only 200 employees. However, the Industrial Revolution greatly increased the number of employees who worked in factories and companies. For example, while only 1.3 million people worked in manufacturing in 1860, that number had quadrupled to 5.3 million by 1890. With factories employing thousands of workers per location, companies then had a need for managers who knew how to organize and make good decisions.

Taylor filled this need for organized decision making by advocating the practice of scientific management. The goal of scientific management was to use systematic study to find the "one best way" of doing each task. In scientific management, managers have four duties or responsibilities. First, "develop a science" for each element of work. Study it. Analyze it. Determine the "one best way" to do the work. For example, one of Taylor's controversial proposals at the time was to give rest breaks to factory workers doing physical labor. Whereas we take morning, lunch, and afternoon breaks for granted, in Taylor's day, factory workers were expected to work without stopping. So when Taylor suggested the idea and said that it would increase worker pro-

ductivity, no one believed him. However, he showed that workers receiving frequent rest breaks were able to quadruple their daily work.

Second, scientifically select, train, teach, and develop workers to help them reach their full potential. Before Taylor, supervisors often hired on the basis of favoritism and nepotism. Who you knew was often more important than what you could do. Similarly, training and development of workers were extremely rare.

Third, cooperate with employees to ensure implementation of the scientific principles. Labor unrest was widespread at the time, with the number of labor strikes against companies doubling between 1893 and 1904. More often than not, workers and management viewed each other as the enemy. Taylor's advice ran contrary to common wisdom of the day. He said:

> The majority of these men [workers and managers] believe that the fundamental interests of employees and employers are necessarily antagonistic. Scientific management, on the contrary, has for its very foundation the firm conviction that the true interests of the two are one and the same; that prosperity for the employer cannot exist through a long term of years unless it is accompanied by prosperity for the employee and vice versa; and that it is possible to give the workman what he most wants—high wages—and the employer what he wants—a low labor cost—for his manufactures.

The fourth responsibility of management, according to scientific management, was to divide the work and the responsibility equally between management and workers. Prior to Taylor, workers alone were held responsible for productivity and performance. But, according to Taylor:

> Almost every act of the workman should be preceded by one or more preparatory acts of the management which enable him to do his work better and quicker than he otherwise could. And each man should daily be taught by and receive the most friendly help from those who are over him, instead of being, at the one extreme, driven or coerced by his bosses, and at the other left to his own unaided devices.

**Sources:** G.R. Butler, "Frederick Winslow Taylor: The Father of Scientific Management and His Philosophy Revisited," *Industrial Management* 33 (1991): 23-26. B. Franklin, "A Letter to Joseph Priestly, 1772," reprinted in B. Franklin, *The Benjamin Franklin Sampler* (New York: Fawcett Publications, 1956). R. Reich, *The Next American Frontier* (New York: Times Books, 1983). T.L. Robinson, "Revisiting the Original Management Primer: Defending a Great Productivity Innovator," *Industrial Management* 34 (1992): 19-21. F.W. Taylor, *The Principles of Scientific Management* (New York: Harper Bros., 1911).

us where we need to be. Hey, almost forgot, you're probably going to have to do some educating here. Most of us in management don't speak "computer geek." Heck, half of the dinosaurs we've got in upper management think computers are $1,500 paper weights—Don't repeat that, O.K.? So be sure to explain in everyday language how we can decide which plans or options are best. Have a rough draft on my desk in three weeks.

When your boss delegated this "computer problem," what he really wanted from you is a rational decision. In other words, you need to define and analyze the problem, and explore alternatives. Furthermore, the solution has to be "optimal," since the department is going to live with the computer equipment you recommend for the next three years.

*After reading these next two sections, you should be able to*
*1. explain the steps to rational decision making.*
*2. discuss the limits to rational decision making.*

## 1. Steps to Rational Decision Making

*Exhibit 6.1 shows the six steps of the rational decision-making process. Let's learn more about each of these steps: 1.1 define the problem, 1.2 identify decision criteria, 1.3 weight the criteria, 1.4 generate alternative courses of action, 1.5 evaluate each alternative, and 1.6 compute the optimal decision.*

---

*EXHIBIT 6.1*

STEPS OF THE RATIONAL DECISION-MAKING PROCESS

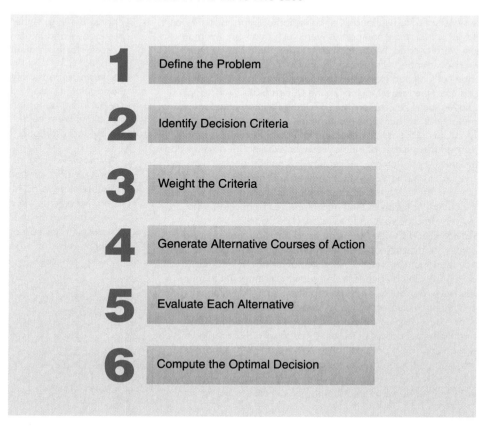

1  Define the Problem

2  Identify Decision Criteria

3  Weight the Criteria

4  Generate Alternative Courses of Action

5  Evaluate Each Alternative

6  Compute the Optimal Decision

## 1.1 Define the Problem

**problem**
a gap between a desired state and an existing state

The first step in decision making is identifying and defining the problem. A **problem** exists when there is a gap between a desired state—what managers want—and an existing state—the situation that the managers are facing. For example, despite being the largest and most popular e-tailing site on the Web with, by far, the highest customer satisfaction ratings, Amazon.com has not been profitable in its first five years. In its fifth year, 20 million customers bought $2.8 billion of books, electronics, video, and music. However, the company lost $1.4 billion making those sales![3]

The existence of a gap between an existing state and a desired state is no guarantee that managers will make decisions to solve problems. Three things must occur for this to happen.[4] First, managers have to be aware of the gap. They have to know there is a problem before they can begin solving it. For example, after noticing that people were spending more money on their pets, a new dog food company created an expensive, high-quality dog food. To emphasize the quality of the product, the dog food was sold in cans and bags with gold labels, red letters, and detailed information about product benefits and nutrients. However, the product didn't sell very well, and the company was out of business in less than a year. Company founders didn't understand why. When they asked a manager at a competing dog food company what their biggest mistake had been, the answer was, "Simple. You didn't have a picture of a dog on the package."[5] This problem would have been easy to solve, if management had only been aware of it.

Being aware of the gap between a desired state and an existing state isn't enough to begin the decision-making process. Managers also have to be motivated to reduce the gap. For example, business people have complained for years about unreasonable workplace regulation. However, Congress was not interested in solving this "problem" until the Congressional Accountability Act subjected Congress to the same laws as private businesses. Now, like any business, Congress must give overtime pay to anyone who works more than 40 hours a week. Legislative and office assistants, all of whom used to work 60 hours a week, are now limited by law to just 40. Ironically, Congress doesn't have the funds for overtime pay. To limit hours, no one is allowed to work during lunch (even if they want to). Computers are turned off. Phones go unanswered. Employees can't even watch C-Span while eating their sandwiches. At 6:00 P.M., office managers walk through the offices, ringing loud bells and turning off lights to force employees who want to keep working to go home. Not surprisingly, these changes have motivated many in Congress to take a second look at the unintended effects that workplace laws and regulations have on businesses.[6]

Finally, it's not enough to be aware of a problem and be motivated to solve it. Managers must also have the knowledge, skills, abilities, and resources to fix the problem. Amazon.com is now going "full out" to reverse the gap between its oversized expenses and its undersized revenues. It has a new accounting system that uses product and shipping costs, the frequency with which products are returned, and 47 other factors to show how much money Amazon makes or loses on each product it sells. For example, this program (which Amazon built internally using 800,000 equations) indicated that, given the difference between retail and wholesale prices, Amazon should have been making a profit on a $10 pack of Polaroid instant film. However, after factoring in all of its costs, from inventory to packing to billing to shipping, Amazon loses $1 each time it sells this product. Since Amazon loses money on this item, the computer then suggested several options to make it profitable: "consider bundling with other items" (to reduce shipping costs), "find another merchant to handle and ship the film," "press vendor for lower costs," or "raise prices."[7]

## 1.2 Identify Decision Criteria

**decision criteria**
the standards used to guide judgments and decisions

**Decision criteria** are the standards used to guide judgments and decisions. Typically, the more criteria that a potential solution meets, the better that solution should be.

Let's return to the employee who was given the responsibility for making a rational decision about the office computer setup. What general kinds of factors would be important when purchasing computers for the office? Reliability, price, warranty, on-site service, and compatibility with existing software, printers, and computers would all be important, wouldn't they? However, you can't buy computer equipment without considering the technical details. So what kinds of specific factors would you want the office computer to have? Well, with technology changing so quickly, you'll probably want to buy computers with as much capability as you can afford. At the minimum, according to *PC Magazine*, you'll probably want a 64-bit 1.5-gigahertz Pentium 4 or Athlon chip, with 256 megs of memory, a 40-gig hard drive, a DVD drive holding 8 gigabytes of data, a 100 megabit per second network card for high speed Internet connections, and a 19-inch monitor—all for a price of $2,000 or less![8] These general and specific factors represent the criteria that could guide the purchase of computer equipment.

### 1.3 Weight the Criteria

After identifying decision criteria, the next step is deciding which criteria are more or less important. For example, despite *PC Magazine*'s advice, a 19-inch monitor and a DVD-ROM drive aren't that important for business computers. In most cases, a lower-cost 17-inch monitor would suffice for office work (word processing, email, and spreadsheets). And, as long as someone on the office network has a DVD-ROM drive that can be accessed from any other computer on the network, then most office computers don't have to have a DVD-ROM drive. A CD-ROM drive in each computer will do. On the other hand, a 1.5-gigahertz Pentium or Athlon computer chip, 256 megabytes of memory, high-speed network/Internet connections, and at least a 40-gigabyte hard drive are "must-haves" for today's desktop corporate computers. (These specifications may be outdated by the time you read this.)

---

**EXHIBIT 6.2**

ABSOLUTE WEIGHTING OF DECISION CRITERIA FOR A CAR PURCHASE

5 critically important
4 important
3 somewhat important
2 not very important
1 completely unimportant

**PERFORMANCE CHARACTERISTICS**

| | 1 | 2 | 3 | 4 | 5 |
|---|---|---|---|---|---|
| 1. starting and acceleration | 1 | 2 | 3 | **4** | 5 |
| 2. fuel economy | 1 | 2 | 3 | 4 | **5** |
| 3. handling and steering | 1 | 2 | **3** | 4 | 5 |
| 4. shifting/transmission | 1 | **2** | 3 | 4 | 5 |
| 5. ride quality | 1 | 2 | **3** | 4 | 5 |
| 6. braking | 1 | 2 | 3 | **4** | 5 |

**DESIGN CHARACTERISTICS**

| | 1 | 2 | 3 | 4 | 5 |
|---|---|---|---|---|---|
| 1. overall design | 1 | 2 | 3 | **4** | 5 |
| 2. interior ergonomics | 1 | 2 | **3** | 4 | 5 |
| 3. seating | 1 | 2 | 3 | 4 | **5** |
| 4. accessories and amenities | **1** | 2 | 3 | 4 | 5 |
| 5. cargo space | 1 | 2 | 3 | 4 | **5** |
| 6. fit and finish | 1 | 2 | **3** | 4 | 5 |

While there are numerous mathematical models for weighting decision criteria, all require the decision maker to provide an initial ranking of the decision criteria. Some use **absolute comparisons**, in which each criterion is compared to a standard or ranked on its own merits. For example, *Consumer's Digest* uses a 12-point checklist when it rates and recommends new cars. Six points address the car's performance (starting and acceleration, fuel economy, handling and steering, shifting/transmission, ride quality, and braking), and six address the car's design (overall design, interior ergonomics, seating, accessories and amenities, cargo space, and fit and finish).[9]

Exhibit 6.2 shows the absolute weights that someone buying a car might use. Because these weights are absolute, each criterion is judged on its own importance, using a five-point scale, with "5" representing "critically important" and "1" representing "completely unimportant." In this instance, fuel economy, seating, and cargo space were rated most important, while shifting/transmission, accessories, and amenities were rated least important.

Another method is **relative comparisons**, in which each criterion is compared directly to every other criterion.[10] For example, moving down the first column of Exhibit 6.3, we see that starting/acceleration has been rated less important (−1) than fuel economy; more important (+1) than handling and steering, shifting/transmission, and ride quality; but just as important as braking (0). Total weights, which are obtained by summing the scores in each column, indicate that fuel economy and starting/acceleration are the most important factors to this car buyer, while handling and steering, shifting/transmission, and ride quality are the least important.

### 1.4 Generate Alternative Courses of Action

After identifying and weighting the criteria that will guide the decision-making process, the next step is to identify possible courses of action that could solve the problem. In general, at this step, the idea is to generate as many alternatives as possible. For instance, let's assume that you're in the insurance industry and that your company wants to reduce costs by moving its headquarters out of Los Angeles. Why? Because real estate costs are astronomical, congested roadways lead to average commuting times of two to three hours per day, and, from your perspective, the regulatory environment is largely anti-business. Not surprisingly, the location of your new headquarters would have to meet the following criteria: a qualified labor force, high quality of life (easy commutes), low operating costs, low cost of living (low real estate costs), and a business-friendly state regulatory environment. After meeting with your staff, you generate a list of alternative

---

### EXHIBIT 6.3

#### RELATIVE COMPARISON FOR CAR PERFORMANCE CHARACTERISTICS

| CAR PERFORMANCE CHARACTERISTICS | STARTING/ ACCELERATION | FUEL ECONOMY | HANDLING AND STEERING | SHIFTING/ TRANSMISSION | RIDE QUALITY | BRAKING |
|---|---|---|---|---|---|---|
| starting/acceleration | | +1 | −1 | −1 | −1 | 0 |
| fuel economy | −1 | | −1 | −1 | −1 | −1 |
| handling and steering | +1 | +1 | | 0 | 0 | +1 |
| shifting/transmission | +1 | +1 | 0 | | 0 | 0 |
| ride quality | +1 | +1 | 0 | 0 | | 0 |
| braking | 0 | +1 | −1 | 0 | 0 | |
| Total Weight | +2 | +5 | −3 | −2 | −2 | 0 |

# BeenThereDoneThat

In this interview, Howard Raiffa and John S. Hammond of Harvard Business School, and Ralph L. Keeney of the University of Southern California, authors of *Smart Choices: A Practical Guide to Making Better Decisions*, explain what the average person does wrong when making decisions and what they can do to make better decisions.

**Q:** What does the average person do wrong in making difficult decisions?

Keeney: One of the most common errors is that they start to solve the wrong problem. They jump at the first characterization of their decision, so their objectives are too narrow, and they consider too few alternatives. They're in a rush to decide and get it over with, rather than backing away from it, seeing it in a broader context, and really focusing on what they should.

**Q:** Why do you think people are so inherently ill-equipped to make good decisions?

Raiffa: I think it's not easy to think hard about making decisions. The easy way out is just to do what comes naturally and not try to question the issues more broadly, and to balance pros and cons. Usually there are lots of conflicting objectives—for example, what is right to make a lot of money may not be right for your family.

**Q:** Take us through that proper decision-making process.

Hammond: Essentially, the process we advocate has eight possible steps in it. [Author's Note: This model is very similar to the rational decision-making model discussed in the text.] You may or may not need every step, depending on your particular situation. But the first thing you need to do is define the "decision problem" that you're facing—what it is that you have to decide. A good solution to a well-posed problem is usually far superior to an outstanding solution to a poorly posed problem.

**Q:** How do we know if we're posing the problem correctly?

Hammond: That's a decision in its own right. You keep coming at it and coming at it and asking yourself, "Is this really what I need to decide?" You ask that at the outset, and as you go along you keep asking yourself, "Am I working on the right problem?" Often while you're in the course of deciding, the situation changes and the problem becomes a new problem. And sometimes the situation hasn't changed, but your insights into the situation have changed. There's no magical way to know that you have the right problem.

Raiffa: A good example is a man named Bill, whom we counseled. Bill, who with a partner was in the soundproofing business, was a little disgruntled with his lifestyle and thought that he'd like to sell out his part of the business. He posed the problem to himself as "How much should I accept for my share of the business?"

Hammond: He said he wanted to talk to us about how he could sell out his half of the business to his partner. Basically, he hadn't formulated his problem very carefully. He thought his problem was getting the right price for his business. He hadn't developed a full range of creative alternatives—the one alternative he was pursuing was selling out to his partner. If selling was his problem, he could have sold out to some-

body else. Or they both could have sold out to somebody else, and his partner could have stayed on and managed the business if he wanted to. But because he hadn't formulated his problem very well, he missed a whole range of other alternatives, including the one he ended up choosing, which was to stay in the business and do something entirely different.

**Q:** It seems to me that our culture celebrates an entrepreneurial way of thinking, which often includes seat-of-the-pants decision making. Entrepreneurs often make quick decisions amidst uncertainty, perhaps without all the relevant information, based on a gut feeling. Do you think poor decision-making habits are being held up as a "model" because some people have been lucky enough to make good decisions with bad information?

Hammond: There are some good intuitive decision makers out there, and we should celebrate them. But the method that we outlined can become intuitive. You can, in just 5 or 10 minutes, go through a checklist, asking, "What's my 'decision problem' (what am I trying to achieve here?)," "What are my alternatives," "How can I think of others," and so on. In other words, quickly ask yourself a series of those simple questions. You can do it over time until it sort of becomes automatic. Eventually, it drives your intuition.

**Q:** What role should emotion play in good decision making?

Raiffa: There's always a debate about where systematic analysis leads and where intuitive analysis leads. What happens if they clash? Should you go with your intuition, or should you go with the more formal analysis? My answer is that if intuition and analysis are in conflict, you should feel uncomfortable. You should review both sides of the ledger to see if your intuition holds up when it is informed with some systematic analysis. And if your analysis seems wrong intuitively, don't accept the analysis, just keep on probing.

**Q:** Can you ever get to the point of feeling certain about decisions?

Raiffa: When I was younger and taught at Columbia, I had an offer at Harvard. I had a very difficult time deciding. Finally, somebody said, "Look, whatever you do, commit yourself partially but not fully. Tell your friends what you're going to do, but don't write any formal acceptance or rejection. Then see how you sleep for a week and let your emotions catch up with it. See how it settles down before you act." I think that's wise advice.

**Q:** So you're saying that at some point emotion has to kick in.

Raiffa: That is very important.

Keeney: The fundamental reason to make decisions is because you care about what consequences may occur. If you don't care, don't bother to make decisions.

**Q:** Probably the most frustrating thing for a small-business owner, an entrepreneur, is that so many decisions are made amidst uncertainty. How can an entrepreneur cope with that uncertainty and still make good decisions?

Raiffa: I think there is a trap here: we're not saying that people should put down probabilities and do quantitative analysis. We encourage people to reflect on the uncertainties, on what might be the possible outcomes, and to trace out the consequences of those outcomes. Sometimes by grappling with uncertainties, by listing what could happen, by ordering the likelihood of the possibilities, you can clarify the problem. It's important to identify what the uncertainties are, what the possible outcomes are, what the consequences are to your lifestyle. Will you sleep well? Or will you have so much anxiety that it will interfere with your sleep or your lifestyle?

Q: Some people would say that some of the best and most interesting business ideas would never have come to be had their originators gone through that process.

Raiffa: Yes, but we make a big distinction. Uncertainty is present between the quality of the decision and the quality of the outcome. You may have a decision that was made by the seat of the pants and was not thought through clearly but that turned out miraculously well by luck. However, I think luck usually goes to the better decision maker.

**Source:** K. Dillon, "The Perfect Decision," *Inc.*, 1 October 1998, 74. This interview was edited for inclusion in this textbook.

locations: Atlanta, Baltimore, Chicago, Des Moines, Kansas City, Milwaukee, Minneapolis, Seattle, St. Louis, and Tampa.

### 1.5 Evaluate Each Alternative

The next step is to systematically evaluate each alternative against each criterion. Because of the amount of information that must be collected, this step can take much longer and be much more expensive than other steps in the decision-making process. For example, in order to evaluate the quality of locations for insurance companies, *Best's Review* (the "bible" for insurance companies) employed a research firm to conduct three in-depth surveys that asked top insurance executives how their locations affected their businesses. The research firm also mailed questionnaires to economic development offices in 25 cities. Those questionnaires contained questions about 50 items specific to the insurance industry (state regulations governing insurance, number of insurance companies, number of insurance workers, etc.).[11]

Once the necessary information has been gathered, use it to evaluate each alternative against each criterion. Exhibit 6.4 shows how each of the 10 cities fared on each criterion

| EXHIBIT 6.4 | | | | | | |
|---|---|---|---|---|---|---|
| CRITERIA RATINGS USED TO EVALUATE THE BEST LOCATIONS FOR INSURANCE COMPANIES | | | | | | |
| CITY | REGULATORY CLIMATE | ACCESSIBILITY | LABOR | LIVING ENVIRONMENT | OPERATING COSTS | WEIGHTED AVERAGE |
| Atlanta | 3 | 5 | 4 | 6 | 4 | 4.35 |
| Baltimore | 5 | 4 | 2 | 4 | 5 | 4 |
| Chicago | 7 | 6 | 6 | 5 | 4 | 5.75 |
| Des Moines | 7 | 1 | 4 | 2 | 7 | 4.2 |
| Kansas City | 5 | 3 | 2 | 4 | 6 | 3.95 |
| Milwaukee | 6 | 2 | 4 | 3 | 5 | 4.05 |
| Minneapolis | 5 | 5 | 4 | 5 | 5 | 4.8 |
| Seattle | 4 | 4 | 3 | 6 | 4 | 4.2 |
| St. Louis | 3 | 5 | 1 | 4 | 5 | 3.5 |
| Tampa | 2 | 3 | 4 | 3 | 7 | 3.55 |

**Source:** K. Galloway, "America's Best Insurance Cities," *Best's Review/Property-Casualty Insurance Edition*, 1 November 1994, 38.

(higher scores are better). For example, Chicago and Des Moines have the best regulatory climates. But because Chicago is a major city, it received the lowest score for operating costs, while Des Moines, which does not have a major airport, received the lowest score for accessibility.

### 1.6 Compute the Optimal Decision

The final step in the decision-making process is to compute the optimal decision by determining each alternative's optimal value. This is done by multiplying the rating for each criterion (Step 5) by the weight for that criterion (Step 3), and then summing those scores for each alternative course of action that you generated (Step 4). For example, *Best's Review* rated the five decision criteria in terms of importance to the final decision: regulatory climate (25 percent), accessibility (20 percent), labor (20 percent), living environment (20 percent), and operating costs (15 percent). Those weights are then multiplied by the ratings in each category. For example, St. Louis's optimal value of 3.5 (i.e., weighted average) is determined using the following calculation:

$$(.25*3) + (.20*5) + (.20*1) + (.20*4) + (.15*5) = 3.5$$

Exhibit 6.5 shows that Chicago is clearly the best location for insurance companies, no doubt because of its extremely good accessibility, labor, and regulatory climate. By contrast, St. Louis was the worst location, by virtue of its poor regulatory climate and weak labor force.

## Review 1
### Steps to Rational Decision Making

Rational decision making is a six-step process in which managers define problems, evaluate alternatives, and compute optimal solutions. The first step is identifying and defining the problem. Problems exist where there is a gap between desired and existing states. Managers won't begin the decision-making process unless they are aware of the gap, motivated to reduce it, and possess the necessary resources to fix it. The second step is defining the decision criteria that are used when judging alternatives. In Step 3, an absolute or relative comparison process is used to rate the importance of decision criteria. Step 4 involves generating as many possible courses of action (i.e., solutions) as possible. Potential solutions

192

---

| EXHIBIT 6.5 |
| --- |

**CITIES RANKED BY OPTIMAL VALUE**

| **OPTIMAL VALUES** | |
| --- | --- |
| 1. Chicago | 5.75 |
| 2. Minneapolis | 4.80 |
| 3. Atlanta | 4.35 |
| 4. Des Moines | 4.20 |
| 5. Seattle | 4.20 |
| 6. Milwaukee | 4.05 |
| 7. Baltimore | 4.00 |
| 8. Kansas City | 3.95 |
| 9. Tampa | 3.55 |
| 10. St. Louis | 3.50 |

**Source:** K. Galloway, "America's Best Insurance Cities," *Best's Review/Property-Casualty Insurance Edition*, 1 November 1994, 38.

are assessed in Step 5 by systematically gathering information and evaluating each alternative against each criterion. In Step 6, criterion ratings and weights are used to compute the optimal value for each alternative course of action. Rational managers then choose the alternative with the highest optimal value.

# 2. Limits to Rational Decision Making

In general, managers who diligently complete all six steps of the rational decision-making model will make better decisions than those who don't. So, when they can, managers should try to follow the steps in the rational decision-making model, especially for big decisions with long-range consequences.

However, it's highly doubtful that rational decision making can help managers choose *optimal* solutions that provide *maximum* benefits to their organizations. The terms "optimal" and "maximum" suggest that rational decision making leads to perfect or near-perfect decisions. Of course, for managers to make perfect decisions, they have to operate in perfect worlds with no real-world constraints. For example, in an optimal world, the manager who was given three weeks to define, analyze, and fix computer problems in the office would have followed *PC Magazine*'s advice to buy all employees the "perfect personal computer" (i.e., 1-gigahertz chip, 256 megabytes of memory, etc.). And in arriving at that decision, our manager would not have been constrained by price ("$5,000 per computer? Sure, no problem.") or time ("Need six more months to decide? Sure, take as long as you need."). Furthermore, without any constraints, our manager could identify and weight an extensive list of decision criteria, generate a complete list of possible solutions, and then test and evaluate each computer against each decision criterion. Finally, our manager would have the necessary experience and knowledge with computers to easily make sense of all these sophisticated tests and information.

*Of course, it never works like that in the real world. Managers face time and money constraints. They often don't have time to make extensive lists of decision criteria. And they often don't have the resources to test all possible solutions against all possible criteria. Let's see how 2.1 bounded rationality, 2.2 risk and risky decisions, and 2.3 common decision-making mistakes make it difficult for managers to make completely rational, optimal decisions.*

## 2.1 Bounded Rationality

The rational decision-making model describes the way decisions *should* be made. In other words, decision makers wanting to make optimal decisions *should not* have to face time and costs constraints. They *should* have unlimited resources and time to generate and test all alternative solutions against all decision criteria. And they *should* be willing to recommend any decision that produces optimal benefits for the company, even if that decision would harm their own jobs or departments. Of course, very few managers actually make rational decisions like they *should*. The way in which managers actually make decisions is more accurately described as "bounded (or limited) rationality."

**bounded rationality**
decision-making process restricted in the real world by limited resources, incomplete and imperfect information, and managers' limited decision-making capabilities

**Bounded rationality** means that managers try to take a rational approach to decision making, but are restricted by real-world constraints, incomplete and imperfect information, and their own limited decision-making capabilities. More specifically, as shown in Exhibit 6.6, at least four problems prevent managers from making rational decisions.[12] First, as described above, limited resources often prevent managers from making rational decisions. Managers only have so much time, so much money, and so many people, machines, or offices to devote to a specific problem. When resources increase or decrease, managers change their decisions. For example, when the economy slowed down, Jiffy-Tite, and auto parts manufacturer, cut back on capital spending for expensive new product testing equipment. CEO Jeff Zillig said, "We had planned on the worst . . . and cut the spending budget for testing equipment in half to $100,000." Less than a year later, however, finances improved, so Zillig said, "We're going back to our original budget."

EXHIBIT 6.6

PROBLEMS ASSOCIATED WITH BOUNDED RATIONALITY

Therefore, Jiffy-Tite bought the new testing equipment.[13] Because of limited resources, there is almost always a difference between what managers would like to do (i.e., rational decision making) and what they can do (i.e., bounded rationality).

Second, attention problems limit the information that a decision maker can pay attention to at any one time. Often, attention problems stem from **information overload**, or too much information. For example, since *PC Magazine* uses 24 specific decision criteria to describe the "perfect PC," and since it typically tests approximately 50 computers every time it conducts a review, our rational decision maker would have to process 1,200 different pieces of information. This is simply too much information for one person to make sense of. Even 10 decision criteria and 10 computers would be too much.

Third, memory problems make it difficult to recall or retrieve stored information. Managers forget important facts and details. Companies don't always keep the best records. Since the new computer equipment has to be compatible with the old computer equipment, our manager's first task would be to find out what equipment the company already owns. However, if detailed records have not been kept, and if employees don't know the configuration of their computers ("Does it have an Athlon, or a Pentium chip? What speed is the chip, 1-, 1.3-, or 1.5-gigahertz?"), then each computer will have to be manually inspected to gather this information. Furthermore, information retrieval is not free. It costs time and money.

Fourth, expertise problems make it difficult for decision makers to organize, summarize, and fully comprehend all the information that is available for making the decision. Realistically, even though our manager is a self-professed computer "geek," he or she probably doesn't have the required experience or knowledge to make sense of all of

**information overload**
situation in which decision makers have too much information to attend to

194

## Email Filter Saves Manager from Drowning!

Drowning in email and information overload? If so, you're not alone. With group mailing lists, anyone can send email to hundreds with just one click. The result? The number of emails sent and received has skyrocketed. Consequently, although much of it is irrelevant or worthless, it's increasingly common to spend two-to-three hours a day reading and responding to email. One way to stay afloat is to use the email filter in your email software. Type in the names and topics (keywords) that you don't want to read about. The email filter keeps them from popping up on your screen. Be careful, though. Don't filter the boss.

**Source:** F. Diekmann, "E(nough) Mail," *Credit Union Journal*, 23 July 2001, 1.

**maximizing**
choosing the best alternative

**satisficing**
choosing a "good enough" alternative

**conditions of certainty**
conditions in which decision makers have complete information and knowledge of all possible outcomes

**conditions of risk**
conditions in which decision makers face a very real possibility of making the wrong decision

the test results and determine which computer is the "perfect PC." The difficulty of this task is illustrated by the fact that *PC Magazine* employs 30 full-time staffers in two research labs stuffed with hundreds of thousands of dollars of equipment to make such decisions. No one, not even managers, can possess expert knowledge about everything.

In theory, fully rational decision makers **maximize** decisions by choosing the optimal solution. However, limited resources, along with attention, memory, and expertise problems, make it nearly impossible for managers to maximize decisions. Consequently, most managers don't maximize—they "satisfice." Whereas maximizing is choosing the best alternative, **satisficing** is choosing a "good enough" alternative. With 24 decision criteria, 50 alternative computers to choose from, two computer labs with hundreds of thousands of dollars of equipment, and unlimited time and money, our manager could test all alternatives against all decision criteria and choose the "perfect PC." However, our manager's limited time, money, and expertise mean that only a few alternatives will be assessed against a few decision criteria. In practice, our manager will visit two or three computer or electronic stores, read a couple of recent computer reviews, and then get three or four bids from local computer stores that sell complete computer systems at competitive prices. The decision will be complete when our manager finds a "good enough" computer that meets a few decision criteria, most likely low price, a 1.5-gigahertz chip, a 40-gigabyte hard drive, and 256 megabytes of memory.

### 2.2 Risk and Decision Making under Risky Conditions

Step 5 of the rational decision-making model assumes that managers can gaze into their crystal balls and accurately predict how well a potential solution will fix a problem. Furthermore, it assumes that managers make decisions under **conditions of certainty**, with complete information and knowledge of all possible outcomes. It's like knowing who won the last 10 Super Bowls and then traveling 10 years back in time with $1,000 in your pocket. Because you already know who won, deciding which team to bet on is easy. You're a guaranteed winner.

Of course, if decision making were this easy, companies wouldn't need very many managers. In most situations, managers make decisions under **conditions of risk**, with a very real possibility of losing (making the wrong decision). Thus, risk and risky conditions make it difficult for managers to make completely rational, optimal decisions.

Furthermore, risk has a significant effect on how decision makers define and solve problems. Consider this problem from Max Bazerman's book *Judgment in Managerial Decision Making*:

A large car manufacturer has recently been hit with a number of economic difficulties, and it appears as if three plants need to be closed and 6,000 employees laid off. The vice president of production has been exploring alternative ways to avoid this crisis. She has developed two plans:

Plan A: This plan will save one of three plants and 2,000 jobs.
Plan B: This plan has a one-third probability of saving all three plants and 6,000 jobs, but has a two-thirds probability of saving no plants and no jobs.

Did you choose Plan A? According to Bazerman, 80 percent of people given these choices choose Plan A rather than Plan B. What would you have done if you were faced with the following choices to the same problem?

195

Plan C: This plan will result in the loss of two of the three plants and 4,000 jobs.

Plan D: This plan has a two-thirds probability of resulting in the loss of all three plants and all 6,000 jobs, but has a one-third probability of losing no plants and no jobs.

This time, did you choose Plan D? Again, according to Bazerman, 80 percent choose Plan D. However, if you look closely at both sets of choices, you can see that Plans A and C both save 2,000 jobs, and Plans B and D both provide a two-thirds chance of losing all 6,000 jobs. So why would 80 percent of decision makers choose Plan A in the first context, while only 20 percent chose its equivalent, Plan C, in the second? Likewise, why would 20 percent of decision makers choose Plan B in the first context, while 80 percent chose its equivalent, Plan D, in the second?

The critical difference is how the problem is framed. A **positive frame** is the presentation of a problem in terms of a gain. When you begin with the belief that 6,000 people will lose their jobs, Plan A's ability to keep 2,000 jobs is clearly a gain. When faced with the prospect of a gain, decision makers tend to become risk-averse. In gambling terms, it's like quitting while you're ahead. You don't want to risk losing what you've already won. And in this situation, you start with 6,000 lost jobs, but Plan A helps you win 2,000 back. So most decision makers don't want to put that gain at risk.

By contrast, a **negative frame**, such as that shown in Plan D, is the presentation of a problem in terms of a loss. With nothing left to lose (i.e., there's already a two-thirds chance of losing all 6,000 jobs), most decision makers become risk-seeking. In other words, if it's your last night in Las Vegas, and you've lost $900 of the $1,000 you brought to town, why not put your last $100 in a $100 slot machine? You only get one chance, but if it pays off, you'll get all of your money back and more. And if you lose, it doesn't really matter, you were going to lose that money anyway. In sum, risk not only affects how decision makers define problems, but it also affects the solutions they choose to fix those problems.

Managers also make decisions under **conditions of uncertainty**. How is uncertainty different from risk? With risk, a gambler knows there is a 1 in 52 chance of drawing a particular card, say, the ace of spades. But with uncertainty, you don't know how many cards there are, and you don't know how many aces of spades are in the deck or whether the deck even has an ace of spades. So under conditions of uncertainty, you can lose, but you don't even know the odds of winning or losing.[14]

Very few people are willing to bet years of their lives and their own money under conditions of uncertainty. After all, why make the bet if you have no idea what your odds of success are? However, people differ in their willingness to embrace risks. For example, would you be willing to bungee jump off a bridge? Some, including me, wouldn't do it for all the money in the world. However, others would do it in a heartbeat. **Risk propensity** is a person's tendency to take or avoid risks. And it usually takes an individual with a high risk propensity to be willing to take risks under conditions of uncertainty. One such person is Bill Gross, founder and CEO of Idealab, an Internet business incubator that started the Internet companies eToys, Citysearch, Netzero, CarsDirect, Cooking.com, FreePC, Tickets.com, and GoTo.com. Idealab generates ideas for new businesses (mostly from Bill Gross), specs out the business plans and the business models, hires the managers to run the new businesses, gets the company Web sites running, gets venture capital funding to get the businesses running, and then takes the companies public with an initial public offering of stock. For the first few years, as the Internet took off, Idealab and its companies were wildly successful. But as dotcoms turned into dot bombs, Gross and Idealab burned through $800 million in funding in eight months! Even then, as eToys went bankrupt, CarsDirect blew through $200 million, and Gross's companies' stock prices fell 90 percent in value, Gross was undeterred. Idealab, he proclaimed, would bounce back with "several multi-billion dollar ideas." GoTo.com, whose stock had fallen from $80 to $10, "could be

**positive frame**
couching a problem in terms of a gain, thus influencing decision makers toward becoming risk-averse

**negative frame**
couching a problem in terms of a loss, thus influencing decision makers toward becoming risk-seeking

**conditions of uncertainty**
conditions in which decision makers don't know the odds of winning or losing

196

**risk propensity**
a person's tendency to take or avoid risks

**Don't Worry About Being Perfect**

Is it always best to strive for optimal decisions? Probably not. Shooting for perfect solutions can freeze decision makers into inaction. They become so afraid of not making the perfect decision that they create "paralysis by analysis," where gathering data and information becomes more important than making decisions and taking action. Sometimes, it's better to make decisions, risk mistakes, and then learn from the mistakes when you make them. After all, the saying isn't "decisions make perfect," it's "practice makes perfect."

**Sources:** S. Harper, "Timing: The Bedrock of Anticipatory Management," *Business Horizons* 43 no. 1 (2000): 75.

a $100 stock if they show profitability." Only someone like Gross, who started all of these companies and managed to nurse Idealab through all those failures, could be comfortable in the face of such uncertainties.[15]

### 2.3 Common Decision-Making Mistakes

Another reason that managers have difficulty making rational decisions is that, like all decision makers, they are susceptible to the common mistakes shown in Exhibit 6.7: overreliance on intuition, availability bias, representative bias, and anchoring and adjustment bias.[16]

Have you ever had an "A Ha!" experience, in which the solution to a problem you've been working on jumps into your head when you weren't thinking about it? If so, you've experienced intuition. While it's widely believed that scientists and business people only use logical, analytical, research-based methods, it's actually quite common for intuition to play a large role in the decisions and discoveries of both professions. For example, physicist Albert Einstein, discoverer of the law of relativity, claimed, "I did not arrive at my understanding of the fundamental laws of the universe through my rational mind." Robert Pittman, CEO of Time Warner Enterprises, who helped create MTV and Nickelodeon's "Nick at Nite," said, "Research is not policy making. People make policy. Research just answers some questions. At the end of the day, it's a gut decision."[17]

Intuition works best for experienced decision makers who can quickly analyze patterns of problems that they've seen before. Unfortunately, overreliance on intuition can lead even experienced decision makers to become overconfident, careless, and inconsistent. For example, nine radiologists participated in a study in which they examined 96 cases of possible stomach ulcers. Their task was to determine the likelihood that the ulcers were malignant. One week after initially reviewing these cases, the radiologists were shown the same cases again, but in a different order. Amazingly, these highly trained professionals, who knew

This photo of Bill Gross was placed in *Fortune* magazine, with the quote, "I lost $800 million in eight months. Why am I still smiling?" Indeed, the founder of Idealab clearly has a high risk propensity.

© JEFF MINTON

197

EXHIBIT 6.7

COMMON DECISION MAKING MISTAKES

| Common | Decision | Making | Mistakes |
|---|---|---|---|
| Overreliance on Intuition | Availability Bias | Representative Bias | Anchoring & Adjustment Bias |

that the purpose of the research was to study their diagnostic skills, arrived at different conclusions (malignant versus benign) for nearly one out of four patients in the second week of the study.[18] Put another way, if all 96 patients actually had cancer, 22 of the 96 would have been wrongly diagnosed as disease-free in the second week of the study.

The second common mistake occurs because decision makers have an availability bias when judging the frequency, probability, or causes of an event. The **availability bias** is the tendency of decision makers to give preference to recent information, vivid images that evoke emotions, and specific acts and behaviors that they personally observed. For example, in the last decade, there has been a steady significant decline in the total number of crimes committed in the United States. In particular, murders are down by 42 percent nationwide. However, during this same period, Americans actually *increased* their spending on security-related items from $39 to $55 billion a year. What accounts for this discrepancy? Television and the availability bias. Jason Knott, editor of *Security Sales* magazine, said, "The best advertising a security company has is the local television news." And, according to the Center for Media & Public Affairs, network news has increased its coverage of murders by 700 percent during the same period.[19] So, despite the fact that most people are actually much safer today than they were 10 years ago, they continue to purchase car alarms and home security systems because their minds are filled with the vivid images of murders that are televised to their homes via the local news.

The third common decision-making mistake is the **representative bias**, in which decision makers judge the likelihood of an event's occurrence based on its similarity to previous events and their likelihood of occurrence. For example, if a manager hired a graduate of ABC University, and that person just didn't work out, then that manager might tend to avoid hiring any other ABC graduates. In other words, in the manager's mind, one ABC graduate represents all ABC graduates. If one didn't succeed in the job, then the manager's unconscious expectation may be that others likely wouldn't succeed in the job either.

As another example, consider this riddle:

> A father and son are en route to a baseball game when their car stalls on the railroad tracks. The father can't restart the car. An oncoming train hits the car. The father dies. An ambulance rushes the boy to a nearby hospital. In the emergency room, the surgeon takes one look and says: "I can't operate on this child; he's my son."[20]

**availability bias**
unrecognized tendency of decision makers to give preference to recent information, vivid images that evoke emotions, and specific acts and behaviors that they personally observed

198

**representative bias**
unrecognized tendency of decision makers to judge the likelihood of an event's occurrence based on its similarity to previous events

# "headline news"

## Sex Change a Major Decision—For the Employer

Sex change surgery is not the kind of decision you would expect to find discussed in a corporate boardroom, but that's pretty much what happened in San Francisco. The city's Board of Supervisors, an elected body of 11 members, decided in May 2001 by a 9 to 2 vote to extend health care benefits for sex-change surgery to the city's transsexual employees. All city employees, however, would be required to chip in to pay for it.

The decision has supporters thrilled and critics outraged. The maximum lifetime benefit of $50,000 would cover not only surgery, but ongoing hormone therapies for transsexual patients. "I'm very pleased that we're doing it," board president Tom Ammiano said. "We have a noticeable transgender population in San Francisco, and many are city employees." In fact, Susan Stryker, executive director of the Gay, Lesbian, Bisexual, Transgender Historical Society of Northern California, counts the San Francisco transgender population at about 15,000.

If many of those 15,000 are city employees, as Ammiano's comment suggests, that would seem to indicate a huge upcoming expense for the city. But there seems to be some confusion over the final cost. Insurance actuaries are estimating a cost of about $1.75 million, based on 35 employees requesting surgery and using the lifetime benefit. Supporters of the initiative say that $1.75 million is far too high, considering that the city employs only 14 transsexuals, most of which have already had transgender surgeries. The health insurance payroll deduction will increase for all of San Francisco's 37,000 city employees by $1.70 per month.

Critics of the decision say it is nothing more than pandering to a very small, select group of people and does nothing to further "equal benefits for equal work," the contention of the bill's sponsor, Supervisor Mark Leno. If that were the case, critics argue that the bill would be more comprehensive, covering all workers' elective surgeries, as well as pre-existing conditions, such as heart disease, anorexia, and obesity.

The sex-change decision is proving to have legs. Soon after deciding to approve the sex-change benefit, the Board of Supervisors introduced legislation to require all city contractors to pro-

vide health insurance to their employees. The only alternative is to pay into a fund that finances health care for the uninsured. San Francisco's Chamber of Commerce was blindsided by the announcement. It considers the plan to be too confusing and expects the burden to be too high for many of the city's small- and medium-sized contractors, causing some to go under.

The cost to the contractors is still unclear because the city has not yet defined what benefits must be covered. The sex-change benefit may just be one of those benefits that the city requires its contractors to underwrite. After all, there are 14,986 transsexuals not employed by the city.

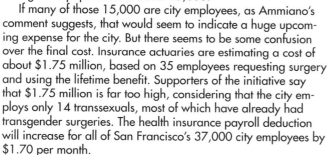

1. Evaluate the decision by the San Francisco Board of Supervisors to provide transgender surgeries as part of its health care benefit. Does it seem to be a political decision alone, or part of a greater commitment to the Bay City's living wage program?

2. What do you think were the key elements in this decision-making process? If you were to apply different decision-making heuristics to the same variables, would you come up with the same decision?

3. Including all employees' elective surgeries on the surface seems more in line with San Francisco's comprehensive living wage and quality of life programs. Why do you think the Board of Supervisors did not consider addressing coverage of pre-existing conditions and other elective surgeries in its decision?

**Sources:** J. Appleby, "San Francisco May Require Firms to Offer Health Coverage," *USA Today*, 25 May 2001, B05. J. Bacon and K. Johnson, "San Francisco Votes to Offer Workers Sex Change Benefits," *USA Today*, 1 May 2001, A03. M. Dornauer, "Debate—Why Cover Workers' Elective Surgeries," *USA Today*, 7 May 2001, A13. L. McLynn and W. Garnett, "The Rights of Man, Woman and Transsexual," *The Times of London*, 20 January 2001, Law 5. J. Ritter, "Sex-Change Benefit Considered," *USA Today*, 30 April 2001, A03. "San Francisco Expected to Approve Sex-Change Benefits," *Amarillo Globe-News*, 19 February 2001, http://amarillonet.com/stories/021901/hea_sexchange.shtml. http://www.ci.sf.ca.us.

199

Researchers have found that it's common for people to invent strange scenarios—some involving extraterrestrials—to explain how this scenario could happen. However, since most surgeons are male, the representative bias prevents most people from considering the simple explanation that the surgeon is the boy's mother.

The fourth common decision-making mistake is the **anchoring and adjustment bias**, in which judgment (good-bad, large-small, yes-no, etc.) is "anchored" by an initial value. Once the anchor is "dropped," two things happen: (1) all subsequent experiences are judged by their similarity to the anchor, and (2) all possible decision alternatives tend

**anchoring and adjustment bias**
unrecognized tendency of decision makers to use an initial value or experience as a basis of comparison throughout the decision process

to cluster around the anchor. For example, if you were accidentally bumped up from coach to first-class seating the first time you flew to Europe on business, the fine food, free drinks, attentive service, and fully reclining seats would make every subsequent trans-Atlantic trip in coach seating seem miserable. Likewise, when negotiating salaries or selling prices, the first number discussed tends to serve as the anchor for the entire negotiation. For example, in house shopping, the "listing price" stated by the house seller is typically the anchor value for negotiations. Consequently, buyers and sellers tend to judge whether they got a "good deal" by how close the selling price was to the listing price.

### Review 2
#### Limits to Rational Decision Making

The rational decision-making model describes how decisions should be made in an ideal world without limits. However, bounded rationality recognizes that in the real world, managers' decision-making processes are restricted by limited resources, incomplete and imperfect information, and managers' limited decision-making capabilities. These limitations often prevent managers from being rational decision makers. So do common decision-making mistakes, such as overreliance on intuition and the availability, representative, and anchoring and adjustment biases. The rational decision-making model assumes that decisions are made under conditions of certainty. However, most managerial decisions are made under conditions of risk, where there is limited information and knowledge and a very real chance of making a bad decision. Risk also affects how decision makers define and solve problems. Positive frames encourage decision makers to be risk averse, whereas negative frames encourage them to be risk-seeking. Finally, managers also make decisions under conditions of uncertainty, in which the odds of winning or losing are unknown. It takes a high risk propensity to be willing to take risks under conditions of uncertainty.

## Improving Decision Making

What's the biggest decision you've ever made? Was it choosing where to go to college? Was it choosing a major? Or was it a personal decision, such as deciding whether to get married, where to live, or which car or house to buy? Considering the lasting effect that decisions like these have on our lives, wouldn't it be great if we could learn how to make them better? Managers struggle with decisions, too. They wring their hands over who to hire or promote, or when and how somebody should be fired. They fret about which suppliers the company should do business with. They lose sleep over who should get how much for pay raises or how to change the company strategy to respond to aggressive competitors. And, considering the lasting effect that these decisions have on themselves and their companies, managers also want to learn how to make better decisions.

*After reading these next two sections, you should be able to*
3. *describe how individual decision making can be improved.*
4. *explain how group decisions and group decision-making techniques can improve decision-making.*

## 3. Improving Individual Decision Making

*In theory, rational decision making leads to optimal decisions. However, in practice, we know that real-world constraints, common decision-making mistakes, and risky situations make fully rational decisions difficult to achieve. Consequently, in the business world, managers are much more likely to satisfice and make "good enough" decisions than they are to maximize and make "optimal" decisions. Let's see how managers can make better decisions by using 3.1 decision rules, 3.2 multivariable testing, and 3.3 decision software, and by avoiding a common post-decision-making error called 3.4 escalation of commitment.*

## 3.1 Decision Rules

decision rule
set of criteria that alternative solutions must meet to be acceptable to the decision maker

A **decision rule** is a set of criteria that alternative solutions must meet to be acceptable to the decision maker. [21] If an alternative doesn't meet the criteria in the decision rule, it is rejected. Nearly every kind of business uses basic decision rules. In restaurants, the general pricing decision rule is to price food at three times its cost, beer at four times its cost, and hard liquor at six times its cost. In clothing stores, the rule is to sell clothing for 60 percent over wholesale, and then reduce that price by 20 percent every two weeks until the clothing has been sold. Decision rules improve decision making because they are easy to understand and simple to follow. Managers who don't have the time or resources to use the complete rational decision-making model can use simpler decision rules instead.

dictionary rule
decision rule that requires decision makers to rank criteria in order of importance and then test alternative solutions against those criteria in rank order, so that alternatives that meet the most important criterion must then meet the second most important criterion, and so on

There are two general kinds of decision rules: the dictionary rule and the threshold rule. In much the same way that a dictionary sorts words by their first letter and then their second letter, and so forth, the **dictionary rule** encourages decision makers to rank their criteria in order of importance and then assess alternative solutions against these criteria in rank order. Specifically, alternatives that meet the most important criterion must then meet the second most important criterion, and so on. For example, the first house that my wife and I owned had a living room and a family room. We found that the living room went basically unused, except when we had guests. So as our family grew and we started shopping for a larger house, the first thing we told the realtor was, "Don't show us any houses with two living areas. We want a house with one large living room." Second, because we've got three kids, "It would be great to have four bedrooms." We were willing to look at any houses that met those criteria.

minimum threshold rule
decision rule that requires alternative solutions to meet all of the established minimum decision criteria

Sometimes decision makers need to make yes/no or accept/reject decisions. Should a bank accept or reject a mortgage application? Should MasterCard approve or deny a jeweler's request to charge your card $3,500 for a jewelry purchase? When these kinds of decisions must be made, companies often use the **minimum threshold rule**, which requires an alternative to pass all the established minimum decision criteria. For example, one of the most common problems seen in emergency rooms is injured ankles. However, only 15 percent of the five million ankle x-rays taken each year indicate fractures. In other words, doctors are ordering expensive x-rays much more than they need to. Recently, clinical research has resulted in the development of the "Ottawa rule," which states that physicians should send patients with ankle injuries for confirmatory x-rays only if there is (1) pain near the ankle joint, *and* (2) bone tenderness, *and* (3) an inability to bear weight on the ankle. All three criteria must be met before sending patients to have their ankles x-rayed. Studies showed that physicians using the Ottawa rule correctly ordered x-rays for 100 percent of the patients who fractured their ankles. Also, the Ottawa rule helped reduce the overall number of ankle x-rays by 34 percent. [22]

## 3.2 Multivariable Testing

multivariable testing
a systematic approach of experimentation used to analyze and evaluate potential solutions

In practice, analyzing alternatives is one of the weakest steps in the decision-making process. Much of the "analysis" that gets done is based on guesswork ("We think that Plan E has a 90 percent chance of working.") rather than on actual tests of possible solutions. Because it is based on data from small experiments rather than guesswork, **multivariable testing** (MVT) helps managers take a much more systematic approach to analyzing and evaluating potential solutions. At Southwestern Bell, where MVT is widely used, the vice president of information services said, "It takes the 'I believe' out of [decision making]. It broadens your problem-solving ability; puts some rigor in your thinking." [23] Dwight Glover, CEO of Evans Clay, a small manufacturing company, said, "What I like about [MVT] is it provides data instead of opinions. It involves employees throughout the organization. You are using the brainpower that you have." [24]

Multivariable testing improves decision making in a number of important ways. First, instead of letting arguments determine what the best solution is (I really like that plan that manufacturing came up with because . . ."), MVT encourages managers to conduct small-scale experiments and let the data decide. Says MVT consultant and trainer Charles Holland, "The power of experimental design is not only its efficiency with data, but that it forces a team to make decisions based on facts. Hierarchy, politics, or emotions are refuted with data."[25] For example, the marketing team of a mail-order catalog company wanted to improve sales. Rather than debating what might or might not increase sales, the team came up with 12 ideas that might work, such as adding more expensive white fiberfill in pillows, adding a price grid for easy reference on each page, or printing the background of the catalog with white ink (instead of just using the natural color of the paper for the catalog background). Instead of arguing about what might work, the marketing team tested all 12 ideas separately by printing up 16 different catalog inserts for one mailing.[26]

Second, traditional scientific experimentation typically relies on controlled testing, in which all potential influences, except the ones you want to test, are controlled. This sounds simple enough, but the 12 ideas that the marketing team came up with to improve mail-order catalog sales would require 4,096 different experiments to test all possible combinations of those 12 variables (i.e., ideas). The advantage of MVT is that it saves time and money by using a mathematical shortcut so that just a few quick tests can get you 70 percent of the information that you'd get if you tested all possible combinations of variables. Rather than running 4,096 possible combinations of ideas that would improve catalog sales, the marketing team only had to use 16 different tests for their 12 ideas. After mailing out 386,000 catalogs, they found that 7 of the 12 ideas made a difference. For instance, it turns out that the more expensive white fiberfill in pillows made no difference in sales. The company saved $300,000 by switching back to cheaper, gray fiberfill. However, the price grid on each page allowed more photo space to feature items, resulting in an increase of $500,000 in sales. In all, by quickly testing all meaningful combinations of their 12 ideas in one printing of the catalog, MVT earned the company more than a million dollars in increased sales and lower costs.[27]

Exhibit 6.8 shows a simple multivariable testing experiment that a small amusement park might use to increase park attendance on Tuesdays, typically the slowest day in the park. On the first Tuesday, Test 1, no changes are made. The park earns a profit of $4,000. On the next Tuesday, Test 2, the park runs a 2-for-1 admission special and gives everyone who enters the park a coupon for a free hotdog and a Coke between 11:00 A.M. and 1:00 P.M. The park earns just $2,000, losing money on all the free lunches it gave away to all those people who were admitted for free. On the next Tuesday, Test 3, parking is free and everyone who enters the park gets a free lunch coupon. The park makes $9,000. Finally, on the fourth Tuesday, the park again offers 2-for-1 admission, but this time with free parking. Profits this time are $5,000. What's the answer? It's obvious: Offer free parking and free lunch on Tuesdays.

---

EXHIBIT 6.8

MULTIVARIABLE TESTING TO INCREASE AMUSEMENT PARK ATTENDANCE ON TUESDAYS

| TEST | 2-FOR-1 | FREE LUNCH | FREE PARKING | PROFITS |
|------|---------|------------|--------------|---------|
| Test 1 | | | | $4,000 |
| Test 2 | X | X | | $2,000 |
| Test 3 | | X | X | $9,000 |
| Test 4 | X | | X | $5,000 |

MVT can be used in all kinds of businesses for many kinds of decisions. However, managers and employees will need to be trained how to design simple experiments and how to gather and analyze basic statistical data. Nonetheless, despite its cost, MVT allows managers to test and evaluate potential solutions before committing large amounts of money to their use. So instead of arguing about what you "think" the best solution might be, use MVT to test alternative solutions.

### 3.3 Staying Rational: Decision Software

Most decision makers satisfice, accepting the first "good enough" solution that comes to mind. Furthermore, because of time pressures and situational limitations, intuitive, unstructured decision making is the norm rather than the exception. Together, these factors make it nearly impossible for managers and business people to "stay rational" and maximize decisions.

Computer software, however, may do for decision making what it did for the nasty tasks of balancing your checkbook and doing your taxes—make it simpler, faster, and easier. If you've got a computer, you probably use Quicken (or a similar program) to balance your checkbook and stick to a budget. Likewise, if you do your own taxes, you probably use Turbo-Tax (or a similar program) to figure out how much money you owe Uncle Sam (or, if you're lucky, how much he owes you). Millions of people swear by these programs. According to Walter Mossberg, who writes the Personal Technology column for *The Wall Street Journal*, one such program, *DecideRight*, "does a far better job of organizing your options in a decision, and then ranking them by criteria you choose, than the traditional yellow legal pad with columns labeled 'pro' and 'con'—the method used by millions."[28]

Here's how it works. *DecideRight* starts with its QuickBuild tool, which, in an interview-like style, walks decision makers through the decision-making process. Step 1, label the decision. "What bank should we choose for the business?" Step 2, enter the decision criteria. "Location, hours, fees, and so forth." Step 3, enter the options you're considering. "Bank One, Central Bank & Trust and so on." Step 4, weight the decision criteria. For example, click on "location" and then drag and drop it on the high, medium, or low importance button on your screen. Step 5, rate each option against each decision criterion. Again, all you do is drag and drop. If Central Bank & Trust is just right around the corner from your business, click on "Central Bank & Trust" and then drag and drop it onto the "excellent" button on your screen for location. Step 6, the ranking of alternatives is performed automatically. There's no math involved (unless you choose this option).

Not only does *DecideRight* automatically rank alternatives, it also generates a report with charts and tables that explains why and how the decision was made. The report even explains why one alternative was chosen over another. Decision-making software like *DecideRight* is no guarantee of good decisions. After all, Quicken can't guarantee that you'll always have money in the bank, and TurboTax can't guarantee a tax refund. But to the extent that decision software tools like *DecideRight* (**http://www. performancesolutionstech.com**), iDecide (**http://www.definitivesoftware.com**), and ExpertChoice (**http://www.expertchoice.com**) encourage managers to work through the steps of the rational decision-making model, it should help them make *better* decisions.[29]

### 3.4 After the Decision: Avoiding Escalation of Commitment

In Section 2.3, you learned about the common mistakes that occur when managers are in the process of *making decisions*: overreliance on intuition, availability bias, representative bias, and the anchoring and adjustment bias. However, individuals and organizations often make a serious *post-decision* mistake called "escalation of commitment." **Escalation of commitment** is the tendency for a person who has already made a decision to more strongly support that original decision despite negative information that clearly indicates it was wrong.[30] For example, one of the reasons that Montgomery Ward's closed

**escalation of commitment**
the tendency for a person who has already made a decision to more strongly support that original decision despite negative information that clearly indicates it was wrong

A Chicago-area Ward's store displays a "Total Liquidation" sign following the news that the national department store chain declared bankruptcy. Sewell Avery's decision not to build new Ward's stores in the suburbs ultimately collapsed the 252-store chain.

after more than a century in business is that it sat on $607 million in on-hand cash and never opened a new store—not one—between 1941 and 1957. Ward's chairman at the time, Sewell Avery, had created a chart that showed that every World War since the time of Napoleon had been followed by a major economic depression. After World War II ended in 1945, Sewell declared, "Who am I to argue with history? Why build $14-per-foot buildings when we soon can do it for $3 per foot?" So, as post-war Americans moved in mass from the cities to the suburbs, Ward's sat back and watched Sears and JCPenney build hundreds of new stores in suburbs and malls. Montgomery Ward's tried to catch up by building similar stores in the 1970s and 1980s, but unlike Sears and Penney's, it never had enough stores in enough good locations to survive. Avery's obviously wrong decision to not build any new stores, which he stuck to for 16 years, eventually led to Ward's closing half a century later.[31]

Besides committing to a failing course of action, like Ward's chairman Sewell Avery, escalation of commitment often involves an increased commitment of resources (i.e., time, money, and people) to try to save the failed effort or decision. For example, the Shoreham Nuclear Power Plant in Shoreham, New York, estimated to cost $75 million, ended up costing $5 billion over 23 years, as its project managers repeatedly kept revising and increasing cost estimates and completion times. Amazingly, the plant never even began operations.[32] Rather than cutting losses and stopping the spending, managers became trapped in escalation of commitment and compounded their original wrong decisions by spending even more money to try to prove that they were right. Professor Barry Staw, a leading researcher on escalation of commitment, said, "Typically the leader is defensive and doesn't want to hear that he might be wrong. Then comes a social process in which other people's careers get staked to his course of action—even if it's wrong, they think they have to defend it or they'll lose their jobs. It's like propping up a defunct government."[33]

While nothing is failsafe, here are a few suggestions for avoiding the traps associated with escalation of commitment. To minimize escalation of commitment from the start, organizations should require frequent, detailed progress reports to make managers compare actual and planned spending, performance, and progress. If there are differences, they should explain why.[34] A second way to minimize escalation from the start is to hire an independent auditor to provide an objective assessment. Independent auditors have no psychological or financial investment in the decisions or projects they audit and are generally not directly affected by internal company politics. Their job is to provide a fresh set of eyes and to communicate a third-party perspective. And, if a project is failing, seriously behind schedule, or over cost, auditors should also be asked to suggest alternative courses of action to continued funding or investment in the project. Furthermore, the presence of an auditor is often enough to encourage managers to be more realistic about the progress or success of their decisions.[35]

Finally, several things can be done to minimize the damage and cost if escalation of commitment does occur. One of the most effective is to change managers. Like independent auditors, new managers with a fresh perspective are much more likely to discontinue decisions resulting in huge cost overruns or unproductive returns. For example, when Williams Catacosinos replaced Charles Pierce as manager of the Shoreham Nuclear Power Plant project, he told the managers who had been running the plant, "I want the plant to open, but I'm not married to it. I don't have the emotional attachment to it that you guys do."[36] Within three years, he had negotiated with the state of New York to shut down the project.[37]

A second way to deal with escalation of commitment is to label the decision as an "experiment." Calling a failed decision or project an "experiment" indicates that failure was a possibility, that the project was designed to help the company learn something, and that there was no permanent commitment to the decision. This gets the company off the hook, permits managers associated with the failed decision to save face, and in general makes it easier to stop or shut down a failed decision or project.[38] For example, after the Priceline WebHouse Club lost $363 million selling gasoline and groceries using Priceline's "name your price" strategy, Priceline.com announced that it was shutting down the Priceline WebHouse Club.[39] Jay Walker, Priceline founder, said this about the closing:[40]

- "In scale and scope the WebHouse Club was a business opportunity with great potential but with real risks. [Translation: "We weren't sure it would work."]
- "We specifically structured the WebHouse Club as a separate company from Priceline.com so that private investors, not Priceline.com shareholders, would bear that risk." [Translation: "Because we weren't sure it would work, we kept it separate from the main business, Priceline.com."]
- "All of us here at WebHouse Club are terribly disappointed, but I am proud of what we accomplished since we commenced operations." [Translation: "We tried our best, but we're hemorrhaging money, so we're going to close this down."]
- "In light of the weakness of the current capital market environment, the WebHouse Club executive team has reluctantly concluded that it was unlikely to be able to raise the additional capital the WebHouse Club would need next year to achieve the necessary scale and our goal of profitability. Accordingly, we have determined that the prudent course of action is to wind down our operations on an orderly basis while fully satisfying all of the WebHouse Club's obligations to customers, employees, and suppliers." [Translation: "We didn't have enough money to keep absorbing these tremendous losses. WebHouse is no more."]

## Review 3
### Improving Individual Decision Making

Decision rules are a relatively simple method of improving decision making. The dictionary rule helps decision makers choose among multiple alternative solutions, whereas the threshold rule helps decision makers make yes/no or accept/reject decisions. Managers use multivariable testing to do a better job of analyzing and evaluating potential solutions. The basic idea is to experimentally test several potential solutions at the same time and let data, rather than beliefs, guide decision making. While most decision makers "satisfice," accepting the first "good enough" solution that comes to mind, decision software (such as

*DecideRight,* which prompts managers to identify and weight decision criteria, generate alternative solutions, and then rank those solutions by their decision weights) can help them be better decision makers by working through the steps of the rational decision-making model. Escalation of commitment occurs when someone continues to strongly support a decision with funding and resources despite negative information that shows the decision was wrong. The damage and costs associated with escalation of commitment can be minimized by asking managers to make detailed progress reports comparing actual and planned spending and progress, hiring independent auditors, replacing managers who made the original decisions with new managers, and being willing to label the failed decision an "experiment," thus making it easier to end support for that decision.

## 4. Using Groups to Improve Decision Making

According to a study reported in *Fortune* magazine, 91 percent of U.S. companies use teams and groups to solve specific problems (i.e., make decisions).[41] Likewise, companies are increasingly using global teams and groups to solve problems and make decisions. For example, at Hewlett Packard, Radha Basu manages a group of software engineers located across 15 time zones and five countries: Japan, India, Germany, Australia, and the United States (Colorado). To make sure the group works well, she physically brings the team together once a year and visits each member four times, racking up more than 100,000 air miles each year. Why put up with the difficulties of trying to manage such a spread out group? Because working together, they've cut new product development time in half. Because working together, they can write and test code 22 hours a day. And, because working together, they can better support customers all over the world.[42]

*When done properly, like at Hewlett Packard, group decision making can lead to much better decisions than individual decision making. In fact, numerous studies show that groups consistently outperform individuals on complex tasks. Let's explore the 4.1 advantages and pitfalls of group decision making and see how the following group decision-making methods—4.2 structured conflict, 4.3 the nominal group technique, 4.4 the Delphi technique, 4.5 the stepladder technique, and 4.6 electronic brainstorming—can be used to improve decision making.*

### 4.1 Advantages and Pitfalls of Group Decision Making

Groups can do a much better job than individuals in two important steps of the decision-making process: defining the problem and generating alternative solutions. Four reasons explain why.

First, because group members usually possess different knowledge, skills, abilities, and experiences, groups will be able to view problems from multiple perspectives. Being able to view problems from multiple sources, in turn, can help groups perform better on complex tasks and make better decisions than individuals.[43] In fact, groups comprised of members with a greater diversity of knowledge, skills, abilities, and experiences will typically outperform groups with less diversity on those dimensions. For example, companies with more women in top management had better financial performance during initial public offerings, that is, the very first time a company publicly sells stock to investors (IPOs). Companies with top management groups composed of 10 percent females had IPO stock prices 4.6 percent higher than companies with no women in top management jobs. And, when women held half of the top management positions in a company, IPO stock prices were 23 percent higher. Company performance and stock prices were higher after the initial public offering, too. Professor Theresa Welbourne, who conducted the study, said, "When you have diversity in top management, you have people looking at data differently, and that brings better decision making overall."[44]

Second, groups can find and access much more information than can individuals. For example, Cough, Harbour & Associates, an engineering consulting firm, uses a

### Want to Help? Shhhhhh, Chew Your Nails

Managers sometimes impede group decision making by beginning the process by saying what they think should be done. Group members tend to place more importance on what their leaders say than on what other members say. This can impair group decision making by leading to premature acceptance of alternatives and decision criteria. So the best thing to do as a manager is to keep quiet. Do what this manager did when group members said, "Why don't you just tell us what to do so we can move on?" Her response? "I sat on my hands. Chewed on my fingernails."

**Sources:** S. Sherman, "Secrets of HP's 'Muddled' Team," *Fortune*, 18 March 1996, 116-120.

**groupthink**
a barrier to good decision making caused by pressure within the group for members to agree with each other

hiring team for interviewing potential employees. The company's director of human resources said, "We think we make better hiring decisions when we get a number of people involved. It's like working a crossword puzzle. If you get four people together, their chances of solving the puzzle are greater than if the four work separately."[45]

Third, the increased knowledge and information available to groups make it easier for them to generate more alternative solutions. Studies show that generating lots of alternative solutions is a critical part of improving the quality of decisions. Fourth, if groups are involved in the decision-making process, group members will be more committed to making chosen solutions work.

Although groups can do a better job of defining problems and generating alternative solutions, group decision making is subject to some pitfalls that can quickly erase these gains. One possible pitfall is groupthink. **Groupthink** occurs in highly cohesive groups when group members feel intense pressure to agree with each other, so that the group can approve a proposed solution.[46] Because groupthink leads to consideration of a limited number of solutions and because it restricts discussion of any considered solutions it usually results in poor decisions. Groupthink is most likely to occur under the following conditions:

- The group is insulated from others with different perspectives.
- The group leader begins by expressing strong preference for a particular decision.
- There is no established procedure for systematically defining problems and exploring alternatives.
- Group members have similar backgrounds and experiences.[47]

NASA's decision to launch the ill-fated space shuttle Challenger is an example of groupthink. Despite cold weather conditions that would normally have postponed a launch, NASA placed heavy pressure on Morton Thiokol (maker of the o-rings) and other engineering firms involved in the launch decision to give their approval to launch. After being told twice that a launch was not recommended, NASA administrators pressured Morton Thiokol one last time for an OK. Because of the pressure and time constraints, Thiokol reversed its decision. Tragically, as Thiokol had originally feared, the o-rings failed, and the shuttle exploded, killing all aboard.[48]

A second potential problem with group decision making is that it takes considerable time. It takes time to reconcile schedules (so that group members can meet). Furthermore, it's a rare group that consistently holds productive task-oriented meetings to effectively work through the decision process. Some of the most common complaints about meetings (and thus decision making) are that the meeting's purpose is unclear, meeting participants are unprepared, critical people are absent or late, conversation doesn't stay focused on the problem, and no one follows up on the decisions that were made. Not surprisingly, given these difficulties, the *Valley News Dispatch*, a small paper in Tarentum, Pennsylvania, has this sign in the company conference room: "Are you lonely? Working on your own? Hate making decisions? HOLD A MEETING!"[49]

A third possible pitfall is that sometimes just one or two people, perhaps the boss or a strong-willed, vocal group member, dominate group discussion, restricting consideration of different problem definitions and alternative solutions. Another possible problem is that, unlike their own decisions and actions, group members often don't feel accountable for the decisions made and actions taken by the group.

While these pitfalls can lead to poor decision making, this doesn't mean that managers should avoid using groups to make decisions. When done properly, group decision making can lead to much better decisions. The pitfalls of group decision making are not inevitable. Most of them can be overcome through good management. Let's see how

207

Group decision making can put pressure on group members to follow the majority. Such pressure was exerted on Morton Thiokol to approve the launch of the space shuttle, Challenger, despite cold-weather warnings. The wreckage of the fatal explosion which resulted is seen being returned to Cape Canaveral.

© CORBIS

structured conflict, the nominal group technique, the Delphi technique, the stepladder technique, and electronic brainstorming help managers improve group decision making.

### 4.2 Structured Conflict

**c-type conflict (cognitive conflict)**
disagreement that focuses on problem- and issue-related differences of opinion

Most people view conflict negatively. However, the right kind of conflict can lead to much better group decision making. **C-type conflict**, or "cognitive conflict," focuses on problem- and issue-related differences of opinion.[50] In c-type conflict, group members disagree because their different experiences and expertise lead them to different views of the problem and its potential solutions. However, c-type conflict is also characterized by a willingness to examine, compare, and reconcile those differences to produce the best possible solution. Alteon WebSystems, now a division of Nortel Networks, makes critical use of c-type conflict. Top manager Dominic Orr described Alteon's c-type conflict this way:

> There's no silent disagreement, and no getting personal, and definitely no "let's take it offline" mentality. Our goal is to make each major decision in a single meeting. People arrive with a proposal or a solution—and with the facts to support it. After an idea is presented, we open the floor to objective, and often withering, critiques. And if the idea collapses under scrutiny, we move on to another: no hard feelings. We're judging the idea, not the person. At the same time, we don't really try to regulate emotions. Passionate conflict means that we're getting somewhere, not that the discussion is out of control. But one person does act as referee—by asking basic questions like "Is this good for the customer?" or "Does it keep our time-to-market advantage intact?" By focusing relentlessly on the facts, we're able to see the strengths and weaknesses of an idea clearly and quickly.[51]

**a-type conflict (affective conflict)**
disagreement that focuses on individual- or personally-oriented issues

By contrast, **a-type conflict**, meaning "affective conflict," refers to the emotional reactions that can occur when disagreements become personal rather than professional. A-type conflict often results in hostility, anger, resentment, distrust, cynicism, and apathy. Unlike c-type conflict, a-type conflict undermines team effectiveness by preventing teams from engaging in the activities characteristic of c-type conflict that are critical to team effectiveness. Examples of a-type conflict statements are "your idea," "our idea," "my department," "you don't know what you are talking about," or "you don't understand our situation." Rather than focusing on issues and ideas, these statements focus on individuals.[52]

**devil's advocacy**
a decision-making method in which an individual or a subgroup is assigned the role of a critic

Devil's advocacy and dialectical inquiry are two methods that introduce structured c-type conflict into the group decision-making process. **Devil's advocacy** creates c-type conflict by assigning an individual or a subgroup the role of critic. The following five steps establish a devil's advocacy program:

1. Generate a potential solution.
2. Assign a devil's advocate to criticize and question the solution.
3. Present the critique of the potential solution to key decision makers.
4. Gather additional relevant information.
5. Decide whether to use, change, or not use the originally proposed solution.[53]

**dialectical inquiry**
a decision-making method in which decision makers state the assumptions of a proposed solution (a thesis) and generate a solution that is the opposite (antithesis) of that solution

**Dialectical inquiry** creates c-type conflict by forcing decision makers to state the assumptions of a proposed solution (a thesis) and to then generate a solution that is the opposite (antithesis) of the proposed solution. The following are the five steps of the dialectical inquiry process:

1. Generate a potential solution.
2. Identify the assumptions underlying the potential solution.
3. Generate a conflicting counterproposal based on the opposite assumptions.
4. Have advocates of each position present their arguments and engage in a debate in front of key decision makers.
5. Decide whether to use, change, or not use the originally proposed solution.[54]

When properly used, both the devil's advocacy and dialectical inquiry approaches introduce c-type conflict into the decision-making process. Further, contrary to the common belief that conflict is bad, studies show that these methods lead to less a-type conflict, improved decision quality, and greater acceptance of decisions once they have been made.[55] See the "What Really Works" feature for more information on both techniques.

## 4.3 Nominal Group Technique

**nominal group technique**
a decision-making method that begins and ends by having group members quietly write down and evaluate ideas to be shared with the group

"Nominal" means "in name only." Accordingly, the **nominal group technique** received its name because it begins with "quiet time," in which group members independently write down as many problem definitions and alternative solutions as possible. In other words, the nominal group technique begins by having group members act as individuals. After the "quiet time," the group leader asks each group member to share one idea at a time with the group. As they are read aloud, ideas are posted on flipcharts or wallboards for all to see. This step continues until all ideas have been shared. The next step involves a discussion of the advantages and disadvantages of these ideas. The nominal group technique closes with a second "quiet time," in which group members independently rank the ideas presented. Group members then read their rankings aloud, and the idea with the highest average rank is selected.[56]

The nominal group technique improves group decision making by decreasing a-type conflict. However, in doing so, it also restricts c-type conflict. Consequently, the nominal group technique typically produces poorer-quality decisions than do the devil's advocacy or dialectical inquiry approaches. Nonetheless, more than 80 studies have found that nominal groups produce better-quality ideas than traditional group decisions.[57]

## 4.4 Delphi Technique

**Delphi technique**
a decision-making method in which a panel of experts responds to questions and to each other until reaching agreement on an issue

The **Delphi technique** is a decision-making method in which a panel of experts respond to questions and to each other until reaching agreement on an issue. The first step is to assemble a panel of experts. However, unlike other approaches to group decision making, it isn't necessary to bring the panel together in one place. Since the Delphi technique does not require the experts to leave their offices or disrupt their schedules, they are more likely to participate in the process. For example, a colleague and I were asked to conduct a Delphi technique assessment of the "10 most important steps for small

209

# WhatReallyWorks

## Devil's Advocacy and Dialectical Inquiry

Ninety percent of the decisions managers face are well-structured problems that recur frequently under conditions of certainty. For example, showing up at an airline ticket counter without your ticket is a well-structured problem. It happens every day (recurs frequently), and it's easy to determine if you have your ticket or not (conditions of certainty).

Well-structured problems are solved with programmed decisions, in which a policy, procedure, or rule clearly specifies how to solve the problem. Thus, there's no mystery about what to do when someone shows up without a ticket. After you present identification to prove who you are, and after you pay a transaction fee (around $75), the airline gives you another ticket.

In some sense, programmed decisions really aren't decisions, because anyone with any experience knows what to do. There's no thought involved. What keeps managers up at night is the other 10 percent of problems. Ill-structured problems that are novel (no one's seen them before) and exist under conditions of uncertainty are solved with nonprogrammed decisions. Nonprogrammed decisions do not involve standard methods of resolution. Every time managers make a nonprogrammed decision, they have to figure out a new way of handling a new problem. That's what makes them so tough.

Both the devil's advocacy and dialectical inquiry approaches to decision making can be used to improve nonprogrammed decision making. Both approaches work because they force decision makers to identify and criticize the assumptions underlying the nonprogrammed decisions that they hope will solve ill-structured problems.

### Devil's Advocacy

There is a 58 percent chance that decision makers who use the devil's-advocacy approach to criticize and question their solutions will produce better-quality decisions than decisions based on the advice of experts.

**Devil's Advocacy**

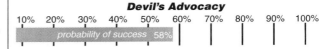

### Dialectical Inquiry

There is a 55 percent chance that decision makers who use the dialectical-inquiry approach to criticize and question their solutions will produce better-quality decisions than decisions based on the advice of experts.

**Dialectical Inquiry**

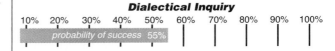

Note that each technique has been compared to decisions obtained by following experts' advice. So, while these probabilities of success, 55 percent and 58 percent, seem small, they very likely *understate* the effects of both techniques. In other words, the probabilities of success would have been much larger if both techniques had been compared to unstructured decision-making processes.

**Source:** C.R. Schwenk, "Effects of Devil's Advocacy and Dialectical Inquiry on Decision Making: A Meta-Analysis," *Organizational Behavior and Human Decision Performance* 47 (1990): 161-176.

businesses." With the help of the dean of my business school and a former mayor of the city, we assembled a panel of local top-level managers and CEOs.

The second step is to create a questionnaire consisting of a series of open-ended questions for the experts. For example, we asked our panel to answer these questions: "What is the most common mistake made by small-business persons?" "Right now, what do you think is the biggest threat to the survival of most small businesses?" "If you had one piece of advice to give to the owner of a small business, what would it be?"

In Step 3, panel members' written responses are analyzed, summarized, and fed back to the panel for reactions until panel members reach agreement. In our Delphi study, it took about a month to get the panel members' written responses to the first three questions. Then we summarized and typed their written responses into a brief report (no more than two pages). We sent the summary to the panel members and asked them to explain why they agreed or disagreed with these conclusions from the first round of questions. Asking why they agreed or disagreed is important, because it helps uncover panel members' unstated assumptions and beliefs. Again, this process of summarizing panel feedback and obtaining reactions to that feedback continues until panel members reach agreement. For our study, it took just one more round for panel members' views to reach a consensus. In all, it took approximately three-and-a-half months to complete our Delphi study.

The Delphi technique is not an approach that managers should use for common decisions. Because it is a time-consuming, labor-intensive, and expensive process, the Delphi technique is best reserved for important long-term issues and problems. Nonetheless, the judgments and conclusions obtained from it are typically better than those you would get from one expert.

## 4.5 Stepladder Technique

**stepladder technique**
when group members are added to a group discussion one at a time (i.e., like a stepladder), the existing group members first take the time to listen to each new member's thoughts, ideas, and recommendations, and then the group, in turn, shares the ideas and suggestions that it had already considered, discusses the new and old ideas, and then makes a decision

The stepladder technique improves group decision making by making sure that each group member's contributions are independent, are considered, and are discussed. As shown in Exhibit 6.9, the **stepladder technique** begins with discussion between two group members, each of whom presents to the other their thoughts, ideas, and recommendations before jointly making a tentative decision. At each step, as other group members are added to the discussion one at a time, like a stepladder, the existing group members take the time to listen to each new member's thoughts, ideas, and recommendations. The group then shares the ideas and suggestions that it had already considered, discusses the new and old ideas, and then makes a tentative decision. This process (new member's ideas are heard, group shares previous ideas and suggestions, discussion is held, tentative group decision is made) continues until each group member's ideas have been discussed.

For the stepladder technique to work, group members must have enough time to consider the problem or decision on their own, to present their ideas to the group, and to thoroughly discuss all ideas and alternatives with the group at each step. Rushing through each step destroys the advantages of this technique. Also, groups must make sure that subsequent group members are completely unaware of previous discussions and suggestions. This will ensure that each member who joins the group brings truly independent thoughts and suggestions, thus greatly increasing the chances of making better decisions.

---

**EXHIBIT 6.9**

STEPLADDER TECHNIQUE FOR GROUP DECISION MAKING

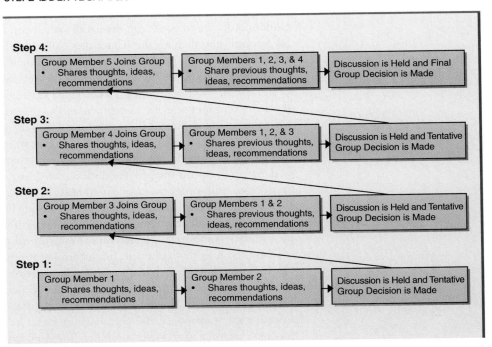

One study found that compared to traditional groups in which all group members are present for the entire discussion, groups using the stepladder technique produced significantly better decisions. Moreover, the stepladder groups performed better than the best individual member of their group 56 percent of the time, while traditional groups only outperformed the best individual member of their group 13 percent of the time.[58] Besides better performance, groups using the stepladder technique also generated more ideas and were more satisfied with the decision-making process.

### 4.6 Electronic Brainstorming

**brainstorming**
a decision-making method in which group members build on each others' ideas to generate as many alternative solutions as possible

**Brainstorming**, in which group members build on others' ideas, is a technique for generating a large number of alternative solutions. Brainstorming has four rules:

1. The more ideas, the better.
2. All ideas are acceptable, no matter how wild or crazy they might be.
3. Other group members' ideas should be used to come up with even more ideas.
4. Criticism or evaluation of ideas is not allowed.

**electronic brainstorming**
a decision-making method in which group members use computers to build on each others' ideas and generate many alternative solutions

**production blocking**
a disadvantage of face-to-face brainstorming in which a group member must wait to share an idea because another member is presenting an idea

**evaluation apprehension**
fear of what others will think of your ideas

While brainstorming is great fun and can help managers generate a large number of alternative solutions, it does have a number of disadvantages. Fortunately, **electronic brainstorming**, in which group members use computers to communicate and generate alternative solutions, overcomes the disadvantages associated with face-to-face brainstorming.[59]

The first disadvantage that electronic brainstorming overcomes is **production blocking**, which occurs when you have an idea, but you have to wait to share it because someone else is already describing an idea to the group. This short delay may make you forget your idea or decide that it really wasn't worth sharing. But with electronic brainstorming, production blocking doesn't happen. With all group members seated at computers, everyone can type in their ideas whenever they occur. There's no "waiting your turn" to be heard by the group.

The second disadvantage that electronic brainstorming overcomes is **evaluation apprehension**, that is, being afraid of what others will think of your ideas. However, with electronic brainstorming, all ideas are anonymous. When you type in an idea and hit the "Enter" key to share it with the group, group members see only the idea. Furthermore, many brainstorming software programs also protect anonymity by displaying ideas in random order. So, if you laugh maniacally when you type "Cut top management's pay by 50 percent!" and then hit the "Enter" key, it won't show up immediately on everyone's screen. This makes it doubly difficult to determine which comments belong to whom.

Exhibit 6.10 shows the typical layout for electronic brainstorming. All participants sit in front of computers around a U-shaped table. This configuration allows them to see their computer screens, each other, and a large main screen. Exhibit 6.11 shows what the typical electronic brainstorming group member will see on his or her computer screen. The first step in electronic brainstorming is to anonymously generate as many ideas as possible. It's common for groups to generate 100 ideas in a half-hour period. Step 2 is to edit the generated ideas, categorize them, and eliminate redundancies. Step 3 is to rank-order the categorized ideas in terms of quality. Step 4, the last step, has three parts: generate a series of action steps, decide the best order for accomplishing these steps, and identify who is responsible for each step. All four steps are accomplished with computers and electronic brainstorming software.[60]

Studies show that electronic brainstorming is much more productive than face-to-face brainstorming. Compared to regular four-person brainstorming groups, the same-sized electronic brainstorming groups produce 25 percent to 50 percent more ideas. Compared to regular 12-person brainstorming groups, the same-sized electronic brainstorming groups produce 200 percent more ideas! In fact, because production blocking (i.e., waiting your turn) is not a problem for electronic brainstorming, the number and quality of ideas generally increases with group size.[61]

EXHIBIT 6.10

TYPICAL LAYOUT FOR AN ELECTRONIC BRAINSTORMING ROOM

**Source:** "GroupSystems Tour Stop 4: Developing Consensus," Ventana Web Site. [Online] Available http://www.ventana.com/html/vc_tour_stop_4__group_consensu.html, 12 January 1999.

Even though it works much better than traditional brainstorming, electronic brainstorming has disadvantages, too. An obvious problem is the expense of computers, networks, software, etc. As these costs continue to drop, however, electronic brainstorming will become cheaper.

Another problem is that the anonymity of ideas may bother people who are used to having their ideas accepted by virtue of their position (i.e., the boss). On the other hand, one CEO said, "Because the process is anonymous, the sky's the limit in terms of what you can say, and as a result it is more thought-provoking. As a CEO, you'll probably discover things you might not want to hear but need to be aware of."[62]

A third disadvantage is that outgoing individuals who are more comfortable expressing themselves verbally may find it difficult to express themselves in writing. Finally, the most obvious problem is that participants have to be able to type. Those who can't type,

EXHIBIT 6.11

WHAT YOU SEE ON THE COMPUTER DURING ELECTRONIC BRAINSTORMING

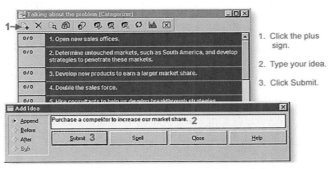

**Source:** "GroupSystems Tour Stop 2: Generating a List of Ideas," Ventana Web Site. [Online] Available http://www.ventana.com/html/vc_tour_stop_2__categorizer.html, 12 January 1999.

or who type slowly, may be easily frustrated and find themselves at a disadvantage to experienced typists. For example, one meeting facilitator was tipped off that an especially fast typist was pretending to be more than one person. Said the facilitator, "He'd type 'Oh, I agree' and then 'Ditto, ditto' or 'What a great idea,' all in quick succession, using different variations of uppercase and lowercase letters and punctuation. He tried to make it seem like a lot of people were concurring, but it was just him." Eventually, the person sitting next to him got suspicious and began watching his screen.[63]

## Review **4**
### Using Groups to Improve Decision Making

When groups view problems from multiple perspectives, use more information, have a diversity of knowledge and experience, and become committed to solutions they help choose, they can produce better solutions than individual decision makers. However, group decisions suffer from these disadvantages: groupthink, slowness, discussions dominated by just a few individuals, and unfelt responsibility for decisions. Group decisions work best when group members encourage c-type conflict. However, group decisions don't work as well when groups become mired in a-type conflict. The devil's-advocacy and dialectical-inquiry approaches improve group decisions because they bring structured c-type conflict into the decision-making process. By contrast, the nominal group technique and the Delphi technique both improve decision making by reducing a-type conflict through limited interactions between group members. The stepladder technique improves group decision making by adding each group member's independent contributions to the discussion one at a time. Finally, because it overcomes the problems of production blocking and evaluation apprehension, electronic brainstorming is a more effective method of generating alternatives than face-to-face brainstorming.

## What Really Happened?

The cleanliness of the rational decision-making model (defining the problem, defining and weighting decision criteria, generating and evaluating alternative courses of action, and computing the optimal decision) rarely matches up with the messiness of real-world decision making. Indeed, at the beginning of this chapter, you heard one manager say, "I just know how disillusioning and frustrating it is to be hit with problems and conflicts all day and not be able to solve them very cleanly." BP Amoco was faced with a messy, tough decision about whether to invest millions in deepwater drilling. Let's find out what really happened at BP Amoco as it struggled with this difficult decision.

**Well, any way that you look at it, you're convinced that deepwater drilling is a good bet, but how can you demonstrate that to top management, especially con-** **sidering the risks involved and the tough economic conditions?**
The rational decision-making model assumes that managers can gaze into crystal balls and accurately predict whether a potential solution will fix a problem. The model also assumes that managers make decisions under conditions of certainty, with complete information and knowledge of all possible outcomes and their likelihood. Under those assumptions, it should be easy to demonstrate to top management that investing in deepwater drilling is the right thing to do. In fact, under conditions of certainty (you know precisely whether various alternatives will work), it should be self-evident.

This was certainly, no pun intended, not the case when BP Amoco was trying to decide whether to invest millions, if not billions, of dollars in deepwater drilling. Indeed, deepwater drilling was unproven at the time, and the risks were great. When an onshore well comes up dry, it only costs the company $1 million. By contrast, when a deepwater well comes up dry, it costs the company $50 million! In short, like most big decisions, BP Amoco was making a multimillion-dollar choice under conditions of uncertainty, not knowing the precise odds of winning or losing.

Today, however, BP Amoco is using technology to increase its chances of hitting a wet (i.e., oil producing) deepwater well. Before spending $50 million on a new deepwater well, it has teams of geologists, engineers, and drillers work together in a room called the "hive" to view and analyze 3D images of rock and shale formations at the bottom of the sea. It used to take months to analyze enough information to have a reasonable certainty of hitting a wet deepwater well, but thanks to teamwork and improvements in technology, today it only takes BP Amoco one day to decide whether to spend $50 million on a new deepwater well.

214

In part, it will depend on how averse to risk top managers are. Are they willing to spend huge sums of money to potentially put BP Amoco in front of its competitors for years to come, or are they averse to risk, wanting to sit back and see whether other oil companies have success with deepwater drilling first? Risk propensity is a person's tendency to take or avoid risks. Managers differ greatly in terms of risk propensity. Some people have a high risk propensity and are willing to bet years of their lives and lots of money under conditions of uncertainty. However, others with a low risk propensity say to themselves, "Why take a chance if you don't know what your odds of success are?"

At BP Amoco, CEO Sir John Browne developed a high risk propensity early in his career when he worked in Prudhoe Bay, Alaska, the site of BP's huge 14-million-barrel oilfield. However, Browne learned an important lesson: building the pipeline to carry the crude oil 800 miles to the sea to be picked up by oil tankers increased the cost of the oil by a factor of 10. Fortunately, he said, "the price of oil went up by a factor of five." After that, when he became chief financial officer of BP's Sohio division, he concluded that BP's Alaskan oilfields would never yield a meaningful profit. So, when BP geologist Jack Golden started to talk about his new ideas on deepwater exploration, Browne was interested, but knew that the economics of this even more expensive drilling would have to be right for BP to make a profit. Still, he decided to gamble and took Sohio's entire $50 million exploration budget and diverted it to deepwater drilling. He said, "The key was to take a position in advance of the then-fashionable theory. It wasn't a 'bet-the-company' strategy, but it was clear that if it didn't work, our position in North America would be limited to Alaska." However, Browne hedged his bet by investing the $50 million to purchase a share in two deepwater projects that Shell Oil had just begun.

When Shell's deepwater wells paid off, Brown and BP invested millions more in deepwater drilling and went further out into the Gulf of Mexico in search of bigger fields. Again, this increased BP's risk, but by going further out, the company could purchase nine square mile tracts of underwater land for only $150,000, compared to $20 million closer to shore. So the higher cost and risk associated with drilling farther from shore was greatly reduced by the much lower cost of purchasing underwater land for drilling. If Sir John Browne's bets on deepwater drilling pay off (two huge oilfields have been found thus far), BP should surpass Shell oil as the second largest oil company in the world and might even knock ExxonMobil from its number one position.

Interestingly, ExxonMobil's drilling strategy, which stems from its risk-averse CEO, Lee Raymond, is to let other oil companies move into a potential oil-producing location first. Once large oil fields have been found, Exxon then moves in with its resources. Using this strategy, Exxon's oil field production has fallen 8 percent over the last few years. By contrast, thanks to the risk propensity of CEO John Browne, BP Amoco's oil field production has increased by 10 percent over the same time and is expected to increase by another 6 percent over the next two years. The key issue, discussed next, is whether those additional reserves will improve company performance.

**Finally, it may come down to something as simple as how the problem is defined. Is the problem cutting costs to restore profitability, or is the problem investing company funds in smartly calculated risks that might pay off in huge increases in oil revenue? In the end, though, you don't want to just convince upper management to do what you want; you want to be right, too.**
The first step in decision making is defining the problem, that is, figuring out what's going wrong. Typically, this means looking for gaps between desired states and existing states. When gasoline dropped below $1 a gallon and a barrel of crude oil below $15, the gap on which everyone in the oil industry was focused was profits, which, for most oil companies, had turned into losses because of the low prices.

One way to define that gap is to conclude that costs are too high. For example, ExxonMobil has focused on keeping costs down, cutting 7,000 employees over the last seven years. In fact, Exxon's earnings were up 27 percent during that time, largely because its operating expenses have not increased. However, another way to define the profit gap is to conclude that revenues are too low. This is why BP Amoco has focused on finding large, offshore deepwater oilfields to greatly increase the oil and gas available to sell.

As mentioned above, BP's oil production is up 10 percent in the last few years and is expected to climb another 6 percent over the next two years. However, because BP was an early player, it was much cheaper to acquire oil rights through deepwater drilling (i.e., $150,000 for a nine square mile tract of deepwater land, compared to $20 million to acquire typical offshore sites). In fact, BP owns as much as 40 percent of the deepwater oil reserves in the Gulf of Mexico. Jack Golden, who heads BP's exploration unit, said, "We managed to come from nowhere over the course of the decade." Furthermore, despite costing as much as $1 billion to develop a deepwater oil field, the low cost of acquisition and BP's technology make deepwater oil fields much less expensive than land-based oilfields. BP can produce a barrel of deepwater oil for about $5 to $6 a barrel. So even if oil drops below $15 a barrel, as it did several years ago when gas dropped below $1 per gallon, BP will still make close to $10 a barrel. Said Jack Golden, deepwater oil "improves the financial characteristics of the whole business."

**Sources:** J. Biers, "Drilling's Leviathans Stumble to Sea: New Generation Rigs, Ships Born in Rough Waters," *Houston Chronicle*, 17 October 1999, Business 6. D. Fisher, "How Sir John Browne Turned BP Amoco into the Hottest Prospect in the Oil Patch," *Forbes*, 2 April 2001, 110. D. Ivanovich, "The New 2000 Millennium—World May Learn to Wean Itself from Oil: The Search for Crude Deepens, As Does the Concern over Its Future," *Houston Chronicle*, 24 October 1999, 1. S. Liesman & A. Sullivan, "Mystery Man—Exxon Mobil Merger Positions an Enigma at Oil Giant's Helm: Hardly a Household Name, Mr. Raymond Fostered a Revolution Quietly Playing Everyman at Valdez," *The Wall Street Journal*, 1 December 1999. "petroleum production" *Encyclopædia Britannica Online*. <http://search.eb.com/bol/topic?artcl=110684&seq_nbr=1&page=n&isctn=6> [Accessed 18 August 2001]. D. Soils, "Oil Discovery Called Largest Ever in Gulf: BP Amoco, Mobil Share in Billion Barrel Fined," *Dallas Morning News*, 16 July 1999, 1D. Staff Reports, "Giant in the Gulf: BP Amoco's Massive Oil Drilling Platform Has Begun Pumping with 5 Wells in Gulf," *The New Orleans Times Picayune*, 3 December 1999, C1. K. Williams, "Transocean at Standoff on Drill Ship," *Houston Chronicle*, 10 June 2001, Business 2.

## Key Terms

absolute comparisons *(179)*
anchoring and adjustment bias *(189)*
a-type conflict (affective conflict) *(198)*
availability bias *(188)*
bounded rationality *(183)*
brainstorming *(202)*
conditions of certainty *(185)*
conditions of risk *(185)*
conditions of uncertainty *(186)*
c-type conflict (cognitive conflict) *(198)*
decision criteria *(177)*
decision making *(174)*

decision rule *(191)*
Delphi technique *(199)*
devil's advocacy *(199)*
dialectical inquiry *(199)*
dictionary rule *(191)*
electronic brainstorming *(202)*
escalation of commitment *(193)*
evaluation apprehension *(202)*
groupthink *(197)*
information overload *(184)*
maximizing *(185)*
minimum threshold rule *(191)*

multivariable testing *(191)*
negative frame *(186)*
nominal group technique *(199)*
positive frame *(186)*
problem *(177)*
production blocking *(202)*
rational decision making *(174)*
relative comparisons *(179)*
representative bias *(188)*
risk propensity *(186)*
satisficing *(185)*
stepladder technique *(201)*

## What Would You Do-II

### What Do You Say?

As the director of human resources for a large, publicly traded manufacturing firm, you are privy to all types of corporate information regarding employee issues. Just yesterday, you attended a meeting with the CEO, president, vice president, and other top-level executives to discuss a proposed merger with a large competing firm. As a result of the merger, slated to be announced in approximately three weeks, a total of 8 percent of the employees at your firm will be laid-off in an effort to combine overlapping jobs and reduce costs. At this same meeting, you were given a tentative list of the affected employees. All members present at the meeting were instructed to not mention a word of the proposed merger or layoff until it has been released by the corporate office. Early release of the confidential information could result in widespread panic among the firm's employees, drastically reduce the company's stock price, and possibly violate the Securities Exchange Act of 1934, which controls how investment information regarding mergers, acquisitions, and tender offers are to be released to the public. If an employee or investor receives information regarding the proposed merger before it is publicly released and uses that information to make investment decisions, that person and the individual who leaked the information may be prosecuted by the Securities Exchange Commission (SEC) for practicing insider trading. Therefore, keeping this information private is extremely important.

This morning, as you were walking across the parking lot, Jim, an employee of the firm and a long-time friend of your family, approached you for some advice. He and his wife have been married for less than a year and are looking to purchase a home. Jim tells you that the bank will be calling your office soon to verify his employment and salary information as part of the prequalification process. Jim also asks you for your personal opinion regarding the amount that he should provide as a down payment on the home. He tells you that as a first-time home buyer, he can qualify for the loan by providing only 3 percent of the total purchase price as a down payment. However, he and his wife have amassed a significant nest egg in the last six months, and, as a result, are able to put approximately 10 percent down on the home. Additionally, Jim tells you that he and his wife Maggie recently learned that she is pregnant and will deliver in approximately seven months.

Suddenly, you have a sinking feeling in your stomach. Yesterday, as you briefly glanced over the list of employees to be cut, you noticed that Jim was one of the affected employees. In order to buy some time, you tell Jim that you are late for an important meeting but that you will call him as soon as you are free to discuss his home-buying dilemma. As you turn to walk toward your office, Jim comments, "I'll wait for your call before making my decision. Maggie and I really trust your advice and experience." As you reach your office door, you think to yourself, I can't tell him that he is about to lose his job. Nor can I honestly tell him to invest his savings into a home, knowing that he has a baby on the way and will soon have no job. You sink into your executive, leather, high-back chair, and you ponder how you will

decide what information to give Jim and his wife without jeopardizing the company's interest and your personal friendship. **As the director of human resources for this firm, choose a decision-making process and determine what information you can honestly and professionally provide to Jim.**

**Source:** J. Seglin, "When an Employee About to Be Axed Asks for Advice," *Fortune,* 23 July 2001.

## Management Decisions

### Sugar-Free Kool-Aid: Let's Brainstorm!

What comes to mind when you think of Kool-Aid? Summer? Pool parties and picnics? Third grade? Kool-pops that you made, poured into molds, and froze in the freezer? Was one of these flavors your favorite: Black Cherry, Cherry, Grape, Incrediberry, Kickin'-Kiwi-Lime, Lemonade, Lemon-Lime, Man-o-Mangoberry, Oh-Yeah Orange-Pineapple, Orange, Pina-Pineapple, Pink Lemonade, Pink Swimmingo, Purplesaurus Rex, Raspberry, Rock-a-dile Red, Slammin' Strawberry-Kiwi, Strawberry, Strawberry-Raspberry, Tropical Punch, or Watermelon-Cherry?

When most people think of Kool-Aid, they think of kids. Just over a decade ago, Kool-Aid sales started to decline. In part, this was due to long-term demographic changes. Families were simply having fewer children. Since the makers of Kool-Aid obviously couldn't do anything to change demographic trends, the next best thing was to encourage groups other than kids, such as teens and adults, to drink more Kool-Aid. With the explosion in popularity of diet-drinks, the answer seemed simple: Sugar-Free Kool-Aid. However, Kool-Aid's management knew that it would still have a tough time convincing teens and adults to make Sugar-Free Kool-Aid their drink of choice. So, to figure out how they might do this, Kool-Aid sponsored a contest for MBA students at the top business schools in the nation. MBA student teams submitted their

ideas, and the teams with the most promising proposals were flown to New York to make formal presentations. Unfortunately, their suggestions were not very creative. Kool-Aid management was extremely disappointed with the results.

The purpose of this in-class management-decision activity is to correct that problem by using brainstorming to generate as many ideas as possible for selling Sugar-Free Kool-Aid to teens and adults. Keep in mind the following rules of brainstorming:

- The more ideas, the better.
- All ideas are acceptable, no matter how wild or crazy they might be.
- Other group members' ideas should be used to come up with even more ideas.
- Criticism or evaluation of ideas is not allowed.

Remember, creativity requires playfulness. Make this fun! Be wild and crazy! And, most important, don't criticize others' ideas. No moaning, groaning, or commenting allowed (or aloud). The first step in brainstorming is to generate as many different ideas as possible. Evaluation comes later.

#### Question
1. Think of as many ways as possible to get teens and adults to buy and use Sugar-Free Kool-Aid.

## Management Decisions

### Cafeteria or Gym?

Due to a record-breaking year, your company posted profits of 24 percent above analysts' expectations. In an attempt to retain qualified employees and to continue to provide an atmosphere of innovation and creativity, a decision was made to allot $1 million of retained earnings toward improving employee incentives. Upon announcing the program, a memo was circulated describing the rationale behind this decision. The memo encouraged employees to submit proposals for ideas regarding what type of incentives to spend money on. A minimum threshold rule was imposed on all proposals to be submitted. In order to be considered, the proposal must provide a tangible return for the organization through an increase

in productivity, aesthetic beauty, functionality, morale, or profitability. Additionally, the proposal must benefit a majority of stakeholders within the company.

A total of 36 ideas were submitted. After analyzing each of the proposals, determining their feasibility, and weighing them against the minimum threshold rule, 10 ideas were chosen to be further reviewed, discussed, and ranked. Several meetings were held discussing the pros and cons of each proposal, and a second memo was circulated asking all employees to rank the proposals from least to most desired. The results showed that the two proposals favored most by employees appear to be the construction of a cafeteria and the construction of a gymnasium / workout center. Both ideas received an equal ranking of importance. You have been chosen to decide which proposal should be implemented.

The cafeteria, as described in the proposal, would include both working and nonworking areas for employees. The working areas would have, in addition to the normal tables and chairs, erasable marker boards, flipcharts, networked computer workstations and projection devices, telephones, and teleconferencing equipment. The nonworking area, separated by a glass partition, would house the normal tables and chairs, along with a big-screen television and a CD-jukebox. The cafeteria would serve a daily special in addition to "on-demand" items, such as hamburgers, hot dogs, salads, burritos, and other common food items. Food would be provided at a reduced price for all employees. Additionally, employees who regularly take clients and representatives out for business lunches would be allowed to charge their meals to their expense account, thus providing a savings for the company through reduced meal expenses.

Proponents of this plan claim that innovativeness, creativity, and profitability would be increased because most employees (whether they realize it or not) would be inclined to discuss work-related matters during their lunch hour. By assembling diverse groups of employees in a common area, these discussions could evolve into new projects or the improvement of existing ones. Having technology-enhanced components available in the working area would provide employees with the tools necessary to perform further research of their ideas during active discussions. The ideas could then be presented and discussed on markerboards or through the computer's LCD projector. Proponents also stated that the cafeteria could im-

prove employee morale since having an on-site cafeteria would reduce the hassle of fighting traffic and crowds during the lunch-time rush and would increase productivity by ensuring that employees do not spend more than their allotted time during lunch.

The proposed gymnasium / workout center would include a half-court basketball area with goal, two racquetball courts, and a complete workout area, containing items such as stairmasters, rowing machines, stationary bikes, nautilus equipment, locker rooms, showers, and hottubs. Proponents of this plan state that employee morale and productivity would be enhanced as studies show that exercise helps eliminate stress and boosts energy levels. Proponents further claim that the increased productivity would, in time, translate into increased profits for the firm. In addition, healthier employees would reduce health insurance costs over the long run. To avoid congestion, timeslots for the use of the workout center would be available by reservation. In order not to impact work time, employees would be encouraged to use the workout center before work, during their lunch break, or after work.

### Questions

1. If you were the manager in question, which proposal would you choose to implement and why?
2. Looking back at the proposal not chosen, did you fall prey to one of the common decision-making mistakes (intuition, availability bias, representative bias, or anchoring and adjustment bias) in not choosing this proposal? Explain.

**Source:** M. Schrage, "I'll Have the Pasta Primavera, With a Side of Strategy", *Fortune*, 8 January 2001.

## Develop Your Managerial Potential

### Making Better Decisions

Modern research shows that managers who make the best decisions don't overanalyze things by relying on rational decision-making models, nor do they oversimplify them by relying solely on their intuition. Instead, many managers utilize a concept referred to as "recognitional decision making." Recognitional decision making leads to quicker decisions than rational decision making because it integrates the use of memory in connection with the context of a situation in order to develop an immediate feel of the current situation. Recurrences from previous experiences help provide sample solutions to current problems. Managers then subconsciously combine these recurrences with their intuition and imagination to help develop potential solutions for the current dilemma. Once a manager has a potential solution(s) in mind, he or she then begins to practice a mental game to see how the situation will play out. This approach is often compared to the strategies used by professional chess players when analyzing their next move. Professional chess players calculate each possible move and the subsequent move(s) of their opponents in their heads. By analyzing the opponent's expected move, chess players narrow their options for

moves until one results in the best possible option (or least negative consequence), given the current situation. Unfortunately, making good decisions, like becoming a master chess player, requires a lot of experience and practice. Managers and potential managers can improve their decision-making skills by practicing the following activities:

First, define your decision criteria for a given situation. For example, if when making decisions under the pressure of a deadline, you often underestimate the length of time it takes to accomplish a task, you should begin by dissecting the situation to see if certain patterns exist. By knowing the components of the decision and by determining which components give you the most trouble, chances are that you can determine the best approach to simplify your choices should this type of decision recur. To reinforce your decision-making ability, intentionally place yourself into situations where these commonalities exist. Doing so will provide further experience and help strengthen your decision-making ability.

Second, obtain feedback regarding current and previous decisions you have made. For example, if part of your job involves scheduling tasks, you can obtain feedback concerning your decisions by logging the expected time to complete a task and comparing that to the actual time taken. Analyzing the factors that attributed to the difference will help you recall them in the future, thus increasing your accuracy. Keep in mind that in most cases, feedback will not occur on its own; it has to be collected.

Third, practice decision making by reading case studies of actual problems and placing yourself in the shoes of the decision maker. This textbook reinforces this approach by offering two "What Would You Do?" case scenarios for each chapter. The scenarios build upon information presented in the text and discuss current problems of real-world situations. By comparing your answer to the "What Really Happened" answer, you can determine your decision-making ability and see if you understood and retained the information from the chapter.

Fourth, practice decision making under conditions of uncertainty. Recall some previous decisions that you have made. Was uncertainty present, and if so, how did you handle it? What steps did you take, or could you have taken, that would have helped reduce the uncertainty or ambiguity involved?

Lastly, improve recognitional decision making by using the expertise of others. If you respect and admire others for their ability to make quick, competent decisions, approach those people and ask them how they were able to arrive at their deci-

sions. Also, ask what clues directed them to the solution that they chose.

Making decisions is a skill not unlike many other skills that you have learned. The more you practice, the better decisions you will make. As your skill progresses, you'll notice that you now quickly and effortlessly make decisions that previously caused you grief. Additionally, you will be able to recognize patterns and recall potential solutions due to your increased decision-making experience.

**Exercise**

Recall a tough decision involving conditions of uncertainty that you recently made. Some examples include finding a roommate, buying a car, or picking your classes for next semester. The decision you select for this exercise should be one that you felt could have been improved. Analyze that decision using the five activities discussed above. After you analyze the decision, determine what steps might you take in the future to improve your decision-making ability, should this type of situation arise again.

**Source:** G. Klein & K. Weick, "Decisions: Making the Right Ones. Learning from the Wrong Ones." *Across the Board,* June 2000.

## Study Tip

Find a study partner and have him or her quiz you using the end-of-chapter materials and the quizzes on your *Management* CD-ROM. Instead of giving the simple answer, try to give the rationale also.

# CHAPTER 7

# Control

## What Would You Do?

**Regal Cinemas Headquarters, Knoxville, Tennessee.** How things have changed in this business! You can remember when every small town had a movie theater. And when the weather warmed, usually between Memorial Day and Labor Day, the local drive-in movie theater would open. Most of those had two screens. Come sundown, cars filled with families, teenagers (some hiding in the trunk to avoid paying), and couples on dates would drive in, park the front wheels of their cars on the top of a three-foot dirt mound in each row (to point their car window slightly upward toward the screen), roll their car windows halfway down, reach for the movie speakers hanging on the metal pole next to their cars, hang those speakers on the car window, and then click on the speakers that provided the tinny sound that accompanied the grainy image projected onto a huge outdoor screen half a block away.

Today, however, you'll be lucky to find a place that still has a downtown theater, not to mention a drive-in. Most disappeared 15 years ago as theater chains like Carmike Cinemas bought them, shut them down, and then replaced them with brand new four- and six-screen theaters with large parking lots designed to handle the larger crowds that flocked to these new multi-screen theaters. As big as those changes were, they pale compared to what's gone on in the last 10 years, when movie theater companies built a record number of new theaters and movie screens.

Twenty years ago, most theater seats were only 17 to 19 inches wide and were utilitarian at best. By contrast, in today's new theaters, seats are plush, comfortable, 21 to 24 inches wide, and equipped with cup holders designed for 44-ounce drinks. Pure and simple, the newer, plusher, wider seats were designed to encourage moviegoers to come to the theater rather than choose the cheaper alternative of renting a video at Blockbuster. And, frankly, those seats were needed because today's moviegoers are quite a bit older and, ahem, wider than in previous years—all that buttered popcorn! Another big change that led to new construction was the move to stadium seating. In larger, luxurious stadium seats, moviegoers, like sports fans, sit in seats placed on steep inclines that are designed to bring everyone closer to the screen and to seat each viewer well above the person in the row ahead of them—no heads to look over or around as in older theaters. The final change that led to record construction was the creation of theater megaplexes in which thousands of moviegoers at a time could choose from two-dozen to 30 movies in one location. While built at a cost of approximately $25 million to $30 million each, attendance at each individual movie screen in such megaplexes was 38 percent higher than traditional theaters. Moreover, with higher food sales, revenues were 10 percent higher per person, even without raising ticket prices. In all, this meant that megaplex theaters had operating cash flows that were 12.5 percent higher.

As the fourteenth largest movie theater company in the United States, Regal Cinemas has had great success during this time, growing from zero to 349 movie screens in just four years. But as competitors build 25- to 30-screen megaplexes with plush stadium seating, does Regal need to consider building its own megaplexes in order to continue its growth? If you decide to follow the competition and build huge megaplex theaters, what key resources will you need to be successful? Finally, Regal Cinemas has always had a reputation for controlling costs and being well managed. Would fast expansion and building of megaplex theaters weaken that part of the company?

If you were in charge at Regal Cinemas, what would you do?

**Sources:** D. Costello, "Hollywood Journal: Movie Seats: Thumbs Down? Fancy New Theaters Promise Big Seats, But How Big? Here's the Tale of the Tape," *The Wall Street Journal*, 6 October 2000, W6. K. Helliker, "Movies: Monster Movie Theaters Invade the Cinema Landscape," *The Wall Street Journal*, 13 May 1997, B1. B. Howard, "Commercial Real Estate Demand Steep for Stadium Seat Theaters: Owners Are Hoping to Sell More Movie Tickets by Promising Unobstructed Views," *Los Angeles Times*, 31 July 2001, C8. B. Orwall & G. Zuckerman, "Box-Office Blues: Regal Cinemas Joined Megaplex Frenzy, Ended Up in Back Row—Investors KKR, Hicks Muse Focused on Fast Growth; Now, Lots of Empty Seats—Stuck with 'B and C Sites'," *The Wall Street Journal*, 27 September 2000, A1. A. Steinhauer, "2 Buyout Firms Eye Theater Chains: Regal Cinemas' Rivals May Be Bought by Mark Pittman," *San Antonio News* [Bloomberg], 15 October 2000, J1. M. Walsh, "Easy on the Popcorn!" *Forbes*, 26 September 1994, 126-127.

**control**
a regulatory process of establishing standards to achieve organizational goals, comparing actual performance against the standards, and taking corrective action, when necessary

**Control** is a regulatory process of establishing standards to achieve organizational goals, compare actual performance against standards, and take corrective action when necessary to restore performance to those standards.

Control is achieved when behavior and work procedures conform to standards and company goals are accomplished.[1] However, control is not just an after-the-fact process. Preventive measures are also a form of control. In fact, we should remember that control is the last step in the first function of management, making things happen. To review, making things happen is a function of planning what you want to accomplish (Chapter 4), gathering and managing the information needed to make good decisions (Chapter 5), deciding how to achieve those plans (Chapter 6), and controlling behavior and processes through preventive or corrective action (Chapter 7).

We begin this chapter by examining the basic control process used in organizations. Then we examine whether control is always necessary or possible (it isn't). In the third part of the chapter, we go beyond the basics to an in-depth examination of the different methods that companies use to achieve control. We finish the chapter by taking a look at the things that companies choose to control (i.e., finances, product quality, customer retention, etc.).

# Basics of Control

If you wanted to control traffic speeds in your town, how would you do it? Well, most municipalities put in speed bumps, lower speed limits, put up traffic lights, or write more speeding tickets. However, the city of Culemborg in the Netherlands is planning to use sheep to slow down speeding cars on its neighborhood streets. Why sheep? One of the city council members, who had observed the driving patterns on country roads in rural England, said, "After all, it's impossible to speed past the sheep [in the middle of the road] if you drive in the Yorkshire Dales." When animal rights groups complained that this was a bad idea, the city responded by erecting a special kind of fence to prevent the sheep from wandering onto busier, high-speed roads where they would clearly be endangered. However, Culemborg's city leaders were apparently not familiar with the tradition of some Yorkshire locals who "accidentally" hit sheep, hoping to make off with a free supply of lamb chops.[2] The city plans to release five or six sheep at first. If motorists actually do slow down, as many as 100 sheep may eventually be released onto city streets.

*After reading the next two sections, you should be able to*
1. *describe the basic control process.*
2. *be able to answer the question: Is control necessary or possible?*

## 1. The Control Process

*The basic control process 1.1 begins with the establishment of clear standards of performance, 1.2 involves a comparison of actual performance to desired performance, 1.3 takes corrective action, if needed, to repair performance deficiencies, 1.4 is a dynamic, cybernetic process, and 1.5 consists of three basic methods: feedback control, concurrent control, and feedforward control.*

The city of Culemborg in the Netherlands devised a rather creative form of traffic control: the use of sheep in the road.

© PATRICK WARD/CORBIS

**standards**
a basis of comparison when measuring the extent to which various kinds of organizational performance are satisfactory or unsatisfactory

## 1.1 Standards

The control process begins when managers set goals, like satisfying 90 percent of customers, or increasing sales by 5 percent. Companies then specify the performance standards that must be met to accomplish those goals. **Standards** are a basis of comparison for measuring the extent to which organizational performance is satisfactory or unsatisfactory. For example, many pizzerias use 30 minutes as the standard for delivery times. Since anything longer than that is viewed as unsatisfactory, they'll typically reduce their prices if they can't deliver a hot pizza to you in 30 minutes or less.

So how do managers set standards? How do they decide which levels of performance are satisfactory and which are unsatisfactory? The first criterion for a good standard is that it must enable goal achievement. If you're meeting the standard, but still not achieving company goals, then the standard may have to be changed. For example, Best Buy, which sells electronics and appliances, used to allow customers to return or exchange goods without receipts. However, the company lost a substantial amount of money when, without making a purchase, people would take goods directly from store shelves to the service counter to exchange or get a cash refund. Today, Best Buy's new standard is "No refunds or exchanges without a receipt. Period."[3]

Companies also determine standards by listening to customers or observing competitors. While study after study has indicated that customers preferred Burger King's Whopper sandwich to McDonald's Big Mac, those studies also showed that customers clearly preferred McDonald's French fries. Burger King spokesperson Rob Doughty admitted that its fries were "soggy, they would get cold easily, they were limp, they weren't competitive." So, after taking two years to develop a crispier French fry, Burger King spent $70 million on a marketing campaign and gave away 15 million free orders of fries on "Free Fryday" to convince consumers that its new fries were better tasting than McDonald's.[4]

Also, as you learned in Chapter 4, standards can be determined by benchmarking other companies. *Benchmarking* is the process of determining how well other companies (though typically not competitors) perform business functions or tasks. In other words, benchmarking is the process of determining other companies' standards.

The first step in setting standards is to determine what to benchmark. Companies can benchmark anything, from cycle time (how fast) to quality (how well). The next step is to identify the companies against which to benchmark your standards. Since this can require a significant commitment on the part of the benchmarked company, it can take time to identify and get agreement from them to be benchmarked. The last step is to collect data to determine other companies' performance standards. For example, countless companies have visited MBNA, the credit card company, to learn how to respond quickly, if not immediately, to customer requests. Indeed, visitors learn that MBNA answers its phones by the second ring 98.5 percent of the time, and that it takes no more than 30 minutes to approve (or deny) customer requests for higher credit limits.[5]

### 1.2 Comparison to Standards

The next step in the control process is to compare actual performance to performance standards. While this sounds straightforward, the quality of the comparison largely depends on the measurement and information systems a company uses to keep track of performance. The better the system, the easier it is for companies to track their progress and identify problems that need to be fixed. For example, because it is so difficult to gather detailed information about how actual customers are treated when they interact with store employees, retail stores spend $435 million a year to hire "secret shoppers," who visit their stores to determine whether their employees provide helpful customer service. In fact, the "secret shoppers" aren't shoppers at all. They're hired consultants who, acting like customers, make detailed observations of the service provided (or not) by employees. For instance, on visiting a grocery store, a "secret shopper" gave a bagboy positive points for hustle, but negative points for wearing his hat backwards. More negative points are tallied when the store clerk in the produce department fails to greet the "secret shopper," when a service counter employee is chewing gum, and when a cashier enters an incorrect price code for an item that the scanner couldn't pick up. Giant Grocery store manager Jim Parker said, "As a tool, it's tremendous. The quiet guy in the corner . . . the others that don't stick out but do a great job . . . their names can surface. It's pretty great."[6]

### 1.3 Corrective Action

The next step in the control process is to identify performance deviations, analyze those deviations, and then develop and implement programs to correct them. This is similar to the planning process discussed in Chapter 4: regular, frequent performance feedback allows workers and managers to track their performance and make adjustments in effort, direction, and strategies.

One example of identifying and correcting performance deviations is the service-quality audit conducted by a prestigious New York City hotel known for its first-class service. The purpose of the quality audit was to identify the frequency and cost of service errors and what it would cost to prevent them. The most common error, occurring nearly 70 times per day at an annual cost of nearly a quarter million dollars, was not posting minibar and phone charges to guests' bills. Following discussions with managers and employees, the hotel took the following steps to correct the problem: (1) During check-in, verify whether guests in the same room have separate bills and charges. (2) Have the night clerk double-check all the phone and minibar charges for guests checking out the next morning. (3) Include a list of phone, minibar, and other charges (and when they were incurred) with the bill provided to guests in their rooms on the morning they checkout. (4) Reduce checkout times and errors by providing the front desk a master list of all of the minibar, phone, and extra charges for guests checking out that day. Importantly, it only cost the hotel $25,000 to implement these corrective actions and begin reducing the $250,000 annual cost of these mistakes.[7]

### 1.4 Dynamic, Cybernetic Process

As shown in Exhibit 7.1, control is a continuous, dynamic, cybernetic process. It begins with actual performance and measures of that performance. Managers then compare performance to the pre-established standards. If they identify deviations from standard performance, they analyze the deviations and develop corrective programs. Then imple-

EXHIBIT 7.1

CYBERNETIC CONTROL PROCESS

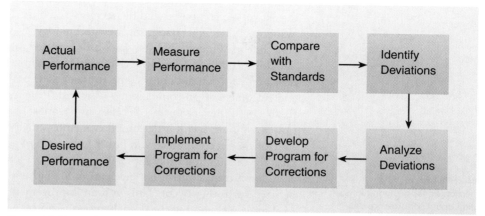

**Source:** H. Koontz & R.W. Bradspies, "Managing through Feedforward Control: A Future Directed View," *Business Horizons,* June 1972, 25-36.

menting the programs (hopefully) achieves the desired performance. Managers must repeat the entire process again and again in an endless feedback loop (a continuous process). So control is not a one-time achievement or result. It continues over time (a dynamic process) and requires daily, weekly, and monthly attention from managers to maintain performance levels at the standard (i.e., cybernetic). **Cybernetic** takes its meaning from the Greek word *kubernetes*, which means "steersman," that is, one who steers or keeps on course.[8] Therefore, the control process shown in Exhibit 7.1 is cybernetic because of the feedback loop in which actual performance is compared to standards to minimize or correct deviations from that standard.

Keeping control of business expenses is an example of a continuous, dynamic, cybernetic process. Companies that don't closely monitor expenses usually find that they can quickly get out of control, even for the most unlikely things. For example, a number of years ago, American Airlines determined that its expenses were too high and that it needed to do some things to cut costs. Figuring that no one would notice, American's CEO decided to remove one olive from every salad it served, saving the company $40,000 a year! Likewise, United Airlines saved $50,000 a year by no longer offering grapefruit juice, lemon peels, and olives as drink condiments. Or consider the cost-cutting at Student Advantage, a marketing company. Kenneth Goldman, chief financial officer, said, "We're not saying, 'Stay at Motel 6 and eat at McDonald's,' and we're not attacking compensation, benefits, or any of the things that make for real quality of life, but you can drink filtered water instead of bottled, and you can be happy at a Holiday Inn instead of a Marriott. And not everyone needs a cell phone, and no one needs a limo."[9]

Sure, it's a cliche, but it's just as true in business as it is in sports: If you take your eye off the ball, you're going to strike out. Control is an ongoing, dynamic, cybernetic process.

### 1.5 Feedback, Concurrent, and Feedforward Control

There are three basic control methods: feedback control, concurrent control, and feedforward control.[10] **Feedback control** is a mechanism for gathering information about performance deficiencies after they occur. This information is then used to correct or prevent performance deficiencies. Study after study has clearly shown that feedback improves both individual and organizational performance. In most instances, any feedback

**cybernetic**
the process of steering or keeping on course

**feedback control**
a mechanism for gathering information about performance deficiencies after they occur

225

is better than no feedback. However, if there is a downside to feedback, it is that it sometimes occurs too late. Sometimes it comes after big mistakes have been made.

For example, while everyone knows about Microsoft's success with its Windows operating system, relatively few know that Microsoft's first try at writing operating software for networked computers and file servers was a bust. This program—the early version of Windows NT ("NT" stands for "new technology")—was huge and painfully slow. (The core code in Windows NT has since been updated, upgraded, and developed into the Windows 2000 and Windows XP operating systems.) Unfortunately, the Windows NT development team did not become aware of these problems until the product shipped and customers began complaining. Why hadn't the team gotten any early indication (i.e., feedback) of these problems? Because, unlike most of their customers who were running slower computers with little computer memory, the NT development team used fast, state-of-the-art computers with nearly four times more memory.[11] So Windows NT ran great for them, but terribly for regular users.

**Concurrent control** is a mechanism for gathering information about performance deficiencies as they occur. Thus, it is an improvement over feedback, because it attempts to eliminate or shorten the delay between performance and feedback about the performance. Because it had not been aware of the slow speed (and other problems) in the initial version of Windows NT, the NT development team abandoned its reliance on late-coming customer feedback and quickly adopted a development model based on concurrent control and feedforward control (discussed below).

For example, rather than waiting for customer complaints to come to them, the NT software team developed concurrent controls by establishing systematic, ongoing relationships between the team engineers and NT customers. When there was a problem, they heard about it immediately. Furthermore, NT programmers took turns answering the help line that NT customers called for technical support. They also traveled to companies using NT, so that they could talk to customers directly and find out how they were using NT and where its performance fell short. Microsoft sent thousands of test copies of redesigned NT software to officially approved beta-testers who, through regular phone calls and emails, told the development team what they liked and didn't like.

**Feedforward control** is a mechanism for gathering information about performance deficiencies before they occur. In contrast to feedback and concurrent control, which provide feedback on the basis of outcomes and results, feedforward control provides information about performance deficiencies by monitoring inputs, not outputs. Thus, feedforward seeks to prevent or minimize performance deficiencies before they occur. So rather than waiting for customer feedback, the Windows NT team used feedforward controls by establishing a special 16-member team of programmers whose sole job was to inspect the underlying computer code (the input). Then, literally step by step, they rewrote, redesigned, or created new computer code to make Windows NT run faster. It worked. Newer versions of the Windows NT software grew from 6.1 to 16.5 million lines of code, but it ran eight times faster than the original, and used one-third less memory. Exhibit 7.2 lists guidelines that companies can follow to get the most out of feedforward control.

## Review 1
### The Control Process

The first step in the control process is to set goals and performance standards. The second is to compare actual performance to performance standards. The better a company's information and measurement systems, the easier it is to make these comparisons. The last step is to identify and correct performance deviations. However, control is a continuous, dynamic, cybernetic process, not a one-time achievement or result. Control requires frequent managerial attention. The three basic control methods are feedback control (after the fact performance information), concurrent control (simultaneous performance information), and feedforward control (preventive performance information).

**concurrent control**
a mechanism for gathering information about performance deficiencies as they occur, eliminating or shortening the delay between performance and feedback

**feedforward control**
a mechanism for monitoring performance inputs rather than outputs to prevent or minimize performance deficiencies before they occur

226

EXHIBIT 7.2

GUIDELINES FOR USING FEEDFORWARD CONTROL

1. Thorough planning and analysis are required.
2. Careful discrimination must be applied in selecting input variables.
3. The feedforward system must be kept dynamic.
4. A model of the control system should be developed.
5. Data on input variables must be regularly collected.
6. Data on input variables must be regularly assessed.
7. Feedforward control requires action.

**Source:** H. Koontz & R.W. Bradspies, "Managing through Feedforward Control: A Future Directed View," *Business Horizons,* June 1972, 25-36.

## 2. Is Control Necessary or Possible?

**control loss**
situation in which behavior and work procedures do not conform to standards

Control is achieved when behavior and work procedures conform to standards and goals are accomplished. By contrast, **control loss** occurs when behavior and work procedures do not conform to standards.[12] Control loss usually prevents goal achievement. Mirage Resorts, which runs the Mirage and Bellagio casinos and hotels in Las Vegas, is one of the best known and most profitable gambling companies in the world. But when it built the state-of-the-art Beau Rivage casino and hotel in Biloxi, Mississippi, control loss was rampant as the company spent $680 million, twice the original budget, to build the complex. One of the cost overruns came in the form of 15 75-year old oak trees, costing $67,000 each, that were purchased and then transplanted to line the drive into the casino. Encouraged by the CEO to build "the finest casino that could be built," expensive Italian marble was used throughout, the number of planned rooms quickly grew from 1,200 to 1,780, while the number of restaurants grew from four to 13, and $10 million was spent building a 31-boat marina—nearly $322,000 per slip—out of imported Brazilian hard

Better control would have helped the Beau Rivage Casino and Hotel keep costs in check. It may take a while for investors to recover from the $340 million in excess spending.

© PHILIP GOULD/CORBIS

## Gain Control—Lower Your Expectations

Control loss occurs when performance falls short of standards. When this happens, the automatic response is to put in more hours and do everything possible to meet the standard. But remember: One way to maintain control is to change goals. This may seem like an admission of failure. But in many cases, it's just being realistic. You can't excel at everything. Disappointed because you're 10 pounds over your high school weight? Celebrate that it's *only* 10 pounds and not 20. Bummed because you didn't get that raise? Be glad you've still got your job. Selectively lower your expectations and regain control.

**degree of dependence**
the extent to which a company needs a particular resource to accomplish its goals

**resources**
the assets, capabilities, processes, information, and knowledge that an organization uses to improve its effectiveness and efficiency, to create and sustain competitive advantage, and to fulfill a need or solve a problem

**resource flow**
the extent to which companies have access to critical resources

woods. Paul Harvey, who heads the Mississippi Gaming Commission, said, "Nobody's ever spent that kind of money here."[13]

*When control losses occur, managers need to find out what they could have done, if anything, to prevent these mistakes from occurring. In Mirage Resort's case, there was a straightforward solution: Closely monitor and check actual building expenses against planned building expenses, and then stick to them. In general, when control loss occurs, managers need to ask three questions: 2.1 Is more control necessary? 2.2 Is more control possible? and 2.3 If more control is necessary but not possible, what should we do instead?*

### 2.1 Is More Control Necessary?

Two factors can help managers determine whether more (or different) control is necessary: the degree of dependence and resource flows.[14] **Degree of dependence** is the extent to which a company needs a particular resource to accomplish its goals. The more important a resource is for meeting organizational standards and goals, the more necessary it is to control that resource.

Note, however, that resources are more than just raw materials. A **resource** is anything that can be used to fulfill a need or solve a problem. Thus, resources can include employee skills, space, intellectual capability, capital (dollars), specialized know-how, a cohesive corporate culture, and so forth. Basically, critical resources, whatever form they take, make it easier for managers and employees to carry out the work processes that conform to standards and lead to goal accomplishment.

For example, a key to profitability in the airline industry is the proportion of filled seats on each flight. With enormous fixed expenses, it costs an airline almost as much money to fly a plane empty as it does to fly it full. So one of the keys to success is to put more people on each plane.[15] Today, computerized yield management systems are the *key resource* that airlines use to make sure their flights are as full as possible. Without them (i.e., a high degree of dependence), most airlines could not compete or earn a profit. Sophisticated computerized yield management systems fill seats (i.e., the key need or problem) by constantly raising and lowering prices in response to customer demand and competitor pricing. If done right, most planes will only be partially full several weeks before departure. Then, at the last minute, the airline can fill the remaining seats with business travelers who, unlike leisure travelers, are willing to pay much higher prices for immediate travel.

The second factor that determines whether more control is necessary is resource flow. **Resource flow** is the extent to which companies have easy access to critical resources. For example, after a year-long drought, the city council of San Antonio, Texas, did what city councils normally do when facing a drought: They placed restrictions on lawn and landscape watering. However, the drought had become so bad that the council discussed restricting the amount of water that homeowners could use in existing pools and even considered forbidding the construction of new pools. Leif Zars, owner of Gary's Pools in San Antonio, immediately recognized that this could put his company out of business. In other words, the city council was just about to cut off the flow of his key resource, water.[16] After all, who would want a pool without water?

When companies have a difficult time getting the critical resources they need, they usually try to increase resource flows by creating or obtaining some form of control over them. For Leif Zars, the question was how could he control the amount of water that the city made available to homeowners? Well, the straight answer is that he couldn't. Nor could he exert much control or influence over the city council, at least probably not more than any other San Antonio resident. But what Leif Zars could do was help pool owners control the amount of water evaporation in their pools. And if he could do that, perhaps the city council could be convinced not to stop the construction of new pools.

# "headline news"

## A Kinder, Gentler IRS

When the Internal Revenue Service was called on the carpet in 1998 for years of alleged taxpayer abuses, the result was a series of congressional hearings in which victims told stories that painted IRS officials as stormtroopers. As citizen after citizen came to testify, it became clear that something had to be done to change the agency in charge of collecting taxes. After all, the government's only supply of money is through the taxpayers, so angering them wouldn't be in the best interest of the federal budget.

After the lengthy hearings, Charles Rossotti, the IRS commissioner, ushered in a new era of customer service. Personnel were shifted from audits to taxpayer hotlines, and all employees are now kept in line by a strict list of taxpayer rights. Staffers now face harsh penalties for mistreating customers. Even the harsh letter threatening to interview neighbors, employers, and other third parties about your tax situation has been replaced with a more straightforward letter that doesn't leave taxpayers terror-stricken after reading it.

The result has been much happier taxpayers, especially those who owed back taxes. Don Otto owed $650,000 in back taxes and penalties dating to the mid-1980s and lived in perpetual fear of mail from the despised agency. After the winds changed, however, he happily discovered that things weren't so bad. In fact, he struck a deal whereby he paid off his full tax bill for only $58,000. And he is not alone. In 2000, the IRS wrote off roughly $2.5 billion in debt owed by 668,018 taxpayers (in 1998, only 98 taxpayers had their cases written off). The assistant deputy commissioner David Mader says that dropped cases are too small to be worth going after.

Since 1992, the IRS staff has been reduced by one-sixth. This means less personnel dedicated to control, so the agency has

sharply curtailed audits (down 66 percent) and other kinds of enforcement. Property seizures to pay back taxes are now nearly nonexistent, having dropped 99 percent. The economic boom times of the 1990's may be partly responsible for the recent leniency. Even though the IRS accepted only $315 million in payments against back-tax debts of $2.6 billion, the tax coffers swelled to a mind-boggling $1.9 trillion.

Some consider the problem to be not so much the refocus on customer service, but that the agency's $9.4 billion budget allotment of that $1.9 trillion is woefully inadequate to achieve customer service *and* control. Somehow, American taxpayers, whose Tax Freedom Day—the day where you have worked enough to pay all of your taxes for the year—is somewhere in June, may not see it that way.

*1. Is more control needed here? Is it possible?*

*2. After you finish reading the chapter, consider whether it is possible to build a balanced scorecard for the IRS. Try. Consider that taxpayers are equivalent to shareholders AND to customers. (The discussion of the balanced scorecard begins on page 240.)*

**Sources:** "IRS Pays Billions to Big Biz," *Earth Island Journal*, Summer 2001 (16:12) 16. InfoTrac Article A73712274. D. C. Johnston, "A Smaller IRS Gives Up on Billions in Back Taxes," *New York Times*, 13 April 2001, A1. J. Raymond, "A Kinder, Gentler Face for the IRS: Who Knew?" *Newsweek*, 16 April 2001, 44. InfoTrac Article A73063002. M. Songini, "IRS Call Center Upgrade Aims to Boost Tax-Time Services," *Computerworld*, 16 April 2001, 6. InfoTrac Article A75559514. "Tax Audits: Uncle Sam Lightens Up," *National Post*, 35 March 1999, D04.

Since most pool owners were unwilling to use expensive, unwieldy tarps to cover their pools, Zars invented cheap, easy-to-use evaporation shields. It only took about 12 lightweight plastic shields, which cost just $3 apiece, to cover most pools. And when used, they reduced water loss to nearly nothing. So rather than restricting new pool construction, Zars wanted the city council to mandate that all pool owners reduce water use by covering their pools to reduce water evaporation.

### 2.2 Is More Control Possible?

**regulation costs**
the costs associated with implementing or maintaining control

Degree of dependence and resource flow can help determine whether control is needed. However, the cost of control and cybernetic feasibility help determine whether control is possible. First, to determine whether more control is possible (or worthwhile), managers need to carefully assess **regulation costs**, that is, whether the costs and unintended consequences of control exceed its benefits. For example, one of the reasons that the number of U.S. pharmaceutical companies producing major vaccines has dropped significantly is that the cost of controlling legal risk (through liability insurance and in-house legal staffs) is just too high.[17] Indeed, the threat of lawsuits has led 47 percent of companies to drop one or more products, has encouraged 25 percent of companies to drop research and development programs, and stopped 39 percent of companies from bringing new products to market.[18] Likewise, over the last 25 years, doctors and nurses have told soon-to-be parents that natural childbirth is much better for the mother and the baby. However, nearly 30 percent of all babies are delivered via cesarean section. Why? Because of the threat of lawsuits. Dr. Robin Richman said, "The No. 1 reason for the lawsuits against ob-gyns is failure to perform a timely C-section. They feel the best way to protect themselves from a lawsuit is to go to a caesarean sooner rather than later."[19] Before choosing to implement control, managers should be confident that the benefits exceed the costs.

An often-overlooked factor in determining the cost of control is the set of unintended consequences that sometimes accompany increased control. Control systems help companies, managers, and workers accomplish their goals, but at the same time that they help solve some problems, they can create others. For example, Delta Airlines set a goal of reducing its costs from 9.76 cents per seat-mile to 7.5 cents per seat-mile. In many respects, Delta succeeded, lowering its costs and returning to solid profitability. However, in some places, the cost-cutting was so deep that Delta's performance suffered in other key areas. For example, Delta used to keep one mechanic at each gate to fix minor problems between flights. After cost-cutting, it only assigned one mechanic to every three or four gates. Because the mechanic could only repair one plane at a time, the unintended consequence was that many flights were delayed. At the time, this caused Delta to fall to last among domestic airlines in on-time arrivals.[20]

The second factor that helps managers determine whether control is possible is cybernetic feasibility. **Cybernetic feasibility** is the extent to which it is possible to implement each step in the control process: clear standards of performance, comparison of performance to standards, and corrective action. If one or more steps cannot be implemented, then maintaining effective control may be difficult or impossible.

**cybernetic feasibility**
the extent to which it is possible to implement each step in the control process

For example, companies have traditionally had a very tough time making employees follow corporate travel procedures (i.e., clear standards, but poor corrective action). Instead of calling the officially approved company travel agency, employees typically make their own reservations or call their own travel agents. American Express, which in addition to its charge-card business is one of the world's largest travel companies, estimates that American companies lose $15 billion a year because managers and employee don't follow travel policies. Online travel agencies, such as Travelocity.com and Expedia.com, have made it even easier for employees to get around company policies and book their own travel.[21]

However, the cybernetic feasibility of corporate travel programs has improved significantly now that many companies have begun using Web-based corporate travel systems that actually force employees to follow company travel policies. Rusty Carpenter of American Express Consulting Services said, "Online corporate booking systems have passed the experimental stage. Companies are incorporating them into their cost-containment programs as recognized, proven tools—not only to cut airfares but also to slash the administrative cost of booking."[22] Web-based tools, such as Oracle's eTravel, feel and look like Web-based travel reservation systems such as Travelocity.com or Expedia.com. However, each company's travel policies and preferences are coded into each eTravel system so that employees who use it to arrange their travel end up using the company's preferred airlines, hotel chains, and rental car agencies (all of which have negotiated much cheaper corporate rates for air fares, hotel rooms, and car rentals in order to gain preferred corporate status). eTravel also keeps track of travel policy compliance, that is, whether employee travel and travel expenses are consistent with corporate travel policy.[23] So thanks to information technology, it is now cybernetically feasible to closely monitor and control corporate travel.

## 2.3 Quasi-Control: When Control Isn't Possible

**quasi-control**
reducing dependence or restructuring dependence when control is necessary but not possible

**reducing dependence**
abandoning or changing organizational goals to reduce dependence on critical resources

**restructuring dependence**
exchanging dependence on one critical resource for dependence on another

If control is necessary but not possible because of costs or cybernetic infeasibility, then managers can use two **quasi-control** options: reducing dependence or restructuring dependence.

**Reducing dependence** involves an explicit choice to abandon or change organizational goals by reducing dependence on critical resources. Companies are likely to choose to reduce dependence under the same conditions that they would choose control. The difference, however, is that companies choose to reduce dependence when control is not possible, that is, when the cost is too high or cybernetic feasibility is near zero. For example, computer maker Compaq Corporation announced that it would no longer sell computer servers (i.e., changing a goal) based on its 64-bit Alpha computer chips, which it will no longer manufacture (i.e., reducing dependence on a resource). Compaq will license the Alpha chip and its manufacturing facility to Intel, the leading computer chip maker, and several hundred Compaq engineers who work on the Alpha will become Intel employees. Compaq's CEO indicated that the choice to quit selling Alpha servers and to reduce dependence on manufacturing the Alpha chip will "lower our costs significantly."[24]

Instead of reducing dependence when control is not possible, companies can choose to **restructure dependence**—exchange dependence on one critical resource for dependence on another. One area in which companies are exchanging resources is to substitute private planes for commercial air travel. Surprisingly, traveling by private plane has a number of advantages over traveling via commercial airlines. To start, compared to last-minute business class tickets, which are much more expensive now than just a few years ago and approximately three to five times the cost of coach class tickets, corporate planes can be cheaper to fly. Tim Quinn, who owns a construction company, saw his monthly air-travel expenses drop almost in half, from $11,000 to $6000, even after making the monthly payments for his company plane.

Another advantage of exchanging private plane travel for commercial air travel is that private planes can get to many more destinations. While commercial airlines fly into 550 airports nationwide, smaller, private planes can fly into more than 5,500 different airports. Also, private planes are useful tools, not the fancy perks that most people believe them to be. Maytag spokesperson Tom Schwartz said that Maytag's two jets "don't have legroom, you can't stand up, and there's no lavatory." He said, "It would be a mistake to think of this as an executive perk."[25]

There are three advantages to restructuring dependence. First, like private planes, the new critical resource may be more controllable. Second, even better, the new critical resource may not require any control at all. Third, the company does not have to change its goals.

### Review 2
#### Is Control Necessary or Possible?

Exhibit 7.3 summarizes the questions that managers should answer to determine if control is necessary or possible. First, if the degree of dependence on a critical resource is high, or if resource flows are poor, managers will want to initiate greater control over critical resources. However, if resource flows and the degree of dependence are low, managers do not need to do anything to increase control. Next, if cybernetics (i.e., the basic control process) is feasible, managers should determine if the cost of control is acceptable. If it is, then managers should choose to regulate or control the degree of dependence on critical resources. However, if cybernetics is not feasible, the next step is deciding whether goals can be changed. If goals are fixed and unchangeable, then managers should restructure their dependence on critical resources by exchanging dependence on one critical resource for dependence on another. On the other hand, if goals can be changed, then managers should reduce dependence on critical resources by abandoning or changing key goals.

231

EXHIBIT 7.3

## IS CONTROL NECESSARY OR POSSIBLE?

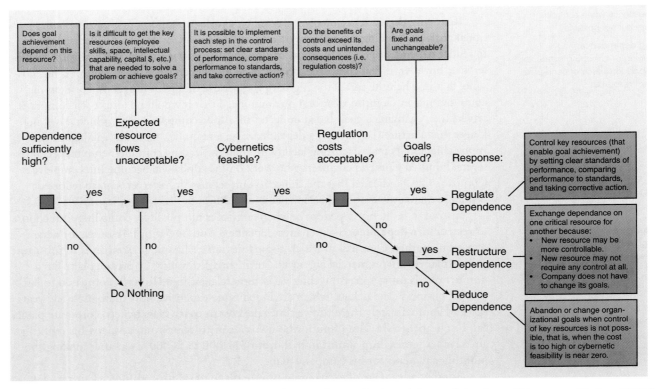

**Source:** S.G. Green & M.A. Welsh, "Cybernetics and Dependence: Reframing the Control Concept," *Academy of Management Review*, 13 (1988): 287-301.

## How and What to Control

Have you developed a taste for gourmet coffee? With gourmet coffee seemingly everywhere, chances are you or someone in your office has. However, the popularity of specialty coffees and coffee shops has created a problem in many offices: the long coffee break. Instead of wandering down the hall to brew a fresh pot of regular coffee and chat with coworkers during a 15-minute coffee break, workers are now running out of their offices to find the nearest gourmet coffee shop. In the marketing department for the Pittsburgh Symphony, the department manager declared coffee shops off-limits after finding five department staffers missing well beyond their regular coffee breaks. [26]

The question for aspiring managers is how would you handle this situation? Should you declare coffee shops off-limits? Should you simply discuss it with employees and rely on them to exercise their own judgment? Should you closely watch for potential violators and then punish them? And then there is the question of whether long coffee breaks are something that managers should even try to control. Paul Ivers, who works for Lotus Development Corporation, believes that there's nothing wrong with trips to the coffee shop. He said, "It's not good to be doing something straight for nine to 10 hours." Likewise, Carol Raymer, a manager at Federal Express (who gets six to eight cups a day from

# BlastFromThePast

## From 1870 to the Present—Five Eras of Management Control

According to researchers Stephen Barley and Gideon Kunda, there have been five eras of management control since 1870: industrial betterment, scientific management, human relations, systems rationalization, and organizational culture and quality.

### Industrial Betterment, 1870-1900

Industrial betterment, which was preceded by an era in which employers did not care about the general welfare or working conditions of employees, is best characterized as paternalistic. Just as parents provide for their children, many large companies sought to provide and care for their employees during this time. Some companies practiced industrial betterment by building libraries, parks, gymnasiums, and subsidized housing for employees. Others improved horrid working conditions by making unsanitary and unsafe factory jobs clean and safe. Still others paid for social clubs and established profit-sharing and benefit plans not found in companies before that time. YMCAs, the Young Men's Christian Associations, were established by railroad companies to attend to the physical and spiritual needs of the employees who rode the rails from coast to coast. Although "industrial betterment" sounds virtuous, it had the larger goal of attracting and producing a reliable workforce. For example, the railroads hoped that in ministering to its workers, YMCAs would also reduce the widespread drunkenness that created an unstable, unreliable, unsafe workforce.

### Scientific Management, 1900-1922

By contrast to the paternalistic view of industrial betterment, scientific management, founded by Frederick W. Taylor (see "Blast from the Past" in Chapter 6), was concerned with efficiency, finding the most efficient combination of procedures to produce a product. Scientific management was built on three ideas. First, controlled, scientific study of work would lead to greater efficiency. Second, all employees are rational. If shown a superior way to do the work, they will embrace it. Third, employees are primarily motivated by money.

Building on these beliefs, Taylor introduced the then-novel idea of piece-rate payment plans, in which workers were paid according to their output. Not surprisingly, Taylor held little respect for industrial betterment. He said, "No self-respecting workman wants to be given things; every man wants to earn things."

### Human Relations, 1925-1955

Unlike the efficiency focus of scientific management, the human relations approach to control assumed that social interaction and the need to belong to work groups were more important to employees than money. The human relations approach advocated the importance of supervisor training, communication, and group dynamics and processes. So rather than just paying workers to work harder, this approach assumed that workers would be more motivated if supervisors treated employees better, if work groups participated in decision making, and if jobs were redesigned to allow rather than restrict social interaction between employees. Although this approach bears similarities to industrial betterment, there is one key difference: Industrial betterment sought to improve the company workforce, whereas human relations took as its goal the improvement of the company itself.

### Systems Rationalization, 1955-1980

In contrast to human relations, which placed employee considerations at the heart of its control philosophy, the systems rationalization, or systems approach, chose to ignore employees to focus exclusively on seeking universal principles or functions that would help an entire organization run like a smooth machine. Using ideas from electrical engineering and computer science, the systems approach sought ways to plan, forecast, and control the performance of the entire organization. Managers focused on organizational inputs and outputs. Supervisor training was unimportant, because it was the larger management system in the company, not its supervisors, which determined success or failure.

### Organizational Culture and Quality, 1980-Present

Finally, in contrast to the sterile approach of systems rationalization, the pendulum of organization control swung the other way to embrace organizational culture and quality. Here, rather than focusing on efficiency or on units of the company as parts of a larger system, leaders and companies maintained control through the shared beliefs, values, and actions of their managers and workers. Concerns shifted from input and output to employee commitment and motivation, teamwork, values, vision, and morale. The goal was to have employees perceive that the organization was committed to producing a quality product or service. Inspired by this vision or goal, employees and managers would work harder and with greater commitment to the company and its customers.

With recent downsizings and the loss of millions of corporate jobs, some would argue that companies have already left the era of culture and quality. Indeed, Barley and Kunda argue that historically, control philosophies have cycled between rational, efficiency-based approaches (scientific management and systems rationalism) and employee-based approaches (industrial betterment, human relations, and corporate culture and quality).

**Source:** S.R. Barley & G. Kunda, "Design and Devotion: Surges of Rational and Normative Ideologies of Control in Management Discourse," *Administrative Science Quarterly* 37 (1992): 363-399.

the coffee shop in her office building!), said, "You talk to customers and issues come up. It's a good networking place."

*After reading the next two sections, you should be able to*
3. *discuss the various methods that managers can use to maintain control.*
4. *describe the behaviors, processes, and outcomes that today's managers are choosing to control their organizations.*

## 3. Control Methods

*There are five different methods that managers can use to achieve control in their organizations: 3.1 bureaucratic, 3.2 objective, 3.3 normative, 3.4 concertive, and 3.5 self-control.*

### 3.1 Bureaucratic Control

When most people think of managerial control, what they have in mind is bureaucratic control. **Bureaucratic control** is top-down control, in which managers try to influence employee behavior by rewarding or punishing employees for compliance or noncompliance with organizational policies, rules, and procedures. However, most employees would argue that bureaucratic managers emphasize punishment for noncompliance much more than rewards for compliance. For instance, when visiting the company's regional offices and managers, the president of a training company, who was known for his temper and for micromanaging others, would get some toilet paper from the restrooms and aggressively ask, "What's this?" When the managers answered, "Toilet paper," he would scream that it was two-ply toilet paper that the company couldn't afford. When told of a cracked toilet seat in one of the women's restrooms, he said, "If you don't like sitting on that seat, you can stand up like I do!"[27]

Ironically, bureaucratic management and control were created to prevent just this type of managerial behavior. By encouraging managers to apply well-thought-out rules, policies, and procedures in an impartial, consistent manner to everyone in the organization, bureaucratic control is supposed to make companies more efficient, effective, and fair. Perversely, it frequently has just the opposite effect. Managers who use bureaucratic control often put following the rules above all else. When an employee collapsed from chest pains, her boss, fearing a heart attack, helped carry her to an ambulance. Yet, when the employee was thankfully diagnosed with indigestion and not a heart attack and returned to work several hours later, her boss filed a disciplinary action accusing her of an unexcused absence. Employees complained to the company CEO, who then took steps to correct the situation. The boss subsequently apologized to the employee and to his entire 25-person staff, explaining that he was wrong for taking the company's absence policy "too literally."[28]

Another characteristic of bureaucratically controlled companies is that due to their rule- and policy-driven decision making, they are highly resistant to change and slow to respond to customers and competitors. Even Max Weber, the German philosopher who is largely credited with popularizing bureaucratic ideals in the late nineteenth century, referred to bureaucracy as the "iron cage." He said, "Once fully established, bureaucracy is among those social structures which are the hardest to destroy."[29] Of course, the federal government, with hundreds of bureaus, agencies, and departments, is typically the largest bureaucracy in most countries. And, because of the thousands of career bureaucrats who staff those offices, even presidents and Congress have difficulty creating change. When General Dwight Eisenhower became president after Harry Truman, Truman, who as president had dealt with government bureaucracies, quipped, "Poor Ike. It won't be a bit like the army. He'll sit here and he'll say, 'Do this, do that,' and nothing will happen."[30]

**bureaucratic control**
use of hierarchical authority to influence employee behavior by rewarding or punishing employees for compliance or noncompliance with organizational policies, rules, and procedures

234

## 3.2 Objective Control

**objective control**
use of observable measures of worker behavior or outputs to assess performance and influence behavior

In many companies, bureaucratic control has evolved into **objective control**, which is the use of observable measures of employee behavior or output to assess performance and influence behavior. Whereas bureaucratic control focuses on whether policies and rules are followed, objective control focuses on the observation or measurement of worker behavior or output. For example, measuring whether sales representatives filed expense reports within 30 days, as specified by company policy, would be an example of bureaucratic control, while measuring whether they met their sales quotas or returned phone calls in a timely manner would be examples of objective control. There are two kinds of objective control: behavior control and output control.

**behavior control**
regulation of the behaviors and actions that workers perform on the job

**Behavior control** is regulating behaviors and actions that workers perform on the job. The basic assumption of behavior control is that if you do the right things (i.e., the right behaviors) every day, then those things should lead to goal achievement. However, behavior control is still management-based, which means that managers are responsible for monitoring, rewarding, and punishing workers for exhibiting desired or undesired behaviors. When Alan Greenberg, the then-CEO of Bear Stearns, a Wall Street investment company, wrote the following memo to his firm's managing partners, he was enacting behavioral control about the importance of always being available:

> Bear Stearns is moving forward at an accelerated rate and everyone is contributing. It is absolutely essential for us to be able to talk to our [the firm's] partners at all times. All of us are entitled to eat lunch, play golf and go on vacation. But you must leave word with your secretary or associates where you can be reached at all times. Decisions have to be made and your input can be important!
>
> I conducted a study of the 200 firms that have disappeared from Wall Street over the last few years, and I discovered that 62.349 percent went out of business because the important people did not leave word where they went when they left their desk if even for 10 minutes.
>
> That idiocy will not occur here![31]

Greenberg has also written pointed memos to his "troops" about not returning phone calls ("Do you realize what a negative effect not returning a call has on an associate or client?"), the expense of overusing Federal Express to mail documents ("I can assure you that future use of Federal Express is going to be very closely monitored. The fact that it wasn't up to now is my fault, and I take full blame."), and the importance of reporting any suspicious behavior that might violate Bear Stearns' standards of honesty and integrity ("If you think somebody is doing something off the wall or his/her decision making stinks, go around the person, and that includes me."). All are examples of attempts to initiate behavioral control.

**output control**
regulation of worker results or outputs through rewards and incentives

Instead of measuring what managers and workers do, **output control** measures the results of their efforts. Whereas behavior control regulates, guides, and measures how workers behave on the job, output control gives managers and workers the freedom to behave as they see fit as long as it leads to the accomplishment of pre-specified, measurable results. Output control is often coupled with rewards and incentives. However, three things must occur for output control and rewards to lead to improved business results.

First, output control measures must be reliable, fair, and accurate. Second, employees and managers must believe that they can produce the desired results. At Global Dining in Japan, a stylish chain of Tex-Mex, Italian, and Asian restaurants, every six months, restaurant managers get a performance bonus based on restaurant sales. The bonus can range from zero to as much as 18 months' salary. It all depends on whether restaurant sales were below or above sales goals. For most of his 14 years with Global Dining, restaurant manager Koki Ohta regularly received some of the largest bonuses awarded by the company. Yet, when management asked him to manage a new restaurant for families with young children, La Boheme Con Bambino, the new restaurant format failed. In fact, the company has abandoned the format. Ohta, who, because of failed sales numbers, received no bonus, said, "You can't always measure everything by numbers. I was experimenting with something entirely new [a new restaurant format]. But I was judged on the same playing field as everybody else. I didn't think that was really fair."[32] Ohta has since left Global Dining for another job.

Third, the rewards or incentives tied to outcome control measures must truly be dependent on achieving established standards of performance. When auto parts manufacturer, Dana Corporation saw its sales drop 6 percent, its profits drop 44 percent, and its stock value drop by more than half, CEO Joseph Magliochetti saw his pay drop, too. Don't shed tears for him yet: Magliochetti still earned an $850,000 salary. His board of directors denied him a bonus and a stock grant that had been worth $1.8 million the year before. Therefore, because the company did not meet its goals for net income growth and return on investment, his pay was reduced by roughly 60 percent.[33] So for output control to work with rewards, the rewards must truly be at risk if performance doesn't measure up.

### 3.3 Normative Control

normative control
regulation of workers' behavior and decisions through widely shared organizational values and beliefs

Rather than monitoring rules, behavior, or output, another way to control what goes on in organizations is to shape the beliefs and values of the people who work there through normative control. With **normative controls**, a company's widely shared values and beliefs guide workers' behavior and decisions. For example, at Nordstrom, a Seattle-based department store chain, one value permeates the entire workforce from top to bottom: extraordinary customer service. On the first day of work at Nordstrom, trainees begin their transformation to the "Nordstrom way" by reading the employee handbook. Sounds boring, doesn't it? But Nordstrom's handbook is printed on one side of a 3" × 5" note card. In its entirety, it reads:

> Welcome to Nordstrom's. We're glad to have you with our company. Our Number One goal is to provide outstanding customer service. Set both your personal and professional goals high. We have great confidence in your ability to achieve them. Nordstrom Rules: Rule #1: Use your good judgment in all situations. There will be no additional rules. Please feel free to ask your department manager, store manager or division general manager any question at any time.[34]

That's it. No lengthy rules. No specifics about what behavior is or is not appropriate. Use your judgment.

Normative controls are created in two ways. First, companies that use normative controls are very careful about whom they hire. While many companies screen potential applicants on the basis of their abilities, normatively controlled companies are just as likely to screen potential applicants based on their attitudes and values. For example, before building stores in a new city, Nordstrom will send its human resource team into town to interview prospective applicants. In those few instances in which it could not find enough qualified applicants, applicants who would embody the service attitudes and values that Nordstrom is known for, the company has canceled its expansion plans in those cities. Nordstrom would rather give up potential sales in lucrative markets than do business using people who could not provide Nordstrom's level of service.[35]

Second, with normative controls, managers and employees learn what they should and should not do by observing experienced employees and by listening to the stories they tell about the company. At Nordstrom, they even have a name for these stories, "heroics," many of which are inspired by the company motto, "Respond to Unreasonable Customer Requests!"[36]

"Nordies," as Nordstrom employees call themselves, like to tell the story about a customer who just had to have a pair of burgundy Donna Karan slacks that had gone on sale. However, she could not find her size. The sales associate, who was helping her, contacted five nearby Nordstrom stores. She could not find the customer's size. So rather than leave the customer dissatisfied with her shopping experience, the sales associate went to her manager for petty cash and then went across the street and paid full price for the slacks at a competitor's store. She then resold them to the customer at Nordstrom's lower sale price.[37] Obviously, Nordstrom would quickly go out of business if this were the norm. However, this story makes clear the attitude that drives employee performance at Nordstrom in ways that rules, behavioral guidelines, or output controls could not.

### 3.4 Concertive Control

Whereas normative controls are based on the strongly held, widely shared beliefs throughout a company, **concertive controls** are based on beliefs that are shaped and negotiated by work groups.[38] So while normative controls are driven by strong organizational cultures, concertive controls usually arise when companies give autonomous work groups complete responsibility for task completion. **Autonomous work groups** are groups that operate without managers and are completely responsible for controlling work group processes, outputs, and behavior. These groups do their own hiring, firing, worker discipline, work schedules, materials ordering, budget making and meeting, and decision making.

Concertive control is not established overnight. Autonomous work groups evolve through two phases as they develop concertive control. In phase one, autonomous work group members learn to work with each other, supervise each other's work, and develop the values and beliefs that will guide and control their behavior. And because they develop these values and beliefs themselves, work group members feel strongly about following them. You will learn more about groups in Chapter 13, Managing Teams.

For example, a member of an autonomous team at ISE Electronics, a small manufacturer of electronic boards, said, "I feel bad, believe it or not. Last Friday, we missed a shipment. I feel like *I* missed the shipment since I'm the last person that sees what goes to ship. But Friday we missed the shipment by two boards and it shouldn't have been missed. But it was and I felt bad because it's me. It's a reflection on me, too, for not getting the boards out the door."[39] Another member of the same team said, "Under the old system [management-led bureaucratic control], who gave a hoot if the boards shipped today or not? We just did our jobs. Now, we have more buy-in by the team members. We feel more personal responsibility for the product."[40]

The second phase in the development of concertive control is the emergence and formalization of objective rules to guide and control behavior. The beliefs and values developed in phase one usually develop into more objective rules as new members join teams. The clearer those rules, the easier it becomes for new members to figure out how and how not to behave.

For example, a team member at ISE electronics described how the team dealt with members showing up late to work: "Well, we had some disciplinary thing, you know. We had a few certain people who didn't show up on time and made a habit of coming in late. So the team got together and kinda set some guidelines and we told them, you know, 'If you come in late the third time and you don't wanna do anything to correct it, you're gone.' That was a team decision that this was a guideline that we were gonna follow."[41] Again, the key difference in concertive control is that the teams and not management enforced these rules.

Ironically, concertive control may lead to even more stress for workers to conform to expectations than bureaucratic control. Under bureaucratic control, most workers only have to worry about pleasing the boss. But with concertive control, they have to keep the rest of their team members satisfied with their behavior. For example, one team member said, "I don't have to sit there and look for the boss to be around; and if the boss is not

## Learn to Say No!

Control is not just setting standards and identifying performance discrepancies. A key issue in control is deciding what to control and what to ignore. We can't do everything, and that means that sometimes we have to say no when we're asked to participate. Here are four tips for saying no. First, listen to show interest and understanding. Second, say no immediately to avoid raising false expectations concerning your involvement. Three, explain why you can't, so that the reasons for your refusal are understood. Fourth, offer alternatives to your participation: "I can't, but you should contact Mary Smith. Mary knows how to do this."

**Sources:** R. Keenan, "Women Urging Others to 'Just Say No,' Don't Enjoy Just Saying 'Yes,'" *Detroit News*, 23 August 2000, 1.

**self-control (self-management)**
control system in which managers and workers control their own behavior by setting their own goals, monitoring their own progress, and rewarding themselves for goal achievement

around, I can sit there and talk to my neighbor or do what I want. Now the whole team is around me and the whole team is observing what I'm doing."[42] Plus, with concertive control, team members have a second, much more stressful role to perform—that of making sure that their team members adhere to team values and rules.

### 3.5 Self-Control

**Self-control**, also known as **self-management**, is a control system in which managers and workers control their own behavior.[43] However, self-control is not anarchy in which everyone gets to do whatever they want. In self-control or self-management, leaders and managers provide workers with clear boundaries within which they may guide and control their own goals and behaviors.[44] Leaders and managers also contribute to self-control by teaching others the skills they need to maximize and monitor their own work effectiveness. In turn, individuals who manage and lead themselves establish self-control by setting their own goals, monitoring their own progress, rewarding or punishing themselves for achieving or for not achieving their self-set goals, and constructing positive thought patterns that remind them of the importance of their goals and their ability to accomplish them.[45]

One technique for reminding yourself of your goals is daily affirmation, in which you write down or speak your goals aloud to yourself several times a day. Skeptics contend that daily affirmations are nothing more than positive thinking. However, an affirmation is just a simple way to help control what you think about and how you spend your time. Basically, it's a technique to prevent (i.e., control) you from getting sidetracked on unimportant thoughts and activities.

Scott Adams, who illustrates the cartoon strip "Dilbert," was skeptical that affirmations would work, but he gave them a try. His first affirmations were to see the price of a company's stock rise and to impress a particular woman. Both happened. Then when he was getting ready to take the GMAT test to get into an MBA program, every day he wrote that he wanted a score of a 94. His score was a 94. When he began affirming, "I will be the best cartoonist on the planet," "Dilbert" ballooned in popularity. Where it once appeared in only 100 newspapers, it now appears in more than 1,100. What's he affirming now? "I will win a Pulitzer Prize."[46] Now it's your turn; start writing, "I will get an 'A' in Management. I will get an 'A' in Management. . . ."

### Review 3
#### Control Methods

There are five methods of control: bureaucratic, objective, normative, concertive, and self-control (self-management). Bureaucratic and objective controls are top-down, management- and measurement-based. Normative and concertive controls represent shared forms of control, because they evolve from companywide or team-based beliefs and values. Self-control, or self-management, is a control system in which managers largely, but not completely, turn control over to the individuals themselves.

Bureaucratic control is based on organizational policies, rules, and procedures. Objective controls are based on reliable measures of behavior or outputs. Normative control is based on strong corporate beliefs and careful hiring practices. Concertive control is based on the development of values, beliefs, and rules in autonomous work groups. Self-control is based on individuals' setting their own goals, monitoring themselves, and rewarding or punishing themselves with respect to goal achievement.

We end this section by noting that there are more or less appropriate circumstances for using each of these control methods. Examine Exhibit 7.4 to find out when each of these five control methods should be used.

EXHIBIT 7.4

WHEN TO USE DIFFERENT METHODS OF CONTROL

## BUREAUCRATIC CONTROL

- when it is necessary to standardize operating procedures
- when it is necessary to establish limits

## BEHAVIOR CONTROL

- when it is easier to measure what workers do on the job than what they accomplish on the job
- when "cause-effect" relationships are clear, that is, when companies know which behaviors will lead to success and which won't
- when good measures of worker behavior can be created

## OUTPUT CONTROL

- when it is easier to measure what workers accomplish on the job than what they do on the job
- when good measures of worker output can be created
- when it is possible to set clear goals and standards for worker output
- when "cause-effect" relationships are unclear

## NORMATIVE CONTROL

- when organizational culture, values, and beliefs are strong
- when it is difficult to create good measures of worker behavior
- when it is difficult to create good measures of worker output

## CONCERTIVE CONTROL

- when responsibility for task accomplishment is given to autonomous work groups
- when management wants workers to take "ownership" of their behavior and outputs
- when management desires a strong form of worker-based control

## SELF-CONTROL

- when workers are intrinsically motivated to do their jobs well
- when it is difficult to create good measures of worker behavior
- when it is difficult to create good measures of worker output
- when workers have or are taught self-control and self-leadership skills

**Sources:** L.J. Kirsch, "The Management of Complex Tasks in Organizations: Controlling the Systems Development Process," *Organization Science 7* (1996): 1-21. S.A. Snell, "Control Theory in Strategic Human Resource Management: The Mediating Effect of Administrative Information," *Academy of Management Journal* 35 (1992): 292-327.

## 4. What to Control?

In the second part of this chapter we asked, "Is control necessary or possible?" In part three we asked, "How should control be obtained?" In this fourth and final section, we ask the equally important question "What should managers control?" The way managers answer this question has critical implications for most businesses. In the midst of an economic slowdown, a medium-sized financial company created a huge upheaval when it tried to cut costs by eliminating company-paid-for cell phones. Salespeople were furious, claiming that "no other group in the company had their cell phone use restricted." Lynda Ford, a consultant who was working with the company at the time, said that canceling cell phones "became the straw that broke the camel's back." As a result, salespeople started quitting and productivity dropped significantly. Several months later, after finally realizing it was wrong, the company reinstated company cell phones.[47]

This financial company lost sales people and productivity because it only worried about (i.e., controlled) one thing—reducing costs. Companies need to have a clear vision. They can't be everything to everybody. However, most companies successfully carry out their visions and missions by finding a balance that comes from doing a multitude of small things right, like managing costs, providing value, and keeping customers and employees satisfied.

*After reading this section, you should be able to explain 4.1 the balanced scorecard approach to control, and how companies can achieve balanced control of company performance by choosing to control 4.2 economic value added, 4.3 customer defections, 4.4 quality, and 4.5 waste and pollution.*

### 4.1 The Balanced Scorecard

In most companies, performance is measured using standard financial and accounting measures, such as return on capital, return on assets, return on investments, cash flow, net income, net margins, and so forth. That's why employees at Americas Marketing and Refining (AM&R), the largest division of Mobil Oil Corporation, were not looking forward to their quarterly meeting with their tough division vice president. On most of these traditional measures, division performance had been poor, and lower-level employees and managers expected to be blasted for their poor performance. In the past, poor financial performance usually led to firings and layoffs. So no one wanted to go to the meeting.

However, this time it was different. After opening the meeting with a discussion of the poor financial results, the meeting turned positive. Market share had improved. Operating expenses were down. And employees, as measured by a recent attitudinal survey, were satisfied with their jobs and their bosses. The VP declared, "In all the areas we could control, we moved the needle in the right direction." The employees, who expected to be handed their heads, were shocked by the praise. Greg Berry, the division's manager of business and performance analysis, said, "It was a total departure from the past. Here was a Mobil executive saying, 'Hey, we didn't make any money, but I feel good about where the business is going.'"[48]

**balanced scorecard**
measurement of organizational performance in four equally important areas: finances, customers, internal operations, and innovation and learning

The **balanced scorecard** encourages managers to look beyond traditional financial measures to four different perspectives on company performance. How do customers see us (the customer perspective)? What must we excel at (the internal perspective)? Can we continue to improve and create value (the innovation and learning perspective)? How do we look to shareholders (the financial perspective)?[49]

The balanced scorecard has several advantages over traditional control processes that rely solely on financial measures. First, it forces managers at each level of the company to set specific goals and measure performance in each of the four areas. For example, Mobil Oil's AM&R division uses 23 different measures in its balanced scorecard. Of those 23, only five are standard financial measures of performance.

Exhibit 7.5 shows the balanced scorecard used by a large semiconductor company. This company does measure its performance in traditional financial terms—cash flows, quarterly sales growth, and increased market share and return on equity. But it also measures the percentage of sales from new products and on-time deliveries (customer perspective), unit costs and whether the company met the projected schedule for new product introductions (internal business perspective), and how long it takes to develop the next generation of new products and how well it rolls out new products compared to its competition (innovation and learning perspective).

**suboptimization**
performance improvement in one part of an organization but only at the expense of decreased performance in another part

The second major advantage of the balanced scorecard approach to control is that it minimizes the chances of **suboptimization**, which occurs when performance improves in one area, but only at the expense of decreased performance in others. For example, at Mobil Oil's AM&R division, everyone in the plant now measures performance based on the balanced scorecard. When the division's executive team meets, all managers must bring their copy of the balanced scorecard to explain how their actions will affect finances, customers, internal business, and innovation and learning. AM&R's

EXHIBIT 7.5

EXAMPLE OF A BALANCED SCORECARD

### FINANCIAL PERSPECTIVE

| GOALS | MEASURES |
|---|---|
| Survive | Cash flow |
| Succeed | Quarterly sales growth and operating income by division |
| Prosper | Increased market share and ROE (return on equity) |

### CUSTOMER PERSPECTIVE

| GOALS | MEASURES |
|---|---|
| New Products | Percent of sales from new products |
| | Percent of sales from proprietary products |
| Responsive supply | On-time delivery |
| Preferred customer | Share of key accounts' purchases |
| Customer partnership | Number of cooperative engineering efforts |

### INTERNAL BUSINESS PERSPECTIVE

| GOALS | MEASURES |
|---|---|
| Technology capability | Manufacturing geometry vs. competition |
| Manufacturing excellence | Cycle time, Unit cost |
| Design productivity | Silicon efficiency, Engineering efficiency |

### INNOVATION AND LEARNING PERSPECTIVE

| GOALS | MEASURES |
|---|---|
| Technology leadership | Time to develop next generation product |
| Product focus | Percent of products equaling 80 percent sales |
| Time to market | New product introduction vs. competition |

**Source**: R.S. Kaplan & D.P. Norton, "The Balanced Scorecard: Measures that Drive Performance," *Harvard Business Review,* January-February 1992, 71-79.

---

**cash flow analysis**
type of analysis that predicts how changes in a business will affect its ability to take in more cash than it pays out

**balance sheets**
accounting sheets that provide a snapshot of a company's financial position at a particular time

**income statements**
types of statements, also called "profit and loss statements," that show what has happened to an organization's income, expenses, and net profit over a period of time

**financial ratios**
calculations typically used to track a business's liquidity (cash), efficiency, and profitability over time compared to other businesses in its industry

**budgets**
qualitative plans through which managers decide how to allocate available money to best accomplish company goals

vice president said, "It's the basis of every conversation. When I go out in the field and talk with a guy running a coker on the midnight shift at one of our refineries, he can tell me what he's doing to impact the scorecard."[50]

Let's examine some of the ways in which companies are controlling the four basic parts of the balanced scorecard: the financial perspective (economic value added), the customer perspective (customer defections), the internal perspective (total quality management), and the innovation and learning perspective (waste and pollution).

### 4.2 The Financial Perspective: Controlling Economic Value Added

The traditional approach to controlling financial performance focuses on accounting tools, such as cash flow analysis, balance sheets, income statements, financial ratios, and budgets. **Cash flow analysis** predicts how changes in a business will affect its ability to take in more cash than it pays out. **Balance sheets** provide a snapshot of a company's financial position at a particular time (but not the future). **Income statements**, also called profit and loss statements, show what has happened to an organization's income, expenses, and net profit (income less expenses) over a period of time. Exhibit 7.6 shows the basic steps or parts for cash flow analyses, balance sheets, and income statements. **Financial ratios** are typically used to track a business's liquidity (cash), efficiency, and profitability over time compared to other businesses in its industry. Exhibit 7.7 lists a few of the most common financial ratios and explains how they are calculated, what they mean, and when to use them. Finally, **budgets** are used to project costs and revenues, to prioritize and control spending, and to ensure that expenses don't exceed available funds and revenues. Exhibit 7.8 reviews the different kinds of budgets managers can use to track and control company finances.

EXHIBIT 7.6

BASIC ACCOUNTING TOOLS FOR CONTROLLING FINANCIAL PERFORMANCE

### STEPS FOR A BASIC CASH FLOW ANALYSIS

1. Forecast sales (steady, up, or down)
2. Project changes in anticipated cash inflows (as a result of changes)
3. Project anticipated cash outflows (as a result of changes)
4. Project net cash flows by combining anticipated cash inflows and outflows

### PARTS OF A BASIC BALANCE SHEET (ASSETS = LIABILITIES + OWNER'S EQUITY)

1. Assets
   a. Current Assets (cash, short-term investment, marketable securities, accounts receivable, etc.)
   b. Fixed Assets (land, buildings, machinery, equipment, etc.)
2. Liabilities
   a. Current Liabilities (accounts payable, notes payable, taxes payable, etc.)
   b. Long-term Liabilities (long-term debt, deferred income taxes, etc.)
3. Owner's Equity
   a. Preferred stock and common stock
   b. Additional paid-in capital
   c. Retained earnings

### BASIC INCOME STATEMENT

SALES REVENUE
- sales returns and allowances
+ other income
= NET REVENUE
- cost of goods sold [beginning inventory, costs of goods purchased, ending inventory]
= GROSS PROFIT
- total operating expenses [selling, general, and administrative expenses]
= INCOME FROM OPERATIONS
- interest expense
= PRETAX INCOME
- income taxes
= NET INCOME

By themselves, none of these tools—cash flow analyses, balance sheets, income statements, financial, ratios, or budgets—tell the whole financial story of a business. They must be used together when assessing a company's financial performance. Since these tools are reviewed in detail in your accounting and finance classes, only a brief overview is provided here. Still, these are necessary tools for controlling organizational finances and expenses, and they should be part of your business toolbox. Unfortunately, most managers don't (but should) have a good understanding of these accounting tools.[51] When the new chief financial officer of Boeing, the passenger jet manufacturer, attended her first company retreat, she began her presentation to the other Boeing executives in attendance, figuring that her discussion of financial ratios, just like those shown in Exhibit 7.7, would be nothing but a boring review for everyone present. Afterwards, she was shocked when dozens of the 280 executives attending the retreat told her that for the very first time they finally understood what the formulas meant.[52]

EXHIBIT 7.7

COMMON FINANCIAL RATIOS

| RATIOS | FORMULA | WHAT IT MEANS | WHEN TO USE |
|---|---|---|---|
| **LIQUIDITY RATIOS** | | | |
| Current Ratio | Current Assets ÷ Current Liabilities | • Whether you have enough assets on hand to pay for short-term bills and obligations.<br>• Higher is better.<br>• Recommended level is two times as many current assets as current liabilities. | • Track monthly and quarterly.<br>• Basic measure of your company's health. |
| Quick (Acid Test) Ratio | Current Assets— Inventories ÷ Current Liabilities | • Stricter than current ratio.<br>• Whether you have enough liquid assets (i.e., cash) to pay short-term bills and obligations.<br>• Higher is better.<br>• Recommended level is one or higher. | • Track monthly.<br>• Also calculate quick ratio with potential customers to evaluate whether they're likely to pay you in a timely manner. |
| **LEVERAGE RATIOS** | | | |
| Debt to Equity | Total Liabilities ÷ Total Equity | • Indicates how much the company is leveraged (in debt) by comparing what is owed (liabilities) to what is owned (equity).<br>• Lower is better. A high debt-to-equity ratio could indicate that the company has too much debt.<br>• Recommended level depends on industry. | • Track monthly.<br>• Lenders often use this to determine the credit worthiness of a business (i.e., whether to approve additional loans). |
| Debt Coverage | Net Profit + Non-cash Expenses ÷ Debt | • Indicates how well cash flow covers debt payments.<br>• Higher is better. | • Track monthly.<br>• Lenders look at this ratio to determine if there is adequate cash to make loan payments. |
| **EFFICIENCY RATIOS** | | | |
| Inventory Turnover | Cost of Goods Sold ÷ Average Value of Inventory | • Whether you're making efficient use of inventory.<br>• Higher is better, indicating that inventory (dollars) isn't purchased (spent) until needed.<br>• Recommended level depends on industry. | • Track monthly by using a 12-month rolling average. |
| Average Collections Period | Accounts Receivable ÷ (Annual Net Credit Sales Divided by 365) | • Shows on average how quickly your customers are paying their bills.<br>• Recommended level is no more than 15 days longer than credit terms. If payment credit is net 30 days, then average should not be longer than 45 days. | • Track monthly.<br>• Use to determine how long company's money is being tied up in customer credit. |
| **PROFITABILITY RATIOS** | | | |
| Gross Profit Margin | Gross Profit ÷ Total Sales | • Shows how efficiently a business is using its materials and labor in the production process.<br>• Higher is better, indicating that a profit can be made if fixed costs are controlled. | • Track monthly.<br>• Analyze when unsure about product or service pricing. Low margin compared to competitors means you're underpricing. |
| Return on Equity | Net Income ÷ Owner's Equity | • Shows what was earned on your investment in the business during a particular period. Often called "return on investment."<br>• Higher is better. | • Track quarterly and annually.<br>• Use to compare what you might have earned on the stock market, bonds, or government treasury bills during the same period. |

243

EXHIBIT 7.8

COMMON KINDS OF BUDGETS

**Revenue Budgets**—used to project or forecast future sales.
* Accuracy of projection depends on economy, competitors, sales force estimates, etc.
* Determined by estimating future sales volume and sales prices for all products and services.

**Expense Budgets**—used within departments and divisions to determine how much will be spent on various supplies, projects, or activities.
* One of the first places that companies look for cuts when trying to lower expenses.

**Profit Budgets**—used by profit centers which have "profit and loss" responsibility.
* Profit budgets combine revenue and expense budgets into one budget.
* Typically used in large businesses with multiple plants and divisions.

**Cash Budgets**—used to forecast how much cash a company will have on hand to meet expenses.
* Similar to cash flow analyses.
* Used to identify cash shortfalls, which much be covered to pay bills, or cash excesses, which should be invested for a higher return.

**Capital Expenditure Budgets**—used to forecast large, long-lasting investments in equipment, buildings, and property.
* Helps managers identify funding it will take to pay for future expansion or strategic moves designed to increase competitive advantage.

**Variable Budgets**—used to project costs across varying levels of sales and revenues.
* Important because it is difficult to accurately predict sales revenue and volume.
* Leads to more accurate budgeting with respect to labor, materials, and administrative expenses, which vary with sales volume and revenues.
* Builds flexibility into the budgeting process.

---

So, if, like those experienced executives, you struggle to understand how these financial ratios can be used where you work, you might find help in the following books: *Accounting the Easy Way,* by Peter J. Eisen; *Accounting for Dummies* and *How to Read a Financial Report: Wringing Vital Signs Out of the Numbers,* both by John A. Tracy; *Schaum's Quick Guide to Business Formulas: 201 Decision-Making Tools for Business, Finance, and Accounting Students,* by Joel G. Siegel, Jae K. Shim, and Stephen W. Hartman; *The Vest-Pocket Guide to Business Ratios,* by Michael R. Tyran; *Essential Managers: Managing Budgets,* by Stephen Brookson; or *Forecasting Budgets: 25 Keys to Successful Planning (The New York Times Pocket MBA Series),* by Norman Moore and Grover Gardner.

While no one would dispute the importance of cash flow analyses, balance sheets, income statements, financial ratios, or budgets for determining the financial health of a business, accounting research also indicates that the complexity and sheer amount of information contained in these accounting tools can shut down the brains and glaze over the eyes of even the most experienced managers.[53] Sometimes, there's simply too much information to make sense of. The balanced scorecard simplifies things by focusing on one simple question when it comes to finances: How do we look to shareholders? One of the best ways to answer that question is through something called economic value added.

Conceptually, **economic value added (EVA)** is fairly easy for managers and workers to understand. EVA is more than just profits. It is the amount by which profits exceed the cost of capital in a given year. It is based on the simple idea that it takes capital to run a business, and capital comes at a cost. While most people think of capital as

**economic value added (EVA)**
the amount by which company profits (revenues, minus expenses, minus taxes) exceed the cost of capital in a given year

EXHIBIT 7.9

## CALCULATING ECONOMIC VALUE ADDED (EVA)

| | |
|---|---|
| 1. Calculate Net Operating Profit After Tax (NOPAT) | $3,500,000 |
| 2. Identify how much capital the company has invested (i.e., spent) | $16,800,000 |
| 3. Determine the cost (i.e., rate) paid for capital (usually between 10 percent and 13 percent) | 10 % |
| 4. Multiply capital used (Step 2) times cost of capital (Step 3) | (10 % × $16,800,000) = $1,680,000 |
| 5. Subtract total dollar cost of capital from net profit after taxes | $3,500,000 Net Operating Profit After Tax <br> −$1,680,000 Total Cost of Capital <br> $1,820,000 Economic Value Added |

cash, capital, once invested (i.e., spent), is more likely to be found in a business in the form of computers, manufacturing plants, employees, raw materials, and so forth. And just like the interest that a homeowner pays on a mortgage or that a college student pays on a student loan, there is a cost to that capital.

The most common costs of capital are the interest paid on long-term bank loans used to buy all those resources, the interest paid to bondholders (who lend organizations their money), and the dividends (cash payments) and growth in stock value that accrue to shareholders. EVA is positive when company profits (revenues minus expenses, minus taxes) exceed the cost of capital in a given year. In other words, if a business is to truly grow, its revenues must be large enough to cover both short-term costs (annual expenses and taxes) and long-term costs (the cost of borrowing capital from bondholders and shareholders). If you're a bit confused, the late Roberto Goizueta, the former CEO of Coca-Cola, explained it this way: "You borrow money at a certain rate and invest it at a higher rate and pocket the difference. It is simple. It is the essence of banking."[54]

Exhibit 7.9 shows how to calculate EVA. First, starting with a company's income statement, you calculate Net Operating Profit after Taxes (NOPAT) by subtracting taxes owed from Income from Operations (see Exhibit 7.5 for a review of an income statement). The NOPAT shown in Exhibit 7.9 is $3,500,000.00. Second, identify how much capital the company has invested (i.e., spent). Total liabilities (what the company owes), less accounts payable and less accrued expenses, neither of which you pay interest on, provides a rough approximation of this amount. In Exhibit 7.9, total capital invested in our example is $16,800,000. Third, calculate the cost (i.e., rate) paid for capital by determining the interest paid to bondholders (who lend organizations their money), which is usually somewhere between 5 percent and 8 percent, and the return that stockholders want in terms of dividends and stock price appreciation, which is historically about 13 percent. Take a weighted average of the two to determine the overall rate cost of capital. In Exhibit 7.9, the cost of capital is 10 percent. Fourth, multiply the total capital ($16,800,000) from Step 2 by the cost of capital (10 percent) from step 3. In Exhibit 7.9, this amount is $1,680,000. Fifth, subtract the total dollar cost of capital in Step 4 from net profit after taxes in Step 1. In Exhibit 7.9, this value is $1,820,000, which means that our example company has created economic value or wealth this year. If our EVA number had been negative, meaning that the company didn't make enough profit to cover the cost of capital from bondholders and shareholders, then the company would have destroyed economic value or wealth by taking in more money than it returned.[55]

# BeenThereDoneThat

## Economic Value Added at Armstrong World Industries

Armstrong World Industries is a manufacturer of floor coverings, building products, and furniture. In this interview, CEO George Lorch explains how the company uses economic value added (EVA) to guide company decisions and align corporate and shareholder interests.

**Q:** How does economic value added (EVA) give Armstrong better analysis than conventional measurements?

**A:** It more closely aligns us to the shareholders' interests, number one. It takes into account our cost of debt and equity capital and really reflects what we need to provide to the shareholder as an adequate return. All the elements that go into that calculation force us to focus on important things: growth, which is profitable sales revenue; our margins, which we arrive at after we take into account our cost; the operating assets it takes to drive that profitability; and taxes.

**Q:** Will EVA ever replace more traditional ways of measuring financial performance?

**A:** No. There is no one measurement system that is absolutely the best. A company has to look at what it is trying to do and pick the best system. EVA holds a company accountable for the cost of capital it uses to expand and operate its business and attempts to show whether a company is creating real value for its shareholders.

**Q:** Your salaried people are on incentive-based compensation.

**A:** Every salaried person is on EVA as a measurement. One hundred percent of my incentive compensation is based on how well we do against our EVA target. Take my assistant. Her incentive compensation is also based 100 percent on our ability to generate the targeted EVA. A president of one of our worldwide businesses—30 percent of his or her incentive would be based on the corporate EVA. Fifty percent would be based on the operation's EVA for that business. The balance would be on personal objectives, all of which are tied specifically to things they must do to drive the financial performance of the business.

**Q:** Did it take you a long time to set this up?

**A:** It took us a few months.

**Q:** Did you have any people who were less than enthusiastic about this?

**A:** No. The greatest apprehension on the part of senior management group was where the EVA target would be set for [each manager's] business. Would we be fair, or would we put them in Never Never Land, where they wouldn't have a chance to make any decent bonus money? Once they understood what the numbers were and compared them to the ROA target, they said, "Yeah. That looks fair."

The farther into the organization you go, the greater the percentage payout is tied directly to that business and the personal objectives. You put the incentive money as close to the target as you can. Somebody who is, let's say, a product manager in our flooring business in North America will be driven by actions that they can control within their business. So, that's what we want to have the incentive follow.

**Q:** Can you cite an example?

**A:** The leader of our worldwide flooring business or building products business is an executive officer of this company and one of the five top-paid guys. You want those guys to be rewarded based on how well the total company does. In our executive compensation plan that follows this measurement, we have benchmarked ourselves against peer companies in our group and [against] a cross-section of American business. We tried to put more opportunity into the incentive side of compensation, so that we really drive performance to align us more closely with what the shareholder wants. If we really do well, as we did last year, our people at all levels of this incentive thing make a lot of money. When we don't do very well, they won't make much money. Under the old plan, the threshold to begin to earn incentive compensation was 4 percent ROA. The threshold under the new plan is 7.1 percent. So, you see, we gave up mediocre performance for extraordinary performance, because under the old plan, there was a cap on how much incentive money you could earn. We've taken the cap off the incentive.

**Q:** But, they've got to work a lot harder.

**A:** They will work a lot harder and a lot smarter, because the reward will be there if they're able to perform. Last year—I'm going to go from memory, now—our performance, ROA-wise, was 10.4 percent against a target of 8 percent. If we do as well this year as we did last year, there's going to be some very handsome rewards out there.

**Q:** Your incentive compensation is 100 percent based on the total performance of the company. What happens if you've got great performance across various sectors, and one falls off the face of the earth?

**A:** My incentive compensation is based on the total company. So, if we've got six business units that do great and one that doesn't, and if it pulls us below the target level, I don't get anything. I like to think that better than 60 percent of my compensation is at risk all the time.

**Q:** Is there too much concentration, then, on the short-term bottom line to the detriment of longer-term factors?

**A:** No. They have long-term incentive compensation in stock options and performance-restricted shares. The longer, term-restricted shares reflect a three-year performance relative to total appreciation of our stock plus the reinvested dividends, measured against the Standard & Poor's 500 performance. Accountability is the important issue, but even more important is that these incentive plans change behavior. They give people a sense of urgency, and they force people to focus on the things that really matter.

So why is EVA so important? First and most importantly, since it includes the cost of capital, it shows whether a business, division, department, or profit center is really paying for itself. For example, soon after Goizueta became Coke's CEO, Coke management used EVA to take a hard look at its fountain business (selling coke concentrate to restaurants). Goizueta said, "And we found out that we're making much less than our cost of capital, which at that time, with no debt, was about 16 percent. So what we thought was a great business [using the traditional accounting and financial measures] was, in fact, a lousy business."[56] In other words, the business was destroying value and wealth, rather than creating it.

Second, because EVA can easily be determined for subsets of a company, such as divisions, regional offices, manufacturing plants, and sometimes even departments, it makes managers at all levels pay much closer attention to how they run their segment of the business. For example, at Coke, when the managers of the fountain business realized that they weren't even covering the cost of capital (i.e., a negative EVA), they looked for ways to do more with less capital. They determined that instead of delivering Coke concentrate in thousands of small 20-gallon steel containers, they could save money by delivering it to restaurants in huge tanker trucks.[57] In other words, EVA motivates all managers to think like small business owners who must scramble to contain costs and generate enough business to meet their bills each month.

Finally, unlike many kinds of financial controls, EVA doesn't specify what should or should not be done to improve performance. Thus, it encourages managers and workers to be creative as they try to find ways to improve EVA performance.

For example, CSX Intermodal uses trains to transport cargo containers across the country to waiting trucks or ships. When CSX managers found out that the company had an EVA of negative $70 million, they started making changes. CSX used to use four engine cars to pull a regularly scheduled train from New Orleans to Jacksonville at an average speed of 28 mph. However, the train usually arrived six to eight hours before it was to be unloaded. So managers made better use of their capital by using only three engine cars, which pulled the train at an average speed of 25 mph. The train still arrived three hours before it was scheduled to be unloaded, but with three rather than four engines, it used 25 percent less fuel.[58]

Exhibit 7.10 shows the top 10 companies in terms of EVA and for market value added (MVA). Remember that EVA is the amount by which profits exceed the cost of capital in a given year. So the more that EVA exceeds the total dollar cost of capital, the better a company is using investors' money that year. MVA is simply the cumulative EVA created by a company over time. Thus, MVA indicates how much value or wealth a company has created or destroyed in total during its existence. As measured by the MVA figures shown in Exhibit 7.10, the top 10 companies have created considerable wealth over time, returning substantially more money than they took in, ranging from $177 billion at Wal-Mart to $502 billion at General Electric. Furthermore, nine of the top 10 in MVA has positive EVAs in the last year. Only American International Group had a difficult year, falling $119 million short in a disappointing year.

EXHIBIT 7.10

LEADING COMPANIES BY MARKET VALUE ADDED AND ECONOMIC VALUE ADDED

| MVA RANKING IN 2000 | MVA RANKING IN 1999 | COMPANY | MARKET VALUE ADDED ($MILLIONS) | ECONOMIC VALUE ADDED ($MILLIONS) |
|---|---|---|---|---|
| 1 | 2 | General Electric | $502,307 | $3,499 |
| 2 | 1 | Microsoft | $388,922 | $5,796 |
| 3 | 3 | Cisco Systems | $377,883 | $ 182 |
| 4 | 5 | Intel | $281,832 | $4,695 |
| 5 | 21 | Pfizer | $260,984 | $1,953 |
| 6 | 12 | Merck | $193,348 | $3,449 |
| 7 | 23 | EMC | $191,904 | $ 668 |
| 8 | 8 | Oracle | $180,885 | $ 605 |
| 9 | 19 | American International Group | $177,982 | ($ 119) |
| 10 | 4 | Wal-Mart Stores | $177,450 | $1,528 |

**Source:** G. Colvin, "America's Best & Worst Wealth Creators: The Real Champions Aren't Always Who You Think. Here's an Eye-Opening Look at Which Companies Produce and Destroy the Most Money for Investors—Plus a New Tool for Spotting Future Winners," *Fortune*, 18 December 2000, 207.

### 4.3 The Customer Perspective: Controlling Customer Defections

The second aspect of organizational performance that the balanced scorecard helps managers monitor is customers. It does so by forcing managers to address the question, "How do customers see us?" Unfortunately, most companies try to answer this question through customer satisfaction surveys that are often misleadingly positive. Most customers are reluctant to talk about their problems, because they don't know who to complain to, or they don't think that complaining will do any good. Indeed, a study by the federal Office of Consumer Affairs indicated that 96 percent of unhappy customers never complain to anyone in the company.[59]

Another reason that customer satisfaction surveys can be misleading is that sometimes even very satisfied customers will leave to do business with competitors. Dave Nichol, founder of the President's Choice brand, explained why: "Customer loyalty is the absence of something better."[60] So even if customers are pleased, they may go elsewhere if they believe they can get a better product or service.

Finally, customer satisfaction surveys can be misleading because they greatly overestimate the degree to which customers will buy from a company again. For example, it's common for automakers to advertise that "90 percent of customers are satisfied with their cars." But what they don't say in their advertising is that only 30 percent to 40 percent of car buyers purchase their next car from the same company.[61]

Rather than pouring over customer satisfaction surveys from current customers, studies indicate that companies may do a better job of answering the question "How do customers see us?" by closely monitoring **customer defections**, that is, by identifying which customers are leaving the company and measuring the rate at which they are leaving. In contrast to customer satisfaction surveys, customer defections and retention have a much greater effect on profits.

For example, very few managers realize that it costs five times as much to obtain a new customer as it does to keep a current one. In fact, the cost of replacing old customers with new ones is so great that most companies could double their profits by

**customer defections**
performance assessment in which companies identify which customers are leaving and measure the rate at which they are leaving

increasing the rate of customer retention by just 5 to 10 percent per year.[62] And, if a company can keep a customer for life, the benefits are even larger. For Taco Bell, keeping a customer is worth $11,000 in lifetime sales. For a Cadillac dealer, the value is $332,000. For a grocery store, it can approach $200,000.[63] For an industrial manufacturer like Rolls-Royce, which manufacturers IAE V2500 jet engines that cost over $2 million each, the lifetime value can approach tens of millions of dollars.

Beyond the clear benefits to the bottom line, the second reason to study customer defections is that customers who have defected to other companies are much more likely than current customers to tell you what you are doing wrong. Perhaps the best way to tap into this source of good feedback is to have top-level managers from various departments talk directly to customers who have left. It's also worthwhile to have top managers talk to dissatisfied customers who are still with the company. Every day, John Chambers, CEO of Cisco Systems, listens to 15 to 20 voice mails that have been forwarded to him from dissatisfied Cisco customers. Chambers said, "Email would be more efficient, but I want to hear the emotion, I want to hear the frustration, I want to hear the caller's level of comfort with the strategy we're employing. I can't get that through email." Likewise, at Vanguard, a leading investment fund company, CEO Jack Brennan visits the customer call center and, working alongside call representatives, answers customer questions and addresses customer complaints.[64] Some might argue that it's a waste of valuable executive time to have upper-level managers make or listen to these calls, but there's no faster way to get the people in charge to realize what needs to be done than to hear it directly from customers who decided that their company's performance was lacking.

Finally, companies that understand why customers leave can not only take steps to fix ongoing problems, but can also identify which customers are likely to leave and make changes to prevent them from leaving. For example, a large bank discovered that departing customers would send signals that they were getting ready to leave. A small business that made regular overnight deposits would make them less frequently. Or a customer with a personal bank account who withdrew money each Friday might only withdraw money once or twice a month. Since these changes usually occurred before customers left, the bank used its computers to create a daily "retention alert" that would identify customers whose regular interaction patterns had changed. Then, each of those customers would receive a personal phone call from bank account managers to determine what could be done to solve their problems and keep their business.[65]

Likewise, Citibank mails postcards to credit card holders when their credit card usage suddenly drops. The postcards say, "Call 1-800 . . . now and tell us why, and we'll make you an offer that will make your card even more valuable to you." When a customer called to explain that his Discover Card paid a cashback bonus, Citibank kept the customer's business by offering him an identical cashback deal.[66]

### 4.4 The Internal Perspective: Controlling Quality

The third part of the balanced scorecard, the internal perspective, consists of the processes, decisions, and actions that managers and workers make within the organization. In contrast to the financial perspective of EVA and the outward-looking customer perspective, the internal perspective asks the question "What must we excel at?" For McDonald's, the answer would be quick, low-cost food. For America Online, the answer would be reliability—when your modem dials, the network should be up and running, and you should be able to connect without getting a busy signal. Yet no matter what area a company chooses, the key is to excel in that area. Consequently, the internal perspective of the balanced scorecard usually leads managers to a focus on quality.

Quality is typically defined and measured in three ways: excellence, value, and conformance to expectations.[67] When the company defines its quality goal as *excellence*, then managers must try to produce a product or service of unsurpassed performance and features. For example, by almost any count, Singapore International Airlines (SIA) is "the best" airline in the world. It has been named so 11 years in a row by readers of *Conde Nast Traveler* magazine.[68] It has also received various "best airline" awards from the *Asian Wall Street Journal, Business Traveler International, Germany Business Traveler, Travel and Leisure,* and *Fortune.*[69] Even SIA's competitors recognize its excellence. *Air Transport World*, the magazine read by those who work in the airline industry, stated, "SIA aimed to be the best and most successful airline in the world."[70] SIA was the first airline to introduce a choice of meals, complementary drinks, and earphones in coach class in the 1970s. Today, it continues to innovate, introducing the first worldwide video, news, telephone, and fax service on any airline. This system offers 40 video channels with movies, news, and documentaries, 12 audio channels, and 50 different games which are viewed on 10.4 inch monitors. AC power is available for laptop computers, as is live Internet access. SIA is also introducing the "SpaceBed," which is a business class seat that converts into the longest and widest "business bed" in the industry.[71]

**value**
customer perception that the product quality is excellent for the price offered

**Value** is the customer perception that the product quality is excellent for the price offered. At a higher price, for example, customers may perceive the product to be less of a value. When a company emphasizes value as its quality goal, managers must simultaneously control excellence, price, durability, or other features of a product or service that customers strongly associate with value. One company that has put value at the core of everything it does is Lands' End, the catalog company that sells quality clothing and accessories at reasonable prices. In its advertising, Lands' End said, "Value is more than price. Value is the combination of product quality, world class customer service, and a fair price." Lands' End puts its commitment to value into practice through its eight principles of doing business, which are shown in Exhibit 7.11.

When a company defines its quality goal as conformance to specifications, employees must base decisions and actions on whether services and products measure up to standard specifications. In contrast to excellence and value-based definitions of quality that can be somewhat ambiguous, measuring whether products and services are "in spec" is relatively easy. Furthermore, while conformance to specifications is usually associated with manufacturing, it can be used equally well to control quality in nonmanufacturing jobs. Exhibit 7.12 shows a quality checklist that a cook or restaurant owner would use to ensure quality when buying fresh fish.

The way in which a company defines quality affects the methods and measures that workers use to control quality. Accordingly, Exhibit 7.13 (See p. 252) shows the advantages and disadvantages associated with the excellence, value, and conformance to specification definitions of quality.

### 4.5 The Innovation and Learning Perspective: Controlling Waste and Pollution

The last part of the balance scorecard, the innovation and learning perspective, addresses the question "Can we continue to improve and create value?" Thus, the innovation and learning perspective is concerned with new product development (discussed in Chapter 4), continuous improvement in ongoing products and services (discussed in Chapter 15), and relearning and redesigning the processes by which products and services are created (discussed in Chapter 10). Since all three categories are discussed in more detail elsewhere in the text, this section reviews an increasingly important topic, waste and pollution minimization, which is affected by all three of these issues.

As shown in Exhibit 7.14, (See p. 253) there are four levels of waste minimization, with waste prevention and reduction producing the greatest minimization of waste, and waste disposal producing the smallest minimization of waste.[72] The top level is *waste prevention and reduction,* in which the goals are to prevent waste and pollution before they occur, or to reduce them when they do occur. There are three strategies for waste prevention and reduction.

EXHIBIT 7.11

### THE LANDS' END PRINCIPLES OF DOING BUSINESS

Principle 1.    We do everything we can to make our products better. We improve material, and add back features and construction details that others have taken out over the years. We never reduce the quality of a product to make it cheaper.

Principle 2.    We price our products fairly and honestly. We do not, have not, and will not participate in the common retailing practice of inflating mark-ups to set up a future phony "sale."

Principle 3.    We accept any return for any reason, at any time. Our products are guaranteed. No fine print. No arguments. We mean exactly what we say: GUARANTEED. PERIOD.

Principle 4.    We ship faster than anyone we know of. We ship items in stock the day after we receive the order. At the height of the last Christmas season, the longest time an order was in the house was 36 hours, excepting monograms which took another 12 hours.

Principle 5.    We believe that what is best for our customer is best for all of us. Everyone here understands that concept. Our sales and service people are trained to know our products, and to be friendly and helpful. They are urged to take all the time necessary to take care of you. We even pay for your call, for whatever reason you call.

Principle 6.    We are able to sell at lower prices because we have eliminated middlemen; because we don't buy branded merchandise with high protected mark-ups; and because we have placed our contracts with manufacturers who have proven that they are cost conscious and efficient.

Principle 7.    We are able to sell at lower prices because we operate efficiently. Our people are hard-working, intelligent, and share in the success of the company.

Principle 8.    We are able to sell at lower prices because we support no fancy emporiums with their high overhead. Our main location is in the middle of a 40-acre cornfield in rural Wisconsin.

**Source:** "The Lands' End Principles of Doing Business," Lands' End Web Site. [Online] Available http://www.landsend.com/cd/fp/help/ 0,2471,1_26215_26859_26906_,00.html?sid=0999527403537, 3 September 2001.

EXHIBIT 7.12

### CONFORMANCE TO SPECIFICATIONS CHECKLIST FOR BUYING FRESH FISH

**QUALITY CHECKLIST FOR BUYING FRESH FISH**

| FRESH WHOLE FISH | ACCEPTABLE | NOT ACCEPTABLE |
| --- | --- | --- |
| Eyes | clear, bright, bulging, black pupils | dull, sunken, cloudy, gray pupils |
| Gills | bright red, free of slime, clear mucus | brown to grayish, thick, yellow mucus |
| Flesh | firm and elastic to touch, tight to the bone | soft and flabby, separating from the bone |
| Smell | inoffensive, slight ocean smell | ammonia, putrid smell |
| Skin | opalescent sheen, scales adhere tightly to skin | dull or faded color, scales missing, or easily removed |
| Belly Cavity | no viscera or blood visible, lining intact, no bone protruding | incomplete evisceration, cuts or protruding bones, off-odor |

**Sources:** "A Closer Look: Buy It Fresh, Keep It Fresh," *Consumer Reports Online.* [Online] http://www.seagrant.sunysb.edu/SeafoodTechnology/ SeafoodMedia/CR02-2001/CR-SeafoodII020101.htm, 3 September 2001. Philipps, "Turn to Pros for Fish Buying Tips," *Cincinnati Post,* 2 September 2000, 3C. "How to Purchase: Buying Fish," *AboutSeaFood* Web Site. [Online] http://www.aboutseafood.com/faqs/purchase1.html, 3 September 2001.

251

EXHIBIT 7.13

ADVANTAGES AND DISADVANTAGES OF DIFFERENT MEASURES OF QUALITY

## QUALITY AS EXCELLENCE

| ADVANTAGES | DISADVANTAGES |
|---|---|
| Promotes clear organizational vision. | Provides little practical guidance for managers. |
| Being/providing the "best" motivates and inspires managers and employees. | Excellence is ambiguous. What is it? Who defines it? |
| Appeals to customers, who "know excellence when they see it." | Difficult to measure and control. |

## QUALITY AS VALUE

| ADVANTAGES | DISADVANTAGES |
|---|---|
| Customers recognize differences in value. | Can be difficult to determine what factors influence whether a product/service is seen as having value. |
| Easier to measure and compare whether products/services differ in value. | Controlling the balance between excellence and cost (i.e., affordable excellence) can be difficult. |

## QUALITY AS CONFORMANCE TO SPECIFICATIONS

| ADVANTAGES | DISADVANTAGES |
|---|---|
| If specifications can be written, conformance to specifications is usually measurable. | Many products/services cannot be easily evaluated in terms of conformance to specifications. |
| Should lead to increased efficiency. | Promotes standardization, so may hurt performance when adapting to changes is more important. |
| Promotes consistency in quality. | May be less appropriate for services, which are dependent on a high degree of human contact. |

**Source:** C.A. Reeves & D.A. Bednar, "Defining Quality: Alternatives and Implications," *Academy of Management Review* 19 (1994): 419-445.

1. *Good housekeeping*—regularly scheduled preventive maintenance for offices, plants, and equipment. Making sure to quickly fix leaky valves, or making sure machines are running properly so they don't use more fuel than necessary are examples of good housekeeping. For example, the commercial dishwashing machine is often the most expensive item in a restaurant, from the initial cost of the machine itself, to its use of water and electricity. Checking that rinse nozzles are clear of food debris, that water pressure and temperatures are within specifications, and that pumps and hoses don't leak are just some of the basic maintenance steps that are needed to keep energy and water waste to a minimum.[73]

2. *Material/product substitution*—replacing toxic or hazardous materials with less harmful materials. As part of its Pollution Prevention Pays program over the last 25 years, Minnesota Mining & Manufacturing (3M) eliminated 800,000 tons of hazardous waste by using benign substitutes for toxic solvents in its manufacturing processes. And, counting only the first year of savings from these changes, 3M has saved $827 million in the process.[74]

3. *Process modification*—changing steps or procedures to eliminate or reduce waste. For example, Coors found ways to make its beer bottles thinner. The results were annual savings of $2 million and a 38-million-pound reduction in the amount of glass used each year to bottle Coors beer.[75] Similarly, by changing the manufacturing process at its Midland, Michigan plant, Dow Chemical was able to reduce chloromethane gas waste by 97 percent. And by not having to treat the gas to turn it into a safe, inert compound, it's saving $3.3 million per year.[76]

EXHIBIT 7.14

FOUR LEVELS OF WASTE MINIMIZATION

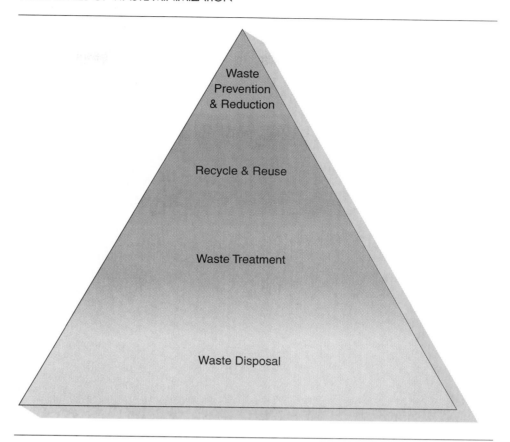

Waste
Prevention
& Reduction

Recycle & Reuse

Waste Treatment

Waste Disposal

**Source:** D.R. May & B.L. Flannery, "Cutting Waste with Employee Involvement Teams," *Business Horizons,* September-October 1995, 28-38.

The second level of the waste minimization is *recycle and reuse*. At this level, wastes are reduced by reusing materials as long as possible or by collecting materials for on- or off-site recycling. Sears recycles the 90 million clothes hangers used at its 860 stores each year. The hangers are collected, boxed up, and then shipped to Sears' distribution centers where they are reused or processed for recycling. Last year, Sears also recycled 48,000 tons of corrugated cardboard, 1,000 tons of plastic bags and coverings, and 995,000 plastic rachets. Over the last eight years, Sears has reduced waste by 60 percent. Plus, 48 percent of its waste each year is now recycled.[77]

A growing trend in recycling is a process called "design for disassembly," where products are redesigned from the start for easy disassembly, recycling, and reuse once they are no longer usable. For example, by 2003, the European Union will not allow companies to sell products unless the entire product and its packaging can be recovered for recycling. Companies, not consumers, will be held responsible for recycling the products they manufacture. Consequently, cereal makers, car companies, appliance makers, and so forth, must design their products from the start with recycling in mind.[78] At reclamation centers throughout Europe, companies will have to be able to recover and recycle 80 percent of the parts that go into their original products.[79] One company that already does this in part is Bosch in Germany. Bosch takes back old auto alternators, remanufactures them, and then resells them by certifying and warranting them as being as good as new.[80]

Waste disposal is becoming an increasingly important issue for several businesses, particularly computer manufacturers. At Hewlett Packard's computer recycling operation, computer cases are sorted into bins for crushing after parts have been removed.

AP PHOTO/BOB GALBRAITH

The third level of waste minimization is *waste treatment*, where companies use biological, chemical, or other processes to turn potentially harmful waste into harmless compounds or useful by-products. For example, one of the processes in the manufacture of steel sheets is called "pickling." Pickling is simply bathing the steel in an acid solution to clean impurities and oxides (that would rust) from the surface of the steel sheet. Getting rid of the "pickle juice" has always been a problem. Not only is the juice an acid, but it also contains ferric chloride and other metals that prevent steel makers from dumping it into local water supplies. Fortunately, Magnetics International has found a safe, profitable way to treat the pickle juice. It sprays the juice into a 100-foot high chamber at 1,200 degrees Fahrenheit. The iron chloride in the juice reacts with oxygen at that temperature to form pure iron oxide, which can be transformed into a useful magnetic powder. Inland Steel is now using this process to transform pickle juice into 25,000 tons of magnetic powder that can be reused in electric motors, stereo speakers, and refrigerator gaskets.[81]

The fourth and last level of the waste minimization is *waste disposal*. Wastes that cannot be prevented, reduced, recycled, reused, or treated should be safely disposed of in processing plants or in environmentally secure landfills that prevent leakage and damage to soil and underground water supplies. Contrary to common belief, all businesses, not just manufacturing firms, have waste-disposal problems. For example, although the fluorescent lights used in most businesses are environmentally friendly because they last longer and use less electricity, burned out fluorescent bulbs contain Mercury, a hazardous waste.[82] And with the average computer lasting just three years, somewhere between 20 and 30 million computers come out of service each year, creating disposal problems for offices all over the world. But with cathode ray tubes in the monitors that contain lead, toxic metals in the circuit boards, paint-coated plastic, and metal coatings that can contaminate ground water, organizations can't just throw old computers away.[83] Many companies give old computers and computer equipment to local computer recycling centers that distribute usable computers to nonprofit organizations or correctly dispose of lead and other toxic materials. However, Hewlett-Packard has started a unique computer disposal program that allows individual computer users to recycle PCs and electronic equipment. Prices range from $13 to $34 per item. The service is available at **http://www.hp.com/recycle.** HP makes no profit on this service. With three clicks and a credit card number, HP will arrange to pick up the old PC equipment and properly dispose of it.[84]

## Review 4
### What to Control?

Deciding what to control is just as important as deciding whether to control or how to control. In most companies, performance is measured using financial measures alone. However, the balanced scorecard encourages managers to measure and control company performance from four perspectives: financial, customers, internal operations, and innovation and learning. Traditionally, financial control has been achieved through cash flow analysis, balance sheets, income statements, financial ratios, and budgets. However, another way to measure and control financial performance is through economic value added (EVA). Unlike traditional financial measures, EVA helps managers assess whether they are performing well enough to pay the cost of the capital needed to run the business. Instead of using customer satisfaction surveys to measure customer performance, companies should pay attention to customer defectors, who are more likely to speak up about what the company is doing wrong. Performance of internal operations is often measured in terms of quality, which is defined in three ways: excellence, value, and conformance to expectations.[85] Minimization of waste has become an important part of innovation and learning in companies. The four levels of waste minimization are waste prevention and reduction, recycling and reuse, waste treatment, and waste disposal.

## What Really Happened?

At the beginning of the chapter, you learned about the incredible changes in the movie theater business in the last 20 years, from a downtown theater and drive-in theater in each small town, followed by four- to six-screen cinemas, followed by gargantuan 25- to 30-screen megaplexes with plush stadium seating and state-of-the art sound systems. Let's find out what really happened at Regal Cinemas and what decisions it made.

**As the fourteenth largest movie theater company in the United States, Regal Cinemas has had great success during this time, growing from zero to 349 movie screens in just four years. But as competitors build 25- to 30-screen megaplexes with plush stadium seating, does Regal need to consider building its own megaplexes in order to continue its growth?**

Control is a process of establishing standards that will achieve organizational goals, comparing actual performance to those standards, and then, if necessary, taking corrective action to restore performance to those standards. The growth, profits, and positive reaction stemming from the first 25-screen megaplexes were so fantastic that Regal Cinema's management couldn't ignore the numbers. For example, even though the average cost was about $1 million per screen, or $25 million to $30 million per megaplex, the first few megaplexes generated huge sales and 30 percent returns. AMC's 25-screen Grand Cinema in Dallas, Texas, attracted 3 million moviegoers per year! So many people visited it that seven new restaurants were built within walking distance. Attendance at each of the Grand Cinema's 25 screens was 38 percent higher than traditional movie screens, and revenue was 10 percent higher per person, even without higher ticket prices.

Customer reactions were extremely positive, too. At AMC's Grand Cinema in Dallas, 60 percent of moviegoers indicated that they intended to see two movies per visit. A teenager said,

"We used to go to the mall but now we come here." Californian Diane Filipowski and her friends regularly visit a 21-screen theater because they can meet without choosing a movie ahead of time. With so many choices and so many starting times, they can easily find something to watch after arriving. And if they can't agree on which movie to see, they can split up and meet afterwards. Indeed, attendance was initially so high at the megaplexes that golf carts were used to haul moviegoers from their cars to the theater. But with staffs ranging from 150 to 175 people, ticket and concession stand lines still moved quickly.

The problem for Regal Cinema was that these huge megaplexes with plush stadium seating were being built soon after it spent six years buying up older theaters. In short, Regal's management felt that its theaters were in danger of becoming obsolete. So with sizable funds from private investing companies, KKR and Hicks Muse, it spent nearly $700 million over the next three years building 111 new theaters with 1,754 screens to catch up with its competitors.

**If you decide to follow the competition and build huge megaplex theaters, what key resources will you need to be successful?**

Two factors help managers determine whether more control is necessary to achieve organizational goals: the degree of dependence and resource flows. Degree of dependence is the extent to which a company needs a particular resource to accomplish its goals. The more important a resource is for meeting organizational standards and goals, the more necessary it is to control that resource, and resources are anything that can be used to fulfill a need or solve a problem. The second factor that determines whether more control is necessary is resource flow, which is the extent to which companies have easy access to critical resources. So for Regal Cinemas, the key was determining which re-

sources were needed to be successful and whether they could gain access to them.

Given the quick move from four- to six-screen multiplex theaters to 24-screen megaplexes, Regal and its investors, KKR and Hicks Muse, figured that money was the most important resource that Regal needed to compete in this game. Accordingly, as mentioned above, KKR and Hicks Muse plowed nearly $700 million over three years into building Regal 111 new theaters with 1,754 screens. But what Regal, KKR, and Hicks Muse overlooked was that location was also a key resource. And by being the third or fourth large movie chain to build megaplexes in nearly each market, it typically bought and built new megaplexes in weak locations. Why was Regal nearly always the third or fourth megaplex to be built in most markets? Because the other movie theater chains were also flush with cash from investors, allowing them to beat Regal to the best building locations. Indeed, Raymond Syufy, CEO of Century Theaters in California, said this about Regal's megaplex locations: "Those were all B and C sites that other exhibitors had passed on. We didn't have faith in those sites. They built nice theaters. But that's not enough today."

So while Regal was able to gain access to one key resource, money, it was largely unable to gain access to the other key resource, great locations. As a result of its rapid expansion, it now finds itself $1.9 billion in debt with megaplex theaters that, because of their poor locations, don't have enough customers.

**Finally, Regal Cinemas has always had a reputation for controlling costs and being well managed. Would fast expansion and building of megaplex theaters weaken that part of the company?**

Despite building 111 new megaplexes and accumulating $1.9 billion in debt, Regal Cinemas actually has a reputation for controlling costs and being well managed. To keep costs down,

Regal uses its information system to keep close track of concessions, which are typically where theaters make most of their profits. If a Regal theater misplaces or damages a box of paper drink cups, Regal uses its computer system to charge the theater manager the full retail price of the drink, not just the replacement cost of the cups. With an information system this accurate, Regal's theater managers and employees don't waste cups, popcorn, popcorn oil, or anything else. However, it's important to point out that Regal's information system isn't used just to track negative performance discrepancies. Indeed, Regal managers who exceed company standards can earn bonuses as large as half the amount of their base salaries.

The problem for Regal is that controlling costs, being well managed, and doing a good job of motivating managers and employees may not matter. If, because of poor locations, its theaters don't have enough customers to generate the revenues they need to pay current bills (i.e., to cover operating costs), they're surely not going to generate the money needed to pay off its long-term debt, which stands at $1.9 billion. In fact, Regal was losing so much money that it has had to close 14 percent of the theaters it was operating. Plus, competition is likely to get even more intense as owners of four- to six-screen multiplex theaters spend the money to retrofit these small theaters to modern stadium seating. Ironically for Regal, the cost of retrofitting is substantially lower. For example, retrofitting only costs about $100,000 per movie screen/auditorium, about one-tenth of what it cost Regal to build stadium seating for each new screen in its 111 megaplex theaters.

One thing is clear, Regal and its investors, KKR and Hicks Muse, seem to have lost sight of a key principle in the balanced scorecard, economic value added (EVA). EVA is more than just profits. It is the amount by which profits exceed the cost of capital in a given year. It is based on the simple idea that it takes capital to run a business, and capital comes at a cost. EVA is positive when company profits (revenues minus expenses, minus taxes) exceed the cost of capital in a given year. In other words, if a business is to truly grow, its revenues must be large enough to cover both short-term costs (annual expenses and taxes) and long-term costs (the cost of borrowing capital from bondholders and shareholders). Basically, EVA says that companies need to be wealth creators, not wealth destroyers. They need to return more money than they take in. Unfortunately, at this point, the KKR and Hicks Muse investment in Regal Cinemas has been a wealth destroyer. With Regal bonds selling for 12 cents per dollar (!), one debt analyst speculated, "Regal files for bankruptcy before the first of the year. I just don't see any other way around it."

**Sources:** D. Costello, "Hollywood Journal: Movie Seats: Thumbs Down? Fancy New Theaters Promise Big Seats, But How Big? Here's the Tale of the Tape," *The Wall Street Journal*, 6 October 2000, W6. K. Helliker, "Movies: Monster Movie Theaters Invade the Cinema Landscape," *The Wall Street Journal*, 13 May 1997, B1. B. Howard, "Commercial Real Estate Demand Steep for Stadium Seat Theaters: Owners Are Hoping to Sell More Movie Tickets by Promising Unobstructed Views," *Los Angeles Times*, 31 July 2001, C8. B. Orwall & G. Zuckerman, "Box-Office Blues: Regal Cinemas Joined Megaplex Frenzy, Ended Up in Back Row—Investors KKR, Hicks Muse Focused on Fast Growth; Now, Lots of Empty Seats—Stuck with 'B and C Sites'," *The Wall Street Journal*, 27 September 2000, A1. M. Pittman & A. Steinhauer, "2 Buyout Firms Eye Theater Chains: Regal Cinemas' Rivals May Be Bought" *San Antonio News* [Bloomberg], 15 October 2000, J1. M. Walsh, "Easy on the Popcorn!" *Forbes*, 26 September 1994, 126-127.

## Key Terms

autonomous work groups *(237)*
balanced scorecard *(240)*
balance sheets *(241)*
behavior control *(235)*
budgets *(241)*
bureaucratic control *(234)*
cash flow analysis *(241)*
concertive control *(237)*
concurrent control *(226)*
control *(222)*
control loss *(227)*

customer defections *(248)*
cybernetic *(225)*
cybernetic feasibility *(230)*
degree of dependence *(228)*
economic value added *(244)*
feedback control *(225)*
feedforward control *(226)*
financial ratios *(241)*
income statements *(241)*
normative control *(236)*
objective control *(235)*

output control *(235)*
quasi-control *(231)*
reducing dependence *(231)*
regulation costs *(229)*
resource flow *(228)*
resources *(228)*
restructuring dependence *(231)*
self-control (self-management) *(238)*
standards *(223)*
suboptimization *(240)*
value *(250)*

## What Would You Do-II?

### "Spit Happens"

As the owner of a fast-food franchise, you have plenty of problems to worry about. Problems you face on a daily basis include meeting or exceeding minimum profitability requirements imposed by the franchisor, constantly battling employee turnover (typically exceeding 200 percent at times), employee scheduling, employee morale, customer satisfaction . . . the list goes on and on. Selecting and retaining qualified people has always been difficult because you cannot afford to pay much more than minimum wage and there aren't many opportunities for advancement within your company. In addition, the majority of your employees are young, immature, and either currently in school or fresh out of school.

Despite the negative aspects of the fast-food industry, you are happy with your restaurant's success and are considering expanding by opening another store across town. As you peruse today's newspaper, you read an article that could have detrimental effects on you and your restaurant. The article discusses police becoming the victims of disgruntled teens working at fast-food establishments. Some uniformed police officers have reported instances when their food was tampered with. For instance, one policeman claimed that a fast-food employee spit in his hamburger. The officer could tell by the look on the boy's face that he was up to something, and the policeman opened the bun to inspect the burger. A crime lab confirmed that the slimy substance found inside the hamburger was, indeed, saliva. The employee was immediately fired and the officer was given an undisclosed cash settlement by the restaurant owner.

Unfortunately, spit isn't the only thing that officers have ingested. The article explained that one officer became violently ill after eating at a fast-food restaurant. Tests later confirmed that the food the officer ingested was tainted with urine and an oven cleanser. As a result, the officer has filed a $13.5 million civil suit against Burger King, the franchisee, and two of its employees. As you begin to digest the information from the article, you wonder if this situation could happen to you and your business. Many police officers frequent your establishment, and you like the security that they provide while dining. You are also aware that you cannot constantly watch your employees 24 hours a day, seven days a week. In order to control your employees' output, what standards could you set, and once you set them how will you measure them? How will you ensure that your employees do not intentionally harm your customers? Additionally, which method of control would work the best in your situation (bureaucratic, objective, or concertive)? **If you were the manager of a fast-food restaurant, what would you do?**

**Source:** J. Ordonez, "Spit Happens: Police in Uniform Are Leary of Fast-Food Places", *The Wall Street Journal,* 23 May 2001.

## Management Decisions

### Preventing Piracy

Point, click, and pirate. Software piracy, which includes the unauthorized copying, use, or distribution of software, costs the computer industry approximately $12 billion dollars each year in lost licensing revenue. Software piracy is a problem in the United States (accounting for 27 percent of the worldwide total); however, it appears to be worse in other parts of the world such as South America and Asia. According to a recent study by the Business Software Alliance (BAS), six out of 10 computers operating in Mexico contain pirated software. Unfortunately, the numbers are just as dreary in China and elsewhere across the globe. As the director of piracy for Microsoft, you feel as though your job is a never-ending battle. In order to crack down on piracy in the United States, you and your staff have begun discussions aimed at coming up with solutions to the piracy problem. Piracy occurs in both private homes and in businesses, yet a recent study by the Software & Information Industry Association (SIIA) suggests that one quarter of piracy committed in the United States occurs in high-tech companies.

One factor that leads to piracy among businesses today is expansion. Most businesses start out by purchasing legal copies of software for their firms. As a firm grows, however, some businesses choose to purchase additional computers and copy their existing software onto the new machines. Another common act of piracy involves "soft-loading." Soft-loading occurs when a firm purchases one legal copy of software and installs it on the local area network (LAN). By installing the software on the server, one copy can support hundreds of machines through a network connection.

Although the SIIA and the BSA conduct routine audits in large companies looking for piracy violations, you and your staff want to step up efforts to identify companies engaging in piracy. Some of the computer manufacturers to which you supply software have notified you recently that there has been an increase in the number of "naked" computer system orders. A computer system is "naked" when it is ordered without any operating system software. Although there are several reasons for ordering a naked system (for example, perhaps a company wants to use a competitor's operating software, such as Linux), you suspect that companies are beginning to pirate operating software in addition to application software. Software piracy not only costs your company money through a loss of revenue, but is also a violation of copyright law, and is therefore illegal.

### Questions

1. What policies or plans could you implement that might help control or diminish piracy of your operating system software within American businesses?
2. How vigorously will you pursue offenders once you identify them? Remember, there is a cost to control.

**Sources:** R. Buckman, "Microsoft Offers Prizes to Identify Orders of PCs Without Windows," *The Wall Street Journal,* 2 May 2001. B. Kruger, "High-Tech Firms Get Piracy Alert," *Electronic News,* 7 February 2000. J. Stevenson, "Piracy Plague," *Business Mexico,* November 2000. Z. Thomas, "High Tech's Dirty Little Software Piracy Secret," *Electronic Business,* November 2000. F. Gallegos, "Software Piracy: Some Facts, Figures, and Issues," *Information System Security,* Winter 2000.

## Management Decisions

### Talkin' Trash About Recycling?

To reduce the amount of waste being generated at landfills and to save natural resources, businesses have been recycling for years. This idea has become so important that the Environmental Protection Agency (EPA) wants each state to recycle a minimum of 25 percent of its garbage. Many states have adopted higher goals. New Jersey currently has a goal of 60 percent and Rhode Island has a 70-percent goal. The recycling movement has grown in recent years. More than 7,000 curbside recycling programs are in operation today, a dramatic increase over the 1,000 available in 1988. Currently, the most common item recycled is paper; however, some firms have adopted measures to recycle other items, including cardboard, plastic, glass, aluminum, scrap-iron, computers, and peripherals. Without nationwide recycling efforts, natural resources would be wasted. For example, a printing of the Sunday *New York Times* uses enough pulp to consume 75,000 trees.

The Target Corporation has adopted a company-wide recycling program at their headquarters in Minneapolis. This program contains a recycling center on each floor, located adjacent to the freight elevator lobby. Within each recycling center are bins for recyclable materials, such as newspaper, office paper, computer paper, cardboard, glass, plastic, and aluminum. At the end of the day, the bins are emptied, sorted, bundled, and sold to various recycling centers in the city. The profits earned through the sale of recycled materials are used to offset the cost and perpetuate the system.

Despite the successes of recycling, critics argue that the costs outweigh the benefits. According to a recent study, it costs $400 to recycle a ton of garbage, versus $70 a ton to dump it in a local landfill. Critics further argue that recycling activities cause more damage to the environment than they prevent. For instance, during the recycling process of glass and some plastics, minute amounts of chemicals can be released into the air. Additionally, the recycling process requires the use of energy (electricity, natural gas, water, etc.), which in turn uses up valuable natural resources. A former official with the EPA claims that using a Styrofoam coffee cup and disposing of the cup in a local landfill is likely less damaging to the environment than using and reusing a porcelain coffee mug since the coffee mug must be washed in hot soapy water, thus incurring additional pollution.

### Questions

1. From your perspective, what are the advantages and disadvantages of recycling in the workplace?
2. Choose one item that can be recycled (e.g., paper, aluminum, cardboard, glass) and research the cost and benefit of recycling this item by using your school's library or searching online. Is it worth the cost?

**Sources:** J. Diconsiglio, "Rethinking Recycling," *Scholastic Update,* 21 March 1997. S. Miller, "Talking Trash: Recycling at Work," *Office Solutions,* March 2001. G. Barrett, "It May Be Time to Toss Old Ideas on Recycling," *USA Today,* 2 July 2001.

## Develop Your Managerial Potential

### Learning from Failure

**"There is the greatest practical benefit of making a few failures early in life."** —T.H. Huxley

No one wants to fail. Everyone wants to succeed. However, some business people believe that failure can have enormous value. At Microsoft, founder and CEO Bill Gates encourages his managers to hire people who have made mistakes in their jobs or careers. A Microsoft vice president said, "We look for somebody who learns, adapts, and is active in the process of learning from mistakes. We always ask, what was a major failure you had? What did you learn from it?" Another reason that failure is viewed positively is that it is often a sign of risk taking and experimentation, both of which are in short supply in many companies. John Kotter, a Harvard Business School professor says, "I can imagine a group of executives 20 years ago discussing a candidate for a top job and saying, 'This guy had a big failure when he was 32.' Everyone else would say, 'Yep, yep, that's a bad sign.' I can imagine that same group considering a candidate today and saying, 'What worries me about this guy is that he's never failed.'" Jack Matson, who teaches a class at the University of Michigan called Failure 101, said, "If you are doing something innovative, you are going to trip and fumble. So the more failing you do faster, the quicker you can get to success."

One of the most common mistakes that occurs after failure is the *attribution error.* An *attribution* is to assign blame or credit. When we succeed, we take credit for the success by owning up to our strategies, how we behaved, and how hard we worked. However, when we fail, we ignore our strategies, or how we behaved, or how hard we worked (or didn't). Instead, when we fail, we assign the blame to other people, or to the circumstances, or to bad luck. In other words, the basic attribution error is that success is our fault but failure isn't. The disappointment we feel when we fail often prevents us from learning from our failures.

What this means is that attribution errors disrupt the control process. The three basic steps of control are to set goals and performance standards, to compare actual performance to performance standards, and to identify and correct performance deviations. When we put all of the blame on external forces rather than our own actions, we stop ourselves from identifying and correcting performance deviations. Furthermore, by not learning from our mistakes, we make it even more likely that we will fail again.

Your task in this "Developing Your Management Potential" is to begin the process of learning from failure. This is not an easy thing to do. When *Fortune* magazine writer Patricia Sellers wrote an article called "So You Fail," she found most of the people she contacted reluctant to talk about their failures. She wrote,

> Compiling this story required months of pleading and letter writing to dozens of people who failed and came back. 'If it weren't for the 'F' word, I'd talk,' lamented one senior executive who got fired twice, reformed his know-it-all management style, and considered bragging about his current hot streak. Others cringed at hearing the word "failure" in the same breath as "your career."

**Questions**

1. Identify and describe a point in your life when you failed. Don't write about simple or silly mistakes. The difference between a failure and a mistake is how badly you felt afterwards. Years afterwards, a real failure still makes you cringe when you think about it. What was the situation? What were your goals? And how did it turn out?

2. Describe your initial reaction to the failure. Were you shocked, surprised, angry, or depressed? Initially, who or what did you blame for the failure? Explain.

3. One purpose of control is to identify and correct performance deviations. With that in mind, describe three mistakes that you made that contributed to your failure. Now that you've had time to think about it, what would you have done differently to prevent these mistakes? Finally, summarize what you learned from your mistakes that will increase your chances of success the next time around.

**Sources:** S. Caulkin, "If You Want to Stay a Winner, Learn from Your Mistakes," *The Observer,* 3 March 1996, 7. J. Hyatt, "Failure 101," *Inc.,* January 1989, 18. B. McMenamin, "The Virtue of Making Mistakes," *Forbes,* 9 May 1994, 192-194. P. Sellers, "So You Fail," *Fortune,* 1 May 1995, 48-66. P. Sellers, "Where Failures Get Fixed," *Fortune,* 1 May 1995, 64. B. Weiner, I. Freize, A. Kukla, L. Reed, S. Rest, & R.M. Rosenbaum, "Perceiving the Causes of Success and Failure," in *Attribution: Perceiving the Causes of Behavior,* eds. E. Jones, D. Kanouse, H. Kelley, R. Nesbitt, S. Valins, and B. Weiner (Morristown, NJ: General Learning Press, 1971), 45-61.

## Study Tip

The list of key terms on page 257 can be a valuable study aid. Write down the definition of each term on a separate piece of paper and without consulting the margin terms in the chapter. Cement your understanding by also writing an example if possible.

# 3
PART

## Meeting the Competition

# CHAPTER 8

## outline

# eight

# Global Management

## What Would You Do?

**Wal-Mart Headquarters, Bentonville, Arkansas**. The first Wal-Mart opened in Rogers, Arkansas, in 1962. Four decades later, with 1,657 stores, 1,016 Wal-Mart Supercenters (Wal-Marts that have grocery stores), 486 Sam's Stores, 962,000 employees, and $191 billion in annual sales, Wal-Mart is clearly the dominant retailer in the United States. Guided by founder Sam Walton's passion for customer satisfaction and a focused mission of "Every Day Low Prices," Wal-Mart was named "Retailer of the Century" by *Discount Store News,* was recognized by *Fortune* magazine as one of the "Most Admired Companies in America" and one of the "100 Best Companies To Work For," and was ranked by the *Financial Times* on its "Most Respected in the World" list.

Ironically, despite these enormous domestic achievements, Wal-Mart has stumbled outside U.S. borders. In fact, Wal-Mart's international performance has been so bad that Toby Radford, an industry analyst for JP Morgan, called Wal-Mart's international strategy "rudderless." For example, when Wal-Mart first entered Mexico, it was so set in its U.S. ways that it filled its Mexican stores with ice skates, riding lawn mowers, fishing tackle, and clay pigeons for skeet shooting, none of which—to anyone's surprise—were very popular items. And when Mexican store managers managed to sell all of these items at heavy discounts, Wal-Mart's computerized inventory system compounded the mistake by automatically reordering all of these "sold out" items.

Although in the United States Wal-Mart clearly outnumbers and outmuscles its competitors, internationally Wal-Mart is just another kid on the block. In fact, the dominant player around the world is not Wal-Mart, but a French-based company called Carrefour. Carrefour, the world's second largest retailer (Wal-Mart is the largest, but only because of its dominant position in the United States), is the top retailer in France, Spain, Portugal, and Greece, and is number two in Italy. Wal-Mart has no stores in those countries. Furthermore, Carrefour is well established in Latin America, Asia, and has 22 stores in nine major cities in China, the largest growth market in the world. In addition to being well ahead of Wal-Mart in key countries around the world, Carrefour is very careful about the new markets it enters, usually taking a year to investigate before making new commitments. But once that commitment is made, Carrefour is quickly up and running. To start, nearly every Carrefour store in the world has the same basic layout, with wide aisles and signature white tiles. While the stores look the same, the food in each Carrefour store is different since 90 percent of the foods come from local suppliers. Carrefour's chairman and CEO says, "You have to adapt your food and other products to the local culture." In short, according to Jamie Vasquez, an industry analyst at Salomon Smith Barney, "Carrefour is the world's most successful international retailer. Wal-Mart has no track record outside North America."

Of course, your boss, Wal-Mart's CEO, doesn't really care what Jamie Vasquez thinks. In fact, he says it's your job as head of Wal-Mart International to prove Vasquez wrong, to begin making Wal-Mart the world's most successful retailer. The question is how. Initial successes came easily in Canada, but not in Mexico. So which countries should Wal-Mart enter? At some time, Wal-Mart and Carrefour are likely to cross paths. And while Carrefour is now the leading international retailer, just how fierce a competitor will Carrefour be in the long run when lined up against Wal-Mart's experience and deep pockets? In other words, what kind of competition is Wal-Mart likely to find when it crosses swords directly with Carrefour? Also, what impact will free trade agreements in North America (NAFTA), Europe (the Maastricht Treaty), Asia (APEC and ASEAN), and South America (FTAA), likely have on Wal-Mart's international expansion?

Finally, should Wal-Mart focus on global consistency, doing around the world what it does in the United States, or like Carrefour, should it adapt what it sells throughout the world?

**If you were head of Wal-Mart International, what would you do?**

**Sources:** W. Boston, & A. Zimmerman, "Wal-Mart Girds for Major German Expansion—U.S. Retail Giant to Stress Internal Growth in Push to Add 50 New Stores," *The Wall Street Journal*, 20 July 2000, A21. Business Brief, "Wal-Mart Stores, Inc.: Retailer Expects to Open Six New Stores in China," *The Wall Street Journal*, 4 June 1988, B10. Business Brief, "Wal-Mart Stores Inc.: New Supermarkets Expected to Add 27,000 British Jobs," *The Wall Street Journal*, 11 January 2000. J. Friedland, & L. Lee, "Foreign Aisles: The Wal-Mart Way Sometimes Gets Lost in Translation Overseas—Chain Changes Some Tactics to Meet Local Tastes; Competitors Are Tough—But Brazil's 'Market Is Ripe'," *The Wall Street Journal*, 8 October 1997, A1. M. Jordan, "Wal-Mart Gets Aggressive about Brazil—New Neighborhood Store Is Latest Step to Seize Bigger Market Share," *The Wall Street Journal*, 25 May 2001, A8. L. Lee, & C. Rohwedder, "Wal-Mart to Acquire German Retailer, Moving into Europe for the First Time," *The Wall Street Journal*, 19 December 1997, A2. D. Luhnow, "Crossover Success: How NAFTA Helped Wal-Mart Reshape the Mexican Market—Lower Tariffs, Retail Muscle Translate into Big Sales; Middlemen Are Squeezed—'Like Shopping in the U.S.'," *The Wall Street Journal*, 31 August 2001, A1. F. McCarthy, "Chimera Wal-Mart Struggles Abroad," *Economist*, 18 May 2000. R. Tomlinson, "Who's Afraid of Wal-Mart? Not Carrefour. The World's Second-Largest Retailer Is Bounding Ahead of the Bentonville Behemoth in Most Markets Outside North America. But Can the French Titan Hold Its Lead?" *Fortune*, 26 June 2000, 186.

Wal-Mart's international expansion is an example of the key issue in global business: How can you be sure that the way you run your business in one country is the right way to run that business in another? This chapter discusses how organizations make those decisions. We will start by examining global business in two ways: first, by exploring its impact on U.S. businesses; and second, by reviewing the basic rules and agreements that govern global trade. Next, we will examine how and when companies go global by examining the tradeoff between consistency and adaptation and by discussing how to organize a global company. Finally, we will look at how companies decide where to expand globally. Here, we will examine how to find the best business climate, how to adapt to cultural differences, and how to better prepare employees for international assignments.

## What Is Global Business?

**global business**
the buying and selling of goods and services by people from different countries

Business is the buying and selling of goods or services. Buying this textbook was a business transaction. So was selling your first car. So was getting paid for babysitting or for mowing lawns. **Global business** is the buying and selling of goods and services by people from different countries. The Timex watch on my wrist as I write this chapter was purchased at a Wal-Mart in Texas. But since it was made in the Philippines, I participated in global business when I wrote Wal-Mart a check. Wal-Mart, in turn, had already paid Timex, which had paid the company that employs the Filipino managers and workers who made my watch.

*Of course, there is more to global business than buying imported products at Wal-Mart. After reading these next two sections, you should be able to*
1. *describe the impact of global business on the United States.*
2. *discuss the trade rules and agreements that govern global trade.*

### 1. Impact of Global Business

You are shopping at the local mall. Someone with a clipboard asks you to respond to this short questionnaire about global business. Mark your answers true or false.

*1.1.* *"Foreigners" are buying up American companies at an astounding rate and now control a large part of our economy.*

*1.2.* *American companies are no longer competitive in the world market, especially in high-tech industries.*

*1.3.* *If given a choice, Americans will buy American-made goods rather than foreign-made goods.*

National polls show that nearly half of all Americans want to prevent foreign companies from buying U.S. companies that have developed new technologies. The polls also show that 62 percent of Americans want to protect U.S. companies from foreign competition and that more than 87 percent believe that countries, such as Japan, are ahead of the United States in exporting high-technology products. Of the Americans polled, 85 percent say they will try to buy American-made products when they have a choice.[1] Overall, 58 to 68 percent believe that foreign trade has been bad for the U.S. economy "because cheap imports have cost wages and jobs here."[2] More specifically, when asked, "Do you think trade agreements with low-wage countries such as China and Mexico lead to higher or lower wages for Americans?", 19 percent said "higher wages," while 68 percent said "lower wages." Pollster David Iannelli said of these results, "Americans continue to think locally as their economy expands globally. A continued us-vs.-them outlook would help explain why in these good economic times, Americans see the international economy as a threat rather than an opportunity."[3]

So if you responded like most Americans, you probably answered "true" to each question. However, none of the statements in our short questionnaire accurately describes the influence of global business in the United States. Let's see why.

### 1.1 "Foreigners" Are Buying up American Companies at an Astounding Rate, and Now Control a Large Part of Our Economy.

**direct foreign investment**
a method of investment in which a company builds a new business or buys an existing business in a foreign county

**Direct foreign investment** is a method of investment in which a company builds a new business or buys an existing business in a foreign country. Kao Corporation, maker of Japanese laundry detergent and body soaps and shampoos, made a direct foreign investment when it purchased Andrew Jergens Company, which makes hair- and skin-care products.

Polls show that 64 percent of Americans believe that Asian countries engage in unfair trading practices. Moreover, 47 percent of Americans believe that European countries engage in unfair practices, too. And with large foreign companies buying American companies, such as Sony's (Japan) purchase of Columbia and Tri-Star Studios (movies) and with Bertelsmann AG's (Germany) purchase of two well-known American book publishers, Bantam Doubleday and Random House, it's not surprising that newspapers periodically run stories proclaiming that the "Japanese and Germans Are Buying America."[4]

In reality, though, the headlines should read, "Foreign Invasion: The World Buys America," because companies from Germany, Belgium, England, Canada, Mexico, and many other countries own businesses in the United States. Exhibit 8.1 (p. 266) shows that companies from the United Kingdom, Germany, Netherlands, Canada, and France have the largest direct foreign investment in the United States. And Japanese companies, which popular opinion typically puts at the top of this list, are just the sixth largest direct foreign investors in the United States.

However, direct foreign investment in the United States is just half the picture. U.S. companies also have made large direct foreign investments in businesses throughout the world. Exhibit 8.2 (p. 267) shows that U.S. companies have made their largest direct foreign investments in the United Kingdom, Canada, the Netherlands, Germany, Japan, Bermuda, France, and Switzerland. These figures make it clear that Americans have misplaced fears about direct foreign investment. Perhaps the newspaper headlines should also read, "Yankee Invasion: U.S.A. Buys the World."

Overall, direct foreign investment throughout the world is now worth $1 trillion dollars a year![5] In fact, over the last 20 years, direct foreign investment involving the purchase or existence of businesses in another country, like Bertelsmann buying Random House, has increased by 42 percent per year.[6] So whether foreign companies invest in the United States or U.S. companies invest abroad, direct foreign investment is an increasingly important and common method of conducting global business.

EXHIBIT 8.1

AVERAGE DIRECT FOREIGN INVESTMENT IN THE U.S., 1994–1999

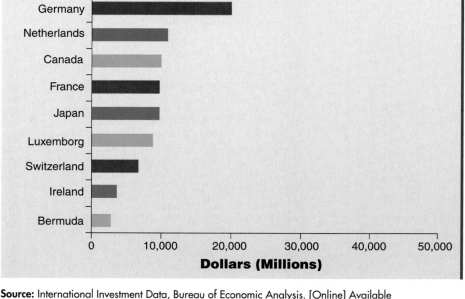

**Source:** International Investment Data, Bureau of Economic Analysis. [Online] Available http://www.bea.doc.gov/bea/di/fdicap-99.htm, 1 November 2000.

*1.2 American Companies Are No Longer Competitive in the World Market, Especially in High-Tech Industries.*

Nearly 90 percent of Americans consider this a serious problem. However, data from the National Science Board, shown in Exhibit 8.3, show that U.S. companies lead Japan, Germany, France, the United Kingdom, China, and South Korea in global high technology market share.[7] The United States has a 31 percent average share of the global high-technology market over the last five years, compared to 22 percent for Japan, 7 percent for Germany, and 6 percent for China. In fact, U.S. high-tech companies are market leaders in four out of the seven global high-technology industries: aircraft, scientific instruments, computers and office equipment, and pharmaceuticals. Indeed, a National Science Foundation report concluded that "U.S. producers are leading suppliers of high-technology products to the global market."[8]

So why do most Americans believe that the United States is falling behind the rest of the world? It may be because U.S. companies once dominated global markets. Immediately following World War II, U.S. companies accounted for 50 percent of the **world gross national product** (GNP).[9] World GNP is the value of all the goods and services produced annually worldwide. While U.S. companies continued to dominate world trade through the early 1960s, today U.S. companies now produce approximately 29 percent of the world's gross national product.[10]

To many Americans, the drop from 50 percent to 29 percent of world GNP is proof of U.S. industrial decline. However, these figures suggest much more about the rest of the world's economy than they do about the U.S. economy. After the war, U.S. companies faced little competition. Bombing had destroyed factories throughout Japan, Europe, and Russia. By contrast, not one manufacturing plant was destroyed in the continental United States. With foreign competitors having to rebuild, literally from the ground up, is it any wonder that U.S. companies dominated the world market then?

**world gross national product**
the value of all the goods and services produced annually worldwide

266

EXHIBIT 8.2

AVERAGE U.S. DIRECT FOREIGN INVESTMENT ABROAD, 1994–1999

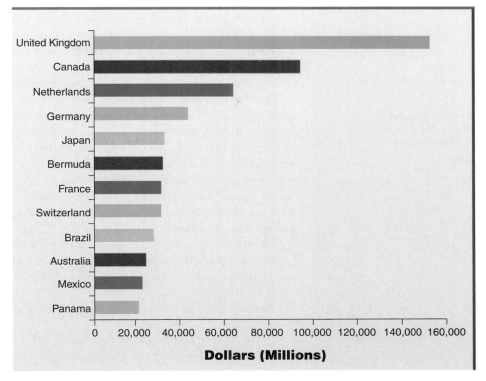

**Source:** International Accounts Data: U.S. Direct Investment Abroad, Bureau of Economic Analysis. [Online] Available http://www.bea.doc.gov/bea/di/dia-ctry.htm, 1 November 2000.

EXHIBIT 8.3

GLOBAL HIGH-TECHNOLOGY MARKET SHARE (AVERAGE GLOBAL HIGH TECHNOLOGY MARKET SHARE, 1993–1997)

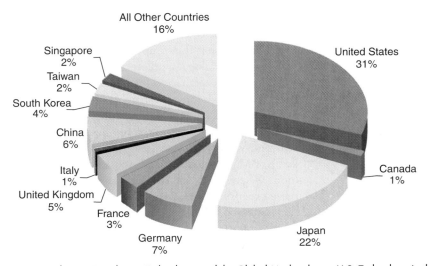

**Source:** "Chapter 7: Industry, Technology, and the Global Marketplace—U.S. Technology in the Marketplace," *Science and Engineering Indicators 2000.* [Online] Available http://www.nsf.gov/sbe/srs/seind00/append/c7/at07-04.xls, 8 September 2001.

Today, in contrast to the postwar global economy, U.S. companies face stiff competition throughout the world. The economies of France, Germany, Italy, Japan, Russia, and the United Kingdom, which the war decimated, now account for the same portion of world GNP controlled by the United States after World War II. Together, these countries, along with the United States and Canada, are part of a group of eight countries called the G8 that meet annually to discuss economic and political issues. And, because of the tremendous growth of international business over the last 25 years, the financial side of the G8 has now been expanded to the G20, meaning that 20 countries send finance ministers and central bank governors to discuss shared financial issues.[11]

Another sign of increased competition in world markets is the *number* of multinational corporations and the location of their headquarters. **Multinational corporations** are corporations that own businesses in two or more countries. In 1970, more than half the world's 7,000 multinational corporations were headquartered in just two countries: the United States and Britain. Today, there are 63,459 multinational corporations, more than twice as many as in 1970, with only 3,387, or 5.3 percent based in the United States.[12] In contrast to 1970, when less than 50 percent of multinationals were based outside the United States and Britain, today 45,404 multinationals, or 71.5 percent, are based in other developed countries, (i.e., Germany, Italy, Canada, Japan, etc.); 12,518, or 19.7 percent, of multinationals are based in developing countries; and 2,150, or 3.4 percent, are based in central and eastern Europe. So, today, multinational companies can be found by the thousands all over the world!

**multinational corporation**
corporation that owns businesses in two or more countries

### 1.3 If Given a Choice, Americans Will Buy American-Made Goods Rather Than Foreign-Made Goods.

Americans say they prefer to "buy American," but if they do, why does the demand for imported products increase year after year?[13] There are a number of potential explanations.[14] The first is that consumers often don't know or pay attention to **country of manufacture** when making purchases. Stop reading for a minute. Take your shoes off. Where were they made? What about the DVD player in your house, or your computer, or your backpack? Did you learn where these products were manufactured before you purchased them? Chances are, you didn't. Many consumers don't know or care about country of manufacture.

**country of manufacture**
country where product is made and assembled

A second explanation for rising imports is that consumers want to buy American and think they are buying American but, in fact, are unknowingly buying imported products. For example, take your Uncle Fred, who bleeds red, white, and blue. That Chrysler minivan in his driveway—he bought it because it was a good "American" car. However, Chrysler assembles most of its minivans in Canada. That Honda Accord Uncle Fred's been giving you a hard time about—it was made in Marysville, Ohio. Uncle Fred has confused the country of manufacture, where the product is made, with the **country of origin**, which is the company's home country. However, this is an easy mistake to make in today's global marketplace.

**country of origin**
the home country for a company, where its headquarters is located

The third explanation for the continued increases in sales of imported products is that consumers know that many products they purchase are imported, but they just don't care, especially if they're getting significantly better quality or much lower prices. For example, Cadillac was the top luxury automobile for six decades, that is, until the last three years when its sales dropped behind four foreign luxury auto manufacturers, Lexus, BMW, Mercedes, and Acura.[15] The same holds true for everyday items like food. When asked whether she'd continue to buy imported apples rather than much more expensive Japanese apples, Sadako Watanabe, a Japanese grandmother, said, "If they taste good, I'll keep buying them."[16] Mark Sneed, President of Phillips Foods, which imports blue crab from its Asian processing factories at one-third the cost of crab caught and processed in the United States, said, "I've never once had a customer ask me if we served domestic or imported crabs, just like they never ask if we have foreign shrimp."[17] Peter Germano, a New York jeweler who sells diamonds, said people don't care where the diamonds are from; they "just want to know which is cheaper."[18] Finally, Luis de Anda, who visits one of Wal-Mart's Sam's Wholesale Clubs in Mexico once a month to purchase diapers and toilet paper in bulk for his family and friends, said, "Why should I care where they're from? With the money I save, I take my family to the movies."[19]

### Review 1
#### Impact of Global Business

Contrary to common opinion, foreigners don't "own" a disproportionate share of U.S. assets. American companies are competitive in world markets, and consumers are less concerned with patriotism than value. In the last decade, direct foreign investment has grown by 42 percent per year, making world markets much more competitive than they used to be. Yet despite this competition, American companies (and German companies, and Japanese companies, and . . . ) continue to expand to meet the demands of consumer-driven world markets.

## 2. Trade Rules and Agreements

*The rules governing global trade are many and complex, and have changed tremendously in the last few years. Let's learn about 2.1 the various kinds of tariff and nontariff trade barriers, 2.2 the global and regional trade agreements that are reducing trade barriers worldwide, and 2.3 consumers' responses to these unprecedented changes in trade rules and agreements.*

### 2.1 Trade Barriers

**trade barriers**
government-imposed regulations that increase the cost and restrict the number of imported goods

Although most consumers don't especially care where the products they buy come from, national governments have preferred that consumers buy domestically made products in hopes that such purchases would increase the number of domestic businesses and workers. However, governments have done much more than hope that you buy from domestic companies. Historically, governments have actively used **trade barriers** to make it much more difficult or expensive (or sometimes impossible) for you to buy imported goods. For example, the Canadian government placed an 80 percent excise tax on the Canadian editions of U.S. magazines. Many "Canadian" magazines, such as *Time* or *Newsweek*, are simply U.S. editions that have been repackaged for the Canadian market by replacing a few U.S. stories with a few Canadian stories. Canadian magazine publishers encouraged their government to enact the excise tax. They knew that given a choice between a Canadian sports magazine and *Sports Illustrated Canada*, which now costs nearly twice as much, thanks to the excise tax, most Canadian sports fans would buy the Canadian magazine. In fact, because of this excise tax, the Canadian edition of *Sports Illustrated Canada* is no longer published. By establishing this tax, the Canadian government engaged in **protectionism**, which is the use of trade barriers to protect local companies and their workers from foreign competition.[20]

**protectionism**
a government's use of trade barriers to shield domestic companies and their workers from foreign competition

Governments have used two general kinds of trade barriers: tariff and nontariff barriers. A **tariff** is a direct tax on imported goods. Like the Canadian excise tax on U.S. magazines, tariffs increase the cost of imported goods relative to domestic goods. For example, the U.S. import tax on trucks is 25 percent. This means that U.S. buyers will pay $25,000 for a $20,000 Toyota T-1 truck, with the $5,000 tariff going to the U.S. government. **Nontariff barriers** are nontax methods of increasing the cost or reducing the volume of imported goods. There are five types of nontariff barriers: quotas, voluntary export restraints, government import standards, government subsidies, and customs valuation/classification. Because there are so many different kinds of nontariff barriers, they can be an even more potent method of shielding domestic industries from foreign competition.

**tariff**
a direct tax on imported goods

**nontariff barriers**
nontax methods of increasing the cost or reducing the volume of imported goods

**quota**
limit on the number or volume of imported products

**Quotas** are specific limits on the number or volume of imported products. For example, the United States places quotas on the number of Chinese area rugs that can be

269

© ANDY SACKS/GETTY IMAGES/STONE

Excessively stringent standards that exceed normally accepted industry practices are a way for countries to control imports. The Chinese requirement that all imported wheat be 100% fungus-free is a means to protect the country's wheat farmers.

imported each year. Yet demand for these rugs is so strong that the quota limit is often reached in August or September. Once this quota is reached, importation of Chinese rugs is forbidden until January 1 of the next year.

**voluntary export restraints**
voluntarily imposed limits on the number or volume of products exported to a particular country

**Voluntary export restraints** are similar to quotas because they limit how much of a product can be imported annually. The difference is that the exporting country rather than the importing country imposes the limit. However, the "voluntary" offer to limit imports usually occurs because of the implicit threat of forced trade quotas by the importing country. For example, in a move to protect Japanese farmers from cheap and plentiful Chinese agricultural products, the Japanese government is trying to convince China to "voluntarily" restrict the number of Chinese-grown leeks, shitake mushrooms, and rushes (used in making Japanese floor mats) that are imported to Japan each year.[21] However, according to the World Trade Organization (see the discussion on the General Agreement on Trade and Tariffs in Section 2.2 below), voluntary export restraints are illegal and should have been phased out after 1999.[22]

**government import standard**
specified to protect the health and safety of citizens

In theory, **government import standards** are specified to protect the health and safety of citizens. In reality, government import standards are often used to restrict or ban imported goods. For example, China is the only nation in the world that requires U.S.-grown grain to be 100 percent fungus-free. Although preventing the importation of a fungus-infected agricultural product sounds reasonable enough, having a very small percentage of fungus is normal for harvested wheat. Since there is no chance that fungus will spread once wheat has been harvested, and since China is the only nation to insist on this standard, the Chinese government is actually using this government import standard to protect the economic health of its wheat farmers, rather than the physical health of its consumers.[23]

**subsidies**
government loans, grants, and tax deferments given to domestic companies to protect them from foreign competition

Many nations also use **subsidies**, such as long-term, low-interest loans, cash grants, and tax deferments, to develop and protect companies in special industries. European and Japanese governments have invested billions of dollars to develop airplane manufacturers and steel companies, while the U.S. government has provided subsidies for manufacturers of computer chips. Not surprisingly, businesses complain about unfair trade practices when other companies receive government subsidies. For example, before Airbus became a publicly-traded company, Boeing Corporation, the world's largest manufacturer of commercial airplanes, frequently complained to U.S. government officials about the millions of dollars in direct government subsidies that the European manufacturer of commercial airplanes received each year from European governments.[24]

**customs classification**
a classification assigned by government officials that affects the size of the tariff and consideration of import quotas

**General Agreement on Tariffs and Trade (GATT)**
worldwide trade agreement that reduces and eliminates tariffs, limits government subsidies, and protects intellectual property

In Kuala Lumpur, a city hall worker spreads millions of pirated DVDs, software, and CDs on the floor before destroying them. Malaysia has been escalating its crackdown on pirated software following complaints from the U.S.-based Business Software Alliance that counterfeit software has meant an estimated $4.8 million in lost sales.

The last nontariff barrier is **customs classification**. As products are imported into a country, they are examined by customs agents, who must decide into which of nearly 9,000 categories they should classify a product. Classification is important, because the category assigned by customs agents can affect the size of the tariff and consideration of import quotas. For example, the U.S. Customs Service changed the tariff on 33,000 girls' ski jackets because corduroy trim had been sewn on the jackets' sleeves. Without the trim, they would have classified the jackets as "garments designed for rain wear, hunting, fishing, or similar uses," which have a tariff of only 10.6 percent. Yet with the trim, they categorized the jackets as "other girls' wearing apparel" and earned a higher tariff of 27.5 percent.[25]

### 2.2 Trade Agreements

Thanks to the trade barriers described above, buying imported goods has often been much more expensive and difficult than buying domestic goods. However, the regulations governing global trade were transformed in the 1990s. The most significant change was that 124 countries agreed to adopt the **General Agreement on Tariffs and Trade (GATT)**.

Through tremendous decreases in tariff and nontariff barriers, GATT makes it much easier and cheaper for consumers in all countries to buy foreign products. First, by 2005, GATT will cut average tariffs worldwide by 40 percent. Second, GATT eliminates tariffs in 10 specific industries: beer, alcohol, construction equipment, farm machinery, furniture, medical equipment, paper, pharmaceuticals, steel, and toys. Third, GATT puts stricter limits on government subsidies. For example, GATT places limits on how much national governments can subsidize company research in electronic and high-technology

AP PHOTO/TEH ENG KOON

industries. Fourth, GATT protects intellectual property, such as trademarks, patents, and copyrights. Protection of intellectual property has been an increasingly important issue in global trade because of widespread product piracy. For example, Chinese bootleggers were selling illegal copies of Disney's *The Lion King* and *Mulan* videos even *before* Disney could get its official copies to stores in the United States.[26] Product piracy like this costs companies billions in lost revenue each year. Finally, trade disputes between countries will be fully settled by arbitration panels from the World Trade Organization. In the past, countries could ignore arbitration panel rulings by using their veto power to cancel arbitration decisions. For instance, the French government has routinely vetoed rulings that it unfairly subsidized French farmers with extraordinarily large cash grants. However, countries that are members of the World Trade Organization (every country that agrees to GATT is a member) will no longer have veto power. Thus, World Trade Organization rulings will be complete and final. For more information about GATT and the World Trade Association (WTO), go to the WTO Web site at **http://www.wto.org**. Exhibit 8.4 provides a brief overview about the WTO and its functions.

The second major development in the historic move toward reduction of trade barriers has been the creation of **regional trading zones**, in which tariff and nontariff barriers are reduced or eliminated for countries within the trading zone. The largest and most important trading zones are in Europe (the Maastricht Treaty), North America (the North American Free Trade Agreement, or NAFTA), South America (the Free Trade Area of the Americas, or FTAA), and Asia (Association of South East Nations, or ASEAN, and Asia-Pacific Economic Cooperation, or APEC). The map in Exhibit 8.5 shows the extent to which free trade agreements govern global trade.

In 1992, Belgium, Denmark, France, Germany, Greece, Italy, Ireland, Luxembourg, the Netherlands, Portugal, Spain, and the United Kingdom implemented the **Maastricht Treaty of Europe**, thus creating the European Union (EU). The purpose of this treaty and the EU was to transform their 12 different economies and 12 currencies into one

**regional trading zones**
areas in which tariff and nontariff barriers on trade between countries are reduced or eliminated

**Maastricht Treaty of Europe**
regional trade agreement between most European countries

---

EXHIBIT 8.4

WORLD TRADE ORGANIZATION

☑ **FACT FILE**

WORLD TRADE ORGANIZATION

**Location:** Geneva, Switzerland
**Established:** 1 January 1995
**Created by:** Uruguay Round negotiations (1986-94)
**Membership:** 142 countries (as of 26 July 2001)
**Budget:** 127 million Swiss francs for 2000
**Secretariat staff:** 500
**Head:** Mike Moore (director-general)

**Functions:**
• Administering WTO trade agreements
• Forum for trade negotiations
• Handling trade disputes
• Monitoring national trade policies
• Technical assistance and training for developing countries
• Cooperation with other international organizations

**Source:** "WTO: About the Organization," *World Trade Organization.* [Online] Available http://www.wto.org/english/thewto_e/thewto_e.htm, 9 September 2001.

EXHIBIT 8.5

GLOBAL MAP OF REGIONAL TRADE AGREEMENTS

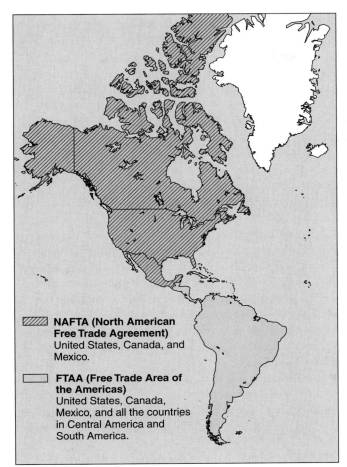

**NAFTA (North American Free Trade Agreement)** United States, Canada, and Mexico.

**FTAA (Free Trade Area of the Americas)** United States, Canada, Mexico, and all the countries in Central America and South America.

**Maastricht Treaty of Europe** Austria, Belgium, Denmark, Finland, France, Germany, Greece, Italy, Ireland, Luxembourg, The Netherlands, Portugal, Spain, Sweden, and the United Kingdom.

**ASEAN** Brunei Darussalam, Cambodia, Indonesia, Laos, Malaysia, Myanmar, the Philippines, Singapore, Thailand, and Vietnam.

**APEC** Australia, Canada, Chile, China, Hong Kong, Japan, Korea, Mexico, New Zealand, Papua New Guinea, Peru, Russia, the United States, and all members of ASEAN except Cambodia, Laos, and Myanmar.

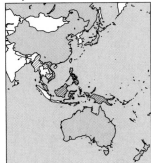

common economic market, called the European Union, and one common currency, the euro. In 1995, Austria, Finland, and Sweden became members, too, bringing total membership to 15 countries.[27] However, 13 other countries have applied and are now being considered for membership: Bulgaria, Cyprus, the Czech Republic, Estonia, Hungary, Latvia, Lithuania, Malta, Poland, Romania, the Slovak Republic, Slovenia, and Turkey.[28]

Prior to the treaty, trucks carrying products were stopped and inspected by customs agents at each border. Furthermore, since the required paperwork, tariffs, and government product specifications could be radically different in each country, companies often had to file 12 different sets of paperwork, pay 12 different tariffs, and produce 12 different versions of their basic product to meet various government specifications.

Likewise, open business travel, which we take for granted in the United States as we travel from state to state, was complicated by inspections at each border crossing. For example, if you lived in Germany, but worked across the border in Luxembourg, your car was stopped and your passport was inspected twice a day, every day, as you traveled to and from work. Also, every business transaction required a currency exchange, for example, from German deutsche marks to Italian lira, or from French francs to British pounds. Imagine all of this happening to millions of trucks, cars, and business people, and you can begin to appreciate the difficulty and cost of conducting business across Europe before the Maastricht Treaty.

For more information about the Maastricht treaty and the European Union, go to **http://europa.eu.int/index-en.htm**. For more about Europe's new currency, the euro, which, by 1 July 2002, will replace the currencies of 12 countries (Austria, Belgium, Finland, France, Germany, Greece, Ireland, Italy, Luxembourg, Netherlands, Portugal, and Spain), see **http://europa.eu.int/euro/html/home5.html?lang=5**.

**NAFTA**, the **North American Free Trade Agreement** between the United States, Canada, and Mexico, went into effect 1 January 1994. More than any other regional trade agreement, NAFTA liberalizes trade between countries so that businesses can plan for one market, North America, rather than for three separate markets, the United States, Canada, and Mexico. One of NAFTA's most important achievements was to eliminate most product tariffs. On 1 January 1994, product tariffs were eliminated on the first and largest group of products traded among the three countries. The result? Just six months after NAFTA went into effect, U.S. exports were up by 10 percent to Canada and 17 percent to Mexico. In fact, initial trade between Mexico and the United States was so strong that more than 2,500 eighteen-wheeler trucks full of U.S. and Mexican products crossed the border at Laredo, Texas, each day.[29] Initial cross-border traffic was also heavy between the United States and Canada. Canadian Pacific, one of Canada's largest railroad companies, saw an immediate 10 percent increase in its north-south shipments after NAFTA went into effect. Overall, both Mexican and Canadian exports to the United States have doubled since NAFTA went into effect.[30] Likewise, U.S. exports to Mexico and Canada have doubled, too, growing twice as fast as U.S. exports to any other part of the world. In fact, U.S. companies now export more to Mexico than to Britain, France, Germany, and Italy combined![31]

The second set of NAFTA product tariffs was eliminated in 1998, with the third and final set to be eliminated in 2003. Importantly, NAFTA also prevents Canada, the United States, and Mexico from increasing existing tariffs or introducing new tariffs. For more information about NAFTA, see the Office of NAFTA & Inter-American Affairs at **http://www.mac.doc.gov/nafta/**.

The goal of the proposed **FTAA, Free Trade Area of the Americas**, is to establish a free trade zone similar to NAFTA throughout the Western Hemisphere. If created, FTAA would likely supplant Mercosur, a free trade agreement between Brazil, Argentina, Uruguay, and Paraguay. FTAA would then become the largest trading zone in the world, consisting of 800 million people in 34 countries in both North and South America with a combined gross domestic product of $11 trillion![32] Similar to NAFTA, FTAA pledges to support trade "without barriers, without subsidies, without unfair practices, and with an increasing stream of productive investments."[33] Leaders from each of the 34 countries have agreed to finish FTAA negotiations by 2005. If that occurs, over the next decade nontariff barriers would be removed, tariffs would gradually be reduced to zero, rules for investing and financial markets would be standardized, and a process would be established to handle trade disputes.[34] For more information about FTAA, see **http://www.ftaa-alca.org**. For more information about Mercosur, see **http://www.mercosur.org/english/default.htm**.

**ASEAN**, the **Association of South East Nations**, and **APEC, Asia-Pacific Economic Cooperation**, are the two largest and most important regional trading groups in Asia. ASEAN is a trade agreement between Brunei Darussalam, Cambodia, Indonesia, Laos, Malaysia, Myanmar, the Philippines, Singapore, Thailand, and Vietnam. Together, these countries form a market of more than 330 million people. United States trade with ASEAN countries is sizable, exceeding $75 billion a year. In fact, the United States is ASEAN's largest trading partner, while the member nations of ASEAN are the U.S.'s fifth largest trade group. ASEAN member countries have agreed to create an ASEAN free trade area beginning in 2015 for the six original countries (Brunei Darussalam,

**NAFTA (North American Free Trade Agreement)**
regional trade agreement between the United States, Canada, and Mexico

**FTAA (Free Trade Area of the Americas)**
regional trade agreement that, when signed, will create a regional trading zone encompassing 36 countries in North and South America

**ASEAN (Association of South East Nations)**
regional trade agreement between Brunei Darussalam, Cambodia, Indonesia, Laos, Malaysia, Myanmar, the Philippines, Singapore, Thailand, and Vietnam

**APEC (Asia-Pacific Economic Cooperation)**
regional trade agreement between Australia, Canada, Chile, the People's Republic of China, Hong Kong, Japan, Korea, Mexico, New Zealand, Papua New Guinea, Peru, Russia, the United States, and all the members of ASEAN, except Cambodia, Laos, and Myanmar

274

Indonesia, Malaysia, the Philippines, Singapore, and Thailand) and in 2018 for newer member countries (Cambodia, Laos, Myanmar, and Vietnam).[35] For more information about ASEAN, see **http://www.aseansec.org**.

APEC is a broader agreement between Australia, Canada, Chile, the People's Republic of China, Hong Kong, Japan, Korea, Mexico, New Zealand, Papua New Guinea, Peru, Russia, the United States and all the members of ASEAN, except Cambodia, Laos, and Myanmar.[36] APEC's 21 member countries contain 2.5 billion people, account for 47 percent of all global trade, and have a combined gross domestic product of over $18 trillion. APEC countries began reducing trade barriers in the year 2000, though it will take until 2020 for all trade barrier reductions to be completely phased in. For more information about APEC, see **http://www.apecsec.org.sg**.

### 2.3 Consumers, Trade Barriers, and Trade Agreements

In Tokyo, a Coke costs $2.30. In Geneva, Switzerland, a small cup of regular coffee costs $1.75. In the United States, each of these items costs about a dollar. Likewise, a McDonald's Big Mac sandwich costs an average of $2.54 in the United States, $2.85 in Britain, and $3.65 in Switzerland.[37] While not all products are this much more expensive in other countries (in some they can be cheaper), a Bureau of Labor Statistics study found that American consumers get much more for their money than most other consumers in the world. For example, the average Swiss consumer earns nearly $44,350 a year, compared to the average American who earns $28,020.[38] Yet after both incomes are compared for how much they can buy, the Swiss income is equivalent to just $25,553! So while U.S. incomes are lower, they still buy more for the average American. Other studies find similar results. Despite having larger average annual incomes than American workers, German and Japanese consumers are only able to buy approximately 72 percent and 58 percent, respectively, of what the average American consumer can buy.[39]

Although the connection is not obvious, one reason that Americans get more for their money is that the U.S. marketplace has been one of the easiest for foreign companies to do business. Some U.S. industries, such as textiles, have been heavily protected from foreign competition through many trade barriers. But, for the most part, American consumers (and businesses) have had plentiful choices among American-made and foreign-made products. More important, the high level of competition between foreign and domestic companies that creates these choices helps to keep prices low in the United States. Furthermore, it is precisely this lack of choice and the low level of competition that keeps prices higher in countries that have not been as open to foreign companies and products. For example, Japanese trade barriers are estimated to cost Japanese consumers more than $100 billion a year. This figure is equivalent to a 178 percent increase in cost across the 47 product categories studied by Japanese economists.[40] To illustrate how large this difference can be, consider that a set of golf balls that retails for $19.99 in the United States typically costs a Japanese golfer $72.00! Not surprisingly, polls show that price, not quality, is the most important consideration for Japanese consumers.[41]

### Review 2
#### Trade Rules and Agreements

Tariffs and nontariff trade barriers, such as quotas, voluntary export restraints, government import standards, government subsidies, and customs classifications, have made buying foreign goods much harder or expensive than buying domestically produced products. However, worldwide trade agreements, such as GATT, along with regional trading agreements, like the Maastricht Treaty of Europe, NAFTA, FTAA, ASEAN, and APEC, substantially reduce tariff and nontariff barriers to international trade. Companies have responded by investing in growing markets in Asia, Eastern Europe, and Latin America. Consumers have responded by purchasing products based on value, rather than geography.

Once a company has decided that it *will* go global, it must decide *how* to go global. For example, if you decide to sell in Singapore, should you try to find a local business partner who speaks the language, knows the laws, and understands the customs and norms of Singapore's culture, or should you simply export your products from your home country? What do you do if you are also entering Eastern Europe, perhaps starting in Hungary? Should you use the same approach in Hungary that you used in Singapore?

*While there is no magical formula to answer these questions, after reading these next two sections, you should be able to*
3. *explain why companies choose to standardize or adapt their business procedures.*
4. *explain the different ways that companies can organize to do business globally.*

## 3. Consistency or Adaptation?

In this section, we return to a key issue in the chapter: How can you be sure that the way you run your business in one country is the right way to run that business in another? In other words, how can you strike the right balance between global consistency and local adaptation?

*Global consistency* means that when a multinational company has offices, manufacturing plants, and distribution facilities in different countries, it will run those offices, plants, and facilities based on the same rules, guidelines, policies, and procedures. Managers at company headquarters value global consistency, because it simplifies decisions. For example, IBM's international sales used to be organized by country. Under this system, if a multinational company with offices in 10 different countries wanted to purchase IBM personal computers, it would deal with 10 different IBM offices and would likely get different prices and levels of service from each. Today, multinational customers only have to deal with IBM's central sales office. Once a deal has been cut, they can expect similar prices and service in each location.[42]

A company with a *local adaptation* policy modifies its standard operating procedures to adapt to differences in foreign customers, governments, and regulatory agencies. Local adaptation is typically more important to local managers who are charged with making the international business successful in their countries. In his book, *Blunders in International Business*, David Ricks describes an ill-fated advertising theme used by Sumitomo Corporation of Japan to introduce a new kind of steel pipe to the U.S. market. Following the advice of a Japanese advertising agency, the steel was named "Sumitomo *High Toughness*" and was advertised in full-page advertisements with nearly full-page letters as *SHT*, the steel "made to match its name." Sumitomo could probably have prevented this mistake if they had given some control of their advertising to local managers who understood the culture and language.

Multinational companies struggle to find the correct balance between global consistency and local adaptation. If companies focus too much on local adaptation, they run the risk of losing the cost efficiencies and productivity that result from using standardized rules and procedures throughout the world. If they lean too much toward global consistency, they run the risk of using management procedures poorly suited to particular countries' markets, cultures, and employees. For example, Coca-Cola, which has 51 percent of the world market for soft drinks and gets 80 percent of its profits from outside the United States, has been fined millions of dollars by European governments for violating safety and business regulations. Coke's top 10 European managers, who, in the name of global consistency, were all from Coke's U.S. headquarters in Atlanta, Georgia, were not sensitive to the different regulations in various European countries, nor to Europeans' different views towards business. In fact, lower level managers, all from Europe, wrote a confidential memo criticizing their U.S. managers for their "abrasive, domineering, and unacceptable American behavior." Today, to restore a focus on local adaptation, nine of Coke's top 10 European managers are from Europe, while only one is from the United States. Furthermore, Coke has stopped construction on its European headquarters—a "second Atlanta" for Europe—because its new CEO wants decision-making power to remain in the hands of Coke's key managers in each country.[43]

### Review 3
### Consistency or Adaptation?

Global business requires a balance between global consistency and local adaptation. Global consistency means using the same rules, guidelines, policies, and procedures in each location. Managers at company headquarters like global consistency, because it simplifies decisions. Local adaptation means adapting standard procedures to differences in markets. Local managers prefer a policy of local adaptation, because it gives them more control. Not all businesses need the same combinations of global consistency and local adaptation. Some thrive by emphasizing global consistency and ignoring local adaptation. Others succeed by ignoring global consistency and emphasizing local adaptation.

## 4. Forms for Global Business

*Besides determining whether to adapt organizational policies and procedures, a company must also determine how to organize itself for successful entry into foreign markets. Historically, companies have generally followed the phase model of globalization. This means that companies make the transition from a domestic company to a global company in sequential phases, beginning with 4.1 exporting, followed by 4.2 cooperative contracts, moving next to 4.3 strategic alliances, and finishing with 4.4 wholly owned affiliates. At each step, a company grows much larger, uses those resources to enter more global markets, is less dependent on home country sales, and is more committed in its orientation to global business. However, evidence suggests that some companies do not follow the phase model of globalization.[44] Some skip phases on their way to becoming more global and less domestic. Others, known as 4.5 global new ventures, don't follow the phase model at all. This section reviews these forms of global business.[45]*

### 4.1 Exporting

**exporting**
selling domestically produced products to customers in foreign countries

When companies produce products in their home countries and sell those products to customers in foreign countries, they are **exporting**. For example, can you answer this question: "Which sport uses a 10-yard long cloth folded into six and called Movashi? Is it (a) sumo wrestling, (b) pollet, (c) hurdling, or (d) malkambh?" If you answered (a) sumo wrestling, you would have been correct and had the chance to earn 10 million rupees ($219,000) on India's TV show *Kaun Banega Crorepati?* "Kaun Banega Crorepati?" meaning "*Are You Sure?*" is India's version of *Who Wants To Be A Millionaire?* which originated in Britain. In fact, Britain-based Celador Productions Ltd. has exported nearly identical versions of the show to over 30 different countries.[46]

Exporting has many advantages as a form of global business. It makes the company less dependent on sales in its home market and provides a greater degree of control over research, design, and production decisions. Colman Hutchinson, executive producer of the original *Who Wants to be a Millionaire?* in Britain, said, "The show is pretty much the same the world over." Details, such as construction of the set, the format of questions, the music, and the procedures for choosing contestants, are standardized via a 169-page guide. Consequently, there are only very small differences in the show across countries. For example, while American host Regis Philbin says, "Is that your final answer?" India host Amitabh Bachchan, India's all-time most popular movie star, says, "Shall we lock it?" followed by "Computer, please lock the answer."[47]

While advantageous in a number of ways, exporting also has its disadvantages. The primary disadvantage is that many exported goods are subject to tariff and nontariff barriers that can substantially increase their final cost to consumers. A second disadvantage of

Indian movie star Amitabh Bachchan, right, welcomes participants to the popular television program *Kuan Banega Crorepati?* (*Who Wants To Be A Millionaire?*) in Bombay, India. The Indian version of the successful American program has high ratings, with millions of Indian viewers glued to their television sets from Monday to Thursday.

AP PHOTO

exporting is that transportation costs can significantly increase the price of an exported product. For example, because of special safety requirements, such as maintaining particular temperatures and pressures, the ships that transport liquefied natural gas can cost up to $350 million to build. Consequently, shipping costs account for as much as 20 to 30 percent of the total cost of liquefied natural gas.[48] Another disadvantage of exporting is that companies that export depend on foreign importers for product distribution. For example, if the foreign importer makes a mistake on the paperwork that accompanies a shipment of imported goods, those goods can be returned to the foreign manufacturer at the manufacturer's expense.

### 4.2 Cooperative Contracts

When an organization decides to expand its business globally, but does not want to make large financial commitments to do so, it will sign a **cooperative contract** with a foreign business owner, who pays the company a fee for the right to conduct that business in his or her country. There are two kinds of cooperative contracts: licensing and franchising.

Under a **licensing** agreement, a domestic company, the *licensor*, receives royalty payments for allowing another company, the *licensee*, to produce its product, sell its service, or use its brand name in a particular foreign market. For example, brands such as Peter Paul Mounds and Almond Joy, which consumers associate with American companies, are not really American products. British company Cadbury Schweppes licenses Peter Paul Mounds and Almond Joy candy bars to Hershey foods for U.S. production.

One of the most important advantages of licensing is that it allows companies to earn additional profits without investing more money. As foreign sales increase, the royalties paid to the licensor by the foreign licensee increase. Moreover, the licensee, not the licensor, invests in production equipment and facilities to produce the licensed product. Licensing also helps companies avoid tariff and nontariff barriers. Since the licensee manufactures the product within the foreign country, tariff and nontariff barriers don't apply. For example, Britvic Corona is licensed to bottle and distribute Pepsi-Cola within Great Britain. Because it bottles Pepsi in England, tariff and nontariff barriers do not affect the price or supply of these products.

The biggest disadvantage associated with licensing is that the licensor gives up control over the quality of the product or service sold by the foreign licensee. Other than specific restrictions in the licensing agreement, the licensee controls the entire business,

**cooperative contract**
an agreement in which a foreign business owner pays a company a fee for the right to conduct that business in his or her country

278

**licensing**
agreement in which a domestic company, the licensor, receives royalty payments for allowing another company, the licensee, to produce its product, sell its service, or use its brand name in a specified foreign market

from production, to marketing, to final sales. Many licensors include inspection clauses in their license contracts, but closely monitoring product or service quality from thousands of miles away can be difficult. An additional disadvantage is that licensees can eventually become competitors, especially when a licensing agreement includes access to important technology or proprietary business knowledge.

A **franchise** is a collection of networked firms in which the manufacturer or marketer of a product or service, the *franchiser,* licenses the entire business to another person or organization, the *franchisee.* For the price of an initial franchise fee plus royalties, franchisers provide franchisees training, help with marketing and advertising, and an exclusive right to conduct business in a particular location. Most franchise fees run between $5,000 and $35,000. Franchisees pay McDonald's, one of the largest franchisers in the world, an initial franchise fee of $45,000. Another $450,000 to $750,000 is needed beyond that to help pay for food inventory, kitchen equipment, construction, landscaping, and so forth. While franchisees typically borrow from a bank to pay some of the expenses, McDonald's requires that franchisers invest $175,000 of their own money into new McDonald's restaurants.[49] Since typical royalties range from 2 percent to 12.5 percent of gross sales, franchisers are well rewarded for the help they provide to franchisees.[50] Well over 400 U.S. companies franchise their businesses to foreign franchise partners.

Overall, franchising is a fast way to enter foreign markets. Over the last 20 years, U.S. franchisers have more than doubled their global franchises for a total of more than 100,000 global franchise units! Because it gives the franchiser additional cash flows from franchisee fees and royalties, franchising can be a good strategy when a company's domestic sales have slowed. For example, Tricon Global Restaurants, which owns and runs Pizza Hut, Taco Bell, and Kentucky Fried Chicken, is accepting very few new U.S. franchises because the U.S. market is saturated with fast-food outlets. McDonald's is only adding about 1 to 2 percent more U.S. stores per year through franchising. By contrast, these restaurants are experiencing phenomenal growth in global franchises. In the last decade, McDonald's has nearly doubled its number of overseas stores. Between Pizza Hut, Taco Bell, and KFC, Tricon Global Restaurants opens nearly 800 new international franchise stores a year.[51]

Despite its many advantages, franchisers face a loss of control when they sell businesses to franchisees who are thousands of miles away. Although there are successful exceptions, franchising success may be somewhat culture-bound. In other words, because most global franchisers begin by franchising their businesses in similar countries or regions (Canada is by far the first choice for American companies taking their first step into global franchising), and because 65 percent of franchisers make absolutely no change in their business for overseas franchisees, that success may not generalize to cultures with different lifestyles, values, preferences, and technological infrastructures. For example, it would be a mistake for Office Depot to franchise its standard American store, that is, wide aisles and large volume purchases, along with American office supplies, such as 8 1/2 by 11 paper and Scotch tape, to other countries. Management consultant Dennis Custage said, "The number one mistake companies make is trying to run everything the way it was in their home country, with a bunch of expatriates."[52] Instead, because Japanese customers buy in small quantities, Office Depot's franchise stores in Japan are smaller with slimmer aisles and smaller volume packages. Likewise, overseas, Office Depot mostly sells "A-4" paper, which is a little bit longer and narrower than the standard 8½ by 11 paper sold in the U.S. Finally, if you wandered into an Office Depot in Britain and asked for "Scotch" tape, they wouldn't know what you wanted because most British people use a similar product called "Tesa tape" instead.[53]

### 4.3 Strategic Alliances

Companies forming **strategic alliances** combine key resources, costs, risks, technology, and people. The most common strategic alliance is a **joint venture,** which occurs when

**franchise**
a collection of networked firms in which the manufacturer or marketer of a product or service, the franchisor, licenses the entire business to another person or organization, the franchisee

**strategic alliance**
agreement in which companies combine key resources, costs, risk, technology, and people

**joint venture**
a strategic alliance in which two existing companies collaborate to form a third, independent company

# BeenThereDoneThat

## Would You Like Fries with That?

Former McDonald's CEO Michael R. Quinlan talks about McDonald's international business. With 13,000 restaurants in the United States, and 15,000 restaurants in 119 other countries, McDonald's, an icon of American fast food, has become a truly global company.

**Q:** Sixty percent of your earnings now come from outside the United States. Can you sustain your target of 20 percent growth in the international field?

**A:** We can come close. In the overseas market, Westernization of eating habits plays to our strengths. We have an extremely powerful brand. When we open in a new country, we typically get record volumes. They really claw the doors open. I don't know what our potential is at the end of the day. I only know that it's greater than what it is today.

What do you need for growth? You need demand for your products. You need capital, people, infrastructure, the ability to market, and the right market conditions. If you don't pay attention to which of those facets are missing or need to be shored up, you can grow for the sake of growth. You could end up going out on a limb the wrong way and actually retarding your ability to grow effectively. I don't want to make that mistake in international. I saw that mistake made in the United States years ago where the economics were still a little sketchy in an area. The ability of the staff to support and train in an effective fashion was outstripped by the efforts of the site development folks.

You can grow as quickly as you can grow effectively taking all factors into consideration. We will open about 1,800 or 1,900 restaurants globally in the next year. Could I do 2,500? 2,600? Yes, I could, no question. Would I like what I got? Probably not.

We're making individual decisions on growth in each country based on readiness. We evaluate all the factors: the strength of the people, the purchasing and licensing infrastructure, our ability to market effectively, the avenues open to us, the avenues that are not, and, of course, the economics in that country at that point in time. We make decisions on capital spending based on where this balance deposits us on a growth curve.

**Q:** What is the biggest limiting factor?

**A:** There's a different answer in each country. You can have as many managers as you want, but you cannot fabricate experience. One strength of our international organization is in helping the new country managers get up to speed quickly, make fewer mistakes, and find creative solutions. But we can't do that blindly. You have to watch how fast you move it along, as well as decisions on sites and real estate deals.

I can make location decisions more aggressively in England because I have more knowledge in that market than I do in a brand new country. Looking at the global landscape right now, we're going at about the right pace just about everywhere. And we tune this up and down, according to conditions. We have had years when we have cut back in a country and then reaccelerated two years later.

**Q:** What prompts you to do that?

**A:** The results. We expanded quickly in East Germany, but we've throttled down because the purchasing power is not coming along as fast as we thought it might. Disposable income is a factor, but it's got to be combined with cultural habits and eating habits. Sometimes the supply infrastructure holds us back.

In any country, a few big factors determine success. On an individual store basis, it's gross profit; food, paper, and distribution costs; labor, both direct labor and social charges; and occupancy costs. Those are the biggies. And while one country might have high food costs, if it's balanced off with lower labor, you're okay. You've got to make decisions on whether you can attack this cost category or that one. Then you have to marry that up with import or export duties and balance the trade restrictions. Should you batch the purchases in Belgium with the purchases in France to drop another 10 percent off the price? You can't just flip a switch and have it all go on automatic.

**Q:** Recent reports show that international operating margins are under pressure.

**A:** It ebbs and flows. There is some impact from one restaurant to another when we expand, and you have to watch that carefully. You can't alter your occupancy costs at a given location, only with future deals and renegotiated deals. That's put a bit of pressure on us, and then we've had some tough economic cycles. Germany and France have been tough. Japan's been a bit tough. Brazil is not booming to the extent that it was a year and a half ago. We had some great growth years in Australia, and matching those figures is tough right now. In Canada, disposable income, the attitude of the consumer, taxes—particularly in eastern Canada—are all coming together to make it pretty rough sledding right now. How long will it last? I have differing opinions on different countries, but while we'll have challenges next year, I expect us to have a very good year in international.

**Q:** You serve 109 countries, yet 55 percent of your international business comes from seven countries.

**A:** That's changing. Our countries are in three tiers: brand new countries, developing countries, and established countries. The developing countries are going through a maturation phase where their margins are coming up. We don't go into China, for example, thinking that we have to make money from day one. We still haven't made any money in China, and we have 160 restaurants there now. Conversely, we're very profitable in Taiwan. But China's moving forward, and I'm patient. It took us six years of working on purchasing before we opened a restaurant there. But now we're set, and the organization is capable of growth, because all the factors that contribute to balance now exist.

**Q:** How is international growth changing the character of this company?

**A:** I would predict that the McDonald's board over the years will evolve to have more of an international knowledge base and expertise as opportunities present themselves. Already, some of our board members have international experience. We do an excellent job at being respectful and attentive to the differences between the countries so that we are not just an American interloper. We're a Chinese-run company in China, and we're a company that takes care of our own and promotes from within to the greatest extent possible.

**Q:** How translatable are your products?

**A:** Good question. As long as the products are of the same category as a McDonald's hamburger, easy to eat, great value, and great quality products that lend themselves to handheld consumption—not only in-store, but takeaway—we're fine. I don't want to be all things to all people, but the concept of brand extensions and also promotional products that add variety and excitement are very live concepts. We do have local adaptations. In southeast Asia, our aggregated chicken products—chicken nuggets, chicken sandwiches, and chicken wing promotions—are high in the product mix. A teriyaki burger made out of ground pork is our second or third best seller in Japan.

**Source:** J.P. Donlon, "Quinlan Fries Harder (Interview with McDonald's CEO Michael Quinlan)," *Chief Executive (U.S.)*, Jan-Feb 1998, 44. This interview was edited for inclusion in this textbook.

two existing companies collaborate to form a third company. The two founding companies remain intact and unchanged, except that, together, they now own the newly created joint venture.

One of the oldest, most successful global joint ventures is Fuji-Xerox, which is a joint venture between Fuji Photo Film of Japan and Xerox Corporation, based in the United States, which makes copiers and automated office systems. More than 35 years after its creation, Fuji-Xerox employs nearly 15,000 employees and has close to $2.5 billion in revenues. Fuji-Xerox is largely responsible for copier sales in Asia, whereas Xerox is responsible for North American sales. Rank Xerox, a Xerox subsidiary, is responsible for sales in Europe.[54]

One of the advantages of global joint ventures is that, like licensing and franchising, they help companies avoid tariff and nontariff barriers to entry. Another advantage is that companies participating in a joint venture bear only part of the costs and the risks of that business. Many companies find this attractive because of the expense of entering foreign markets or developing new products. For example, MTU Aero Engines of Hanover, Germany, has formed several global joint ventures because of the extremely high cost of developing new jet engines. MTU is developing a geared-fan jet engine with Pratt & Whitney Canada. It is also developing a low pollution emissions jet engine, code named CLEAN, with France-based SNECMA and other European aviation parts manufacturers.[55]

Global joint ventures can be especially advantageous to smaller local partners that link up with larger, more-experienced foreign firms that can bring advanced management, resources, and business skills to the joint venture. For instance, SasolChevron is a global joint venture between Sasol, a small South African oil company with expertise in turning natural gas into liquid fuel and gas, and Chevron, the second largest U.S. oil company [which has now merged with Texaco] with 28,000 employees in 90 countries worldwide. SasolChevron's management explained why the companies combined forces:

> SasolChevron was formed in order to take advantage of the synergies of Sasol's and Chevron's gas-to-liquids strengths. Sasol has the world's most advanced Fischer-Tropsch technology. Chevron has extensive global experience with respect to natural gas utilization, product marketing, and hydrotreating technology. Part of Sasol's vision is "To be a respected global enterprise . . . in applying unique, innovative, and competitive technologies." Part of Chevron's strategic drive is to "develop new growth opportunities globally." The SasolChevron joint venture will support the strategic drives of both Sasol and Chevron.[56]

Global joint ventures are not without problems, though. Because companies share costs and risk with their joint venture partners, they must also share their profits. At one time, sharing of profits created some tension between Fuji Color Film, Xerox, and their joint venture Fuji-Xerox. In fact, Xerox has struggled for so long that business experts joke that Fuji-Xerox, which has been highly profitable, should purchase Xerox.[57]

Global joint ventures can also be difficult to manage, because they represent a merging of four cultures: the country and organizational cultures of the first partner, and the country and the organizational cultures of the second partner. Oftentimes, to be "fair" to all involved, each partner in the global joint venture will have equal ownership and power. But this creates power struggles and a lack of leadership. For example, AT&T and British Telecom, two of the largest telecommunication companies in the world, invested $3 billion each to form a joint venture called Concert to provide communication services to multinational corporations. According to industry analyst Jim Rawitsch, Concert struggled because "Whenever you go into a situation where power is equally shared, it becomes like a marriage. In order for anything to happen, both have to agree. If one partner had 51 percent, it would be easier."[58]

Because of these problems, companies forming global joint ventures should carefully develop detailed contracts that specify the obligations of each party. Toshiba, which participated in its first global joint ventures in the early 1900s by making light bulb filaments with General Electric, treats joint ventures like a marriage of two companies and views the contract as a prenuptial agreement.[59] In other words, the joint venture contract specifies how much each company will invest, what its rights and responsibilities are, and what it is entitled to if the joint venture does not work out. These steps are important, because it is estimated that the rate of failure for global joint ventures is as high as 33 percent to 50 percent.[60]

### 4.4 Wholly Owned Affiliates (Build or Buy)

**wholly owned affiliates**
foreign offices, facilities, and manufacturing plants that are 100 percent owned by the parent company

Approximately one-third of multinational companies enter foreign markets through wholly owned affiliates. Unlike licensing, franchising, or joint ventures, **wholly owned affiliates** are 100 percent owned by the parent company. For example, Honda Motors of America in Marysville, Ohio, is 100 percent owned by Honda Motors of Japan. Ford Motor of Germany in Cologne is 100 percent owned by the Ford Motor Company in Detroit, Michigan.

The primary advantage of wholly owned businesses is that they give parent companies all of the profits and complete control over foreign facilities. The biggest disadvantage is the expense of building new operations or buying existing businesses. While the payoff can be enormous if wholly owned affiliates succeed, the losses can be immense if they fail. For example, when Volkswagen spent over a quarter of a billion dollars to purchase and modernize an auto manufacturing plant from Chrysler, everyone, including the state of Pennsylvania that lured Volkswagen to Pennsylvania with a $63 million tax break, thought Volkswagen would be wildly successful. However, nearly a decade later, Volkswagen sales had dropped and the plant, which was running at only 40 percent of capacity, was losing $120 million a year. Twenty-five hundred workers lost their jobs when Volkswagen closed the plant for good.[61]

Acquiring foreign businesses is sometimes resented by local businesses, customers, or workers. In fact, worker resentment may have contributed to Volkswagen's plant shutdown. Volkswagen's U.S. auto workers walked off their jobs and shut down the plant to protest being paid $1 to a $1.50 less an hour than other U.S. auto workers.[62]

### 4.5 Global New Ventures

Companies used to slowly evolve from being small and selling in their home markets to being large and selling to foreign markets. Furthermore, as companies went global, they usually followed the phase model of globalization. However, three trends have combined to allow companies to skip the phase model when going global. First, quick, reliable air travel can transport people to nearly any point in the world within one day. Second, low-

**global new ventures**
new companies with sales, employees, and financing in different countries that are founded with an active global strategy

cost communication technologies, such as international email, teleconferencing, and phone conferencing, make it easier to communicate with global customers, suppliers, managers, and employees. Third, there is now a critical mass of business people with extensive personal experience in all aspects of global business.[63] This combination of events has made it possible to start companies that are global from inception. With sales, employees, and financing in different countries, **global new ventures** are new companies founded with an active global strategy.[64]

While there are several different kinds of global new ventures, all share two common factors. First, the company founders successfully develop and communicate the company's global vision. For example, unlike many large investment firms that began and specialized in transactions within a particular country, the International Investment Group was founded to help global clients and businesses. IIG helps with global trading and offers global investment advice to clients in the United States, India, France, Switzerland, and Great Britain.[65]

Second, rather than going global one country at a time, new global ventures bring a product or service to market in several foreign markets at the same time. Just three years old, Lastminute.com, is a travel site that offers last minute deals on vacations, flights, hotel rooms, restaurants, theater tickets, and so forth, from over 9,000 suppliers. Its mission is to "encourage spontaneous, romantic and sometimes adventurous behavior by offering people the chance to live their dreams at unbeatable prices!" London-based Lastminute.com was global from inception and offers its services to people in the United Kingdom, the United States, the Netherlands, Italy, Spain, Germany, Sweden, France, South Africa, and Australia. Lastminute.com buys tickets and rooms at fixed prices, marks up the still low price, and consistent with its name, sells most of its bookings only a week in advance.[66]

### Review 4
#### Forms for Global Business
The phase model of globalization says that as companies move from a domestic to a global orientation, they use these organizational forms in sequence: exporting, cooperative contracts (licensing and franchising), strategic alliances, and wholly owned affiliates. Yet not all companies follow the phase model. For example, global new ventures are global from their inception.

## Where To Go Global?

*Deciding where to go global is just as important as deciding how your company will go global. After reading these next three sections, you should be able to*
5. *explain how to find a favorable business climate.*
6. *discuss the importance of identifying and adapting to cultural differences.*
7. *explain how to successfully prepare workers for international assignments.*

## 5. Finding the Best Business Climate

*When deciding where to go global, companies try to find countries or regions with promising business climates. An attractive global business climate 5.1 positions the company for easy access to growing markets, 5.2 is an effective but cost-efficient place to build an office or manufacturing site, and 5.3 minimizes the political risk to the company.*

### 5.1 Growing Markets
The most important factor in an attractive business climate is access to a growing market. For example, no product is known and purchased by as many people throughout the world as Coca-Cola. Yet, even Coke, which is available in 195 countries, still has tremendous potential for further global growth. Presently, the Coca-Cola Company gets about

80 percent of its sales from its 16 largest markets. The remaining 20 percent is spread across the other 200 countries in which Coke does business. Coke's former CEO said, "We have really just begun reaching out to the 95 percent of the world's population that lives outside the U.S."[67]

**purchasing power**
a comparison of the relative cost of a standard set of goods and services in different countries

Two factors help companies determine the growth potential of foreign markets: purchasing power and foreign competitors. **Purchasing power** is measured by comparing the relative cost of a standard set of goods and services in different countries. Earlier in the chapter we noted that a Coke costs $2.30 in Tokyo. But because a Coke only costs about $1.00 in the United States, the average American would have more purchasing power. Purchasing power is surprisingly strong in countries like Mexico, India, and China, which have low average levels of income. This is because consumers still have money to spend after paying for basic living expenses, such as food, shelter, and transportation, which are very inexpensive in those countries. To illustrate, the average Chinese household spends only 5 percent of household income on basic living expenses, while the average American household spends 45 percent to 50 percent.[68] Because basic living expenses are so small in China, Mexico, and India, purchasing power is strong, and millions of Chinese, Mexican, and Indian consumers increasingly have extra money to spend on what they want, in addition to what they need.

Consequently, countries with high and growing levels of purchasing power are good choices for companies looking for attractive global markets. As shown in Exhibit 8.6, Coke has found that the per capita consumption of Coca-Cola, or how many Cokes a person drinks per year, rises directly with purchasing power. For example, in Eastern

---

**EXHIBIT 8.6**

HOW CONSUMPTION OF COCA-COLA VARIES WITH PURCHASING POWER AROUND THE WORLD

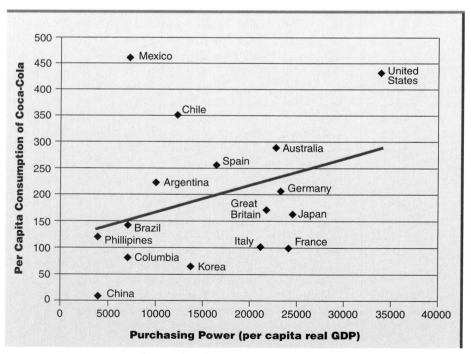

**Sources:** "GDP—Per Capita," *The World Factbook.* [Online] Available http://www.cia.gov/cia/publications/factbook/fields/gdp_-_per_capita.html, 15 September 2001. "Operations Review: Selected Market Results," *The Coca-Cola Company 2000 Annual Report.* [Online] Available http://annualreport2000.coca-cola.com/operations/selected.html, 15 September 2001.

Europe, as countries began to embrace capitalism after the fall of communism, per capita consumption of Coke increased from 20 to 31 Cokes in just two years, and, now, more than a decade later, it is at 46 Cokes per year.[69]

The second part of assessing growing global markets is analyzing the degree of global competition, which is determined by the number and quality of companies that already compete in foreign markets. Before deciding to invest in Europe, American theme park companies like Disney and Six Flags sent teams to scout the competition. Throughout Europe, they found older theme parks like Tivoli Gardens in Copenhagen, Denmark, which had been entertaining European families since 1843. They found older facilities, gentile rides, and shows (ballet, jazz, and symphonies) usually associated with cultural districts rather than theme parks. So, over the last decade, a half-dozen brand new, American-style theme parks—wild rides, fireworks, cotton candy, lively song-and-dance shows, and American food—were built across Europe, and another four are still under construction. Though it took a few years to make it happen, the new theme parks, such as Universal Studios Port Aventura near Barcelona, Spain, and Six Flags Belgium, have been extremely successful. In fact, Disneyland Paris has become the single biggest tourist destination in Europe.[70]

### 5.2 Choosing an Office/Manufacturing Location

Companies do not have to establish an office or manufacturing location in each country they enter. They can license, franchise, or export to foreign markets, or they can serve a larger region from one country. Thus, the criteria for choosing an office/manufacturing location are different from the criteria for entering a foreign market.

Rather than focusing on costs alone, companies should consider both qualitative and quantitative factors. Two key qualitative factors are work force quality and company strategy. Work force quality is important because it is often difficult to find workers with the specific skills, abilities, and experience that a company needs to run its business. Work force quality is one reason that many companies doing business in Europe locate their customer call centers in the Netherlands. As shown in Exhibit 8.7, workers in the Netherlands are the most linguistically gifted in Europe, with 73 percent speaking two languages, 44 percent speaking three languages, and 12 percent speaking four languages. Of course, with call center employees who speak more languages, call centers located in the Netherlands can handle calls from more countries and generally employ 30 to 50 percent fewer employees than those located in other parts of Europe. Another advantage of locating a call center in the Netherlands is that 60 percent of call center workers have university or advanced degrees in technology or management.[71]

EXHIBIT 8.7

QUALITY OF NETHERLANDS WORKFORCE FOR CALL CENTER JOBS

**Source:** "Fact Sheet, Call Center Solutions: How Call Centers Can Work for You," *The Netherlands Foreign Investment Agency*. [Online] Available http://www.nfia.com/html/solution/fact.html, 15 September 2001.

A company's strategy is also important when choosing a location. For example, a company pursuing a low-cost strategy may need plentiful raw materials, low-cost transportation, and low-cost labor. A company pursuing a differentiation strategy (typically a higher priced, better product or service) may need access to fine-quality materials and a highly skilled and educated work force.

Quantitative factors, such as the kind of facility being built, tariff and nontariff barriers, exchange rates, and transportation and labor costs, should also be considered when choosing an office/manufacturing location. Regarding the kind of facility being built, a real estate specialist in company location decisions said, "If it's an assembly plant, a company might be inclined to look for incentives that would subsidize its hiring. With a distribution facility, an adequate transportation network will likely be critical. A corporate headquarters will need a good communications network, a multilingual labor force, and easy access by air. On the other hand, a research and development operation will require proximity to a high-tech infrastructure and access to good universities."

Exhibit 8.8 shows *Fortune* magazine's rankings for the world's top cities for global business. This information is a good starting point if your company is trying to decide where to put an international office or manufacturing plant.

### 5.3 Minimizing Political Risk

When managers think about political risk in global business, they envision burning factories and riots in the streets. Although political events such as these receive dramatic and extended coverage from the press, the political risks that most companies face

---

### EXHIBIT 8.8

#### WORLD'S BEST CITIES FOR BUSINESS

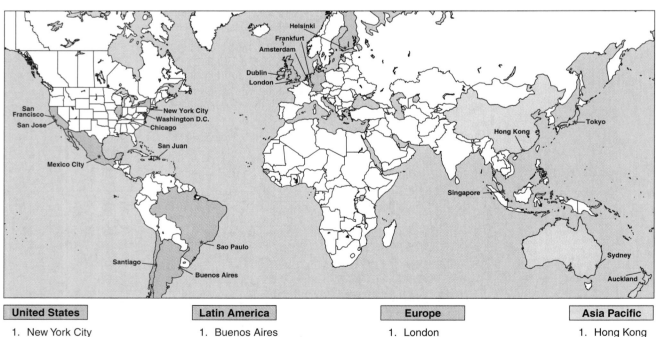

| United States | Latin America | Europe | Asia Pacific |
|---|---|---|---|
| 1. New York City | 1. Buenos Aires | 1. London | 1. Hong Kong |
| 2. San Francisco | 2. San Juan | 2. Frankfurt | 2. Sydney |
| 3. Chicago | 3. Mexico City | 3. Helsinki | 3. Singapore |
| 4. Washington D.C. area | 4. Sao Paulo | 4. Amsterdam | 4. Auckland |
| 5. San Jose | 5. Santiago | 5. Dublin | 5. Tokyo |

**Source:** M. Borden, "The Best Cities for Business: Big, Established, Monied Metropolises—With a Tech Twist—Top FORTUNE's Annual Ranking at the Turn of the Century," *Fortune*, 27 November 2000, 218. C. Murphy, "Winners of the World," *Fortune*, 27 November 2000, 232.

# "headline news"

## Are Starbucks' Expansion Plans Overcaffeinated?

In 1999, Howard Schultz, founder and CEO of Starbucks, announced to Wall Street his plan to transform the coffee giant into an Internet lifestyle portal. Analysts thought he was drunk on his own Venti Mocha Lattes, and the company's stock plummeted.

It didn't take long for Schultz to wake up and smell his own coffee. Now concentrating on its core business, the company has experienced phenomenal growth in a relatively short period of time. With only 17 stores at the end of 1987, Starbucks now boasts over 3,800 stores, half of which opened in a two-year period. International expansion is a big part of this.

Starbucks opened its first overseas store in Toyko in 1996. Now Starbucks has more than 200 stores in Japan and is well on its way to reaching its goal of 500 Japanese stores by 2004. The ambitious Japanese plan is part of Starbucks' overall goal of launching over 800 outlets in the Pacific Rim. Korea is also a main component of this plan. By the end of 2001, 32 Starbucks coffee shops thrived in Korea, 20 percent of Starbucks' goal of 150 shops by 2005. With those 32 shops, Starbucks controls 40 percent of Korea's specialty coffee market, and that number is expected to improve as the company begins to add more middle-aged customers to its core customer base of younger (mid-twenties and younger) coffee drinkers.

The Pacific Rim, however, is not the only bean in the blend. Starbucks is also aggressively expanding in the Middle East, New Zealand, and Europe. The British have long succumbed to the charms of Starbucks, but continental Europe may be a tougher nut to crack. The first store opened there in Zurich in 2001, and Starbucks' new stores in Germany and France soon followed, with taste-sensitive Italy lagging behind.

Still, some countries are worried, and charges of cultural imperialism are being bantered about. A Chinese newspaper criticized Starbucks for operating a kiosk in Bejing's Forbidden City. The chamber of commerce in Trieste, home of one of Italy's most prominent coffee companies, formed an association of historic cafés to seek protection. "Whatever is coming from the States—Cokes, hamburgers—it always seems like an invasion," says an official of the Trieste chamber. In Seoul, Starbucks opened up shop in the Insadong area of the city, famous for Korean an-

tiques and crafts. Even though the company sign is in Korean—unlike the standard board in English posted throughout the world—owners of other shops in the district were upset. They posted signs of their own reading, "Starbucks' invasion of Korea's pride, Insadong." The French just scoff. "An American chain," laughs the barman of the Bar du Marché in Paris. "We are unique! This is Paris!"

When expanding into new countries, Starbucks always seeks a local business partner. (For example, in Japan, it's Sazaby; in Korea, Shinsegae Company.) Before a full-blown expansion in an overseas market, Starbucks tests its formula in a handful of trendy districts. New baristas go to Seattle for a 13-week training course. Once the pilot stores prove successful, only then does Starbucks open stores by the dozens. Even though the coffee menu doesn't change, the food menu conforms to local tastes. The stores themselves are not even identical, each respecting the architecture of the building it occupies.

Howard Behar, president of Starbucks International, couldn't be more pleased with the fact that his division is profitable two years ahead of schedule, and he won't even rule out Italy. "Italy didn't create coffee," Behar says. "Nobody owns coffee." It may be that nobody owns coffee, but Starbucks sure has a lock on it—in North America and, more and more, around the world—with 4,700 stores selling $4.90 Venti Cappuccinos. That's a lot of latte.

1. *What are the risks to Starbucks' aggressive global expansion plans?*

**Sources:** C. Mee-young, "Starbucks Likely to Expand Asia Plan," *Reuters English News Service,* 23 August 2001, *WSJ Interactive,* http://www.wsj.com. "Starbucks Coffee Japan, Ltd.," *The Food Institute Report,* 19 March 2001, 6. Info-Trac Article A72522778. "Starbucks Expansion Continues," *The Food Institute Report,* 19 February 2001, 3. Info-Trac Article A71018604. "Starbucks Launches Café, Looks Towards International Expansion," *The Food Institute Report,* 14 September 1998. Info-Trac Article A53105388. "Trouble Brewing: To Perk Up Sales, Starbucks Has Big Plans to Expand on the Internet and Overseas," *Newsweek,* 19 June 1999, 40. Info-Trac Article A55145746. D. J. Yang, "An American (Coffee) in Paris—and Rome," *U.S. News & World Report,* 19 February 2001, 47. Info-Trac Article A70397036.

**political uncertainty**
the risk of major changes in political regimes that can result from war, revolution, death of political leaders, social unrest, or other influential events

**policy uncertainty**
the risk associated with changes in laws and government policies that directly affect the way foreign companies conduct business

usually will not be covered as breaking stories on CNN. However, the negative consequences of ordinary political risk can be just as devastating to companies that fail to identify and minimize those risks.[72]

When conducting global business, companies should attempt to identify two types of political risk: political uncertainty and policy uncertainty.[73] **Political uncertainty** is associated with the risk of major changes in political regimes that can result from war, revolution, death of political leaders, social unrest, or other influential events. **Policy uncertainty** refers to the risk associated with changes in laws and government policies that directly affect the way foreign companies conduct business. This is the most common form of political risk in global business and perhaps the most frustrating. For example, the government of the People's Republic of China now requires foreign companies to indicate the type of software they use to encrypt and protect data transfers on the Internet. This could range from basic Web browsers, such as Netscape and Internet Explorer, to standard email clients like Microsoft Outlook. Companies must let the Chinese government know which employees use such encryption software, the locations of their computers, their email addresses, and telephone numbers. Plus, "no organization or individual can sell foreign commercial encryption products," including the routers and servers that are the backbone of the Internet, all of which use encryption software. Patrick Power, director of China operations for the U.S. China Business Council, said, "This is sending the wrong message to foreign investors. The foreign business community is deeply concerned." If strictly enforced, many technology companies will have to quit selling basic technologies in China, despite selling them everywhere else. Furthermore, many worry that such information will be used by the Chinese government to spy on businesses to uncover proprietary business knowledge or secrets. Many businesses that rely on these basic software tools (i.e., browsers and email) may choose to relocate offices outside of China to maintain security.[74]

Several strategies can be used to minimize or adapt to the political risk inherent to global business. An *avoidance strategy* is used when the political risks associated with a foreign country or region are viewed as too great. If firms are already invested in high-risk areas, they may divest or sell their businesses. If they have not yet invested, they will likely postpone their investment until the risk shrinks. Exhibit 8.9 (p. 289) provides two lists from the International Country Risk Guide and the Coplin-O'Leary Risk Ratings of the countries who are the most and least politically risky. The following factors, which are used to compile these ratings, would indicate greater political risk: government instability, poor socioeconomic conditions, internal or external conflict, military involvement in politics, religious and ethnic tensions, foreign debt as a percent of gross domestic product, exchange rate instability, and high inflation.[75] An avoidance strategy would likely be used for many of the 10 riskiest countries shown in Exhibit 8.9, but would certainly not be needed for the 10 least risky countries. Risk conditions and factors change, so be sure to make risk decisions with the latest available information from resources such as the PRS Group, **http://www.prsgroup.com**, which supplies information about political risk to 80 percent of *Fortune 500* companies.

*Control* is an active strategy to prevent or reduce political risks. Firms using a control strategy will lobby foreign governments or international trade agencies to change laws, regulations, or trade barriers that hurt their business in that country.

Another method for dealing with political risk is *cooperation*, which makes use of joint ventures and collaborative contracts, such as franchising and licensing. Although cooperation does not eliminate political risk of doing business in a country, it does limit the risk associated with foreign ownership of a business. For example, a German company forming a joint venture with a Chinese company to do business in China may structure the joint venture contract so that the Chinese company owns 51 percent or more of the joint venture. Doing so qualifies the newly formed joint venture as a Chinese company and exempts it from Chinese laws that apply to foreign-owned businesses.[76]

## Review 5
### Finding the Best Business Climate

The first step in deciding where to take your company global is finding an attractive business climate. Be sure to look for a growing market where consumers have strong purchasing power and foreign competitors are weak. When locating an office or manufacturing facility, consider both qualitative and quantitative factors. In assessing political risk, be sure to examine political uncertainty and policy uncertainty. If the location you choose has considerable political risk, you can avoid it, try to control the risk, or use a cooperation strategy.

EXHIBIT 8.9

POLITICAL RISK: THE 10 RISKIEST AND 10 LEAST RISKY COUNTRIES

| INTERNATIONAL COUNTRY RISK GUIDE | COPLIN-O'LEARY RISK RATINGS |
| --- | --- |
| **TEN RISKIEST COUNTRIES** | **TEN RISKIEST COUNTRIES** |
| 1. Sierra Leone | 1. Ecuador |
| 2. Yugoslavia | 2. Iraq |
| 3. Somalia | 3. Cuba |
| 4. Guinea-Bissau | 4. Russia |
| 5. Zimbabwe | 5. Myanmar |
| 6. Congo, Democratic Republic | 6. Sudan |
| 7. Iraq | 7. Vietnam |
| 8. Moldova | 8. Cameroon |
| 9. Korea, D.P.R. | 9. Pakistan |
| 10. Liberia | 10. Nigeria |
| **TEN LEAST RISKY COUNTRIES** | **TEN LEAST RISKY COUNTRIES** |
| 1. Singapore | 1. Switzerland |
| 2. Norway | 2. Bulgaria |
| 3. Switzerland | 3. Singapore |
| 4. Luxembourg | 4. Belgium |
| 5. Netherlands | 5. Ireland |
| 6. Finland | 6. Finland |
| 7. Brunei | 7. Austria |
| 8. Denmark | 8. Canada |
| 9. Canada | 9. Netherlands |
| 10. Sweden | 10. United Kingdom |

**Source:** "Top Ranked Countries," *The PRS Group.* [Online] Available http://www.prsgroup.com/, 16 September 2001 or http://www.countrydata.com.

## 6. Becoming Aware of Cultural Differences

Some of the more interesting and amusing aspects of global business are the unexpected confrontations that people have with cultural differences, "the way they do things over there." For example, as part of a class assignment in global business, a high-school class in Dearborn, Michigan, and a high-school class in Valle, Spain, agreed to form a global "joint venture." The two classes agreed that the U.S. students would buy Spanish products from the Spanish high school students and resell them at a profit to other American students. Likewise, the Spanish students would purchase American products from the American students and then resell them at a profit to their Spanish friends. Now, what to buy from each other? The American students decided to buy giant beach towels showing teenaged Spanish lovers. One of the towels showed a boy helping his girlfriend remove her shirt. Another showed him unzipping her jeans. In Spain's culture, which is much more relaxed about sexuality than American culture, no one gives these towels a second thought. Of course, despite protestations of censorship, the U.S. high school teacher vetoed the towels as too suggestive.[77]

However, U.S. sensitivities about sexual issues are nothing compared to those in Iran's Islamic culture. All Iranian advertising must be approved by the conservative (at least from an American perspective) Ministry of Islamic Guidance, whose job is to prevent anything of a sexual or Western nature from being displayed. For example, a

A veiled Muslim woman travels past a large billboard advertising a film that catalogues the plight of a middle-class Cairo family as it tries to come to terms with the pregnancy of its teenage daughter. The film captures the prevailing mood of contemporary urban Egypt struggling to balance tradition and modernity, religion and science.

**national culture**
the set of shared values and beliefs that affects the perceptions, decisions, and behavior of the people from a particular country

**290**

billboard ad for women's underwear consisted of a picture of a green box with nothing more than the words "soft and delicate" written on it. Not surprisingly, no one knew what the ad was about. Despite approval by the Ministry of Islamic Guidance, billboards displaying giant red lips, which were used to advertise Goldstar televisions from South Korea, were burned down twice by Iranians who felt the ad was too sexual.[78]

**National culture** is the set of shared values and beliefs that affects the perceptions, decisions, and behavior of the people from a particular country. The first step in dealing with culture is to recognize that there are meaningful differences in national cultures. Geert Hofstede has spent the last 20 years studying cultural differences in 53 different countries. His research shows that there are five consistent cultural dimensions across countries: power distance, individualism, masculinity, uncertainty avoidance, and short-term versus long-term orientation.[79]

*Power distance* is the extent to which people in a country accept that power is distributed unequally in society and organizations. In countries where power distance is weak, such as Denmark and Sweden, employees don't like their organizations or their bosses to have power over them or to tell them what to do. They want to have a say in decisions that affect them. As shown in Exhibit 8.10, Russia and China, with scores of 95 and 80, are much stronger in power distance than Germany (35), the Netherlands (38), and the United States (40).

*Individualism* is the degree to which societies believe that individuals should be self-sufficient. In individualistic societies, employees put loyalty to themselves first, and loyalty to their company and work group second. The United States (91), the Netherlands (80), France (71), and Germany (67) are the strongest in individualism, while West Africa (20), China (20), and Indonesia (14) are the weakest.

*Masculinity* and *femininity* capture the difference between highly assertive and highly nurturing cultures. Masculine cultures emphasize assertiveness, competition,

EXHIBIT 8.10

## HOFSTEDE'S FIVE CULTURAL DIMENSIONS

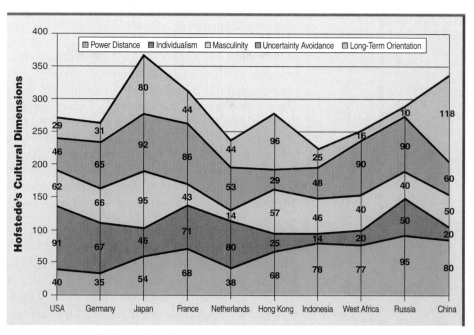

**Source**: Geert H. Hofstede, "Cultural Constraints in Management Theories," *Academy of Management Executive 7* no. 1 (1993): 81-94.

material success, and achievement, whereas feminine cultures emphasize the importance of relationships, modesty, caring for the weak, and quality of life. Japan (95), Germany (66), and the United States (62) have the most masculine orientations, while the Netherlands (14) has the most feminine orientation.

The cultural difference of *uncertainty avoidance* is the degree to which people in a country are uncomfortable with unstructured, ambiguous, unpredictable situations. In countries with strong uncertainty avoidance, like Greece and Portugal, people are aggressive, emotional, and seek security (rather than uncertainty). Japan (92), France (86), West Africa (90), and Russia (90) are strongest in uncertainty avoidance, while Hong Kong (29) is the weakest.

*Short-term/long-term orientation* addresses whether cultures are oriented to the present and seek immediate gratification, or to the future and defer gratification. Not surprisingly, countries with short-term orientations are consumer driven, whereas countries with long-term orientations are savings driven. China (118) and Hong Kong (96) have very strong long-term orientations, while West Africa (16) Indonesia (25), the United States (29), and Germany (31) have very strong short-term orientations.

Cultural differences affect perceptions, understanding, and behavior. Recognizing cultural differences is critical to succeeding in global business. However, Hofstede said we should recognize that these cultural differences are based on averages—the average level of uncertainty avoidance in Portugal, or the average level of power distance in Argentina, and so forth. Hofstede said, "If you are going to spend time with a Japanese colleague, you shouldn't assume that overall cultural statements about Japanese society automatically apply to this person."[80]

After becoming aware of cultural differences, the second step is deciding how to adapt your company to those cultural differences. Unfortunately, studies investigating the effects of cultural differences on management practice point more to difficulties than to easy solutions. One problem is that different cultures will probably perceive management policies and practices differently. For example, blue-collar workers in France and Argentina, all of whom performed the same factory jobs for the same multinational company, perceived the company's corporate-wide safety policy differently.[81] French workers perceived that safety wasn't very important to the company, but Argentine workers thought that it was. The fact that something as simple as a safety policy can be perceived differently across cultures shows just how difficult it can be to standardize management practices across different countries and cultures.

Another difficulty is that cultural values are changing, albeit slowly, in many parts of the world. The fall of communism in Eastern Europe, the former Soviet Republic, and the broad economic reforms in China have combined to produce sweeping changes on two continents in the last decade. Thanks to increased global trade resulting from GATT and other regional free trade agreements, major economic transformations are also underway in India, Mexico, Central America, and South America. The difficulty that companies face when trying to adapt management practices to cultural differences is that they may be basing their adaptations on outdated and incorrect assumptions about a country's culture.

### Review 6
#### Becoming Aware of Cultural Differences

National culture is the set of shared values and beliefs that affects the perceptions, decisions, and behavior of the people from a particular country. The first step in dealing with culture is to recognize meaningful differences, such as power distance, individualism, masculinity, uncertainty avoidance, and short-term/long-term orientation. Cultural differences should be carefully interpreted, because they are based on averages, not individuals. Adapting managerial practices to cultural differences is difficult, because policies and practices can be perceived differently in different cultures. Another difficulty is that cultural values may be changing in many parts of the world. Consequently, when companies try to adapt management practices to cultural differences, they need to be sure that those changes are not based on outdated assumptions about a country's culture.

## 7. Preparing for an International Assignment

Around a conference table in a large U.S. office tower, three American executives sat with their new boss, Mr. Akiro Kusumoto, the newly appointed head of a Japanese firm's American subsidiary, and two of his Japanese lieutenants. The meeting was called to discuss ideas for reducing operating costs. Mr. Kusumoto began by outlining his company's aspiration for its long-term U.S. presence. He then turned to the budgetary matter. One Japanese manager politely offered one suggestion, and an American then proposed another. After gingerly discussing the alternatives for quite some time, the then exasperated American blurted out: "Look, that idea is just not going to have much impact. Look at the numbers!" In the face of such bluntness, uncommon and unacceptable in Japan, Mr. Kudumoto fell silent. He leaned back, drew air between his teeth, and felt a deep longing to return east. He realized his life in this country would be filled with many such jarring encounters and lamented his posting to a land of such rudeness.[82]

Mr. Kusumoto is a Japanese **expatriate**, someone who lives and works outside his or her native country. The cultural shock that he was experiencing is common. The difficulty of adjusting to language, cultural, and social differences is the primary reason that so many expatriates fail in overseas assignments. For example, it is estimated that 10 to 45 percent of American expatriates sent abroad by their companies will return to the United States before they have successfully completed their international assignments.[83] Of those who do complete their international assignments, as many as 30 to

**expatriate**
someone who lives and works outside his or her native country

50 percent are judged by their companies to be no better than marginally effective.[84]

*Since the average cost of sending an employee on an international assignment can run between $200,000 and $1.2 million, failure in those assignments can be extraordinarily expensive.[85] However, the chances for a successful international assignment can be increased through 7.1 language and cross-cultural training and 7.2 consideration of spouse, family, and dual-career issues.*

### 7.1 Language and Cross-Cultural Training

The purpose of predeparture language and cross-cultural training is to reduce the uncertainty that expatriates feel, the misunderstandings that take place between expatriates and natives, and the inappropriate behaviors that expatriates unknowingly commit when they travel to a foreign country. Indeed, simple things like using a phone, finding a public toilet, asking for directions, knowing how much things cost, exchanging greetings, or ordering in a restaurant can become tremendously complex when expatriates don't know a foreign language or a country's customs and cultures. In his book *Blunders in International Business*, David Ricks tells the story of an American couple in Asia. After a walk with their dog, the Americans had dinner at a local restaurant. Since the waiters and waitresses did not speak English, they ordered by pointing to items on the menu. Because their dog was hungry, they pointed to the dog and to the kitchen. The waiter had trouble understanding, but finally took the dog to the kitchen. The American couple assumed that this meant the dog could not be fed in the dining room, but was going to be fed in the kitchen. Unfortunately, to the couple's dismay, the waiter and the chef returned later to proudly show them how well they had cooked the poodle.

Expatriates who receive predeparture language and cross-cultural training make faster adjustments to foreign cultures and perform better on their international assignments (and are better at ordering in foreign restaurants!).[86] Unfortunately, only a third of the managers who go on international assignments receive any kind of predeparture training. This is somewhat surprising given the failure rates for expatriates and the high cost of those failures. It is also surprising because, with the exception of some language courses, predeparture training is not particularly expensive nor difficult to provide.

For example, a U.S. electronics manufacturer prepared workers for assignments in South Korea by using a combination of documentary training, cultural simulations, and field experiences. *Documentary training* focuses on identifying the critical specific differences between various cultures. Trainees learned that U.S. subordinates will normally look their boss in the eye, whereas Korean subordinates avoid eye contact unless their boss asks them a question. Trainees also learned about other differences between the United States and South Korea, such as how to greet business people, how to behave toward South Korean women or elders, and how to respect privacy.

After learning critical specific differences in documentary training, trainees participated in a *cultural simulation,* in which they had the opportunity to practice adapting to cultural differences. For example, the trainees participated in a simulated cocktail party in which company managers who had spent time in South Korea posed as South Korean business people and their spouses. Trainees practiced South Korean greetings, introductions, and communication styles, and then received feedback on their performance.

*Field simulation* training, a technique made popular by the U.S. Peace Corps, places trainees in an ethnic neighborhood for three to four hours to talk to residents about cultural differences. In this instance, trainees explored a nearby South Korean neighborhood, talking to shopkeepers and people on the street about South Korean politics, family orientation, and day-to-day living practices.

# WhatReallyWorks

## Cross-Cultural Training

Most expatriates will tell you that cross-cultural training helped them adjust to foreign cultures. However, anecdotal data is not as convincing as systematic studies. Twenty-one studies, with a combined total of 1,611 participants, have examined whether cross-cultural training affects the self-development, perceptions, relationships, adjustment, and job performance of expatriates. Overall, they show that cross-cultural training works extremely well in most instances.

### Self-Development

When you first live in another country, you must learn how to make decisions that you took for granted in your home country: how to get to work, how to get to the grocery, how to pay your bills, and so on. If you've generally been confident about your self and your abilities, an overseas assignment can challenge that sense of self. However, cross-cultural training helps expatriates deal with these and other challenges. Expatriates who receive cross-cultural training are 79 percent more likely to report healthy psychological well-being and self-development than those who don't receive training.

*Psychological Well-Being & Self Development*

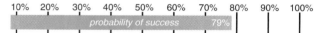

### Fostering Relationships

One of the most important parts of an overseas assignment is establishing and maintaining relationships with host nationals. If you're in Brazil, you need to make friends with Brazilians. However, many expatriates make the mistake of making friends only with expatriates from their home country. In effect, they become social isolates in a foreign country. They work and live there, but as much as they can, they speak their native language, eat their native foods, and socialize with other expatriates from their home country. Cross-cultural training makes a big difference in whether expatriates establish relationships with host nationals. Expatriates who receive cross-cultural training are 74 percent more likely to have established such relationships.

*Fostering Relationships with Native Citizens*

### Accurate Perceptions of Culture

Another thing that distinguishes successful from unsuccessful expatriates is that they understand the cultural norms and practices of the host country. For example, many Americans do not understand the famous pictures they have seen of Japanese troops turning their backs to American military commanders on V-J day, the day that Japan surrendered to the United States in World War II. Americans viewed this as a lack of respect, when in fact in Japan, turning one's back in this way is a sign of respect. Cross-cultural training makes a big difference in the accuracy of perceptions concerning host country norms and practices. Expatriates who receive cross-cultural training are 74 percent more likely to have accurate perceptions.

*Accurate Cultural Perceptions*

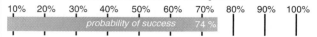

### Rapid Adjustment

New employees are most likely to quit in the first six months, because this initial period requires the most adjustment: learning new names, new faces, new procedures, and new information. It's tough. Of course, expatriates have a much tougher time making a successful adjustment, because besides learning new names, faces, procedures, and information, expatriates are learning new languages, new foods, new customs, and often new lifestyles. Expatriates who receive cross-cultural training are 74 percent more likely to make a rapid adjustment to a foreign country.

*Rapid Adjustment to Foreign Cultures and Countries*

### Job Performance

It's good that cross-cultural training improves self-development, fosters relationships, improves the accuracy of perceptions, and helps expatriates make rapid adjustments to foreign cultures. However, from an organizational standpoint, the ultimate test of cross-cultural training is whether it improves expatriates' job performance. The evidence shows that cross-cultural training makes a significant difference in expatriates' job performance. This is not quite as big a difference as for the other factors. However, it is estimated that cross-cultural training for 100 managers could bring about $390,000 worth of benefits to a company, nearly $4,000 per manager. This is an outstanding return on investment, especially when you consider the high rate of failure for expatriates. Expatriates who have received cross-cultural training are 71 percent more likely to have better on-the-job performance than those who did not receive cross-cultural training.

*On-the-Job Performance*

**Source:** S.P. Deshpande & C. Viswesvaran, "Is Cross-Cultural Training of Expatriate Managers Effective: A Meta-Analysis," *International Journal of Intercultural Relations* 16, no. 3 (1992): 295-310.

## 7.2 Spouse, Family, and Dual-Career Issues

At the request of his company, "Sam" and his wife "Janet" moved to London for Sam's international assignment. Their plush apartment was across the street from the world-famous Harrods department store and was also close to London's best parks, museums, and gardens. The company also paid them enough to afford full-time childcare. By most accounts, Sam and Janet should have had a wonderful experience in London. However, Janet was miserable. Consequently, so was Sam. Their social life was active but revolved around Sam's business clients. Janet was lonely. She missed her job, which she gave up to come to London. She also missed her friends in Atlanta. Sam and Janet divorced after returning to the United States.[87]

Not all international assignments turn out so badly for expatriates and their families, but the evidence clearly shows that how well an expatriate's spouse and family adjust to the foreign culture is the most important factor in determining the success or failure of an international assignment.[88] Unfortunately, despite its importance, there has been little systematic research on what does and does not help expatriates' families successfully adapt. However, a number of companies have found that adaptability screening and intercultural training for families can lead to more successful overseas adjustment.

*Adaptability screening* is used to assess how well managers and their families are likely to adjust to foreign cultures. For example, Prudential Relocation Management's international division has developed an "Overseas Assignment Inventory" to assess spouse and family's open-mindedness, respect for others' beliefs, sense of humor, and marital communication. Likewise, AMP, based in Pennsylvania, conducts extensive psychological screening on expatriates and their spouses when making international assignments. But adaptability screening is not just companies assessing employees; it can also mean that employees screen international assignments for desirability. Since more employees are becoming aware of the costs of international assignments (spouses having to give up or change jobs, children having to change schools, having to learn a new language, etc.), some companies are willing to pay for a preassignment trip for the employee and his or her spouse to investigate the country *before* accepting the international assignment.[89]

Language and cross-cultural training for families is just as important as language and cross-cultural training for expatriates. In fact, it may be more important, because unlike expatriates, whose professional jobs often shield them from the full force of a country's culture, spouses and children are often fully immersed in foreign neighborhoods and schools. Households must be run, shopping must be done, and bills must be paid. Likewise, children and their parents must deal with different cultural beliefs and practices about discipline, alcohol, dating, and other issues. For example, 15-year-old Holly Timmons from Lilburn, Georgia, fought with her parents about moving to China when her dad's company, John Deere, gave him a new assignment. In tears, she told him, "No, Dad. I want you to go. I just don't see why I have to go, too." Holly began to feel better about moving to China after the company arranged for her to talk to Cee Kung, a 17-year-old Canadian already attending Holly's new school in China. Holly learned that she would be able to play on the girls' basketball team, buy her favorite jeans (for less), and still be able to get U.S. fast food. Holly, who had thoughts about running away from home to avoid the move, said that talking to Cee Kung "took a lot of my fears away. I was worried that school would be a lot harder [in Beijing]. If I hadn't gotten to talk to Cee . . . I probably would have done something crazy the night before we got [ready] to go."[90] In short, language and cross-cultural training is just as important for families of expatriates as it is for expatriates themselves. Language and cross-cultural training can help reduce uncertainty about how to act and decrease misunderstandings between expatriates, their families, and locals.

## Review 7
### Preparing for an International Assignment

Many expatriates return prematurely from international assignments because of poor performance. However, this is much less likely to happen if employees receive language

## What Really Happened?

At the beginning of the chapter, you learned that it took Wal-Mart only four decades to become the dominant retailer in the United States. However, you also learned that Wal-Mart's success in the United States did not automatically translate to other countries. Despite its initial missteps, Wal-Mart continued to invest in international markets. Let's find out what really happened to see if Wal-Mart became more successful in other places around the world.

### Initial successes came easily in Canada, but not in Mexico. So which countries should Wal-Mart enter?

An attractive global-business climate positions a company for easy access to growing markets, chooses effective but cost-efficient places to build offices or manufacturing sites, and minimizes the political risk to the company. In particular, it's important to look for a growing market where consumers have strong purchasing power and foreign competitors are weak. So on the basis of these criteria, which countries did Wal-Mart enter?

Besides Mexico (see the discussion on NAFTA and free trade agreements below), Wal-Mart chose to enter Germany, Britain, and Brazil (see the next question for a discussion of Brazil). While Germany's general retail markets are competitive, competition is very weak in food retailing. In general, German supermarkets don't have cheaper store brands (like Wal-Mart Cola), do a poor job of managing and reordering inventory, and, unlike Wal-Mart, struggle to keep costs low. Keith Wills, an industry analyst with Goldman Sachs, said, "Germany is a backward, nearly old-fashioned market in terms of retail

development. If I were a U.S. retailer interested in Europe, I would absolutely go to Germany first. It is way behind others in Europe, and it has room for a lot of people." Wal-Mart entered Germany by buying two German retailers, Wertkauf GmbH and Spar Handels AG, both of which have hypermarket stores (retail and groceries combined). Wal-Mart is still losing money in Germany, but expects profits soon. Now that Wal-Mart is in charge of these stores, Manfred Siwek, a German shopper, said, "It's much better than before. Prices are lower, and the service is friendlier."

And, for similar reasons (i.e., lack of strong competition), Wal-Mart has also expanded aggressively into the United Kingdom, paying $10.84 billion to acquire ASDA Group PLC and its 229 stores. Furthermore, it has cut prices to U.S. levels, which are typically much lower than in the United Kingdom. Wal-Mart also says it will add 27,000 ASDA jobs over the next five years because of extremely strong sales growth in existing stores and construction of new ASDA stores.

### While Carrefour is now the leading international retailer, just how fierce a competitor will Carrefour be in the long run when lined up against Wal-Mart's experience and deep pockets? In other words, what kind of competition is Wal-Mart likely to find when it crosses swords directly with Carrefour?

The most important factor in an attractive international business climate is access to a growing market. Two factors help companies determine the growth potential of foreign markets: purchasing power and foreign competitors. Purchasing power is measured by comparing the relative cost of a standard set of goods and services in different countries. The greater the purchasing power in a country, the better the potential business climate, but only if there isn't strong business competition, too. Therefore, the second part of assessing growing global markets is to analyze the degree of global competition, which is determined by the number and quality of companies that already compete in particular foreign markets.

While Wal-Mart's incredible success in the United States gives it the resources and deep pockets that it will need to be successful internationally, Carrefour is its fiercest competitor, period. (Carrefour is presently the largest *international* retailer in the world. Wal-Mart is the largest retailer in the world due to its domestic U.S. sales, not its relatively small international sales.) For example, in Brazil, customers see little difference between the standard goods and prices offered at Wal-Mart and Carrefour. Because Carrefour has so many stores in South America (and Brazil), its purchasing power with suppliers is as good, if not better, than Wal-Mart's. Therefore, in Brazil Wal-Mart finds it difficult to gain business by cutting prices. Tomas Gallegos, who managed a Wal-Mart store in Texas before coming to Brazil, says, "Geez, is the competition aggressive." In fact, just hours after Wal-Mart distributes fliers advertising bargains, Carrefour offers the same products for just a few cents less. And because it has been in international markets for years, if not decades, before Wal-Mart, its large number of stores gives Carrefour the capability to match Wal-Mart's prices worldwide. Finally, Carrefour is better at some things. Carrefour's CEO said, "They [Wal-Mart] learn from us in fresh food and merchandising," the latter meaning the attractive display of retail items.

**What impact, if any, are free trade agreements likely to have on Wal-Mart's international expansion?**

In addition to GATT, the General Agreement on Tariffs and Trade, the second major development in the historic move toward reduction of trade barriers has been the creation of regional trading zones, in which tariff and nontariff barriers are reduced or eliminated for countries within the trading zone.

Today, Wal-Mart has 520 stores, $9 billion in revenues, and $1.1 billion in profits in Mexico. It's fair to say that it wouldn't have achieved this success in Mexico without the advantages of free trade provided by NAFTA. Here's why.

Before NAFTA, in the early 1990s, Wal-Mart had to use expensive middlemen to distribute goods to its stores. Furthermore, it sometimes took months for deliveries to clear customs at the border. Paperwork for imports into Mexico was torturous and burdensome. And Mexican officials often pressured Wal-Mart managers for bribes. All of this is different with NAFTA. Take the example of Act II popcorn, a product that Wal-Mart buys from U.S.-based ConAgra. Wal-Mart has ConAgra pack the popcorn in Spanish-labeled packages and then ships the popcorn to a Wal-Mart distribution center on the Mexican boarder in Laredo, Texas, where it is picked up and taken across the border by a Mexican trucking company hired by Wal-Mart. The next day, the popcorn is on the shelf at Sam's and Wal-Mart stores for the same price that the popcorn costs in the United States. By contrast, Wal-Mart's competitors are still forced to buy Act II popcorn through more expensive Mexican distributors. Or take the example of 29-inch Sony Wegas flat-screen TVs from Japan, which, thanks to a 23 percent tariff (since it was imported from Japan), Wal-Mart sold for $1,600 each. However, because of NAFTA, Sony built a new Wegas factory in Mexico, which allows it to ship the TVs duty free anywhere in the United States, Canada, or Mexico.

With shipping costs now next to nothing and the 23 percent tariff eliminated, today Wal-Mart sells the 29-inch, flat-screen TVs for $600, or approximately what they sell for in the United States.

**Finally, should Wal-Mart focus on global consistency, doing around the world what it does in the United States, or should it adapt what it sells throughout the world (like Carrefour)?**

Global consistency means that when a multinational company has offices, manufacturing plants, and distribution facilities in different countries, it will run those offices, plants, and facilities based on the same rules, guidelines, policies, and procedures. Managers at company headquarters value global consistency, because it simplifies decisions. Local adaptation is a company policy to modify its standard operating procedures to adapt to differences in foreign customers, governments, and regulatory agencies. Local adaptation is typically more important to local managers who are charged with making the international business successful in their countries. Multinational companies struggle to find the correct balance between global consistency and local adaptation. If companies focus too much on local adaptation, they run the risk of losing the cost efficiencies and productivity that result from using standardized rules and procedures throughout the world. If they lean too much towards global consistency, they run the risk of using management procedures poorly suited to particular countries' markets, cultures, and employees.

Early on, Wal-Mart focused too little on local adaptation and too much on global consistency. This was evident in the way in which it ordered store items that its U.S. customers would want, but not necessarily what its international customers would want. For example, when Wal-Mart first entered Mexico, it filled its stores with ice skates, riding lawn mowers, fishing tackle, and clay pigeons for skeet shooting. And when Mexican store managers managed to sell all of these items at heavy discounts, Wal-Mart's computerized inventory system compounded the mistake by automatically reordering all of these "sold out" items. Wal-Mart made the same mistake in South America, ordering live trout, American footballs, cordless tools, and leaf blowers, none of which South Americans use. But Wal-Mart learned to listen to local managers. Consequently, sushi, soccer balls, and feijoada (a mix of beef, pork, and black beans) are now available in its South American stores.

However, because of its vast purchasing power around the world, Wal-Mart hasn't given up completely on global consistency. Why? Franciso Martinez, chief financial officer of Comercial Mexicana SA, Wal-Mart's key rival in Mexico, says, "I buy 20,000 plastic toys, and Wal-Mart buys 20 million. Who do you think gets them cheaper?" So, to systematically take advantage of this purchasing power, Wal-Mart has formed a new global sourcing team of 100 people who work together at its Bentonville, Arkansas, headquarters to buy common global products like laundry detergent. The risk, of course, is that the global sourcing team may overlook local tastes and preferences. However, if these standard products are accepted by the locals, they'll be much, much cheaper than anything Wal-Mart's competition, even Carrefour, which is one-third Wal-Mart's size, has to offer. For instance, one person on the global sourcing team could buy Tide detergent from Procter & Gamble for all of Wal-Mart's 4,000 stores around the world. Jay Allen, a Wal-Mart spokesperson, said, "There are economies of scale all the way around. We want to make sure we're getting the best deal. Global sourcing is a big opportunity for us. [But] we're not there yet."

**Sources:** W. Boston, & A. Zimmerman, "Wal-Mart Girds for Major German Expansion—U.S. Retail Giant to Stress Internal Growth in Push to Add 50 New Stores," *The Wall Street Journal*, 20 July 2000, A21. "Wal-Mart Stores, Inc.: Retailer Expects to Open Six New Stores in China," *The Wall Street Journal*, 4 June 1988, B10. "Wal-Mart Stores Inc.: New

297

Supermarkets Expected to Add 27,000 British Jobs," *The Wall Street Journal*, 11 January 2000. J. Friedland, & L. Lee, "Foreign Aisles: The Wal-Mart Way Sometimes Gets Lost in Translation Overseas—Chain Changes Some Tactics to Meet Local Tastes; Competitors Are Tough—But Brazil's 'Market Is Ripe'," *The Wall Street Journal*, 8 October 1997, A1. M. Jordan, "Wal-Mart Gets Aggressive about Brazil—New Neighborhood Store Is Latest Step

to Seize Bigger Market Share," *The Wall Street Journal*, 25 May 2001, A8. L. Lee, & C. Rohwedder, "Wal-Mart to Acquire German Retailer, Moving into Europe for the First Time," *The Wall Street Journal*, 19 December 1997, A2. D. Luhnow, "Crossover Success: How NAFTA Helped Wal-Mart Reshape the Mexican Market—Lower Tariffs, Retail Muscle Translate into Big Sales; Middlemen Are Squeezed—'Like Shopping in the U.S.'," *The Wall Street*

*Journal*, 31 August 2001, A1. F. McCarthy, "Chimera Wal-Mart Struggles Abroad," *Economist*, 18 May 2000. R. Tomlinson, "Who's Afraid of Wal-Mart? Not Carrefour. The World's Second-Largest Retailer Is Bounding Ahead of the Bentonville Behemoth in Most Markets Outside North America. But Can the French Titan Hold Its Lead?" *Fortune*, 26 June 2000, 186.

## Key Terms

APEC (Asia-Pacific Economic Cooperation) *(274)*

ASEAN (Association of South East Nations) *(274)*

cooperative contract *(278)*

country of manufacture *(268)*

country of origin *(268)*

customs classification *(271)*

direct foreign investment *(265)*

expatriate *(292)*

exporting *(277)*

franchise *(279)*

FTAA (Free Trade Area of the Americas) *(274)*

GATT (General Agreement on Tariffs and Trade) *(271)*

global business *(264)*

global new ventures *(283)*

government import standards *(270)*

joint venture *(279)*

licensing *(278)*

Maastricht Treaty of Europe *(272)*

multinational corporation *(268)*

NAFTA (North American Free Trade Agreement) *(274)*

national culture *(290)*

nontariff barriers *(269)*

policy uncertainty *(287)*

political uncertainty *(287)*

protectionism *(269)*

purchasing power *(284)*

quota *(269)*

regional trading zones *(272)*

strategic alliance *(279)*

subsidies *(270)*

tariff *(269)*

trade barriers *(269)*

voluntary export restraints *(270)*

wholly owned affiliates *(282)*

world gross national product *(266)*

## What Would You Do-II

### JCPenney and Brazil

"Here we go again" was your initial thought as you read the memo just delivered from the CEO's office. As the president of international operations with JCPenney for the last seven years, you've opened stores in several overseas markets. However, recent economic conditions both at home and abroad have forced your company to relax its pursuit of expansion and focus on strengthening sales and reducing costs. At the beginning of the year, JCPenney announced that it would be closing 44 stores across the nation and reducing the workforce by more than 5,500. As a result, you were dumbfounded by the tone of the memo claiming that the latest data from a recent marketing survey shows that Brazil appears to be a haven for retailers and that your unit should look into a proposed expansion for that market. The survey, which was attached to the memo, shows that despite conditions of economic and political uncertainty in the area, Latin America is a largely untapped market. Latin America has approximately 270 million active consumers, compared to only 180 million in the United States. Additionally, Latin America appears to have one of the youngest populations in the world, with a median age of 24 years compared to 36 years in the United States. The most alluring part of the survey illustrated that the average sales per meter for shopping centers in Latin America is $4,174, compared to only $2,528 in the United States.

From what you've just read, you agree that this might be an area worth considering. Unfortunately, you know that it can't be that easy. International JCPenney stores haven't fared well in the past. In fact, not long ago, JCPenney began to divest itself of some international stores, including stores in Chile, Indonesia, and the Philippines. The question that immediately pops into your mind is "What went wrong with the previous international stores?" If this data is reflective of the area, the two JCPenney stores in Chile should have prospered. Unfortunately, due to labor problems and poor sales, JCPenney pulled out of the Chilean market at the end of 1999.

So would you recommend moving into the retail market in Brazil based on the data presented in the marketing survey? Why or why not? Assuming you do propose to enter the market, what information would you acquire and what form of global business would you recommend to ensure that this global venture succeeds?

**As the president of international operations for JCPenney, what would you do?**

**Sources:** M. Jordan, "Penney Blends Two Business Cultures," *The Wall Street Journal*, 5 April 2000. "Latin America Remains a Retail Market Untapped by U.S., Analysts Say," *Knight-Ridder/Tribune Business News*, 5 October 1999. G. Brown, "New Tricks for an Old Chilean Store," *Business Week*, 26 June 2000. "Penney Faces Charge of Five Cents a Share to Shed Chile Store," *The Wall Street Journal*, 7 October 1999.

## Management Decisions

### Hearts at Home and Going Native

In the last five years, your company has considerably improved the way in which it prepares employees for international assignments. Except in emergencies, employees are typically given four to five months' notice before being sent abroad. Employees, their spouses, and their families are carefully screened and selected. Moreover, all employees and their families receive two months of extensive language and cultural training before beginning an international assignment. Although these steps have greatly improved the success and performance of your company's expatriates, you're still running into two serious problems.

Problem number one is the expatriate who "goes native." Expatriates who go native are strongly committed to doing what is right for the foreign office, even at the expense of ignoring parent company policy. For example, Gary, a manager who had spent half his 15 years with a company on three different overseas assignments, stated, "My first commitment is to the unit here [in France]. In fact, half the time I feel as if corporate is a competitor I must fight rather than a benevolent parent I can look to for support." While he had only six months remaining on his French assignment, Gary had already asked the home office for an extended stay.

Problem number two is the expatriate whose heart is still at home. Consider Earl, who, after two decades with the parent company, was promoted to managing director of European head-

quarters. This was Earl's first international assignment. Consequently, his allegiance was first and foremost to the parent company rather than the European office. In fact, when his two years as managing director are up, he is going straight back to the states.

Expatriates who go native make it very difficult for companies to achieve global consistency in their operations. Expatriates whose hearts are at home ignore the importance of local adaptation. As one senior manager put it, "How can we get expatriate managers who are committed to the local overseas operation during their international assignments, but who remain loyal to the parent firm?"

#### Questions

1. What steps would you take to reduce the chances that an expatriate would go native?
2. What steps would you take to reduce the chances that an expatriate would leave his or her heart at home?
3. What steps could be taken to encourage expatriates to develop a dual allegiance to the parent company *and* the overseas operation?

**Sources:** J.S. Black, "Serving Two Masters: Managing the Dual Allegiance of Expatriate Employees," *Sloan Management Review,* Summer 1992, 61-71. H.B. Gregersen, "Commitments to a Parent Company and a Local Work Unit during Repatriation," *Personnel Psychology* 45 (1992): 29-54. J. Kaufman, "In China, John Aliberti Gets VIP Treatment; At Home, Grass Grows in the Patio," *The Wall Street Journal,* 19 November 1996, A1.

## Management Decisions

### Men or Women, Who Goes Abroad?

As the regional vice president of sales for a multinational corporation with offices located in almost every continent on the globe, you've made some tough decisions throughout your career. Unfortunately, you feel that today's decision might possibly be your hardest yet. Sales in New Zealand have been dropping lately and you've been charged with choosing one of your best salespersons to take over as the new regional manager for that area. Two potential salespeople immediately come to mind. Laura has been a sales representative for the North American region for seven years. She has a master's degree in business administration and was a foreign exchange student in Sidney, Australia, for two years during college. She is extremely competent, knowledgeable, and confident. Adam has been with the North American region for only four years, but also served three and one-half years as a sales representative with the European region of a well-known competitor. He too is qualified, with a master's degree in business and considerable experience in international assignments. Since the primary language spoken in New Zealand is English, language will not be a factor in your decision. You truly believe that either candidate would succeed in this position and work to improve conditions in the New Zealand region.

However, a conversation with a colleague from a few days back lingers in the back of your mind. You and John, a fellow V.P., were discussing international assignments and the subject of sending women abroad came up. John stated that from his experience, women did not make good expatriate candidates for several reasons. One, they are not as willing as males to take assignments in foreign countries due to family obligations and other personal reasons. Second, women are typically not as successful as males in foreign assignments because they may be viewed as being inferior to males in certain cultures. Lastly, John stated that women could more likely be subjected to discrimination or sexual harassment issues than a male candidate. Although you initially agreed with John and his perception, you later concluded that times have changed: After all, the world is a much smaller and more culturally diverse place today than it was when you went on your first international assignment.

You can't stop thinking about John's comments. As you weigh the pros and cons of each candidate, you wonder if Laura would be accepted by her New Zealand counterparts. As the vice president of sales, whom would you choose as the next New Zealand regional manager, Laura or Adam? Why?

**Source:** L. Stroh, "Why Are Women Left at Home: Are They Unwilling to Go on International Assignments?", *Journal of World Business,* Fall 2000.

# Develop Your Managerial Potential

## Are you Nationminded or Worldminded?

There are three parts to this assignment. Step 1: Complete the questionnaire shown below. Step 2: Determine your score. Step 3: Develop a plan to increase your global managerial potential.

**Step 1:** Use the six-point rating scale to complete the questionnaire shown below.

### Rating Scale

| | |
|---|---|
| 6 Strongly Agree | 3 Mildly Disagree |
| 5 Agree | 2 Disagree |
| 4 Mildly Agree | 1 Strongly Disagree |

____ 1. Our country should have the right to prohibit certain racial and religious groups from entering it to live.

____ 2. Immigrants should not be permitted to come into our country if they compete with our own workers.

____ 3. It would be a dangerous procedure if every person in the world had equal rights which were guaranteed by an international charter.

____ 4. All prices for exported food and manufactured goods should be set by an international trade committee.

____ 5. Our country is probably no better than many others.

____ 6. Race prejudice may be a good thing for us because it keeps many undesirable foreigners from coming into this country.

____ 7. It would be a mistake for us to encourage certain racial groups to become well educated because they might use their knowledge against us.

____ 8. We should be willing to fight for our country without questioning whether it is right or wrong.

____ 9. Foreigners are particularly obnoxious because of their religious beliefs.

____ 10. Immigration should be controlled by an global organization rather than by each country on its own.

____ 11. We ought to have a world government to guarantee the welfare of all nations irrespective of the rights of any one.

____ 12. Our country should not cooperate in any global trade agreements which attempt to better world economic conditions at our expense.

____ 13. It would be better to be a citizen of the world than of any particular country.

____ 14. Our responsibility to people of other races ought to be as great as our responsibility to people of our own race.

____ 15. A global committee on education should have full control over what is taught in all countries about history and politics.

____ 16. Our country should refuse to cooperate in a total disarmament program even if some other nations agreed to it.

____ 17. It would be dangerous for our country to make international agreements with nations whose religious beliefs are antagonistic to ours.

____ 18. Any healthy individual, regardless of race or religion, should be allowed to live wherever he or she wants to in the world.

____ 19. Our country should not participate in any global organization that requires that we give up any of our national rights or freedom of action.

____ 20. If necessary, we ought to be willing to lower our standard of living to cooperate with other countries in getting an equal standard for every person in the world.

____ 21. We should strive for loyalty to our country before we can afford to consider world brotherhood.

____ 22. Some races ought to be considered naturally less intelligent than ours.

____ 23. Our schools should teach the history of the whole world rather than of our own country.

____ 24. A global police force ought to be the only group in the world allowed to have armaments.

____ 25. It would be dangerous for us to guarantee by international agreement that every person in the world should have complete religious freedom.

____ 26. Our country should permit the immigration of foreign peoples, even if it lowers our standard of living.

____ 27. All national governments ought to be abolished and replaced by one central world government.

____ 28. It would not be wise for us to agree that working conditions in all countries should be subject to international control.

____ 29. Patriotism should be a primary aim of education so our children will believe our country is the best in the world.

____ 30. It would be a good idea if all the races were to intermarry until there was only one race in the world.

____ 31. We should teach our children to uphold the welfare of all people everywhere, even though it may be against the best interests of our own country.

____ 32. War should never be justifiable, even if it is the only way to protect our national rights and honor.

**Step 2:** Determine your score by entering your response to each survey item below, as follows. In blanks that say *regular score,* simply enter your response for that item. If your response was a 4, place a 4 in the *regular score* blank. In blanks that say *reverse score,* subtract your response from 6 and enter the result. So if your response was a 4, place a 2 (6 − 4 = 2) in the *reverse score* blank.

| | | | |
|---|---|---|---|
| 1. reverse score | ____ | 12. reverse score | ____ |
| 2. reverse score | ____ | 13. regular score | ____ |
| 3. reverse score | ____ | 14. regular score | ____ |
| 4. regular score | ____ | 15. regular score | ____ |
| 5. regular score | ____ | 16. reverse score | ____ |
| 6. reverse score | ____ | 17. reverse score | ____ |
| 7. reverse score | ____ | 18. regular score | ____ |
| 8. reverse scorez | ____ | 19. reverse score | ____ |
| 9. reverse score | ____ | 20. regular score | ____ |
| 10. regular score | ____ | 21. reverse score | ____ |
| 11. regular score | ____ | 22. reverse score | ____ |

23. regular score \_\_\_\_
24. regular score \_\_\_\_
25. reverse score \_\_\_\_
26. regular score \_\_\_\_
27. regular score \_\_\_\_

28. reverse score \_\_\_\_
29. reverse score \_\_\_\_
30. regular score \_\_\_\_
31. regular score \_\_\_\_
32. regular score \_\_\_\_

Total your scores from items 1–16 \_\_\_\_
Total your scores from items 17–32 \_\_\_\_
Add together to compute *total score* \_\_\_\_
Higher scores show greater worldmindedness.

**Step 3:** Develop a plan to increase your global managerial potential.

People don't change from being nationminded to world-minded overnight. Below you'll find the outlines of a plan to increase your worldmindedness. You need to fill in the details to make it work. This plan is based on foreign languages, living overseas, global news and television, and your openness to the different cultural experiences available right where you live!

**3A. Language.** How many languages do you speak fluently? If you're an average American student, you speak one language, American English. Develop a plan to become fluent in another language. Specify the courses you would need to take to become conversationally fluent. A minimum of two years is recommended. Even better is minoring in a language! What courses would you have to take to complete a minor?

**3B. Living overseas.** Develop a plan to study overseas. List the facts for two different overseas study programs available at your university or another university. Be sure to specify how long the program lasts, whether you would receive language training, where you would live, the activities in which you would participate, and any other important details.

**3C. Global news and television.** Another way to increase your worldmindedness is to increase the diversity of your news sources. Most Americans get their news from local TV and radio, or from the major networks, ABC, NBC, and CBS. Luckily, you don't have to leave the country to gain access to foreign news sources. Furthermore, you don't have to speak a foreign language. Many foreign newspapers and television and radio shows are presented in English. List the foreign newspapers and television and radio shows available to you where you live. Hint: Check your university library, CNN, PBS, and the Internet. Be sure to indicate where you can find the newspapers, the day and time the shows are on, and whether the newspapers or TV shows are in English or a foreign language.

**3D. Local cultural experiences.** Many American students wrongly assume that they have to travel overseas to gain exposure to foreign cultures. Fortunately, many American cities and universities are rich in such experiences. Ethnic neighborhoods, restaurants, festivals, foreign films, and art displays, along with ethnic Americans who continue to live and celebrate their heritage, present ample opportunities to sample and learn about foreign cultures right here in our own backyards. Specify a plan of foreign restaurants, ethnic neighborhoods, and cultural events that you could attend this year.

**Sources:** R. W. Boatler, "Study Abroad: Impact on Student Worldmindedness," *Journal of Teaching in International Business* 2, no. 2 (1990):17-13. R.W. Boatler, "Worldminded Attitude Change in a Study Abroad Program: Contact and Content Issues," *Journal of Teaching in International Business* 3, no. 4 (1992): 59-68. H. Lancaster, "Learning to Manage in a Global Workplace (You're on Your Own)," *The Wall Street Journal*, 2 June 1998, B1. D.L. Sampson & H.P. Smith, "A Scale to Measure Worldminded Attitudes," *Journal of Social Psychology* 45, 1957, 99-106.

## Study Tip

Review your class notes. Do they give you enough information? If they are lacking, visit your campus study center to learn how to take good notes. For this chapter, you have an Xtra! CNN clip with case and solutions on your CD. Watch the segment on the World Trade Organization and work hour regulations and then read the case.

CHAPTER

9

# Organizational Strategy

## What Would You Do?

**General Motors Headquarters, Detroit, Michigan.** When General Motors (GM) dominated the U.S. auto industry and the U.S. economy, people used to say that "What was good for General Motors was good for the country." With GM now holding a 28 percent market share, down from 38 percent ten years ago and from 50 percent twenty-five years ago, nobody says that any more.

Many of GM's products appeal to older rather than younger buyers who, by contrast, look first to newly designed, foreign-made cars. For example, in the 20- to 29-year-old age bracket for first-time car buyers, Volkswagen has scored with its two-year-old retro Beetle and the market-leading Jetta (a four-year-old design), while Toyota is marketing the two and one-half-year-old Echo, and Honda is selling a completely redesigned Civic (an 18-month old design). By contrast, GM is still trying to woo first-time buyers with Saturn cars based on an 11-year-old design and Chevy Cavaliers based on a seven-year-old design.

With the largest car and truck lineup in the auto industry, including seven divisions (Cadillac, Chevrolet, Buick, GMC, Oldsmobile, Pontiac, and Saturn) and 80 different car models in the United States alone, GM just doesn't have the resources to redesign and update its cars as often as its competitors. As a result, some of GM's best and most profitable divisions, Cadillac and Oldsmobile, are now struggling. Cadillac, which had dominated the market for luxury cars for six decades, is now sixth in the market behind Toyota's Lexus, BMW, Mercedes-Benz, Ford's Lincoln, and Honda's Acura. And despite hundreds of millions of dollars in advertising (i.e., "This isn't your father's Oldsmobile."), Oldsmobile sales, once at a million cars per year, have dropped by 80 percent to just over 200,000 cars annually.

Competitive conditions in the auto industry certainly won't make things any easier for GM. The biggest problem is that automakers now have the capacity to make 80 million cars a year, more than double the worldwide demand. And with Japanese and European auto manufacturers planning to build 11 more factories in the United States over the next five years, things will get even worse. For now, rather than shutting down factories and laying off workers, GM is propping up sales by cutting prices, by offering rebates worth thousands of dollars, and by offering cut-rate financing. For example, to spur Oldsmobile sales, GM is offering consumers no money down, no monthly payments, and no interest for 12 months. Competitors joke that Oldsmo-bile is the perfect car if your doctor has just told you that you've only got a year to live. The problem with this approach is that it not only destroys current profits (auto manufacturers often make most of their profits on auto financing); it hurts future profits by encouraging customers to buy cars now, reducing profitable sales at a future date.

If GM is to compete in the long term, it must develop a strategy that addresses these key questions. First, how can GM create a sustainable advantage over its competitors? Second, are there potential business opportunities among the obvious and numerous threats to GM business? Finally, what should GM's new strategy be? Should it be growth, stability, or retrenchment/recovery?

**If you were in charge of GM's strategy, what would you do?**

**Sources:** G. White, "Hitting the Brakes: In Order to Grow, GM Finds That the Order of the Day Is Cutbacks—For CEO Rick Wagoner, Killing Off Oldsmobile Was Just the Beginning—Banking on Hot New Cars," *The Wall Street Journal*, 18 December 2000, A1. G. White, J. White, & S. Freeman, "What's a Cool Car? The Question Is Driving U.S. Auto Makers Wild—Beyond Focus Groups, Officials Hang Out in Video Arcades and Chat Up Snowboarders," *The Wall Street Journal*, 9 August 2000, B1. G. White, "Half-Full Tank: After Gloomy Winter, Big-Three Car Makers Grow Warily Optimistic—Sales Data Suggest Economy Isn't Spooking Consumers to Extent Industry Feared—Minivan for a Baby on the Way," *The Wall Street Journal*, 4 April 2001, A1.

J. White, G. White, & N. Shirouzu, "Passing Era: Soon, The Big Three Won't Be, As Foreigners Make Inroads in U.S.—Toyota Draws Near Chrysler as Investments Pay Off; Dealers Shift Loyalties—'A Life-Threatening Disease'," *The Wall Street Journal*, 13 August 2001, A1. A. Taylor, III. & F. Garcia, "Bumpy Roads for Global Automakers: Forget This Year's Record Sales—DaimlerChrysler Is in Chaos, And Price Wars Are Eating Profits at Most Other Companies—Life in the Fast Lane Is About to Get Rougher," *Fortune*, 28 December 2000, 278.

After years of weakening brands and dwindling market share, General Motors President and CEO Rick Wagoner (left, pictured with Ron Zarrella, president of GM North America) announced that the floundering Detroit automaker would kill its Oldsmobile brand over several years. In addition, GM will reduce salaried employment by 10 percent in North America and Europe.

AP PHOTO/PAUL SANCYA

In Chapter 4, you learned that *strategic plans* are overall company plans that clarify how a company intends to serve customers and position itself against competitors over the next two to five years. General Motors' problems show that picking the wrong strategic plan can have devastating consequences. This chapter begins with an in-depth look at how managers create and use strategies to obtain a sustainable competitive advantage. Then you will learn the three steps of the strategy-making process. Next, you will learn about corporate-level strategies that help managers answer the question: What business or businesses should we be in? You will then examine the industry-level competitive strategies that help managers determine how to compete successfully within a particular line of business. The chapter finishes with a review of the firm-level strategies of direct competition and entrepreneurship.

## Basics of Organizational Strategy

It should have been a time of celebration for Steve Case, founder and CEO of America Online (AOL), the leading online computer company, which provides services such as email, Internet access, chat rooms, and so forth. Under Case's guidance, AOL had grown from being one of the smallest online service providers to the largest in less than a decade. The last few years, in particular, had been especially good, because AOL quadrupled its customer base and achieved consistently good profits. In fact, AOL's success enabled it to buy the much larger Time Warner, which owns Time Magazine (among others), HBO, Cinemax, CNN, and numerous providers of cable television and high-speed Internet services. However, several years later, AOL's stock price is just one-third of what it was before becoming AOL Time Warner.[1] And while AOL now has 25 million subscribers (MSN, the Microsoft Network, and Earthlink, its two closest competitors, trail with 6 million and 5 million subscribers each), AOL's market share among Internet service providers has actually shrunk from above 52 percent to 40 percent![2]

How can a company like AOL, which dominates an industry, keep its competitive advantage? What steps can AOL and other companies take to better manage the strategy-making process?

*After reading the next two sections, you should be able to*
1. *explain the components of sustainable competitive advantage and why it is important.*
2. *describe the steps involved in the strategy-making process.*

## 1. Sustainable Competitive Advantage

**resources**
the assets, capabilities, processes, information, and knowledge that an organization uses to improve its effectiveness and efficiency, to create and sustain competitive advantage, and to fulfill a need or solve a problem

An organization's **resources** are the assets, capabilities, processes, information, and knowledge that the organization controls. Firms use their resources to improve organizational effectiveness and efficiency. Resources are critical to organizational strategy, because they can help companies create and sustain an advantage over competitors.[3]

**competitive advantage**
providing greater value for customers than competitors can

Organizations can achieve a **competitive advantage** by using their resources to provide greater value for customers than competitors can. For example, prior to its recent troubles, AOL created competitive advantage for itself and value for its customers through its simplicity. To get online with AOL, you put its software disk in your computer, typed "Install," and followed the directions (enter your name, credit card number, etc.) as the software automatically dials AOL's free sign-up number.[4] In less than five minutes, you were an AOL subscriber with 10 to 100 free hours of full access. Furthermore, the software's simple-to-understand menus, icons, and instructions made AOL's service easy and intuitive, even for those who knew little about computers. AOL customer George LeMien of Bethel, Connecticut, said, "I like [AOL's] ease of use, especially how it helps guide me around the Net."[5] Other online services were more difficult to use.

**sustainable competitive advantage**
a competitive advantage that other companies have tried unsuccessfully to duplicate and have, for the moment, stopped trying to duplicate

A competitive advantage becomes a **sustainable competitive advantage** when other companies cannot duplicate the value a firm is providing to customers. Importantly, sustainable competitive advantage is not the same as a long-lasting competitive advantage, though companies obviously want a competitive advantage to last a long time. Instead, a competitive advantage is *sustained* if that advantage still exists after competitors have tried unsuccessfully to duplicate the advantage and have, for the moment, stopped trying to duplicate it. For example, CompuServe lost $100 million dollars trying to establish WOW!, an easy-to-use online service that was similar in ways to AOL. However, WOW!, which was supposed to give parents much more control over what their children could view online, only attracted 100,000 subscribers. Unable to duplicate America Online's success, CompuServe shut down WOW! less than a year after it began.[6] In fact, AOL now owns and runs CompuServe. Today, to compete with AOL, both MSN and Earthlink have created simple software interfaces, MSN Explorer and Earthlink 5.0, for much easier email, Web browsing, chat and messaging software, and file uploads and downloads. Two years in a row, CNET (**http://www.cnet.com**), one of the leading online sources of computer and technology information, has awarded Earthlink 5.0 its Editor's Choice Award.[7] So the competitive advantage that AOL created with its easy-to-use software has thus far been a sustainable competitive advantage. But that sustained competitive advantage may be slipping.

As shown in Exhibit 9.1, four conditions must be met if a firm's resources are to be used to achieve a sustainable competitive advantage. The resources must be valuable, rare, imperfectly imitable, *and* nonsubstitutable.

**valuable resource**
a resource that allows companies to improve efficiency and effectiveness

**Valuable resources** allow companies to improve their efficiency and effectiveness. Unfortunately, changes in customer demand and preferences, competitors' actions, and technology can make once-valuable resources much less valuable. For example, when America Online charged $9.95 a month for five online hours and $2.95 for every additional hour, it had sufficient resources, meaning phone lines, network computers, and available support staff, to successfully handle the business growth it was experiencing. However, when it first switched to a $19.95 flat-rate plan with unlimited connection hours, those once-valuable resources became an obstacle to efficiency and effectiveness, because they could not keep up with surging customer demand for online access.

**rare resource**
a resource that is not controlled or possessed by many competing firms

For sustained competitive advantage, valuable resources must also be rare resources. Think about it. How can a company sustain a competitive advantage if all of its competitors have similar resources and capabilities? Consequently, **rare resources**, resources

305

EXHIBIT 9.1

FOUR REQUIREMENTS FOR SUSTAINABLE COMPETITIVE ADVANTAGE.

| Valuable Resources | Rare Resources | Imperfectly Imitable Resources | Non-Substitutable Resources |

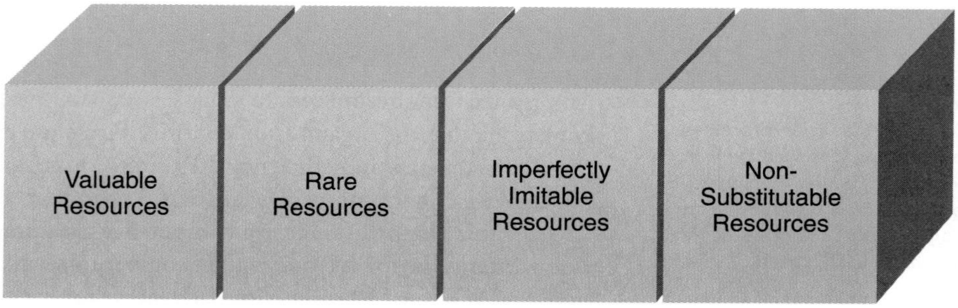

that are not controlled or possessed by many competing firms, are necessary to sustain a competitive advantage. When America Online first created the ability to automatically charge monthly bills to customers' credit cards, none of its competitors were offering this service. However, any competitive advantage gained from this was short-lived, because within months, CompuServe, Prodigy, and other online services and Internet providers soon had the same capability. What was initially a rare resource, the capability to bill to credit cards, had become commonplace.

**imperfectly imitable resource**
a resource that is impossible or extremely costly or difficult for other firms to duplicate

As the previous example shows, valuable, rare resources can create temporary competitive advantage. However, for sustained competitive advantage, other firms must be unable to imitate or find substitutes for those valuable, rare resources. **Imperfectly imitable resources** are impossible or extremely costly or difficult to duplicate. For example, despite numerous attempts by competitors, such as CompuServe, AOL's ease-of-use and simplicity has, thus far, been an imperfectly imitable resource. *PC Magazine* said, "AOL's graphical interface, with menus made up of single-click art icons, folders, and other documents, is a best-of-breed design. The total effect is coherent and easy to navigate. Some interface elements are even animated, adding still more visual appeal."[8] Indeed, over the first decade in the online service business, it was AOL's ease-of-use and intuitive design, shown in Exhibit 9.2, that helped it displace CompuServe and then Prodigy as industry leaders. However, its current competitors, Microsoft and its MSN Explorer (shown in Exhibit 9.3) and Earthlink and its Earthlink 5.0 software (shown in Exhibit 9.4 on page 308) are now much easier to use than before. Carefully compare AOL, MSN Explorer, and Earthlink 5.0 in Exhibits 9.2, 9.3, and 9.4, and you begin to see how AOL's imperfectly imitable resources, intuitive design and ease-of-use, aren't that different from its competitors anymore.

**nonsubstitutable resource**
a resource, without equivalent substitutes or replacements, that produces value or competitive advantage

Valuable, rare, imperfectly imitable resources can produce sustainable competitive advantage only if they are also **nonsubstitutable resources**, meaning that no other resources can replace them and produce similar value or competitive advantage. For example, as described above, the resource that has brought AOL its strongest competitive advantage is its simplicity and ease-of-use. In the online/Internet service business, this resource has proved valuable, rare, and imperfectly imitable. However, AOL's service and connectivity problems (i.e., constant busy signals) have made customers aware that local Internet Service Providers (ISPs) are potential substitutes for online access. ISPs do one thing—provide access to the Internet. That's it. Unlike AOL, there's no award-winning, easy-to-use software. (Typically, you have to download the software on your own.) And, ISPs generally don't offer extensive, proprietary content for members.

So what do local ISPs have in the way of resources than can substitute for everything AOL has to offer? First, most ISPs have direct links to Internet sites that allow their customers to download free, simple-to-use software for email and browsing the Web, the most popular tasks on the Internet. While not as easy to use as AOL, most people can be up and running within minutes of activating their Internet accounts. The second substitute for AOL's resources is the level of customer support that some local

306

EXHIBIT 9.2

AMERICAN ONLINE 6.0'S DESIGN INTERFACE

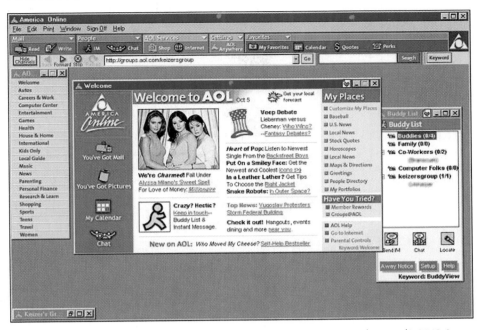

**Source:** "America Online 6.0," *Cnet.* [Online] Available http://www.cnet.com/internet/0-3762-8-4951560-8.html?tag=st.is.3762-8-4951560-7.SP.3762-8-4951560-8, 23 September 2001.

EXHIBIT 9.3

MSN EXPLORER'S DESIGN INTERFACE

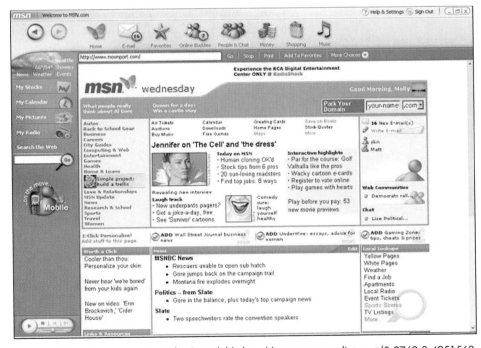

**Source:** "MSN Explorer," *Cnet.* [Online] Available http://www.cnet.com/internet/0-3762-8-4951560-11.html?tag=st.is.3762-8-4951560-9.SP.3762-8-4951560-11, 23 September 2001.

EXHIBIT 9.4

### EARTHLINK 5.0'S DESIGN INTERFACE

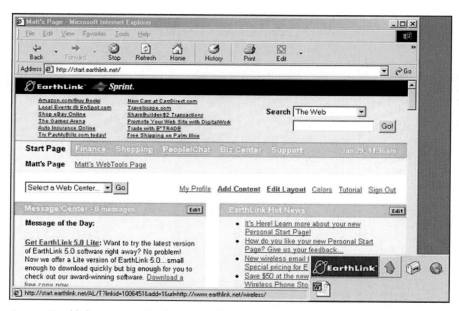

**Source:** "Earthlink 5.0," *Cnet*. [Online] Available, http://www.cnet.com/internet/0-3762-8-4951560-5.html?tag=st.is.3762-8-4951560-4.SP.3762-8-4951560-5, 23 September 2001.

ISPs provide. John "Zeke" Brumage, who runs Zeke's General Store Internet Services in Arizona, said, "My wife and I answer the phones 24 hours a day. It rings at the house and we call-forward to the cell phone when we're traveling." Likewise, Ed Fineran, president of Atlantech Online, in Silver Spring, Maryland, said, "When our customers call up, we typically know them by name."[9]

In summary, AOL's resources that provide customers with simplicity and ease-of-use have been valuable, rare, and imperfectly imitable. However, if customers decide that the Internet access provided by ISPs is an acceptable substitute, then AOL will not have a sustainable competitive advantage. Indeed, Exhibit 9.5 shows the results of *PC Magazine's* latest survey of Internet Service Provider (ISP) customers. Across the top and across the board, America Online customers were clearly the most dissatisfied, from initial setup to technical support to connections during evening hours to download speed and email service. In fact, another study indicated that 30 percent of AOL users plan to change ISPs in the next 12 months.[10]

## Review 1
### Sustainable Competitive Advantage

Firms can use their resources to create and sustain a competitive advantage, that is, to provide greater value for customers than competitors can. A competitive advantage becomes sustainable when other companies cannot duplicate the benefits it provides and have, for now, stopped trying. To provide a sustainable competitive advantage, the firm's resources must be valuable (capable of improving efficiency and effectiveness), rare (not possessed by many competing firms), imperfectly imitable (extremely costly or difficult to duplicate), and nonsubstitutable (competitors cannot substitute other resources to produce similar value).

## 2. Strategy-Making Process

*Companies use a strategy-making process to create strategies that produce sustainable competitive advantage.[11] Exhibit 9.6 displays the three steps of the strategy-making*

# EXHIBIT 9.5

## PC MAGAZINE SURVEY OF INTERNET SERVICE PROVIDER CUSTOMERS

⬆ Significantly better than average
● Average
⬇ Significantly worse than average

| | Overall satisfaction | Initial setup | Rates | Technical support | Connection during business hours | Connection during evening hours | Connects at the highest speed | Connection reliability | Speed of page downloads | E-mail service | Top reasons for choosing |
|---|---|---|---|---|---|---|---|---|---|---|---|
| **America Online (541 responses)** | ⬇ | ⬇ | ⬇ | ⬇ | ⬇ | ⬇ | ⬇ | ⬇ | ⬇ | ⬇ | Reputation, availability of local phone numbers, price |
| AT&T Worldnet (190) | ⬆ | ⬆ | ⬆ | ⬆ | ● | ● | ● | ● | ⬆ | ⬆ | Reputation, price, speed of access |
| **BellSouth Internet Services (73)** | ● | ● | ● | ● | ⬆ | ● | ● | ⬆ | ● | ● | Speed of access, price, reputation |
| EarthLink/Mindspring (333) | ● | ⬆ | ● | ⬆ | ● | ● | ● | ● | ⬇ | ● | Reputation, price, availability of local phone numbers |
| Excite@Home (376) | ⬆ | ● | ⬇ | ● | ⬆ | ⬆ | ⬆ | ⬆ | ⬆ | ● | Speed of access, price, recommendation from friend |
| Juno/Juno Web (66) | ⬇ | ● | ⬆ | ● | ⬇ | ⬇ | ⬇ | ⬇ | ⬇ | ● | Price, free/local calls for access, availability of local phone numbers |
| MSN Internet Access (163) | ⬇ | ⬇ | ⬇ | ● | ⬇ | ⬇ | ⬇ | ⬇ | ⬇ | ● | Reputation, price, availability of local phone numbers |
| Prodigy Internet (90) | ● | ● | ● | ● | ● | ● | ⬇ | ● | ⬇ | ● | Availability of local phone numbers, price, free/local calls for access |
| Quest Net (53) | ● | ● | ● | ● | ● | ● | ● | ⬆ | ⬆ | ● | Speed of access, price, availability of local phone numbers |
| Road Runner (250) | ⬆ | ⬆ | ⬇ | ⬆ | ⬆ | ⬆ | ⬆ | ⬆ | ⬆ | ● | Speed of access, price, reputation |
| Verizon Online (91) | ● | ⬇ | ● | ⬇ | ● | ● | ● | ● | ⬆ | ⬇ | Speed of access, price, availability of local phone numbers |
| Local ISPs (642) | ● | ⬆ | ⬆ | ⬆ | ● | ● | ● | ● | ⬇ | ⬆ | Price, availability of local phone numbers, free/local calls for access |
| **AVERAGE** | 7.6* | 6.9* | 6.9* | 7.1* | 8.4* | 7.9* | 7.2* | 7.8* | 6.9* | 7.9* | |

GREEN text denotes Readers' Choice

**Source:** B. Howard, M. Muchmore, & B. Gottesman, "14th Annual Reader's Survey: Service & Reliability, ISPs," *PC Magazine*, August 2001, 126.

# EXHIBIT 9.6

## THREE STEPS OF THE STRATEGY-MAKING PROCESS

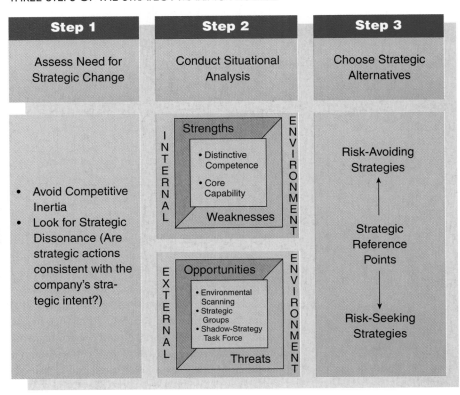

**Step 1** — Assess Need for Strategic Change
- Avoid Competitive Inertia
- Look for Strategic Dissonance (Are strategic actions consistent with the company's strategic intent?)

**Step 2** — Conduct Situational Analysis
- INTERNAL ENVIRONMENT: Strengths (Distinctive Competence, Core Capability) / Weaknesses
- EXTERNAL ENVIRONMENT: Opportunities (Environmental Scanning, Strategic Groups, Shadow-Strategy Task Force) / Threats

**Step 3** — Choose Strategic Alternatives
- Risk-Avoiding Strategies
- Strategic Reference Points
- Risk-Seeking Strategies

# WhatReallyWorks

## Strategy-Making for Firms, Big *and* Small

The strategy-making process (assessing the need for strategic change, conducting a situational analysis, and choosing strategic alternatives) is the method by which companies create strategies that produce sustainable competitive advantage. For years, it had been thought that strategy-making was something that only large firms could do well. It

was believed that small firms did not have the time, knowledge, or staff to do a good job of strategy-making. However, two meta-analyses indicate that strategy-making can improve the profits, sales growth, and return on investment of both big *and* small firms.

### Strategy-Making for Big Firms

There is a 72 percent chance that big companies that engage in the strategy-making process will be more profitable than big companies that don't. However, strategy-making not only improves profits, but also helps companies grow. Specifically, there is a 75 percent chance that big companies that engage in the strategy-making process will have greater sales and earnings growth than big companies that don't. Thus, in practical terms, the strategy-making process can make a significant difference in a big company's profits and growth.

**Strategic Planning & Profits for Big Companies**

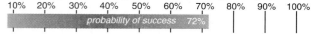

**Strategic Planning & Growth for Big Companies**

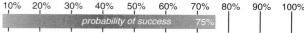

### Strategy-Making for Small Firms

Strategy-making can also improve the performance of small firms. There is a 61 percent chance that small firms that engage

in the strategy-making process will have more sales growth than small firms that don't. Likewise, there is a 62 percent chance that small firms that engage in the strategy-making process will have a larger return on investment than small companies that don't. Thus, in practical terms, the strategy-making process can make a significant difference in a small company's profits and growth, too.

**Strategic Planning & Sales Growth for Small Companies**

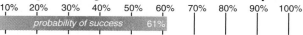

**Strategic Planning & Return on Investment for Small Companies**

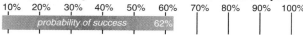

**Sources:** S. Hart & C. Banbury, "How Strategy-Making Processes Can Make a Difference," *Strategic Management Journal* 15 (1994): 251-269. C.C. Miller & L.B. Cardinal, "Strategic Planning and Firm Performance: A Synthesis of More Than Two Decades of Research," *Academy of Management Journal* 37 (1994): 1649-1665. C.R. Schwenk, "Effects of Formal Strategic Planning on Financial Performance in Small Firms: A Meta-Analysis," *Entrepreneurship Theory and Practice*, Spring 1993, 53-64.

process. Step one is to 2.1 assess the need for strategic change. Step two is to 2.2 conduct a situational analysis. Step three is to 2.3 choose strategic alternatives. Let's examine each of these steps in more detail.

### 2.1 Assessing the Need for Strategic Change

The external business environment is much more turbulent than it used to be. With customers' needs constantly growing and changing, and with competitors working harder, faster, and smarter to meet those needs, the first step in strategy-making is determining the need for strategic change. In other words, the company should determine whether it needs to change its strategy to sustain a competitive advantage.[12]

Determining the need for strategic change might seem easy to do, but in reality, it's not. There's a great deal of uncertainty in strategic business environments. Furthermore, top-level managers are often slow to recognize the need for strategic change, especially at successful companies that have created and sustained competitive advantages. Because

## Thinking Strategically? Be Foolish!

You've all heard "Don't be foolish! This is serious!" However, being foolish occasionally may actually be a good thing, because it encourages you to challenge conventional thinking and see things you might normally miss. For example, as a researcher at AT&T's Bell Labs, David Isenberg dressed as a court jester while holding a conference called "What If Minutes Were Free?" At the time, many in AT&T thought the conference foolish. But with the advent of free Internet phone calls, Isenberg no longer looks the fool. So next time you're thinking strategically, be foolish! It may help you and your company see the need for strategic change.

**Sources:** T. Petzinger, Jr., "A Smart Business Model Is Seen in a 'Stupid Network,' Somebody Had to Play the Fool, and David Isenberg Figured It Might as Well Be Him," *The Wall Street Journal Interactive Edition*, 20 February 1998.

**competitive inertia**
a reluctance to change strategies or competitive practices that have been successful in the past

**strategic dissonance**
a discrepancy between upper management's intended strategy and the strategy actually implemented by lower levels of management

**situational (SWOT) analysis**
an assessment of the strengths and weaknesses in an organization's internal environment and the opportunities and threats in its external environment

they are acutely aware of the strategies that made their companies successful, they continue to rely on them, even as the competition changes. In other words, success often leads to **competitive inertia**—a reluctance to change strategies or competitive practices that have been successful in the past.

For example, just a few years ago, no one in the cable TV industry believed that direct broadcast satellite dishes would threaten their business. With huge satellite dishes costing over $1,000, why would the 70 million Americans who already had cable TV in their homes pay more than $1,500 to install an unsightly ten-foot-diameter satellite dish in their yard to get the same number of channels that they could get from their local cable company for only a $50 installation fee and $50 a month? Managers of cable TV companies laughed that "DBS" (direct broadcast satellite) really stood for "Don't Be Stupid." However, now that satellite dishes are smaller (two feet in diameter), cost less than $150, and offer 200 channels, compared to the 40 or fewer channels available on most cable systems, no one who manages a cable company is laughing anymore. Indeed, over the last five years, DBS raised its market share from 6 percent to 20 percent by increasing the number of DBS subscribers from four to 16 million.[13]

So, besides being aware of the dangers of competitive inertia, what can managers do to improve the speed and accuracy with which they determine the need for strategic change? One method is to actively look for signs of strategic dissonance. **Strategic dissonance** is a discrepancy between upper management's intended strategy and the strategy actually implemented by the lower levels of management. Upper management sets overall company strategy, but middle- and lower-level managers must carry out the strategy. Middle- and lower-level managers are held directly responsible for meeting customers' needs and responding to competitors' actions. While strategic dissonance can indicate that these managers are not doing what they should to carry out company strategy, it can also mean that the intended strategy is out of date and needs to be changed.

For example, over the last five years, the Coca-Cola Company used a centralized strategy in which most key product and market decisions, such as which products should be sold in which markets, were made by those in or directly associated with Coke's Atlanta, Georgia, headquarters. And with headquarters running the show, the goal was to push sales of Coke's carbonated beverages to record levels worldwide. During that time, however, Coke's growth, which had been among the fastest of Fortune 500 companies, slowed tremendously. Profits dropped consistently for the first time in more than a quarter century. Coke's new CEO Doug Daft, who had previously headed Coke's Asia team, recognized the problem instantly. In Japan, which accounted for 20 percent of Coke's profits, Daft and his management team generated two-thirds of those profits by selling canned coffee and canned tea instead of Coke's leading carbonated drinks. So when he became CEO, Daft changed the focus from centralized control to local control and local decision making. Hundreds of people from Coke's headquarters have now been reassigned to local offices in countries throughout the world. Furthermore, as you learned in Chapter 8, Global Management, Daft replaced nine out of Coke's 10 top European managers, all of whom were Americans, with local, European managers who were more familiar with local tastes, cultures, and customs. Said Daft, "With the world changing more quickly than ever, we must move decision making closer to the local markets."[14]

Determining the need for strategic change is a difficult process, but can be improved by actively looking for signs of strategic dissonance, a difference between the intended strategy and what managers are actually doing.

### 2.2 Situational Analysis

A situational analysis can also help managers determine the need for strategic change. A **situational analysis**, also called a **SWOT analysis** for *strengths, weaknesses,*

311

*opportunities,* and *threats,* is an assessment of the strengths and weaknesses in an organization's internal environment and the opportunities and threats in its external environment.[15] Ideally, as shown in Step 2 of Exhibit 9.6, a SWOT analysis helps a company determine how to increase internal strengths and minimize internal weaknesses while maximizing external opportunities and minimizing external threats. A basic situational analysis of Kodak, the camera, film, and photo-processing company, shows this is not always easy to do. For most of the 20th century, Kodak dominated the photography business. But with five restructurings and layoffs of 40,000 employees over the last five years, Kodak is clearly struggling. Unfortunately, many believe that digital photography will darken Kodak's future even more. With film-based photography, Kodak makes money selling film, cameras, developing equipment, film development chemicals, and photographic paper. But digital camera users can snap pictures and transfer them to a personal computer for viewing in just minutes. With digital photography, consumers don't need Kodak film, Kodak photographic paper, Kodak chemicals (for film labs), or Kodak film and print-developing equipment (for film labs) to view digital pictures. The opportunity for Kodak, if there is one, is that its reputation and long history in the photography business may help it sell digital cameras. Unfortunately, competition in digital photography from Canon, Olympus, Nikon, and others has been fierce. And while Kodak has done well, it's certainly not the market leader in digital cameras at this time.[16]

As Kodak's experience shows, competitive advantages can erode over time if internal strengths eventually become weaknesses. Consequently, an analysis of an organization's internal environment, that is, a company's strengths and weaknesses, begins with an assessment of distinctive competencies and core capabilities. A **distinctive competence** is something that a company can make, do, or perform better than its competitors. For example, *Consumer Reports* magazine consistently ranks Toyota cars number one in quality and reliability. Likewise, for 10 of the last 11 years, *PC Magazine* readers have ranked Dell's desktop computers best in terms of service and reliability.[17]

While distinctive competencies are tangible—for example, a product or service is faster, cheaper, or better—the core capabilities that produce distinctive competencies are not. **Core capabilities** are the less-visible, internal decision-making routines, problem-solving processes, and organizational cultures that determine how efficiently inputs can be turned into outputs.[18] Distinctive competencies cannot be sustained for long without superior core capabilities. Southwest Airline's unique corporate culture is a core capability that helps it achieve its distinctive competencies in airline performance. At Southwest, employees know that company management truly values them. One example of that value occurs each year on the busiest flying day of the year, the Wednesday before Thanksgiving. On that day, Chairman Herb Kelleher and other top managers show their support for Southwest's employees by helping exhausted ground crews load baggage onto planes. Southwest's employees, in turn, work even smarter, harder, and longer than most employees. Consequently, at Southwest, the corporate culture is *the* core capability that enables Southwest to create distinctive competencies in on-time performance, baggage handling, and customer satisfaction.[19]

After examining internal strengths and weaknesses, the second part of a situational analysis is to look outside the company and assess the opportunities and threats in the external environment. In Chapter 2, you learned that *environmental scanning* is searching the environment for important events or issues that might affect the organization. With environmental scanning, managers usually scan the environment to stay up-to-date on important factors in their environment, such as pricing trends and technology changes in the industry. However, in a situational analysis, managers use environmental scanning to identify specific opportunities and threats that can either improve or harm the company's ability to sustain its competitive advantage. Identification of strategic groups and formation of shadow-strategy task forces are two ways to do this.

Strategic groups are not "actual" groups, but are groups selected for study by managers. A **strategic group** is a group of other companies within an industry that top man-

**distinctive competence**
what a company can make, do, or perform better than its competitors

**core capabilities**
the internal decision-making routines, problem-solving processes, and organizational cultures that determine how efficiently inputs can be turned into outputs

312

**strategic group**
a group of companies within an industry that top managers choose to compare, evaluate, and benchmark strategic threats and opportunities

In order to bolster waning demand for its traditional film products, Kodak has teamed with Maytag Corp. to roll out thousands of camera-and-film vending machines over the next three years. Kodak is targeting consumers with instant cravings for a must-have snapshot at places like the beach, theme parks, and ski resorts.

AP PHOTO/EASTMAN KODAK CO.

agers choose for comparing, evaluating, and benchmarking their company's strategic threats and opportunities.[20] Typically, managers include companies as part of their strategic group if they compete directly with those companies for customers or if those companies use strategies similar to theirs. For example, it's likely that the managers at Gannett Company, the largest U.S. newspaper publisher (97 daily newspapers and *USA Today*), assess strategic threats and opportunities by comparing themselves to a strategic group consisting of the other major newspaper companies.[21] This would probably include the Tribune Company (the *Chicago Tribune*, the *Ft. Lauderdale Sun-Sentinel*, *Orlando Sentinel*, *Newsday*, the *Los Angeles Times*, and many other newspapers) and Knight-Ridder (32 daily newspapers, including the *Detroit Free Press*, the *Philadelphia Inquirer*, and the *Miami Herald*).[22] By contrast, given that Gannett owns 97 daily newspapers in 43 states with a total circulation approaching 7.8 million readers, it's unlikely that Gannett management worries much about *The Arkansas Democrat Gazette*. The *Gazette* is a fine paper, having won numerous awards for its writing and news coverage, but with a total circulation of 175,000, mostly within Arkansas, managers at Gannett would probably not include it in their strategic group.

In fact, when scanning the environment for strategic threats and opportunities, managers tend to categorize the different companies in their industries into several kinds of strategic groups: core, secondary, and transient firms.[23] The first kind of strategic group consists of **core firms**, that is, central companies in a strategic group. Gannett's core firms would be the Tribune Company and Knight-Ridder publishing. When most managers scan their environments for strategic threats and opportunities, they do so by primarily scanning the strategic actions of core firms.

**Secondary firms** are firms that use related but somewhat different strategies than core firms. For Gannett, this might be the New York Times Company, which publishes the *New York Times*, the *Boston Globe*, and 14 other small newspapers. However, the New York Times Company is somewhat different in that it also publishes magazines, runs eight network-affiliated TV stations and two radio stations, operates two paper mill companies, and sells wire and photo services to other newspapers publishers.[24]

**core firms**
the central companies in a strategic group

**secondary firms**
the firms in a strategic group that follow related, but somewhat different, strategies than do the core firms

313

Managers are aware of the potential threats and opportunities posed by secondary firms. However, they spend more time assessing the threats and opportunities associated with core firms.

**Transient firms** are companies whose strategies are changing from one strategic position to another. With the *Wall Street Journal* and *Barron's*, the Dow Jones company has been a publisher of daily and weekly financial news since its inception. While those publications continue to thrive, in the last decade Dow Jones has considerably broadened its business, starting SmartMoney, a monthly personal investment magazine, and moving into television as a co-owner of CNBC, the leading business and financial cable TV channel in the United States, Europe, and Asia.[25] Because their strategies are changing, managers may not know what to think about transient firms. Consequently, managers may often overlook or be wrong about the potential threats and opportunities posed by transient firms.

Since a strategic group is a group of other companies within an industry that top managers choose for comparing, evaluating, and benchmarking their company's strategic threats and opportunities, Exhibit 9.7 displays the number of newspapers, TV stations, Web sites, and other businesses that Gannett has in comparison to the Tribune Company, Knight Ridder, and the New York Times Company. Knight Ridder is clearly the closest to Gannett and would probably be classified as the core firm in Gannett's strategic group. And while the Tribune Company has as many TV stations as Gannett, it has fewer newspapers and Web sites and would be classified as a secondary firm in Gannett's strategic group. Because it has such a small number of Web sites, the New York Times Company bears little resemblance to Gannett and might not be included as part of Gannett's strategic group. No doubt Gannett would monitor what the New York Times Company does, but it would make more sense to monitor Knight Ridder and the Tribune Company instead. Finally, Dow Jones, the transient company in Gannett's strategic group because it has been changing its strategy, is actually becoming a miniGannett, concentrating its resources in newspapers and Web sites.

So, what external threats and opportunities did Gannett see after assessing its strategic groups? In terms of threats, Gannett saw little chance for growth in several

## EXHIBIT 9.7

### STRATEGIC GROUPS FOR GANNETT COMPANY

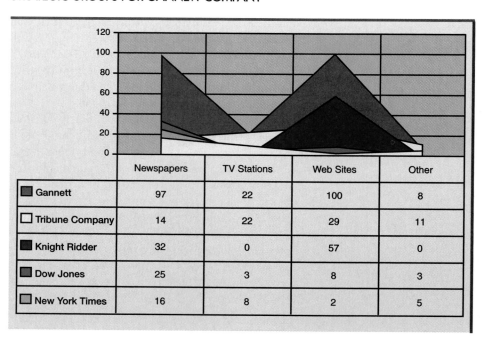

| | Newspapers | TV Stations | Web Sites | Other |
|---|---|---|---|---|
| Gannett | 97 | 22 | 100 | 8 |
| Tribune Company | 14 | 22 | 29 | 11 |
| Knight Ridder | 32 | 0 | 57 | 0 |
| Dow Jones | 25 | 3 | 8 | 3 |
| New York Times | 16 | 8 | 2 | 5 |

areas, selling all five of its remaining radio stations and its outdoor advertising company (i.e., billboards). In terms of opportunities, Gannett has focused on technology and television, establishing InfiNet, an Internet access and service company designed to help newspapers go online, and purchasing five television stations in the last few years. It has also expanded overseas, purchasing Newsquest plc, one of the largest regional publishers in England with 11 daily newspapers, as well as Newscom, which has four papers in the United Kingdom. Finally, continuing to focus on its core business, Gannett acquired 19 daily newspapers in Wisconsin, Ohio, Louisiana, Maryland, and Utah. It also bought two new flagship papers, the *Arizona Republic* and *The Indianapolis Star*.[26]

**shadow-strategy task force**
a committee within the company that analyzes the company's own weaknesses to determine how competitors could exploit them for competitive advantage

Because top managers tend to limit their attention to the core firms in their strategic group, some companies have started using shadow-strategy task forces to more aggressively scan their environments for strategic threats and opportunities. The goal of a **shadow-strategy task force** is to actively seek out its own company's weaknesses and then, thinking like a competitor, determine how other companies could exploit them for competitive advantage.[27] Furthermore, to make sure that the task force challenges conventional thinking, its members should be independent-minded, come from a variety of company functions and levels, and have the access and authority to question the company's current strategic actions and intent. For example, Ciba-Geigy's Industrial Dye division makes color dyes used in carpet manufacturing. One of the difficulties in this business is ensuring color consistency, that is, making sure that the dark gray carpet manufactured today looks the same color as the dark gray carpet manufactured next week. Ciba-Geigy's shadow-strategy task force determined that if its competitors could find ways to consistently, precisely, and cheaply match color carpet dyes (so that carpet colors looked the same regardless of when and where they were manufactured), Ciba-Geigy would be at a considerable competitive disadvantage. After the shadow-strategy task force challenged top management with its conclusions, the company went about developing distinctive competencies in dye research and manufacturing, which allowed it to make dyes with scientific preciseness.[28]

In short, there are two basic parts to a situational analysis. The first is to examine internal strengths and weaknesses by focusing on distinctive competencies and core capabilities. The second is to examine external opportunities and threats by focusing on environmental scanning, strategic groups, and shadow-strategy task forces.

### 2.3 Choosing Strategic Alternatives

After determining the need for strategic change and conducting a situational analysis, the last step in the strategy-making process is to choose strategic alternatives that will help the company create or maintain a sustainable competitive advantage. According to Strategic Reference Point Theory, managers choose between two basic alternative strategies. They can choose a conservative, *risk-avoiding strategy* that aims to protect an existing competitive advantage. Or they can choose an aggressive, *risk-seeking strategy* that aims to extend or create a sustainable competitive advantage. For example, Menards is a hardware store chain with 160 locations throughout the Midwest. When hardware giant Home Depot entered the Midwest, Menards faced a basic choice: avoid risk by continuing with the strategy it had in place before Home Depot's arrival, or seek risk by trying to further its competitive advantage against Home Depot, which is six times its size. Some of its competitors decided to fold. Kmart closed all of its Builder's Square hardware stores when Home Depot came to Minneapolis. Handy Andy liquidated its 74 stores when Home Depot came to the Midwest. But Menards decided to fight, spending millions to open 35 new stores at the same time that Home Depot was opening 44 of its new stores.[29]

**strategic reference points**
the strategic targets managers use to measure whether a firm has developed the core competencies it needs to achieve a sustainable competitive advantage

The choice to be risk-seeking or risk-avoiding typically depends on whether top management views the company as falling above or below strategic reference points. **Strategic reference points** are the targets that managers use to measure whether their firm has developed the core competencies that it needs to achieve a sustainable competitive advantage. For example, if a hotel chain decided to compete by providing superior quality and

315

CHAPTER 9   ORGANIZATIONAL STRATEGY

service, then top management would track the success of this strategy through customer surveys or published hotel ratings, such as those provided by the prestigious *Mobil Travel Guide*. By contrast, if a hotel chain decided to compete on price, it would regularly conduct market surveys to check the prices of other hotels. The competitors' prices are the hotel managers' strategic reference points against which to compare their own pricing strategy. If competitors can consistently underprice them, then the managers need to determine whether their staff and resources have the core competencies to compete on price.

As shown in Exhibit 9.8, when companies are performing above or better than their strategic reference points, top management will typically be satisfied with company strategy. Ironically, this satisfaction tends to make top management conservative and risk-averse. After all, since the company already has a sustainable competitive advantage, the worst thing that could happen would be to lose it. Consequently, new issues or changes in the company's external environments are viewed as threats. But when companies are performing below or worse than their strategic reference points, top management will typically be dissatisfied with company strategy. However, in this instance, managers are much more likely to choose a daring, risk-taking strategy. After all, if the current strategy is producing substandard results, what has the company got to lose by switching to risky new strategies in the hopes that it can create a sustainable competitive advantage? Consequently, for companies in this situation, new issues or changes in external environments are viewed as opportunities for potential gain.

However, Strategic Reference Point Theory is not deterministic. Managers are not predestined to choose risk-averse or risk-seeking strategies for their companies. Indeed, one of the most important points in Strategic Reference Point Theory is that managers *can* influence the strategies chosen at their companies by *actively changing and adjusting* the strategic reference points they use to judge strategic performance. To illustrate, if a company has be-

---

EXHIBIT 9.8

STRATEGIC REFERENCE POINTS

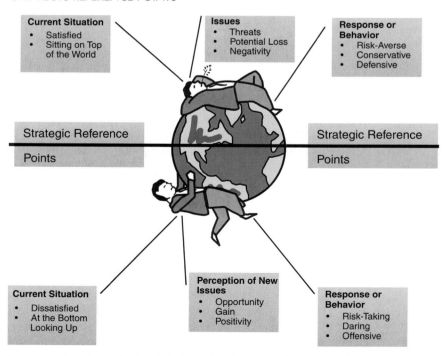

**Current Situation**
- Satisfied
- Sitting on Top of the World

**Issues**
- Threats
- Potential Loss
- Negativity

**Response or Behavior**
- Risk-Averse
- Conservative
- Defensive

Strategic Reference Points

Strategic Reference Points

**Current Situation**
- Dissatisfied
- At the Bottom Looking Up

**Perception of New Issues**
- Opportunity
- Gain
- Positivity

**Response or Behavior**
- Risk-Taking
- Daring
- Offensive

**Source:** A. Fiegenbaum, S. Hart, & D. Schendel, "Strategic Reference Point Theory," *Strategic Management Journal* 17 (1996): 219-235.

One of the most difficult steps in strategy making is getting top managers to recognize the need for strategic change. Professor Gary Hamel advises senior executives to answer two questions. First, over time, have you become more or less willing to challenge conventional thinking about your business? Second, have you become more or less curious about the changes taking place outside your industry? Ralph Waldo Emerson wrote, "There are always two parties, the party of the past and the party of the future; the establishment and the movement." Hamel, paraphrasing Emerson, asks top managers, "To which party do you belong? The past or the future?"

**Source:** G. Hamel, "Strategy as Revolution," *Harvard Business Review*, July-August 1996, 69-82.

come complacent after consistently surpassing its strategic reference points, then top management can change the company's strategic risk orientation from risk-averse to risk-taking by raising the standards of performance (i.e., strategic reference points). Indeed, this is what happened at Menards.

Instead of being satisfied with just protecting its existing stores (a risk-averse strategy), founder John Menard changed the strategic referent points the company had been using to assess strategic performance. To encourage a daring, offensive-minded strategy that would allow the company to open nearly as many new stores as Home Depot, he determined that Menards would have to beat Home Depot on not one or two, but four strategic reference points: price, products, sales per square foot, and "friendly accessibility." Preliminary data indicate that the Menard's strategy is well on its way to succeeding. In terms of price, market research indicates that a 100-item shopping cart of goods is consistently cheaper at Menards.[30] In terms of products, Menards sells 50,000 products per store, the same as Home Depot. In terms of sales per square foot, Menards ($360 per square foot) strongly outsells Home Depot ($290 per square foot). Finally, unlike Home Depot's warehouse-like stores, Menards' stores are built to resemble grocery stores. Shiny tiled floors, wide aisles, and easy-to-reach products all make Menards a "friendlier" place for shoppers.[31]

So even when (perhaps *especially* when) companies have achieved a sustainable competitive advantage, top managers must adjust or change strategic reference points to challenge themselves and their employees to develop new core competencies for the future. In the long run, effective organizations will frequently revise their strategic reference points to better focus managers' attention on the new challenges and opportunities that occur in their ever-changing business environments.

### Review 2
#### Strategy-Making Process

The first step in strategy making is determining whether a strategy needs to be changed in order to sustain a competitive advantage. Because uncertainty and competitive inertia make this difficult to determine, managers can improve the speed and accuracy of this step by looking for differences between top management's intended strategy and the strategy actually implemented by lower-level managers (i.e., strategic dissonance). The second step is to conduct a situational analysis that examines internal strengths and weaknesses (distinctive competencies and core capabilities), as well as external threats and opportunities (environmental scanning, strategic groups, and shadow-strategy task forces). In the third step of strategy making, Strategic Reference Point Theory suggests that when companies are performing better than their strategic reference points, top management will typically choose a risk-averse strategy. When performance is below strategic reference points, risk-seeking strategies are more likely to be chosen. Importantly, however, managers *can* influence the choice of strategic alternatives by actively changing and adjusting the strategic reference points they use to judge strategic performance.

## Corporate, Industry, and Firm-Level Strategies

Several years ago, Walter Young received a call from an investment banker who wanted to know if he was interested in running Champion Enterprises, maker of recreational vehicles, recreational buses, and manufactured homes and seller of home insurance, home financing, and numerous other products and services. Despite the fact that Champion had lost $30 million over the last five years, Young decided to take the job. The first question he asked himself and Champion's managers was "What business are we in?" Were they in the money-lending business? No. Were they in the property-selling business? No. What about housing parts or insurance? No, not those either. After serious consideration, Walter Young and his managers decided that Champion Enterprises should only be in one business, "supplying affordable housing." So Champion stopped selling property. Plus, it got out of the housing component, insurance, and RV businesses, selling them to others. As a result, Champion now has one focus: selling low-cost, premanufactured housing.

With its business, supplying affordable housing, now clear, Young and his managers asked themselves a second important question: "How should we compete in this industry?" At first, the answer was "cut costs." Accordingly, Young lowered Champion's expenses, cutting the number of staffers at corporate headquarters from 260 to 12. Then, he further cut costs by reducing the number of different models of manufactured houses that the company would build. After bringing costs in line, the answer was growth. In the last four years, Champion has strengthened its core business by purchasing seven other premanufactured housing companies. Together, these moves have doubled Champion's revenues and increased its market share, making it second only to industry leader Redman Industries. [32]

What business are we in? How should we compete in this industry? Who are our competitors and how should we respond to them? These simple, but powerful questions are at the heart of corporate-, industry-, and firm-level strategies.

*After reading the next three sections, you should be able to*
*3. explain the different kinds of corporate-level strategies.*
*4. describe the different kinds of industry-level strategies.*
*5. explain the components and kinds of firm-level strategies.*

## 3. Corporate-Level Strategies

**corporate-level strategy**
the overall organizational strategy that addresses the question "What business or businesses are we in or should we be in?"

**Corporate-level strategy** is the overall organizational strategy that addresses the question "What business or businesses are we in or should we be in?" For example, after five years of diversifying its business, Intel has gone back to basics by refocusing on its core business of making integrated computer chips. It sold off its interactive media-services division, closed iCat, a business that managed Web sites for small businesses, and shut down a business that streamed video and audio content for other companies. CEO Craig Barrett admitted that Intel had "screwed up" by focusing too much on these other businesses. By refocusing on integrated computer chips, Barrett said, "We're prioritizing our investments—you allocate your resources into the areas of highest return. The core competency has always been integrated circuits."[33]

*Exhibit 9.9 shows the two major approaches to corporate-level strategy, **3.1** portfolio strategy and **3.2** grand strategies, that companies use to decide which businesses they should be in.*

### 3.1 Portfolio Strategy [34]

**diversification**
a strategy for reducing risk by buying a variety of items (stocks or, in the case of a corporation, types of businesses), so that the failure of one stock or one business does not doom the entire portfolio

One of the standard strategies for stock market investors is **diversification**: buy stocks in a variety of companies in different industries. The purpose of this strategy is to reduce risk in the overall stock portfolio (i.e., the entire collection of stocks). The basic idea is simple: If you invest in 10 companies in 10 different industries, you won't lose your entire investment if one company performs poorly. Furthermore, because they're in different industries, one company's losses are likely to be offset by another company's gains. Portfolio strategy is based on these same ideas.

**portfolio strategy**
corporate-level strategy that minimizes risk by diversifying investment among various businesses or product lines

**Portfolio strategy** is a corporate-level strategy that minimizes risk by diversifying investment among various businesses or product lines. Like an investor who invests in a variety of stocks, portfolio strategy guides the strategic decisions of corporations that compete in a variety of businesses. For example, it could be used to guide the strategy of a company like 3M, which makes 50,000 products for 16 different industries. Similarly, it could be used by Johnson & Johnson, which has 170 divisions making health care

EXHIBIT 9.9

## CORPORATE-LEVEL STRATEGIES

| **PORTFOLIO STRATEGY** | **GRAND STRATEGIES** |
| --- | --- |

**PORTFOLIO STRATEGY**
- Acquisitions, unrelated diversification, related diversification, single businesses
- Boston Consulting Group Matrix
  - ❑ Stars
  - ❑ Question marks
  - ❑ Cash cows
  - ❑ Dogs

**GRAND STRATEGIES**
- Growth
- Stability
- Retrenchment/recovery

---

products for the pharmaceuticals, diagnostics, consumers, and health care professionals markets. And, just as investors consider the mix of stocks in their stock portfolio when deciding which stocks to buy or sell, portfolio strategy provides the following guidelines to help managers acquire companies that fit well with the rest of their corporate portfolio and sell those that don't.

First, the more businesses in which a corporation competes, the smaller its overall chances of failing. Think of a corporation as a stool and its businesses as the legs of the stool. The more legs or businesses added to the stool, the less likely it is to tip over. Using this analogy, portfolio strategy reduces 3M's risk of failing, because the corporation's survival depends on essentially 16 different businesses. Because the emphasis is on adding "legs to the stool," managers who use portfolio strategy are often on the lookout for **acquisitions**, that is, other companies to buy.

Second, beyond adding new businesses to the corporate portfolio, portfolio strategy can reduce risk even more through **unrelated diversification**—creating or acquiring companies in completely unrelated businesses. If the businesses are unrelated, then losses in one business or industry will have minimal effect on the performance of other companies in the corporate portfolio. One of the best examples of unrelated diversification is Samsung Corporation of Korea. Samsung has eight businesses in electronics (video and audio products, appliances, information systems, computers, and semiconductors), four companies in its machinery business group (power plants, waste-treatment facilities, infrastructure, and material-handling systems), five companies in chemicals (high-polymer composites, engineering plastics, and specialty chemicals), five companies in finance and insurance (life, property, and casualty insurance, as well as credit cards and securities), and 16 other companies in businesses ranging from automobiles to hotels to entertainment. Because most internally grown businesses tend to be related to existing products or services, acquiring new businesses is the preferred method of unrelated diversification.

Third, investing the profits and cash flows from mature, slow-growth businesses into newer, faster-growing businesses can reduce long-term risk. The best known portfolio strategy for guiding investment in a corporation's businesses is the Boston Consulting Group (BCG) matrix. The **BCG matrix** is a portfolio strategy that managers use to categorize their corporation's businesses by growth rate and relative market share, helping them decide how to invest corporate funds. The matrix, shown in Exhibit 9.10, separates businesses into four categories based on how fast the market is growing (high-growth or low-growth) and the size of the business's share of that market (small or large). **Stars** are companies that have a large share of a fast-growing market. To take advantage of a star's fast-growing market and its strength in that market (large share), the corporation must invest substantially in it. However, the investment is usually worthwhile, because many stars produce sizable future profits. **Question marks** are companies that have a small

**acquisition**
purchase of a company by another company

**unrelated diversification**
creating or acquiring companies in completely unrelated businesses

**BCG matrix**
A portfolio strategy, developed by the Boston Consulting Group, that managers use to categorize the corporation's businesses by growth rate and relative market share, helping them decide how to invest corporate funds

**star**
a company with a large share of a fast-growing market

**question mark**
a company with a small share of a fast-growing market

319

EXHIBIT 9.10

BOSTON CONSULTING GROUP MATRIX

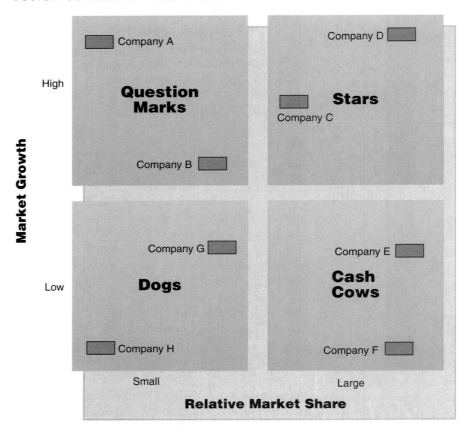

**cash cow**
a company with a large share of a
slow-growing market

**dog**
a company with a small share of a
slow-growing market

share of a fast-growing market. If the corporation invests in these companies, they may eventually become stars, but their relative weakness in the market (small share) makes investing in question marks more risky than investing in stars. **Cash cows** are companies that have a large share of a slow-growing market. Companies in this situation are often highly profitable, hence the name "cash cow." Finally, **dogs** are companies that have a small share of a slow-growing market. As the name "dogs" suggests, having a small share of a slow-growth market is often not profitable.

Since the idea is to redirect investment from slow-growing to fast-growing companies, the Boston Consulting Group matrix starts by recommending that, while they last, the substantial cash flows from cash cows should be reinvested in stars to help them grow even faster and obtain even more market share. Using this strategy, current profits help produce future profits. Cash flows should also be directed to some question marks. Though riskier than stars, question marks have great potential because of their fast-growing market. However, managers must decide which question marks are most likely to turn into stars and therefore warrant further investment, and which ones are too risky and should be sold. Finally, because dogs lose money, the corporation should "find them new owners" or "take them to the pound." In other words, dogs should be sold to other companies, or should be closed down and liquidated for their assets.

While the BCG matrix and other forms of portfolio strategy are relatively popular among managers, portfolio strategy has some drawbacks. The most significant is that the evidence does not support the usefulness of acquiring unrelated businesses. As shown in

Exhibit 9.11, there is a U-shaped relationship between diversification and risk. The left side of the curve shows that single businesses with no diversification are extremely risky (if the single business fails, the entire business fails). So, in part, the portfolio strategy of diversifying is correct—competing in a variety of different businesses can lower risk. However, portfolio strategy is partly wrong, too—the right side of the curve shows that conglomerates composed of completely unrelated businesses are even riskier than single, undiversified businesses.

The second set of problems with portfolio strategy has to do with the dysfunctional consequences that occur when companies are categorized as stars, cash cows, question marks, or dogs. Contrary to expectations, the BCG matrix often yields incorrect judgments about a company's future potential. This is because it relies on past performance (i.e., previous market share and previous market growth), which is a notoriously poor predictor of future company performance. For example, for the first 50 years of its existence, Krispy Kreme doughnuts was a small, regional chain of doughnut shops in the southeastern United States. Sales, profits, and growth were respectable, but Krispy Kreme was clearly not a player in a highly competitive business thoroughly dominated by Dunkin Donuts and its 1,000 U.S. stores. With a small share of a slowly growing market, Krispy Kreme was a "dog," according to the BCG matrix. However, in the last decade, Krispy Kreme has had remarkable success, quadrupling from 100 to more than 400 stores, increasing sales and profits at an annual average of over 25 percent, and becoming one of the more popular growth stocks on Wall Street.[35]

Furthermore, using the BCG matrix can also weaken the strongest performer in the corporate portfolio, the cash cow. As funds are redirected from cash cows to stars, corporate managers essentially take away the resources needed to take advantage of the cash

*EXHIBIT 9.11*

321

U-SHAPED RELATIONSHIP BETWEEN DIVERSIFICATION AND RISK

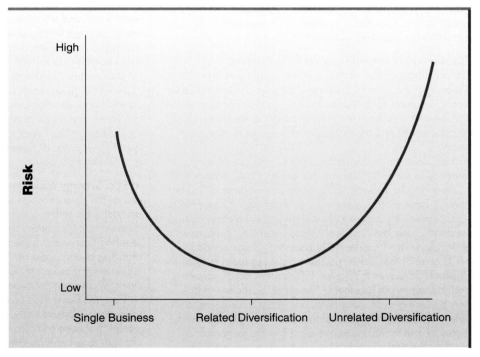

**Source:** M. Lubatkin & P.J. Lane, "Psst . . . The Merger Mavens Still Have It Wrong!" *Academy of Management Executive* 10 (1996): 21-39.

# BlastFromThePast

## Five Decades of Diversification Strategies

According to Michael Gold and Kathleen Luchs, there have been four distinct periods of thought about corporate diversification strategies: conglomerates and general management skills in the 1950s and 1960s; corporate strategy and portfolio planning in the 1970s; restructuring and value-based planning in the 1980s; and synergy and "core" portfolios in the 1990s.

### 1950s & 1960s: Conglomerates and General Management Skills

The 1950s and 1960s saw the rise of "professional managers," who were assumed capable of managing any organization in any industry. Supposedly, general management skills made managers interchangeable. If a manager was successful at an insurance company, then that success should be transferable to a steel company or a hospital. Human and conceptual skills, not specific work experience or knowledge, were thought to be the keys to good management.

Of course, if the same management skills and principles could be used to ensure success in any industry, then it didn't really matter what business you were in. Consequently, unquestioned faith in general management skills led to the rise of conglomerates, large collections of unrelated businesses under one company name. One of the largest conglomerates was ITT Corporation. As its name—International Telephone and Telegraph—suggests, ITT began as an international phone company and manufacturer. However, when Harold Geneen became ITT's president in 1959, he began a decade-long acquisition binge that ended with ITT owning 300 different companies. In one board meeting alone, Mr. Geneen suggested buying a baking company, a glassmaker, a company that taught speedwriting, and a company that manufactured hydraulic equipment for ships. During this time, ITT also bought Avis, Sheraton Hotels, Hartford Insurance, Levitt & Sons home builders, a TV company in England, and a cosmetics company in France.

### 1970s: Corporate Strategy and Portfolio Planning

By the end of the 1960s, enthusiasm for conglomerates and general management skills dimmed considerably. Studies indicated that conglomerates following a strategy of unrelated diversification were able to grow revenues and build market share, but were significantly less profitable and efficient than most other companies.

In the 1970s, three key ideas about diversification emerged in response to the failings of conglomerates. First, strategy was more than long-term planning. It was a way of determining a company's basic direction and taking advantage of future opportunities. Second, the purpose of strategy was to help top managers decide what business they should be in (i.e., corporate-level strategy). Third, unlike the haphazard, almost random diversification in the 1960s, portfolio planning tools, such as the GE Business Screen or the Boston Consulting Group matrix, helped managers put together a "balanced portfolio" of businesses. By selling weak companies and shifting resources from mature to promising companies, managers hoped to ensure future growth and to maximize overall corporate performance rather than the performance of any single business unit. One CEO said, "I was finding it very difficult to manage and understand so many different products and markets. I just grabbed at portfolio planning, because it provided me with a way to organize my thinking about our businesses and the resource allocation issues facing the total company. I became and still am very enthusiastic." Indeed, it's estimated that nearly half of Fortune 500 companies used portfolio planning during this time.

### 1980s: Restructuring and Value-Based Planning

By the end of the 1970s, top managers realized that managing a "balanced" portfolio of different companies was much more difficult than they had thought. The most serious mistake was applying the same management systems (i.e., financial planning, capital investment, incentive systems, and strategy-making processes) to very different business subunits. The lesson learned was that different types of businesses had to be managed differently.

In large part, diversification strategies in the 1980s were used to "correct" the excesses of the conglomerate-based, unrelated diversification of the 1960s and 1970s. The first correction was to cut headquarters costs, mostly by cutting the large number of headquarters staffers who had been needed to help manage large portfolios of companies. The second correction was to evaluate company value using stock market and economic measures, such as discounted cash flows and return on equity, rather than revenue growth and market share. Using these tools, managers discovered a huge "value gap" between what accounting book values indicated their corporate assets (i.e., business units) were worth and what the stock market indicated they were worth. In other words, in direct contrast to the 1960s and 1970s, managers now believed that different business units would be more valuable apart than together. These views produced the third correction, corporate restructuring, which let managers "fully value" these assets by selling the business units acquired during the acquisition binges of the 1960s and 1970s. The last correction was that managers came to believe that the most successful companies "stuck to their knitting," focusing on achieving quality, low costs, and excellence in just one business or in several related businesses.

### 1990s: Synergy and "Core" Portfolios

Just as the diversification strategies of the 1970s can be seen as an attempt to refine and improve the strategies of the 1960s, the diversification strategies in the 1990s can be seen as an attempt to refine and improve the strategies of the 1980s. With the dismantling of corporate conglomerates largely complete, diversification strategies in the 1990s have revolved around three ideas: synergy, core competencies, and dominant logic.

First, the basic idea of synergy is that related diversification works best. Consequently, acquisitions should be limited to companies that have complementary parts that make the companies stronger together than they were apart. In other words, synergy occurs when 1 + 1 = 3. Second, corporate portfolios are not collections of businesses, but collections of core competencies, meaning unique skills and capabilities. Walter Kiechel of *Fortune* magazine wrote, "To the extent that such skills can be exploited by each of the company's businesses, they represent a reason for having all of those businesses under one corporate umbrella." Third, dominant logic is the general way in which managers perceive and think about the business and its problems. Dominant logic influences the opportunities and threats that managers see and the strategic alternatives they consider. So, to improve the chances that diversification will work, managers should strive for good "fit," and they should acquire companies in industries that have similar dominant logic. For example, a poor "fit" would probably occur if the dominant logic of corporate management was growth and the dominant logic of the acquired firm was retrenchment.

For now, synergy, core competencies, and dominant logic are the leading beliefs about corporate diversification. However, in time, just as with conglomerates, portfolio planning, and restructuring and value-based planning, these ideas are likely to be challenged as well.

## 2000s: Too Early to Tell

With numerous business challenges in the technology, Internet, and telecommunication industries, some might argue that consolidation is the early pattern, that is, surviving companies purchasing competitors in the same line of business. At this point, though, it's much too early to tell what key patterns and themes will develop with respect to corporate diversification this decade.

**Sources:** D. Dowling, "On the March, ITT Sets Breakaway Pace: Firm Loosens the Conglomerate Grip," *The Star-Ledger Newark*, 26 November 1995. M. Goold & K. Luchs, "Why Diversify? Four Decades of Management Thinking," *Academy of Management Executive* 7 (1993): 7–25. R.G. Hamermesh, *Making Strategy Work* (New York: John Wiley & Sons, 1986). B. Orwall, R.L. Rundle, & F. Rose, "Hilton and ITT Took Two Different Paths to this Confrontation, But Both Companies Wrestled with a Similar Demon: A Serious Lack of Focus," *The Wall Street Journal Europe*, 30 January 1997.

cow's new business opportunities. The result is that the cash cow becomes less aggressive in seeking new business or in defending its present business. For example, Procter & Gamble's Tide, the laundry detergent that P&G brought to market in 1946, is clearly a cash cow, accounting for billions in worldwide profits. However, in a bid to bring new products to market—P&G hasn't successfully introduced a top-selling new product since Pampers in 1961—the company is diverting up to a half billion dollars from cash cows like Tide to promote potential product blockbusters (i.e., stars) such as Febreze, a spray that eliminates odors; Dryel, which dry cleans clothes at home; Fit, a spray that kills bacteria; and Impress, a high-tech plastic wrap.[36] Finally, labeling a top performer as a cash cow can harm employee morale. Instead of working for themselves, cash cow employees realize that they have inferior status because their successes are now being used to fund the growth of stars and question marks.

So, what kind of portfolio strategy does the best job of helping managers decide which companies to buy or sell? The U-shaped curve in Exhibit 9.11 indicates that the best approach is probably **related diversification**, in which the different business units share similar products, manufacturing, marketing, technology, or cultures. The key to related diversification is to acquire or create new companies with core capabilities that complement the core capabilities of businesses already in the corporate portfolio. We began this section with the example of 3M and how its 50,000 products are sold in over 16 different industries. While seemingly different, most of 3M's product divisions are based in some fashion on its distinctive competencies in adhesives and tape (i.e., wet or dry sandpaper, Post-It notes, Scotchgard fabric protector, transdermal skin patches, reflective material used in traffic signs, etc.). Furthermore, all of 3M's divisions share its strong corporate culture that promotes and encourages risk-taking and innovation. In sum, in contrast to single, undiversified businesses or unrelated diversification, related diversification reduces risk, because the different businesses can work as a team, relying on each other for needed experience, expertise, and support.

Exhibit 9.12 details the problems associated with portfolio strategy and recommends ways that managers can increase their chances of success through related diversification.

**related diversification**
creating or acquiring companies that share similar products, manufacturing, marketing, technology, or cultures

### 3.2 Grand Strategies

A **grand strategy** is a broad strategic plan used to help an organization achieve its strategic goals.[37] Grand strategies guide the strategic alternatives that managers of individual businesses or subunits may use. There are three kinds of grand strategies: growth, stability, and retrenchment/recovery.

**grand strategy**
a broad corporate-level strategic plan used to achieve strategic goals and guide the strategic alternatives that managers of individual businesses or subunits may use

EXHIBIT 9.12

PORTFOLIO STRATEGY: PROBLEMS AND RECOMMENDATIONS

| PROBLEMS WITH PORTFOLIO STRATEGY | RECOMMENDATIONS FOR MAKING PORTFOLIO STRATEGY WORK |
|---|---|
| • Unrelated diversification does not reduce risk.<br>• Present performance is used to predict future performance.<br>• Assessments of a business's growth potential are often inaccurate.<br>• Cash cows fail to aggressively pursue opportunities and defend themselves from threats.<br>• Being labeled a "cash cow" can hurt employee morale.<br>• Companies often overpay to acquire stars.<br>• Acquiring firms often treat acquired stars as "conquered foes." Key stars' managers, who once controlled their own destiny, often leave because they are now treated as relatively unimportant middle managers. | • Don't be so quick to sell dogs or question marks. Instead, management should commit to the markets in which it competes by strengthening core capabilities.<br>• Put your "eggs in similar (not different) baskets" by acquiring companies in related businesses.<br>• Acquire companies with complementary core capabilities.<br>• Encourage collaboration and cooperation between related firms and businesses within the company.<br>• "Date before you marry." Work with a business before deciding to acquire it.<br>• When in doubt, don't acquire new businesses. Mergers and acquisitions are inherently risky and difficult to make work. Only acquire firms that can help create or extend a sustainable competitive advantage. |

Sources: M. Lubatkin, "Value-Creating Mergers: Fact or Folklore?" *Academy of Management Executive* 2 (1988): 295-302. M. Lubatkin & S. Chatterjee, "Extending Modern Portfolio Theory into the Domain of Corporate Diversification: Does It Apply?" *Academy of Management Journal* 37 (1994): 109-136. M.H. Lubatkin & P.J. Lane, "Psst . . . The Merger Mavens Still Have It Wrong!" *Academy of Management Executive* 10 (1996): 21-39.

**growth strategy**
strategy that focuses on increasing profits, revenues, market share, or the number of places in which the company does business

The purpose of a **growth strategy** is to increase profits, revenues, market share, or the number of places (store, offices, locations) in which the company does business. Companies can grow in several ways. They can grow externally by merging with or acquiring other companies. In recent years, some of the largest mergers and acquisitions were JDS Uniphase acquiring SDL (fiber optics), Chevron acquiring Texaco (oil), America Online acquiring Time Warner (multimedia publishing), Chase acquiring J.P. Morgan (investment banking), and Bertelsman acquiring Random House (publishing).[38]

Another way to grow is internally, directly expanding the company's existing business or creating and growing new businesses. For example, over the last decade, Walgreen's, one of the largest pharmacy chains in the United States, opened approximately 100 stores a year. With baby boomers aging and the need for pharmacies to sell more prescription drugs rapidly growing, Walgreen's opened 344 new stores last year and will shoot for 500 this year. In fact, with 3,300 stores in 43 states, it hopes to add 500 stores a year and reach 6,000 Walgreen's stores within the next six years. Walgreen's CEO said, "Growth is a huge challenge, but it's the right thing to do. And this is absolutely the right time in our history to do it." Since its stores tend to draw customers from only a one- to two-mile radius, each additional store should add significant revenues and profits without cannibalizing existing stores' sales.[39]

**stability strategy**
strategy that focuses on improving the way in which the company sells the same products or services to the same customers

The purpose of a **stability strategy** is to continue doing what the company has been doing, but just do it better. Consequently, companies following a stability strategy try to improve the way in which they sell the same products or services to the same customers. For example, Subaru has been making four-wheel drive station wagons for 30 years. But over the last decade, it strengthened this focus by only manufacturing all-wheel drive vehicles, like the Subaru Legacy or Outback (both come in four-door sedans or two-door coupes), which are popular in snowy and mountainous regions. Subaru's extremely loyal customers have rewarded the company with an average 7 percent annual increase in sales (which is extremely high for the auto industry) over the last five years. In turn, the company is bringing out new and improved all-wheel drive vehicles, like the WRX, which goes from 0 to 60 miles per hour in 6.1 seconds.[40] Companies often choose a stability

# "headline news"

## No Room for Go in Playhouse Disney

Disney's Go.com has hit a red light. After two years of trying to build a successful portal, Disney has finally pulled the plug on Go.com. When Disney acquired Infoseek in 1999, it bought the cornerstone on which it built Go.com, a Web site that integrated Disney-owned ABC's Internet activities with the Infoseek search engine. With all the resources Disney put behind it, it seemed to be a good bet, and Wall Street even applauded the company's efforts. "It shows Wall Street that the company is serious about its Internet strategy. This is an Internet property that has its future in front of it," said analyst Barry Hyman of Ehrenkrantz King Nussbaum.

Hyman couldn't have been more wrong. Go.com was slow off the starting line, arriving late to the portal game and facing off against formidable competition: Internet giants Yahoo!, AOL, and Microsoft's MSN. For analysts, hindsight is twenty-twenty vision. "Disney tried to enter the portal game at a time when the window for portal ventures had effectively been shut, and that was probably one of the tougher—one of the biggest—hurdles for Go.com," says Mark Mooradian, a senior analyst with Jupiter Communications. Another problem was that success in the portal business has hinged on the need for a portal itself to be neutral. Users don't want to feel that they are being pushed to certain sites. Go.com integrated Disney's ABC content; therefore, it "could never be a successful distribution partner for CBS Sportsline, so there was a serious conflict of interest there that doesn't exist with an AOL or a Yahoo," as Arem Sinnreich, senior analyst at Jupiter Media Metrix, explained. AOL may now face similar problems since its merger with TimeWarner.

Faced with an impotent portal strategy, Disney decided to relaunch Go as a Web guide that focused on entertainment, recreation, and leisure. But a collapsing Internet economy and an ongoing lawsuit against GoTo.com would keep Go.com's new strategy from shifting into high gear. Once Internet advertising tanked, Go suffered insurmountable pro forma losses of $402 million on $368 million in revenue, not counting a $1.23 billion write-off of intangible assets—all in its last fiscal year. Disney Internet Group (DIG) President Steve Wadsworth said he decided to close the portal in an effort to not distract from established Disney brands like ESPN.com and ABC.com, but clearly the financials had something to do with it. "This is a difficult decision, as it impacts both our employees and Go.com users," DIG chairman Steve Bornstein explained. "However, the Internet environment has continued to shift and change, and therefore our strategies must also change."

Why would Disney media executives sitting on a goldmine in established brands feel that they had to rush into the uncharted territory of the Internet? Perhaps they just forgot what business they were really in—mass media. Disney has a treasure-trove of content designed for and distributed to very large audiences. The Internet really runs in the opposite vein, reaching thousands—even millions—of tiny audiences with very specific needs. It really only seems the same if you have Internet fever, something that DIG executives contracted the minute they bought Infoseek.

1. Create a BCG matrix that maps out Disney's portfolio of holdings. Consult **http://disney.go.com/corporate/investors. html** to help identify the complete list of Disney holdings and their contribution to the company's bottom line.
2. What problems did Disney have with Go.com in terms of Disney's overall portfolio strategy?

**Sources:** "Disney to Buy Infoseek, Form Go.com," Bloomberg News, 12 July 1999, http://news.cnet.com/news/0,10000,0-1005-200-344656,00.html. G. Du Bois, "Disney's Go.com Site Goes No More," *eWeek*, 5 February 2001, 42. Info-Trac Article A69980846. M. Graser, "Mouse Gives Go the Heave-Ho," *Variety*, 5 February 2001, 27. Info-Trac Article A70637439. K. Kerschbaumer, "Disney's No Go," *Broadcasting & Cable*, 5 February 2001, 40. Info-Trac Article A70429777. R. Smith, "Mass Media Miss the Point on Web," *Variety*, 19 March 2001, 5. Info-Trac Article A72503313.

strategy when their external environment doesn't change much, or after they have struggled with periods of explosive growth.

**retrenchment strategy**
strategy that focuses on turning around very poor company performance by shrinking the size or scope of the business

The purpose of a **retrenchment strategy** is to turn around very poor company performance by shrinking the size or scope of the business. The first step of a typical retrenchment strategy might include significant cost reductions, layoffs of employees, closing of poorly performing stores, offices, or manufacturing plants, or closing or selling entire lines of products or services.[41] Because of a slowing economy, American, United, U.S. Air, Northwest, and Continental airlines had already lost several billion dollars prior to the terrorist attack on the World Trade Center in New York City. However, after terrorists collapsed the World Trade Center towers by flying two passenger jets into the buildings, security-conscious Americans simply quit flying. In the weeks immediately after the bombing, flights were, at best, only about 40 percent full. As a result, every airline, with the exception of Southwest, quickly reduced its flight schedule by 20

# BeenThereDoneThat

## Nestlé CEO, Helmut Maucher, Discusses Strategy

Twenty years ago, half of Nestlé's profits came from one product, Nescafé instant coffee. Likewise, most of its revenues came from one market, Europe. However, today, after a decade of worldwide acquisitions, Nestlé is the most global food company in the world. In fact, Nestlé sells more than 8,500 food products in over 100 countries. Some of

its best-known products are Nescafé and Taster's Choice instant coffees, Perrier mineral water, Nestea iced tea, Coffee-Mate coffee creamer, Stouffer's frozen foods, the Nestlé Crunch candy bar, and Friskies cat food. CEO Helmut Maucher, who oversaw this expansion, talks about Nestlé's past and future strategies.

**Q:** How can Nestlé hope to maintain the momentum and the earnings growth that the company has enjoyed over the past decade?

**A:** In the past 15 years, we put Nestlé on a new footing to prepare for competition and the global markets of the future. We believe we have more or less done our homework: We are now in all the big markets, and we're in all those product areas that we want to be in. We've streamlined our organization and focused it in terms of strategic direction. Acquisitions will still be part of our future strategy, but to a lesser extent. Internal growth from the assets we now have in our hands will play a much more important role.

**Q:** What can be done to reduce the risks of currency fluctuation against the Swiss franc and the ups and downs of commodities from which your products are made?

**A:** When I started here we relied heavily on Europe, and half of our profit came from Nescafé instant coffee. If anything were to have happened to coffee, we would really have been in trouble. Now we've expanded into pet food, ice cream, water and other areas. Our policy has been to spread risks over different countries and product areas, without embarking on serious diversification: We're still 95 percent concentrated on food products. Commodities do certainly fluctuate, but coffee and cocoa prices have much less of an effect on us than in the past, because of a widening of our activities. This will never endanger our profit-and-loss account.

**Q:** In the past decade two-thirds of Nestlé's growth came from acquisitions. But now the emphasis seems to be on organic, internal growth. Are you turning away from acquisitions because prices are too high or because there's nothing left to buy?

**A:** Two big strategic items are now behind us: getting into certain countries, and [getting a presence in] product areas

where we were weak. That's why there's no longer the same need to be acquisitive. We made a few big decisions about major acquisitions that will take us into the next century, but now we don't need to do any more of these. But now we have all the elements in our hands to provide us with the organic growth we need.

**Q:** Financial markets are schizophrenic: They like to see signs of long-term strategic thinking, but they also demand very short-term performance. What do you say to investors who demand near-term results at the expense of long-term vision?

**A:** Back in the days when everyone was praising the so-called stakeholder approach, I always said, "Please don't forget shareholders, because they are our main priority." We are there to get long-term results for our shareholders. But if an investor from New York presses me to produce returns over the next two months, I'll reply: "No. I can't satisfy people whose interest is simply to see an increase in the value of Nestlé shares because they need to sell again." I have a responsibility to those long-term shareholders in Nestlé who feel a sense of ownership. I just can't afford to get nervous about some of these short-term games.

**Q:** How do you ensure a smooth second stage of sales growth in emerging markets?

**A:** The greatest growth potential for us comes in countries with per capita incomes between $2,000 and $20,000. In China, for example, the level is $350 per capita, which means we have a huge population moving into that growth zone. They'll eat more chocolate, drink more Nescafé and buy better-tasting, quality food, including convenience food. Once countries like China and India find themselves at the upper end of that growth zone, we might have annual sales of 200 billion Swiss Francs.

**Source:** R. House, "Helmut Maucher of Nestlé: Sweet Success," *Institutional Investor* 25, no. 2 (January 1997). This interview was edited for inclusion in this textbook.

---

percent and laid off thousands of workers—40,000 combined at American and United Airlines—in hopes of saving money. Because of their huge fixed costs (labor, the high cost of planes, the loans to pay for those planes, etc.), the airlines only make money when their flights are 65 percent full. And with passenger loads running at 40 percent, the airlines were losing millions of dollars a day. A top manager at American Airlines said, "There is no posturing going on here. We see a sharp decline in demand. We see the cash flying out the window, and no revenue coming in." Consequently, in an unprecedented move, nearly every company in the airline industry engaged in significant and simultaneous retrenchment in hopes of surviving the crisis.[42]

recovery
the strategic actions taken after
retrenchment to return to a growth
strategy

After cutting costs and reducing a business's size or scope, the second step in a retrenchment strategy is recovery. **Recovery** consists of the strategic actions that a company takes to return to a growth strategy. This two-step process of cutting and recovery is analogous to pruning roses. Prior to each growing season, roses should be cut back to two-thirds their normal size. However, pruning doesn't damage the roses; it makes them stronger and more likely to produce beautiful, fragrant flowers. The retrenchment-and-recovery process is similar. Cost reductions, layoffs, and plant closings are sometimes necessary to restore companies to "good health." When a dozen of PeopleSoft's top managers met to decide which 10 percent of its employees should be laid off, Larry Butler, vice president of human resources, asked them, "How do you feel?" When a manager ignored the question and began discussing how PeopleSoft should handle the layoffs, Butler stopped him and repeated his question to the group. "No," he said, "How do you feel?" At that point, half the managers in the room began crying. Tina Cox, manager of employee communications, said nearly everyone believed that layoffs "could never happen at PeopleSoft."[43] But like pruning, those cuts are intended to allow companies to eventually return to growth strategies (i.e., recovery). Indeed, two years later, after the layoffs and after instituting other controls, such as making sure managers stayed within their budgets, requiring that purchases over $100,000 have the CEO's approval, and stopping free bagels for all employees (annual cost, $2 million), PeopleSoft was profitable and growing again.[44] As these examples show, when company performance drops significantly, a strategy of retrenchment and recovery may help companies return to a successful growth strategy.

### Review 3
### Corporate-Level Strategies

Corporate-level strategies, such as portfolio strategy and grand strategies, help managers determine what businesses they should be in. Portfolio strategy focuses on lowering business risk by being in multiple, unrelated businesses and by investing the cash flows from slow-growth businesses into faster growing businesses. One portfolio strategy, the BCG matrix, suggests that cash flows from cash cows should be reinvested in stars and in carefully chosen question marks. Dogs should be sold or liquidated. However, portfolio strategy has several problems. Acquiring unrelated businesses actually increases risk rather than lowering it. The BCG matrix is often wrong when predicting companies' (i.e., dogs, cash cows, etc.) future potential. And redirecting cash flows can seriously weaken cash cows. The most successful way to use the portfolio approach to corporate strategy is to reduce risk through related diversification.

The three kinds of grand strategies are growth, stability, and retrenchment/recovery. Companies can grow externally by merging with or acquiring other companies, or they can grow internally through direct expansion or creating new businesses. Companies choose a stability strategy—selling the same products or services to the same customers—when their external environment changes very little or after they have dealt with periods of explosive growth. Retrenchment strategy, shrinking the size or scope of a business, is used to turn around poor performance. If retrenchment works, it is often followed by a recovery strategy that focuses on growing the business again.

## 4. Industry-Level Strategies

industry-level strategy
corporate strategy that addresses
the question "How should we compete in this industry?"

**Industry-level strategy** is a corporate strategy that addresses the question "How should we compete in this industry?" For example, the strategy of most nursing homes has been to provide medical care for elderly people who were no longer able to physically take care of themselves. However, in recent years, nursing homes have had to compete with assisted-living facilities. Assisted-living facilities don't offer the serious medical support available at most nursing homes. Although they provide assistance with things such as bathing and dressing, they have a different goal: to help residents be independent and active for as long as possible. Consequently, assisted-living facilities are much

327

EXHIBIT 9.13

## INDUSTRY-LEVEL STRATEGIES

**FIVE INDUSTRY FORCES**
- Character of rivalry
- Threat of new entrants
- Threat of substitute products or services
- Bargaining power of suppliers
- Bargaining power of buyers

**POSITIONING STRATEGIES**
- Cost leadership
- Differentiation
- Focus

**ADAPTIVE STRATEGIES**
- Defenders
- Analyzers
- Prospectors
- Reactors

more livable than traditional nursing homes. For example, all of Sunrise Assisted Living's facilities resemble Victorian mansions. Open porches, lots of big windows, curved staircases, carpeted floors, and comfortable couches and living areas replace the dark lighting, tile floors, and narrow hallways found in most nursing homes.[45]

*Let's find out more about industry-level strategies, shown in Exhibit 9.13, by discussing* **4.1** *the five industry forces that determine overall levels of competition in an industry and* **4.2** *the positioning strategies and* **4.3** *adaptive strategies that companies can use to achieve sustained competitive advantage and above-average profits.*

### 4.1 Five Industry Forces

According to Harvard professor Michael Porter, five industry forces—character of rivalry, threat of new entrants, threat of substitute products or services, bargaining power of suppliers, and bargaining power of buyers—determine an industry's overall attractiveness and potential for long-term profitability. The stronger these forces, the less attractive the industry becomes to corporate investors, because it is more difficult for companies to be profitable. Porter's industry forces are illustrated in Exhibit 9.14. Let's examine how these industry forces are bringing changes to several kinds of industries.

**character of the rivalry**
a measure of the intensity of competitive behavior between companies in an industry

**Character of the rivalry** is a measure of the intensity of competitive behavior between companies in an industry. Is the competition among firms aggressive and cutthroat, or do competitors focus more on serving customers than attacking each other? Both industry attractiveness and profitability decrease when rivalry is cutthroat. For example, selling cars is a highly competitive business. Pick up a local newspaper on Friday, Saturday, or Sunday morning, and you'll find dozens of pages of car advertising ("Anniversary Sale-A-Bration," "Ford March Savings!" and "$99 Down, You Choose!"). In fact, competition is so intense that if it weren't for used car sales, repair work, and replacement parts, many auto dealers would actually lose money.

**threat of new entrants**
a measure of the degree to which barriers to entry make it easy or difficult for new companies to get started in an industry

The **threat of new entrants** is a measure of the degree to which barriers to entry make it easy or difficult for new companies to get started in an industry. If it is easy for new companies to get started in the industry, then competition will increase and prices and profits will fall. However, if there are sufficient barriers to entry, such as large capital requirements to buy expensive equipment or plant facilities or the need for specialized knowledge, then competition will be weaker and prices and profits will generally be higher. For instance, high costs and intense competition make it very difficult to successfully enter the airline business. With even small passenger jets costing $20 million and larger jets costing $100 million and up, new airlines must have access to huge amounts of money just to buy planes. And, even if they have the money for planes, they still need to get certifications from the Department of Transportation (DOT) and the Federal Aviation Administration (FAA). If they overcome that hurdle, which is high because the DOT and FAA are charged with ensuring passenger safety, then they have to lease or buy hard-to-get landing slots at congested airports. Not surprisingly, given these barriers to entry, over the last 20 years only two out of 51 new airlines, America West and Jet Blue, managed to succeed, and that was after barely surviving bankruptcy.[46]

328

EXHIBIT 9.14

PORTER'S FIVE INDUSTRY FORCES

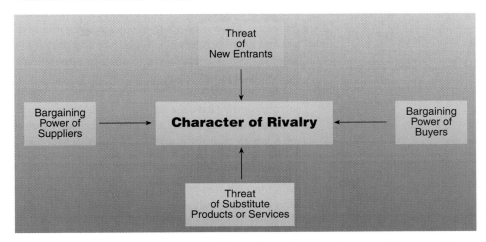

**Source:** M.E. Porter, *Competitive Strategy: Techniques for Analyzing Industries and Competitors* (New York: Free Press, 1980).

**threat of substitute products or services**
a measure of the ease with which customers can find substitutes for an industry's products or services

The **threat of substitute products or services** is a measure of the ease with which customers can find substitutes for an industry's products or services. If customers can easily find substitute products or services, the competition will be greater and profits will be lower. If there are few or no substitutes, competition will be weaker and profits will be higher. Generic medicines are some of the best-known examples of substitute products. Under U.S. patent law, a company that develops a drug has exclusive rights to produce and market that drug for 20 years. During this time, if the drug sells well, prices and profits are generally high. However, at the end of 20 years, after the patent has expired, any pharmaceutical company can manufacture and sell the same drug. When this happens, drug prices drop substantially, and the company that developed the drug typically sees its revenues drop sharply. For example, Prozac, a medication that fights depression, cost $30 a pill and returned $2.7 billion in sales revenues to Eli Lilly & Company the last year it was under patent. However, fluoxetine, a generic version of Prozac made by Merck-Medco that became available the day the patent for Prozac expired, costs, by contrast, only $5 per pill. In fact, the threat of generic substitutes is so strong in the pharmaceutical industry that pharmaceutical companies Warner-Lambert, Upjohn, Syntex, Sandoz, Ciba-Geigy, Rhone-Poulenc, and Hoechst have all had to merge with other pharmaceutical companies in order to survive. Their research labs could not come up with enough new strong selling, patented drugs to replace sales lost to generic drugs.[47]

**bargaining power of suppliers**
a measure of the influence that suppliers of parts, materials, and services to firms in an industry have on the prices of these inputs

**Bargaining power of suppliers** is a measure of the influence that suppliers of parts, materials, and services to firms in an industry have on the prices of these inputs. If an industry has numerous suppliers from whom to buy parts, materials, and services, companies will be able to bargain with suppliers to keep prices low. On the other hand, if there are few suppliers, or if a company is dependent on a supplier with specialized skills and knowledge, then suppliers will have the bargaining power to dictate price levels. Intel, which supplies more than an 75 percent of the microprocessors used in personal computers, has clearly had much more bargaining power than manufacturers of personal computers, who have had little choice but to buy their computer chips from Intel. As a result of this dominance, Intel clearly controlled the pricing of microprocessors and became one of the most profitable companies in the computer industry. Today, however, Intel's bargaining power is greatly reduced thanks to strong competition from AMD, which sells computer chips that are cheaper and as fast, if not faster, than Intel's leading computer chips. As a result, Intel has had to aggressively cut prices to maintain its dominant position as market leader.[48]

329

**Bargaining power of buyers** is a measure of the influence that customers have on the firm's prices. If a company is dependent on just a few high-volume buyers, those buyers will typically have enough bargaining power to dictate prices. By contrast, if a company sells a popular product or service to multiple buyers, then the company has more power to set prices. When it comes to purchasing cars, one of the ways in which consumers are increasing their bargaining power is to concentrate it in the hands of vehicle-buying services now available at credit unions, Sam's Discount Warehouses, or AAA. For example, AAA Auto Club operates a free, no-haggle buyer's service in which it prenegotiates car prices for its members. A toll-free phone call to AAA starts the process. AAA then contacts local dealers to see if they have the car that the customer wants. If they do, and the AAA member wants to buy, they simply sign a prenegotiated purchase agreement that guarantees a low price, which typically averages $100 over dealer cost for U.S. models and $400 over dealer cost for foreign models.[49] No haggling. No tricky negotiating ploys by salespeople.

### 4.2 Positioning Strategies

After analyzing industry forces, the next step in industry-level strategy is to effectively protect your company from the negative effects of industry-wide competition and to create a sustainable competitive advantage. According to Michael Porter, there are three positioning strategies: cost leadership, differentiation, and focus.

**cost leadership**
the positioning strategy of producing a product or service of acceptable quality at consistently lower production costs than competitors can, so that the firm can offer the product or service at the lowest price in the industry

**Cost leadership** means producing a product or service of acceptable quality at consistently lower production costs than competitors, so that the firm can offer the product or service at the lowest price in the industry. Cost leadership protects companies from industry forces by deterring new entrants, who will have to match low costs and prices. Cost leadership also forces down the prices of substitute products and services, attracts bargain-seeking buyers, and increases bargaining power with suppliers, who have to keep their prices low if they want to do business with the cost leader. AirTran airlines is an example of a cost leadership strategy. Its founders started the company based on one simple fact and two simple questions. The fact: Twenty million people drive to Florida each year for vacation. The questions: If prices were low enough, wouldn't they rather fly? And where else would they like to fly if prices were low enough? How low are AirTran's prices? President Lewis Jordan said, "It wouldn't take a lot to study our costs and figure out that if we wanted to cut our fares in half, we could run for a long time on the cash we have built up and be very competitive. If a big carrier was going to match us across the board, they would have to bleed hundreds of millions of dollars" to put AirTran out of business.[50]

**differentiation**
the positioning strategy of providing a product or service that is sufficiently different from competitors' offerings such that customers are willing to pay a premium price for it

**Differentiation** means making your product or service sufficiently different from competitors' offerings so that customers are willing to pay a premium price for the extra value or performance that it provides. Differentiation protects companies from industry forces by reducing the threat of substitute products. It also protects companies by making it easier to retain customers and more difficult for new entrants trying to attract new customers. Home Box Office (HBO), the subscription cable TV movie channel, relies on a differentiation strategy to set itself apart from its competitors such as Starz and Showtime. Like its competitors, HBO spends half a billion dollars a year to acquire the rights to broadcast first-run movies. However, it differentiates itself by spending an additional half billion dollars to develop its own programming, such as the popular *Dennis Miller Live*, *Sex and the City*, *The Sopranos*, as well as *Band of Brothers*, the 10-part World War II miniseries on which it spent $120 million, twice what it cost Steven Spielberg to make *Saving Private Ryan*. As a result, 90 percent of cable and satellite customers who pay for premium TV services subscribe to HBO. In turn, HBO is more profitable than the ABC, CBS, NBC, and Fox television networks put together.[51]

**focus strategy**
the positioning strategy of using cost leadership or differentiation to produce a specialized product or service for a limited, specially targeted group of customers in a particular geographic region or market segment

A **focus strategy** means that a company uses either cost leadership or differentiation to produce a specialized product or service for a limited, specially targeted group of customers in a particular geographic region or market segment. Focus strategies typically work in market niches that competitors have overlooked or have difficulty serving. Alpine Log Homes is a company that follows a focus strategy. First, as its name indicates, Alpine Log Homes serves a specialized niche in the home construction industry: manu-

330

facturing log houses. However, Alpine is even more focused than that. With the average Alpine log home running 6,500 square feet and costing $1.2 million, Alpine serves just the high end of the log home market. Other than price, what differentiates Alpine's log homes is the number of options available (indoor swimming pools, movie theaters, heated indoor parking) and the fact that its logs are hand-hewn (most logs in log homes are cut and shaped in factories). Finally, Alpine maintains its differentiation focus strategy by building only 75 log homes per year.[52]

### 4.3 Adaptive Strategies

Adaptive strategies are another set of industry-level strategies. While the aim of positioning strategies is to minimize the effects of industry competition and build a sustainable competitive advantage, the purpose of adaptive strategies is to choose an industry-level strategy that is best suited to changes in the organization's external environment. There are four kinds of adaptive strategies: defenders, prospectors, analyzers, and reactors.[53]

**defenders**
an adaptive strategy aimed at defending strategic positions by seeking moderate, steady growth and by offering a limited range of high-quality products and services to a well-defined set of customers

**Defenders** seek moderate, steady growth by offering a limited range of products and services to a well-defined set of customers. In other words, defenders aggressively "defend" their current strategic position by doing the best job they can to hold on to customers in a particular market segment. LanChile, Latin America's most successful airline, gets 43 percent of its revenues from cargo and 57 percent of revenues from passengers. Its planes transport Columbian flowers, Ecuadorian fish, Peruvian asparagus, as well as 100 tons of fresh Pacific salmon to Miami, Florida, every day. The planes return full of U.S.-made products, such as cell phones, high technology components, and chemicals. When Continental Airlines started a nonstop flight from Santiago, Chile, to New York, LanChile aggressively defended its business by switching to smaller planes to cut costs and then matched Continental's low prices. After a frustrated Continental eventually left the market, CEO Enrique Cueto said, "If someday one of the huge U.S. companies wants to enter the region, they have two alternatives. Either they compete with us or they join us."[54]

**prospectors**
an adaptive strategy that seeks fast growth by searching for new market opportunities, encouraging risk-taking, and being the first to bring innovative new products to market

**Prospectors** seek fast growth by searching for new market opportunities, encouraging risk taking, and being the first to bring innovative new products to market. Prospectors are analogous to gold miners who "prospect" for gold nuggets (i.e., new products) in hopes that it will lead them to a mine that has a rich deposit of gold (i.e., fast growth). Minnesota Mining & Manufacturing (3M), has long been known for its innovative products, particularly in the areas of adhesives where, beginning in 1904, it invented sandpaper, followed by masking, cellophane, electrical, and scotch tapes, as well the first commercially available audio and video tapes and its most famous invention, Post-it notes. 3M is also a leader in lighting technologies and has invented a film that increases the brightness of LCD displays on laptop and handheld computers, as well as a similar product that improves the visibility of road signs, making them visible even in heavy fog. In packing technology, 3M's new Inflata-Pak can now be used to protect items for shipping. Simply place an item inside the Inflata-Pak plastic bag, blow air in to inflate the walls, and then pinch the inflation valve for a tight seal. Once filled with air, the double-walled plastic provides a strong and durable cushion to protect fragile items. And, unlike foam peanuts or bubble wrap, the Inflata-Pak plastic bag lies flat and takes up little space until inflated for shipping. Finally, returning to its first product, 3M has improved sandpaper so that it sands three times faster and lasts three times longer. It has also color-coded sandpapers with variations in grit (i.e., light or heavy sanding paper) to make it easy to know which sand paper should be or is being used to complete a sanding job.[55]

**analyzers**
an adaptive strategy that seeks to minimize risk and maximize profits by following or imitating the proven successes of prospectors

**Analyzers** are a blend of the defender and prospector strategies. Analyzers seek moderate, steady growth *and* limited opportunities for fast growth. Analyzers are rarely first to market with new products or services. Instead, they try to simultaneously minimize risk and maximize profits by following or imitating the proven successes of prospectors. For example, while 75 percent of personal computers are made by the 20 largest PC manufacturers (Compaq, Dell, IBM, Gateway, etc.), the remaining 25 percent are made by 100,000 small manufacturers, most of which use an analyzer strategy. One such company is Adam Computers, which manufactures and sells 7,000 computers a year in Dallas.

Two television shows featuring bowling are boosting the reactor strategy of alley owners. NBC's hit comedy "Ed" and a new hit show, "Let's Bowl!" aired on Comedy Central give the sport the most media coverage in recent memory. "Let's Bowl!" puts such a kitschy twist on the old PBA King of Bowling shows that it may just bring people back to the lanes.

**reactors**
an adaptive strategy of not following a consistent strategy, but instead reacting to changes in the external environment after they occur

Rather than trying to design new computer products (a prospector strategy), Adam typically makes computers with the same options and configurations as the large PC manufacturers offer. However, Adam Computers distinguishes itself by offering personal service. Instead of impersonal Web sites and 24-hour phone support, small manufacturers like Adam Computers frequently send service technicians to customers' homes to make repairs. Likewise, when customers call with a question, they can often talk directly to the technician who manufactured their computer.[56]

Finally, unlike defenders, prospectors, or analyzers, **reactors** do not follow a consistent strategy. Furthermore, rather than anticipating and preparing for external opportunities and threats, reactors tend to "react" to changes in their external environment after they occur. Not surprisingly, reactors tend to be poorer performers than defenders, prospectors, or analyzers. One likely example of a reactor is your local bowling alley. Bowling peaked in popularity in the early 1970s. At that time, 10 million Americans eagerly signed up to participate in regular bowling leagues lasting 35 weeks a year. However, twenty years later, only five million Americans count themselves as regular bowlers. As would be expected, many bowling alleys have gone out of business. Consistent with a reactor strategy, the surviving bowling alleys have only recently begun to take actions to reverse these declines. Bowling alley owners can only hope that innovations such as "no gutter" bowling for small children (on weekends), traditional leagues for retirees (on week days), and "cosmic bowling" with pounding music, glow-in-the-dark pins, laser lights, and fog machines (for teenagers on weekend nights) will bring customers back.[57]

## Review 4
### Industry-Level Strategies

Industry-level strategies focus on how companies choose to compete in their industry. Five industry forces determine an industry's overall attractiveness to corporate investors and potential for long-term profitability. Together, a high level of new entrants, substitute products or services, bargaining power of suppliers, bargaining power of buyers, and rivalry between competitors combine to increase competition and decrease profits. Three positioning strategies can help companies protect themselves from the negative effects of industry-wide competition. Under a cost leadership strategy, firms try to keep production costs low, so that they can sell products at prices lower than competitors'. Differentiation is a strategy aimed at making a product or service sufficiently different from competitors' that it can command a premium price. Using a focus strategy, firms seek to produce a specialized product or service for a limited, specially targeted group of customers. The four adaptive strategies help companies adapt to changes in the external environment. Defenders want to "defend" their current strategic positions. Prospectors look for new market opportunities by bringing innovative new products to market. Analyzers minimize risk by following the proven successes of prospectors. Reactors do not follow a consistent strategy, but instead react to changes in their external environment after they occur.

## 5. Firm-Level Strategies

**firm-level strategy**
corporate strategy that addresses the question "How should we compete against a particular firm?"

**Firm-level strategy** addresses the question "How should we compete against a particular firm?" For example, over the last two decades, McDonald's has dominated its nearest rival Burger King in terms of sales, profits, market share, and growth. Consequently, McDonald's is twice Burger King's size. However, over the last few years, Burger King has become the attacker and McDonald's the nervous follower. Burger King started its attack by heavily advertising that its Whopper sandwich was bigger than McDonald's Big Mac. McDonald's responded by creating larger, more expensive deluxe sandwiches like the Arch Deluxe hamburger. When it did, Burger King's sales (not McDonald's) increased by 11 percent. To keep weight and health-conscious customers coming in, Burger King created a grilled chicken sandwich. Several years later, McDonald's did the same. Then, Burger King attacked McDonald's stranglehold on the fast-food breakfast business, introducing its own croissant and biscuit breakfast sandwiches and selling them for 20 to 25 cents less than McDonald's better-known Egg McMuffin and Sausage McMuffin sandwiches. Moreover, Burger King was able to lower prices on items across its entire menu at the same time that McDonald's food prices increased by 4 percent to 8 percent.[58]

All told, Burger King's aggressive attacks have worked. Burger King's sales are increasing while McDonald's are decreasing. Indeed, an internal McDonald's memo indicated that price cuts might be needed because of an "overt competitive attack by BK."[59]

*Let's find out more about the firm-level strategies (i.e., direct competition between companies) shown in Exhibit 9.15 by reading about 5.1 the basics of direct competition, 5.2 the strategic moves involved in direct competition between companies, and 5.3 the firm-level strategy of entrepreneurship and intrapreneurship.*

### 5.1 Direct Competition

While Porter's five industry forces indicate the overall level of competition in an industry, most companies do not compete directly with all the firms in their industry. For example, McDonald's and Red Lobster are both in the restaurant business, but no one would characterize them as competitors. McDonald's offers low-cost, convenient fast food in a "seat yourself" restaurant, while Red Lobster offers mid-priced, sit-down seafood dinners complete with servers and a bar.

EXHIBIT 9.15

FIRM-LEVEL STRATEGIES (DIRECT COMPETITION)

| DIRECT COMPETITION | STRATEGIC MOVES OF DIRECT COMPETITION | ENTREPRENEURIAL/INTRAPRENEURIAL ORIENTATION |
|---|---|---|
| • Market commonality<br>• Resource similarity | • Attack<br>• Response | • Autonomy<br>• Innovativeness<br>• Risk-taking<br>• Proactiveness<br>• Competitive aggressiveness |

**direct competition**
the rivalry between two companies
that offer similar products and services, acknowledge each other as
rivals, and act and react to each
other's strategic actions

**market commonality**
the degree to which two companies
have overlapping products, services,
or customers in multiple markets

**resource similarity**
the extent to which a competitor
has similar amounts and kinds of
resources

Instead of "competing" with the industry, most firms compete directly with just a few companies. **Direct competition** is the rivalry between two companies offering similar products and services that acknowledge each other as rivals and take offensive and defensive positions as they act and react to each other's strategic actions.[60] Two factors determine the extent to which firms will be in direct competition with each other: market commonality and resource similarity. **Market commonality** is the degree to which two companies have overlapping products, services, or customers in multiple markets. The more markets in which there is product, service, or customer overlap, the more intense the direct competition between the two companies. **Resource similarity** is the extent to which a competitor has similar amounts and kinds of resources, that is, similar assets, capabilities, processes, information, and knowledge used to create and sustain an advantage over competitors. From a competitive standpoint, resource similarity means that the strategic actions that your company takes can probably be matched by your direct competitors.

Exhibit 9.16 shows how market commonality and resource similarity interact to determine when and where companies are in direct competition.[61] The overlapping area in each quadrant (between the triangle and the rectangle, or between the differently colored rectangles) depicts market commonality. The larger the overlap, the greater the market commonality. Shapes depict resource similarity, with rectangles representing one set of competitive resources and triangles representing another. Quadrant I shows two companies in direct competition, because they have similar resources at their disposal and a high degree of market commonality. This reflects the fact that they try to sell similar products and services to similar customers. McDonald's and Burger King would clearly fit here as direct competitors.

In Quadrant II, the overlapping parts of the triangle and rectangle show two companies going after similar customers with some similar products or services, but doing so with different competitive resources. McDonald's and Wendy's restaurants would fit here. Wendy's is after the same lunchtime and dinner crowds that McDonald's is. How-

---

**EXHIBIT 9.16**

A FRAMEWORK OF DIRECT COMPETITION

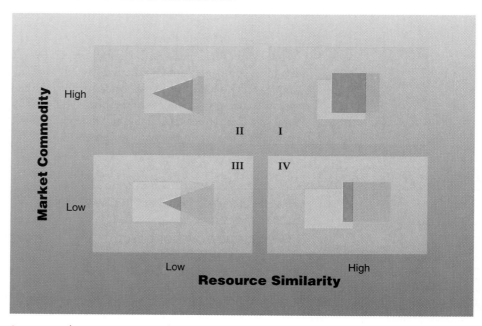

**Source:** M. Chen, "Competitor Analysis and Interfirm Rivalry: Toward a Theoretical Integration," *Academy of Management Review* 21 (1996): 100-134.

ever, it is less of a direct competitor to McDonald's than Burger King is, because Wendy's hamburgers, fries, and shakes are more expensive. A representative from Wendy's said, "We believe you win customers by consistently offering a better product at a strong, everyday value." Plus, Wendy's is now competing less with McDonald's as it expands its Tim Horton's chain. Tim Horton's is a baked-goods store that also serves bagels, soups, deli sandwiches, cookies, and soft drinks.[62]

In Quadrant III, the very small overlap shows two companies with different competitive resources and little market commonality. McDonald's and Luby's cafeteria fit here. Although both are in the fast-food business, there's almost no overlap in terms of products and customers. For example, Luby's sells baked chicken, turkey, roasts, meat loaf, and vegetables, none of which are available at McDonald's. Furthermore, Luby's customers aren't likely to eat at McDonald's. In fact, Luby's is not really competing with other fast-food restaurants, but with eating at home. Company surveys show that close to half of its customers would have eaten at home, not at another restaurant, if they hadn't come to Luby's.[63]

Finally, in Quadrant IV, the small overlap between the two rectangles shows two companies competing with similar resources but with little market commonality. Surprisingly, McDonald's and Burger King fit here, too. The major difference from Quadrant I is that Quadrant IV represents direct competition between McDonald's and Burger King in Japan, not the United States. Both sell burgers and fries in Japan (i.e., similar products). However, unlike the U.S. market, market commonality is low, because of Burger King's small size and because few Japanese fast-food customers have ever heard of it. Jun Fujita, an assistant manager at a Tokyo McDonald's, said, "We don't see them as a threat at all. Who has ever heard of Burger King?"[64] This example also illustrates the point that even between direct competitors, competition in each market (i.e., geographic regions, particular products or services, etc.) is unique. Furthermore, direct competitors have different strengths and weaknesses in different markets. For example, although Burger King has been gaining on McDonald's in the United States, McDonald's is clearly dominant in Japan. McDonald's has been in Japan for 25 years and has over 2,000 restaurants. By contrast, Burger King hopes to open 200 restaurants in Japan over the next five years.

## 5.2 Strategic Moves of Direct Competition

While corporate-level strategies help managers decide what business to be in and business-level strategies help them determine how to compete within an industry, firm-level strategies help managers determine when, where, and what strategic actions should be taken against a direct competitor. There are two basic strategic moves in direct competition between firms: attacks and responses.

**attack**
a competitive move designed to reduce a rival's market share or profits

An **attack** is a competitive move designed to reduce a rival's market share or profits. For example, Dallas-based Legend airlines replaced all the coach seats in its DC-9 airplanes with first-class seats, but sold them at business-class prices. Legend's plan was simple. Instead of being a discount flyer like Southwest Airlines, its plan was to go after American Airline's best customers (American accounts for 70 percent of the flights at nearby DFW International Airport), business travelers who fly frequently and are willing to pay top dollar for business-class tickets purchased at the last minute before traveling. And by flying from Dallas to New York, Los Angeles, Washington, and Las Vegas, it attacked American on its most profitable routes. So why would customers fly Legend instead? Consider that a roundtrip business-class ticket between Dallas and New York cost about $2,000 with either American or Legend. But at Legend, that $2,000 ticket bought a first-class seat and first-class amenities. At American, it only bought you business-class seating and business-class amenities.[65]

**response**
a competitive countermove, prompted by a rival's attack, to defend or improve a company's market share or profit

A **response** is a countermove, prompted by a rival's attack, designed to defend or improve a company's market share or profit. For example, in an extremely aggressive response to Legend Airlines, American Airlines sued the city of Dallas, the U.S. government, and Legend itself to prevent it from flying out of Dallas's Love Field. Though it prevailed, fighting these lawsuits cost Legend $2 million in legal fees. When the lawsuits failed, American leased an abandoned terminal at Love Field to prevent Legend from

## Competitive Intelligence, Shopping the Competition

One of the best ways to keep abreast of the need for strategic change is to "shop the competition." Every time the Wal-Mart CEO visits a local Wal-Mart store, he also visits the nearby Kmart or Target store. When FedEx wants to benchmark its delivery services against the competition, it has FedEx employees, posing as customers, mail identical packages with identical destinations at FedEx and UPS offices. Likewise, when Burger King wants to study the efficiency of its drive-through windows, it sends researchers through the drive-through windows at Burger King, McDonald's, and Wendy's. Curious about what your competitors are up to? Go shopping.

**Sources:** J. Frontier, "Spies Like Us: You Don't Need to Be James Bond or IBM to Use Competitive Intelligence. Here's How It Works," *Business Week*, 12 June 2000, F24.

obtaining access to those airline gates. As a result, Legend had to spend $21 million to build a new terminal and parking garage. And when Legend began calling on companies to sell discounted corporate packages, American had beaten them to the punch by huge incentives that took effect only if company employees and managers flew just with American. Said T. Allan McArtor, Legend's CEO, "Everything American did here over the last several years had one purpose: To run Legend Airlines out of business." In fact, American Airlines' counterattack was so strong that Legend filed for bankruptcy after spending $62 million of its $70 million in funding on legal battles.[66]

Attacks and responses can include smaller, more tactical moves, like price cuts, specially advertised sales or promotions, or improvements in service. However, they can also include resource-intensive strategic moves, such as expanding service and production facilities, introducing new products or services within the firm's existing business, or entering a completely new line of business for the first time. Of these, market entries and exits are probably the most important kinds of attacks and responses. Entering a new market is a clear offensive signal to an attacking or responding firm that your company is committed to gaining or defending market share and profits at their expense. By contrast, exiting a market is an equally clear defensive signal that your company is retreating.[67] For example, in response to tremendous competition from Cisco Systems, 3Com exited the high-end networking business for the routers and switches used to run the Internet. It also sold its dial-up modem division, where competition had increased. 3Com will now focus on providing high-speed cable modems, wireless networks, and home networking products for small- and medium-sized businesses, network service providers, and high-end home users. 3Com's president said, "We're going to narrow our focus on markets, products, and technologies where we can lead."[68]

Exhibit 9.17 shows that market commonality and resource similarity determine the likelihood of an attack or response, that is, whether a company is likely to attack a direct competitor or to strike back with a strong response when attacked. When market commonality is strong and companies have overlapping products, services, or customers in multiple markets, there is less motivation to attack and more motivation to respond to an attack. The reason for this is straightforward: When firms are direct competitors in a large number of markets, there is much more at stake. If Kmart cuts prices in its lawn-and-garden department so that they're 10 percent lower than Wal-Mart's prices, it knows that Wal-Mart, which has a store within several miles of nearly every Kmart store, will

336

### EXHIBIT 9.17

#### LIKELIHOOD OF ATTACKS AND RESPONSES IN DIRECT COMPETITION

| Competitor Analysis | Interfirm Rivalry: Action and Response |
|---|---|
| Strong Market Commonality | Less Likelihood of an Attack |
| Weak Market Commonality | Greater Likelihood of an Attack |
| High Resource Similarity | Greater Likelihood of a Response |
| Low Resource Similarity | Less Likelihood of a Response |

**Source:** M. Chen, "Competitor Analysis and Interfirm Rivalry: Toward a Theoretical Integration," *Academy of Management Review* 21 (1996): 100-134.

strike back by immediately cutting its lawn-and-garden prices so that its prices are cheaper. The result is that both Kmart and Wal-Mart will sacrifice profits from the lawn-and-garden department in thousands of stores.

While market commonality affects the likelihood of an attack or a response to an attack, resource similarity largely affects response capability, that is, how quickly and forcefully a company can respond to an attack. When resource similarity is strong, the responding firm will generally be able to match the strategic moves of the attacking firm. Consequently, firms are less likely to attack firms with similar levels of resources, because they're unlikely to gain any sustained advantage when the responding firm strikes back. On the other hand, if one firm is substantially stronger than another (i.e., low resource similarity), then a competitive attack is more likely to produce sustained competitive advantage. For example, CVS drugstores, which has 4,000 stores, is one of the fastest growing drugstore chains. CVS attacks competitors, mostly weaker, independently owned and operated pharmacies, by quickly opening up several nearby stores. Then, to lure shoppers to its stores and away from competitors, it negotiates sole-provider contracts with local health maintenance organizations. Consequently, HMO members who get their prescriptions filled at CVS pay less money out of their own pockets. Finally, CVS pressures its rivals with repeated buyout offers. One competitor, Jack Morgan, watched helplessly as his former customers began going to a nearby CVS store to fill their prescriptions. With his sales cut in half, he sold out to CVS. "I didn't have much choice," Mr. Morgan said. "You can't compete with CVS."[69]

In general, the greater the number of moves (i.e., attacks) a company initiates against direct competitors, and the greater a firm's tendency to respond when attacked, the better its performance. More specifically, attackers and early responders (companies that are quick to launch a retaliatory attack) tend to gain market share and profits at the expense of late responders. This is not to suggest that a "full-attack" strategy always works best. In fact, attacks can provoke harsh retaliatory responses. Indeed, under the gun from falling profits and intense competition from Vauxhall, Volkswagen, and MG Rover, Britain's largest car manufacturer, Ford Motor Company, struck back with a blistering 20 percent cut in automobile list prices.[70] Consequently, when deciding when, where, and what strategic actions to take against a direct competitor, managers should always consider the possibility of retaliation.

## 5.3 Entrepreneurship and Intrapreneurship: A Firm-Level Strategy

Firm-level strategy addresses how one company should compete against another. Furthermore, of the various kinds of attacks and responses used in direct competition, market entry is perhaps the most forceful attack or response, because it sends the clear signal that the company is committed to gaining or defending market share and profits at a direct competitor's expense.

**entrepreneurship**
the process of entering new or established markets with new goods or services

**intrapreneurship**
entrepreneurship within an existing organization

Since **entrepreneurship** is the process of entering new or established markets with new goods or services, entrepreneurship is also a firm-level strategy. In fact, the basic strategic act of entrepreneurship is new entry—creating a new business from a brand new startup firm. However, existing firms can also enter new or established markets with new goods or services. In other words, established firms can be entrepreneurial, too. However, when existing companies are entrepreneurial, it's called **intrapreneurship**.[71] For example, each year 5 million pounds of formulated insecticide are used to protect potato crops from pests and diseases. However, instead of applying agricultural chemicals, farmers can now simply plant Monsanto Corporation's NewLeaf Plus potatoes, which, thanks to biotechnology engineering, are pest and disease resistant. Because Monsanto has been in the agricultural chemical business for decades, its new biotech products, like the NewLeaf Plus potato, are strong evidence that the company is now using an intrapreneurial strategy to enter brand new markets with brand new products and services.[72]

While the goal of an intrapreneurial strategy is new entry, the process of carrying out an intrapreneurial strategy depends on the ability of the company's founders or existing managers to foster an entrepreneurial orientation (remember, intrapreneurship is entre-

**entrepreneurial orientation**
the set of processes, practices, and decision-making activities that lead to new entry, characterized by five dimensions: autonomy, innovativeness, risk-taking, proactiveness, and competitive aggressiveness

preneurship in an existing organization). An **entrepreneurial orientation** is the set of processes, practices, and decision-making activities that lead to new entry. Five key dimensions characterize an entrepreneurial orientation: autonomy, innovativeness, risk-taking, proactiveness, and competitive aggressiveness.[73] Without these, an entrepreneurial orientation is unlikely to be created, and an intrapreneurial strategy is unlikely to succeed.

1. *Autonomy.* If a firm wants to successfully develop new products or services to enter new markets, it must foster creativity among employees. To be creative, employees need the freedom and control to develop a new idea into a new product or service opportunities without interference from others. In other words, they need autonomy. For example, when IBM was developing its first personal computer in the early 1980s, it created a dozen design teams, gave them complete freedom to design what they wanted, and sent them to different locations away from IBM's regular offices. In fact, the winning team worked out of an old rundown manufacturing plant in Boca Raton, Florida. Furthermore, to prevent interference or influence from IBM's existing business, almost no one in the company knew these teams existed.

2. *Innovativeness.* Entrepreneurial firms also foster innovativeness by supporting new ideas, experimentation, and creative processes that might produce new products, services, or technological processes. One example is Great Plains Software, which makes accounting software for small companies. With 63 other firms also producing accounting software, the obvious question was how to make the company's accounting software stand out in a crowded market. The answer was to provide extensive phone support to customers who purchased the software. The innovation was to charge for that support, something that no software company had dared try. In fact, Great Plains found that customers were more than willing to pay a fixed amount for unlimited support, because Great Plains was not only helping them learn to use its software, but was also helping them set up their accounts and ledgers correctly. Today, customers who pay a fixed annual fee for support are guaranteed to be called back in 30 minutes by their own personal support representative.[74]

3. *Risk taking.* Entrepreneurial firms are also willing to take some risks, by making large resource commitments that may result in costly failure.[75] Another way to conceptualize risk taking is to think of it as managers' preferences for bold rather than cautious acts. For example, after travelling to Italy and noticing that Italians cooked pasta for their dogs, Richard Thompson decided to start Pet Pasta Products. With Americans spending over $9 billion a year on pet food, and much of that for premium brands that look tasty and promise superior nutritional benefits, Thompson figured that products like Pasta Plus dog food would be fast sellers. However, in four years of business, the company has spent $30 million and not yet earned a profit. Thompson, however, is not deterred. He said, "I'm the only one with the guts to take on these guys [Purina, Heinz, and Mars pet foods]. . . . I've gambled my fortune that this will work!"[76]

4. *Proactiveness.* Entrepreneurial firms have the ability to anticipate future problems, needs, or changes by developing new products or services that may not be related to their current business, by introducing new products or services before the competition does, and by dropping products or services that are declining (and likely to be replaced by new products or services).[77] Internet Security Systems (ISS) anticipated the security risks associated with corporate email, Internet access, and company intranets by developing software that helps companies protect company data and computer systems. For example, ISS's software scans company password databases, looking for 25,000 easy-to-crack account passwords, like "Spot," "Steelers," and "Star Trek." When it finds them, users must then submit a more-secure password. In all, ISS's software can shut down over 200 computer hacker tricks that compromise corporate computer security. Christopher Klaus, the 23-year-old company founder, said, "We make sure all the windows are closed and the doors are locked."[78]

5. *Competitive aggressiveness.* Because new entrants are more likely to fail than are existing firms, they must be aggressive if they want to succeed. A new firm often must be will-

ing to use unconventional methods to directly challenge competitors for their customers and market share. A new company called Fresh Picks is using this approach to enter the highly competitive retail business of selling music CDs to consumers. In recent years, music stores like Wherehouse Entertainment and Camelot Music have ended up in bankruptcy, losing business to the likes of Wal-Mart, Kmart, and Circuit City. So instead of setting up music stores, Fresh Picks wants to sell CDs in grocery stores by setting up CD display cases holding up to 400 different selections. Why grocery stores? In France, supermarkets already sell half of all CDs. In the United Kingdom, it's roughly 12 percent. Fresh Picks' president Michael Rigby said, "Customers go into a supermarket with an open shopping list and a 100 percent intent to spend."[79]

## Review 5
### Firm-Level Strategies

Firm-level strategies are concerned with direct competition between firms. Market commonality and resource similarity determine whether firms are in direct competition and thus likely to attack each other or respond to each other's attacks. In general, the more markets in which there is product, service, or customer overlap, and the greater the resource similarity between two firms, the more intense the direct competition between them. When firms are direct competitors in a large number of markets, attacks are less likely, because responding firms are highly motivated to quickly and forcefully defend their profits and market share. By contrast, resource similarity affects response capability, meaning how quickly and forcefully a company responds to an attack. When resource similarity is strong, attacks are much less likely to produce a sustained advantage, because the responding firm is capable of striking back with equal force. Market entries and exits are the most important kinds of attacks and responses. Entering a new market is a clear offensive signal, while exiting a market is a clear signal that a company is retreating. In general, attackers and early responders gain market share and profits at the expense of late responders. However, attacks must be carefully planned and carried out, because they can provoke harsh retaliatory responses. Firm-level strategy addresses how one company should compete against another. Of the various kinds of attacks and responses used in direct competition, market entry is perhaps the most forceful attack or response, because it sends the clear signal that the company is committed to gaining or defending market share and profits at a direct competitor's expense. Finally, the basic strategic act of entrepreneurship is new entry. To carry out an entrepreneurial strategy, a company must create an entrepreneurial orientation by encouraging autonomy, innovativeness, risk-taking, proactiveness, and competitive aggressiveness.

## What Really Happened?

At the beginning of the chapter, you learned that General Motors once dominated the U.S. auto industry with a 50 percent share of the market. However, 10 years ago, GM's market share had dropped to 38 percent, and today, it has dropped all the way to 28 percent. Let's find out what really happened to see the strategic plans GM is putting in place to turn the company around.

### First, how can GM create a sustainable advantage over its competitors?

To provide a sustainable competitive advantage, firm resources must im-prove efficiency and effectiveness (i.e., value), must not be possessed by many competing firms (i.e., rare), must be extremely costly or difficult to duplicate (i.e., imperfectly imitable), and must be nonsubstitutable (i.e., competitors cannot substitute other resources to produce similar value). The two most common forms of competitive advantage in the auto industry are cost and quality. GM does not have a competitive cost advantage, as Kia and Hyundai, two Korean auto manufacturers, charge much lower prices for their cars than GM does. On the other hand, GM has significantly improved the reliability of its cars in recent years. Guy Briggs, GM's top manufacturing executive, said, "We're attacking it like a life-threatening disease." However, according to the J.D. Power & Associates survey of auto quality and reliability, GM still trails Toyota, Honda, and Nissan. So while GM has made significant improvements, it still has a lot of work to do to create some kind of sustainable competitive advantage.

### Second, are there potential business opportunities among the obvious and numerous threats to GM business?

The key question in industry-level strategy is "How should we compete in this industry?" One answer is cost leadership, which means producing a product or service of acceptable quality at consistently lower production costs than competitors, so that the firm can offer the product or service at the lowest price in the industry. However, as discussed above, GM is unlikely to have success with a cost leadership strategy. Another answer is differentiation, making your product or service sufficiently different from competitors' offerings so that customers are willing to pay a premium price for the extra value or performance that it provides. Differentiation protects companies from industry forces by reducing the threat of substitute products. It also protects companies by making it easier to retain customers and more difficult for new entrants trying to attract new customers.

GM hopes to reduce costs, not enough to compete using a cost leadership strategy, but enough to be able to shift cost savings into a differentiation strategy in which significant investments from cost savings lead to quicker development of hot new cars and trucks that customers are clamoring to buy. It should be noted that GM is not pursuing a pure differentiation strategy. People are willing to pay much more for a Lexus, BMW, or Acura because the luxury, performance, and quality are so much better than other cars (i.e., differentiation). By contrast, GM hopes to follow a limited differentiation strategy in which it hopes to make and sell new, different, reliable cars at a good price. In this sense, GM's limited differentiation strategy is actually closer to Honda's than to Lexus, BMW, or Acura.

However, GM will have to avoid past mistakes if this strategy is to work in the future. For example, it took GM more than a decade to realize that consumers were dumping station wagons by the thousands for more versatile mini-vans. Chrysler and Ford had sold 1 million mini-vans before GM had a product on the market. More recently, GM spent millions to develop the Pontiac Aztec, a boxy looking sports utility vehicle that has been a sales dud. A differentiation strategy only works if customers are willing to pay more for a different product. Unfortunately, the Pontiac Aztec was too different and customers have stayed away. Another way in which GM hopes to pursue a differentiation strategy is by expanding its auto parts and service unit, where its profit margins are twice what it earns when manufacturing cars. GM hopes to increase revenues in this parts and service by 30 percent to $12 billion a year. GM's executive vice president Ron Zarella said, "We've got a plan. Now it's a question of do we have the guts to execute?"

## Finally, what should GM's new strategy be? Should it be growth, stability, or retrenchment/recovery?

A grand strategy is a broad strategic plan used to help an organization achieve its strategic goals. Grand strategies guide the strategic alternatives that managers of individual businesses or subunits may use. There are three kinds of grand strategies: growth, stability, and retrenchment/recovery.

GM's ultimate goal is to return to regular growth by following the limited differentiation strategy discussed above. However, before returning to growth, it is first pursuing a radical retrenchment strategy, the purpose of which is to turn around very poor company performance by shrinking the size or scope of the business. The first step of a typical retrenchment strategy might include significant cost reductions, employee layoffs, closing of poorly performing stores, offices, or manufacturing plants, or closing or selling entire lines of products or services. Consistent with these steps, GM's CEO Rick Wagoner has already announced that GM is killing its Oldsmobile division and cutting 15,000 jobs. It will also close 15 percent of its European factories. Within three years, it plans to cut the number of cars it offers, currently 80 models, by 20 percent. GM has also cut several car platforms (each platform is the building block for several car models),

saving hundreds of millions of dollars in associated material, engineering, and factory costs. Put together, these cutbacks mean that GM will need 10 percent fewer engineers and administrators, so additional layoffs will be coming for GM's white collar work force. The cost savings should amount to $100,000 per worker. However, the goal is not just cost savings, but to put a shock to GM's culture that results in immediate changes. Rick Wagoner, GM's CEO said, "[You] don't sit here with a ten-year plan and say things are going to be great in years nine and ten. If you don't get years one through three right, you won't have a chance to execute those." GM's executive vice president Ron Zarella, echoed that sentiment, saying, "Damn it, once and for all, we're going to get the business turned [around], we're going to get our brands stronger, we're going to get the [market] share turned [around], we're going to take cost out of the business to make the best returns in the industry."

Only time will tell if GM's retrenchment strategy is successful.

**Sources:** G. White, "Hitting the Brakes: In Order to Grow, GM Finds That the Order of the Day Is Cutbacks—For CEO Rick Wagoner, Killing Off Oldsmobile Was Just the Beginning—Banking on Hot New Cars," *The Wall Street Journal*, 18 December 2000, A1. G. White, J. White, & S. Freeman, "What's a Cool Car? The Question Is Driving U.S. Auto Makers Wild—Beyond Focus Groups, Officials Hang Out in Video Arcades and Chat Up Snowboarders," *The Wall Street Journal*, 9 August 2000, B1. G. White, "Half-Full Tank: After Gloomy Winter, Big-Three Car Makers Grow Warily Optimistic—Sales Data Suggest Economy Isn't Spooking Consumers to Extent Industry Feared—Minivan for a Baby on the Way," *The Wall Street Journal*, 4 April 2001, A1. J. White, G. White, & N. Shirouzu, "Passing Era: Soon, The Big Three Won't Be, As Foreigners Make Inroads in U.S.—Toyota Draws Near Chrysler as Investments Pay Off; Dealers Shift Loyalties—'A Life-Threatening Disease,'" *The Wall Street Journal*, 13 August 2001, A1. A. Taylor, III., & F. Garcia, "Bumpy Roads for Global Automakers: Forget This Year's Record Sales—DaimlerChrysler Is in Chaos, And Price Wars Are Eating Profits at Most Other Companies—Life in the Fast Lane Is About to Get Rougher," *Fortune*, 28 December 2000, 278.

# Key Terms

# What Would You Do-II

## Olestra's Slippery Strategy

Thanks in part to a dwindling economy, your employer, Procter & Gamble, has been struggling for the last 18 months. Because of the recent downturn, a decision was made at yesterday's board meeting to reduce the company's workforce of 110,000 by 10 percent initially, up to a maximum of 20 percent if problems continue to plague the company. At the same meeting, the board grilled top executives for not ending failed projects early. Many board members expressed concern that failing projects were allowed to continue operating at a loss for long periods of time, and that now, the company and the employees are paying a price for those losses.

As a result of the meeting, you've been given a directive: Make the Olestra project profitable or dump it altogether. Olestra is a fat substitute, developed by P&G approximately 25 years ago, and used in snacks such as fat-free Pringles and Frito Lay's WOW! Chips. Olestra, which has been marketed by P&G under the name Olean, passes through the body without leaving any fat or calories behind. Unfortunately, Olestra has suffered negative publicity since its introduction because the Food and Drug Administration (FDA) requires the product to carry a warning label informing consumers of the potential for abdominal cramping and loose stools. As a result of this warning and several exposés on television shows such as Primetime and Dateline, sales of Olestra have not fared well. Over the years, approximately $500 million has been spent developing and marketing the product, including the construction of a $200 million plant exclusively for the production of Olestra. Unfortunately, Olestra-related sales have only amounted to $200 million a year, much lower than original expectations, and, as of yet, the project has not returned initial research and development costs.

P&G has countered the FDA's claim of abdominal problems by researching the product's side effects. Research shows that Olestra causes no more digestive problems than other products such as prunes and bran fiber. P&G has presented its findings and is currently waiting on the FDA to lift its requirement of the warning. However, unless a new strategy is developed in which Olestra can be useful and turn a profit, P&G may not need the FDA's blessing. As the director of the Olestra product, you are accountable for the success or failure of your brand, which operates as an independent unit similar to a company. What kind of corporate-level strategy should Olestra pursue? In short, what would you propose to save your flailing brand? **If you were the director of the Olestra product, what would you do?**

**Sources:** N. Hellmich and B. Horovitz, "Fat Substitute Olestra Eyed as Hazardous-Waste Cleaner," *USA Today*, 31 May 2001. E. Nelson, "P&G Expects to Restore Growth; Will Pull the Plug on Failed Projects," *The Wall Street Journal*, 18 June 2001. E. Nelson, "Procter & Gamble May Cut Work Force by 10% to 20%," *The Wall Street Journal*, 21 March 2001.

## Management Decisions

### Absolutely, Positively Overnight

It begins at 11 P.M. each night. Every 90 seconds an orange, blue, and white FedEx cargo plane lands at the Memphis airport. By 1 A.M., all the planes have arrived. As FedEx workers scurry between planes, loading and unloading packages and cargo containers, activity is everywhere. The scene is not unlike a busy colony of ants lucky enough to find itself underneath a park picnic table. Before the planes return to the runway several hours later, stuffed to the cockpit with packages guaranteed to be delivered to their final destinations "absolutely, positively overnight," FedEx's 9,000 Memphis workers will have sorted one million packages in less than four hours. However, the daily numbers for the entire company are even more impressive: 562 cargo planes and 372,000 vans delivering 2.5 million packages in 211 countries.

Thanks to the increasing pace of the business world (and the human tendency to want immediate gratification, despite determined procrastination), FedEx has had unparalleled growth over the last two decades. Revenues have grown from zero, when FedEx invented the overnight delivery business a quarter century ago, to more than $10 billion a year. But can FedEx achieve the same explosive growth in the next 25 years that it had in its first 25? Unlike 1973, when founder and CEO Fred Smith started the company, FedEx faces numerous competitors, as well as technology (e.g., faxes and the Internet) that no one had even imagined a quarter-century ago.

**Additional Internet Resources**

- FedEx Home Page
  (**http://www.fedex.com**). This site contains information about FedEx's services, software, tracking, and delivery services.

- United Parcel Service Home Page
  (**http://www.ups.com**). This site contains information about UPS's services, software, tracking, and delivery services.
- U.S. Postal Service Home Page
  (**http://www.usps.gov**). This site contains information about the United States Postal Service. In particular, be sure to check out "Express Mail" and information about postal rates, especially for express mail.

**Questions**

1. Conduct a situational analysis for FedEx. What are its internal strengths (i.e., core competencies) and weaknesses? What strategic opportunities and threats does it face?
2. Assume that CEO Fred Smith has made you head of FedEx's shadow-strategy task force. Thinking like a competitor, actively determine FedEx's weaknesses and how a competitor could exploit them for competitive advantage.

**Sources:** D.A. Blackmon, "FedEx Plans to Establish a Marketplace in Cyber Space–Shipper Aims to Deliver the Goods as It Moves into Internet Commerce," *The Wall Street Journal*, 9 October 1996. D.A. Blackmon, "Federal Express Sees Strong 4Q, Backs Yr View above $3/Shr," *Dow Jones News Service*, 31 March 1997. D.A. Blackmon, "Federal Express Plans 3-Day Service to Challenge UPS," *The Wall Street Journal*, 2 April 1997. "Dietzgen's New Same-Day Satellite Document Delivery Service for Architectural and Engineering Blueprints Takes Direct Aim at Overnight Courier Business," *Business Wire*, 21 March 1997. T. Lappin, "FedEx: The Airline of the Internet," *Wired Magazine*, December 1996.

## Management Decisions

### How About a "Cuppa?"

In Great Britain, when someone asks, "How about a cuppa?" they're asking if you want a cup of tea. And with an average of 3.6 "cuppas" a day per person, Great Britain, which has a population just one-fourth the size of the U.S., consumes an amazing 10 percent of the world's tea each year—more than North America and Europe put together. In Great Britain, people of all ages and economic levels drink tea, bringing annual sales to more than $750 million per year. Indeed, the British drink so much tea that market researchers estimate that tea accounts for 42 percent of all liquid intake in Great Britain.

Yet even in tea-crazed Britain, tea is not as popular as it once was. Tea still outsells coffee and soft drinks combined, but tea sales are no longer growing. By contrast, coffee sales, especially among young professionals, are increasing approximately 4 percent per year. Mark Beales, a coffee marketing manager at Nestlé Foods, said, "It's seen to be more sophisticated than tea now. Out-of-home consumption is being driven by the increas-

ing number of quality café bars, which improves the perception of coffee and makes it more widely available." With sales of soft drinks increasing, too, especially among children and teens, the long-term prospects for tea don't look promising.

**Questions**

1. Using Michael Porters' Industry Forces model, explain how each of the five forces will affect the tea industry's overall attractiveness and potential for long-term profitability.
2. If you worked for one of the leading tea companies in Britain (tea bags account for 83 percent of all tea sold by these companies), what industry-level strategy would you recommend to the company? Would it be focus, cost-leadership, differentiation, defender, prospector, analyzer, reactor, or a combination of these strategies? Explain which you recommend, why you recommend it, and how the company should use that strategy to gain competitive advantage.

**Sources:** E. Beck, "New 3-D Tea Bag Rattles Some Tea Cups in the U.K.," *The Wall Street Journal Interactive Edition*, 24 March 1997. L. Bray, "Boiling Points: Life Is Not an Easy Ride for Tea and Coffee Manufacturers These Days, with Innovation in Other Beverage Categories Increasing All the Time," *Grocer*, 16 November 1996, 45-46. N. Clayton, "Workforce Is Showing Bags of Innovation," *The Times of London*, 2 October 1994. R. Mulholland, "Storm Brewing in Britain's Teacups," *Agence France-Presse*, 24 February 1996. R. Turcsik, "A Bounty of Teas," *Supermarket News*, 13 November 1995, 42-43.

## Develop Your Managerial Potential

### An Individual SWOT Analysis

In order to maintain and sustain a competitive advantage, companies continue to analyze their overall strategy in light of their current situation. In doing so, a SWOT analysis is often used. The SWOT analysis focuses on the strengths and weaknesses evident in the firm's internal environment and the opportunities and threats present in the firm's external environment. One way to gain experience in conducting a SWOT analysis is to perform one on yourself—in other words, conduct a personal SWOT analysis.

Assume you have just completed your college education and are ready to apply for a job as a manager of a small to medium-sized facility. Perform a personal SWOT analysis to determine if your current situation matches your overall strategy. Identifying your strengths will most likely be the easiest step in the analysis. However, as you analyze your strengths, be sure to keep them realistic and honest. Your strengths will most likely be the skills, abilities, experience, and knowledge that help differentiate you from your competitors.

One way of recognizing both strengths and weaknesses can be found by looking at previous job evaluation comments and by speaking to former and present employers and coworkers. Their comments will typically focus on objective strengths and weaknesses that you exhibit or exhibited while on the job. You may also gather information about your strengths and weaknesses by analyzing your personal interests and learning more about your personality style. Most college placement offices have software to help students identify their interests and personality styles and then match that information to certain career paths. This type of assessment can help ensure that you do not choose a career path that is incongruent with your personality and interests.

Probably the hardest portion of the personal SWOT analysis will be the identification of personal weaknesses. As humans, we are often not willing to pronounce our deficiencies; however, being aware of potential weaknesses can help us reduce them or improve upon them. Since you are focusing on a career in management, you should research what skills, abilities, knowledge, and experience are needed in order to be a successful manager. Comparing your personal inventory to those needed as a manager can help illustrate potential weaknesses. Once you identify weaknesses, develop a plan to help you overcome those weaknesses. Remember that most annual evaluations will include both strengths and weaknesses, so don't forget to include this valuable piece of information in your analysis.

Opportunities can be chosen by looking at various employment possibilities for entry-level managers at this particular point in time. In this part of the analysis, it helps to match personal strengths with opportunities. For example, if you have experience in manufacturing, you may choose to initially apply only to manufacturing-type businesses.

The last step of the analysis involves identifying potential threats. Threats are barriers that can prevent you from obtaining your goals. Threats may include items such as an economic recession that reduces the number of job openings for entry-level managers. By knowing what the barriers are and by assembling proactive plans to help deal with them, you can reduce the possibility of your strategy becoming ineffective.

Focusing on a personal SWOT analysis can be a practical way to prepare for an actual company analysis, plus it allows you to learn more about yourself and your long-term plans.

### Questions

1. In light of the SWOT analysis, what plans might you propose for yourself that will help you maximize your strengths, exploit your opportunities, and minimize your weaknesses and threats? Write three S.M.A.R.T. goals (remember Chapter 4) that will help you implement your plans.
2. How might this assignment prepare you for both your academic and your professional career?

**Source:** P. Buhler, "Managing Your Career: No Longer Your Company's Responsibility", *Supervision*, May 1997.

## Study Tip

Pick up a recent copy of *The Wall Street Journal* and read several articles. List the strategy issues facing the companies you read about. Watch the Xtra! CNN clip on P&G's acquisition of Clairol and read the case.

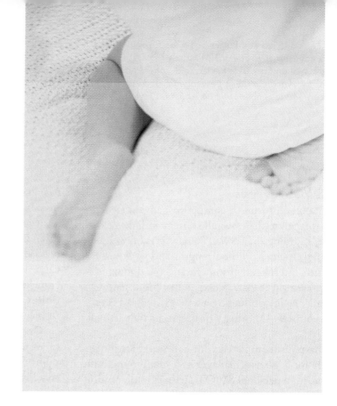

# CHAPTER 10

## Innovation and Change

### What Would You Do?

**Kimberly-Clark Headquarters, Dallas, Texas.** "Innovation? Yeah, right" was the disbelieving response that you got when you proposed that the company use innovative products to pull ahead of the competition. "Innovative diapers? Innovative wipes? Innovative toilet paper? How can you be innovative with those products?" was the sarcastic response. But what else was Kimberly-Clark going to do, especially with a larger competitor like Procter & Gamble determined to keep it in second place?

Take the diaper business, for example. From birth to potty training, which typically lasts about three years, the average child uses 6,000 disposable diapers. At about $30 a week, the total cost of diapers comes to about $4,700 per child. Even better, the market has grown to the point where disposable diapers now cover 94 percent of U.S. babies' bottoms. Yes, it's a good business to be in, but it's a cutthroat business. Your company Kimberly-Clark has been battling with market leader Procter & Gamble (P&G) for nearly three decades. The battle began when P&G introduced Pampers, the first disposable diaper, in 1961. Seven years later, Kimberly-Clark produced its first disposable, Kimbies. In the 1970s, P&G

innovated by adding tape closures to Pampers to replace the safety pins that parents used to keep disposable diapers on babies. P&G also introduced sizes for toddlers and premature infants. These aggressive moves killed Kimbies' sales, forcing Kimberly-Clark to pull Kimbies from the market. However, in 1978, Kimberly-Clark introduced Huggies, diapers with elastic around the legs to prevent leakage. Then, in 1983, Kimberly-Clark added refastenable tape closures to Huggies. Now parents could unfasten the diaper to see if it was dirty and then refasten it for continued use if it wasn't. The result: P&G's profits and market share dropped significantly. However, three years later, P&G responded with Pampers Ultras, ultra-absorbent diapers that were half the thickness of regular disposable diapers. A year later, Kimberly-Clark followed with Huggies SuperTrim.

In short, no matter what you came up with, every Kimberly-Clark move was countered by a quick response from Procter & Gamble. Furthermore, even if you can find a way to innovate products like toilet paper, can you convince consumers that the innovation matters more than price? After all, many people in the company believe that consumers treat all toilet paper brands as interchangeable and simply shop on price. For example,

Wal-Mart sells its own cheaper brand, White Cloud toilet tissue, by displaying open rolls that consumers can touch. Convinced that the cheaper White Cloud tissue was no worse than other brands, this simple sales technique increased White Cloud sales by 83 percent in Wal-Mart stores. So even if you did come up with a better toilet paper through innovation and creativity, how could you tastefully convince consumers to buy it?

Well, if you're going to pursue these ideas, you're going to have to convince some people in the company that there's a method to your madness. The first question you'll have to address is "Why does innovation matter?", especially in a humdrum, boring business like toilet papers and diapers. Second, how do you know when to try for an innovation home run (that is, go for an entirely new design or technology that is dramatically better than existing products), or when to simply take the existing technology or products and make them incrementally better? Lastly, if you wanted to swing for the fences and hit an innovation home run, just how would Kimberly-Clark do that?

**If you were in charge of product innovation at Kimberly-Clark, what would you do?**

**Sources:** N. Byrnes, D. Foust, S. Anderson, W. Symonds, & J. Weber, "Brands in a Bind: Many Household Names Are Hurting—And Taking a Cue from High Techs Outfits," *Business Week*, 28 August 2000, 234. S. Marta, "Cre-ating Fresh Products: Old Favorites Are Being Reinvented for a New Market," *Dallas Morning News*, 25 August 2001, 1F. E. Nelson, "Toilet-Paper War Heats Up with New, Wet Roll," *The Wall Street Journal*, 17 January 2001, B1. T. Parker-Pope, "The Tricky Business of Rolling Out a New Toilet Paper," *The Wall Street Journal*, 12 January 1998, B1. D. Starkman, "Hefty's Plastic Zipper Bag Is Rapping Rivals," *The Wall Street Journal*, 16 April 1999, B1.

**organizational innovation**
the successful implementation of creative ideas in organizations

**creativity**
the production of novel and useful ideas

**organizational change**
a difference in the form, quality, or condition of an organization over time

We begin this chapter by reviewing the issues associated with organizational innovation. **Organizational innovation**, the problem facing Kimberly-Clark, is the successful implementation of creative ideas in an organization.[1] **Creativity**, which is a form of organizational innovation, is the production of novel and useful ideas.[2] In the first part of this chapter, you will learn why innovation matters and how to manage innovation to create and sustain a competitive advantage.

In the second half of this chapter, you will learn about organizational change. **Organizational change** is a difference in the form, quality, or condition of an organization over time.[3] For example, for most people, the name "Olivetti" brings to mind typewriters, the product by which Olivetti first made its name internationally. However, over the years Olivetti moved away from typewriters to become a technology company. In fact, the Olivetti M20 was one of the very first personal computers. However, Olivetti changed again, selling its computer division, and refocusing on telecommunications, becoming the sixth largest provider of fixed and mobile phone services in the world (and the largest in Italy).[4] In each instance, from typewriters to computers and then computers to telecommunications, Olivetti changed significantly in form, quality, and condition. In the second half of this chapter, you will learn why changes like these occur. You will also learn about the risk of not changing, the different kinds of change, and the ways in which companies can manage change.

## Organizational Innovation

Do you remember the first time, probably as a child, that you saw a blimp floating overhead? It moved slowly, was clearly visible for miles, and held your attention as it got closer, passed overhead, and then floated away. Interestingly, the things that make blimps fascinating to kids also make them great for advertising (i.e., slow, visible, holds attention). For example, Goodyear Tires, Anheuser-Busch (Budweiser Beer), and Blockbuster Video use blimps to advertise their products. Company names are clearly displayed on the side of their blimps at sporting events that are attended by thousands and seen by millions on TV. Blimps are so commonplace that major sporting events such as Monday Night Football, the Superbowl, the U.S. Open Golf Tournament, and the World Series would seem incomplete without traditional overhead camera shots from the blimp. Even when games occur inside domed stadiums, blimp-mounted cameras are still used to transmit pictures of city skylines or nearby mountains, oceans, or deserts.

Today, however, the "Lightship," an innovative blimp made by the American Blimp Company, is revolutionizing the blimp business and the advertising revenues that go with it. Lightships have several advantages over traditional blimps. To start, they're much smaller and cheaper. A typical, full-size blimp costs about $300,000 a month to operate. Most of that cost is for the 24 people who work in the blimp's ground and flight crews. Because American Blimp's Lightships are smaller, it takes only 14 people to staff the ground and flight crews. Consequently, monthly costs run around $200,000, one-third less than full-size blimps. Another advantage is that Lightships are lighted from the inside. So, when it gets dark, the company name and logo on the side of the blimp are still visible! Since most sporting events take place at night, this is critical to maximizing the size of their TV audience.[5]

*Organizational innovation*, like American Blimp's new Lightships, is the successful implementation of creative ideas in an organization.[6]

*After reading the next two sections on organizational innovation, you should be able to*
1. *explain why innovation matters to companies.*
2. *discuss the different methods that managers can use to effectively manage innovation in their organizations.*

# 1. Why Innovation Matters

When was the last time you used a record player to listen to music, tuned up your car, baked cookies from scratch, or manually changed the channel on your TV? Because of product innovations and advances in technology, it's hard to remember, isn't it? In fact, since compact discs began replacing vinyl record albums nearly a decade ago, many of you may *never* have played a record album. Lots of people used to tune up their own cars because it was easy, quick, and cheap. Change the points, spark plugs, and distributor cap, and your car was good for another six months or 12,000 miles. Today, with advanced technology and computerized components, almost no one tunes up their cars anymore. It's far too complex for weekend mechanics. Hardly anybody makes cookies from scratch anymore, either. Millions of kids think that baking cookies means adding water to a powered mix or getting pre-made cookie dough out of the refrigerator. As for manually changing the channels on your TV, you may have done that recently, but only because you couldn't find the remote.

We can only guess what changes technological innovations will bring in the next 20 years. Maybe we'll be listening to compact chips rather than compact discs. Maybe cars won't need tune-ups. Maybe we'll use the Internet to have cookies delivered hot to our homes like pizza. And maybe TVs will be voice-activated, so it doesn't matter if you lose the remote (just don't lose your voice). Who knows? The only thing we do know about the next 20 years is that innovation will continue to change our lives. For a fuller appreciation of how technological innovation has changed our lives, see the "Blast from the Past" on technological innovation in the 20th century.

*Let's begin our discussion of innovation by learning about 1.1 technology cycles and 1.2 innovation streams.*

## 1.1 Technology Cycles

**technology cycle**
cycle that begins with the "birth" of a new technology and ends when that technology reaches its limits and is replaced by a newer, substantially better technology

**S-curve pattern of innovation**
a pattern of technological innovation characterized by slow initial progress, then rapid progress, and then again by slow progress as a technology matures and reaches its limits

In Chapter 2, you learned that *technology* is the knowledge, tools, and techniques used to transform inputs (raw materials, information, etc.) into outputs (products and services). A **technology cycle** begins with the "birth" of a new technology and ends when that technology reaches its limits and "dies" as it is replaced by a newer, substantially better technology.[7] For example, technology cycles occurred when air conditioning supplanted fans, when Henry Ford's Model T replaced horse-drawn carriages, when planes replaced trains as a means of cross-country travel, when vaccines that prevented diseases replaced medicines designed to treat them, and when battery-powered wristwatches replaced mechanically powered, stem-wound wristwatches.

From Gutenberg's invention of the printing press in the 1400s to the rapid advance of the Internet in the last few years, studies of hundreds of technological innovations have shown that nearly all technology cycles follow the typical **S-curve pattern of innovation** shown in Exhibit 10.1 (see p. 349).[8] Early in a technology cycle, there is still much to learn and progress is slow, as depicted by point A on the S-curve. The flat slope indicates that increased effort (i.e., money, research and development) brings only small improvements in technological performance. Intel's technology cycles have followed this pattern. Intel spends billions to develop new computer chips and to build new production facilities to produce them. Intel has found that the technology cycle for its integrated circuits (that power personal computers) is about three years. In each three-year cycle, Intel introduces a new chip, improves the chip by making it a little bit faster each year, and then replaces

# BlastFromThePast

## Technological Innovation in the 20th Century

There's no better way to understand how technology has repeatedly and deeply changed modern life than to read a year-by-year list of innovations in the 20th century. The first time through the list, simply appreciate the amount of change that has occurred in the last century. It's astonishing. However, the second time through, look at each invention and ask yourself two questions: What brand new business or industry was created by this innovation? And, what old business or industry was made obsolete by this innovation?

### 1900–1910
- electric typewriter
- air conditioner
- airplane
- reinforced concrete skyscraper
- vacuum tube
- plastic
- chemotherapy
- electric washing machine

### 1911–1920
- artificial kidney
- mammography
- 35mm camera
- zipper
- sonar
- tank
- Band-Aid
- submachine gun

### 1921–1930
- self-winding watch
- TB vaccine
- frozen food
- commercial fax service
- talking movies
- black and white television
- penicillin
- jet engine
- supermarket

### 1931–1940
- defibrillator
- radar
- Kodachrome film
- helicopter
- nylon
- ballpoint pen
- first working computer
- fluorescent lighting
- color television

### 1941–1950
- aerosol can
- nuclear reactor
- atomic bomb
- first modern herbicide
- microwave oven
- bikini
- disposable diaper
- ENIAC computer
- mobile phone
- transistor
- credit card

### 1951–1960
- Salk's polio vaccine
- DNA
- oral contraceptive
- solar power
- Tylenol
- Sputnik
- integrated circuit
- breast implant

### 1961–1970
- measles vaccine
- navigation satellite
- miniskirt
- video recorder
- soft contact lenses
- coronary bypass
- handheld calculator
- computer mouse
- Arpanet (prototype Internet)
- bar-code scanner
- lunar landing

### 1971–1980
- compact disc
- Pong (first computer game)
- word processor
- gene splicing
- Post-It note
- Ethernet (computer network)
- laser printer
- personal computer
- VHS video recording
- fiber-optics
- linked ATMs
- magnetic resonance imaging

### 1981–1990
- MS-DOS
- space shuttle
- clone of IBM personal computer
- cellular-phone network
- computer virus
- human embryo transfer
- CD-ROM
- Windows software
- 3-D video game

- disposable contact lenses
- Doppler radar
- RU-486 (abortion pill)
- global positioning system by satellite
- stealth bomber
- World Wide Web

## 1991–2000
- baboon-human liver transplant
- taxol (cancer drug)
- mapping of the male chromosome
- Pentium processor
- channel tunnel opens

- HIV protease inhibitor
- gene for obesity discovered
- Java (computer language)
- cloning of an adult mammal

## 2001–Today
- mapping of human genome
- first cloning of human embryo

**Source:** T. Gideonse, "Decade by Decade: A Rich Century of Better Mousetraps," *Newsweek Special Issue: The Power of Invention,* Winter 1997-1998, 12-15.

that chip at the end of the cycle with a brand new chip that is substantially faster than the old chip. But, at first, the billions Intel spends typically produce only small improvements in performance. For instance, as shown in Exhibit 10.2, Intel's first 60 megahertz (MHz) Pentium processors ran at a speed of 51 based on the iComp Index.[9] (The iComp Index is a benchmark test for measuring relative computer speed. For example, a computer with an iComp score of 200 is twice as fast as a computer with an iComp score of 100.) Yet, six months later, Intel's new 75 MHz Pentium was only slightly faster, with an iComp speed of 67.

Fortunately, as the technology matures, researchers figure out how to get better performance from the new technology. This is represented by point B of the S-curve in Exhibit 10.1. The steeper slope indicates that small amounts of effort will result in significant increases in performance. Again, Intel's technology cycles have followed this

---

*EXHIBIT 10.1*

S-CURVES AND TECHNOLOGICAL INNOVATION

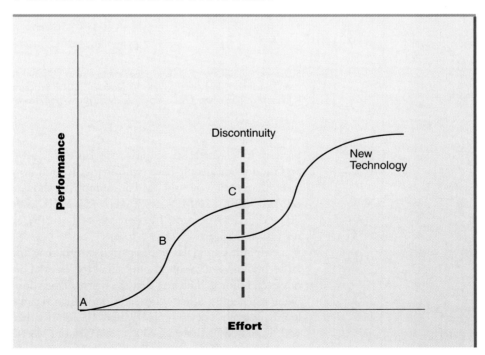

**Source:** R.N. Foster, *Innovation: The Attacker's Advantage* (New York: Summit, 1986).

EXHIBIT 10.2

## ICOMP INDEX 2.0 COMPARING THE RELATIVE PERFORMANCE OF DIFFERENT INTEL MICROPROCESSORS

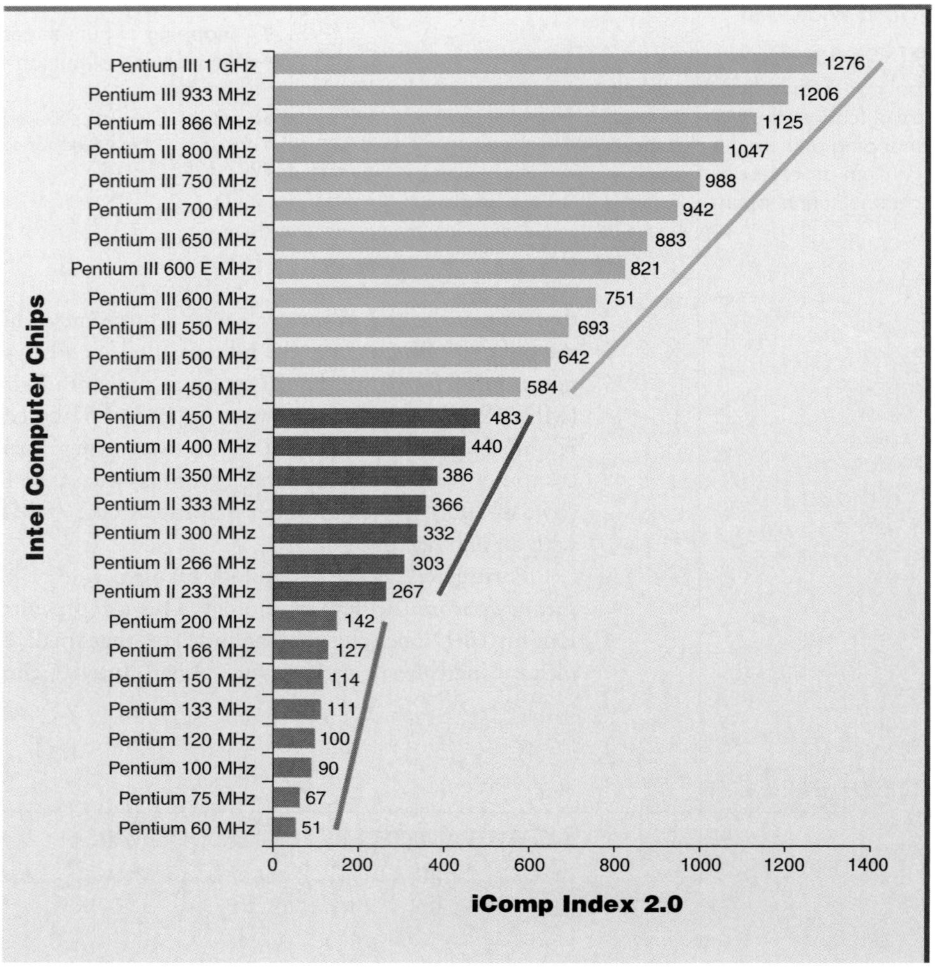

**Sources:** "Intel iCOMP (Full List)," Ideas International. [Online] Available http://www.ideasinternational. com/benchmark/intel/icomp.html, 13 October 2001. "Benchmark Resources: iCOMP Index3.0," Intel. [Online] Available http://developer.intel.com/procs/perf/icomp/index.htm, 13 October 2001.

pattern. In fact, after six months to a year with a new chip design, Intel's engineering and production people have typically figured out how to make the new chips much faster than they were initially. For example, as shown in Exhibit 10.2, Intel soon rolled out 100 MHz, 120 MHz, 133 MHz, 150 MHz, and 166 MHz Pentium chips that were 76 percent, 117 percent, 124 percent, 149 percent, and 178 percent faster than its original 60 MHz speed.

At point C, the flat slope again indicates that further efforts to develop this particular technology will result in only small increases in performance. More importantly, however, point C indicates that the performance limits of that particular technology are being reached. In other words, additional significant improvements in performance are highly unlikely. For example, Exhibit 10.2 shows that with iComp speeds of 127 and 142, Intel's 166 MHz and 200 MHz Pentiums were 2.49 and 2.78 times faster than its original 60 MHz Pentiums. Yet, despite these impressive gains in performance, Intel was unable to make its Pentium chips run any faster, because the basic Pentium design had reached its limits.

After a technology has reached its limits at the top of the S-curve, significant improvements in performance usually come from radical new designs or new performance-enhancing materials. In Exhibit 10.1, that new technology is represented by the second S-curve. The changeover or discontinuity between the new and old technologies is represented by the dotted line. At first, the new and old technologies will likely coexist. Eventually, however, the new technology will replace the old technology. When that happens, the old technology cycle will be complete and a new one will have started. The changeover between Intel's Pentium processors, the old technology, and its Pentium II processors, the new technology (these chips are significantly different technologies despite their similar names), took approximately one year. Exhibit 10.2 shows this changeover or discontinuity between the two technologies. With an iComp speed of 267, the first Pentium II (233 MHz) was 88 percent faster than the last and fastest 200 MHz Pentium processor. And because their design and performance are significantly different (and faster) than Pentium II chips, Intel's Pentium III chips represented the beginning of yet another S-curve technology cycle in integrated circuits. This can be seen by the fact that a 450 MHz Pentium III processor is 21 percent faster than a 450 MHz Pentium II chip. Over time, improving existing technology (tweaking the performance of the current technology cycle), combined with replacing old technology with new technology cycles (i.e., the Pentium III replacing the Pentium II which replaced the Pentium) has increased the speed of computer processors by a factor of 255 in just 15 years!

While the evolution of Intel's Pentium chips has been used to illustrate the idea of S-curves and technology cycles, it's important to note that technology cycles and technological innovation don't necessarily mean "high technology." Remember, *technology* is simply the knowledge, tools, and techniques used to transform inputs (raw materials, information, etc.) into outputs (products and services). So a technology cycle occurs whenever there are major advances or changes in the *knowledge, tools,* and *techniques* of a field or discipline. For example, one of the most important technology cycles in the history of civilization occurred in 1859, when 1,300 miles of central sewer line were constructed throughout London to carry human waste to the sea more than 11 miles away. This extensive sewer system replaced the widespread practice of directly dumping raw sewage into streets, where people walked through it and where it drained into public wells that supplied drinking water. Though the relationship wasn't known at the time, preventing waste runoff from contaminating water supplies stopped the spread of cholera that had killed millions of people for centuries in cities throughout the world.[10] Safe water supplies immediately translated into better health and longer life expectancies. Indeed, the water you drink today is safe thanks to this "technology" breakthrough. So when you think about technology cycles, don't automatically think "high technology." Instead, broaden your perspective by considering advances or changes in knowledge, tools, and techniques.

### 1.2 Innovation Streams

In Chapter 9, you learned that organizations can create *competitive advantage* for themselves if they have a *distinctive competence* that allows them to make, do, or perform something better than their competitors. Furthermore, a competitive advantage becomes sustainable if other companies cannot duplicate the benefits obtained from that distinctive competence. Technological innovation, however, makes it possible not only to duplicate the benefits obtained from a company's distinctive advantage, but also to quickly turn a company's competitive advantage into a competitive disadvantage. For example, through the 1970s, National Cash Register (NCR) was the leading U.S. producer of, well, cash registers. But in 1971, NCR announced that it was taking a $140 million write-off for millions of brand new cash registers. If the cash registers were brand new, why couldn't NCR sell them? NCR's cash registers were electromechanical and had been made obsolete by newer, more powerful, and cheaper electrical cash registers.[11] Technological innovation had turned NCR's competitive advantage into a competitive disadvantage. And, in the last decade, the same electrical cash registers that began NCR's

EXHIBIT 10.3

INNOVATION STREAMS: TECHNOLOGY CYCLES OVER TIME

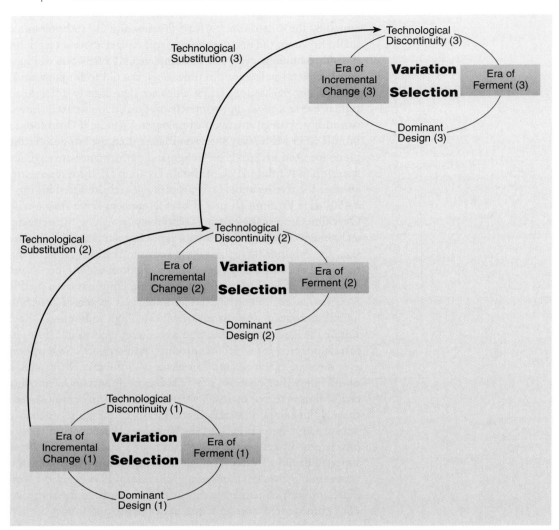

**Source:** M.L. Tushman, P.C. Anderson, & C. O'Reilly, "Technology Cycles, Innovation Streams, and Ambidextrous Organizations: Organization Renewal Through Innovation Streams and Strategic Change," in *Managing Strategic Innovation and Change,* eds. M.L. Tushman & P. Anderson (1997), 3-23.

**352**

**innovation streams**
patterns of innovation over time that can create sustainable competitive advantage

**technological discontinuity**
scientific advance or unique combination of existing technologies that creates a significant breakthrough in performance or function

downfall were themselves made obsolete by scanners that automatically scanned prices and product information from bar codes into computerized cash registers.

As NCR's example shows, companies that want to sustain a competitive advantage must understand and protect themselves from the strategic threats of innovation. Over the long run, the best way to do that is for a company to create a stream of its own innovative ideas and products year after year. Consequently, we define **innovation streams** as patterns of innovation over time that can create sustainable competitive advantage.[12] Exhibit 10.3 shows a typical innovation consisting of a series of technology cycles. Recall that technological cycles begin with a new technology and end when that technology is replaced by a newer, substantially better technology. The innovation stream in Exhibit 10.3 shows three such technology cycles.

An innovation stream begins with a **technological discontinuity**, in which a scientific advance or a unique combination of existing technologies creates a significant breakthrough in performance or function. For example, coronary bypass surgery, which is a common treatment for heart attacks, has saved millions of lives. Because of the intrusive nature of the surgery—an incision is made from the belly button to the middle of the chest, the breast bone is sawed through, and then a metal ratchet is used to spread the rib cage open—it takes anywhere from three to six months to recover from the operation. However, thanks to miniature lights, cameras, and surgical tools, surgeons can now do bypass operations by making several small, key-sized holes in the chest. The trauma associated with this new technique is so small that people can be back at work or on the golf course three to four days after the surgery.[13]

Technological discontinuities are followed by an **era of ferment,** characterized by technological substitution and design competition. **Technological substitution** occurs when customers purchase new technologies to replace older technologies. For example, in the first half of the 1800s, letters, messages, and news traveled slowly by boat, train, or horseback, such as the famous Pony Express that, using a large number of fresh riders and fresh horses, could deliver mail from St. Joseph, Missouri, to Sacramento, California, in 10 days.[14] However, between 1840 and 1860, many businesses began using the telegraph, because it allowed messages and news to be sent cross-country (or even around the world) in minutes rather than days, weeks, or months.[15] Indeed, telegraph companies were so successful that the Pony Express went out of business almost immediately after the completion of the transcontinental telegraph, which linked telegraph systems from coast to coast.

An era of ferment is also characterized by **design competition,** in which the old technology and several different new technologies compete to establish a new technological standard or dominant design. Because of large investments in old technology, and because the new and old technologies are often incompatible with each other, companies and consumers are reluctant to switch to a different technology during design competition. Indeed, the telegraph was so widely used as a means of communication in the late 1800s that, at first, almost no one understood why telephones would be a better way to communicate. In his book *Interactive Excellence: Defining and Developing New Standards for the Twenty-first Century*, Edwin Schlossberg wrote, "People could not imagine why they would want or need to talk immediately to someone who was across town or, even more absurdly, in another town. Although people could write letters to one another, and some could send telegraph messages, the idea of sending one's voice to another place and then instantly hearing another voice in return was simply not a model that existed in people's experience. They also did not think it was worth the money to accelerate sending or hearing a message."[16] Also, during design competition, the changeover from older to newer technologies is often slowed by the fact that older technology usually improves significantly in response to the competitive threat from the new technologies.

An era of ferment is followed by the emergence of a **dominant design**, which becomes the accepted market standard for technology.[17] Dominant designs emerge in several ways. One is critical mass, meaning that a particular technology can become the dominant design simply because most people use it. Since millions more people bought VCRs that used VHS tapes, larger VHS tapes that provided twice as much recording time, beat out Sony's smaller Beta format, which had shorter recording times, to become the dominant design for VCRs. Likewise, a design can become dominant if it solves a practical problem. For example, the QWERTY keyboard (look at the top left line of letters on a keyboard) became the dominant design for typewriters, because it slowed typists who, by typing too fast, caused mechanical typewriter keys to jam. Ironically, despite the fact that computers can easily be switched to the DVORAK keyboard layout, which doubles typing speed and cuts typing errors by half, QWERTY lives on as the standard keyboard. Thus, the best technology doesn't always become the dominant design.

Another way in which dominant designs emerge is through independent standards bodies. The International Telecommunication Union (**http://www.itu.ch/**) is an independent organization that establishes standards for the communications industry. The ITU was founded in Paris in 1865, because all the countries in Europe had different

**era of ferment**
phase of a technology cycle characterized by technological substitution and design competition

**technological substitution**
purchase of new technologies to replace older ones

**design competition**
competition between old and new technologies to establish a new technological standard or dominant design

**dominant design**
a new technological design or process that becomes the accepted market standard

telegraph systems that could not communicate with each other. Messages crossing borders had to be transcribed from one country's system before they could be coded and delivered on another. After three months of negotiations, 20 countries signed the International Telegraph Convention that standardized equipment and instructions, so that telegraph messages could flow seamlessly from country to country. Today, as in 1865, various standards are proposed, discussed, negotiated, and changed until agreement is reached on a final set of standards that communication industries (i.e., Internet, telephony, satellites, radio, etc.) will follow worldwide. For example, within a few years, multi-beam, or spot-beam, technology should double or triple the speed and capacity with which satellites deliver data streams to users on earth.[18] Likewise, China has developed a new standard for third generation (3G) mobile-phone networks that are fast enough for graphics, video, and other high-speed Internet functions.[19] With both technologies, satellites and 3G mobile phones, the ITU will choose an official standard from several competing standards.

Yet, no matter how they occur, the emergence of a dominant design is a key event in an innovation stream. First, emergence of a dominant design indicates that there are winners and losers. Technological innovation is both competence enhancing and competence destroying. Companies that bet on the wrong design or on the old technology often struggle, while companies that bet on the now-dominant design usually prosper. In fact, more companies are likely to go out of business in an era of ferment than in an economic recession or slowdown. Second, the emergence of a dominant design signals a change away from design experimentation and competition to **incremental change**, a phase in which companies innovate by lowering the cost and improving the functioning and performance of the dominant design. For example, during a technology cycle, manufacturing efficiencies let Intel cut the costs of its chips by half to two-thirds, all while doubling or tripling the chips' speed. This focus on improving the dominant design continues until the next technological discontinuity occurs.

**incremental change**
the phase of a technology cycle in which companies innovate by lowering costs and improving the functioning and performance of the dominant technological design

### Review 1
#### Why Innovation Matters
Technology cycles typically follow an S-curve pattern of innovation. Early in the cycle, technological progress is slow and improvements in technological performance are small. However, as a technology matures, performance improves quickly. Finally, small improvements occur as the limits of a technology are reached. At this point, significant improvements in performance must come from new technologies.

The best way to protect a competitive advantage is to create a stream of innovative ideas and products. Innovation streams begin with technological discontinuities that create significant breakthroughs in performance or function. Technological discontinuities are followed by an era of ferment, in which customers purchase new technologies (technological substitution) and companies compete to establish the new dominant design (design competition). Dominant designs emerge because of critical mass, because they solve a practical problem, or because of the negotiations of independent standards bodies. Because technological innovation is both competence-enhancing and competence-destroying, companies that bet on the wrong design often struggle, while companies that bet on the eventual dominant design usually prosper. Emergence of a dominant design leads to a focus on incremental change, lowering costs, and small, but steady, improvements in the dominant design. This focus continues until the next technological discontinuity occurs.

## 2. Managing Innovation

The previous discussion of technology cycles and innovation streams showed that managers must be equally good at managing innovation in two very different circumstances. First, during eras of ferment, companies must find a way to anticipate and survive the technological discontinuities that can suddenly transform industry leaders into losers and industry unknowns into industry powerhouses. Companies that can't manage inno-

# "headline news"

## How Much Innovation Is Too Much?

It didn't come rolling out to the Stone's "Start Me Up," but that does not mean that Microsoft's newest operating system entered the market without fanfare. It was just clouded by looming antitrust issues and upgrade fatigue. With stripped down PCs selling for under $1,000, home purchases have surpassed purchases for business. The result is a nearly saturated market. Today's PC users are reluctant to shell out any more money—even at the rock-bottom prices created by recent price wars—for only modest improvements.

Microsoft is betting it can revive innovation-weary consumers with its new XP operating system. XP, for "experience," adds new audio functionality, creates a steadier platform, and increases the Internet integration of the Millennium (Me) edition. New experiences, Microsoft contends, drive growth, and growth will lift the PC market out of impending doldrums.

Carrying an R&D price tag of $1 billion, XP is evidence of the trend in computer innovation that is sweeping the industry. Led by Dell, which spends only about 1.5 percent of sales on R&D, hardware manufacturers are reducing the scope—and expense—of their R&D activities and increasing their dependence on software and microprocessor manufacturers to pick up the slack. In 2001, Microsoft spent roughly $4.8 billion on research, and Intel spent nearly $4 billion, or 15 percent of sales. Such expenditures are not going to software alone. Microsoft has developed a portable device which can store notes written long-hand with a stylus and has built-in wireless communications, called Tablet PC, which Compaq will release in 2002. Since PC manufacturers are sacrificing innovation to prices, the PC is becoming a standard item whose only novelties are cosmetic (like new color panels). Leave it to Intel to share its map for a PC makeover with the industry.

At the center of the innovation stall is value. "The only way we can encourage people to upgrade is if they find value," says Jeff Raike, Microsoft's group vice president for productivity and business services. "We spend a lot of R&D to create that value." Indeed, modest changes in PCs and the software that powers them are akin to the latest model car: Not much has changed of substance, but the difference is there. Incremental change has consumers keeping their wallets in their pockets. In the 1990s, people replaced PCs every three years on average. Currently, it's every four years. PCs are becoming durable goods, and that does not bode well for either hardware or software manufacturers.

For Microsoft, the XP stakes are even higher than overcoming upgrade fatigue. XP is the opening salvo in a new technology war with AOL. More than just a routine upgrade, XP sets the stage for Microsoft's .Net Internet-era business plan, which entails a shift away from the company's existing business plan toward one dependent on recurring subscription and transaction fees. Today, most Internet links and information are free, but sooner or later Internet players will need to wean themselves from advertising revenue as a sole source of income. With XP, Microsoft will be ready. Want a stock quote? XP will gladly link you to a Microsoft-run financial service. Want to download a new song? (Napster is not an option.) XP links to Microsoft's Media Player and takes a transaction fee in the process.

The shift in Microsoft's business plan indicates that it is aware of the environmental factors at play in the computer industry, namely, the saturation of the market with PCs, not to mention the consumer with upgrades. Whereas archrival AOL is a consumer-marketing company that uses technology, Microsoft is using XP to transform itself into a technology company that uses consumer-marketing. It all amounts to one small step for the operating platform and one giant step for Microsoft.

1. Where is Microsoft's XP on the innovation stream? Can you identify where personal computers are on the S-curve, depicted in Exhibit 10.1?
2. If Microsoft does not rethink its traditional business model, which generates revenue from software purchases and licenses, is it necessarily going to spin into organizational decline?

**Sources:** S. Alsop, "Microsoft Will Falter—In 2020," *Fortune*, 9 July 2001, 44. Info-Trac Article A75915595. P. Galli, "Pushing Forward—Despite Injunction Threats, Microsoft Plots XP Upgrade," *eWeek*, 23 July 2001, 11. Info-Trac Article A76854326. P. Lewis, "AOL vs. Microsoft: Now It's War," *Fortune*, 23 July 2001, 88. Info-Trac Article A76474325. —, "Soup It Up—Or Trade It In," *Fortune*, 9 July 2001, 260. Info-Trac Article A76474339. G. McWilliams, "Computer Trouble: As More Buyers Suffer from Upgrade Fatigue, PC Sales Are Falling," *The Wall Street Journal*, 24 August 2001, A1.

355

vation following technological discontinuities risk quick organizational decline and dissolution. Second, after a new dominant design emerges following an era of ferment, companies must manage the very different process of incremental improvement and innovation. Companies that can't manage incremental innovation slowly deteriorate as they fall farther behind industry leaders.

*Unfortunately, what works well when managing innovation after technological discontinuities doesn't work well when managing innovation during periods of incremental*

## Cultivate Your Most Demanding Customer

Once successful, it can be difficult to change. One way to battle complacency is to cultivate demanding customers, those who always want more. PPG Industries shoots dead chickens at 850 mph into aircraft windshields to simulate the impact of birds hitting an airplane. Boeing and Airbus won't buy from PPG unless its windshields withstand these tests. PPG also tests antitheft glass for automobiles by seeing how many hits it takes before a glass window layered with special plastic breaks. Luxury automakers that purchase from PPG asked it to develop this new product. So, to force yourself to keep changing, cultivate a demanding customer!

**Source**: A. Moore, "Torture Testing Manufacturers Pound, Punish, And Even Destroy Products to Test Them to and Beyond Their Limits. New Techniques Make Lab Tests Much Better, But Field Testing Is Still Critical," *Fortune*, 2 October 2000, 244.

---

change (and vice versa). Consequently, to successfully manage innovation streams, companies need to be good at three things: *2.1 managing the sources of innovation, 2.2 managing innovation during discontinuous change,* and *2.3 managing innovation during incremental change.*

### 2.1 Managing Sources of Innovation

Innovation comes from great ideas. So a starting point for managing innovation is to manage the sources of innovation, that is, where new ideas come from. One place that new ideas originate is with brilliant inventors. For example, do you know who invented the telephone, the light bulb, electricity, air conditioning, radio, television, automobiles, the jet engine, computers, and the Internet? Respectively, these innovations were created by Alexander Graham Bell, Thomas Edison, Pieter van Musschenbroek, Willis Carrier, Guglielmo Marconi, John Baird and Philo T. Farnsworth, Gottlieb Daimler and Wilhelm Maybach, Sir Frank Whittle, Charles Babbage, and Vint Cerf and Robert Kahn. These innovators and their innovations forever changed the course of modern life. However, only a few companies have the likes of an Edison, Marconi, or Graham Bell working for them. Given that great thinkers and inventors are in short supply, what might companies do to ensure a steady flow of good ideas?

Well, when we say that innovation begins with great ideas, we're really saying that innovation begins with creativity. *Creativity* is the production of novel and useful ideas.[20] While companies can't command creativity from employees ("You *will* be more creative!"), they can jump-start innovation by building **creative work environments,** in which workers perceive that creative thoughts and ideas are welcomed and valued. As shown in Exhibit 10.4, creative work environments have five components that encourage creativity: challenging work, organizational encouragement, supervisory encouragement, work group encouragement, and freedom. A sixth component, organizational impediments, must be managed so as not to discourage creativity.[21]

**creative work environments**
workplace cultures in which workers perceive that new ideas are welcomed, valued, and encouraged

---

356

Managing innovation is a critical part of building sustainable competitive advantage. Microsoft has done this extremely well over its 30-year history. It remains to be seen, however, whether the markets where Microsoft competes will continue to support such quick innovation by buying new and upgraded products.

© REUTERS NEWMEDIA INC./CORBIS

EXHIBIT 10.4

COMPONENTS OF CREATIVE WORK ENVIRONMENTS

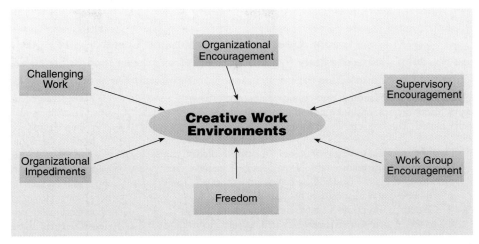

**Source:** T.M. Amabile, R. Conti, H. Coon, J. Lazenby, & M. Herron, "Assessing the Work Environment for Creativity," *Academy of Management Journal* 39 (1996): 1154-1184.

**flow**
a psychological state of effortlessness, in which you become completely absorbed in what you're doing and time seems to pass quickly

Work is *challenging* when it requires hard work, demands attention and focus, and is seen as important to others in the organization. Researcher Mihaly Csikszentmihalyi (pronounced ME-high-ee CHICK-sent-me-high-ee) said that challenging work promotes creativity because it creates a rewarding psychological experience known as "flow." **Flow** is a psychological state of effortlessness, in which you become completely absorbed in what you're doing and time seems to fly. (You begin work, become absorbed in it, and then suddenly realize that several hours have passed.) When flow occurs, who you are and what you're doing become one. Csikszentmihalyi first encountered flow when studying artists. He said, "What struck me by looking at artists at work was their tremendous focus on the work, this enormous involvement, this forgetting of time and body. It wasn't justified by expectation of rewards, like, 'Aha, I'm going to sell this painting.'"[22] Csikszentmihalyi has found that chess players, rock climbers, dancers, surgeons, and athletes regularly experience flow, too. A key part of creating flow experiences, and thus creative work environments, is to achieve a balance between skills and task challenge. When workers can do more than what is required of them, they become bored. Anxiety occurs when workers' skills aren't sufficient to accomplish a task. However, when skills and task challenge are balanced, flow and creativity can occur.

A creative work environment requires three kinds of encouragement: organizational, supervisory, and work group encouragement. *Organizational encouragement* of creativity occurs when management encourages risk taking and new ideas, supports and fairly evaluates new ideas, rewards and recognizes creativity, and encourages the sharing of new ideas throughout different parts of the company. *Supervisory encouragement* of creativity occurs when supervisors provide clear goals, encourage open interaction with subordinates, and actively support development teams' work and ideas. *Work group encouragement* occurs when work group members have diverse experience, education, and backgrounds; when there is a mutual openness to ideas; when there is positive, constructive challenge to ideas; and when there is shared commitment to ideas. See Chapter 13, "Managing Teams," for further discussion of the importance of these ideas.

An example of organizational and supervisory encouragement can be found at Toro Corporation, which makes lawn mowers and equipment. Toro tried to encourage innovation by announcing that innovative ideas that failed would not be punished.

357

# BeenThereDoneThat

## "No More Mistakes and You're Through!":

### John Cleese on Innovation and Creativity in Organizations

For years, John Cleese of Monty Python, star/writer of movies such as "A Fish Called Wanda," has also created management and marketing training videos for the corporate world (see http://www.videoarts.com). Cleese, widely regarded as a creative and comic genius, shared his thoughts about organizational innovation and creativity in a speech entitled "The Importance of Mistakes":

I want to suggest to you that unless we have a tolerant attitude toward mistakes—I might almost say a positive attitude toward them—we shall be behaving irrationally, unscientifically, and unsuccessfully.

Of course, if you now say to me, "Look here, you weird limey, are you seriously advocating relaunching the Edsel?" I will reply, "No, Mac. There are mistakes and mistakes." There are true copper-bottomed mistakes like wearing a black bra under a white blouse, or, to take a more masculine example, starting a land war in Asia. I'm talking about mistakes that at the time they were committed did have a chance.

Let's first concentrate on taking the risk of making a mistake. Has it occurred to you that if you don't take this risk, you can't do or say anything useful?

For example, if you ask me now "What is the time?" I could give you the following guaranteed-true answer. "It is between five o'clock in the morning and midnight." Right? You can't argue with that. No chance of error there. Or I could tell you that it is 23 minutes of 2, when it is in fact 24 minutes of 2. Which of those is more useful to you? The true one or the mistake?

It's self-evident that if we can't take the risk of saying or doing something wrong, our creativity goes right out the window. Because the essence of creativity is not the possession of some special talent, it is much more the ability to "play." MacKinnon's research at Berkeley in the 1960s and 1970s on professionals rated by their colleagues as "highly creative" showed they were no different in intelligence from their less creative colleagues—but that they took longer to study problems and "played with them" more. Highly creative people know better how to get themselves into a mode where they are able to respond more spontaneously to their intuitions, to explore out of pure curiosity, to follow little impulses with interest without immediately imposing critical thought.

For a group to function more creatively, people must lose their inhibitions. They must gain the confidence to contribute spontaneously to what's happening, and the inhibition arises because of the fear of looking foolish. Yes! It's nothing more than the fear of making mistakes. While people are held back by this fear, while they go over each thought they had six times before expressing it in case someone will think it's "wrong," nothing useful can happen creatively.

Now, to come to the second half of my argument, a positive attitude toward mistakes will allow them to be corrected rapidly when they occur.

In organizations where mistakes are not allowed, you get two types of counterproductive behavior. First, since mistakes are "bad," if they're committed by people at the top, the feedback arising from those mistakes has to be ignored or selectively reinterpreted, in order that those top people can pretend that no mistake has been made. So it doesn't get fixed. Second, if they're committed by people lower down in the organization, mistakes get concealed.

Taking concealment first, Peter Parker, the very successful former head of British Rail, said recently, "The hardest thing in management is the mistake concealer. If someone walks into my office saying, 'I screwed up,' I say, 'Come on in.'"

In the healthiest organizations, the taboo is not on making mistakes, it's on concealing them. But in a mistake-denying culture, they are concealed and therefore not corrected. Worse, lies have to be told.

This is the essence of a particular form of comedy that has traditionally been popular in Europe—the farce. In America, you have a similar form of entertainment, usually called Something-Gate, where entire departments of government officials pass their working days trying unsuccessfully to conceal one key mistake. This type of comedy is less successful in Britain, simply because the government there has much greater power to suppress the best jokes in the name of national security.

Next, let's see what happens if the people at the top of organizations are determined to show they are infallible. Peter Drucker has a nice example of ignored feedback when he refers to a product he calls the "investment in managerial ego." This is a product that the manager believed in, nay, fought for and which has been repackaged, its salesmen retrained, it advertising changed and then the agency subsequently sacked, which was then relaunched as a seasonal product—but which has never actually sold. The manager has always reinterpreted the feedback from the marketplace so as to avoid acknowledging that the product has been a mistake.

If the corporate ego is so huge and unrealistic that failures have to be repackaged as successes, then disaster cannot be very far down the road. If the heads of organizations cannot bear to receive feedback that may suggest that mistakes have been made and need correction, then they will increasingly be surrounded by yes-men and will be increasingly cut off from the feedback they need to stay on course. (I still treasure, incidentally, Sam Goldwyn's memo: "I don't want any yes-men in this organization. I want people to speak their minds—even if it does cost them their jobs.")

So once the corporate ethos is that the corporation cannot have made a mistake, then it's going to go further and further off course. The CEO becomes a bit like a pilot in an aircraft who says to the altimeter, "What's the height?" And hears the altimeter reply, "What would you like it to be?"

The leading philosopher of science of this century, Karl Popper, says that scientists do not sit around dispassionately observing clusters of phenomena and then come up with rational explanations of them. He suggests that scientists really get "hunches" and then look around for examples to fit in with their ideas. And that, therefore, in the pursuit of scientific truth, when they have worked out their hypothesis, they should test it, not with tests to prove it right, but with tests specifically designed to prove it wrong. In Popper's words, falsifiable. All of which shows that current philosophical and scientific thought has arrived at the startling realization that we learn only from our mistakes.

Now we reach the real problem. If all the evidence from business, science, and psychology suggests that the best results are obtained by risking mistakes, and by having a positive attitude toward them when they occur, why are we all so nervous about making them?

I'm sure that the answer is quite simply that we all have these ridiculous things called egos. Once you've got an ego, you want to be right. I've noticed this even in my 3-year-old daughter. If I ask her a question and she doesn't know the answer, she doesn't want to guess in

case she makes a mistake. She changes the subject, even though I tell her it doesn't matter.

How can we solve this problem? You may be able to persuade yourself and others that admitting small mistakes right away protects your ego more efficiently than running the risk of making a far greater and more painful mistake later.

For example, I chose to show my latest film here in New York in a rough form, and actually encouraged people to damage my ego by criticizing it, so that I can eliminate some of the mistakes and improve it. I feel safer doing this than sheltering myself from adverse criticism now only to run the risk of discovering in a few months' time that it's Britain's answer to Heaven's Gate. People say nobody likes criticism. True, but I feel safer getting the pain up front.

Finally, the most effective way that we can create an atmosphere of tolerance and positiveness toward mistakes is, of course, to model it. In the early stages of a discussion, say that you don't know the solution, throw up a couple of ideas that, after examination, you casually discard saying, "Okay, I don't think that was very useful." Better still, discuss a couple of recent mistakes that you've made and learned from.

Any ego-loss suffered is more than compensated for in my experience by the ego-gain in showing you're the kind of guy who's big enough to admit when he's wrong.

**Source:** D. Machan, "No More Mistakes and You're Through!" (Importance of mistakes in business, excerpts from speech by British comedian John Cleese) (transcript), *Forbes*, 16 May 1988.

Encouraged by this announcement, a team of engineers used an experimental molding technique to cut the cost and time it took to make the metal hoods for Toro riding lawn mowers. The experimental molding technique worked great in the lab, but failed miserably at the fast speeds required in Toro's production facilities. Despite the company's pronouncements that innovation would not be punished, all the team members expected to be fired when Toro's CEO asked for a meeting with them. On arriving at the CEO's office, instead of finding pink slips, they found balloons, cake, and a pleased CEO who wanted to celebrate their efforts.[23] For more on creativity and failure, see the "Been There, Done That" feature about British comedian John Cleese's thoughts on creativity and the importance of making mistakes.

*Freedom* means having autonomy over one's day-to-day work, and a sense of ownership and control over one's ideas. Numerous studies have indicated that creative ideas thrive under conditions of freedom. At 3M, engineers and scientists can spend 10 percent of their time, roughly a half day per week, doing whatever they want, as long as it's related to innovation and new product development. At DuPont, engineers and scientists are given a full day per week to do the same: Read, stay home, surf the Internet, visit competitors, or take a class—as long as it has something to do with innovative ideas. Phone company Bell Atlantic takes the idea of freedom even further with its Champion program. Employees who qualify as "idea champions" take a fully paid leave from their regular jobs to be trained on how to write a business plan, organize a development schedule, and spend the money the company gives them to develop their idea into a product or business. Champions are also allowed to invest 10 percent of their salary in their projects and can choose to give up their annual bonus in exchange for 5 percent of the revenues from their ideas, should they ever become profitable. In its first three years,

**Listen to All Ideas, Big and Small**

Companies can encourage innovation by listening to all ideas, big and small. The Great Harvest Bread Company, which is a franchisor of bakery stores, encourages all of its franchisees and their employees to share ideas on its internal "Breadboard" Web site. Ideas are shared about recipes, promotions, and marketing. Successful ideas with detailed instructions are written up as case studies and published on the Breadboard for all to see. Likewise, American Airlines has saved millions from the thousands of ideas generated by employees through its "IdeAAs in Action" suggestion program. Big or small, the next breakthrough idea could come from anyone or anywhere in your company. Listen hard or you may miss it.

**Source:** M. Hopkins, "Inc. Case Study: Great Harvest Bread Co. Runs Itself," *Inc.*, 1 November 2000, 54.

the Champion program has led to two government patents, with 11 more patents pending. [24]

Work environments that generally foster creativity may also have some impediments to creativity. Internal conflict and power struggles, rigid management structures, and a conservative bias toward the status quo can all discourage creativity. They create the perception that others in the organization will decide which ideas are acceptable and deserve support. One way in which many companies avoid a conservative, anti-innovation bias is to ask their customers for ideas. After all, if customers are enthusiastic about new ideas, it's harder to discount them. For example, Sportime International sold a million Hands-On basketballs with color-coded markings that show kids where to place their hands for better shooting accuracy. The idea was suggested by nine-year-old Chris Haas, who has made $35,000 in royalties thus far from the suggestion. Spinmaster started selling its Proshops line of simple, unassembled skateboards and bicycles that kids could put together themselves with interchangeable parts. The idea came from its "kids' advisory board." The unassembled Proshops products and bikes far outsell its already assembled products.[25]

## 2.2 Managing Innovation during Discontinuous Change

A study of 72 product development projects (i.e., innovation) in 36 computer companies across the United States, Europe, and Asia found that companies that succeeded in periods of discontinuous change (in which a technological discontinuity created a significant breakthrough in performance or function) typically followed an experiential approach to innovation.[26] The **experiential approach to innovation** assumes that innovation is occurring within a highly uncertain environment, and that the key to fast product innovation is to use intuition, flexible options, and hands-on experience to reduce uncertainty and accelerate learning and understanding. There are five parts to the experiential approach to innovation: design iterations, testing, milestones, multifunctional teams, and powerful leaders.[27]

An "iteration" is a repetition. So, a **design iteration** is a cycle of repetition in which a company tests a prototype of a new product or service, improves on the design, and then builds and tests the improved product or service prototype. As you learned in Chapter 4, a product prototype is a full-scale working model that is being tested for design, function, and reliability. **Testing** is a systematic comparison of different product designs or design iterations. Companies that want to create a new dominant design following a technological discontinuity quickly build, test, improve, and retest a series of different product prototypes.

For example, it took a number of design iterations for Starbucks and its suppliers to successfully create a paper coffee cup that would keep coffee hot but not burn customers' hands. To prevent customers from burning themselves, Starbucks had either stacked two paper cups together or used cardboard sleeves that slid over the outside of the cup. However, customers complained that sleeves fell off or prevented cups from fitting into cup holders and that using two cups was wasteful. As a result, Starbucks and its suppliers worked for three years to come up with a paper cup that was light, cheap, environment-friendly, and heat-insulating. Prototypes ranged from a layered cup that folded and wrapped one long piece of paper into three layers of paper, to a Japanese-designed cup coated with a special plastic. Testing was both practical, using human hands to pick up different cups filled with steaming coffee, and scientific, using an infrared temperature gauge to test cups' external temperatures. The breakthrough cup design, now being tested in Starbucks stores, sandwiches a thin air layer between an inner-polyethylene liner and outer layer of brown recycled paper.[28]

By trying a number of very different designs, or by making successive improvements and changes in the same design, frequent design iterations reduce uncertainty and im-

---

**experiential approach to innovation**
an approach to innovation that assumes a highly uncertain environment, and uses intuition, flexible options, and hands-on experience to reduce uncertainty and accelerate learning and understanding

**design iteration**
a cycle of repetition in which a company tests a prototype of a new product or service, improves on that design, and then builds and tests the improved prototype

**testing**
systematic comparison of different product designs or design iterations

360

### Testing 1-2-3, Testing 1-2-3

Ideas are no substitute for real-world testing. Team New Zealand used daily testing, two identical racing boats, and sophisticated design software to prepare for the America's Cup yacht races. Each day, one boat would use the new design generated by the computer. Then, the two boats would race to determine which was better. Afterwards, the simulation was reprogrammed using data gathered during that race. In the morning, another configuration would be race-tested the same way. The result? Team New Zealand defeated Team USA by the largest margin in history. Not sure which idea is best? Give them a try and put them to the test.

**Source**: M. Iansiti & A. MacCormack, "Developing Products," *Harvard Business Review*, September-October 1997, 108-117.

**milestones**
formal project review points used to assess progress and performance

**multifunctional teams**
work teams composed of people from different departments

prove understanding. Simply put, the more prototypes you build, the more likely you are to learn what works and what doesn't. Plus, building a number of prototypes also means that designers and engineers are less likely to "fall in love" with a particular prototype. Instead, they'll be more concerned with improving the product or technology as much as they can. Testing speeds up and improves the innovation process, too. Testing two very different design prototypes against each other, or testing the new design iteration against the previous iteration, quickly makes product design strengths and weaknesses apparent. Likewise, testing uncovers errors early in the design process when they are easiest to correct. Finally, testing accelerates learning and understanding by forcing engineers and product designers to examine hard data about product performance. When there's hard evidence that prototypes are testing well, the confidence of the design team grows. Also, personal conflict between design team members is less likely when testing focuses on hard measurements and facts rather than personal hunches and preferences.

**Milestones** are formal project review points used to assess progress and performance. For example, a company that has put itself on a 12-month schedule to complete a project might schedule milestones at the three-month, six-month, and nine-month points on the schedule. By making people regularly assess what they're doing, how well they're performing, and whether they need to take corrective action, milestones provide structure to the general chaos that follows technological discontinuities. Milestones also shorten the innovation process by creating a sense of urgency that keeps everyone on task. For example, when Florida Power & Light was building its first nuclear power facility, the company's construction manager passed out 2,000 desk calendars to company employees, construction contractors, vendors, and suppliers, so that everyone involved in the project was aware of the construction timeline. Contractors that regularly missed deadlines were replaced.[29] Finally, milestones are beneficial for innovation, because meeting regular milestones builds momentum by giving people a sense of accomplishment.

**Multifunctional teams** are work teams composed of people from different departments. Multifunctional teams accelerate learning and understanding by mixing and integrating technical, marketing, and manufacturing activities. By involving all key departments in development from the start, multifunctional teams speed innovation through early identification of new ideas or problems that would typically not have been generated or addressed until much later. Kellogg's, the cereal company, isn't known for being a particularly innovative company. After all, its best-selling cereal, Frosted Flakes, was created 50 years ago. Furthermore, after creating its top-selling breakfast food, Pop Tarts, it took Kellogg's nearly three decades to come up with another new kind of breakfast food, NutriGrain cereal bars. Today, however, the company is using multifunctional design teams composed of market researchers, food technologists, engineers, and cooks to develop new cereals and breakfast foods. Each design team is located between a restaurant-quality kitchen to come up with new food ideas and a minimanufacturing line that is used to run test batches. Thus far, the approach seems to be working. In their first month, Kellogg's multifunctional teams came up with 65 new product ideas and 94 new ways to package existing products. Two of the best new ideas are the popular Raisin Bran Crunch, with thick flakes that don't get soggy in milk, and Rice Krispie Treats, which is a cereal version of the marshmallow squares made in millions of home kitchens (melted marshmallows over Rice Krispies, baked in the oven).[30]

*Powerful leaders* provide the vision, discipline, and motivation to keep the innovation process focused, on time, and on target. Powerful leaders are able to get resources when they are needed, are typically more experienced, have high status in the company, and are held directly responsible for product success or failure. On average, powerful

361

Multifunctional work teams are a key part of generating new ideas. When Kellogg's realized that it was experiencing a dearth of new ideas and products, it implemented multifunctional work teams. In their first month, the teams generated 65 new product ideas, including the now-popular prepackaged Rice Krispie Treat.

© JEFF SCIORTINO

leaders can get innovation-related projects done nine months faster than leaders with little power or influence. One such powerful leader is Sherm Mullin, who headed Lockheed Corporation's Advanced Development company, which developed the F-117 Stealth Fighter and is now developing the new Advanced Tactical Fighter jet for the U.S. Air Force. When Mullin brought the ATF design team together, the first slide in his presentation to the group was "Lead, follow, or get the hell out of the way." This was his way of telling them that the project would come in on time and under budget. Furthermore, Mullin runs a tight operation. When developing new planes, he creates small teams of highly motivated workers, gives them demanding schedules and small budgets, and then isolates them from the rest of Lockheed to keep management "off their backs." He said, "You don't let anyone in, and you give them the freedom to do their thing." The key challenge, he said, is "to do it faster and cheaper."[31]

### 2.3 Managing Innovation during Incremental Change

As shown in Exhibit 10.5, the experiential approach is used to manage innovation in highly uncertain environments during periods of discontinuous change. In comparison, the compression approach is used to manage innovation in more certain environments during periods of incremental change. And while the goals of the experiential approach are significant improvements in performance and the establishment of a *new* dominant technology design, the goals of the compression approach are lower costs and incremental improvements in the performance and function of the *existing* technological design. Finally, the general strategies in each approach are different, too. With the experiential approach, the general strategy is to build something new, different, and substantially better. Since there's so much uncertainty—no one knows which technology will become the market leader—companies adopt a winner-take-all approach by trying to create the market-leading, dominant design. With the compression approach, the general strategy is to compress the time and steps needed to bring about small, consistent im-

362

EXHIBIT 10.5

## COMPARING THE EXPERIENTIAL AND COMPRESSION APPROACHES TO MANAGING INNOVATION

| APPROACH | EXPERIENTIAL APPROACH TO INNOVATION: MANAGING INNOVATION DURING DISCONTINUOUS CHANGE | COMPRESSION APPROACH TO INNOVATION: MANAGING INNOVATION DURING INCREMENTAL CHANGE |
|---|---|---|
| Assumptions | • Highly uncertain environment<br>  o Era of ferment—technological substitution and design competition<br>• Goals:<br>  o Speed<br>  o Significant improvements in performance<br>  o Establishment of new dominant design<br>• Approach<br>  o Build something new, different, and substantially better | • Certain environment<br>  o Era of incremental change—established technology (i.e., dominant design)<br>• Goals<br>  o Speed<br>  o Lower costs<br>  o Incremental improvements in performance of dominant design<br>• Approach<br>  o Compress time and steps needed to bring about small improvements |
| Steps | • Design iterations<br>• Testing<br>• Milestones<br>• Multifunctional teams<br>• Powerful leaders | • Planning<br>• Supplier involvement<br>• Shortening the time of individual steps<br>• Overlapping steps<br>• Multifunctional teams |

provements in performance and functionality. Because a dominant technology design already exists, the general strategy is to continue improving the existing technology as rapidly as possible.

In short, a **compression approach to innovation** assumes that innovation is a predictable process, that incremental innovation can be planned using a series of steps, and that compressing the time it takes to complete those steps can speed up innovation. There are five parts to the compression approach to innovation: planning, supplier involvement, shortening the time of individual steps, overlapping steps, and multifunctional teams.[32]

In Chapter 4, *planning* was defined as choosing a goal and a method or strategy to achieve that goal. When *planning for incremental innovation*, the goal is to squeeze or compress development time as much as possible, and the general strategy is to create a series of planned steps to accomplish that goal. Planning for incremental innovation helps avoid unnecessary steps. Plus, planning allows developers to sequence steps in the right order to avoid wasted time and shorten the delays between steps. Planning also reduces misunderstandings and decreases coordination problems regarding when and how things are to be done.

Most planning for incremental innovation is based on the idea of generational change. **Generational change** occurs when incremental improvements are made to a dominant technological design such that the improved version of the technology is fully backward compatible with the older version.[33] So unlike technological discontinuities that result in the replacement of older technologies, generational change allows the old and newer versions of the same technological design to coexist in the marketplace. For example, Sony used the idea of generational change to extend the life of its Sony Walkman products. After inventing the Walkman tape player, Sony introduced 250 different

**compression approach to innovation**
an approach to innovation that assumes that incremental innovation can be planned using a series of steps, and that compressing those steps can speed innovation

**generational change**
change based on incremental improvements to a dominant technological design such that the improved technology is fully backward compatible with the older technology

363

kinds of Walkmans over the next decade. However, there were few significant changes in the basic Walkman over that time. In fact, 85 percent of the new models simply represented small improvements (i.e., generational change) based on a four-point plan that Sony developed. First, make the Walkmans smaller. Second, make them cheaper. Third, when possible, add small improvements. For example, while the first Walkman only played audio tapes, subsequent Walkmans added AM/FM stereo radio, auto reverse, Dolby sound, water resistance, TV audio band, digital tuning, and enhanced bass. Finally, make minor cosmetic changes in the Walkman's color and appearance. Together, these generational changes have helped Sony maintain above-average profits and a 50 percent share of this market.[34] Furthermore, Sony has used the same generational approach in designing and selling its personal CD players.

Because the compression approach assumes that innovation can follow a series of preplanned steps, one of the ways to shorten development time is *supplier involvement*. Delegating some of the preplanned steps in the innovation process to outside suppliers reduces the amount of work that internal development teams must do. Plus, suppliers provide an alternative source of ideas and expertise that can lead to better designs. For example, when Whirlpool, a leading manufacturer of appliances, decided to completely redesign its products, it involved one of its key partners, Inland Steel, from the start. Inland used its expertise in metals to help Whirlpool tear down and analyze each component of its competitors' washers, dryers, and refrigerators.

Supplier involvement also takes advantage of distinctive competencies by allowing both the development team and the suppliers to do what they do best. Said Whirlpool manager Jack Crank, "We know how to make the world's best appliances, but that doesn't mean we are also experts in metallurgy or all of the processes necessary to get maximum benefit from a particular metal. They [Inland] test materials, help us set specifications for metals, make steel that exactly fits our needs, and get it to us on time—all of which saves us money and raises the quality of our products."[35] In general, the earlier suppliers are involved, the quicker they catch and prevent future problems, such as unrealistic designs or mismatched product specifications.

Another way to shorten development time is to simply *shorten the time of individual steps* in the innovation process. One of the most common ways to do that is through computer-aided design (CAD). CAD speeds up the design process by allowing designers and engineers to make and test design changes using computer models. In many steps of the design process, Ford found that CAD models and computer simulations can replace physical testing of expensive automobile prototypes. And since computer-based CAD systems store design specifications and characteristics in computer files (the same way that a personal computer stores word processing files), CAD speeds innovation by making it easy to access and reuse previous designs. At Ford, product designers and engineers use desktop and laptop computers to access a design knowledge base containing standard parts, standard design guides (that walk designers through the process of creating new parts), and detailed performance and testing information. The design knowledge base is accessible to any computer connected to Ford's company network. Finally, CAD systems improve communication and organization by making sure that all design team members work with the latest design iteration. If the engineers in charge of engine design change the size of an engine from four to six cylinders, those changes are automatically registered in what Ford calls the "common total vehicle data model." So when the designers in charge of the car's suspension system log on, they'll find that the engine has been changed and can make the necessary changes to the car's suspension system.[36]

In a sequential design process, each step must be completed before the next step begins. But sometimes multiple development steps can be performed at the same time. *Overlapping steps* shortens the development process by reducing the delays or waiting time between steps. By using overlapping rather than sequential steps, most car companies have reduced the time it takes to develop a brand new car from five years to three years. However, they still develop new models sequentially. First, they design and build, say, a four-door sedan. Then, after perfecting the design and manufacture of the sedan, two or three years later they introduce the two-door coupe. A couple of years after that, they introduce the station wagon version of the same model. Toyota, however, takes the notion of overlapping steps even further by developing all three versions (four-door sedan, two-door coupe, and station wagon) simultaneously. By overlapping model development in 2001, Toyota cut its total development time for all three models in half! This helped Toyota bring 18 new or redesigned cars to market in just two years. And its new Picnic and Corolla Spacio models went into production just 14½ months after designs were approved, well under the three years it normally takes to develop a new car.[37] Today, however, Toyota has squeezed development time even more, cutting the time between initial design and production to just 12 months![38]

## Review 2
### Managing Innovation

To successfully manage innovation streams, companies must manage the sources of innovation and learn to manage innovation during both discontinuous and incremental change. Since innovation begins with creativity, companies can manage the sources of innovation by supporting a creative work environment in which creative thoughts and ideas are welcomed, valued, and encouraged. Creative work environments provide challenging work; offer organizational, supervisory, and work group encouragement; allow significant freedom; and remove organizational impediments to creativity.

Companies that succeed in periods of discontinuous change typically follow an experiential approach to innovation. The experiential approach assumes that intuition, flexible options, and hands-on experience can reduce uncertainty and accelerate learning and understanding. This approach involves frequent design iterations, frequent testing, regular milestones, creation of multifunctional teams, and use of powerful leaders to guide the innovation process.

A compression approach to innovation works best during periods of incremental change. This approach assumes that innovation can be planned using a series of steps and that compressing the time it takes to complete those steps can speed up innovation. The five parts to the compression approach are planning (generational change), supplier involvement, shortening the time of individual steps (computer-aided design), overlapping steps, and multifunctional teams.

# Organizational Change

The idea was simple. Instead of going to the store to get your groceries, Webvan would bring your groceries to you. No more having to find a parking spot. No more waiting in the checkout line. And no more having to carry your groceries to your car and then, minutes later, from your car to your house. Simply order your groceries online today and Webvan would bring them to your house tomorrow, all for about the same cost of going to the store yourself. Customers like Lisa Dana, a busy doctor with three kids, loved Webvan. Every five days, a Webvan truck would come to her house with $120 to $140 worth of groceries for her family. She said, "They [Webvan] go out of business, I go out of business. We would not be able to do without it."[39] Unfortunately, though, Webvan did go out of business because it lost money on each order. Although it actually made good money on the groceries themselves (for example, on a $112 grocery order, $30 was profit, about the same profit earned by a typical grocery store), it lost money delivering those orders, well beyond any profits it earned on groceries. In fact, Webvan was losing so much money that it burned through $200 million in cash during its last six months in business.

The problem wasn't surprise or ignorance. Webvan knew it was hemorrhaging cash. The problem was that Webvan was unable to change its business to stop the bleeding.

That inability to change, to figure out ways to bring in more customers and to be more efficient, eventually led to its demise.

*After reading the next two sections on organizational change, you should be able to*
*3. discuss why change occurs and why it matters.*
*4. discuss the different methods that managers can use to better manage change as it occurs.*

## 3. Why Change Occurs and Why It Matters

*Businesses operate in a constantly changing environment. Recognizing and adapting to internal and external changes can mean the difference between continued success and going out of business. Let's learn 3.1 how change forces and resistance forces bring about change and 3.2 and how companies that fail to change run the risk of organizational decline.[40]*

### 3.1 Change Forces and Resistance Forces

**change forces**
forces that produce differences in the form, quality, or condition of an organization over time

**resistance forces**
forces that support the existing state of conditions in organizations

According to social psychologist Kurt Lewin, change is a function of the forces that promote change and the opposing forces that slow or resist change.[41] **Change forces** lead to differences in the form, quality, or condition of an organization over time. By contrast, **resistance forces** support the status quo, that is, the existing state of conditions in organizations.

Exhibit 10.6 illustrates how the relative strengths of resistance and change forces interact to bring about different levels of change. Change can be nonexistent, sporadic, continuous, or discontinuous, depending on whether change forces are stronger or weaker than resistance forces. At one extreme, when resistance forces are strong and changes forces are weak, there is *no change*. For example, the United Way is the best-known charity in the United States. It works by collecting donations from companies and their employees and then redistributing those funds to local charities. Over the last decade, however, it has been a much less effective organization. A dozen years ago, donations to the United Way accounted for 3.16 percent of all charitable giving in the United States. Today, only 1.98 percent of all charitable giving goes to the United Way. Furthermore, over the same period, while the percentage of personal income donated to charities increased 8.2 percent, contributions to the United Way actually dropped 29 percent! Yet, despite these problems, there is tremendous resistance to change within the United Way. One example involves the United Way's use of confusing and highly inefficient paper pledge forms. When national president Betty Beene tried to get all 1,400 local United Way offices to computerize their United Way pledge forms to reduce the work associated with pledging, the offices complained, fearing a loss of power, and withheld their dues to the national office, before finally having Beene removed from office. *Fortune* magazine characterized the United Way's problems this way: "It [Getting Beene removed] seems a Pyrrhic victory at best. The rebels have toppled a leader who was pushing for necessary transformation." In short, resistance forces were strong and changes forces were weak. No change occurred at the United Way.[42]

**sporadic change**
change that occurs in random patterns or for accidental reasons

When resistance and change forces are both weak, chance events can lead to **sporadic change** that occurs in random patterns or for accidental reasons. For example, Ontrack Data International became a successful small company by writing software that allowed computer manufacturers (or anyone installing a new hard drive) to shorten the time it takes to install and format computer hard drives from 24 hours to less than one hour. Today, however, Ontrack accidentally finds itself in the "disk doctor" business. Why? Because Ontrack was so good at fixing hard drives and retrieving data from crashed drives, the disk drive manufacturers themselves began referring customers with hard drive problems to Ontrack. Now, Ontrack gets more than 60 percent of its revenues from "disk doctoring" and only 20 percent of its revenues from its original software products.[43]

EXHIBIT 10.6

HOW CHANGE AND RESISTANCE FORCES CREATE CHANGE

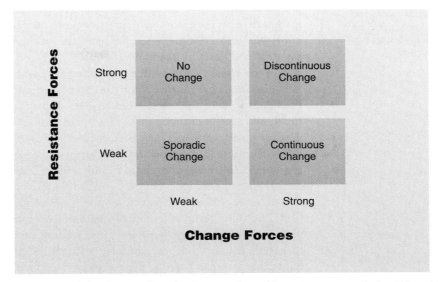

**Source:** P. Strebel, "Choosing the Right Change Path," *California Management Review,* Winter 1994, 29-51.

**continuous change**
change that occurs when change forces are strong and resistance forces are weak

When change forces are strong and resistance forces are weak, **continuous change** occurs, as organizations are forced to adapt to ongoing change forces. Over the last three decades, companies have clearly struggled to keep up with the continuous changes in computer technology. For example, Intel's first microprocessor computed 60,000 instructions per second. However, by the year 2010, it's estimated that Intel's microprocessors will be capable of computing more than 100 billion instructions per second.[44] Not surprisingly, companies have had to increase the amount of money they spend on technology. It's now estimated that 41 percent of capital investments (i.e., money spent for long-term improvement of the firm) is spent on information technology, compared to just 31 percent five years ago."[45]

**discontinuous change**
sudden change that occurs when change and resistance forces are strong and resistance forces can no longer hold back the change forces

If both change and resistance forces are strong and the resistance forces can no longer hold back the change forces, sudden **discontinuous change** can occur. Discontinuous change is similar to an arm-wrestling match between two 250-pound men. Both men are strong, but after a while, one is likely to tire or lose his grip. When that happens, the match will end seconds later, as the winner suddenly overpowers the loser. Eisnor Interactive, a start-up company that specializes in promoting and marketing Web sites, experienced wrenching, discontinuous change. One morning, when founder Di-Ann Eisnor was having breakfast with its biggest client, Bertelsmann Online (BOL), BOL's president suddenly announced that it was scrapping its online bookstore project and would no longer need Eisnor and the eight people who worked for her. With BOL accounting for 80 percent of Eisnor Interactive's revenues, Eisnor feared that her company would go out of business. As it turned out, the company managed to survive, but only because Eisnor and her staff acted immediately by changing its strategy, targeting existing companies with new online divisions (Barnes & Noble, Priceline.com, Federal Express, Office Depot, and MTV Online) and hiring a press relations firm of its own to publicize its services. Within a year of these sudden, discontinuous changes, Eisnor Interactive had 19 clients on retainer and was doing projects for 15 others.[46]

367

**organization decline**
a large decrease in organizational performance that occurs when companies don't anticipate, recognize, neutralize, or adapt to the internal or external pressures that threaten their survival

**Organization decline** occurs when companies don't anticipate, recognize, neutralize, or adapt to the internal or external pressures that threaten their survival.[47] In other words, decline occurs when organizations don't recognize the need for change. GM's loss of market share in the automobile industry (from 50 percent to 28 percent) is an example of organizational decline. There are five stages of organizational decline: blinded, inaction, faulty action, crisis, and dissolution.[48]

In the *blinded stage*, decline begins because key managers don't recognize the internal or external changes that will harm their organizations. This "blindness" may be due to a simple lack of awareness about changes. It may stem from an inability to understand the significance of changes. Or, it may simply come from the overconfidence that can develop when companies have been successful. For example, Barney's started as a tiny men's discount clothing store on 17th Street and Seventh Avenue in New York City and grew into a collection of stores in Beverly Hills, Chicago, London, and Tokyo (and a dozen other international cities). Barney's sold some of the most expensive and fashionable designer clothes in the world until the overconfidence of the founder's grandsons, Gene and Bob Pressman, eventually led to the company's demise.[49] In his book *The Rise and Fall of The House of Barneys: A Family Tale of Chutzpah*, Joshua Levine of *Forbes* magazine described how overconfidence led the Pressmans to spend more time working out at the gym than running the company.[50] Confident of their success, the Pressmans blindly overspent and overbuilt the company. Indeed, just three years after opening a luxurious $270 million store on Madison Avenue in New York City, complete with marble floors, silver-plated windows, and an extravagantly priced restaurant, expresso bar, beauty salon, and health club, Barney's filed for bankruptcy.

In the *inaction stage*, as organizational performance problems become more visible, management may recognize the need to change but still take no action. The managers may be waiting to see if the problems will correct themselves. Or, they may find it difficult to change previous practices and policies that once led to success. Another possible reason is that they wrongly assume that they can make changes to correct problems, so they don't feel the problems are urgent. For example, when Barney's expanded from

The risk of not changing can be great, as the managers of Barney's found out. As costs spiraled out of control on a new building for women's clothing, pictured here, top managers at the trendy department store still maintained a "What's money?" attitude. When the company adopted more stringent cash management measures, it was too little, too late.

© ROBERT HOLMES/CORBIS

men's into women's clothing, management budgeted $12 million to buy and convert a building into a 70,000 square foot store for women's clothing. However, management ended up spending $25 million, more than double the estimated cost. While most managers would have been worried sick about spending twice their budget for a project like this, one of Barney's top managers exclaimed, "What's money?"[51]

In the *faulty action stage*, due to rising costs and decreasing profits and market share, management will announce "belt-tightening" plans designed to cut costs, increase efficiency, and restore profits. In other words, rather than recognizing the need for fundamental changes, managers assume that if they just run a "tighter ship," company performance will return to previous levels. Barney's fit this pattern, too. Rather than reexamine the basic need for change, Barney's management focused on cost cutting. Company managers and staff were no longer allowed to spend hundreds of thousands of dollars a year on perks such as cellular phones, cars, and entertainment. In fact, clothing allowances for some senior managers had been as much as $20,000 a year.[52] Unfortunately for Barney's, even this belt-tightening was too little too late.

In the *crisis stage*, bankruptcy or dissolution (i.e., breaking up and selling the different parts of the company) is likely to occur unless the company completely reorganizes the way it does business. At this point, however, companies typically lack the resources needed to fully change how they run their businesses. Cutbacks and layoffs will have reduced the level of talent among employees. Furthermore, talented managers who were savvy enough to see the crisis coming will have begun taking jobs with other companies (often with competitors). Because of rising costs and lower sales, cash is tight. And, lenders and suppliers are unlikely to extend further loans or credit to ease the cash crunch. For example, after giving Barney's more than $180 million in loans, Barney's bankers refused to loan the company any more money.

In the *dissolution stage*, after failing to make the changes needed to sustain the organization, the company is dissolved through bankruptcy proceedings or by selling assets in order to pay suppliers, banks, and creditors. At this point, a new CEO may be brought in to oversee the closing of stores, offices, and manufacturing facilities, the final layoff of managers and employees, and the sale of assets to pay bills and loans. In fact, after filing for bankruptcy, Barney's closed four stores, including the original Barney's at Seventh Avenue and 17th Street.[53] Then, three years later, Barney's was sold to two investment companies that brought in new management to rebuild the company.[54]

Finally, because decline is reversible at each of the first four stages, not all companies in decline reach final dissolution like Barney's did. For example, after nearly a decade in decline, GM has cut costs, stabilized its market share, and had several consecutive years of small profits.

## Review 3
### Why Change Occurs and Why It Matters

Change is a function of the relative strength of the change forces and resistance forces that occur inside and outside of organizations. Change can be nonexistent, sporadic, continuous, or discontinuous, depending on whether change forces are stronger or weaker than resistance forces. The five-stage process of organizational decline begins when organizations don't recognize the need for change. In the blinded stage, managers don't recognize the changes that threaten their organization's survival. In the inaction stage, management recognizes the need to change, but doesn't act, hoping that the problems will correct themselves. In the faulty action stage, management focuses on cost cutting and efficiency rather than facing up to fundamental changes needed to insure survival. In the crisis stage, failure is likely unless fundamental reorganization occurs. Finally, in the dissolution stage, the company is dissolved through bankruptcy proceedings, by selling assets to pay creditors, or through the closing of stores, offices, and facilities. However, if companies recognize the need to change early enough, dissolution may be avoided.

# 4. Managing Change

Atwaters is a fancy restaurant on top of the 30-story U.S. Bancorp tower in Portland, Oregon. With great views, fine service, and good food, Atwaters "wanted to be the best restaurant in town and didn't care how much it cost." However, under new manager Stephen Earnhart, Atwaters' new goal was to make a profit *and* be the best restaurant in town. To attract younger customers, waiters replaced their tuxedos with dressy, but still casual, white aprons and ties. Instead of a team of waiters at each table (waiters, back waiters, and maitre d's), service was personalized by having each waiter take responsibility for particular tables in the dining room. When it was slow in the bar, bartenders were asked to help out in the dining room. When it was slow in the dining room, waiters were asked to help out in the bar. Within weeks, employees began to complain. "That's not my job." "That's not what I was hired for." "You're asking me to do more, but you're not paying me for it." As employee dissatisfaction with the changes grew stronger, food began disappearing from the kitchen. Bartenders gave away drinks. The reservation book vanished on busy nights. Stephen Gagnon, a former Atwaters bartender, summed things up, saying, "Employee morale went to hell with all the changes."[55]

**Resistance to change**, like that shown by Atwaters' employees, is caused by self-interest, misunderstanding and distrust, and a general intolerance for change.[56] People resist change out of *self-interest*, because they fear that change will cost or deprive them of something they value. For example, resistance might stem from a fear that the changes will result in a loss of pay, power, responsibility, or even perhaps one's job. People also resist change because of *misunderstanding and distrust*. That is, they don't understand the change or the reasons for it, or they distrust the people, typically management, behind the change. For example, James Selby, a former waiter at Atwaters, said, "A lot of us felt the changes were unjustified."[57] However, resistance isn't always visible at first. In fact, some of the strongest resisters may initially support the changes in public, nodding and smiling their agreement, but then ignore the changes in private and just do their jobs as they always have. Management consultant Michael Hammer calls this deadly form of resistance the "Kiss of Yes."[58]

Resistance may also come from a generally low tolerance for change. Some people are simply less capable of handling change than others. People with a *low tolerance for change* are threatened by the uncertainty associated with change and worry that they won't be able to learn the new skills and behaviors needed to successfully negotiate change in their companies.

*Because resistance to change is inevitable, successful change efforts require careful management. So, in this section you will learn about 4.1 managing resistance to change, 4.2 different change tools and techniques, 4.3 managing conversations to promote change, and, finally, 4.4 what not to do when leading organizational change.*

## 4.1 Managing Resistance to Change

According to Kurt Lewin, managing organizational change is a basic process of unfreezing, change intervention, and refreezing. **Unfreezing** is getting the people affected by change to believe that change is needed. During the **change intervention** itself, workers and managers change their behavior and work practices. **Refreezing** is supporting and reinforcing the new changes so they "stick."

Resistance to change, as shown by Atwaters' employees, is an example of frozen behavior. Given the choice between changing and not changing, most people would rather not change. Because resistance to change is natural and inevitable, managers need to unfreeze resistance to change to create successful change programs. As shown in Exhibit 10.7, the following methods can be used to manage resistance to change: education and communication, participation, negotiation, top management support, and coercion.[59]

When resistance to change is based on insufficient, incorrect, or misleading information, managers should *educate* employees about the need for change and *communicate* change-related information to them. Managers must also supply the information and

EXHIBIT 10.7

MANAGING RESISTANCE TO CHANGE.

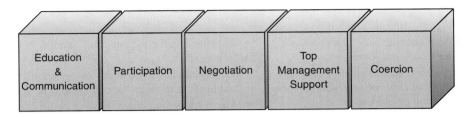

| Education & Communication | Participation | Negotiation | Top Management Support | Coercion |

funding or other support employees need to make changes. For example, resistance to change can be particularly strong when one company buys another company. Jeff Boyd, who worked for a large Canadian company, described the first meeting between the people in his department (the company that was acquired) and the people in the same department from the acquiring company: "It wasn't a friendly meeting. It wasn't hostile or anything like that, but everybody was on their guard a little bit. Right now, everybody's wondering if they'll be able to get along with the other employees, because there's a big difference in both companies' cultures and in the way both companies operate." Boyd concluded, "There's a lot of tension down at the employee level. We're still being kept in the dark about certain things. Everything seems to be up in the air right now."[60] By contrast, New York Presbyterian Health System reduced resistance to change by designating mentors to coach individuals, groups, and departments in newly acquired companies about its procedures and practices. New York Presbyterian's Diane Iorfida said, "Keeping employees informed every step of the way is so important. It's also important to tell the truth, whatever you do. If you don't know, say you don't know."[61]

Another way to reduce resistance to change is to have those affected by the change *participate in planning and implementing the change process.* Employees who participate have a better understanding of change and the need for it. Furthermore, employee concerns about change can be addressed as they occur if employees participate in the planning and implementation process. For example, when Avis, the car rental company, became employee-owned, it made hundreds of significant changes in the way the company was run. This degree of change would be difficult for any company. But Avis handled it by creating more than 150 employee-participation groups. On the first Thursday of every month, these groups meet to discuss specific problems and find ways to increase company productivity. Because other Avis employees elect the people who attend as representatives, there is typically little resistance to the changes and recommendations made by Avis's employee-participation groups.[62]

Employees are less likely to resist change if they are allowed *to discuss and agree on who will do what* after change occurs. For example, construction projects are notoriously hard to manage. It's difficult to get clients, architects, contractors, and subcontractors to agree on things like prices, materials, schedules, or who should be held responsible for unexpected changes and expenses. Often, lawsuits have to be filed to force reluctant parties to fulfill their responsibilities. However, McDevitt Street Bovis (MSB), a major building contractor, avoids these problems by meeting to negotiate an agreement in which MSB, its clients, and its subcontractors put each other's expectations and obligations into writing before construction begins. This way, when problems or changes occur, the parties involved are much more likely to fulfill their responsibilities. The power of this negotiating procedure is evident in a single fact: Unlike most building contractors, MSB has never been sued by a client when it negotiates an agreement ahead of time.[63]

Resistance to change also decreases when change efforts receive *significant managerial support.* Top managers must do more than talk about the importance of change. They must provide the training, resources, and autonomy needed to make change happen. For

371

EXHIBIT 10.8

## WHAT TO DO WHEN EMPLOYEES RESIST CHANGE

**UNFREEZING**

- **Share Reasons:** Share the reasons for change with employees.
- **Empathize:** Be empathetic to the difficulties that change will create for managers and employees.
- **Communicate:** Communicate the details simply, clearly, extensively, verbally, and in writing.

**CHANGE**

- **Benefits:** Explain the benefits, "What's in it for them."
- **Champion:** Identify a highly respected manager to manage the change effort.
- **Input:** Allow the people who will be affected by change to express their needs and offer their input.
- **Timing:** Don't begin change at a bad time, for example, during the busiest part of the year or month.
- **Security:** If possible, maintain employees' job security to minimize fear of change.
- **Training:** Offer training to ensure that employees are both confident and competent to handle new requirements.
- **Pace:** Change at a manageable pace. Don't rush.

**REFREEZING**

- **Top Management Support:** Send consistent messages and free resources.
- **Publicize Success:** Let others know when and where change is working.
- **Employee Services:** Offer counseling or other services to help employees deal with the stress of change.

**Source:** G.J. Iskat & J. Liebowitz, "What to Do When Employees Resist Change," *Supervision*, 1 August 1996.

**coercion**
using formal power and authority to force others to change

example, at Monarch Marking Systems, Elfie Winter's team was responsible for redesigning how the company manufactured its price-marking tool (which is used to put price tags on items in stores). Her boss demonstrated managerial support by making Winters' team fully responsible for designing a solution, for working out the necessary changes with other departments, and for making arrangements with company suppliers. He told Winters and her once-resistant coworkers, "Go make it happen and then tells us about it." When Winters and her coworkers were finished, they had reduced the amount of space it takes to assemble the product by 70 percent, cut inventory by $127,000, reduced late shipments by 90 percent, and doubled productivity.[64]

Finally, use of formal power and authority to force others to change is called **coercion**. Because of the intense negative reactions it can create (i.e., fear, stress, resentment, sabotage of company products), coercion should only be used when a crisis exists or when all other attempts to reduce resistance to change have failed.

Exhibit 10.8 summarizes some additional suggestions for what managers can do when employees resist change.

### 4.2 Change Tools and Techniques

Imagine your boss came to you and said, "Alright, genius, you wanted it. You're in charge of turning around the division." How would you start? Where would you begin? How would you encourage change-resistant managers to change? What would you do to include others in the change process? How would you get the change process off to a quick start? Finally, what long-term approach would you use to promote long-term effectiveness and performance? Results-driven change, the General Electric workout, transition management teams, and organizational development are different change tools and techniques that can be used to address these issues.

One of the reasons that organizational change efforts fail is that they are activity-oriented, meaning that they primarily focus on changing company procedures, manage-

372

ment philosophy, or employee behavior. Typically, there is much buildup and preparation as consultants are brought in, presentations are made, books are read, and employees and managers are trained. There's a tremendous emphasis on "doing things the new way." But for all the focus on activities, on "doing," there's almost no focus on results, on seeing if all this activity has actually made a difference.

**results-driven change**
change created quickly by focusing on the measurement and improvement of results

By contrast, **results-driven change** supplants the sole emphasis on activity with a laser-like focus on quickly measuring and improving results.[65] For example, at Monarch Marking Systems, quality-assurance engineer Steve Schneider guided the company's results-driven change process by first identifying everything in Monarch's factory that could be measured easily. He found 162 measures in all.[66] He further emphasized the importance of quick results by declaring that problem-solving teams had only 30 days to solve a particular problem. He encouraged workers to get to it, saying, "It's a project, not a process."

Another advantage of results-driven change is that managers introduce changes in procedures, philosophy, or behavior only if they are likely to improve measured performance. In other words, managers actually test to see if changes make a difference. Consistent with this approach, Schneider announced that Monarch's problem-solving teams could make any permanent changes they wanted, as long as those changes improved one of the 162 different measures of performance.

A third advantage of results-driven change is that quick, visible improvements motivate employees to continue to make additional changes to improve measured performance. For example, one team at Monarch used cross-training to reduce the number of job categories from 120 to 32. Another, encouraged by the success of 90 other problem-solving teams, trained machine operators how to enter production data directly into the computer on the factory floor, eliminating the 7,600 hours of staff work that it used to take to enter those data from paper records. Consequently, unlike most change efforts, the quick successes associated with results-driven change were particularly effective at reducing resistance to change. Exhibit 10.9 describes the basic steps of results-driven change.

**General Electric Workout**
a three-day meeting in which managers and employees from different levels and parts of an organization quickly generate and act on solutions to specific business problems

The **General Electric Workout** is a special kind of results-driven change. It is a three-day meeting that brings together managers and employees from different levels and parts of an organization to quickly generate and act on solutions to specific business problems.[67] On the first morning of a workout, the boss discusses the agenda and targets specific business problems that the group is to try to solve. Then, the boss leaves, and an outside facilitator breaks the group, typically 30 to 40 people, into five or six teams and helps them spend the next day and a half discussing and debating solutions. On day

*EXHIBIT 10.9*

RESULTS-DRIVEN CHANGE PROGRAMS

1. Management should create measurable, short-term goals to improve performance.
2. Management should use action steps only if they are likely to improve measured performance.
3. Management should stress the importance of immediate improvements.
4. Consultants and staffers should help managers and employees achieve quick improvements in performance.
5. Managers and employees should test action steps to see if they actually yield improvements. Action steps that don't should be discarded.
6. It takes few resources to get results-driven change started.

**Source:** R.H. Schaffer & H.A. Thomson, J.D, "Successful Change Programs Begin with Results," *Harvard Business Review on Change* (Boston: Harvard Business School Publishing, 1998), 189-213.

three, in what GE calls a "town meeting," the teams present specific solutions to their boss, who has been gone since day one. As each team spokesperson makes specific suggestions, the boss has only three options: agree on the spot, say no, or ask for more information so that a decision can be made by a specific, agreed-on date. Amand Lauzon was a GE boss who sweated his way through a town meeting. To encourage him to say yes, his workers set up the meeting room so that he couldn't make eye contact with his boss. He said, "I was wringing wet within half an hour. They had 108 proposals, I had about a minute to say yes or no to each one, and I couldn't make eye contact with my boss without turning around, which would show everyone in the room that I was chicken."[68] In the end, Lauzon agreed to all but eight suggestions. Furthermore, once those decisions were made, no one at GE was allowed to overrule them.

While the GE Workout clearly speeds up change, it may fragment change, as different managers approve different suggestions in different town meetings across a company. By contrast, a transition management team provides a way to coordinate change throughout an organization. A **transition management team** (TMT) is a team of eight to 12 people whose full-time job is to manage and coordinate a company's change process.[69] One member of the TMT is assigned the task of anticipating and managing the emotions and behaviors related to resistance to change. Despite their importance, many companies overlook the impact that negative emotions and resistant behaviors can have on the change process. Also, TMTs report to the CEO every day, decide which change projects are approved and funded, select and evaluate the people in charge of different change projects, and make sure that different change projects complement one another. Microsoft is relying on a TMT to implement its .Net strategy, in which major parts of its Windows operating system and its Office software programs are redesigned to work seamlessly through the Internet. Microsoft's TMT, a small, close-knit group of software and technical engineers, advises founder Bill Gates on Microsoft's key strategies and products. At the time this chapter was written, Microsoft's TMT consisted of Eric Rudder, Gate's key technical advisor; Craig Mundie, Microsoft's consumer strategist; Paul Flessner, who was in charge of Microsoft's database products; Jim Allchin, who supervised development of operating systems (Windows 2000 and Windows XP), and David Cole, who ran Microsoft's Internet services (Hotmail and MSN). Michael Cusumano, author of *Microsoft Secrets*, said that, "This is the way Bill [Gates] has always liked to operate. Key decisions are made informally, and there are [only a] few people [i.e., Microsoft's TMT] close to him whom he trusts."[70]

It is also important to say what a TMT is not. A TMT is not an extra layer of management further separating upper management from lower managers and employees. Indeed, at Microsoft, nearly all the members of the TMT already head key divisions or departments. So their participation on the TMT does not create another layer of management. A TMT is not a steering committee that creates plans for others to carry out. Instead, the members of the TMT are fully involved with making change happen on a daily basis. Furthermore, it's not the TMT's job to determine how and why the company will change. That responsibility belongs to the CEO and upper management. Again, at Microsoft, founder and Chairman Bill Gates asks his TMT members to fiercely debate the advantages and disadvantages of potential Microsoft strategies. Responsibility for final decisions on key changes, though, falls to Gates. Once decided, it is the TMT's responsibility to accomplish those changes and make them stick. Finally, a TMT is not permanent. Once the company has successfully changed, the TMT is disbanded. At Microsoft, TMTs have been created and disbanded twice before, when the company was founded and again in the early 1990s. And when Microsoft successfully implements its .Net strategy, its TMT will be disbanded until needed again. Exhibit 10.10 lists the primary responsibilities of TMTs.

**Organizational development** is a philosophy and collection of planned change interventions designed to improve an organization's long-term health and performance. Organizational development takes a long-range approach to change, assumes that top management support is necessary for change to succeed, creates change by educating

EXHIBIT 10.10

## THE PRIMARY RESPONSIBILITIES OF TRANSITION MANAGEMENT TEAMS

1. Establish context for change and provide guidance.
2. Stimulate conversation.
3. Provide appropriate resources.
4. Coordinate and align projects.
5. Ensure congruence of messages, activities, policies, and behaviors.
6. Provide opportunities for joint creation.
7. Anticipate, identify, and address people problems.
8. Prepare the critical mass.

**Source:** J.D. Duck, "Managing Change: The Art of Balancing," *Harvard Business Review on Change* (Boston: Harvard Business School Publishing, 1998) 55-81.

**change agent**
the person formally in charge of guiding a change effort

workers and managers to change ideas, beliefs, and behaviors so problems can be solved in new ways, and emphasizes employee participation in diagnosing, solving, and evaluating problems.[71] As shown in Exhibit 10.11, organizational development interventions begin with recognition of a problem. Then, the company designates a **change agent** to be formally in charge of guiding the change effort. This person can be someone from the company or a professional consultant. The change agent clarifies the problem, gathers information, works with decision makers to create and implement an action plan, helps to evaluate the plan's effectiveness, implements the plan throughout the company, and then leaves only after making sure the change intervention will continue to work. Hajime Oba is a change agent and one of the key reasons that Toyota cars are tops in quality and reliability. Oba's job is to work closely with Toyota suppliers, showing them how to increase quality and decrease costs. For example, Michigan Summit Polymers installed a $280,000 paint system with robots and a paint oven to bake paint onto the dashboard vents that went into Toyota cars. However, Oba showed them that a $12 hair dryer did

375

EXHIBIT 10.11

### GENERAL STEPS FOR ORGANIZATIONAL DEVELOPMENT INTERVENTIONS

| | |
|---|---|
| 1. Entry | A problem is discovered and the need for change becomes apparent. Search begins for someone to deal with the problem and facilitate change. |
| 2. Start-up | A change agent enters the picture and works to clarify the problem and gain commitment to a change effort. |
| 3. Assessment and Feedback | The change agent gathers information about the problem and provides feedback about it to decision makers and those affected by it. |
| 4. Action Planning | The change agent works with decision makers to develop an action plan. |
| 5. Intervention | The action plan, or organizational development intervention, is carried out. |
| 6. Evaluation | The change agent helps decision makers assess the effectiveness of the intervention. |
| 7. Adoption | Organizational members accept ownership and responsibility for the change, which is then carried out through the entire organization. |
| 8. Separation | The change agent leaves the organization after first ensuring that the change intervention will continue to work. |

**Source:** W.J. Rothwell, R. Sullivan, & G.M. McLean, *Practicing Organizational Development: A Guide For Consultants* (San Diego: Pfeiffer & Company, 1995).

the job better and faster in just three minutes compared to the 90 minutes it took with robots and the special paint oven process. Because of Oba's demonstration, Summit replaced the robots with simple, but effective $150 spray guns and the paint oven with intense light bulbs. Overall, Oba has helped Summit cut its defects to less than 60 parts per million, down from 3,000 parts per million five years ago.[72] Oba's efforts as a change agent have significantly improved the quality of parts at Toyota's suppliers. That, in turn, has helped put Toyota at the top of quality rankings issued by J.D. Power and Associates and *Consumer Reports* magazine.[73]

Organizational development interventions are aimed at changing large systems, small groups, or people.[74] More specifically, the purpose of *large system interventions* is to change the character and performance of an organization, business unit, or department. The purpose of a *small group intervention* is to assess how a group functions, and help it work more effectively toward the accomplishment of its goals. The purpose of a *person-focused intervention* is to help people become aware of their attitudes and behaviors and acquire new skills and knowledge to increase interpersonal effectiveness. Exhibit 10.12 describes the most frequently used organizational development interventions for large systems, small groups, and people. For additional information about changing systems, groups, and people, see "What Really Works: Change the Work Setting or Change the People? Do Both!"

### 4.3 Managing Conversations to Promote Change

Think about where you have worked. How well and often did managers, especially top management, talk to you and other employees? Was it one-way, top-down communication, or did management listen and respond to the ideas of lower-level managers and employees? How did people from different parts of the company talk to each other? Did they try to understand each other, or did they talk past each other by using terms and ideas particular to their jobs or departments?

**organizational dialogue**
the process by which people in an organization learn to talk effectively and constructively with each other

**Organizational dialogue** is the process by which people in an organization learn to talk effectively and constructively with each other.[75] Unfortunately, in most companies, the quality of organizational dialogue isn't very good. But when change forces are strong

---

376

| EXHIBIT 10.12 | DIFFERENT KINDS OF ORGANIZATIONAL DEVELOPMENT INTERVENTIONS |
|---|---|

**LARGE SYSTEM INTERVENTIONS**

| | |
|---|---|
| Sociotechnical Systems | An intervention designed to improve how well employees use and adjust to the work technology used in an organization. |
| Survey Feedback | An intervention that uses surveys to collect information from organizational members, reports the results of that survey to organizational members, and then uses those results to develop action plans for improvement. |

**SMALL GROUP INTERVENTIONS**

| | |
|---|---|
| Team Building | An intervention designed to increase the cohesion and cooperation of work group members. |
| Unit Goal Setting | An intervention designed to help a work group establish short- and long-term goals. |

**PERSON-FOCUSED INTERVENTIONS**

| | |
|---|---|
| Counseling/Coaching | An intervention designed so that a formal helper or coach listens to managers or employees and advises them how to deal with work or interpersonal problems. |
| Training | An intervention designed to provide individuals the knowledge, skills, or attitudes they need to become more effective at their jobs. |

**Source:** W.J. Rothwell, R. Sullivan, & G.M. McLean, *Practicing Organizational Development: A Guide For Consultants* (San Diego: Pfeiffer & Company, 1995).

# WhatReallyWorks

## Change the Work Setting or Change the People? Do Both!

Let's assume that you believe that your company needs to change. Congratulations! Just recognizing the need for change puts you ahead of 80 percent of the companies in your industry. But now that you've recognized the need for change, how do you make change happen? Should you focus on changing the work setting or the behavior of the

people who work in that setting? It's a classic chicken or egg type of question. Which would you do?

A recent meta-analysis based on 52 studies and a combined total of 29,611 study participants indicated that it's probably best to do both!

### Changing the Work Setting

An organizational work setting has four parts: organizing arrangements (control and reward systems, organizational structure), social factors (people, culture, patterns of interaction), technology (how inputs are transformed into outputs), and the physical setting (the actual physical space in which people work).

Overall, there is a 55 percent chance that organizational change efforts will successfully bring changes to a company's work setting. While the odds are still 55-45 in your favor, this is undoubtedly a much lower probability of success than you've seen with the management techniques discussed in other chapters. This simply reflects how strong resistance to change is in most companies.

**Probability of Success**

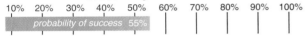

### Changing the People

Changing people means changing individual work behavior. The idea is powerful. Change the decisions people make. Change the activities they perform. Change the information they share with others. And change the initiatives they take on their own. Change these individual behaviors and collectively you change the entire company. Overall, there is a 57 percent

chance that organizational change efforts will successfully change people's individual work behavior. If you're wondering why the odds aren't higher, consider how difficult it is to simply change personal behavior. It's incredibly difficult to quit smoking, change your diet, or maintain a daily exercise program. Not surprisingly, changing personal behavior at work is also difficult. Thus, viewed in this context, a 57 percent chance of success is a notable achievement.

**Probability of Success**

### Changing Individual Behavior and Organizational Performance

The point of changing individual behavior is to improve organizational performance (i.e., higher profits, market share, and productivity, and lower costs). Overall, there is a 76 percent chance that changes in individual behavior will produce changes in organizational outcomes. So if you want to improve your company's profits, market share, or productivity, focus on changing the way that your people behave at work.

**Probability of Success**

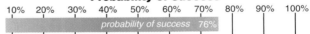

**Source:** P.J. Robertson, D.R. Roberts, & J.I. Porras, "Dynamics of Planned Organizational Change: Assessing Empirical Support for a Theoretical Model," *Academy of Management Journal* 36 (1993): 619-634.

and managers and workers are stressed, organizational dialogue can be nonexistent. Consequently, the way managers and workers talk (or don't talk) to each other can be a significant barrier to successful change efforts.

According to this line of thinking, talk is not cheap. Conversations shape attitudes, intentions, and actions. What is said or not said really matters. So when organizational dialogue breaks down, change efforts break down, too. From this perspective, managing change is akin to managing the conversations that make up organizational dialogue.

The dark-colored boxes in Exhibit 10.13 show the four kinds of conversations that managers can use to influence change in organizations.[76] When change efforts work, change begins with initiative conversations. These are followed by conversations about understanding, performance, and closure. However, the light-colored boxes in Exhibit 10.13 show that each of those conversations is subject to potential breakdowns: nothing happens, unclear conditions of satisfaction, agreement isn't action, lack of rigor, and omitting closure. When breakdowns happen, change may fail. Let's examine each of

EXHIBIT 10.13

## MANAGING CONVERSATIONS TO INITIATE CHANGE

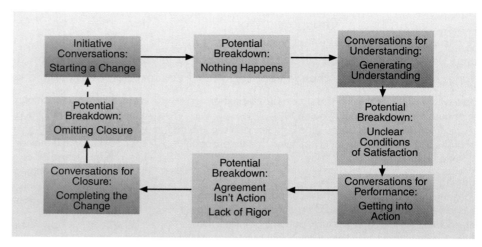

**Source:** J. Ford & L.W. Ford, "The Role of Conversations in Producing Intentional Change in Organizations," *Academy of Management Review* 20 (1995): 541-570.

**initiative conversations**
conversations that start the change process by discussing what should or needs to be done to bring about change

these change conversations and breakdowns in more detail. As we do so, refer to Exhibit 10.14, which shows a conversation among hospital managers who are discussing the need for a quality-improvement plan.

**Initiative conversations** start the change process by discussing what should or needs to be done to bring about change. Initiative conversations begin with phrases like "I propose," "Tell me what we should do about," "We should stop . . . and start," "It is time we undertake," and "What do you think about." For example, in Exhibit 10.14, the hospital CEO begins an initiative conversation by stating, "I want us to implement a quality-improvement program."

Naturally, talking about change only matters if it leads to action to promote change. Consequently, if *nothing happens* after talking about what needs to be done to bring about change, then the change process will stop. This kind of breakdown occurs for two reasons. First, the people who want to initiate change may be unable to actually make change happen. Second, if previous initiatives for change have been ignored or dismissed as unimportant, the people who have initiative conversations about what changes need to occur may not tell anyone with the power or authority to make change happen. In both instances, despite the fact that change clearly needs to occur, frustration sets in, because nothing happens.

**conversations for understanding**
conversations that generate a deeper understanding of why change is needed, what problems have been occurring, and what might be done to solve those problems

If a breakdown is avoided, initiative conversations should be followed by conversations for understanding. **Conversations for understanding** generate a deeper understanding of why change is needed, what problems have been occurring, and what might be done to solve those problems. For example, in the conversation of understanding shown in Exhibit 10.14, the hospital managers discuss why change is needed ("First, we are getting far too many complaints from our patients.") and try to figure out why problems have been occurring ("The staff may be doing a better job as individual workers but not as a team. There must be some reason for the complaints.")

**conditions of satisfaction**
a statement of the specific, measurable, and observable conditions that must be met in order for change to be successful

A conversation for understanding breaks down when *there is no clear understanding of the conditions of satisfaction.* Conditions of satisfaction are similar to the S.M.A.R.T. goals criteria discussed in Chapter 4 on Planning. Recall that S.M.A.R.T. goals are **S**pecific, **M**easurable, **A**ttainable, **R**ealistic, and **T**imely.[77] Likewise, **conditions of satisfaction** are the specific, measurable, and observable conditions that must be met in order for someone to judge whether change has been successful. For example, in Exhibit

EXHIBIT 10.14

A HOSPITAL STAFF'S CHANGE CONVERSATIONS ABOUT CHANGE

| CONVERSATION | STATEMENTS |
|---|---|
| Initiative | CEO: I want us to implement a quality-improvement program. |
| Understanding | Director of Administration: What's this all about? |
| | CEO: Several things. First, we are getting far too many complaints from our patients. Second, the current climate for reform makes quality essential, and, third, I am convinced we can deliver better care. |
| | Director of Nursing: I'm not sure we need to improve quality. We have a well-trained staff and they do a good job. The average performance ratings of the nurses are up, and any changes would just give them more work to do. |
| | CEO: The staff may be doing a better job as individual workers but not as a team. There must be some reason for the complaints. |
| | CEO: Okay, so we are all agreed that we should undertake a quality-improvement program. Now, how will we know if the program works? |
| | Director of Administration: What if we used the number of formal complaints received to tell? We received over 100 complaints last month, both written and verbal. That translates into about three complaints per thousand patients. |
| (Condition of satisfaction) | Director of Nursing: Okay, so if the number of complaints is less than one per thousand per month by the end of this calendar year, we will say the program worked. |
| Performance | CEO to Director of Administration: Will you contact each of the department heads and ask them to generate a list of things they think could contribute to us getting fewer complaints and then to bring that list with them to a meeting on the sixth of this month at 1 P.M.? |
| | Director of Administration: Yes. Do you want us to make a list also? |
| | CEO: No. |
| | Director of Nursing: I will meet with my supervisors and ask them to generate a similar list and ask them to bring the list to a meeting on the eighth of this month starting at 3 P.M. |
| | CEO: Great. Then, at the meetings, we will identify things that can be done and assign them to some project teams. |
| Closure | CEO: I want to thank each of you for the work you did here today. Your willingness to press in on the issue made it possible for us to see what is needed to get our quality program well-defined. Does anyone have anything to say about the meeting or what happened here? |

**Source:** J. Ford & L.W. Ford, "The Role of Conversations in Producing Intentional Change in Organizations," *Academy of Management Review* 20 (1995): 541-570.

379

10.14, the Director of Nursing clearly describes the conditions of satisfaction by stating, "Okay, so if the number of complaints is less than one per thousand per month by the end of the calendar year, we will say the program worked." Without clear conditions of satisfaction, people are not sure about what to do or what to change. Furthermore, they're unable to determine if what they're doing or changing is working.

If the conditions of satisfaction can be clearly stated, the next step is a conversation for performance. **Conversations for performance** are conversations about action plans, in which managers and workers make specific requests and promise specific results. For example, in Exhibit 10.14, the CEO made a specific performance-related request with this statement: "Will you contact each of the department heads and ask them to generate a list of things they think could contribute to us getting fewer complaints." The Director of Nursing promised a specific result when she said, "I will meet with my supervisors and ask them to generate a similar list and ask them to bring the list to a meeting on the eighth of this month starting at 3 P.M." If done properly, the specific requests and

**conversations for performance** conversations about action plans, in which managers and workers make specific requests and promise specific results

promises discussed in performance conversations will be closely linked to the specific, measurable, and observable conditions set forth in the conditions of satisfaction.

Conversations for performance break down in two ways. The first breakdown is that managers may not realize that *agreement isn't action*. In fact, many managers rely exclusively on conversations for understanding when managing change processes. Unfortunately, a general understanding about why change is needed is not enough to produce change-related actions. For example, just because the hospital managers (Exhibit 10.14) agree that the number of complaints per 1,000 patients needs to be reduced, it doesn't mean they'll take any specific actions to reduce it. If managers want specific changes to occur, then the specific requests and promises that occur in conversations for performance must follow agreement and understanding.

The second kind of breakdown at this point is the *lack of rigor* used when managing conversations for performance. Specifically, managers may assume that people know what they should be doing and may not ask them to take specific actions or ask them to indicate what specific actions they intend to take. Consequently, people just "do their best." Furthermore, managers compound this breakdown by not specifying the deadline for that result. In the end, workers get around to the change "as soon as possible" or "when they have the time." From this perspective, breakdowns don't occur because of resistance to change, but from managers not being clear about what specific actions will be taken, who will do them, and when they will be done.

If conversations for performance have focused on specific requests and promises and specific actions have been taken to create successful change, then the last step in this process is a conversation for closure. **Conversations for closure** end the change process by indicating that the work is done. Congratulations may be expressed if the change was successful. Regrets may be expressed if it was not. Yet, regardless of the results, the process is declared complete. In fact, closure is so important that *omitting closure* is the last possible breakdown in the change process. When it becomes obvious to everyone that the intended results have been achieved or that they will not be achieved, (or at least not on schedule), managers need to express thanks for what has been accomplished. When successes, losses, creativity, and hard work are not recognized, people feel unappreciated. Even worse, they may become resentful, cynical, and unlikely to fully participate in future change efforts.

One way to achieve closure is to celebrate the successes, losses, creativity, and hard work of the people and groups involved in the change process. For example, Southwest Airlines celebrates each time it begins flying to a new city (a change process that takes between three and six months to complete). When Southwest began flights at Chicago's Midway Airport, it threw a party at which Chicago's mayor and Southwest's CEO fastened a 10-foot seatbelt together to signify the importance of Southwest coming to Chicago. When Southwest opened service at Baltimore/Washington International Airport, it celebrated its $49 one-way ticket prices by flying 49 Baltimore fifth-graders to Cleveland to spend a day at the Cleveland Zoo. Celebrations publicize outstanding performance, renew and energize employees, and allow people throughout the company to build relationships in an informal setting.[78] Celebrations bring closure to change processes, because they mark beginnings, ends, and milestones. See Exhibit 10.15 for more reasons why Southwest Airlines celebrates change.

### 4.5 What Not to Do When Leading Change

So far, you've learned about the basic change process (unfreezing, change, refreezing), managing resistance to change, the four kinds of change tools and techniques (results-driven change, the GE Workout, transition management teams, and organizational development), and using conversations to promote change. However, John Kotter of the Harvard Business School argues that knowing what *not* to do is just as important as knowing what to do when it comes to achieving successful organizational change.[79]

Exhibit 10.16 (see p. 382) shows the most common errors that managers make when they lead change. The first two errors occur during the unfreezing phase, in which managers try to get the people affected by change to believe that change is really needed. The first and

**conversations for closure**
conversations that end the change process by indicating that the work is done and the change process is complete

EXHIBIT 10.15

WHY SOUTHWEST AIRLINES CELEBRATES CHANGE

1. Celebration provides an opportunity for building relationships.
2. Celebration gives us a sense of history.
3. Celebration helps us envision the future.
4. Celebration is a way of recognizing major milestones.
5. Celebration helps reduce stress.
6. Celebration inspires motivation and reenergizes people.
7. Celebration builds self-confidence and removes fear.
8. Celebration helps us mourn the losses associated with change.

**Source:** K. Freiberg & J. Freiberg, *Nuts! Southwest Airlines' Crazy Recipe for Business and Personal Success* (Austin, TX: Bard Press, 1996).

potentially most serious of these errors is *not establishing a great enough sense of urgency*. Indeed, Kotter estimates that more than half of all change efforts fail because the people affected by change are just not convinced that change is necessary. However, people will feel a greater sense of urgency about change if a leader in the company makes a public, candid assessment of the company's problems and weaknesses. For example, Continental Airlines CEO Gordon Bethune said, "We had a crappy product, and we were trying to discount ourselves into profitability. Nobody wants to eat a crummy pizza, no matter if it's 99 cents."[80] Plus, by sharing extensive (and depressing) financial information with Continental's workers, Bethune made it clear that the company was truly at risk of going bankrupt. And because employees knew that neither Pan Am nor Eastern Airlines ever recovered after declaring bankruptcy, resistance to change evaporated at Continental as employees concluded that accepting change was the only reasonable option.[81]

The second mistake that occurs in the unfreezing process is *not creating a powerful enough coalition*. Change often starts with one or two people, but in order to build enough momentum to change an entire department, division, or company, change has to be supported by a critical and growing group of people. Besides top management, Kotter recommends that key employees, managers, board members, customers, and even union leaders be members of a *core change coalition,* which guides and supports organizational change. Furthermore, it's important to strengthen this group's resolve by periodically bringing its members together for off-site retreats. At Merck, a leading pharmaceutical firm, CEO Raymond Gilmartin uses off-site retreats to break down barriers and build confidence. He said, "What goes on during the breaks and during the dinners or lunches is often just as important" as what is discussed in the meetings. Likewise, to encourage an openness to change, IBM's CEO takes his top 40 managers to an off-site retreat every six weeks. The purpose? To get IBM's managers to challenge their thinking and to learn to view IBM's business from different perspectives.[82]

The next four errors that managers make occur during the change phase, in which a change intervention is used to try to get workers and managers to change their behavior and work practices.

*Lacking a vision* for change is a significant error at this point. As you learned in Chapter 4, a *vision* is a statement of a company's purpose or reason for existing. A vision for change makes clear where a company or department is headed and why the change is occurring. Change efforts that lack vision tend to be confused, chaotic, and contradictory. By contrast, change efforts guided by visions are clear, easy to understand, and can be effectively explained in five minutes or less. At Continental Airlines, the initial change vision was simple: "getting passengers where they were supposed to be on time."[83] With

EXHIBIT 10.16

ERRORS MANAGERS MAKE WHEN LEADING CHANGE

### UNFREEZING

1. Not establishing a great enough sense of urgency.
2. Not creating a powerful enough guiding coalition.

### CHANGE

3. Lacking a vision.
4. Undercommunicating the vision by a factor of ten.
5. Not removing obstacles to the new vision.
6. Not systematically planning for and creating short-term wins.

### REFREEZING

7. Declaring victory too soon.
8. Not anchoring changes in the corporation's culture.

**Source:** J.P. Kotter, "Leading Change: Why Transformation Efforts Fail," *Harvard Business Review* 73, no. 2 (March-April 1995): 59.

this clear-cut vision focusing managers and workers, Continental now ranks first in on-time arrivals and second in baggage handling. Previously, it had ranked 10th on both.[84] These improved results also explain why Continental has ranked first or second in the J.D. Power airline customer satisfaction ratings over the last five years.

*Undercommunicating the vision by a factor of ten* is another mistake in the change phase. According to Kotter, companies mistakenly hold just one meeting to announce the vision. Or, if the new vision receives heavy emphasis in executive speeches or company newsletters, senior management then undercuts the vision by behaving in ways contrary to it. Successful communication of the vision requires that top managers link everything the company does to the new vision and that they "walk the talk" by behaving in ways consistent with the vision. Furthermore, even companies that begin change with a clear vision sometimes make the mistake of *not removing obstacles to the new vision.* Insisting on change, but then failing to redesign jobs, pay plans, and technology to support the new way of doing things, leaves formidable barriers to change in place. One way Continental removed obstacles to its new vision was by completely rewriting its employee policy manual. CEO Bethune said, "And we don't call it a manual anymore; we call it guidelines. The new guidelines are supposed to help employees solve problems—give them a sense of where the boundaries are when they run into trouble. But in the general pursuit of their jobs, we want them to use their heads and use their resources." In short, "if you find yourself in the middle of something complicated, something unusual, something that just doesn't fit, then use your head and make the best decision you can."[85]

Similar to results-driven change, another error in the change phase is *not systematically planning for and creating short-term wins.* Most people don't have the discipline and patience to wait two years to see if the new change effort works. Change is threatening and uncomfortable, so for people to continue to support it, they need to see an immediate payoff. Kotter recommends that managers create short-term wins by actively picking people and projects that are likely to work extremely well early in the change process. The short-term wins at Continental came in the form of $65 checks. Bethune told managers and employees that every employee would get a check for $65 each month that Continental finished in the top five in on-time arrivals (as rated by the Department of Transportation). The first time that Continental made it into the top five, it sent out $2.5 million worth of $65 checks to its employees. Bethune said, "We didn't just drop 65 extra dollars into their paychecks and have the whole impact of their bonus disappear.

Nor did we let them start calculating how much of it they lost to taxes. We gave each employee $65 in a special check—we took the withholding out of their regular paychecks so they got 65 actual dollars."[86] In all, Continental has spent more than $100 million for on-time bonuses to reward and remind its employees that getting customers to their travel destinations on time is one of the most important things it does.[87]

The last two errors that managers make occur during the refreezing phase, when attempts are made to support and reinforce changes so they "stick." *Declaring victory too soon* is a tempting mistake in the refreezing phase. Managers typically declare victory right after the first large-scale success in the change process. For instance, it would have been easy for Continental to declare victory the first time that it made it into the top five in on-time arrivals. Ironically, declaring success too early has the same effect as draining the gasoline out of a car. It stops change efforts dead in their tracks. With success declared, supporters of the change process stop pushing to make change happen. After all, why "push" when success has been achieved? Rather than declaring victory, managers should use the momentum from short-term wins to push for even bigger or faster changes. This maintains urgency and prevents change supporters from slacking off before the changes are frozen into the company's culture. For example, after quickly moving into the top five in on-time arrivals, Continental maintained urgency by raising the requirements for monthly, on-time bonuses. Now, instead of the top five, Continental had to finish third or higher in on-time arrival. However, when it raised the bar, it also raised the reward, increasing the on-time bonus from $65 to $100. Moreover, CEO Bethune instituted a reward system that maintained urgency among company managers by awarding bonuses only if all of Continental's top 25 executives met their goals. Bethune said, "We had to have all these people working collectively. We put in a compensation program for the 20 top executives that meant they were paid on meeting quarterly budget results and getting 25 percent of your bonus each quarter. You miss the number, you can't get the money back. It kept us all really focused for three months at a time. We never missed our number, and either we all got paid or none of us did. Marketing could not fight with sales; it just ended internecine warfare."[88]

The last mistake that managers make is *not anchoring changes in the corporation's culture*. An o*rganization's culture* is the set of key values, beliefs, and attitudes shared by organizational members that determines the "accepted way of doing things" in a company. As you learned in Chapter 2, cultures are extremely difficult and slow to change. Kotter said that two things help anchor changes in a corporation's culture. The first is directly showing people that the changes have actually improved performance. At Continental, this was easily demonstrated by the company's improved Department of Transportation rankings for on-time arrival and baggage handling. The second is to make sure that the people who get promoted fit the new culture. If they don't, it's a clear sign that the changes were only temporary.

When did CEO Gordon Bethune know that the changes he was seeking were anchored in Continental's culture? He was getting on a Continental flight at the last minute, right as the gate agent was scrambling to get the plane out of the gate on time. Bethune, whose back was to the agent, heard him say, " Excuse me, sir, you'll have to sit down. The plane has to leave." The flight attendant became upset and said to the agent, "Do you know who that is? That's Mr. Bethune!" The agent responded, "That's very nice, but we gotta go. Tell him to sit down." Bethune said that this "is how Continental Airlines stays on time—and how it has changed for the better."[89]

## Review 4
### Managing Change

The basic change process is unfreezing, change, and refreezing. Resistance to change, which stems from self-interest, misunderstanding and distrust, and a general intolerance for change, can be managed through education and communication, participation, negotiation, coercion, and top management support. When change efforts work, change begins with initiative conversations and is followed by conversations about understanding, performance, and closure. But when conversations break down, change efforts break down, too. Change conversations can break down in five ways: nothing happens, unclear conditions of satisfaction, agreement instead of action, lack of rigor, and omitting closure.

Managers can use a number of change techniques. Results-driven change and the GE Workout reduce resistance to change by getting change efforts off to a fast start. Transition management teams, which manage a company's change process, coordinate change efforts throughout an organization. Organizational development is a collection of planned change interventions (large system, small group, person-focused), guided by a change agent, that are designed to improve an organization's long-term health and performance. Finally, knowing what *not* to do is as important as knowing what to do to achieve successful change. Managers should avoid these errors when leading change: not establishing urgency, not creating a guiding coalition, lacking a vision, undercommunicating the vision, not removing obstacles to the vision, not creating short-term wins, declaring victory too soon, and not anchoring changes in the corporation's culture.

## What Really Happened?

At the beginning of the chapter, you learned that Kimberly-Clark was having difficulty creating a sustainable competitive advantage. Let's find out what really happened and see how Kimberly-Clark is using innovation to try to create that competitive advantage over its primary rival, Procter & Gamble.

**The first question you'll have to address is "Why does innovation matter?", especially in a hum-drum, boring business like toilet papers and diapers.**
Organizations can create competitive advantage for themselves if they have a distinctive competence that allows them to make, do, or perform something better than their competitors. Furthermore, a competitive advantage becomes sustainable if other companies cannot duplicate the benefits obtained from that distinctive competence. Technological innovation, however, makes it possible not only to duplicate the benefits obtained from a company's distinctive advantage, but also to quickly turn a company's competitive advantage into a competitive disadvantage. For example, soon after Kimberly-Clark produced its first disposable, Kimbies, which was a copycat product based on Procter & Gamble's Pampers, P&G innovated by adding tape closures to Pampers to replace the safety pins that parents used to keep disposable diapers on babies. P&G also introduced sizes for toddlers and pre-

mature infants. These aggressive moves, based on product innovation, killed Kimbies' sales, forcing Kimberly-Clark to pull Kimbies from the market. However, Kimberly-Clark came back by introducing Huggies, diapers with elastic around the legs to prevent leakage. It then improved Huggies by adding refastenable tape closures that let parents unfasten the diaper to see if it was dirty and then refasten it for continued use if it wasn't. The result: P&G's profits and market share dropped significantly. However, three years later, P&G responded with another product innovation, Pampers Ultras, ultra-absorbent diapers that were half the thickness of regular disposable diapers. A year later, Kimberly-Clark followed with Huggies SuperTrim.

As these examples show, companies that want to sustain a competitive advantage must understand and protect themselves from the strategic threats of innovation. Over the long run, the best way to do that is for a company to create a stream of its own innovative ideas and products year after year. Indeed, that's precisely the issue for Kimberly-Clark. How can it use innovation to create and then keep a competitive advantage over its primary competitor, Procter & Gamble?

**Second, how do you know when to try for an innovation home run (that is, go for an entirely new design or technology that is dramatically better than existing products), or when to simply take the ex-**isting technology or products and make them incrementally better?**
The best way to protect a competitive advantage is to create a stream of innovative ideas and products. Innovation streams begin with technological discontinuities (i.e., technological home runs) that create significant breakthroughs in performance or function. Technological discontinuities are followed by an era of ferment, in which customers purchase new technologies (technological substitution) and companies compete to establish the new dominant design (design competition). Because technological innovation is both competence-enhancing and competence-destroying, companies that bet on the wrong design often struggle, while companies that bet on the eventual dominant design usually prosper. Emergence of a dominant design leads to a focus on incremental change, lowering costs, and small, but steady improvements in the dominant design. This focus continues until the next technological discontinuity occurs. So, if the dominant design (i.e., a technology or product design) is relatively new, companies should focus on incremental improvements. However, if the dominant design is mature or aging, then much could be gained by trying to come up with a new, superior design.

This is just what Kimberly-Clark tried to do when it came up with Cottonelle Fresh Rollwipes. Kimberly-

Clark spent three years and $100 million to create the first roll of "pre-moistened" toilet paper. Cottonelle Fresh Rollwipes are basically baby wipes in a special toilet paper dispenser (instead of a box, like most baby wipes). The dispenser holds two rolls of toilet paper, a regular roll on the bottom, and a roll of Cottonelle Fresh Rollwipes on the top, which is enclosed by a plastic cover that keeps in the moisture. With 24 percent of the $4.5 billion U.S. toilet paper market compared to Procter & Gamble's 29 percent share, Kimberly-Clark is hoping that Cotton Fresh Rollwipes are a significantly better toilet paper for much of the buying public. In fact, its research shows that one-third of its wet wipe customers are adults and not infants. Furthermore, 63 percent of consumers occasionally use something wet, such as a baby wipe, or sprinkling water on regular toilet paper, and 27 percent do so daily. So, there appears to be a market for this product. But, importantly, Kimberly-Clark didn't just take baby wipes and put them on a roll. What makes this product significantly different is that it disperses or breaks apart into small fibers when immersed in water. Therefore, unlike standard baby wipes, Cottonelle Fresh Roll Wipes won't clog your toilet or your pipes. This explains why Kimberly-Clark has filed 30 patents to protect this product.

**Last, if you wanted to swing for the fences and hit an innovation home run, just how would Kimberly-Clark do that?**
To successfully manage innovation streams, companies must manage the sources of innovation and learn to manage innovation during both discontinuous and incremental change. Since innovation begins with creativity, companies can manage the sources of innovation by supporting a creative work environment, in which creative thoughts and ideas are welcomed, valued, and encouraged. Creative work environments provide challenging work; offer organizational, supervisory, and work group encouragement; allow significant freedom; and remove organizational impediments to creativity. Companies that succeed in periods of discontinuous change typically follow an experiential approach to innovation. The experiential approach assumes that intuition, flexible options, and hands-on experience can reduce uncertainty and accelerate learning and understanding. This approach involves frequent design iterations, frequent testing, regular milestones, creation of multifunctional teams, and use of powerful leaders to guide the innovation process.

Over the years, Kimberly-Clark has used this method consistently to swing for the fences with brand new designs for everyday products. Indeed, Tom Falk, Kimberly-Clark's president and COO, said, "If we have a large share of a business and it's not growing, we ask ourselves what we can do to make the market grow." For example, Kimberly-Clark invented "pull-ups," training-pants that toddlers could take on or off themselves as they were learning to be potty-trained. It now controls 76 percent of this $845 million market. Likewise, the company was the first to introduce products such as Depends and Poise for adult incontinence. Kimberly-Clark dominates this market, too. Finally, it has also succeeded by significantly improving the technology behind existing personal care products. For instance, its market share in feminine hygiene products increased from 25 percent to 43 percent in Korea after it introduced proprietary absorbency materials. These advances are now in use in similar products around the world.

**Sources:** N. Byrnes, D. Foust, S. Anderson, W. Symonds, & J. Weber, "Brands in a Bind: Many Household Names Are Hurting—And Taking a Cue from High Techs Outfits," *Business Week*, 28 August 2000, 234. S. Marta, "Creating Fresh Products: Old Favorites Are Being Reinvented for a New Market," *Dallas Morning News*, 25 August 2001, 1F. E. Nelson, "Toilet-Paper War Heats Up with New, Wet Roll," *The Wall Street Journal*, 17 January 2001, B1. T. Parker-Pope, "The Tricky Business of Rolling Out a New Toilet Paper," *The Wall Street Journal*, 12 January 1998, B1. D. Starkman, "Hefty's Plastic Zipper Bag Is Rapping Rivals," *The Wall Street Journal*, 16 April 1999, B1.

385

## Key Terms

change agent *(375)*
change forces *(366)*
change intervention *(370)*
coercion *(372)*
compression approach to innovation *(363)*
conditions of satisfaction *(378)*
continuous change *(367)*
conversations for closure *(380)*
conversations for performance *(379)*
conversations for understanding *(378)*
creative work environments *(356)*
creativity *(346)*
design competition *(353)*
design iteration *(360)*
discontinuous change *(367)*

dominant design *(353)*
era of ferment *(353)*
experiential approach to innovation *(360)*
flow *(357)*
General Electric Workout *(373)*
generational change *(363)*
incremental change *(354)*
initiative conversations *(378)*
innovation streams *(352)*
milestones *(361)*
multifunctional teams *(361)*
organizational change *(346)*
organization decline *(368)*
organizational development *(374)*
organizational dialogue *(376)*

organizational innovation *(346)*
refreezing *(370)*
resistance forces *(366)*
resistance to change *(370)*
results-driven change *(373)*
S-curve pattern of innovation *(347)*
sporadic change *(366)*
technological discontinuity *(352)*
technological substitution *(353)*
technology cycle *(347)*
testing *(360)*
transition management team *(374)*
unfreezing *(370)*

# What Would You Do-II

## Lego

As you look over your calendar, your hands automatically begin to rub your temples. The annual Toy Fair is right around the corner, and newspapers and magazines around the world are publishing their lists of the most successful toys of last year and their predictions of what will be hot next year. Unfortunately, you pretty much know that none of your company's products will be on any of them. Founded nearly 70 years ago by your grandfather, Lego has a long history in the toy industry, but it can't seem to keep up with today's kids' (or even yesterday's kids') thirst for so-called interactive toys. Technically, Lego's are interactive, but nowadays that means battery-operated, software-driven, and done-for-you rather than do-it-yourself. Today's children grow up in an entertainment-saturated environment, and open-ended, self-guided play is fading into a nostalgic memory.

The Lego name was created in 1934 by Ole Kirk Christiansen, a Danish toymaker who introduced the first plastic Lego brick in 1949. His son Godtfred Kirk Christiansen then designed an entire system of play around the bricks in the mid-1950s. Since these revolutionary moments, the only real innovation at Lego was the introduction of themed sets, like towns, farms, and space stations, which didn't start until the 1970s. The formula for making the plastic bricks hasn't even changed since then! My, how time flies, you think to yourself.

The only thing brighter and more enduring than Lego's vividly colored blocks is the company's core value of inspiring and nurturing creativity and play. One extension of this is the fact that you refuse to produce any toy that resembles a twentieth-century weapon. Holding onto such admirable values, however, doesn't seem to be helping the company succeed. Your company hasn't had a toy in the list of top 20 U.S. sellers in the last seven years, and this year doesn't look to be any different. And one could argue that the themed Lego sets already signal a departure from open-ended play. After all, some sets have pages and pages of instructions on how to build the set "right."

Lego is the seventh most powerful worldwide brand among families, behind such giants as Coca-Cola and Disney (you know because you closely follow the research), but Lego hasn't changed the way kids play, let alone the way they learn, for a long time. Can Lego be that kind of leader again, and if so, how? Will you have to change your company values and management, or just your products? What are the risks of not changing?

**As Kirk Kjeld Kristiansen (his name was misspelled on his birth certificate), CEO of Lego, what would you do?**

**Sources:** "Bestsellers," *U.S. News & World* Report, 19 February 2001, 66. C. Fishman, "Why Can't Lego Click?" *Fast Company*, September 2001, http://www.fastcompany.com/online/50/lego.html. S. Jarvis, "New Lego Creation Marketing Up a Storm," *Marketing News*, 9 October 2001, http://www.marketingpower.com. N. Montfort, "Some Creativity Required," *Technology Review*, July 2000, 110. F. Witsil, "Toy Stores Have Tough Time Keeping Lego-Made Bionicles in Stock," *Tampa Tribune*, 21 October 2001, http://www.wsj.com.

# Management Decisions

## Heads, You Change. Tails, You Change

You are the general manager of a medium-sized appliance manufacturing facility in Dayton, Ohio. You've just received a phone call that you have been expecting for some time now. Your boss just informed you that if your plant doesn't show markedly better results (in productivity, profitability, etc.) within six months, it will be closed down and relocated to Ciudad Juarez, an industrial Mexican city across the border from El Paso, Texas. Of course, this news is no surprise to you. Your plant is one of only a few left producing appliances in the United States. Due to lower wages, closer proximity to suppliers, and favorable tax treatments, many U.S. factories have closed their American doors and reopened as Maquiladoras within Mexico's borders. If your plant follows the same road, most of the production workers will lose their jobs. The supervisory, middle, and top-level management positions, however, will be transferred to the new location.

Moving your managers would be a challenge. Even the carrot of job security may not be enough to overcome resistance. Many of your management staff have lived in or around Dayton their whole lives, have close family ties to the area, or have children who are entrenched in their schools and social lives. The alternative—turning the plant around in six months—is no more attractive. This would require all employees to rethink how work is done and to re-engineer work processes, in short to change the very way they all think about working at your company.

The typical employee at your plant is like Tom, your assistant and best friend, who would probably be very resistant to *any* kind of change. Tom eats the same kind of sandwich everyday. He is never receptive to new ideas or radical change. And he has worked at the plant since he returned to Dayton after college.

You really don't want to move to Mexico, and you'd like to keep the 500 production jobs at your plant in Dayton. But there are so many ways to implement change. Which one would be best-suited to your situation?

### Questions

1. Jot down the pros and cons of each change tool and technique presented in the chapter and determine what seems to fit this situation the best. Which one(s) did you choose and why?

2. You are going to have to internally promote whatever option you chose. Outline change conversations that you might have with the typical employee, say Tom, for example. How can you avoid breakdowns in change initiatives during your conversations?

3. If your change initiatives fail to bring the plant into corporate expectations, you will have to handle the equally tough situation of convincing managers to follow the company to Mexico. How will you do this? What can you do as their supervisor to calm their fears and minimize their resistance to this type of change?

## Management Decisions

### Hot Spots

Repeatedly throughout history, entire industries have become associated with particular regions, locations, or cities. For example, in the mid 15th century, because of nearby silver and soft metal mines, the German towns of Augsberg, Regensburg, Ulm, and Nuremburg became the center of Europe's metalworking industry. In the 17th century, the British Navigation Act of 1651 required that all trade with England or its numerous colonies throughout the New World be conducted using British ships. The result was that London became the busiest seaport in the world and thus the center of international trade in tobacco, spices, tea, and other goods. Today, we continue to associate particular industries with particular locations: Paris with the fashion industry, New York and Wall Street with finance, Detroit with the automobile, and Hollywood with the entertainment industry.

The development of a particular industry in a particular location is known as a "hot spot." Hot spots are regional clusters of companies in the same industry that require similar kinds of resources and that grow faster than the industry average. Hot spots are thought to be especially important to the development and growth of technology companies, whose success depends on the ability to create innovative products and technologies. Indeed, the standard service for innovation- or technology-based companies is that they be located in or near high-tech hot spots. For example, Silicon Valley in northern California, near Palo Alto, Santa Clara, and San Jose, is still perhaps the best-known hot spot in the world for the computer hardware industry. There are more major computer companies (e.g., Intel, Cisco, Hewlett-Packard) and more hardware computer start-up companies in Silicon Valley than anywhere else in the world.

However, the wisdom of locating innovation-based companies in geographical hot spots is now being questioned. Critics claim that the disadvantages of locating in hot spots can easily outweigh the advantages. Furthermore, as hot spots "burn out," the advantages that once made them great places to start and grow a business may actually become serious disadvantages.

To gain some experience with the idea of "hot spots," imagine that you started a computer-related business while in college. Now that you've graduated, you have to decide where to formally locate your business. After some initial consideration, you limit your final choices to three locations: Silicon Valley (San Jose, California), still hanging on as a hot spot; Austin, Texas, an up-and-coming hot spot; and Seattle, Washington, another hot spot on the rise. As you decide where to locate your company, you'll want to consider the following factors:

cost of living, cost of office space, availability and cost of employees, and access to customers and important business partners or suppliers. Use the Internet resources shown below to research each of these locations. Then answer the questions to explain your reasons for your choice.

#### Additional Internet Resources

* *Money* magazine's Best Places to Live (**http://www.money.com/money/depts/real_estate/bplive/**). This site's screening tool helps you sort through America's 300 largest metro areas to find the best spot to live, work, or play. Also, while you are there, check for this year's best places to live. Be sure to enter "San Jose," "Seattle," and "Austin" into the City Search search engine to learn more about each of these cities.
* *Money* magazine's Cost of Living Comparator (**http://www.homefair.com/calc/salcalc.html?NETSCAPE_LIVEWIRE.src=mm_salcal**). Use the Cost of Living Comparator to compare San Jose, Seattle, and Austin.
* *Fortune* magazine's Best Cities for Business (**http://www.fortune.com**). Use the "Search Fortune" box and enter "best cities for business." Choose the most current year regarding Fortune's perception of these top cities.

#### Questions

1. What were the two most important criteria that you used when deciding where to locate your company? Why? What were the two least important criteria you used? Why?
2. Which location did you choose? Explain your choice by writing a brief paragraph about each location—Silicon Valley, Austin, and Seattle—that explains the advantages and disadvantages each offers your business.
3. Did you uncover any other hot spots in the course of your research?

**Sources:** K. Alesandrini, "In Search of Greener Valleys," *Computer Shopper,* 1 December 1997. C.M. Anders, "Santa Clara No Longer Hot—Its Insane Housing Prices Skyrocketing in Silicon Valley," *San Francisco Examiner,* 6 July 1997. J. Burke, *The Day the Universe Changed* (Boston: Little, Brown, and Company, 1985). M. Dickerson, "Phoenix Ascending: Southwest Boomtown Rides Diversified Industries; Arizona's Valley of the Sun Shines in Reinventing Itself as a Hotbed of Startup and Tech Companies," *Austin American-Statesman,* 21 December 1997. R. Pouder & C.H. St. John, "Hot Spots and Blind Spots: Geographical Clusters of Firms and Innovation," *Academy of Management Journal* 21 (1996): 1192-1225. C. Rosen, "The Best Locations: Hot Today, Cold Tomorrow? Industry Executives Weigh the Pros and Cons of Establishing Roots in Different Regions," *Electronic Buyers' News,* 17 February 1997.

# Develop Your Managerial Potential

## A Personal Force Field Analysis

In the "What Really Works" section of this chapter, you learned that when people change their behavior in the workplace, there is a 76 percent chance that organizational profits, market share, and productivity can be improved. However, you also learned that organization-wide change efforts have only a 57 percent chance of successfully changing people's work behavior. So changing people's behavior works great for company improvement. The hard part is figuring out how to get them to change their behavior. This "Develop Your Managerial Potential" assignment reviews how you can use a personal force field analysis to change your behavior at work.

At the beginning of this chapter, you learned that organizational change is a function of change forces and resistance forces. Change forces lead to differences in the form, quality, or condition of an organization over time. Resistance forces support the status quo, that is, the existing state of conditions in organizations. One of the ways that managers prepare for specific organizational change is to carefully conduct an organizational force field analysis by listing the change and resistance forces that support and oppose that change. For example, Exhibit 10.17 lists the resistance forces and change forces that oppose and support the possibility of changing a company's corporate headquarters from New York City to Dallas.

Listing resistance and change forces is also a useful way to conduct a personal force field analysis. The first step of a personal force field analysis is to clearly describe how or what behavior you intend to change. For example, if you're always late with your expense reports, you might write, "I will turn in my expense reports within three days of return-ing from a business trip." In Chapter 4, you learned that to be effective, goals need to be S.M.A.R.T.: specific, measurable, attainable, realistic, and timely. Descriptions of the behaviors you intend to change should follow the S.M.A.R.T. guidelines, too.

The second step of a personal force field analysis is to list and describe resistance forces, that is, the reasons that make it difficult for you to change your behavior. Since resistance to change is caused by self-interest, misunderstanding and distrust, and a general intolerance for change, be sure to assess whether these factors are making it difficult for you to change your behavior. For example, are you turning your expense reports in late because turning them in on time will cost or deprive you of something of value (i.e., self-interest)? Probably not, because if you turned the expense reports in on time, you'd get your money back sooner.

Are you turning in your expense reports late because you misunderstand or distrust the reasons for turning in your expense report on time or distrust the people who review the expenses? Well, we might be on to something here. Misunderstanding probably isn't the problem. What's to misunderstand about an expense report? You fill it out, turn it in, and get reimbursed. In this case, it's more likely that your resistance stems from distrust of the people who review the reports. Perhaps, in the past, you felt that you weren't fairly reimbursed. If so, why turn in your expense report on time when you don't expect to get back all the money you're owed?

Finally, are you turning in your expense reports late because you have a low tolerance for change? In this case, however, a low tolerance for change probably has more to do with habitual behavior than with any uncertainty associated with the change process.

388

### EXHIBIT 10.17

#### RESISTANCE AND CHANGE FORCES

**POSSIBLE CHANGE:**

Moving Corporate Headquarters from New York City to Dallas

*Resistance Forces*

- Many employees may not want or be able to move.
- Large expense of making the move, buying or building new headquarters, and selling old headquarters.
- Negative publicity from local press generated by just considering the move.
- New York City officials may offer incentives to encourage firm to stay.

*Change Forces*

- Much lower cost of living and no state income tax will make it easier to attract and retain a talented work force.
- Lower real estate and energy costs will significantly lower the cost of maintaining corporate headquarters.
- Significant customer base has developed in the south, southwest, and western regions of the country.
- Dallas city officials may offer incentives to encourage firm to move.

The final step of a personal force field analysis is to list the change forces, that is, the reasons prompting you to consider changing your behavior. At this step, it can be useful to separate your reasons by category, such as personal or organizational benefits, or personal or organizational consequences (i.e., the negative consequences associated with not changing your behavior). For example, turning in your expense report on time gets you your money faster, a personal benefit; helps the organization stay current with its expenses, an organizational benefit; and helps you avoid getting yelled at by your boss for being late with the expense report, which is a personal negative consequence.

Now use these steps to conduct a personal force field analysis.

**Questions**

1. Clearly describe how or what behavior you intend to change. Be sure your description is S.M.A.R.T.: specific, measurable, attainable, realistic, and timely.

2. List and describe the resistance forces that make it difficult for you to change this behavior. Do these reasons have anything to do with

- *Self-interest?* Will the change cost or deprive you of something you value?
- *Misunderstanding and distrust?* Do you not understand the change or the reasons for it? Do you distrust the people behind the change? In other words, is someone other than yourself pressuring you to make this change?
- *A general intolerance for change?* Are you simply less capable of handling change than others? Are you worried that you won't be able to learn the new skills and behaviors needed to successfully negotiate this behavior change?

3. List and describe the change forces that are leading you to consider changing your behavior. Separate your reasons into personal or organizational benefits, or personal or organizational consequences (i.e., the negative consequences associated with not changing your behavior).

## Study Tip

On a separate sheet, write the titles of the exhibits in this chapter. Then, with your book closed, try to reproduce the diagrams exactly as they are in the text. Write a short description of what the diagram depicts, then open your book to check your work. Remember you can use the exhibit worksheets on your Xtra! CD-ROM as well.

For this chapter you also have an Xtra! CNN clip about concept cars on your CD-ROM. Watch the segment, read the case, and work the questions.

# CHAPTER 11

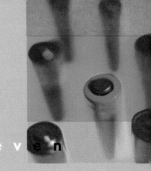

# eleven

# Designing Adaptive Organizations

## What Would You Do?

**Exide Technologies Headquarters, Princeton, New Jersey**. "Geez, I can't believe we can't figure this out! In 1898, didn't we supply the batteries for the U.S. Navy's first submarine? In 1901, weren't the first transcontinental telephone and telegraph services powered by Exide batteries? In 1934, whom did Commander Byrd look to when he needed power to establish a military base on Antarctica? In 1969, didn't we build the batteries for NASA's Apollo space missions and its first lunar landing? And in 1991, during Operation Desert Storm, didn't we make tank and ordinance batteries for the U.S. Army? If we're good enough to make products that have been critical to so many historical events, then why can't we figure out how to organize this company?"

Certainly, designing the right organizational structure should be easier than designing new products, but as CEO of Exide Technologies, it doesn't seem that way to you. Your management consultants assure you that Exide's difficulties in choosing the right organizational structure put it in good company. The more global a company, they say—and Exide is in 89 countries—the more difficult it is figuring out who should have responsibility for what and who should

report to whom. For example, under the "Ford 2000" plan, Ford tried to consolidate its functional departments, such as new car development, which had separate departments in Europe (Merkenich, Germany) and North America (Detroit, Michigan) into one global department. Unfortunately, results were mixed. While Ford initially saved $5 billion after reorganizing, it also saw its market share slip significantly in Europe, from 13 percent to 8.8 percent, over the same time.

Likewise, Procter & Gamble's "Organization 2005" plan was designed to take employees who had been organized by geographical markets (i.e., North America, South America, Europe, Mid-East, Asia, etc.) into five global business units (GBU), such as the "beauty-care GBU" or the "food and beverage GBU." After the changes, food and beverage managers, most of whom were located in Cincinnati, reported to the GBU president in Caracas, Venezuela. Laundry and household employees, most of whom were also located in Cincinnati, reported to their GBU president in Brussels, Belgium. Besides separating managers from subordinates, "Organization 2005" also created personal upheaval for P&G managers, half of whom were assigned new jobs. Furthermore, 1,000 managers and employees were transferred from various points across Europe to Geneva, Switzerland.

Similar numbers of people were moved to other locations. Following the changes, 25 percent of P&G's marketing managers left the company, and market share and financial performance dropped significantly.

Unfortunately, with its geographical structure Exide has found itself in situations eerily similar to Ford and P&G. First, despite being the world's largest producer of industrial and automotive batteries, financial losses are increasing, the company share price is dropping, and the company's debt load is soaring. Second, like Ford and P&G, Exide is organized geographically, with "country managers" in charge of Exide operations in each country. Unfortunately, this has led to competition as company managers try to steal business from each other. For instance, Mark Stevenson, the company's managing director for Britain, argued with the country manager for Germany who was upset that the British unit sold batteries in Austria for 10 percent to 15 percent less. Third, the geographical organization encouraged country managers to build their own fiefdoms, adding offices and manufacturing plants, whether needed or not. In short, said Mark Stevenson, the managing director for Britain, country managers "acted like barons."

Which organizational structure should Exide use? Should it stay with a geographical structure, but tinker with it to fix the problems? What would be the advantages or disadvantages of that approach? Or should it use a product structure—what P&G called "global business units"—to standardize what it does around the world? What would be the advantages or disadvantages of this approach? When will Exide know when it has found the right organizational structure?

**If you were the CEO at Exide Technologies, what would you do?**

**Sources:** E. Nelson, "Rallying the Troops at P&G—New CEO Lafley Aims to End Upheaval by Revamping Program of Globalization," *The Wall Street Journal*, 31 August 2000, B1. "Exide Technologies Announces Restructuring: Focuses on Global Customer Business Units," Exide Technologies. [Online] Available http://www.exide.com/ 11 November 2001. J. Lublin, "Division Problem, Place Vs. Product: It's Tough

to Choose a Management Model—Exide Tore Up System Based on Countries for One Centered on Battery Lines—Rolling over European Fiefs," *The Wall Street Journal*, 27 June 2001, A1. R. Simison, "Ford Hopes Its New Focus Will Be a Global Bestseller—Escort's Replacement Offers Improvements for Same Price," *The Wall Street Journal*, 8 October 1998, B10. "The History of Exide Technologies," Exide Technologies. [Online] Available http://www.exide.com/ 11 November 2001.

No one builds a house without first looking at the design. Put a window there. Take out a wall here. Soon you've got the design you want. Only then do you start building. These days, the design of a company is just as important as the design of a house. As the Exide Technologies case shows, if you don't have the right design, the company's performance can quickly fall apart like a house of cards.

This chapter begins by reviewing the traditional organizational structure approach to organizational design. **Organizational structure** is the vertical and horizontal configuration of departments, authority, and jobs within a company. For example, Exhibit 11.1 shows Microsoft's organizational chart. From this chart, you can see the vertical dimensions of the company—who reports to whom, the number of management levels, who has authority over what, and so forth. Founder Bill Gates is the chairman and chief software architect. In this role, Gates focuses on Microsoft's product and technology strategies. He has left the running of the company to CEO Steve Ballmer, who reports directly to him.[1] Five group vice presidents report directly to Ballmer. In turn, each group vice president oversees a number of divisions. For instance, the vice president of the Personal Services Group works with managers and employees to make it easier for consumers and businesses to connect online (via the Mobility and MSN Internet Access Divisions) and to deliver software as a service on a variety of devices (via the Services Platform, Consumer Devices, and User Interface Platforms Divisions).

The organizational chart also displays Microsoft's horizontal dimensions—who does what jobs, the number of different departments, and so forth. For instance, in addition to the Personal Services Group, Microsoft has groups in Platforms (where software such as Windows 98, NT, and XP are written); Operations (manufacturing, delivery, and corporate functions); Worldwide Sales, Marketing, & Services (for all customers, application developers, and for product support services); and Productivity & Business Services (which is responsible for Microsoft Office software, as well as emerging technologies, business tools, and business applications). In the first half of the chapter, you will learn about the traditional vertical and horizontal approaches to organizational structure, including departmentalization, organizational authority, and job design.

In the second half of the chapter, you will learn how contemporary organizations are becoming more adaptive by redesigning their internal and external processes. An **organizational process** is the collection of activities that transforms inputs into outputs that customers value.[2] For example, Exhibit 11.2 shows the basic internal and external processes that Microsoft uses to write computer software. The process starts when Microsoft gets feedback from customers through Internet newsgroups, email, phone calls, or letters. This information helps Microsoft understand customers' needs and problems and identify important software issues and needed changes and functions. Microsoft then rewrites the software, testing it internally at the company and then externally through its beta-testing process. In beta testing, early versions of software are distributed to beta testers (i.e., customers who volunteer or are selected by Microsoft), who give the company extensive feedback, which is then used to make

**organizational structure**
the vertical and horizontal configuration of departments, authority, and jobs within a company

**organizational process**
the collection of activities that transforms inputs into outputs that customers value

392

EXHIBIT 11.1

MICROSOFT CORPORATION'S ORGANIZATIONAL CHART

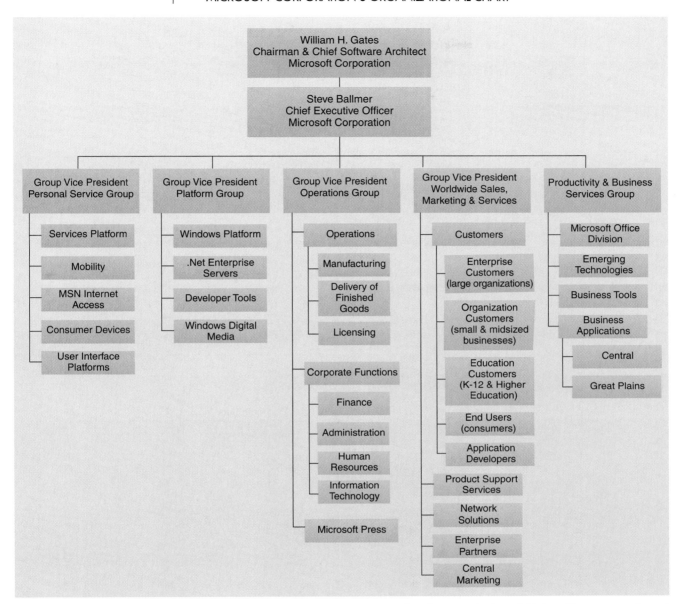

**Source:** "Microsoft Corporate Profile and Organizational Structure Overview," Microsoft Web site. [Online] Available http://www.microsoft.com/presspass/corpprofile.asp, 3 November 2001.

improvements. The beta-testing process may take as long as a year and involve thousands of customers. After "final" corrections are made to the software, the company distri-butes and sells it to customers, who start the process again by giving Microsoft more feedback.

This process view of Microsoft, which focuses on how things get done, is very different from the hierarchical view of Microsoft (go back to Microsoft's organizational chart in Exhibit 11.1), which focuses on accountability, responsibility, and position within the chain of command. In the second half of the chapter, you will learn how companies are using reengineering, empowerment, and behavior informality to redesign their internal organizational processes. The chapter ends with a discussion about the ways in which companies are redesigning their external processes, that is, how they are

EXHIBIT 11.2

PROCESS VIEW OF MICROSOFT'S ORGANIZATION

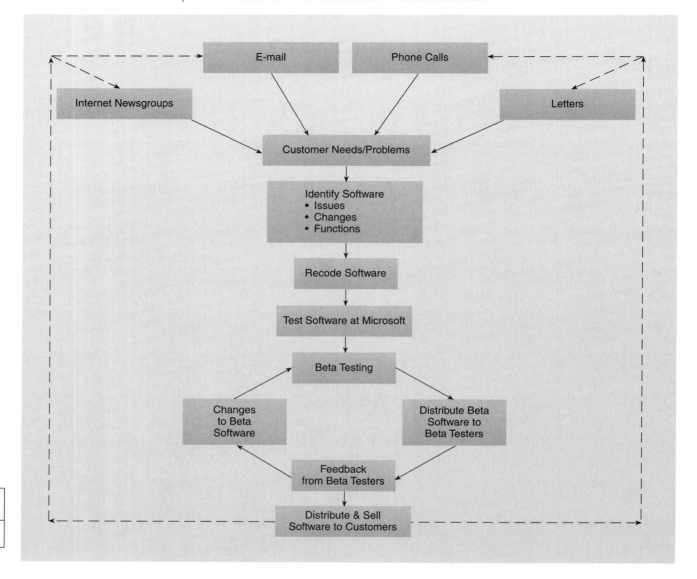

changing to improve their interactions with those outside the company. In that discussion, you will explore the basics of modular, virtual, and boundaryless organizations.

## Designing Organizational Structures

With 345 Borders bookstores, 860 Waldenbooks stores, 32 "Books etc." stores in the United Kingdom and 30,000 employees, Borders is one of the largest sellers of books in the world. In hopes of improving sales growth, Borders is replacing its division structure with a product structure. Formerly, each retail division (Borders, Waldenbooks, and Borders.com) had its own purchasing, accounting, merchandising, and marketing departments. In the new product structure, each product category (books, children's, multimedia, gifts and stationery, periodicals, café, and calendars) will have its own purchasing, accounting, merchandising, and marketing departments. Borders' CEO expressed hope that the product structure would improve the ability to track the various product lines and to "specifically address consumer needs in these categories."[3]

Why would a large company like Borders, with 30,000 employees and $3.3 billion in annual revenues, completely restructure its organizational design? What does it expect to gain as a result of this change?

*After reading these next three sections, you'll have a better understanding of the importance of organizational structure, because you should be able to*
1. *describe the departmentalization approach to organizational structure.*
2. *explain organizational authority.*
3. *discuss the different methods for job design.*

# 1. Departmentalization

**departmentalization**
subdividing work and workers into separate organizational units responsible for completing particular tasks

Traditionally, organizational structures have been based on some form of departmentalization. **Departmentalization** is a method of subdividing work and workers into separate organizational units that take responsibility for completing particular tasks.[4] For example, the Sony Corporation has separate departments or divisions for electronics, music, movies, computer games, and theaters.[5] Likewise, Bayer, a German-based company, has separate departments or divisions for healthcare, agriculture, polymers, and chemicals.[6]

*Traditionally, organizational structures have been created by departmentalizing work according to five methods: 1.1 functional, 1.2 product, 1.3 customer, 1.4 geographic, and 1.5 matrix.*

## 1.1 Functional Departmentalization

**functional departmentalization**
organizing work and workers into separate units responsible for particular business functions or areas of expertise

The most common organizational structure is functional departmentalization. Companies tend to use this structure when they are small or just starting out. **Functional departmentalization** organizes work and workers into separate units responsible for particular business functions or areas of expertise. For example, a common set of functions would consist of accounting, sales, marketing, production, and human resources departments.

However, not all functionally departmentalized companies have the same functions. For example, Exhibit 11.3 shows functional structures for an insurance company and an advertising agency. The lightly colored boxes indicate that both companies have sales, accounting, human resources, and information systems departments. The darker boxes are different for each company. As would be expected, the insurance company has separate departments for life, auto, home, and health insurance. By contrast, the advertising agency has departments for artwork, creative work, print advertising, and radio advertising. So the kind of functional departments in a functional structure depends, in part, on the business or industry a company is in.

Functional departmentalization has some advantages. First, it allows work to be done by highly qualified specialists. While the accountants in the accounting department take responsibility for producing accurate revenue and expense figures, the engineers in research and development can focus their efforts on designing a product that is reliable and simple to manufacture. Second, it lowers costs by reducing duplication. When the engineers in research and development come up with that fantastic new product, they don't have to worry about creating an aggressive advertising campaign to sell it. That task belongs to the advertising experts and sales representatives in marketing. Third, with everyone in the same department having similar work experience or training, communication and coordination are less problematic for departmental managers.

However, functional departmentalization has a number of disadvantages, too. To start, cross-department coordination can be difficult. Managers and employees are often more interested in doing what's right for their function than in doing what's right for the entire organization. A good example is the traditional conflict between marketing and manufacturing. Marketing typically pushes for spending more money to make more products with more accessories and capabilities to meet customer needs. By contrast,

EXHIBIT 11.3

FUNCTIONAL DEPARTMENTALIZATION

Insurance Company

| | |
|---|---|
| Sales | Information Systems |
| Accounting | Human Resources |
| Life Insurance | Auto Insurance |
| Home Insurance | Health Insurance |

Advertising Agency

| | |
|---|---|
| Sales | Information Systems |
| Accounting | Human Resources |
| Art Department | Print Advertising |
| Creative Department | Radio Advertising |

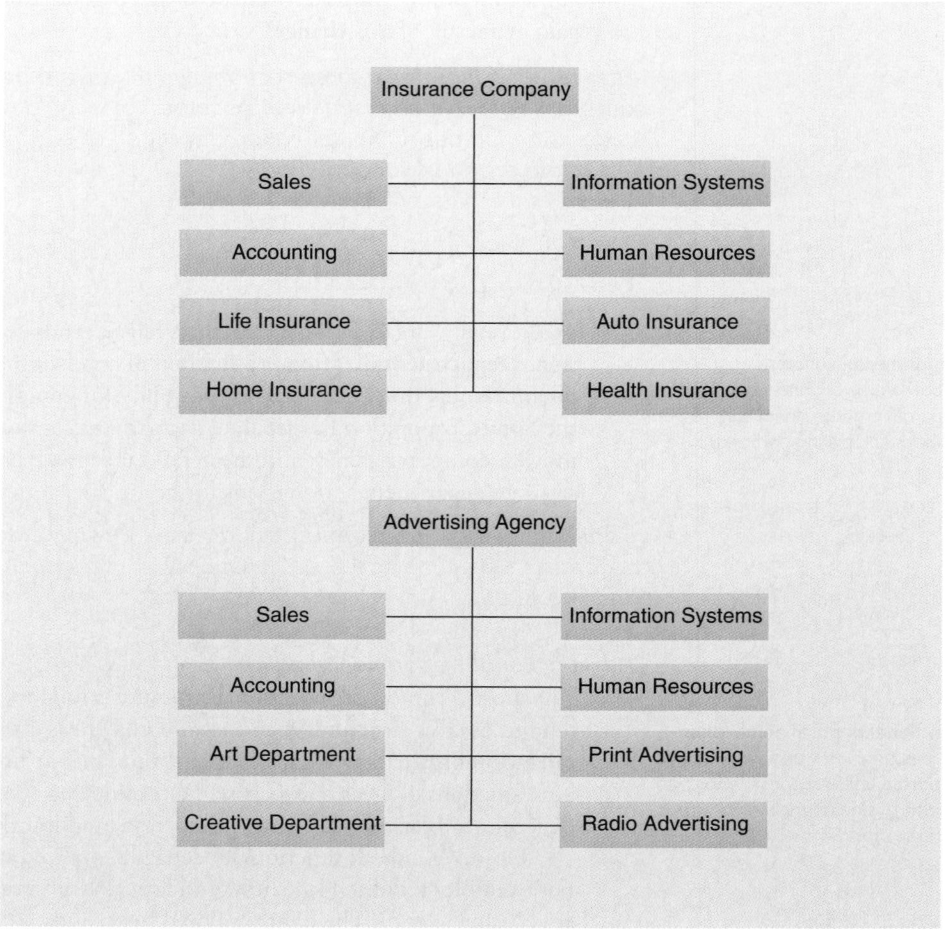

manufacturing pushes for fewer products with simpler designs, so that manufacturing facilities can ship finished products on time and keep costs within expense budgets. As companies grow, functional departmentalization may also lead to slower decision-making, and produce managers and workers with narrow experience and expertise.

### 1.2 Product Departmentalization

**product departmentalization**
organizing work and workers into separate units responsible for producing particular products or services

**Product departmentalization** organizes work and workers into separate units responsible for producing particular products or services. Exhibit 11.4 shows the product departmentalization structure used by the General Electric Corporation. GE is organized along nine different product lines: aircraft engines, appliances, capital services, lighting, technical products and services (i.e., medical systems), NBC television, plastics, power systems, and industrial products and systems.

One of the advantages of product departmentalization is that, like functional departmentalization, it allows managers and workers to specialize in one area of expertise. However, unlike the narrow expertise and experiences in functional departmentalization, managers and workers develop a broader set of experiences and expertise related to an entire product line. Likewise, product departmentalization makes it easier for top managers to assess work-unit performance. For example, because of their clear separation, it is a relatively straightforward process for GE's top managers to evaluate the performance of their nine different product divisions. For instance, GE's Aircraft Engines product division outperformed GE's Industrial Products and Systems division. Both had similar revenues,

EXHIBIT 11.4

PRODUCT DEPARTMENTALIZATION: GENERAL ELECTRIC CORPORATION

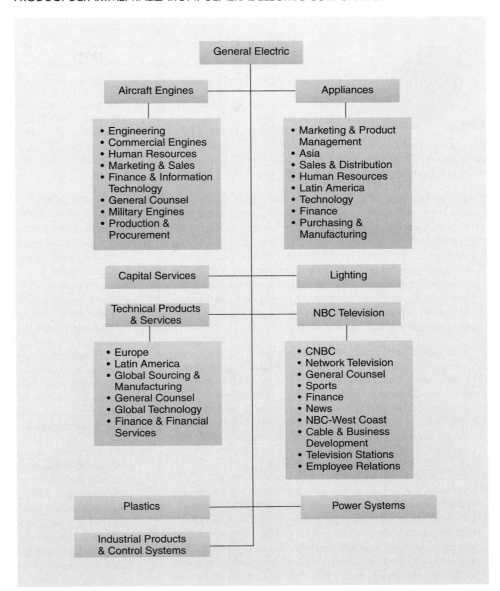

**Source:** GE Annual Report. [Online] Available http://www.ge.com/, 3 November 2001.

$10.78 billion for Aircraft Engines and $11.85 billion for Power Systems, but Aircraft Engines had a larger profit of $2.46 billion, while Industrial Products and Systems had a smaller profit of just $2.19 billion.[7] Finally, because managers and workers are responsible for the entire product line rather than for separate functional departments, decision-making should be faster, because there are fewer conflicts (compared to functional departmentalization).

The primary disadvantage of product departmentalization is duplication. For example, you can see in Exhibit 11.4 that the Aircraft Engines and Appliances divisions both have human resources, finance, and sales departments. Likewise, the Medical Systems and NBC Television divisions both have finance and general counsel departments. Duplication like this often results in higher costs.

A second disadvantage is that it can be difficult to achieve coordination across the different product departments. For example, GE would probably have difficulty standardizing

# BeenThereDoneThat

## igus and the Solar System

Frank Blasé is CEO of the igus corporation (http://www.igus.de/index.html and http://www.igus.com) in Cologne, Germany. igus designs, manufactures, and sells products (bearings, chainflex cables, and energy chain systems) that carry and protect cables and hoses on machines. igus products are used on items ranging from factory machines to robots to 10-story cranes to medical lab equipment to network television cameras at sporting events. In the interview below Frank discusses the unique organizational design used at igus.

**Q:** After getting your MBA, you worked for a large Fortune 500 firm. Then, out of frustration with the company, you quit to return to Germany to help your father run igus. How did it go at first?

**A:** (He laughs.) The first three years were totally unexpected. Nothing I did worked. Nobody bought products. We tried to establish a presence abroad with a U.S. business partner. Unfortunately, after spending lots of money on advertising, the partnership only lasted three weeks. In all, the first three years were humbling and frustrating.

**Q:** What did you do? How did you fix things?

**A:** The key was customers. We knew we needed to get our customers more involved with igus. And, in turn, we needed to find a way to get our employees to pay more attention to customers, to be glad to take a $5 order, or to hear customer complaints. In short, when we did things right, there was an energy, almost a light, you might say, that came directly from customers.

**Q:** Okay. So how did you create a focus on customers?

**A:** By creating an organization structure based on the solar system. The planets in a solar system rotate around the sun. Well, in igus' solar system, the sun is the customer and the planets were teams of igus workers (from tooling, injection molding, product assembly, and accounting). Since the sun gives off energy and all things need energy to survive, the basic idea of this solar system structure was to make sure that everyone in igus had regular, consistent exposure to customers. It's just like a planet's orbit. Of course, some employee teams, such as in-house services, maintenance and repairs, and factory planning may have less interaction (i.e., longer orbits), while others like sales people may have more frequent interaction (i.e., shorter orbits). And, unlike hierarchical organizations in which everyone gets their orders from top management, here at igus with this solar system structure, we get our orders and direction from customers.

**Q:** I noticed that you even have a large solar system chiseled into the building near the front entrance.

**A:** That's by design. British architect Nicholas Grimshaw, who is known for his high-tech designs, used the ideas behind this solar system structure when planning the building. For example, there is total transparency through the entire building. The offices are not separated from the factory. Likewise, thanks to glass walls, you can see from the factory into the offices (and vice versa), as well as from one end of the factory to another.

**Q:** That's really different. In most companies, it's rare for office workers and factory workers to see each other, or much less interact with each other.

**A:** Well, we wanted to make sure that everyone was treated the same. Every office, including mine, has the same industrial furniture kit. The same wooden table that I use as my desk is the same kind of wooden table that is used to pack boxes for shipping products. The chairs, whether they're in the offices or out in the factory, are all alike. Furthermore, we all have the same social areas. The cafeteria, which provides free food for all, opens as early as 5:30 A.M. to encourage everyone to interact from the beginning of the day to the end of the day. Finally, there's just one bathroom area that is used by both office and factory workers. Surprisingly, it's a place you run into people that you might not otherwise see. Having one bathroom area (though it's not unisex) actually leads to better communication.

**Q:** Is there anything else you do at igus to reinforce this egalitarian culture and the importance of customers?

**A:** First, we send out a weekly newsletter. I write this every Saturday and then email it to everyone in the company. This newsletter covers what's new, the trade shows igus will be going to, the percentage increases and decreases in sales and market share, and so forth. Though both good and bad news can be found in the newsletter, we do try to stress the positive. Even when we make a mistake, it can still be presented as "see what we learned." Second, all serious job applicants must spend an unpaid day with the company before they are hired. Because we're different, we want them to know us and us to know them before making a job offer. This alone tends to screen out most applicants. Only 10 to 15 percent agree to do this. We make sure that applicants talk to the employees, that they learn about our culture, and that they learn about vacations, overtime, and other official things like that. We're bluntly honest because we don't want people to have false hopes. We want them to know what they're getting into. Finally, at the end of the day, there's a team appraisal. If the team with which an applicant will be working doesn't like the job candidate, they don't get hired. So not only are our teams highly involved with customers, we also make sure that they play a critical role in deciding who gets hired.

its policies and procedures in product departments as different as the Lighting (light bulbs and lighting products for homes, offices, and factories) and Capital Services (corporate debt and equity financing, commercial real estate, insurance, and personal credit and financing) divisions.

### 1.3 Customer Departmentalization

**customer departmentalization**
organizing work and workers into separate units responsible for particular kinds of customers

**Customer departmentalization** organizes work and workers into separate units responsible for particular kinds of customers. For example, Exhibit 11.5 (see p. 400) shows that American Express is organized into departments that cater to consumers, travelers, investors, and businesspeople: cards, travel and entertainment, financial services, and business services respectively.[8]

The primary advantage to customer departmentalization is that it focuses the organization on customer needs rather than on products or business functions. Furthermore, creating separate departments to serve specific kinds of customers allows companies to specialize and adapt their products and services to customer needs and problems.

The primary disadvantage of customer departmentalization is that, like product departmentalization, it leads to duplication of resources. Furthermore, like product departmentalization, it can be difficult to achieve coordination across different customer departments. Finally, the emphasis on meeting customers' needs may lead workers to make decisions that please customers but hurt the business.

### 1.4 Geographic Departmentalization

**geographic departmentalization**
organizing work and workers into separate units responsible for doing business in particular geographical areas

**Geographic departmentalization** organizes work and workers into separate units responsible for doing business in particular geographical areas. For example, Exhibit 11.6 (see p. 401) shows the geographic departmentalization used by Coca-Cola Enterprises (CCE), the largest bottler and distributor of Coca-Cola products in the world. (The Coca-Cola Company develops and advertises soft drinks. CCE, which is a separate company with its own stock, buys the soft drink concentrate from the Coca-Cola Company, combines it with other ingredients, and then distributes the final product in cans, bottles, or fountain containers.) As shown in Exhibit 11.6, CCE has two regional groups: North America and Europe. The table below Exhibit 11.6 shows that each of these regions would be a sizable company by itself. For example, the European group serves a population of 143 million people in Belgium, France, Great Britain, Luxembourg, and the Netherlands, sells more than 900 million cases of soft drinks a year, employs 10,000 people, runs 30 bottling facilities, and has a customer base that drinks an average of 152 soft drinks per year per person.

The primary advantage of geographic departmentalization is that it helps companies respond to the demands of different markets. This can be especially important when selling in different countries. For example, CCE's geographic divisions sell products suited to the taste preferences in different countries. CCE bottles and distributes the following products in Europe but not in the United States: Aquarius, Bonaqua, Burn, Canada Dry, Coca-Cola light, Cresta flavors, Five Alive, Kia-Ora, Kinley, Lilt, Malvern, and Oasis.[9] Another advantage is that geographic departmentalization can reduce costs by locating unique organizational resources closer to customers. For instance, it is much cheaper for CCE to build bottling plants in Belgium than to bottle Coke in England and then transport it across the English Channel.

The primary disadvantage of geographic departmentalization is that it can lead to duplication of resources. For example, while it may be necessary to adapt products and marketing to different geographic locations, it's doubtful that CCE needs significantly different inventory tracking systems from location to location. Also, even more so than with the other forms of departmentalization, it can be especially difficult to coordinate departments that are literally thousands of miles from each other and whose managers have very limited contact with each other.

EXHIBIT 11.5

CUSTOMER DEPARTMENTALIZATION: AMERICAN EXPRESS CORPORATION

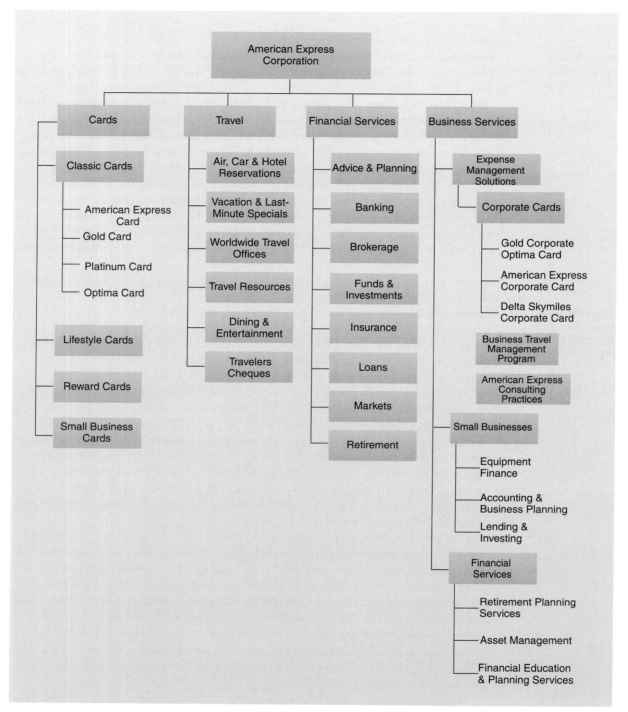

**Source:** "About American Express," American Express Web Site. [Online] Available http://www.americanexpress.com/corp/?aexp_nav=hp_corp, 11 January 1999.

EXHIBIT 11.6

GEOGRAPHIC DEPARTMENTALIZATION: COCA-COLA ENTERPRISES

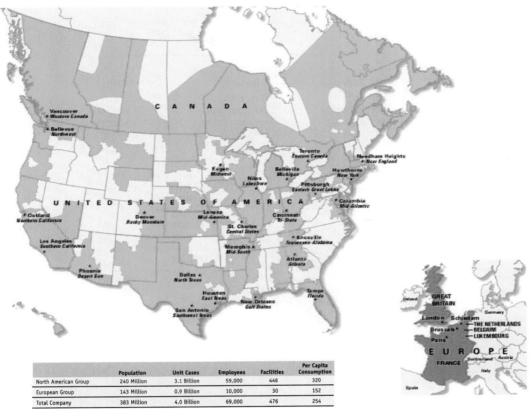

| | Population | Unit Cases | Employees | Facilities | Per Capita Consumption |
|---|---|---|---|---|---|
| North American Group | 240 Million | 3.1 Billion | 59,000 | 446 | 320 |
| European Group | 143 Million | 0.9 Billion | 10,000 | 30 | 152 |
| Total Company | 383 Million | 4.0 Billion | 69,000 | 476 | 254 |

*Facilities include 22 production, 378 sales/distribution, and 46 combination centers in North America and 5 production, 15 sales/distribution, and 10 combination centers in Europe.

**Source**: Territories. Coca-Cola Enterprises. [Online] Available http://www.cokecce.com/, 4 November 2001.

## 1.5 Matrix Departmentalization

**matrix departmentalization**
a hybrid organizational structure in which two or more forms of departmentalization, most often product and functional, are used together

**Matrix departmentalization** is a hybrid structure in which two or more forms of departmentalization are used together. The most common matrix combines product and functional forms of departmentalization. Exhibit 11.7 (see p.402) shows the matrix structure used by Pharmacia & Upjohn, a pharmaceutical company. Across the top of Exhibit 11.7, you can see that the company uses a functional structure (research, development, manufacturing, and marketing) *within* each of its three largest geographic markets, the United States, Europe, and Japan. However, down the left side of the figure, notice that the company is using a product structure to research and develop drugs for the central nervous system, infectious diseases, metabolic and inflammatory diseases, as well as thrombosis, women's health, ophthalmology, critical care, urology, and oncology.

The boxes in the figure represent the matrix structure, created by the combination of the functional/geographic and product structures. For example, in Europe, the Metabolic Diseases group has four functional departments: Research, Development, Manufacturing, and Marketing. In the United States, the Oncology group has the same set of functional departments.

EXHIBIT 11.7

MATRIX DEPARTMENTALIZATION: PHARMACIA & UPJOHN

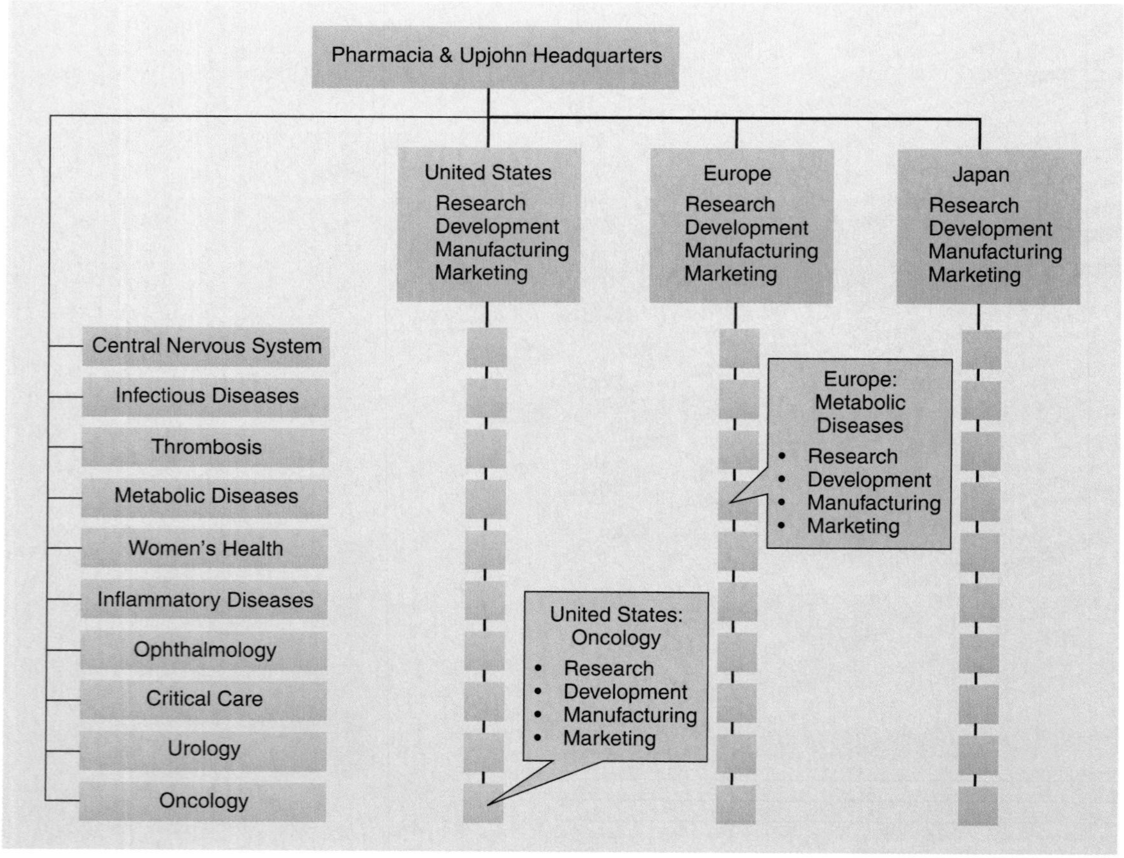

**Source:** "Financial Reports," Pharmacia & Upjohn Annual Report. [Online] Available http://www.upjohn.com/, 11 January 1999.

402

Several things distinguish matrix departmentalization from the other traditional forms of departmentalization.[10] First, most employees report to two bosses, a functional boss and a project or product boss. For example, in Exhibit 11.7, a research employee in the European Metabolic Diseases group would have a boss from the European Research department and a boss from the European Metabolic Diseases product group. Second, by virtue of the function-by-project design, matrix structures lead to much more cross-functional interaction than other forms of departmentalization. In fact, while matrix workers are members of only one functional department (based on their work experience and expertise), it is common for them to be members of several ongoing project groups. Third, because of the high level of cross-functional interaction, matrix departmentalization requires significant coordination between functional and project managers. In particular, these managers have the complex job of tracking and managing the multiple project and functional demands on employees' time.

The primary advantage of matrix departmentalization is that it allows companies to efficiently manage large, complex tasks like researching, developing, and marketing pharmaceuticals. Efficiency comes from avoiding duplication. For example, rather than having an entire marketing function for each project, the company simply assigns and reassigns workers from the marketing department as they are needed at various stages of product completion. More specifically, an employee from a department may simultane-

# "headline news"

When companies take a nose dive, there's a chance for a great turnaround, but usually at a cost to the status quo. JCPenney is one such candidate. With its stock languishing at under $10 per share, off highs of around $78 a share, JCPenney hired Allen Questrom, the first outside CEO in the company's 99-year history, to nurse it back to health.

And that is no small feat. Nearly everything about the JCPenney organization needed revamping. It didn't take long, however, to shake up the insular organization. Questrom quickly imported a staff of executives and managers from other successful retailers and began to make significant changes.

Penney's difficulties can be attributed to one thing—the store has slid off the radar of young consumers, largely due to the store's dowdy image and blasé merchandise. JCPenney used to have a centralized merchandising organization that would broadcast next season's fashions from a soundstage in the company's Plano, Texas, headquarters. In an effort to give individual stores more control over their product, JCPenney decentralized the merchandising function, hoping that store managers would tailor their offerings to regional tastes. What sounded good in theory was terrible in practice. Decision making was left up to people who didn't necessarily know what would be hot next year, only what sold well this year. The result was stores full of unappealing and dated merchandise.

To reverse this trend, JCPenney reinstated centralized merchandising, but with a twist. The Plano merchandising staff of 1,300 is supported by a group of newly hired outside merchandisers with expertise in specific product categories. Vanessa Castagna, who joined the company from Wal-Mart, is responsible for initiating the change. Other changes to the retailing organization included revamping the Penney's catalog, with the help of John Irvin from Spiegel, and beefing up the Web site. In fact, the e-commerce part of the organization is flourishing, offering more product than the stores and servicing an average of two million unique visitors a month.

For all the changes, however, a Penney's turnaround is not a sure bet. Even Fortune magazine refused to take sides. Because of a hung jury of editors, the magazine's editors decided to leave it off their "comeback kid" list in a March 2001 article.

Generating less than half the sales dollars per square foot of retail space than its biggest competitors, Target and Kohl's, JCPenney has a long way to go to return to its former glory. How far? The company's best performing U.S. store, Store 43, is in Puerto Rico, where the JCPenney is the only department store on the island.

1. *What kind of organizational departmentalization would you recommend for JCPenney? Go to http://www.JCPenney.net for more information about the corporation and its holdings.*
2. *Will organizational restructuring solve JCPenney's problems, or are there other issues that the company needs to address? Visit the nearest JCPenney and the company Web site to make this determination.*

**Sources:** L. Clifford, "When to Believe the Spin on Turnarounds," *Fortune*, 19 March 2001, 192. Info-Trac Article A71352270. J. Doherty, "Texas Two-Step: A Retail Whiz Strives to Dust off J.C. Penney," *Barron's*, 20 August 2001, 18. "Traditional Retailers Convert Customers to E-Commerce," *Internet Business News*, 3 August 2001, NA. Info-Trac Article A76952763. A. Wheat, "Retail Champs: Where Are the Best Stores in the United States?" *Fortune*, 16 April 2001, 196. Info-Trac Article A73681369. http://www.jcpenney.net.

**403**

ously be part of five different ongoing projects, but may only be actively completing work on a few projects at a time.

Another advantage is the ability to carry out large, complex tasks. Because of the ability to quickly pull in expert help from all the functional areas of the company, matrix project managers have a much more diverse set of expertise and experience at their disposal than do managers in the other forms of departmentalization.

The primary disadvantage of matrix departmentalization is the high level of coordination required to manage the complexity involved with running large, ongoing projects at various levels of completion. Matrix structures are notorious for confusion and conflict between project bosses, or between project and functional bosses. Disagreements or misunderstanding about project schedules, budgets, available resources, and the availability of employees with particular functional expertise are common. Another disadvantage is that matrix structures require much more management skill than the other forms of departmentalization.

**simple matrix**
a form of matrix departmentalization in which project and functional managers negotiate conflicts and resources

**complex matrix**
a form of matrix departmentalization in which project and functional managers report to matrix managers, who help them sort out conflicts and problems

Because of these problems, many matrix structures evolve from the **simple matrix**, in which project and functional managers negotiate conflicts and resources directly, to the **complex matrix**, in which specialized matrix managers and departments are added to the organizational structure. In the complex matrix, project and functional managers report to the same matrix manager, who helps them sort out conflicts and problems.

Sometimes, however, even these steps aren't enough to alleviate the problems that can occur in matrix structures. For example, European-based Unilever, maker and marketer of such well-known products as Dove soap, Vaseline Intensive Care lotions, Hellman's Mayonnaise, I Can't Believe It's Not Butter, Lipton teas, Wish-Bone salad dressings, Skippy peanut butter, and Lawry's seasonings, was run using a complex matrix structure. In fact, the company even had dual headquarters in Rotterdam in the Netherlands, and in London, England. Because of the confusion and conflict associated with two sets of management located in two headquarters, Unilever has now switched to a product structure with two global divisions: foods and home personal care.[11] Because everyone now reports to just one boss, Unilever's management believes that "This structure allows improved focus on foods and home and personal care activities at both the regional and global levels. It allows for faster decision making and strengthens our capacity for innovation by more effectively integrating research into the divisional structure."[12]

### Review 1
#### Departmentalization

There are five traditional departmental structures: functional, product, customer, geographic, and matrix. Functional departmentalization is based on the different business functions or expertise used to run a business. Product departmentalization is organized according to the different products or services a company sells. Customer departmentalization focuses its divisions on the different kinds of customers that companies have. Geographic departmentalization is based on the different geographical areas or markets in which the company does business. Matrix departmentalization is a hybrid form that combines two or more forms of departmentalization, the most common being the product and functional forms. There is no "best" departmental structure. Each structure has advantages and disadvantages.

## 2. Organizational Authority

*The second part of traditional organizational structures is authority.* **Authority** *is the right to give commands, take action, and make decisions to achieve organizational objectives.*[13] *Traditionally, organizational authority has been characterized by the following dimensions: 2.1 chain of command, 2.2 line versus staff authority, 2.3 delegation of authority, and 2.4 degree of centralization.*

**authority**
the right to give commands, take action, and make decisions to achieve organizational objectives

### 2.1 Chain of Command

Turn back a few pages to Microsoft's organizational chart in Exhibit 11.1. If you place your finger on any position in the chart, say, the Director of Human Resources (under Corporate Functions in the Operations Group), you can trace a line upward to the company CEO, Steve Ballmer. This line, which vertically connects every job in the company to higher levels of management, represents the chain of command. The **chain of command** is the vertical line of authority that clarifies who reports to whom throughout the organization. People higher in the chain of command have the right, *if they so choose,* to give commands, take action, and make decisions concerning activities occurring anywhere below them in the chain. In the following discussion about delegation and decentralization, you will learn that managers don't always choose to exercise their authority directly.[14]

One of the key assumptions underlying the chain of command is **unity of command**, which means that workers should report to just one boss.[15] In practical terms, this means that only one person can be in charge at a time. Matrix organizations, in which employees have two bosses, or—as in the Unilever example you just read about—two headquar-

**chain of command**
the vertical line of authority that clarifies who reports to whom throughout the organization

**unity of command**
a management principle that workers should report to just one boss

ters, automatically violate this principle. This is one of the primary reasons that matrix organizations are difficult to manage. The purpose of unity of command is to prevent the confusion that might arise when an employee receives conflicting commands from two different bosses. For example, if someone walks into an emergency room describing symptoms similar to a heart attack, the first person in charge, most likely a nurse, makes the initial assessment, assigns the patient to a treatment room, and gets the necessary doctors, nurses, and equipment to begin evaluation and treatment. Then the emergency room physician, who is higher than the nurse in the chain of command, takes charge and begins the process of determining whether the patient is really having a heart attack by conducting an examination, ordering tests, and taking the patient's medical history. If the physician calls in a cardiologist for consultation, the cardiologist becomes the person in charge, and makes the final treatment decision. Despite the number of people involved in the process, it's clear who is in charge at each point, because the emergency room follows the principle of unity of command.

### 2.2 Line Versus Staff Authority

**line authority**
the right to command immediate subordinates in the chain of command

A second dimension of authority is the distinction between line and staff authority. **Line authority** is the right to command immediate subordinates in the chain of command. For example, in the Microsoft organizational chart in Exhibit 11.1, CEO Steve Ballmer has line authority over the manager of the Personal Services Group. Ballmer can issue orders to that group vice president and expect them to be carried out. In turn, the Personal Services Group vice president can issue orders to the managers in charge of the Service Platform, Mobility, MSN Internet Access, Consumer Device, and User Interface Platform divisions and expect them to be carried out.

**staff authority**
the right to advise, but not command, others who are not subordinates in the chain of command

**Staff authority** is the right to advise but not command others who are not subordinates in the chain of command. For example, at Microsoft, a manager in human resources might advise the vice president of the Personal Services Group in making a hiring decision but cannot order him or her to hire a certain applicant.

**line function**
an activity that contributes directly to creating or selling the company's products

**staff function**
an activity that does not contribute directly to creating or selling the company's products, but instead supports line activities

The terms "line" and "staff" are also used to describe different functions within the organization. A **line function** is an activity that contributes directly to creating or selling the company's products. So, for example, activities that take place within the manufacturing and marketing departments would be considered line functions. A **staff function** is one that does not contribute directly to creating or selling the company's products, but instead supports line activities. Typical staff functions within an organization are accounting, human resources, and legal services. For example, marketing managers might consult with the legal staff to make sure the wording of a particular advertisement is legal.

### 2.3 Delegation of Authority

**delegation of authority**
the assignment of direct authority and responsibility to a subordinate to complete tasks for which the manager is normally responsible

Managers can exercise their authority directly by completing the tasks themselves, or they can choose to pass on some of their authority to subordinates. **Delegation of authority** is the assignment of direct authority and responsibility to a subordinate to complete tasks for which the manager is normally responsible.

When a manager delegates work, three transfers occur, as illustrated in Exhibit 11.8. First, the manager transfers full responsibility for the assignment to the subordinate. Many managers find giving up full responsibility somewhat difficult. For example, Joseph Liemandt, CEO of Trilogy Development Group, said, "You always hate to delegate something that you like to do, but you have no choice if the company is going to grow."[16] Indeed, most managers have way too much to do. So, from a practical perspective, they can't assume new responsibilities that come with change and growth until they fully delegate old ones.

Another problem is that managers often fear that the task won't be done as well if they don't do it themselves. However, Liemandt said, "If you can delegate a task to somebody who can do it 75 percent to 80 percent as well as you can today, you delegate it immediately." Why? Because many tasks needn't be done perfectly; they just need to be

*EXHIBIT 11.8*

DELEGATION: RESPONSIBILITY, AUTHORITY, AND ACCOUNTABILITY

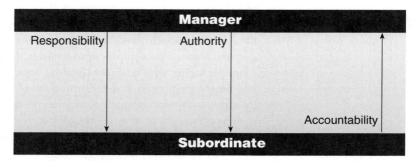

**Source:** C.D. Pringle, D.F. Jennings, and J.G. Longenecker, *Managing Organizations: Functions and Behaviors* (Columbus, OH: Merrill Publishing, 1988), 210.

done. And delegating tasks that someone can already do frees managers to assume other important responsibilities.

Sometimes managers delegate "full responsibility" only to later interfere with how the employee is performing the task. "Why are you doing it that way? That's not the way I do it." In short, delegating full responsibility means that the employee—not the manager—is now completely responsible for task completion.

Second, delegation transfers to the subordinate full authority over the budget, resources, and personnel needed to do the job. To do the job effectively, subordinates must have the same tools and information at their disposal that managers had when they were responsible for the same task. In other words, for delegation to work, delegated authority must be commensurate with delegated responsibility. This can be seen in the case of Brinker International, a company that runs nine restaurant chains, including Chili's, On the Border, and Macaroni Grill. As part of a cost-cutting effort several years ago, CEO Ronald McDougall ordered food portions cut in all restaurants. But when customers complained and business dropped, McDougall changed course and delegated the cost cutting to the managers in charge of each restaurant chain. He gave each a cost-cutting goal, and told them they could accomplish it any way they wanted. So the chain man-

**406**

When unilateral reduction of food portions angered Chili's customers, company CEO Ron McDougall delegated control over cost cutting to individual restaurant chains. Now restaurant managers are more innovative in identifying areas where they can trim costs without sacrificing customer satisfaction.

© INDEX STOCK IMAGERY/STEWART COHEN

EXHIBIT 11.9

## HOW TO BE A MORE EFFECTIVE DELEGATOR

1. Trust your staff to do a good job. Recognize that others have the talent and ability to complete projects.
2. Avoid seeking perfection. Establish a standard of quality and provide a time frame for reaching it.
3. Give effective job instructions. Make sure employees have enough information to complete the job successfully.
4. Know your true interests. Delegation is difficult for some people who actually prefer doing the work themselves rather than managing it.
5. Follow up on progress. Build in checkpoints to help identify potential problems.
6. Praise the efforts of your staff.
7. Don't wait to the last minute to delegate. Avoid crisis management by routinely delegating work.
8. Ask questions, expect answers, and assist employees to help them complete the work assignments as expected.
9. Provide the resources you would expect if you were doing an assignment yourself.
10. Delegate to the lowest possible level to make the best possible use of organizational resources, energy, and knowledge.

**Source:** S.B. Wilson, "Are You an Effective Delegator?" *Female Executive,* 1 November 1994, 19.

agers returned to regular-sized portions and then cut costs by trimming low-profit menu items and by training staff to increase employee retention (and cut costs). Delegating to the chain managers worked so well, that McDougall gave them even more freedom. He says, "They're now more like local entrepreneurs."[17]

The third transfer that occurs with delegation is the transfer of accountability. The subordinate now has the authority and responsibility to do the job and is then accountable for getting the job done. In other words, managers give subordinates their managerial authority and responsibility in exchange for results. *Forbes* magazine columnist John Rutledge called delegation "MBB," Managing by Belly Button. He said, "The belly button is the person whose belly you point your finger at when you want to know how the work is proceeding, i.e., the person who will actually be accountable for each step. . . . The belly button is not a scapegoat—a person to blame later when things go wrong. He or she is the person who makes sure that things go right."[18] Exhibit 11.9 gives some tips on how to be an effective delegator.

### 2.4 Degree of Centralization

Companies A and B both sell computers directly to the public via the Internet and free 1-800 sales lines. At Company A, when a customer calls to complain that the computer monitor doesn't work, the customer service representatives are not authorized to handle the situation. They must forward the call to their manager, who handles the situation. In such instances, the average customer waits on hold an additional 10 to 20 minutes, because the manager of the customer service department is dealing with other customers' problems, too. By contrast, when the same thing happens at Company B, the customer representatives walk the customer through an installation checklist to determine if the monitor is set up correctly. Then, convinced that the monitor is indeed broken, the customer representatives immediately instruct the company ordering system to ship a new monitor, overnight, at no cost to the customer. Furthermore, representatives immediately fax or email packing instructions and account authorization numbers to the customer, so that the broken monitor can be picked up, again, at no expense to the customer, when UPS delivers the new one the next morning. Total elapsed time to handle the problem: less than 10 minutes.

The primary difference between Companies A and B is the location of authority in the organization. Company A, where the customer representative must "kick" the customer problem "upstairs" to management, is an example of centralization. **Centralization of authority** is the location of most authority at the upper levels of the organization. In a centralized organization, managers make most decisions, even the relatively small ones. By

**centralization of authority**
the location of most authority at the upper levels of the organization

**decentralization**
the location of a significant amount of authority in the lower levels of the organization

contrast, the approach used in Company B, where the customer representatives handle the entire problem without any input or consultation from company management, is an example of decentralization. **Decentralization** is the location of a significant amount of authority in the lower levels of the organization. An organization is decentralized if it has a high degree of delegation at all levels. In a decentralized organization, workers closest to problems are authorized to make the decisions necessary to solve the problems on their own.

Decentralization has a number of advantages. It develops employee capabilities throughout the company and leads to faster decision making and more satisfied customers and employees. Furthermore, a study of 1,000 large companies found that companies with a high degree of decentralization outperformed those with a low degree of decentralization in terms of return on assets (6.9 percent versus 4.7 percent), return on investment (14.6 percent versus 9 percent), return on equity (22.8 percent versus 16.6 percent), and return on sales (10.3 percent versus 6.3 percent). Ironically, however, the same study found that few large companies are actually decentralized. Specifically, only 31 percent of employees in these 1,000 companies were responsible for recommending improvements to management. Overall, just 10 percent of employees received the training and information needed to support a truly decentralized approach to management.[19]

With results like these, the key question is no longer whether companies should decentralize, but where they should decentralize. One rule of thumb is to stay centralized where standardization is important and to decentralize where standardization is unimportant. **Standardization** is solving problems by consistently applying the same rules, procedures, and processes. Children's Orchard is a franchise chain of stores that sells children's clothing, toys, accessories, and furniture. Under the company's original management, Children's Orchard franchisees could buy whatever they wanted, market it how they saw fit, and set their own prices. The result was that Children's Orchard stores had different merchandise, different marketing promotions, and different management practices. But when Walter Hamilton bought the company, he decided that Children's Orchard could not become a powerful brand name unless there was some standardization from store to store. Consequently, he standardized the purchasing process, requiring the franchisees who owned each store to buy quality merchandise from a list of approved vendors. He also standardized advertising and promotions, producing clip art, predesigned ads, and other promotions materials for franchisees to use.[20] The result is consistent promotions and merchandise from store to store.

**standardization**
solving problems by consistently applying the same rules, procedures, and processes

## Review **2**
### Organizational Authority

Organizational authority is determined by the chain of command, line versus staff authority, delegation, and the degree of centralization in a company. The chain of command vertically connects every job in the company to higher levels of management and makes clear who reports to whom. Managers have line authority to command employees below them in the chain of command, but have only staff or advisory authority over employees not below them in the chain of command. Managers delegate authority by transferring to subordinates the authority and responsibility needed to do a task, and, in exchange, subordinates become accountable for task completion. In centralized companies, most authority to make decisions lies with managers in the upper levels of the company. In decentralized companies, much of the authority is delegated to the workers closest to problems, who can then make the decisions necessary for solving the problems themselves. Centralization works best for tasks that require standardized decision making. When standardization isn't important, decentralization can lead to faster decisions, greater employee and customer satisfaction, and significantly better financial performance.

## 3. Job Design

Imagine that McDonald's decided to pay $50,000 a year to its drive-through window cashiers. $50,000 for saying, "Welcome to McDonald's. May I have your order please?"

Would you take the job? Sure you would. Work a couple of years. Make a hundred grand. Why not? However, let's assume that to get this outrageous salary, you have to be a full-time drive-through McDonald's window cashier for the next ten years. Would you still take the job? Just imagine, 40 to 60 times an hour, you repeat the same basic process:

1. "Welcome to McDonald's. May I have your order please?"
2. Listen to the order. Repeat it for accuracy. State the total cost. "Please drive to the second window."
3. Take the money. Make change.
4. Give customers drinks, straws, and napkins.
5. Give customers food.
6. "Thank you for coming to McDonald's."

Could you stand to do the same simple tasks an average of 50 times per hour, 400 times per day, 2,000 times per week, or 8,000 times per month? Few can. It's rare for fast-food workers to stay on the job more than six months. Indeed, McDonald's and other fast-food restaurants have well over 100 percent employee turnover each year.[21]

**job design**
the number, kind, and variety of tasks that individual workers perform in doing their jobs

*In this next section, you will learn about **job design**—the number, kind, and variety of tasks that individual workers perform in doing their jobs. You will learn 3.1 why companies continue to use specialized jobs like the McDonald's drive-through job, and 3.2 how job rotation, job enlargement, job enrichment, and the 3.3 job characteristics model are being used to overcome the problems associated with job specialization.*

### 3.1 Job Specialization

**job specialization**
a job composed of a small part of a larger task or process

**Job specialization** is a job composed of a small part of a larger task or process. Specialized jobs are characterized by simple, easy-to-learn steps, low variety, and high repetition, like the McDonald's drive-through window job described above. One of the clear disadvantages of specialized jobs is that, being so easy to learn, they quickly become boring. This, in turn, can lead to low job satisfaction and high absenteeism and employee turnover, all of which are very costly to organizations.

Why, then, do companies continue to create and use specialized jobs? The primary reason is that specialized jobs are very economical. Once a job has been specialized, it takes little time to learn and master. Consequently, when experienced workers quit or are absent, the company loses little productivity when replacing them with a new employee. For example, next time you're at McDonald's, notice the pictures of the food on the cash registers. These pictures make it easy for McDonald's trainees to quickly learn to take orders. Likewise, to simplify and speed operations, the drink dispensers behind the counter are set to automatically fill drink cups. Put a medium cup below the dispenser. Punch the medium drink button. The soft drink machine then fills the cup to within a half-inch of the top, while that same worker goes to get your fries. At McDonald's, every task has been simplified in this way. Because the work is designed to be simple, wages can remain low, since it isn't necessary to pay high salaries to attract highly experienced, educated, or trained workers.

### 3.2 Job Rotation, Enlargement, and Enrichment

Because of the efficiency of specialized jobs, companies are often reluctant to eliminate them. Consequently, job redesign efforts have focused on modifying jobs to keep the benefits of specialized jobs, but to reduce their obvious costs and disadvantages. Three methods, job rotation, job enlargement, and job enrichment, have been used to try to improve specialized jobs.[22]

In factory work or even some office jobs, many workers perform the same task all day long. For example, if you attach side mirrors in an auto factory, you probably complete this task 45 to 60 times an hour. If you work as the cashier at a grocery store, you check out a different customer every two to three minutes. And if you work as an office receptionist, you may answer and direct phone calls up to 200 times an hour.

# BlastFromThePast

## From Farms to Factories to Telecommuting

An 8 A.M. to 5 P.M. workday, coffee breaks, lunch hours, crushing rush-hour traffic, and punching a time clock are things we associate with work. However, work hasn't always been this way. In fact, the design of jobs and organizations has changed dramatically over the last 500 years.

For most of humankind's history, people didn't commute to work. In fact, travel of any kind was arduous and extremely rare. Work usually occurred in homes or on farms. For example, in 1720, 4¼ million of the 5½ million people in England lived and worked in the country. As recently as 1870, two-thirds of Americans earned their living from agriculture. However, even most of those who didn't earn their living from agriculture still didn't commute to work. Skilled tradesmen or craftsmen, such as blacksmiths, furniture makers, and leather goods makers, who formed trade guilds (the historical predecessors of labor unions) in England as early as 1093, typically worked out of shops in or next to their homes. Likewise, cottage workers worked with each other out of small homes (i.e., cottages) that were often built in a semicircle. Families in each cottage would complete different production steps, passing work from one cottage to the next until production was complete. For example, textile work was a common "cottage industry." Families in different cottages would shear the sheep, clean the wool, and then comb, spin, weave, bleach, and dye the wool to turn it into yarn. Cottage work was very different from today's jobs and companies. There was no commute, no bosses (workers determined the amount and pace of their work), and no common building (from the time of the ancient Greeks, Romans, and Egyptians through the middle of the 19th century, it was rare for more than 12 people to actually work together under one roof).

However, during the industrial revolution (1750–1900), jobs and organizations changed dramatically. First, thanks to the availability of power (steam engines and later electricity) and numerous inventions, such as Darby's coke-smelting process and Cort's puddling and rolling process (both for making iron) and Hargreave's Jenny and Arkwright's water frame (both for spinning cotton), low-paid, unskilled laborers running machines began to replace high-paid, skilled craftsmen. Craftsmen handmade entire goods by themselves. This new production system was based on a division of labor in which each worker, interacting with machines, performed separate, highly specialized tasks that were but a small part of all the steps required to make manufactured goods. Mass production was born as rope- and chain-driven assembly lines moved work to stationary workers, who concentrated on performing one small task over and over again.

As a result, productivity skyrocketed. At Ford Motor Company, the time required to assemble a car dropped from 12½ worker-hours to just 93 worker-minutes.

Second, instead of being performed in fields, homes, or small shops, jobs occurred in large, formal organizations in which hundreds, if not thousands, of people worked under one roof. For example, with just 123 workers in 1849, Chicago Harvester (predecessor of International Harvester) ran the largest factory in the United States. Yet, by 1913, Henry Ford employed 12,000 employees in his Highland Park, Michigan, factory. Between 1860 and 1890, the number of Americans working in factories quintupled, while the number of people working in cities grew even faster. Chicago's population grew from 109,620 in 1860 to 2.2 million in 1910.

Finally, with factories employing so many workers, companies now had a need for disciplinary rules (to impose order and structure) and, for the first time, managers who knew how to organize, work with employees, and make good decisions.

Today, of course, agriculture and manufacturing comprise only about 20 percent of all jobs. In fact, 70 percent of today's jobs are service-based jobs in which customers pay someone else to do something (i.e., lawn care, house painting, financial advice, child care) that they cannot do or choose not to do for themselves. However, history has come full circle in at least one way as computers and the Internet allow an estimated 23 million telecommuters to work from home, much like farm and craft workers did 400 years ago.

**Sources:** J. Burke, *The Day the Universe Changed* (Boston: Little, Brown, and Company, 1985). "Current Telecommuting Survey Data Shows Strong Growth," *Telecommuting Review: The Gordon Report*, 1 November 1998. From *Britannica Online*, "History of the Organization of Work: Organization of Work in Preindustrial Times" the following articles: "From the 16th to the 18th Century," (http://www.eb.com); "The Ancient World," (http://www.eb.com); "Medieval Industry," (http://www.eb.com), all available 15 January 1999. R.B. Reich, *The Next American Frontier* (New York: Times Books, 1983). S. Wells, "Making Telecommuting Work," *HR Magazine* October (2001): 34. J.B. White, "The Line Starts Here: Mass Production Techniques Changed the Way People Work and Live throughout the World," *The Wall Street Journal*, 11 January 1999, R25.

**410**

**job rotation**
periodically moving workers from one specialized job to another to give them more variety and the opportunity to use different skills

**Job rotation** attempts to overcome the disadvantages of job specialization by periodically moving workers from one specialized job to another to give them more variety and the opportunity to use different skills. For example, the office receptionist who does nothing but answer phones could be systematically rotated to a different job, such as typing, filing, or data entry, every day or two. Likewise, the "mirror attacher" in the automobile plant might attach mirrors in the first half of the day's work shift and then install bumpers during the second half. Because employees simply switch from one specialized job to another, job rotation allows companies to retain the economic benefits of specialized work. However, the greater variety of tasks makes the work less boring and more satisfying for workers.

Another way to counter the disadvantages of specialization is to enlarge the job. **Job enlargement** is increasing the number of different tasks that a worker performs within one particular job. So, instead of having to perform just one task, workers with enlarged jobs would be given several tasks to perform. For example, an enlarged "mirror attacher" job might include attaching the mirror, checking to see that the mirror's power adjustment controls work, and then cleaning the mirror's surface. While job enlargement increases variety, many workers report feeling more stress when their jobs are enlarged. Consequently, many workers view enlarged jobs as simply "more work," especially if they are not given additional time to complete the additional tasks.

**Job enrichment** attempts to overcome the deficiencies in specialized work by increasing the number of tasks *and* by giving workers the authority and control to make meaningful decisions about their work.[23] For example, at AES, an independent power company that sells electricity to public utilities and steam (for power) to industrial organizations, workers have been given an extraordinary level of authority and control. For example, with his hands still blackened after unloading coal from a barge, employee Jeff Hatch calls a broker to determine which Treasury bills the company should buy to maximize the short-term return on its available cash. Hatch asks his broker, "What kind of rate can you give me for $10 million at 30 days?" When the broker tells him, "6.09 percent," he responds, "But I just got a 6.13 percent quote from Chase."[24] Indeed, at AES, ordinary plant technicians are given budgets worth several million dollars and are trusted to purchase everything from mops to gas turbines. In most companies, such tasks would only be entrusted to managers. CEO Dennis Bakke said, "The more you increase individual responsibility, the better the chances for incremental improvements in operations." Paul Burdick, an engineer entrusted with the ability to purchase billions of dollars of coal agrees, saying, "You're given a lot of leeway and a low of rope. You can use it to climb or you can hang yourself."[25]

### 3.3 Job Characteristics Model

In contrast to job rotation, job enlargement, and job enrichment, which focus on providing variety in job tasks, the **job characteristics model (JCM)** is an approach to job redesign that seeks to formulate jobs in ways that motivate workers and lead to positive work outcomes.[26] As shown in Exhibit 11.10, the primary goal of the model is to create jobs that result in positive personal and work outcomes such as internal work motivation, satisfaction with one's job, and work effectiveness. Of these, the central outcome of the JCM is internal motivation. **Internal motivation** is motivation that comes from the job itself rather than from outside rewards, such as a raise or praise from the boss. If workers feel that performing the job well is itself rewarding, then the job has internal motivation. Statements such as "I get a nice sense of accomplishment" or "I feel good about myself and what I'm producing" are examples of internal motivation.

Moving to the left in Exhibit 11.10, you can see that the JCM specifies three critical psychological states that must occur for work to be internally motivating. First, workers must *experience the work as meaningful*, that is, they must view their job as being important. Second, they must *experience responsibility for work outcomes*—they must feel personally responsible for the work being done well. Third, workers must have *knowledge of results*, that is, know how well they are performing their jobs. All three critical psychological states must occur for work to be internally motivating.

For example, let's return to our grocery store cashier. Cashiers usually have knowledge of results. When you're slow, your checkout line grows long. If you make a mistake, customers point it out: "No, I think that's on sale for $2.99, not $3.99." Likewise, cashiers experience responsibility for work outcomes. At the end of the day, the register is totaled and the money is counted. Ideally, the money matches the total sales

---

**job enlargement**
increasing the number of different tasks that a worker performs within one particular job

**job enrichment**
increasing the number of tasks in a particular job and giving workers the authority and control to make meaningful decisions about their work

**job characteristics model (JCM)**
an approach to job redesign that seeks to formulate jobs in ways that motivate workers and lead to positive work outcomes

**internal motivation**
motivation that comes from the job itself rather than from outside rewards

411

## JOB CHARACTERISTICS MODEL

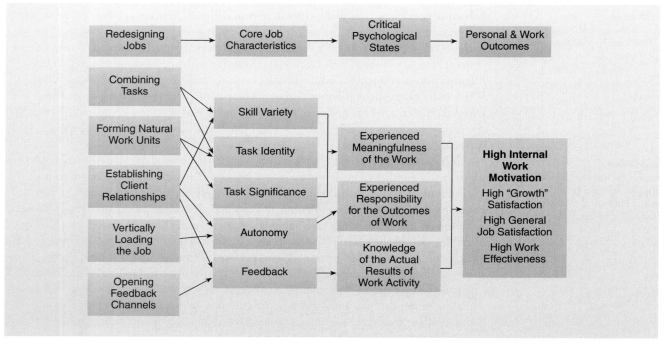

**Source:** J.R. Hackman and G.R. Oldham, *Work Redesign* (Reading, MA: Addison-Wesley, 1980). Reprinted with permission.

in the register. However, if the money in the till is less than what's recorded in the register, most stores make the cashier pay the difference. Consequently, most cashiers are very careful to avoid being caught "short" at the end of the day. However, despite knowing results and experiencing responsibility for work outcomes, most grocery store cashiers (at least where I shop) aren't internally motivated, because they don't experience the work as meaningful. With scanners, it takes little skill to learn or do the job. Anyone can do it. In addition, cashiers have few decisions to make. Plus, the job is highly repetitive.

Of course, this raises the question: What kinds of jobs produce the three critical psychological states? Again, moving to the left in Exhibit 11.10, the JCM specifies that the three critical psychological states arise from jobs that are strong on five core job characteristics: skill variety, task identity, task significance, autonomy, and feedback. **Skill variety** is the number of different activities performed in a job. **Task identity** is the degree to which a job requires completion of a whole and identifiable piece of work, from beginning to end. **Task significance** is the degree to which a job is perceived to have a substantial impact on others inside or outside the organization. **Autonomy** is the degree to which a job gives workers the discretion, freedom, and independence to decide how and when to accomplish the job. Finally, **feedback** is the amount of information the job provides to workers about their work performance.

To illustrate how the core job characteristics work together, let's use them to more thoroughly assess why the McDonald's drive-through window job is not particularly satisfying or motivating. To start, skill variety is low. Except for the size of an order or special requests (no onions), the process is the same for each customer. At best, task identity is moderate. Although you take the order, handle the money, and deliver the food, others are responsible for a larger part of the process, preparing the food. However, task identity will be even lower if a McDonald's has two drive-through windows.

412

**skill variety**
the number of different activities performed in a job

**task identity**
the degree to which a job requires, from beginning to end, the completion of a whole and identifiable piece of work

**task significance**
the degree to which a job is perceived to have a substantial impact on others inside or outside the organization

**autonomy**
the degree to which a job gives workers the discretion, freedom, and independence to decide how and when to accomplish the job

**feedback**
the amount of information the job provides to workers about their work performance

When this is the case, each drive-through window worker has an even more specialized task. The first is limited to taking the order and making change, while the second just delivers the food. Task significance, the impact you have on others, is probably low. Autonomy is also very low. McDonald's has strict rules about dress, cleanliness, and procedures. But the job does provide immediate feedback, such as positive and negative customer comments, car horns honking, amount of time it takes to process orders, and the number of cars in the drive-through. With the exception of feedback, the core job characteristics show why the drive-through window job is not internally motivating for many workers.

So, what can managers do when jobs aren't internally motivating? The far left column of Exhibit 11.10 lists five job redesign techniques that managers can use to strengthen a job's core characteristics. *Combining tasks* increases skill variety and task identity by joining separate, specialized tasks into larger work modules. For example, some trucking firms are now requiring truck drivers to drive and load their rigs. The hope is that involving drivers in loading will ensure that trucks are properly loaded, thus reducing damage claims.

Work can be formed into *natural work units* by arranging tasks according to logical or meaningful groups. Many trucking companies simply assign any driver to any truck. However, some have begun assigning drivers to particular geographic locations (i.e., the northeast or southwest) or to truckloads that require special driving skill when being transported (i.e., oversized loads, chemicals, etc.). Forming natural work units increases task identity and task significance.

*Establishing client relationships* increases skill variety, autonomy, and feedback by giving employees direct contact with clients and customers. In some companies, truck drivers are expected to establish business relationships with their regular customers. When something goes wrong with a shipment, customers are told to call drivers directly.

*Vertical loading* means pushing some managerial authority down to workers. For truck drivers, this means that they have the same authority that managers would have to resolve customer problems. In some companies, this means that if a late shipment causes problems for a customer, the driver has the ability to fully refund the cost of that shipment (without first requiring management's approval).

The last job redesign technique offered by the model, *opening feedback channels,* means finding additional ways to give employees direct, frequent feedback about their job performance. For example, with advances in electronics, many truck drivers get instantaneous data as to whether they're on schedule and driving their rigs in a fuel-efficient manner. Likewise, the increased contact with customers also means that many drivers now receive monthly data on customer satisfaction. For additional information on the JCM, see "What Really Works: The Job Characteristics Model."

## Review 3
### Job Design

Companies use specialized jobs because they are economical, easy to learn, and don't require highly paid workers. However, specialized jobs aren't motivating or particularly satisfying for employees. Companies have used job rotation, job enlargement, job enrichment, and the job characteristics model to make specialized jobs more interesting and motivating. With job rotation, workers move from one specialized job to another. Job enlargement simply increases the number of different tasks within a particular job. Job enrichment increases the number of tasks in a job and gives workers authority and control over their work. The goal of the job characteristics model is to make jobs intrinsically motivating. For this to happen, jobs must be strong on five core job characteristics (skill variety, task identity, task significance, autonomy, and feedback), and workers must experience three critical psychological states (knowledge of results, responsibility for work outcomes, and meaningful work). If jobs aren't internally motivating, they can be redesigned by combining tasks, forming natural work units, establishing client relationships, vertical loading, and opening feedback channels.

# WhatReallyWorks

## The Job Characteristics Model: Making Jobs More Interesting and Motivating

Think of the worst job you ever had. Was it factory work in which you repeated the same task every few minutes? Was it an office job requiring a lot of meaningless paperwork? Or was it a job so specialized that it took no effort or thinking whatsoever to do?

The job characteristics model reviewed in this chapter suggests that workers will be more motivated or satisfied with their work if their jobs have greater task identity, task significance, skill variety, autonomy, and feedback. Eighty-four studies, with a combined total of 22,472 study participants, indicated that, on average, these core job characteristics make jobs more satisfying for most workers. However, jobs rich with the five core job characteristics are especially satisfying for workers who possess an individual characteristic called *growth need strength*. Read on to see how well the job characteristics model really increases job satisfaction and reduces workplace absenteeism.

### Job Satisfaction

There is a 66 percent chance that workers will be more satisfied with their work when their jobs have task identity, the chance to complete an entire job from beginning to end, than when they don't.

#### Task Identity and Job Satisfaction

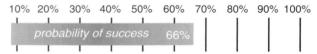

On average, there is a 69 percent chance that workers will be more satisfied with their work when their jobs have task significance, meaning a substantial impact on others, than when they don't.

#### Task Significance and Job Satisfaction

On average, there is a 70 percent chance that workers will be more satisfied with their work when their jobs have skill variety, meaning a variety of different activities, skills, and talents, than when they don't.

#### Skill Variety and Job Satisfaction

On average, there is a 73 percent chance that workers will be more satisfied with their work when their jobs have autonomy, meaning the discretion to decide how and when to accomplish the jobs, than when they don't.

#### Autonomy and Job Satisfaction

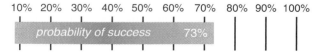

On average, there is a 70 percent chance that workers will be more satisfied with their work when their jobs have feedback, meaning knowledge about their work performance, than when they don't.

#### Feedback and Job Satisfaction

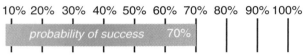

The statistics presented above indicate that, on average, the job characteristics model has, at worst, a 66 percent chance of improving workers' job satisfaction. In all, this is impressive evidence that the model works. In general, you can expect these results when redesigning jobs based on the job characteristics model.

However, we can be more accurate about the effects of the job characteristics model if we split workers into two groups, those with high growth need strength and those with low growth need strength. *Growth need strength* is the need or desire to achieve personal growth and development through your job. Workers high in growth need strength respond well to jobs designed according to the job characteristics model, because they enjoy work that challenges them and allows them to learn new skills and knowledge. In fact, there is an 84 percent chance that workers with high growth need strength will be more satisfied with their work when their jobs are redesigned according to the job characteristics model.

#### High Growth Need Strength and Job Satisfaction

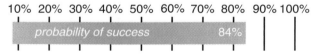

By comparison, because they aren't as interested in being challenged or learning new things at work, there is only a 69 percent chance that workers low in growth need strength will be satisfied with jobs that have been redesigned according to the principles of the job characteristics model. This is still a favorable percentage, but weaker than the 84 percent chance of job satisfaction that occurs for workers high in growth need strength.

#### Low Growth Need Strength and Job Satisfaction

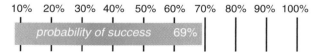

### Workplace Absenteeism

Although not shown in the job characteristics model displayed in Exhibit 11.10, workplace absenteeism is an important personal or work outcome affected by a job's core job characteristics. In general, the "richer" your job is with task identity, task significance, skill variety, autonomy, and feedback, the more likely you are to show up for work every day.

414

Workers are 63 percent more likely to attend work when their jobs have task identity, the chance to complete an entire job from beginning to end, than when they don't.

### Task Identity and Absenteeism

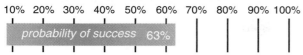

Workers are 68 percent more likely to attend work when their jobs have task significance, meaning a substantial impact on others, than when they don't.

### Task Significance and Absenteeism

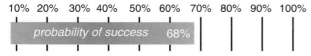

Workers are 72 percent more likely to attend work when their jobs have skill variety, meaning a variety of different activities, skills, and talents, than when they don't.

### Skill Variety and Absenteeism

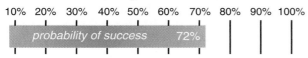

Workers are 74 percent more likely to attend work when their jobs have autonomy, meaning the discretion to decide how and when to accomplish a job, than when they don't.

### Autonomy and Absenteeism

Workers are 72 percent more likely to attend work when their jobs have feedback, meaning knowledge about their work performance, than when they don't.

### Feedback and Absenteeism

**Sources:** Y. Fried & G.R. Ferris, "The Validity of the Job Characteristics Model: A Review and Meta-Analysis," *Personnel Psychology* 40 (1987): 287-322. B.T. Loher, R.A. Noe, N.L. Moeller, & M.P. Fitzgerald, "A Meta-Analysis of the Relation of Job Characteristics to Job Satisfaction," *Journal of Applied Psychology* 70 (1985): 280-289.

## Designing Organizational Processes

**mechanistic organization**
organization characterized by specialized jobs and responsibilities, precisely defined, unchanging roles, and a rigid chain of command based on centralized authority and vertical communication

**organic organization**
organization characterized by broadly defined jobs and responsibility, loosely defined, frequently changing roles, and decentralized authority and horizontal communication based on task knowledge

Nearly 40 years ago, Tom Burns and G.M. Stalker described how two kinds of organizational designs, mechanistic and organic, are appropriate for different kinds of organizational environments.[27] **Mechanistic organizations** are characterized by specialized jobs and responsibilities, precisely defined, unchanging roles, and a rigid chain of command based on centralized authority and vertical communication. This type of organization works best in stable, unchanging business environments. By contrast, **organic organizations** are characterized by broadly defined jobs and responsibility, loosely defined, frequently changing roles, and decentralized authority and horizontal communication based on task knowledge. This type of organization works best in dynamic, changing business environments.

The organizational design techniques described in the first half of this chapter, departmentalization, authority, and job design, are methods better suited for mechanistic organizations and the stable business environments that were more prevalent before 1980. However, the organizational design techniques discussed here in the second part of the chapter are more appropriate for organic organizations and the increasingly dynamic environments in which today's businesses compete.

*The key difference between these approaches is that while mechanistic organizational designs focus on organizational structure, organic organizational designs are concerned with organizational processes, the collection of activities that transforms inputs into outputs valued by customers. After reading these next two sections, you should be able to*

*4. explain the methods that companies are using to redesign internal organizational processes (i.e., intraorganizational processes).*
*5. describe the methods that companies are using to redesign external organizational processes (i.e., interorganizational processes).*

415

# 4. Intraorganizational Processes

**intraorganizational process**
the collection of activities that take place within an organization to transform inputs into outputs that customers value

An **intraorganizational process** is the collection of activities that take place within an organization to transform inputs into outputs that customers value. The steps involved in an automobile insurance claim are a good example of an intraorganizational process:

1. Document the loss (i.e., the accident).
2. Assign an appraiser to determine the dollar amount of damage.
3. Make an appointment to inspect the vehicle.
4. Inspect the vehicle.
5. Write an appraisal and get the repair shop to agree to the damage estimate.
6. Pay for the repair work.
7. Return the repaired car to the customer.

*Let's take a look at how companies are using 4.1 reengineering, 4.2 empowerment, and 4.3 behavioral informality to redesign internal organizational processes like these.*

## 4.1 Reengineering

**reengineering**
fundamental rethinking and radical redesign of business processes to achieve dramatic improvements in critical measures of performance, such as cost, quality, service, and speed

In their best-selling book *Reengineering the Corporation,* Michael Hammer and James Champy defined **reengineering** as "the *fundamental* rethinking and *radical* redesign of business *processes* to achieve *dramatic* improvements in critical, contemporary measures of performance, such as cost, quality, service and speed."[28] Hammer and Champy further explained the four key words shown in italics in this definition. The first key word is "fundamental." When reengineering organizational designs, managers must ask themselves, "Why do we do what we do?" and "Why do we do it the way we do?" The usual answer is "Because that's the way we've always done it." The second key word is "radical." Reengineering is about significant change, about starting over by throwing out the old ways of getting work done. The third key word is "processes." Hammer and Champy noted that "Most business people are not process oriented; they are focused on tasks, on jobs, on people, on structures, but not on processes." The fourth key word is "dramatic." Reengineering is about achieving "quantum" improvements in company performance.

An example from IBM's Credit operation illustrates how work can be reengineered.[29] IBM Credit loans businesses money to buy IBM computers. Previously, the loan process began when an IBM salesperson called needing credit approval for a customer's purchase. The first department involved in the process took the credit information over the phone from the salesperson and recorded it on the credit form. Then, the credit form was sent to a separate credit checking department, and then to a separate pricing department (where the interest rate was determined), and so on. In all, it took five departments six days to approve or deny the customer's loan. Of course, this delay cost IBM business. Some customers got their loans elsewhere. Others, frustrated by the wait, simply canceled their orders.

Finally, two IBM managers decided to walk a loan straight through to each of the five departments involved in the process. At each step, they asked the workers to stop what they were doing and immediately process their loan application. They were shocked by what they found. From start to stop the entire process took just 90 minutes! It turns out that the average time of six days was created by delays that occurred in handing off the work from one department to another. The solution: IBM redesigned the process so that one person, not five in five separate departments, handled the entire loan approval process by themselves without any handoffs. The results were "dramatic." Reengineering the credit process reduced approval time from six days to four hours and allowed IBM Credit to increase the number of loans it handled by a factor of 100!

Reengineering changes an organization's orientation from vertical to horizontal. Instead of "taking orders" from upper management, lower- and middle-level managers and workers "take orders" from a customer who is at the beginning and end of each process. Instead of running independent functional departments, managers and workers in different departments take ownership of cross-functional processes. Instead of simplifying

416

**task interdependence**
the extent to which collective action is required to complete an entire piece of work

**pooled interdependence**
work completed by having each job or department independently contribute to the whole

**sequential interdependence**
work completed in succession, with one group or job's outputs becoming the inputs for the next group or job

work so that it becomes increasingly specialized, reengineering complicates work by giving workers increased autonomy and responsibility for complete processes.

In essence, reengineering changes work by changing **task interdependence**, the extent to which collective action is required to complete an entire piece of work. As shown in Exhibit 11.11, there are three kinds of task interdependence.[30] In **pooled interdependence**, each job or department independently contributes to the whole. In **sequential interdependence**, work must be performed in succession, as one group or job's outputs become the inputs for the next group or job. Finally, in **reciprocal interdependence**, different jobs or groups work together in a back-and-forth manner to complete the process. By reducing the handoffs between different jobs or groups, reengineering decreases sequential interdependence. Likewise,

## EXHIBIT 11.11

### REENGINEERING AND TASK INTERDEPENDENCE

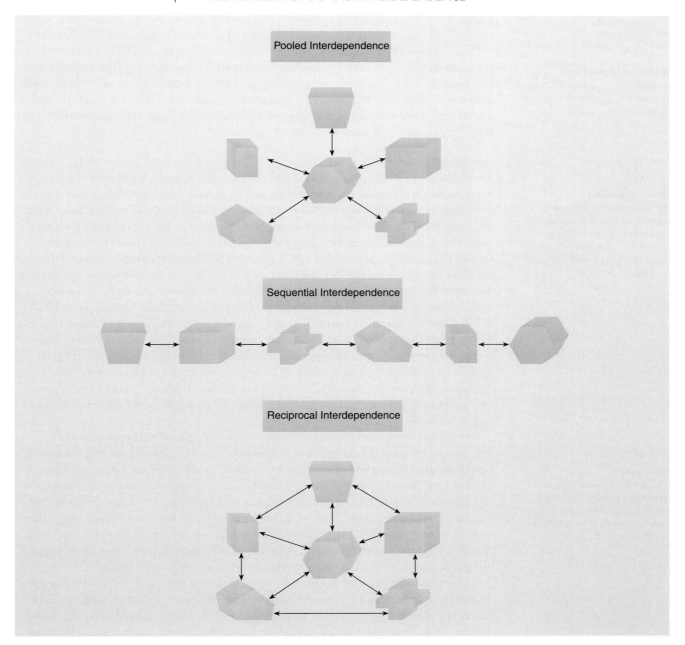

Pooled Interdependence

Sequential Interdependence

Reciprocal Interdependence

**Singles, Not Home Runs**

Reengineering, the radical redesign of business processes, can dramatically improve business performance. However, when you swing for home runs, you strike out a lot (i.e., the 70 percent failure rate of reengineering projects). Dana Corporation, a maker of car parts, swings for singles, not home runs, by focusing on daily, continuous improvement. Every day, teams are encouraged to question how things are done. Employees submit two ideas (in writing) each month for improving manufacturing processes. And when small improvements occur, company management celebrates with free barbecue and soft drinks for all. Swing for singles every day, and you're much more likely to get a hit.

**Source**: J. Byrne, "PepsiCo's New Formula: How Roger Enrico Is Remaking the Company ...," *Business Week*, 10 April 2000, 172.

**reciprocal interdependence**
work completed by different jobs or groups working together in a back-and-forth manner

**empowering workers**
permanently passing decision-making authority and responsibility from managers to workers by giving them the information and resources they need to make and carry out good decisions

418

**empowerment**
feelings of intrinsic motivation, in which workers perceive their work to have impact and meaning, and perceive themselves to be competent and capable of self-determination

reengineering decreases pooled interdependence by redesigning work so that formerly independent jobs or departments now work together to complete processes. Finally, reengineering increases reciprocal interdependence by making groups or individuals responsible for larger, more complete processes in which several steps may be accomplished at the same time.

As an organizational design tool, reengineering promises big rewards. However, it has come under severe criticism, too. The most serious complaint is that since it allows a few workers to do the work formerly done by many, reengineering is simply a corporate code word for cost cutting and worker layoffs. Likewise, for that reason, detractors claim that reengineering hurts morale and performance. For example, despite reducing ordering times from three weeks to three days, Levi Strauss ended an $850 million reengineering project because of the fear and turmoil it created in its work force. One of the low points occurred when Levi management, encouraged by its reengineering consultants, told 4,000 workers that they would have to "reapply for their jobs" as the company shifted from its traditional vertical structure to a process-based form of organizing. Thomas Kasten, Levi's vice president for reengineering and customer service, said, "We felt the pressure building up [over reengineering efforts], and we were worried about the business."[31] Today, even reengineering gurus Hammer and Champy admit that roughly 70 percent of all reengineering projects fail because of the effects on people in the workplace. Said Hammer, "I wasn't smart enough about that [the people issues]. I was reflecting my engineering background and was insufficiently appreciative of the human dimension. I've learned [now] that's critical."[32]

### 4.2 Empowerment

Another way of redesigning interorganizational processes is through empowerment. **Empowering workers** means permanently passing decision-making authority and responsibility from managers to workers. However, for workers to be fully empowered, companies must give them the information and resources they need to make and carry out good decisions, and then reward them for taking individual initiative.[33] Unfortunately, this doesn't happen often enough. Michael Schrage, author and MIT researcher wrote, "A warehouse employee can see on the intranet that a shipment is late but has no authority to accelerate its delivery. A project manager knows—and can mathematically demonstrate—that a seemingly minor spec change will bust both her budget and her schedule. The spec must be changed anyway. An airline reservations agent tells the Executive Platinum Premier frequent flier that first class appears wide open for an upgrade. However, the airline's yield management software won't permit any upgrades until just four hours before the flight, frequent fliers (and reservations) be damned. In all these cases, the employee has access to valuable information. Each one possesses the 'knowledge' to do the job better. But the knowledge and information are irrelevant and useless. Knowledge isn't power; the ability to act on knowledge is power."[34]

However, when workers are given the proper information and resources and allowed to act to make good decisions, they experience strong feelings of empowerment. **Empowerment** is a feeling of intrinsic motivation, in which workers perceive their work to have meaning, and perceive themselves to be competent, having an impact, and capable of self-determination.[35] Work has meaning when it is consistent with personal standards and beliefs. Workers feel competent when they believe they can perform an activity with skill. The belief that they are having an impact comes from a feeling that they can affect work outcomes. A feeling of self-determination arises from workers' belief that they have the autonomy to choose how best to do their work.

Empowerment can lead to changes in organizational processes, because meaning, competence, impact, and self-determination produce empowered employees who take active, rather than passive, roles in their work. At CSX, a large railroad company, accidents, such as knocking railroad cars off the tracks or into each other, were all too com-

At CSX, company employees were empowered to manage the company's safety programs. As a result, train accidents dropped by 20 percent and dismissals resulting from accidents and safety violations fell 65.7 percent.

AP PHOTO/CHRIS GARDNER

mon. When they occurred, management would typically charge employees with wrongdoing and often dismiss them from their jobs. However, in an abrupt turn, CSX has now empowered employees to be completely responsible for safety. Employees, rather than managers, elect other employees to safety committees that are responsible for reviewing accidents. And, instead of charging and dismissing employees who commit accidents, those employee-run safety committees now sit down with employees who were involved in accidents to "casually discuss" what happened. In most cases, employees return to their jobs unpunished. Fearing the company had gone soft, veteran managers expected accident rates to rise. But instead, under the new program, accident rates have fallen by 20 percent and suspensions and dismissals have fallen from 70 to 24 in just one year since CSX empowered employees to improve company safety.[36]

### 4.3 Behavioral Informality

How would you describe the atmosphere in the office in which you last worked? Was it a formal, by-the-book, follow-the-rules, address-each-other-by-last-names atmosphere? Or was it more informal, with an emphasis on results rather than rules, casual business dress rather than suits, and first names rather than last names and titles? Or was it somewhere in between?

Behavioral informality (or formality) is a third influence on intraorganizational processes. **Behavioral informality** refers to workplace situations characterized by spontaneity, casualness, and interpersonal familiarity. By contrast, **behavioral formality** refers to workplace situations characterized by routine and regimen, specific rules about how to behave, and impersonal detachment. Exhibit 11.12 shows that behavioral formality and informality are characterized by four factors: language usage, conversational turn taking and topic selection, emotional and proxemic gestures, and physical and contextual cues. Let's examine each in more detail. [37]

Compared to formal work atmospheres, the language in informal workplaces is often slurred ("Whatcha doin'?"), elliptical ("Coffee?" versus "Would you like some coffee?"), and filled with slang terms and vivid descriptions. People use first names and perhaps nicknames to address each other, rather than Mr., Ms., Dr., or formal titles. When it comes to conversations in informal workplaces, people jump right in when they have something to say (i.e., unregulated turn taking), conversations shift from topic to topic, many of which are unrelated to business, and joking and laughter are common. From joy

**behavioral informality**
workplace atmosphere characterized by spontaneity, casualness, and interpersonal familiarity

**behavioral formality**
workplace atmosphere characterized by routine and regimen, specific rules about how to behave, and interpersonal detachment

EXHIBIT 11.12

DIFFERENCES BETWEEN FORMAL AND INFORMAL WORKPLACES

| FORMAL | INFORMAL |
|---|---|
| **LANGUAGE USAGE** | |
| Fully articulated speech ("What are you doing?") | Phonological slurring ("Whatcha doin'?") |
| Grammatically complete phrasing ("Would you like some coffee?") | Use of elliptical expressions ("Coffee?") |
| Use of formal word choices ("Would you care to dine?") | Use of colloquial and slang expressions ("Wanna grab a bite to eat?") |
| Use of honorifics ("Ms.," "Sir," "Dr.") | Use of the vivid present ("So I come down the stairs, and she says…") |
| Elimination of "I" and "you" (It is requested that…") | First name, in-group names ("Mac," "Bud") |
| **CONVERSATIONAL TURN TAKING AND TOPIC SELECTION** | |
| Turn taking well regulated | Turn taking relatively unregulated |
| Few interruptions or overlaps | Many interruptions or overlaps |
| Few changes of topic | Many shifts of topic possible |
| Seriousness of topic | Joking or conversational levity possible |
| **EMOTIONAL AND PROXEMIC GESTURES** | |
| Sober facial demeanor | Greater latitude of emotional expression |
| Much interpersonal distance | Small interpersonal distance |
| No touching, postural attention | Touching, postural relaxation allowed |
| **PHYSICAL AND CONTEXTUAL CUES** | |
| Formal clothing, shoes, etc. | Informal clothing, shoes, etc. |
| Central focus of attention | Decentralized, multiple centers of attention possible |
| Symmetric arrangement of chairs/furniture | Asymmetric arrangement of chairs/furniture |
| Artifacts related to official status | Informal trappings: flowers, art, food, soft furniture |
| Hushed atmosphere, little background noise | Background noise acceptable |

**Source:** D.A. Morland, "The Role of Behavioral Formality and Informality in the Enactment of Bureaucratic Versus Organic Organizations," *Academy of Management Review* 20 (1995): 831–872. Reproduced by permission of the publisher via Copyright Clearance Center, Inc.

to disappointment, people show much more emotion in informal workplaces. In addition, relaxed expressions, such as putting your feet on your desk or congregating in hallways for impromptu discussions, are more common, too. In terms of physical and contextual cues, informal workplaces de-emphasize differences in hierarchical status or rank to encourage more frequent interaction between organizational members. Consequently, to make their organizations feel less formal, many companies have eliminated what used to be considered "management perks," things like executive dining rooms, reserved parking spaces, and large corner offices separated from most workers because they were located on a higher floor of the company building (the higher the floor, the greater one's status).

Casual dress policies and open office systems are two of the most popular methods for increasing behavioral informality. In fact, a survey conducted by the Society for Human Resource Management indicates that casual dress policies (no suits, ties, jackets,

## Dress for Success the Casual Way

Dressing for success used to be easy. Conservative suits, shirts, blouses, and ties were the norm. Yet, with the popularity of casual dress, many are now unsure what to wear to work. In general, women should not wear denim, leggings, sneakers, tank tops, plunging necklines, or short skirts. Men should not wear jeans, shorts, T-shirts, gym shoes, or sandals. In general, women can wear flat shoes, blazers, and linen slacks or full-skirted dresses. Men can wear pleated pants (i.e., Dockers) with a polo or dress shirt. To be safe, though, always check with coworkers and read your company's casual dress policy.

**Sources:** C. Daniels, "On the Job—Wall Street, Unbuttoned: The Man in the Tan Khaki Pants," *Fortune*, 1 May 2000, 338.

**open office systems**
offices in which the physical barriers that separate workers have been removed in order to increase communication and interaction

**shared spaces**
spaces used by and open to all employees

**private spaces**
spaces used by and open to just one employee

dresses, or formal clothing required) are extremely popular.[38] Today 86 percent of companies have some form of casual dress code compared to 63 percent five years ago. Similarly, 42 percent of all companies permit casual dress at least one day a week compared to 17 percent five years ago. Moreover, compared to 20 percent five years ago, 33 percent of companies permit casual dress every day of the week. Amazingly, even staid, stuffy IBM, known as "Big Blue," in part for the dark blue suits and white shirts traditionally worn by its employees, has gone business casual. So has AT&T. Burke Stinson, an AT&T spokesperson, explained that "Brainpower is more important than appearance, and brainpower is what makes you productive, not a gray flannel suit."[39] Many managers seem to agree. In fact, 85 percent of human resources directors believe that casual dress can improve office morale. Moreover, nearly two-thirds of them believe that casual dress policies are an important tool for attracting qualified employees in tight labor markets. Michael Losey, president of the Society for Human Resource Management, concluded that "for the majority of corporations and industries, allowing casual dress can have clear advantages at virtually no cost."[40]

While casual dress increases behavioral informality by having managers and workers at all levels dress in a more relaxed manner, open office systems increase behavioral informality by significantly increasing the level of communication and interaction among employees. By definition, **open office systems** try to increase interaction by removing physical barriers that separate workers. One characteristic of open office systems is that they have much more shared space than private space. In contrast, **shared spaces** are used by and open to all employees. Cubicles with low-to-the-ground partitions, offices with no doors or with glass walls, collections of comfortable furniture that encourage people to congregate, and common areas with tables and chairs that encourage people to meet, work, or eat together are examples of shared space. **Private spaces**, such as a private office with a door, are used by and open to just one employee.

The advantage of this much-shared space in open offices is that it dramatically increases the amount of unplanned, spontaneous, and chance communication between employees.[41] People are much more likely to plan meetings and work together when numerous "collaboration spaces" with conference tables, white boards, and computers are readily available. With no office walls, with inviting common areas, and with different departments mixed together in large open spaces, spontaneous communication occurs more often. Kit Tuveson of Hewlett-Packard said that open environments encourage "more momentary interaction [than private-office plans] because when people are more easily seen, they are perceived to be more accessible."[42] Also, open office systems increase chance communication by making it much more likely that people from different departments or areas will run into each other. When Alcoa moved its headquarters from a 31-story building with traditional offices to a six-story building with open offices, glass-walled conferences, family-style kitchens on each floor, and escalators instead of elevators, the transformation was dramatic. Then-CEO Paul O'Neill said, "I'd run into three people in the elevator [in the old building] and that's how many people I saw each day—except for those I had scheduled appointments with." But in the new open office design, he says, "I take the escalator down and I see 50 people or 50 people can see me."[43]

However, not everyone is enthusiastic about open offices. For instance, Michael McKay works for an Internet service company and finds it almost impossible to get work done, especially when three of his nearby coworkers all use speakerphones to participate in the same conference call. He said, "You get this stereophonic effect of hearing one person's voice live, and then hearing it coming out of someone else's speakerphone two or three cubes over."[44] Because of disruptions like these, Sun Microsystems and Microsoft give employees private offices so they can concentrate on their work. William Agnello, Sun's vice president of real estate and the workplace, said, "We have researched the heck out of this. Our studies show that, for our engineers, there are just too many distractions and interruptions."[45] Said Microsoft's John Pinette, "Private offices allow our

421

### Hot Desks and Big Savings?

With "hot desks," workers no longer have permanent offices or desks. Using central storage for personal belongings, networks that permit access to work files from any computer, and phone systems that forward permanent phone numbers to any phone, workers are simply assigned to the next empty desk when they arrive for work. Because you sit next to somebody different each day, "hot desks" improve communication. And, in offices where people spend time with customers or working from home, overall office space can be reduced by 30 percent to 45 percent. Would you be willing to give up your desk to achieve these savings?

**Sources:** G. Gordon, "The Hot Desk Shuffle," *The Scotsman,* 15 June 2000, 10.

employees to concentrate on their work and to avoid unnecessary distractions—[which is] obviously critical when you're doing something that requires as much focus as developing software does."[46]

Indeed, because there is so much shared space and so little private space, companies with open systems have to take a number of steps to give employees privacy when they need to concentrate on individual work. One step is to simply use taller cubicles. Indeed, Herman Miller, a manufacturer of office furniture and systems, has seen sales of its 62-inch high cubicle panels increase by 18 percent while sales of its 46-inch high panels have dropped by 19 percent. Another approach is to install white noise machines to prevent voices and other noises from disrupting others.[47] At Procter & Gamble headquarters in Cincinnati the company uses white noise from two interior waterfalls to prevent voices and other noises from disrupting others. In contrast to traditional offices, many employees reserve conference rooms when they need private time to work. Advertising agency GSD&M built 43 conference rooms of varying sizes to give its workers privacy when they needed it. Since most of its employees use laptop computers, they simply unplug from their cubicles and plug back in after reaching the conference room. Account director Nancy Ryan uses the small conference rooms as much as eight times per day to make phone calls, to write, or to have private conversations with employees or clients.[48] At Steelcase, employees and managers can put privacy screens around their work stations (the equivalent of shutting your door in a traditional office), display large "do not disturb" signs, or wear brightly colored earplugs.[49]

### Review 4
#### Intraorganizational Processes

Today, companies are using reengineering, empowerment, and behavioral informality to change their intraorganizational processes. Through fundamental rethinking and radical redesign of business processes, reengineering changes an organization's orientation from vertical to horizontal. Reengineering changes work processes by decreasing sequential and pooled interdependence and by increasing reciprocal interdependence. Reengineering promises dramatic increases in productivity and customer satisfaction, but has been criticized as simply an excuse to cut costs and lay off workers. Empowering workers means taking decision-making authority and responsibility from managers and giving it to workers. Empowered workers develop feelings of competence and self-determination and believe their work to have meaning and impact. Workplaces characterized by behavioral informality are spontaneous and casual. The formality or informality of a workplace depends on four factors: language usage, conversational turn taking and topic selection, emotional and proxemic gestures, and physical and contextual cues. Casual dress policies and open office systems are two of the most popular methods for increasing behavioral informality.

## 5. Interorganizational Processes

**interorganizational process**
a collection of activities that take place among companies to transform inputs into outputs that customers value

An **interorganizational process** is a collection of activities that occur *among companies* to transform inputs into outputs that customers value. In other words, many companies work together to create a product or service that keeps customers happy. For example, when someone purchases a Bennetton sweater at the mall, they're not just buying from Bennetton. A network of small companies supplies Bennetton's factories. And while Bennetton performs weaving, cutting, dyeing, and quality control, another network of small companies provides labor for production tasks, such as tailoring, finishing, and ironing. A worldwide network of retail sales agents selects the Bennetton designs that they feel will sell best in their local markets. In turn, those agents supply Bennetton products to retailers who sell them to consumers. While this network design originated in Italy, it is repeated throughout the world. For example, Bennetton Hungary coordinates the network of production companies in Hungary, Ukraine, the Czech Republic, Poland, Moldavia, Bulgaria, and Romania.[50]

*In this section, you'll explore interorganizational processes by learning about 5.1 modular organizations, 5.2 virtual organizations, and 5.3 boundaryless organizations.[51]*

### 5.1 Modular Organizations

**modular organization**
an organization that outsources noncore business activities to outside companies, suppliers, specialists, or consultants

Except for the core business activities that they can perform better, faster, and cheaper than others, **modular organizations** outsource all remaining business activities to outside companies, suppliers, specialists, or consultants. The term "modular" is used because the business activities purchased from outside companies can be added and dropped as needed, much like adding pieces to a three-dimensional puzzle. Exhibit 11.13 depicts a modular organization in which the company has chosen to keep training, human resources, sales, research and development, information technology, product design, customer service, and manufacturing as core business activities. However, it has chosen to outsource the noncore activities of product distribution, Web page design, advertising, payroll, accounting, and packaging.

Modular organizations have several advantages. First, because modular organizations pay for outsourced labor, expertise, or manufacturing capabilities only when needed, they can cost significantly less to run than traditional organizations. When you buy a

EXHIBIT 11.13

MODULAR ORGANIZATIONS

Outsourced Noncore Business Activities

Product Distribution

Web Page Design

Advertising

Training

Research & Development

Payroll

Human Resources

Information Technology

Customer Service

Accounting

Sales

Product Design

Manufacturing

Packaging

Core Business Activities

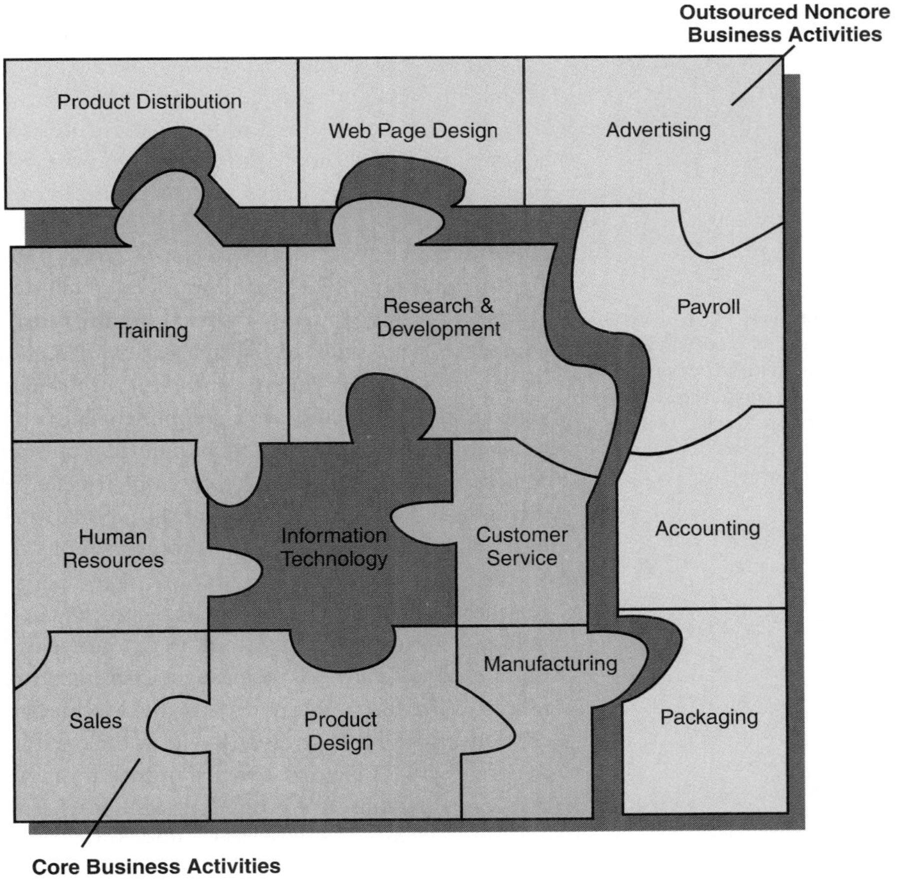

laptop computer from Dell, Gateway, Hewlett-Packard, Apple, or Compaq, the chances are very good that you're really buying a Quanta, a laptop made by Taiwan-based Quanta Computer, the world's largest laptop manufacturer. Why have all of these mainstream computer companies taken a modular approach by using Quanta to manufacture most of their laptops? Because it lets them focus on their core competencies, marketing and order-taking, and because Quanta uses its sophisticated logistics system and design engineers to squeeze costs better than they can. Some computer companies, like Dell, still design their laptops, but leave production and shipping to Quanta. Others prefer to let Quanta do it all. T.J. Fang, Quanta's chief of production, said that some "don't even see the computer. They just sell their brand and collect the money."[52] As for HP, worldwide supply-chain director Jim Burns says that outsourcing to Quanta "saved our business. It was the biggest turnaround in HP's history."[53]

However, to obtain these advantages, several preconditions must be met. The most important is that modular organizations need to work closely with reliable partners, that is, vendors and suppliers that they can trust. While Quanta is able to manufacture laptops more cheaply than Dell, Gateway, Packard-Packard, Apple, or Compaq, these companies would not stay with Quanta if it couldn't quickly deliver high-quality laptops. To consistently meet that goal, Quanta must, in turn, rely on its suppliers. Danny Lin, one of Quanta's production managers said, "If any supplier has a problem, it will destroy your [production] plans."[54] For instance, Quanta used to buy memory chips from Fairchild Semiconductor in Portland, Maine. But because it needed the flexibility of a local supplier, it dropped Fairchild and began purchasing memory chips from Acbel Polytech in Taipei, China. But Acbel understands that if Quanta calls with special orders, it must deliver that order the same day. Danis Yang of Acbel Polytech said, "If I want to get the customer [Quanta], I have to follow the rules. It's very hard."[55]

However, modular organizations have disadvantages, too. The primary disadvantage is the loss of control that occurs when key business activities are outsourced to other companies. Also, companies may reduce their competitive advantage in two ways if they mistakenly outsource a core business activity. First, competitive and technological change may produce a situation in which the noncore business activities a company has outsourced suddenly become the basis for competitive advantage. Second, related to that point, companies to which work is outsourced can sometimes become competitors.

### 5.2 Virtual Organizations

**virtual organization**
an organization that is part of a network in which many companies share skills, costs, capabilities, markets, and customers to collectively solve customer problems or provide specific products or services

By contrast to modular organizations in which the interorganizational process revolves around a central company, a **virtual organization** is part of a network in which many companies share skills, costs, capabilities, markets, and customers with each other. Researchers Eva Kasper-Fuehrer and Neal M. Ashkanasy give this example of a virtual organization: "An executive in a components distribution company based in Germany has to project-manage a new product requiring outsourced manufacture of 150 parts. To achieve this, she enters the Web site of Virtuelle Fabrik Euregic Bodensee (**http://www. virtuelle-fabrik.org**), a virtual infrastructure that facilitates dynamic creation of temporary interorganizational virtual organizations capable of fulfilling complex orders. Virtuelle Fabrik consists of a network of companies centered on the Bodensee region in central-western Europe that facilitates project communication through computer technology. Through Virtuelle Fabrik the executive is able to establish clear roles and responsibilities for all partners, including a legal framework for participating in virtual collaborations. Virtuelle Fabrik notes that this is achieved through 'the development of a partner relationship and thence of trust within the organization.'"[56]

Exhibit 11.14 shows a virtual organization in which, for "today," the parts of a virtual company consist of product design, purchasing, manufacturing, advertising, and information technology. However, unlike modular organizations, in which outside organizations are tightly linked to one central company, virtual organizations work with some

EXHIBIT 11.14

NETWORK ORGANIZATION

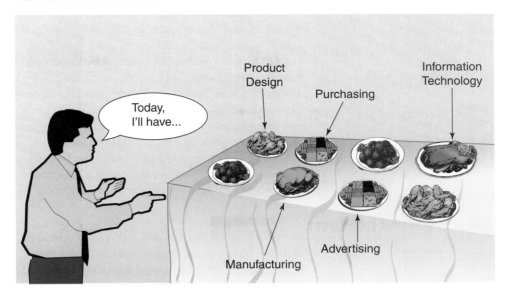

companies in the network alliance, but not with all. So, whereas a puzzle with various pieces is a fitting metaphor for modular organizations, a potluck dinner is an appropriate metaphor for virtual organizations. Everyone brings their finest food dish, but only eats what they want.

Another difference is that the working relationships between modular organizations and outside companies tend to be more stable and longer lasting than the shorter, often temporary relationships found among the virtual companies in a network alliance. Thus, the composition of a virtual organization is always changing. The combination of network partners that a virtual corporation has at any one time simply depends on the expertise needed to solve a particular problem or provide a specific product or service. This is why the businessperson in the network organization shown in Exhibit 11.14 said, "Today, I'll have. . ." Tomorrow, the business could want something completely different. In this sense, the term "virtual organization" means the organization that exists "at the moment." For example, 19 small companies in Pennsylvania have formed a network of virtual organizations that they call the "Agile Web." Together, the companies have expertise in product development and design, machining, metal fabrication, diecasting, plastic-injection molding, finishing and coating, and the design and manufacture of electronic components. Tony Nickel, who coordinates business opportunities for the 19 Web members, said, "We do have multiple machine shops and multiple sheet-metal shops. If only one is needed, I make the decision based on the nature of the [customer's] request and the areas of specialization of the member firms." He added that, "We've already had one occasion where, while negotiating with a customer, we discovered that we really didn't have the right Web member for a particular part—so we changed members."[57]

Virtual organizations have a number of advantages. They let companies share costs. And, because members can quickly combine their efforts to meet customers' needs, they are fast and flexible. For example, Tony Nickel of the Agile Web said, "Where we think we really can have rapid response is when a customer wants help in the design and building of an assembly or system. Then I can bring members of the Web to the table—or to the customer's facility—right away; the next day, if required. We are able to assemble a team from the Web within 24 hours if that is what the customer wants."[58] Finally,

425

because each member of the network alliance is the "best" at what it does, in theory, virtual organizations should provide better products and services in all respects.

Like modular organizations, a disadvantage of virtual organizations is that once work has been outsourced, it can be difficult to control the quality of work done by network partners. However, the greatest disadvantage is that it requires tremendous managerial skills to make a network of independent organizations work well together, especially since their relationships tend to be shorter and task- or project-based. However, virtual organizations are using two methods to solve this problem. The first is to use a *broker*, like Tony Nickel. In traditional, hierarchical organizations, managers plan, organize, and control. But with the horizontal, interorganizational processes that characterize virtual organizations, the job of a broker is to create and assemble the knowledge, skills, and resources from different companies for outside parties, such as customers.[59] The second way to make networks of virtual organizations more manageable is to use a *virtual organization agreement* that, somewhat like a contract, specifies the schedules, responsibilities, costs, and payouts to participating organizations.[60]

### 5.3 Boundaryless Organizations

Former General Electric CEO Jack Welch coined the term "boundaryless organization" in an annual letter to GE shareholders. Welch wrote, "Our dream . . . is a boundaryless company, a company where we knock down the walls that separate us from each other on the inside and from our constituencies on the outside." Why was Welch, arguably one of the most effective CEOs of the last two decades, so concerned with boundaries? Steve Kerr, GE's former vice president of Leadership Development, explained: "Boundaries determine how an organization operates. There are vertical boundaries like floors and ceilings that separate levels of the organization; there are inside walls that separate departments from each other; and there are outside walls that separate the firm from its environment, from its customers, outside regulators, suppliers, and other constituencies."[61] Thus, a **boundaryless organization** would break down the vertical, horizontal, external, and geographic boundaries in organizations.[62]

Exhibit 11.15 shows how a boundaryless organization might work. First, notice that inside the company, in the internal environment, there are no vertical or horizontal relationships. Now, this doesn't mean that there are literally no bosses in boundaryless organizations. It also doesn't mean that lower-level managers and workers aren't responsible to upper-level managers. They are. What it does mean is that in boundaryless organizations the emphasis is on speed, responsiveness, and flexibility rather than who you report to. GE's Steve Kerr said, "In a hierarchy, you're always asking who is the boss. In a boundaryless company, you don't ask that question. It stops being relevant. You ask who has the information that would improve the decision."[63] Second, notice that in Exhibit 11.15, the organization's external boundary, represented by the dotted line, is permeable. Again, the point here is to remove the boundary separating the organization's internal environment from its external environment (i.e., industry regulation, suppliers, customers, competitors, and advocacy groups).

By focusing on results rather than on reporting relationships, boundaryless organizations make much better use of employee knowledge, skills, and abilities. Instead of asking what department or job is "responsible" for a problem, employees ask, "Who inside or outside the company can best solve this problem?" Another advantage is that boundaryless organizations lead to much closer relationships with the components of the company's external environment. For example, one of the ways that GE has made external boundaries more permeable is by putting key managers "on loan" to outside companies. So, instead of reporting to work at a GE office in a GE building, these "on loan" managers report to work at offices that are permanently located in customers' or suppliers' offices or buildings.

However, boundaryless organizations have significant disadvantages as well. To start, managers and employees often find the transition to boundaryless organizations threatening. Managers and workers who are used to the clear accountability and reporting relationships of vertical hierarchies often struggle with the new emphasis on speed and flexibility. However, the biggest disadvantage to boundaryless organizations is that there is no clear

EXHIBIT 11.15

BOUNDARYLESS ORGANIZATIONS

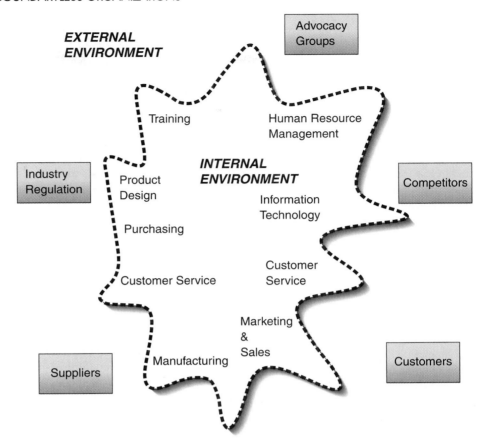

**Source:** Adapted from G.G. Dess, A.M.A. Rasheed, K.J. McLaughlin, & R.L. Priem, "The New Corporate Architecture," *Academy of Management Executive* 9 (1995): 7-18.

427

way to achieve them. The suggested methods read like a list of ingredients: create interdivisional committees, establish communication flows, create mutually beneficial relationships with suppliers and customers, build trust with employees, and so on. Unfortunately, there is little advice on how best to combine and "cook" them.[64]

## Review 5

### Interorganizational Processes

Organizations are using modular, virtual, and boundaryless organizations to change interorganizational processes. Because modular organizations outsource all noncore activities to other businesses, they are less expensive to run than traditional companies. However, modular organizations require extremely close relationships with suppliers, may result in a loss of control, and could create new competitors if the wrong business activities are outsourced. Virtual organizations participate in a network in which they share skills, costs, capabilities, markets, and customers. As customer problems, products, or services change, the combination of virtual organizations that work together changes. Virtual organizations reduce costs, respond quickly, and, if they can successfully coordinate their efforts, can produce outstanding products and service. By breaking down internal and external boundaries, boundaryless organizations try to increase organizational speed, flexibility, and responsiveness. However, boundaryless organizations are threatening to managers and workers, and are difficult to create.

## What Really Happened?

At the beginning of the chapter, you learned that Exide Technologies was having difficulty selecting the correct organizational structure for its business. However, you also learned that such problems weren't unique, that Ford Motor Company's "Ford 2000" plan and that Procter & Gamble's "Organization 2005" plan both intended to establish the correct organizational structure for their companies, but created just as many problems as they solved. Let's find out what really happened at Exide to see if it avoided similar problems when it chose a new organizational structure.

**Which organizational structure should Exide use? Should it stay with a geographical structure, but tinker with it to fix the problems? What would be the advantages or disadvantages of that approach?**

Geographic departmentalization organizes work and workers into separate units responsible for doing business in particular geographical areas. At Exide, this organizing was done by country. For example, Europe, France, Germany, Spain, and Britain all had their own country managers who were responsible for selling and manufacturing Exide batteries. The primary advantage of geographic departmentalization is that it helps companies respond to the demands of different markets. This can be especially important when selling in different countries. However, it wasn't all that important for Exide, whose country managers often sold identical products in regions throughout the world. This was why Mark Stevenson, Exide's country manager for Britain, was able to sell the same batteries in Austria as Exide's country manager for Germany. Indeed, while there were some differences from country to country, those differences were much less important than the larger differences in products across regions, such as Europe, North America, Asia, and South America. Another advantage of geographic departmentalization is that it can re-duce costs by locating unique organizational resources closer to customers.

The primary disadvantage of geographic departmentalization is that it can lead to duplication of resources. This was especially problematic for Exide. Most of Exide's 89 countries had a country manager, production plants, marketing budgets, human resource departments, and so forth. And, despite the duplication that was apparent to everyone, country managers were reluctant to see the problem in their own backyards. For example, Albrecht Leuschner, country manager for Germany's six Exide factories, said, "My region was in good shape. [By changing,] I was afraid we would destroy structure and that would damage the [German] business."

Also, even more so than with the other forms of departmentalization, it can be especially difficult to coordinate geographic departments that are literally thousands of miles from each other or whose managers have very limited contact with each other. In fact, because of its country-based system, Exide had created a geographic structure that encouraged its country managers to maximize their country's profits, even at the expense of Exide's other country managers. For example, with 10 country organizations in Europe alone, the temptation to undercut each other's prices was too tempting. Chairman Robert Lutz said, "[They were] driven to maximize their own results—even if it was at the price of their next-door neighbor, who also was Exide. The guys were poking each other in the eye."

**Or should it use a product structure— what P&G called "global business units"—to standardize what it does around the world? What would be the advantages or disadvantages of this approach?**

Product departmentalization organizes work and workers into separate units responsible for producing particular products or services. One advantage of product departmentalization is that, like functional departmentalization, it allows managers and workers to special-ize in one area of expertise. However, unlike the narrow expertise and experiences in functional departmentalization, managers and workers develop a broader set of experiences and expertise related to an entire product line. Likewise, product departmentalization makes it easier for top managers to assess work-unit performance. Finally, because managers and workers are responsible for the entire product line rather than for separate functional departments, decision making should be faster because there are fewer conflicts.

The primary disadvantage of product departmentalization is duplication. A second disadvantage is that it can be difficult to achieve coordination across the different product departments.

After dumping its country-based geographic structure, Exide implemented a product structure around global business units based on its two core product lines, industrial applications and transportation. Industrial applications included (A) network-power batteries for telecommunications systems, fuel-cell load leveling, electric utilities, railroads, photovoltaic (solar-power related), and uninterruptible power supply (UPS) markets, and (B) motive-power batteries for a broad range of equipment uses, including lift trucks, mining vehicles and commercial vehicles. Transportation uses included (C) automotive, heavy-duty truck, agricultural, marine and other batteries; and (D) new technologies developed for hybrid vehicles and new 42-volt automotive applications.

However, just like Ford and Procter & Gamble, Exide seemed to overlook the effect a switch from country management to a product structure would have on its managers. For instance, after the change, most of its country managers were demoted to the job of local coordinator, which was a huge step down for people used to running their own areas. When Chairman Lutz announced, "We don't have 100 percent consensus yet. . . . But I'm going to make a decision, and we are going to go to a global business unit structure," his decision was greeted with immediate dissatisfaction. When Lutz asked a forlorn Eduardo Garnica, Exide's country manager in Spain, "Why don't you give it a try?" Garnica responded, "No, I'm out of here," and soon quit his job with the company. At dinner that same evening, Giovani Mele, Exide's country manager for Italy told two other country managers, "Being a country manager is my life. It's something I've worked for my whole life. I don't see how I'll have a role going forward." Furthermore, after Exide reduced his role, it moved his job from Italy to Frankfurt, Germany. His family, which refused to leave Italy, has remained in Naples.

### When will Exide know when it has found the right organizational structure?

Ironically, Exide's new global business unit structure (i.e., product structure) only lasted six weeks. Albrecht Leuschner from Germany was one of the few country managers promoted to head a global business unit. He said, "For six weeks, I was emperor of the world." But then Exide bought GNB Technologies, another international manufacturer of batteries. Because Exide did not want to lose Mitchell Bregman, president of GNB's industrial-battery division, it changed its organizational structure once again to provide him a role with significant responsibilities. Said Chairman Robert Lutz, "If we had been rigid about our organizational framework, we would have broken up GNB."

Lutz's solution was to choose an organizational structure that swung back to a focus on geography. But instead of returning to a country-based structure, Exide's six new global business units (i.e., product structures) were rearranged into five global divisions, North America, South America, Europe, Asia, and Africa. However, this organizational structure was in place for less than a year before the company replaced it with three "global power groups," which returned the company full circle to a strict product structure. The Global Network Power Group, based in Lombard, Illinois, provides unique product and service solutions to the communications and data, industrial and security, and government segments of the network-power market, including stationary hybrid electric-power generation applications. Mitchell S. Bregman, who was with GNB Technologies has been named president. The Global Motive Power Group, based in Manchester, England, provides unique, total energy management solutions to the original-equipment and aftermarket segments of the material handling, access equipment, and electric-powered vehicle markets. Last, the Global Transportation Business Group, based in Atlanta, Georgia, provides unique products and services to both the original-equipment and aftermarket segments of the automotive, heavy truck, agriculture, construction, and marine markets. This division will also will lead Exide's efforts in developing system solutions

for emerging 42-volt and hybrid energy management applications.

According to Chairman Lutz, the latest reorganization is "definitely working far better than what we had." But when will Exide know that it has the right structure? In general, companies know they have the right structure when responsibilities are clear to those in and out of the company, when problems are quickly solved, when efficiencies increase, and when people in the company become comfortable in their roles. But, as Exide's experiences shows, finding a proper organizational structure can be difficult. In fact, President Craig Mulhauser said, "Come back a year from now and we will look different. We were searching for the Holy Grail. But there isn't one."

**Sources:** E. Nelson, "Rallying the Troops at P&G—New CEO Lafley Aims to End Upheaval by Revamping Program of Globalization," *The Wall Street Journal*, 31 August 2000, B1. "Exide Technologies Announces Restructuring: Focuses on Global Customer Business Units," *Exide Technologies.* [Online] Available http://www.exide.com/news/pressrelease/general/20011017_exide_restructuring.html, 11 November 2001. J. Lublin, "Division Problem, Place Vs. Product: It's Tough to Choose a Management Model—Exide Tore Up System Based on Countries for One Centered on Battery Lines—Rolling over European Fiefs," *The Wall Street Journal*, 27 June 2001, A1. R. Simison, "Ford Hopes Its New Focus Will Be a Global Bestseller—Escort's Replacement Offers Improvements for Same Price," *The Wall Street Journal*, 8 October 1998, B10. "The History of Exide Technologies," *Exide Technologies.* [Online] Available http://www.exide.com/about/history.html, 11 November 2001.

## Key Terms

authority *(404)*
autonomy *(412)*
behavioral formality *(419)*
behavioral informality *(419)*
boundaryless organization *(426)*
centralization of authority *(407)*
chain of command *(404)*
complex matrix *(404)*
customer departmentalization *(399)*
decentralization *(408)*
delegation of authority *(405)*
departmentalization *(395)*

empowering workers *(418)*
empowerment *(418)*
feedback *(412)*
functional departmentalization *(395)*
geographic departmentalization *(399)*
internal motivation *(411)*
interorganizational process *(422)*
intraorganizational process *(416)*
job characteristics model (JCM) *(411)*
job design *(409)*
job enlargement *(411)*
job enrichment *(411)*

job rotation *(410)*
job specialization *(409)*
line authority *(405)*
line function *(405)*
matrix departmentalization *(401)*
mechanistic organization *(415)*
modular organization *(423)*
open office systems *(421)*
organic organization *(415)*
organizational process *(392)*
organizational structure *(392)*
pooled interdependence *(417)*

## What Would You Do-II

### Clear Organization Structure?

Spent much time stuck in traffic lately? Chances are, you have. Over the last 30 years, the U.S. population has grown by 23 percent, the number of cars per household has increased by 49 percent, and the number of daily car trips has increased by 82 percent. Put that all together, stir and mix, and the number of vehicles on the road has increased by 128 percent! While drivers and passengers hate traffic jams, radio stations and advertisers love them because they create a captive audience that turns to the radio for entertainment (and yes, traffic reports).

Thanks to recent mergers with AMFM Radio, Inc. and Katz Media, Clear Channel Radio is one of the largest radio companies in the United States. Clear Channel's 1,170 radio stations reach 110 million people each week in 47 of the United States's top 50 radio markets, offering everything from news/talk to country to new wave formats. Clear Channel's mission is to broadcast the best programming to the broadest audience while providing the best value to advertisers.

Because of its size and reach, Clear Channel has several advantages over its competitors. First, advertisers like Budweiser, Procter & Gamble, and General Motors can cheaply reach a national market by advertising with one company instead of thousands of separate radio stations. Second, in addition to its national reach, Clear Channel also allows advertisers to target particular market segments, such as news/talk, easy listening,

country, and so forth. For instance, Bose, which directly markets high-end radio and stereo equipment to consumers, has had great success advertising on radio stations using the news/talk format. Finally, Clear Channel balances national and market segment advertising with local advertising.

Although the mergers have given Clear Channel national broadcast coverage in a variety of formats, organizing a vast, new radio empire into a workable structure has its challenges. President and COO John Hogan knows this only too well. He must design a new organization for Clear Channel that will make sense for such a large company. Should he consider a geographic form of departmentalization (since Clear Channel is a national company), or a product form that will organize stations according to formats? Maybe another form makes even more sense, like dividing music, advertising, and technology functions. Which form of departmentalization is most appropriate? Whatever the choice, it needs to be hashed out soon: The board of directors is meeting next week to review Hogan's proposal and the rationale behind it. What should Hogan recommend? **If you were the COO of Clear Channel, which structure would you recommend?**

**Sources:** "Clear Channel: Radio," *Clear Channel.* [Online] Available http://www.clearchannel.com/radio/index.html, January 6, 2002. J. Hiestand, "Clear Channel Restructures Radio Advertising Operations," *Hollywood Reporter*, 28 August 2001, 47. D. Trigoboff, "Clearheadedly Restructuring," *Broadcasting & Cable*, 3 September 2001, 12.

## Management Decisions

### Outsource or Not?

As you gaze out the windshield of your car while stopped at a red light, you think back on how simple life used to be. Several years ago when you started your small manufacturing company, life was tough, but it wasn't as hectic as it is today. You started your company, which builds partially assembled furniture and components, on a shoestring with only a few employees. Even though everyone worked 15-hour days, six or seven days a week, things still seemed easier back then. Now that your firm has grown and is finally turning a healthy profit, your average workday has dropped to around 10 hours per day. Because of sustained growth, you have distanced yourself from the physical production of the product. Instead, you now spend your time wandering around the factory, looking for ways to streamline the production process, speed up delivery time, improve quality, and solve any other logistical or systems problems that crop up.

One area that is in need of immediate attention is the customer service department. It seems that customer service issues

and questions quadrupled overnight. In the beginning, you and your spouse used to take turns returning the occasional customer complaint, question, or request for additional information. When the volume of customer service requests began to consume a large portion of both your work routines, you hired a full-time customer service representative to take over. Today, the company has four full-time customer service reps on staff and is still experiencing long periods of delays and complaints because customers can't get through in a timely basis.

Of course, one easy solution is to outsource the customer service function to an outside agency. An external agency that specializes in customer service is likely better prepared to handle the ever-increasing number of customer service calls and could possibly do so for the same cost you are paying now. Outsourcing is not new to you. During the enormous growth cycle your company has experienced over the last two years, you have outsourced a number of functions within the firm, including accounting, personnel, payroll, and maintenance. You thought those were easy decisions because each required only a little time each month to perform. In addition, the cost to you of staffing and performing those functions internally significantly outweighed any benefits received. Since you made your decision to outsource those areas, you have been delighted with the service that you receive and have not had to micromanage the providers' results.

Unfortunately, you believe customer service is different. It is a daily activity—sometimes a 24/7 activity—not to mention that it requires specific and detailed knowledge of the 115 products you produce. Your customer service reps are not only well-versed in your product lines, but they are also able to decipher the sometimes-incomprehensible instructions that accompany your products, a critical part of resolving many customer-related issues. You take pride in the fact that two of the four customer service reps have been with you from the start and are good at defusing potentially bad situations. These two individuals can usually turn a disgruntled customer into a happy one and do it without giving away the store. You're afraid that if you outsource the CS department, you'll lose that ability and jeopardize the loyalty of these two employees. On the other hand, you see your market share declining as frustrated customers flock to the competition. You've got to decide.

**Questions**

1. What factors would you consider before determining whether to outsource the customer service department or not? What advantages and disadvantages are there to outsourcing activities?
2. What would you do? Why?
3. If you choose to outsource the customer service department, how could you control the performance of the outsourcing agency?

**Sources:** S. Bothe, "Outsourcing for Small and Mid-Sized Businesses," *The CPA Journal*, May 2001. J. Bowles, "Build or Outsource?," *Customer Interface*, June 2001. E. Garaventa and T. Tellefsen, "Outsourcing: The Hidden Costs," *Review of Business*, Spring 2001.

## Management Decisions

### Plush Management Perks: Partaking or Pruning?

"They do, too!" "*They do not!*" "You don't know what you're talking about." "*See, it's attitudes like yours that prove my point!*"

Ah, nothing like watching your two top executives argue during lunch to raise your blood pressure. You knew that Sam, the VP of Sales, was going to get mad when Catherine, the VP of Human Resources, suggested getting rid of executive perks (the private dining room, company cars, first-class air travel, etc.). It took Sam 25 years to become a vice president and nobody, including Sam, wants to see his or her perks and rewards reduced. However, you didn't think it was possible for someone to get that mad that fast. Given the way Sam's face instantly turned beet red when Catherine suggested that the reserved parking spaces be eliminated, it's a good thing she caught him between bites or he might have choked on his shrimp salad.

Well, with executive perks topping the agenda for the annual executive retreat next weekend, Sam and Catherine's argument has given you something to think about. Is Catherine right? Do all executive perks need to be eliminated? Or is Sam right? Do the executive perks need to be left alone? After all, even Catherine got defensive when Sam asked her how happy she'd be if the company closed its on-site day care. When she responded, "They wouldn't dare do that," Sam barked, "That's exactly the way I feel about your recommendations!"

Well, you need to get your thoughts sorted out. A good place to start is with the list of executive perks currently being offered by the company:

- company cars
- reserved parking spaces
- company cellular phones
- personal financial counseling
- personal liability insurance
- executive dining room
- first-class air travel
- spouse travel on extended business trips
- signing bonuses
- stock options
- country club memberships
- large, expensively furnished private offices
- home security systems
- home computer/office equipment

**Questions**

1. Of the perks listed above, choose three that your managers are most likely to desire. In other words, which three executive perks would your managers scream the most about if you took them away? Explain your reasoning for each of your three choices.
2. Of the perks listed above, which three probably create the most resentment among your work force (i.e., nonmanagers)? In other words, which three executive perks anger your work force the most? Explain your reasoning for each of your three choices.
3. Of the options below (a, b, or c) choose one that is likely to benefit the company most in the long run:

    a. eliminate all executive perks
    b. retain all executive perks
    c. selectively eliminate perks

    Explain your reasoning behind your choice. If you choose option "c," specify the perks you kept and why you kept them.

**Sources:** M. Budman, "The Persistence of Perks," *Across the Board*, 1 February 1994. L. Fleeson, "In Today's Efficient, Egalitarian Offices, Plush Perks Are Passe," *The News Tribune*, 10 July 1994. S. Lohr, "Cubicle or Cavern? Egalitarian Work Space Duels with Need for Privacy Among Brainy Folks in High-Tech Firms," *Rocky Mountain News*, 7 September 1997. T. Schellhardt, "Executive Pay (A Special Report)—Passing of Perks: Company Cars, Country Club Memberships, Executive Dining Rooms; Where Have All the Goodies Gone?" *The Wall Street Journal*, 13 April 1994.

# Develop Your Managerial Potential

## "Work" in Someone Else's Shoes

Why is learning to see things from someone else's perspective one of the most difficult things to do in today's workplace? Sometimes, the inability to see things as others see them has to do with the people involved. Inexperience, ignorance, and self-ishness can all play a role. However, in most organizations, the inability to see things from someone else's perspective results from the jobs themselves, not the people who do them. Because jobs limit who we talk to, what we talk about, what we think about, and what we care about at work, it should not be a sur-prise that people who perform different jobs have very different views about each other and the workplace.

For example, at Southwest Airlines the pilots who fly the planes and the ground crews who unload, load, and refuel them had little appreciation for each other. The ground crews felt that the pilots treated them like second-class citizens. The pilots couldn't understand why the ground crews weren't doing more to get their planes out of the gates and in the air as fast as possi-ble. To improve understanding and help them see things from each other's perspective, Southwest created a program called the "Cutting Edge," in which the captains and ground crews learned a lot about each other's jobs. For example, the pilots brought the ground crews into their cockpits and showed them the detailed processes they were required to follow to get planes ready for departure. The pilots, on the other hand, gained ap-preciation and understanding by actually working as members of Southwest's ground crews. After several days of demanding ground crew work, Southwest pilot Captain Mark Boyter said:

> I remember one time when I was working the ramp [as a member of a ground crew] in Los Angeles. I was dead tired. I had flown that morning and had a couple of legs in, so I got out of my uniform and jumped into my ramp clothes. That afternoon was very hot. It was in the 80s—I can't imagine how they do it on a 120-degree day in Phoenix. I was tired and hungry and hadn't had a break. Then I saw this pilot sitting up there in the cockpit eating his frozen yogurt. I said to myself, "Man, I'd like to be up there now." Then I caught myself. I'm up there every day. Now, I know that pilot has been up since

3:00 in the morning. I know that he's been flying an airplane since 6:00 A.M. I know it's 3:00 in the after-noon and he hasn't had a chance to get off and have a meal yet today. I know all that, and yet, the yogurt still looks really good to me. Then I thought, "How can a ramp agent [on the ground crew] in Los Ange-les who works his butt off for two or three years, working double shifts two or three times a week, un-derstand this? It hit me that there's a big gap in un-derstanding here.

The misunderstandings between Southwest's pilots and ground crews are not unique. All organizations experience them. Nurses and doctors, teachers and students, and managers and employees all have difficulty seeing things from each other's perspective. However, as Southwest's Cutting Edge pro-gram shows, you can minimize differences and build under-standing by "working" in someone else's shoes.

## Questions

1. Describe the job-related differences or tensions where you work. Who is involved? What jobs do they do? Explain why the job-related differences or tensions exist.
2. Since the best way to see things from someone else's perspec-tive is to "work" in his or her shoes, see if you can spend a day, a morning, or even two hours performing one of these jobs. If that's not possible, spend some time carefully observ-ing the jobs and then interview several people who perform them. Describe your boss's reaction to this request. Was he or she supportive or not? Why?
3. Answer the following questions after you have worked the job or conducted your interviews. What most surprised you about this job? What was easiest? What was hardest? Ex-plain. Now that you've had the chance to see things as others see them, what do you think would happen, good or bad, from letting other people in your organization work in someone else's shoes? Explain.

**Sources:** K. Freiberg & J. Freiberg, *Nuts! Southwest Airlines' Crazy Recipe for Business and Personal Success* (Austin, TX: Bard Press, 1996).

## Study Tip

Take advantage of all the review opportunities on the *Manage-ment* Web site at **http://williams.swcollege.com**. Write up a list of questions you have about concepts you don't understand and visit your professor or TA during office hours. For this chapter, you have an Xtra! CNN clip with case and solutions on your CD. Watch the segment on seeking patents for business models, then work the case and its questions.

# 4 PART

## Organizing People, Projects, and Processes

# 12

CHAPTER

*outline*

# twelve

# Managing Individuals and a Diverse Work Force

## What Would You Do?

**Denny's Restaurants.** It's 1:00 in the morning. Thirty-two African-American high-school students arrive at a Denny's restaurant after attending an NAACP-sponsored (National Association for the Advancement of Colored People) conference about college life at nearby San Jose State University. After letting the restaurant staff know that they had an oversized group, the manager tells the students that the restaurant has a "pre-payment policy," allegedly because some late-night customers eat and then leave without paying, and that there was also a $2 cover charge for each person. However, white customers in nearby booths are not asked to pay a cover charge nor to prepay.

Twenty-one uniformed Secret Service agents, on their way to the Naval Academy in Annapolis, Maryland, to set up security for then-President Bill Clinton, enter an uncrowded Denny's restaurant around 7:00 A.M. Seven of the 21 are African American. All 21 Secret Service agents are seated in the same section of the restaurant. Everyone's food is quickly delivered, except for the food ordered by the six African-American Secret Service agents sitting together at one table. After half an hour, Agent Robin Thompson enquires twice about their food. Each time

the waitress rolls her eyes as she walks away. After 45 minutes, they are still without food, while white customers who entered the restaurant 30 minutes later are already eating. As they leave the restaurant, having not eaten, the agents ask the manager for the address and phone number of the Denny's regional office.

Rachel Thompson, an African-American youth, asks her family to celebrate her thirteenth birthday at Denny's so she can have waffles and an ice cream sundae for dinner. Rachel's parents and her two younger brothers arrive to a nearly empty restaurant. Because Denny's is promoting "free food on your birthday," they have brought Rachel's baptism certificate as proof that she turned 13 that day. The waitress, who doesn't greet them, demands to know what they want to eat. When they present Rachel's baptism certificate so that her meal can be free, the waitress storms off to get the manager. The manager demands proof of Rachel's birthdate, but refuses to take the certificate offered by Rachel's mother. He demands to see Rachel's school I.D. and then refuses it when offered. When the increasingly angry manager begins yelling, the distraught family leaves the restaurant. Rachel's mother, Susan, later said, "I was angry, outraged at what happened. I felt insulted. You have to have lived it to know how it felt. . . . The pain [was] too great,

especially on my daughter's thirteenth birthday, her first as a teenager."

Unfortunately, just before you became CEO of Advantica, the company that now owns Denny's, dozens of stories like this were reported. In fact, after news stories broke about the Secret Service agents being denied service, comedian Jay Leno joked on the *Tonight Show*, "Denny's is offering a new sandwich called the Discriminator. It's a hamburger, and you order, and then they don't serve it to you." Following these incidents and the intense negative publicity, lawsuits were filed. Flagstar Companies, which owned Denny's restaurants at the time, settled the suits out of court, eventually paying a total of $54 million in damages. While the payouts took care of those situations, the core problems still remain. For instance, you just received reports that some Denny's restaurant managers use the term "blackout" as a code word to indicate to employees that there are "too many" African-American customers in the restaurant. Compounding the problem, some of Denny's district managers have told their restaurant managers to "start cracking down and get rid of some of those blackouts."

As Advantica's new CEO, you were hired to change the company's reputation and its culture. But what should you do?

Should you focus on diversity? Many people aren't sure what "diversity" means. Ask 10 different people and you're likely to get 10 different answers. If you can't explain what diversity means, how can you make effective changes throughout the company? What kinds of things go into a diversity plan? Are there key ideas or principles that you could follow? Finally, what initial steps could you take as a leader to communicate that things will change and that all Denny's customers are entitled to excellent food and service?

**If you were the new CEO at Advantica, what would you do?**

**Sources:** J. Adamson, R. McNatt, R. McNatt, *The Denny's Story: How a Company in Crisis Resurrected Its Good Name* (New York: Wiley, 2000).C. Chen, J. Jonathan, E. LeBlanc, L. Vanderkam, & K. VellaZarb, "America's 50 Best Companies for Minorities," *Fortune*, 10 July 2000, 190. F. Esposito, S. Garman, J. Hickman, N. Watson, & A. Wheat, "America's 50 Best Companies for Minorities," *Fortune*, 9 July 2001, 122. B. Holden, "Denny's Chain Settles Suits by Minorities," *The Wall Street Journal*, 24 May 1994, A3. A. Lengel, "Denny's Daring Entree: Eatery, NE Hope to Improve Image," *Washington Post*, 21 September 2000, A1. J. Mitchell, "Los Angeles Family Sues Denny's, Alleges Bias Court: Suit Says Large Group Was Denied Service as Whites Were Being Seated," *Los Angeles Times*, 24 August 2001. P. Ridge, "A Special Background Report on Trends in Industry," *The Wall Street Journal*, 27 April 2000, A1. D. Segal, "Denny's Serves Up a Sensitive Image: Restaurant Chain Launches PR Drive to Show Minorities It Has Changed Its Ways," *Washington Post*, 7 April 1999, E1.

As we begin a new millennium, predictions abound about advances in medicine and computer technology, the possibility of finding life on other planets, and the chances of another world war. However, one prediction that is already beginning to come true is that workplace diversity will increase dramatically in this new millennium.

For example, Exhibit 12.1 shows estimates from the U.S. Bureau of the Census that indicate that the percentage of white, non-Hispanic Americans in the general

---

**EXHIBIT 12.1**

PREDICTED U.S. POPULATION, DISTRIBUTED BY RACE, 2000 TO 2070

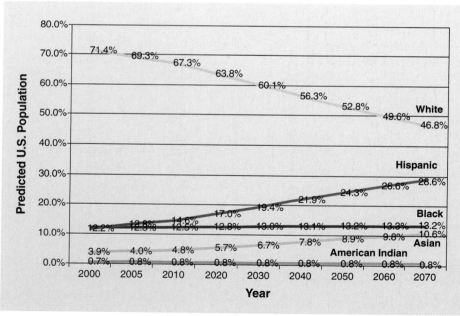

**Sources:** "Projections of the Resident Population by Race, Hispanic Origin, and Nativity: Middle Series, 1999 and 2000, 2001-2005, 2006-2010, 2011-2015, 2016-2020, 2025-2045, 2050-2070," U.S. Census Bureau. [Online] Available http://www.census.gov/population/projections/nation/summary/np-t5-a.txt, http://www.census.gov/population/projections/nation/summary/np-t5-b.txt, http://www.census.gov/population/projections/nation/summary/np-t5-c.txt, http://www.census.gov/population/projections/nation/summary/np-t5-e.txt, http://www.census.gov/population/projections/nation/summary/np-t5-f.txt, http://www.census.gov/population/projections/nation/summary/np-t5-g.txt.

population will decline from 71.4 percent in 2000 to 46.8 percent by the year 2070. By contrast, the percentage of African Americans in the general population will increase from 12.2 percent to 13.2 percent over the same period. The proportion of American Indians (0.7 percent to 0.8 percent) and Asians (3.9 percent to 10.6 percent) is also increasing. The fastest growing group by far, though, is Hispanics, who will increase from 11.8 percent of the total population in 2000 to an estimated 28.6 percent by 2070.

Other significant changes are expected, too. For example, women will hold half the jobs in the United States by 2005, up from 38.2 percent in 1970.[1] Furthermore, the percentage of white males in the work force, who comprised 63.9 percent of all workers in 1950, will drop to just 38.2 percent of the total work force by 2005.[2]

These represent rather dramatic changes in a relatively short time. And these trends clearly show that the work force of the near future will be more Hispanic, Asian, African American, and female. However, it will also be older, as the average "baby boomer" approaches the age of 60 around 2010. Since many of these boomers are likely to postpone retirement and work well into their 70s in order to offset predicted reductions in Social Security and Medicare benefits, the work force may become even older than expected.[3]

This chapter begins with a review of work force diversity—what it is and why it matters. Next, you will learn about two basic dimensions of diversity: surface-level diversity, or how age, gender, race/ethnicity, and mental and physical disabilities affect people at work; and deep-level diversity, how core personality differences influence behavior and attitudes. In the last section, you will learn how diversity can be managed. Here, you'll read about diversity paradigms, principles, and practices that help managers strengthen the diversity *and* the competitiveness of their organizations.

# Diversity and Why It Matters

**diversity**
a variety of demographic, cultural, and personal differences among an organization's employees and the customers

Diversity means variety. Therefore, **diversity** exists in organizations when there is a variety of demographic, cultural, and personal differences among the people who work there and the customers who do business there. For example, step into Longo Toyota in El Monte, California, one of Toyota's top-selling dealerships, and you'll find diversity in the form of salespeople who speak Spanish, Korean, Arabic, Vietnamese, Hebrew, and Mandarin Chinese. In fact, the 60 salespeople at Longo Toyota speak 20 different languages. Surprisingly, this level of diversity was achieved without a formal diversity plan in place.[4]

By contrast, some companies lack diversity, either in their work force or their customers. For example, as you learned in the chapter introduction, Advantica, the parent company of Denny's restaurants, paid $54.4 million to settle a class-action lawsuit alleging discriminatory treatment of black customers at Denny's restaurants. Shoney's, another restaurant company, paid $132.8 million for wrongly rejecting job applicants on the basis of race. Edison International, a California-based utility company, paid more than $11 million for the same mistake. And phone company Bell Atlantic paid a whopping $500 million to black employees who were unfairly passed over for promotions.[5] (Bell Atlantic and GTE have now merged and become Verizon Communications.)

Today, however, Advantica, Shoney's, Bell Atlantic, and Edison International have made great improvements in their level of diversity. At Advantica, all the company's charitable contributions now go to organizations that benefit minorities. At Shoney's, Bell Atlantic, and Edison International, minorities now comprise 30 percent, 17 percent, and 25 percent, respectively, of all managers. In fact, Advantica, Shoney's, Edison International, and Bell Atlantic have increased their diversity so much that all recently made *Fortune* magazine's list of 50 best companies for minorities.[6]

*After reading this next section, you should be able to*
1. describe diversity and why it matters.

# 1. Diversity: Differences That Matter

*You'll begin your exploration of diversity by learning 1.1 that diversity is not affirmative action and 1.2 how to build a business case for diversity.*

## 1.1 Diversity Is Not Affirmative Action

**affirmative action**
purposeful steps taken by an organization to create employment opportunities for minorities and women

A common misconception is that workplace diversity and affirmative action are the same. However, diversity and affirmative action are different in several critical ways. To start, **affirmative action** is purposeful steps taken by an organization to create employment opportunities for minorities and women.[7] By contrast, diversity exists in organizations when there is a variety of demographic, cultural, and personal differences among the people who work there and the customers who do business there. So one key difference is that affirmative action is more narrowly focused on demographics such as gender and race, while diversity has a broader focus that includes demographic, cultural, and personal differences. Furthermore, diversity can exist even if organizations don't take purposeful steps to create it. For example, you learned that the 60 salespeople at Longo Toyota speak 20 different languages. However, Longo Toyota achieved this level of diversity without using a formal affirmative action program. Likewise, a local restaurant located near a university in a major city is likely to have a more diverse group of employees than one located in a small town. So, organizations can achieve diversity without affirmative action. Likewise, organizations that take affirmative action to create employment opportunities for women and minorities may not yet have diverse work forces.

Another important difference is that affirmative action is required by law for private employers with 15 or more employees, while diversity is not. Affirmative action originated with the 1964 Civil Rights Act that bans discrimination in voting, public places, federal government programs, federally supported public education, and employment. Title VII of the Civil Rights Act (**http://www.eeoc.gov/laws/vii.html**) requires that workers have equal employment opportunities when being hired or promoted. More specifically, Title VII prohibits companies from discriminating on the basis of race, color, religion, sex, or national origin. Furthermore, Title VII created the Equal Employment Opportunity Commission (**http://www.eeoc.gov**) to administer these laws. By contrast, there is no federal law or agency to oversee diversity. Organizations that pursue diversity goals and programs do so voluntarily. For example, Fannie Mae, an organization that makes it easier and cheaper for lower-income families to purchase mortgages for home ownership, has pursued a diverse work force and customer base because, in the words of its CEO Jim Johnson, it is "morally right."[8]

Affirmative action programs and diversity programs also have different purposes. The purpose of affirmative action programs is to compensate for past discrimination, which was widespread when legislation was introduced in the 1960s; to prevent ongoing discrimination; and to provide equal opportunities to all, regardless of race, color, religion, gender, or national origin. Organizations that fail to uphold these laws may be required to

- hire, promote, or give back pay to those not hired or promoted;
- reinstate those who were wrongly terminated;
- pay attorneys' fees and court costs for those who brought charges against them; or
- take other actions that make individuals whole by returning them to the condition or place they would have been had it not been for discrimination.[9]

Consequently, affirmative action is basically a punitive approach.[10] By contrast, as shown in Exhibit 12.2, the general purpose of diversity programs is to create a positive work environment where no one is advantaged or disadvantaged, where "we" is everyone, where everyone can do their best work, where differences are respected and not ignored, and

EXHIBIT 12.2

## GENERAL PURPOSE OF DIVERSITY PROGRAMS

To create a positive work environment where

- no one is advantaged or disadvantaged.
- "we" is everyone.
- everyone can do their best work.
- differences are respected and not ignored.
- everyone feels comfortable.

**Source:** T. Roosevelt, "From Affirmative Action to Affirming Diversity," *Harvard Business Review* 68, no. 2 (1990): 107-117.

where everyone feels comfortable.[11] So, unlike affirmative action, which punishes companies for not achieving specific gender and race ratios in their work forces, diversity programs seek to benefit both organizations and their employees by encouraging organizations to value all kinds of differences.

At this time, affirmative action programs are substantially more controversial than diversity programs.[12] Despite their overall success in making workplaces much fairer than they used to be,[13] many people, including the courts (see *Hopwood v. State of Texas*[14]) and some states, have viewed some affirmative action programs as offering preferential treatment to females and minorities at the expense of other employees. For example, California Proposition 209, approved by state voters, bans race- and gender-based affirmative action in college admissions, government hiring, and government contracting programs. Jake Weiss, a white worker in Jericho, New York, said, "It used to be if you were white, you got everything in America and that wasn't right. But now [with affirmative action], all that's left for people like me are the crumbs."[15] Christopher Katzenback, an attorney in a San Francisco law firm, said, "I think people want to be evaluated on their merits, not their race or gender, and that is the driving force behind a lot of this [reverse discrimination] litigation."[16]

**439**

Affirmative action programs are substantially more controversial than diversity programs, but the former are finding some surprising proponents. Members of the group called "Angry White Guys for Affirmative Action" ostensibly support affirmative action because without it, reverse discrimination lawsuits lose some strength. The group publicly opposed California Proposition 209.

AP PHOTO/BOB GALBRAITH

# BeenThereDoneThat

## Diversity at 7-Eleven

Jeanne Hitchcock is Southland Corporation's manager of urban affairs. In this interview, she discusses how Southland manages diversity at its headquarters and its thousands of 7-Eleven stores.

**Q:** Sometimes the whole topic of diversity gets bogged down in a heavy, sociopolitical debate about affirmative action. Is managing diversity as unpleasant as the controversy that sometimes surrounds it?

**A:** No. We have fun at 7-Eleven. It's a new 7-Eleven. We've been able to capture and profit from the differences of our various constituencies. I'd say to other corporations who are standing on the sidelines: try it, you'll like it!

**Q:** Is diversity a business imperative?

**A:** Absolutely. We certainly recognize that at 7-Eleven. If you are a forward-thinking company, if you want to be profitable, if you want growth, if you want efficiency in your operation, if you want an intelligent, skilled work force, then you are going to have to learn to manage a work force and service a consumer base that are becoming increasingly diverse. The question lies not so much in your philosophy regarding race relations or affirmative action and those kinds of principles, but how well can you manage change? How well can you identify it? And how well can you adjust to it? For those who can't, I suggest that they will not be successful entrepreneurs in the 21st century.

**Q:** Isn't that part of how you came to the Southland Corporation, as an agent of change?

**A:** No. Southland has been profitable over the years because it has always been willing to identify and adjust to change. Everything about our business principles continues to reflect that today. We have a new look, a new merchandising system, and a new distribution system, and we have been a diverse franchise system for a long, long time. Over 40 percent of our franchisees are ethnic minorities and over half are women. So Southland was a pioneer in managing diversity before it became popular to do so. It wasn't a hard sell for me to agree to join the Southland team when I could look around and see diversity as a natural part of the way we do business.

**Q:** We still hear talk about the corporate glass ceiling, which forces the best women and minorities to leave a company because the environment does not foster or promote their own growth. Can diversity training programs help alleviate these problems? Is that a good place to start?

**A:** It is, if that's what's needed. Southland did that in the '80s. Everyone from the CEO all the way down through the organization went through diversity training. But diversity training for management has evolved over the years. What we're looking to do now is manage diversity from a skill set. There are varying groups of people coming from different religions and different ethnic persuasions, different ages and genders. You must be able to look beyond these physical characteristics and determine their unique skill sets. Then you can manage toward those skill sets to get the best out of that person, get their best performance, and benefit from their creative thinking. That's the best approach to creating an effective and efficient business environment where people of different cultures, colors and genders work together.

**Q:** How do the kinds of products and services 7-Eleven offers today differ from the past?

**A:** One easy example is in our merchandising program. You'll notice the difference in the health and beauty aids category line. We carry stockings, cosmetics and hair products targeted toward women of color. You will also find differences in merchandising in the soft drink category. Individuals in different parts of the country prefer different flavors. You will find a very targeted approach to satisfying what our customers want—as between men and women, as between young and old, as between ethnic groups. It's a function of each franchisee knowing exactly who his or her customers are and adjusting the product selection accordingly.

**Source:** T. Barnes, "The Art of Diversity at 7-Eleven," *Franchising World* 27 (1995): 14–17. This interview was edited for inclusion in this textbook.

Furthermore, research clearly shows that people who have gotten a job or promotion as a result of affirmative action are frequently viewed as unqualified, even when clear evidence of their qualifications exists.[17] For example, one woman said, "I won a major prize [in my field], and some of the guys in my lab said it was because I was a woman. I'm certain they didn't choose me because I was a woman. But it gave some disgruntled guys who didn't get the prize a convenient excuse."[18] So, while affirmative action programs have created opportunities for minorities and women, those same minorities and women are frequently presumed to be unqualified when it is believed that their jobs were obtained as a result of affirmative action.

**Employment Practices Liability Insurance**

If company policy makes clear that discrimination won't be tolerated, and if you train employees to recognize discrimination, designate at least one person to handle complaints, and investigate promptly and fairly, you greatly reduce the chance of being sued for discrimination. You can reduce the threat even more with employment practices liability insurance (EPLI). EPLI covers claims against sexual harassment and age, gender, race, religion, or disability discrimination. Are you covered by EPLI? With the average lawsuit costing $675,000, can you afford not to be?

**Source:** A. Genn, "Taking Cover against Employee Lawsuits," *LI Business News* 12 April 2001, 31A. R. Rupp, "In EPLI Market Evolution, One Size Does Not Fit All Clients," *National Underwriter Property & Casualty-Risk & Benefits Management*, 21 May 2001, 3.

In summary, affirmative action and diversity are not the same thing. Not only are they fundamentally different, but they also differ in purpose, practice, and the reactions they produce.

### 1.2 Diversity Makes Good Business Sense

Those who support the idea of diversity in organizations often ignore its business aspects altogether, claiming instead that diversity is simply the "right thing to do." However, diversity actually makes good business sense in several ways: cost savings, attracting and retaining talent, and driving business growth.[19]

Diversity helps companies with *cost savings* by reducing turnover, decreasing absenteeism, and avoiding expensive lawsuits. Because of lost productivity and the cost of recruiting and selecting new workers, companies lose substantial amounts of money when employees quit their jobs. In fact, turnover costs typically amount to more than 90 percent of employees' salaries. So if an executive who makes $100,000 leaves an organization, it would cost approximately $90,000 to find a replacement. Using the 90 percent estimate, even the lowest-paid hourly workers can cost companies as much as $10,000 when they quit. Since the turnover rates for blacks average 40 percent higher than for whites, and since women quit their jobs at twice the rate men do, companies that manage diverse work forces well can cut costs by reducing the turnover rates of these employees.[20] And, with women absent from work 60 percent more often than men, primarily because of family responsibilities, diversity programs that address the needs of female workers can also reduce the substantial costs of absenteeism.

Diversity programs also save companies money by avoiding discrimination lawsuits, which have increased by a factor of 20 since 1970 and quadrupled just since 1995. Indeed, because companies lose two-thirds of all discrimination cases that go to trial, the best strategy from a business perspective is not to be sued for discrimination at all. And when companies lose, the average settlement costs more than $600,000.[21] Of course, this is just an average. Settlement costs can be substantially larger. For example, Coca-Cola paid $192.5 million to settle a class-action lawsuit filed by 2,200 African-American workers who claimed they were discriminated against in pay, promotions, and performance reviews.[22] Similar charges prompted Texaco to pay $176 million to settle a class-action lawsuit filed by 1,300 African-American workers.[23] State Farm Insurance paid $157 million to 814 women who were not given the chance to be hired or promoted into its key sales agent jobs in California.[24] Home Depot paid $65 million to settle a gender discrimination lawsuit with 25,000 female employees who were paid less and not promoted because they were women.[25] Finally, Ford Motor paid $17.5 million to settle a sexual harassment lawsuit filed by female workers at its two Chicago factories.[26]

Diversity also makes business sense by helping companies *attract and retain talented workers*.[27] And in today's job markets, where job seekers have more choice and opportunity than ever before, diversity-friendly companies are attracting better *and* more diverse job applicants. Very simply, diversity begets more diversity. Companies that make *Fortune* magazine's list of 50 best companies for minorities already attract a diverse and talented pool of job applicants. But after being recognized by *Fortune* for their efforts, they experience even bigger increases in both the quality and diversity of people who apply for jobs. Indeed, research shows that companies with acclaimed diversity programs not only attract more talented workers, but they also have higher stock market performance.[28]

Just as important, however, is that these companies also create opportunities that encourage workers to stay. For example, Anne Shen Smith, vice president of support services for Pacific Enterprises, a California-based utility holding company, said that the company created opportunities by replacing the "old boy network," in which only bosses could nominate employees for promotions, with a program called "Readiness

441

for Management," in which employees nominate themselves. Workers begin the process by taking a number of self-assessment tests to determine their strengths and weaknesses. Then they take training courses to improve their skills and knowledge. The Readiness for Management Program works because it gives people who were previously overlooked a chance to move up and because it makes employees responsible for improving their skills and knowledge.[29] Employees who don't take that responsibility don't get promoted.

The third way in which diversity makes business sense is by *driving business growth*. Diversity helps companies grow by improving marketplace understanding. When companies have diverse work forces, they are better able to understand the needs of their increasingly diverse customer bases. Exhibit 12.3 indicates just how diverse customers are becoming. For example, there are 134 million women in the United States with a total annual purchasing power of $1.1 trillion! Moreover, seven million women own businesses that generate annual business revenues of $2.3 trillion. Similarly impressive numbers appear for gays and lesbians, and African, Hispanic, and Asian Americans. Indeed, according to U.S. Secretary of Commerce Norman Mineta, "America's population will increase 50 percent over the next 50 years, with almost 90 percent of that increase in the minority community." [30] Accordingly, he concluded, "Both Fortune 1,000 and minority businesses need to pay attention to the consumer purchasing power that will result from that growth."[31] Companies such as SBC Communications are already taking note, trying to match the diversity of their work force to the diversity of their customer base.[32] William Howell, former chairman of JCPenney, said, "If we don't have people of diverse backgrounds in the back, how in the world can we satisfy the diversity of people coming in through the front door?"[33] In fact, a survey of 34 U.S. multinational organizations found that tapping into "diverse customers and markets" was the number one reason managers gave for implementing diversity programs.[34]

Diversity also helps companies grow through higher quality problem solving. While diverse groups initially have more difficulty working together than homogeneous groups, after several months, diverse groups do a better job of identifying problems and generating alternative solutions, the two most important steps in problem solving.[35] Ernest Drew, former CEO of Hoechst Celanese, a chemical company, recalled a company conference in which the company's top 125 managers, mostly white males, were joined by 50 lower-level employees, mostly minorities and women. Problem-solving teams were formed to discuss how the company's corporate culture affected business and how it could be changed. Half the teams were composed of white males, while the other half

| EXHIBIT 12.3 | | | |
|---|---|---|---|

RISING CUSTOMER DIVERSITY BY POPULATION, PURCHASING POWER, BUSINESS OWNERSHIP, AND BUSINESS REVENUE

| | U.S. POPULATION | PURCHASING POWER | BUSINESS OWNERS | ANNUAL BUSINESS REVENUE |
|---|---|---|---|---|
| Women | 134,000,000 | $ 1,100,000,000,000 | 7,000,000 | 2,300,000,000,000 |
| Gays & Lesbians | 20,000,000 | $ 514,000,000 | 2,200,000 | 37,000,000,000 |
| People with Disabilities | 49,000,000 | $ 100,000,000,000 | not available | not available |
| African Americans | 34,000,000 | $ 400,000,000,000 | 621,000 | 32,000,000,000 |
| Asian Americans | 10,000,000 | $ 150,000,000,000 | 706,000 | 1,000,000,000,000 |
| Hispanic Americans | 28,000,000 | $ 235,000,000,000 | 1,500,000 | 200,000,000,000 |

**Source:** K. Ellison & N. Bond, "Diversity: The Bottom Line for Small Business," *Inc.*, 19 May 1998, D1.

were of mixed gender and race. Drew said, "It was so obvious that the diverse teams had the broader solutions. They had ideas I hadn't even thought of. For the first time, we realized that diversity is a strength as it relates to problem solving. Before, we just thought of diversity as the total number of minorities and women in the company, like affirmative action. Now we knew we needed diversity at every level of the company where decisions are made."[36]

In short, says Virginia Clarke, of Spencer Stuart, an executive search firm, "There is a strong business case [for diversity] now."[37]

## Review 1
### Diversity: Differences That Matter

Diversity exists in organizations when there is a variety of demographic, cultural, and personal differences among the people who work there and the customers who do business there. A common misconception is that workplace diversity and affirmative action are the same. However, affirmative action is more narrowly focused on demographics, is required by law, and is used to punish companies that discriminate on the basis of race, color, religion, gender, or national origin. By contrast, diversity is broader in focus (going beyond demographics), voluntary, more positive in that it encourages companies to value all kinds of differences, and, at this time, substantially less controversial than affirmative action. So, affirmative action and diversity differ in purpose, practice, and the reactions they produce. Diversity also makes good business sense in terms of cost savings (reducing turnover, decreasing absenteeism, and avoiding lawsuits), attracting and retaining talent, and driving business growth (improving marketplace understanding and higher-quality problem solving).

# Diversity and Individual Differences

Want a glimpse into the world of diversity? Try the men's bathroom in any American factory. For whatever reason, the bathroom wall remains the broadsheet of the blue-collar male. What a shock the day in March that I checked out our plant's men's room at the urging of a concerned employee. Every imaginable racial and ethnic slur was scrawled across the surface of the largest stall. I asked myself, Is this what people really think? How are they ever going to work together if they feel this way?

Wandering the factory floor, though, you'd never guess the writing on the wall. Anglos bend over machines helping Spanish-speaking workers repair timing belts. Koreans mix inks for African-American printing-press operators. Women and men spell one another on the packing lines. Everyone seems to be working together to get the job done at our vegetable-bag printing plant.[38]

Kevin Kelly, a former *Business Week* reporter who now works at Emerald Packaging in Union City, California, wrote this description of diversity. Did you notice that he described his workers in terms of ethnicity (Anglos and African-Americans), national origin (Koreans and Spanish-speaking workers) and gender (men and women)? Kelly's description of the diversity of his workers is fairly typical. A survey found that when managers were asked, "What is meant by diversity to decision-makers in your organization?" they most frequently mentioned race, culture, gender, national origin, age, religion, and regional origin.[39]

When managers describe workers this way, they are focusing on surface-level diversity. **Surface-level diversity**, as illustrated in Exhibit 12.4, consists of differences that are immediately observable, typically unchangeable, and easy to measure.[40] In other words,

**surface-level diversity** differences such as age, gender, race/ethnicity, and physical disabilities that are observable, typically unchangeable, and easy to measure

EXHIBIT 12.4

SURFACE- AND DEEP-LEVEL DIVERSITY

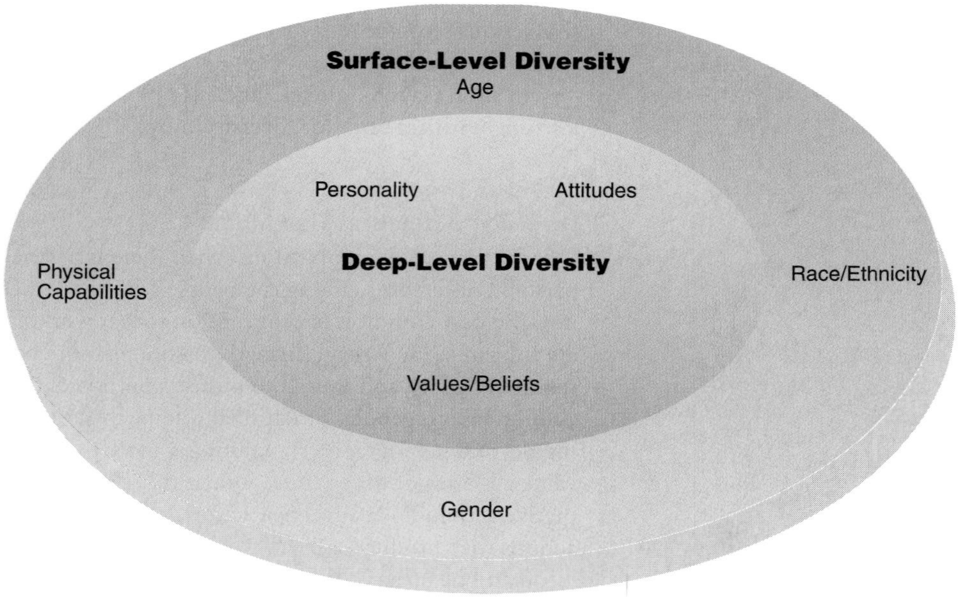

independent observers can usually agree on dimensions of surface-level diversity, such as another person's age, gender, race/ethnicity, or mental or physical disabilities.

Did you also notice that when Kelly's employees at Emerald Packaging actually worked with each other, the surface-level differences such as race/ethnicity, national origin, and gender didn't seem to matter as much? In fact, Kelly said, "Everyone seems to be *working together to get the job done* at our vegetable-bag printing plant" [emphasis added].

This, too, is more typical than you'd think. In fact, the good news is that while most people start by using easily observable characteristics, such as surface-level diversity, to categorize or stereotype other people, those initial, superficial categorizations typically give way to deeper impressions formed from knowledge of others' behavior and psychological characteristics, such as personality or attitudes. When you think of others this way, you are focusing on deep-level diversity. **Deep-level diversity** consists of differences communicated through verbal and nonverbal behaviors that are learned only through extended interaction with others.[41] Examples of deep-level diversity include personality differences, attitudes, beliefs, and values. In other words, as people in diverse workplaces get to know each other, the initial focus on surface-level differences such as age, race/ethnicity, gender, and physical capabilities is replaced by deeper, more accurate knowledge of coworkers.

If managed properly, the shift from surface- to deep-level diversity can accomplish two things.[42] First, coming to know and understand each other better can result in reduced prejudice and conflict. Second, it can lead to stronger social integration. **Social integration** is the degree to which group members are psychologically attracted to working with each other to accomplish a common objective, or, as Kevin Kelly described it, "working together to get the job done."

*After reading the next two sections, you should be able to*

*2. understand the special challenges that the dimensions of surface-level diversity pose for managers.*

*3. explain how the dimensions of deep-level diversity affect individual behavior and interactions in the workplace.*

**deep-level diversity**
differences communicated through verbal and nonverbal behaviors, such as personality and attitudes, that are learned only through extended interaction with others

**social integration**
the degree to which group members are psychologically attracted to working with each other to accomplish a common objective

444

# 2. Surface-Level Diversity

Because age, gender, race/ethnicity, and disabilities are usually immediately observable, many managers and workers use these dimensions of surface-level diversity to form initial impressions and categorizations of coworkers, bosses, customers, or job applicants. Whether intentional or not, sometimes those initial categorizations and impressions lead to decisions or behaviors that discriminate. Consequently, these dimensions of surface-level diversity post special challenges for managers who are trying to create positive work environments where everyone feels comfortable and no one is advantaged or disadvantaged.

*Let's learn more about those challenges and the ways that 2.1 age, 2.2 gender, 2.3 race/ethnicity, and 2.4 mental or physical disabilities can affect decisions and behaviors in organizations.*

## 2.1 Age

**age discrimination**
treating people differently (e.g., in hiring and firing, promotion, and compensation decisions) because of their age

**Age discrimination** is treating people differently (e.g., in hiring and firing, promotion, and compensation decisions) because of their age. Since age discrimination almost always occurs against "older" workers, no cliché captures the basic idea behind age discrimination as well as "You can't teach an old dog new tricks." It's commonly believed that older workers are unable to learn how to use computers and technology, are incapable of adapting to change, are sick more often, and, in general, are much more expensive to employ than younger workers. One manager explained his preference for younger workers over older workers this way: "The way I look at it, for $40,000 or $50,000, I can get a smart, raw kid right out of undergrad who's going to work seven days a week for me for the next two years. I'll train him the way I want him, he'll grow with me, and I'll pay him long-term options so I own him, for lack of a better word. He'll do exactly what I want—and if he doesn't, I'll fire him. . . . The alternative is to pay twice as much for some 40-year-old who does half the amount of work, has been trained improperly, and doesn't listen to what I say."[43]

Unfortunately, attitudes like this are all too common. For example, 80 percent of human resource managers surveyed by *Personnel Management* magazine said that age discrimination was a major problem in their organizations and that older employees were not receiving the same training and promotional opportunities as younger workers.[44] Likewise, two-thirds of the 10,000 people surveyed by the American Association for Retired People (AARP) felt that they had been wrongly discharged from a job because of their age. In fact, a study by the Society for Human Resource Management found that 20 percent of all companies had been sued for age discrimination in the last five years. However, the actual incidence of age discrimination may be even higher, given that 90 percent of age discrimination cases are settled before official complaints are registered with the Equal Employment Opportunity Commission (EEOC) and then the courts. Plaintiffs, though, have won more than 90 percent of the cases that have gone to court in recent years.[45]

So, what's reality and what's myth? Do older employees actually cost more? In some ways, they do. The older people are and the longer they stay with a company, the more the company pays for salaries, pension plans, and vacation time. However, older workers cost companies less, too, because they show better judgment, care more about the quality of their work, and are less likely to quit, show up late, or be absent, the cost of which can be substantial.[46] A survey by Chicago outplacement firm Challenger, Gray & Christmas found that only 3 percent of employees age 50 or over changed jobs in any given year compared to 10 percent of the entire work force and 12 percent of workers ages 25 to 34. The study also found that while older workers make up about 14 percent of the work force, they suffer only 10 percent of all workplace injuries and use fewer health care benefits than younger workers with school-age children.[47] As for the widespread belief that job performance declines with age, the scientific evidence clearly refutes this stereotype. Performance does not decline with age, regardless of the type of job.[48]

Accusations of age discrimination have multiplied recently and include companies of all sizes and industries. These two Visteon employees, along with six others, filed suit against the company based of statistics they say show that Visteon cut 30 percent of workers 56 and older and 15 percent of workers 51 to 55 (for a total of 45 percent of the work force over 51 years of age). They contend the company only cut 6 percent of workers under 40.

AP PHOTO/PAUL SANCYA

What can companies do to reduce age discrimination?[49] To start, managers need to recognize that age discrimination is much more pervasive than they probably think. While "old" used to mean mid-50s, in today's workplace, "old" is closer to 40. When 773 CEOs were asked, "At what age does a worker's productivity peak?" the average age was 43. So, age discrimination may affect more workers simply because perceptions about age have changed. However, with the aging of baby boomers, age discrimination is more likely simply because there really are millions more older workers than there used to be. And, because studies show that interviewers rate younger job candidates as more qualified (even when they aren't), companies need to train managers and recruiters to make hiring and promotion decisions on the basis of qualifications, not age. Companies also need to monitor the extent to which older workers receive training. The Bureau of Labor Statistics indicates that the number of training courses and number of hours spent in training drops dramatically after employees reach the age of 44. Finally, companies need to ensure that younger and older workers interact with each other. One study found that younger workers generally hold positive views of older workers, and that the more time they spent working with older coworkers, the more positive their attitudes became.[50]

### 2.2 Gender

**gender discrimination**
treating people differently because of their gender

**glass ceiling**
the invisible barrier that prevents women and minorities from advancing to the top jobs in organizations

**Gender discrimination** means treating people differently because of their gender. Gender discrimination and racial/ethnic discrimination (discussed in the next section) are often associated with the **glass ceiling**, the so-called invisible barrier that prevents women and minorities from advancing to the top jobs in organizations. To what extent do women face gender discrimination in the workplace? In some ways, there is much less gender discrimination than there used to be. For example, while women held only 17 percent of managerial jobs in 1972, today they hold nearly 49.5 percent percent of managerial jobs, a number that exceeds the percentage of women (46.5 percent) in the work force. Likewise, women own 38 percent of all U.S. businesses.[51] Women owned 700,000

EXHIBIT 12.5

## WOMEN'S EARNINGS AS A PERCENT OF MEN'S

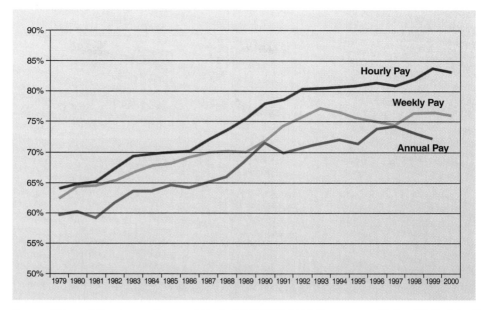

**Source:** "Women's Earnings as Percent of Men's, 1979-2000," U.S. Department of Labor. [Online] Available http://www.dol.gov/dol/wb/public/wb_pubs/2000.htm, 26 November 2001.

businesses in 1977, 4.1 million businesses in 1987, and 9.1 million businesses in 1999![52] Finally, while women still earn less than men on average, Exhibit 12.5 shows that women paid an hourly wage earn 83 percent of what men did in 2000, up from 64 percent in 1979; that women paid on a weekly basis earn 76 percent of what men did in 2000, up from 63 percent in 1979; and that in terms of annual earnings, women earn 72 percent of what men did in 2000, up from 60 percent in 1979.

Although progress is being made, however, gender discrimination continues to operate via the glass ceiling at higher levels in organizations. For instance, as shown in Exhibit 12.6 (see p. 448), a woman had the highest salary (i.e., was a top earner) in only 4.1 percent of Fortune 500 companies, up from 1.2 percent in 1995. Only 12.5 percent of corporate officers (i.e., top management) were women in 2000, up from 8.7 percent in 1995. Indeed, out of the 500 largest companies in the United States, only five have women CEOs.[53] Membership on corporate boards of directors is similar, as women hold 11.7 percent of all board memberships in the United States, up from 9.5 percent in 1995.[54]

Unfortunately, contrary to popular opinion, women are actually worse off in Europe than in the United States. While women make up 41 percent of the European work force, they hold only 29 percent of all management jobs, no more than 2 percent of top management jobs, and just 1 percent of board membership positions, far worse than the 11.7 percent of board seats held by American women. Furthermore, while 95 percent of the 100 largest U.S. companies have at least one female on their board of directors, the percentage is far less in most European countries. For example, only 41 percent of the 100 largest British companies have a female board member.[55]

Is gender discrimination the sole reason for the slow rate at which women have been promoted to mid and upper levels of management and corporate boards? Some studies indicate that it's not. In some instances, the slow progress appears to be due to career and job choices. Unlike men, whose career and job choices are often driven by the search for higher pay and advancement, women are more likely to choose jobs or careers that also give them a greater sense of accomplishment, more control over their work schedules,

447

EXHIBIT 12.6

WOMEN AT FORTUNE 500 COMPANIES

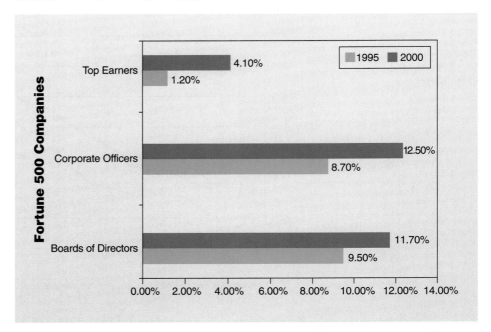

**Source:** "Fact Sheet: 2000 Catalyst Census of Women Corporate Officers and Top Earners of the Fortune 500," *Catalyst.* [Online] Available http://www.catalystwomen.org/press/factsheets/factscote00.html, 26 November 2001.

and easier movement in and out of the workplace.[56] Furthermore, women are historically much more likely than men to prioritize family over work at some time in their careers. Gilberte Beaux, CEO of Paris-based Basic Petroleum International and one of France's most accomplished female managers, managed to have both a successful career and a family, but said, "It's hard to drop out for a family if you want to get to the top." As to why so many women choose families over careers, she said, "Women should be able to do what they want in life . . . just like men."[57]

However, beyond these reasons, it's likely that gender discrimination plays a major role in the slow advancement of women into higher levels of management. And even if you don't think so, many of the women you work with probably do. Indeed, one study found that more than 90 percent of executive women believed that the glass ceiling had hurt their careers.[58] In another study, 80 percent of women said they left their last organization because the glass ceiling had limited their chances for advancement.[59] A third study indicated that the glass ceiling is prompting more and more women to leave companies to start their own businesses.[60] Anita Borg, a senior researcher at Digital Equipment Corp., summed up the frustrations of many professional women when she said, "You run into subtle sexism every day. It's like water torture. It wears you down."[61]

What can companies do to make sure that women have the same opportunities for development and advancement as men? One strategy is mentoring, to pair promising female executives with senior executives with whom they can talk and seek advice and support. A vice president at a utility company said, "I think it's the single most critical piece to women advancing career-wise. In my experience you need somebody to help guide you and . . . go to bat for you."[62] In fact, 91 percent of female executives had a mentor at some point and felt their mentor was critical to their advancement.

Another strategy is to make sure that a male-dominated activity doesn't unintentionally exclude women. For example, at Avon, the CEO stopped the annual hunting trips,

Lynn Pendergrass and Paula Burris both participate in GE mentoring, a unique program that pairs industrious women and minorities with seasoned GE professionals. Through special mentoring relationships, like the one Paula has with Lynn, employees gain the support and guidance they need to further their careers.

COURTESY OF GE

**WHEN PAULA BURRIS CAME TO GE, SHE WAS GIVEN AN OFFICE, A LAPTOP AND A VICE PRESIDENT.**

Paula is one of hundreds of promising employees who participate in GE Mentoring, a unique program that pairs industrious women and minorities with seasoned GE professionals. Through special mentoring

relationships, like the one Paula has with Lynn Pendergrass at GE Appliances, employees gain the support and guidance they need to further their careers. Because at GE, everyone can be a success story.

FOR MORE INFORMATION, VISIT US AT WWW.GE.COM.

*We bring good things to life.*

during which top managers would drink and play cards all night.[63] One final strategy is to designate a "go-to person," other than employees' supervisors, that women can talk to if they believe that they are being held back or discriminated against because of their gender. Make sure this person has the knowledge and authority to conduct a fair, confidential internal investigation.[64]

### 2.3 Race/Ethnicity

**racial and ethnic discrimination**
treating people differently because of their race or ethnicity

**Racial and ethnic discrimination** means treating people differently because of their race or ethnicity. To what extent is racial and ethnic discrimination a factor in the workplace? Thanks to the 1964 Civil Rights Act and Title VII, there is much less racial and ethnic discrimination than there used to be. For example, the number of African Americans and Hispanics in top management positions increased 200 percent in Fortune 1,000 firms between 1979 and 1989.[65] However, strong racial and ethnic disparities still exist. For instance, while about 12 percent of Americans are black, only 6 percent of managers and less than 1 percent of top managers are black.[66] Similarly, while 11 percent of Americans are Hispanic, only 5 percent of all managers are Hispanic.

What accounts for the disparities between the percentages of African, Hispanic, and Asian Americans in the general population and their smaller representation in management positions? Sometimes studies show that the disparities are due to pre-existing differences in training, education, and skills, and that when African, Hispanic, Asian, and white Americans have similar skills, training, and education, they are much more likely to have similar jobs and salaries.[67]

However, other studies provide increasingly strong direct evidence of racial or ethnic discrimination in the workplace. For example, one study directly tested hiring discrimination by sending pairs of black and white males and pairs of Hispanic and non-Hispanic males to apply for the same jobs. Each pair had résumés with identical qualifications, and all were trained to present themselves in similar ways to minimize differences during interviews. The researchers found that white males got three times as many

**Form a Friendly Supper Club**

For two decades, blacks and whites have come to the Piccadilly Cafeteria in Montgomery, Alabama, for the monthly meeting of the Friendly Supper Club. The goal is simple: To get people to talk. There are no agendas, no club officers, and no speeches. One member said, "We are people who come to dinner just to enjoy each other." The result is significantly improved race relations in a town once thick with racial tensions. To improve things in your corner of our diverse world, start a Friendly Supper Club and make a habit of inviting someone different to dinner. You might find out how much you have in common.

**Source:** R. Thurow, "Can Liver and Onions Lead People to Peace and Understanding? Just Ask the Friendlies, Who Have Been Dining for Years on Racial Reconciliation," *The Wall Street Journal*, 17 December 1998, A1.

job offers as black males, and that non-Hispanic males got three times as many job offers as Hispanic males.[68]

Another study, which used similar methods to test hiring procedures at 149 different companies, found that whites received 10 percent more interviews than blacks. Of those interviewed, half of whites received job offers as compared to only 11 percent of blacks. And when job offers were made, blacks were much more likely to be offered lower-level positions, while whites were more likely to be offered jobs that were at higher levels than the jobs they had applied for.[69]

Critics of these studies point out that it's nearly impossible to train different applicants to give identical responses in job interviews and that differences in interviewing skills may have somehow accounted for the results. However, British researchers found similar kinds of discrimination just by sending letters of inquiry to prospective employers. As before, the letters sent to employers were identical except for the applicant's race. Employers frequently responded to letters from Afro-Caribbean, Indian, or Pakistani "applicants" by indicating that the positions had been filled. By contrast, they often responded to white, Anglo-Saxon "applicants" by inviting them to face-to-face interviews. Similar results were found with Vietnamese and Greek "applicants" in Australia.[70] In short, the evidence strongly indicates that there is strong and persistent racial and ethnic discrimination in the hiring processes of many organizations.

What can companies do to make sure that people of all racial and ethnic backgrounds have the same opportunities?[71] Start by looking at the numbers. Compare the hiring rates of whites to the hiring rates for different racial and ethnic applicants. Do the same thing for promotions within the company. See if nonwhite workers quit the company at higher rates than white workers. Also, survey employees to compare white and nonwhite employees' satisfaction with jobs, bosses, and the company, as well as perceptions concerning equal treatment. Next, if the numbers indicate racial or ethnic disparities, consider a test of your hiring system by employing a private firm to have applicants of different races with identical qualifications apply for jobs in your company.[72] Although disparities aren't proof of discrimination, it's much better to investigate hiring and promotion disparities yourself than to have the EEOC or a plaintiff's lawyer do it for you, especially since nearly half of the discrimination charges filed with the EEOC in the last six years were related to race and ethnicity (which the EEOC calls "national origin").[73]

Another step is to eliminate unclear selection and promotion criteria. Vague hiring and promotion criteria allow decision makers to focus on non-job-related characteristics that may unintentionally lead to employment discrimination. Instead, selection and promotion criteria should spell out the specific knowledge, skills, abilities, education, and experience needed to perform a job well.

Finally, train managers and others who make hiring and promotion decisions. At Tower Records, the human resources staff assembles on a giant game board that covers a conference room floor. Tower store managers then answer questions about hiring situations. If they answer a question correctly, they move forward on the board. If they answer it incorrectly, they stay in place, and the group discusses what should have been done instead. The number of grievances about hiring procedures has dropped significantly since the training began.[74]

### 2.4 Mental or Physical Disabilities

**disability**
a mental or physical impairment that substantially limits one or more major life activities

**disability discrimination**
treating people differently because of their disabilities

Back problems, foot pain, depression, alcoholism, epilepsy, paralysis, AIDS, cancer, learning disabilities, and substantial hearing or visual impairments: What do all these things have in common? Each is a disability. According to the Americans with Disabilities Act (**http://www.usdoj.gov/crt/ada/adahom1.htm**), a **disability** is a mental or physical impairment that substantially limits one or more major life activities.[75] One out of five Americans, or more than 52 million people, have a disability. **Disability discrimination** means treating people differently because of their disabilities.

450

To what extent is disability discrimination a factor in the workplace? According to the U.S. Census Bureau, 80 percent of able people have jobs, compared to only 77 percent of those with nonsevere disabilities and 26 percent of those with severe disabilities. More specifically, only 64 percent of those who have difficulty hearing, 44 percent of those who have difficulty seeing, 41 percent of those with a mental disability, and 34 percent of those who have difficulty walking have jobs.[76] Furthermore, people with disabilities are disproportionately employed in low-status or part-time jobs, have little chance for advancement, and, on average, have incomes 35 percent smaller than able people.[77] Numerous studies also indicate that managers and the general public believe that discrimination against people with disabilities is common and widespread.[78]

What accounts for the disparities between the employment and income levels of able people and people with disabilities? Contrary to popular opinion, it has nothing to do with the ability of people with disabilities to do their jobs well. Studies show that as long as companies make reasonable accommodations for disabilities (i.e., changes in procedures or equipment, etc.), people with disabilities perform their jobs just as well as able people. Furthermore, they have better safety records and are not any more likely to be absent or quit their jobs.[79] Plus, most accommodations for disabilities are relatively inexpensive. The medium cost of accommodations is $250, but 20 percent of accommodations cost nothing and 51 percent of accommodations cost less than $500.[80] For example, after Michael Kuster lost all vision in his right eye and some in his left, his employer, Walgreen's, accommodated his disability by adding lights in his office and giving him a 21-inch monitor for his computer and a magnifying glass to read printed material.[81] Sears spends an average of just $45 to accommodate employees with disabilities. In fact, 75 percent of the accommodations it makes cost nothing at all. For example, when a saleswoman indicated that she was allergic to nylon, Sears simply waived the requirement that she wear panty hose. Hamilton Davis, Sears' assistant general counsel of employment practices, said, "The bulk of our accommodations are common sense and any company should be able to provide them."[82]

In most cases, whether intentional or not, discrimination toward people with disabilities results from incorrect stereotypes, incorrect expectations, and the emotional responses that people have when interacting with people with disabilities.[83] **Stereotypes** are negative, false, overgeneralized beliefs about people in particular categories.[84] People with disabilities are often thought to be shy, honest, helpless, hypersensitive, depressed, unappealing, bitter, unaggressive, insecure, dependent, or less competent. Inaccurate stereotypes of people with disabilities can lead to inaccurate expectations about on-the-job performance. For example, the stereotypes listed above lead to the expectation that people with disabilities are less qualified and have difficulty interacting with others. Consistent with these expectations, people with disabilities are less likely to be hired or recommended for promotion. Also, it's well established that people react emotionally to others' physical or mental disabilities. Reactions, which range from simple discomfort to negative attitudes to revulsion, can lead organizational decision makers to overlook people with disabilities for promotion or hiring.

What can companies do to make sure that people with disabilities have the same opportunities as everyone else? Beyond educational efforts to address incorrect stereotypes and expectations, a good place to start is to commit to reasonable workplace accommodations. Examples include changing work schedules, reassigning jobs, acquiring or modifying equipment, or providing assistance when needed. Furthermore, as discussed above, accommodations needn't be expensive. For example, rather than rebuild its offices, the U.S. Postal Service used inexpensive ramps to raise wheelchair-bound clerks to counter level so they could wait on customers. For further information about reasonable accommodations, contact the Job Accommodations Network of the President's Committee on Employment of People with Disabilities (**http://janweb.icdi.wvu.edu/**), which provides free help and has a

**stereotypes**
negative, false, overgeneralized beliefs about people in particular categories

451

EXHIBIT 12.7

REASONABLE ACCOMMODATIONS FOR DISABLED WORKERS

- Physical changes, such as installing a ramp or modifying a workspace or restroom;
- A quieter workspace or other changes that reduce noisy distractions for someone with a mental disability;
- Training and other written materials in an accessible format, such as in Braille, on audio tape, or on computer disk;
- TTYs for use with telephones by people who are deaf, and hardware and software that make computers accessible to people with vision impairments or who have difficulty using their hands; and
- Time off for someone who needs treatment for a disability.

**Source:** "Americans with Disabilities Act: A Guide for People with Disabilities Seeking Employment," U.S. Department of Justice. [Online] Available http://www.usdoj.gov/crt/ada/workta.htm, 27 November 2001.

database of 26,000 successful accommodations.[85] Exhibit 12.7 provides a list of common, inexpensive accommodations that companies can make for disabled workers.

Another effective strategy is to provide *assistive technology* that gives workers with disabilities the tools they need to overcome their disabilities. According to the National Council on Disability, 92 percent of workers with disabilities who use assistive technology reported that it helps them work faster and better, 81 percent indicated that it helps them work longer hours, and 67 percent said that it is critical to getting a job.[86] To learn about assistive technologies that can help workers with disabilities, see Abledata (**http://www.abledata.com/**), which lists 25,000 products from 3,000 organizations, or the National Rehabilitation Information Center (**http://www.naric.com/**), which provides information for specific disabilities.

Finally, companies should actively recruit qualified workers with disabilities. Numerous organizations, such as Mainstream, Kidder Resources, Just One Break (**http://www. justonebreak.org/**), the American Council of the Blind (**http://www.acb.org/**), the National Federation of the Blind (**http://www.nfb.org/**), the National Association for the Deaf (**http://www.nad.org/**), the Epilepsy Foundation of America (**http://www.efa.org/**), and the National Amputation Foundation (**http://www.nationalamputation.org/**), actively work with employers to find jobs for qualified people with disabilities. Companies can also place advertisements in publications, such as *Careers and the Disabled*, that specifically target workers with disabilities.[87]

### Review 2
### Surface-Level Diversity

Age, gender, race/ethnicity, and physical and mental disabilities are dimensions of surface-level diversity. Because those dimensions are (usually) easily observed, managers and workers tend to rely on them to form initial impressions and stereotypes of others. Sometimes, this can lead to age, gender, racial/ethnic, or disability discrimination (i.e., treating people differently) in the workplace. In general, older workers, women, people of color or different national origins, and people with disabilities are much less likely to be hired or promoted than white males. This disparity is often due to incorrect beliefs or stereotypes, such as "job performance declines with age," or "females aren't willing to travel on business," or "workers with disabilities aren't as competent as able workers." To reduce discrimination, companies can determine the hiring and promotion rates for different groups, train managers to make hiring and promotion decisions on the basis of specific criteria, and make sure that everyone has equal access to training, mentors, reasonable work accommodations, and assistive technology. Finally, companies need to designate a "go-to person" that employees can talk to if they believe they have suffered discrimination.

# 3. Deep-Level Diversity

Have you ever just disliked someone from the minute you met him or her—the way the person talked, acted, or treated you? But then after spending some time working or interacting with this person, you decided that your initial impressions were wrong and that he or she wasn't so bad after all?

If you've had this experience, then you understand the difference between surface- and deep-level diversity. As you just learned, people often use the dimensions of surface-level diversity to form initial impressions about others. However, over time, as people have a chance to get to know each other, initial impressions based on age, gender, race/ethnicity, and mental or physical disabilities give way to deeper impressions based on behavior and psychological characteristics. When we think of others this way, we are focusing on deep-level diversity. *Deep-level diversity* represents differences that can only be learned through extended interaction with others. Examples of deep-level diversity include personality differences, attitudes, beliefs, and values. In short, deep-level diversity means getting to know and understand one another better. And that matters, because it can result in less prejudice, discrimination, and conflict in the workplace. These changes can then lead to better *social integration*, the degree to which organizational or group members are psychologically attracted to working with each other to accomplish a common objective.

*Let's examine deep-level diversity by exploring 3.1 the "Big Five" dimensions of personality and 3.2 other significant work-related aspects of personality.*

## 3.1 Big Five Dimensions of Personality

Stop for a second and think about your boss (or the boss you had in your last job). What words would you use to describe him or her? Is your boss introverted or extraverted? Emotionally stable or unstable? Agreeable or disagreeable? Organized or disorganized? Open or closed to new experiences? When you describe your boss or others this way, what you're really doing is describing dispositions and personality.

**disposition**
the tendency to respond to situations and events in a predetermined manner

**personality**
the relatively stable set of behaviors, attitudes, and emotions displayed over time that makes people different from each other

A **disposition** is the tendency to respond to situations and events in a predetermined manner. **Personality** is the relatively stable set of behaviors, attitudes, and emotions displayed over time that makes people different from each other.[88] For example, think of your closest friends. Among them, is there someone you trust enough to invest your money for you? Chances are, there's not. Why? It could be that this friend doesn't know any more about investing than you do. Or, it could be that he or she just doesn't have the personality or disposition to do this well. In fact, the people who run multibillion-dollar investment funds are typically introverted, make decisions on the basis of data rather than intuitive hunches, are swayed by thinking and analysis rather than emotion, and are single-minded in their jobs (i.e., improving fund performance). It makes sense, doesn't it? After all, would you invest in a fund in which the fund manager made decisions on hunches, was swayed more by emotion than analysis, and wasn't solely devoted to improving the return on your investments? People with these personality traits may make great friends, but you probably wouldn't want them to invest your money.[89]

For years, personality researchers studied thousands of different ways to describe people's personalities. However, in the last decade, personality research conducted in different cultures, different settings, and different languages indicates that five basic dimensions of personality account for most of the differences in peoples' behaviors, attitudes, and emotions (or for why your boss is the way he or she is!). The *Big Five Personality Dimensions* are extraversion, emotional stability, agreeableness, conscientiousness, and openness to experience.[90]

**extraversion**
the degree to which someone is active, assertive, gregarious, sociable, talkative, and energized by others

**Extraversion** is the degree to which someone is active, assertive, gregarious, sociable, talkative, and energized by others. In contrast to extraverts, introverts are less active, prefer to be alone, and are shy, quiet, and reserved. For the best results in the workplace, introverts and extraverts should be correctly matched to their jobs. For example, the Peabody Hotel in Memphis, Tennessee, solved one of its problems by having job applicants complete an introversion/extraversion personality measure. Ken Hamko, a manager at the hotel, said, "We had hostesses who wouldn't stay by the door or greet guests or smile. When we gave them the personality profile, we found they didn't like being in front of people. So we moved them into other positions and replaced them with extraverts."[91]

**Emotional stability** is the degree to which someone is angry, depressed, anxious, emotional, insecure, and excitable. People who are emotionally stable respond well to stress. In other words, they can maintain a calm, problem-solving attitude in even the toughest situations (i.e., conflict, hostility, dangerous conditions, or extreme time pressures). By contrast, under moderately stressful situations, emotionally unstable people are unable to handle the most basic demands of their jobs, and become distraught, tearful, self-doubting, and anxious. Emotional stability is particularly important for high-stress jobs, such as police work, fire fighting, emergency medical treatment, or piloting planes. John S. Blonsick, a captain with Delta Air Lines, said, "From the first day of flight training, pilot aspirants are tested for their ability to separate their emotions from their operational environment. The process allows a pilot to erect psychological barriers to avoid distractions in an environment that commands superior mental diligence and responses—an environment in which the decision-making process is conducted at slightly under the speed of sound. . . . Abnormal and emergency situations are handled in a cool and professional manner. Voice-recorder transcripts of accidents invariably read like training manuals, despite the life-threatening situations they depict. Crew members are focused and actively working to correct the situation as they have been trained to do right up to the very last moment before impact."[92]

As you learned in Chapter 1, emotional stability is also important for managers. Indeed, the number one mistake managers make is intimidating, bullying, and being abrasive to the people who work for them.

**Agreeableness** is the degree to which someone is cooperative, polite, flexible, forgiving, good-natured, tolerant, and trusting. Basically, agreeable people are easy to work with and be around, while disagreeable people are distrusting and difficult to work with and be around. A number of companies have made general attitude or agreeableness the most important factor in their hiring decisions. Hal Rosenbluth, CEO of Rosenbluth International, one of the nation's largest travel companies, said, "We try to attract and hire great human beings with the prerequisite of being nice . . . [because] when nice people work together they're effective and they have fun."[93] Likewise, Southwest Airlines chairman Herb Kelleher said, "At Southwest, we hire attitudes. We can teach someone anything they need to know, but they must start with the right attitude."[94] Sherry Phelps, Southwest's director of corporate employment, explained that attitude (i.e., agreeableness) is a key hiring criterion for pilots, too. Speaking about a pilot who applied for a job, she said, "He came highly recommended, had won several flying awards while in the military and was an excellent candidate in terms of technical skills. But we didn't hire him. Because although he interviewed well with the recruiters, we found out he was rude to the flight attendants and customer-service agents he came in contact with on the way to the interview. We hire people who want to please everyone they meet, not just the audience they think they have to perform for."[95]

**Conscientiousness** is the degree to which someone is organized, hardworking, responsible, persevering, thorough, and achievement-oriented. One management consultant wrote about his experiences with high- and low-conscientiousness employees. He said:

> Many of the latter were charming individuals; they were often laid back, relaxed, and hard to ruffle. One once told me, "I don't sweat the small stuff." He might have added: "Even many of the things that you think are critical!" One highly conscientious subordinate was all business. He arrived at our first meeting with a typed copy of his daily schedule, a sheet bearing his home and office phone numbers, addresses, and his email address. At his request, we established a timetable for meetings for the next four months. He showed up on time every time, day planner in hand, and carefully listed tasks and due dates. He questioned me exhaustively if

454

# WhatReallyWorks

## Conscientiousness: The Organized, Hard-Working, Responsible Personality

Conscientious people are organized, hardworking, responsible, persevering, thorough, and achievement-oriented. Who wouldn't want to hire people with these personality traits? Indeed, 92 studies across five occupational groups (professionals, police, managers, sales, and skilled/semi-skilled) with a combined total of 12,893 study participants indicated that, on average, conscientious people are inherently more motivated and are better at their jobs.

### Motivational Effort

There is a 71 percent chance that conscientious workers will be more motivated and will work harder than less conscientious workers.

**Probability of Success**

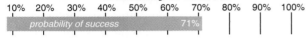

### Job Performance

There is a 66 percent chance that conscientious workers will be better at their jobs than less-conscientious workers.

**Probability of Success**

**Sources:** M.R. Barrick & M.K. Mount, "The Big Five Personality Dimensions and Job Performance," *Personnel Psychology* 44 (1991): 1-26. M.K. Mount & M.R. Barrick, "The Big Five Personality Dimensions: Implications for Research and Practice in Human Resource Management," *Research in Personnel and Human Resources Management* 13 (1995): 153-200. M.K. Mount & M.R. Barrick, "Five Reasons Why the 'Big Five' Article Has Been Frequently Cited," *Personnel Psychology* 51 (1998): 849-857. D.S. Ones, M.K. Mount, M.R. Barrick, & J.E. Hunter, "Personality and Job Performance: A Critique of the Tett, Jackson, and Rothstein (1991) Meta-Analysis," *Personnel Psychology* 47 (1994): 147-156.

he didn't understand an assignment and returned on schedule with the completed work or with a clear explanation as to why it wasn't done.[96]

How accurately do measures of conscientiousness categorize employees? The U.S. Department of Defense sponsored a study in which it asked 320 upper-level, white-collar employees (in organizations ranging from banks to government agencies to a state university) and 329 white-collar criminals (in 23 federal prisons) to complete a battery of personality tests to learn what, if any, personality differences existed between the two groups. Of all the personality tests given, conscientiousness was by far the strongest differentiator of the two groups. Only 18 percent of the criminals scored high on the conscientiousness scales, compared to 88 percent of the white-collar employees.[97]

**openness to experience**
the degree to which someone is curious, broad-minded, and open to new ideas, things, and experiences; is spontaneous; and has a high tolerance for ambiguity

**Openness to experience** is the degree to which someone is curious, broad-minded, and open to new ideas, things, and experiences; is spontaneous; and has a high tolerance for ambiguity. Most companies need people with personalities both strong and weak in terms of openness to experience. People in marketing, advertising, research, or other creative jobs need to be curious, open to new ideas, and spontaneous. By contrast, openness to experience is not particularly important to accountants, who need to consistently apply stringent rules and formulas to make sense out of complex financial information.

Which of the Big Five Personality Dimensions has the largest impact on behavior in organizations? The cumulative results across 117 studies indicate that conscientiousness is related to job performance across five different occupational groups (professionals, police, managers, sales, and skilled or semi-skilled).[98] In short, people "who are dependable, persistent, goal directed, and organized tend to be higher performers on virtually any job; viewed negatively, those who are careless, irresponsible, low-achievement striving, and impulsive tend to be lower performers on virtually any job."[99] However, the results also indicate that extraversion is related to performance in jobs, such as sales and management, in which there is significant interaction with others. In people-intensive jobs like these, it helps to be sociable, assertive, and talkative and to have energy and be able to energize others. Finally, people who are extraverted and open to experience seem to do much better in training. Being curious and open to new experiences, as well as sociable, assertive, talkative, and full of energy helps people perform better in learning situations.[100]

455

Does the way you keep your desk reveal something about your personality? Lots of people think so. For example, people with ultra-neat desks tend to believe that a desk buried under mounds of paper, food wrappers, and old magazines is a sign that its owner is lazy, disorganized, undependable, and a dreamer. On the other hand, people with messy desks believe that a spotless desk with everything in its place is a sign that its owner is impatient, critical, controlling, analytical, and a perfectionist. Who knows, maybe if your desk is somewhere between "operating-room clean" and the "aftermath of a tornado," it is a sign that you have a good-natured, flexible, and fun-loving personality.[101]

Although studies indicate that extraversion, emotional stability, agreeableness, conscientiousness, and openness to experience are the five basic dimensions of personality in any culture, setting, or language, research has also identified additional personality dimensions that directly affect workplace attitudes and behaviors. These additional personality dimensions are authoritarianism, Machiavellian tendencies, Type A/B personality, self-monitoring, locus of control, and positive/negative affectivity.

**Authoritarianism** is the extent to which an individual believes there should be power and status differences within the organization.[102] Authoritarian employees are likely to prefer a direct leadership style, in which the boss tells them exactly what to do. While this sounds desirable, one disadvantage is that even when they know a better solution or are aware of problems, authoritarian employees may simply carry out their boss's orders without question. Also, authoritarian employees may not perform well on ambiguous tasks, or for managers who encourage employees to use their own initiative and judgment.

Authoritarian leaders are highly demanding and expect employees to unquestioningly obey their orders. T.J. Rodgers, CEO of Cypress Semiconductor, is considered Silicon Valley's toughest boss. Rodgers starts every meeting with a complaint, for example, noting at a recent meeting that a competitor had achieved 98% on-time deliveries and was "kicking our a\*\*." When he feared that good employees would be hired away by competitors, he ordered his managers to take stock options away from poor performers and give them to his best ones. Said Rodgers, "I'm more concerned about stars not getting enough stock than I am about turkeys not getting any." And, consistent with his authoritarian style, Rodgers' office contains a replica of an aircraft bomb labeled with the names of Cypress's competitors.[103]

People with **Machiavellian** personalities believe that virtually any type of behavior is acceptable if it helps satisfy needs or accomplish goals.[104] In other words, people with Machiavellian personalities believe that the ends justify the means. For example, "high Machs" are generally more willing to use lies and deceit to get their way than are "low Machs," even in high-pressure situations where the chances of being caught in a lie are high.[105] High Machs believe that most people are gullible and can be manipulated. High Machs also are more effective in persuading others than are low Machs, and tend to be resistant to others' efforts to persuade them.[106] One reason high Machs are more effective in persuading others is that low Machs (meaning most people) may be distracted by emotions or issues unrelated to winning. By contrast, high Machs are difficult to persuade, because they ignore emotions and secondary issues and focus only on the things that move them closer to their goals.

Richard Hatch, winner of the first *Survivor* reality TV show, is one of the best-known Machiavellian personalities in recent years. Hatch, who schemed, scratched, and clawed his way through the 33-day game, only cared about one thing: figuring out how to win the $1 million prize. For example, after making himself indispensable by being the only person to regularly catch fish (to add to the meager portions of rice provided to the contestants), Hatch leaned toward the camera and explained that he was going to control the other game players by purposely catching fewer fish. Furthermore, Hatch worked hard to thoroughly understand each of his competitors, not because he wanted to be friends, but to better manipulate them. He said, "Maintaining some kind of thumb on all these different people's personalities that I care very little about, is exhaust-

**authoritarianism**
the extent to which an individual believes that there should be power and status differences within organizations

456

**Machiavellianism**
the extent to which individuals believe that virtually any type of behavior is acceptable in trying to satisfy their needs or meet their goals

ing."[107] And, when necessary, Hatch would lie. When the game was over, he even lied to his sister and his son about winning the million dollar prize. He said, "My sister, my son, I lied to both of them. Blatantly, outright lied to them, told them I wasn't the winner, just to stop the continuous probing and let them enjoy watching the show, and that was just really fun. They both thought I hadn't."[108]

Also, because they are out for themselves and no one else, high Machs don't do well in work teams. High Machs often cause conflicts within teams and sometimes cause teams to break up. For example, a businessman in Alexandria, Virginia worked with two of his oldest friends to build a small company that eventually grew into a multimillion dollar business. After his friends actively encouraged him to take a six-week paternity leave following the birth of his baby, they then fired him to reduce his negotiating leverage and force him to take a lower price for his shares of the business! Said the businessman, "I was suddenly fired, broke, humiliated and facing a whole new life with a new baby. These [people] are Machiavellian, but this extreme I never anticipated."[109] Finally, high Machs can have a devastating effect on trust in the workplace. As soon as people realize that a high Mach has used them, there are likely to be interpersonal problems and conflict.[110]

The **Type A/B personality dimension** is the extent to which people tend toward impatience, hurriedness, competitiveness, and hostility.[111] **Type A personalities** try to complete as many tasks as possible in the shortest possible time and are hard-driving, competitive, impatient, perfectionistic, angry, and unable to relax.[112] Type A's are also likely to be aggressive, self-confident, dominant, and extraverted, and have a high need for achievement. For example, John Chatwin, a sales representative for EMC, a maker of large-scale computer data storage devices, is a classic Type A personality. John treats nearly all parts of his life as a contest. Each morning, he races up the stairs to see how many he can climb before the office door closes behind him. Chatwin also works incredibly long hours and hasn't missed more than two days of work since he and his wife vacationed in Hawaii three years ago. Even then, Chatwin was so dedicated to succeeding at his sales job that he would get up in the middle of the night while in Hawaii to call customers on the U.S. mainland (where it was morning). Chatwin's monstrous work hours, combined with his penchant for playing ice hockey and softball several evenings a week, leaves little time for his family. Said Chatwin, "I want to win at everything I do."[113]

In contrast to Chatwin's hurried Type A tendencies, **Type B personalities** are easygoing, patient, and able to relax and engage in leisure activities. Unlike Type A personalities, they are neither highly competitive nor excessively driven to accomplishment. What do we know about the Type A/B personality dimension and the workplace? Contrary to what you'd expect, Type A's don't always outperform Type B's on the job. Type A's tend to perform better on tasks that demand quick decisions made at a rapid work pace under time pressure, but Type B's tend to perform better at tasks requiring well-thought-out decisions in which there is little time pressure. And despite their ambition to succeed, top managers are much more likely to have Type B personalities than Type A personalities.[114] Ironically, the task complexity and psychological challenge inherent in management jobs actually works against many Type A managers by dramatically increasing their stress levels.[115] Type B's, on the other hand, do a much better job of handling and responding to the stress of managerial jobs. Joe Torre, manager of baseball's New York Yankees who led his team to four World Series victories in five years, is the quintessential Type B manager. Torre easily handles the stress in his high-pressure job managing the Yankees, the most successful team in the history of professional sports. But, just as importantly, he helps his players handle the stress inherent in their jobs, too. Said right fielder Paul O'Neill, "Joe doesn't put added pressure on you or act differently toward you because you're not hitting well or playing well." Catcher Joe Girardi said, "Joe never panics, and you never see him berating a player. You never see him dropping his head in disgust." *Fortune* magazine summarized Torre's calming, Type B style this way: "As the situation grows more tense, he grows outwardly calmer, his mannerisms becoming even more deliberate. (Yankees general manager Brian Cashman calls these displays calm bombs.)"[116]

**Type A/B personality dimension**
the extent to which people tend toward impatience, hurriedness, competitiveness, and hostility

**Type A personality**
a person who tries to complete as many tasks as possible in the shortest possible time and is hard driving, competitive, impatient, perfectionistic, angry, and unable to relax

**Type B personality**
a person who is relaxed, easygoing, and able to engage in leisure activities without worrying about work

457

New York Yankees manager Joe Torre congratulates Alfonso Soriano after winning a game in the 2001 American League Championship series. The team eventually won the Championship but fell to Arizona in the World Series. Despite the loss. Torre's Type B personality allowed him to stay calm and to continue to encourage his players.

AP PHOTO/ELAINE THOMPSON

The Type A/B personality dimension is also known for its well-established link to heart attacks.[117] However, it is the hostility and anger of Type A personalities that increase the risk of heart attack, and not impatience, hurriedness, or competitiveness. In fact, a long-term study at Duke University followed a group of lawyers for 25 years and found that those with higher hostility scores were 4.2 times as likely to have died over that period as those with low scores.[118]

**Self-monitoring** refers to the ability to adjust one's behavior to different situations and environments.[119] High self-monitors have the ability to adapt when situational expectations change, while low self-monitors are more likely to insist on behaving in the same way, regardless of the situation. More specifically, high self-monitors are very sensitive to cues from others concerning appropriate behavior. In other words, they are able to adjust their own behavior to suit the situation. By contrast, low self-monitors are controlled from within by their feelings and attitudes. When interacting with others, high self-monitors ask themselves, "Who does this situation want me to be and how can I be that person?" whereas low self-monitors ask themselves "Who am I and how can I be me in this situation?"[120]

For example, you're in an interview situation and you're asked what your strengths and weaknesses are. How do you respond? If you're a high self-monitor, you sense that the interviewer doesn't want to hire an egomaniac and is looking for a balanced description of your capabilities, so you describe your strengths and a few weaknesses (but nothing that would torpedo your chances of getting the job). If you're a low self-monitor and intent on portraying yourself in the best possible way (to increase your chances of getting the job), you miss this cue and respond by describing your strengths and then declaring, "I don't have any major weaknesses." The result? The high self-monitor gets the job offer and the low self-monitor does not.

Studies also show that high self-monitors do better than low self-monitors at boundary-spanning jobs that require interactions with others across and outside organizations, that they often emerge as leaders in work groups, and that they are more likely to resolve conflicts through compromise or collaboration.[121] Because of their ability to adapt to the

**self-monitoring**
the ability to adjust one's behavior to different situations and environments

458

demands of different situations and circumstances, high self-monitors are also much more likely to be promoted or to receive job offers from outside companies.[122] And once promoted, high self-monitors are generally better performers. Indeed, a comparison of average and high-performing managers found that high-performing managers were higher self-monitors, more adaptable, and more self-aware than average managers.[123] Of course, one downside of excessive self-monitoring is that people may be seen as unreliable and inconsistent.[124]

**Locus of control** is the degree to which people believe that their actions influence what happens to them. **Internal locus of control** is the belief that what happens to you is largely under your control. **External locus of control** is the belief that what happens to you is primarily due to factors beyond your control, such as luck, chance, or other powerful people.[125] For example, two decades ago, at the age of 36, James Sweeney came up with the idea for the home healthcare business (in which patients are treated at home rather than in hospitals). McGaw Laboratories, the company he worked for, rejected his idea and fired him. If Sweeney were an "external," he might have given up his dream. However, being an "internal," Sweeney immediately started his home healthcare business. Indeed, Warren Bennis, a leading management author, said that internals, unlike externals, view failures as "false starts, stumbles, or steps to greatness."[126] In fact, eight years later, Sweeney sold his business for nearly $600 million. Ironically, he then used that money to purchase McGaw Labs, the company that had rejected his idea and fired him. Then, when the home healthcare business he started and sold began to struggle, he bought it back for half of what he sold it for.[127]

Besides believing that what happens to them is largely under their control, internals have been found to be easier to motivate (especially when rewards are linked to performance), more difficult to lead, more independent, and better able to handle complex information and solve complex problems.[128] On the other hand, externals are more compliant and conforming and therefore are easier to lead than internals. For example, internals may question directives from their managers, while externals are likely to quietly accept them. Finally, internals are likely to perform better on complex tasks that require initiative and independent decision making, whereas externals tend to perform better on simple, repetitive tasks that are well structured.

**Affectivity** is the stable tendency to experience positive or negative moods and to react to things in a generally positive or negative way.[129] People with **positive affectivity** consistently notice and focus on the positive aspects of themselves and their environments. In other words, they seem to be in a good mood most of the time and are predisposed to being optimistic, cheerful, and cordial. By contrast, people with **negative affectivity** consistently notice and focus on the negative in themselves and their environments. They are frequently in bad moods, consistently expect the worst to happen, and are often irritated or pessimistic.

How stable are the positive or negative moods associated with positive/negative affectivity? A 10-year study by the National Institute of Aging found that even when people changed jobs or companies, the people who were the happiest at the beginning of the study were still the happiest people 10 years later at the end of the study.[130] Likewise, the results of a much longer study found that high school counselors' ratings of student cheerfulness predicted how satisfied these people were with their jobs 30 years later.[131] Since dispositions toward positive or negative affectivity are long lasting and very stable, some companies have begun measuring affectivity during the hiring process. Elsie Houck, who oversees 1,200 employees at 72 bank centers for Bank One Dallas, said, "The biggest thing we're focusing on in this market is customer service. We want to make sure that we're really providing world-class service to our customers so we can retain them. My motto when we're hiring employees is, we've got to hire the right people in the right job. We look for people with a twinkle in their eye, a spring in their step, and a smile in their voice. It's important that they have a positive attitude [and are] filled with high energy and enthusiasm. If they have those qualities, we're going to provide world-class service to our customers."[132]

**locus of control**
the degree to which individuals believe that their actions can influence what happens to them

**internal locus of control**
the belief that what happens to you is largely the result of your own actions

**external locus of control**
the belief that what happens to you is largely the result of factors beyond your control

**affectivity**
the stable tendency to experience positive or negative moods and to react to things in a generally positive or negative way

**positive affectivity**
personality trait in which individuals tend to notice and focus on the positive aspects of themselves and their environments

**negative affectivity**
personality trait in which individuals tend to notice and focus on the negative aspects of themselves and their environments

mood linkage
a phenomenon in which one
worker's negative affectivity and
bad moods can spread to others

Studies also show that employees with positive affectivity are absent less often, report feeling less stress, are less likely to be injured in workplace accidents, and are less likely to retaliate against management and the company when they believe that they have been treated unfairly.[133] Affectivity is also important because of **mood linkage**, a phenomenon where one worker's negative affectivity and bad moods can spread to others. Studies of nurses and accountants show a strong relationship between individual workers' moods and the moods of their coworkers.[134] Finally, people with positive affectivity are better decision makers, are rated as having much higher managerial potential, and are more successful in sales jobs.[135]

## Review 3
### Deep-Level Diversity

Deep-level diversity matters because it can reduce prejudice, discrimination, and conflict while increasing social integration. It consists of dispositional and personality differences that can be learned only through extended interaction with others. Research conducted in different cultures, settings, and languages indicates that there are five basic dimensions of personality: extraversion, emotional stability, agreeableness, conscientiousness, and openness to experience. Of these, conscientiousness is the perhaps most important, because conscientious workers tend to be higher performers on virtually any job. Extraversion is also related to performance in jobs that require significant interaction with others. Studies also show that the personality dimensions of authoritarianism, Machiavellian tendencies, Type A/B personality, self-monitoring, locus of control, and positive/negative affectivity are important in the workplace. These personality dimensions are related to honesty, trust, teamwork, persuasive abilities, job performance, decision making, stress, heart disease, adaptability, promotions, interpersonal skills, motivation, initiative, job satisfaction, absenteeism, accidents, retaliatory behavior, mood linkage, and management potential.

# How Can Diversity Be Managed?

How much should companies change their standard business practices to accommodate the diversity of their workers? For example, at Whirlpool Corporation's Lavergne, Tennessee, appliance factory, 10 percent of the work force is Muslim. Many Muslim men have long beards and wear skullcaps, while Muslim women wear flowing headscarves and modest, loose-fitting, form-hiding clothes. For safety reasons, long hair, hats of any kind, and loose clothing are prohibited on the factory floor. (Imagine any of these getting caught in moving machinery.) How should Whirlpool's managers deal with the obvious conflict between the Muslim religious practices and the company's safety procedures that are designed to prevent injury? Furthermore, at noon on Fridays, all Muslims attend 45- to 90-minute religious services at their mosques. With a typical Monday to Friday workweek and lunch breaks of just 30 minutes, how can Whirlpool's managers accommodate this Friday service without hurting the production schedule and without giving the Muslims special treatment (that may be resented by the 90 percent of workers who aren't Muslim)?[136]

Likewise, what do you do when a talented top executive has a drinking problem that only seems to affect his behavior at company business parties (for entertaining clients), where he made inappropriate advances toward female employees? What do you do when, despite aggressive company policies against racial discrimination, employees continue to tell racial jokes and publicly post cartoons displaying racial humor? And, since many people confuse diversity with affirmative action, what do you do to make sure that your company's diversity practices and policies are viewed as benefiting all workers and not just some workers?

No doubt about it, questions like these make managing diversity one of the toughest challenges that managers face.[137] However, there are steps companies can take to begin to address these issues.

4. *explain the basic principles and practices that can be used to manage diversity.*

## 4. Managing Diversity

*As discussed earlier, diversity programs try to create a positive work environment where no one is advantaged or disadvantaged, where "we" is everyone, where everyone can do their best work, where differences are respected and not ignored, and where everyone feels comfortable. Let's begin to address those goals by learning about 4.1 different diversity paradigms, 4.2 diversity principles, and 4.3 diversity training and practices.*

### 4.1 Diversity Paradigms

As shown in Exhibit 12.8, there are several different methods or paradigms for managing diversity: the discrimination and fairness paradigm, the access and legitimacy paradigm, and the learning and effectiveness paradigm.[138] The *discrimination and fairness paradigm*, which is the most common method of approaching diversity, focuses on equal opportunity, fair treatment, recruitment of minorities, and strict compliance with the equal employment opportunity laws. Under this approach, success is usually measured by how well companies achieve recruitment, promotion, and retention goals for women, people of different racial/ethnic backgrounds, or other underrepresented groups. For example, one manager said, "I do know that if you don't measure something, it doesn't count. You measure your market share. You measure your profitability. The same should be true for diversity. There has to be some way of measuring whether you did, in fact, cast your net widely, and whether the company is better off today in terms of the experience of people of color than it was a few years ago. I measure my market share and my profitability. Why not this?"[139] The primary benefit of the discrimination and fairness paradigm is that it generally brings about fairer treatment of employees and increases demographic diversity. The primary limitation is that the focus of diversity remains on the surface-level diversity dimensions of gender, race, and ethnicity.

---

**EXHIBIT 12.8**

PARADIGMS FOR MANAGING DIVERSITY

| DIVERSITY PARADIGM | FOCUS | SUCCESS MEASURED BY | BENEFITS | LIMITATIONS |
|---|---|---|---|---|
| Discrimination & Fairness | • Equal opportunity<br>• Fair treatment<br>• Recruitment of minorities<br>• Strict compliance with laws | • Recruitment, promotion, & retention goals for underrepresented groups | • Fairer treatment<br>• Increased demographic diversity | • Focus on surface-level diversity |
| Access & Legitimacy | • Acceptance & celebration of differences | • Diversity in company matches diversity of primary stakeholders | • Establishes a clear business reason for diversity | • Focus on surface-level diversity |
| Learning & Effectiveness | • Integrating deep-level differences into organization | • Valuing people on the basis of individual knowledge, skills, and abilities | • Values common ground<br>• Distinction between individual and group differences<br>• Less conflict, backlash, and divisiveness<br>• Bringing different talents and perspectives together | • Focus on deep-level diversity is more difficult to measure and quantify |

The *access and legitimacy paradigm* focuses on the acceptance and celebration of differences, so that the diversity within the company matches the diversity found among primary stakeholders, such as customers, suppliers, and local communities. This is similar to the *business growth* advantage of diversity discussed earlier in the chapter. The basic idea behind this approach is "We are living in an increasingly multicultural country, and new ethnic groups are quickly gaining consumer power. Our company needs a demographically more diverse work force to help us gain access to these differentiated segments."[140] Consistent with this goal, Margaret Cerrudo, senior vice president at phone company SBC Communications, said, "Our goal is not to mirror the civilian labor force but the population we serve."[141] The primary benefit of this approach is that it establishes a clear business reason for diversity. However, like the discrimination and fairness paradigm, it does no more than focus on the surface-level diversity dimensions of gender, race, and ethnicity. Furthermore, employees who are assigned responsibility for customers and stakeholders on the basis of their gender, race, or ethnicity may eventually feel frustrated and exploited.

While the discrimination and fairness paradigm focuses on assimilation (having a demographically representative work force), and the access and legitimacy paradigm focuses on differentiation (where demographic differences inside the company match those of key customers and stakeholders), the *learning and effectiveness paradigm* focuses on integrating deep-level diversity differences, such as personality, attitudes, beliefs, and values, into the actual work of the organization. Under this approach, people are valued not only on the basis of surface-level diversity (i.e., gender, race/ethnicity), but also for all of their knowledge, skills, abilities, and experiences. For example, Bedie Kohake didn't become a plant manager for Catalytica Pharmaceuticals, which makes Sudafed for Warner-Lambert and the HIV drug AZT for GlaxoSmithKline, because she's female. She got the job because she graduated summa cum laude with a degree in chemical engineering and had a decade of experience working in manufacturing facilities for companies like Du Pont Chemical, where she managed to increase production by 60 percent. Kohake, who manages 10 production areas and 100 workers, technicians, and chemical engineers, said, "I've never had any disadvantage here, because Catalytica practices diversity."[142] Exhibit 12.9 shows the necessary preconditions for creating a learning and effectiveness diversity paradigm within an organization.

## EXHIBIT 12.9

### CREATING A LEARNING AND EFFECTIVENESS DIVERSITY PARADIGM IN AN ORGANIZATION

1. The leadership must understand that a diverse work force will embody different perspectives and approaches to work, and must truly value variety of opinion and insight.
2. The leadership must recognize both the learning opportunities and the challenges that the expression of different perspectives presents for an organization.
3. The organizational culture must create an expectation of high standards of performance for everyone.
4. The organizational culture must stimulate personal development.
5. The organizational culture must encourage openness and a high tolerance for debate, and support constructive conflict on work-related matters.
6. The culture must make workers feel valued.
7. The organization must have a well-articulated and widely understood mission. This keeps discussions about work differences from degenerating into debates about the validity of people's perspectives.
8. The organization must have a relatively egalitarian, nonbureaucratic structure.

**Source:** D.A. Thomas & R.J. Ely, "Making Differences Matter: A New Paradigm for Managing Diversity," *Harvard Business Review* 74 (September/October 1996): 79-90.

In other words, the learning and effectiveness paradigm is consistent with achieving organizational plurality. **Organizational plurality** is a work environment where (1) all members are empowered to contribute in a way that maximizes the benefits to the organization, customers, and themselves, and (2) the individuality of each member is respected by not segmenting or polarizing people on the basis of their membership in a particular group.[143]

There are four benefits to the learning and effectiveness diversity paradigm.[144] First, it values common ground. Dave Thomas of the Harvard Business School said, "Like the fairness paradigm, it promotes equal opportunity for all individuals. And like the access paradigm, it acknowledges cultural differences among people and recognizes the value in those differences. Yet this new model for managing diversity lets the organization internalize differences among employees so that it learns and grows because of them. Indeed, with the model fully in place, members of the organization can say, 'We are all on the same team, with our differences—not despite them.'"[145]

Second, it makes a distinction between individual and group differences. When diversity focuses only on differences between groups, such as females versus white males, large differences within groups are ignored.[146] For example, think of the women you know at work. Now, think for a second about what they have in common. After that, think about how they're different. If your situation is typical, the list of differences should be just as long, if not longer, than the list of commonalties. In short, managers can achieve a greater understanding of diversity and their employees by treating them as individuals and by realizing that not all African Americans, Hispanics, women, or white males want the same things at work.[147]

Third, because the focus is on individual differences, the learning and effectiveness paradigm is less likely to encounter the conflict, backlash, and divisiveness sometimes associated with diversity programs that just focus on group differences. Taylor Cox, one of the leading management writers on diversity, said, "We are concerned here with these more destructive forms of conflict which may be present with diverse work forces due to language barriers, cultural clash, or resentment by majority-group members of what they may perceive as preferential and unwarranted treatment of minority-group members."[148] Ray Haines, a consultant who has helped companies deal with the aftermath of diversity programs that became divisive, said, "There's a large amount of backlash related to diversity training. It stirs up a lot of hostility, anguish, and resentment but doesn't give people tools to deal with [the backlash]. You have people come in and talk about their specific ax to grind."[149] Certainly, not all diversity programs are divisive or lead to conflict. But, by focusing on individual rather than group differences, the learning and effectiveness paradigm helps to minimize these potential problems.

Finally, unlike the other diversity paradigms that simply focus on the value of being different (primarily in terms of surface-level diversity), there is a focus on bringing different talents and perspectives *together* (i.e., deep-level diversity) to make the best organizational decisions and to produce innovative, competitive products and services.

### 4.2 Diversity Principles

While diversity paradigms represent general approaches or strategies for managing diversity, the following diversity principles, shown in Exhibit 12.10, will help managers do a better job of *managing company diversity programs,* no matter which diversity paradigm they choose.[150]

In terms of diversity principles, begin by *carefully and faithfully following and enforcing federal and state laws regarding equal opportunity employment.* Diversity programs can't and won't succeed if the company is being sued for discriminatory actions and behavior. Faithfully following the law will also reduce the time and expense associated with EEOC investigations or lawsuits. Start by learning more at the EEOC Web site (**http://www.eeoc.gov**). Following the law also means strictly and fairly enforcing company policies. Kevin Kelly, the former *Business Week* reporter whose workers were writing racial slurs on the stalls of the company bathroom, said:

EXHIBIT 12.10

### DIVERSITY PRINCIPLES

1. Carefully and faithfully follow and enforce federal and state laws regarding equal employment opportunity.
2. Treat group differences as important, but not special.
3. Find the common ground.
4. Tailor opportunities to individuals, not groups.
5. Reexamine, but maintain, high standards.
6. Solicit negatives as well as positive feedback.
7. Set high but realistic goals.

**Source:** L.S. Gottfredson, "Dilemmas in Developing Diversity Programs," in *Diversity in the Workplace,* eds. S.E. Jackson and Associates (New York: Guildford Press, 1992).

Last year, at the urging of our labor attorney, we assembled an employee handbook, the first few pages of which spell out tough harassment and equal opportunity policies. We passed out literature on sexual harassment and adopted formal investigation procedures for any bias complaint. Anybody found guilty of breaking the rules is dealt with harshly. This seems to have improved things considerably. Employees on one shift, it turned out, felt they had been putting up with racially insensitive jokes of a foreman. With the new policy, a few men felt free to complain, which prompted an investigation in which the foreman cooperated. We suspended him without pay for two weeks, enrolled him in a class on managing a multicultural work force, and told him if he broke the rules again, he'd be fired. It seems to have worked.[151]

*Treat group differences as important, but not special.* Surface-level diversity dimensions such as age, gender, and race/ethnicity should be respected, but should not be treated as more important than other kinds of differences (i.e., deep-level diversity). Remember, the shift from surface- to deep-level diversity helps people know and understand each other better, reduces prejudice and conflict, and leads to stronger social integration with people wanting to work together and get the job done. Also, *find the common ground.* While respecting differences is important, it's just as important, especially with diverse work forces, to actively find ways for employees to see and share commonalties.

*Tailor opportunities to individuals, not groups.* Special programs for training, development, mentoring, or promotions should be based on individual strengths and weaknesses, not on group status. Instead of making mentoring available just for one group of workers, create mentoring opportunities for everyone who wants to be mentored. For example, at Pacific Enterprises, all programs, including the Career Conversations forums, in which upper level managers are publicly interviewed about themselves and how they got their jobs, are open to all employees.[152]

*Reexamine, but maintain high standards.* Companies have a legal and moral obligation to make sure that their hiring and promotion procedures and standards are fair to all. However, in today's competitive markets, companies should not lower standards because of diversity. This not only hurts organizations, but also feeds stereotypes that applicants who are hired or promoted in the name of affirmative action or diversity are less qualified. For example, at the Marriott Marquis Hotel in New York's Time Square, where the hotel's 1,700 employees come from 70 countries and speak 47 different languages, managers are taught to cope with diversity by focusing on job performance. Jessica Brown, a quality-assurance manager who checks the cleanliness of rooms, said, "I don't lower my standards for anybody."[153]

*Solicit negative as well as positive feedback.* Diversity is one of the most difficult management issues. No company or manager gets it right from the start. Consequently, companies should aggressively seek positive and negative feedback about their diversity pro-

**464**

grams. For example, Allstate Insurance surveys all 50,000 of its employees on a quarterly basis to compile a "diversity index" that indicates whether customers are receiving bias-free service and managers are showing respect for employees and following the company's diversity policies.[154]

*Set high but realistic goals.* Just because diversity is difficult doesn't mean that organizations shouldn't try to accomplish as much as possible. The general purpose of diversity programs is to try to create a positive work environment where no one is advantaged or disadvantaged, where "we" is everyone, where everyone can do their best work, where differences are respected and not ignored, and where everyone feels comfortable. Even if progress is slow, companies should not shrink from these goals.

## 4.3 Diversity Training and Practices

**awareness training**
training that is designed to raise employees' awareness of diversity issues and to challenge the underlying assumptions or stereotypes they may have about others

**skills-based diversity training**
training that teaches employees the practical skills they need for managing a diverse work force, such as flexibility and adaptability, negotiation, problem solving, and conflict resolution

**diversity audits**
formal assessments that measure employee and management attitudes, investigate the extent to which people are advantaged or disadvantaged with respect to hiring and promotions, and review companies' diversity-related policies and procedures

**diversity pairing**
mentoring program in which people of different cultural backgrounds, genders, or races/ethnicities are paired together to get to know each other and change stereotypical beliefs and attitudes

Organizations use diversity training and several common diversity practices to manage diversity. There are two basic types of diversity training programs. **Awareness training** is designed to raise employees' awareness of diversity issues, such as the dimensions discussed in this chapter, and to get employees to challenge underlying assumptions or stereotypes they may have about others. For example, in Texaco's awareness training, employees "get in touch with their negative assumptions" and learn how their behavior affects others.[155] By contrast, **skills-based diversity training** teaches employees the practical skills they need for managing a diverse work force, such as flexibility and adaptability, negotiation, problem solving, and conflict resolution.[156]

Companies also use these diversity practices to better manage diversity: diversity audits, diversity pairing, and minority experiences for top executives. **Diversity audits** are formal assessments that measure employee and management attitudes, investigate the extent to which people are advantaged or disadvantaged with respect to hiring and promotions, and review companies' diversity-related policies and procedures. For example, the results of a formal diversity audit prompted BRW, an architecture and engineering firm, to increase job advertising in minority publications, to set up a diversity committee to provide recommendations to upper management, to provide diversity training for all employees, and to rewrite the company handbook to make a stronger statement about the company's commitment to a diverse work force.[157]

Earlier in the chapter you learned that *mentoring*, pairing a junior employee with a senior employee, is a common strategy for creating learning and promotional opportunities for women. Diversity pairing is a special kind of mentoring. **Diversity pairing** is pairing people of different cultural backgrounds, genders, or races/ethnicities for mentoring. The hope is that stereotypical beliefs and attitudes will change as people get to know each other as individuals.[158] Procter & Gamble uses diversity pairing in its "Mentor Up" program, which pairs senior men with junior women. But unlike traditional mentoring programs, the Mentor Up program is designed to have the junior women mentor the senior men. The basic idea is to change the culture among P&G's executives one manager at a time. Lisa Gevelber, a 29-year-old detergent brand manager who was paired with Rob Steele, a 43-year-old vice president and general manager of cleaning products, said, "I provide him a lot of perspective on what issues are hot among young women in the company today."[159]

Finally, because top managers are still overwhelmingly white and male, a number of companies believe that it is worthwhile to *have top executives experience what it is like to be in the minority.* This can be done by having top managers go to places or events in which nearly everyone else is of a different gender or racial/ethnic background. At Hoechst Celanese, top managers must join two organizations in which they are a minority. For instance, the CEO, who is white and male, joined the board of Hampton University, an historically African-American college, and Jobs for Progress, a Hispanic organization that helps people prepare for jobs. As a result of his experiences, he said, "The only way to break out of comfort zones is to be exposed to other people. When we are, it becomes clear that all people are similar." A Hoechst vice president who joined three organizations in which he was in the minority said, "Joining these organizations has been more helpful to me than two weeks of diversity training.[160]

465

# "headline news"

## Banking on Diversity? Mentoring Is the Way to Go.

For business today and in the future, diversity matters. Corporations have taken long steps to improve the work life of minority employees, but in a sea of failing efforts, mentoring alone has been proven successful in accomplishing this. In her new book, *Be Your Own Mentor*, Sheila Wellington writes, "Mentors are more important to career success than hard work, more important than talent, more important than intelligence. Mentors can show you the ropes. And pull strings."

Some might argue that Wellington's statement is on the side of hyperbole, but Pat Carmichael, a senior vice president at Chase Bank overseeing Long Island and Queens branches—and an African American—would probably say it's on par. Carmichael has been a mentor throughout her 30-year banking career, and her current slate of 10 mentees routinely takes advantage of her experience and advice.

She counsels minorities climbing the corporate ladder to ask for tough assignments—and feedback: "Minority employees have to take the initiative and say to their bosses 'What do I need to grow?'" Wellington's research of women in corporate leadership throughout the United States, Canada, and the United Kingdom confirms this. Women in Wellington's study say that keys to success are seeking high-profile assignments and having a mentor. Finding a style with which male colleagues and supervisors are comfortable is also important.

Mentoring isn't just for minorities, nor is it all about individual career guidance, at least not for Carmichael. One of her mentees is John Imperiale, a 25-year-old white assistant branch manager. Carmichael sought out this relationship when she noticed that the quiet Imperiale was too comfortable just crunching numbers. It was she who encouraged him to diversify himself by stepping into the more interpersonal role of branch manager. She hopes that the exposure Imperiale has to her will give him insights when he is working with or managing a diverse group of employees in the future.

Like Pat Carmichael, Bob Knowling takes his role as a mentor seriously, particularly in developing the technology skills of minority employees. He has found that he can provide valuable coaching even to college-educated employees who may not have a personal network of family or friends with business savvy on which to rely. This is particularly important in light of concerns about the digital divide and about an economy that is shifting more and more toward technology-based jobs.

Mentoring does more than develop employees. It can help retain them. Dinah Moore, one of Carmichael's mentees, says mentoring at Chase is one of the reasons she has stayed at Chase. With a tight labor market and the cost of employees increasing, mentoring can positively affect the bottom line. And that's money in the bank.

1. Can a successful minority mentoring program obviate the need for other types of diversity training?
2. Outline the steps you might follow to create a mentoring program at your firm.

**Sources:** E. Alleman and D.L. Clarke, "Accountability: Measuring Mentoring and Its Bottom Line Impact," *Review of Business*, Spring 2000 (2:1) 62. Info-Trac Article A73182593. S. Mehta, "Why Mentoring Works," *Fortune*, 9 July 2001, 119. Info-Trac Article A75915627. M. Messner, "Establishing a Mentoring Program," *Business Credit*, May 2000 (102:5) 44. Info-Trac Article A62929268. E. Alt Powell, "Mentors Key for Female Execs, Expert Says," *Cincinnati Enquirer*, 23 July 2001, B5.

## Review 4
### Managing Diversity

The three paradigms for managing diversity are the discrimination and fairness paradigm (equal opportunity, fair treatment, strict compliance with the law), the access and legitimacy paradigm (matching internal diversity to external diversity), and the learning and effectiveness paradigm (achieving organizational plurality by integrating deep-level diversity into the work of the organization). Unlike the other paradigms that focus on surface-level differences, the learning and effectiveness program values common ground, distinguishes between individual and group differences, minimizes conflict and divisiveness, and focuses on bringing different talents and perspectives together. What principles can companies use when managing diversity? Follow and enforce federal and state laws regarding equal employment opportunity. Treat group differences as important, but not special. Find the common ground. Tailor opportunities to individuals, not groups. Reexamine, but maintain, high standards. Solicit negative as well as positive feedback. Set high but realistic goals. The two types of diversity training are awareness training and skills-based diversity training. Companies also manage diversity through diversity audits, diversity pairing, and by having top executives experience what it is like to be a minority.

## What Really Happened?

With adverse publicity, numerous lawsuits, multimillion dollar out-of-court settlements, and late-night talk-show comics lampooning it, Denny's restaurants picked up a reputation as a business that discriminates against African-American customers. Advantica's new CEO Jim Adamson said, "The combination of hundreds of complaints, a growing number of lawsuits, and relentless publicity had turned Denny's restaurants, one of the country's largest restaurant chains, into what one person called 'a poster child for racism.'" However, in less than five years, Adamson and his management team instituted significant changes that led to Denny's being ranked as America's best company for minorities two years running by *Fortune* magazine. Let's find out what really happened at Advantica/Denny's as it made this amazing turnaround.

**As Advantica's new CEO (Advantica now owns Denny's), you were hired to change the company's reputation and its culture. But what should you do? Should you focus on diversity? Many people aren't sure what "diversity" means. Ask 10 different people and you're likely to get 10 different answers. If you can't explain what diversity means, how can you make effective changes throughout the company?**

Diversity exists in organizations when there is a variety of demographic, cultural, and personal differences among the employees and the customers. A common misconception is that workplace diversity and affirmative action are the same. However, affirmative action is more narrowly focused on demographics, is required by law, and is used to punish companies that discriminate on the basis of race, color, religion, gender, or national origin. By contrast, diversity is broader in focus (going beyond demographics), voluntary, more positive in that it encourages companies to value all kinds of differences, and, at this time, substantially less controversial than affirmative ac-

tion. Diversity also makes good business sense in terms of cost savings (reducing turnover, decreasing absenteeism, and avoiding lawsuits), attracting and retaining talent, and driving business growth (improving marketplace understanding and higher-quality problem solving).

Less than a decade ago, Denny's was not a very diverse business. However, it has made dramatic improvement in a short time. Previously, none of its suppliers were minority-owned firms. Today, Denny's spends $125 million a year, approximately 18 percent of its total purchases, with minority-owned suppliers. Likewise, of its 46,000 employees, 31 percent are now Hispanic, 11 percent are African American, and 6 percent are of Asian-Pacific origin. In addition, one-third of its managers are now minorities, and minorities now own 35 percent of Denny's franchise restaurants. Diversity continues at the top with its board of directors. Three of its 12 board members are black and one is Hispanic. As a result of these changes and others, Denny's now has a much more diverse customer base, gaining more than a million black customers in the last few years. Much of that gain comes from building new, minority-owned restaurants in inner cities. Olivia Johnson, who lives in Washington D.C., said, "We were very surprised to see them come to this neighborhood, with all the bad feelings and racism." And while people were skeptical at first, attitudes are changing. Olivia's husband James said, "We're very pleased." Likewise, in inner city Houston, Texas, new customer Silas McGee said, "It's really been needed here. It's great."

So Denny's, once known for discrimination, is now one of the most diverse businesses in the United States. As a result of these astonishing changes, *Fortune* magazine has ranked Denny's as the best American company for minorities two years in a row. Denny's is also ranked twelfth in the United States by *Working Woman* magazine for opportunities for women. Fi-

nally, according to *Asian-Enterprise* magazine, Denny's is also a top-10 best company for Asian Americans.

**What kinds of things go into a diversity plan? Are there key ideas or principles that you could follow?**

The three paradigms for managing diversity are the discrimination and fairness paradigm (equal opportunity, fair treatment, strict compliance with the law), the access and legitimacy paradigm (matching internal diversity to external diversity), and the learning and effectiveness paradigm (achieving deep-level diversity by focusing on common ground and bringing different talents and perspectives together). What principles can companies use when managing diversity? Follow and enforce federal and state laws regarding equal employment opportunity. Treat group differences as important, but not special. Find the common ground. Tailor opportunities to individuals, not groups. Reexamine, but maintain, high standards. Solicit negative as well as positive feedback. Set high but realistic goals.

In making its largest initial changes, Denny's relied heavily on the discrimination and fairness paradigm. It signed a consent decree with the Justice Department that specifically forbade discrimination. That decree contains 15 specific guidelines that must be followed by all Denny's employees. For instance, "Do not refuse to seat, take meal orders, or serve any guest on the basis of race, color, or national origin," or "Do not require any guest to wait longer, or provide inferior services to any guest on the basis of race, color, or national origin." Furthermore, all employees and managers were required to sign and return a statement indicating that they had read and understood the guidelines and that failure to follow them could lead to sanctions or termination. Denny's diversity officer said that prior to the decree, "There were no clear-cut policies against discrimination. And there was no racial-sensitivity training." But now, with the decree, according to CEO Jim Adamson, "If you discriminate, you're fired."

Denny's strongly reinforces the decree in two ways. First, 25 percent of top managers' pay is linked to meeting diversity goals, such as finding minority franchise buyers or minority suppliers. Second, all Denny's managers and employees participate in several days of diversity training where the key message is that all customers must be treated the same. Even small details aren't overlooked. For example, to avoid implying disrespect, servers are told to put money into customers' hands when returning change. Managers and the wait staff are also taught to communicate with customers to avoid misunderstandings. If there is a wait for tables, they must explain why. If a small group that arrived later is seated before a larger group that arrived earlier, the larger group must be told that only a small table was available at that time.

**Finally, what initial steps could you take as a leader to communicate that things will change and that all Denny's customers are entitled to excellent food and service?**

When Jim Adamson became CEO of Advantica (which owns Denny's), one of his first steps was to hold a meeting his first week in the company auditorium. At that meeting, he made several key announcements. First, no discrimination of any kind would be tolerated. He told the assembled audience of managers and employees, "If you discriminate, we will fire you. Period." Secondly, he sent a message about openness and access by making the top floor of the building, where his offices were located, accessible to everyone who worked there. In the past, only Adamson and the chief financial officer had card keys to gain access to the top floor. Adamson had engineers reprogram the card keys so everyone could enter the top floor, and then invited everyone to visit. He said, "The people in our corporate headquarters were so amazed at this gesture that Dory [his assistant] and I ended up giving tours of the executive floors. . . . Employees visited our floors at regular intervals for about four months." Two weeks later, Adamson sent another significant signal, declaring that Dr. Martin Luther King, Jr.'s birthday would now be an official company holiday. He said, "So I declared the day a holiday at headquarters. I didn't take away any of the existing holiday schedule, either, in the way that some companies do. I just added a day." Finally, in addition to those changes, Adamson and his staff began putting together the plans for the diversity training, mentioned above, that all Denny's managers and employees must attend. Denny's calls this training "We Can," with the "Can" standing for "Consistently Attend to guests' Needs."

**Sources:** J. Adamson, R. McNatt, R. McNatt, *The Denny's Story: How a Company in Crisis Resurrected Its Good Name* (New York: Wiley, 2000). C. Chen, J. Jonathan, E. LeBlanc, L. Vanderkam, & K. VellaZarb, "America's 50 Best Companies for Minorities," *Fortune*, 10 July 2000, 190. F. Esposito, S. Garman, J. Hickman, N. Watson, & A. Wheat, "America's 50 Best Companies for Minorities," *Fortune*, 9 July 2001, 122. B. Holden, "Denny's Chain Settles Suits by Minorities," *The Wall Street Journal*, 24 May 1994, A3. A. Lengel, "Denny's Daring Entree; Eatery, NE Hope to Improve Image," *Washington Post*, 21 September 2000, A1. J. Mitchell, "Los Angeles Family Sues Denny's, Alleges Bias Court: Suit Says Large Group Was Denied Service as Whites Were Being Seated," *Los Angeles Times*, 24 August 2001. P. Ridge, "A Special Background Report on Trends in Industry," *The Wall Street Journal*, 27 April, 2000, A1. D. Segal, "Denny's Serves up a Sensitive Image; Restaurant Chain Launches PR Drive to Show Minorities It Has Changed Its Ways," *Washington Post*, 7 April 1999, E1.

## Key Terms

affectivity *(459)*

affirmative action *(438)*

age discrimination *(445)*

agreeableness *(454)*

authoritarianism *(456)*

awareness training *(465)*

conscientiousness *(454)*

deep-level diversity *(444)*

disability *(450)*

disability discrimination *(450)*

disposition *(453)*

diversity *(437)*

diversity audits *(465)*

diversity pairing *(465)*

emotional stability *(454)*

external locus of control *(459)*

extraversion *(453)*

gender discrimination *(446)*

glass ceiling *(446)*

internal locus of control *(459)*

locus of control *(459)*

Machiavellianism *(456)*

mood linkage *(460)*

negative affectivity *(459)*

openness to experience *(455)*

organizational plurality *(463)*

personality *(453)*

positive affectivity *(459)*

racial and ethnic discrimination *(449)*

self-monitoring *(458)*

skills-based diversity training *(465)*

social integration *(444)*

stereotypes *(451)*

surface-level diversity *(443)*

Type A personality *(457)*

Type A/B personality dimension *(457)*

Type B personality *(457)*

## What Would You Do-II

### Diversity at Coke: Is It the Real Thing?

For years, your company, Coca-Cola, has been lauded for its successes in creating and maintaining an environment of diversity. In order to continue Coke's promotion of diversity, a formal program was established to recruit and train women and minorities. A key component of this program involved the identification, recruitment, training, and mentoring of women and minorities to prepare them for senior positions within the firm. Further, Coca-Cola has been a continued sponsor of the annual National Black MBA Conference and other diversity-related organizations and has historically tied management incentives to the achievement of specific diversity-related goals in recruitment and promotion. Unfortunately, nothing lasts forever.

Today, your company received a memo about a class action lawsuit, involving 2,200 current and former employees, alleging racial discrimination in the areas of compensation, evaluation, promotion, and termination. The memo pointed to a Web site devoted to the lawsuit, which is promoting a nationwide boycott of all Coca-Cola products. The Web site (**http://www. corporatejustice.org**) not only lists the boycott theme "NO JUSTICE! NO COKE!," but it also lists a comparison of management positions held by African Americans and whites. To top it off, the attorney leading the lawsuit is Cyrus Mehri, the attorney responsible for securing the recent racial discrimination settlement of $176 million against Texaco. According to the lawsuit, black employees are underpaid in comparison to their white counterparts and are typically moved into departments such as human resources or community affairs, which generally have less responsibility and career opportunities than other departments primarily staffed by whites. When you visit the Web site, you find posted average salaries at Coke for the last three years split out by ethnicity groups. It shows that the mean salary among African Americans in 1998 was $45,215, compared to a mean of $72,045 for Caucasians, a whopping difference of $26,830. Attorneys for the plaintiff further claim that the major problem with Coca-Cola is the existence of a good-old-boy network led by white middle- and senior-level managers who promote familiar faces.

This is not the first time you have heard about racial issues within your firm. Several of the plaintiffs claim that when confronted with past racial inequities, Coke managers did not take the issue seriously. Now, the situation is sure to gain national attention, and you wonder what effect this news may have on the company's stock price and current market share. After all, Coca-Cola currently holds the most diverse group of consumers among all soft-drink brands.

Clearly, the emphasis at this point is not only to salvage the company's reputation, but also to make changes so that this type of situation does not reoccur. Is implementing an affirmative action program the answer? After all, the issue here *is* racial discrimination, and the more general diversity program that you had in place failed somewhere (or else you wouldn't be getting sued). Maybe instead of revamping your program you can refine it—or implement it better. You need to figure out just what to do quickly and decisively. **As the CEO of Coca-Cola, what would you do?**

**Sources:** A. King, "Coca-Cola Takes the High Road," *Black Enterprise*, February 2001. S. Reed, "Taking It to the Web," *American Prospect*, January 2001. "Courting Favor," *Progressive Grocer*, May 2000. "Coca-Cola Agrees to Pay Black Workers $192.5 Million in Discrimination Settlement," *Jet*, 4 December 2000. A. Harrington, "Prevention Is the Best Defense," *Fortune*, 10 July 2000. C. Cooper, "Coca-Cola Loses Its Perfect Harmony," *People Management*, 22 June 2000.

## Management Decisions

### To Hire or Not to Hire

You are the manager of a small practice that provides accounting, auditing, and consulting services both for private individuals and for several large firms. When your firm consults with its business clients, it is typically done at their location, so office space and appearance has not been an issue in the past. Since the bulk of the company's clientele has been large businesses, the firm has operated out of an older building in the downtown area. In an attempt to increase the number of private clients, you recently opened a small, remote office located in a retail shopping center in a newer part of town. You are in the process of screening applicants for a business auditor position at the downtown office. This morning, you interviewed an outstanding applicant at the shopping center location, where your office is located. This applicant not only has the minimal requirement of a BBA in Accounting, but has also successfully passed the CPA exam and has four years of full-time experience as a practicing accountant/auditor. From all respects, both on paper and in person, this applicant looks like the best person for the job. But you are hesitant because this applicant arrived for the interview in a wheelchair. Although you did not discuss her disability during the interview, it was readily apparent that she was not able to maneuver without the use of the chair.

The downtown office, where the candidate will work, is an older building with an elevated lower level. Because of its age, it does not have a ramp that would allow a physically challenged person to gain access to the front or rear doors, which, until now, has not been a problem since virtually no clients visit the downtown office. Additionally, from your recollection, even if it had a wheelchair ramp, the door frames, bathrooms, and hallways are not designed to accommodate a wheelchair.

Your brother-in-law is a contractor and is familiar with the downtown office. You give him a call to see what it would cost to build a wheelchair ramp, enlarge the door openings, and remodel the bathroom to become ADA compliant. He estimates a cost of around $10,000 to $15,000 and would take approximately two or three weeks to complete. While on the phone, your brother-in-law reminds you that since your firm employs only 12 employees, it does not fall under the jurisdiction of the Equal Employment Opportunity Commission (EEOC), and therefore is not subject to the requirements of the Americans with Disabilities Act (ADA).

You really want to hire this candidate, since she has all of the requisite skills, knowledge, and abilities you are looking for; however, your firm has recently just opened a second office and at this time cannot afford another construction project. To complicate matters, the new office is barely large enough to accommodate you and your present assistant, so moving in another accountant would not work either.

**Questions**
1. Would you hire the physically disabled accountant and spend the money to remodel the downtown office or would you hire the next-best qualified candidate (who is a close second)?

2. If you choose to hire the wheelchair-bound candidate, are there alternatives to remodeling the downtown offices?
3. What other factors might you consider in making your decision?

**Source:** S. Wells, "Is the ADA Working?," *HR Magazine*, April 2001. Equal Employment Opportunity Commission. [Online] Available http://www.eeoc.gov.

## Management Decisions

### Family-Friendly or Discrimination?

Flexible work schedules, a daycare center, extended health coverage for families, and generous parental leaves (when babies are born or adopted): When these benefits were announced last year, company management had the public relations people work their contacts to make sure that there was plenty of coverage from the local press about the "family-friendly" workplace it was creating. At that time, everyone praised these "socially responsible" policies.

However, over the last 18 months, an increasing number of employees have griped about how unfair these policies are to people without kids. One common complaint is that whenever there are critical deadlines, the people without kids seem to be expected to stay, while the people with children get to go home. Likewise, in the factory, the complaint is that people with families are more likely to get the highly prized day shift, while people without kids are more likely to be assigned to the evening and midnight shifts. Another employee complained that she wasn't allowed to leave early one day to take a hurt friend to the hospital but that her boss left at 5:00 *every* day to pick up her children from daycare. Her boss's response was, "Why can't someone else take her?"

At first, you thought these were just isolated complaints, but after some research, you found out that this kind of resentment is much more common than you thought. For example, according to the U.S. Bureau of Labor, only 38 percent of workers have children at home under the age of 18. In other words, a clear majority of workers, 62 percent, do not benefit from these family-friendly policies. In fact, women with children under six only comprise 8 percent of the work force. Not surprisingly, a Conference Board survey found that 56 percent of companies report that childless employees resent the "special treatment" given to workers with children. Leslie Lafayette, founder of the Childfree Network, which has 38 chapters and 5,000 members, said, "To expect other people to, in effect, subsidize you for having your own children, I think is really off the mark." Lafayette went on to say, "I feel that there should be equal treatment for all, whether or not you are a parent. It's not business's place to put a value on parenting, or to judge and reward you because you are a parent, but the workplace is set up to do just that."

**Questions**
1. Do family-friendly policies discriminate against people who don't have children? Explain.
2. What should the company do with its family-friendly policies: leave them alone, eliminate them, or change them? Explain the reasons behind your choice.

**Sources:** V. Frazee, "When the Team Takes Advantage of Single Employees," *Personnel Journal* 75 (November 1996): 103. L. Jenner, "Family-Friendly Backlash," *Management Review* 83 (May 1994): 7. M. Picard, "No Kids? Get Back to Work!" *Training* 34 (September 1997): 33-40. D. Seligman, "Who Needs Family-Friendly Companies? A Contrarian View: It Sounds Lovely to Help Out Workers with Families, Except Then You Are Discriminating against Singles," *Forbes*, 11 January 1999, 72.

## Develop Your Managerial Potential

### From Majority to Minority and Back Again

Do you know what it feels like to walk into a room where, because of your gender, race/ethnicity, religion, language, or some other dimension, you are intensely aware of being different from everyone else? Some of you do. Most of you probably don't. And, since most managers are white and male, it's a good bet that they don't know either. It can be unsettling, especially the first time you experience it.

Some companies have begun broadening perspectives and understanding by having their managers join groups or attend events in which they are different from everyone else. As you read in section 4.3, at Hoechst Celanese, the CEO, who is white and male, joined the board of Hampton University, an historically African-American college, and Jobs for Progress, a Hispanic organization that helps people prepare for jobs.

For more than 30 years, United Parcel Service has required its top managers to participate in community service programs in inner cities or poor rural areas. James Casey, UPS's founder, started the program in 1968 to expose his white male managers to diverse experiences, people, and communities. Casey also hoped that the experience would increase empathy, break down stereotypes, and encourage volunteer and community service. The program works by assigning managers with 10 to 30 years of experience to community service tasks in inner cities or rural areas. Don Wofford, who directs the program, said, "We choose managers on the fast track, people who'll be positioned to influence their work force and the community for years to come." UPS managers spend two weeks doing community service, followed by a weekend at their homes, and then two more weeks of community service. Wofford said, "This format gives them a chance to digest the experience—they tend to come back renewed after the break, with a new focus, sometimes even more bewildered, but still ready to go for it."

Your assignment for this Develop Your Managerial Potential is to attend an event, meeting, or activity in which your are different from almost everyone else in terms of your gender, race/ethnicity, religion, language, or some other dimension. You can choose a church service, local community group, volunteer organization, or student group on campus. Ask your professor for ideas. You should probably contact the group beforehand to arrange your visit. Answer the following questions after your visit.

**Questions**

1. Describe the event, meeting, activity, and/or organization you visited.
2. How were you different from others in attendance? Describe what it was like to be different from everyone else.
3. In what ways was this event, meeting, activity, and/or organization actually similar to previous experiences that you've had? In other words, while Question 2 focuses on differences, this question focuses on similarities and commonalties.
4. What did you learn from this experience?

**Sources:** M. Crowe, "UPS Managers Trained in the Real World to Deliver Results," *The Business Journal—San Jose,* 21 September 1998, 26. F. Rice, "How to Make Diversity Pay," *Fortune,* 8 August 1994, 78.

## Study Tip

In the margin next to each paragraph or section in the chapter, write the question that the section answers. For example, "What is the difference between surface- and deep-level diversity?" could go on page 444. Once you have questions throughout the chapter, you can quiz yourself by using a blank piece of paper to cover the content. To check yourself, reveal each paragraph after you have answered the corresponding question.

# CHAPTER 13

# thirteen

# Managing Teams

## What Would You Do?

**GE Aircraft Engines, Durham, N.C.**
In 1917, when the United States entered World War I, the U.S. government was looking for a company that could develop the first airplane engine "booster" or turbo supercharger. Under wartime secrecy, General Electric began testing and developing various engine designs. Months later, at Pike's Peak, 14,000 feet above sea level, GE demonstrated a 350-horsepower, turbo supercharged Liberty aircraft engine for the U.S. government. GE landed the federal contract and went full time into the aircraft engine business. Today, GE Aircraft Engines, with revenues of nearly $11 billion, develops and manufactures jet engines for military and commercial aircraft. Indeed, nearly half of the aircraft flown by the U.S. military, as well as half of the aircraft flown by commercial airlines, are powered by GE jet engines. GE's jet engines are so reliable that its CF6-80C2 jet engine was selected to power Air Force One, the Boeing 747 used to fly the President of the United States.

Today, you and your management team are responsible for planning a new factory to build the GE90, one of GE's most popular commercial jet engines. The location has already been decided: an empty GE manufacturing plant in Durham, North Carolina. However, all other decisions are up to you and your managers. Fortunately, you have designed and started a new plant from the ground up before, what the management consultants call a "greenfield site." You think to yourself, "This is a great opportunity. But we're going to have to be very careful, because whatever we establish from the start will be perpetuated. Fortunately, though, starting a culture is so much easier than changing a culture." The question, of course, is what to create?

Well, one way to answer that is to hit the road and visit well-run factories at other companies. You're bound to come up with good ideas that way. One of your managers has an interesting suggestion, too. She thinks that everyone who is hired to work in the plant should have an FAA mechanic's license. In other words, the people who are building GE's jet engines should be capable of repairing any kind of jet engine. She says, "That would mean we'd start with a better caliber of employee, and we wouldn't have to spend time in fundamental training." And you say, thinking out loud, "We might just want to consider using teams to run everything." As you look around the room, you can sense mixed reactions. One of your managers says, "Boy, I just don't know. At the GE plant where I used to work, we switched to teams and the employee turnover rate, which was near zero, jumped to double digits." Another manager says, "Levi Strauss tried teams, too, and had horrible results."

You respond, "I understand your reluctance. Teams can be tricky. But they hold a lot of promise, too. If we do teams properly, productivity, quality, and employee satisfaction should rise, and costs should decrease. Well, we don't have to decide today. As we travel and visit other factories, let's see if we can't answer these questions. First, when does it make sense to use teams and when does it make sense to not? Second, if we determine that teams would be appropriate for our factory, what kind of teams should we use and why? Third, how should people who work on teams be paid? We've got to find a way to encourage individual initiative, while encouraging people to work together. Get your airline tickets and we'll meet back here in two weeks to make our decision."

**If you were the manager at GE Aircraft Engines' new Durham, North Carolina, plant, what would you do?**

**Sources:** "About GEAE / History," *GE Aircraft Engines.* [Online] Available http://www.geae.com/aboutgeae/history.html, 21 January 2002. "About GEAE / Locations," *GE Aircraft Engines.* [Online] Available http://www.geae.com/aboutgeae/location.html, 21 January 2002. C. Fishman, "Engines of Democracy," *Fast Company,* 1 October 1999, 174. C. Fishman, "How Teamwork Took Flight: This Team Built a Commercial Engine—And Self-Managing GE Plant—From Scratch," *Fast Company,* 1 October 1999, 188.

EXHIBIT 13.1

WHEN SELECTED COMPANIES FIRST BEGAN USING WORK TEAMS

| | |
|---|---|
| Boeing | 1987 |
| Caterpillar | 1986 |
| Champion International | 1985 |
| Cummings Engine | 1973 |
| Digital Equipment | 1982 |
| Ford | 1982 |
| General Electric | 1985 |
| LTV Steel | 1985 |
| Procter & Gamble | 1962 |

**Source:** J. Hoerr, "The Payoff from Teamwork—The Gains in Quality Are Substantial—So Why Isn't It Spreading Faster?" *Business Week,* 10 July 1989, 56.

A growing number of organizations are significantly improving their effectiveness by establishing work teams. In fact, 91 percent of U.S. companies use teams and groups of one kind or another to solve specific problems.[1] However, Exhibit 13.1 shows that with the exception of Procter & Gamble, which began using teams in 1962, work teams were not established in many companies until the mid- to late-1980s. And since many of the companies shown in Exhibit 13.1 were early adopters, teams really haven't been in place at most companies for more than 10 to 15 years, if that long. In other words, teams are a relatively new phenomenon in companies, and there's still much for organizations to learn about managing them.

We begin this chapter by reviewing the advantages and disadvantages of teams and exploring when companies should use them over more traditional approaches. Next, we discuss the different types of work teams and the characteristics common to all teams. The chapter ends by focusing on the practical steps to managing teams—team goals and priorities and organizing, training, and compensating teams.

## Why Work Teams

**474**

**work team**
a small number of people with complementary skills who hold themselves mutually accountable for pursuing a common purpose, achieving performance goals, and improving interdependent work processes

**Work teams** consist of a small number of people with complementary skills who hold themselves mutually accountable for pursuing a common purpose, achieving performance goals, and improving interdependent work processes.[2] By this definition, computer programmers working on separate projects in the same department of a company would not be considered a team. To be a team, the programmers would have to be interdependent and share responsibility and accountability for the quality and amount of computer code they produced.[3]

Julia Garcia is a member of a work team in a Frito-Lay snack plant in Lubbock, Texas. Prior to the establishment of teams at the plant, Garcia and her coworkers never paid any attention to the quality and cost data posted on company bulletin boards and rarely concerned themselves with ways to improve the running of the plant. Today, however, Garcia and her teammates receive weekly updates on costs, quality, and performance and take as much responsibility for quality standards and performance as company management does. When products don't meet Frito-Lay's quality standards, Garcia and her teammates reject them. When machines are shut down for maintenance and too many workers are sitting around with nothing to do, Garcia and her teammates keep costs down by deciding who should be sent home until the machines are working.

Since the move to teams, the number of managers at the Frito-Lay plant has dropped from 38 to 13, while the number of hourly workers (i.e., team members) has increased by 20 percent to more than 220. More importantly, the teams have produced double-digit decreases in costs and such huge improvements in quality that the plant is now ranked sixth out of 48 plants by Frito management, up from the bottom 20 where it was previously ranked. Furthermore, Garcia and her coworkers are thriving in the team atmosphere. She said, "It kind of frightened me at first. I thought, 'I'm not going to be able to decide anything.' [But now] I really enjoy [the team approach] because it gives me a sense of pride. I know my work and what we need to do. . . . It's more fun. It used to be it was just the 'same-ol-same-ol,' [but] now there are more things happening."[4]

The success that Julia Garcia and Frito-Lay experienced with teams is not uncommon. In many industries, teams are growing in importance because they help organizations respond to specific problems and challenges. For Frito-Lay, the challenges were to increase product quality and lower costs. For a service business, like a restaurant or an airline, the challenge may be to increase customer satisfaction or employee motivation. While work teams are not the answer for every situation or organization, if the right teams are used properly and in the right settings, teams can dramatically improve company performance over more traditional management approaches and instill a sense of vitality in the workplace that is otherwise difficult to achieve.

*After reading the next two sections, you should be able to*

1. *explain the good and bad of using teams.*
2. *recognize and understand the different kinds of teams.*

## 1. The Good and Bad of Using Teams

*Let's begin our discussion of teams by learning about 1.1 the advantages of teams, 1.2 the disadvantages of teams, and 1.3 when to use and not use teams.*

### 1.1 The Advantages of Teams

Companies are making greater use of teams because teams have been shown to increase customer satisfaction, product and service quality, speed and efficiency in product development, and employee job satisfaction.[5] Teams help businesses increase *customer satisfaction* in several ways. One way is to create work teams that are trained to meet the needs of specific customer groups. When Kodak reengineered its customer service center, it created specific teams to field calls from the general public (based on the geographic location of the caller), scientific users, and corporate users. Under this system, customers were immediately directed to the team trained to meet their needs. Within a year, the work teams doubled the rate at which Kodak solved customer problems on the first phone call.[6]

Businesses also create problem-solving teams and employee-involvement teams to study ways to improve overall customer satisfaction and make recommendations for improvements. Teams like these typically meet on a weekly or monthly basis. Every day at the Longaberger Company, 2,500 skilled weavers make over 40,000 high-quality baskets (which sell for $30 to $260). But when productivity began to drop, management turned to an employee involvement group to solve the problem. After studying 40 basket makers for three weeks, the team came up with a solution that made sure that the different kinds of wood veneers used to make different baskets went to the right weavers (who were often stuck with the wrong materials). Before the new system, workers ran out of the proper materials 53 times per day. But with the new system, that only happens nine times per day. And, because the new system has also cut scrap (i.e., leftover, unusable materials) by 75 percent, the company is saving $3 million per year.[7]

Teams also help firms improve *product and service quality* in several ways.[8] In contrast to traditional organizational structures where management is responsible for organizational outcomes and performance, teams take direct responsibility for the quality of the products and service they produce. At the Boulders Resort, an upscale hotel, management created and trained housekeepers to form three-person teams that were completely responsible for assigning work, evaluating room quality, and conducting room inspections. As a result, rooms are ready for use faster than before, there are fewer intrusions and interruptions for guests, and the job satisfaction and retention of housekeepers has increased.[9] At Whole Foods, a supermarket chain that sells groceries and health foods, the 10 teams that manage each store are not only responsible for store quality and performance, but they are also directly accountable, since the size of their team bonus depends on it.[10] And making teams directly responsible for service and production quality pays off. A survey by *Industry Week* indicates that 42 percent of the companies who use teams report revenues of more than $250,000 per employee, compared to only 25 percent of the companies that don't use teams.[11]

As you learned in Chapter 10, companies that are slow to innovate or integrate new features and technologies into their products are at a competitive disadvantage. Therefore, a third reason that teams are increasingly popular is *the need for speed and efficiency when designing and manufacturing products.*[12] Traditional product design proceeds sequentially, meaning that one department has to finish its work on the design of a product before the next department can start. Unfortunately, this is not only slow, but it also encourages departments to work in isolation from one another.[13] For example, with sequential design processes, it's common for different departments, such as manufacturing, to work for months on their part of the product design only to have it rejected by another department, such as marketing, which was never consulted as the work was being done.

As you learned in Chapter 4, *overlapping development phases* is a faster and better way to design products and is often made possible through the use of teams. With overlapping development phases, teams of employees, consisting of members from the different functional areas in a firm (i.e., engineering, manufacturing, and marketing), work on the product design at the same time. Because each of the different functional areas is involved in the design process from the start, the company can avoid most of the delays and frustration associated with sequential development. Industrial Light & Magic (ILM), founded by George Lucas, the originator and producer of *Star Wars*, has won 14 Academy Awards for visual effects and technical achievement. ILM uses overlapping development phases to quickly produce specialized, computer effects for movies. Teams of artists and animators work on different movie scenes simultaneously to speed up production. Visual-effects producer Jacqui Lopez said, "When we get down to the wire, our artists need every second they can get in front of their computers."[14] Oftentimes, she said, "Being late is not an option. The publicity is already locked in, and the studios have schedules to keep. We can't be late."[15] And ILM has *never* been late. Indeed, whether it was for *Titanic* or *Harry Potter*, when film studios and directors fall behind, they regularly come to ILM to avoid missing deadlines.

Another reason for using teams is that teamwork often leads to increased job satisfaction.[16] One reason that teamwork can be more satisfying than traditional work is that it gives workers a chance to improve their skills. This is often accomplished through **cross training**, in which team members are taught how to do all or most of the jobs performed by the other team members. Mary Keene used to stand in one spot for eight hours a day using a powered chisel to chip cast iron from Ford automobile engines. She said, "You thought your arms would fall off. It was the worst job I had there." Today, thanks to cross training, Mary and her Plant 2 coworkers at Ford's Brook Park, Ohio, manufacturing facility perform seven different jobs each shift, such as installing ignition coils, taking apart engines, restarting machinery after it breaks down, and contacting suppliers if engine parts are sub par in quality.[17] The advantage for the organization is that cross training allows teams to function normally when one member is absent or a team member quits or is transferred. The advantage for workers is that cross training broadens their skills and makes them more capable while also making their work more varied and interesting. Indeed, Ford's Mary Keene said, "Plant 2 is the best we've ever had it." Huck Granakis, the United Auto Worker's building chairman and a member of

**cross training**
training team members how to do all or most of the jobs performed by the other team members

Plant 2's operating committee, said, "They love it. I know of no one who has quit to go to another job."[18]

Participation in work teams also increases job satisfaction by providing team members unique opportunities that would otherwise not be available to them. Again, at Ford's engine Plant 2 in Brook Park, Ohio, Mary Keene and her teammates contact suppliers if engine parts are sub par in quality.[19] In most manufacturing facilities, this would be the supervisor's job.

Also, work teams often receive proprietary business information that is only available to managers at most companies. For example, at Whole Foods, the supermarket chain that sells groceries and health foods, team members are given full access to their store's financial information and everyone's salaries, including the store manager and the CEO.[20] Each day, next to the time clock, Whole Foods employees can see the previous day's sales for each team, as well as the sales on the same day from the previous year. Each week, team members can examine the same information, broken down by team, for all of the Whole Foods stores in their regions. And each month, store managers review information on profitability, including sales, product costs, wages, and operating profits, with each team in the store. Since team members decide how much to spend, what to order, what things should cost, and how many team members should work each day, this information is critical to making teams work at Whole Foods.[21]

Team members often gain job satisfaction from unique leadership responsibilities that would typically not be available in traditional organizations. For example, at Colgate-Palmolive, work teams are responsible for determining their own work assignments, scheduling overtime, scheduling vacations, performing preventive equipment maintenance, and assuring quality control. For each work team, the position of team leader rotates, giving different team members the opportunity to build leadership skills.[22]

Teams share many of the advantages of group decision making discussed in Chapter 6. For instance, because team members possess different knowledge, skills, abilities, and experiences, teams will be able to view problems from multiple perspectives. This diversity of viewpoints increases the odds that team decisions will solve the underlying causes of problems rather than simply address the symptoms. The increased knowledge and information available to teams also makes it easier for them to generate more alternative solutions, which is a critical part of improving the quality of decisions. Finally, because teams members are involved in decision-making processes, they should be more committed to making those decisions work. In short, teams can do a much better job than individuals in two important steps of the decision-making process: defining the problem and generating alternative solutions. Exhibit 13.2 summarizes the advantages and disadvantages of teams, the latter of which is discussed next in Section 1.2

477

---

EXHIBIT 13.2

## ADVANTAGES AND DISADVANTAGES OF TEAMS

| ADVANTAGES OF TEAMS | DISADVANTAGES OF TEAMS |
|---|---|
| • Customer satisfaction | • Initially high employee turnover |
| • Product and service quality | • Social loafing |
| • Speed and efficiency in product development | • Self-limiting behavior |
| • Employee job satisfaction | • Legal risk (National Labor Relations Act) |
| • Better decision making and problem solving (multiple perspectives, more alternative solutions, increased commitment to decisions) | • Disadvantages of group decision making (groupthink, inefficient meetings, minority domination, lack of accountability) |

## 1.2 The Disadvantages of Teams

Although teams can significantly increase customer satisfaction, product and service quality, speed and efficiency in product development, and employee job satisfaction, using teams does not guarantee these positive outcomes. In fact, if you've ever participated in team projects in your classes, you're probably already aware of some of the problems inherent in work teams. Despite all of their promise, teams and teamwork are also prone to these significant disadvantages: initially high turnover, social loafing, self-limiting behavior, and legal risk.

The first disadvantage of work teams is *initially high turnover*. Teams aren't for everyone, and some workers will balk at the responsibility, effort, and learning required in team settings. When General Electric's Salisbury plant switched to teams, the turnover rate, which was near zero, jumped to 14 percent. Plant manager Roger Gasaway said of teams and teamwork, "It's not all wonderful stuff."[23] Other people may quit because they object to the way in which team members closely scrutinize each other's job performance, particularly when teams are small. Randy Savage, who works for Eaton Corp., a manufacturer of car and truck parts, said, "They say there are no bosses here, but if you screw up, you find one pretty fast." Beverly Reynolds, who quit Eaton's team-based system after nine months, said her coworkers "weren't standing watching me, but from afar, they were watching me." And even though her teammates were willing to help her improve her job performance, she concluded, "As it turns out, it just wasn't for me at all."[24]

Social loafing is another disadvantage of work teams. **Social loafing** occurs when workers withhold their efforts and fail to perform their share of the work. A nineteenth-century German scientist named Ringleman first documented social loafing when he found that one person pulling on a rope alone exerted an average of 63 kg of force on the rope. In groups of three, the average force dropped to 53 kg. In groups of eight, the average dropped to just 31 kg. Ringleman concluded that the larger the team, the smaller the individual effort. In fact, social loafing is more likely to occur in larger groups where it can be difficult to identify and monitor the efforts of individual team members.[25] In other words, social loafers count on being able to blend into the background, so that their lack of effort isn't easily spotted. Because of team-based class projects, most students already know about social loafers or "slackers," who contribute poor, little, or no work whatsoever. Not surprisingly, research with 250 student teams clearly shows that the most talented students are typically the least satisfied with teamwork because of having to carry "slackers" and having to do a disproportionate share of their team's work.[26]

Self-limiting behavior is another disadvantage of teams. **Self-limiting behavior** occurs whenever team members choose to limit their involvement in the team's work.[27] Of course, self-limiting behavior, such as daydreaming, doodling, thinking about tasks other than work, withholding opinions, or not participating in meetings, reduces team performance. While similar to social loafing, there is a difference. Social loafers try to make sure that no one detects that they are withholding their efforts. The payoff is that they get away with it. Self-limiters have a different motivation. They reduce their involvement in team activities because they just don't see any payoff to participating. For example, one manager said, "The last time we went through this process, it was just an exercise in futility—no one listened to our suggestions. Why fight or argue the point? This is a meaningless exercise anyway."[28] Self-limiters just don't see the point. They give up.

How prevalent is self-limiting behavior? One study found that when team activities were not mandatory, 25 percent of manufacturing workers volunteered to join problem-solving teams, 70 percent were quiet, passive supporters (i.e., self-limiters), and 5 percent were opposed to these activities.[29] Another study found that self-limiting behavior was somewhat less prevalent among managers. Still, 56 percent of managers, more than half, engaged in self-limiting behavior in management teams. Exhibit 13.3 lists the factors that encourage self-limiting behavior in teams.

Another disadvantage of teams is that they can present a legal risk to companies that violate the National Labor Relations Act (NRLA), which is the primary law governing relationships between unions and employers in the private sector.[30] With respect to

**social loafing**
behavior in which team members withhold their efforts and fail to perform their share of the work

**self-limiting behavior**
behavior in which team members choose to limit their involvement in a team's work

478

EXHIBIT 13.3

## FACTORS THAT ENCOURAGE SELF-LIMITING BEHAVIOR IN TEAMS

1. *The presence of someone with expertise.* Team members will self-limit when another team member is highly qualified to make a decision or comment on an issue.

2. *The presentation of a compelling argument.* Team members will self-limit if the arguments for a course of action are very persuasive or similar to their own thinking.

3. *Lacking confidence in one's ability to contribute.* Team members will self-limit if they are unsure about their ability to contribute to discussions, activities, or decisions. This is especially so for high-profile decisions.

4. *An unimportant or meaningless decision.* Team members will self-limit by mentally withdrawing or adopting a "who cares" attitude if decisions don't affect them or their units, or if they don't see a connection between their efforts and their team's successes or failures.

5. *A dysfunctional decision-making climate.* Team members will self-limit if other team members are frustrated or indifferent or if a team is floundering or disorganized.

**Source:** P.W. Mulvey, J.F. Veiga, & P.M. Elsass, "When Teammates Raise a White Flag," *Academy of Management Executive* 10, no. 1 (1996): 40-49.

teams, the National Labor Relations Board (NLRB) (**http://www.nlrb.gov/**), which administers the NLRA, looks for two things. First, it determines whether the company's work teams can be categorized as a *labor organization*, which it defines as "any organization of any kind, or any agency or employee representation committee or plan, in which employees participate and which exists for the purpose . . . of dealing with employers concerning grievances, labor disputes, wages, rates of pay, hours of employment or conditions of work." Since many work teams control or have a large say on these issues, teams in many companies can be categorized as labor organizations. Second, if teams can be categorized as labor organizations, then the NLRA tries to determine if the company controlled or dominated the teams by having management participate on the teams, by financially supporting the teams, or by determining team membership. As we will discuss later in the chapter, management is likely to do all of these things in one way or another to make teams run more efficiently and effectively.

How much of a legal risk does the NLRA represent to companies that use teams? It's hard to say. Thus far, only a handful of companies, including EFCO, Polaroid, NCR, and Dillon Stores, have violated the NLRA by using teams in these ways. So with teams of some kind in use at more than 80 percent of companies, the absolute risk is relatively low. However, there's no way of knowing how many companies have not used teams or have restricted the way they use teams because of this legal threat.

What scares managers away is that the companies that have violated the NLRA have done so using teams for relatively straightforward business purposes. For example, at EFCO Corporation, participation on teams and committees was completely voluntary. Moreover, the EFCO committees that were disbanded following the NLRB's ruling were the employee policy review committee, the safety committee, the employee suggestion screening committee, and the employee benefit committee.[31] Even more foreboding is that the NLRB has also ruled that employers using teams can violate the NLRA even when employees aren't members of unions and even if the company takes steps to comply with the law. For example, Polaroid changed its teams and participation programs to make sure that they did not violate the NLRA, but was still found in violation because the work teams "represented" the views of other workers and therefore constituted a "labor organization." Like EFCO, the members of Polaroid's Employee Owner Influence Council were picked from a pool of volunteers. The council, which received office space and supplies from the company, served as a sounding board for management by offering opinions on pay, benefits, and other issues.[32] Exhibit 13.4 provides some guidelines for minimizing the legal risks that teams pose for companies at this time.

EXHIBIT 13.4

### MINIMIZING THE LEGAL RISKS ASSOCIATED WITH TEAMS AND THE NATIONAL LABOR RELATIONS ACT

1. *Suggestion boxes.* Use suggestion boxes that invite all employees to share their thoughts and feelings with management.
2. *Greater worker control.* Establish teams that give workers greater direct control over their own work.
3. *Don't overrule.* If teams are used to settle workplace grievances or make other decisions concerning workers, don't overrule those decisions or influence the autonomy of the groups making them. Doing so may lead to charges that management is dominating the teams or committees.
4. *Don't turn teams into representative bodies.* One of the key complaints in terms of the NLRA is that teams or committees "represent" the views and opinions of other employees and thus usurp the role of labor unions. So make sure that teams and committees don't speak for all groups or all employees in a representational manner.
5. *Timing is important.* Don't form teams when a labor union is trying to convince your employees to consider union representation. Forming teams at that time could be viewed as illegal management interference.

**Source:** M.E. Pivec & H.Z. Robbins, "Employee Involvement Remains Controversial," *HRMagazine* 41, no. 11 (1996): 145-150.

Finally, teams share many of the disadvantages of group decision making discussed in Chapter 6. This includes *groupthink,* in which group members in highly cohesive groups feel intense pressure not to disagree with each other so that the group can approve a proposed solution. Because groupthink restricts discussion and leads to consideration of a limited number of alternative solutions, it usually results in poor decisions. Also, team decision making takes considerable time. Furthermore, it's the rare team that consistently holds productive task-oriented meetings to effectively work through the decision process. Another possible pitfall is that sometimes just one or two people dominate team discussions, restricting consideration of different problem definitions and alternative solutions. Last, team members may not feel accountable for the decisions and actions taken by the "team."

### 1.3 When to Use Teams

The two previous subsections make clear that teams have significant advantages *and* disadvantages. Therefore, the question is not whether to use teams, but when and where to use teams for maximum benefit and minimum cost. Doug Johnson, associate director at the Center for the Study of Work Teams, said, "Teams are a means to an end, not an end in themselves. You have to ask yourself questions first. Does the work require interdependence? Will the team philosophy fit company strategy? Will management make a long-term commitment to this process?"[33] Exhibit 13.5 provides some additional guidelines on when to use or not use teams.[34]

First, teams should be used where there is a clear, engaging reason or purpose for using them. Too many companies use teams because they're popular or because they assume that teams can fix all problems. Teams are much more likely to succeed if they know why they exist and what they are supposed to accomplish, and more likely to fail if they don't. For example, because headquarters did not stress the importance of cost savings, the platform teams that develop new cars at DaimlerChrysler didn't communicate with one another about the possibility of using identical parts on different cars to cut costs and increase efficiency. For example, the Dodge Durango and Chrysler Jeep are similar kinds of sport utility vehicles, but they use completely different windshield wipers. As a result, overall costs are higher since Chrysler buys smaller volumes of each kind of windshield wiper. Furthermore, five different platform teams chose three different kinds of corrosion protection for a simple piece of steel used in all automobile bumpers. The resulting cost was $1 or $2 higher for each part. Multiply that by 3 million cars a year, and Chrysler's costs increased by $3 million to $6 million because it wasn't made clear to the teams that cost savings were one of their objectives.[35]

EXHIBIT 13.5

WHEN TO USE OR NOT USE TEAMS

| USE TEAMS WHEN . . . | DON'T USE TEAMS WHEN . . . |
|---|---|
| 1. there is a clear, engaging reason or purpose. | 1. there isn't a clear, engaging reason or purpose. |
| 2. the job can't be done unless people work together. | 2. the job can be done by people working independently. |
| 3. rewards can be provided for teamwork and team performance. | 3. rewards are provided for individual effort and performance. |
| 4. ample resources are available. | 4. the necessary resources are not available. |
| 5. teams will have clear authority to manage and change how work gets done. | 5. management will continue to monitor and influence how work gets done. |

**Sources:** R. Wageman, "Critical Success Factors for Creating Superb Self-Managing Teams," *Organizational Dynamics* 26, no. 1 (1997): 49-61.

Second, teams should be used when the job can't be done unless people work together. This typically means that teams are required when tasks are complex, require multiple perspectives, or require repeated interaction with others to complete. For example, contrary to stories of legendary programmers who write software programs by themselves, Microsoft uses teams to write computer code because of the enormous complexity of today's software. Most software simply has too many options and features for one person (or even one team) to complete it all. Likewise, Microsoft uses teams because writing good software requires repeated interaction with others. Microsoft ensures this interaction by having its teams "check in" their computer code every few days. The different pieces of code written by the different teams are then compiled to create an updated working build or prototype of the software. Then, beginning the next day, all the teams and team members begin testing and debugging the new build. Over and over again, the computer code is compiled, then sent back to the teams to be tested and improved, and then compiled and tested again.[36]

However, if tasks are simple and don't require multiple perspectives or repeated interaction with others, teams should not be used. For instance, production levels dropped by 23 percent when Levi Strauss introduced teams in its factories. Levi's mistake was assuming that teams were appropriate for garment work, where workers performed single, specialized tasks, like sewing zippers or belt loops. Because this kind of work does not require interaction with others, Levi's unwittingly pitted the faster workers against the slower workers in each team. Arguments, infighting, insults, and threats were common between faster workers and the slower workers who held back team performance. One seamstress even had to physically restrain an angry coworker who was about to throw a chair at a faster worker who constantly nagged her about her slow pace.[37]

Third, teams should be used when rewards can be provided for teamwork and team performance. Team rewards that depend on team performance rather than individual performance are the key to rewarding team behaviors and efforts. You'll read more about team rewards later in the chapter, but for now it's enough to know that if the level of rewards (individual vs. team) is not matched to the level of performance (individual vs. team), groups won't work. As discussed above, this was the case with Levi's, where a team structure was superimposed on individual jobs that didn't require interaction between workers. After the switch to teams, faster workers placed tremendous pressure on slower workers to increase their production speed. And since pay was determined by team performance, top individual performers saw their pay drop by several dollars an hour, while slower workers saw their pay increase by several dollars an hour, all while overall productivity dropped in the plant.[38]

Fourth, teams should be used when ample resources are available. The resources that teams need include training (discussed later in the chapter), sufficient time and a place or method to work together, job-specific tools, and consistent information and feedback concerning team work processes and job performance. Susan Cohen, a professor at the University of Southern California's Center for Effective Organizations, said, "People keep doing it [teams] because it is popular, a fad, a thing to do. But then they find that they run into problems because these things do require considerable care and feeding. Companies have to invest some resources in making them succeed."[39] At Levi's, team members complained that there were few resources, such as training, to support the transition from independent, individual-based work to team-based work. They also complained about not being given enough time to learn how to run the new machines to which they were assigned on the team system.

Another key problem with resources is management resistance. Managers who have been in charge are often reluctant to help teams or turn over resources to them. At Levi's, when team members would ask supervisors for assistance, a common reaction was "Y'all are empowered; y'all decide."[40]

Finally, teams should be used when they have clear authority to manage and change how the work gets done. This means that teams—not managers—decide what problem to tackle next, when to schedule time for maintenance or training, or how to solve customer problems. Research clearly shows that teams with the authority to manage their own work strongly outperform teams that don't.[41] Unfortunately, managers can undermine teams' authority by closely monitoring their work, asking teams to change their decisions, or directly ignoring or overruling team decisions. Jeffrey Pfeffer, a Stanford professor and management consultant/author, said, "The fact is, the people doing the work know better how to do it. Get the managers out of the way and you will do better."[42]

## Review 1
### The Good and Bad of Using Teams

In many industries, teams are growing in importance because they help organizations respond to specific problems and challenges. Teams have been shown to increase customer satisfaction (specific customer teams), product and service quality (direct responsibility), speed and efficiency in product development (overlapping development phases), and employee job satisfaction (cross training, unique opportunities, and leadership responsibilities). While teams can produce significant improvements in these areas, using teams does not guarantee these positive outcomes. Teams and teamwork have the disadvantages of initially high turnover, social loafing (especially in large groups), self-limiting behavior, and legal risk (National Labor Relations Act). Teams also share many of the advantages (multiple perspectives, generation of more alternatives, and more commitment) and disadvantages (groupthink, time, poorly run meetings, domination by a few team members, and weak accountability) of group decision making. Finally, teams should be used for a clear purpose, when the work requires that people work together, when rewards can be provided for both teamwork and team performance, when ample resources can be provided, and when teams can be given clear authority over their work.

## 2. Kinds of Teams

Companies use different kinds of teams for different purposes. For example, Merck, a leading pharmaceutical firm, found that it was taking much too long to bring new drugs to market following final Federal Drug Administration approval. Merck now has teams of marketing, manufacturing, and research people who are responsible for speeding up this process. Wendy Dixon, a marketing vice president who managed the launch of Vioxx, a new pain killer, said, "We carved four to five weeks off the normal product launch process."[43] Likewise, at Maytag's Cleveland, Tennessee, manufacturing plant, which makes gas and electric stoves, the use of teams has helped cut production costs by $7 million and reduce inventory by $10 million.[44]

*Let's continue our discussion of teams by learning about the different kinds of teams that companies like Merck and Maytag use to make themselves more competitive. Let's start by looking at 2.1 how teams differ in terms of autonomy, which is the key dimension that makes one team different from another, and finish by examining 2.2 some special kinds of teams.*

### 2.1 Autonomy, the Key Dimension

Teams can be classified in a number of ways, such as permanent or temporary, or functional or cross-functional. However, studies indicate that the amount of autonomy possessed by a team is the key dimension that makes teams different from each another.[45] *Autonomy* is the degree to which workers have the discretion, freedom, and independence to decide how and when to accomplish their jobs.

Exhibit 13.6 displays an autonomy continuum that shows how five kinds of teams differ in terms of autonomy. Moving left to right at the top of Exhibit 13.6, notice that traditional work groups and employee involvement groups have the lowest levels of autonomy, followed by semi-autonomous work groups, which have a higher level of autonomy, and then self-managing teams and self-designing teams, which have the highest levels of autonomy. Moving from top to bottom along the left side of Exhibit 13.6, note that the number of responsibilities given to each kind of team increases directly with that team's autonomy. Let's review each of these teams and their autonomy and responsibilities in more detail.

The smallest amount of autonomy is found in **traditional work groups**, where two or more people work together to achieve a shared goal. In these groups, workers do not have direct responsibility or control over their work, but are responsible for doing the work or "executing the task." Workers report to managers, who are responsible for their

**traditional work group**
group composed of two or more people who work together to achieve a shared goal

---

### EXHIBIT 13.6

**TEAM AUTONOMY CONTINUUM**

LOW TEAM AUTONOMY ← → HIGH TEAM AUTONOMY

| RESPONSIBILITIES | TRADITIONAL WORK GROUPS | EMPLOYEE INVOLVEMENT GROUPS | SEMI-AUTONOMOUS WORK GROUPS | SELF-MANAGING TEAMS | SELF-DESIGNING TEAMS |
|---|---|---|---|---|---|
| Execute Task | ✓ | ✓ | ✓ | ✓ | ✓ |
| Give Advice/Make Suggestions | | ✓ | ✓ | ✓ | ✓ |
| Information | | | ✓ | ✓ | ✓ |
| Major Production/Service Tasks: | | | | | |
|   Make Decisions | | | ✓ | ✓ | ✓ |
|   Solve Problems | | | ✓ | ✓ | ✓ |
| All Production/Service Tasks: | | | | | |
|   Make Decisions | | | | ✓ | ✓ |
|   Solve Problems | | | | ✓ | ✓ |
| Control Design: | | | | | |
|   Team | | | | | ✓ |
|   Tasks | | | | | ✓ |
|   Membership | | | | | ✓ |

**Sources:** R.D. Banker, J.M. Field, R.G. Schroeder, & K.K. Sinha, "Impact of Work Teams on Manufacturing Performance: A Longitudinal Field Study," *Academy of Management Journal* 39 (1996): 867-890. J.R. Hackman, "The Psychology of Self-Management in Organizations," in *Psychology and Work: Productivity, Change, and Employment*, eds. M.S. Pallak & R. Perloff (Washington, D.C.: American Psychological Association), 85-136.

performance and have the authority to hire and fire them, make job assignments, and control resources. For instance, take the situation of an experienced worker who blatantly refuses to do his share of the work, saying, "I've done my time. Let the younger employees do the work." In a team with high autonomy, the responsibility of getting this employee to put forth his fair share of effort would belong to his teammates. But in traditional work groups, the responsibility of telling this employee that his "sitting days are over" belongs to the boss or supervisor. In fact, the supervisor in this situation calmly confronted this employee and told him, "We need your talent, [and] your knowledge of these machines. But if you won't work, you'll have to go elsewhere." Within days, the employee's behavior improved.[46]

**Employee involvement teams**, which have somewhat more autonomy, meet on company time on a weekly or monthly basis to provide advice or make suggestions to management concerning specific issues, such as plant safety, customer relations, or product quality.[47] While they offer advice and suggestions, they do not have the authority to make decisions. Membership on these teams is often voluntary, but members may be selected because of their expertise. The idea behind employee involvement teams is that the people closest to the problem or situation are best able to recommend solutions. Commercial Casework, a woodworking and cabinetry company in Fremont, California, used an employee involvement team consisting of seven volunteers to research and suggest possibilities for the company bonus plan. Commercial Casework manager Bill Palmer said, "They learned a whole lot more about what it means to give and get a bonus. They saw how difficult it was and wound up really taking ownership of the process."[48]

**Semi-autonomous work groups** not only provide advice and suggestions to management, but they also have the authority to make decisions and solve problems related to the major tasks required to produce a product or service. Semi-autonomous groups regularly receive information about budgets, work quality and performance, as well as competitors' products. Furthermore, members of semi-autonomous work groups are typically cross-trained in a number of different skills and tasks. In short, semi-autonomous work groups give employees the autonomy to make decisions that are typically made by supervisors and managers.

However, that authority is not complete. Managers still play a role, though much reduced compared to traditional work groups, in supporting the work of semi-autonomous work groups. At the Ritz-Carlton, Kansas City, where semi-autonomous work groups were implemented, long-time manager Sandi Shartzer, director of housekeeping, said, "I had attendants who for 22 years had been told where to go, what to do. Now they're being told to do it on their own. Sure, the staff still runs to me occasionally, but they're learning to 'own' their own responsibility. I even had one worker tell me today that she's setting goals for herself." Hotel manager Bob Schrader reinforced Shartzer's view of the Ritz's semi-autonomous work groups. Schrader said, "My role is to be out on the floor, not sit in my office and look at paperwork. I attend team meetings and try to get people comfortable about approaching me on issues, but then a lot of my job is directing people back to their teams for solutions. A lot of what I should be doing now is asking questions instead of dictating methods."[49]

**Self-managing teams** are different from semi-autonomous work groups in that team members manage and control *all* of the major tasks directly related to production of a product or service without first getting approval from management. This includes managing and controlling the acquisition of materials, making a product or providing a service, and ensuring timely delivery. For example, when Ford was bringing out its new version of the Ford Escort, "product specialist" Tom Arnold was part of a self-managing team that consisted of engineers, car designers, and auto suppliers. Compared to the limited authority he had before, Arnold said, "I've had so many freedoms, it's unbelievable. I never had this experience until I got here. This [self-managing team] has been fantastic." Mike Oblack, a United Auto Workers officer who was part of another self-managing team at Ford, said, "What Ford has discovered is that by allowing us to make mistakes and work through them, the company benefits."[50]

# BeenThereDoneThat

## AAL: A Pioneer in the Use of Self-Managed Teams

The Aid Association for Lutherans (AAL) is the largest fraternal benefit society in the United States in terms of assets ($18.7 billion) and insurance ($82 billion). In this interview, Charles Dull, senior vice president and chief quality officer for AAL, discusses AAL's pioneering use of self-managed teams.

### "Everyone won when the field team won."

**Q:** The self-managed team concept at AAL was a very innovative approach, especially for an organization in the financial services industry. Tell me about your involvement in that.

**A:** During a major corporate transformation, I was asked to provide leadership for the insurance operations of AAL. There were over 500 people in its service operation. We had an interesting challenge in that we were in a downsizing mode, while trying to get closer to our customers. We were able to reduce our layers of management from eight to three. We did it by creating self-managed teams. A group of our employees borrowed this concept from the manufacturing world and challenged us to use it to get closer to our customers and improve our response times.

**Q:** During this restructuring, were positions eliminated through attrition?

**A:** Yes. We were able to find places for most of the management and supervisory people that were displaced. They were very good people. After all, we had promoted talented people into those supervisory positions. During a four-year period, we reduced our entire home office workforce by 250, or over 15 percent. At the same time, we increased our business volume by about 50 percent.

**Q:** Let's go back to these self-managed teams. What were some of the results that they accomplished?

**A:** We have about 2,400 men and women in our field organization and each home office business team partnered with a group of those field people. The field people's satisfaction level with our service just took off after that. We keep track of satisfaction data, and the level dramatically increased—almost overnight. We moved from a controlling and somewhat adversarial relationship to more of a helping, supporting relationship with our colleagues in the field. Everyone won when the field team won.

Response time improved. By having all the work done by one team, we reduced hand-off time. Teams were cross-trained so the products and services got out the door much faster. We had one group of people who literally could service a problem immediately after it arrived at the home office.

**Q:** Do you remember any of the numbers, like productivity improvement?

**A:** Service time was reduced by 75 percent in some processes. In fact, through downsizing and other factors, the overall productivity of those service teams increased by about 40 percent over a five-year period.

**Q:** So that had to be good news for the whole corporation, as well as for your board and your members, correct?

**A:** It was a significant factor that contributed to our recognition as one of the lowest-cost providers in the entire financial services industry.

**Q:** How extensive was the self-managed concept at AAL?

**A:** We really did transfer this social technology throughout the insurance division. We were the only large group that went that far in our industry during the late '80s. A number of other financial service organizations, here and abroad, are, of course, also adopting some version of self-managed teams.

**Q:** Now I suppose you have all the other insurers coming up to Appleton, Wisconsin? [Appleton is the location of AAL's headquarters.]

**A:** We've had over 250 organizations visit us in the past three years. And we were selected as a benchmark organization by General Electric because of our approach to self-managed teams.

**Q:** That's interesting that General Electric used you, a fraternal insurance organization, as their best practice for self-managed teams.

**A:** That's correct.

**Q:** Chuck, we all hear the success stories, including AAL's success. But could you tell me what some of the problems have been?

**A:** We've certainly had our share of problems. As I mentioned earlier, we moved to self-managed teams to get closer to the customer. We wanted to gain more flexibility in our staff so that we could handle the rise and fall of the business cycle better and build a partnership with our field organization. But what we didn't do right away was change our compensation structure. What we had was a classic individual merit pay system that did not reward people operating in teams. It rewarded people for individual effort and accomplishment. The result was that we were into the team structure for more than a year before we realized our reward system was working at cross purposes with this. Finally, we created a performance-based compensation structure that rewarded people for applied knowledge in a group setting.

**Q:** Do you feel that, under that team approach, you were able to objectively determine the group reward? Did the groups buy into that?

**A:** I'd say it was a mixed bag at first. The high performer was feeling dragged down, if you will, by the lower performer, because it was the team totals that triggered the rewards. We went through a period of refining the system to gain the appropriate balance among organization, group, and individual measures.

The way we solved performance-management challenges was quite different from our traditional approach. The teams wanted a manager to come in and fix things. But the new managers were more facilitators than experts in the particular processes under their supervision. So they turned this challenge back to the team for resolution.

**Q:** In other words, management held fast and said, "It's your problem, you resolve it." That's why you're doing self-managed teams.

**A:** That's right. And some people—not a lot—said, "I didn't sign up for this kind of responsibility. I don't mind receiving the compensation of my ex-managers, but I'm not sure I want their managerial responsibility."

**Q:** Did those people self-select out, or are they still there?

**A:** A few moved out. It just wasn't a good fit for some employees. Most of the unhappy folks elected to move elsewhere in the organization to an area that wasn't self-managed. In very few cases, they elected to leave the organization. However, except for these few, nearly all our employees soon embraced the concept.

**Source:** F. Luthans, "A Conversation with Charles Dull," *Organizational Dynamics* 18, no. 7 (1993): 57-70. This interview was edited for inclusion in this textbook.

**self-designing team**
team that has the characteristics of self-managing teams but that also controls team design, work tasks, and team membership

**Self-designing teams** have all the characteristics of self-managing teams, but they can also control and change the design of the teams themselves, the tasks they do and how they do them, and who belongs to the teams. At Saturn, a division of General Motors, self-designing teams of about 10 people each build Saturn cars. Each team determines work schedules, vacation time, and even how assembly jobs are to be performed. Furthermore, the teams determine team membership by conducting the hiring interviews.[51]

### 2.2 Special Kinds of Teams

There are a number of other kinds of teams that can't be easily categorized in terms of autonomy. In other words, depending on how these teams are designed, they can be either low- or high-autonomy teams. Nonetheless, companies are increasingly using these special kinds of teams: cross-functional teams, virtual teams, and project teams.

**cross-functional team**
team composed of employees from different functional areas of the organization

**Cross-functional teams** are purposively composed of employees from different functional areas of the organization.[52] Because their members have different functional backgrounds, education, and experience, cross-functional teams usually attack problems from multiple perspectives and generate more ideas and alternative solutions, all of which are especially important when trying to innovate or do creative problem solving.[53] Cross-functional teams can be used almost anywhere in an organization and are often used in conjunction with matrix and product organizational structures. They can also be used with either part-time or temporary team assignments, or they can be used with full-time, long-term teams. What does a cross-functional team look like in practice? Charles Parnell of Miller Brewing Company explained how a cross-functional team might work at Miller:

> If marketing wants to launch a group of new products, they will set up a task force and call in someone from finance, human resources, and operations.
>
> The operations people will explain to the marketing group the realities of brewing, packaging, and shipping more than 40 brands of beer in more than twenty-eight hundred different can, bottle, keg, package, and label configurations. This means that if marketing had been thinking about introducing 10 new brands next year, they will understand that's a virtual impossibility for the operations people and *they will know why* [italics added].
>
> Based on these discussions, they mutually agree on just how many new products Miller can introduce in an effective, profitable manner.[54]

**virtual team**
team composed of geographically and/or organizationally dispersed coworkers who use telecommunication and information technologies to accomplish an organizational task

**Virtual teams** are groups of geographically and/or organizationally dispersed co-workers who use a combination of telecommunications and information technologies to accomplish an organizational task.[55] In other words, members of virtual teams rarely meet face-to-face. The idea of virtual teams is relatively new and has been made possible by advances in communications and technology, such as email, the World Wide Web, videoconferencing, and other products. Virtual teams can be employee involvement

486

Telecommunications and information technology allow geographically dispersed virtual teams to work together to accomplish organizational tasks.

© WAYNE R. BELENDUKE/GETTY IMAGES/STONE

teams, self-managing teams, or nearly any kind of team discussed in this chapter. Virtual teams are often (but not necessarily) temporary teams that are set up to accomplish a specific task.[56]

Because the team members don't meet in a physical location, one of the unique qualities of virtual teams is that it is much easier to include other key stakeholders, such as suppliers and customers. The development of the Boeing 777 was largely a virtual team effort. Boeing developed the 777 through the combined efforts of 238 design teams. The 238 teams used a network of 1,700 individual computer systems, which had links to Japan; Wichita, Kansas; Philadelphia; Boeing's headquarters, then near Seattle; and other locations. Virtual project teams worked on the 777 in each location and used computer technology to communicate with each other, including airlines that had purchased the 777 and suppliers who provided key expertise and parts.[57]

The principle advantage of virtual teams is that they are very flexible. Employees can work with each other, regardless of physical location, time zone, or organizational affiliation.[58] Plus, virtual teams have certain efficiency advantages over traditional team structures. Because the teammates do not meet face to face, the time commitment involved in participating in a virtual team is typically not as great as for a traditional team. Moreover, employees can fulfill the responsibilities of their virtual team membership from the comfort of their own offices, without the travel time or downtime typically required by face-to-face meetings. [59]

A drawback of virtual teams is that the team members must learn to express themselves in new contexts.[60] For example, the give-and-take that naturally occurs in face-to-face meetings is more difficult to achieve through videoconferencing or other methods of virtual teaming. In addition, several studies have shown that physical proximity enhances information processing.[61] Therefore, some companies bring virtual team members together on a regular basis. Pat O'day is the manager of a five-person virtual team at KPMG. O'day, whose virtual team members live in Washington, Maryland, and Texas, said, "We communicate through email and conference calls and meet in person four times a year."[62] Exhibit 13.7 provides a number of tips for successfully managing virtual teams.

**project team**
team created to complete specific, one-time projects or tasks within a limited time

**Project teams** are created to complete specific, one-time projects or tasks within a limited time.[63] Project teams are often used to develop new products, to significantly improve existing products, to roll out new information systems, or to build new factories or offices. The project team is typically led by a project manager, who has the overall responsibility for planning, staffing, and managing the team.

EXHIBIT 13.7

## TIPS FOR MANAGING SUCCESSFUL VIRTUAL TEAMS

- Select people who are self-starters and strong communicators.
- Keep the team focused by establishing clear, specific goals and by explaining the consequences and importance of meeting these goals.
- Provide frequent feedback so team members can measure their progress.
- Keep team interactions upbeat and action-oriented by expressing appreciation for good work and completed tasks.
- "Personalize" the virtual team by periodically bringing team members together and by encouraging team members to share information with each other about their personal lives.
- Improve communication through increased telephone calls, emails, and Internet messaging and videoconference sessions.
- Periodically ask team members how well the team is working and what can be done to improve performance.

**Sources:** C. Solomon, "Managing Virtual Teams," *Workforce* 80 (June 2001), 60. W.F. Cascio, "Managing a Virtual Workplace," *Academy of Management Executive* 14 (2000): 81-90.

Because project tasks are often unique, project teams are often staffed by employees from different functional areas and may also include members from the company's suppliers or customers. USAir, a major airline, used a project team when it decided to start its own low-fare airline. The team included a pilot, the driver of a catering truck (that delivers food to planes), an aircraft cleaner, a ramp supervisor, a mechanic, a flight attendant, a dispatcher, a reservation agent, and others. Relieved of their regular jobs for four months, the members of the project team flew to Virginia each week to plan a low-fare airline to compete with Southwest Airlines, which had begun flying into Baltimore; Providence, Rhode Island; and other East Coast destinations where USAir flies. After making hundreds of flights on other airlines to scout the competition, team members decided almost everything about the new airline, from whether it would have first class seats (no) to where freezers should be stationed so that food could be quickly loaded onto planes. At the end of the four months, the team disbanded after completing a detailed business plan for MetroJet, USAir's low-fare airline.[64]

One advantage of project teams is that drawing employees from different functional areas can reduce or eliminate communication barriers. In turn, as long as team members feel free to express their ideas, thoughts, and concerns, free-flowing communication encourages cooperation among separate departments and typically speeds up the design process.[65] For example, GE Global eXchange Services used a cross-functional team to design its Web site so that it would have the same simple, intuitive-looking feel in English, French, Spanish, German, and Italian. This Web site is equally effective across all of these languages and cultures because, according to GE employee Doug Irwin, the company used a "cross-functional, cross-geography tiger team" during development. Said Irwin, "Every Wednesday morning for an hour, we'd meet on a global conference call. There were five to 15 of us, from all areas of the business and from all across the globe."[66] Today, in 58 countries, GE Global eXchange Services uses its Web site (**http://www.geis.com/gxs/home**) to operate one of the largest business-to-business e-commerce networks in the world, with more than 100,000 trading partners.

Another advantage of project teams is their flexibility. When projects are finished, project team members either move on to the next project or return to their functional units. For example, after designing the new low-fare airline the members of USAir's MetroJet project team returned to their jobs as pilots, flight attendants, baggage handlers, and so forth. Publication of this book required designers, editors, page makeup artists, and Web designers, among others. When the task was finished, these people applied their skills to other text assignments. Because of this flexibility, project teams are often used with the matrix organizational designs discussed in Chapter 11.

## Review 2
### Kinds of Teams

Companies use different kinds of teams to make themselves more competitive. Autonomy is the key dimension that makes teams different. Traditional work groups (that execute tasks) and employee involvement groups (that make suggestions) have the lowest levels of autonomy. Semi-autonomous work groups (that control major, direct tasks) have more autonomy, followed by self-managing teams (that control all direct tasks) and self-designing teams (that control membership and how tasks are done), which have the highest levels of autonomy. Cross-functional, virtual, and project teams are common, but not easily categorized in terms of autonomy. Cross-functional teams combine employees from different functional areas to help teams attack problems from multiple perspectives and generate more ideas and solutions. Virtual teams use telecommunications and information technologies to bring coworkers "together," regardless of physical location or time zone. Virtual teams reduce travel and work time, but communication may suffer since team members don't work face-to-face. Finally, project teams are used for specific, one-time projects or tasks that must be completed within a limited time. Project teams reduce communication barriers and promote flexibility; teams and team members are reassigned to their department or new projects as old projects are completed.

# Managing Work Teams

Operations manager: Why did I ever let you talk me into teams? They're nothing but trouble. I have to spend all my time in training and meetings, and we're behind on our production schedule.

Human resources manager: Hey, you were the one who wanted to try teams, remember? We went to visit that car company and you fell in love with their program.

Operations manager: I know, but obviously there's something wrong here. Maybe the car people were giving us a song and dance.

HR manager: I don't know about that. Maybe we ought to look at ourselves. What is it we're doing that's causing the problem?[67]

"Why did I ever let you talk me into teams?" Lots of managers have this reaction after making the move to teams. However, many don't realize that this reaction is normal, both for them and for workers. In fact, such a reaction is characteristic of the *storming* stage of team development (discussed in Section 3.5). Managers who are familiar with these stages and with the other important characteristics of teams will be better prepared to manage the predictable changes that occur when companies make the switch to team-based structures.

*After reading the next two sections, you should be able to*

3. *understand the general characteristics of work teams*
4. *explain how to enhance work team effectiveness*

## 3. Work Team Characteristics

*Understanding the characteristics of work teams is a requirement for making teams an effective part of an organization. Therefore, in this section you'll learn about 3.1 team norms, 3.2 team cohesiveness, 3.3 team size, 3.4 team conflict, and 3.5 stages of team development.*

### 3.1 Team Norms

**norms**
informally agreed-upon standards that regulate team behavior

Over time, teams develop **norms**, informally agreed-upon standards that regulate team behavior.[68] Norms are valuable because they let team members know what is expected of them. At Nucor Steel, work groups expect their members to get to work on time. To reinforce this norm, if someone is late to work, he or she cannot receive the team bonus for that day (assuming the team is productive). If the worker is more than 30 minutes late, he or she cannot receive the team bonus for the entire week. At Nucor this matters, since bonuses can double the size of a worker's take-home pay.[69]

Studies indicate that norms are one of the most powerful influences on work behavior. Team norms are often associated with positive outcomes, such as stronger organizational commitment, more trust in management, and stronger job and organizational satisfaction.[70] In general, effective work teams develop norms about the quality and timeliness of job performance, absenteeism, safety, and honest expression of ideas and opinions. The power of norms also comes from the fact that they regulate the everyday kinds of behaviors that allow teams to function effectively. Since the switch to self-directed teams at Lucent Technologies, it is now the norm for team members to identify and solve manufacturing problems on their own. When Phil Daily realized that it would only take 25 percent more staff to increase output of digital transmitting stations by 33 percent, he simply borrowed workers from other teams—all without management approval. Furthermore, any Lucent worker can change any procedure or process as long as the workers who are affected okay them. In fact, because they feel so much responsibility for what goes on, teams put pressure on teammates who miss important meetings.[71]

Norms can also influence team behavior in negative ways. For example, most people would agree that damaging organizational property; saying or doing something to hurt someone at work; intentionally doing one's work badly, incorrectly, or slowly; griping about coworkers; deliberately bending or breaking rules; or doing something to harm the company or boss are negative behaviors. However, a study of workers from 34 teams in 20 different organizations found that teams with negative norms strongly influenced their team members to engage in these negative behaviors. In fact, the longer they were a member of a team with negative norms and the more frequently they interacted with their teammates, the more likely individual team members were to perform negative behaviors. Since team norms typically develop early in the life of a team, these results indicate how important it is for teams to establish positive norms from the outset.[72]

### 3.2 Team Cohesiveness

490

**cohesiveness**
the extent to which team members are attracted to a team and motivated to remain in it

Cohesiveness is another important characteristic of work teams. **Cohesiveness** is the extent to which team members are attracted to a team and motivated to remain in it.[73] Burlington Northern Railroad's intermodal team, which was charged with finding efficient ways to combine transportation through trucks and trains, was a particularly cohesive team. Dave Burns, a member of that team, said, "In my mind, the key word to this team was 'shared.' We shared everything. There was a complete openness among us. And the biggest thing that we shared was an objective and a strategy that we had put together jointly. That was our benchmark every day. Were we doing things in support of *our* plan?"[74]

The level of cohesiveness that exists in a group is important for several reasons. To start, cohesive groups have a better chance of retaining their members. As a result, cohesive groups typically experience lower turnover.[75] In addition, team cohesiveness promotes cooperative behavior, generosity, and a willingness on the part of team members to assist each other.[76] When team cohesiveness is high, team members are more motivated to contribute to the team, because they want to gain the approval of other team members. As a result of these reasons and others, studies have clearly established that cohesive teams consistently perform better.[77] Furthermore, cohesive teams quickly achieve high levels of performance. By contrast, it takes teams low in cohesion much longer to reach the same levels of performance.[78]

What can be done to promote team cohesiveness? First, make sure that all team members are present at team meetings and activities. Team cohesiveness suffers when

# WhatReallyWorks

## Cohesion and Team Performance

Have you ever worked in a really cohesive group where everyone really liked and enjoyed each other and was glad to be part of the group? It's great. By contrast, have you ever worked in a group where everyone really disliked each other and was unhappy to be a part of the group? It's terrible. Anyone who has had either of these experiences can

appreciate how important group cohesion is and the effect it can have on team performance. Indeed, 46 studies based on 1,279 groups confirm that cohesion does matter.

### Team Performance

On average, there is a 66 percent chance that cohesive teams will outperform less cohesive teams.

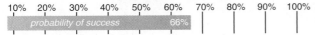

### Team Performance with Interdependent Tasks

Teams work best for interdependent tasks that require people to work together to get the job done. When teams perform interdependent tasks, there is a 73 percent chance that cohesive teams will outperform less cohesive teams.

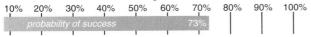

### Team Performance with Independent Tasks

Teams are generally not suited for independent tasks in which people can accomplish the job by themselves. When teams

perform independent tasks, there is a only a 60 percent chance that cohesive teams will outperform less cohesive teams.

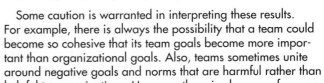

Some caution is warranted in interpreting these results. For example, there is always the possibility that a team could become so cohesive that its team goals become more important than organizational goals. Also, teams sometimes unite around negative goals and norms that are harmful rather than helpful to organizations. However, there is also room for even more optimism about cohesive teams. Teams that are cohesive *and* committed to the goals they are asked to achieve should have an even higher probability of success than the numbers shown here.

**Sources:** S.M. Gully, D.S. Devine, and D.J. Whitney, "A Meta-Analysis of Cohesion and Performance: Effects of Level of Analysis and Task Interdependence," *Small Group Research* 26, no. 4 (1995): 497-520.

members are allowed to withdraw from the team and miss team meetings and events.[79] Second, create additional opportunities for teammates to work together by rearranging work schedules and creating common workspaces. When task interdependence is high and team members have lots of chances to work together, team cohesiveness tends to increase.[80] Third, engaging in nonwork activities as a team can help build cohesion. At Cambridge Technology Partners, where teams put in extraordinarily long hours coding computer software, the software teams maintained cohesion by doing "fun stuff" together. Team leader Tammy Urban said, "We went on team outings at least once a week. We'd play darts, shoot pool. Teams work best when you get to know each other outside of work—what people's interests are, who they are. Personal connections go a long way when you're developing complex applications in our kind of time frames."[81] Finally, companies build team cohesiveness by making employees feel that they are part of a "special" organization. For example, all the new hires at Disney World in Orlando are required to take a course entitled "Traditions One," in which they learn the traditions and history of the Walt Disney Company (including the names of the seven dwarfs!). The purpose of Traditions One is to instill a sense of team pride in working for Disney.

### 3.3 Team Size

There appears to be a curvilinear relationship between team size and performance. In other words, very small or very large teams may not perform as well as moderately sized teams. For most teams, the right size is somewhere between six and nine members.[82] This size is conducive to high team cohesion, which has a positive affect on team performance,

Rescue workers at the World Trade Center terrorist attack site provide an example of a team with a high level of cohesiveness. This quickly formed team was composed of thousands of people from all over the country who focused intently on the task at hand—find any survivors.

© AFP/CORBIS

as discussed above. Teams of this size are small enough for the team members get to know each other and for each member to have an opportunity to contribute in a meaningful way to the success of the team. However, they're also large enough to take advantage of team members' diverse skills, knowledge, and perspectives. It is also easier to instill a sense of responsibility and mutual accountability in teams of this size.[83]

By contrast, when teams get too large, team members find it difficult to get to know one another and may splinter into smaller subgroups. When this occurs, subgroups sometimes argue and disagree, weakening overall team cohesion. As teams grow, there is a greater chance of *minority domination*, where just a few team members dominate team discussions. Even if minority domination doesn't occur, there still isn't as much time in larger groups for all team members to share their input. And when team members feel that their contributions are unimportant or not needed, the result is less involvement, effort, and accountability to the team.[84] Large teams also face logistical problems, such as finding an appropriate time or place to meet. Finally, the incidence of social loafing, discussed earlier in the chapter, is much higher in large teams. All of these factors indicate how large teams can have a negative impact on team performance.

While teams should not be too large, it's also important that they not be too small. Teams with just a few people may lack the diversity of skills and knowledge found in larger teams. Also, teams that are too small are unlikely to gain the advantages of team decision making (i.e., multiple perspectives, generating more ideas and alternative solutions, and stronger commitment) found in larger teams.

What signs indicate that a team's size needs to be changed? If decisions are taking too long, if it is difficult for the team to make decisions or take action, if the team is dominated by a few members, or if the commitment or efforts of team members are weak, chances are the team is too big. However, if a team is having difficulty coming up with ideas or generating solutions, or if the team does not have the expertise to address a specific problem, chances are the team is too small.

### 3.4 Team Conflict

Conflict and disagreement are inevitable in most teams. But this shouldn't surprise anyone. From time to time, people who work together are going to disagree about what and how things get done. What causes conflict in teams? While almost anything can lead to conflict—casual remarks that unintentionally offend a team member or fighting over scarce resources—the primary cause of team conflict is disagreement over team goals and priorities.[85] Other common causes of team conflict include disagreements over task-related issues, interpersonal incompatibilities, and simple fatigue.

While most people view conflict negatively, the key to dealing with team conflict is not avoiding conflict, but making sure that teams experience the right kind of conflict. In Chapter 6, you learned about *c-type conflict*, or *cognitive conflict*, which focuses on problem-related differences of opinion; and *a-type conflict*, or *affective conflict*, which refers to the emotional reactions that can occur when disagreements become personal rather than professional.[86] Cognitive conflict is strongly associated with improvements in team performance, while affective conflict is strongly associated with decreases in team performance.[87] Why does this happen? With cognitive conflict, team members disagree because their different experiences and expertise lead them to different views of the problem and solutions. Indeed, managers who participated on teams that emphasized cognitive conflict described their teammates as "smart," "team players," and "best in the business." They described their teams as "open," "fun," and "productive." One manager summed up the positive attitude that team members had about cognitive conflict by saying, "We scream a lot, then laugh, and then resolve the issue."[88] Thus, cognitive conflict is also characterized by a willingness to examine, compare, and reconcile differences to produce the best possible solution.

By contrast, affective conflict often results in hostility, anger, resentment, distrust, cynicism, and apathy. Managers who participated on teams that emphasized affective conflict described their teammates as "manipulative," "secretive," "burned out," and "political."[89] Not surprisingly, affective conflict can make people uncomfortable and cause them to withdraw and decrease their commitment to a team.[90] Affective conflict also lowers the satisfaction of team members, may lead to personal hostility between coworkers, and can decrease team cohesiveness.[91] So, unlike cognitive conflict, affective conflict undermines team effectiveness by preventing teams from engaging in the kinds of activities that are critical to team effectiveness.

So, what can managers do to manage team conflict? First, managers need to realize that emphasizing cognitive conflict alone won't be enough. Studies show that cognitive and affective conflicts often occur together in the same teams! Therefore, sincere attempts to reach agreement on a difficult issue can quickly deteriorate from cognitive to affective conflict if the discussion turns personal and tempers and emotions flare. So while cognitive conflict is clearly the better approach to take, efforts to engage in cognitive conflict should be approached with caution.

493

---

**EXHIBIT 13.8**

### HOW TEAMS CAN HAVE A GOOD FIGHT

1. Work with more, rather than less, information.
2. Develop multiple alternatives to enrich debate.
3. Establish common goals.
4. Inject humor into the workplace.
5. Maintain a balance of power.
6. Resolve issues without forcing a consensus.

**Source:** K.M. Eisenhardt, J.L. Kahwajy, & L.J. Bourgeois, III, "How Management Teams Can Have a Good Fight," *Harvard Business Review* 75, no. 4 (July/August 1997): 77-87.

Can teams disagree and still get along? Fortunately, they can. In an attempt to study this issue, researchers examined team conflict in 12 high-tech companies. In four of the 12 companies, work teams used cognitive conflict to address work problems but did so in a way that minimized the occurrence of affective conflict. Exhibit 13.8 shows what steps these teams took to be able to have a "good fight." [92]

First, work with more, rather than less, information. If data are plentiful, objective, and up-to-date, teams will focus on issues, not personalities. Second, develop multiple alternatives to enrich debate. Focusing on multiple solutions diffuses conflict by getting teams to keep searching for a better solution. Positions and opinions are naturally more flexible with five alternatives than with just two. Third, establish common goals. Remember, most team conflict arises from disagreements over team goals and priorities. Therefore, common goals encourage collaboration and minimize conflict over a team's purpose. Steve Jobs, CEO of Apple Computer, explained it this way: "It's okay to spend a lot of time arguing about which route to take to San Francisco when everyone wants to end up there, but a lot of time gets wasted in such arguments if one person wants to go to San Francisco and another secretly wants to go to San Diego." [93] Fourth, inject humor into the workplace. Humor relieves tension, builds cohesion, and just makes being in teams fun. Fifth, maintain a balance of power by involving as many people as possible in the decision process. And sixth, resolve issues without forcing a consensus. Consensus means that everyone must agree before decisions are finalized. Effectively, consensus gives everyone on the team veto power. Nothing gets done until everyone agrees, which, of course, is nearly impossible. The result is that consensus usually promotes affective rather than cognitive conflict. If team members can't agree after constructively discussing their options, it's better to have the team leader make the final choice. Most team members can accept the team leader's choice if they've been thoroughly involved in the decision process.

### 3.5 Stages of Team Development

As teams develop and grow, they pass through four stages of development. As shown in Exhibit 13.9, those stages are forming, storming, norming, and performing. [94] While not every team passes through each of these stages, teams that do tend to be better performers. [95] This holds true even for teams composed of seasoned executives. However, after a period of time, if not managed well, performance may start to deteriorate as teams begin a process of decline, in which they progress through the stages of de-norming, de-storming, and de-forming. [96]

**Forming** is the initial stage of team development. This is the getting-acquainted stage, where team members first meet each other, form initial impressions, and try to get a sense of what it will be like to be part of the team. Some of the first team norms will be established during this stage, as team members begin to find out what behaviors will and won't be accepted by the team. Team leaders should allow enough time for team members to get to know each other during this stage, should set early ground rules, and should begin to set up a preliminary team structure.

Conflicts and disagreements often characterize the second stage of team development, **storming**. As team members begin working together, different personalities and work styles may clash. Team members become more assertive at this stage and more willing to state opinions. This is also the stage when team members jockey for position and try to establish a favorable role for themselves in the team. In addition, team members are likely to disagree about what the group should do and how it should do it. Team performance is still relatively low, given that team cohesion is weak and team members are still reluctant to support each other. Since teams that get stuck in the storming stage are almost always ineffective, it is important for team leaders to focus the team on team goals and on improving team performance. Team members need to be particularly patient and tolerant with each other in this stage.

During **norming**, the third stage of team development, team members begin to settle into their roles as team members. Positive team norms will have developed by this stage, and teammates should know what to expect from each other. Petty differences

---

494

**forming**
the first stage of team development in which team members meet each other, form initial impressions, and begin to establish team norms

**storming**
the second stage of team development, characterized by conflict and disagreement, in which team members disagree over what the team should do and how it should do it

**norming**
the third stage of team development, in which team members begin to settle into their roles, group cohesion grows, and positive team norms develop

EXHIBIT 13.9

STAGES OF TEAM DEVELOPMENT

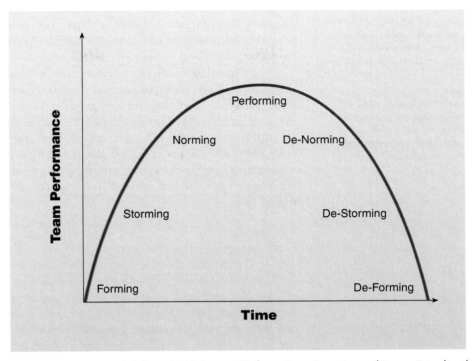

**Sources:** J.F. McGrew, J.G. Bilotta, & J.M. Deeney, "Software Team Formation and Decay: Extending the Standard Model for Small Groups," *Small Group Research* 30, no. 2 (1999): 209-234. B.W. Tuckman, "Development Sequence in Small Groups," *Psychological Bulletin* 63, no. 6 (1965): 384-399.

should also have been resolved, friendships will have developed, and group cohesion will be relatively strong. At this point, team members will have accepted team goals, will be operating as a unit, and, as indicated by the increase in performance, be working together effectively. This stage can be very short and is often characterized by someone in the team saying, "I think things are finally coming together." However, teams may also cycle back and forth between storming and norming several times before finally settling into norming.

In the last stage of team development, **performing**, performance improves because the team has finally matured into an effective, fully functioning team. At this point, members should be fully committed to the team and think of themselves as "members of a team" and not just "employees." Team members often become intensely loyal to one another at this stage and feel mutual accountability for team successes and failures. Trivial disagreements, which can take time and energy away from the work of the team, should be rare. At this stage, teams get a lot of work done, and it is fun to be a team member.

However, after a period of time, if not managed well, performance may begin to decline, as teams progress through the stages of de-norming, de-storming, and de-forming.[97] Indeed, John Puckett, manufacturing vice president for circuit board maker XEL Communications, said, "The books all say you start in this state of chaos and march through these various stages, and you end up in this state of ultimate self-direction, where everything is going just great. They never tell you it can go back in the other direction, sometimes just as quickly."[98]

In **de-norming**, which is a reversal of the norming stage, team performance begins to decline as the size, scope, goal, or members of the team change. With new members joining the group, older members may become defensive as established ways of doing

**performing**
the fourth and final stage of team development, in which performance improves because the team has matured into an effective, fully functioning team

**de-norming**
a reversal of the norming stage, in which team performance begins to decline as the size, scope, goal, or members of the team change

things are questioned and challenged. Expression of ideas and opinions becomes less open. New members change team norms by actively rejecting or passively neglecting previously established team roles and behaviors.

In **de-storming**, which is a reversal of the storming phase, the team's comfort level decreases. Team cohesion weakens as more group members resist conforming to team norms and quit participating in team activities. Angry emotions flare as the group explodes in conflict and moves into the final stage of de-forming.

In **de-forming**, which is a reversal of the forming stage, team members position themselves to gain control of pieces of the team. Team members begin to avoid each other and isolate themselves from team leaders. Team performance rapidly declines as the team quits caring about even minimal requirements of team performance.

If teams are actively managed, decline is not inevitable. However, managers need to recognize that the forces at work in the de-norming, de-storming, and de-forming stages represent a powerful, disruptive, and real threat to teams that have finally made it to the performing stage. Getting to the performing stage is half the battle. Staying there is the second half.

**de-storming**
a reversal of the storming phase, in which the team's comfort level decreases, team cohesion weakens, and angry emotions and conflict may flare

**de-forming**
a reversal of the forming stage, in which team members position themselves to control pieces of the team, avoid each other, and isolate themselves from team leaders

## Review 3
### Work Team Characteristics

The most important characteristics of work teams are team norms, cohesiveness, size, conflict, and development. Norms let team members know what is expected of them and can influence team behavior in positive and negative ways. Positive team norms are associated with organizational commitment, trust, and job satisfaction. Team cohesiveness helps teams retain members, promotes cooperative behavior, increases motivation, and facilitates team performance. Attending team meetings and activities, creating opportunities to work together, and engaging in nonwork activities can increase cohesiveness. Team size has a curvilinear relationship with team performance, such that very small or very large teams do not perform as well as moderately sized teams of six to nine members. Teams of this size are cohesive and small enough for team members to get to know each other and contribute in a meaningful way, but are large enough to take advantage of team members' diverse skills, knowledge, and perspectives. Conflict and disagreement are inevitable in most teams. The key to dealing with team conflict is to maximize cognitive conflict, which focuses on issue-related differences, and minimize affective conflict, the emotional reactions that occur when disagreements become personal rather than professional. As teams develop and grow, they pass through four stages of development: forming, storming, norming, and performing. However, after a period of time, if not managed well, performance may decline, as teams progress through the stages of de-norming, de-storming, and de-forming.

# 4. Enhancing Work Team Effectiveness

*Making teams work is a challenging and difficult process. However, companies can increase the likelihood that teams will succeed by carefully managing 4.1 the setting of team goals and priorities, and how work team members are 4.2 selected, 4.3 trained, and 4.4 compensated.[99]*

## 4.1 Setting Team Goals and Priorities

In Chapter 4, you learned that specific, measurable, attainable, realistic, and timely (i.e., S.M.A.R.T.) goals are one of the most effective means for improving individual job performance. Fortunately, team goals also improve team performance. In fact, team goals lead to much higher team performance 93 percent of the time.[100] For example, Nucor Steel sets specific, challenging goals for each of its production teams, which consist of first-line supervisors and production and maintenance workers. Each day these teams are challenged to produce a specific number of tons of high-quality steel.[101] Teams that meet their goals earn daily bonuses that can double their base salaries.

If you want to establish a team mentality in employees, what better way than to create a conference room that reminds them of the role of teamwork? At the Chicago law firm of Bartlit Beck Herman Palenchar & Scott, that's just what the partners did. Philip Beck's office opens onto an arena-style conference room with regulation keys and a three-point line woven into the carpet. The Forum, as the room is called, is also equipped with tables, chairs, and white boards for trial preparation. The idea was to encourage teamwork and make the senior partners available to younger lawyers.

Why is setting specific, challenging team goals so critical to team success? One reason is that increasing a team's performance is inherently more complex than just increasing one individual's job performance. For instance, consider that for any team there are likely to be at least four different kinds of goals: each member's goal for the team, each member's goal for himself or herself on the team, the team's goal for each member, and the team's goal for itself.[102] In other words, without a specific, challenging goal for the team itself (the last of the four goals listed), these other goals may encourage team members to head off in twelve different directions at once. Consequently, setting a specific, challenging goal *for the team* clarifies team priorities by providing a clear focus and purpose.

Specific, challenging team goals also regulate how hard team members work. In particular, challenging team goals greatly reduce the incidence of social loafing. When faced with difficult goals, team members simply expect everyone to contribute. Consequently, they are much more likely to notice and complain if a teammate isn't doing his or her share. In fact, when teammates know each other well, when team goals are specific, when team communication is good, and when teams are rewarded for team performance (discussed below), there is only a one in 16 chance that teammates will be social loafers. [103]

What can companies and teams do to ensure that team goals lead to superior team performance? One increasingly popular approach is to give teams stretch goals. In Chapter 4, you learned that *stretch goals* are extremely ambitious goals that workers don't know how to reach.[104] The purpose of stretch goals is to achieve extraordinary improvements in performance by forcing managers and workers to throw away old comfortable solutions and adopt radical, never-used solutions. Some of IBM's stretch goals are to significantly increase the speed, shrink the size, and reduce the cost of the $4 billion worth of computer chips it sells each year. To achieve these stretch goals, its research scientists have experimented with materials ranging from copper to aluminum. With its latest new material, which it calls "strained silicon," IBM has managed to increase processing speeds by 35 percent, all without increasing the size or thickness of these new computer chips. And because the size of the chips won't change, existing manufacturing technologies can be used to make these significantly faster computer chips, which means that costs won't increase.[105]

Four things must occur for stretch goals to effectively motivate teams.[106] First, teams must have a high degree of autonomy or control over how they achieve their goals. At CSX's railroad division, top management challenged the new management team at its Cumberland, Maryland, office to increase productivity by 16 percent. The goal was specific and challenging: Ship the same amount of coal each month, but do it with 4,200 rail cars instead of 5,000 rail cars. The local team, consisting of five new managers, quickly figured out that the trains were spending too much time sitting idly in the rail yards. Finance director Peter Mills said, "We'd look out our office windows at the tracks and wonder, 'Why aren't the cars moving?'" The problem? Headquarters wouldn't let the trains run until they had 160 full rail cars to pull, a process that could take nearly a week to complete. But since the local management team had the autonomy to pay for the extra crews to run the trains more frequently, it started running the trains with as few as 78 cars. Now, since coal cars never wait more than a day to be transported to customers, rail productivity has skyrocketed.[107]

Second, teams must be empowered with control resources, such as budgets, workspaces, computers, or whatever they need to do their jobs. Steve Kerr, General Electric's former "Chief Learning Officer," said, "We have a moral obligation to try to give people the tools to meet tough goals. I think it's totally wrong if you don't give employees the tools to succeed, then punish them when they fail."[108]

Third, teams need structural accommodation. **Structural accommodation** means giving teams the ability to change organizational structures, policies, and practices if it helps them meet their stretch goals. When Hewlett-Packard imposed tough goals on its customer service teams, one of the unintended consequences was a big increase in work stress from being called to customer sites on weekends and at all hours of the night. As a result, overworked customer service engineers began quitting their jobs, making it unlikely that the teams could achieve their stretch goals. HP responded by giving teams the ability to "reinvent work" in a way that would meet the stretch goals, but reduce worker stress. The teams decided to throw out existing policies on employee work hours and to simply ask who would be willing to work Fridays through Mondays and who would be willing to work Tuesdays through Fridays. Stress dropped immediately, and employees stopped quitting their jobs.[109]

Finally, teams need bureaucratic immunity. **Bureaucratic immunity** means that teams no longer have to go through the frustratingly slow process of multilevel reviews and sign offs to get management approval before making changes. Once granted bureaucratic immunity, teams are immune from the influence of various organizational groups and are only accountable to top management. Therefore, teams can act quickly and even experiment with little fear of failure. Climate Engineering Corp. gave its self-directed work teams bureaucratic immunity so they could have more control over their work and provide better service to customers. Although others in the company strongly resisted, President Eric Bindner told each repair service team (which services heating and air-conditioning systems) that they were free to schedule regular maintenance, day-to-day jobs and repairs, emergency nighttime and weekend repairs, as well as their own vacation time. They were also given complete control over recruiting new team members and structuring and running each team.[110]

### 4.2 Selecting People for Teamwork

University of Southern California professor Edward Lawler said, "People are very naive about how easy it is to create a team. Teams are the Ferraris of work design. They're high performance but high maintenance and expensive."[111] It's almost impossible to make effective work teams without carefully selecting people who are suited for teamwork or for working on a particular team. A preference for teamwork, team elevation, and team diversity can help companies choose the right team members.[112]

**structural accommodation**
the ability to change organizational structures, policies, and practices in order to meet stretch goals

**498**

**bureaucratic immunity**
the ability to make changes without first getting approval from managers or other parts of an organization

# BlastFromThePast

## Work Teams: Just Horsing Around

**The Hawthorne studies were the first large-scale, systematic study of work groups. Conducted by Elton Mayo in the 1920s and 1930s, the Hawthorne studies indicated that work groups form strong "informal" norms, and that these norms are not always positive. For example, in one of the factories in Mayo's studies, managers posted the daily**

output of individual workers for all to see, hoping to stimulate competition and increase production. What happened instead was that the workers used this information to punish the best workers. Their motivation was simple. They punished the best workers because they didn't want management to think that everyone could and should do more work. Mayo and his researchers used this finding to warn managers about the unintended effects that can occur in workplace groups and teams.

Historians believe that the term "work team" was first used in the 15th century to refer to teams of horses that were put together to increase their ability to pull heavy loads. However, Eric Trist was the first to use the term "work team" to describe groups in business organizations. Trist was studying the work processes in British mines when a dramatic change occurred in the way that the miners performed their jobs. An improvement in hydraulic jack technology made it possible for the miners to work in small areas (15 to 150 feet), rather than in tunnels that were several hundred feet long. The new method was called "shortwall" mining, while the old method was called "longwall" mining. The miners responded to this change by asking to be put into small, autonomous groups to work the short mines. Trist found that the miners that worked in small groups were more productive and committed to their work than the miners that who did not work in groups.

Finally, the term "skunk works" entered our vocabulary in the 1970s. "Skunk Works" was the nickname for the group that Lockheed (now Lockheed Martin) used in 1943 to design the U.S. Army's first generation of jet airplanes. The urgency of the war effort in Europe demanded that a prototype aircraft be delivered in 180 days. To accomplish this task, Lockheed formed a team of 23 engineers and 103 shop mechanics, and separated them from the rest of the company in a windowless facility in the corner of the Burbank, California, airport. The Skunk Works team completed the XP-80, nicknamed the Lulu-belle, in just 143 days, 37 days ahead of schedule. The initial success of the Skunk Works and its continuing successes have been studied by many team-based organizations. Today, the term "skunk works" is commonly used to denote a work team that has been "set apart" from a corporation's normal hierarchy to try to accomplish an extraordinary task in a relatively short period of time.

**Sources:** M.M. Beyerlein, "The History of Work Teams," in *Handbook of Best Practices for Teams*, Volume 1, ed. Glenn M. Parker (Amherst, MA: Irwin, 1996), 13-19. R.A. Guzzo, "Fundamental Considerations about Work Groups," in *Handbook of Work Group Psychology*, ed. Michael A. West (New York: John Wiley & Sons, 1996), 3-21.

---

**individualism-collectivism**
the degree to which a person believes that people should be self-sufficient and that loyalty to one's self is more important than loyalty to team or company

Are you more comfortable working alone or with others? If you strongly prefer to work alone, you may not be well suited for teamwork. Indeed, studies show that job satisfaction is higher in teams when team members prefer working with others.[113] An indirect way to measure someone's *preference for teamwork* is to assess the person's degree of individualism or collectivism. **Individualism-collectivism** is the degree to which a person believes that people should be self-sufficient and that loyalty to one's self is more important than loyalty to one's team or company.[114] *Individualists*, who put their welfare and interests first, generally prefer independent tasks in which they work alone. On the other hand, *collectivists*, who put group or team interests ahead of self-interests, generally prefer interdependent tasks in which they work with others. Collectivists would also rather cooperate than compete and are fearful of disappointing team members or of being ostracized from teams. Given these differences, it makes sense to select team members who are collectivists rather than individualists. Indeed, many companies use individualism-collectivism as an initial screening device for team members. However, as discussed below, individualists may be appropriate if team diversity is desired. To determine your preference for teamwork, take the Team Player Inventory shown in Exhibit 13.10.

**team level**
the average level of ability, experience, personality, or any other factor on a team

**Team level** is the average level of ability, experience, personality, or any other factor on a team. For example, a high level of team experience means that a team has particularly experienced team members. This does not mean that every member of the team has considerable experience, but that enough team members do to significantly raise the average level of experience on the team. Team level is used to guide selection of teammates when teams need a particular set of skills or capabilities to do their jobs well. For instance, in retail sales jobs, teams with high average levels of conscientiousness, agreeableness, and

EXHIBIT 13.10

THE TEAM PLAYER INVENTORY

| | STRONGLY DISAGREE 1 2 3 4 5 | STRONGLY AGREE |
|---|---|---|
| 1. I enjoy working on team/group projects. | 1 2 3 4 5 | |
| 2. Team/group project work easily allows others to not "pull their weight." | 1 2 3 4 5 | |
| 3. Work that is done as a team/group is better than the work done individually. | 1 2 3 4 5 | |
| 4. I do my best work alone rather than in a team/group. | 1 2 3 4 5 | |
| 5. Team/group work is overrated in terms of the actual results produced. | 1 2 3 4 5 | |
| 6. Working in a team/group gets me to think more creatively. | 1 2 3 4 5 | |
| 7. Team/groups are used too often, when individual work would be more effective. | 1 2 3 4 5 | |
| 8. My own work is enhanced when I am in a team/group situation. | 1 2 3 4 5 | |
| 9. My experiences working in team/group situations have been primarily negative. | 1 2 3 4 5 | |
| 10. More solutions/ideas are generated when working in a team/group situation than when working alone. | 1 2 3 4 5 | |

Reverse score items 2, 4, 5, 7, and 9. Then add the scores for items 1 to 10. Higher scores indicate a preference for teamwork, while lower total scores indicate a preference for individual work.

**Source:** T.J.B. Kline, "The Team Player Inventory: Reliability and Validity of a Measure of Predisposition Toward Organizational Team-Working Environments," *Journal for Specialists in Group Work* 24, no. 1 (1999): 102-112.

openness to experience have much higher sales than teams with low average levels on these dimensions.[115]

While team level represents the average level or capability on a team, **team diversity** represents the variances or differences in ability, experience, personality, or any other factor on a team. For example, teams with strong team diversity on job experience would have a mix of team members, ranging from seasoned veterans to people with three or four years of experience to rookies with little or no experience. Team diversity is used to guide selection of teammates when teams are asked to complete a wide range of different tasks or when tasks are particularly complex.

Delta Dental Plan in Medford, Massachusetts, used the principle of team diversity to select the team members who service its largest account. Tom Raffio, senior vice president, explained that the company wanted a team of people whose strengths complemented each other. The first step was to administer personality inventories to potential team members. Raffio said, "We were looking for a combination of introverts and extroverts, people who reflect on things and people who close on things, and people who could process claims efficiently on a daily basis, as well as those who could keep in mind the long-term vision of the company." The next step was to make sure there was a mixture of language capabilities on the team: English, Spanish, and French. Finally, the company wanted a mix of experience, including seasoned employees who understood the company culture and new employees who brought outside ideas and perspectives. Accordingly, team members were recruited from both inside and outside the company.[116]

### 4.3 Team Training

Organizations that create work teams often underestimate the amount of training required to make teams effective. This mistake occurs frequently in successful organizations, where managers assume that if employees can work effectively on their own, they can work effectively in teams. However, companies that successfully use teams provide thousands of hours of training to make sure that teams work. Ames Rubber provided more than 17,000 hours of training in communication, quality improvement, and prob-

**team diversity**
the variances or differences in ability, experience, personality, or any other factor on a team

lem solving to its 445 team members. As a result, Ames' defect rate fell from 30,000 parts per million to just 11 parts per million. Productivity rose 43 percent and teams' ideas saved the company more than $3 million, or an average of $2,700 per employee.[117] At General Motors' brand new automobile assembly plant in Lansing, Michigan, each employee working on the assembly line will receive 250 classroom hours of training, most of it in problem solving. According to Tim Lee, the group director of manufacturing for GM's North American car group, "Problem solving is not an easy task. Typically, in a plant we treat the symptoms, not the problem."[118]

The most common type of training provided to members of work teams is training in interpersonal skills. **Interpersonal skills**, such as listening, communicating, questioning, and providing feedback, enable people to have effective working relationships with others. When Super Sack, a maker of heavy-duty plastic bags for the food and pharmaceutical industries, first used teams, it failed. David Kellenberger, Super Sack's vice president of manufacturing, said, "One of our greatest mistakes at the beginning was our failure to recognize how important training was. You need to make a huge commitment of time and resources for training people in communication, goal-setting, and general team-building skills to make a successful transition [to teams]."[119] Experiences like these are why Wilson Sporting Goods provides all of its first-year team members 26 hours of training on team interaction skills and how to run meetings.[120]

Because of their autonomy and responsibility, many companies give teams training in decision-making and problem-solving skills to help them do a better job of cutting costs and improving quality and customer service. Stacy Myers, a consultant who helps companies implement teams, said, "When we help companies move to teams, we also require that employees take basic quality and business knowledge classes as well. Teams must know how their work affects the company, and how their success will be measured."[121] Many organizations also teach teams conflict resolution skills. Coldwater Machine Company formed teams but waited several months to provide conflict resolution training. Ken Meyer, Coldwater's coordinator of work groups, said, "People are starting to encounter differences right now, so we're starting conflict resolution training. We think work group members will appreciate the training more now that they're in particular situations and see the relevance."[122]

Firms must also provide team members the technical training they need to do their jobs, particularly if they are expected to perform all of the different jobs on the team (i.e., cross training). Before teams were created at Milwaukee Mutual Insurance, separate employees performed the tasks of rating, underwriting, and processing insurance policies. However, after extensive cross training, each team member can now do all three jobs.[123] Cross training is less appropriate for teams of highly skilled workers. For instance, it is unlikely that a group of engineers, computer programmers, and systems analysts would be cross-trained for each other's jobs.

Finally, companies need to provide training for team leaders, who often feel unprepared for their new duties. Exhibit 13.11 shows the top 10 problems reported by new team leaders. These range from confusion about their new roles as team leaders (compared to their old jobs as managers or employees), to not knowing where to go for help when their teams have problems. The solution is extensive training for team leaders.

### 4.4 Team Compensation and Recognition

Compensating teams correctly is very difficult. For instance, one survey found that only 37 percent of companies were satisfied with their team compensation plans and even fewer, just 10 percent, reported being "very positive."[124] One of the problems, according to Monty Mohrman of the Center for Effective Organizations, is that "There is a very strong set of beliefs in most organizations that people should be paid for how well they do. So when people first get put into team-based organizations, they really balk at being paid for how well the team does. It sounds illogical to them. It sounds like their individuality and their sense of self-worth are being threatened."[125] Consequently, companies need to carefully choose a team compensation plan and then fully explain how teams will be rewarded.

501

EXHIBIT 13.11

TOP 10 PROBLEMS REPORTED BY TEAM LEADERS

1. Confusion about their new roles and about what they should be doing differently.
2. Feeling they've lost control.
3. Not knowing what it means to coach or empower.
4. Having personal doubts about whether the team concept will really work.
5. Uncertainty about how to deal with employees' doubts about the team concept.
6. Confusion about when a team is ready for more responsibility.
7. Confusion about how to share responsibility and accountability with the team.
8. Concern about promotional opportunities, especially about whether the "team leader" title carries any prestige.
9. Uncertainty about the strategic aspects of the leader's role as teams mature.
10. Not knowing where to turn for help with team problems, since few, if any, of their organization's leaders have led teams.

**Source:** B. Filipczak, M. Hequet, C. Lee, M. Picard, & D. Stamps, "More Trouble with Teams," *Training*, October 1996, 21.

One basic requirement is that the level of rewards (individual vs. team) must match the level of performance (individual vs. team) for team compensation to work.

There are three methods of compensating employees for team participation and accomplishments. The first is called skill-based pay. **Skill-based pay** programs pay employees for learning additional skills or knowledge.[126] These programs encourage employees to acquire the additional skills they will need to perform multiple jobs within a team. For example, at XEL Communications, the number of skills each employee has mastered determines his or her individual pay. An employee who takes a class and on the job training in advanced soldering (XEL makes circuit boards) will earn 30 cents more per hour. Passing a written test or satisfactorily performing a skill or job for a supervisor or trainer certifies mastery of new skills and results in increased pay. Eastman Chemical uses a similar approach with its teams. But in Eastman's case, team members also have to demonstrate that they use their new skills at least 10 percent of the time. Otherwise, they lose their pay increase.[127]

The second approach to compensating employees for team participation is through **gainsharing** programs, in which companies share the financial value of performance gains, such as productivity, cost savings, or quality, with their workers.[128] The first month that gainsharing was used at Rogan Corporation, a maker of plastic handles and knobs, employee teams saved the company $23,424, earning an additional $11,712 for themselves. They earned slightly more the second month. Since its inception, gainsharing has added 16 to 22 percent to the salaries of Rogan's employees, typically $3,000 to $5,000 per employee per year. But the company has benefited as well. Before gainsharing, employees produced an average of 95,000 knobs per employee each year. After gainsharing, employees produced at more than twice that rate, turning out an average of 206,000 knobs per employee per year.[129]

Nonfinancial rewards are another way to reward teams for their performance. These rewards, which can range from vacation trips to T-shirts, plaques, and coffee mugs, are especially effective when coupled with management recognition, such as awards, certificates, and praise.[130] Nonfinancial awards tend to be most effective when teams or team-based interventions, such as total quality management (see Chapter 15), are first introduced.[131]

**skill-based pay**
compensation system that pays employees for learning additional skills or knowledge

**gainsharing**
compensation system in which companies share the financial value of performance gains, such as productivity, cost savings, or quality, with their workers

# "headline news"

## From the Cool to the Bizarre—All in the Name of Teamwork

What would you do to build a sense of camaraderie among your colleagues at work? Walk across a bed of nails together? Hot coals? Finding your way out of a cornfield maze? What about putting together a circus complete with trapeze and high wire, or a rodeo with mechanical bulls and cattle branding? Although these may sound farfetched, they are some of the tamest of the odd feats companies are asking employees to perform (beyond sitting in a corporate training facility for two days), all in the name of teamwork.

EMC, Burger King, Genentech, Adobe Systems, Pepsi, Goodyear, and Hewlett-Packard have all sent employees to some pretty wacky (and pretty fun) teambuilding camps. Burger King enrolls employees in a fire-walking seminar; they also march across a bed of nails and smash their hands against inch-thick boards. Adobe and Genentech have sponsored work team circuses, and Pepsi, Goodyear, and HP have sent employees to Mid-Ohio Speedway for race-car driving seminars. If these exercises are too tame, **http://Teambuildinginc.com** offers team beekeeping and honey gathering, rattlesnake hunts, skydiving, bull riding, and paint-ball wars. If you crave a more intensely realistic experience, you can sign up your team for simulated hostage negotiations. Stylish teams can stomp grapes and make Merlot. If you really need something outlandish, try Barbie Heroism, offered by a consulting company called Total Rebound, in which four employees use cranks and pulleys to operate a toy helicopter in an effort to rescue a school of floating Barbies from deadly plastic sharks.

But if you really want to immerse employees in a teambuilding exercise run by an organization that knows the absolute vital nature of teamwork, send your teams to NASA's Corporate Space Academy in Huntsville, Alabama. The government agency with the longest history of teamwork (besides the military, of course) is coaching businesses on how to build reliable, workable teams. Business teams try to launch a shuttle three times, and each time many simulated crises are thrown at them to see how they function as a team. In an environment that is unfamiliar and where team members have no expertise, the focus is on how well developed (or underdeveloped) their team skills and crisis management skills are.

As the shuttle-launch director at John F. Kennedy Space Center, Michael Leinbach leads a team of about 500 people. For him, "the most critical element of a successful shuttle-launch team is an open channel of communication from each team member to the team leader." Part of this involves team members taking responsibility for speaking up if something is not going right. Nobody wants to be the person who says that a launch should be scrubbed, but if a team member can't stand up and say, "There's a glitch in my work—no go," then the results can be catastrophic. Leinbach said, "I make it clear that nobody should ever feel bad about being the reason that we scrub a launch. If we didn't launch that day, it's because we put safety first—and that's what's really important."

For Leinbach, what makes a team work is communication. For Ray Ogelthorpe, president of AOL Technologies, it's size (ideally seven to nine people). For Jeanie Duck, senior vice president of Boston Consulting Group, it's spending the time to set up the team properly. For Millard Fuller, founder and president of Habitat for Humanity, it's having a cause that everyone buys into. For Thomas Leppert, chairman and CEO of Turner Corporation (builders of stadiums and highrises), it's mutual respect among team members and a common vision about where the team is going.

Despite the fact that these exercises vary widely in their effectiveness, companies are still shelling out big bucks for team coaching, proving that teamwork is seen as an essential part of the management toolkit. Though some employees might balk at the rattlesnake hunt or the beekeeping exercise, it's probably not too difficult to rally the troops around the race-car driving or NASA seminars. Anything in the name of teamwork.

1. Do the activities above qualify as team training? Why or why not?

2. Based on the limited descriptions given, try to rank the activities listed above according to how well you think they a) teach teamwork skills and b) foster team spirit. Your two lists may not be the same. Explain your rankings. Are some activities more appropriate for certain kinds of teams, for example circus activities for cross-functional teams or making Merlot for self-managing teams?

**Sources:** R. F. Maruca, "What Makes Teams Work?" *Fast Company*, November 2000, http://www.fastcompany.com. R. Rivenburg, "Extreme Management," *Los Angeles Times*, http://www.latimes.com/features/lifestyle/la-000092598nov20.story, 20 November 2001.

503

Which team compensation plan should your company use? In general, skill-based pay is most effective for self-managing and self-directing teams performing complex tasks. In these situations, the more each team member knows and can do, the better the whole team performs. By contrast, gainsharing works best in relatively stable environments where employees can focus on improving the productivity, cost savings, or quality of their current work system.

Finally, given the level of dissatisfaction with most team compensation systems, what compensation plans would today's managers like to use with the teams in their companies? Forty percent of managers would directly link merit pay increases to team performance, but allow adjustments within teams for differences in individual performance. By contrast, 13.7 percent would link merit-based increases directly to team performance, but would give each team member an equal share of the team's merit-based reward. 19 percent would use gainsharing plans based on quality, delivery, productivity, or cost reduction, and then provide equal payouts to all teams and team members. 14.5 percent would use gainsharing, but would vary the team gainsharing award, depending on how much money the team saved the company. Payouts would still be equally distributed within teams. Finally, 12.2 percent of managers would opt for plantwide profit-sharing plans tied to overall company or division performance.[132] In this case, there would be no payout distinctions between or within teams.

## Review 4
### Enhancing Work Team Performance

Companies can make teams more effective by setting team goals and managing how team members are selected, trained, and compensated. Team goals provide a clear focus and purpose, reduce the incidence of social loafing, and lead to higher team performance 93 percent of the time. Extremely difficult stretch goals can be used to motivate teams as long as teams have autonomy, control over resources, structural accommodation, and bureaucratic immunity. Not everyone is suited for teamwork. When selecting team members, companies should select people who have a preference for teamwork (individualism-collectivism) and should consider the importance of team level (average ability on a team) and team diversity (different abilities on a team). Organizations that successfully use teams provide thousands of hours of training to make sure that teams work. The most common types of team training are for interpersonal skills, decision-making and problem-solving skills, conflict resolution, technical training to help team members learn multiple jobs (i.e., cross-training), and training for team leaders. There are three methods of compensating employees for team participation and accomplishments: skill-based pay, gainsharing, and nonfinancial rewards.

## What Really Happened?

GE has been in the aircraft engine business for eight decades. Over the last 25 years, as business increased, it often turned to existing manufacturing plants to handle the load. So, when GE Aircraft Engines decided to build a brand new jet engine facility in an empty GE manufacturing plant in Durham, North Carolina, it had the opportunity to completely redesign the way in which it manufactured jet engines. The question, of course, was what should it do? Should it use teams or not? If so, what kinds of teams should be used, and how should they be paid? Let's find out what really happened at GE Aircraft Engines' new manufacturing facility.

**Well, we don't have to decide today. As we travel and visit other factories, let's see if we can't answer these questions. First, when does it make sense to use teams and when does it make sense to use a traditional structure?**

Teams should be used when there is a clear, engaging reason or purpose for using them. Too many companies use teams just because they're popular. They should be used when the job can't be done unless people work together. This typically means that teams are required when tasks are complex, require multiple perspectives, or require repeated interaction with others to complete. Teams should be used when rewards can be provided for teamwork and team performance. Team rewards that depend on team performance rather than individual performance are the key to rewarding team behaviors and efforts. Finally, teams should be used when ample resources are available. The resources that teams need include training, sufficient time and a place or method to work together, job-specific tools, and consistent information and feedback concerning team work processes and job performance.

Because building jet engines is such a complex task, GE was very careful when it hired the people who work in the plant. Everyone had to have an FAA-certified mechanic's license (which requires two years of classroom training before taking the FAA licensing exam), something that no other GE jet engine plant requires. Following that, all applicants were tested in 11 different areas, only one of which involved those technical skills. Keith McKee, who works at the plant, said, "You have to be above the bar in all 11 of the areas: helping skills, team skills, communication skills, diversity, flexibility, coaching ability, work ethic, and so forth. Even if just one thing out of the 11 knocks you down, you don't come to work here."

Once hired, everyone received extensive training on how to work well as a group. Duane Williams, who has worked at the plant since its inception, said, "Everybody doesn't see things in the same way. But we've had training on how to reach consensus. We've had training on how to live with ideas that we might not necessarily agree with. All the things you normally fuss and moan about to yourself and your buddies—well, we have a chance to do something about them. I can't say, 'They' don't know what's going on, or, 'They' made a bad decision. I am 'they.'"

Finally, everyone in the plant receives feedback concerning teamwork processes and job performance, even Paula Sims, the plant manager. (Sims is the only manager for all 170 employees.) Sims said, "We call this the feedback capital of the world. Not long after I started here, an employee came to me and said, 'Paula, you realize that you don't need to follow up with us to make sure we're doing what we agreed to do. If we say we'll do something, we'll do it. You don't need to micro-

manage us.' I sat back and thought, 'Wow. That's so simple. I'm sending the message that I don't trust people, because I always follow up.' I took that to heart. This was a technician, and I had been at the plant less than 30 days. I appreciated that he felt comfortable enough to tell me this. And I thought, this is really a different place."

When asked to summarize why the plant works, Sims said, "One, we have a layerless organization: There is just one classification of worker. Two, people are paid according to their skills. Three, everyone is an FAA power-plant mechanic—meaning that he or she comes highly skilled. And four, this is a team environment that requires a highly involved workforce."

### Second, if we determine that teams would be appropriate for our factory, what kind of teams should we use and why?

Autonomy is the key dimension that makes teams different. Traditional work groups (that execute tasks) and employee involvement groups (that make suggestions) have the lowest levels of autonomy. Semi-autonomous work groups (that control major, direct tasks) have more autonomy, followed by self-managing teams (that control all direct tasks) and self-designing teams (that control membership and how tasks are done), which have the highest levels of autonomy. Cross-functional, virtual, and project teams are common, but not easily categorized in terms of autonomy. Cross-functional teams combine employees from different functional areas to help teams attack problems from multiple perspectives and generate more ideas and solutions. Virtual teams use telecommunication and information technologies to bring coworkers together, regardless of physical location or time zone. Project teams are used for specific, one-time projects or tasks that must be completed within a limited time.

In its new Durham, North Carolina, manufacturing plant, GE Aerospace Engines used a combination of self-designing teams, which have the highest levels of autonomy, and cross-functional teams, in which employees

in different functional areas attack problems from multiple perspectives. In terms of each team's autonomy, nobody punches a time clock. If workers want to go to their kids' band concerts or soccer games, they go. All workers have email addresses, access to the Internet, their own voicemail boxes, business cards, and their own desks, all of which are extremely uncommon for factory workers. Furthermore, at one time or another, everyone serves on work councils that handle plant-wide problems with suppliers, engineering issues, computers, discipline, and rewards. Team member Duane Williams said, "We had to come up with a schedule. We had the chance to order tools, tool carts, and so on. We had to figure out the flow of the assembly line that makes the engine. We were put on councils for every part of the business." Williams goes on to say, "I was never valued that much as an employee in my life. I had never been at the point where I couldn't wait to get to work. Here, I couldn't wait to get to work every day. That's no BS!"

### Third, how should people who work on teams be paid? We've got to find a way to encourage individual initiative, while encouraging people to work together.

There are three methods of compensating employees for team participation and accomplishments: skill-based pay, gainsharing, and nonfinancial rewards. Skill-based pay programs pay employees for learning additional skills or knowledge. These programs encourage employees to acquire the additional skills they will need to perform multiple jobs within a team. The second approach to compensating employees for team participation is through gainsharing programs, in which companies share the financial value of performance gains, such as productivity, cost savings, or quality, with their workers. Nonfinancial rewards are another way to reward teams for their performance. These awards, which can range from vacation trips to T-shirts, plaques, and coffee mugs, are especially effective when coupled with management recognition such as awards, certificates, and praise. In general, skill-based pay is most effective for self-managing and self-directing teams that perform complex tasks. In these situations, the more each team member knows and can do, the better the team performs. By contrast, gainsharing works best in relatively stable environments where employees can focus on improving the productivity, cost savings, or quality of their current work system.

GE Aerospace Engines chose to pay their team members using a skill-based pay program, which it calls multiskilling. In GE's system, workers are paid according to their skill level: technical level 1, technical level 2, or technical level 3. While pay increases with the technical level, everyone at the same technical level is paid the same. Team member Derrick McCoy said, "Multiskilling is how the place is kept together. You don't hoard your skills. That way, when I'm on vacation, the low pressure

turbine can still be built without me." Because of multiskilling, every worker has a variety of tasks to do every day.

So how effective is this teamwork? On average, only 25 percent of the engines produced at the Durham, North Carolina, plant have just one defect, which is usually cosmetic, like a scratch. The other 75 percent of the engines produced at the plant are perfect. Furthermore, every single engine produced at the plant has been delivered on time for 38 straight months. In addition, the cost of producing GE90 jet engines at the plant has dropped by 10 percent or more every year for the last five years. In fact, it costs 50 percent less to produce the GE90 engine than it did five years ago. Likewise, the teams at the plant have reduced the cost of the CF6 engine, which has been in production for 20 years, by more than 30 percent over the last five years. Plant manager Paula Sims said, "We're very close to producing twice the out-

put of CF6s from this plant with the same number of employees as when I came here." Finally, the Durham, North Carolina, plant significantly outperforms other GE jet engine plants. Bob McEwen is the plant manager of GE's jet engine facility at Evendale, Ohio. McEwen said, "They had been producing the CFM engine for eight weeks. In Evendale, we've been producing it for years and years. And in Durham, they're already producing it for 12 percent to 13 percent less cost than we are here."

**Sources:** "About GEAE / History," GE Aircraft Engines. [Online] Available http://www.geae.com/aboutgeae/history.html, 21 January 2002. "About GEAE / Locations," GE Aircraft Engines. [Online] Available http://www.geae.com/aboutgeae/location.html, 21 January 2002. C. Fishman, "Engines of Democracy," *Fast Company,* 1 October 1999, 174. C. Fishman, "How Teamwork Took Flight: This Team Built a Commercial Engine—and Self-Managing GE Plant—From Scratch," *Fast Company,* 1 October 1999, 188.

## Key Terms

bureaucratic immunity *(498)*
cohesiveness *(490)*
cross-functional team *(486)*
cross training *(476)*
de-forming *(496*
de-norming *(495)*
de-storming *(496)*
employee involvement team *(484)*
forming *(494)*
gainsharing *(502)*

individualism-collectivism *(499)*
interpersonal skills *(501)*
norming *(494)*
norms *(490)*
performing *(495)*
project team *(487)*
self-designing team *(486)*
self-limiting behavior *(478)*
self-managing team *(484)*
semi-autonomous work group *(484)*

skill-based pay *(502)*
social loafing *(478)*
storming *(494)*
structural accommodation *(498)*
team diversity *(500)*
team level *(499)*
traditional work group *(483)*
virtual team *(486)*
work team *(474)*

506

## What Would You Do-II

### Pistons Exploding under Pressure
You probably shouldn't have left before the final buzzer, but it was clear that the fat lady had sung well before the final act. In another lackluster performance, your team, the Detroit Pistons, fell to the Portland Trailblazers. But you're not really surprised. Your team hasn't finished a season noticeably over .500 in years, and no one except the most exuberant of fans expects the team to make the playoffs. The worst part is that the lack of performance isn't related to lack of talent. You managed to sign Grant Hill

right out of college. He was ecstatic about coming to Detroit, claiming that he wanted to spend his whole career with you. And you lured Jerry Stackhouse away from the 76ers to be the strong sixth man on your team. You've also got Christian Laettner, Lindsey Hunter, Jerome Williams, Bison Dele, and a deep bench.

For all their talent, though, team members aren't executing: They're not playing well with others, on or off the court. The root problem is not a mystery to you. Disagreements among team members are boiling over and name-calling and back-biting has begun to infect morale. And this is starting to affect the economics of the franchise and the morale of the fans. Who wants to support—mentally or financially—a team whose members are constantly passing the buck? Other teams in the league are having teamwork problems as well, but that doesn't seem to be affecting their stats. Larry Brown and Allen Iverson are in the press daily, or at least it seems that way. But Iverson's habitual tardiness and absence at practices doesn't seem to be affecting the 76ers.

Knowing that last night's game won't be mentioned in your new edition of *The Sporting News*, you collapse into your chair with a cup of coffee and begin to flip through your magazine. You stare in horror at an article that exposes in grand fashion everything you've just been thinking about. Your players are starting to share their frustrations with the press. This is bad any way you look at it.

Hill called Dele a wimp and was quoted as saying, "If Bison doesn't want to put out the effort and the energy, we should sit him down." Even better, Hill said that he'd prefer to play with a guy not good enough to stay on the roster (i.e., Mikki Moore) than with a guy incapable of earning his $45 million-a-year salary. For his turn, Stackhouse called Hill a "ball hog" and

said that Hill's scoring tear hasn't "been so great for our team. I think we become stagnant watching him . . . I want the ball more."

You grab your roster and start to think about next season. (Forget the rest of this one.) The team is the essence of your business, but it doesn't seem to be working. What's plaguing the Pistons? Do you have too many superstars and not enough players? Maybe it's that the team is too young (as a team) to have figured out how to play together to win. But shouldn't the veterans be helping along the younger players? What you do know is that in-fighting has to stop. If you're going to regain the glory of the late 1980s and early 1990s, you are going to have to do something in the off-season.

**If you were the owner of the Detroit Pistons, what would you do?**

**Sources:** D. D'Alessandro, "Pistons Must Keep Fighting, But Not Among Themselves," *The Sporting News*, 1 March 1999, 16. D. Howerton, "Chemistry 101: National Basketball Association Is Forgetting the Idea of Team Building and the Effect of Interpersonal Chemistry on a Team," *Sport*, December 1998, 74. M.L. Sachs, "Is 'TEAM' a Four-Letter Word?" *USA Today Magazine*, January 2002, 58. http://www.nba.com/pistons.

## Management Decisions

### A Team Leader's Worst Nightmare

"OK, Ted, tell me one more time what happened." Ted Knight, a new employee just assigned to the Hard Disk Assembly Team, is sitting in your office on a Friday afternoon, and you can't believe what you're hearing.

Each member of the Hard Disk Assembly Team is responsible for assembling and testing hard disks that go into PCs. As a way of creating healthy competition among the team's six members, you've been recording each member's production output each day and posting it near the team's work area. At the end of each week, the team member who has assembled the most hard disks without a quality failure receives a $50 bonus.

You always thought that the competition had worked well. Several different team members had won the $50 bonus, production numbers were inching up, and no one had complained about the availability of extra cash. But Ted's story was making you heartsick. Ted joined the Hard Disk Assembly Team three weeks ago. His first two weeks were primarily training. But this week, Ted had a workstation of his own on the factory floor. Ted is a quick learner, which is one of the reasons you hired him. According to Ted, two of his teammates cornered him in a quiet corner of the snack room during his afternoon break. They told him that under no circumstances was he to assemble more than 30 hard disks during a single day. One of the employees, who Ted was not willing to identify, told him, "We all work at a comfortable pace around here. If you assemble more than 30 hard disks a day, the team

leader will expect us all to." Ted went on to say that the second employee told him, "And by the way, no one gets to win the weekly production award until they've been around for awhile. If you are leading toward the end of the week, I'll let you know so you can slow down some."

You took a deep breath and looked Ted straight in the eye. "Ted, thanks for letting me know what's going on. I honestly had no idea that anything like this was happening. Give me the weekend, and on Monday morning I'll let you know what I am going to do."

### Questions

1. If you were the team leader, what would you do? Would you call a team meeting and deal directly with this problem, or would you try a more subtle approach?
2. What about Ted? If you go to Ted's teammates and reveal what he told you, will he ever be accepted as a member of the team? Also, what about the weekly production award? Should you cancel it, allow it to continue as is, or change it in some way?

**Sources:** J. George, "Extrinsic and Intrinsic Origins of Perceived Social Loafing in Organizations," *Academy of Management Journal* 35 (1992): 191-202. R.E. Kidwell, Jr. & N. Bennett, "Employee Propensity to Withhold Effort: A Conceptual Model to Intersect Three Avenues Research," *Academy of Management Review* 18, no. 3 (1993): 429-456. P.W. Mulvey, J.F. Veiga, & P.M. Elsass, "When Teammates Raise a White Flag," *Academy of Management Executive* 10, no. 1 (1996): 40-49.

### You Thought That Awarding Bonuses Would Be Easy. Think Again.

You've just reread the fifth email message this month about the new team bonus plan. None of them has been positive. Two years ago, you switched your Credit Card Customer Service Center to a team-based design. Prior to the switch, your employees had been assigned to traditional functional areas. But hoping to increase customer service and decrease costs, you eliminated the traditional departments and put your employees into teams. Now you have five teams to service your credit card customers. The teams are as follows:

Team 1    Handles routine requests for personal accounts
Team 2    Handles routine requests for corporate accounts
Team 3    Investigates requests for credit line increases
Team 4    Sells credit card protection insurance
Team 5    Investigates disputed charges

After you created work teams, your employees complained about the lack of team incentives. Basically, you were still paying employees an individually based merit increase plus a cost-of-living adjustment. Six months ago you decided to give team incentives a try. You challenged each team to increase its productivity by 5 percent per month. According to the new plan, teams that increased productivity by that amount would receive a $500 bonus to split among its team members.

But it hasn't worked. Here's the problem. Teams 1, 2, and 3 have won the bonus for each of the six months that the bonus has been in existence. Teams 4 and 5 have never won the bonus. You're getting the same complaint from every member of Teams 4 and 5 that you talk to. What they keep telling you is that it is easier for Teams 1, 2, and 3 to increase their productivity than it is for them. Teams 1 and 2 handle hundreds

of routine calls every day. To increase productivity, all they have to do is move more quickly through their calls. Team 3 investigates requests for credit line increases. Because interest rates have been going down, they have gotten numerous requests and have been able to approve the majority of them. So these teams have been steadily increasing their productivity and have been awarded the $500 bonus each month.

However, according to members of Teams 4 and 5, it is not as easy for them to increase their productivity. Team 4 sells credit card protection insurance, which is a tough product to sell. Team 5 investigates disputed charges. It can sometimes take weeks to get to the bottom of a disputed charge. It is not a process that is easily rushed. As a result, despite their efforts, Teams 4 and 5 have never won the award. Instead, they continue to complain that the bonus program just isn't fair.

As you look up from your desk, a group of employees from Team 4 is waiting to see you. They had called earlier in the day and asked if they could stop by to talk about the bonus program. You are really tiring of this. You thought that awarding bonuses would be easy. What should you tell them?

#### Questions

1. Is the bonus compensation program fair? If not, would you scrap the program or revise it in some way?
2. Was the implementation of the bonus compensation plan handled appropriately in the first place? What could have been done initially to create a more equitable plan?

**Sources:** Anonymous, "AT&T Universal Card Services," *Business America* 113, no. 22 (1992): 12-13. S.E. Gross, *Compensation for Teams* (New York: American Management Association, 1995). P.A. Murphy, "It's No Longer Just Teleservices," *Credit Card Management* 11, no. 1 (1998): 115-119.

## Develop Your Managerial Potential

### A Quick Check of Your Team Skills

To be part of an effective team, you have to be a good team member. However, sometimes it's hard to objectively judge our contributions in a team or group effort. Think about one of your most important team experiences. Were you an effective team member? Take the following test to find out. After you take the test, answer the questions below to begin thinking about how you can improve.

#### Instructions:

Step 1:   Answer the following questions the way that you think other members of your team would if they were describing your actions.
Step 2:   Total your score for each section. Then transfer all totals to the "Quick Check of My Team Skills" section at the conclusion of the exercise.

**Scale:**    1 = Almost never
              2 = Seldom
              3 = Sometimes
              4 = Usually
              5 = Almost always

#### I. Honor team values and agreements.

**As a team member, I**                                      **Your score:**

a. show appreciation for other team members' ideas.    _____

b. help other team members cope with change.    _____

c. encourage others to use their strengths.    _____

d. help the team develop a productive relationship with other teams.    _____

e. willingly assume a leadership role
when needed.

**Your score:** _____

Total: _____

## II. Promote team development.

**As a team member, I**

**Your score:**

a. volunteer for all types of tasks, including
the hard ones. _____
b. help orient and train new team members. _____
c. help organize and run effective meetings. _____
d. help examine how we are doing as a team
and make any necessary changes in the
way we work together. _____
e. help identify milestones and
mini-successes to celebrate. _____

Total: _____

## III. Help make team decisions.

**As a team member, I**

**Your score:**

a. analyze what a decision entails. _____
b. ensure that the team selects and includes
the appropriate people in the decision
process. _____
c. clearly state my concerns. _____
d. search for common ground when team
members have different views. _____
e. actively support the team's decisions. _____

Total: _____

## IV. Coordinate and carry out team tasks.

**As a team member, I**

**Your score:**

a. help identify the information, skills, and
resources necessary to accomplish team tasks. _____
b. help formulate and agree on a plan to
meet performance goals. _____
c. stay abreast of what is happening in other
parts of the organization and bring that
information to the team. _____
d. find innovative ways to meet the needs of
the team and of others in the organization. _____

e. maintain a win-win outlook in all
dealings with other teams.

**Your score:** _____

Total: _____

## V. Handle difficult issues with the team.

**As a team member, I**

**Your score:**

a. bring team issues and problems to the
team's attention. _____
b. encourage others on the team to state
their views. _____
c. help build trust among team members by
speaking openly about the team's problems. _____
d. give specific, constructive, and timely
feedback to others. _____
e. admit when I've made a mistake. _____

Total: _____

## A Quick Check of My Team Skills

| Category | Total Score |
|---|---|
| Honor team values and agreements. | _____ |
| Promote team development. | _____ |
| Help make team decisions. | _____ |
| Coordinate and carry our team tasks. | _____ |
| Handle difficult issues with the team. | _____ |

## Interpreting Scores

- A score of 20 or above in any activity indicates an area of
strength.
- A score of 20 or below in any activity indicates an area that
needs more attention.

## Questions to Ask Yourself

Looking at your scores, what areas are strengths? How can you
maintain these strengths? What areas are weaknesses? What
steps can you take to turn these areas into strengths?

**Source:** M. A. West, ed., *Handbook of Work Group Psychology*
(Chichester, UK: Wiley, 1996).

## Study Tip

Make up a crossword puzzle using the key terms in this
chapter. Writing the clues will help you remember the
definition and the context of each concept. Make
photocopies for exam time and for your study group.

# CHAPTER 14

*outline*

# Managing Human Resource Systems

## What Would You Do?

**MGM-Mirage Resorts Headquarters, Las Vegas, Nevada.** MGM-Mirage runs some of the most famous Las Vegas hotels in the world: the MGM Grand, the Mirage, Treasure Island, the Golden Nugget, and New York, New York. Its latest hotel is the Bellagio, a spectacular and sumptuous 36-story hotel that is a recreation of the small town with the same name that overlooks Lake Como in Italy. The Bellagio has 3,000 rooms, 21 upscale restaurants, and an eight-acre artificial lake (i.e., Lake Como) circled by hundreds of choreographed fountains that shoot water 200 feet into the air, synchronized to opera music. When it opens, the Bellagio may turn out to be the most lavish resort in Las Vegas.

Your job as vice president of human resources is to hire a staff of 9,600 managers and workers capable of providing service as lavish as the resort itself. The only catch is that 100,000 people are expected to apply, and you've only got 24 weeks to screen 100,000 résumés, conduct 25,000 interviews, and hire and train the final staff of 9,600. But how do you process that many people that quickly—nearly 4,200 people per day—and still do a good job of selecting the best applicants? Clearly, you'll have to rely on electronic forms and processing. And since everything in human resources is now run using paper and pencil forms, how can you

expect to develop a fully electronic hiring and screening system at the same time you're trying to hire 9,600 people?

In addition to developing a process that can screen over 4,000 people per day, you also need to develop a brand new, standardized interview system that managers are comfortable with, that only takes 30 minutes to conduct, and that does a better job of screening and selecting candidates than traditional interviews. The information that you've read shows that traditional interviews are barely better than chance at selecting the best job applicants. Unfortunately, in traditional interviews, most managers jump to conclusions and make up their minds about job candidates within the first two minutes of the interview. Furthermore, because managers naturally look for information that would disqualify applicants (especially when there are so many people to interview), they tend to give negative information, information that reflects poorly on the job applicant, much more weight than positive information. Finally, interviews tend to be unreliable simply because of the difficulty of comparing one job applicant's performance in an interview to another's. This occurs because managers are inconsistent when they conduct interviews. Different managers typically ask applicants different questions. Furthermore, individual managers tend to ask different questions when interviewing different applicants. A manager may

ask a job applicant about A, B, and C in the morning and then ask a different job applicant about X, Y, and Z in the afternoon, making it difficult, if not impossible, to compare the two interviews.

Finally, once your managers have decided which 9,600 people to hire, you need to conduct thorough background checks before making job offers. With millions of dollars to be spent and gambled at the Bellagio each day, it's critical that you hire honest people. In other words, you need people who don't lie about their qualifications on their résumés, people who won't be tempted to pocket money for themselves, and people without criminal backgrounds that could put the Bellagio or its guests at risk.

**If you were the vice president of human resources at the Bellagio casino and resort and had 24 weeks to review 100,000 résumés, conduct 25,000 interviews, and hire and train a final staff of 9,600 people, what would you do?**

**Sources:** B. Breen, "Full House: Executives at Las Vegas's Bellagio Hotel Screened 84,000 Candidates, Did 27,000 Interviews, And Hired 9,600 People—In 24 Weeks. Now Cisco Wants to Know How They Did It," *Fast Company*, 1 January 2000, 110. B. Carlino, "At Your Service: Fine-Dining Operators Hone Segment's Hospitality Hallmark," *Nation's Restaurant News*, 24 November 1997, 65. R. Hughes, "Wynn Win?" *Time*, 26 October 1998, 76. D. Muret, "Attitude: The Major Ingredient in Obtaining a New Job," *Amusement Business*, 14 December 1998, 38. J. Shapiro, "Employers Look to the Joint to Fill Jobs," *U.S. News & World Report*, 6 November 2000, 70.

Unfortunately, the basic hiring issues faced by the Bellagio casino and resort, effectively attracting and selecting qualified job applicants, are all too common. For example, when Erler Industries, a small industrial painting and finishing company, signed a contract for a large amount of work with Dell Computers, it grew from six to 175 people almost overnight to meet the increased workload. Co-owner Linda Erler said, "We were so desperate for employees that if we could see the whites of your eyes and it looked as if blood was running through your veins, [you were offered a job]." Linda explained that this approach didn't always translate into successful hiring, like the time that a group of new hires all came to work with "whiskey in their soda cans." And even though new employees could earn bonuses if they stayed for just 30 days, she said, "We had tremendous turnover. Everyone had to be replaced five or six times before we found a person who really wanted to work."[1]

**human resource management**
the process of finding, developing, and keeping the right people to form a qualified work force

The experiences of the Bellagio and Erler Industries indicate that **human resource management (HRM)**, the process of finding, developing, and keeping the right people to form a qualified work force, remains one of the most difficult and important of all management tasks. This chapter is organized around the four parts of the human resource management process shown in Exhibit 14.1: determining human resource needs and attracting, developing, and keeping a qualified work force.

Accordingly, the chapter begins by reviewing how human resource planning determines human resource needs, such as the kind and number of employees a company requires to meet its strategic plans and objectives. Next, we explore how companies use recruiting and selection techniques to attract and hire qualified employees to fulfill those needs. The third part of the chapter reviews how training and performance appraisal can develop the knowledge, skills, and abilities of the work force. The chapter concludes with a review of compensation and employee separation, that is, how companies can keep their best workers through effective compensation practices, and how they can manage the separation process when employees leave the organization.

## Determining Human Resource Needs

Should we hire more workers? What should we pay our current employees to slow employee turnover? What kinds of training do our new employees need to be prepared to do a good job, and what's the best way to deliver that training? In other words, what are our human resource needs and what's the best way to address them?

Managers often treat these questions as separate issues. However, the human resource process illustrated in Exhibit 14.1 shows that attracting (recruiting and selecting), developing (training and evaluating performance), and keeping or losing employees (compensation and employee separation) are interdependent issues. You can't solve one problem without considering its impact on the others. More specifically, Exhibit 14.1 indicates that human resource needs affect how the company uses recruiting and selection to attract employees. In turn, the kind and number of employees hired influence the orientation, training, performance appraisal, and compensation strategies the company uses, which then affect who stays and who leaves. Finally, as indicated by the feedback loop, the process comes full circle, as the number and kind of employees who leave the company affect its human resource needs and planning.

You can see how the HR process works by examining what hospitals are doing to address the shortage of qualified nurses around the world. How acute is this shortage? Hospitals in London, England, find it so difficult to attract British nurses that they send managers all the way to Jamaica to recruit English-speaking nurses. In turn, Jamaica has lost so many nurses to English hospitals that it now prevents the British government (which runs the health system in Britain) from hiring its nurses. And why do British hospitals have such a hard time finding nurses? Because Canadian nurses take higher-paying jobs in the United States, which forces Canadian hospitals to hire British nurses and British hospitals to hire nurses from Ghana (since they can no longer hire Jamaican

EXHIBIT 14.1

THE HUMAN RESOURCE MANAGEMENT PROCESS

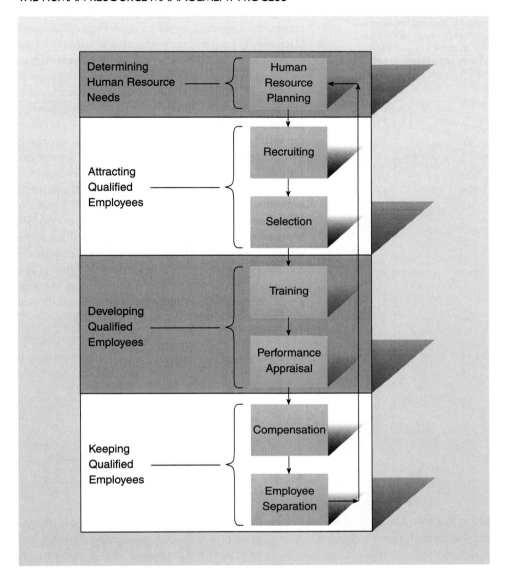

nurses). However, the nursing shortage is so strong worldwide that even American hospitals now recruit directly in many countries. In South Africa, nurses are encouraged to come to the United States with ads that say, "Nurses! Think of it as your seat in America. Gain invaluable experience, learn the latest medical techniques, and live a fuller life in a relaxed environment."[2] And, like all workers, nurses who work in poor conditions for poor pay are even willing to move to other countries for better-paying jobs in good companies. So, for the hospitals around the world that struggle to hire nurses, the HRM process, as shown in Exhibit 14.1, comes full circle as attracting, developing, and keeping qualified nurses affects their human resource needs.

Fortunately, there are steps that companies can take to begin to address the employee shortfalls among experienced nurses in the healthcare industry.

*After reading the next two sections, you should be able to*
1. *describe the basic steps involved in human resource planning.*
2. *explain how different employment laws affect human resource practice.*

# 1. Human Resource Planning

**human resource planning (HRP)**
using an organization's goals and strategy to forecast the organization's human resource needs in terms of attracting, developing, and keeping a qualified work force

**Human resource planning (HRP)** is the process of using an organization's goals and strategy to forecast the organization's human resource needs in terms of attracting, developing, and keeping a qualified work force.[3] Companies that don't use HRP or that do HRP poorly may end up with either a surplus of employees and have to use layoffs to correct the surplus, or a shortage of employees that leads to increased overtime costs and an inability to meet demand for the company's product or service.

The HRP process begins with a consideration of the organization's mission, strategy, and objectives. Therefore, HRP is directly related to and should be considered part of an organization's strategic planning process.[4] Dell Computer makes sure that the HRP process is tied to its mission and strategy by splitting its HR function into two departments. "HR Operations" has a service center that takes care of all "transactional" activities for Dell employees, such as benefits and compensation. HR Operations rarely has direct contact with Dell's business units. Its job is to serve Dell's individual employees. By contrast, the HR staffers in Dell's "HR Management" department report directly to the vice president of HR *and* the vice president of a Dell business unit (e.g., procurement, higher education sales, etc.). The HR staffers then attend that business unit's staff meetings, help to develop that unit's leadership team, and then create a specific HR strategy for that part of Dell's business.[5] Dell's HR Management team also helps business units identify personnel needs, assess training needs, and determine the best organizational structure for reporting relationships (i.e., the organizational chart).

*Let's explore human resource planning by examining how to 1.1 forecast the supply and demand of human resources, and 1.2 use human resource information systems to improve those forecasts.*

# BlastFromThePast

## The First HR Department

**During the late 1800s and early 1900s, the predecessors of today's human resource departments began to emerge from the brand new field of industrial psychology, in which psychologists were beginning to apply their knowledge to factory settings. Hugo Munsterberg (1863-1916), the "Father of Industrial Psychology," established a psychology**

laboratory at Harvard University in 1892 that became the foundation of the industrial psychology movement. In 1913, he published a book entitled *Psychology and Industrial Efficiency*, in which he discusses the demands that jobs make on people and the importance of matching individuals to jobs. He was also one of the first people to suggest using tests to select workers. And in 1913, Munsterberg met with President Wilson, the secretary of commerce, and the secretary of labor in an attempt to convince them to establish a government research center that would examine the application of psychology to industrial problems. The center was never established, but Munsterberg continued to conduct research on employee motivation and methods for reducing employee fatigue. His work and that of his colleagues resulted in more concern for the human factors in work.

In 1900, the B.F. Goodrich Company established the first human resource department. Goodrich's "Employment Department" performed a limited number of functions, such as handling employee discipline, keeping performance records, and administering compensation. In 1914, Henry Ford formed one

of the earliest personnel departments in his Detroit automobile plant, calling it the "Sociological Department." When a $5-per-day minimum wage was established, Ford hired 100 investigators, called "advisors," to visit employees' homes to make sure the homes were neat and clean and that the employees didn't drink too much. Ford was concerned that with a $5-per-day income, which was enormous for that time, employees might go astray and spend their money irresponsibly. And, similar to the wellness benefits offered by many companies today, Ford's Sociological Department also employed social workers to help employees with family or other nonwork problems.

**Sources:** "Industrial Relations," *Encyclopædia Britannica Online.* [Online] Available http://www.eb.com:, 5 June 1999. H. Munsterberg, *Psychology and Industrial Efficiency* (Boston: Houghton-Mifflin Company, 1913). L. Baritz, *The Servants of Power* (New York: John Wiley & Sons, 1960). D.A. Wren, *The Evolution of Management Thought*, 2nd ed. (New York: John Wiley and Sons, 1979).

**work force forecasting**
the process of predicting the number and kind of workers with specific skills and abilities that an organization will need in the future

**Work force forecasting** is the process of predicting the number and kind of workers with specific skills and abilities that an organization will need in the future.[6] There are two kinds of work force forecasts, internal and external forecasts, and three kinds of forecasting methods, direct managerial input, best guess, and statistical/historical ratios.

*Internal forecasts* are projections about factors within the organization that affect the supply and demand for human resources. These factors include the financial performance of the organization, productivity, the organization's mission, changes in technology or the way the work is performed, and the termination, promotion, transfer, retirement, resignation, and death of current employees. For example, a drop in profits prompted Union Pacific Corp., a railroad company, to use attrition and an early retirement program to cut 2,000 workers. However, it didn't layoff train dispatchers who, through effective scheduling of company trains and cargo, have a huge effect on company productivity. Barbara Schaefer, Union Pacific's senior vice president for human resources, said, "They're not being offered the pension enhancement. We can't afford to lose them."[7] Exhibit 14.2 provides a more complete list of factors that influence internal forecasts.

*External forecasts* are projections about factors outside the organization that affect the supply and demand for human resources. These factors include the labor supply for specific types of workers, the economy (unemployment rate), labor unions, demographics of the labor force (e.g., proportion of labor force in various age groups), geographic movement of the labor force, strength of competitors, and growth in particular businesses and markets. For example, when the economy slowed, Behlen Manufacturing switched its 400 factory workers from full time to part time work and cut the pay of its salaried workers by 10 percent. CEO Tony Raymundo said, "This year, we've been reducing hours and telling people we believed it was short-term. We think we saved a lot of jobs by doing that."[8] Then, when the economy strengthened and sales began increasing again, he quickly switched his factory workers back to full-time hours and removed the 10 percent pay cut. Exhibit 14.2 provides a more complete list of factors that influence external forecasts.

Three kinds of forecasting methods—direct managerial input, best guess, and statistical/historical ratios—are often used to predict the number and kind of workers with

515

---

| EXHIBIT 14.2 | |
|---|---|

INTERNAL AND EXTERNAL FACTORS THAT INFLUENCE WORK FORCE FORECASTING

| **INTERNAL FACTORS** | **EXTERNAL FACTORS** |
|---|---|
| • New positions | • Demographics of labor supply |
| • New equipment and technology | • Geographic population shifts |
| • Eliminated positions | • Shift from manufacturing- to service- to information-based economy |
| • Terminations | • General economic conditions |
| • Retirements | • Unemployment rate |
| • Resignations | • Labor unions |
| • Turnover | • Availability of applicants with specific skills and education |
| • Transfers | • Technological advances |
| • Deaths | • Strength and number of competitors |
| • Promotions | • Growth in particular businesses and markets |
| • Organization's mission | |
| • Productivity of current employees | |
| • Skills/education of current employees | |

specific skills and abilities that an organization will need in the future.[9] The most common forecasting method, *direct managerial input*, is based on straightforward projections of cash flows, expenses, or financial measures, such as return on capital. While financial indicators are relatively quick to calculate and can help managers determine how many workers they might need, they don't help managers decide which critical skills new employees should possess.

The *best guess* forecasting method is based on managers' assessment of current headcount, plus a best guess of how internal factors and external factors will affect that head count. Totalling these produces the overall projection. Dell Computer, in part, uses a best guess system to forecast the kinds of people it would like to hire. Steve Price, Dell's vice president of human resources for its Public and Americas International Group, said, "We look at the people who have been given the biggest merit increases, the best appraisals and so forth, and then we interview against these competencies."[10]

Finally, the *statistical/historical ratios* forecasting method uses statistical methods, such as multiple regression, in combination with historical data, to predict the number and kind of workers a company should hire. For example, a manager might run a regression analysis using data from the last two years. In that regression equation, the number of employees that need to be hired is the dependent (predicted) variable, and the number of items manufactured, number of clients, or average increase in sales, and so forth, are the independent (predictor) variables. The regression analysis produces a simple equation that indicates how many more employees should be added for each increase in the independent variables, such as items manufactured or increased sales. This approach takes advantage of existing data and can be much more accurate than best guess predictions, but only if a company's internal and external environments have not changed significantly.

Dell also uses statistical/historical ratios to help predict its work force needs. Andy Esparza, vice president of staffing for Dell's companywide staffing function, said, "One of the things this [HR planning process] maps into is a set of key job openings that we can use to start forecasting and sourcing people in advance." More specifically, Dell's Web-based HR planning process allows managers to play "what if?" with work force predictions. Kathleen Woodhouse, an HR manager who supports Dell's preferred accounts division, said, "Managers use our intranet to complete HR functions, like appraisals; our appraisal system also feeds into the financial system so they can play with figures if they need to."[11]

## 1.2 Human Resource Information Systems

**Human resource information systems (HRISs)** are computerized systems for gathering, analyzing, storing, and disseminating information related to attracting, developing, and keeping a qualified work force.[12] Exhibit 14.3 shows some of the data that are commonly used in HR information systems, such as personal and educational data, company employment history, performance appraisal information, work history, and promotions.

Human resource information systems can be used for transaction processing, employee self-service, and decision support. For HRIS systems, *transaction processing* usually involves employee payroll checks, taxes, and benefit deductions. Tenet Healthcare Corp. uses a HRIS to keep track of the payroll information for the 113,000 employees who work in its 116 hospitals in 17 states.[13] Tenet switched to a centralized HRIS because lists of employees and their pay and benefits were being kept in 85 different data locations. Regarding its new centralized HRIS, Alan Ewalt, Tenet's senior vice president of human resources, said, "This will combine everything in one automated system. Once we enter the employees' names upon hiring them, the system will continually be updated with each payroll change and know exactly where they're located, what department they're in, and how many hours they are working."[14] The advantage of this system is that it will quickly provide accurate, up-to-date information about staff compensation in one complete database. HRISs can also reduce administrative costs by preparing certain routine reports, such as the EEOC (Equal Employment Opportunity Commission) or OSHA (Occupational Safety and Health Administration) reports that are required of many companies.

**human resource information systems (HRIS)**
computerized systems for gathering, analyzing, storing, and disseminating information related to the HRM process

EXHIBIT 14.3

COMMON DATA CATEGORIES IN HUMAN RESOURCE INFORMATION SYSTEMS

### PERSONAL DATA

- Name
- Address/Telephone Number
- Employee Identification Number
- Social Security Number
- Medical Plan/Coverage
- Retirement/Investment Plan

### COMPANY EMPLOYMENT HISTORY

- Previous Job Assignments
- Current Position
- Date of Initial Employment
- Seniority Date
- Salary/Pay History
- Current Salary/Pay
- Fringe Benefit Package
- Last Pay Raise

### WORK HISTORY

- Previous Employers
- Previous Positions
- Duties in Previous Positions
- Supervisory Experience

### EDUCATIONAL DATA

- High School Diploma
- College Degrees
- Special Courses/Training

### PERFORMANCE APPRAISAL

- Date of Last Performance Appraisal
- Productivity Measures
- Disciplinary Action
- Tardiness
- Absenteeism
- Last Performance Rating
- Quality Measures

### PROMOTION DATA

- Geographic Preferences
- Personal Interests
- Awards
- Job Preferences
- Special Skills/Knowledge
- Foreign Language(s)

While human resource information systems are typically used to give managers and HR staffers access to human resource data, the flip side of today's Web-based HRISs is that they also give employees immediate, 24-hour *self-service* access to personal data, such as benefits and retirement packages. With secure, Web-based systems, employees need to enter only a username and password to access and change their medical insurance plan, adjust the mix of investments in their 401(k) retirement plan, or check on the status of medical or childcare reimbursements.[15] According to benefits coordinator Priscilla Craven, the primary advantage of self-service systems is that "You no longer need to call a person when an office is open to get a form or make an enrollment choice." And with access available 24 hours a day, companies have also begun eliminating restricted "open enrollment" periods, in which employees have to make (and then not change) all of their benefit decisions for the entire year at one time. With Web-based systems, employees can make changes whenever they want. Dick Quinn, director of performance and rewards at Public Service Electric & Gas Company of New Jersey, said, "Our intent next year is to have completely eliminated the concept of annual open enrollment. This will eliminate all of the printing and communication costs associated with the annual sign-up period. When employees know they aren't locked into a healthcare choice for a full year, it will make all of our managed-care choices more attractive."[16]

Human resource information systems are not only useful for gathering and storing information, but they also help managers by serving as decision support systems for critical human resource decisions.[17] In Chapter 5, you learned that *decision support systems* (DSS) help managers understand problems and potential solutions by acquiring and analyzing information with sophisticated models and tools. For instance, a HRIS can help managers make human resource decisions from the moment that job applicants submit résumés to the company. Those résumés are scanned, turned into text via optimal character recognition software, and then fed into the HRIS, where they are analyzed for the quality of the writing and for key words that match the organization's job database. John Reese, founder of an Internet recruiting site, said, "Whatever the media—paper, email, the Web, or fax—we can scan a résumé into a database, reformat it according to our specifications, and then make it available to the hiring manager or HR manager anywhere in a company, anywhere in the world. An applicant can send in an application on Thursday and have an interview by Monday."[18]

A HRIS can even be used to do pre-employment testing or background screening. Elaine Daily, marketing director for Qwiz, Inc., which sells computerized employment tests to companies, said, "We can do remote testing through a Web site or through software installed on a PC. This saves the company from having to bring in a candidate to headquarters before deciding whether the person is technically competent."[19]

HRISs can also be used effectively to screen internal applicants on particular qualifications, to match the qualifications of external applicants against those of internal applicants, to compare salaries within and between departments, and to review and change employees' salaries instantaneously without lengthy paperwork. In short, today's HRISs can help managers make any number of critical human resource decisions.

### Review 1
### Human Resource Planning

Human resource planning (HRP) uses organizational goals and strategies to determine what needs to be done to attract, develop, and keep a qualified work force. Work force forecasts are used to predict the number and kind of workers with specific skills and abilities that an organization needs. Work force forecasts consider both internal and external factors that affect the supply and demand for workers and can be formulated using three kinds of forecasting methods: direct managerial input, best guess, and statistical/historical ratios. Computerized human resource information systems improve human resource planning by gathering, analyzing, storing, and disseminating information (personal, educational, work history, performance, and promotions) related to human resource management activities. Human resource information systems can be used for transaction processing (payroll checks and routine reports), employee self-service (24-hour Web access allowing instant changes to benefit and retirement packages), and decision support for human resource decisions (analyzing résumés, background screening, and pre-employment testing).

## 2. Employment Legislation

Since their inception, Hooters restaurants have hired only female servers. Moreover, consistent with the company's marketing theme, it has its female servers wear short nylon shorts and cutoff T-shirts that show their midriffs. The Equal Employment Opportunity Commission (EEOC) began an investigation of Hooters when a Chicago man filed a gender-based discrimination charge. The man alleged that he had applied for a server's job at a Hooters restaurant and was rejected because of his gender. The dispute between Hooters and the EEOC quickly gained national attention. One sarcastic letter to the EEOC printed in *Fortune* magazine read as follows:

> Dear EEOC:
> Hi! I just wanted to thank you for investigating those Hooters restaurants, where the waitresses wear those shorty shorts and midriffy T-shirts. I think it's a great idea that you have decided to make Hooters hire men as—how do you say it?—waitpersons. Gee, I never knew so many men wanted to be waitpersons at Hooters. No reason to let them sue on their own either. You're right, the government needs to take the lead on this one.[20]

This photo epitomizes how ludicrous the public thought the EEOC suit against Hooters was. A group of men calling themselves "Hooter Guys," dressed like the female employees of the popular restaurant as part of their entry in the Boulder Kinetic Sculpture Challenge. Despite favorable ruling, Hooters was still required to create more support jobs that would be open to men.

© LAYNE KENNEDY/CORBIS

This letter characterized public sentiment at the time. With a backlog of 100,000 job discrimination cases, many wondered why the EEOC didn't have better things to do with its scarce resources.

Three years after the initial complaint, the EEOC ruled that Hooters had violated antidiscrimination laws. The EEOC offered Hooters a settlement, which demanded that the company pay $22 million to the EEOC for distribution to male victims of the "Hooters Girl" hiring policy, establish a scholarship fund to enhance opportunities or education for men, and provide sensitivity training to teach Hooters' employees how to be more sensitive to men's needs. Hooters responded with a $1 million publicity campaign, chastising the EEOC for its investigation. Billboards featuring "Vince," a male dressed in a Hooters Girl uniform and blond wig sprang up all over the country. Hooters customers were given postcards to send complaints to the EEOC. Of course, Hooters paid the postage. As a result of the publicity campaign, restaurant sales increased by 10 percent. Soon thereafter, the EEOC announced that it would not pursue discriminatory hiring charges against Hooters.[21] However, the company still ended up paying $3.75 million to settle a class action suit brought by seven men who claimed that not being able to get a job at Hooters violated federal law.[22] The settlement still allowed Hooters to maintain its women-only policy for server jobs, but the company was required to create additional support jobs, such as hosts and bartenders, that would also be open to men.

*As the Hooters example illustrates, the human resource planning process occurs in a very complicated legal environment. Let's explore employment legislation by reviewing 2.1 the major federal employment laws that affect human resource practice, 2.2 how the concept of adverse impact is related to employment discrimination, and 2.3 the laws regarding sexual harassment in the workplace.*

### 2.1 Federal Employment Laws

Exhibit 14.4 lists the major federal employment laws as well as their Web sites, where you can find more detailed information. The general result of this body of law, which is still evolving through court decisions, is that employers may not discriminate in employment decisions on the basis of gender, age, religion, color, national origin, race, or disability. The intent is to make these factors irrelevant in employment decisions. Stated another way,

EXHIBIT 14.4

## SUMMARY OF MAJOR FEDERAL EMPLOYMENT LAWS

**Equal Pay Act of 1963**
http://www.eeoc.gov/laws/epa.html

Prohibits unequal pay for males and females doing substantially similar work.

**Civil Rights Act of 1964**
http://www.eeoc.gov/laws/vii.html

Prohibits discrimination on the basis of race, color, religion, gender, or national origin.

**Age Discrimination in Employment Act of 1967**
http://www.eeoc.gov/laws/adea.html

Prohibits discrimination in employment decisions against persons age 40 and over.

**Pregnancy Discrimination Act of 1978**
http://www.eeoc.gov/facts/fs-preg.html

Prohibits discrimination in employment against pregnant women.

**Americans with Disabilities Act of 1990**
http://www.eeoc.gov/laws/ada.html

Prohibits discrimination on the basis of physical or mental disabilities.

**Civil Rights Act of 1991**
http://www.eeoc.gov/laws/cra91.html

Strengthened the provisions of the Civil Rights Act of 1964 by providing for jury trials and punitive compensation.

**Family and Medical Leave Act of 1993**
http://www.dol.gov/dol/esa/fmla.htm

Permits workers to take up to 12 weeks of unpaid leave for pregnancy and/or birth of a new child, adoption or foster care of a new child, illness of an immediate family member, or personal medical leave.

---

**bona fide occupational qualification (BFOQ)**
an exception in employment law that permits gender, age, religion, and so forth, to be used when making employment decisions, but only if they are "reasonably necessary to the normal operation of that particular business." BFOQs are strictly monitored by the Equal Employment Opportunity Commission.

520

employment decisions should be based on factors that are "job related," "reasonably necessary," or a "business necessity" for successful job performance. The only time that gender, age, religion, and so forth can be used to make employment decisions is when they are considered a bona fide occupational qualification.[23] Title VII of the 1964 Civil Rights Act says that it is not unlawful to hire and employ someone on the basis of their gender, religion, or national origin when there is a **bona fide occupational qualification (BFOQ)** that is "reasonably necessary to the normal operation of that particular business." For example, a Baptist church hiring a new minister can reasonably specify that being a Baptist rather than a Catholic or Presbyterian is a BFOQ for Baptist ministers. However, it's unlikely that a church could specify race or national origin as a BFOQ. In general, the courts and the EEOC take a hard look when a business claims that gender, age, religion, color, national origin, race, or disability are BFOQs. For instance, the EEOC disagreed with Hooters' claim that it was "in the business of providing vicarious sexual recreation" and that "female sexuality is a bona fide occupational qualification."[24]

It is important to understand, however, that these laws don't just apply to selection decisions (i.e., hiring and promotion), but rather to the entire HRM process. Thus, these laws cover all training and development activities, performance appraisals, terminations, and compensation decisions.

Except for the Department of Labor (**http://www.dol.gov**), which administers the Family and Medical Leave Act, all of these laws are administered by the EEOC (**http://www.eeoc.gov**). Employers who use gender, age, race, or religion to make employment-related decisions when those factors are unrelated to an applicant's or employee's ability to perform a job may face charges of discrimination from employee lawsuits or the EEOC. For example, five women sued Met Life, a large insurance company, accusing it of gender discrimination in hiring, pay, and promotions. The lawyer representing the women said that only 25 percent of the company's 6,000 sales representatives were women, that only 7 percent of branch managers and managing directors were women, and that there were no women vice presidents at the highest levels of sales management. Likewise, Ford Motor Company settled a lawsuit after being sued for age discrimination when it switched to a new employee evaluation system in which 10 percent of workers received A grades, 80 percent received B's, and 10 percent received C's. If you received a C, you wouldn't get a pay raise or a bonus. If you got a C two years in a row, you were to be demoted or asked to leave the company. The lawyer representing the workers who sued Ford said, "We believe the new evaluation system was deliberately designed to reduce Ford's work force based on age."[25]

In addition to the laws presented in Exhibit 14.4 there are two other important sets of federal laws. Labor laws regulate the interaction between management and labor unions that represent groups of employees. These laws guarantee employees the right to form and join unions of their own choosing. For more information about labor laws, see the National Labor Relations Board at **http://www.nlrb.gov**. The Occupational Safety and Health Act (OSHA) requires that employers provide employees with a workplace that is "free from recognized hazards that are causing or are likely to cause death or serious physical harm." OSHA sets safety and health standards for employers and conducts inspections to determine whether those standards are being met. Employers who do not meet OSHA standards may be fined.[26] For example, OSHA fined Rocky Mountain Steel Mills twice for violating workplace safety standards, such as having elevated platforms without guardrails and electricians using the wrong kind of gloves. The first fine was for $1.1 million and the second was for $487,000. At the company's most recent inspection, which was prompted by two employee deaths over the last nine months, OSHA investigators found 22 repeat violations that had not been corrected, 74 new safety violations, and 11 new health violations.[27] For more information about OSHA, see **http://www.osha.gov**.

### 2.2 Adverse Impact and Employment Discrimination

The EEOC has investigatory, enforcement, and informational responsibilities. Therefore, it investigates charges of discrimination, enforces the provisions of these laws in federal court, and publishes guidelines that organizations can use to ensure they are in compliance with the law. One of the most important guidelines jointly issued by the EEOC, the Department of Labor, the U.S. Justice Department, and the federal Office of Personnel Management is the *Uniform Guidelines on Employee Selection Procedures*, which can be read in their entirety at **http://www2.dol.gov/dol/esa/public/regs/cfr/41cfr/ toc_Chapt60/60_3_toc.htm**. These guidelines define two important criteria, disparate treatment and adverse impact, that are used in deciding whether companies have participated in discriminatory hiring and promotion practices.

Discrimination means treating people differently. **Disparate treatment**, which is intentional discrimination, occurs when people, because of their race, sex, ethnic group, national origin, religious beliefs, and so forth, are purposively not given the same hiring, promotion, or membership opportunities as other employees, despite being qualified.[28] For example, in Chapter 12, you learned that Coca-Cola paid $192.5 million to settle a class action disparate treatment lawsuit in which it was accused of purposely not giving African-American employees equal opportunities in pay, promotions, and performance reviews.[29] Likewise, Rent-A-Center paid $12.3 million to settle a class action disparate treatment lawsuit in which it was accused of not providing fair hiring and promotion opportunities to 4,600 female employees and job applicants.[30]

Legally, one of the key parts of discrimination lawsuits is establishing motive, meaning that the employer intended to discriminate. If no motive can be established, then a case of disparate treatment may actually be a case of adverse impact. **Adverse impact**, which is unintentional discrimination, is a substantially different rate of selection in hiring, promotion, or other employment decisions that works to the disadvantage of members of a particular race, sex, or ethnic group. The courts and federal enforcement agencies use the **four-fifths (or 80 percent) rule** to determine if adverse impact has occurred. Adverse impact occurs if the selection rate for a protected group of people is less than four-fifths (or 80%) of the selection rate for a nonprotected group (usually white males). So, if 100 white applicants and 100 black applicants apply for entry-level jobs, and 60 white applicants are hired (60/100 = 60%), but only 20 black applicants

**disparate treatment**
intentional discrimination that occurs when people are purposely not given the same hiring, promotion, or membership opportunities because of their race, sex, age, ethnic group, national origin, or religious beliefs

**adverse impact**
unintentional discrimination in which there is a substantially different rate of selection in hiring, promotion, or other employment decisions that works to the disadvantage of members of a particular race, sex, age, ethnicity, or protected group

**four-fifths (or 80 percent) rule**
a rule of thumb used by the courts and the EEOC to determine whether there is evidence of disparate impact. A violation of this rule occurs when the selection rate for a protected group is less than 80 percent or four-fifths of the selection rate for a nonprotected group.

are hired (20/100 = 20%), adverse impact will have occurred (0.20/0.60 = 0.33). The criterion for the four-fifths rule in this situation is 0.48: 0.60 × 0.80 = 0.48. Since 0.33 is less than 0.48, then the four-fifths rule has been violated.

However, violation of the four-fifths rule is not an automatic indication of discrimination. If an employer can demonstrate that a selection procedure or test is valid, meaning that the test accurately predicts job performance or that the test is job related because it assesses applicants on specific tasks actually used in the job, then the organization may continue to use the test. However, if validity cannot be established, then a violation of the four-fifths rule may likely result in a lawsuit brought by employees, job applicants, or the EEOC itself.

### 2.3 Sexual Harassment

**sexual harassment**
form of discrimination in which unwelcome sexual advances, requests for sexual favors, or other verbal or physical conduct of a sexual nature occur while performing one's job

**quid pro quo sexual harassment**
form of sexual harassment in which employment outcomes, such as hiring, promotion, or simply keeping one's job, depend on whether an individual submits to sexual harassment

**hostile work environment**
form of sexual harassment in which unwelcome and demeaning sexually related behavior creates an intimidating and offensive work environment

According to the EEOC, **sexual harassment** is a form of discrimination in which unwelcome sexual advances, requests for sexual favors, or other verbal or physical conduct of a sexual nature occur. From a legal perspective, there are two kinds of sexual harassment, quid pro quo and hostile work environment.[31]

**Quid pro quo sexual harassment** occurs when employment outcomes, such as hiring, promotion, or simply keeping one's job, depend on whether an individual submits to being sexually harassed. For example, in a quid pro quo sexual harassment lawsuit against Prudential Insurance, a female employee alleged that her boss repeatedly propositioned her for sexual favors and that when she refused, he said that "she would not amount to anything in this business without his help."[32] By contrast, a **hostile work environment** occurs when unwelcome and demeaning sexually related behavior creates an intimidating, hostile, and offensive work environment. One example of a hostile work environment was a Sears manager who would ask his female subordinates to step into his office to look at close-up photos of women's breasts and bottoms that he had taken while on vacation at a beach.[33] Or at Prudential, the same manager who was alleged to have engaged in quid pro quo harassment was also alleged to have made inappropriate sexual comments about women in front of female workers, to have allowed the display of pornographic material on company computers, and to have permitted the posting of a sign saying, "Sexual harassment will not be tolerated, it will be graded."[34]

What common mistakes do managers make when it comes to sexual harassment laws?[35] First, many assume that the victim and harasser must be of the opposite sex. According to the courts, they do not. Sexual harassment can also occur between people of the same sex. Second, it is assumed that sexual harassment can occur only between coworkers or between supervisors and subordinates. Not so. Sexual harassers can also include agents of employers, such as consultants, and can even include nonemployees. The key is not employee status but whether the harassment takes place while conducting company business. Third, it is often assumed that only people who have themselves been harassed can file complaints or lawsuits. In fact, especially in hostile work environments, anyone affected by offensive conduct can file a complaint or lawsuit.

Finally, what should companies do to make sure that sexual harassment laws are followed and not violated?[36] First, respond immediately when sexual harassment is reported. A quick response encourages victims of sexual harassment to report problems to management rather than to lawyers or the EEOC. Furthermore, a quick and fair investigation may serve as a deterrent to future harassment. A lawyer for the EEOC said, "Worse than having no sexual harassment policy is a policy that is not followed. It's merely window dressing. You wind up with destroyed morale when people who come forward are ignored, ridiculed, retaliated against, or nothing happens to the harasser."[37] Next, take the time to write a clear, understandable sexual harassment policy that is strongly worded, gives specific examples of what constitutes sexual harassment, spells outs sanctions and punishments, and is widely publicized within the company. This lets potential harassers and victims know what will not be tolerated and how the firm will deal with harassment should it occur. Exhibit 14.5 provides an example of such a sexual harassment policy.

EXHIBIT 14.5

EXAMPLE OF A SEXUAL HARASSMENT POLICY

Sexual harassment is a form of sexual discrimination. Sexual harassment negatively affects job performance, productivity, morale, and employment opportunities. Sexual harassment negatively affects (*your company's*) goodwill, community standing, and profitability. Sexual harassment is offensive, inappropriate, and illegal. (*your company*) prohibits the sexual harassment of its employees by management, coworkers, independent contractors, nonemployees, vendors, and visitors. Sexual harassment will not be tolerated. Violators of our sexual harassment policy will be subject to disciplinary action, up to and including discharge.

Sexual harassment includes unwelcome sexual advances, requests for sexual favors, and other verbal and physical conduct of a sexual nature. Sexual harassment includes conduct that is based on a person's sex and alters the terms and conditions of that person's employment. Sexual harassment includes inappropriate conduct, irrespective of whether the harasser and the person harassed are of different sexes or are of the same sex. Examples of sexual harassment include the following:

Employment decisions that are based on the submission to or the rejection of unwelcome sexual advances or requests for sexual favor;

Conduct of a sexual nature that unreasonably interferes with work performance;

Conduct of a sexual nature that creates an intimidating, hostile, or offensive work environment, including unwelcome verbal comments, jokes, suggestions, or derogatory remarks based on sex; unwelcome leering, whistling, physical touching, pats, squeezes, repeated brushing against, or the impeding or blocking of one's movement; references regarding an individual's sex life or comments about an individual's sexual activities, deficiencies, or prowess; unwelcome visual harassment, sexually suggestive or derogatory pictures, drawings, or cartoons; and unwelcome communications, notes, phone calls, and email.

Employees are encouraged to take action when sexual harassment occurs.

Any employee who believes that he/she is being harassed should take the following action:

1. Where appropriate, express your discomfort to the harasser. Speak to the harasser about his/her conduct or behavior. State firmly and specifically what action you find objectionable and what you want stopped. Please respond immediately to the offending conduct or behavior. Do NOT ignore the problem.

2. Where appropriate, notify your supervisor or manager immediately. We want to respond to and remedy your problem. By notifying us of improper conduct, we can respond more quickly.

NOTE: You should always feel free to bypass your supervisor and report instances of sexual harassment to (*name, address, and telephone number of senior management*). This individual is also available to provide information and to answer questions about our sexual harassment policy.

3. If a nonemployee harasses you, immediately report the incident to your supervisor. Sexual harassment by nonemployees, including visitors, vendors, or customers, will not be tolerated.

4. Keep your supervisor or (*member of management*) informed of any repeat occurrences after the harasser has been notified that his/her conduct is offensive.

The creation of a harassment-free workplace is the responsibility of all managers, supervisors, and employees. You should be aware of how fellow employees react to your comments and actions. If a fellow employee objects to or seems uncomfortable with your conduct, heed the objection and discontinue the conduct that may be objectionable. Remember that what is acceptable behavior to some employees may not be acceptable to others.

Any manager, supervisor, or employee who witnesses or becomes aware of instances of sexual harassment must report such instances to his/her supervisor or to senior management. Violations of this reporting requirement may be grounds for disciplinary action, up to and including discharge.

Retaliation against an individual for reporting an instance of sexual harassment, for cooperating in an investigation, or for helping to achieve the purposes of this policy is prohibited and may be grounds for disciplinary action, up to and including discharge.

All complaints of sexual harassment will be investigated promptly and thoroughly. To the extent practicable under the circumstance, information related to the complaint will be held in confidence and will only be disclosed on a "need-to-know" basis. If an investigation reveals that sexual harassment has occurred, disciplinary action will be taken to stop the harassment and to prevent harassment in the future.

No action will be taken against any individual who makes a good faith complaint or against any individual participating in the investigation or the enforcement of this policy. However, any individual who knowingly makes a false claim of sexual harassment may be subject to appropriate disciplinary action, up to and including discharge.

If you have any questions or comments, please contact (*member of management*).

**Source:** Anonymous, "XYZ Printing Sexual Harassment," *American Printer* 222, no. 1 (1998): 166-167.

# "headline news"

## White House Pastry Chef Cooks Up Trouble

White House Head Pastry Chef Roland Mesnier has apparently tried to cook up more than just dessert in the White House kitchen. In September 2000, his assistant Franette McCulloch filed a lawsuit against him alleging sexual harassment.

McCulloch studied under Mesnier at l'Académie de Cuisine and began her career at the White House in 1983. She routinely participated in baking the presidential and first family birthday cakes, as well as working on state dinners and other high-profile assignments throughout the Reagan, Bush, and Clinton presidencies, but that slowed soon after the alleged sexual harassment began in 1991. McCulloch's suit claimed that Mesnier suggestively asked her to feel under his apron to see how aroused he was, attempted to kiss her, and left messages on her home answering machine demanding sex. When she spurned his advances, he became hostile and rude, "screaming at her for refusing to have sex." She also says he excluded her from designing desserts and once assigned her to peel eight crates of kiwi instead.

Finally, in 1997 McCulloch was diagnosed with stress-related depression, so she took a leave of absence. After a year, she had run through her savings and really wanted to return to the White House kitchen—but not with Mesnier. She consulted an attorney who filed the suit on her behalf.

Mesnier was not the only target: The suit also named then-President Bill Clinton as a codefendant. No stranger to sexual harassment allegations, lawsuits, and hearings, Clinton was only a defendant in this instance because he allegedly failed to carry out his duty under the 1996 Presidential and Executive Office Accountability Act (PEOAA). PEOAA was enacted to make sure that the executive branch was subject to the same kinds of employment laws as companies in the private sector. In the McCulloch case, Clinton was effectively the top-level manager who did not ensure that his company—the White House—protected the civil rights of its employees. The head of any federal agency is

**CNN VIDEO**

typically named in suits brought against the agency. This suit sought $1 million from Mesnier and $1 million from Clinton.

McCulloch's lawyer was shocked to find out that the White House lawyers did not seem to be aware of PEOAA when he contacted them a month before filing the suit. "The White House has remained frozen in the headlights," he said. "I'm not only surprised. I'm shocked . . . It's bizarre. Who's in charge?" According to PEOAA, it should have been Bill Clinton. Asked why she waited until 2000 to file a suit when harassment began in 1991, McCulloch says that she was "deliberately misled" into believing she could not pursue her allegations. In fact, she claims that she was told that she could either remain in her position with Mesnier as her supervisor or quit her job.

The White House kitchen is no second-rate operation. Everything prepared in its pastry kitchen is original, no recipe is ever repeated, and no cookbooks are ever used. It is no wonder that McCulloch held on so long under such unconscionable circumstances and that she wanted to return to her prestigious and exciting position.

1. How accountable should upper-level managers be for the conduct of managers and employees that are not their direct reports? In other words, should Bill Clinton have been named in this suit?
2. Could the White House have avoided this harassment suit? How?

**Sources:** R. Mikkelsen, "White House Pastry Chef Sues Her Boss and President," *National Post*, 14 September 2000, A02. E.Nakashima, "White House Chef Accuses Boss of Sexual Harassment," *The Washington Post*, 14 September 2000, A33. "White House Chef Alleges Sexual Harassment," *CNN.com/Associated Press*, Published on CNN.com 13 September 2000. "A Tradition of Service," *The Working White House Today*, 28 August 2001, http://clinton3.nara.gov/WH/kids/inside/html/trad2.html.

Next, establish clear reporting procedures that indicate how, where, and to whom incidents of sexual harassment can be reported. The best procedures ensure a quick response, that impartial parties will handle the complaint, and that the privacy of the accused and accusers will be protected. At Dupont, AT&T, Avon, and Texas Industries, employees can call a confidential hotline 24 hours a day, 365 days a year.[38]

Finally, managers should also be aware that most states and many cities or local governments have their own employment-related laws and enforcement agencies. So, compliance with federal law is often not enough. In fact, organizations can be in full compliance with federal law, while at the same time violating state or local sexual harassment laws.

Human resource management is subject to the following major federal employment laws: Equal Pay Act, Civil Rights Acts of 1964 and 1991, Age Discrimination in Employment Act, Pregnancy Discrimination Act, Americans with Disabilities Act, and Family and Medical Leave Act. HR management is also subject to review by these federal agencies: Equal Employment Opportunity Commission, Department of Labor, Occupational Safety and Health Administration, and National Labor Relations Board. In general, these laws indicate that gender, age, religion, color, national origin, race, disability, and pregnancy may not be considered in employment decisions unless these factors reasonably qualify as a BFOQ. Two important criteria, disparate treatment (intentional discrimination) and adverse impact (unintentional discrimination), are used to decide whether companies have wrongly discriminated against someone. While motive is a key part of determining disparate treatment, the courts and federal enforcement agencies use the four-fifths rule to determine if adverse impact has occurred.

The two kinds of sexual harassment are quid pro quo and hostile work environment. Managers often wrongly assume that the victim and harasser must be of the opposite sex, that sexual harassment can only occur between coworkers or between supervisors and their employees, and that only people who have themselves been harassed can file complaints or lawsuits. To make sure that sexual harassment laws are followed, companies should respond immediately when harassment is reported, write a clear, understandable sexual harassment policy; establish clear reporting procedures; and be aware of and follow city and state laws concerning sexual harassment.

# Finding Qualified Workers

Ironically, despite record sales, Technical Materials, which sells electroplating and metal-bonding processes to car manufacturers and high tech industries, could not find enough qualified employees to work in its factories. Its pool of prospective employees was so weak that the number of applicants who failed its drug test had increased from one out of 25 to one out of six. Company president Al Lubrano made numerous strong job offers, added more pay and benefits to those offers when applicants asked for more, and still, they couldn't hire anybody. Finally, Lubrano said, "When it got ridiculous, we walked away."[39] A few years ago, the situation was just as desperate on Wall Street, where Charles Schwab Corp., a stock brokerage firm, paid $94,500 for a full-page advertisement in *The Wall Street Journal* to try to recruit the 1,000 new workers that it needed to meet the incredible growth of its online Internet service and its traditional branch offices. "We do need lots of employees, and we continue to grow on all fronts," said Schwab Co-Chief Executive David S. Pottruck.[40]

As these examples illustrate, finding qualified workers can be an increasingly difficult task. However, finding qualified applicants is just the first step. Selecting which applicants to hire is the second. CEO John Chambers of Cisco Systems, the leading designer and manufacturer of high-tech equipment that serves as the backbone of the Internet, said, "Cisco has an overall goal of getting the top 10 to 15 percent of people in our industry. Our philosophy is very simple—if you get the best people in the industry to fit into your culture and you motivate them properly, then you're going to be an industry leader."[41]

*After reading the next two sections, you should be able to*
3. *explain how companies use recruiting to find qualified job applicants.*
4. *describe the selection techniques and procedures that companies use when deciding which applicants should receive job offers.*

525

# 3. Recruiting

*Recruiting* is the process of developing a pool of qualified job applicants. Let's examine 3.1 what job analysis is and how it is used in recruiting, and how companies use 3.2 internal recruitment and 3.3 external recruiting to find qualified job applicants.

## 3.1 Job Analysis and Recruiting

**recruiting**
the process of developing a pool of qualified job applicants

**job analysis**
a purposeful, systematic process for collecting information on the important work-related aspects of a job

**Job analysis** is a "purposeful, systematic process for collecting information on the important work-related aspects of a job."[42] Typically, a job analysis collects four kinds of information:

- work activities, such as what workers do and how, when, and why they do it,
- the tools and equipment used to do the job,
- the context in which the job is performed, such as the actual working conditions or schedule, and
- the personnel requirements for performing the job, meaning the knowledge, skills, and abilities needed to do a job well.[43]

---

EXHIBIT 14.6

**JOB DESCRIPTION AND JOB SPECIFICATIONS FOR A GENERAL RECREATION LEADER FOR THE CITY OF SEATTLE'S PARKS AND RECREATION DEPARTMENT**

---

### JOB DESCRIPTION FOR GENERAL RECREATION LEADER (40 HRS/WK):

General recreation leaders are responsible for a broad range of programs, including but not limited to indoor/outdoor recreation activities (educational and recreational), athletic skills development and competitions, aquatics, special events and family programs, drop-in activities, and seasonal and major community gatherings. Leaders will organize, plan, implement, and lead activities; handle all administrative aspects, including registration, financial administration and budgeting, collection of performance measures and other statistics, and evaluation. Leaders will have lead responsibilities for Recreation Attendants, seasonal workers, and volunteers assigned. They will maintain personal contacts with the public, including interaction with participants, parents, volunteers, and employees of off-site program locations, and staff at other departments or community agencies to coordinate program activities or facility use. General leaders will be required to meet the performance measures for their program area and support the facility efforts to achieve performance measures.

### JOB SPECIFICATIONS FOR GENERAL RECREATION LEADER (40 HRS/WK):

*Required Qualifications:* The equivalent of one year of experience in a community-based recreation program and an Associate Degree in Recreation, Therapeutic Recreation, or related field (or a combination of education and/or training and/or experience which provides an equivalent background required to perform the work of the class). Washington State Driver's License.

*Desired Qualifications:* One year of experience in planning and implementing a program budget; developing programmatic timelines; anticipating all aspects of events and programs; collecting fees and registering participants; keeping accurate financial, demographic, and programmatic statistics; evaluating programs; and seeking assistance from outside resources. Competitive candidates will be able to demonstrate a history of developing programs to meet the community needs of a diverse, urban population, and possess skills in the following areas: conflict resolution, use of computer programs, customer service, and proficiency in a language other than English. Knowledge of youth development and marketing/publicity is important. Food Handler's Permit, Red Cross First Aid and Community CPR certification.

---

**Source:** City of Seattle Parks and Recreation Department, "Recreation Leader." [Online] Available http://www.ci.seattle.wa.us/jobs/Prks%20Rec%20Leader.htm, 25 May 1999. Anewer classification can be found at http://www.c.seattle.wa.US/personnel/classcomp/detail.asp?Schematic=3200504

**job description**
a written description of the basic tasks, duties, and responsibilities required of an employee holding a particular job

**job specifications**
a written summary of the qualifications needed to successfully perform a particular job

Job analysis information can be collected by having job incumbents and/or supervisors complete questionnaires about their jobs, by direct observation, by interviews, or by filming employees as they perform their jobs.

Job descriptions and job specifications are two of the most important results of a job analysis. A **job description** is a written description of the basic tasks, duties, and responsibilities required of an employee holding a particular job. **Job specifications**, which are often included as a separate section of a job description, are a summary of the qualifications needed to successfully perform the job. Exhibit 14.6 shows a job description and the job specifications for a general recreation leader for the City of Seattle's Parks and Recreation Department.

Because a job analysis clearly specifies what a job entails, as well as the knowledge, skills, and abilities that are needed to do a job well, companies must complete a job analysis *before* beginning to recruit job applicants. Exhibit 14.7 shows that job analysis, job descriptions, and job specifications are the foundation on which all critical human resource activities are built. They are used during recruiting and selection to match applicant qualifications with the requirements of the job. They are used throughout the staffing process to ensure that selection devices and the decisions based on these devices are job related. For example, the questions asked in an interview should be based on the most important work activities identified by a job analysis. Likewise, during performance appraisals, employees should be evaluated in areas that a job analysis has identified as the most important in a job.

Job analyses, job descriptions, and job specifications also help companies meet the legal requirement that their human resource decisions be job related. To be judged *job related,* recruitment, selection, training, performance appraisals, and employee separations must be valid and be directly related to the important aspects of the job, as identified by a careful job analysis. In fact, in *Griggs v. Duke Power Co.* and *Albemarle Paper Co. v. Moody*, the U.S. Supreme Court ruled that job analyses should be used to help

---

**EXHIBIT 14.7**

IMPORTANCE OF JOB ANALYSIS TO HUMAN RESOURCE MANAGEMENT

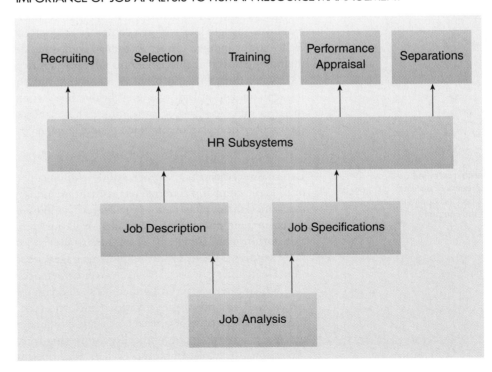

companies establish the job relatedness of their human resource procedures.[44] The EEOC's *Uniform Guidelines on Employee Selection Procedures* also recommend that companies base their human resource procedures on job analysis.

## 3.2 Internal Recruiting

**internal recruiting**
the process of developing a pool of qualified job applicants from people who already work in the company

**Internal recruiting** is the process of developing a pool of qualified job applicants from people who already work in the company. Internal recruiting, sometimes called "promotion from within," improves employee commitment, morale, and motivation. Recruiting current employees also reduces recruitment startup time and costs and, because employees are already familiar with the company's culture and procedures, generally increases workers' chances of success in new jobs. Kotak Mahindra Finance, a Japanese company, cuts costs by using internal recruitment first before looking outside the company for qualified applicants. GlaxoSmithKline, a pharmaceutical and healthcare company, internally recruits 20 first-level managers each year to keep recruiting costs low and to keep talented people in the company.[45] Job posting and career paths are two methods of internal recruiting.

*Job posting* is a procedure for advertising job openings within the company to existing employees. A job description and requirements are typically posted on a bulletin board, in a company newsletter, or in an internal computerized job bank that is only accessible to employees. For example, Japan-based Fujisawa Pharmaceuticals has a "Job Challenge" policy whereby all Fujisawa departments and divisions recruit internally by posting job openings to the company's intranet for all employees to see.[46] Job posting helps organizations discover hidden talent, allows employees to take responsibility for career planning, and makes it easier for companies to retain talented workers who are dissatisfied in their current jobs and would otherwise leave the company.[47] Fujisawa Pharmaceuticals also has a "Free Agent" policy, which encourages employees who want to change jobs to post their résumés to the same intranet. So when Fujisawa's departments and divisions have openings, the first place they look to fill those openings is the company intranet.[48]

A *career path* is a planned sequence of jobs through which employees may advance within an organization. For example, a person who starts as a sales representative may then move up to sales manager, and then to district or regional sales manager. Career paths help employees focus on long-term goals and development while also helping companies do succession or replacement planning. For instance, one of the disadvantages of internal recruitment is that it sets off a domino effect of job changes. When an internal employee changes jobs within a company, this person fills one job opening but automatically creates another. Career paths help companies deal with these changes by quickly identifying possible replacements as job openings ricochet through an organization. Coca-Cola deals with this problem by making sure that all of its managers are developing replacements at least two levels below their current position. Ian Pinto, senior HR manager for Coca-Cola of India, said, "This enables us to cut the costs associated with scrambling for replacements when people leave, or are moved up or sideways."[49]

## 3.3 External Recruiting

**external recruiting**
the process of developing a pool of qualified job applicants from outside the company

**External recruiting** is the process of developing a pool of qualified job applicants from outside the company. External recruitment methods include advertising (newspapers, magazines, direct mail, radio, or television), employee referrals (asking current employees to recommend possible job applicants), walk-ins (people who apply on their own), outside organizations (universities, technical/trade schools, professional societies), employment services (state or private employment agencies, temporary agencies, and professional search firms), special events (career conferences or job fairs), and Internet job sites.

Which external recruiting method should you use? Studies show that employee referrals, walk-ins, newspaper advertisements, and state employment agencies tend to be used most frequently for office/clerical and production/service employees. By contrast, newspaper advertisements and college/university recruiting are used most frequently for professional/technical employees. When recruiting managers, organizations tend to rely most heavily on newspaper advertisements, employee referrals, and search firms.[50]

However, in the last few years the biggest changes in external recruiting have come as a result of the Internet. For example, Cisco Systems no longer runs newspaper help-wanted ads. Instead, it takes out simple newspaper ads that direct recruits to its Web site (**http://www.cisco.com/jobs**), where they can see hundreds of job descriptions, learn in detail about Cisco's highly competitive benefits, and submit an online résumé.[51] In addition to extensive job information on corporate Web sites, some companies have begun subscribing to Internet job sites, such as Monster.com (**http://www.monster.com**), Hotjobs.com (**http.www.hotjobs.com**), and CareerBuilder (**http://www.careerbuilder.com**). For just about $200, a company can post a job opening for 30 days on one of these Internet job sites, about half of what it costs for an advertisement to appear just once in a Sunday newspaper. Another problem, according to Marcia Wheatley, H.R. director for the American College Personnel Association, is that with a tiny print advertisement in a Sunday newspaper, "We just can't compete with the big company box ads."[52] By contrast, when she posts a job opening on an Internet Web site, she said, "Instead of a tiny ad that says, 'ACPA needs an accountant,' I get a whole page to describe the job, give information about the association, and include a link to our Web site." Plus, she says she gets better responses from the Internet ad, getting nine times as many résumés as she does from one ad in the Sunday newspaper. Finally, she believes it's faster and easier to post ads online. She types them herself, doesn't have to talk to anyone to put the ad online, and the ads appear in less than one day. With the newspaper, however, you have to call by 3:00 P.M. on Thursday to dictate the ad to someone so it can appear on Sunday.

Despite its promise, there are some disadvantages to Internet recruiting. The main drawback (which some companies consider a plus) is that Internet recruiting is unlikely to reach recruits who don't use or have access to the Internet. And, since it is so easy for applicants to apply, companies may receive hundreds, if not thousands, of applications from unqualified applicants, which increases the importance of proper screening and selection. Furthermore, if the proper security precautions aren't taken, there is also the danger of violating employee/applicant privacy.[53] Despite these disadvantages, companies are expected

Job fairs are a common method of external recruiting, allowing applicants to visit several companies at a time and companies to meet hundreds of applicants and advertise themselves as workplaces. At a career fair held annually in Philadelphia, members of Accenture's recruiting team, pictured here, discuss the status of the job market after the terrorist attacks of 2001 with potential applicants.

© AP/World Photos

to make even more use of the Internet for external recruiting. It's predicted that 20 percent of all external job recruiting will be done via the Internet by 2005.

### Review 3
### Recruiting

Recruiting is the process of finding qualified job applicants. The first step in recruiting is to conduct a job analysis to collect information about the important work-related aspects of the job. The job analysis is then used to write a job description of basic tasks, duties, and responsibilities and to write job specifications indicating the knowledge, skills, and abilities needed to perform the job. Job analyses, descriptions, and specifications help companies meet the legal requirement that their human resource decisions be job related. Internal recruiting, or finding qualified job applicants from inside the company, can be done through job posting and career paths. External recruiting, or finding qualified job applicants from outside the company, is done through advertising, employee referrals, walk-ins, outside organizations, employment services, special events, and Internet job sites. The Internet is a particularly promising method of external recruiting because of its low cost, wide reach, and ability to communicate and receive unlimited information.

## 4. Selection

Once the recruitment process has produced a pool of qualified applicants, the selection process is used to determine which applicants have the best chance of performing well on the job. Tom Blangiardo, president of Basic Education and Training Associations (BETA group) in Fishers, Indiana, uses a fairly typical selection process to hire telemarketers to sell the company's educational videos. "For every ad we place, we get about 100 applicants. I interview everyone over the phone, because the way you come across on the phone is very important here. I evaluate voice tone, friendliness, and persuasiveness." Around 30 to 40 candidates are then chosen for group interviews. Managers explain BETA Group's philosophy and benefits and show the candidates examples of the videos they'll be selling. After the group interviews, nine candidates are typically eliminated, six receive immediate job offers, and 15 go on to individual interviews with Human Resource Director John Brown. During the individual interview, candidates are asked to role play a sales call. Another seven applicants are lost at this stage. The 10 to 15 survivors are hired and put through a one-week orientation program that includes product and technology training, practice taking live calls, and more role playing. "We put people on the hot seat to see how they behave," says Kara O'Connor, BETA Group's employee training manager. After 30 to 60 days, about half of these survivors leave because it's either too intense for them, or they're just not selling enough.[54]

As this example illustrates, **selection** is the process of gathering information about job applicants to decide who should be offered a job. To make sure that selection decisions are accurate and legally defensible, the *Uniform Guidelines on Employee Selection Procedures* recommend that all selection procedures be validated. **Validation** is the process of determining how well a selection test or procedure predicts future job performance. The better or more accurate the prediction of future job performance, the more valid a test is said to be. See the "What Really Works" section of this chapter for more on the validity of common selections tests and procedures.

*Let's examine common selection procedures, such as 4.1 application forms and résumés, 4.2 references and background checks, 4.3 selection tests, and 4.4 interviews.*

### 4.1 Application Forms and Résumés

The first selection devices that most job applicants encounter when they seek a job are application forms and résumés. Both contain similar information about job applicants, such as name, address, job and educational history, and so forth. While an organization's application form often asks for information already provided by the résumé, most orga-

**selection**
the process of gathering information about job applicants to decide who should be offered a job

**validation**
the process of determining how well a selection test or procedure predicts future job performance. The better or more accurate the prediction of future job performance, the more valid a test is said to be

530

nizations prefer to collect this information in their own format for entry into a human resource information system.

Employment-related laws apply to application forms, as they do all selection devices. Application forms may ask applicants only about valid, job-related information. However, application forms commonly ask applicants to report non-job-related information, such as marital status, maiden name, age, or date of high school graduation. Indeed, one study found that 73 percent of organizations have application forms that violate at least one federal or state law.[55] Exhibit 14.8 presents a list of the kinds of information that companies may not request in application forms, during job interviews, or in any other part of the selection process. Attorney Tiberio Trimmer said, "Your objective is to hire someone qualified to perform the requirements of the job. Not asking things that are peripheral to the work itself helps you to stay on the right side of the law."[56]

However, employment laws in other countries are different with respect to these issues. For instance, in France, employers may ask about non-job-related personal issues such as your age or the number of children that you have. And most French employers expect you to include a picture of yourself with your curriculum vitae (i.e., résumé ).[57] Consequently, most companies should closely examine their application forms, interview questions, and other selection procedures for compliance with the law wherever they do business.

Résumés also pose problems for companies, but in a different way. Studies show as many as one out of every three job applicants falsifies some information on his or her résumé. The items most frequently falsified are job responsibilities, job titles, previous

---

| EXHIBIT 14.8 | TOPICS THAT EMPLOYERS SHOULD AVOID IN APPLICATION FORMS, INTERVIEWS, OR OTHER PARTS OF THE SELECTION PROCESS |

1. *Children*—Don't ask applicants if they have children, plan to have them, or have or need childcare. Questions about children can unintentionally single out women.
2. *Age*—Because of the Age Discrimination Act, employers cannot ask job applicants their age during the hiring process. Since most people graduate high school at the age of 18, even asking for high school graduation dates could violate the law.
3. *Disabilities*—Don't ask if applicants have physical or mental disabilities. According to the Americans with Disabilities Act, disabilities (and reasonable accommodations for them) cannot be discussed until a job offer has been made.
4. *Physical Characteristics*—Don't ask for information about height, weight, or other physical characteristics. Questions about weight could somehow be construed as leading to discrimination toward overweight people, who studies show are less likely to be hired in general.
5. *Name*—Yes, you can ask people for their name, but you cannot ask female applicants for their maiden name because it indicates marital status. Asking for a maiden name could also lead to charges that the organization was trying to establish a candidate's ethnic background.
6. *Citizenship*—Asking applicants about citizenship could lead to claims of discrimination on the basis of national origin. However, according to the Immigration Reform and Control Act, companies may ask applicants if they have a legal right to work in the United States.
7. *Lawsuits*—Applicants may not be asked if they have ever filed a lawsuit against an employer. Federal and state laws prevent this so that whistleblowers may be protected from retaliation by future employers.
8. *Arrest Records*—Applicants cannot be asked about their arrest records. Arrests don't have legal standing. However, applicants can be asked whether they have been convicted of a crime.
9. *Smoking*—Applicants cannot be asked if they smoke. Smokers might be able to claim that they weren't hired because of fears of higher absenteeism and medical costs. However, they can be asked if they are aware of company policies that restrict smoking at work.
10. *AIDS/HIV*—Applicants can't be asked about AIDS, HIV, or any other medical condition. Questions of this nature would violate the Americans with Disabilities Act, as well as federal and state civil rights laws.

**Source:** J.S. Pouliot, "Topics to Avoid with Applicants," *Nation's Business* 80, no. 7 (1992): 57.

531

**Using a Reference Release Form**

Employment references are often reluctant to talk. Encourage them to share information by having applicants sign a reference release form like this.

I have applied for employment with [company name] and have listed you as a reference. Please provide answers to the following questions and return this form to [company contact] in the enclosed envelope. By this authorization, I hereby release you from any liability or action based upon the content of your answers.

Thank you for your cooperation and assistance.

Sincerely yours,

[candidate signature]

[date]

And when references talk, listen carefully to how they answer the questions (e.g., hesitancy, damning with faint praise).

**Source:** B. Weinstein, "Tips for Getting References to Talk," *Career.WSJ.Com.* [Online] Available at http://www.careerjournal.com/jobhunting/resumes/19980909-weinstein.html.

**employment references**
sources such as previous employers or co-workers who can provide job-related information about job candidates

**background checks**
procedures used to verify the truthfulness and accuracy of information that applicants provide about themselves and to uncover negative, job-related background information not provided by applicants

salary, and the length of employment on previous jobs. Other frequently falsified information includes educational background, academic degrees, and college majors and minors.[58] Therefore, managers should verify the information collected via résumés and application forms by comparing it with additional information collected during interviews and other stages of the selection process. Another way to check résumé information is to hire a private firm to do it. Costs vary but can often be as low as $50 per person. Cynthia Myers, who runs a company that verifies résumé information, said that companies can discourage false résumés by including this warning in their application forms and recruiting literature: "All information on this form is checked by a national agency that specializes in checking credentials. If any false claims are uncovered, that applicant will no longer be considered for a position."[59]

### 4.2 References and Background Checks

Nearly all companies ask applicants to provide **employment references,** such as previous employers or coworkers, that they can contact to learn more about job candidates. **Background checks** are used to verify the truthfulness and accuracy of information that applicants provide about themselves and to uncover negative, job-related background information not provided by applicants. Background checks are conducted by contacting "educational institutions, prior employers, court records, police and governmental agencies, and other informational sources, either by telephone, mail, remote computer access, or through in-person investigations."[60]

Unfortunately, previous employers are increasingly reluctant to provide references or background check information for fear of being sued by previous employees for defamation. If former employers provide potential employers with unsubstantiated information that damages applicants' chances of being hired, applicants can (and do) sue for defamation. As a result, many employers are reluctant to provide information about previous employees. Many provide only dates of employment, positions held, and date of separation.

When previous employers decline to provide meaningful references or background information, they put other employers at risk of *negligent hiring* lawsuits, in which employers are held liable for the actions of employees who should not have been hired had employers conducted thorough reference searches and background checks. In Florida, the Tallahassee Furniture Co. hired a worker to make home furniture deliveries, but did not have him complete an application form and did not conduct a background check. After being hired, he attacked a woman in her home with a knife. When she sued the company, it found out that he had a background of drug use, violent assault, and mental illness. The courts awarded the woman $2.5 million in damages.[61]

With previous employers generally unwilling to give full, candid references and with negligent hiring lawsuits awaiting companies that don't get full, candid references and background information, what can companies do? Dig deeper for more information. Ask references to provide references. Voca Corporation, based in Columbus, Ohio, has 2,500 employees in six states who care for people with mental retardation and developmental disabilities. Hilary Franklin, director of human resources, said she not only checks references, but she also asks the references to provide references, and asks those references for still others. She said, "As you get two or three times removed, you get more detailed, honest information."

Next, ask in writing before checking references or running a background check. Before Voca runs a background check, it asks applicants if there is anything they would like the company to know. This, in itself, is often enough to get applicants to share information that they previously withheld. Voca also keeps its findings confidential to minimize the chances of a defamation charge.[62]

Always document all reference and background checks, who was called and what information was obtained. And to reduce the success of negligent hiring lawsuits, it's particularly important to document which companies and people refused to share reference check and background information.

Finally, consider hiring private investigators to conduct background checks. They can often uncover surprising information not revealed by traditional background checks. When an American Investment Company was looking for a Japanese manager to run its Tokyo office, it quickly found a strong applicant who claimed to have experience with dozens of initial public offerings (the process of bringing privately held companies public so that shares of company stock can be sold in financial markets). In multiple interviews, this applicant clearly had detailed information about each IPO deal. However, a background check had soon revealed that he was the Japanese translator and not the financier behind each deal.[63]

### 4.3 Selection Tests

Why do some people do well in jobs while other people do poorly? If only you could know before deciding who to hire! Selection tests give organizational decision makers a chance to know who will likely do well in a job and who won't. The basic idea behind selection testing is to have applicants take a test that measures something directly or indirectly related to doing well on the job. The selection tests discussed here are specific ability tests, cognitive ability tests, biographical data, personality tests, work sample tests, and assessment centers.

**Specific ability tests** are tests that measure the extent to which an applicant possesses the particular kind of ability needed to do a job well. Specific ability tests are also called **aptitude tests**, because they measure aptitude for doing a particular task well. For example, if you took the SAT to get into college, then you've taken the aptly named Scholastic Aptitude Test, which is one of the best predictors of how well students will do in college (i.e., scholastic performance). Specific ability tests also exist for mechanical, clerical, sales, and physical work. For example, clerical workers have to be good at accurately reading and scanning numbers as they type or enter data. Exhibit 14.9 shows items similar to the Minnesota Clerical Test, in which applicants have only a short time to determine if the two columns of numbers and letters are identical. Applicants who are good at this would likely be better clerical or data-entry workers.

**Cognitive ability tests** measure the extent to which applicants have abilities in perceptual speed, verbal comprehension, numerical aptitude, general reasoning, and spatial aptitude. In other words, these tests indicate how quickly and how well people understand words, numbers, logic, and spatial dimensions. While specific ability tests

**specific ability tests (aptitude tests)**
tests that measure the extent to which an applicant possesses the particular kind of ability needed to do a job well

**cognitive ability tests**
tests that measure the extent to which applicants have abilities in perceptual speed, verbal comprehension, numerical aptitude, general reasoning, and spatial aptitude

533

---

### EXHIBIT 14.9

EXAMPLE CLERICAL TEST ITEMS, SIMILAR TO THOSE FOUND ON THE MINNESOTA CLERICAL TEST

| | NUMBERS/LETTERS | | SAME | |
|---|---|---|---|---|
| 1. | 3468251 | 3467251 | Yes | No |
| 2. | 4681371 | 4681371 | Yes | No |
| 3. | 7218510 | 7218520 | Yes | No |
| 4. | ZXYAZAB | ZXYAZAB | Yes | No |
| 5. | ALZYXMN | ALZYXNM | Yes | No |
| 6 | PRQZYMN | PRQZYMN | Yes | No |

**Source:** N.W. Schmitt & R.J. Klimoski, *Research Methods in Human Resources Management* (Cincinnati, OH: South-Western Publishing Co., 1991).

predict job performance in only particular types of jobs, cognitive ability tests accurately predict job performance in almost all kinds of jobs.[64] Why is this so? Because people with strong cognitive or mental abilities are usually good at learning new things, processing complex information, solving problems, and making decisions, and these abilities are important in almost all jobs. In fact, cognitive ability tests are almost always the best predictors of job performance. Consequently, if you were allowed to use just one selection test, cognitive ability tests would be the one to use. (In practice, though, companies use a battery of different tests, because this leads to much more accurate selection decisions.)

**Biographical data**, or **biodata**, are extensive surveys that ask applicants questions about their personal backgrounds and life experiences. The basic idea behind biodata is that past behavior (personal background and life experience) is the best predictor of future behavior. For example, during World War II, the U.S. Air Force had to quickly test tens of thousands of men without flying experience to determine who was likely to be a good pilot. Since flight training took several months and was very expensive, selecting the right people for training was important. After examining extensive biodata, it found that one of the best predictors of success in flight school was whether flight students had ever built model airplanes that actually flew. This one biodata item was almost as good a predictor as the entire set of selection tests that the Air Force was using at the time.[65]

Most biodata questionnaires have over 100 items that gather information about habits and attitudes, health, interpersonal relations, money, what it was like growing up in your family (parents, siblings, childhood years, teen years), personal habits, current home (spouse, children), hobbies, education and training, values, preferences, and work.[66] In general, biodata are very good predictors of future job performance, especially in entry-level jobs.

You may have noticed that some of the information requested in biodata surveys also appears in Exhibit 14.8 as topics employers should avoid in applications, interviews, or other parts of the selection process. This information can be requested in biodata questionnaires provided that companies can demonstrate that the information is job related (i.e., valid) and does not result in adverse impact against protected groups of job applicants. Biodata surveys should be validated and tested for adverse impact before using them to make selection decisions.[67]

*Personality* is the relatively stable set of behaviors, attitudes, and emotions displayed over time that makes people different from each other. **Personality tests** measure the extent to which applicants possess different kinds of job-related personality dimensions. In Chapter 12, you learned that there are five major personality dimensions (the Big 5)—extraversion, emotional stability, agreeableness, conscientiousness, and openness to experience—that are related to work behavior.[68] Of these, only conscientiousness, the degree to which someone is organized, hardworking, responsible, persevering, thorough, and achievement-oriented, predicts job performance across a wide variety of jobs. Conscientiousness works especially well in combination with cognitive ability tests, allowing companies to select applicants who are organized, hardworking, responsible, and smart!

**Work sample tests**, also called *performance tests*, require applicants to perform tasks that are actually done on the job. So unlike specific ability, cognitive ability, biographical data, and personality tests, which are indirect predictors of job performance, work sample tests directly measure job applicants' capability to do the job. At Microtraining Plus, a Norwalk, Connecticut, company that does computer training, employee-trainers have to be able to get up in front of people they don't know and present complex information in a clear, interesting way. Therefore, CEO David Knise uses work sample tests by having job candidates make hour-long presentations to his eight-person staff on any topic other than computers. He believes that since they're all computer people, they'd focus too much on content and not on delivery. By asking applicants to give an hour-long presentation, "We see how applicants organize their thoughts, if they've given themselves enough time to cover the material, and if they have overall command of a classroom."[69]

**biographical data (biodata)**
extensive surveys that ask applicants questions about their personal backgrounds and life experiences

**personality tests**
tests that measure the extent to which applicants possess different kinds of job-related personality dimensions

**work sample tests**
tests that require applicants to perform tasks that are actually done on the job

These work sample presentations give Microtraining direct evidence of whether job candidates can do the job if they are hired. Work sample tests generally do a very good job of predicting future job performance; however, they can be expensive to administer and can be used for only one kind of job. For example, at an auto dealership, a work sample test for mechanics could not be used as a selection test for sales representatives.

**assessment centers**
a series of managerial simulations, graded by trained observers, that are used to determine applicants' capability for managerial work

**Assessment centers** use a series of job-specific simulations that are graded by multiple trained observers to determine the extent to which applicants can perform managerial work. So, unlike the previously described selection tests commonly used for specific jobs or entry-level jobs, assessment centers are most often used to select applicants who have high potential to be good managers. Assessment centers often last two to five days and require participants to complete a number of tests and exercises that simulate managerial work.

Some of the more common assessment center exercises are in-basket exercises, role plays, small-group presentations, and leaderless group discussion. An *in-basket exercise* is a paper-and-pencil test in which an applicant is given the contents of a manager's "in-basket," which contains memos, phone messages, organizational policies, and other communication normally received by and available to managers. Applicants have a limited time to read through the in-basket, prioritize the items, and decide how to deal with each item. Experienced managers then score applicants' decisions and recommendations. Exhibit 14.10 shows an item that could be used in an assessment center for assessing applicants for the job of high school principal.

In a *leaderless group discussion*, which is another common assessment center exercise, a group of six applicants is given approximately two hours to solve a problem, but no one is put in charge (hence the name "leaderless" group discussion). Trained observers watch and score each participant on the extent to which he or she facilitates discussion, listens, leads, persuades, and works well with others.

Are tests perfect predictors of job performance? No, they aren't. Some people who do well on selection tests will do poorly in their jobs. Likewise, some people who do poorly on selection tests (and should have been hired, but weren't) would have been very good performers. However, valid tests will minimize these selection errors (hiring people who should not have been hired, and not hiring people who should have been hired) while maximizing correct selection decisions (hiring people who should have been hired,

535

EXHIBIT 14.10

IN-BASKET ITEM FOR AN ASSESSMENT CENTER FOR HIGH SCHOOL PRINCIPALS

February 28

R.A. Howard, Principal
Avon High School

Dear Mr. Principal,

I have observed a number of high school students smoking dope on my property during and after school hours.

Yesterday, I was startled to see a group of students amusing themselves by breaking pop bottles in the empty lot adjacent to my home. I went outside and yelled to them to get off of my property.

If you don't take any action, I'm going to the police. I'm fed up with this!

Sincerely,

Jean Wagner

**Source:** N.W. Schmitt & R.J. Klimoski, *Research Methods in Human Resources Management* (Cincinnati, OH: South-Western Publishing Co., 1991).

**Preparing for Structured Interviews**

Structured interviews assume that past performance predicts future performance. Therefore, structured interview questions often begin with "Tell me about a time when . . ." or "Give me an example of . . ." Use the P-A-R (Problem-Action-Result) technique to prepare for structured interviews. Go through the job description and your résumé line by line to think up examples and stories. Then write, edit, and rehearse them in the P-A-R format. And for variety, use the R-A-P approach, too. Start by describing your results. Then describe your actions. Finish by describing the problem you solved. You're less likely to be stumped by questions if you prepare in this way.

**Source:** A. Hirsh, "Tricky Questions Reign in Behavioral Interviews," *National Business Employment Weekly* (posted on Careers.WSJ.com). [Online] Available http://www.career-journal.com/jobhunting/interviewing/19990420-hirsch.html, 5 February 2002.

**interviews**
selection tool in which company representatives ask job applicants job-related questions to determine whether they are qualified for the job

**structured interviews**
interviews in which all applicants are asked the same set of standardized questions, usually including situational, behavioral, background, and job-knowledge questions

and not hiring people who should not have been hired). In short, tests increase the chances that you'll hire the right person for the job, that is, someone who turns out to be a good performer. So, while tests aren't perfect, almost nothing predicts future job performance as well as the selection tests discussed here. For more on how well selection tests increase the odds of hiring the right person for the job, see the "What Really Works" section of this chapter.

### 4.4 Interviews

In **interviews**, company representatives ask job applicants job-related questions to determine whether they are qualified for the job. Interviews are probably the most frequently used and relied on selection device. There are several basic kinds of interviews: unstructured, structured, and semistructured.

In *unstructured interviews*, interviewers are free to ask applicants anything they want, and studies show that they do. For instance, because interviewers often disagree about which questions should be asked during interviews, different interviewers tend to ask applicants very different questions.[70] Furthermore, individual interviewers even seem to have a tough time asking the same questions from one interview to the next. This high level of inconsistency lowers the validity of unstructured interviews as a selection device, because it becomes difficult to compare applicant responses. As a result, unstructured interviews do about half as well as structured interviews in accurately predicting which job applicants should be hired.

By contrast, with **structured interviews**, standardized interview questions are prepared ahead of time, so that all applicants are asked the same job-related questions. Four kinds of questions are typically asked in structured interviews:

- *situational questions,* which ask applicants how they would respond in a hypothetical situation (e.g., "What would you do if . . . ?"),
- *behavioral questions,* which ask applicants what they did in previous jobs that were similar to the job for which they are applying (e.g., "In your previous jobs, tell me about . . . ?"),
- *background questions,* which ask applicants about their work experience, education, and other qualifications (e.g., "Tell me about the training you received at . . ."),
- *job-knowledge questions,* which ask applicants to demonstrate their job knowledge (e.g., for nurses, "Give me an example of a time when one of your patients had a severe reaction to a medication. How did you handle it?").[71]

The primary advantage of structured interviews is that asking all applicants the same questions makes comparing applicants a much easier process. Structuring interviews also ensures that interviewers only ask for important, job-related information. These advantages not only improve the accuracy, usefulness, and validity of the interview, but also reduce the chances that interviewers will ask questions about topics that violate employment laws (go back to Exhibit 14.8 for a list of these topics).

*Semistructured interviews* lie somewhere in between structured and unstructured interviews. A major part of the semistructured interview (perhaps as much as 80 percent) is based on structured questions. However, some time is set aside for unstructured interviewing to allow interviewers to probe into ambiguous or missing information uncovered during the structured portion of the interview.

How well do interviews predict future job performance? Contrary to what you've probably heard, recent evidence indicates that even unstructured interviews do a fairly good job. When conducted properly, however, structured interviews can lead to much more accurate hiring decisions than unstructured interviews. In some cases, the validity of structured interviews can rival that of cognitive ability tests. But even more important, since interviews are

# WhatReallyWorks

## Using Selection Tests to Hire Good Workers

Hiring new employees always seems like a gamble. When you speak the words, "We'd like to offer you a job," you never know how it's going to turn out. However, the selection tests discussed in this chapter and reviewed in this section go a long way toward helping employers take the gambling aspect out of the hiring process. Indeed, more than

1,000 studies based on over 100,000 study participants strongly indicate that selection tests can give employers a much better than average (50-50) chance of hiring the right workers. In fact, if you had odds like these working for you in Las Vegas, you'd make so much money the casinos wouldn't let you in the door.

### Cognitive Ability Tests

There is a 76 percent chance that workers who do well on cognitive ability tests will be much better performers in their jobs than employees who did not do well on such tests.

**Probability of Success**

### Work Sample Tests

There is a 77 percent chance that workers who do well on work sample tests will be much better performers in their jobs than employees who did not do well on such tests.

**Probability of Success**

### Assessment Centers

There is a 69 percent chance that workers who do well on assessment center exercises will be much better managers than employees who did not do well on such exercises.

**Probability of Success**

### Structured Interviews

There is a 76 percent chance that workers who do well in structured interviews will be much better performers in their jobs than employees who did not do well in structured interviews.

**Probability of Success**

### Cognitive Ability + Work Sample Tests

When deciding who to hire, most companies use a number of tests together to make even more accurate selection decisions. There is an 82 percent chance that workers who do well on a combination of cognitive ability tests and work sample tests will be much better performers in their jobs than employees who did not do well on both tests.

**Probability of Success**

### Cognitive Ability + Integrity Tests

There is an 83 percent chance that workers who do well on a combination of cognitive ability tests and integrity tests (see Chapter 3 for a discussion of integrity tests) will be much better performers in their jobs than employees who did not do well on both tests.

**Probability of Success**

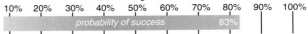

### Cognitive Ability + Structured Interviews

There is an 82 percent chance that workers who do well on a combination of cognitive ability tests and structured interviews will be much better performers in their jobs than employees who did not do well on both tests.

**Probability of Success**

**Sources:** F.L. Schmidt & J.E. Hunter, "The Validity and Utility of Selection Methods in Personnel Psychology: Practical and Theoretical Implications of 85 Years of Research Findings," *Psychological Bulletin* 124, no. 2 (1998): 262-274.

537

especially good at assessing applicants' interpersonal skills, they work especially well with cognitive ability tests. The combination (i.e., smart people who work well with others) leads to even better selection decisions than using either alone. Exhibit 14.11 provides a set of guidelines for conducting effective structured employment interviews.

EXHIBIT 14.11

GUIDELINES FOR CONDUCTING EFFECTIVE STRUCTURED INTERVIEWS

### PLANNING THE INTERVIEW

- Identify and define the knowledge, skills, abilities and other (KSAO) characteristics needed for successful job performance.
- For each essential KSAO, develop key behavioral questions that will elicit examples of past accomplishments, activities, and performance.
- For each KSAO, develop a list of things to look for in applicants' responses to key questions.

### CONDUCTING THE INTERVIEW

- Create a relaxed, nonstressful interview atmosphere.
- Review applicants' application forms, résumés, and other information.
- Allocate enough time to complete the interview without interruption.
- Put the applicant at ease; don't jump right into heavy questioning.
- Tell the applicant what to expect. Explain the interview process.
- Obtain job-related information from the applicant by asking those questions prepared for each KSAO.
- Describe the job and the organization to applicants. Applicants need adequate information to make a selection decision about the organization.

### AFTER THE INTERVIEW

- Immediately after the interview, review your notes and make sure they are complete.
- Evaluate applicants on each essential KSAO.
- Determine each applicant's probability of success and make a hiring decision.

**Source:** B.M. Farrell, "The Art and Science of Employment Interviews," *Personnel Journal* 65 (1986): 91-94.

## Review 4
### Selection

Selection is the process of gathering information about job applicants to decide who should be offered a job. Accurate selection procedures are valid, are legally defendable, and improve organizational performance. Application forms and résumés are the most common selection devices. Because many application forms request illegal, non-job-related information, and because as many as one-third of job applicants falsify information on résumés, these procedures can sometimes be of little value when making hiring decisions. References and background checks can also be problematic, given that previous employers are reluctant to provide such information for fear of being sued for defamation. Unfortunately, the lack of this information puts other employers at risk of negligent hiring lawsuits. Selection tests generally do the best job of predicting applicants' future job performance. In general, cognitive ability tests, work sample tests, biographical data, and assessment centers are the most valid tests, followed by personality tests and specific ability tests, which are still good predictors. Selection tests aren't perfect predictors of job performance, but almost nothing predicts future job performance as well as selection tests. The three kinds of job interviews are unstructured, structured, and semistructured interviews. Of these, structured interviews work best, because they ensure that all applicants are consistently asked the same situational, behavioral, background, or job-knowledge questions.

## Developing Qualified Workers

Harmon Industries, which makes signaling and communications equipment for the railway and transit industries, has a new training center where its employees learn engineering, safety, teamwork, time management, and other workplace skills. Ron Breshears,

Harmon's vice president of human resources and safety, said, "Training is an investment, not a cost. Once you see that, you see that you get a good return on your investment."[72] At Sprint, the telecommunications company, 50,000 out of 62,000 employees received training last year. Sprint's University of Excellence has 400 employees who provide classroom and on-the-job training in 20 cities. Said Brad Harsha, assistant vice president of Sprint's University of Excellence, "Our philosophy is that Sprint supports continuous learning. Our training doesn't stop with orientation to the company. It's a lifelong learning commitment."[73]

Why are Harmon Industries and Sprint spending so much time and money to train their workers? Because, according to the American Society for Training and Development (ASTD), an investment in training increases productivity by an average of 17 percent, reduces employee turnover, and makes companies more profitable.[74]

However, giving employees the knowledge and skills they need to improve their performance is just the first step in developing employees. The second step is giving employees formal feedback about their actual job performance. For example, at his last performance appraisal, Thomas Loarie, CEO of KeraVision, a company that invented a patented vision correction procedure, learned that he needed to be more realistic about his sales plans and that he needed to hold his subordinates more accountable for their work.[75] Gilbert Amelio, Apple Computer's former CEO, said, "CEOs really want the feedback about how we're doing and what we can be doing to improve what's going on."[76] Peter Bastone, CEO of a hospital in Mission Viejo, California, agreed: "I'm evaluated annually by the [hospital] board's executive committee, and it is extremely helpful because the committee has a big picture of my effectiveness."[77] So, in today's competitive business environment, even CEOs understand the importance of formal performance feedback.

*After reading the next two sections, you should be able to*
*5. describe how to determine training needs and select the appropriate training methods.*
*6. discuss how to use performance appraisal to give meaningful performance feedback.*

## 5. Training

*Training* *means providing opportunities for employees to develop the job-specific skills, experience, and knowledge they need to do their jobs or improve their performance. American companies spend more than $60 billion a year on training. To make sure those training dollars are well spent, companies need to 5.1 determine specific training needs, 5.2 select appropriate training methods, and 5.3 evaluate training.*

### 5.1 Determining Training Needs

**training**
developing the skills, experience, and knowledge employees need to perform their jobs or improve their performance

**needs assessment**
the process of identifying and prioritizing the learning needs of employees

**Needs assessment** is the process of identifying and prioritizing the learning needs of employees. Needs assessments can be conducted by identifying performance deficiencies, listening to customer complaints, surveying employees and managers, or formally testing employees' skills and knowledge.

The Work Keys method created by American College Testing in Iowa City, Iowa, (makers of the ACT test used for college admissions) is a needs assessment tool being used by more than 1,400 companies nationwide.[78] Work Keys is a series of tests that determine the knowledge and skill levels that an organization's employees have in communication (listening, reading for information, and writing), problem-solving (applied mathematics, applied technology, locating information, and observation), and interpersonal skills (teamwork). A needs assessment using Work Keys begins with a job analysis (what ACT calls "job profiling") to determine the knowledge and skill levels required to perform a job successfully. For example, Exhibit 14.12 shows that the job of customer service representative requires strong listening, reading, and writing skills, but only moderate capabilities in locating information, applied technology, and teamwork. Following the job analysis, employees are tested and their skill levels are compared to the

EXHIBIT 14.12

WORK KEYS NEEDS ASSESSMENT FOR A CUSTOMER SERVICE REPRESENTATIVE JOB

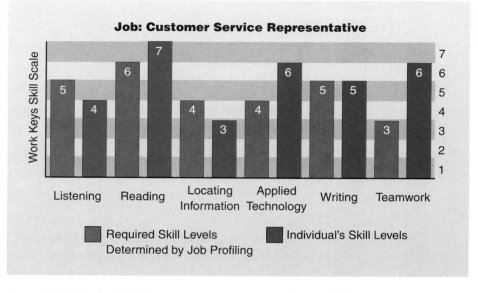

**Source:** "Work Keys in Action," *Introduction to Work Keys.* [Online] Available http://www.act.org/workkeys/, 31 May 1999.

requirements for the job. The greater the difference between an employee's skill levels and those required, the greater the need for training. Exhibit 14.12 shows the current skill levels in each area for one individual. Based on the Work Keys needs assessment, this employee needs some training in listening and locating information.

Note that training should never be conducted without first performing a needs assessment. Sometimes, training isn't needed at all or isn't needed for all employees. Since the needs assessment shown in Exhibit 14.12 indicates that the customer service representative has reading, applied technology, and teamwork skills that exceed those required for the job, it would be a waste of time and money to send this employee for training in these skills. Unfortunately, however, many organizations simply require all employees to attend training, whether they need to or not. The result is that employees who are not interested or don't need the training may react negatively during or after training. Likewise, employees who should be sent for training but aren't may also react negatively. Consequently, a needs assessment is an important tool for deciding who should or should not attend training. In fact, employment law restricts employers from discriminating on the basis of age, sex, race, color, religion, national origin, or handicap when selecting training participants. Instead, just like hiring decisions, the selection of training participants should be based on job-related information.

### 5.2 Training Methods

Assume that you're a training director for a bank, and that you're in charge of making sure that all bank employees know what to do in case of a robbery. Exhibit 14.13 lists a number of training methods you could use: films and videos, lectures, planned readings, case studies, coaching and mentoring, group discussions, on-the-job training, role playing, simulations and games, vestibule training, and computer-based learning. Which method would be best?

To choose the best method, you should consider a number of factors, such as the number of people to be trained, the cost of training, and the objectives of the training. For instance, if the training objective is to impart information or knowledge to trainees,

Internet training and e-learning are gaining momentum mostly because of the flexibility they offer. This flexibility (like allowing employees to train when it fits their schedules) can translate into increased productivity and decreased stress.

then you should use films and videos, lectures, and planned readings. In our robbery training example, trainees would hear, see, or read about what to do in case of a robbery.

If developing analytical and problem-solving skills is the objective, then use case studies, group discussions, and coaching and mentoring. In our example, trainees would read about a real robbery, discuss what to do, and then talk to people who had been through robberies before.

If practicing, learning, or changing job behaviors is the objective, then use on-the-job training, role-playing, simulations and games, and vestibule training. In our example, trainees would learn about robbery situations on the job, pretend that they were in a robbery situation, or participate in a highly realistic mock robbery.

If training is supposed to meet more than one of these objectives, then your best choice may be to combine one of the previous methods with computer-based training. Customer service representatives at Aetna Healthcare attend training by logging onto the personal computers in their offices. Aetna's trainees, who learn together from their offices in California, North Carolina, Ohio, and Texas, simply click a computer icon to get a live feed of their training instructor from Aetna's Hartford, Connecticut, headquarters.[79]

These days, many more companies are adopting Internet training or "e-learning." For instance, DaimlerChrysler now has the ability to provide electronic learning or training to all 4,500 of its U.S. dealers. There can be several advantages to Internet training or e-learning. Because employees don't need to leave their jobs, travel costs are greatly reduced. Also, because employees can take training modules when it is convenient (in other words, they don't have to fall behind at their jobs to attend week-long training courses), workplace productivity should increase and employee stress should decrease. Finally, if the company's technology infrastructure can support it, Internet training and e-learning can be much faster than traditional training methods. For example, nearly 25 percent of Cambridge Technology's 4,400 employees had completed a 10-hour Internet training course on their own just six weeks after it was first made available. After three months, the company expects all employees to have completed this training. CEO Jack

541

*EXHIBIT 14.13*

TRAINING OBJECTIVES AND METHODS

### TRAINING OBJECTIVE: IMPART INFORMATION OR KNOWLEDGE

- *Films and Videos:* Films and videos share information, illustrate problems and solutions, and effectively hold trainees' attention.
- *Lecture:* Instructors present oral presentations to trainees.
- *Planned Readings:* Trainees read about concepts or ideas before attending training.

### TRAINING OBJECTIVE: DEVELOP ANALYTICAL AND PROBLEM-SOLVING SKILLS

- *Case Studies:* Cases are analyzed and discussed in small groups. The cases present a specific problem or decision and trainees develop methods for solving the problem or making the decision.
- *Coaching and Mentoring:* Coaching and mentoring of trainees by managers involves informal advice, suggestions, and guidance. This method is helpful for reinforcing other kinds of training and for trainees who benefit from support and personal encouragement.
- *Group Discussions:* Small groups of trainees actively discuss specific topics. Instructor may perform the role of discussion leader.

### TRAINING OBJECTIVE: PRACTICE, LEARN, OR CHANGE JOB BEHAVIORS

- *On-the-Job Training (OJT):* New employees are assigned to experienced employees. The trainee is expected to learn by watching the experienced employee perform the job, and eventually by working along side the experienced employee. Gradually, the trainee is left on his or her own to perform the job.
- *Role Playing:* Trainees assume job-related roles and practice new behaviors by acting out what they would do in job-related situations.
- *Simulations and Games:* Experiential exercises place trainees in realistic job-related situations and give them the opportunity to experience a job-related condition in a relatively low-cost setting. The trainee benefits from "hands-on experience" before actually performing the job where mistakes may be more costly.
- *Vestibule Training:* Procedures and equipment similar to those used in the actual job are set up in a special area called a "vestibule." The trainee is then taught how to perform the job at his or her own pace without disrupting the actual flow of work, making costly mistakes, or exposing the trainee and others to dangerous conditions.

### TRAINING OBJECTIVE: IMPART INFORMATION OR KNOWLEDGE; DEVELOP ANALYTICAL AND PROBLEM-SOLVING SKILLS; PRACTICE, LEARN, OR CHANGE JOB BEHAVIORS

- *Computer-Based Learning:* Interactive videos, software, CD-ROMs, personal computers, teleconferencing, and the Internet may be combined to present multimedia-based training.

**Source:** A. Fowler, "How to Decide on Training Methods," *People Management* 25, no. 1 (1995): 36.

542

Messman said, "To train the entire company the old way would take a year. Now it takes us less than a quarter. When you're moving at Internet speed, that important."[80]

There are, however, several disadvantages to Internet training or e-learning. First, despite its increasing popularity, it's not always the appropriate training method. Internet training can be a good way to impart information, but it isn't nearly as effective for changing job behaviors or developing problem-solving and analytical skills. Second, e-learning requires a significant investment in computers and high-speed Internet and network connections for all employees. Finally, because it is new, it's too early to know whether Internet training and e-learning actually produce better training results.

### 5.3 Evaluating Training

After selecting a training method and conducting the training, the last step is to evaluate the training. Training can be evaluated in four ways: on *reactions*, how satisfied trainees were with the program; on *learning*, how much employees improved their knowledge or skills; on *behavior*, how much employees actually changed their on-the-job behavior because of training; or on *results*, how much training improved job performance, such as increased sales or quality, or decreased costs.[81] For example, Aetna Healthcare found that its computer-based training led to higher levels of learning and saved the company $5 million a year in travel costs.[82]

## Review 5
### Training

Training is used to give employees the job-specific skills, experience, and knowledge they need to do their jobs or improve their job performance. To make sure training dollars are well spent, companies need to determine specific training needs, select appropriate training methods, and then evaluate the training. Needs assessments can be conducted by identifying performance deficiencies, listening to customer complaints, surveying employees and managers, or formally testing employees' skills and knowledge. Selection of an appropriate training method depends on a number of factors, such as the number of people to be trained, the cost of training, and the objectives of the training. If the objective is to impart information or knowledge, then films and videos, lectures, and planned readings should be used. If developing analytical and problem-solving skills is the objective, then case studies, group discussions, and coaching and mentoring should be used. If practicing, learning, or changing job behaviors is the objective, then on-the-job training, role-playing, simulations and games, and vestibule training would be used. If training is supposed to meet more than one of these objectives, then it may be best to combine one of the previous methods with computer-based training. Training can be evaluated on reactions, learning, behavior, or results.

## 6. Performance Appraisal

**performance appraisal**
the process of assessing how well employees are doing their jobs

**Performance appraisal** is the process of assessing how well employees are doing their jobs. Most employees and managers intensely dislike the performance appraisal process. One manager said, "I hate annual performance reviews. I hated them when I used to get them, and I hate them now that I give them. If I had to choose between performance reviews and paper cuts, I'd take paper cuts every time. I'd even take razor burns and the sound of fingernails on a blackboard."[83] Unfortunately, attitudes like this are all too common. In fact, seven out of 10 employees are dissatisfied with the performance appraisal process in their companies. Likewise, according to the Society for Human Resource Management, 90 percent of human resource managers are dissatisfied with the performance appraisal systems used by their companies.[84]

Because they are used for so many important purposes, companies with poor performance appraisal systems face tremendous problems. For example, performance appraisals are used as a basis for compensation, promotion, and training decisions. In human resource planning, performance appraisals are used for career planning and for making termination decisions.[85] And because of their key role in so many organizational decisions, performance appraisals are also central to many of the lawsuits that employees (or former employees) file against employers.

*Let's explore how companies can avoid some of these problems with performance appraisals by 6.1 accurately measuring job performance and 6.2 effectively sharing performance feedback with employees.*

### 6.1 Accurately Measuring Job Performance

Workers often have strong doubts about the accuracy of their performance appraisals. And they may be right. For example, it's widely known that assessors are prone to errors when rating worker performance. Three of the most common rating errors are central tendency, halo, and leniency. *Central tendency* error occurs when assessors rate all workers as average or in the middle of the scale. *Halo error* occurs when assessors rate all workers as performing at the same level (good, bad, or average) in all parts of their jobs. *Leniency error* occurs when assessors rate all workers as performing particularly well. One of the reasons that managers make these errors is that they often don't spend enough time gathering or reviewing performance data. Winston Connor, the former vice president of

543

human resources at Huntsman Chemical, said, "Most of the time, it's just a ritual that managers go through. They pull out last year's review, update it and do it quickly."[86]

What can be done to minimize rating errors and improve the accuracy with which job performance is measured? In general, two approaches have been used: improving performance appraisal measures themselves and training performance raters to be more accurate.

One of the ways in which companies try to improve performance appraisal measures is to use as many objective performance measures as possible. **Objective performance measures** are measures of performance that are easily and directly counted or quantified. Common objective performance measures include output, scrap, waste, sales, customer complaints, or rejection rates.

But when objective performance measures aren't available, and frequently they aren't, subjective performance measures have to be used instead. **Subjective performance measures** require that someone judge or assess a worker's performance. The most common kind of subjective performance measure is the trait rating scale shown in Exhibit 14.14. **Trait rating scales** ask raters to indicate the extent to which a worker possesses a particular trait or characteristic, such as reliability or honesty. However, trait rating scales, also called *graphic rating scales*, are typically inaccurate measures of performance. To start, managers are notoriously poor judges of employee traits. Second, traits are not related to job performance in any meaningful way.

So instead of using trait rating scales, subjective performance should be measured using behavioral observation scales. **Behavioral observation scales (BOSs)** ask raters to rate the frequency with which workers perform specific behaviors representative of the job dimensions that are critical to successful job performance. Exhibit 14.14 shows a BOS for two important job dimensions for a retail salesperson: customer service and money handling. Notice that each dimension lists several specific behaviors characteristic of a worker who excels in that dimension of job performance. (Normally, the scale would list seven to 12 items, not three, as shown in the table.)

Not only do BOSs work well for rating critical dimensions of performance, but studies also show that managers strongly prefer BOSs for giving performance feedback; accurately differentiating between poor, average, and good workers; identifying training needs; and accurately measuring performance. And in response to the statement, "If I were defending a company, this rating format would be an asset to my case," attorneys strongly preferred BOSs over other kinds of subjective performance appraisal scales.[87]

The second approach to improving the measurement of workers' job performance appraisal is rater training. **Rater training** is the process of training performance raters how to avoid rating errors (i.e., central tendency, halo, and leniency) and how to increase rating accuracy. In rater training designed to minimize rating errors, trainees view videotapes of managers observing an employee performing some aspect of a job. Following each video, trainees are asked how they would have rated the worker's performance and how the manager on the tape would have rated it. Each videotape, however, is an example of the different kinds of rating errors. So trainees have a chance to actually observe rating errors being made (by the manager in the videotape) and then discuss how to avoid those errors.

Another common form of rater training stresses rater accuracy (rather than minimizing errors). Here, raters closely examine the key dimensions of job performance (e.g., customer service and money handling for the retail salesperson in our example) and discuss specific behaviors representative of each dimension. Trainees may then be asked to role-play examples of these behaviors or to watch videos containing behavioral examples of each dimension of job performance. Both kinds of rater training are effective.[88]

### 6.2 Sharing Performance Feedback

After gathering accurate performance data, the next step is to share performance feedback with employees. Unfortunately, even when performance appraisal ratings are accurate, the appraisal process often breaks down at the feedback stage. Employees become

---

**objective performance measures**
measures of job performance that are easily and directly counted or quantified

**subjective performance measures**
measures of job performance that require someone to judge or assess a worker's performance

**trait rating scales**
a rating scale that indicates the extent to which a worker possesses particular traits or characteristics

**behavioral observation scales (BOS)**
rating scales that indicate the frequency with which workers perform specific behaviors that are representative of the job dimensions critical to successful job performance

**544**

**rater training**
training performance appraisal raters in how to avoid rating errors and increase rating accuracy

EXHIBIT 14.14

## SUBJECTIVE PERFORMANCE APPRAISAL SCALES

### TRAIT RATING SCALE

|  | Strongly Disagree | 1 2 3 4 5 | Strongly Agree |
|---|---|---|---|
| 1. Employee is a hard worker. |  | 1 2 3 4 5 |  |
| 2. Employee is reliable. |  | 1 2 3 4 5 |  |
| 3. Employee is trustworthy. |  | 1 2 3 4 5 |  |

### BEHAVIORAL OBSERVATION SCALE

| *Dimension: Customer Service* | Almost Never | 1 2 3 4 5 | Almost Always |
|---|---|---|---|
| 1. Greets customers with a smile and a "hello." |  | 1 2 3 4 5 |  |
| 2. Calls other stores to help customers find merchandise that is not in stock. |  | 1 2 3 4 5 |  |
| 3. Promptly handles customer concerns and complaints. |  | 1 2 3 4 5 |  |

| *Dimension: Money Handling* | Almost Never | 1 2 3 4 5 | Almost Always |
|---|---|---|---|
| 1. Accurately makes change from customer transactions. |  | 1 2 3 4 5 |  |
| 2. Accounts balance at the end of the day, no shortages or surpluses. |  | 1 2 3 4 5 |  |
| 3. Accurately records transactions in computer system. |  | 1 2 3 4 5 |  |

**360-degree feedback**
a performance appraisal process in which feedback is obtained from the boss, subordinates, peers and coworkers, and the employees themselves

defensive and dislike hearing any negative assessments of their work, no matter how small. Managers become defensive, too, and dislike giving appraisal feedback as much as employees dislike receiving it. One manager said, "I myself don't go as far as those who say performance reviews are inherently destructive and ought to be abolished, but I agree that the typical annual-review process does nothing but harm. It creates divisions. It undermines morale. It makes people angry, jealous, and cynical. It unleashes a whole lot of negative energy, and the organization gets nothing in return."[89]

So what can be done to overcome the inherent difficulties in performance appraisal feedback sessions? Since performance appraisal ratings have traditionally been the judgments of just one person, the boss, one approach is to use **360-degree feedback**. In this approach, feedback comes from four sources: the boss, subordinates, peers and coworkers, and the employees themselves. The data, which are obtained anonymously (except for the boss), are then compiled into a feedback report comparing the employee's self-ratings to those of the boss, subordinates, and peers and coworkers. Usually, a consultant or human resource specialist discusses the results with the employee. The advantage of 360-degree programs is that negative feedback ("You don't listen.") is often more credible if heard from several people. For example, one boss who received 360-degree feedback thought he was a great writer, so he regularly criticized and corrected his subordinates' reports. Though the subordinates never discussed it among themselves, they all complained about his writing in the 360-degree feedback and mentioned that he should quit rewriting their reports. After receiving the feedback, he apologized and stopped.[90]

A word of caution, though. About half of the companies using 360-degree feedback for performance appraisal now use the feedback only for developmental purposes. They found that sometimes with raises and promotions on the line, peers and subordinates would sometimes give high ratings in order to get high ratings from others and that they would also distort ratings to harm competitors or help people they liked. A senior manager at a New York City marketing company agreed, saying that 360-degree feedback "also allows people to vent their frustrations and anger on bosses and colleagues in an insensitive way."[91] On the other hand, studies clearly show that ratees prefer to receive feedback from multiple raters, so 360-degree feedback is likely to continue to grow in popularity.[92]

Herbert Meyer, who has been studying performance appraisal feedback for more than 30 years, made the following specific recommendations for sharing performance feedback with employees.[93] First, managers should separate developmental feedback, which is designed to improve future performance, from administrative feedback, which is used as a reward for past performance, such as for raises. When managers give developmental feedback, they're acting as coaches, but when they give administrative feedback, they're acting as judges. These roles, coaches and judges, are clearly incompatible. As coaches, managers are encouraging, pointing out opportunities for growth and improvement, and employees are typically open and receptive to feedback. But as judges, managers are evaluative, and employees are typically defensive and closed to feedback. Jean Gatz, a training expert in Baton Rouge, said, "Most of us don't like to sit down and hear where we're lacking and where we need to improve. It's like sitting down with your mom and dad and they're telling you, 'We know what's best.'"[94]

Second, Meyer suggests that performance appraisal feedback sessions be based on self-appraisals, in which employees carefully assess their own strengths, weaknesses, successes, and failures in writing. Because employees play an active role in the review of their performance, managers can be coaches rather than judges. Also, because the focus is on future goals and development, both employees and managers are likely to be more satisfied with the process and more committed to future plans and changes. See Exhibit 14.15 for the list of topics that Meyer recommends for discussion in performance appraisal feedback sessions.

One concern about self-appraisals is that employees will be overly positive when evaluating their performance. However, when the focus is on development and not administrative assessment, studies show that self-appraisals lead to more candid self-assessments than traditional supervisory reviews.[95]

Third, Meyer suggests eliminating the "grading" aspect of performance appraisal, in which employees are ranked on a 1 to 5 scale or are scored as below average, average, above average, or exceptional. He says that "Assigning a numerical or adjectival grade, such as 'satisfactory,' 'excellent,' 'adequate,' 'outstanding,' or 'poor' to overall performance or specific performance tends to obstruct rather than facilitate constructive discussion. It treats a mature person like a school child. The administrative action taken, such as the amount of salary increase or a promotion, will communicate an overall appraisal better than will a grade."[96]

---

**EXHIBIT 14.15**

WHAT TO DISCUSS IN A PERFORMANCE APPRAISAL FEEDBACK SESSION

1. Overall progress—an analysis of accomplishments and shortcomings.
2. Problems encountered in meeting job requirements.
3. Opportunities to improve performance.
4. Long-range plans, opportunities—for the job and for the individual's career.
5. General discussion of possible plans and goals for the coming year.

**Source:** H.H. Meyer, "A Solution to the Performance Appraisal Feedback Enigma," *Academy of Management Executive 5*, no. 1 (1991): 68-76.

Most employees and managers intensely dislike the performance appraisal process. However, some of the problems associated with appraisals can be avoided by accurately measuring job performance and effectively sharing performance feedback with employees. Managers are prone to three kinds of rating errors: central tendency, halo, and leniency error. One way to minimize rating errors is to use better appraisal measures, such as objective measures of performance or behavioral observation scales. Another method is to directly train performance raters to minimize errors and more accurately rate the important dimensions of job performance.

After gathering accurate performance data, the next step is to share performance feedback with employees. One way to overcome the inherent difficulties in performance appraisal feedback is to provide 360-degree feedback, in which feedback is obtained from four sources: the boss, subordinates, peers and coworkers, and the employees themselves. Feedback tends to be more credible if heard from several sources. Traditional performance appraisal feedback sessions can be improved by separating developmental and administrative feedback, by basing feedback discussions on employee self-appraisals, and by eliminating the "grading" aspect.

# Keeping Qualified Workers

When Toyota built a huge new truck factory in the small town of Princeton, Indiana, and began offering incredible benefits and paying workers $19 an hour, it sent a shockwave through the pay scales of employers in the area. Not surprisingly, more than 50,000 people applied for the 1,300 jobs at Toyota's plant. Of course, many of the highly skilled workers that Toyota hired used to work for other employers for much less pay. As a result, to keep workers from jumping ship to Toyota and other high-paying companies in the area (Alcoa pays $16.50 an hour), companies throughout the Princeton area responded by increasing their pay and benefits.[97]

Gene Weisheit, director of human resources at Evansville Veneer & Lumber Company, said that increasing wages is the only way to not be left "scraping the bottom of the barrel in a strong economy." Accordingly, his company just raised its starting pay by 50 cents to $9 an hour. His more experienced workers now earn more than $11 an hour. However, other companies, like Flanders Electric Motor Service, have focused on increasing benefits to retain workers. While Flanders Electric always sponsored one bowling team, it now sponsors several teams in men's and women's bowling leagues. It also pays for health club memberships at the local YMCA and conducts blood pressure screening during work hours. Flanders coowner David Patterson said, "We didn't get intense with our wellness and other programs until we started to lose people to Toyota."

Unfortunately, keeping their employees will become even more difficult when Toyota hires another 1,000 well-paid workers to build a sports utility vehicle at the same manufacturing plant.

*After reading this next two sections, you should be able to*
*7. describe basic compensation strategies and how they affect human resource practice.*
*8. discuss the four kinds of employee separations: termination, downsizing, retirements, and turnover.*

## 7. Compensation

*__Compensation__ includes both the financial and nonfinancial rewards that organizations give employees in exchange for their work. Let's learn more about compensation by examining the 7.1 compensation decisions that managers must make and 7.2 the role that employment benefits play in compensating today's employees.*

EXHIBIT 14.16

KINDS OF COMPENSATION DECISIONS

| Pay Level | Pay Variability | Pay Structure | Employment Benefits |
|---|---|---|---|
| Job Evaluation | Piecework | Hierarchical | Cafeteria Plans |
| | Commission | Compressed | Flexible Plans |
| | Profit Sharing | | Payroll Deductions |
| | Employee Stock Ownership Plans | | |
| | Stock Options | | |

## 7.1 Compensation Decisions

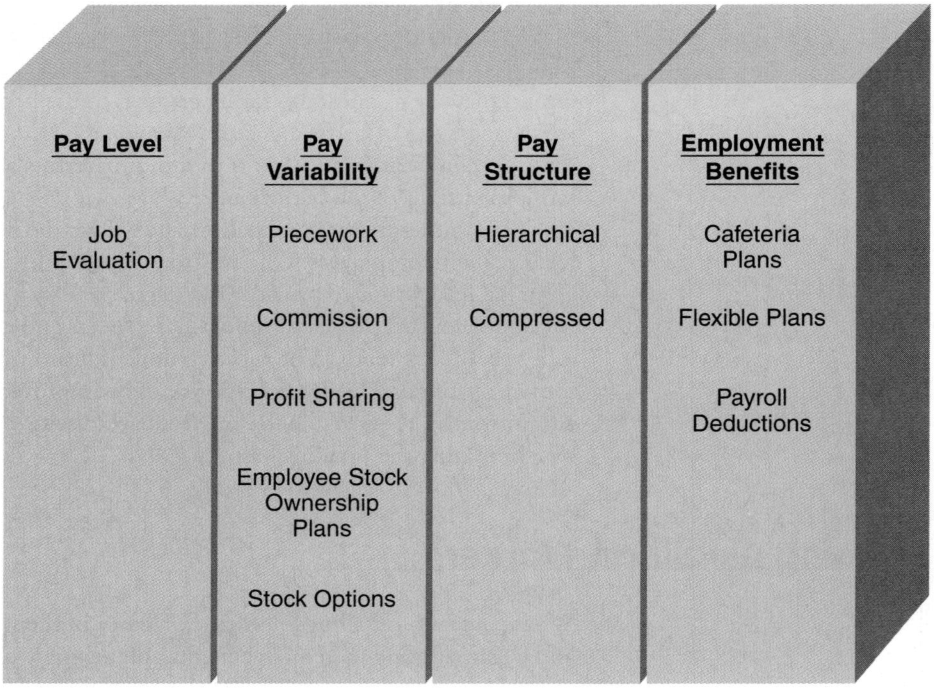

**compensation**
the financial and nonfinancial rewards that organizations give employees in exchange for their work

**job evaluation**
a process that determines the worth of each job in a company by evaluating the market value of the knowledge, skills, and requirements needed to perform it

As shown in Exhibit 14.16, there are four basic kinds of compensation decisions: pay level, pay variability, pay structure, and employment benefits. We'll discuss employment benefits in the next subsection.[98]

*Pay-level decisions* are decisions about whether to pay workers at a level that is below, above, or at current market wages. Companies use job evaluation to set their pay structures. **Job evaluation** determines the worth of each job by determining the market value of the knowledge, skills, and requirements needed to perform it. After conducting a job evaluation, most companies try to pay the "going rate," meaning the current market wage. There are always companies, however, such as Evansville Veneer & Lumber Company and Flanders Electric Motor Service mentioned above, whose financial situation leads them to pay considerably less than current market wages. The childcare industry, for example, has chronic difficulties filling jobs, because it pays well below market wages. Also, because wages are so low ($10,000 to $19,000 a year), the applicants it attracts are increasingly less qualified. Donna Krause, who runs Creative Learning and Child Care in Dundalk, Maryland, lost five childcare teachers one August when all were hired away by higher paying public school systems. While the teachers who left all had college degrees, none of their replacements did.[99]

Some companies choose to pay above-average wages to attract and keep employees. *Above-market wages* can attract a larger, more qualified pool of job applicants, increase the rate of job acceptance, decrease the time it takes to fill positions, and increase how long employees stay.[100] Of course, it's very difficult to attract and keep good employees when your company has to compete with the likes of Toyota that intentionally pays above-market wages. Government agencies, which typically pay well below market wages, find that it can take months and sometimes years to fill job openings, as applicants go to the private sector for much more money. Tom Cunningham, senior economist at the Federal Reserve Bank of Atlanta, summed it up when he said, "In a tight labor market, no one wants to inspect pig farms" for the government for poor wages.[101]

*Pay-variability decisions* are decisions concerning the extent to which employees' pay varies with individual and organizational performance. Linking pay to organizational performance is intended to increase employee motivation, effort, and job performance. Piecework, sales commission, profit sharing, employee stock ownership plans, and stock options are common pay-variability options. For instance, under **piecework** pay plans, employees are paid a set rate for each item produced up to some standard (e.g., $0.35 per item produced for output up to 100 units per day). Once productivity exceeds the standard, employees are paid a set amount for each unit of output over the standard (e.g., $0.45 for each unit above 100 units). Sales **commission** is another kind of pay variability, in which salespeople are paid a percentage of the purchase price of items they sell. The more they sell, the more they earn.

Because pay plans such as piecework and commissions are based on individual performance, they can reduce the incentive that people have to work together. Therefore, companies also use group incentives (discussed in Chapter 13) and organizational incentives, such as profit sharing, employee stock ownership plans, and stock options, to encourage teamwork and cooperation.

**Profit sharing** is the payment of a portion of the organization's profits to employees over and above their regular compensation. The more profitable the company, the more profit is shared. In 2000, when Ford Motor Company reported record profits, each of its automobile assembly workers received a profit-sharing check of approximately $8,000. However, in 2001, when Ford lost money, no one got checks since there wasn't a profit to distribute.[102]

**Employee stock ownership plans (ESOPs)** compensate employees by awarding them shares of the company stock in addition to their regular compensation. At McKay Nursery in Waterloo, Wisconsin, Joe Hernandez, a 41-year-old migrant worker, makes $20,000 a year working from April to November. But Joe also gets an additional 20 to 25 percent in company stock. So far, he's accumulated more than $80,000 through the company ESOP.

**Stock options** give employees the right to purchase shares of stock at a set price. It works like this. Let's say that you are awarded the right (or option) to buy 100 shares of stock from the company for $5 a share. If the company's stock price rises to $15 a share, you can exercise your options and make $1000. Because of your stock options, you pay the company $500, 100 shares for $5 a share. However, since the stock sells for $15 in the stock market, you've made $1,000 (100 shares which have increased $10 in value, from $5 to $15). Of course, as company profits and share values increase, stock options become even more valuable to employees. However, stock options have no value if a company's stock falls below the stock option "grant price," the price at which options have been issued to you. For instance, the options you have on 100 shares of stock with a grant price of $5 aren't going to do you a lot of good if the company's stock is worth $2.50. Why exercise your stock options and pay $5 a share for stock that sells for $2.50 a share in the stock market? (Stock options are said to be "underwater" when the grant price for a stock is lower than the market price for a stock.) Proponents of stock options argue that this gives employees and managers a strong incentive to work hard to make the company successful. If they do, the company's profits and stock price increase, and their stock options increase in value. If they don't, profits stagnate or turn into losses, and their stock options decrease in value or become worthless. To learn more about ESOPs and stock options, see The National Center for Employee Ownership (**http://www.nceo.org**).

*Pay-structure decisions* are concerned with internal pay distributions, meaning the extent to which people in the company receive very different levels of pay.[102] With *hierarchical pay structures*, there are big differences from one pay level to another. The largest pay levels are for people near the top of the pay distribution. The basic idea behind hierarchical pay structures is that large differences in pay between jobs or organizational levels should motivate people to work harder to obtain those higher-paying jobs.

---

**piecework**
a compensation system in which employees are paid a set rate for each item they produce

**commission**
a compensation system in which employees earn a percentage of each sale they make

**profit sharing**
a compensation system in which a percentage of company profits is paid to employees in addition to their regular compensation

**employee stock ownership plans (ESOPs)**
a compensation system that awards employees shares of company stock in addition to their regular compensation

**stock options**
a compensation system that gives employees the right to purchase shares of stock at a set price, even if the value of the stock increases above that price

549

# BeenThereDoneThat

## GE's Legendary CEO Jack Welch Discusses How to Motivate Employees with Performance Feedback and Stock Options

For two decades, CEO Jack Welch, now retired, made General Electric the best-run and most profitable corporation in the world. In this *Wall Street Journal* article, Welch discusses how to motivate workers with straightforward performance feedback and stock options. In general, Welch says, "You have to go along with a can of fertilizer in one hand and water in the other and constantly throw both on the flowers. If they grow, you have a beautiful garden. If they don't, you cut them out. That's what management is all about."

**Q:** How much time do you spend on people issues?

**A:** At least 50 percent of my time. I'll show you. [He pulls out a huge notebook filled with charts that rate each professional in one unit.] Here would be the vitality rating. Everyone knows where they are.

1's are the top 10 percent. These are the top people. 2's are the next-strongest 15 percent. 3's are the middle 50 percent. The ones in the middle have a real future. Then 4's are the cautionary 15 percent. They can move to the left. 5's are the least effective 10 percent. We've got to get rid of them. We don't want to see these people again.

On every performance appraisal, they are being told, "You are at 1, 2, 3, 4, or 5." So no one will ever come in with any chance to say, "I was always told I was great. And now you are telling me I am not great."

**Q:** And your rating affects your chance at stock options, right?

**A:** All the 1's will get options. About 90 percent—plus of the 2's will get options. About half of the 3's will get options. And the 4's get no stock options.

See, there's an option chart in here. Who got options? Who didn't? Here it says what happens. . . . Are they out? How did you reward these people? Do you want to love and hug these people? Kiss them? Nurture them? Give them everything?

**Q:** What is that like for them? In a sense, they are all up against each other then. Doesn't that put a lot of stress on them?

**A:** No. There is plenty of room. See, 3's are okay. This is not punishing 3's. This is not at all that. I don't know if this is more rigorous than other companies. But I think it is our product.

**Q:** In this example, it's broken down evenly: 10 percent are 1, 15 percent are 2, 50 percent are 3, 15 percent are 4 and 10 percent are 5. Do you always grade on a curve?

**A:** We demand it of every group. Because every group will fight like hell to say, "I have all 1's." If I get 10 people, one is a 1 and one is a 5.

**Q:** How do you know when to cut somebody loose?

**A:** With the 5's, it is clear as a bell. I think they know it. And you know it. It isn't even a hard conversation.

It is better for everyone. They go on to a new place, a new life, a new start.

The decision is harder with the 4's. The difference between a 1 and a 3, though, is not that little a jump. It is 10 people. It is 15 people. When you get the top 10 percent performers, their output and energizing impact is overwhelming compared to 4's.

**Q:** How do you motivate those average employees?

**A:** By telling them they can get to be 2's and 1's, and telling them they are eligible for options. But only the best of them will get options.

**Q:** How many actually get options?

**A:** We have about 85,000 professionals. And we give options to 10,000 to 12,000 a year—but not always to the same people. So about one-third of our people, about 29,000, have gotten options, although not all in any one year.

**Q:** How do you get your message down through the ranks?

**A:** I would never want to run this company without Crotonville [GE's management training center in Crotonville, New York]. About 5,000 people go through there each year. I will see about 1,000 myself for four hours, plus another two hours at the bar.

**Q:** When it comes to recognizing employees, what counts more, financial rewards or the personal touch?

**A:** I think showering rewards on people for excellence is an important part of the management process. There's nothing I like more than giving big raises. I don't want anyone with their nose against the glass, I want them to go right through the glass—maybe because I had my nose against the glass.

You have to get rewarded in the soul and the wallet.

The money isn't enough, but a plaque isn't enough either. Years ago I worked for somebody who was giving out medals to employees who got patents. I wanted to give them more cash. This guy was a fat cat who had a lot of money. He said money is so crass, just give them the medal. I just thought that was wrong; you have to give both.

**Q:** How do you evaluate your top executives? Do you rate them against each other?

**A:** I compare them against their competition and never against each other. We have one plan where half the reward executives get is for the performance of their business and half for the performance of the whole company. But if the company doesn't make it and the business has a greater performance, the bonus is zero—because no boats get to the shore if the Titanic sinks.

**Source:** C. Hymowitz & M. Murray, "Boss Talk: Raises and Praise or Out the Door—How GE's Chief Rates and Spurs His Employees," *The Wall Street Journal*, 21 June 1999, B1. This interview was edited for inclusion in this textbook.

Many publicly owned companies have hierarchical pay structures by virtue of the huge amounts they pay their top managers and CEOs. For example, the average CEO now makes 475 times more than the average blue-collar worker. This enormous difference in pay occurs because CEOs almost always receive much larger annual pay increases than regular workers. For instance, from 1998 to 2000, CEO pay rose by 36 percent, 17 percent, and 6 percent, compared to an average of just 2 to 4 percent per year for blue-collar and white-collar workers.[104]

By contrast, *compressed pay structures* typically have fewer pay levels and smaller differences in pay between pay levels. Pay is less dispersed and more similar across jobs in the company. The basic idea behind compressed pay structures is that similar pay levels should lead to higher levels of cooperation, feelings of fairness and a common purpose, and better group and team performance.

So should companies choose hierarchical or compressed pay structures? The evidence isn't straightforward, but studies seem to indicate that there are significant problems with the hierarchical approach. The most damaging is that there appears to be little link between organizational performance and the pay of top managers.[105] Furthermore, studies of professional athletes indicate that hierarchical pay structures (e.g., paying superstars 40 to 50 times more than the lowest-paid athlete on the team) hurt the performance of teams and individual players.[106] For now, the key seems to be that hierarchical pay structures work best for independent work, where it's easy to determine the contributions of individual performers and where little coordination with others is needed to get the job done. In other words, hierarchical pay structures work best when clear links can be drawn between individual performance and individual rewards. By contrast, compressed pay structures, that is, paying everyone similar amounts of money, seem to work best for interdependent work, in which employees must work with each other. But some companies are pursuing a middle ground, in which they try to balance hierarchical and compressed pay structures by giving ordinary workers the chance to earn more through ESOPs, stock options, and profit sharing.

## 7.2 Employment Benefits

**employment benefits**
a method of rewarding employees that includes virtually any kind of compensation other than wages or salaries

**Employment benefits** include virtually any kind of compensation other than direct wages paid to employees.[107] Three employee benefits are mandated by law: social security, worker's compensation, and unemployment insurance. However, to attract and retain a good work force, most organizations offer a wide variety of benefits, including retirement plans and pensions, paid holidays, paid vacations, sick leave, health insurance, life insurance, dental care, eye care, daycare facilities, paid personal days, legal assistance, physical fitness facilities, educational assistance, and discounts on company products and services. Currently, benefits cost organizations about 27 percent of their payroll, with an average cost per employee of $10,720 for a basic benefits plan.[108]

Managers should understand that benefits are not likely to improve employee motivation and performance. However, benefits do affect job satisfaction, employee decisions about staying or leaving the company, and the company's attractiveness to job applicants.[109] One way in which organizations make their benefit plans more attractive is through **cafeteria benefit plans** or **flexible benefit plans**, which allow employees to choose which benefits they receive, up to a certain dollar value.[110] Many cafeteria or flexible benefit plans start with a core of benefits, such as health insurance and life insurance that are available to all employees. Then employees are allowed to select other benefits that best fit their needs, up to a predetermined dollar amount. Some organizations provide several packages of benefits from which employees may choose. Each package is of equivalent value; however, the mix of benefits differs. For example, older employees may prefer more benefit dollars spent on retirement plans, while younger employees may prefer additional vacation days.

**cafeteria benefit plans (flexible benefit plans)**
plans that allow employees to choose which benefits they receive, up to a certain dollar value

Payroll deductions are one of the more popular benefits options, especially for small companies. With payroll deductions, organizations pass their buying power on to employees. For example, some employees can save as much as 20 percent on auto insurance if they purchase it through their employer. Furthermore, since the fees are automatically taken out of their checks, employees don't have to worry about setting aside the money to pay their premium every six months. The advantage for employers is that they don't pay for the benefit; employees do. The advantages for employees are low costs and an easy payment method via automatic payroll deductions.[111]

The drawback to flexible benefit plans has been the high cost of administering these programs. However, with advances in information processing technology and HRISs, the cost of administering benefits has begun to drop in recent years.

### Review 7
#### Compensation

Compensation includes both the financial and nonfinancial rewards that organizations give employees in exchange for their work. There are four basic kinds of compensation decisions: pay level, pay variability, pay structure, and employment benefits. Pay-level decisions determine whether workers will receive wages below, above, or at current market levels. Pay-variability decisions concern the extent to which pay varies with individual and organizational performance. Piecework, sales commission, profit sharing, employee stock ownership plans, and stock options are common pay-variability options. Pay-structure decisions concern the extent to which people in the company receive very different levels of pay. Hierarchical pay structures work best for independent work, while compressed pay structures work best for interdependent work.

Employee benefits include virtually any kind of compensation other than direct wages paid to employees. Flexible or cafeteria benefits plans offer employees a wide variety of benefits, improve job satisfaction, increase the chances that employees will stay with companies, and make organizations more attractive to job applicants. The cost of administering benefits has begun to drop in recent years.

## 8. Employee Separations

**employee separation**
the voluntary or involuntary loss of an employee

**Employee separation** is a broad term covering the loss of an employee for any reason. *Involuntary separation* occurs when employers decide to terminate or lay off employees. *Voluntary separation* occurs when employees decide to quit or retire. Because employee separations affect recruiting, selection, training, and compensation, organizations should forecast the number of employees they expect to lose through terminations, layoffs, turnover, or retirements when doing human resource planning.

*Let's explore employee separation by examining 8.1 terminations, 8.2 downsizing, 8.3 retirements, and 8.4 turnover.*

### 8.1 Terminating Employees

Hopefully, the words "You're fired!" have never been directed at you. Lots of people hear them, however, as more than 400,000 people a year get fired from their jobs. Getting fired is a terrible thing, but many managers make it even worse by bungling the firing process, needlessly provoking the people who were fired, and unintentionally inviting lawsuits. For example, one worker found out he had been fired after a restaurant told him that his company credit card was no longer active. The top office manager for a professional sports team returned to the office to find his parking space taken by someone interviewing for his job. The CEO of a clothing store company gave all of his top managers a fruit basket every holiday season, except his top finance manager who was soon fired.[112] Finally, workers at a high-tech company know that they've been fired when their security codes no longer open their office doors or the front door to their office buildings.[113] How would you feel if you had been fired in one of these ways? While firing is never pleasant (and managers hate firings nearly as much as employees do), there are several things managers can do to minimize the problems inherent in firing employees.

First, in most firing situations, firing should not be the first option. Instead, employees should be given a chance to change their behavior. When problems arise, em-

552

ployees should have ample warning and must be specifically informed as to the nature and seriousness of the trouble they're in. After being notified, they should be given sufficient time to change. If the problems continue, they should again be counseled about their job performance, what could be done to improve it, and the possible consequences if things don't change (e.g., written reprimand, suspension without pay, or firing). Sometimes this is enough to solve the problem. Outplacement specialist Laurence Stybel tells about a large hospital that was getting ready to fire its director of radiology because of his bad attitude and increasing rudeness to coworkers. Rather than fire him, hospital management put him on probation and hired a consultant to counsel him about working with others. Within weeks, his attitude and behavior changed, and the hospital avoided firing him and the expense of replacing him (which could have included a lawsuit).[114] However, after several rounds of warnings and discussions, if the problem isn't corrected, the employee may be terminated.[115]

Second, employees should be fired for a good reason. Employers used to hire and fire employees under the legal principle of "employment at will," which allowed them to fire employees for a good reason, a bad reason, or no reason at all. (Employees could also quit for good reason, bad reason, or no reason whenever they desired.) However, as employees began contesting their firings in court, the principle of wrongful discharge emerged. **Wrongful discharge** is a legal doctrine that requires employers to have a job-related reason to terminate employees. In other words, just like other major human resource decisions, termination decisions should be made on the basis of job-related factors, such as violating company rules or consistently poor performance. And with former employees winning 68 percent of wrongful discharge cases, managers should record the job-related reasons for the termination, document specific instances of rule violations or continued poor performance, and keep notes and documents from the counseling sessions held with employees.[116]

Finally, to reduce the chances of a wrongful discharge suit, employees should always be fired in private. State the reason for discharge, but don't go into detail or engage in a lengthy discussion with the employee. Make every attempt to be as kind and respectful as possible when informing someone that they're being fired. It is permissible, and sometimes a good idea, to have a witness present. However, this person should be from human resources or part of the employees' chain of command, such as their supervisor's boss. Company security may be nearby, but should not be in the room unless an employee has made direct threats toward others. Finally, managers should be careful not to publicly criticize the employee who has just been fired, as this can also lead to wrongful discharge lawsuit. In general, unless someone has a "business reason to know" why someone was fired, the reasons and details related to someone's firing should remain confidential.[117]

### 8.2 Downsizing

**Downsizing** is the planned elimination of jobs in a company. Whether it's because of cost cutting, declining market share, or over-aggressive hiring and growth, it's estimated that companies eliminate more than 3 million jobs a year.[118] Two-thirds of companies that downsize will downsize a second time within a year. For example, Applied Materials, based in California's Silicon Valley, downsized 1,500 workers the first time it downsized, followed by another 2,000 workers less than three months later.[119]

Does downsizing work? In theory, downsizing is supposed to lead to higher productivity and profits, better stock performance, and increased organizational flexibility. However, numerous studies demonstrate that it doesn't. For instance, a 15-year study of downsizing found that downsizing 10 percent of a company's work force only produces a 1.5 percent decrease in costs, that firms that downsized increased their stock price by 4.7 percent over three years, compared to 34.3 percent for firms that didn't, and that profitability and productivity were generally not improved by downsizing.[120] These results make it clear that the best strategy is to conduct effective human resource planning and avoid downsizing altogether. Indeed, downsizing should always be used as a measure of last resort.

However, if companies do find themselves in financial or strategic situations where downsizing is required for survival, they should train managers how to break the news to

**wrongful discharge**
a legal doctrine that requires employers to have a job-related reason to terminate employees

**downsizing**
the planned elimination of jobs in a company

553

EXHIBIT 14.17

GUIDELINES FOR CONDUCTING LAYOFFS

1. Provide clear reasons and explanations for the layoffs.
2. To avoid laying off employees with critical or irreplaceable skills, knowledge, and expertise, get input from human resources, the legal department, and several levels of management.
3. Train managers how to tell employees that they are being laid off (i.e., stay calm; make the meeting short; explain why, but don't be personal; and provide information about the immediate concerns, such as benefits, job search, and collecting personal goods).
4. Give employees the bad news early in the day, and try to avoid laying off employees before holidays.
5. Provide outplacement services and counseling to help laid-off employees find new jobs.
6. Communicate with survivors to explain how the company and their jobs will change.

**Source:** M. Boyle, "The Not-So-Fine Art of the Layoff," *Fortune*, 19 March 2001, 209.

**outplacement services**
employment-counseling services offered to employees who are losing their jobs because of downsizing

downsized employees, have senior managers explain in detail why downsizing is necessary, and time the announcement so employees hear it from the company and not from other sources, such as TV or newspaper reports.[121] Finally, companies should do everything they can to help downsized employees find other jobs. One of the best ways to do this is to use **outplacement services** that provide employment-counseling services for employees faced with downsizing. Outplacement services often include advice and training in preparing résumés and getting ready for job interviews, and even identifying job opportunities in other companies. Exhibit 14.17 provides additional guidelines for conducting layoffs.

Extensive outplacement programs not only help laid off employees, but also help the company maintain a positive image in the community affected by downsizing. Steps such as these also help employees remain productive during their final days at the company. For example, when faced with sluggish sales, the E.D. Smith manufacturing company decided to close its Byhalia, Mississippi, plant. One hundred and twenty employees, some of whom had worked there for 30 years, found themselves without jobs. Two months before the plant closed, the company brought in a national outplacement firm to help employees find new jobs. A job development center was established within the plant to provide training in job search techniques, interviewing skills, and résumé writing. In addition, hundreds of job openings were posted at the center. The company also advertised the availability of its employees by sending letters to prospective employers. The letter stated, in part, "These employees are skilled in such areas as purchasing, quality assurance, shipping and receiving, forklift operations, production, inventory control, process cooks, and blenders. These employees are loyal, reliable, and dedicated. They have extensive experience in a fast-paced production environment."[122]

Companies also need to pay attention to remaining employees, the "survivors," after layoffs have occurred. Susan Bowman, executive vice president for human resources at Genuity, an Internet company that went through significant downsizing, said, "These are the people who are left running the company. Intuitively you have to know that people are distracted by these events."[123] Management consultant Diane Durken said, "The people who are left behind start looking behind their backs and saying, 'Am I next?' They need to be rejuvenated, so they can refocus on the future. Honesty and integrity are the core of this."[124] The key to working with layoff survivors is communication, communication, and communication. "The worst thing managers can do is what they want to do, which is hide in the office," says management consultant Joan Caruso. Therefore, immediately following the layoffs at Genuity, managers met with small groups of employees to talk about how the company and their jobs would be affected.[125]

## 8.3 Retirement

**early retirement incentive programs (ERIPs)**

programs that offer financial benefits to employees to encourage them to retire early

**Early retirement incentive programs (ERIPs)** offer financial benefits to employees to encourage them to retire early. Companies use ERIPs to reduce the number of employees in the organization, to lower costs by eliminating positions after employees retire, to lower costs by replacing high-paid retirees with lower-paid, less-experienced employees, or to create openings and job opportunities for people inside the company. For example, the state of Wyoming offered its employees a lump-sum bonus, additional insurance benefits, and increased monthly retirement payments to encourage early retirement. Its ERIP must have been fairly attractive because 56 percent of the state employees eligible for early retirement accepted. Thirty percent of the 437 positions vacated by early retirees remained empty, saving the state $23.2 million over the first 46 months of the program and a projected $65 million over eight years. After accounting for the costs of the increased early retirement benefits, the predicted savings came to more than $148,000 per retiree.[126]

The biggest problem with most ERIPs is accurately predicting who and how many will accept early retirement. The company will likely lose both good and poor performers and sometimes more workers than they expect. For example, Ameritech Corporation, the largest telephone company in the Midwest, offered an ERIP consisting of a $5,000 educational assistance program to retrain workers, financial planning counseling, and outplacement advice and guidance. Since most pension benefits are based on a formula including years of service and employee age, the core of Ameritech's program was the "three-plus-three enhancement," which added three years to the employees' age and three years to their years of service to help them qualify for greater retirement benefits. Ameritech carefully identified the number of employees near retirement age and estimated that 5,000 to 6,000 of its 48,000 employees would take advantage of the program. Instead, nearly 22,000 employees accepted the ERIP offer and applied for early retirement![127]

## 8.4 Employee Turnover

**employee turnover**

loss of employees who voluntarily choose to leave the company

**functional turnover**

loss of poor-performing employees who voluntarily choose to leave a company

**dysfunctional turnover**

loss of high-performing employees who voluntarily choose to leave a company

**Employee turnover** is the loss of employees who voluntarily choose to leave the company. In general, most companies try to keep the rate of employee turnover low to reduce recruiting, hiring, training, and replacement costs. However, not all kinds of employee turnover are bad for organizations. In fact, some turnover can actually be good. For instance, **functional turnover** is the loss of poor-performing employees who choose to leave the organization.[128] Functional turnover gives the organization a chance to replace poor performers with better replacements. In fact, one study found that simply replacing poor-performing leavers with average replacements would increase the revenues produced by retail salespeople in an upscale department store by $112,000 per person per year.[129] By contrast, **dysfunctional turnover**, the loss of high performers who choose to leave, is a costly loss to the organization.

Employee turnover should be carefully analyzed to determine exactly who is choosing to leave the organization, good or poor performers. If the company is losing too many high performers, managers should determine the reasons and find ways to reduce the loss of valuable employees. The company may have to raise salary levels, offer enhanced benefits, or improve working conditions to retain skilled workers. One of the best ways to influence functional and dysfunctional turnover is to link pay directly to performance. A study of four sales forces found that when pay was strongly linked to performance via sales commissions and bonuses, poor performers were much more likely to leave (i.e., functional turnover). By contrast, poor performers were much more likely to stay when paid large, guaranteed monthly salaries and small sales commissions and bonuses.[130]

## Review 8
### Employee Separations

Employee separation is the loss of an employee, which can occur voluntarily or involuntarily. Before firing or terminating employees, managers should give employees a chance to improve. If firing becomes necessary, it should be done because of job-related factors, such as violating company rules or consistently performing poorly. Downsizing is supposed to

555

lead to higher productivity and profits, better stock performance, and increased organizational flexibility, but studies show that it doesn't. The best strategy is to downsize only as a last resort. Companies that do downsize should offer outplacement services to help employees find other jobs. Companies use early retirement incentive programs to reduce the number of employees in the organization, lower costs, and create openings and job opportunities for people inside the company. The biggest problem with ERIPs is accurately predicting who and how many will accept early retirement. Companies generally try to keep the rate of employee turnover low to reduce costs. However, functional turnover can be good for organizations, because it offers the chance to replace poor performers with better workers. Managers should analyze employee turnover to determine who is resigning and take steps to reduce the loss of good performers.

## What Really Happened?

The Bellagio Hotel, one of the most lavish resorts in Las Vegas, has been in business for several years and is a smashing success. Critics and customers alike rave about the service, its fantastic restaurants, and the beauty of the hotel itself. However, just 24 weeks before it opened, success was anything but guaranteed. At that point, Arte Nathan, the Bellagio's vice president of human resources, had to find a way to review 100,000 résumés, conduct 25,000 interviews, and hire and train a final staff of 9,600 people. Let's find out what really happened at the Bellagio casino and resort when Nathan had to screen, interview, hire, and train so many people in such a short time.

**Your job is to hire a staff of 9,600 managers and workers, capable of providing service as lavish as the resort itself. The only catch is that 100,000 people are expected to apply, and you've only got 24 weeks to screen 100,000 résumés, conduct 25,000 interviews, and hire and train the final staff of 9,600. But since everything is now run using paper and pencil forms, how can you expect to develop a fully electronic hiring and screening system at the same time you're trying to hire 9,600 people?** Computerized human resource information systems (HRISs) improve human resource planning by gathering, analyzing, storing, and disseminating information (personal, educational, work history, performance, and pro-

motions) related to human resource management activities. Human resource information systems can be used for transaction processing, such as payroll checks and routine reports, and for employee self-service transactions, such as 24-hour Web access allowing instant changes to benefit and retirement packages. But the Bellagio needed an HRIS for human resource decision support, such as analyzing résumés, background screening, and pre-employment testing.

Arte Nathan said, "The only way that we could hire so many so fast was to move everything online—the entire application process, plus all of the personnel files that resulted from hiring 9,600 people. That meant we had to build one of the first fully integrated online job-application and HR systems. I told our managers that this technology would give them hire-and-fire responsibility, which they say they want. It would give them complete authority, which they rarely get. And it would make them 100 percent accountable for their decisions, which they never want. Going online would take out of the loop the people who shouldn't be there: human resources. I'm an HR guy, but I firmly believe that my job is to give our managers the tools that they need to perform—and then get out of the way."

The only problem, of course, was that Nathan and his people had to build their human resource information system from scratch. So Nathan

taught himself about client-server technology and open database architecture. He took computer classes and visited Microsoft, IBM, and other technology companies. Then, when his team was prepared with a thorough plan, they approached Bellagio's CEO, as well as the chief financial officer and chief information officer of MGM-Mirage Resorts. "I told them that I needed $1 million to hire a bunch of people and to build a paperless HR system," Nathan said. I promised that we would deliver the ROI within two years. Bellagio cost $1.6 billion to build. I blew another million. Asking for an extra million, under any circumstances, is serious."

However, Nathan and his team spent the money well, developing a computerized application with 168 questions covering 633 different kinds of jobs, from card dealers and hotel maids, to accountants and vice presidents. By bringing in 100 people at a time to test the computerized application system, the development team was able to make 2,800 improvements that simplified the process for applicants, allowing them to complete the application in just 48 minutes. This allowed the Bellagio to process approximately 1,200 job applications per day.

**In addition to developing a process that can screen over 4,000 people per day, you also need to develop a brand new, standardized interview system that managers are comfortable with, that only takes 30 minutes to conduct, and that**

does a better job of screening and selecting candidates than traditional interviews.

In unstructured interviews, interviewers are free to ask applicants anything they want, and studies show that they do. For instance, because interviewers often disagree about which questions should be asked during interviews, different interviewers tend to ask applicants very different questions. Furthermore, individual interviewers even seem to have a tough time asking the same questions from one interview to the next. This high level of inconsistency lowers the validity of unstructured interviews as a selection device, because it becomes difficult to compare applicant responses. As a result, unstructured interviews do about half as well as structured interviews in accurately predicting which job applicants should be hired. By contrast, with structured interviews, standardized interview questions are prepared ahead of time, so that all applicants for the same kinds of jobs are asked the same job-related questions.

Like many companies these days, the Bellagio used structured interviews and behavioral interview questions (which ask applicants what they did in previous jobs that were similar to the job for which they are applying) to interview the one out of every four job applicants who made it through résumé screening. However, unlike most managers, the Bellagio's managers could sit at their desks and use the computerized résumé scoring system to schedule the three highest applicants for job interviews.

Nathan said, "For the interviews, hiring managers asked a set of questions [i.e., structured interviews] that we had developed for this process. They were behavioral questions, like 'Tell me about a time when you were working at the front desk, and a guest was late. What did you do when you couldn't find the reservation?' Managers had a PC embedded in their desktops, so the computers were unobtrusive, and the monitors displayed a rating sheet. Candidates were scored based on their answers, which were again ranked in numerical order and fed into the database. We had to use a formal system: If we had left it up to 180 managers to follow their own formats, we'd still be interviewing candidates today." By using a computerized, structured interview process, 180 managers were able to conduct 740 interviews per day. Managers received a week of training and were taught how to complete the interviews in just 30 minutes. Why 30 minutes? Because managers had only 10 weeks in which to conduct all of their interviews. Adding just 10 minutes per interview would have set the hiring process far behind schedule.

**Finally, once your managers have decided which 9,600 people to hire, you need to conduct thorough background checks before making them job offers. With millions of dollars to be spent and gambled at the Bellagio each day, it's critical that you hire honest people. In other words, you need people who don't lie about their qualifications on their résumés, people who won't be tempted to pocket money for themselves, and people without criminal backgrounds that could put the Bellagio or its guests at risk.**

Nearly all companies ask applicants to provide employment references, such as previous employers or coworkers, whom they can contact to learn more about job candidates. Background checks are used to verify the truthfulness and accuracy of information that applicants provide about themselves and to uncover negative, job-related background information not provided by applicants. Background checks are conducted by contacting educational institutions, prior employers, court records, police and governmental agencies, and other informational sources, either by telephone, mail, remote computer access, or in-person investigations.

At the Bellagio, if a job applicant had made it through résumé screening (a one in four chance), and then made it through the job interview process (a one in three chance), then only one step, a background check, remained before the company made a job offer. Arte Nathan said, "If a manager wanted to hire you, he would call up your file and click on 'Conduct a background check.' I had 18 law-enforcement officials looking into candidates' backgrounds. They'd get your application online and then check your employment, military, and education history to make sure that everything was okay. We rejected about 8 percent of our candidates at this stage for various reasons, such as lying on their applications. If you passed the background check and a drug test, the manager would then make the final hiring decision. If he clicked 'Yes' on your form, one of our HR staffers would invite you to a job-offer meeting."

In the end, what started out as a $1 million experiment to computerize résumé screening, interviews, and background checks, ended up saving the company $1.9 million. The human resource information system developed by the Bellagio is now being used at 15 other MGM resort properties. In fact, the system is so advanced that Cisco, the high-tech company that makes the routers that run the Internet, wants to create a system just like it for its managers.

**Sources:** B. Breen, "Full House: Executives at Las Vegas's Bellagio Hotel Screened 84,000 Candidates, Did 27,000 Interviews, And Hired 9,600 People—In 24 Weeks. Now Cisco Wants to Know How They Did It," *Fast Company*, 1 January 2000, 110. B. Carlino, "At Your Service: Fine-Dining Operators Hone Segment's Hospitality Hallmark," *Nation's Restaurant News*, 24 November 1997, 65. R. Hughes, "Wynn Win?" *Time*, 26 October 1998, 76. D. Muret, "Attitude: The Major Ingredient in Obtaining a New Job," *Amusement Business*, 14 December 1998, 38. J. Shapiro, "Employers Look to the Joint to Fill Jobs," *U.S. News & World Report*, 6 November 2000, 70.

557

360-degree feedback *(545)*
adverse impact *(521)*
assessment centers *(535)*
background checks *(532)*
behavioral observation scales (BOS) *(544)*
biographical data (biodata) *(534)*
bona fide occupational qualification (BFOQ) *(520)*
cafeteria benefit plans (flexible benefit plans) *(551)*
cognitive ability tests *(533)*
commission *(549)*
compensation *(548)*
disparate treatment *(521)*
downsizing *(553)*
dysfunctional turnover *(555)*
early retirement incentive programs (ERIPs) *(555)*
employee separation *(552)*
employee stock ownership plans (ESOPs) *(549)*

employee turnover *(555)*
employment benefits *(551)*
employment references *(532)*
external recruiting *(528)*
four-fifths (or 80 percent) rule *(521)*
functional turnover *(555)*
hostile work environment *(522)*
human resource information systems (HRIS) *(516)*
human resource management *(HRM) (512)*
human resource planning (HRP) *(514)*
internal recruiting *(528)*
interviews *(536)*
job analysis *(526)*
job description *(527)*
job evaluation *(548)*
job specifications *(527)*
needs assessment *(539)*
objective performance measures *(544)*
outplacement services *(554)*
performance appraisal *(543)*

personality tests *(534)*
piecework *(549)*
profit sharing *(549)*
quid pro quo sexual harassment *(522)*
rater training *(544)*
recruiting *(526)*
selection *(530)*
sexual harassment *(522)*
specific ability tests (aptitude tests) *(533)*
stock options *(549)*
structured interviews *(536)*
subjective performance measures *(544)*
training *(539)*
trait rating scales *(544)*
validation *(530)*
work force forecasting *(515)*
work sample tests *(534)*
wrongful discharge *(553)*

## What Would You Do-II

### A Bumpy Ride for Ford

Evaluating employees is something that you have grappled with for years, even before you became the CEO of Ford Motor Company. Particularly difficult has been measuring and evaluating the performance of your senior and middle-level managers in a fair and equitable way, while ensuring that managers are motivated and actually performing to preset standards. The system formerly used at Ford produced overly inflated evaluations, as managers were not informed of their deficiencies, nor given constructive feedback on how to improve their performance. This system proved problematic when economic factors created a need to downsize the managerial pool. Based on the old system's inadequacies, good-performing managers were just as likely to be laid off as poor-performing managers.

After several trial and error attempts, you thought you had come up with the perfect system. This system, modeled after one used at General Electric, is a top-down system in which managers are assembled into groups of 30 or 50 and are assigned a ranking based on their peers. Within this group, the managers are ranked according to the bell-curve, a statistical phenomenon used to approximate a "normal-distribution" from a random sample. Within the employee ranking system at Ford, once the 18,000 managers have been assigned to their specific groups, higher-level managers rank the employees, placing them into one of three categories. For this year's performance evaluations, you have mandated that the top 10 percent get an "A," the middle 80 percent a "B," and the bottom 10 percent a "C." Those employees ranked "B" or better will be rewarded with bonuses, salary increases, and stock options. For those who receive a "C,"

there will be no pay raise, and, if managers receive a "C" ranking for a second consecutive year, they will either be demoted or terminated. Under this system, those who receive a "C" ranking in the first year will be teamed up with a coach or mentor who will assist them in improving their deficiencies, thereby potentially improving their subsequent evaluations.

After months of discussion and weighing the pros and cons, this performance evaluation system was put in place. It is now in its second year, and you have just received word of a class-action age-discrimination lawsuit filed by 30 middle-aged white Ford managers. They claim that Ford is using this system to weed out older, higher-paid white managers. According to the lawsuit, Ford is so intent on pursuing racial and ethnic diversity, that older white males are disproportionately ranked in the bottom 10 percent. Further, the lawsuit contends that many managers are unfairly evaluated when ranked with their peers. Attorneys for the disgruntled managers claim that a few managers from a highly talented pool will be ranked at the bottom, whereas mediocre managers from an average pool may receive a "B" ranking. One manager in particular claims that there is no way that the performance evaluation method is fair since nine out of the 12 managers who ranked him had no idea who he was or what his skills and abilities were. Another claims that when he does his job correctly, there are no problems. However, when there are no problems, he is not visible and, therefore, is assumed to not be performing. This manager claims that the performance evaluation system leads to politicking in order to stay visible and be perceived by higher-level managers as a performer.

Given the debacle with Firestone tires and the Ford Explorer, stalled sales in an uncertain economy, and reduced revenue from your financial service arm (0 percent financing doesn't make the company any money), you certainly don't need any more rough roads, especially not internally. It's clear that you'll have to respond quickly *and* thoughtfully. You wonder how it is that GE hasn't had similar problems with its system. How can such a simple, random, bell-curve evaluation system be discriminatory? Maybe it's not the appraisal system that is the problem; maybe the company needs better proce- dures to deal with employee separation. But for the moment, the issue is about performance appraisals. You've got to evaluate managers somehow. Can you modify the year-old evaluation program, or do you have to start over from scratch? **If you were the CEO of Ford Motor Company, what would you do?**

**Sources:** D. Kiley and D. Jones, "Ford Alters Worker Evaluation Process," *USA Today*, 11 July 2001. D. Jones, "More Firms Cut Workers Ranked at Bottom to Make Way for Talent," *USA Today*, 30 May 2001. C. Hymowitz, "Ranking Systems Gain Popularity but Have Many Staffers Riled," *Wall Street Journal*, 15 May 2001.

## Management Decisions

### Job Analysis

Job analysis is a foundation for many of the HRM subsystems. Even though you may never have to actually conduct a job analysis and write job descriptions, you should be familiar with the process to better understand how to use this information in selection decisions. Pick a relatively simple job that you can observe without interrupting the employee. You should observe this job at least twice at different times (e.g., once in the morning and once in the afternoon) for approximately 30 minutes each time. The goal is to observe a representative performance of this job.

Copy or recreate the form below and use it to perform a job analysis of this job. Remember, your goal is to identify the most important activities, responsibilities, and duties, as well as any special equipment or tools that are used or any significant customer/ client/coworker contact. If you are working in teams, have two or three team members observe the same job. When you've finished, write a job description and job specifications for this job.

On the job analysis form below, the column headings stand for I = Importance of the activity, T = Time spent performing the activity (e.g., percentage of each day on average), and D = Difficulty of this activity. Use the following rating scales for these factors:

*Importance of Activity*
1 Very Unimportant
2 Slightly Unimportant
3 Slightly Important
4 Fairly Important
5 Very Important

*Time Spent on Average*
1 0–19% of each day
2 20–39% of each day
3 40–59% of each day
4 60–79% of each day
5 80–100% of each day

*Difficulty of Activity*
1 Extremely Easy
2 Fairly Easy
3 Average Difficulty
4 Above Average Difficulty
5 High Difficulty

After rating each activity, add the scores in each column and the total score. These scores can be used to compare relative values of different jobs to the company. If you are working in teams, average the scores from your group members to come up with a total for the job.

| Activity | I | T | D | I+T+D |
|---|---|---|---|---|
| | | | | |
| | | | | |
| | | | | |
| | | | | |
| | | | | |
| | | | | |
| | | | | |
| | | | | |
| | | | | |
| | | | | |
| | | | | |
| | | | | |
| | | | | |

TOTAL _____

Job Description:

Job Specifications:

## Management Decisions

### A Behavioral Interview for Your Professor?

Interviews are by far the most frequently used selection procedure. In fact, it's rare for people to be hired without first being interviewed. But, as you learned in the chapter, most managers conduct unstructured interviews, in which they are free to ask applicants anything they want, and studies show that they do. Indeed, studies show that because interviewers often disagree about which questions should be asked during interviews, different interviewers tend to ask applicants very different questions. Individual interviewers even seem to have a tough time asking the same questions from one interview to the next. This high level of inconsistency lowers the validity of interviews as a selection device, because it becomes difficult to compare applicant responses. As a result, unstructured interviews do about half as well as structured interviews in accurately predicting which job applicants should be hired.

By contrast, with structured interviews, standardized interview questions are prepared ahead of time, so that all applicants may be asked the same job-related questions. The primary advantage of structured interviews is that asking all applicants the same questions makes comparing applicants a much easier process. Also, structuring interviews ensures that interviewers will ask for only important, job-related information. These advantages significantly improve the accuracy, usefulness, and validity of interviews as a selection procedure. Since you're likely to use interviewing more than any other selection procedure, the purpose of this assignment is to give you some experience creating questions for structured interviews.

You'll be writing questions for the job of college professor, a job with which all of you should be familiar (having observed each of your instructors for an average of 40 hours per college class). Your job is to write 12 questions that you would ask applicants who wanted to teach at your university. Remember, four kinds of questions are typically asked in structured interviews. You'll be writing three questions for each of the four kinds of questions shown below.

- *Situational questions* ask applicants how they would respond in a hypothetical situation (e.g., "What would you do if . . . ?").

- *Behavioral questions* ask applicants what they did in previous jobs that were similar to the job for which they are applying (e.g., "In your previous jobs, can you tell me about . . . ?").
- *Background questions* ask applicants about their work experience, education, and other qualifications (e.g., "Tell me about the training you received at . . .").
- *Job-knowledge questions* ask applicants to demonstrate their job knowledge (e.g., for nurses, "Give me an example of a time in which one of your patients had a severe reaction to a medication. How did you handle it?").

Always ask open-ended questions, not closed-ended questions that can be answered with a "yes" or a "no." The point of the interview is to get applicants to talk about themselves, so that you can make a good hiring decision. Also, make sure your questions are job related. Finally, remember that if you were actually using this interview to hire college professors, every person interviewing for the job would be asked these 12 questions. So try to pick questions that would help you differentiate good instructors from bad instructors. For example, asking candidates where they received their Ph.D., which is a research degree, would probably not help you determine which candidates are most qualified to teach.

**Assignment**
Write three questions of each type (situational, behavioral, background, and job-knowledge) that you would like to ask someone who wanted to teach at your university.

## Develop Your Managerial Potential

### 360-Degree Feedback

While most performance appraisal ratings have traditionally come from just one person, the boss, 360-degree feedback is obtained from four sources: the boss, subordinates, peers and coworkers, and the employees themselves. In this assignment, you will be gathering 360-degree feedback from people that you work with or from a team or group that you're a member of for a class.

Here are some guidelines for obtaining your 360-degree feedback:

- *Carefully select respondents.* One of the keys to good 360-degree feedback is getting feedback from the right people. In general, the people you ask for feedback should interact with you on a regular basis and should have the chance to regularly observe your behavior. Also, be sure to get a representative sample of opinions from a similar number of coworkers and subordinates (assuming you have some).
- *Get a large enough number of responses.* Except for the boss, you should have a minimum of three respondents to give you feedback in each category (peers and subordinates). Five or six respondents per category is even better.
- *Ensure confidentiality.* Respondents are much more likely to be honest if they know that their comments are confidential and anonymous. So, when you ask respondents for feedback, have them return their comments to someone other than

yourself. Have this person, we'll call the person your "feedback facilitator," remove the names and any other information that would identify who made particular comments.
- *Explain how the 360-degree feedback will be used.* In this case, explain that the feedback is for a class assignment, that the results will be used for your own personal growth and development, and that the feedback they give you will not affect your grade or formal assessment at work.
- *Ask them to make their feedback as specific as possible.* For instance, writing "bad attitude" isn't very good feedback. However, writing "won't listen to others' suggestions" is much better feedback, because it would let you know how to improve your behavior. Have your respondents use the feedback form shown below to provide your feedback.

Here's what you need to turn in for this assignment:

1. The names and relationships (boss, peers, subordinates, classmates, teammates) of those whom you've asked for feedback.
2. The name of the person you've asked to be your feedback facilitator.
3. Copies of all written feedback that was returned to you.
4. A one-page summary of the written feedback.
5. A one-page plan in which you describe specific goals and action plans for responding to the feedback you received.

# 360-DEGREE FEEDBACK FORM

As part of a class assignment, I, _____, am collecting feedback from you about my performance. What you say or write will not affect my grade. The purpose of this assignment is for me to receive honest feedback from the people I work with in order to identify the things I'm doing well and the things that I need to improve. So please be honest and direct in your evaluation.

When you have completed this feedback form, please return it to _____. He or she has been selected as my feedback facilitator and is responsible for ensuring that your confidentiality and anonymity are maintained. After all feedback forms have been returned to _____, he or she will make sure that your particular responses cannot be identified. Only then will the feedback be shared with me.

Please provide the following feedback.

**CONTINUE DOING. . .**

Describe 3 things that _____ is doing that are a positive part of his or her performance and that you want him or her to continue doing.

1.

2.

3.

**START DOING . . .**

Describe 3 things that _____ needs to start doing that would significantly improve his or her performance.

1.

2.

3.

Please make your feedback as specific and behavioral as possible. For instance, writing "needs to adjust attitude" isn't very good feedback. However, writing "needs to begin listening to others' suggestions" is much better feedback because the person now knows exactly how he or she should change his or her behavior. So please be specific. Also, please write more than one sentence per comment. This will help feedback recipients better understand your comments.

## Study Tip

Use the chapter outline on page 510 as a study tool. After reading the whole chapter, return to the list and write a summary for each objective. Check your work by reading the actual review paragraphs on pages 525, 538, 547, and 555. For this chapter, you have Xtra! CNN clips with cases and solutions on your CD. Watch the segments on temporary workers and on the cost of keeping an employee, then read the cases and work the questions.

**CHAPTER 15**

*outline*

# fifteen

# Managing Service and Manufacturing Operations

## What Would You Do?

**Huffman Corporation, 1050 Huffman Way, Clover, South Carolina.** Stanley Huffman founded his company in 1961, distributing others' machine tools, the machines that make the parts that every manufacturer uses when assembling products. For example, machine tools are used to cut, carve, and polish the pistons in your car engine, the medical tools that surgeons use, the steel blades in electricity-generating turbines used by utility companies, and the parts of compressors that make new refrigerators and air conditioners much more energy efficient than they used to be. By 1969, Huffman Corporation began designing, producing, and selling its own line of machine tools.

Over the years, the machine tool industry has been a very tough business. Competition is intense and profits and market share are hard to come by. The last three years have been particularly tough for the industry. Ralph Nappi, president of the American Machine Tool Distributors' Association, said, "We're off 60 percent from where we were at our peak three years ago. We are going to drag anchor on the bottom a little while longer, but things will only improve from here." Robert Gardner, a spokesman for the Association for Manufacturing Technology, said, "Year-to-date orders are off 33 percent, and we've been in the doldrums for two or three years. We're down from a year ago, 2000 was down from '99, and that was substantially off from '98." Ralph Nappi concluded, "The one positive thing I can say is that we're at the bottom and it's not going to get any worse."

Of course, that doesn't mean things will get better either. But it's your job to help your management team figure out how to make that happen. Unfortunately, no one agrees on what to do. The marketing vice president insists that cut-rate financing will spur sales. He says that if customers pay less for the loans they take out to buy your expensive machine tools, business will improve. The company's chief financial officer is recommending that Huffman either merge with a major competitor or purchase a number of key competitors. But with hundreds of small companies in the industry, that could take a lot of time and cash to accomplish. The company's vice president for manufacturing, the quietest person on the executive team, keeps repeating one word like a mantra, "productivity, productivity, productivity." She says that if Huffman can simply do more with less, profits and market share will follow. Moreover, she sites the example of the U.S. defense industry, which increased productivity by reducing the number of parts in its products (from 41 to 27 subassemblies per plane) and by making sure that 81 percent of its workers were directly involved in manufacturing fighter jets, tanks, and other products (compared to 71 percent of workers at European defense contractors). As a result of increased productivity, U.S. defense companies sold better products for less money, more than doubling their market share from 25 percent to 57 percent over the last decade.

Her plan to improve productivity sounds great, but you've got your doubts. For instance, what's the best way to measure and improve productivity? If it's hard to define, much less measure, it won't make sense to try to track and improve productivity. Also, so what if we improve productivity? She makes improving productivity sound like a cure-all. Can improving productivity really make that much of a difference for one company, especially a company that has a very small share of the market and that would have to steal market share from several hundred competitors in order to grow? And will improved productivity really matter much to our competitors and customers? After all, aren't the effects of productivity fairly limited from company to company?

**If you were in charge of productivity at Huffman Corporation, what would you do?**

**Sources:** Interview with Don Carlson, "The Old Economy Is the New Economy," *Business Week*, 13 November 2000, 42H. S. Liesman, "Crucial Driver of U.S. Productivity Gains May Be Improvements in Machine Tools," *The Wall Street Journal*, 28 September 2000, A2.

S. Liesman, "Better Machine Tools Give Manufacturers Newfound Resilience," *The Wall Street Journal*, 15 February 2001, A1. S. Modic & J. McKenna, "Machine Tool Executives 'Crystal Ball' Future," *Tooling & Production*, 1 April 2000, 58. G. Rosenberger, "Com-

mercial Aircraft Business, The One Shining Light, Evaporating—Little Ramp Up for Military Contractors As Yet—Strong Car Sales Ironically Hinder Capital Investment," *Market News International*, 26 November 2000, no page numbers available.

The problems that Huffman Corporation faces in manufacturing its products are not unique to the machine tool industry. Airlines, auto manufacturers, hospitals, restaurants, and many other kinds of businesses also struggle to find ways to efficiently produce quality products and services and then deliver them in a timely manner.

**operations management**
managing the daily production of goods and services

In this chapter, you will learn about **operations management**—managing the daily production of goods and services. You will begin by learning about the basics of operations management: productivity and quality. Next, you will read about managing operations, beginning with service operations, turning next to manufacturing operations, and finishing with an examination of the types, measures, costs, and methods for managing inventory.

## Managing for Productivity and Quality

You're "crossing the pond" in June to visit your company's European offices and suppliers. Because business is down, your boss has given you a limited budget of $1,500 for airfare. Fortunately, your roundtrip ticket from Chicago to London cost just $800 on American Airlines. However, because there are fewer airlines to choose from in Europe, you expect travel to be somewhat more expensive. Your first flight from London to Dublin, Ireland, just barely over an hour long, costs $311 on British Airways. Ouch! Then, you're off from Dublin to Brussels, Belgium, at a cost of $487 on Aer Lingus, Ireland's national airline. From Brussels, you visit your Italian supplier in Venice at a cost of $572 on Lufthansa. Finally, you fly from Venice back to London on Alitalia, Italy's national airline, for $572. The total cost of your European travel is $1,942, $442 more than your budget and 2.4 times the cost of your roundtrip flight from the states! Your boss won't approve that.

At lunch, you're griping about the cost of European air travel when the company intern tells you to check out Ryanair, which saved her money when she was backpacking in Europe last summer. So, after lunch, you surf to **www.ryanair.com** to check out flight prices on the same dates and times. You discover that Ryanair's prices are dramatically lower. London to Dublin is $53. Dublin to Brussels is $25. Brussels to Venice is $50, and Venice to London is $98. Your total cost via Ryanair is $226, well below your budget, and just 11 percent of the cost of the same flights on Europe's major airlines!

Modeled after U.S.-based Southwest Airlines, Ryanair achieves dramatically lower prices through aggressive price-cutting, much higher productivity, and quality customer service. Want a frequent-flier plan? You won't find one at Ryanair. It's too expensive. Want a meal on your flight? Pack a lunch. Ryanair doesn't even serve peanuts because it takes too much time (i.e., expense) to get them out of the seat cushions. And, because it's quicker and cheaper, it uses old-fashioned, rolling stairs instead of extendable boarding gates, to get customers on and off their planes. As a result of this and other cost-cutting moves, Ryanair does more with less and thus has higher productivity. For example, most airlines break even on their flights when they're 75 percent full. By contrast, even with its incredibly low prices, Ryanair's productivity means that it breaks even when its planes are only half full. And with this low break-even point, Ryanair attracts plenty of customers who allow it to fill most of its seats and earn 20 percent net profit margins. Finally, because of its extremely low prices (and its competitors' extremely high prices), it has increased passenger traffic for nine straight years.[1]

564

*After reading these next two sections, you should be able to*
1. *discuss the kinds of productivity and their importance in managing operations.*
2. *explain the role that quality plays in managing operations.*

# 1. Productivity

**productivity**
a measure of performance that indicates how many inputs it takes to produce or create an output

At their core, organizations are production systems. Companies combine inputs, such as labor, raw materials, capital, and knowledge, to produce outputs in the form of finished products or services. **Productivity** is a measure of performance that indicates how many inputs it takes to produce or create an output.

$$\text{Productivity} = \frac{\text{Outputs}}{\text{Inputs}}$$

The fewer inputs it takes to create an output (or the greater the output from one input), the higher the productivity. For example, a car's gas mileage is a common measure of productivity. A car that gets 35 miles (output) per gallon (input) is more productive and fuel efficient than a car that gets 18 miles per gallon.

*Let's examine 1.1 why productivity matters and 1.2 the different kinds of productivity.*

## 1.1 Why Productivity Matters

Why does productivity matter? For companies, higher productivity, that is, doing more with less, results in lower costs. In turn, doing more with less can lead to lower prices, faster service, higher market share, and higher profits. For example, at fast-food restaurants, every second saved in the drive-through lane increases sales by 1 percent. Furthermore, increasing the efficiency of drive-through service by 10 percent adds nearly 10 percent to a fast-food restaurant's sales. And with 65 percent of all fast-food restaurant sales coming from the drive-through window, it's no wonder that Wendy's (average drive-through time of 150.3 seconds), McDonald's (average time of 167 seconds), and Burger King (average time of 171.3 seconds) continue to find ways to shorten the time it takes to process a drive-through order.[2]

For countries, productivity matters because it produces a higher standard of living. One way productivity leads to a higher standard of living is through increased wages. When companies can do more with less, they can raise employee wages without increasing prices or sacrificing normal profits. For instance, when I wrote this chapter, recent government economic data indicated that companies were paying workers 4.1 percent more than they were the previous year. But, since workers produced 2.8 percent more than they had the year before, real labor costs only rose 1.3 percent, one of the smallest increases in several years. How much of a difference can productivity increases make to wages and standards of living? If productivity grew just 1 percent a year, it would take 70 years to double the standard of living. However, if productivity grew 2 percent per year, it would only take 35 years to double the standard of living. One way to demonstrate this is to examine the effect that productivity has on wages. For example, the average American family earned approximately $44,500 in 1997. If productivity grew 1 percent a year, that family's income would grow to $56,000 in 2020. But if productivity grew 2 percent a year, their annual income would grow to more than $70,000 in 2020, more than $14,000 greater, and that's without working longer hours.[3] Thanks to long-term increases in business productivity, the average American family today earns 20 percent more than the average family in 1980 and 50 percent more than the average family in 1950—and that's after accounting for inflation.[4]

Rising income stemming from increased productivity creates numerous other benefits as well. For example, with productivity increases hovering over 2 percent per year during the 1990s, the U.S. economy created 20 million new jobs. And when more people have jobs that pay more, they give more to charity. For example, in 1999, Americans

565

donated over $190 billion to charities, 41 percent more than they donated in 1995. Had Americans become more thoughtful, caring, conscientious, and giving between 1995 and 1999? Probably not. Yet, because of strong increases in productivity during that time, the average American family saw its income increase by 15 percent and its net worth increase by 28 percent. Because more people earned more money, they were able to share their good fortune with others by giving more to charity.[5] Likewise, when productivity increased and incomes rose, medical coverage became more widely available. Today, more than 85 percent of Americans are covered by some form of medical insurance, compared to just 70 percent in 1960.

Another way that productivity increases the standard of living is by making products more affordable or better. For example, while inflation has pushed the average cost of a car to more than $23,000, increases in productivity have actually made cars cheaper. In 1960, the average family needed 26 weeks of income to pay for the average car. Today, the average family needs only 23 weeks of income—and today's car is loaded with accessories, like airbags, power steering and brakes, power windows, cruise control, stereo/CD players, and air conditioning, features that weren't even available in 1960.[6] So, in terms of real purchasing power, productivity gains have actually made the $23,000 car of today cheaper than the $2,000 car of 1960.

### 1.2 Kinds of Productivity

Two common measures of productivity are partial productivity and multifactor productivity. **Partial productivity** indicates how much of a particular kind of input it takes to produce an output.

**partial productivity**
a measure of performance that indicates how much of a particular kind of input it takes to produce an output

$$\text{Partial Productivity} = \frac{\text{Outputs}}{\text{Single Kind of Input}}$$

Labor is one kind of input that is frequently used when determining partial productivity. *Labor productivity* typically indicates the cost or number of hours of labor it takes to produce an output. In other words, the smaller the cost of the labor to produce a unit of output, or the less time it takes to produce a unit of output, the higher the labor productivity. For example, the automobile industry often measures labor productivity by determining the average number of hours of labor it takes to completely assemble a car. The three most productive auto manufacturers can assemble a car with 31 or fewer hours of labor. Nissan assembles a car in only 27.63 hours of labor. Honda does it in 29.11 hours, and Toyota in 31.06 hours. By comparison, Nissan, Toyota, and Honda have much higher labor productivity than Ford, which needs 39.94 hours of labor to assemble a car, General Motors, which needs 40.52 hours, or Chrysler, which needs 44 hours.[7] In terms of labor costs, this means that Nissan pays $1,332 less for labor per car than does Ford. In turn, Ford pays $507 less for labor per car than does Chrysler.[8]

Partial productivity assesses how efficiently companies use only one input, such as labor, when creating outputs. Multifactor productivity is an overall measure of productivity that assesses how efficiently companies use all the inputs it takes to make outputs. More specifically, **multifactor productivity** indicates how much labor, capital, materials, and energy it takes to produce an output.[9]

**multifactor productivity**
an overall measure of performance that indicates how much labor, capital, materials, and energy it takes to produce an output

$$\text{Multifactor Productivity} = \frac{\text{Outputs}}{\text{Labor + Capital + Materials + Energy}}$$

Exhibit 15.1 shows the trends in multifactor productivity across a number of different U.S. industries since 1987. With a six-fold increase (from the starting point scaled at 100 in 1987 to a productivity level of 631 in 1999), the growth in multifactor productivity in the electronics components and accessories industry far exceeded the productiv-

566

EXHIBIT 15.1

MULTIFACTOR PRODUCTIVITY GROWTH ACROSS INDUSTRIES

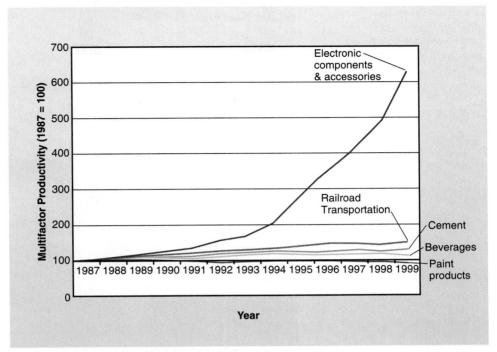

**Source:** "Industry Multifactor Productivity Indexes (1987=100)," *Bureau of Labor Statistics.* [Online] Available ftp://ftp.bls.gov/pub/special.requests/opt/dipts/indmfp2.txt, 21 February 2002.

ity growth in the railroad, cement, beverage, and paint products industries, as well most other industries tracked by the U.S. federal government.

Of course, the surge in productivity in the electronics industry isn't a surprise. Each round of technology advances brings significantly smaller and cheaper, yet much more powerful electronic devices. It takes significantly less labor, capital, materials, and energy to produce electronic products today (i.e., computers and their components, computer game devices such as the PlayStation 2, cellphones, Palm PCs, and so forth) than it did in the past. An examination of some of the components of multifactor productivity shows how members of the electronics industry, such as Dell Computers, have obtained such large increases in productivity.

First, with respect to labor, every time that Dell Computers opens a new factory, it increases productivity by producing more computers with fewer factory workers. John Egan, who directs manufacturing and distribution for one of Dell's most popular computer lines, said, "Every time [we open a new plant,] we get more and more efficient."[10] In fact, Dell's new plant on Parmer Lane in Austin, Texas, is twice as productive as the plant it replaced. Likewise, Dell saves on labor costs since 95 percent of the orders processed by this plant are handled automatically when customers place their orders on the Internet.

Second, with respect to capital, multifactor productivity assesses how efficiently a company uses the money it spends on equipment, facilities (offices and operating plants), inventories, and land. Dell has greatly increased the productivity of its assembly plants by aggressively cutting costs and by building them twice as fast as its competitors. For instance, when Dell built a new assembly plant in Lebanon, Tennessee, it only took 62 days from beginning to end. Dell cut two weeks out of the construction process by picking the architectural firm in one morning and then by working with the architects

567

You can see from this photo how efficient Dell really is. When Dell opens new manufacturing plants, it increases productivity by producing more computers with fewer factory workers. In this photo of the new Parmer Lane plant, the ratio of computers to workers is extremely high.

COURTESY OF DELL COMPUTER CORP.

from noon till midnight on that same day to put together a construction schedule and budget.[11]

Finally, in terms of materials, that is, the components used to manufacture Dell Computers, Dell's new factories have almost no parts or finished product inventory. Computer parts are ordered when customers complete their orders. And, according to Sharon Boyle, who manages Dell's new Parmer Lane plant, "More than 95 percent of the orders received are shipped within eight hours." In fact, when the plant was designed, the company completely eliminated space that would normally hold parts and finished goods.[12]

The electronics industry is not only much more productive than it used to be, but the products it produces are sometimes thousands of times better in terms of processing power, storage, battery life, and functionality. For instance, IBM introduced the first personal computer, the IBM PC XT in 1983. For $4,995 ($8,800 in today's dollars), you got an Intel 4.77 mhz processor, 128k RAM, a 360k floppy drive, a 10-megabyte hard drive, and a 12.5 inch monochrome monitor. By contrast, the day I wrote this, $1,000 would buy a computer with a 1.6 gigahertz processor (1,595 times faster than the IBM PC XT), 256 megabytes of RAM (2,046 times more memory), a 1.44 megabyte floppy drive (3.1 times more floppy storage), a CD drive/burner (1,819 times more storage than a floppy), a 20-gigabyte hard drive (2,046 times more hard drive storage), and a 17-inch color monitor (nearly twice the viewable screen area—and in color, not monochrome). Today's computer also comes with operating system software, as well as office suite software, all of which cost an additional $600 on the original IBM PC XT.

Should managers use multiple or partial productivity measures? In general, they should use both. Multifactor productivity indicates a company's overall level of productivity relative to its competitors. In the end, that's what counts most. However, multifactor productivity measures don't indicate the specific contributions that labor, capital, materials, or energy make to overall productivity. To analyze the contributions of these individual components, managers need to use partial productivity measures.

## Review 1
### Productivity

At their core, companies are production systems that combine inputs, such as labor, raw materials, capital, and knowledge to produce outputs, such as finished products or services. Productivity is a measure of how many inputs it takes to produce or create an output. The greater the output from one input, or the fewer inputs it takes to create an output, the higher the productivity. Partial productivity measures how much of a single kind of input, such as labor, is needed to produce an output. Multifactor productivity is an overall measure of productivity that indicates how much labor, capital, materials, and energy are needed to produce an output. Increased productivity helps companies lower costs, which can lead to lower prices, higher market share, and higher profits. Increased productivity helps countries by leading to higher wages, lower product prices, and a higher standard of living.

## 2. Quality

With the average car costing more than $23,000, car buyers want to make sure that they're getting good quality for their money. Fortunately, as indicated by the number of problems per 100 cars (PP100), today's cars are of much higher quality than earlier models. In 1981, Japanese cars averaged 240 PP100. GM averaged 670, Ford averaged 740, and Chrysler averaged 870 PP100! In other words, as measured by PP100, the quality of American cars was three to four times worse than Japanese cars. However, by 1992, U.S. carmakers had made great strides, significantly reducing the number of problems to an average of 155 PP100. Japanese vehicles had improved, too, averaging just 125 PP100. Exhibit 15.2 shows the 2001 results of the J.D. Power survey of initial car quality. Lexus, with just 85 PP100, had the best quality, while Kia, with 267 PP100, had the worst. The overall average was 147 PP100. However, American auto companies continue to close the quality gap with Japanese auto companies. While Ford had 162 PP100, Chrysler, with 137 PP100, and Chevrolet (GM), with 146 PP100, were close to Honda, 135 PP100, and better than Nissan, which had 148 PP100. Toyota, however, still had only 121 PP100.

**quality**
a product or service free of deficiencies, or the characteristics of a product or service that satisfy customer needs

The American Society for Quality gives two meanings for **quality**. First, it can mean a product or service free of deficiencies, such as the number of problems per 100 cars. Second, quality can mean the characteristics of a product or service that satisfy customer needs.[13] In this sense, today's cars are of higher quality because of the additional standard features (power brakes and steering, stereo/CD player, power windows and locks, rear defrosters, cruise control, etc.) they have compared to 20 years ago.

*In this part of the chapter, you will learn about 2.1 quality-related product characteristics, 2.2 quality-related service characteristics, 2.3 ISO 9000, 2.4 the Baldrige National Quality Award, and 2.5 Total Quality Management.*

### 2.1 Quality-Related Product Characteristics

As shown in Exhibit 15.3, quality products usually possess three characteristics: reliability, serviceability, and durability.[14] A breakdown occurs when a product quits working or doesn't do what it was designed to do. The longer it takes for a product to break down, or the longer the time between breakdowns, the more reliable the product. Consequently, many companies define *product reliability* in terms of the average time between breakdowns. For example, Quantum Corporation sells a computer product called the DLT 8000 tape drive that customers can use to back up 70 gigabytes of data. The DLT 8000 is so reliable that the estimated mean time between breakdowns is 250,000 hours, or more than 28.5 years![15] Of course, this is just an average. Some DLT 8000 tape drives will break down much sooner. However, some will last even longer than 28.5 years before breaking down.

*Serviceability* refers to how easy or difficult it is to fix a product. The easier it is to maintain a working product or fix a broken product, the more serviceable that product

EXHIBIT 15.2

## 2001 J.D. POWER SURVEY OF INITIAL CAR QUALITY

| Make | Score |
|------|-------|
| Kia | 267 |
| Suzuki | 234 |
| Mazda | 209 |
| Land Rover | 207 |
| Isuzu | 192 |
| Hyundai | 192 |
| Subaru | 183 |
| Daewoo | 176 |
| Dodge | 170 |
| Mitsubishi | 169 |
| Volkswagen | 165 |
| Pontiac | 165 |
| Ford | 162 |
| Oldsmobile | 159 |
| Jeep | 155 |
| Volvo | 154 |
| GMC | 153 |
| Lincoln | 149 |
| Nissan | 148 |
| Chevrolet | 146 |
| Plymouth | 145 |
| Mercury | 143 |
| Porsche | 140 |
| Audi | 140 |
| Saturn | 139 |
| Chrysler | 137 |
| Honda | 135 |
| Mercedes | 129 |
| Cadillac | 126 |
| Infiniti | 123 |
| Buick | 123 |
| Toyota | 121 |
| Saab | 121 |
| BMW | 119 |
| Acura | 118 |
| Jaguar | 108 |
| Lexus | 85 |

**Source:** J.D. Powers Initial Quality Survey, cited by K. Schweitzer, "Rising to the Occasion; Japanese, European Cars Still Lead in the Quality Race, but the Domestics Are Closing in Fast," *Chicago Tribune*, 28 October 2001, Transportation 1.

EXHIBIT 15.3

## CHARACTERISTICS OF QUALITY PRODUCTS

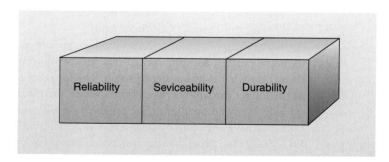

is. For example, few people realize that over the life of a car, they'll spend more for car insurance than for gas. The Saturn division of General Motors decided that one way to lower the cost of car ownership is to make cars easier to repair after they've been in collisions. Charles Sollar of State Farm Insurance said, "Fixing a conventional car requires

# "headline news"

Tony Alexander of Miami, Florida, has had persistent problems with his new Jeep Cherokee leaking water into the interior of the car. The dealer has been unable to fix the perpetually water-logged car, so Alexander is suing DaimlerChrysler under Florida's strict lemon law. Since there has been no recall of Jeeps for this problem, he considers his car a lemon, and he wants the company to buy it back.

This might sound extreme, but manufacturers buy back roughly 75,000 problem-plagued cars out of the average 45 million cars sold per year. These buy-backs are then sold to dealers at auction for drastically lower prices, after which they re-enter the market as used cars, only to be sold to unsuspecting car shoppers. Some shoppers, however, should know better.

Greg Hunter, a consumer correspondent for ABC News, bought a new Monte Carlo that turned out to be a lemon. He eventually sold it back to the Florida dealer without much fuss, but not before marking his name in the trunk and turning the situation into a news story. Hunter tracked the car and found out that it was sold to Connie Bagwell in South Carolina. Her husband, who sells cars for a living, bought the car at an auction, but received no disclosure of lemon status. When Hunter caught up to them, the Bagwell's were astounded to find out that they paid $13,600 for a certified lemon. Although their title was not branded before the report, discovery of the car's lemon status meant that the car would have to be retitled a lemon, according to their state's lemon law, which effectively cut the car's value in half. A branded title clearly indicates that the car is a lemon so that future buyers know what they are getting.

Each state has different standards for determining a lemon. In Pennsylvania, home to Kimmel and Silverman, the second largest lemon-law legal practice in the country, a defect is defined as any problem that substantially impairs the use, value, or safety of the vehicle. Car makers have three chances to fix the defect, but that doesn't mean that the car has to be in the shop three times: It has to be in the shop three times for the same repair. And not all cars are covered. Leased vehicles are not because they are generally considered the property of the dealer.

How can you protect yourself from getting squeezed into a lemon to begin with? An online service called Carfax.com has an extensive database of used car information. Simply enter the Vehicle Identification Number and it creates a detailed history of the car, including owners, wrecks, and repairs.

As car warranties have extended from 12 months to 36 months to 10 years, it's easy to think that quality has improved. After all, if the company is willing to pay for repairs out 10 years, it must have great confidence in its product. In fact, the expected cost of warranty repairs is built into the purchase price, so the buyer is just paying up front for them, to the tune of 15 to 30 percent of the car's sticker. But even 30 percent of the sticker price on his new Jeep was not enough to cover the damage to Alexander's Cherokee. With a dealer who cannot fix it and a manufacturer who will not buy it back, he sees his only recourse as suing under Florida lemon-law statutes. Although Chrysler accuses him of playing litigation lotto, Alexander is just trying to juice his lemon.

1. Should manufacturers and dealers be responsible for after-market lemons, or is it just a case of caveat emptor (let the buyer beware)?
2. With 75,000 cars on average per year being bought back, does the automotive industry have a systemic quality problem?

**Sources:** L. Clifford, "Why You Can Safely Ignore Six Sigma," *Fortune*, 22 January 2001, p.140. Info-Trac Article A68972059. "Database Records Detail Vehicle History for Potential Buyers," *Online Product News*, March 2000 (19: 3), p. NA. Info-Trac Article A59492172. G. Hunter, report for *Good Morning America* as seen on http://www.lemonlawamerica.com. P. Sabatini, "State's Auto Lemon Law Can Relieve a Car Buyer's Sour Experience," *Post-Gazette.com*, 26 February 2001, http://www.post-gazette.com/yourbiz/20010226main2.asp. http://www.carfax.com. http://www.ita.doc.gov/td/auto/qfact.html. http://www.jdpa.com. http://www.lemonlawamerica.com

straightening or replacing steel panels that are welded together. Saturn adopted a whole new approach—mounting plastic door skins, front fenders and quarter panels to the car with screws instead of welds. When a repair was necessary, panels could be replaced by simply unscrewing the attachment fasteners. This approach yields significant repair-cost savings." Saturn also improved serviceability and reduced collision repair costs by moving expensive components and the car battery away from high impact areas. Jack Ribbens, who works for Allstate Insurance, said, "The second concern is removing expensive components from the most vulnerable areas under the hood. For example, we convinced Saturn engineers to relocate their power train control module—a very expensive part—from the left-front corner of the car to a safer location under the dash. Batteries aren't expensive to replace. But you don't want them in vulnerable areas because they can spray acid with disastrous results. It's not unusual for a crushed battery to ruin the transmission case and the wiring harness."[16]

A product breakdown assumes that a product can be repaired. However, some products don't break down—they fail. *Product failure* means products can't be repaired. They can only be replaced. Thus, durability is a quality characteristic that applies to products that *can't be repaired*. *Durability* is defined as the mean time to failure. A product for which durability matters is the defibrillation equipment used by emergency medical technicians, doctors, and nurses to restart patients' hearts. Imagine the lost lives (and lawsuits) that would occur if this equipment were prone to frequent failure. Dick Martin, president of Medtronic Physio-Control, which manufactures 80 percent of the defibrillation units in use today, said, "We know there are people alive today who wouldn't be if we weren't in business. If anybody in the world ought to be preoccupied with quality, it is this company."[17] The mean time between failures for Physio-Control's defibrillation units is 20 years. However, if a Physio-Control "LIFEPAK" does break, the company replaces it within 24 hours.

### 2.2 Quality-Related Service Characteristics

Reliability, serviceability, and durability characterize high-quality products. However, services and products are different. With services, there's no point in assessing durability. Unlike products, services don't last. Services are consumed the minute they're performed. For example, once a lawn service has mowed your lawn, the job is done until the mowers come back next week to do it again. Likewise, services don't have serviceability. You can't maintain or fix a service. If a service wasn't performed correctly, all you can do is perform the service again. Finally, the quality of service interactions often depends on how the service provider interacts with the customer. Was the service provider friendly, rude, or helpful? Consequently, as shown in Exhibit 15.4, five characteristics—reliability, tangibles, responsiveness, assurance, and empathy—typically distinguish a quality service.[18]

*Service reliability* is the ability to consistently perform a service well. Studies clearly show that reliability matters more to customers than anything else when buying services. Also, while services themselves are not tangible (you can't see or touch them), services are provided in tangible places. Thus, *tangibles* refer to the appearance of the offices, equipment, and personnel involved with the delivery of a service. *Responsiveness* is the promptness and willingness with which service providers give good service. *Assurance* is the confidence that service providers are knowledgeable, courteous, and trustworthy. *Empathy* is the extent to which service providers give individual attention and care to customers' concerns and problems.

EMC makes highly reliable computers that are used by some of the largest companies in the world (banks, phone companies, auto manufacturers, etc.). If EMC's equip-

---

EXHIBIT 15.4

CHARACTERISTICS OF QUALITY SERVICE

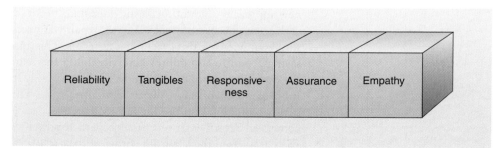

Reliability | Tangibles | Responsiveness | Assurance | Empathy

ment goes down even for a few minutes, its customers can lose millions from vanished sales. While its equipment is incredibly reliable, what distinguishes EMC from its competition is the level of service it provides when problems occur. In other words, EMC is a standout performer in terms of *service reliability*, the ability to consistently perform a service well. Because of its excellent service, EMC retains an amazing 99 percent of its customers from year to year. When Carl Howe of Forrester Research, a marketing research firm, asked 50 large Fortune 500 companies about the technology companies they worked with, "EMC came out looking like God." Howe said that EMC "had the best customer-service reviews we have ever seen, in any industry."[19]

EMC also excels in terms of *responsiveness*, the promptness and willingness with which service providers give good service. When a Wisconsin bank lost access to its data (no account numbers, no deposits, no withdrawals, nada!), which was stored on an EMC machine, EMC service engineers were on the problem within minutes (EMC's computers "call home" automatically whenever there are problems). After four hours EMC had created a setup identical to the bank's in a $1 billion facility designed for such purposes. After examining the bank's software and data, both of which it had automatically backed up, and after involving the engineers who designed the machines used by the bank, it finally found a problem in the machine's operating system and put together a software patch that had the bank up and running by the end of the day.[20]

EMC provides quality service by virtue of clear *assurance* that it can be trusted. Every customer knows that the company follows a disciplined procedure for addressing customer problems. First, every EMC system does a self-check every two hours to make sure it is running the way it's supposed to. If even the slightest thing is wrong, it "phones home" to tell EMC's engineers what's happening. EMC gets 3,500 such "calls" from its machines and systems every day. Second, if a problem isn't fixed within four hours, Leo Colborne, the vice president of global technical support is notified. After six hours, Colborne's boss, the senior vice president of global customer services is contacted. After eight hours, the company's CEO and Chairman are notified. And, in most cases, the CEO will leave immediately to visit the customer, to apologize for the problem, to reassure the customer that everything is being done to solve the problem, and to begin working with the customer to put in procedures or solutions to prevent the problem from recurring in the future.[21]

Finally, EMC provides quality service because of the *empathy* it has for its customers' problems. Indeed, early in the company's history, its customers' businesses were suffering because EMC could not figure out why one of its best-selling systems had unexpectedly become unreliable. And with key information systems frozen up, business ground to a halt for key customers. Rather than make excuses or empty promises, EMC solved the problem at great cost to itself by putting itself in its customers' shoes. It told customers that they had a choice. EMC would send them a brand new EMC computer system, or it would install a similar system, made by EMC's competitor, IBM. At the height of its problems, EMC installed more of IBM's machines than its own. But rather than undermining the company and its products, customers realized that EMC would do almost anything to solve their problems. And, as EMC solved the problems with that machine, customers trusted the company enough to begin ordering from EMC again. EMC's CEO said, "What that proved to me, to all of us, was that when a customer believes in you, and you go to great lengths to preserve that relationship, they'll stick with you almost no matter what. It opened our eyes to the power of customer service."[22]

**ISO 9000**
a series of five international standards, from ISO 9000 to ISO 9004, for achieving consistency in quality management and quality assurance in companies throughout the world

## 2.3 ISO 9000

*ISO*, pronounced *ice-o*, comes from the Greek word *isos*, meaning *equal, similar, alike,* or *identical.* Thus, **ISO 9000** is a series of five international standards, from ISO 9000 to ISO 9004, for achieving consistency in quality management and quality assurance in companies throughout the world. The ISO 9000 standards were created by the International Organization of Standards, an international agency that helps set standards for 91 countries. The purpose of this agency is to develop and publish standards that facilitate the international exchange of goods and services.[23]

The ISO 9000 standards publications, which can be purchased from the American National Standards Institute (**http://web.ansi.org**) for about $400, are general and can be used for manufacturing any kind of product or delivering any kind of service. Importantly, the ISO 9000 standards don't describe how to make a better quality car, computer, or widget. Instead, they describe how companies can extensively document (and thus standardize) the steps they take to create and improve the quality of their products.

Why should companies go to the trouble to achieve ISO 9000 certification? Because, increasingly, their customers want them to. Du Pont, General Electric, Eastman Kodak, British Telecom, and Philips Electronics are some of the Fortune 500 companies that are telling their suppliers to achieve ISO 9000 certification. John Yates, G.E.'s general manager of global sourcing, said, "There is absolutely no negotiation. If you want to work with us, you have to get it."[24]

Typically, "getting" ISO 9000 means having your company certified for ISO 9000 registration by an accredited third party. The process is similar to having a certified accountant indicate that a company's financial accounts are up-to-date and accurate. But in this case, the certification is for quality, not accounting procedures. To become certified, a process that can take months, companies must show that they are following their own procedures for improving production, updating design plans and specifications, keeping machinery in top condition, educating and training workers, and satisfactorily dealing with customer complaints.[25]

Once a company has been certified as ISO 9000 compliant, the accredited third party will issue an ISO 9000 certificate that the company can use in its advertising and publications. This is the quality equivalent of the "Good Housekeeping Seal of Approval." However, ISO 9000 certification is not guaranteed. Accredited third parties typically conduct periodic audits to make sure quality procedures continue to be followed. Companies that don't follow their quality systems have their certifications suspended or cancelled.

It's estimated that more than half of mid-sized U.S. manufacturers have achieved ISO 9000 certification. In fact, two-thirds of companies that already have achieved ISO 9000 certification said they did so because it increases customer satisfaction. Most advertise their ISO certification in their promotional materials. A spokesperson for Hyundai Electronics Americas said, "We always mention our certification when we can."[26] See the American National Standard Institute (**http://web.ansi.org**) and the American Society for Quality (**http://www.asq.org/**) for additional information on ISO 9000 guidelines and procedures.

### 2.4 Baldrige National Quality Award

The Baldrige National Quality Award was established in 1987 to honor the late Malcolm Baldrige, a former secretary of commerce. The purpose of the award, which is administered by the U.S. government's National Institute for Standards and Technology, is "to recognize U.S. companies for their achievements in quality and business performance and to raise awareness about the importance of quality and performance excellence as a competitive edge."[27] Each year, three awards may be given in five categories: manufacturing, service, and small business, as well as education and health, which were added in 1999. Exhibit 15.5 lists the 1993 to 2001 Baldrige Award winners for manufacturing, service, and small business.

The cost of applying for the Baldrige Award is $4,500 for large businesses, $2,000 for small businesses, and as little as $300 for nonprofit organizations.[28] At a minimum, each company that applies receives an extensive report based on 300 hours of assessment from at least eight business and quality experts. At $5 an hour for small businesses and $15 an hour for large businesses, the *Journal for Quality and Participation* called the Baldrige feedback report "the best bargain in consulting in America."[29] Roger Milliken, CEO of Milliken & Company, a Baldrige Award winner, said, "Applying for the Baldrige and getting the feedback they give you is of incredible value to a company."[30]

EXHIBIT 15.5

**BALDRIGE NATIONAL QUALITY AWARD RECIPIENTS (1993–2001)**

## MANUFACTURING

Clarke American Checks (2001)
Dana Corporation—Spicer Driveshaft Division (2000)
STMicroelectronics, Inc.—Region Americas (1999)
Boeing Airlift and Tanker Programs (1998)
3M Dental Products Division (1997)
Solectron Corporation (1997)
ADAC Laboratories (1996)
Armstrong World Industries Building Products Operations (1995)
Corning Incorporated, Telecommunications Products Division (1995)
Eastman Chemical Company (1993)

## SERVICE

Operations Management International (2000)
BI (1999)
The Ritz-Carlton Hotel Company (1999)
Merrill Lynch Credit Corporation (1997)
Xerox Business Services (1997)
Dana Commercial Credit Corporation (1996)
AT&T Consumer Communications Services (1994) (now part of AT&T Consumer Markets Division)
GTE Directories Corporation (1994)

## SMALL BUSINESS

Pal's Sudden Service (2001)
Los Alamos National Bank (2000)
Sunny Fresh Foods (1999)
Texas Nameplate Company (1998)
Custom Research, Inc. (1996)
Trident Precision Manufacturing, Inc. (1996)
Wainwright Industries, Inc. (1994)
Ames Rubber Corporation (1993)

**Source::** "1988–2001 Award Recipients' Contacts and Profiles," *National Institute for Standards and Technology.* [Online] Available http://www.quality.nist.gov, 25 February 2002.

575

As shown in Exhibit 15.6, companies that apply for the Baldrige Award are judged on a 1,000-point scale based on seven criteria: leadership, strategic planning, customer and market focus, information and analysis, human resource focus, process management, and business results.[31] But with 450 out of 1,000 points, "business results" are clearly the most important. In other words, in addition to the six other criteria, companies must show that they have achieved superior quality when it comes to customers, financial performance, market share, treatment of employees, and organizational effectiveness, such as productivity and efficiency. This emphasis on "results" is what differentiates the Baldrige Award from the ISO 9000 standards. The Baldrige Award indicates the extent to which companies have actually achieved world-class quality. ISO 9000 standards simply indicate whether a company is following the management system it put in place to improve quality. In fact, ISO 9000 certification covers less than 10 percent of the requirements for the Baldrige Award.[32]

Why should companies go to the trouble of applying for the Baldrige Award? Earnest Deavenport, Chairman and CEO of Eastman Chemical, said, "Eastman, like

EXHIBIT 15.6

CRITERIA FOR THE BALDRIGE NATIONAL QUALITY AWARD

| 2002 CATEGORIES/ITEMS | POINT VALUES |
|---|---|
| **1 LEADERSHIP** | **(120)** |
| Organizational Leadership | 80 |
| Public Responsibility and Citizenship | 40 |
| **2 STRATEGIC PLANNING** | **(85)** |
| Strategy Development Process | 40 |
| Strategy Deployment | 45 |
| **3 CUSTOMER AND MARKET FOCUS** | **(85)** |
| Customer and Market Knowledge | 40 |
| Customer Relationships and Satisfaction | 45 |
| **4 INFORMATION AND ANALYSIS** | **(90)** |
| Measurement and Analysis of Organizational Performance | 50 |
| Information Management | 40 |
| **5 HUMAN RESOURCE FOCUS** | **(85)** |
| Work Systems | 35 |
| Employee Education, Training, and Development | 25 |
| Employee Well-Being and Satisfaction | 25 |
| **6 PROCESS MANAGEMENT** | **(85)** |
| Product and Service Processes | 45 |
| Business Processes | 25 |
| Support Processes | 15 |
| **7 BUSINESS RESULTS** | **(450)** |
| Customer-Focused Results | 125 |
| Financial and Market Results | 125 |
| Human Resource Results | 80 |
| Organizational Effectiveness Results | 120 |
| **TOTAL POINTS** | **1000** |

**Source:** "Criteria for Performance Excellence," *Baldrige National Quality Program 2002.* [Online] Available http://www.quality.nist.gov, 25 February 2002.

other Baldrige Award winners, didn't apply the concepts of total quality management to win an award. We did it to win customers. We did it to grow. We did it to prosper and to remain competitive in a world marketplace."[33] Furthermore, the companies that have won the Baldrige Award have achieved superior financial returns. Since 1988, an investment in Baldrige Award winners would have out-performed the Standard & Poor's 500 stock index by nearly 4.4 to 1. The return on investment from the Baldrige Award winners was 685 percent, compared to 163 percent for the Standard & Poor's stock index.[34] For additional information about the Baldrige Award, see the National Institute of Standards and Technology Web site at **http://www.quality.nist.gov**.

### 2.5 Total Quality Management

**total quality management (TQM)**
an integrated, principle-based, organization-wide strategy for improving product and service quality

**Total quality management (TQM)** is an integrated organization-wide strategy for improving product and service quality.[35] TQM is not a specific tool or technique. Rather, TQM is a philosophy or overall approach to management that is characterized by three

**Continuous Improvement? Ask for Feedback.**

"Continuous improvement" is usually associated with manufacturing operations, but can also be used to improve your job performance and career opportunities. Begin with a candid evaluation of where your job performance needs improvement. Next, after a thorough self-assessment, ask your boss, trusted coworkers, and key customers to identify what they'd like you to do differently. Ask for only a few suggestions per person. The point is to generate specific targets for improvement, not put you into a depression. Then, phase in changes by taking action on only two or three things at time. Finally, repeat this process periodically to ensure continuous improvement.

**Source:** M. Barkley, "Passed Over for Promotion? Take the High Road, Prepare Yourself for Success Next Time," *Greensboro News & Record,* 18 November 2001, F1.

**customer focus**
an organizational goal to concentrate on meeting customers' needs at all levels of the organization

**customer satisfaction**
an organizational goal to provide products or services that meet or exceed customers' expectations

principles: customer focus and satisfaction, continuous improvement, and teamwork.[36]

Contrary to most economists, accountants, and financiers who argue that companies exist to earn profits for shareholders, TQM suggests that customer focus and customer satisfaction should be a company's primary goals. **Customer focus** means the entire organization, from top to bottom, should be focused on meeting customers' needs. For example, La Madeleine, is a Dallas-based restaurant chain that models itself after a French bakery and café. Wood floors and exposed beams provide the feel of a kitchen, library, or wine cave. Each new store manager is sent to France for extensive training. And while La Madeleine offers a variety of popular salads, soups, and sandwiches for lunch and dinner, it is best known for its breakfast menu featuring freshly baked bread, croissants, and French Roast coffee. Despite its initial success, the company has struggled lately and has newly rededicated itself to better serving its customers. Consequently, the company has held more focus groups (in which customers were asked to discuss positive and negative experiences) in the last 18 months than it did in its first 16 years. Customer input has resulted in numerous changes. For instance, wine glasses have been replaced with stylish, larger drinking glasses. Though emblematic of France, wine glasses tended to fall from food trays and were easily knocked off tables. Also, customers wanted to be able to drink more than four ounces at a time. CEO John Corcoran said that customers told them, "You can strike a balance between some of the hallmarks that make La Madeleine unique yet be functional."[37]

**Customer satisfaction** is an organizational goal to make products or deliver services that meet or exceed customers' expectations. And at companies where TQM is taken seriously, such as Cisco Systems, a leading provider of the routers used to run the Internet, paychecks depend on keeping customers satisfied. For example, Cisco surveys clients each year about 60 different performance criteria. CEO John Chambers said, "We pay every manager on customer satisfaction. It's amazing how that works. Once you say it's going to

Valassis is in the business of stuffing your Sunday newspaper with discount-coupon circulars. Employee teams also stuff the company suggestion box with cost-cutting and quality ideas, so much so that the company was able to avoid layoffs during recession. Valassis is regularly one of *Fortune's* Best Companies to Work For.

© KRISTINE LARSEN 2001

be part of their compensation, people say, 'This must really be important,' and secondly, 'John's going to ask me about it all the time.' And for either reason, they respond very well."[38] And Cisco is serious about tying rewards to customer satisfaction. According to CEO Chambers, "If a manager improves his or her [customer satisfaction] scores, he or she can get a fair amount [of a financial bonus]. But if the scores go down, we'll take money out of the manager's pocket."[39] Not surprisingly, this emphasis on quality increased the number of completely satisfied Cisco customers from 81 percent to 85 percent in just one year.

**Continuous improvement** is an ongoing commitment to increase product and service quality by constantly assessing and improving the processes and procedures used to create those products and services. How do companies know whether they're achieving continuous improvement? Besides higher customer satisfaction, continuous improvement is usually associated with a reduction in variation. **Variation** is a deviation in the form, condition, or appearance of a product from the quality standard for that product. The less a product varies from the quality standard, or the more consistently a company's products meet a quality standard, the higher the quality. At Visteon Corporation, an auto parts supplier, continuous improvement means shooting for a goal of "six sigma" quality, meaning just 3.4 defective or nonstandard parts per million (PPM). Achieving this goal would eliminate almost all product variation. Last year, Visteon made 360 million auto parts with a defect rate of 65 PPM. As shown in Exhibit 15.7, this puts Visteon well past "five sigma," or 230 defective PPM. Furthermore, this represents significant improvement from several years ago when Visteon was averaging 1,000 defective PPM. And, with a goal of just 30 defective PPM, Visteon expects the quality of its parts to continue to improve.

The third principle of TQM is teamwork. **Teamwork** means collaboration between managers and nonmanagers, across business functions, and between the company and its customers and suppliers. In short, quality improves when everyone in the company is given the incentive to work together and the responsibility and authority to make improvements and solve problems. Thanks to team members' suggestions at a Maytag plant in Cleveland, Tennessee, production has doubled, production costs have dropped by $7 million per year, and on-hand inventory of parts and finished goods has been reduced by

**continuous improvement**
an organization's ongoing commitment to constantly assess and improve the processes and procedures used to create products and services

**variation**
a deviation in the form, condition, or appearance of a product from the quality standard for that product

**teamwork**
collaboration between managers and nonmanagers, across business functions, and between companies, customers, and suppliers

EXHIBIT 15.7

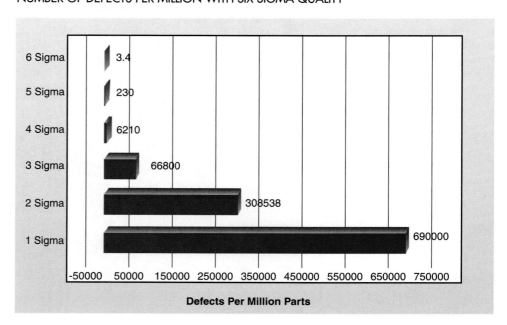

NUMBER OF DEFECTS PER MILLION WITH SIX SIGMA QUALITY

| | Defects |
|---|---|
| 6 Sigma | 3.4 |
| 5 Sigma | 230 |
| 4 Sigma | 6210 |
| 3 Sigma | 66800 |
| 2 Sigma | 308538 |
| 1 Sigma | 690000 |

**Defects Per Million Parts**

$10 million.[40] Likewise, at Valassis, a printing company long famous for its use of teams, management turned to employees for additional suggestions when business fell during a recession. Teams offered so many ideas to cut costs and raise quality that the company was able to avoid layoffs.[41]

Together, customer focus and satisfaction, continuous improvement, and teamwork mutually reinforce each other to improve quality throughout a company. Customer-focused continuous improvement is necessary to increase customer satisfaction. However, continuous improvement depends on teamwork from different functional and hierarchical parts of the company.

### Review 2
### Quality

Quality can mean a product or service free of deficiencies or the characteristics of a product or service that satisfy customer needs. Quality products usually possess three characteristics: reliability, serviceability, and durability. Quality service means reliability, tangibles, responsiveness, assurance, and empathy. ISO 9000 is a series of five international standards for achieving consistency in quality management and quality assurance. The ISO 9000 standards can be used for any product or service, because they ensure that companies carefully document the steps they take to create and improve quality. ISO 9000 certification is awarded following a quality audit from an accredited third party. The Baldrige National Quality Award recognizes U.S. companies for their achievements in quality and business performance. Each year, three Baldrige Awards may be given for manufacturing, service, small business, education, and health. Companies that apply for the Baldrige Award are judged on a 1,000-point scale based on leadership, strategic planning, customer and market focus, information and analysis, human resource focus, process management, and business results. Total quality management (TQM) is an integrated organization-wide strategy for improving product and service quality. TQM is based on three mutually reinforcing principles: customer focus and satisfaction, continuous improvement, and teamwork.

## Managing Operations

At the start of this chapter, you learned that operations management means managing the daily production of goods and services. Then you learned that to manage production, you must oversee the factors that affect productivity and quality. In this half of the chapter, you will learn about managing operations in service and manufacturing businesses. The chapter ends with a discussion of inventory management, a key factor in a company's profitability.

*After reading these next three sections, you should be able to*
3. *explain the essentials of managing a service business.*
4. *describe the different kinds of manufacturing operations.*
5. *describe why and how companies should manage inventory levels.*

### 3. Service Operations

Imagine that your trusty five-year-old VCR breaks down as you try to record your favorite TV show. You've got two choices. You can run to Wal-Mart and spend $50 to $90 to purchase a new VCR. Or, you can spend somewhere between $35 and $50 (you hope) to have it fixed at a repair shop. With either choice, you end up with the same thing, a working VCR. However, the first choice, getting a new VCR, involves buying a physical product (a "good"), while the second, dealing with a repair shop, involves buying a service.

Services are different from goods in several ways. First, goods are produced or made, but services are performed. In other words, services are almost always labor-intensive: Someone typically has to perform the service for you. A repair shop could give you the parts needed to repair your old VCR, but without the technician to perform the repairs, you're still going to have a broken VCR. Second, goods are tangible, but services are intangible. You can touch and see that new VCR. But you can't touch or see the service provided by the technician who fixed your old VCR. All you can "see" is that the VCR works. Third, services are perishable and unstorable. If you don't use them when they're available, they're wasted. For example, if your VCR repair shop is backlogged on repair jobs, then you'll just have to wait until next week to get your VCR repaired. You can't store an unused service and use it when you like. By contrast, you can purchase a good, such as motor oil, and store it until you're ready to use it.

*Because services are different from goods, managing a service operation is different from managing a manufacturing or production operation. Let's look at 3.1 the service-profit chain and 3.2 service recovery and empowerment.*

### 3.1 The Service-Profit Chain

One of the key assumptions in the service business is that success depends on how well employees, that is, service providers, deliver their services to customers. However, the concept of the service-profit chain, depicted in Exhibit 15.8, suggests that in service businesses, success begins with how well management treats service employees.[42]

The first step in the service-profit chain is *internal service quality*, meaning the quality of treatment that employees receive from a company's internal service providers, such as management, payroll and benefits, human resources, and so forth. For example, Southwest Airlines is legendary for its positive culture and, to the surprise of many, its excellent customer service. Southwest's Chairman Herb Kelleher said, "In the old days, my mother told me that in business school they'd say, 'This is a real conundrum: Who comes first, your employees, your shareholders, or your customers?' My mother taught me that your employees come first. If you treat them well, then they treat the customers well, and that means your customers come back and your shareholders are happy." Gordon Bethune, Kelleher's counterpart at Continental Airlines, which has topped the J.D. Powers airline customer satisfaction survey the last five years, believes the same thing. Said Bethune, "Why are we successful, when year after year our competitors are not doing as well? It's because of the culture we have maintained. The way you do that is to act consistently: You come to work every day feeling good about the way you are going to be treated, and knowing how you are going to be treated." Bethune concluded, "The only other airline in America where people actually like coming to work is Southwest. We are superior in customer satisfaction because we are superior in employee satisfaction. That's it."[43]

Exhibit 15.9 defines the elements that constitute good internal service quality. For employees to do a good job serving customers, management must implement policies and procedures that support good customer service; provide workers the tools and training they need to do their jobs; reward, recognize, communicate, and support good customer service; and encourage people and departments to work together as teams to accomplish company goals with respect to internal service quality and customer service. CVS, a large drugstore chain, has developed a special monthly scorecard to measure and reward internal service quality for 19 different areas in the company. Larry Merlo, executive vice president of stores, said, "Let's use distribution as an example of how this operates. A store manager might say, 'Please make certain the truck delivery [from the CVS warehouse to a CVS pharmacy] is on time today, because I've got two people waiting to unload it and another three waiting to put that order up.' Being on time keeps boxes off the floor and products on the shelves. However, if that truck is two or three hours late, you've significantly impacted that store manager's ability to perform."[44] Since the program began, internal service quality ratings are up by 30 percent. Merlo said, "If we have engaged, satisfied employees who are delivering internal service at a high level to those who are serving the end customers, then customer satisfaction and profitability will follow."[45]

As depicted in Exhibit 15.8, good internal service leads to employee satisfaction and service capability. *Employee satisfaction* occurs when companies treat employees in a way

EXHIBIT 15.8

SERVICE-PROFIT CHAIN

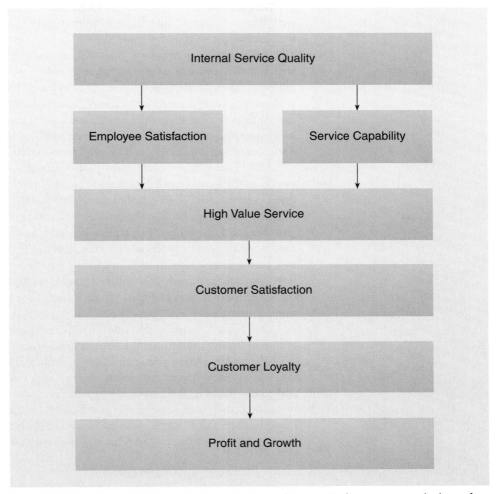

**Source:** R. Hallowell, L.A. Schlesinger, & J. Zornitsky, "Internal Service Quality, Customer and Job Satisfaction: Linkages and Implications for Management," *Human Resource Planning* 19 (1996): 20–31. J.L. Heskett, T.O. Jones, G.W. Loveman, W.E. Sasser, Jr., & L.A. Schlesinger, "Putting the Service-Profit Chain to Work," *Harvard Business Review,* March-April 1994, 164–174.

581

EXHIBIT 15.9

COMPONENTS OF INTERNAL SERVICE QUALITY

| | |
|---|---|
| Policies and Procedures | Do policies and procedures facilitate serving customers? |
| Tools | Has the organization provided service employees the tools they need to serve customers? |
| Effective Training | Is effective, useful, job-specific training made available in a timely fashion? |
| Rewards and Recognition | Are individuals rewarded and/or recognized for good performance? |
| Communication | Does necessary communication occur both vertically and horizontally throughout the organization? |
| Management Support | Does management aid (versus hinder) employees' ability to serve customers? |
| Goal Alignment | Are the goals of senior management aligned with the goals of frontline service employees? |
| Teamwork | Does teamwork occur among individuals and between departments when necessary? |

**Source::** R. Hallowell, L.A. Schlesinger, & J. Zornitsky, "Internal Service Quality, Customer and Job Satisfaction: Linkages and Implications for Management," *Human Resource Planning* 19 (1996): 20–31.

that meets or exceeds their expectations. In other words, the better employees are treated, the more satisfied they are, and the more likely they are to give high-value service to satisfy customers.

*Service capability* is an employee's perception of his or her ability to serve customers well. When an organization serves its employees in ways that help them to do their jobs well, employees, in turn, are more likely to believe that they can and ought to provide high-value service to customers. Again, Southwest Airlines not only treats its employees well, but also takes a number of direct steps to strengthen the service capability of its employees. Chairman Herb Kelleher said, "I can't anticipate all of the situations that will arise at the stations [airport terminals] across our system. So what we tell our people is, 'Hey, we can't anticipate all of these things; *you* handle them the best way possible. *You* make a judgement and use *your* discretion; we trust you'll do the right thing. If we think you've done something erroneous, we'll let you know—without criticism, without backbiting.'"[46]

Finally, according to the service-profit chain shown in Exhibit 15.8, high-value service leads to customer satisfaction and customer loyalty, which, in turn, lead to long-term profits and growth. What's the link between customer satisfaction and loyalty and profits? To start, the average business keeps only 70 to 90 percent of its existing customers each year. No big deal, you say? Just replace leaving customers with new customers. Well, there's one significant problem with that solution. It costs five times as much to find a new customer as it does to keep an existing customer. Also, new customers typically buy only 20 percent as much as established customers. In fact, keeping existing customers is so cost-effective that most businesses could double their profits by simply keeping 5 percent more customers per year![47]

One service company that understands the relationship between high-value service, customer loyalty, and profits is USAA, a Texas-based finance/insurance company. When USAA's customers have young children, it sends them booklets on how to save for a college education. When its customers near the age of 50, it contacts them about retirement and estate planning. And when it issues credit cards to college students, it takes the time to teach them how to manage their credit and avoid excessive credit card debt. Says USAA vice president Phyllis Stahle, "We build loyalty by convincing [customers] we're loyal to them."[48] Indeed, USAA has a 97 percent customer retention rate!

### 3.2 Service Recovery and Empowerment

Many service businesses organize themselves like manufacturing companies. Tasks and jobs are simplified and separated, creating a clear division of labor. Equipment and technology are substituted for people whenever possible. Strict guidelines and rules take the place of employee authority and discretion. This production-line approach to running a service business is still widely used today in businesses that sell a high-volume, low-cost service in which there is a brief, simple transaction between customers and service providers.[49]

While the production-line model excels at efficiency and low costs, it doesn't work well when mistakes are made and customers have become dissatisfied with the service they've received. When this occurs, service businesses must switch from the process of service delivery to the process of **service recovery**, that is, restoring customer satisfaction to strongly dissatisfied customers.[50] Sometimes, service recovery requires service employees to not only fix whatever mistake was made, but also perform "heroic" service acts that "delight" highly dissatisfied customers by far surpassing their expectations of fair treatment. For example, Continental Airlines lost a Scottish customer's luggage, containing rare Irish and Scottish books. Continental's Judy Dyar explained that when they couldn't locate the luggage, "One of our resourceful baggage tracers called publishers and bookstores and managed to replace the books and get them to the customer in a reasonable time."[51] Likewise, when a plane full of tired travelers was diverted from Houston to Corpus Christi, Texas, because of bad weather, the plane's captain ordered pizza which was served hot to customers when the plane arrived at the Corpus Christi airport. Continental awarded the pilot its new "Customer Care Outstanding Service Award." Said Continental's Judy Dyar, "We wanted to recognize when employees go above and be-

**service recovery**
restoring customer satisfaction to strongly dissatisfied customers

yond the call of duty, so other employees would know the importance of doing that and know it's OK to step outside the box sometimes." In both instances, Continental's employees performed service recovery by surpassing customers' expectations with an act meant to make up for poor service or unexpected problems.

Unfortunately, when mistakes occur under a production-line system, service employees typically don't have the discretion to resolve customer complaints. Customers who want service employees to correct or make up for poor service are frequently told, "I'm not allowed to do that," "I'm just following company rules," or "I'm sorry, only managers are allowed to make changes of any kind." In other words, the production-line system prevents them from engaging in acts of service recovery meant to turn dissatisfied customers back into satisfied customers. The result is frustration for customers and service employees and lost customers for the company.

Because production-line systems make it difficult for service employees to do service recovery, many companies are now empowering their service employees.[52] In Chapter 11, you learned that *empowering workers* means permanently passing decision-making authority and responsibility from managers to workers. With respect to service recovery, empowering workers means giving service employees the authority and responsibility to make decisions that immediately solve customer problems.[53] For example, when its trains are delayed, the employees riding Amtrak trains are "empowered" to engage in service recovery. Amtrak manager James Drummond said that employees are empowered to do "whatever it takes to make sure guests have a smile on their face, even if it's an unfortunate trip." On train routes that experience frequent delays, extra staffers ride the trains or stay at train terminals until all customer issues have been addressed. Furthermore, employees are empowered to give dissatisfied passengers travel vouchers worth an amount equivalent to the cost of their current ticket. Vouchers can be used to purchase tickets for future Amtrak travel.[54] In short, the purpose of empowering service employees is zero customer defections, that is, to turn dissatisfied customers back into satisfied customers who continue to do business with the company.

Empowering service workers does entail some costs. Exhibit 15.10 describes some costs and benefits of empowering service workers to act in ways that they believe will

---

*EXHIBIT 15.10*

### COSTS AND BENEFITS OF EMPOWERING SERVICE WORKERS FOR SERVICE RECOVERY

#### COSTS

1. Increased cost of selection to find service workers who are capable of solving problems and dealing with upset customers.
2. Increased cost to train service workers how to solve different kinds of problems.
3. Higher wages to attract and keep talented service workers.
4. A focus on service recovery may lead to less emphasis on service reliability, doing it right the first time. Ultimately, this could lead to slower delivery of services.
5. In their quest to please customers, empowered service workers may cost the company money by being too eager to provide "give-aways" to make up for poor or slow service.
6. Empowered service workers may unintentionally treat customers unfairly by occasionally being overly generous to make up for poor or slow service.

#### BENEFITS

1. Quicker responses to customer complaints and problems.
2. Employees feel better about their jobs and themselves.
3. Employee interaction with customers will be warm and enthusiastic.
4. Employees are more likely to offer ideas for improving service or preventing problems.

**Source:** D.E. Bowen & E.E. Lawler, III, "The Empowerment of Service Workers: What, Why, How, and When," *Sloan Management Review* 33 (Spring 1992): 31–39.

accomplish service recovery. The savings to the company of retaining customers usually exceed the costs of empowering workers.

### Review 3
### Service Operations

Services are different from goods. Goods are produced, tangible, and storable. Services are performed, intangible, and perishable. Likewise, managing service operations is different from managing production operations. The service-profit chain indicates that success begins with internal service quality, meaning how well management treats service employees. Internal service quality leads to employee satisfaction and service capability, which, in turn, lead to high-value service to customers, customer satisfaction, customer loyalty, and long-term profits and growth. Many service businesses are organized like manufacturers. While this "production-line" approach is efficient and inexpensive, its strict rules and guidelines make it difficult for service workers to perform service recovery, restoring customer satisfaction to strongly dissatisfied customers. To resolve this problem, some companies are empowering service employees to perform service recovery by giving them the authority and responsibility to immediately solve customer problems. The hope is that empowered service recovery will prevent customer defections.

# 4. Manufacturing Operations

Let's play word association. What do the phrases "chicken and stars," "chicken noodle," "cream of mushroom," and "cream of tomato" make you think of? Well, soup, of course! And, chances are, you thought of Campbell's soup, the world's best-selling soup brand. In fact, Campbell's soup can be found in 93 percent of U.S. households. While Campbell's effective "hmmm-mmmm good" advertisements bring to mind images of home cooking, Campbell's obviously doesn't make its soups in small kitchens. It makes them in large factories, like its 1.4 million square foot facility in Maxton, North Carolina, that produces 4.9 million cans of soup per day! Moreover, this factory can make over 200 different kinds of soup, as well as SpaghettiOs, pork and beans, and different kinds of gravy.[55]

In contrast to soup, Americana Foods makes food that you'd want to eat on a hot day. In its 220,000 square foot facility in Dallas, Americana makes TCBY frozen yogurt, as well as ice cream, frozen yogurt, sorbet, and popsicles for other private label companies. At one million pounds per day, the plant's total capacity is split among three manufacturing lines for hard-pack ice cream, two manufacturing lines for soft-serve frozen yogurt, two manufacturing lines for novelty products (sorbet, popsicles, etc.), and one manufacturing line for flavored syrup.[56]

*Like the Campbell's soup and Americana ice cream/frozen yogurt manufacturing plants described above, all manufacturing operations produce physical goods. But not all manufacturing operations are the same. And, although both produce food, the Campbell's and Americana factories are actually quite different. Let's learn how various manufacturing operations differ in terms of **4.1** the amount of processing that is done to produce and assemble a product and **4.2** the flexibility to change the number, kind, and characteristics of products that are produced.*

### 4.1 Amount of Processing in Manufacturing Operations

Manufacturing operations can be classified according to the amount of processing or assembly that occurs after receiving an order from customers. For example, at regular-sized Burger King restaurants, Whopper sandwiches are not assembled until a customer makes an order. Only then does the cooking crew put a burger on the grill, begin toasting the hamburger buns, and then prepare the sandwich to customer specifications (i.e., "lettuce, tomatoes, and onion, no pickles"). By contrast, at some of Burger King's largest, busiest restaurants, such as those in airports, museums, schools, and university campuses, cheeseburgers, Whoppers, chicken sandwiches, and fries are prepared ahead of time and left out for customers to retrieve and place on their food trays. In this instance, unless a customer makes a special order, no processing occurs after a customer orders.

**make-to-order operation**
manufacturing operation that does not start processing or assembling products until a customer order is received

The highest degree of processing occurs in **make-to-order operations**. A make-to-order operation does not start processing or assembling products until it receives a customer order. In fact, some make-to-order operations may not even order parts until that customer order is received. Not surprisingly, these practices permit make-to-order operations to produce or assemble highly specialized or customized products for customers.

For example, Dell Computers has one of the most advanced make-to-order operations in the computer business. Dell has no finished-goods inventory—it does not build a computer until someone buys it. Because Dell doesn't order parts from suppliers until machines are purchased, its computers always have the latest, most advanced computer components. No one who buys a Dell computer gets stuck with old technology. Also, because prices of computer components tend to fall, Dell's make-to-order operation can pass on price cuts to customers. Plus, Dell can customize all of its orders, big and small. For example, it took Dell just six weeks to make and ship 2,000 personal computers and 4,000 network servers for Wal-Mart. Furthermore, Dell preloaded each of these 6,000 machines with proprietary software that Wal-Mart uses in its stores and offices.[57]

**assemble-to-order operation**
manufacturing operation that divides manufacturing processes into separate parts or modules that are combined to create semi-customized products

A moderate degree of processing occurs in **assemble-to-order operations**. A company using an assemble-to-order operation divides its manufacturing or assembly process into separate parts or modules. They order parts and assemble modules ahead of customer orders. Then, on the basis of actual customer orders or on research forecasting what customers will want, those modules are then combined to create semi-customized products. For example, when a customer orders a new car, General Motors may have already ordered the basic parts or modules it needs from suppliers. In other words, on the basis of sales forecasts, GM may already have ordered enough tires, air-conditioning compressors, brake systems, and seats from suppliers to accommodate nearly all customer orders on a particular day. However, special orders from customers and car dealers are then used to determine the final assembly checklist for particular cars as they move down the assembly line.

Exhibit 15.11 shows the different package options that come with the Chevrolet Suburban. Each option is different and is the equivalent of a different manufacturing module under an assemble-to-order operation. The table, reading left to right, shows some of the additional options that come with the Suburban as buyers upgrade from the Suburban 1500 LS, to the 2500 LT, and finally to the 1500 Z71. For example, all three Suburban models come with power door locks, autotrac automatic 4WD, front and rear air-conditioning, AM/FM stereo with CD player, heated outside mirrors with self-dimming driver side, six-way power driver and front passenger seats, power windows, luggage rack, power-heated mirrors with ground illumination, aluminum wheels, and remote keyless entry. However, the LT model adds automatic climate control, the OnStar satellite communication system, rear-seat audio controls with headphone jacks, leather trim, heated seats, and polished aluminum wheels. Finally, the Z71 adds tube-type side steps, color-keyed grille, bumpers, door handles, and mirrors, a lighted luggage carrier, front fog lights, and special shocks with 17-inch wheels and tires.

**make-to-stock operation**
manufacturing operation that orders parts and assembles standardized products before receiving customer orders

The lowest degree of processing occurs in **make-to-stock operations**. A company using a make-to-stock operation starts ordering parts and assembling finished products before receiving customer orders. These standardized products are typically purchased by consumers at retail stores or directly from the manufacturer. Because parts are ordered and products are assembled before customers order the products, make-to-stock operations are highly dependent on the accuracy of sales forecasts. If sales forecasts are incorrect, make-to-stock operations may end up building too many or too few products, or they may make products with the wrong features or lacking the features that customers want.

These disadvantages led Wilkerson Corporation, a manufacturer of pneumatic devices such as air compressors, to switch to a make-to-order assembly operation. Under its old make-to-stock system, Wilkerson would make large batches of its best-selling products and store them on shelves that reached all the way to the ceiling of its manufacturing plant. Storing unsold inventory was not only expensive (costs ran as high as 30

EXHIBIT 15.11

AN EXAMPLE OF ASSEMBLE-TO-ORDER OPERATIONS: CHEVROLET SUBURBAN PACKAGE OPTIONS

| FEATURES | 1500 LS | 2500 LT | 1500 Z71 |
|---|---|---|---|
| • Power door locks | ✓ | ✓ | ✓ |
| • AM/FM stereo | ✓ | ✓ | ✓ |
| • Autotrac Automatic 4WD | ✓ | ✓ | ✓ |
| • Front and rear air-conditioning | ✓ | ✓ | ✓ |
| • AM/FM with CD player | ✓ | ✓ | ✓ |
| • Heated outside mirrors with self-dimming driver side | ✓ | ✓ | ✓ |
| • Six-way power driver and front passenger seats | ✓ | ✓ | ✓ |
| • Power windows | ✓ | ✓ | ✓ |
| • Luggage rack | ✓ | ✓ | ✓ |
| • Power-heated mirrors with ground illumination | ✓ | ✓ | ✓ |
| • Aluminum wheels | ✓ | ✓ | ✓ |
| • Remote keyless entry | ✓ | ✓ | ✓ |
| • Automatic climate control | | ✓ | ✓ |
| • OnStar communication system | | ✓ | ✓ |
| • Rear-seat audio controls with headphone jacks | | ✓ | ✓ |
| • Leather trim | | ✓ | ✓ |
| • Heated seats | | ✓ | ✓ |
| • Polished aluminum wheels | | ✓ | ✓ |
| • Tube-type side steps | | | ✓ |
| • Color-keyed grille, bumpers, door handles, and mirrors | | | ✓ |
| • A unique light luggage carrier | | | ✓ |
| • Front fog lights | | | ✓ |
| • Specifically tuned shocks | | | ✓ |
| • 17-inch wheels and tires | | | ✓ |

**Source:** "2002 Chevrolet Suburban: Model Line Description," *Carpoint.MSN.com.* [Online] Available http://carpoint.msn.com/Vip/Description/Chevrolet/Suburban/2002.asp, 28 February 2002.

percent of sales), but it also sometimes took six to 18 months to sell off the unsold finished inventory. And because the company was spending all of its time producing large batches of its best-selling products, it was frequently unable to make special, customized products for customers who required them. With a product catalog of more than 50,000 items, it was almost impossible under the made-to-stock system for Wilkerson to have all of its products in stock and ready for delivery.[58]

### 4.2 Flexibility of Manufacturing Operations

**manufacturing flexibility**
degree to which manufacturing operations can easily and quickly change the number, kind, and characteristics of products they produce

A second way to categorize manufacturing operations is by **manufacturing flexibility**, meaning the degree to which manufacturing operations can easily and quickly change the number, kind, and characteristics of products they produce. Flexibility allows companies to respond quickly to changes in the marketplace (i.e., competitors and customers) and to reduce the lead-time between ordering and final delivery of products. However, there is often a tradeoff between flexibility and cost, with the most flexible manufacturing operations frequently having higher costs per unit and the least flexible operations having lower costs per unit.[59] As shown in Exhibit 15.12, the least to most

EXHIBIT 15.12

FLEXIBILITY OF MANUFACTURING OPERATIONS

| Continuous-Flow Production | Line-Flow Production | Batch Production | Job Shops | Project Manufacturing |

**Least Flexible** ←———————————————————→ **Most Flexible**

flexible manufacturing operations are continuous-flow production, line-flow production, batch production, job shops, and project manufacturing.

Most production processes generate finished products at a discrete rate. A product is completed, and then, perhaps a few seconds, minutes, or hours later, another is completed, and so on. For instance, if you stood at the end of an automobile assembly line, it would appear as if nothing much was happening for 55 seconds of every minute. However, in that last 5 seconds, a new car would be started and driven off the assembly line, ready for its new owner. By contrast, in **continuous-flow production**, products are produced at a continuous, rather than discrete rate, in which production of the final product never stops. It's sort of like a water hose that is never turned off. The water (or product) just keeps on flowing. In other words, the product is always and continuously being produced. Liquid chemicals and petroleum products are examples of continuous-flow production. If you're still struggling with this concept (and it can be confusing), think of PlayDoh. Continuous-flow production is similar to squeezing PlayDoh into a toy press and watching the various shapes ooze out of the "PlayDoh Machine." But with continuous-flow production, the PlayDoh machine would never quit oozing or producing rectangle- or triangle-shaped PlayDoh. Because of their complexity, continuous-flow production processes are the most standardized and least flexible manufacturing operations.

**Line-flow production** processes are pre-established, occur in a serial or linear manner, and are dedicated to making one type of product. In this way, the 10 different steps required to make product X can be completed in a separate manufacturing process (with separate machines, parts, treatments, locations, and workers) from the 12 different steps required to make product Y. Line-flow production processes are inflexible, because they are typically dedicated to manufacturing one kind of product. For example, nearly every city has a local bottling plant for soft drinks or beer. The processes or steps in bottling plants are serial, meaning they must occur in a particular order. For example, after empty bottles are sterilized, they are filled with soft drinks or beer using a special dispenser that distributes the liquid down the inside walls of the bottle. This fills the bottle from the bottom up and displaces the air that was in the bottle. The bottles are then crowned or capped, checked for underfilling and missing caps, labeled, inspected a final time for fill levels and missing labels, and then placed in cases that are shrink-wrapped on pallets and put on trucks for delivery.[60]

The next most flexible manufacturing operation is **batch production**, which involves the manufacture of large batches of different products in standard lot sizes. Consequently, a worker in a batch production operation will perform the same manufacturing process on 100 copies of product X, followed by 200 copies of product Y, and then 50 copies of product Q. Furthermore, these "batches" move through each manufacturing department or process in identical order. So if the paint department follows chemical treatment, and chemical treatment is now processing a batch of 50 copies of product Q, then the paint department's next task will be to paint 50 copies of product Q. Batch production is finding increasing use among restaurant chains. To ensure consistency in the taste and quality of their products, many restaurants have central kitchens, or commissaries, that produce

**continuous-flow production**
manufacturing operation that produces goods in a continuous, rather than a discrete, rate

**line-flow production**
manufacturing processes that are pre-established, occur in a serial or linear manner, and are dedicated to making one type of product

**batch production**
manufacturing operation that produces goods in large batches in standard lot sizes

587

batches of food, such as mashed potatoes, stuffing, macaroni and cheese, rice, quiches, chili, and so forth, in volumes ranging from 10 to 200 gallons. These batches are then delivered to restaurants, where the food is served to customers.

The next most flexible manufacturing operation is called a job shop. **Job shops** are typically small manufacturing operations that handle special manufacturing processes or jobs. By contrast to batch production, which handles large batches of different products, job shops typically handle very small batches, some as small as one product or process per "batch." Basically, each "job" in a job shop is different, and once a job is done, the job shop moves on to a completely different job or manufacturing process for, most likely, a different customer. For example, Leggett & Platt Machine Products in Carthage, Missouri, is a job shop that makes coil springs, innerspring units, welded metal grids, and various other parts for mattress manufacturers around the world. Since inception, its 225 employees have made over 25,000 *different* parts, or, in other words, have completed 25,000 different jobs for its customers.[61] Another example of a job shop is Heil Trailer International in Athens, Tennessee. Heil specializes in the production of custom truck trailers that carry petroleum or dry bulk. Heil also makes intermodal trailers that can be pulled by trucks and transported by trains. Steve Slaughter, Heil's general manager, said, "Even when we get orders for multiple trailers, the trailers normally aren't the same. The shape of the tank itself doesn't really change that much. But with all the different weight laws and customer preferences, it's unusual to see two identical trailers going down the same assembly line."[62]

The most flexible manufacturing operation is project manufacturing. **Project manufacturing** is an operation designed to produce large, expensive, specialized products like custom homes; defense weapons, such as aircraft carriers and submarines; and aerospace products, like passenger planes and the space shuttle. Project manufacturing is highly flexible, because each project is usually significantly different from the one before it, even if the projects produce the same general type of product, such as a submarine. Because of each project's size, expense, and high degree of customization, project manufacturing can take an extremely long time to complete. For instance, General Dynamics uses project manufacturing when making new submarines. The U.S. Navy's Virginia class subs, which are its newest and most advanced attack submarines, are 377 feet long and able to attain speeds greater than 25 knots (28 miles per hour/46.3 kilometers per hour). Therefore, they will be significantly quieter and faster than the Los Angeles class submarines that they replace.[63] Project manufacturing is required for submarine construction because of the tremendous cost, $1.6 billion each, the complexity of the subs themselves, and the length of time it takes to complete a new submarine, six years. Because of these enormous challenges, only one new Virginia class submarine is being completed each year.

## Review 4
### Manufacturing Operations

Manufacturing operations produce physical goods. Manufacturing operations can be classified according to the amount of processing or assembly that occurs after receiving an order from customers. Make-to-order operations have the highest degree of processing, in which assembly doesn't begin until products are ordered. The next-highest degree of processing occurs in assemble-to-order operations, in which preassembled modules are combined after orders are received to produce semicustomized products. The lowest degree of processing occurs in make-to-stock operations, in which, on the basis of sales forecasts, standard parts are ordered and assembled before orders occur.

Manufacturing operations can also be classified in terms of flexibility, the degree to which the number, kind, and characteristics of products can easily and quickly be changed. Flexibility allows companies to respond quickly to competitors and customers and to reduce order lead-times, but can also lead to higher unit costs. The least to most flexible manufacturing operations are continuous-flow production, line-flow production, batch production, job shops, and project manufacturing.

---

**job shops**
manufacturing operations that handle custom orders or small batch jobs

**project manufacturing**
manufacturing operations designed to produce large, expensive, specialized products

# 5. Inventory

Heinz, the food company, closed a baby food and soup factory for 10 weeks to reduce inventories and cut costs. During this time, 400 of the plant's 700 workers were temporarily suspended without pay. A company spokesperson called the temporary closure a "one-time adjustment." Said the spokesperson, "It is not related to sales at all. Right now, the focus of the Heinz Corporation is to control costs. What this represents is an attempt to control costs by managing inventory levels."[64] Likewise, when auto sales dropped by 16 percent, General Motors shut down 14 of its 29 assembly plants and laid off half of its workers for periods ranging from one to five weeks. GM had a 116-day supply of new trucks and sport utility vehicles on hand, well over its goal of a 72-day supply. Paul Ballew, who is a general director for market and industry analysis at GM, said, "With sales moderating, the industry had to work through this inventory bubble."[65]

**inventory**
the amount and number of raw materials, parts, and finished products that a company has in its possession

*Inventory* is the amount and number of raw materials, parts, and finished products that a company has in its possession. Both Heinz and General Motors made the mistake of having too much inventory on hand and had to close their factories to let existing sales draw down inventory levels to an acceptable and affordable level. In this section, you will learn about 5.1 the different types of inventory, 5.2 how to measure inventory levels, 5.3 the costs of maintaining an inventory, and 5.4 the different systems for managing inventory.

## 5.1 Types of Inventory

Exhibit 15.13 shows the four kinds of inventory a manufacturer stores: raw materials, component parts, work-in-process, and finished goods. The flow of inventory through a manufacturing plant begins when the purchasing department buys raw materials from vendors. **Raw material inventories** are the basic inputs in the manufacturing process. For example, to begin making a car, automobile manufacturers purchase raw materials like steel, iron, aluminum, copper, rubber, and unprocessed plastic.

**raw material inventories**
the basic inputs in a manufacturing process

**component parts inventories**
the basic parts used in manufacturing that are fabricated from raw materials

Next, raw materials are fabricated or processed into **component parts inventories**, meaning the basic parts used in manufacturing a product. For example, in an automobile plant, steel is fabricated or processed into a car's body panels, and steel and iron are melted and shaped into engine parts like pistons or engine blocks. Component parts inventories are sometimes purchased directly from vendors.

**work-in-process inventories**
partially finished goods consisting of assembled component parts

The component parts are then assembled to make unfinished **work-in-process inventories** (WIP), which are also known as partially finished goods. This process is also called *initial assembly*. For example, steel body panels are welded to each other and to the frame of the car to make a "unibody," which comprises the unpainted interior frame and exterior structure of the car. Likewise, pistons, camshafts, and other engine parts are inserted into the engine block to create a working engine.

**finished goods inventories**
the final outputs of manufacturing operations

Next, all the work-in-process inventories are assembled to create **finished goods inventories**, which are the final outputs of the manufacturing process. This process is also called *final assembly*. So, for a car, the engine, wheels, brake system, suspension, interior, and electrical system are assembled into a car's painted unibody to make the working automobile, which is the factory's finished product. In the last step in the process, the finished goods are sent to field warehouses, distribution centers, or wholesalers, and then to retailers for final sale to customers.

## 5.2 Measuring Inventory

As you'll learn below, uncontrolled inventory can lead to huge costs for a manufacturing operation. Consequently, managers need good measures of inventory to prevent inventory costs from becoming too large. Three basic measures of inventory are average aggregate inventory, weeks of supply, and inventory turnover.

If you've ever worked in a retail store and have had to "take inventory," you probably weren't too excited about the process of counting every item in the store and storeroom. It's an extensive process. Fortunately, "taking inventory" is somewhat easier today because of bar codes that mark items and computers that can count and track them. However, if

EXHIBIT 15.13

TYPES OF INVENTORY

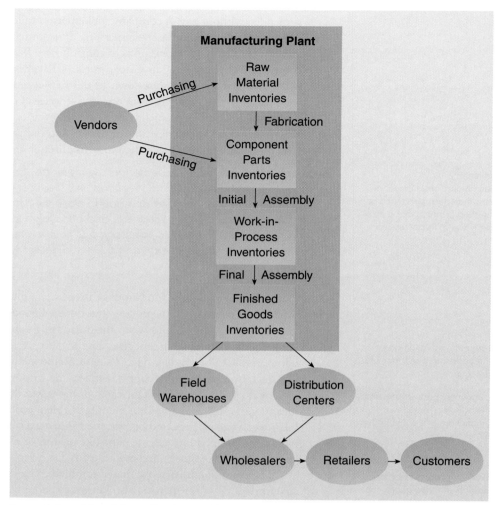

**Source:** Adapted from R.E. Markland, S.K. Vickery, & R.A. Davis, *Operations Management* (Cincinnati, OH: South-Western College Publishing, 1998).

**average aggregate inventory**
average overall inventory during a particular time period

**stockout**
situation in which a company runs out of finished product

you took inventory at the beginning of the month, the inventory count would likely be different from the count at the end of the month. Similar differences in inventory count might occur if inventory was taken on a Friday rather than a Monday. Because of day-to-day differences in inventories, companies often measure **average aggregate inventory**, which is the average overall inventory during a particular time period. Average aggregate inventory for a month can be determined by simply averaging the inventory counts at the end of each business day for that month. One way companies know whether they're carrying too much or too little inventory is to compare their average aggregate inventory to the industry average for aggregate inventory. For example, in the automobile industry, 72 days of inventory is the industry average.

Inventory is also measured in terms of *weeks of supply*, meaning the number of weeks it would take for a company to run out of its current supply of inventory. In general, there is an acceptable number of weeks of inventory for a particular kind of business. Too few weeks of inventory on hand, and a company risks a **stockout**—running out of inventory. For example, Microsoft initially shipped 300,000 Xbox videogame consoles to retailers at the beginning of November 2001. Normally, this would be about two weeks

**Buy High and Sell Low?**

Conventional wisdom in investing says to "buy low and sell high." However, with inventory levels, you should *buy high,* because sellers are more likely to cut prices when they have excess inventory. For example, since 72 days of inventory is the norm in the auto industry, car manufacturers will usually cut car prices when they have 90 or more days of inventory. *The Wall Street Journal* regularly publishes this information. Likewise, you should *sell low,* because when inventories are low, buyers will typically pay more to obtain hard-to-get items. So, to make your hard-earned money go further, remember to *buy high and sell low.*

**inventory turnover**
the number of times per year that a company sells or "turns over" its average inventory

worth of inventory during the busy holiday shopping season. However, Kmart, Wal-Mart, Electronics Boutique, Toys "R" Us, and other retailers sold out all 300,000 Xboxes on the first day they were available in stores. And while Microsoft ultimately sold 1.1 million Xboxes between early November and Christmas, its sales were still much smaller than Sony's PlayStation 2 (PS2). Sony had learned its lesson the previous holiday season when limited PS2 inventory led to stockouts. However, PS2s outsold Xboxes in 2001 because Sony made sure it had more than enough PS2s in stores for all the moms, dads, and kids who wanted one for the holiday season.[66] Too many weeks of inventory on the other hand, and the business incurs high costs (discussed below). For example, companies that make linerboard used for corrugated cardboard boxes typically have too much inventory when they have more than six weeks' supply on hand and about the right amount of inventory when the level drops to four weeks' supply.[67] Anything more than that results in excess inventory, which can only be reduced through price cuts or by temporarily stopping production.

Another common inventory measure, **inventory turnover**, is the number of times per year that a company sells or "turns over" its average inventory. For example, if a company keeps an average of 100 finished widgets in inventory each month, and it sold 1,000 widgets this year, then it "turned" its inventory 10 times this year.

In general, the higher the number of inventory "turns," the better. In practice, a high turnover means that a company can continue its daily operations with just a small amount of inventory on hand. For example, let's take two companies, A and B, which, over the course of a year, have identical inventory levels (520,000 widget parts and raw materials). If company A turns its inventories 26 times a year, it would completely replenish its inventory every two weeks and have an average inventory of 20,000 widgets parts and raw material. By contrast, if company B turned its inventories only 2 times a year, it would completely replenish its inventory every 26 weeks and have an average inventory of 260,000 widget parts and inventory. So by turning its inventory more often, company A has 92 percent less inventory on hand at any one time than company B.

Across all kinds of manufacturing plants, the average number of inventory turns, as shown in Exhibit 15.14, is approximately eight per year.[68] However, the average can be as

591

A line of New York gamers waits on an escalator for their chance to purchase an Xbox game console before the Christmas 2001 season. But at stores like this, Xbox consoles sold out within the first few hours of being released and stocked on store shelves. Microsoft's miscalculation of its inventory resulted in losing sales to Sony's PlayStation 2.

AP/WIDE WORLD PHOTOS

EXHIBIT 15.14

INVENTORY TURN RATES ACROSS INDUSTRIES

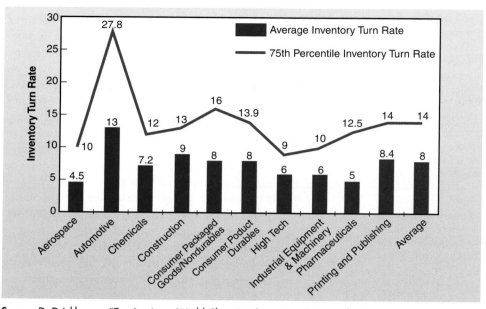

Source: D. Drickhamer, "Zeroing in on World-Class," *Industry Week*, November 2001, 36.

high as 13 inventory turns per year in the automotive industry, where turning inventory more frequently can cut costs by several hundred million dollars per year per company. Exhibit 15.14 also shows the inventory turn rates for some of the best companies in each industry (i.e., 75th percentile). For example, while the average auto company turns its entire industry 13 times per year, some of the best auto companies more than double that rate, turning their total inventory 27.8 times per year, or once every two weeks.[69]

### 5.3 Costs of Maintaining an Inventory

Maintaining an inventory incurs four kinds of costs: ordering, setup, holding, and stockout. **Ordering cost** is not the cost of the inventory itself, but the costs associated with ordering the inventory. It includes the costs of completing paperwork, manually entering data into a computer, making phone calls, getting competing bids, correcting mistakes, and simply determining when and how much new inventory should be reordered. For example, ordering costs are relatively high in the restaurant business, because 80 percent of food service orders (in which restaurants reorder food supplies) are processed manually. However, it's estimated that the food industry could save $6.6 billion if all restaurants converted to electronic data interchange (see Chapter 5), in which purchase and ordering information from one company's computer system is automatically relayed to another company's computer system. In fact, a number of restaurants and food service trade groups have formed an interest group called Efficient Foodservice Response to encourage restaurants and food suppliers to use EDI and other methods of electronic commerce.[70]

**Setup cost** is the cost of changing or adjusting a machine so it can produce a different kind of inventory.[71] For example, 3M uses the same production machinery to make several kinds of industrial tape. However, different adjustments have to be made to the machines for each kind of tape. There are two kinds of setup costs, downtime and lost efficiency. *Downtime* occurs any time a machine is not being used to process inventory. So if it takes five hours to switch a machine from processing one kind of inventory to another, then five hours of downtime have occurred. Downtime is costly, because companies only earn an economic return when machines are actively turning raw materials

**592**

**ordering cost**
the costs associated with ordering inventory, including the cost of data entry, phone calls, obtaining bids, correcting mistakes, and determining when and how much inventory to order

**setup cost**
the costs of downtime and lost efficiency that occur when changing or adjusting a machine to produce a different kind of inventory

# BlastFromThePast

## Guns, Geometry, and Fire: A Brief History of Manufacturing Operations

Today, we take it for granted that manufactured goods will be made with standardized, interchangeable parts; that the design of those parts will be based on specific, detailed plans; and that manufacturing companies will aggressively manage inventories to keep costs low and increase productivity. Surprisingly, these key elements of modern manufacturing operations have some rather strange origins: guns, geometry, and fire.

Since 1526, in Gardone, Italy, the family of Fabbrica d'Armi Pietro Beretta has been making world-renowned Beretta firearms and gun barrels. Throughout most of the company's history, skilled craftsmen handmade the lock, stock, and barrel of Beretta guns. After each part had been handmade, a skilled gun finisher assembled the parts into a complete gun. However, a gun finisher's job was not simply screwing the different parts of a gun together, as is done today. Instead, each handmade part required extensive finishing and adjusting, so it would fit together with the other handmade gun parts. This was necessary because, even if made by the same skilled craftsman, no two parts were alike. In fact, gun finishers played a role similar to that of fine watchmakers, who meticulously assembled expensive watches—without them, the product simply wouldn't work.

However, this all changed in 1791 when the U.S. government, worried about a possible war with France, ordered 40,000 muskets from private gun contractors. Like Beretta, all but one contractor built handmade muskets assembled by skilled gun finishers who made sure that each part fit together. Thus, each musket was unique. If a part broke, a replacement part would have to be handcrafted. But one contractor, Eli Whitney of New Haven, Connecticut, who is better known for his invention of the cotton gin, determined that if gun parts were made accurately enough, guns could be made with standardized, interchangeable parts. So he designed machine tools that allowed unskilled workers to make each gun part the same as the next. Said Whitney, "The tools which I contemplate to make are similar to an engraving on copper plate from which may be taken a great number of impressions perceptibly alike." Years passed before Whitney delivered his 10,000 muskets to the U.S. government. However, in 1801, he demonstrated the superiority of interchangeable parts to President-elect Thomas Jefferson by quickly and easily assembling complete muskets from randomly picked piles of musket parts.

Today, because of Whitney's ideas, most things, from cars to toasters to space shuttles, are manufactured using standardized, interchangeable parts. But even with this advance, manufacturers still faced the significant limitation of not being able to produce a part that they had not seen or examined firsthand. Yet, thanks to Gaspard Monge, a Frenchmen of modest beginnings, this soon changed.

In Monge's time, maps were crude, often inaccurate, and almost never up-to-date. However, in 1762, as a 16-year-old, Monge drew a large-scale map of the town of Beaune, France. He developed new surveying tools and systematic methods of observation, so that everything on the map was in proportion and correctly placed. Monge's advanced skills as a draftsman led to his appointment to the prestigious École Militaire de Mézières, a military institute, where one of his first assignments was to determine the proper placement of cannons for a military fortress. This task normally involved long, complicated mathematical computations, but using the geometrical principles he developed as a draftsman, Monge calculated his estimates so quickly that, at first, commanders refused to believe they were accurate. However, they soon realized the importance of his breakthrough and protected it as a military secret for more than a decade.

However, the book *Descriptive Geometry* was Monge's greatest achievement. In it, he explained techniques for drawing three-dimensional objects on paper. For the first time, such precise drawings permitted manufacturers to make standardized, interchangeable parts without first examining a prototype. Today, thanks to Monge, manufacturers rely on CAD (computer-aided design) and CAM (computer-aided manufacturing) to take three-dimensional designs straight from the computer to the factory floor.

With standardized, interchangeable parts now the norm, and with parts that could be made from design drawings alone, manufacturers ran into a problem that they had never faced before: too much inventory. In fact, it became common for large factories to have as much as two months' parts inventory on hand. Ironically, a solution to this problem was found in 1905 when the Oldsmobile Motor Works in Detroit burned down. At a time when cars were far too expensive for most Americans, Oldsmobile had become the leading automobile manufacturer in the United States by being the first to produce an affordable car. So when the Oldsmobile factory burned down, management rented a new production facility to get production up and running as quickly as possible. However, because the new facility was much smaller (and because the company was short on funds), there was no room to store large stockpiles of inventory, as was the custom of the day. Therefore, the company made do with what it called "hand-to-mouth inventories," in which each production station had only enough parts on hand to do a short production run. Fortunately, since all of its parts suppliers were close by, Oldsmobile could place orders in the morning and receive them in the afternoon (even without telephones), just like today's computerized, just-in-time inventory systems. So, contrary to common belief, just-in-time inventory systems were not invented by Japanese manufacturers. Instead, they were invented out of necessity nearly a century ago because of a fire.

**Sources:** "The Arsenals of Progress," *Economist*, 5 March 1995, 5. C. Behagg, "Mass Production without the Factory: Craft Producers, Guns and Small Firm Innovation, 1790–1815," *Business History* 40, no. 3 (1 July 1998): 1. The Beretta Museum, "Beretta History." [Online] Available http://www.beretta.com, 15 February 1999. *Morning Chronicle*, 11 November 1850. *Household Words* IV (1851/52): 582. Select Committee on Small Arms, QQ. 411–15. M. Schwartz & A. Fish, "Just-in-Time Inventories in Old Detroit," *Business History* 40, no. 3 (July 1998): 48. J.B. White, "The Line Starts Here: Mass Production Techniques Changed the Way People Work and Live Throughout the World. So Whose Idea Was It Anyway?" *The Wall Street Journal*, 11 January 1999, R25. "Whitney, Eli" Britannica Online. [Online] Available http://www.eb.com, 15 February 1999.

593

EXHIBIT 15.15

TRADE-OFF BETWEEN SETUP COSTS AND MANUFACTURING FLEXIBILITY

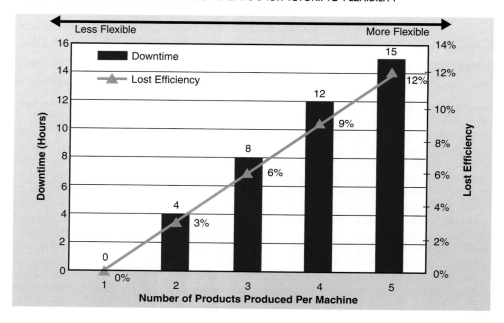

into parts or parts into finished products. The second setup cost is *lost efficiency*. Typically, after a switchover, it takes some time to recalibrate a machine to its optimal settings. It may take several days of fine tuning before a machine finally produces the number of high-quality parts that it is supposed to. Exhibit 15.15 illustrates the trade-off between setup costs, meaning downtime and lost efficiency, and manufacturing flexibility, that is, the number of *different* products (or inventory) that can be processed or assembled on a particular machine. The data in Exhibit 15.15 assume that four hours of downtime and 3 percent lost efficiency occur each time a machine's setup has to be changed from one product to another. So, as shown in Exhibit 15.15, each time a machine has to be changed to handle a different kind of inventory, setup costs (downtime and lost efficiency) rise.

**Holding cost**, also known as *carrying* or *storage cost*, is the cost of keeping inventory until it is used or sold. Holding costs include the cost of storage facilities, insurance to protect inventory from damage or theft, inventory taxes, the cost of obsolescence (holding inventory that is no longer useful to the company), and the opportunity cost of spending money on inventory that could have been spent elsewhere in the company. For example, it's estimated that at any one time, U.S. airlines have a total of $60 billion worth of airplane parts in stock for maintenance, repair, and overhauling their planes. The holding costs for managing, storing, and purchasing these parts is nearly $12.5 billion—or roughly one-fifth of the cost of the parts themselves.[72]

**Stockout costs** are the costs incurred when a company runs out of a product. There are two basic kinds of stockout costs. The first is the transaction costs of overtime work, shipping, and so forth, that are incurred in trying to quickly replace out-of-stock inventories with new inventories. The second and perhaps most damaging cost is the loss of customers' goodwill when a company cannot deliver the products that it promised. And stockouts occur more often than you'd think. Studies indicate that common products, such as yogurt, bottled water, juice, soft drinks, bread, toilet tissue, frozen pizza, and baby diapers, were out of stock at least once per month. On a typical afternoon, 8.2 percent of these items were out of stock. On Sundays, following the busiest shopping day of the week, stockouts of these items rose to 11 percent.[73] Marc Pritchard, vice president

**holding cost**
the cost of keeping inventory until it is used or sold, including storage, insurance, taxes, obsolescence, and opportunity costs

**stockout costs**
the costs incurred when a company runs out of a product, including transaction costs to replace inventory and the loss of customers' goodwill

594

and general manager for Procter & Gamble, said, "Research shows the number-one complaint of mass shoppers is product availability. Twenty-five percent of shoppers walk out of the mass store without a purchase. What's worse is what you'd find in the back of stores and in manufacturers' warehouses—$1.3 billion in inventory, think of that—but we still can't keep the right product in stock."[74]

## 5.4 Managing Inventory

Inventory management has two basic goals. The first is to avoid running out of stock and angering and dissatisfying customers. Consequently, this goal seeks to increase inventory levels to a "safe" level that won't risk stockouts. The second is to efficiently reduce inventory levels and costs as much as possible without impairing daily operations. Thus, this goal seeks a minimum level of inventory. The following inventory management techniques—economic order quantity (EOQ), just-in-time inventory (JIT), and materials requirement planning (MRP)—are different ways of balancing these competing goals.

**Economic order quantity (EOQ)** is a system of formulas that helps determine how much and how often inventory should be ordered. EOQ takes into account the overall demand (D) for a product while trying to minimize ordering costs (O) and holding costs (H). The formula for EOQ is $EOQ = \sqrt{\dfrac{2DO}{H}}$. For example, if a factory uses 40,000 gallons of paint a year (D), and ordering costs (O) are $75 per order, and holding costs (H) are $4 per gallon, then the optimal quantity to order is 1,225 gallons, $EOQ = \sqrt{\dfrac{2(40,000)(75)}{4}} = 1,225$. And, with 40,000 gallons of paint being used per year, the factory uses approximately 110 gallons per day $\left(\dfrac{40,000 \; gallons}{365 \; days} = 110\right)$.

Consequently, the factory would order 1,225 new gallons of paint approximately every 11 days $\left(\dfrac{1,225 \; gallons}{110 \; gallons \; per \; day} = 11.1 \; days\right)$. In general EOQ formulas do a good job of letting managers know what size or amount of inventory they should reorder to minimize ordering and holding costs. However, EOQ formulas and models can become much more complex as adjustments are made for price changes, quantity discounts, setup costs, and many other factors.[75]

While EOQ formulas try to minimize holding and ordering costs, the just-in-time (JIT) approach to inventory management attempts to eliminate holding costs by reducing inventory levels to near zero. A **just-in-time (JIT) inventory system** is a system in which component parts arrive from suppliers just as they are needed at each stage of production. By having parts arrive "just in time," the manufacturer has little inventory on hand, avoiding the costs associated with holding inventory. For example, thanks to its JIT inventory system, Toyota's Georgetown, Kentucky, car factory has only 2.8 hours' worth of inventory on hand at any one time. This low level of inventory saves Toyota millions of dollars a year in inventory expenses.[76] When Ford needs more seats at its Taurus plant in Chicago, it uses an electronic system to give its seat supplier two hours' notice to make its next delivery of seats to the factory.[77]

To have just the right amount of inventory arrive at just the right time requires a tremendous amount of coordination between manufacturing operations and suppliers. One way to promote tight coordination under JIT is close proximity. At Toyota's Georgetown, Kentucky, plant, most parts suppliers are located within 200 miles of the plant. Furthermore, parts are picked up from suppliers and delivered to Toyota as often as 16 times a day.[78]

A second way to promote close coordination under JIT is shared information systems. These systems allow manufacturers and their suppliers to know the quantity and kinds of parts inventory the other has in stock. One way to facilitate information sharing is for factories and suppliers to use the same part numbers and names. Ford's seat

# BeenThereDoneThat

## Lean Manufacturing at Wiremold

Art Byrne is CEO of Wiremold, a manufacturer of wire and cable management systems, power and data quality products, and data/communications connectivity systems. Over the last 10 years, Wiremold aggressively implemented "lean manufacturing" through continuous improvement and just-in-time inventory systems to greatly increase quality and reduce costs.

**Q:** There is no easy or fast way to implement a lean business system, is there?

**A:** This is a physical thing. You can't just reprogram your computer system and, baboom, off you go. That was the promise of MRP. It never worked. It's a lazy man's way of doing it.

This is physical. You're going to have to move every machine in the factory maybe six or eight times. When you say that, you get the following:

"Oh, gee, we don't want to do that because we haven't moved any of these machines for 20 years. You want to move them six or eight times over the next three years?"

"Yes."

"Well, how do you know that?"

"Experience."

"Oh, that sounds like it's going to take a lot of effort and maybe we shouldn't start down that path. Couldn't we do something else?"

Let's talk about setup for a second because it helps to answer your question.

Say you ran a company and it takes three hours to change over and you came and spent a day with us and you went home, got all of your setup guys in a room, and told them: "I've seen it. This is it. It has taken us three hours to change over for the last 25 years, and as of now, I need you all to change over in less than five minutes."

These guys have been running their machines for you for 20 years and you come in and tell them this revelation. What do you think they're going to say to you?

First of all, they'll think you're nuts. They'll say: "Haven't you learned anything in all these years you've been here? You know it takes this long."

When they find out that you're really kind of serious, now you're going to get "The List." This is the list of why it can't be done. And you know what? It will be a pretty good list. It will make a lot of sense. Unless you're good at this, unless you know how specifically to do this and to show them how to do this, it's impossible for you to overcome The List because The List comes out of the guys who do this every day. They're going to tell you why you can't do it. So are you stumped?

This is why people fail. They're stumped.

What are you going to do when they give you The List? How are you going to show them? You can't just tell them. You just tried that and it didn't work. So now you're forced to show them that this can happen. You're forced to make them understand what is possible.

**Q:** How do you get people to take the next step? How do you get them to understand that there are another 20 steps after that?

**A:** The difficulty might be Western economies in general and the difference between Christian and Eastern religions. We

believe in an absolute—a beginning and end. You die, that's it. In Asia, you can come back as a cat, a dog, or a prince. You can come back a lot of times. So there is never an absolute ending.

We translate that into, "I did a kaizen, this is the most perfect way to do it, period. Never go back and look at it again." That's a problem. The Japanese will go back and look at something 40 or 50 times. We've kaizened every part of our business—every cell, every process—multiple times. You just have to keep going back. We are never going to stop. The crazy thing is that maybe the first time through you get a 50 percent productivity gain; the next time through you're going to get 100 percent. That is a mindboggling thing for people to think about.

**Q:** Do you see the same results the eighth time through?

**A:** Yes. With one of our initial cells, we went from eight people down to four, a 50 percent productivity gain. Then we went from four to two, same thing. Then we went from two to one. The percentage gain was much bigger.

**Q:** Can you go from one to none?

**A:** You effectively do that by incorporating other things into their jobs. One person is now doing two or three other rows of tasks.

**Q:** Is the Internet a big deal in all of this? Is it an enabler?

**A:** Not so far. We'd like to be able to get orders over the Internet and that will speed up the information flow, but you still physically have to make the stuff. You physically have to move it. You physically have to buy parts. Things are still done physically.

We buy parts from suppliers based on kanban. The cardboard vendor comes in the morning. He delivers what we ordered yesterday in the afternoon, and we give him a physical fistful of kanban cards. We had gone to this location and done kaizens to show him how to deal with these kanban cards and put them on the next bundle of product. In the afternoon, he'll come back and give us bundles of cardboard with the kanban cards on these bundles that we gave him in the morning.

So what do we need the Internet for? We want to physically give him these cards so he can physically put them on the product so we can keep track of them. In cases like that we don't really need it. But I can see some uses for the Internet with our communication with other suppliers, like our steel supplier, who is farther away. We have to communicate with him electronically.

At the end of the day, it's all physical.

**Q:** Is your inventory-turn figure the key measure for your business?

**A:** We use about five or six measures, and if you want to say that's too many, I would tell you to use only two measures: inventory turns and customer service. If you have customer service going up and inventory turns going up at the same time, I can just about guarantee you that you are doing a good job every place else.

That is the antithesis of how most people think about business. Most people accept low inventory turns as a necessary evil in order to have good customer service. They think about it in the exact opposite way.

We found that the more we can turn inventory, the faster we can turn it, the better our customer service gets. In order to turn it that well and have good customer service, you have to have good quality, good costs, and good productivity because those things are all linked.

In our language internally, we see inventory as the root of all evil because it is. It's only there for bad reasons. If you were better you wouldn't need to have it. When you go to a huge Toyota factory—and huge is like a city—and you ask them how much inventory they have, and they hang their head and say, "We are very baaad today, we have point eight days of inventory and we're supposed to have point five," you just want to go out into the parking lot and shoot yourself. Then you go onto the floor and see it.

People around here are running around with three or four months' worth. Look at a company like Boeing. When they finish their product, it flies away. Not too long ago, they were turning inventory one time—one time. If they turned it 10 times, they would free up $15 billion in cash. And you ask, "What's wrong with management's thinking that they wouldn't be interested in turning it 10 times and generating $15 billion? Why aren't shareholders screaming for that?"

The reason is they don't believe it, and even if they believed it, they don't know how to do it. They've got a whole organization that is telling them it can't be done. How's one CEO going to go against this whole organization that is telling them that this can't be done because they are Boeing, and they are different?

**Source:** R. McCormack, "Breaking the Mold at Wiremold," *Manufacturing News*, 31 January 2002, 1. This interview was edited for inclusion in this textbook.

supplier accomplishes this by sticking a bar code on each seat. Ford then uses the same bar code in its factories to determine when the seat is needed, which car the seat is installed in, and which workstation on the assembly line will install the seat.

Another way to facilitate close coordination between manufacturing operations and their parts suppliers is the Japanese system of kanban. **Kanban**, which is Japanese for "sign," is a simple ticket-based system that indicates when it is time to reorder inventory. Suppliers attach kanban cards to batches of parts. Then, when an assembly line worker uses the first part out of a batch, the kanban card is removed. The cards are then collected, sorted, and quickly returned to the supplier, who begins resupplying the factory with parts that match the order information on the kanban cards. Glenn Uminger, manager of production control and logistics at Toyota's Georgetown, Kentucky, plant, said, "We are placing orders for new parts as the first part is used out of a box." And, because prices and batch sizes are typically agreed to ahead of time, kanban tickets greatly reduce paperwork and ordering costs.[79]

A third method for managing inventory is **materials requirement planning (MRP)**. MRP is a production and inventory system that, from beginning to end, precisely determines the production schedule, production batch sizes, and inventories needed to complete final products. The three key parts of MRP systems are the master production schedule, the bill of materials, and inventory records. The *master production schedule* is a detailed schedule that indicates the quantity of each item to be produced, the planned delivery dates for those items, and the time by which each step of the production process must be completed in order to meet those delivery dates. Based on the quantity and kind of products set forth in the master production schedule, the *bill of materials* identifies all the necessary parts and inventory, the quantity or volume of inventory to be ordered, and the order in which the parts and inventory should be assembled. *Inventory records* indicate the kind, quantity, and location of inventory that is on hand or that has been ordered. When inventory records are combined with the bill of materials, the resulting report indicates what to buy, when to buy it, and what it will cost to order. Today, nearly all MRP systems are available in the form of powerful, flexible computer software.[80]

Which inventory management system should you use? Economic order quantity (EOQ) formulas are intended for use with **independent demand systems**, in which the level of one kind of inventory does not depend on another. For example, because inventory levels for automobile tires are unrelated to the inventory levels of ladies dresses, Sears could use EOQ formulas to calculate separate optimal order quantities for dresses and tires. By contrast, JIT and MRP are used with **dependent demand systems**, in which

**kanban**
a ticket-based JIT system that indicates when to reorder inventory

**materials requirement planning (MRP)**
a production and inventory system that determines the production schedule, production batch sizes, and inventory needed to complete final products

**independent demand system**
inventory system in which the level of one kind of inventory does not depend on another

**dependent demand systems**
inventory system in which the level of inventory depends on the number of finished units to be produced

the level of inventory depends on the number of finished units to be produced. For example, if Yamaha makes 1,000 motorcycles a day, then it will need 1,000 seats, 1,000 gas tanks, and 2,000 wheels and tires each day. So when optimal inventory levels depend on the number of products to be produced, use a JIT or MRP management system.

### Review 5
#### Inventory

There are four kinds of inventory: raw materials, component parts, work-in-process, and finished goods. Because companies incur ordering, setup, holding, and stockout costs when handling inventory, inventory costs can be enormous. To control those costs, companies measure and track inventory in three ways: average aggregate inventory, weeks of supply, and turnover. Companies meet the basic goals of inventory management (avoiding stockouts and reducing inventory without hurting daily operations) through economic order quantity (EOQ) formulas, just-in-time (JIT) inventory systems, and materials requirement planning (MRP). EOQ formulas minimize holding and ordering costs by determining how much and how often inventory should be ordered. By having parts arrive just when they are needed at each stage of production, JIT systems attempt to minimize inventory levels and holding costs. JIT systems often depend on proximity, shared information, and the Japanese system of kanban. MRP precisely determines the production schedule, production batch sizes, and the ordering of inventories needed to complete final products. The three key parts of MRP systems are the master production schedule, the bill of materials, and inventory records. Use EOQ formulas when inventory levels are independent, and JIT and MRP when inventory levels are dependent on the number of products to be produced.

## What Really Happened?

Machine tools are the machines that make the parts that every manufacturer uses when assembling its products. For example, machine tools are used to cut, carve, and polish the pistons in car engines. Huffman Corporation, which has been making machine tools since 1969, is in one of the toughest, most competitive industries in the world. In the United States alone, several hundred small machine tool companies compete against each other for market share and profits. In the last few years, Huffman decided to focus on improving the company's productivity and the productivity of its products. Let's find out what really happened at Huffman Corporation to see if this focus on productivity paid off.

**For instance, what's the best way to measure and improve productivity? If it's hard to define, much less measure, it won't make sense to try to track and improve productivity.**

Productivity is a measure of performance that indicates how many inputs it takes to produce or create an output. The fewer inputs it takes to create an output (or the greater the output from one input), the higher the productivity. There are two basic measures of productivity. Partial productivity indicates how much of a particular kind of input it takes to produce an output. Labor is one kind of input that is frequently used when determining partial productivity. *Labor productivity* typically indicates the cost or number of hours of labor it takes to produce an output. In other words, the smaller the cost of the labor to produce a unit of output, or the less time it takes to produce a unit of output, the higher the labor productivity. By contrast, multifactor productivity is an overall measure of productivity that assesses how efficiently companies use all the inputs it takes to make outputs. More specifically, multifactor productivity indicates how much labor, capital, materials, and energy it takes to produce an output.

As mentioned above, one of the most common ways in which companies measure productivity is labor productivity, the number of hours of labor it takes to produce a product. For example, earlier in the chapter you learned that Nissan assembles a car in only 27.63 hours of labor. By contrast, it takes Huffman 800 hours of labor to produce one of its best-selling machine tools. Does this mean that Huffman is less productive than most automakers? Not necessarily. Machine tools are quite different from cars and are typically much larger and much more expensive. And the key is not whether Huffman is more or less competitive than automakers, but whether it is more or less competitive than in the past or than its competitors. In fact, the 800 hours of labor that it takes Huffman to produce a machine tool is 33 percent less than five years ago. And that increase in productivity allowed Huffman to drop prices by 20 percent and still increase profits.

**Also, so what if we improve productivity? She makes improving productivity sound like a cure-all. Can improving productivity really make that much of a difference for one company, especially a**

company that has a very small share of the market and that would have to steal market share from several hundred competitors in order to grow?

Why does productivity matter? For companies, higher productivity, that is, doing more with less, results in lower costs. In turn, doing more with less can lead to lower prices, faster service, higher market share, and higher profits. For example, at fast-food restaurants, every second saved in the drive-through lane increases sales by 1 percent. Furthermore, increasing the efficiency of drive-through service by 10 percent adds nearly 10 percent to a fast-food restaurant's sales. Similarly, higher productivity allows European-based Ryanair to make a profit when its planes are just half full. By contrast, its European competitors don't break even unless their flights, which are generally five to 10 times more expensive, are 75 percent full.

Because of intense competition that keeps a lid on price increases, Huffman has only increased its annual revenues by approximately 8 percent per year over the last five years. By contrast, significant increases in productivity have allowed Huffman to aggressively cut its costs. As a result, despite moderate increases in sales, Huffman has averaged a 35 percent annual increase in earnings over the last five years, a number that Microsoft would be happy to match. Nearly all of that is due to increases in Huffman's surging productivity, that is, doing more with less. Huffman's president Roger Hayes summarized the positive effects of these improvements in productivity when he stated that the company ended their most recent fiscal year with "record [sales] backlogs and record profits."

**And will improved productivity really matter much to our competitors and customers? After all, aren't the effects of productivity fairly limited from company to company?**

For countries, productivity matters because it produces a higher standard of living. One way productivity leads to a higher standard of living is through increased wages. When companies can do more with less, they can raise employee wages without increasing prices or sacrificing normal profits. However, productivity increases in one company's products can also lead to productivity increases for other companies. This is especially true for machine tools, which are a key component of the productivity of nearly every manufacturing facility that makes its own parts. The more productive machine tools become, the quicker and cheaper it becomes for manufacturers to produce the parts used in their products.

For example, Huffman makes a grinding machine specifically designed to make medical tools and instruments such as a "broach," which is used to carve bones during hip-replacement surgery. Broaches are such complex medical tools that they have typically been carved and shaped by hand. However, Huffman's advanced software and computer controls now allow cheaper and sharper broaches to be made automatically by machine tools. It takes a Huffman machine tool just 11 minutes to make a broach, compared to 222 minutes to make one by hand. Paragon Medical, which designs and manufactures surgical tools, has purchased $5 million worth of machine tools from Huffman over the last four years. Toby Buck, Paragon's CEO, says that each new machine tool lowers his manufacturing costs by 15 to 20 percent. And those medical tools are not only cheaper and faster to make, they're also better tools that improve the productivity of the doctors who use them. Dr. Lawrence Livingston, chief of orthopedic surgery at a New Jersey hospital, said, "You can sculpt the bone with more agility because of the improvements in the instruments." As a result, a typical one-hour hip replacement surgery now takes only 50 minutes.

Advances in machine tools have improved productivity in countless other products over the last five years. Air conditioners are 30 to 40 percent more efficient than they used to be because machine tools are now capable of producing a compressor with parts that can be measured down to 10 microns, or one ten-millionth of a meter. If every American house had one of these new air conditioners, consumers would save $20 billion a year in electricity costs. Likewise, improvements in machine tools have led to productivity increases of 29 percent per year for airplane parts and engine manufacturers. For instance, Huffman makes a special machine tool for manufacturing turbine blades for jet engines or electricity-generating turbines. In the past, each turbine blade was specially fitted in a cumbersome metal holder that was used by workers to push the blade against a grinder to hand make the part. However, Huffman's new machine is so easy to use and so efficient that workers drop each unfinished blade in the machine as easily as dropping quarters into a vending machine. As a result, it now takes just two hours to make all the blades for a turbine, whereas before it took 10 days.

In the end, Huffman Corporation's productivity improvements significantly improved its profits and reduced its costs. However, the improved productivity of Huffman's machine tools also led to dramatic productivity increases in the manufacture of durable goods products like air conditioners and turbines. In turn, those products have become much cheaper and more efficient, resulting in substantially lower costs and improved performance for consumers.

**Sources:** Interview with Don Carlson, "The Old Economy Is the New Economy," *Business Week*, 13 November 2000, 42H. S. Liesman, "Crucial Driver of U.S. Productivity Gains May Be Improvements in Machine Tools," *The Wall Street Journal*, 28 September 2000, A2. S. Liesman, "Better Machine Tools Give Manufacturers Newfound Resilience," *The Wall Street Journal*, 15 February 2001, A1. S. Modic & J. McKenna, "Machine Tool Executives 'Crystal Ball' Future," *Tooling & Production*, 1 April 2000, 58. G. Rosenberger, "Commercial Aircraft Business, The One Shining Light, Evaporating—Little Ramp Up for Military Contractors As Yet—Strong Car Sales Ironically Hinder Capital Investment," *Market News International*, 26 November 2000, no page numbers available.

## Key Terms

assemble-to-order operation *(585)*
average aggregate inventory *(590)*
batch production *(587)*
component parts inventories *(589)*
continuous-flow production *(587)*
continuous improvement *(578)*
customer focus *(577)*
customer satisfaction *(577)*
dependent demand systems *(597)*
economic order quantity (EOQ) *(595)*
finished goods inventories *(589)*
holding cost *(594)*
independent demand system *(597)*
inventory *(589)*

inventory turnover *(591)*
ISO 9000 *(573)*
job shops *(588)*
just-in-time (JIT) inventory system *(595)*
kanban *(597)*
line-flow production *(587)*
make-to-order operation *(585)*
make-to-stock operation *(585)*
manufacturing flexibility *(586)*
materials requirement planning (MRP) *(597)*
multifactor productivity *(566)*
operations management *(564)*
ordering cost *(592)*

partial productivity *(566)*
productivity *(565)*
project manufacturing *(588)*
quality *(569)*
raw material inventories *(589)*
service recovery *(582)*
setup cost *(592)*
stockout *(590)*
stockout costs *(594)*
teamwork *(578)*
total quality management (TQM) *(576)*
variation *(578)*
work-in-process inventories *(589)*

## What Would You Do-II

### Improve the Quality or Turn in Your Keys

You are the manager for the claims processing center for Farmers Insurance Company. Lately, your department has been experiencing pressure from top management to improve the quality of your department's output and decrease the time taken to process claims. The industry average to process a typical automobile accident claim is around five days, with less than 4 percent errors. Your department, on average, takes 10 days to process a claim and has a 10 percent error rate. The problem, as you see it, is an inability to automate the claims-processing function, since a majority of the information needed to process a claim, including photographs, repair estimates, police reports, and statements from customers, are difficult to enter into standardized computer databases.

The typical process of inputting a claim involves receiving the claim form and supporting materials (photographs, police reports, customer statements, repair estimates . . .) in paper form from the sales agent's office, scanning the support materials into an electronic format, retrieving the customer's file from the central database, and inputting all of the items into the system so that it can be forwarded to a claims processing agent. As can be seen, a majority of the work needed to process a claim is tedious, time consuming, and must be done by hand. In fact, an internal report estimates that the 3.7 million claims submitted last year generated approximately 79 million pieces of paper.

Unfortunately, your supervisors aren't concerned with the amount of work or paper generated in the process, they are more focused on industry averages. As a result, you have received a mandate that either your department meet the industry average for processing claims by the end of the year, or face having the entire claims processing function (along with your job) outsourced to an external agency. As the manager of the claims processing center for Farmers Insurance Company, you've got to make changes or take steps to increase the quality of the department's output and increase productivity, that is, decrease the time taken to process claims.

**If you were the manager of Farmers Insurance Company's claims department, what would you do?**

**Sources:** D. Deckmyn, "Farmers Insurance Revamps Claims Processing," *Computerworld*, 9 August 1999, 38. G. McWilliams, "ACS Finds Profits in Business Outsourcing," *Wall Street Journal*, 3 May 2001. G. Mac-Sweeney, "Farmers Tackles Claims Upgrade Challenge," *Insurance & Technology*, Oct. 1999, 29. G. McWilliams, "Small ACS Beat Out Bigger-Name Rivals to Business Process," *Wall Street Journal*, 3 May 2001, B5–6.

## Management Decisions

### Continuous Quality Improvement, Yeah, Right!

You've just been promoted as the manager of customer service for a medium-sized general merchandise retailer. Your boss, the former customer service manager, resigned yesterday, when she realized that her department was not going to meet the company's mandate of increasing customer satisfaction by 15 percent for the quarter. You are glad to get the chance to head up the department, however, you realize that your time may also be limited.

Your company has been suffering from low customer satisfaction since you began working there three years ago. Although customer satisfaction has increased during that time period, the company currently holds a 73 percent satisfaction rate, compared to its closest competitor's satisfaction rate of 92 percent. This rate suggests that only 7.3 out of 10 people are satisfied with their shopping experience. The company has tried many tactics to improve satisfaction in the store, ranging from training sales associates to be more customer-friendly, providing bonuses and pay raises for those who receive favorable evaluations from customers, and demoting or terminating sales associates who receive unfavorable evaluations from customers. Despite these programs, the overall customer satisfaction rate has yet to achieve top management's expectations. As the newly appointed customer service manager, what factors might you consider when attempting to solve the current customer satisfaction dilemma?

**Source:** M. Jordan, "Penney Blends Two Business Cultures," *Wall Street Journal*, 5 April 2001, http://www.wsj.com.

## Management Decisions

### Cycle Time and Quality Improvement

In the pursuit of quality improvement, many service organizations attempt to reduce the cycle time of key processes. "Cycle time" refers to the time taken to complete a key step in the delivery of a service or good. For example, cycle time can be the amount of time it takes the purchasing department to approve a purchase request. The cycle time begins when the purchasing department receives the request and ends when the request has been processed and returned to the individual.

Many organizations attempt to improve cycle time by looking at the processes involved in each department and removing any redundant steps or steps that do not create value for the organization. One organization that seems to have a negative image regarding cycle time is the government. At the local motor vehicle department (MVD), it seems that no matter what time of day or what day of the week you visit, you will end up spending a majority of your time standing in line. Likewise, receiving a tax refund or a passport traditionally have not been quick transactions. Wouldn't it be great if governmental agencies took steps to improve quality and decrease the cycle time of the services that they offer!

Another situation in which customers spend time waiting is at the local college, especially during registration. Many colleges tend to send students from one location to another in order for them to complete the registration process. For example, at one school, new students are required to fill out the admissions application and request for transcripts in the registrar's office. Then students must go down the hall to the business office in order to pay their admission fee. Once the fee has been paid, they must return to the registrar's office and show their receipt in order to complete the admission process. Once admitted, they must then go to an advisor's office to set an appointment in order to register for classes. Since they are new students, the advisor typically wants to see a copy of their transcript, which they typically don't have. If a transcript is on file, they have to return to the registrar's office in order to get a copy. Hopefully, with a copy of their transcript in hand, students are now ready to go back to the advisor's office and register for classes. All of these steps take time and confuse and frustrate the customer (in this case the student). If the whole process were inspected and improved, the majority of this confusion and frustration could be prevented.

Your assignment for this management decision is to think back to your last visit to the MVD, registrar, or other place where you had to either wait for a long time or go through several steps before completing the process. Think about ways to decrease the cycle time between steps, improve the overall flow, and increase customer satisfaction with the entire process.

Begin this exercise by describing the situation that you faced. Then list the steps you would take or the changes you would implement to improve the overall quality and outcome of the situation.

## Develop Your Managerial Potential

### Take a Factory Tour

Imagine that you arrive back at your dorm room one afternoon to find your roommate watching Mister Rogers. When asked why, your roommate simply replies, "Management homework." Crazy? Maybe not. Fred Rogers may possibly have been on more factory tours than anyone in the United States. Over his long career, he has broadcast footage to millions of children showing how Cheerios, plastic drinking straws, graham crackers, pasta, and a host of other familiar products are made. He was even at Crayola when the one-billionth crayon rolled off the production line.

Fred Rogers, however, isn't the only American interested in manufacturing. Each year, thousands visit corporate facilities like these:

- Coca-Cola (**http://www.coke.com**) has an interactive, virtual factory tour where participants try to guess the optimal amount of sugar, water, and secret formula needed to create a batch of Coca-Cola, practice quality inspection, package Coca-Cola for shipment, and much more.
- The JCPenney Museum (**http://www.jcpenney.net/ company/history/archive2.htm**) displays the history and products of James Cash Penney and the company he founded.
- Hershey's Chocolate World in Hershey, Pennsylvania (**http://www.hersheys.com**), is the home of Hershey Food Corporation's free visitor's center with a Disney-like ride through a simulated chocolate factory. If you don't like

chocolate, check out Jelly Belly at **http://www.jellybelly.com/About/Tours/virtual_tour.html**.

- The Boeing Everett Tour Center (**http://www.boeing.com/companyoffices/aboutus/tours/**) introduces visitors to how Boeing makes its 747, 767, and 777 passenger jets.
- Cereal City (**http://www.kelloggscerealcityusa.org/**) shows how Kellogg makes its best-selling cereals.
- Ken Smith Bass Guitars has a photographic virtual factory tour at **http://www.kensmithbasses.com/ft/newtour/factorytourcontents.html**.

In fact, visiting factories has become so popular that there are now two books on the subject, *Watch It Made in the U.S.A.: A Visitor's Guide to the Companies That Make Your Favorite Products*, by Karen Axelrod and Bruce Brumberg (John Muir Publications), and *Inside America: The Great American Industrial Tour Guide, 1,000 Free Industrial Tours Open to the Public Covering More Than 300 Different Industries*, by Jack and Eunice Berger (Heritage Publications).

If you've never toured a factory, you might wonder what the fuss is all about. Author Karen Axelrod said, "Everyone's eyes get bigger when they see the way things work. Everyone becomes a five-year old." Barbara Bernstein of Annapolis, Maryland, said, "I'm interested in how companies make anything, plastic bags for grocery stores, peanut butter, Formica, anything." There's just something magical about watching the manufacture of familiar products like cereal, cars, or candy.

Your assignment for this Develop Your Management Potential is to take a factory tour. Consult one of the books men-

tioned above, visit one of the following Web sites listing factory tours in your region (**http://www.foodfactorytours.com**, **http://www.factorytour.com**, or **http://www.bygpub.com/books/tg2rw/factory-tours.htm**), do a quick Web search on the keywords "factory tour", or simply ask around about a good factory tour near you. When on your tour, gather some literature and ask about the following issues.

1. What steps or procedures does the company take to ensure the quality of its products?
2. How does the company measure productivity and how does its productivity compare to others in the industry?
3. Describe the basic steps used to make the finished products in this factory. As you do this, be sure to describe the raw materials inventories, component parts inventories, and work-in-process inventories used to create the finished products.
4. What did you find most impressive about the factory or manufacturing processes? Also, using the material from the chapter, describe one thing that the company could do differently to improve quality, increase productivity, or reduce inventory.

**Sources:** E. Gehrman, "Factory Facts Show Heart, Soul of America," *Boston Herald*, 29 January 1998. E. Perkins, "Factory Tour Can Be Fun, Not to Mention Real Cheap," *Orlando Sentinel*, 1 February, 1998, L6. L. Singhania (Associated Press), "Breakfast for Battle Creek's New Cereal City," *Grand Rapids Press*, 24 May 1998, F2. C. Quintanilla, "Planning a Vacation? Give Some Thought to Spamtown USA," *The Wall Street Journal*, 30 April 1998, A1.

## Study Tip

Close your book and write a list of the key concepts in this chapter. Or create flashcards for key concepts (concept on one side, explanation and example on the other). Flashcards are great portable study aids that you can use over and over, in a group, with a partner, or on your own. For this chapter, you have an Xtra! CNN clip with case and solutions on your CD about how productivity dropped during the presidential elections of 2000. Read the accompanying case and work the questions.

# 5

**PART**

## Leading

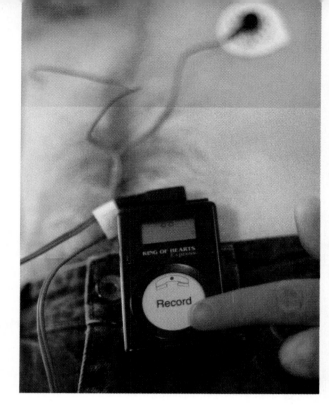

# CHAPTER 16

# Motivation

## What Would You Do?

**Medtronic Headquarters, Minneapolis, Minnesota.** Over the last decade, Medtronic has been one of the leading medical technology companies in the world, conducting business in 120 countries. Medtronic makes automatic defibrillators that untrained people can use to restart the heart of someone having a heart attack in a public place. (Given the possibility that emergency medical teams might not arrive in time, retail stores, airlines, and cities now purchase this product precisely for this use.) The company also makes cardioverter defibrillators that are implanted in peoples' chests to monitor heart rates. If an arrhythmia occurs and a heart beats dangerously fast, this product shocks the heart to restore a regular cardiac rhythm. Another Medtronic device controls the tremors associated with Parkinson's disease. Implanted like a pacemaker, this device delivers a small electrical charge to block brain signals that lead to tremors. Turn it off and the tremors start immediately. Turn it on, and they immediately stop.

Over the last decade, Medtronic has had remarkable business success, increasing sales by 19 percent per year, earnings by 23 percent per year, and market share of its most important product, pacemakers, from 45 percent to 54 percent. Medtronic owes much of its success to its ability to innovate and its willingness to cannibalize existing products with newer, better ones. In fact, every time it starts selling a new product, it has already started work on the next four products that will replace it (a minor upgrade, a major upgrade, and two later products based on newer technology). Overall, Medtronic generates a remarkable 70 percent of its sales from products no more than two years old.

Most companies struggle to be as successful as Medtronic. However, Medtronic's key challenge will be to sustain the success it has achieved. Its business, medical technology, is extremely competitive. Established companies, such as Johnson & Johnson, which invented cardiac stents (special metal tubing used to open arteries and prevent them from clogging), have seen their market shares quickly erased. Furthermore, Bill George, the CEO who led and grew Medtronic, changed its culture, and boosted research spending from 8 percent to 10 percent of sales, has just retired.

His successor, Arthur Collins, who previously served as Chief Operating Officer, is already beginning to make changes, moving the company to a decentralized structure to make product development even faster. However, Collins' biggest challenge will be finding a way to continue to motivate Medtronic's managers and employees. Long-term success has a way of softening a company's competitive edge. Managers become complacent. Employees become satisfied and resistant to change. After a while, fatigue sets in. It happened to IBM, Sears, General Motors, and Xerox, all long-time market leaders who lost their dominance when they lost the hearts and minds of their workers.

The question for Collins and Medtronic is how to prevent the same thing from happening to them. Most winning sports teams start an immediate decline after winning the championship. It's rare for champions to repeat or even "three-peat," so how can Medtronic continue to motivate managers and workers after a decade of incredible success? Often times, successful companies turn into farm clubs for other companies, grooming, and developing talented people, only to have them hired away by other companies just as they reach their potential. How can Medtronic prevent that from happening? Finally, in the long run, what will make people happiest and most productive at work? Is it money, benefits, opportunities for growth, interesting work, or something else altogether different? And with people desiring different things, how can Medtronic keep everyone motivated to continue to "win championships"?

**If you were the new CEO at Medtronic, what would you do?**

**Sources:** D. Emerson, "Holiday Bonuses Drop off Wish List," *Minneapolis-St. Paul City Business*, 15 December 2000, 16. R. Langreth, "Medtronic: Pacing the Field," *Forbes*, 8 January 2001, 142. P. Marsh & C. Bowe,

"Medtronic Needs Health Check from New Executive: Despite Past Success, The Health Device Maker Faces Big Changes," *The Financial Times*, 1 May 2001, 28. J. Niemela, "Med-Tech Mission Overrides Benefits," *Minneapolis-*

*St. Paul City Business*, 4 August 2000, 42. D. Whitford, "A Human Place to Work," *Fortune*, 8 January 2001, 108.

What makes people happiest and most productive at work? Is it money, benefits, opportunities for growth, interesting work, or something else altogether different that motivates people? And with people desiring different things, how can we keep everyone motivated? The set of problems that Medtronic is experiencing illustrates that motivating workers is never easy. It takes insight and hard work to motivate managers and workers to create a successful company. Maintaining that motivation to sustain and continue growing the company is just as difficult, especially after achieving long-term success.

This chapter begins by reviewing the basics of motivation—effort, needs, and intrinsic and extrinsic motivation. We will start with a basic model of motivation and add to it as we progress through each section in the chapter. Next, we will explore how employees' equity perceptions and reward expectations affect their motivation. If you're familiar with the phrase "perception is reality," you're off to a good start in understanding the importance of perceptions and expectations in motivation. The third part of the chapter reviews the role that rewards and goals play in motivating employees. You'll see that finding the right combination of goals and rewards is much harder in practice than it looks. The chapter finishes with a summary of practical, theory-based actions that managers can take to motivate their workers.

## What Is Motivation?

**motivation**
the set of forces that initiates, directs, and makes people persist in their efforts to accomplish a goal

**Motivation** is the set of forces that initiates, directs, and makes people persist in their efforts to accomplish a goal.[1] In terms of this definition, *initiation of effort* is concerned with the choices that people make about how much effort to put forth in their jobs. ("Performance feedback is important. I'm going to schedule an hour to review each file and an hour to write each appraisal." versus "Gosh, I hate writing performance appraisals, so maybe I'll just add a paragraph to last year's appraisals.") *Direction of effort* is concerned with the choices that people make in deciding where to put forth effort in their jobs. ("I'm really excited about the new computer system and can't wait to get started," versus "Yeah, yeah, another new computer system. I'll do what I need to get by with it, but I think my time is better spent working directly with employees and customers.") *Persistence of effort* is concerned with the choices that people make about how long they will put forth effort in their jobs before reducing or eliminating those efforts. ("We're only halfway to our goal with three months to go, but if we all keep working hard, we can do it." versus "We're only halfway to our goal with three months to get it done. We'll never make it, so I'm not going to work at this anymore.") As shown in Exhibit 16.1, initiation, direction, and persistence are at the heart of motivation.

*After reading these next two sections, you should be able to*
1. *explain the basics of motivation.*

## 1. Basics of Motivation

Take your right hand and point the palm toward your face. Keep your thumb and pinky finger straight and bend the three middle fingers so the tips are touching your palm. Now rotate your wrist back and forth. If you were in the Regent Square Tavern in Pittsburgh, Pennsylvania, that hand signal would tell waitress Marjorie Landale that you

EXHIBIT 16.1

THE COMPONENTS OF MOTIVATION

wanted a Yeungling beer. However, Marjorie, who isn't deaf, would not have understood that sign a few years ago. But with a state school for the deaf nearby, the tavern always has its share of deaf customers, so she decided on her own to take classes to learn how to sign. She said, "It occurred to me that I could learn their language more easily than they could learn mine." At first, deaf customers would signal for a pen and paper to write out their orders. But after Marjorie signaled that she was learning to sign, she said, "Their eyes [would] light up, and they [would] finger-spell their order and [then] we've made a connection." The tavern's regular deaf customers teased her in a friendly way about her poor signing skills, but word quickly spread as the students started bringing in their friends, classmates, teachers, and hearing friends, as well. Said Marjorie, "The deaf customers are patient with my amateur signing. They appreciate the effort."[2]

What would motivate an employee like Marjorie to voluntarily learn a new language like the American Sign Language? (Sign language is every bit as much as a language as French or Spanish.) She wasn't paid to take classes in her free time. She chose to do it on her own. And while she undoubtedly makes more tip money with a full bar than with an empty one, it's highly unlikely that she began her classes with the objective of making more money. Just what is it that motivates employees like Marjorie Landale?

*Let's learn more about motivation by building a basic model of motivation out of these parts: 1.1 effort and performance, 1.2 need satisfaction, and 1.3 intrinsic and extrinsic rewards. This section ends with a brief discussion of 1.4 how to motivate people with this basic model of motivation.*

### 1.1 Effort and Performance

When most people think of work motivation, they think that working hard (effort) should lead to doing a good job (performance). Exhibit 16.2 shows a basic model of work motivation and performance, displaying this process.

The first thing to notice about Exhibit 16.2 is that this is a basic model of work motivation *and* performance. In practice, it's almost impossible to talk about one without mentioning the other. Not surprisingly, managers often confuse the two, saying things such as "Your performance was really terrible last quarter. What's the matter? Aren't you as motivated as you used to be?" In fact, motivation is just one of three primary determinants of job performance. In industrial psychology, job performance is frequently represented by this equation:

EXHIBIT 16.2

A BASIC MODEL OF WORK MOTIVATION AND PERFORMANCE

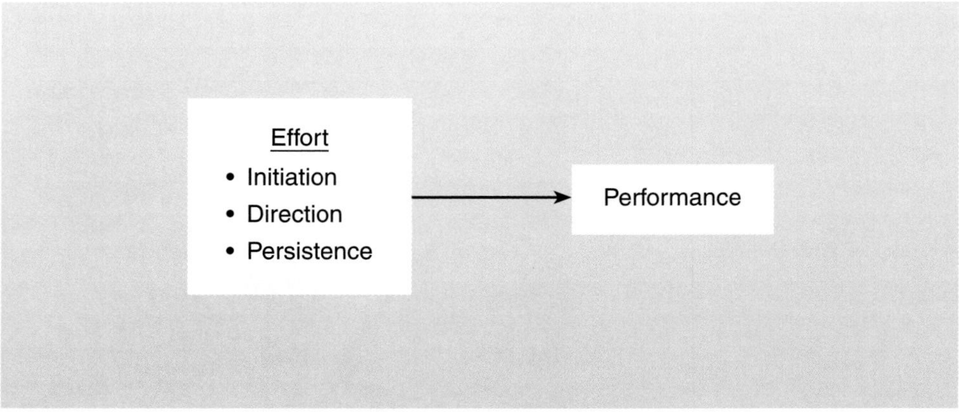

Job Performance = Motivation × Ability × Situational Constraints

In this formula, *job performance* is how well someone performs the requirements of the job. *Motivation*, as defined above, is effort, the degree to which someone works hard to do the job well. *Ability* is the degree to which workers possess the knowledge, skills, and talent needed to do a job well. And, *situational constraints* are factors beyond the control of individual employees, such as tools, policies, and resources that have an effect on job performance.

Since job performance is a multiplicative function of motivation times ability times situational constraints, job performance will suffer if any one of these components is weak. For example, in 1988, the East German bobsled team was fully funded by the East German government and had state-of-the art coaching and equipment (no situational constraints). It also recruited and selected bobsled team members from a wide pool of highly trained athletes (ability) who had trained year-round for most of their lives (motivation) for a chance to make the highly prestigious East German bobsled team. By contrast, consider the Jamaican bobsled team that Disney made famous in the movie *Cool Runnings.* In 1988 at its first winter Olympics, it had limited funding, a coach with bobsledding experience (a five-time U.S. champion) but no coaching experience, and an old bobsled that couldn't compete with the world-class equipment used by the best teams (high situational constraints). It also had a group of drivers and riders raised in tropical Jamaica with almost no bobsledding or winter sports experience (very little ability). However, this group of drivers dreamed of competing in the Olympics and did what little they could to train for several months, considering their limited circumstances (strong motivation).

It's not hard to guess which team did better, is it? With ample motivation, ability, and almost no situational constraints, you'd expect the East Germans to be competitive, and they were—finishing second and third in the two-man competition and second in the four-man competition.[3] By contrast, with strong motivation, little ability, and extremely high situational constraints, the Jamaican two-man team finished in 35th place, while the four-man team crashed spectacularly and had to push the bobsled across the line to complete its final run on the course.

Does this mean that motivation doesn't matter? No, not at all. It just means that all the motivation in the world won't translate into high performance when you have little ability and high situational constraints. In fact, prior to the 1996 Winter Olympics, the Jamaican team spent six weeks working with Sam Bock, who also worked with the elite Canadian team. Bock put the Jamaicans through their paces at a special bobsled training center in Oberhof, Germany. After training for four to eight hours a day in world-class conditions under world-class tutelage, the Jamaican four-man team finished in 14th place, ahead of the Americans, French, Russians, and one of the two Swiss and Italian teams. The two-man team did even better, finishing 10th.[4]

### 1.2 Need Satisfaction

In Exhibit 16.2, we started with a very basic model of motivation in which effort leads to job performance. However, managers want to know, "What leads to effort?" And they will try almost anything they can to find the answer to this question. The employees at Lyon & Associates Creative Services are apparently motivated by money. At the end of the year, 20 percent of company profits are equally distributed among all full-time employees who have worked there for at least one year. Managing Director Susan Lyon said, "Our philosophy is that if you want more money, just help the company make more, and you're guaranteed a chunk of it."[5] And, in addition to profit sharing, Lyon's employees receive annual bonuses of 5 to 10 percent of their annual salaries. However, money isn't everything. Linda Jacobsen, CEO of Global Vision Strategies, which does cross-cultural training for executives, was used to people demanding high salaries when negotiating salary and benefits packages. However, one prospective hire valued time more than money. She asked Jacobsen, who quickly agreed, for $5,000 less than she was earning in her previous job in exchange for 8 weeks of vacation.[6] Likewise, employees at Wilton Connor Packaging, Inc. in Charlotte, North Carolina, can take their laundry to work and have it washed, dried, and folded. The company also employs a handyman, who does free minor household repairs for employees while they're at work. At AutoDesk in San Rafael, California, employees can take their dogs to work.[7] So which of these techniques will motivate employees and lead to increased effort? The answer is all of them and none of them: It depends on employees' needs.

**needs**
the physical or psychological requirements that must be met to ensure survival and well being

**Needs** are the physical or psychological requirements that must be met to ensure survival and well-being.[8] As shown in the left side of Exhibit 16.3, a person's unmet need creates an uncomfortable, internal state of tension that must be resolved. For example, if you normally skip breakfast, but then get stuck working through lunch, chances are you'll be so hungry by late afternoon that the only thing you'll be motivated to do is find something to eat. So, according to needs theories, people are motivated by unmet needs. But once a need is met, it no longer motivates. When this occurs, people become satisfied, as illustrated on the right side of Exhibit 16.3.

Note: Throughout the chapter, as we build on this basic model, the parts of the model that we've already discussed will appear shaded in color. For example, since we've already discussed the effort → performance part of the model, those components are shown with a shaded background. However, when we add new parts to the model, those

---

EXHIBIT 16.3

ADDING NEED SATISFACTION TO THE MODEL

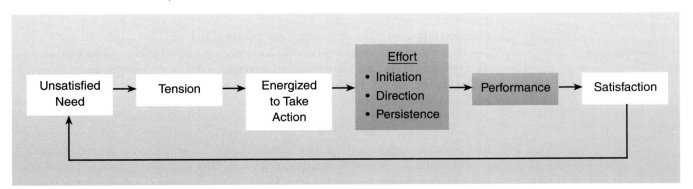

EXHIBIT 16.4

NEEDS CLASSIFICATION OF DIFFERENT THEORIES

| | **MASLOW'S HIERARCHY** | **ALDERFER'S ERG** | **MCCLELLAND'S LEARNED NEEDS** |
|---|---|---|---|
| *Higher-Order Needs* | Self-Actualization<br>Esteem<br>Belongingness | Growth<br>Relatedness | Power<br>Achievement<br>Affiliation |
| *Lower-Order Needs* | Safety<br>Physiological | Existence | |

parts will have a white background. For instance, since we're adding need satisfaction to the model at this step, the need-satisfaction components of unsatisfied need, tension, energized to take action, and satisfaction are shown with a white background. This shading convention should make it easier to understand the work motivation model as we add to it in each section of the chapter.

Since people are motivated by unmet needs, managers must learn what those unmet needs are and address them. However, this is not always a straightforward task, since different needs theories suggest different needs categories. Exhibit 16.4 shows needs from three well-known needs theories. Maslow's Hierarchy of Needs suggests that people are motivated by *physiological* (food and water), *safety* (physical and economic), *belongingness* (friendship, love, social interaction), *esteem* (achievement and recognition), and *self-actualization* (realizing your full potential) needs.[9] Alderfer's ERG theory collapses Maslow's five needs into three: *existence* (safety and physiological needs), *relatedness* (belongingness), and *growth* (esteem and self-actualization).[10] McClelland's Learned Needs Theory suggests that people are motivated by the need for *affiliation* (to be liked and accepted), the need for *achievement* (to accomplish challenging goals), or the need for *power* (to influence others).[11]

Things become even more complicated when we consider the different predictions made by these theories. According to Maslow, needs are arranged in a hierarchy from low (physiological) to high (self-actualization). Within this hierarchy, people are motivated by their lowest unsatisfied need. And, as needs are met, they work their way up the hierarchy from physiological to self-actualization needs. By contrast, Alderfer says that people can be motivated by more than one need at a time. Furthermore, he suggests that people are just as likely to move down the needs hierarchy as up, particularly when unable to achieve satisfaction at the next higher need level. McClelland, on the other hand, argues that the degree to which particular needs motivate varies tremendously from person to person, with some people being motivated primarily by achievement, and others by power or affiliation. Moreover, McClelland says that needs are learned, not innate. For instance, studies show that children whose parents own a small business or hold a managerial position are much more likely to have a high need for achievement.[12]

So with three different sets of needs and three very different ideas about how needs motivate, where does this leave managers who want a practical answer to the question "What leads to effort?" Fortunately, the research evidence simplifies things a bit. To start, studies indicate that there are two basic kinds of needs categories.[13] As shown in Exhibit 16.4, *lower-order needs* are concerned with safety and with physiological and existence requirements, while *higher-order needs* are concerned with relationships (belongingness, relatedness, and affiliation); challenges and accomplishments (esteem, self-actualization, growth, and achievement); and influence (power). Studies generally show that higher-order needs will not motivate people as long as lower order needs remain unsatisfied.

For example, imagine that it's six months since you graduated from college and that you're still looking for your first job. With money running short (you're probably living on your credit cards) and the looming possibility of having to move back in with your parents (if this doesn't motivate you, what will?), your basic needs for food, shelter, and security drive your thoughts, behavior, and choices at this point. But once you land that job, find a great place (of your own!) to live, and put some money in the bank, these basic needs should decrease in importance as you begin to think about making new friends and taking on challenging work assignments. In fact, once lower-order needs are satisfied, it's difficult for managers to predict which higher-order needs will motivate behavior.[14] Some people will be motivated by affiliation, while others will be motivated by growth or esteem. Also, the relative importance of the various needs may change over time, but not necessarily in any predictable pattern.

So, what leads to effort? In part, needs do. Subsection 1.4 discusses how managers can use what we know from need-satisfaction theories to motivate workers.

### 1.3 Extrinsic and Intrinsic Rewards

No discussion of motivation would be complete without considering rewards. Let's add two kinds of rewards, extrinsic and intrinsic, to the model, as shown in Exhibit 16.5.[15]

**Extrinsic rewards** are tangible and visible to others and are given to employees contingent on the performance of specific tasks or behaviors.[16] External agents (managers, for example) determine and control the distribution, frequency, and amount of extrinsic rewards, such as pay, company stock, benefits, and promotions. For example, Edge Software Services uses the "bonus bucket" method to reward its managers and employees. As the company meets profit targets, a percentage of those profits are shared with employees, hence the name "bonus bucket." It works like this. If the first profit target was $2 million, then the bonus shared among employees might be 5 percent, or $100,000. However, employees would share 7.5 percent, or $150,000, of the next $2 million in profit, and so forth. Company president Kevin Clark said, "The incentive has no upside limit. What I wanted to do was create an environment in which people were rewarded."[17] The risk, of course, is that profits can't be shared if they're not made. Indeed, profits were small last year and, according to Clark, "not a lot of bonuses were paid."

Why do companies need extrinsic rewards? To get people to do things they wouldn't otherwise do. Companies use extrinsic rewards to motivate people to perform four basic behaviors: joining the organization, regularly attending their jobs, performing their jobs well, and staying with the organization.[18] Think about it. Would you show up to work

**extrinsic reward**
a reward that is tangible, visible to others, and given to employees contingent on the performance of specific tasks or behaviors

611

EXHIBIT 16.5

ADDING REWARDS TO THE MODEL

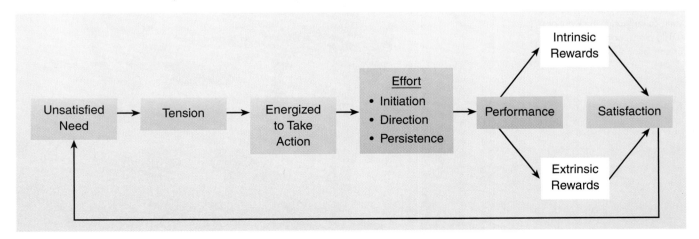

### Let Employees Have Fun!

Creating fun is a great way to motivate. Some companies have "treat days," when managers serve employees coffee, doughnuts, or ice cream. Others ask their managers to bring in baby pictures, so that people can have fun guessing which baby was which manager. Some companies create a "stress-free zone," with a hammock, an inflatable palm tree, and a "stress-reduction dummy"—a large inflatable punching bag. One manager sends employees "stress support kits," which contain chewing gum, aspirin, a comedy cassette, wind-up toys for employees' desks, and a rubber toy for squeezing during tense moments. So if you want to motivate employees, let them have fun.

**Sources:** P. Brotherton, "The Company That Plays Together...," *HR Magazine* 41 (December 1996): 76–82. K. Johnson, "Companies Try New Perks to Keep Stressed Workers Happy," *Lawrence Eagle-Tribune*, 26 September 1995, A1. D. Selinsky, "Happy Campers," *Success*, 1 April 2001, 54.

**intrinsic reward**
a natural reward associated with performing a task or activity for its own sake

every day to do the best possible job that you could just out of the goodness of your heart? Very few people would. This is especially true in the fast-food business where employee turnover averages 200 percent a year and higher. Aylwin Lewis of Tricon Global Restaurants (Pizza Hut, Taco Bell, and Kentucky Fried Chicken) admits, "Not a lot of people wake up and say they want to go into this industry."[19] However, fast-food companies are now offering significantly better external rewards to get more people to take and keep fast-food jobs. For example, in addition to their hourly wages, employees at Burger King's restaurants now have 401(k) retirement plans. Not to be outdone, McDonald's now provides its restaurant employees medical and dental insurance, credit union memberships, discounts on home and car insurance, and money to pay for college textbooks. Likewise, Tricon's store employees are now eligible for stock options. Thanks to these external rewards, turnover rates have dropped from 223 percent to 205 percent at Burger King, from 147 percent to 120 percent at Pizza Hut, and from 243 percent to 200 percent at Taco Bell.[20]

By contrast, **intrinsic rewards** are the natural rewards associated with performing a task or activity for its own sake. For example, aside from the external rewards management offers for doing something well, employees often experience a sense of interest and enjoyment from the activities or tasks they perform. Examples of intrinsic rewards include a sense of accomplishment or achievement, a feeling of responsibility, the chance to learn something new or interact with others, or simply the fun that comes from performing an interesting, challenging, and engaging task.

Which types of rewards are most important to workers in general? A number of surveys suggest that both extrinsic and intrinsic rewards are important. One survey found that the most important rewards were good benefits and health insurance, job security, a week or more of vacation (all extrinsic rewards), interesting work, the opportunity to learn new skills, and independent work situations (all intrinsic rewards). And employee preferences for intrinsic and extrinsic rewards appear to be relatively stable. With little change over the last three decades, employees are twice as likely to indicate that "important and meaningful work" matters more to them than what they are paid.[21]

In some industries, like the fast-food industry, it is difficult to motivate people who occupy positions that offer little in the way of intrinsic motivation. For this reason—and to combat high turnover—many fast-food chains have begun offering rewards more usually found in the white-collar world: stock options, 401(k) plans, and reimbursement for education expenses.

© MICHAEL NEWMAN/PHOTOEDIT

## 1.4 Motivating with the Basics

So, given the basic model of work motivation in Exhibit 16.5, what practical things can managers do to motivate employees to increase their effort?

As shown in Exhibit 16.6, *start by asking people what their needs are.* If managers don't know what workers' needs are, they won't be able to provide them the opportunities and rewards that can satisfy those needs. Linda Connor, vice president of corporate culture at Technology Professionals Corp (TPC) in Grand Rapids, Michigan, keeps careful notes about TPC employees' needs. She said, "I sit down at employees' 30-day reviews and ask specific questions about hobbies and interests for each member of their families."[22] For instance, her notes about top performer Phil Mayrose indicated that he loved college football, oldies music, and, more than anything else, golf. Armed with this information, Connor and TPC rewarded Mayrose with a weekend vacation at a dude ranch with a great golf course. Sometimes, however, meeting employee needs means helping them deal with stress. Here again, Linda Connor's notes helped TPC take care of another of its employees. Connor's notes read, "During stressful periods [she] loses confidence in her ability as a mom, housekeeper, sister, daughter, friend, and aunt. Ideas during high-stress times: lawn-mowing service, housekeeping, hot meals, day away with her son."[23] So if you want to meet employees' needs, do like Linda Connor does and just ask.

*Next, satisfy lower-order needs first.* Since, higher-order needs will not motivate people as long as lower-order needs remain unsatisfied, companies should satisfy lower-order needs first. In practice, this means providing the equipment, training, and knowledge to create a safe workplace free of physical risks, paying employees well enough to provide financial security, and offering a benefits package that will protect employees and their families through good medical coverage and health and disability insurance. Indeed, a survey based on a representative sample of Americans found that when people choose jobs or organizations, three of the four most important factors—starting pay/salary (62 percent), employee benefits (57 percent), and job security (47 percent)—are lower-order needs.[24]

*Expect people's needs to change.* As some needs are satisfied or situations change, managers should expect that employees' needs will change. In other words, what motivated people before may not motivate them again. Likewise, what motivates people to accept a job may not necessarily motivate them once they have the job. For instance, David Stum, president of the Loyalty Institute, said, "The [attractive] power of pay and benefits is only [strong] during the recruitment stage. After employees take the job, pay and benefits become entitlements to them. They think: 'Now that I work here, you owe me that.'"[25] Managers should also expect needs to change as people mature. For employees 40 or older, benefits are more important than pay, which is always ranked as most important by younger employees. Also, employees 40 or older rank job security as more important than personal and family time, which is more important to younger employees.[26]

*Finally, as needs change and lower-order needs are satisfied, satisfy higher-order needs by looking for ways to allow employees to experience intrinsic rewards.* Recall that intrinsic

---

**EXHIBIT 16.6**

### MOTIVATING TO INCREASE EFFORT

- Start by asking people what their needs are.
- Satisfy lower-order needs first.
- Expect people's needs to change.
- As needs change and lower-order needs are satisfied, satisfy higher-order needs by looking for ways to allow employees to experience intrinsic rewards.

---

# "headline news"

In the new economy, job hunters could be selective—even arrogant—when it came to what a company offered in the way of salary and employee perks. Legendary stock option packages ballooned even for relatively standard positions, and employees were quick to evaluate their companies' plans against the competition's offerings. Corporate concierges littered the Silicon Valley landscape, and free food was only a cube away. When the dotcom world crashed, many of these perks withered on the vine. At the very least, the vine was severely pruned. The main perk became getting a paycheck at all.

There's no doubt that cool cars and cruises have gone by the wayside. In fact, according to Buck Consultants, the number of companies with hiring bonuses and stock options was down 5 percent in 2001 from 2000. Furthermore, companies offering bonuses for completing projects fell 2 percent, and companies offering retention bonuses fell a whopping 10 percent. Some experts warn that trimming perks too far can be detrimental to the overall health of the organization. Recommendations? Richard Hadden, author of *Contented Cows Give Better Milk*, said, "If things have to be taken away, take them from the executives first." On his list of things that shouldn't survive a first round of cost-cutting perk reductions are executive trips and toys, non-job-related classes (e.g., yoga), extensive travel, gym memberships, and concierge or convenience services.

Some perks, however, are definite keepers. These are things like childcare programs, job-related training, work/life balance programs (e.g., paid time off, flex time), employee community-builders (e.g., free-bagel Fridays), and business travel reimbursement. All of these sound pretty obvious if not traditional, but companies shouldn't sacrifice creativity in thinking about perks. Despite the tumbling popularity of some of the newly conceived perks (like concierge services and yoga), some of the quirky, dotcom influence still survives.

DevElements, a software design and consulting firm in Reston, Virginia, is a profitable start-up that hasn't taken any outside capital. For today's job hunters, this alone can be the main selling point, but DevElements also sponsors a monthly happy hour, offers cash incentives for employees who refer a job candidate who is hired, and gives employees their birthday off. The Plitt Company, a Chicago seafood business, throws a party for its employees' children to celebrate their good grades. For every "A" earned in school, each child receives $20. About 50 children participate each year, so for the cost of a few thousand dollars, the company strengthens its relationship with its employees and their families. Thixomat, a company in Ann Arbor, Michigan, established a limited liability corporation (LLC) to purchase its new location. All employees were invited to buy shares of the LLC. In return, they receive annual rent checks and the CFO prepares a pamphlet to help them complete the depreciation page of their personal income tax forms.

Cutting perks is a quick way to bolster profits, but it can also have a long-lasting negative effect on a company's internal morale and external reputation. When times get tough, eliminating free-bagel Fridays might seem like a good idea, but the more you cut, the tougher it will be to motivate employees, let alone attract new ones when finances improve.

1. *How can perks, which are usually established as a company benefit, motivate employees?*
2. *How can you keep morale high and motivate your employees when you really need to tighten the corporate finances? What about when the company is flying high?*

**Sources:** N.L. Torres, "Herky-Perky," *Entrepreneur*, July 2001, 19, Info-Trac Article A79826851. "Old Perks, New Twists," *Inc.*, 15 October 1999, 214, Info-Trac Article A57615889. C. Webb, "Digital Capital: Forget the Cars, But Some Shops Still Offer Perks," *The Washington Post*, 22 November 2001, E01. "What! No Car?" *U.S. News & World Report*, 13 August 2001, 8, Info-Trac Article A77014424.

rewards, such as accomplishment, achievement, learning something new, and interacting with others, are the natural rewards associated with performing a task or activity for its own sake. And with the exception of influence (power), intrinsic rewards correspond very closely to higher-order needs that are concerned with relationships (belongingness, relatedness, and affiliation) and challenges and accomplishments (esteem, self-actualization, growth, and achievement). Therefore, one way for managers to meet employees' higher-order needs is to create opportunities for employees to experience intrinsic rewards by providing challenging work, encouraging employees to take greater responsibility for their work, and giving employees the freedom to pursue tasks and projects they find naturally interesting. For example, we began this section by asking, "What would motivate an employee like Marjorie Landale to voluntarily learn the American Sign Language?" Marjorie wasn't paid to do this. In fact, she even spent her own money and free time to learn how to sign. The reason that Marjorie learned how to sign is that doing so met her higher-order needs. It gave her a sense of accomplishment, and it allowed her to interact with deaf customers with whom she had been previously unable to interact. And Marjorie learned how to sign because her boss was smart enough to realize that there was no downside to giving her the freedom to pursue a task or project that she found naturally interesting.

## Review 1
### Basics of Motivation

*Motivation* is the set of forces that initiates, directs, and makes people persist in their efforts over time to accomplish a goal. Managers often confuse motivation and performance. However, since job performance is a multiplicative function of motivation times ability times situational constraints, job performance will suffer if any one of these components is weak. Needs are the physical or psychological requirements that must be met to ensure survival and well-being. When needs are not met, people experience an internal state of tension. But once a particular need is met, it no longer motivates. When this occurs, people become satisfied and are then motivated by other unmet needs. Different motivational theories, such as Maslow's Hierarchy of Needs (physiological, safety, belongingness, esteem, and self-actualization); Alderfer's ERG Theory (existence, relatedness, and growth); and McClelland's Learned Needs Theory (affiliation, achievement, and power), specify a number of different needs. However, studies show that there are only two general kinds of needs, lower-order needs and higher-order needs, and that higher-order needs will not motivate people as long as lower-order needs remain unsatisfied. Both extrinsic and intrinsic rewards motivate people. Extrinsic rewards, which include pay, company stock, benefits, and promotions, are used to motivate people to join organizations and attend and perform their jobs. The basic model of motivation suggests that managers can motivate employees by asking them what their needs are, satisfying lower-order needs first, expecting people's needs to change, and satisfying higher-order needs through intrinsic rewards.

# How Perceptions and Expectations Affect Motivation

On 1 January 2002, Europe's new currency, the euro, replaced the currencies of 11 countries (Austria, Belgium, Finland, France, Germany, Ireland, Italy, Luxembourg, Netherlands, Portugal, and Spain). As a result of that change, European consumers now find it much easier to compare the price of goods from one country to another without having to make cumbersome currency translations. ("Let's see, 100 deutsche marks are worth 335 French francs, and 100 Spanish pesetas are worth 1,164 Italian lira, so that means it's cheaper if I buy it in....").[27] But consumers weren't the only ones making crossborder euro comparisons after the currency changeover. Companies and employees did, too, as they compared salaries and benefits among countries. For example, salaries tended to be much higher in northern than in southern Europe. In Germany, a sales and marketing director in a medium-sized company would be paid about 175,000 euros ($154,350) a year. But in Spain, the same job pays about 110,000 euros ($97,000). Yet even after taxes, which are higher in Germany, the German sales and marketing director takes home 87,500 euros a year ($77,100), while the Spanish sales and marketing director takes home 61,000 euros ($53,800). The difference is a whopping 43 percent.[28]

So with much of Europe's work force now being paid in euros, companies are expecting a firestorm of salary adjustments, as employees, like the Spanish sales and marketing director, complain loudly about the unfairness of their pay. William Scott, who heads the Paris office of Hewitt Associates, a human resources consulting company, said, "We're doing many more crossborder [pay] comparisons. The need to compete and pay on a European-wide basis is quite significant. There will be a pay extravaganza for some folks."[29] And if companies don't make salary adjustments, they can expect some employees to leave for higher pay in other companies or countries, especially multilingual employees who possess technical skills.

After reading the next two sections, you should be able to

2. *use equity theory to explain how employees' perceptions of fairness affect motivation.*

3. *use expectancy theory to describe how workers' expectations about rewards, effort, and the link between rewards and performance influence motivation.*

## 2. Equity Theory

Finnish businessman Jaako Rytsola was out driving in his BMW one evening. "The road was wide and I was feeling good. It was nice to be driving when there was no one in sight." However, Rytsola wasn't really alone. A local policeman pulled him over and issued him a speeding ticket for driving 43 miles per hour in a 25 miles per-hour zone. The cost of the ticket: $71,400! Janne Rajala, a college student, was also pulled over for driving 18 miles per hour over the speed limit. However, Rajala's ticket only cost him $106. The $71,294 difference is because Finland bases traffic fines on the driver's income and the severity of the offense, which in this case is identical.

Quick question: Is Finland fair or unfair in the way it determines speeding fines? Most Americans would argue that Finland's approach is unfair, that fairness means that such fines should be proportional to the offense and that everyone who breaks the law to the same degree should pay the same fine. By contrast, most Finns believe that fines proportional to income are fair. Erkki Wuouma of Finland's Ministry of the Interior said, "This is a Nordic tradition. We have progressive taxation and progressive punishments. So the more you earn, the more you pay." Rytsola pays more because he is a high-earning Internet entrepreneur. Rajala pays less because he's a low-earning college student.[30]

Fairness, or what people perceive to be fair, is also a critical issue in organizations. **Equity theory** says that people will be motivated at work when they *perceive* that they are being treated fairly. In particular, equity theory stresses the importance of perceptions. So, regardless of the actual level of rewards people receive, they must also perceive that, relative to others, they are being treated fairly. For example, you learned in Chapter 14 that the average CEO now makes 475 times more than the average blue-collar worker. This enormous difference in pay occurs because CEOs almost always receive much larger annual pay increases than regular workers. For instance, from 1998 to 2000, CEO pay rose by 36 percent, 17 percent, and 6 percent, compared to an average of just 2 to 4 percent per year for blue-collar and white-collar workers.[31] Many people, particularly leaders of labor unions,

**equity theory**
theory that states that people will be motivated when they perceive that they are being treated fairly

616

Equity theory is not an absolute. It is dependent on many factors, including culture. Jaakko Rytsola, pictured here with his Lamborghini, was fined $71,400 for speeding because in Finland traffic fines are based on a person's income. People of different cultures may not have the same view of equity as the Finnish!

AP/WIDE WORLD PHOTOS

# BeenThereDoneThat

## Let's Pay the CEO $0.00 This Year!

John Lauer is the chairman and CEO of Oglebay Norton Co., which mines, processes, transports, and markets industrial minerals. In one of the most unique pay packages in business history, Lauer insisted that he not be paid an annual salary. Instead, after investing $1.25 million of his own money to buy company stock, he convinced the

Oglebay board of directors to award him 380,174 premium stock options with a strike price of $38 a share. When the options were issued, Oglebay Norton's stock price was $32 a share, just $6 under the strike price. However, on the day I wrote the introduction to this interview, the stock closed at $11.75, meaning that the stock will have to almost quadruple before exceeding $38 a share, the point above which Lauer's stock options begin to have value. Read this interview with John Lauer to learn why he insisted on this pay package and what he thinks of typical CEO compensation plans.

**Q:** Do you think your type of compensation makes sense for the company?

**A:** Well, yes, I do. It's quite similar to the compensation-package model used at privately held companies. The CEO takes the same risk as the founders or investors and is motivated in exactly the same way as they are. A CEO of a privately-owned company is capable of getting huge rewards—but only after the private shareholders win. I don't find that to be the case in most publicly held companies.

**Q:** How does your compensation approach make sense for employees?

**A:** You are investing in yourself, the confidence you have in your own abilities to succeed and perform under certain measurements. Employees recognize that.

It creates a much more interesting dynamic, that "Wow, here's a guy who came into the company [and] invested his own money. If he wins, we are all going to win. I would rather work for a guy like that than somebody maybe who is motivated differently."

That attitude has made a difference in the type of person we attract into management. And it makes a difference in how people relate to management. I receive emails from all over the company and letters from retirees that they really like what I did. They think it is a meaningful way for a CEO to be compensated.

My payday, if I succeed, will be very large: an option on 8 percent of the shares of Oglebay Norton.

My ethic is that if you are willing to take the risk and put your money up there and work hard, it is okay if you get paid really well.

But it is structured in a way that is not a low-risk or no-risk approach to CEO compensation. That means our stock that trades at $26 and change right now [in mid-February 2001] has got to almost double in the next four and one-half years for me to really win big and for the shareholders to win big.

**Q:** When you took the job here, were you a "centimillionaire," a "decamillionaire," or just a multimillionaire?

**A:** I was up there in the deca level.

**Q:** Not everybody is worth $10 million when they become CEOs. Therefore, many want considerable cash.

**A:** I agree. However, it would be hard for me to name one CEO today who, when they became CEOs, couldn't afford to invest in their own company by buying shares. They should be willing to invest enough money that if they lost it, it would hurt. Yet, no one ever seems to do that—in part because the governance structure in the public-company sector doesn't require it.

**Q:** When the board didn't buy your original idea of a pay package tied to a percentage of increased operating profit, you came back with the proposed deal you got instead. How much selling did that take?

**A:** I said, "Look, I want to be able at the end of a successful five-year time frame to own 10 percent of the company." I said, "I am willing to invest some of my own money in the company to start that stake." As a result, I invested well over $1 million. They [matched] the first million with a like amount in value of restricted shares. I have 80 percent of those shares vested right now. The other 20 percent will vest at the end of the fifth year, 1 January 2003.

**Q:** As part of your package, the board asked you to take an annual performance bonus—an idea you rejected at first. What's your view of such bonuses for CEOs? When they don't earn them, they often get something else instead.

**A:** That's right. My interest was in the equity part. The [board] discussion, as described to me, went as follows: "If we give John such an equity package, while clearly aligned with shareholders, he will really not be aligned in any meaningful way to the management [team]. Is there a way we can link those?"

I accepted the premise that it would be important to tie me into the management team's performance. That has worked well. I find I can go to the board and recommend something about a bonus for [other executives] without affecting my own situation. I get listened to more clearly because I am not going to get any more out of this. It is the people that are working for me that I am in there lobbying for. In a more traditional pay setup, if I am seeking more money for the management team, that ratchets me up again.

**Q:** With your share price back in a more normal range, how will you ever make any money from your options?

**A:** The first way is if we achieve our stated performance target of doubling earnings per share in the four-year time frame. That would take our earnings per share to $5-plus. We think we have an opportunity to be able to do that.

**Q:** In addition to your worthless stock options, you have invested $1.25 million in Oglebay Norton shares. You are not being paid any salary. You are getting a very modest bonus. Does this make it hard to get up in the morning? Are you demoralized?

**A:** No.

**Q:** Why wouldn't you take more premium-priced options at this point?

**A:** Because that's not the deal I struck. I knew and understood the risk going in. I didn't expect to come in and create the kind of new Oglebay Norton that we are creating overnight.

I did and continue to expect to be able to create the performance base within five to seven years. If the CEO can't get the job done in five to seven years, he shouldn't be CEO any longer. Again, using my research against myself, I said, "If I can't do it in seven and one-half years, I don't deserve anything."

I have never been frustrated about the stock price. I have been disappointed a few times that the market doesn't reflect the things we do.

When I came in here, if everything [had] worked just perfect—which it never does—I would be out of here . . . .

**Q:** By now!

**A:** There would be a new CEO and I would be off enjoying myself in Europe somewhere.

My agreement is for five years. Directors may say, "Look, we don't want you to leave at the end of five years. Can you give us six or something?"

I would probably say yes. If the board assesses that I can't get the job done I signed up to do, then I ought to be out of here. With my stake in the company, I am not about to sit here because I am dying to continue to be CEO. My objective is to capture the payout, first for shareholders and then for me.

**Q:** Given that you have made so little from your current pay package, are you still a decamillionaire?

**A:** Oh, yes.

**Q:** No thanks to Oglebay Norton.

**A:** Not yet.

**Source:** "Investing in Himself: CEO John Lauer Talks about Why He Chose to Get Paid Only If He Performs—And Why So Few Others Take the Same Risk," *The Wall Street Journal*, 12 April 2001, R10. This interview was edited for inclusion in this textbook.

believe that CEO pay is obscenely high and unfair. Others believe that CEO pay is fair because the supply and demand for executive talent largely determines what CEOs are paid. They argue that if it were easier to find good CEOs, then CEOs would be paid much less. (See the Been There, Done That "Let's Pay the CEO $0.00 This Year!" for more on executive pay.)

As explained below, equity theory doesn't focus on objective equity (i.e., that CEOs make 475 times more than blue-collar workers). Instead, equity theory says that equity, like beauty, is in the eye of the beholder.

*Let's learn more about equity theory by examining 2.1 the components of equity theory, 2.2 how people react to perceived inequities, and 2.3 how to motivate people using equity theory.*

### 2.1 Components of Equity Theory

The basic components of equity theory are inputs, outcomes, and referents. **Inputs** are the contributions employees make to the organization. Inputs include education and training, intelligence, experience, effort, number of hours worked, and ability. **Outcomes** are the rewards employees receive in exchange for their contributions to the organization. Outcomes include pay, fringe benefits, status symbols, job titles and assignments, and even the leadership style of their superiors. And since perceptions of equity depend on how you are being treated compared to others, **referents** are others with whom people compare themselves to determine if they have been treated fairly. Usually, people choose to compare themselves to referents who hold the same or similar jobs or who are otherwise similar, such as in gender, race, age, or tenure.[32] For instance, by any objective measure, it's hard to make the argument that the best professional athletes, who make upwards of $20 million a year (and no doubt more by the time you read this), are treated unfairly, especially when the average American earns $42,148 a year.[33] However, most top athletes' contracts include escalator contracts that specify that if another top player at the same position (i.e., their referent) receives a larger contract, then their contract will automatically be increased to that higher amount.

According to the equity theory process shown in Exhibit 16.7, employees compare inputs, their contributions to the organization, to outcomes, the rewards they receive from the organization in exchange for those inputs. This comparison of outcomes to inputs is called the **outcome/input (O/I) ratio**. After an internal comparison in which they compare their outcomes to their inputs, employees then make an external comparison in

**inputs**
in equity theory, the contributions employees make to the organization

**outcomes**
in equity theory, the rewards employees receive for their contributions to the organization

**referent**
in equity theory, others with whom people compare themselves to determine if they have been treated fairly

**outcome/input (O/I) ratio**
in equity theory, an employee's perception of the comparison between the rewards received from an organization and the employee's contributions to that organization

EXHIBIT 16.7

## OUTCOME/INPUT RATIOS

$$\frac{\text{OUTCOMES}_{\text{SELF}}}{\text{INPUTS}_{\text{SELF}}} = \frac{\text{OUTCOMES}_{\text{REFERENT}}}{\text{INPUTS}_{\text{REFERENT}}}$$

which they compare their O/I ratio with the O/I ratio of a referent.[34] When people perceive that their O/I ratio is equal to the referent's O/I ratio, they conclude that they are being treated fairly. But when people perceive that their O/I ratio is different from their referent's O/I ratio, they conclude that they have been treated inequitably or unfairly.

**underreward**
when the referent you compare yourself to is getting more outcomes relative to their inputs than you are

There are two kinds of inequity, underreward and overreward. **Underreward** occurs when a referent's O/I ratio is better than your O/I ratio. In other words, the referent you compare yourself to is getting more outcomes relative to his or her inputs than you are. When people perceive that they have been underrewarded, they tend to experience anger or frustration. For example, when a manufacturing company received notice that some important contracts had been canceled, management cut employees' pay by 15 percent in one plant but not in another. Just as equity theory predicts, theft doubled in the plant that received the pay cut. Likewise, employee turnover increased from 5 percent to 23 percent.[35]

**overreward**
when you are getting more outcomes relative to your inputs than the referent to whom you compare yourself

By contrast, **overreward** occurs when a referent's O/I ratio is worse than your O/I ratio. In this case, you are getting more outcomes relative to your inputs than your referent is. In theory, when people perceive that they have been overrewarded, they experience guilt. Not surprisingly, people have a very high tolerance for overreward. It takes a tremendous amount of overpayment before people decide that their pay or benefits are more than they deserve.

### 2.2 How People React to Perceived Inequity

As a kid, do you remember the disagreements you'd have while playing with your friends? "That ball was out." "No, it was in." "Out." "In." "OUT!" "IN!" "Do-Over!" "Yeah, why don't you both cool it and we'll have a do-over." Even as children, we have a strong desire for fairness, for being treated equitably. And when this need isn't met, we are strongly motivated to find a way to restore equity and be fair, hence the "do-over." Not surprisingly, equity is just as important at the office as it is on the playground.

So what happens when people perceive that they have been treated inequitably at work? Exhibit 16.8 shows that perceived inequity affects satisfaction. In the case of underreward, this usually translates into frustration or anger, while with overreward, the reaction is guilt. These reactions lead to tension and a strong need to take action to restore equity in some way. At first, a slight inequity may not be strong enough to motivate an employee to take immediate action. However, if the inequity continues or there are multiple inequities, tension may build over time until a point of intolerance is reached, and the person is energized to take action. [36]

There are five ways in which people try to restore equity when they perceive that they have been treated unfairly: reducing inputs, increasing outcomes, rationalizing inputs or outcomes, changing the referent, or simply leaving. These will be discussed in terms of the inequity associated with underreward, which is much more common than the inequity associated with overreward.

People who perceive that they have been underrewarded may try to restore equity by decreasing or withholding their inputs (i.e., effort). For example, over the last 15 years, Alaska Air, the 10th largest U.S. airline, has had tremendous difficulty trying to reach labor agreements with the labor unions representing its pilots, mechanics, and flight attendants. During the last round of negotiations, flight attendants initiated a plan against the

EXHIBIT 16.8

ADDING EQUITY THEORY TO THE MODEL

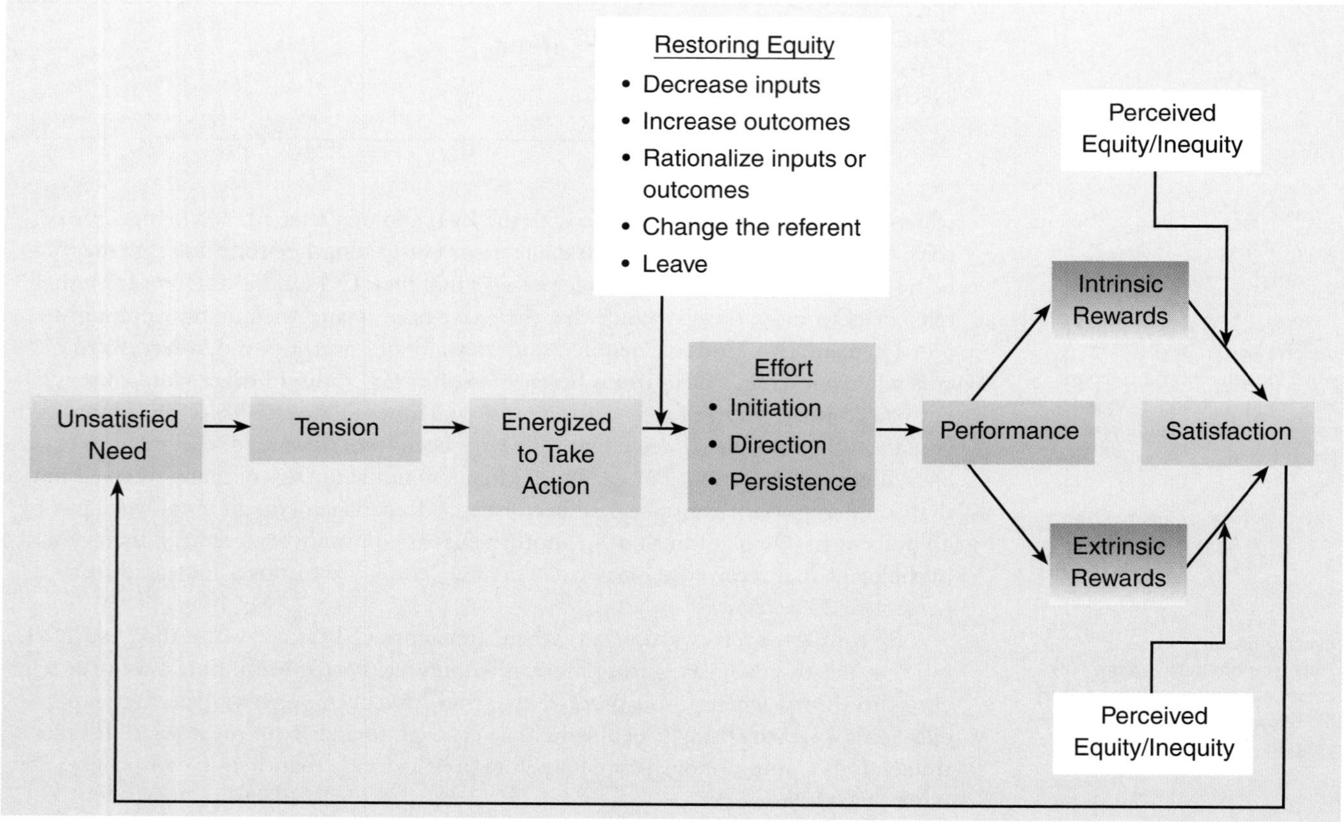

Restoring Equity
• Decrease inputs
• Increase outcomes
• Rationalize inputs or outcomes
• Change the referent
• Leave

Unsatisfied Need → Tension → Energized to Take Action → Effort
• Initiation
• Direction
• Persistence → Performance → Intrinsic Rewards / Extrinsic Rewards → Satisfaction

Perceived Equity/Inequity

Perceived Equity/Inequity

company that they dubbed C.H.A.O.S., create havoc around our system, in which flight attendants simply walked off flights because they thought the company was offering an unfair compensation package. Mechanics used a similar strategy, slowing the rate at which they repaired or completed schedule maintenance work on company planes. Hundreds of flights were delayed as a result.[37]

Increasing outcomes is another way in which people try to restore equity. This might include asking for a raise or pointing out the inequity to the boss and hoping that she takes care of it. Sometimes, however, employees may go to external organizations, such as labor unions, federal agencies, or the courts to get help in increasing outcomes to restore equity. For instance, the U.S. Department of Labor estimates that one in 10 workers is not getting the extra overtime pay they deserve when they work more than 40 hours a week.[38] In fact, there are nearly 20,000 such cases each year and employees win 90 percent of them.[39] For example, the managers of Waffle House restaurants sued the company because they were working an average of 89 hours a week without any overtime pay. The company contended that as managers they were exempt from the Fair Labor Standards Act (FLSA) which mandates that workers be paid time and a half for any work beyond 40 hours a week. (Managers; administrative or staff employees; professionals, such as teachers, engineers, or programmers; and sales people are typically "exempt" from the FLSA. See **http://www.dol.gov/dol/esa/public/regs/compliance/whd/whdfs17.htm** and **http://www.dol.gov/dol/esa/public/regs/compliance/whd/whdfs23.htm** for further explanation.) Waffle House managers, however, acted as grill cooks on busy shifts and substituted for absent hourly employees (who in turn fulfilled the duties of absent managers). Furthermore, the primary goals of Waffle House's management training was to teach each manager "to become a proficient grill operator," and to "gain exposure to the daily management duties and responsibilities." For these reasons, the courts ruled that Waffle House managers were really employees who deserved overtime pay. As a result, they were awarded $2,868,841.50 in back overtime pay.[40]

Another method of restoring equity is to rationalize or distort inputs or outcomes. So instead of actually decreasing inputs or increasing outcomes, employees restore equity by making mental or emotional "adjustments" in their O/I ratios or the O/I ratios of their referents. For example, say a company downsizes 10 percent of its work force. It's likely that the survivors, the people who still have jobs, will be angry or frustrated with company management because of the layoffs. However, if alternative jobs are difficult to find, the employees who are still with the company may rationalize or distort their O/I ratios and conclude, "Well, things could be worse. At least I still have my job." Rationalizing or distorting outcomes may be used when other ways to restore equity aren't available.

Changing the referent is another way of restoring equity. In this case, people compare themselves to someone other than the referent they had been using for previous O/I ratio comparisons. Since people usually choose to compare themselves to others who hold the same or similar jobs or who are otherwise similar, they may change referents to restore equity when their personal situations change, such as a decrease in job status or pay.

Finally, when none of these methods—reducing inputs, increasing outcomes, rationalizing inputs or outcomes, or changing referents—are possible or none restore equity, employees may leave by quitting their jobs, transferring, or increasing absenteeism.[41] For example, the median hourly wage for security guards is $8.45 an hour, which is less than telemarketers, movers, or secretaries earn. Not surprisingly, turnover rates for security guards are typically between 120 and 200 percent per year as security guards quit to take better paying jobs elsewhere.[42] Likewise, attorneys and accountants at the U.S. Government's Securities and Exchange Commission (SEC) quit their jobs at twice the rate found in other federal agencies. Why? Because the SEC's attorneys and accountants are paid 40 percent less than their counterparts at other government agencies. They also leave the SEC because they can get jobs in the private sector that pay $180,000 to $250,000 per year.[43]

### 2.3 Motivating with Equity Theory

What practical things can managers do to use equity theory to motivate employees?

As shown in Exhibit 16.9, *start by looking for and correcting major inequities.* One of the difficulties that equity theory makes us aware of is that an employee's sense of fairness is based on subjective perceptions. So what one employee considers grossly unfair may not affect another employee's perceptions of equity at all. While this makes it difficult for managers to create conditions that satisfy all employees, it's critical that they do their best to take care of major inequities that can energize employees to take disruptive, costly, or harmful actions, such as decreasing inputs or leaving. So, whenever possible, managers should look for and correct major inequities. For example, British-based Zurich Financial Services decided to pay its information technology staff a bonus of an extra year's salary if they agreed to stay with the company for another three years. The total cost of the bonus plan was 17 million pounds ($27.5 million). The company began offering this retention bonus after one quarter of its staff quit to pursue much higher-paying jobs in other companies. Employees who left before the three years were up were asked to completely repay the bonus. Corporate affairs manager Wendy May said, "We are doing what it takes to hold on to these staff. We cannot lock our staff in a cupboard to make them stay, so we are offering them a long-term incentive to stick with us. What it is costing is a small price to pay compared to the catastrophe of losing all our in-house expertise."[44]

621

EXHIBIT 16.9

## MOTIVATING WITH EQUITY THEORY

- Look for and correct major inequities.
- Reduce employees' inputs.
- Make sure decision-making processes are fair.

*Reduce employees' inputs.* Increasing outcomes is often the first and only strategy that companies use to restore equity. This approach is unfortunate, because reducing employee inputs is just as viable a strategy. In fact, with 50-hour weeks, dual-career couples, and working at work *and* home being more the norm than the exception, more and more employees are looking for ways to reduce stress and restore a balance between work and family. In this context, it makes sense to ask employees to do less not more, to have them identify and eliminate the 20 percent of their jobs that don't increase productivity or add value for customers, and to have managers eliminate company-imposed requirements that really aren't critical to managers', employees', or companies' performance (i.e., unnecessary meetings, reports, etc.). The SAS Institute, maker of the Statistical Analysis Software used by nearly every major company in the United States, has been reducing employees' inputs with success for years. Unlike most software companies that expect employees to work 12- to 14-hour days, SAS offices close at 6 P.M. every evening. Also, employees receive unlimited sick days each year. And, to encourage employees to spend time with their families, there's an on-site daycare facility, the company cafeteria has plenty of highchairs and baby seats, and the company even has a seven-hour workday. The payoff? With an employee turnover of just 3.7 percent a year (compared to 20 percent and up for most software companies), the company saves $67 million a year in unnecessary costs and expenses.[45]

*Make sure decision-making processes are fair.* Equity theory focuses on **distributive justice**, the degree to which outcomes and rewards are fairly distributed or allocated. However, **procedural justice**, the fairness of the process used to make reward allocation decisions, is just as important.[46] Procedural justice matters because even when employees are unhappy with their outcomes (i.e., low pay), they're much less likely to be unhappy with company management if they believe that the procedures used to allocate outcomes were fair. For example, employees who are laid off tend to be hostile toward their employer when they perceive that the procedures leading to the layoffs were unfair. By contrast, employees who perceive layoff procedures to be fair tend to continue to support and trust their employers.[47] Also, if employees perceive that their outcomes are unfair (i.e., distributive injustice), but that the decisions and procedures leading to those outcomes were fair (i.e., procedural justice), they are much more likely to seek constructive ways of restoring equity, such as discussing these matters with their manager. In contrast, if employees perceive both distributive and procedural injustice, they may resort to more destructive tactics, such as withholding effort, absenteeism, tardiness, or even sabotage and theft.[48]

## Review 2
### Equity Theory

The basic components of equity theory are inputs, outcomes, and referents. After an internal comparison in which employees compare their outcomes to their inputs, they then make an external comparison in which they compare their O/I ratio with the O/I ratio of a referent, a person who works in a similar job or is otherwise similar. When their O/I ratio is equal to the referent's O/I ratio, employees perceive that they are being treated fairly. But when their O/I ratio is different from their referent's O/I ratio, they perceive that they have been treated inequitably or unfairly. There are two kinds of inequity, underreward and overreward. Underreward occurs when a referent's O/I ratio is better than the employee's O/I ratio. Underreward leads to anger or frustration. Overreward occurs

**distributive justice**
the perceived degree to which outcomes and rewards are fairly distributed or allocated

**procedural justice**
the perceived fairness of the process used to make reward allocation decisions

when a referent's O/I ratio is worse than the employee's O/I ratio. Overreward can lead to guilt, but only when the level of overreward is extreme. When employees perceive that they have been treated inequitably (i.e., underreward), they may try to restore equity by reducing inputs, increasing outcomes, rationalizing inputs or outcomes, changing the referent, or simply leaving. Managers can use equity theory to motivate workers by looking for and correcting major inequities, reducing employees' inputs, and emphasizing procedural as well as distributive justice.

## 3 Expectancy Theory

How attractive would you find the following rewards? A company concierge service that sends someone to be at your house when the cable guy or repair person shows up, or picks up your car from the mechanic? A "7 to 7" travel policy that stipulates that no one has to leave home for business travel before 7 A.M. on Mondays and that everyone should return home from their business travels by 7 P.M. on Fridays? The opportunity to telecommute, so that you can feed your kids breakfast, pick them up after school, and then tuck them into bed at night? A "circle of excellence" award, in which employees nominate coworkers for outstanding work, and the winners get company-paid trips to Hawaii and the Bahamas? A full-sized basketball court with a real wooden floor? Or a sabbatical program that gives employees the chance to take a paid leave, so they can work for local charities?[49]

If you had kids, you might love the chance to telecommute; but if you didn't, you might not be interested. If you didn't travel much on business, you wouldn't be interested in the "7 to 7" travel policy; but if you did, you'd probably love it. One of the hardest things about motivating people is that rewards that are attractive to some employees are unattractive to others. **Expectancy theory** says that people will be motivated to the extent to which they believe that their efforts will lead to good performance, that good performance will be rewarded, and that they are offered attractive rewards.[50]

*Let's learn more about expectancy theory by examining 3.1 the components of expectancy theory and 3.2 how to use expectancy theory as a motivational tool.*

### 3.1 Components of Expectancy Theory

Expectancy theory holds that people make conscious choices about their motivation. The three factors that affect those choices are valence, expectancy, and instrumentality.

**Valence** is simply the attractiveness or desirability of various rewards or outcomes. Expectancy theory recognizes that the same reward or outcome, say, a promotion, will be highly attractive to some people, highly disliked by others, and for some, may not make much difference one way or the other. Accordingly, when people are deciding how much effort to put forth, expectancy theory says that they will consider the valence of all possible rewards and outcomes that they can receive from their jobs. The greater the sum of those valences, each of which could be positive, negative, or neutral, the more effort people will choose to put forth on the job.

**Expectancy** is the perceived relationship between effort and performance. When expectancies are strong, employees believe that their hard work and efforts will result in good performance, so they work harder. By contrast, when expectancies are weak, employees figure that no matter what they do or how hard they work, they won't be able to perform their jobs successfully, so they don't work as hard.

**Instrumentality** is the perceived relationship between performance and rewards. When instrumentality is strong, employees believe that improved performance will lead to better and more rewards, so they will choose to work harder. When instrumentality is weak, employees don't believe that better performance will result in more or better rewards, so they will choose not to work as hard.

Expectancy theory holds that for people to be highly motivated, all three variables—valence, expectancy, and instrumentality—must be high. Thus, expectancy theory can be represented by the following simple equation:

---

**expectancy theory**
theory that states that people will be motivated to the extent to which they believe that their efforts will lead to good performance, that good performance will be rewarded, and that they will be offered attractive rewards

**valence**
the attractiveness or desirability of a reward or outcome

**expectancy**
the perceived relationship between effort and performance

**instrumentality**
the perceived relationship between performance and rewards

$$\text{Motivation} = \text{Valence} \times \text{Instrumentality} \times \text{Expectancy}$$

If any one of these variables (valence, instrumentality, or expectancy) declines, overall motivation will decline, too.

Exhibit 16.10 incorporates the expectancy theory variables into our motivation model. Valence and instrumentality combine to affect employees' willingness to put forth effort (i.e., the degree to which they are energized to take action), while expectancy transforms intended effort ("I'm really going to work hard in this job") into actual effort. If you're offered rewards that you desire and you believe that you will in fact receive these rewards for good performance, you're highly likely to be energized to take action. However, you're not likely to actually exert effort unless you also believe that you can do the job (i.e., that your efforts will lead to successful performance).

Caribou Coffee, which has stores in Minnesota, Illinois, Ohio, Georgia, North Carolina, and Michigan, integrates valence, expectancy, and instrumentality into its employee motivation program. First, Caribou offers a wide variety of rewards, such as employee recognition programs, sales incentives, and company-wide contests, so that all of its employees can receive highly valent rewards that they desire. The company manages employee expectancies by using its "Coffee College" to provide substantial training to new hires and continuing education for long-time employees. Caribou's director of training, Annmarie Lofy, said that the program sets new employees up for success from the very beginning. When they start their new jobs, they're not nervous and unsure, because the training has prepared them to do their jobs well. Finally, Caribou manages instrumentality by linking various rewards to the specific behaviors it wants to reward. In

## EXHIBIT 16.10

### ADDING EXPECTANCY THEORY TO THE MODEL

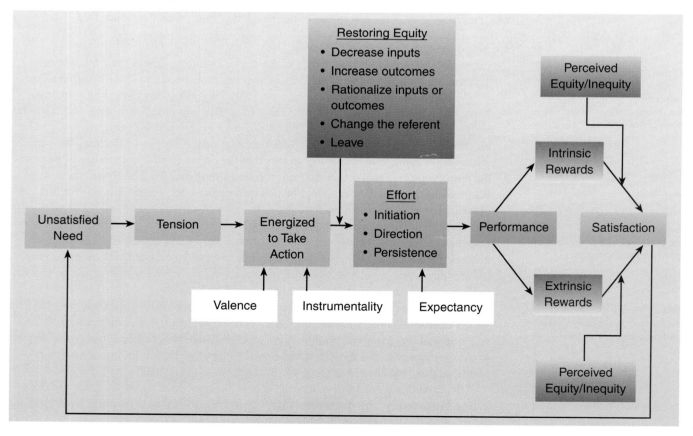

one such program, store employees receive "Bou Bucks" from store managers for performance above and beyond their job descriptions. Bou Bucks are redeemable for merchandise at stores such as Marshall Fields and Foot Locker. One reason Bou Bucks have had such a strong effect on instrumentality perceptions is that Caribou Coffee managers immediately award them when they see employees performing their jobs well. This strengthens employees' perceptions that performance is instrumental to receiving rewards.[51]

### 3.2 Motivating with Expectancy Theory

What practical things can managers do to use expectancy theory to motivate employees?

As shown in Exhibit 16.11, *systematically gather information to find out what employees want from their jobs.* In addition to individual managers directly asking employees what they want from their jobs (see "Motivating with Equity Theory"), companies still need to survey their employees regularly to determine their wants, needs, and dissatisfactions. Since people consider the valence of all the possible rewards and outcomes that they can receive from their jobs, regular identification of wants, needs, and dissatisfaction gives companies the chance to turn negatively valent rewards and outcomes into positively valent rewards and outcomes, thus raising overall motivation and effort. Marc Albin, CEO of Albin Engineering, said, "My experience in managing people is, they're all different. Some people want to be recognized for their cheerful attitude and their ability to spread their cheerful attitude. Some want to be recognized for the quality of their work, some for the quantity of their work. Some like to be recognized individually; others want to be recognized in groups."[52] Therefore, at the end of each employee orientation session (during the first week on the job), he asks them to identify the rewards they want. New employees appreciate his interest in what they want or need. Said Albin, "No one has ever said, 'Just recognize me for anything I do well.'"[53]

*Take specific steps to link rewards to individual performance in a way that is clear and understandable to employees.* Unfortunately, most employees are extremely dissatisfied with the link between pay and performance in their organizations. A study based on a representative sample of Americans found that 80 percent of employees wanted to be paid according to a different kind of pay system! Moreover, only 32 percent of employees were satisfied with how their annual pay raises were determined, while only 22 percent were happy with the way in which companies determined the starting salaries for their jobs.[54] One way to make sure that employees see the connection between pay and performance in their companies (see Chapter 14 for a discussion of compensation strategies) is for managers to publicize the way in which pay decisions are made. For example, at Allstate Insurance, the company compensation team wrote a pamphlet called "Tracking the Clues to Your Pay," which explains how Allstate carefully used market value surveys and analyses to determine employee pay. Importantly, this helped counter the widespread belief that employee pay was determined in some random way. When asked, "To what extent does the pay system competitively reward you for results?" 27 percent more Allstate employees responded "A great deal" or "Quite a bit" after the publication of "Tracking the Clues to Your Pay."[55]

625

EXHIBIT 16.11

### MOTIVATING WITH EXPECTANCY THEORY

- Systematically gather information to find out what employees want from their jobs.
- Take specific steps to link rewards to individual performance in a way that is clear and understandable to employees.
- Empower employees to make decisions if you really want them to believe that their hard work and effort will lead to good performance.

*Empower employees to make decisions if you really want them to believe that their hard work and effort will lead to good performance.* If valent rewards are linked to good performance, people should be energized to take action. However, this works only if they also believe that their efforts will lead to good performance. One of the ways in which managers destroy the expectancy that hard work and effort will lead to good performance is by restricting what employees can do or by ignoring employees' ideas. In Chapter 11, you learned that *empowerment* is a feeling of intrinsic motivation, in which workers perceive their work to have meaning and perceive themselves to be competent, to have an impact, and to be capable of self-determination.[56] So, if managers want workers to have strong expectancies, they should empower them to make decisions. Doing so will motivate employees to take active rather than passive roles in their work. For instance, British billionaire Richard Branson, founder and chief of Virgin Corporation (Virgin Atlantic Airways, Virgin Records, Virgin Rail, etc.), builds strong expectancies in his employees through empowerment. He said:

> Yes. It all comes down to people. There's nothing that comes close. Motivating people, bringing in the best. The girl who opened what will be the best bridal shop in Europe was flying on the airline [Virgin Air] as an air hostess. She came to me with an idea and I said, "Go to it." She did. Now it's Virgin Bride. By having the freedom to prove herself, she has excelled. . . . Praise people—like plants, they must be nurtured—and make it fun. Value them and give them the opportunity to contribute in ways that excite them.[57]

## Review 3
### Expectancy Theory

Expectancy theory holds that three factors affect the conscious choices people make about their motivation: valence, expectancy, and instrumentality. Valence is simply the attractiveness or desirability of various rewards or outcomes. Expectancy is the perceived relationship between effort and performance. Instrumentality is the perceived relationship between performance and rewards. Expectancy theory holds that for people to be highly motivated, all three factors must be high. If any one of these factors declines, overall motivation will decline, too. Managers can use expectancy theory to motivate workers by systematically gathering information to find out what employees want from their jobs, by linking rewards to individual performance in a way that is clear and understandable to employees, and by empowering employees to make decisions, which will increase their expectancies that hard work and effort will lead to good performance.

# How Rewards and Goals Affect Motivation

No matter what management tried, it couldn't find a way to prevent the mechanics at Monsanto's Pensacola, Florida, plant from accidentally dropping heavy machine parts on their toes or the yarn workers from accidentally cutting their fingers. Regular meetings, accident investigations, safety slogans and posters—nothing seemed to work. Finally, management called in psychologists and statisticians to identify the causes and teach workers how to avoid accidents by reinforcing each other's safe behavior. After identifying dozens of possible causes, workers were given "scorecards" to count the number of times they observed other employees performing safe or potentially unsafe behaviors. Employees looked for things like "shortcuts and deviations," "keeping eyes on hands," "avoiding pinch points," and housekeeping issues such as "clutter." Using the feedback obtained from the scorecards, management set specific safety goals and recognized safe workers at weekly meetings and in quarterly reviews. When an entire division improved its safety behavior, everyone won a free lunch or a coffee mug. Plus, safety records were considered in promotion decisions. As a result, Monsanto's safety record improved from 6.5 to just 1.6 injuries per hundred workers. Overall, injuries dropped by more than 75 percent, all without heavy-handed supervision or punishment.[58]

*After reading the next three sections, you should be able to*

*4. explain how reinforcement theory works and how it can be used to motivate.*

*5. describe the components of goal-setting theory and how managers can use them to motivate workers.*

*6. discuss how the entire motivation model can be used to motivate workers.*

## 4. Reinforcement Theory

**reinforcement theory**
theory that states that behavior is a function of its consequences, that behaviors followed by positive consequences will occur more frequently, and that behaviors followed by negative consequences, or not followed by positive consequences, will occur less frequently

**reinforcement**
the process of changing behavior by changing the consequences that follow behavior

**reinforcement contingencies**
cause-and-effect relationships between the performance of specific behaviors and specific consequences

**schedule of reinforcement**
rules that specify which behaviors will be reinforced, which consequences will follow those behaviors, and the schedule by which those consequences will be delivered

**Reinforcement theory** says that behavior is a function of its consequences, that behaviors followed by positive consequences (i.e., reinforced) will occur more frequently, and that behaviors followed by negative consequences, or not followed by positive consequences, will occur less frequently.[59] Therefore, Monsanto decided to reinforce safe behaviors. Chuck Davis, a safety consultant, said, "It's better to recognize a guy for success than beat him up for failure. It's amazing how little reward a guy needs so he doesn't stick his arm in a machine."[60] More specifically, **reinforcement** is the process of changing behavior by changing the consequences that follow behavior.[61]

Reinforcement has two parts: reinforcement contingencies and schedules of reinforcement. **Reinforcement contingencies** are the cause-and-effect relationships between the performance of specific behaviors and specific consequences. For example, if you get docked an hour's pay for being late to work, then a reinforcement contingency exists between a behavior, being late to work, and a consequence, losing an hour's pay. A **schedule of reinforcement** is the set of rules regarding reinforcement contingencies, such as which behaviors will be reinforced, which consequences will follow those behaviors, and the schedule by which those consequences will be delivered.[62]

Exhibit 16.12 incorporates reinforcement contingencies and reinforcement schedules into our motivation model. First, notice that extrinsic rewards and the schedules of reinforcement used to deliver them are the primary method for creating reinforcement contingencies in organizations. In turn, those reward contingencies directly affect valences (the attractiveness of rewards), instrumentality (the perceived link between rewards and performance), and effort (how hard employees will work).

*Let's learn more about reinforcement theory by examining 4.1 the components of reinforcement theory, 4.2 the different schedules for delivering reinforcement, and 4.3 how to motivate with reinforcement theory.*

### 4.1 Components of Reinforcement Theory

*Reinforcement contingencies* are the cause-and-effect relationships between the performance of specific behaviors and specific consequences. The four kinds of reinforcement contingencies are positive reinforcement, negative reinforcement, punishment, and extinction.

**positive reinforcement**
reinforcement that strengthens behavior by following behaviors with desirable consequences

**negative reinforcement**
reinforcement that strengthens behavior by withholding an unpleasant consequence when employees perform a specific behavior

**Positive reinforcement** strengthens behavior (i.e., increases its frequency) by following behaviors with desirable consequences. For example, most people are members of frequent flyer clubs that earn them air miles for flying with a particular airline. In return, those air miles can be used for free first-class upgrades or free airline tickets. While most people dislike frequent business travel because it takes them away from their friends and family, one of the reasons they put up with it is that employers typically let them keep the air miles they earn while traveling for the company. So, every time they travel, they earn air miles that can be used for personal trips or family vacations. In fact, company-earned air miles are so valued by employees that many would leave if their companies tried to keep the air miles for themselves. Chuck Collins, a technology and management consultant, said, if a company "tried to nickel-and-dime me for miles, I'd get my résumé up to date real fast."[63]

**Try Praise**

Positive reinforcement doesn't have to be costly. In fact, praise and recognition are just as important to employees as financial rewards. However, many managers forget to praise employees or simply don't know how. Until praising employees becomes second nature to you, here are some simple ways to make sure you're praising employees effectively. Put praising employees on your to-do list. Set aside 10 minutes at the end of the day to write notes or emails to employees who deserve praise. If you can't be there in person, praise using the telephone, voice mail, or email. Finally, make sure your praise is prompt, sincere, specific, and positive.

**Source:** P. Kitchen, "Appreciation Builds a Better Workplace," *Newsday*, 11 February 2001, F11.

**Negative reinforcement** strengthens behavior by withholding an unpleasant consequence when employees perform a specific behavior. Negative reinforcement is also called *avoidance learning*, because workers perform a behavior to *avoid* a negative consequence. For example, at the Florist Network, a small business in Buffalo, New York, company management instituted a policy in which good attendance is required for employees to receive their annual bonuses. Employee attendance has improved significantly now that poor attendance can result in the loss of $1,500 or more, depending on the size of the annual bonus.[64]

By contrast, **punishment** weakens behavior (i.e., decreases its frequency) by following behaviors with undesirable consequences. For example, the standard disciplinary or punishment process in most companies is an oral warning ("Don't ever do that again."), followed by a written warning ("This letter is to discuss the serious problem you're having with . . ."), followed by three days off without pay ("While you're at home not being paid, we want you to think hard about . . ."), followed by being fired ("This was your last chance. You're fired."). While punishment can weaken behavior, managers have to be careful to avoid the backlash that sometimes occurs when employees

EXHIBIT 16.12

ADDING REINFORCEMENT THEORY TO THE MODEL

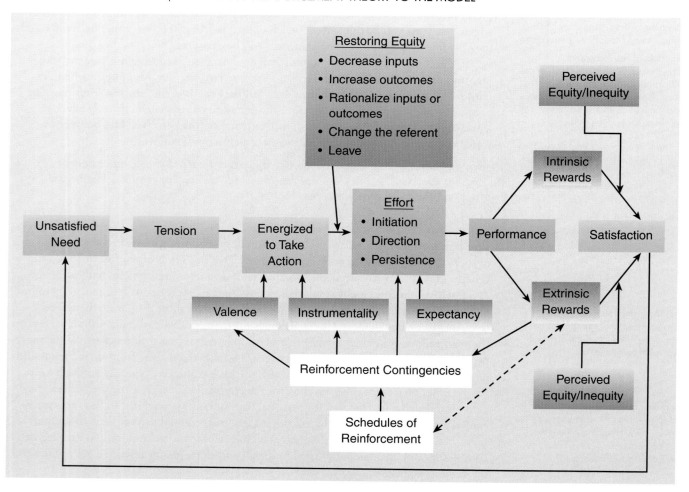

# BlastFromThePast

## Send in the Reinforcements!

Recently the enormous interest in stock options, profit sharing, and other pay-for-performance plans would lead you to believe that reinforcement theory was something new. However, reinforcements have been used (though not widely) to motivate workers for some time. Here are some classic examples of positive reinforcement.

**1972, Michigan Bell Telephone Company.** Because of high rates of absenteeism among its telephone operators, the company decided to provide workers more frequent feedback on how often they missed work. So instead of receiving absence reports on a monthly basis, telephone operators received absence reports on a weekly basis. The combination of more frequent feedback and praise for good attendance dropped the rate of absenteeism from 11 percent to 6.5 percent in just six weeks. E.D. Grady, the general manager in charge of operator services, said, "It has been our experience, over the past 10 years, that when standards are set and feedback provided in a positive manner, performance will reach very high levels—perhaps in the upper 90th percentile in a very short period of time. . . . We have also found that when positive reinforcement is discontinued, performance returns to levels that existed prior to the establishment of feedback."

**1971, Emery Air Freight.** Employees in the customer service department believed they were accomplishing the departmental goal of responding to customer inquiries within 90 minutes at least 90 percent of the time. But without careful measurement and charting of the desired behavior (called "establishing a baseline" in reinforcement terminology), employees were basically guessing about how well they were doing. So when the customer service representatives were given tally sheets and asked to keep track of how long it actually took them to respond to each call, they were shocked to find out that they were actually responding within 90 minutes only 30 percent of the time. In addition to having employees generate feedback by keeping track of their response times, Emery also trained supervisors to provide praise and recognition for employees who met the goal, or whose performance had improved. Supervisors were also taught that if performance did not improve, they should simply remind employees of the goal in a nonpunitive manner. As a result, performance in one office improved from 30 percent of standard to 95 percent in a single day. And, after three years, the department still met the goal 90 to 95 percent of the time.

**1911, Frederick W. Taylor and Bethlehem Steel.** Frederick W. Taylor is known as the "Father of Scientific Management." In his book *The Principles of Scientific Management*, published in 1911, he wrote this about incentives:

The writer repeats, therefore, that in order to have any hope of obtaining the initiative of his workmen the manager must give some special incentive to his men beyond that which is given to the average of the trade. This incentive can be given in several different ways, as, for example, the hope of rapid promotion or advancement; higher wages, either in the form of generous piecework prices or of a premium or bonus of some kind for good and rapid work; shorter hours of labor; better surroundings and working conditions than are ordinarily given, etc., and, above all, this special incentive should be accompanied by that personal consideration for, and friendly contact with, his workmen, which comes only from a genuine and kindly interest in the welfare of those under him. It is only by giving a special

inducement or "incentive" of this kind that the employer can hope even approximately to get the "initiative" of his workmen.

Taylor then proved the effectiveness of incentives by using them to increase productivity among laborers at the Bethlehem Steel Company. The laborers had the job of picking up and loading 92 pound pieces of pig iron (unprocessed iron) into a railroad car. The job was made more difficult by having to carry the pig iron pieces up a steep plank to load them onto the rail car. The average laborer could load about 12.5 tons, or 272 pieces of pig iron per day. However, through studying the workers and the work process, Taylor determined that the average laborer should be able to load 47 tons, or 1,022 pieces of pig iron per day. Of course, the question was how to do it. Taylor also wrote, "And it was further our duty to see that this work was done without bringing on a strike among the men, without any quarrel with the men, and to see that the men were happier and better contented when loading at the new rate of 47 tons than they were when loading at the old rate of 12.5 tons."

Taylor decided that the best way to accomplish this task was through a combination of rest periods and incentive pay, both of which were unheard of at the time. And to prove his point that any man should be able to move 47 tons of pig iron per day, he selected the smallest worker in the group to test his ideas. Taylor increased this worker's pay by 61 percent, from $1.15 a day to $1.85 a day, contingent on loading 47 tons of pig iron. Taylor explained the results this way:

Schmidt [the laborer] started to work, and all day long, and at regular intervals, was told by the man [one of Taylor's associates] who stood over him with a watch, "Now pick up a pig and walk. Now sit down and rest. Now walk—now rest," etc. He worked when he was told to work, and rested when he was told to rest, and at half-past five in the afternoon had his 47.5 tons loaded on the car. And he practically never failed to work at this pace and do the task that was set him during the three years that the writer was at Bethlehem. And throughout this time he averaged a little more than $1.85 per day, whereas before he had never received over $1.15 per day, which was the ruling rate of wages at that time in Bethlehem. That is, he received 60 percent higher wages than were paid to other men who were not working on task work. One man after another was picked out and trained to handle pig iron at the rate of 47.5 tons per day until all of the pig iron was handled at this rate, and the men were receiving 60 per cent more wages than other workmen around them.

**Sources:** E.J. Feeney, "At Emery Air Freight: Positive Reinforcement Boosts Performance," *Organizational Dynamics* 1, no. 3 (1973): 41–50. W.C. Hamner & E.P. Hamner, "Behavior Modification on the Bottom Line," *Organizational Dynamics* 4, no. 4 (1976): 3–21. B.F. Skinner & W.F. Dowling, "Conversation with B.F. Skinner," *Organizational Dynamics* 1, no. 1 (1973): 31–40. F.W. Taylor, *The Principles of Scientific Management* (New York: Harper, 1911).

**punishment**
reinforcement that weakens behavior by following behaviors with undesirable consequences

**extinction**
reinforcement in which a positive consequence is no longer allowed to follow a previously reinforced behavior, thus weakening the behavior

are punished at work. For example, Frito-Lay began getting complaints from customers that they were finding potato chips with obscene messages written on them. Frito-Lay eventually traced the problem to a potato chip plant where supervisors had fired 58 out of the 210 workers for disciplinary reasons over a nine-month period. The remaining employees were so angry over what they saw as unfair treatment from management that they began writing obscene phrases on potato chips with felt-tipped pens.[65] Because of the strong backlash, Frito-Lay abandoned the discipline system in use at that plant and trained supervisors how to talk to employees about performance issues in a problem-focused, nonconfrontational manner.

**Extinction** is a reinforcement strategy in which a positive consequence is no longer allowed to follow a previously reinforced behavior. By removing the positive consequence, extinction weakens the behavior, making it less likely to occur. Based on the idea of positive reinforcement, most companies give company leaders and managers substantial financial rewards when the company performs well. However, based on the idea of extinction, you would expect that leaders and managers would not be rewarded (i.e., removing the positive consequence) when companies perform poorly. If companies really want pay to reinforce the right kinds of behaviors, then rewards have to be removed when company management doesn't produce successful performance. For instance, after the Walt Disney Company's income dropped from $1.9 billion to $920 million in just three years, you would expect, based on the idea of extinction, that the rewards given to company leaders would decline. However, they did not. During those three years of declining performance, Disney rewarded CEO Michael Eisner a large increase in salary, an additional 2 million stock options worth $37.7 million, and an $11.5 million bonus.[66]

### 4.2 Schedules for Delivering Reinforcement

A *schedule of reinforcement* is the set of rules regarding reinforcement contingencies, such as which behaviors will be reinforced, which consequences will follow those behaviors, and the schedule by which those consequences will be delivered. There are two categories of reinforcement schedules: continuous and intermittent.

With **continuous reinforcement schedules**, a consequence follows every instance of a behavior. For example, employees working on a piece-rate pay system earn money (consequence) for every part they manufacture (behavior). The more they produce, the more they earn. By contrast, with **intermittent reinforcement schedules**, consequences are delivered after a specified or average time has elapsed or after a specified or average number of behaviors has occurred. As shown in Exhibit 16.13, there are four types of intermittent reinforcement schedules. Two of these are based on time and are called *interval reinforcement schedules*, while the other two, known as *ratio schedules*, are based on behaviors.

**continuous reinforcement schedule**
schedule that requires a consequence to be administered following every instance of a behavior

**intermittent reinforcement schedule**
schedule in which consequences are delivered after a specified or average time has elapsed or after a specified or average number of behaviors has occurred

**630**

---

**EXHIBIT 16.13**

INTERMITTENT REINFORCEMENT SCHEDULES

| INTERMITTENT REINFORCEMENT SCHEDULES | FIXED | VARIABLE |
|---|---|---|
| INTERVAL (TIME) | Consequences follow behavior after a fixed time has elapsed. | Consequences follow behavior after different times, some shorter and some longer, that vary around a specified average time. |
| RATIO (BEHAVIOR) | Consequences follow a specific number of behaviors. | Consequences follow a different number of behaviors, sometimes more and sometimes less, that vary around a specified average number of behaviors. |

**fixed interval reinforcement schedule**
intermittent schedule in which consequences follow a behavior only after a fixed time has elapsed

**variable interval reinforcement schedule**
intermittent schedule in which the time between a behavior and the following consequences varies around a specified average

**fixed ratio reinforcement schedule**
intermittent schedule in which consequences are delivered following a specific number of behaviors

**variable ratio reinforcement schedule**
intermittent schedule in which consequences are delivered following a different number of behaviors, sometimes more and sometimes less, that vary around a specified average number of behaviors

With **fixed interval reinforcement schedules**, consequences follow a behavior only after a fixed time has elapsed. For example, most people receive their paychecks on a fixed interval schedule (e.g., once or twice per month). As long as they work (behavior) during a specified pay period (interval), they get a paycheck (consequence). With **variable interval reinforcement schedules**, consequences follow a behavior after different times, some shorter and some longer, that vary around a specified average time. On a 90-day variable interval reinforcement schedule, you might receive a bonus after 80 days or perhaps after 100 days, but the average interval between performing your job well (behavior) and receiving your bonus (consequence) would be 90 days.

With **fixed ratio reinforcement schedules**, consequences are delivered following a specific number of behaviors. For example, a car salesperson might receive a $1,000 bonus after every 10 sales. Therefore, a salesperson with only nine sales would not receive the bonus until he or she finally sold a 10th car. With **variable ratio reinforcement schedules**, consequences are delivered following a different number of behaviors, sometimes more and sometimes less, that vary around a specified average number of behaviors. With a 10-car variable ratio reinforcement schedule, a salesperson might receive the bonus after seven car sales, or after 12, 11, or nine sales, but the average number of cars sold before receiving the bonus would be 10 cars.

Students often have trouble envisioning how these schedules could actually be used in a work setting, so a couple of examples will help. In one study, tree planters working for a forestry and logging company were paid to plant bags of tree seedlings (about 1,000 seedlings per bag) to regrow trees that had been cut down. Workers were paid under several different conditions: (1) an hourly wage ($3 an hour), (2) continuous reinforcement in which they were paid $2 for every bag of seedlings they planted, (3) variable ratio reinforcement in which they were paid $4 for planting a bag of tree seedlings and then had to correctly guess what color marble their supervisor had in their hand (supervisors had two differently colored marbles, so workers were correct about half the time, which is equivalent to $2 a bag), and (4) another variable ratio reinforcement schedule in which they were paid $8 for planting a bag of tree seedlings and had to correctly guess the color of two marbles (on average, workers were correct about a quarter of the time, which is equivalent to $2 a bag).[67] In another study designed to increase employee attendance, employees who came to work participated in an innovative variable ratio schedule in which they drew a card from a deck of playing cards. At the end of each week, the employee with the best poker hand from those cards received a $20 bonus.[68]

Which reinforcement schedules work best? In the past, the standard advice was to use continuous reinforcement when employees were learning new behaviors, since reinforcement after each success leads to faster learning. Likewise, the standard advice was to use intermittent reinforcement schedules to maintain behavior after it is learned, since intermittent rewards are supposed to make behavior much less subject to extinction.[69] However, except for interval-based systems, which usually produce weak results, there is little difference between the effectiveness of continuous reinforcement, fixed ratio, or variable ratio schedules.[70] In organizational settings, all three produce consistently large increases over noncontingent reward schedules. So managers should choose whichever of these three is easiest to use in their companies.

### 4.3 Motivating with Reinforcement Theory

What practical things can managers do to use reinforcement theory to motivate employees? Professor Fred Luthans, who has been studying the effects of reinforcement theory in organizations for more than a quarter of a century, says that there are five steps to motivating workers with reinforcement theory. Listed in Exhibit 16.14, those key preliminary steps are to *identify, measure, analyze, intervene,* and *evaluate* critical performance-related behaviors.[71]

*Identify* means identifying critical, observable, performance-related behaviors. These are the behaviors that are most important to successful job performance. However, they

**EXHIBIT 16.14**

### MOTIVATING WITH REINFORCEMENT THEORY

- Identify, measure, analyze, intervene, and evaluate critical performance-related behaviors.
- Don't reinforce the wrong behaviors.
- Correctly administer punishment at the appropriate time.
- Choose the simplest and most effective schedules of reinforcement.

must also be easily observed, so they can be accurately measured. *Measure* means measuring the baseline frequencies of these behaviors. In other words, find out how often workers perform them. *Analyze* means analyzing the causes and consequences of these behaviors. Analyzing the causes helps managers create the conditions that produce these critical behaviors, while analyzing the consequences helps them determine if these behaviors produce the results that they want. *Intervene* means changing the organization by using positive and negative reinforcement to increase the frequency of these critical behaviors. *Evaluate* means evaluating the extent to which the intervention actually changed workers' behavior. This is done by comparing behavior after the intervention to the original baseline of behavior before the intervention. For more on the effectiveness of reinforcement theory, see the "What Really Works?" feature in this chapter.

*Don't reinforce the wrong behaviors.* While reinforcement theory sounds simple, it's actually very difficult to put into practice. One of the most common mistakes is accidentally reinforcing the wrong behaviors. In fact, sometimes managers reinforce behaviors that they don't want! For example, the salary and bonus system was not working correctly at Discovery Communications, which runs the Discovery Channel on cable and satellite TV. Within the same job classifications, top performers' salaries were the same as poor performers' salaries. Also, people doing identical jobs, but in different locations, were paid very differently. Because the company's reward system did not allow managers to give large raises to people who stayed in the same job from year to year, managers used promotions to get workers higher pay and keep them in the company. However, the system was so rigid that they frequently promoted good workers before they were ready or promoted them into jobs for which they weren't qualified. Likewise, employees campaigned to be transferred to locations that paid undeservedly higher salaries. Mark Kozak, senior vice president for administration and operations, said, "People felt that it was unfair."[72]

*Correctly administer punishment at the appropriate time.* Many managers believe that punishment can change workers' behavior and help them improve their job performance. Furthermore, managers believe that fairly punishing workers also lets other workers know what is or isn't acceptable.[73] However, one of the dangers of using punishment is that it can produce a backlash against managers and companies. If administered properly, punishment can weaken the frequency of undesirable behaviors without creating a backlash.[74] For punishment to work, the punishment must be strong enough to stop the undesired behavior and must be administered objectively (same rules applied to everyone), impersonally (without emotion or anger), consistently and contingently (each time improper behavior occurs), and quickly (as soon as possible following the undesirable behavior). In addition, managers should clearly explain what the appropriate behavior is and why the employee is being punished. When administered this way, employees typically respond well to punishment.[75]

*Choose the simplest and most effective schedule of reinforcement.* When choosing a schedule of reinforcement, managers need to balance effectiveness against simplicity. In fact, the more complex the schedule of reinforcement, the more likely it is to be misunderstood and

# WhatReallyWorks

## Financial, Nonfinancial, and Social Rewards

Throughout this chapter, we have been making the point that there is more to motivating people than money. But we haven't yet examined how well financial (money or prizes), nonfinancial (performance feedback), or social (recognition and attention) rewards motivate workers by themselves, or in combination. However, 19 studies based on more than 2,800 people clearly indicate that rewarding and reinforcing employees greatly improves motivation and performance.

### Overall Performance and Rewards

On average, there is a 63 percent chance that employees whose behavior is reinforced in some way will outperform employees whose behavior is not reinforced.

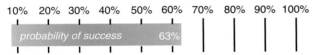

### Performance in Manufacturing Organizations

**Financial rewards.** On average, there is an 84 percent chance that employees in manufacturing organizations whose behavior is reinforced with financial rewards will outperform employees whose behavior is not reinforced.

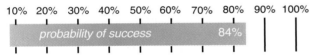

**Nonfinancial rewards.** On average, there is an 87 percent chance that employees in manufacturing organizations whose behavior is reinforced with nonfinancial rewards will outperform employees whose behavior is not reinforced.

**Financial, nonfinancial, and social rewards.** On average, there is a 96 percent chance that employees in manufacturing organizations whose behavior is reinforced with a combination of financial, nonfinancial, and social rewards will outperform employees whose behavior is not reinforced.

### Performance in Service Organizations

**Financial rewards.** On average, there is a 61 percent chance that employees in service organizations whose behavior is reinforced with financial rewards will outperform employees whose behavior is not reinforced.

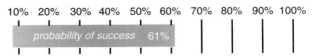

**Nonfinancial rewards.** On average, there is a 54 percent chance that employees in service organizations whose behavior is reinforced with nonfinancial rewards will outperform employees whose behavior is not reinforced.

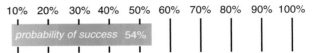

**Social rewards.** On average, there is a 61 percent chance that employees in service organizations whose behavior is reinforced with social rewards will outperform employees whose behavior is not reinforced.

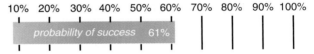

**Financial and nonfinancial rewards.** On average, there is a 72 percent chance that employees in service organizations whose behavior is reinforced with a combination of financial and nonfinancial rewards will outperform employees whose behavior is not reinforced.

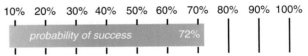

**Nonfinancial and social rewards.** On average, there is a 73 percent chance that employees in service organizations whose behavior is reinforced with a combination of nonfinancial and social rewards will outperform employees whose behavior is not reinforced.

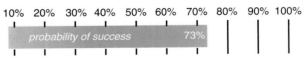

**Sources:** A.D. Stajkovic & F. Luthans, "A Meta-Analysis of the Effects of Organizational Behavior Modification on Task Performance, 1975-95," *Academy of Management Journal* 40, no. 5 (1997): 1122–1149.

resisted by managers and employees. For example, when the forestry and logging company discussed above first paid tree planters to plant bags of tree seedlings, it didn't have much luck with its initial variable ratio schedule. When planters finished planting a bag of seedlings, they got to flip a coin. If they called the coin flip correctly (heads or tails), they were paid $4, double the hourly rate. If they called the coin flip incorrectly, they got nothing. The company began having problems when several workers and a manager, who was a part-time minister, claimed that the coin flip was a form of gambling. Then, one of the workers found that the company was taking out too much money in taxes from their paychecks. Since workers didn't really understand the reinforcement schedule, they blamed the payment plan associated with it and accused the company of trying to cheat them out of their money. After all of these problems, the researchers who implemented the variable ratio schedule concluded that "the results of this study may not be so much an indication of the relative effectiveness of different schedules of reinforcement as they are an indication of the types of problems that one encounters when applying these concepts in an industrial setting."[76] In short, choose the simplest, most effective schedule of reinforcement. Since there is little difference between the effectiveness of continuous reinforcement, fixed ratio, or variable ratio schedules, continuous reinforcement schedules may be the best choice in many instances by virtue of their simplicity.

### Review 4
### Reinforcement Theory

Reinforcement theory says that behavior is a function of its consequences. Reinforcement has two parts: reinforcement contingencies and schedules of reinforcement. The four kinds of reinforcement contingencies are positive reinforcement and negative reinforcement, which strengthen behavior, and punishment and extinction, which weaken behavior. There are two kinds of reinforcement schedules, continuous and intermittent, the latter of which can be separated into fixed and variable interval schedules and fixed and variable ratio schedules. Managers can use reinforcement theory to motivate workers by following five steps (identify, measure, analyze, intervene, and evaluate critical performance-related behaviors); not reinforcing the wrong behaviors; correctly administering punishment at the appropriate time; and choosing a reinforcement schedule, such as continuous reinforcement, that balances simplicity and effectiveness.

## 5. Goal-Setting Theory

Scott Grocki, president of Grocki Magic Studios, believes in the power of setting goals. In his Boca Raton office, he and his performing partner, Jennifer Brown, have more goals than places to put them! Long-term goals ("BROADWAY" and "TELEVISION") are written on the office wall as a constant reminder that they want to appear on television and develop a Broadway show about magic. "ART" is also written on the wall to remind them to strive for "artistic integrity." They keep monthly and six-month goals on file and review them every two weeks. Weekly goals are kept near the office telephone. Every Monday, they set new goals, and Jennifer makes sure that they "match the writing on the wall." In other words, she ensures that each new goal contributes to their long-term goals. Grocki describes the importance of goals in this manner: "When you set a goal, you create something and it becomes real. You write it down. You focus on it, you aspire to it, and that's your motivation."[77]

The basic model of motivation with which we began this chapter showed that individuals feel tension after becoming aware of an unfulfilled need. Once they experience tension, they search for and select courses of action that they believe will eliminate this tension. In other words, they direct their behavior toward something. This something is a goal. A **goal** is a target, objective, or result that someone tries to accomplish. **Goal-setting theory** says that people will be motivated to the extent to which they accept specific, challenging goals and receive feedback that indicates their progress toward goal achievement.

**goal**
a target, objective, or result that someone tries to accomplish

**goal-setting theory**
theory that states that people will be motivated to the extent to which they accept specific, challenging goals and receive feedback that indicates their progress toward goal achievement

*Let's learn more about goal setting by examining the **5.1** components of goal-setting theory and **5.2** how to motivate with goal-setting theory.*

## 5.1 Components of Goal-Setting Theory

**goal specificity**
the extent to which goals are detailed, exact, and unambiguous

The basic components of goal-setting theory are goal specificity, goal difficulty, goal acceptance, and performance feedback.[78] **Goal specificity** is the extent to which goals are detailed, exact, and unambiguous. Specific goals, such as "I'm going to have a 3.0 average this semester," are more motivating than general goals, such as "I'm going to get better grades this semester."

**goal difficulty**
the extent to which a goal is hard or challenging to accomplish

**Goal difficulty** is the extent to which a goal is hard or challenging to accomplish. Difficult goals, such as "I'm going to have a 3.5 average and make the Dean's List this semester," are more motivating than easy goals, such as "I'm going to have a 2.0 average this semester."

**goal acceptance**
the extent to which people consciously understand and agree to goals

**Goal acceptance**, which is similar to the idea of goal commitment discussed in Chapter 4, is the extent to which people consciously understand and agree to goals. Accepted goals, such as "I really want to get a 3.5 average this semester to show my parents how much I've improved," are more motivating than unaccepted goals, such as "My parents really want me to get a 3.5 this semester, but there's so much more I'd rather do on campus than study!"

**performance feedback**
information about the quality or quantity of past performance that indicates whether progress is being made toward the accomplishment of a goal

**Performance feedback** is information about the quality or quantity of past performance and indicates whether progress is being made toward the accomplishment of a goal. Performance feedback, such as "My prof said I need a 92 on the final to get an "A" in the class," is more motivating than no feedback, "I have no idea what my grade is in that class." In short, goal-setting theory says that people will be motivated to the extent to which they accept specific, challenging goals and receive feedback that indicates their progress toward goal achievement.

How does goal setting work? To start, challenging goals focus employees' attention (i.e., direct effort) on the critical aspects of their jobs and away from unimportant areas. Goals also energize behavior. When faced with unaccomplished goals, employees typically develop plans and strategies to reach those goals. Goals also create a tension between the goal, which is the desired future state of affairs, and where the employee or company is now, meaning the current state of affairs. This tension can only be satisfied by achieving or abandoning the goal. Finally, goals influence persistence. Since goals only "go away" when they are accomplished, employees are more likely to persist in their efforts in the presence of goals. Exhibit 16.15 incorporates goals into the motivation model by showing how goals directly affect tension, effort, and the extent to which employees are energized to take action.

## 5.2 Motivating with Goal-Setting Theory

What practical things can managers do to use goal-setting theory to motivate employees?

As listed in Exhibit 16.16, *assign specific, challenging goals.* One of the simplest, most effective ways to motivate workers is to give them specific, challenging goals. However, an amazing number of managers never do this with their employees. One manager who does is Jim Schaefer. When Schaefer's top management asked him to increase profits at his oil refinery plant by $7 million, he turned around and promised them profits of $60 million. Then, with this difficult goal on the line, he met with senior managers and union leaders every 90 days to set specific goals for overall improvement in the plant. He also met with first-level supervisors every 30 days to get them to develop specific goals for improving in their departments. The result? While most oil refineries scratch and claw to find ways to produce 1 percent more oil, thanks to specific, challenging goals, Schaefer's oil refinery increased its production by 20 percent.[79] For more information on assigning specific, challenging goals, see the discussion in Chapter 4 on S.M.A.R.T. goals.

*Make sure workers truly accept organizational goals.* Specific, challenging goals won't motivate workers unless they really accept, understand, and agree to the

635

EXHIBIT 16.15

ADDING GOAL-SETTING THEORY TO THE MODEL

EXHIBIT 16.16

MOTIVATING WITH GOAL-SETTING THEORY

- Assign specific, challenging goals.
- Make sure workers truly accept organizational goals.
- Provide frequent, specific, performance-related feedback.

organization's goals. For this to occur, people must see the goals as fair and reasonable. Plus, they must trust management and believe that managers are using goals to clarify what is expected from them rather than to exploit or threaten them ("If you don't achieve these goals. . ."). However, participative goal setting, in which managers and employees generate goals together, can help increase trust and understanding and thus acceptance of goals. Furthermore, providing workers with training can help increase goal acceptance, particularly when workers don't believe they are capable of reaching the organization's goals.[80]

*Provide frequent, specific, performance-related feedback.* In addition to accepting specific, challenging goals, goal-setting theory also specifies that employees should receive

Setting performance goals and giving regular feedback relative to the progress being made toward those goals lead to stronger motivation. The complexity and the isolation of the offshore oil drilling rig makes safety a critical goal, so managers set high goals and gave weekly feedback on safety-related measurements. The result was decreased accident rates and increased safe behavior by all employees.

frequent performance-related feedback so they can track progress toward goal completion. Feedback leads to stronger motivation and effort in three ways.[81] First, receiving specific feedback that indicates how well you're performing can encourage employees who don't have specific, challenging goals to actually set goals to improve their performance. Second, once people meet goals, performance feedback often encourages them to set higher, more difficult goals. Third, feedback lets people know whether they need to increase their efforts or change strategies in order to accomplish their goals.

For example, in an effort to improve worker safety on offshore oil-drilling platforms, an oil company generated a list of dangerous work behaviors by analyzing previous accident reports, reviewing industry safety manuals, and interviewing and observing workers. Employees then attended training in which they viewed videotapes of workers performing the same task safely and unsafely. Following training, each work crew set goals to engage in safe behaviors 100 percent of the time on each work shift. To help workers track their improvement, management posted weekly safety performance in the galley of each rig, where it was sure to be seen when workers ate meals and gathered for coffee breaks. Prior to training, setting goals, and weekly performance feedback, employees were engaging in safe work behaviors just 76 percent of the time. However, after a year of goal setting (100 percent safe behavior on each shift) and weekly performance feedback at two oil rigs, workers behaved safely over 90 percent of the time. As a result, accident rates dropped from 21.1 percent to 6.1 percent at the first rig and from 14.2 percent to 12.1 percent at the second rig. By contrast, at a third oil rig, where training, goal setting, and feedback were not used, the total accident rate *increased* from 11.6 percent to 20.3 percent over the same time.[82] So, to motivate employees with goal-setting theory, make sure they receive frequent performance-related feedback so they can track progress toward goal completion.

### Review 5
### Goal-Setting Theory

A goal is a target, objective, or result that someone tries to accomplish. Goal-setting theory says that people will be motivated to the extent to which they accept specific, challenging goals and receive feedback that indicates their progress toward goal achievement. The basic components of goal-setting theory are goal specificity, goal difficulty, goal acceptance, and performance feedback. Goal specificity is the extent to which goals are detailed, exact, and unambiguous. Goal difficulty is the extent to which a goal is hard or challenging to accomplish. Goal acceptance is the extent to which people consciously understand and agree to goals. Performance feedback is information about the quality or quantity of past performance and indicates whether progress is being made toward the accomplishment of a goal. Managers can use goal-setting theory to motivate workers by assigning specific, challenging goals, making sure workers truly accept organizational goals, and providing frequent, specific, performance-related feedback.

## 6. Motivating with the Integrated Model

We began this chapter by defining motivation as the set of forces that initiates, directs, and makes people persist in their efforts to accomplish a goal. We also asked the basic question that managers ask when they try to figure out how to motivate their workers: "What leads to effort?" While the answer to that question is likely to be somewhat different for each employee, Exhibit 16.17 helps you begin to answer it by consolidating the practical advice from the theories reviewed in this chapter into one convenient location. So, if you're having difficulty figuring out why people aren't motivated where you work, Exhibit 16.17 provides a useful, theory-based starting point.

---

**EXHIBIT 16.17**

MOTIVATING WITH THE INTEGRATED MODEL

### MOTIVATING WITH THE BASICS
- Ask people what their needs are.
- Satisfy lower-order needs first.
- Expect people's needs to change.
- As needs change and lower-order needs are satisfied, satisfy higher-order needs by looking for ways to allow employees to experience intrinsic rewards.

### MOTIVATING WITH EQUITY THEORY
- Look for and correct major inequities.
- Reduce employees' inputs.
- Make sure decision-making processes are fair.

### MOTIVATING WITH EXPECTANCY THEORY
- Systematically gather information to find out what employees want from their jobs.
- Take specific steps to link rewards to individual performance in a way that is clear and understandable to employees.
- Empower employees to make decisions if you really want them to believe that their hard work and efforts will lead to good performance.

### MOTIVATING WITH REINFORCEMENT THEORY
- Identify, measure, analyze, intervene, and evaluate critical performance-related behaviors.
- Don't reinforce the wrong behaviors.
- Correctly administer punishment at the appropriate time.
- Choose the simplest and most effective schedules of reinforcement.

### MOTIVATING WITH GOAL-SETTING THEORY
- Assign specific, challenging goals.
- Make sure workers truly accept organizational goals.
- Provide frequent, specific, performance-related feedback.

---

## What Really Happened?

At the beginning of this chapter, you read about the unique challenges that Medtronic faces in continuing to motivate its managers and workers after a decade of growth in profits and market share. Long-term success has a way of softening a company's competitive edge. Managers become complacent. Employees become satisfied and resistant to change. IBM, Sears, General Motors, and Xerox were once long-time market leaders. They lost their dominance when they lost the hearts and minds of their workers. Read the answers to the opening case to read what really happened and learn about Medtronic's plans for continuing to motivate its managers and workers.

**Most winning sports teams start an immediate decline after winning the championship. It's rare for champions to repeat or "three-peat," so how can Medtronic continue to motivate managers and workers after a decade of incredible success?**

*Motivation* is the set of forces that initiates, directs, and makes people persist in their efforts over time to accomplish a goal. However, managers want to know, "What leads to effort?" One basic premise of motivation is that people are motivated to fulfill unmet physical or psychological needs. When needs are not met, people experience an internal state of tension. But once a particular need is met, it no longer motivates. When this occurs, people become satisfied and are then motivated by other unmet needs. Since people are motivated by unmet needs, managers must learn what those unmet needs are and address them.

When companies are growing, things are exciting, there are different things to do and challenges to meet, and it's easy to find ways to motivate people. The difficulty for Medtronic is to continue to do that after a decade of incredible success. Fortunately, studies generally show that there are only two general kinds of needs, lower-order needs and higher-order needs, and that higher-order needs will not motivate people as long as lower-order needs remain unsatisfied. Consequently, the first step in Medtronic's plan is to aggressively meet its 21,000 workers' lower-order needs (safety, physiological, and existence). Therefore, it starts by offering workers excellent medical, dental, and life insurance, as well as long-term disability coverage. With these benefits, Medtronic's employees and their families don't have to worry about paying medical bills or losing income because of illness or disability.

However, because of the variety of lower-order needs that must be met in today's work force, Medtronic doesn't stop there. It also provides flexible work schedules to allow families to juggle busy schedules, personal well-being programs to help employees manage and improve their health, an employee assistance program to help with psychological problems or drug or alcohol dependency, elder care assistance for families that care for older loved ones, educational scholarships for employees' children, adoption assistance benefits for employees unable to have their own children, and domestic partner benefits for gay and lesbian employees. Furthermore, some Medtronic offices have on-site fitness centers, massage therapy, meditation rooms, rooms for nursing mothers, and sick child care facilities so that parents don't have to stay home with sick children. Janet Fiola, senior vice president for human resources, said, "We look at it in a holistic way. We try to take all the benefits and address those needs of the employee in an integrated way."

**Often times, successful companies turn into farm clubs for other companies, hiring, grooming, and developing talented people, only to have them hired away by other companies just as they reach their potential. How can Medtronic prevent that from happening?**

One of the best ways for Medtronic to attract, develop, and keep talented people is to provide a competitive set of extrinsic rewards. Extrinsic rewards, such as pay and company stock, are tangible, visible, and are given to employees contingent on the performance of specific tasks or behaviors. Companies use extrinsic rewards to motivate people to join the organization, regularly attend their jobs, perform their jobs well, and stay with the organization. Indeed, Medtronic's extrinsic rewards are so good that few people leave. Sherice Nelson, coordinator of the tachy-arrhythmia group, said, "There's not a lot of turnover here. In fact, it's usually more about people wanting to get in. My husband's been trying to get in for years."

Medtronic provides the following extrinsic rewards. Employees can contribute up to 15 percent of their eligible pre-tax income to a 401 (k) plan and Medtronic will match $0.50 to $1.50 for every dollar employees contribute up to the first 6 percent of pay. The match is made in Medtronic stock and is based on company performance. Medtronic's pension plan provides a monthly income at retirement based on final average pay, age, and years of service. Employees do not have to contribute any income to this plan. All regular employees are automatically enrolled in the plan after one year of service. In addition to the 401 (k) and retirement plans, Medtronic also offers an Employee Stock Ownership Plan (ESOP). Depending on how the company performs, employees annually receive Medtronic stock worth 2.5 to 4 percent of their salaries. Again, employees do not have to contribute any income to pay for this plan. Employees are eligible to participate from their first day of employment. The company also offers an Employee Stock Purchase Plan (ESPP) in which employees can contribute up to 10 percent of their eligible after-tax income to purchase Medtronic stock at a discounted price.

Medtronic also has a number of professional recognition programs in which awards and recognition are provided for technical contributions, patents, and outstanding performance and leadership. The company also provides cash awards for outstanding individual and team performance.

**Finally, in the long run, what will make people happiest and most productive at work? Is it money, benefits, opportunities for growth, interesting work, or something else altogether different? And with people desiring different things, how can Medtronic keep everyone motivated to continue to "win championships"?**

While competitive extrinsic rewards such as pay, benefits, and bonus and stock plans are keys to attracting and retaining a talented, motivated work force, studies show that once people have joined a company, they are much more motivated by intrinsic rewards, the natural rewards associated with performing a task or activity for its own sake. Examples of intrinsic rewards include a sense of accomplishment or achievement, a feeling of responsibility, the chance to learn something new or interact with others, or simply the fun that comes from performing an interesting, challenging, and engaging task. Indeed, three decades of research show that employees are twice as likely to in-

dicate that "important and meaningful work" matters more to them than what they are paid.

Because Medtronic designs and makes life-altering products, it has a built-in opportunity to provide intrinsic rewards for its workers. Every December at the company's holiday party, it flies in six patients to demonstrate that the company is accomplishing its mission to "alleviate pain, restore health, and extend life." Each patient gives testimonials describing the incredible difference that Medtronic's products have made to them and their loved ones. Production supervisor Karen McFadzen said, "We have patients who come in who would be dead if it wasn't for us. I mean, they sit right up there and they tell us what their lives are like. You don't walk away from them not feeling anything." *Fortune* magazine described the annual event this way, "It's a teary, communal reminder that what goes on here day after day is not the same as making VCRs."

While Medtronic's mission is noble, make no mistake: It requires tremendous effort from company management to make sure that work is meaningful on a daily basis. For instance, researcher Mark Rise, one of Medtronic's most creative inventors, could have a more prestigious job at a university or make more money start-

ing his own company. However, Rise doesn't want to test theory or develop marketing plans or raise venture capital. What matters most to him is developing products that make a difference in people's lives. Said Rise, "That's what keeps me tied to what I'm doing now." Indeed, Rise thrives on being able to work with physicians, medical researchers, software developers, and engineers to identify new treatments and to design and manufacture new products.

How successful has Medtronic been at providing intrinsic rewards for managers and employees? Good enough for *Fortune* magazine to rank Medtronic 86th among its "100 best companies to work for." Good enough for 86 percent of its employees to say their work has special meaning, and for 94 percent to take pride in what they accomplish at work.

**Sources:** D. Emerson, "Holiday Bonuses Drop off Wish List," *Minneapolis-St. Paul City Business*, 15 December 2000, 16. R. Langreth, "Medtronic: Pacing the Field," *Forbes*, 8 January 2001, 142. P. Marsh & C. Bowe, "Medtronic Needs Health Check from New Executive: Despite Past Success, The Health Device Maker Faces Big Changes," *The Financial Times*, 1 May 2001, 28. J. Niemela, "Med-Tech Mission Overrides Benefits," *Minneapolis-St. Paul City Business*, 4 August 2000, 42. D. Whitford, "A Human Place to Work," *Fortune*, 8 January 2001, 108.

## Key Terms

continuous reinforcement schedule *(630)*
distributive justice *(622)*
equity theory *(616)*
expectancy *(623)*
expectancy theory *(623)*
extinction *(630)*
extrinsic reward *(611)*
fixed interval reinforcement schedule *(631)*
fixed ratio reinforcement schedule *(631)*
goal *(634)*
goal acceptance *(635)*
goal difficulty *(635)*
goal-setting theory *(634)*

goal specificity *(635)*
inputs *(618)*
instrumentality *(623)*
intermittent reinforcement schedule *(630)*
intrinsic reward *(612)*
motivation *(606)*
needs *(609)*
negative reinforcement *(627)*
outcome/input (O/I) ratio *(618)*
outcomes *(618)*
overreward *(619)*
performance feedback *(635)*
positive reinforcement *(627)*

procedural justice *(622)*
punishment *(630)*
referent *(618)*
reinforcement *(627)*
reinforcement contingencies *(627)*
reinforcement theory *(627)*
schedule of reinforcement *(627)*
underreward *(619)*
valence *(623)*
variable interval reinforcement schedule *(631)*
variable ratio reinforcement schedule *(631)*

## What Would You Do-II

### Motivation in the Call Center

As companies begin selling direct to customers, customer service is becoming increasingly critical. You should know—you are the manager of the customer service contact center for Borders Group, the parent company of Borders Books and Music. You directly supervise approximately 100 customer-service agents in two different states, and your employees are, in many cases, the only contact between Borders and the customer. If a customer experiences an unfriendly customer-service encounter, there is a high probability that the customer will break all ties with the company. Therefore, customer-service agents become Borders' primary spokespeople and set the tone for future relationships between the company and the customer.

Contact centers have become a booming industry in recent years, currently valued at over $45 billion in the United States and growing. They have also gained a reputation for having a high turnover rate and low employee morale. Having been a customer-service agent for six years, you are one of the first to realize that customer-service agents have a tough job. Every day they answer hundreds of phone calls, facing a wide variety of situations, and never knowing who is on the other end of the line or what the question, comment, concern, or complaint may be. Many times, customer-service agents have to diffuse heated situations and turn disgruntled and often hostile customers into satisfied and happy ones. Additionally, most call-center agents work in a cubicle-farm, surrounded by other agents who rarely have the opportunity to leave their stations, except at usual break times.

These challenges, coupled with the fact that most call-center agents receive a starting wage that is slightly above minimum-wage, ensures that you have a steady stream of customer-service agent positions to fill at any given time. Nationwide, the average starting salary is $7.77 and the average turnover rate is 60 percent per year. In addition to low morale and high turnover, the industry also faces a growing absenteeism problem, especially around holidays. Ironically, the weeks before, during, and after holidays—especially Thanksgiving and Christmas—tend to pose the greatest demand for a contact center's staff.

As December approaches, you are concerned about employee burnout. When an extremely dissatisfied (and maybe somewhat abusive) customer is on the line, are your employees paid enough to care? The job isn't easy, the quarters are a bit cramped, and no one would describe the work as glitzy. What could possibly motivate employees to listen to angry customer complaints—often rudely and condescendingly expressed—all day long, five days a week, year after year?

**If you were the manager of the customer-service contact center at Borders, what would you do to reduce turnover and motivate employees at the holidays and throughout the year?**

**Sources:** J. Bowles, "Motivating the Front Line," *Customer Interface*, March 2001. R. Sanbandam, "Phone Reps. Can Make, Break Overall C.S.," *Marketing News*, 7 May 2001. T. Heath, "Study Reveals British Columbia's Low Call-Center Labor Costs," *Site Selection*, January 2001. Bureau of Labor Statistics Web site, http://www.bls.gov. S. Jarvis, "Call Centers Raise Bar on Hiring Criteria," *Marketing News*, 11 September 2000.

## Management Decisions

### What's Wrong with Joe?

You've been the manager of a video rental store for the last three years. Joe, one of your best employees, was the first new employee that you hired. You and Joe have always had a good working relationship, and you have always respected Joe for his dedication, work ethic, and ability to do his job with very little direction or supervision. In fact, Joe has helped train a majority of the new employees that have been hired since you both joined the store. They all seem to respect Joe and turn to him for guidance when they need help. All, that is, with the exception of one.

Bill, the newest employee, doesn't seem to get along with anyone. He habitually comes in late, leaves early, and doesn't do his fair share of the work. You have had several conversations with Bill, but his attitude and work ethic have not changed. Ordinarily, you would fire Bill and hire another employee. Unfortunately, it isn't that easy because Bill is the owner's grandson. Last week, you approached the owner about his grandson's

performance and how it was impacting the other employees. The owner apologized for his grandson's lack of responsibility, but admitted that there was nothing else for him to do. The owner stated that if his grandson lost his job, then he would have to support him altogether. Further, the owner commented, as long as Bill has a job, he can use some of the money he earns to support himself.

You explained to your boss that Bill's lack of responsibility and output was impacting the employees as a group. Joe, your best employee, has called in sick three times in the last month. To the best of your memory, Joe has never missed a day of work due to illness. Likewise, the other employees are beginning to complain about having to do their jobs when Bill doesn't do his. Morale really took a turn for the worse yesterday when Bill bragged to the group that he made more money per hour than all of the other employees. "In fact," he replied, "I make almost as much as the manager." You are afraid that Bill's attitude is going to infect the morale and affect the performance of the store in general.

3. Write a specific and detailed plan to motivate the employees of the video store. Include at least one element from each motivational theory discussed in the chapter.

## Management Decisions

### Employee of the Month!

As you get back to your desk with your third cup of coffee this morning, your boss stops by your office in the middle of his morning rounds. He says, "Hey, you've got a degree in management, don't you? Heck, even if you don't, you're probably more up-to-date on all these new motivational theories and ideas than I am. Here's what I want. We need an employee-of-the-month award for our clerical employees. I want to boost their morale and motivate them to work harder and do their jobs better! Take a couple of weeks and design a basic employee award program, but make sure that it's got an employee-of-the-month award in it. That's the key. Have it on my desk two weeks from Friday." Before you can say yes, he's off to another coworker's desk to give them some assignment that he brainstormed last night. You're not even sure he heard you say, "Sure, Mr. Smith, no problem."

However, what you really wanted to say was, "I don't know, Mr. Smith. I've never seen an employee of the month award

motivate anyone." In fact, no one really seemed to care about being employee of the month in the places you had worked before, even when there was a small amount of cash involved. You think to yourself, "Well, if he wants an employee-of-the-month award, I'll make sure that's in there. But there have got to be better ways to motivate the clerical staff. I'm just going to have to figure out what those are."

**Questions**
1. What is wrong with many employee-of-the-month award programs? Why wouldn't they be particularly effective at motivating employees?
2. Describe the three most important steps you'd take to motivate the clerical staff in your office. Explain what the steps are, the reasoning behind them, and what they're meant to accomplish. Be specific.

## Develop Your Managerial Potential

### Cut Your Costs, Not Your Morale

Management textbooks abound with discussions of the importance of honest and open communication when disseminating negative information to employees. One study suggests that the best way to ruin morale and motivation is to spring bad news on employees without explaining the reasoning or rationale. Yet, despite the need to maintain a high level of motivation and morale during a receding economy, many companies cut perks without communicating the need to their employees. During the technological boom at the end of the twentieth century, many companies implemented programs to increase productivity, motivation, and job satisfaction. Some of the perks provided were minor, including free soft drinks, catered lunches, snacks, and tickets to events such as a baseball games or the opera. Other free perks were more extravagant, including concierge services to help employees run their errands, service their vehicles, and pick up their laundry. Some firms went as far as providing their employees with in-house massages and annual Caribbean cruises. Obviously, cutting these nonvalue-added expenses can save tremendous money for a struggling firm. In fact, many firms not only cut out the extravagant but the basic as a way to conserve much-needed cash. Cutting perks, however, doesn't have to be forever.

Perks can be powerful motivational tools that companies can reintegrate into their performance reward systems.

For this assignment, consider your own budget and expenses in terms of revenue and perks. Imagine that like so many companies, you experience a cash crunch. Your revenue (income) shrinks 25 percent, so you must trim some fat from your budget.

**Exercises**
1. First, you will need to review your expenditures. What "perks" have you built into your budget as a student? (Think pizza and beer.) Make a list of all your nonvalue-added expenses. This includes anything not directly related to your studies (like books, tuition, enrollment fees, pens, paper, etc.) or your fixed expenses (like rent, car payments, insurance, etc.).
2. If you experienced a 25 percent reduction in your income—like numerous firms did after the tech bubble burst—which perks would you eliminate? In addition, are there things that you previously considered necessities that you can cut out? An example would be selling your car (thereby eliminating a car payment and related insurance) and taking public transportation or catching a ride with a friend. What about getting a roommate, moving into the dorms, or living with your parents?

3. Often employees develop a sense of entitlement around perks, and when perks are trimmed, great dissatisfaction can result. Companies even lose employees when perks are cut. In this exercise, let's consider that cutting out your nonvalue-added (i.e., fun) expenditures may put a crimp on your social life. In fact, you may have trouble staying in the loop. What can you do to "retain" your social friends as you cut down your personal perks? Do you think that "retention" will even be an issue for you? Why or why not?

4. Once you have taken the axe to your perks, how can you reincorporate them into your budget, this time as motivational tools? Which perks would motivate you to have perfect attendance in class? To make an "A"? Straight "A"s? Be creative. The purpose is to see if you can modify your own behavior by using your perks.

**Sources:** M. Boyle, "How to Cut Perks without Killing Morale," *Fortune*, 19 February 2001. T. Pollock, "Managing for Better Morale," *Automotive Manufacturing & Production*, February 2001.

## Study Tip

Don't forget to review with your Study Guide. Even more review opportunities are on your *Management* CD-ROM. You can also re-use some of the earlier study tips for Chapter 16 material. For this chapter, you have an Xtra! CNN clip, with a case and solutions on your CD. Check out what companies are doing when they can't offer stock option packages to job candidates. Watch the clip, read the case, then work the questions.

# CHAPTER 17

# seventeen

# Leadership

## What Would You Do?

**Sandler O'Neill & Partners, L.P., New York City.** With clear skies, bright sunshine, and temperatures predicted to reach the mid-70s by afternoon, it's a beautiful Tuesday in September. In New York City, millions of people are streaming into Manhattan by car, subway, trams, or ferries, including your 170 coworkers who are heading to the Sandler O'Neill offices on the 104th floor of Tower Two of the World Trade Center. Sandler O'Neill is a successful, full-service investment-banking firm that helps small and mid-sized companies and banks with strategic planning, interest rate management, mergers and acquisitions, and nearly any other kind of bonds, stocks, or financial transactions. With 1,000 clients and $100 million in annual revenues, Sandler O'Neill has become one of the most successful small firms on Wall Street in its 13 years of existence, and you are one of its three leading partners.

Unlike your coworkers, you're enjoying a rare day off, playing golf at the Bedford Gold and Tennis Club in Westchester, New York, in an attempt to qualify for the U.S. Mid-Amateur Golf Championship tournament. You are on the sixth hole when the call comes, informing you that two planes have flown into Towers One and Two of the World Trade Center. You make it back to the clubhouse just in time to see both buildings collapse on TV. Just in case they forgot where you are, your first call is to your family to let them know that you're okay. You ask yourself who is in the office? Did Chris Quackenbush, head of investment banking and your friend of 25 years, make it out? What about the company founder and your mentor, Herman Sandler? Does anyone know what has happened to him? After spending several hours on the phone trying to find out what happened and trying to begin accounting for the whereabouts of Sandler O'Neill's 170 employees, you grab a train and get back to New York as quickly as you can.

At the Sandler O'Neill offices, on the 104th floor of Tower Two of the World Trade Center, only a few people headed straight to the stairs and the elevators when the first plane crashed into Tower One at 8:46 A.M. Karen Fishman, who helps Sandler O'Neill put together bond offerings for companies, stepped out of her office to hear Chris Quackenbush or Herman Sandler say, "A plane hit the other building." Just then, two other company executives rushed past in the hallway, saying, "We're getting the hell out of here." Fishman went with them. She said, "I don't know why I left. I don't know that it was a conscious decision. It was instinct. So much depended on who you saw right at that moment." Most people, though, didn't panic and stayed at their desks calling family and friends to reassure them they were okay. Why didn't they leave? Because when terrorists exploded a bomb in the basement parking garage of the World Trade Centers in 1993, people who headed down the stairs were swallowed up in smoke, while people who fled to the roof to be rescued froze outside for hours. The people who stayed at their desks were barely affected. Unlike Fishman, who made her way down the stairs, 83 people from Sandler O'Neill stayed on the 104th floor because of that previous experience. Indeed, after the first plane crashed into Tower One, company founder Herman Sandler said, "I think the safest place to be is right here." Still, he announced that, "Whoever wants to leave can leave."

By the time your train reaches Grand Central Station, it is 5 P.M., nearly eight hours after Tower Two collapsed. You literally run toward 48th street, still in your golf clothes, to a small Sandler O'Neill office where employees have gathered during the day. But as you near 46th street, you stop running and think, "I can't run in there all crazed. I need to arrive with a sense of calmness. I know people are going to look to me." Other thoughts stream through your mind. "How many people didn't get out? We're getting panicked calls from family members who haven't yet talked to their loved ones. What do we do if they didn't get out of the building? How will we take care of their families? And with our offices gone, how do we keep the business running? We surely can't take care of families if we don't get back in business." No one has heard from Chris Quackenbush and Herman Sandler, your best friend and your mentor. If they didn't get out, that means you're in charge. Do you have what it takes to be in charge? You've always played the tough guy. But that's not what's needed now. Can you change to provide the right kind of leadership? You just don't know.

**If you were the surviving partner of Sandler O'Neill on September 11, 2001, what would you do?**

**Sources:** K. Brooker, "Starting Over," *Fortune*, 21 January 2002, 50. A. Geller, "Firms Decimated in Attacks Work to Rebuild Their Ranks with Alumni; Widespread Layoffs Help by Providing a Supply of High-Quality Applicants," *St. Louis Post Dispatch (Associated Press)*, 24 October 2001, C1. "Company Information: Our Approach," *Sandler O'Neill & Partners, L.P.,* [Online] Available http://www.sandleroneill.com/sandler/asp/control.asp?RequestingFrame=MAIN&RequestedAction=Approach, 25 March 2002. "Family Support," *Sandler O'Neill & Partners, L.P.* [Online] Available http://sandleroneillfamily.com/, 25 March 2002. "Sandler O'Neill Announces Company Open for Business," *Sandler O'Neill & Partners, L.P.* [Online] Available http://sandleroneillfamily.com/press_releases/press091701.htm, 25 March 2002. R. Smith, "Six Months After: At Sandler, A Client Sees Enormous Strain, Tries to Lend a Hand," *The Wall Street Journal*, 8 March 2002, C11.

Providing for deceased employees' families, struggling to ensure the company's survival with only half of a work force, and replacing the company's top managers were but some of the major leadership challenges facing Jimmy Dunne at Sandler O'Neill. However, Dunne was not alone. Dozens of other companies that had offices in the World Trade Center faced the same problems. And while they normally don't occur in such dire circumstances, leadership-related issues create severe problems for all kinds of companies each year.

We begin this chapter by discussing what leadership is, who leaders are, meaning their traits and characteristics, and what leaders do that makes them different from people who aren't leaders. Next we examine four major contingency theories of leadership that specify which leaders are best suited for which situations or how leaders should change their behavior to lead different people in different circumstances. The chapter ends with a review of strategic leadership issues, such as charismatic and transformational leadership, which are concerned with working with others to meet long-term goals and with creating a viable future for an organization.

## What Is Leadership?

When Cynthia Danaher became general manager of Hewlett-Packard's Medical Products Group, she told her 5,300 employees, "I want to do this job, but it's scary and I need your help." She also told them that they finally have a boss who "knows how to make coffee." After three years of experience as a leader, she now regrets her choice of words. If she had a chance to hold that meeting again, she says that she would emphasize goals and challenge her people to find ways to meet them. She said, "People say they want a leader to be vulnerable just like them, but deep down they want to believe you have the skill to move and fix things they can't. And while anyone who starts something new is bound to feel some anxiety, you don't need to bare your soul." Moreover, she says that for leaders, setting a direction is more important than making employees feel comfortable.[1]

**leadership**
the process of influencing others to achieve group or organizational goals

As H-P's Cynthia Danaher discovered, **leadership** is the process of influencing others to achieve group or organizational goals.

*After reading the next two sections, you should be able to*
1. *explain what leadership is.*
2. *describe who leaders are and what effective leaders do.*

## 1. Leadership

Southwest Airlines flies two-to-three times as many passengers per employee as other airlines at a cost 25 to 40 percent below its competitors.[2] A key part of Southwest's performance is that it empties its planes, refills them with passengers, crews, fuel, and food (peanuts and soft drinks), and has them back on the runway in 20 minutes, compared to an hour for most airlines. This allows Southwest to keep each of its planes filled with paying passengers about three more hours a day. Why is Southwest able to achieve such incredible results? Herb Kelleher, Southwest's Chairman and cofounder, answered the question this way, "We pay just as good wages and benefits as other airlines, but our costs are lower because our productivity is higher, which is achieved through the dedicated energy of our people. It's sheer willpower—no mechanical tricks. We've got exactly the same equipment. The difference is, when a plane pulls into a gate, our people run to meet it. Ponce de Leon was looking for the Fountain of Youth in the wrong place—he should have come to Southwest Airlines." In other words, the people of Southwest Airlines have been successfully influenced to achieve company goals (i.e., leadership).

*Let's learn more about leadership by exploring* **1.1** *the differences between leaders and managers and* **1.2** *substitutes for leadership.*

### 1.1 Leaders Versus Managers

In Chapter 1, we defined *management* as getting work done through others. In other words, managers don't do the work themselves. Managers help others do their jobs better. By contrast, *leadership* is the process of influencing others to achieve group or organizational goals. So what are the key differences between leadership and management?

According to Professor Warren Bennis, the primary difference, as shown in Exhibit 17.1, is that leaders are concerned with doing the right thing, while managers are concerned with doing things right.[3] In other words, leaders will begin with the question, "What should we be doing?" while managers start with "How can we do what already we're doing better?" Leaders focus on vision, mission, goals, and objectives, while managers focus on productivity and efficiency. Managers see themselves as preservers of the status quo, while leaders see themselves as promoters of change, as challengers of the status quo in that they encourage creativity and risk-taking. Carol Bartz, CEO of Autodesk, Inc., a software company, said managers "know how to write business plans, while leaders get companies—and people—to change." She went on to say that, "Human nature says

**EXHIBIT 17.1**

MANAGERS VERSUS LEADERS

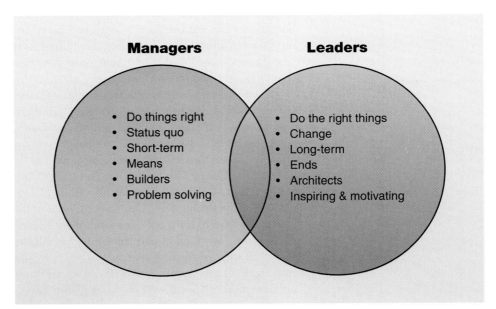

Managers
- Do things right
- Status quo
- Short-term
- Means
- Builders
- Problem solving

Leaders
- Do the right things
- Change
- Long-term
- Ends
- Architects
- Inspiring & motivating

Andrea Jung, CEO of Avon, certainly is concerned with doing the right things, with change, and with developing Avon's long-term strategy. Under Jung, Avon has developed numerous new brands, created mall kiosks to sell them, and put the brand at the JCPenney cosmetic counter. Jung has moved Avon out of the 1950s and given the company relevance in the 21st century.

cling to what you have, whether that's an old coat, a boyfriend, or a way of doing business," but that leaders have to "leave that behind." And since Bartz took over, Autodesk has tripled its revenues to more than $940 million a year.[4] Managers have a relatively short-term perspective, while leaders take a long-term view. Managers are more concerned with *means*, how to get things done, while leaders are more concerned with *ends*, what gets done. Managers are concerned with control and limiting the choices of others, while leaders are more concerned with expanding peoples' choices and options.[5] Finally, managers solve problems so that others can do their work, while leaders inspire and motivate others to find their own solutions.

Let's illustrate the difference between managers and leaders by taking another look at Southwest Airlines. After the federal government deregulated the airline industry, giving airlines the right to determine how many flights they would have and where those flights would go (previously, this was determined by the government), one of the first things Southwest did was reassess its strategic plan and objectives. Howard Putnam, Southwest's CEO at the time, told his top managers, "We aren't going to leave this room until we can write up on the wall, in a hundred words or less, what we are going to be when we grow up." And then, unlike other airlines, which simply tried to improve what they were already doing (i.e., management), Southwest critically examined what it was doing, why it was doing what it was doing, and whether it should continue to do what it had been doing. For instance, unlike most airlines, which have long-haul flights to major airport hubs (Chicago for United Airlines, Dallas-Fort Worth for American Airlines, etc.), Southwest flies short flights to smaller city airports, so that it can cater to higher-paying business travelers. And while most airlines fly a number of different airplanes, for example, American Airlines flies the Airbus A300, the Boeing 727, 737, 757, 767, and 777, and the McDonnell Douglas DC-10, MD-11, and MD-80, Southwest flies only one plane, the Boeing 737. This saves millions of dollars as pilots, flight attendants, and mechanics have to learn only one kind of airplane. Plus, Southwest saves millions by needing only one kind of parts inventory.[6] Finally, instead of paying its competitors to be part of their reservation systems (for example, the Apollo, Amadeus, and SABRE travel reservation systems used by travel agents to book tickets worldwide for dozens of different airlines), Southwest set up its own ticket reservation system and office.[7]

# "headline news"

### Growing Leaders from Private to General—To CEO?

Parallels have long been drawn between military and business leaders. Everyone knows the two strongest business metaphors are sports and war. For the connection between military and corporate to be so strong, there must be some substance behind the image, but what is it? Scholars say that the principles of leadership that drive the military are the same ones that drive business: knowing where you're headed, leading by example, and respecting and inspiring subordinates. And a recent study found that successful business and military leaders both had similar upbringings as children and young adults.

The September 11 terrorist attacks revealed where leadership—both business and civil—was strong and where there were deficits. "A situation like this is not unlike combat," said Ed Vick, the outgoing CEO of Young & Rubicam Advertising and a decorated Vietnam veteran. "You either lead by example, or you don't lead at all." On the Monday following the attacks, Vick stood in the lobby of the company's Manhattan office and greeted his employees as they arrived with a simple, "Welcome back, how are you?" The results were astounding.

With leadership so paramount to a company's success, how can a business be sure that it has good leaders, particularly in this age of early retirement, rapid growth, and high turnover? This question is on the minds of the vast majority of current business leaders around the world. A study by Development Dimension International and Corporate Leadership Council revealed that three-fourths of companies worldwide are not confident in their capability to effectively staff strategic leadership positions over the next five years.

Remedies to this leadership crisis are not out of reach. One way to ensure a stream of good leaders is to grow your own. This is exactly what the military does. No four-star general was ever

hired at that level: After all, the expression "earning your stripes" comes from the military process of moving up the ranks. One tool for growing leaders within an organization is succession planning. Succession planning forces a company to look inside (and outside) the organization to map a future course for when the current leadership retires or steps down. There are as many ways to plan a leadership transition as there are companies. Busken Bakery, a 73-year-old family-run business, has a second-generation CEO, Page Busken, who is approaching retirement age, but his son, Brian Busken, is only 28 years old. Although Brian grew up in the business, he's not yet ready to assume the helm. The company decided to hire an outside CEO for the transition period. Part of the new, experienced CEO's responsibilities is mentoring Brian so that he is ready to take over the business in a few years and lead it to the next generation.

1. *Make a list of what military leaders do and then of what business leaders do. Maybe even consider what political leaders do. Can you make any generalizations from your lists about what leadership is based on? Are there leadership traits on your list of business leadership functions that seem only relevant to the business world and not to the military or civic arenas?*

**Sources:** B. Avolio, "Are Leaders Born or Made?" *Psychology Today*, September 1999, 18, InfoTrac Article A55625479. A. Wheat, "What It Takes: Rudy Guiliani Has It. Gustavus Smith Didn't," *Fortune*, 12 November 2001, 126, InfoTrac article A79613413. "DDI's Byham Tells Firms: Time Is Ripe to 'Grow Your Own,'" *Business Wire*, 25 April 2001, 2341, InfoTrac Article A73618820. S. Marino, "Followers Create the Best Leaders," *Industry Week*, 2 November 1998, 20, InfoTrac Article A53165951. D. Monk, "Guiding a Son's Rise," *Cincinnati Business Courier*, 15 March 2002, 3.

649

While leaders are different from managers, in practice, organizations need them both. Managers are critical to getting out the day-to-day work, and leaders are critical to inspiring employees and setting the organization's long-term direction. The key issue is the extent to which organizations are properly led or properly managed. Warren Bennis summed up the difference between leaders and managers by noting that "American organizations (and probably those in much of the rest of the industrialized world) are underled and overmanaged. They do not pay enough attention to doing the right thing, while they pay too much attention to doing things right."[8]

### 1.2 Substitutes for Leadership: Do Leaders Always Matter?

One of the basic assumptions about leadership is that leaders always matter. The thinking goes that without sound leadership, organizations are sure to fail. In fact, when companies struggle, their leaders are almost always blamed for their poor performance. When Lockheed Martin, an aerospace company, struggled, *The Wall Street Journal* wrote this about Vance Coffman, its chairman and CEO:

As head of Lockheed Martin Corporation's classified government space business over the years, Vance Coffman was known for his engineering savvy and secretive management style.

But now, as chairman and chief executive of the struggling aerospace company, Mr. Coffman's same penchant for secrecy, combined with a string of serious setbacks afflicting some of the programs he once ran directly, has put his leadership into question. Increasingly, many investors, senior Pentagon officials, and even some of his own managers fault Mr. Coffman for failing to promptly disclose, or follow, a consistent strategy in facing the problems that have recently bedeviled the world's largest defense contractor.[9]

However, there are situations and circumstances in which leadership isn't necessary, or is unlikely to make much of a difference, or in which leaders aren't to blame for poor performance. These are known as leadership substitutes and leadership neutralizers.[10] Exhibit 17.2 lists a number of subordinate, task, or organizational characteristics that can act as leadership substitutes or neutralizers (some can act as both) for either task-related or people-related leader behaviors. Leaders' task-related behaviors, such as setting goals, giving directions, and providing resources, affect the extent to which people are

---

**EXHIBIT 17.2**

**LEADERSHIP SUBSTITUTES AND NEUTRALIZERS**

| CHARACTERISTIC | PEOPLE-RELATED LEADERSHIP BEHAVIORS | TASK-RELATED LEADERSHIP BEHAVIORS |
|---|---|---|
| **SUBORDINATE CHARACTERISTICS** | | |
| • Ability, experience, training, knowledge | Neutralize | Substitute, Neutralize |
| • Need for independence | Neutralize | Neutralize |
| • Professional orientation | Substitute, Neutralize | Substitute, Neutralize |
| • Indifference toward organizational rewards | Neutralize | Neutralize |
| **TASK CHARACTERISTICS** | | |
| • Unambiguous and routine tasks | No effect | Substitute, Neutralize |
| • Performance feedback provided by the work itself | No effect | Substitute, Neutralize |
| • Intrinsically satisfying work | Substitute, Neutralize | Neutralize |
| **ORGANIZATIONAL CHARACTERISTICS** | | |
| • Formalization, meaning specific plans, goals, and areas of responsibility | No effect | Neutralize |
| • Inflexibility, meaning rigid, unbending rules and procedures | No effect | Neutralize |
| • Highly specified staff functions | No effect | Neutralize |
| • Cohesive work groups | Substitute, Neutralize | Substitute, Neutralize |
| • Organizational rewards beyond a leader's control | Neutralize | Neutralize |
| • Spatial distance between supervisors and subordinates | Neutralize | Neutralize |

**Source:** S. Kerr & J.M. Jermier, "Substitutes for Leadership: Their Meaning and Measurement," *Organizational Behavior and Human Performance* 22 (1978): 375–403.

able to perform their jobs well. Leaders' people-related behaviors, such as being approachable, supportive, or showing concern for employees, affect how satisfied people are with their jobs.

**leadership substitutes**
subordinate, task, or organizational characteristics that make leaders redundant or unnecessary

**Leadership substitutes** are subordinate, task, or organizational characteristics that make leaders redundant or unnecessary. For instance, when subordinates have ability, experience, training, and knowledge about their jobs (see subordinate characteristics in Exhibit 17.2), task-related leader behavior that specifies goals, task assignments, and how to do the job aren't likely to improve a subordinate's work performance. Think about it. Workers already have the capability to do their jobs. And the job itself provides enough information to let them know how well they're doing their jobs or what they might do to correct performance problems. In situations like this, where leadership substitutes are strong, leaders don't need to tell workers what to do or how to do their jobs.

**leadership neutralizers**
subordinate, task, or organizational characteristics that can interfere with a leader's actions or make it impossible for a leader to influence followers' performance

**Leadership neutralizers** are subordinate, task, or organizational characteristics that can interfere with a leader's actions or make it impossible for a leader to influence followers' performance. Unlike substitutes that simply take the place of leaders, leadership neutralizers create an "influence vacuum." In other words, leadership neutralizers create a need for leadership by ironically preventing leadership from working. For example, when a subordinate is indifferent toward organizational rewards (see subordinate characteristics in Exhibit 17.2), there may be nothing that a leader can do to reward them for good performance. Likewise, inflexible rules and procedures (see organizational characteristics in Exhibit 17.2), such as union contracts that specify that all employees be paid the same, organizational policies that reward employees by seniority, and salary and raise processes that don't give leaders enough money to substantially reward good performers, effectively neutralize the ability of leaders to reward workers. Spatial distance (see organizational characteristics in Exhibit 17.2) can also neutralize leadership. Spatial distance is a situation in which supervisors and subordinates don't work in the same place, such as with telecommuters or people working thousands of miles away in overseas offices. Spatial distance typically means infrequent feedback, little or no face-to-face contact, and being "out of sight and out of mind," all of which make it very difficult for leaders to lead. In fact, some companies find telecommuting to be so disruptive to leadership processes that they require their telecommuters to come into the office at least once or twice a week.

So do leaders *always* matter? Leadership substitutes and neutralizers indicate that sometimes they don't. However, this doesn't mean that leaders don't matter at all. Quite the opposite. Leaders do matter, but they're not superhuman. They can't do it all by themselves. And they can't fix every situation. In short, leadership is very important. But poor leadership isn't the cause of every organizational crisis, and changing leaders isn't the solution to every company problem.

## Review 1
### Leadership

Leadership is the process of influencing others to achieve group or organizational goals. Leaders are different from managers. The primary difference is that leaders are concerned with doing the right thing, while managers are concerned with doing things right. Furthermore, managers have a short-term focus and are concerned with the status quo, with means rather than ends, and with solving others' problems. By contrast, leaders have a long-term focus, are concerned with change, with ends rather than means, and with inspiring and motivating others to solve their own problems. Organizations need both managers and leaders. But, in general, companies are overmanaged and underled. While leadership is important, leadership substitutes and neutralizers create situations in which leadership isn't necessary or is unlikely to make much of a difference. Leadership substitutes are subordinate, task, or organizational characteristics that make leaders redundant or unnecessary. By contrast, leadership neutralizers are subordinate, task, or organizational characteristics that interfere with a leader's actions or make it impossible for a leader to influence followers' performance.

## 2. Who Leaders Are and What Leaders Do

Every year, *Fortune* magazine conducts a survey to determine corporate American's "most admired" companies. And, every few years, as part of that study, it takes a look at the leaders of those companies. However, the last time it did this, it found that the CEOs of its ten most admired companies were surprisingly different. In fact, *Fortune* wrote that "Every conceivable leadership style is represented by these CEOs."[11] General Electric's CEO was described as "combative," as someone who "tilts his head, and thrusts out his chin as if to say, 'Go ahead, take your best shot'—and is never happier than when you do." Southwest Airline's CEO was described as "a prankster and a kisser so unabashedly affectionate that his company's ticker symbol is LUV, so hands-on he has loaded baggage and served peanuts to passengers." In fact, Southwest's CEO admitted that he is terrible at understanding the financial side of business, something that no regular CEO would ever admit. Finally, Coke's CEO was the mirror image of Southwest's CEO. *Fortune* described him as "undemonstrative and a 'financial wizard.'"

*So if the CEOs of Fortune's "most admired" corporations are all different, just what makes a good leader? Let's learn more about who leaders are by investigating 2.1 leadership traits, and 2.2 leadership behavior.*

### 2.1 Leadership Traits

**trait theory**
leadership theory that holds that effective leaders possess a similar set of traits or characteristics

**traits**
relatively stable characteristics, such as abilities, psychological motives, or consistent patterns of behavior

Trait theory is one way to describe who leaders are. **Trait theory** says that effective leaders possess a similar set of traits or characteristics. **Traits** are relatively stable characteristics, such as abilities, psychological motives, or consistent patterns of behavior. For example, according to trait theory, leaders were commonly thought to be taller, more confident, and have greater physical stamina (i.e., higher energy levels). Trait theory is also known as the "great person" theory, because early versions of trait theory stated that leaders were born, not made. In other words, you either had the "right stuff" to be a leader, or you didn't. And if you didn't, there was no way to get "it."

For some time, it was thought that trait theory was wrong, that there were no consistent trait differences between leaders and nonleaders, or between effective and ineffective leaders. However, more recent evidence shows that "successful leaders are not like other people," that successful leaders are indeed different from the rest of us. [12] More specifically, as shown in Exhibit 17.3, leaders are different from nonleaders in the following traits: drive, the desire to lead, honesty/integrity, self-confidence, emotional stability, cognitive ability, and knowledge of the business.[13]

---

EXHIBIT 17.3

LEADERSHIP TRAITS

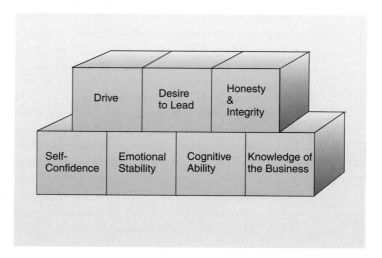

# WhatReallyWorks

## Leadership Traits Do Make a Difference

For decades, researchers assumed that leadership traits, such as drive, emotional stability, cognitive ability, and charisma were *not* related to effective leadership. However, more recent evidence shows that there are reliable trait differences between leaders and nonleaders. In fact, 54 studies based on more than 6,000 people clearly indicate that in terms of leadership traits, "successful leaders are not like other people."

### Traits and Perceptions of Leadership Effectiveness

Several leadership models argue that successful leaders will be viewed by their followers as good leaders. (This is completely different from determining whether leaders actually improve organizational performance.) Consequently, one test of trait theory is whether leaders with particular traits are viewed as more or less effective leaders by their followers.

**Intelligence.** On average, there is a 75 percent chance that intelligent leaders will be seen as better leaders than less intelligent leaders.

**Probability of Success**

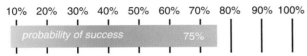

**Dominance.** On average, there is only a 57 percent chance that leaders with highly dominant personalities will be seen as better leaders than those with less dominant personalities.

**Probability of Success**

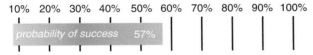

**Extroversion.** On average, there is a 63 percent chance that extroverts will be seen as better leaders than introverts.

**Probability of Success**

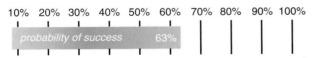

### Charisma and Leadership Effectiveness.

As discussed at the end of the chapter, *charismatic leadership* is the set of behavioral tendencies and personal characteristics of leaders that creates an exceptionally strong relationship between leaders and their followers. More specifically, charismatic leaders articulate a clear vision for the future that is based on strongly held values or morals; model those values by acting in a way consistent with the company's vision, communicate high performance expectations to followers; and display confidence in followers' abilities to achieve the vision.

**Performance and Charisma.** On average, there is a 72 percent chance that charismatic leaders will have better-performing followers and organizations than less charismatic leaders.

**Probability of Success**

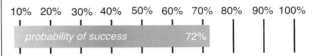

**Charisma and Perceived Leader Effectiveness.** On average, there is an 89 percent chance that charismatic leaders will be perceived as more effective leaders than less charismatic leaders.

**Probability of Success**

**Charisma and Leader Satisfaction.** On average, there is a 90 percent chance that the followers of charismatic leaders will be more satisfied with their leaders than the followers of less charismatic leaders.

**Probability of Success**

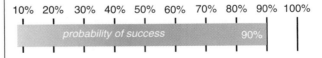

**Sources:** J.B. Fuller, C.E.P. Patterson, K. Hester, & D. Stringer, "A Quantitative Review of Research on Charismatic Leadership," *Psychological Reports* 78 (1996): 271–287. R.G. Lord, C.L. De Vader, & G.M. Alliger, "A Meta-Analysis of the Relation Between Personality Traits and Leadership Perceptions: An Application of Validity Generalization Procedures," *Journal of Applied Psychology* 71, no. 3 (1986): 402–410.

653

*Drive* refers to high levels of effort and is characterized by achievement, motivation, ambition, energy, tenacity, and initiative. In terms of achievement and ambition, leaders always try to make improvements or achieve success in what they're doing, and have strong desires to "get ahead." Leaders typically have more energy, and they have to, given the long hours they put in year after year. Furthermore, leaders don't have the luxury of being "down." Since we tend to take our cues from leaders, we expect them to be positive and "up." Thus, leaders must have physical, mental, and emotional vitality. Leaders are also more tenacious than nonleaders, and are better at overcoming obstacles and problems that would deter most of us. Most change takes place slowly, and leaders need to have a "stick-to-it-iveness" to see changes through. Leaders also show more initiative. For example, GE's former CEO Jack Welch said, "Some CEOs think the day they become CEO is the high point of their careers. They ought to feel they're just beginning." Indeed, legendary investor Warren Buffet said, "Jack feels there's more to do at GE than when he started," more than 20 years ago.[14] So, rather than waiting for others to take action, leaders move forward quickly to promote change or solve problems.

Successful leaders also have a stronger *desire to lead.* They want to be in charge and think about ways to influence or convince others about what should or shouldn't be done. *Honesty/integrity* is also important to leaders. *Honesty,* that is, being truthful with others, is a cornerstone of leadership. Without honesty, leaders won't be trusted. But with it, subordinates are willing to overlook other flaws. For example, one follower said this about the leadership qualities of his manager: "I don't like a lot of the things he does, but he's basically honest. He's a genuine article, and you'll forgive a lot of things because of that. That goes a long way in how much I trust him."[15] *Integrity* is the extent to which leaders do what they said they would do. Leaders may be honest and have good intentions, but if they don't consistently deliver on what they promise, they won't be trusted.

*Self-confidence,* believing in one's abilities, also distinguishes leaders from nonleaders. Self-confidence is critical to leadership. Leaders make risky, long-term decisions and must convince others of the correctness of those decisions. Self-confident leaders are more decisive and assertive and are more likely to gain others' confidence. Moreover, self-confident leaders will admit mistakes, because they view them as learning opportunities rather than a refutation of their leadership capabilities. This also means that leaders have *emotional stability.* Even when things go wrong, they remain even-tempered and consistent in their outlook and in the way they treat others. Leaders who can't control their emotions, who anger quickly or attack and blame others for mistakes are unlikely to be trusted. For example, Steve Jobs, CEO and cofounder of Apple Computers, is well known for his temper and for being an extremely demanding boss. When one of his assistants was late installing a high-speed, T-1 Internet connection, Jobs marched out to his cubicle and said, "No T-1. You're fired." The assistant went home, not sure whether Jobs was serious. Jobs apologized the next morning, but the assistant resigned soon after the incident.[16]

Leaders are also smart. Leaders typically have strong *cognitive abilities.* This doesn't mean that leaders are geniuses, far from it. But it does mean that leaders have the capacity to analyze large amounts of seemingly unrelated, complex information and can see patterns, opportunities, or threats where others might not see them. Finally, leaders also "know their stuff," which means they have superior technical knowledge about the businesses they run. Leaders who have a good *knowledge of the business* understand the key technological decisions and concerns facing their companies. More often than not, studies indicate that effective leaders have long, extensive experience in their industries.

### 2.2 Leadership Behaviors

Thus far, you've read about who leaders are. However, traits alone are not enough to be a successful leader. Traits are a precondition for success. After all, it's hard to imagine a truly successful leader who lacks all of these qualities. Leaders who have these traits (or many of them) must then take actions that encourage people to achieve group or organizational goals.[17] Accordingly, we now examine what leaders do, meaning the behaviors they perform or the actions they take to influence others to achieve group or organizational goals.

Researchers at the University of Michigan, Ohio State University, and the University of Texas examined the specific behaviors that leaders use to improve subordinate satisfaction and performance. Hundreds of studies were conducted and hundreds of leader behaviors were examined. At all three universities, two basic leader behaviors emerged as central to successful leadership: initiating structure (called *job-centered leadership* at the University of Michigan and *concern for production* at the University of Texas) and considerate leader behavior (called *employee-centered leadership* at the University of Michigan and *concern for*

**Monitor These Signs of Failing Leadership**

Successful leaders seem to have a sixth sense that helps them monitor how followers feel about them and their ideas. You can develop your own "sixth sense" by monitoring these signs of failed leadership: (1) performance—not meeting your numbers and goals, (2) execution—not meeting commitments to direct reports, (3) isolation—bad news and problems aren't coming to you, (4) turnover—talented subordinates start leaving because of you or organizational problems, and (5) people problems—not having the emotional strength to confront or replace poor-performing key subordinates. So develop your "sixth sense" and monitor these signs of failed leadership.

**Source:** R. Charan & G. Colvin, "Why CEOs Fail," *Fortune*, 21 June 1999, 69–78.

**initiating structure**
the degree to which a leader structures the roles of followers by setting goals, giving directions, setting deadlines, and assigning tasks

**consideration**
the extent to which a leader is friendly, approachable, supportive, and shows concern for employees

*people* at the University of Texas).[18] In fact, these two leader behaviors form the basis for many of the leadership theories discussed in this chapter.

**Initiating structure** is the degree to which a leader structures the roles of followers by setting goals, giving directions, setting deadlines, and assigning tasks. A leader's ability to initiate structure primarily affects subordinates' job performance. Indeed, in an article entitled "Why CEOs Fail," *Fortune* magazine indicated that CEOs who do initiate structure are likely to succeed, while those who don't are likely to fail and often lose their jobs. *Fortune* wrote, "Watch the likes of [Jack] Welch [GE's former CEO] or EDS's [CEO] Richard Brown or [Lawrence] Bossidy [CEO of Allied Signal] or any other proven implementer in a meeting. Near the end he'll grab a pen and start writing: He's noting exactly what is supposed to be done by whom, by when. He'll go over this with everyone before the meeting closes, and he'll probably send each one a reminder afterward." That, in a nutshell, is initiating structure.[19]

**Consideration** is the extent to which a leader is friendly, approachable, supportive, and shows concern for employees. Consideration primarily affects subordinates' job satisfaction. Specific leader consideration behaviors include listening to employees' problems and concerns, consulting with employees before making decisions, and treating employees as equals. For example, when an explosion killed workers at Ford's Rouge manufacturing facility, Chairman William (Bill) Clay Ford, Jr. rushed to the scene to express regret and provide support. He was later instrumental in the fair way in which the company treated victims' families. Likewise, rather than insulating himself when the Ford Explorer crisis grew (Firestone tires on Ford Explorers blew apart, causing vehicles to flip over), Bill Ford toured company plants to meet with employees and managers. Said Ford at the time, "I got an earful." When Ford became CEO, he continued his considerate leadership style to try to repair strained relationships that existed with employees, managers, suppliers, and car dealers. Ford declared, "We need to be a company that employees want to work for and that they are proud of. We need to be a company of quality products that customers want to buy and feel that they can trust." He also said, "We're being sued by our own employees [over the company performance appraisal system]. That breaks my heart. I will do everything I can to repair those relationships."[20]

While researchers at all three universities generally agreed on the two kinds of basic leader behaviors, initiating structure and consideration, they differed on the interaction and effectiveness of these behaviors. The University of Michigan studies indicated that initiating structure and consideration were mutually exclusive behaviors on opposite ends of the same

655

Nowhere is consideration for employees more in evidence than at Southwest Airlines. Founder and former CEO Herb Kelleher has modeled this style to such an extent that his managers, like Denis Carvill pictured here, jump in to help employees whenever there is backlog in any area of the business. No one is above doing any task such as loading and unloading baggage.

AP/WIDE WORLD PHOTOS

continuum. In other words, leaders who wanted to be more considerate would have to do less initiating of structure (and vice versa). The University of Michigan studies also indicated that only considerate leader behaviors (i.e., employee-centered) were associated with successful leadership. By contrast, researchers at Ohio State University and the University of Texas found that initiating structure and consideration were independent behaviors, meaning that leaders can be considerate and initiate structure at the same time. Additional evidence confirms this finding.[21] The same researchers also concluded that the most effective leaders were strong on both initiating structure and considerate leader behaviors.

This "high-high" approach can be seen in the upper right corner of the Blake and Mouton Leadership Grid, shown in Exhibit 17.4. Blake and Mouton used two leadership behaviors, concern for people (i.e., consideration) and concern for production (i.e., initiating structure), to categorize five different leadership styles. Both behaviors are rated on a nine-point scale with one representing "low" and nine representing "high." Blake and Mouton suggest that a "high-high" or nine-nine leadership style is the best. They call this style *team management,* because leaders who use it display a high concern for people (nine) and a high concern for production (nine). By contrast, leaders use a nine-one *authority-compliance* leadership style when they have a high concern for production and a low concern for people. A one-nine *country club* style occurs when leaders really care about producing a friendly and enjoyable work environment but don't really pay much attention to production or performance. The worst leadership style, according to the grid, is the one-one *impoverished* leader, who shows little concern for people or

EXHIBIT 17.4

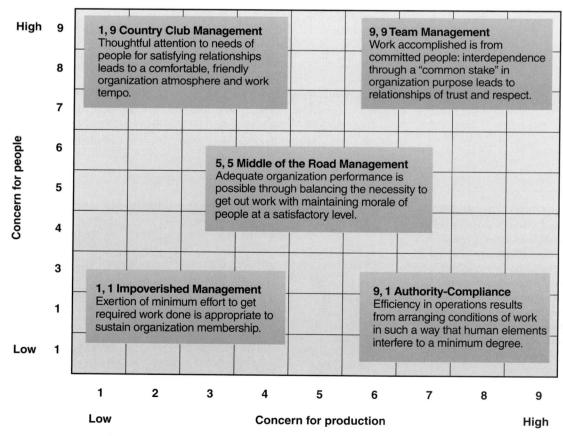

BLAKE/MOUTON LEADERSHIP GRID

**1, 9 Country Club Management**
Thoughtful attention to needs of people for satisfying relationships leads to a comfortable, friendly organization atmosphere and work tempo.

**9, 9 Team Management**
Work accomplished is from committed people: interdependence through a "common stake" in organization purpose leads to relationships of trust and respect.

**5, 5 Middle of the Road Management**
Adequate organization performance is possible through balancing the necessity to get out work with maintaining morale of people at a satisfactory level.

**1, 1 Impoverished Management**
Exertion of minimum effort to get required work done is appropriate to sustain organization membership.

**9, 1 Authority-Compliance**
Efficiency in operations results from arranging conditions of work in such a way that human elements interfere to a minimum degree.

Concern for people — High 9, 8, 7, 6, 5, 4, 3, 1 — Low 1

Concern for production — Low 1, 2, 3, 4, 5, 6, 7, 8, 9 — High

**Source:** R.R. Blake & A.A. McCanse, "The Leadership Grid®," *Leadership Dilemmas—Grid Solutions* (Houston: Gulf Publishing Company), 29. Copyright © 1991, by Scientific Methods, Inc. Reproduced by permission of the owners.

production and does the bare minimum needed to keep his or her job. Finally, the five-five *middle-of-the-road* style occurs when leaders show a moderate amount of concern for people and production.

Is the team management style, with a high concern for production and a high concern for people, the "best" leadership style? Logically, it would seem so. Why wouldn't you want to show high concern for both people and production? However, nearly 50 years' worth of research indicates that there isn't one "best" leadership style. The "best" leadership style depends on the situation. In other words, no one leadership behavior by itself and no one combination of leadership behaviors work well across all situations and employees.

### Review 2
### Who Leaders Are and What Leaders Do

Trait theory says that effective leaders possess traits or characteristics that differentiate them from nonleaders. Those traits are drive, the desire to lead, honesty/integrity, self-confidence, emotional stability, cognitive ability, and knowledge of the business. However, traits aren't enough for successful leadership. Leaders who have these traits (or many of them) must behave in ways that encourage people to achieve group or organizational goals. Two key leader behaviors are initiating structure, which improves subordinate performance, and consideration, which improves subordinate satisfaction. There is no "best" combination of these behaviors. The "best" leadership style depends on the situation.

# Situational Leadership

Imagine that you're the director of emergency medicine at a major hospital and that you've just learned that one of your doctors broke hospital policy by ordering a series of expensive tests for an emergency room patient without first getting approval from the hospital's cardiologist. The tests were for an extremely rare heart condition that could prove fatal if not detected. In fact, you were incensed when you learned that the doctor who broke the policy was a new intern with just two months of job experience. Why would he order an expensive test like this when hospital treatment policies and protocols make clear that this test cannot be ordered without a consulting cardiologist's approval? What a waste of money! This doctor obviously didn't know what he was doing! However, what if the physician who ordered the series of expensive tests was your most experienced emergency room physician? Instead of being angry and doubting the diagnosis, you probably would have thought to yourself, "I wonder what condition or mannerism tipped her off? Something had to be symptomatic of this rare condition or else she wouldn't have ordered this expensive test without first consulting the hospital cardiologist." In other words, you would have reacted differently depending on the situation and the person you were dealing with.

After leader traits and behaviors, situational leadership is the third major approach to the study of leadership. The three major situational leadership theories—Fiedler's contingency theory, path-goal theory, and Vroom and Yetton's normative decision model—all assume that the effectiveness of any **leadership style**, the way a leader generally behaves toward followers, depends on the situation.[22] Accordingly, there is no one "best" leadership style. However, these theories differ in one significant way. Fiedler's contingency theory assumes that leadership styles are consistent and difficult to change. Therefore, leaders must be placed in or "matched" to a situation that fits their leadership style. However, the other two situational theories all assume that leaders are capable of adapting and adjusting their leadership styles to fit the demands of different situations.

*After reading the next four sections, you should be able to*
3. *explain Fiedler's contingency theory.*
4. *describe how path-goal theory works.*
5. *explain the normative decision theory.*

**leadership style**
the way a leader generally behaves
toward followers

657

## 3. Putting Leaders in the Right Situation: Fiedler's Contingency Theory

**contingency theory**
leadership theory that states that in order to maximize work group performance, leaders must be matched to the situation that best fits their leadership style

Fiedler's **contingency theory** states that in order to maximize work group performance, leaders must be matched to the right leadership situation.[23] More specifically, as shown in Exhibit 17.5, the first basic assumption of Fiedler's theory is that leaders are effective when the work groups they lead perform well. So instead of judging leader effectiveness by what a leader does (i.e., initiating structure and consideration) or who the leader is (i.e., trait theory), Fiedler assesses leaders by the conduct and performance of the people they supervise. Second, Fiedler assumes that leaders are generally unable to change their leadership styles and that leaders will be more effective when their leadership styles are matched to the proper situation. Third, Fiedler assumes that the favorableness of a situation for a leader depends on the degree to which the situation permits the leader to influence the behavior of group members. Thus, Fiedler's third assumption is consistent with our definition of leadership, which is the process of influencing others to achieve group or organizational goals.

*Let's learn more about Fiedler's contingency theory by examining 3.1 the least preferred coworker and leadership styles, 3.2 situational favorableness, and 3.3 how to match leadership styles to situations.*

### 3.1 Leadership Style: Least Preferred Coworker

When Fiedler uses the term *leadership style*, he means the way in which a leader generally behaves toward followers. However, Fiedler also assumes that leadership styles are tied to leaders' underlying needs and personalities. And since personality and needs are relatively stable, he assumes that leaders are generally incapable of changing their leadership styles. For example, earlier in the chapter, you read about the hot temper of Apple CEO Steve Jobs and how he fired one of his assistants when a high-speed Internet connection was installed late. However, stories about Jobs' temper have been around for more than 20 years. In fact, his temper is one of the reasons that he was fired from Apple in the 1980s (before returning in the last few years). In other words, over the last two decades, Jobs' leadership style and personality have been remarkably consistent.[24]

Fiedler uses a questionnaire called the Least Preferred Coworker scale (LPC) to measure leadership style. When completing the LPC scale, people are instructed to consider all of the people with whom they have ever worked and then to choose the one person with whom they "have worked LEAST well." Fiedler explains that, "This does not have

---

EXHIBIT 17.5

FIEDLER'S CONTINGENCY THEORY

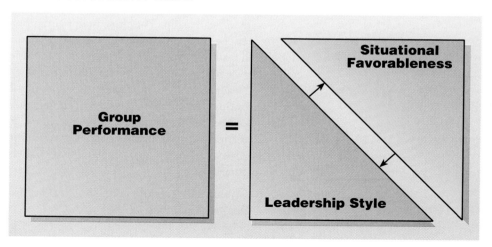

to be the person you liked least well, but should be the one person with whom you have the most trouble getting the job done."[25]

Take a second yourself to identify your LPC. It's usually someone you had a big disagreement with, or, for whatever reason, you couldn't work with. After identifying their LPC, people use the LPC scale shown in Exhibit 17.6 to "describe" their LPC.

EXHIBIT 17.6

## LEAST PREFERRED COWORKER SCALE

| Left | 8 | 7 | 6 | 5 | 4 | 3 | 2 | 1 | Right |
|------|---|---|---|---|---|---|---|---|-------|
| Pleasant | 8 | 7 | 6 | 5 | 4 | 3 | 2 | 1 | Unpleasant |
| Friendly | 8 | 7 | 6 | 5 | 4 | 3 | 2 | 1 | Unfriendly |
| Rejecting | 1 | 2 | 3 | 4 | 5 | 6 | 7 | 8 | Accepting |
| Tense | 1 | 2 | 3 | 4 | 5 | 6 | 7 | 8 | Relaxed |
| Distant | 1 | 2 | 3 | 4 | 5 | 6 | 7 | 8 | Close |
| Cold | 1 | 2 | 3 | 4 | 5 | 6 | 7 | 8 | Warm |
| Supportive | 8 | 7 | 6 | 5 | 4 | 3 | 2 | 1 | Hostile |
| Boring | 1 | 2 | 3 | 4 | 5 | 6 | 7 | 8 | Interesting |
| Quarrelsome | 1 | 2 | 3 | 4 | 5 | 6 | 7 | 8 | Harmonious |
| Gloomy | 1 | 2 | 3 | 4 | 5 | 6 | 7 | 8 | Cheerful |
| Open | 8 | 7 | 6 | 5 | 4 | 3 | 2 | 1 | Guarded |
| Backbiting | 8 | 7 | 6 | 5 | 4 | 3 | 2 | 1 | Loyal |
| Untrustworthy | 8 | 7 | 6 | 5 | 4 | 3 | 2 | 1 | Trustworthy |
| Considerate | 8 | 7 | 6 | 5 | 4 | 3 | 2 | 1 | Inconsiderate |
| Nasty | 8 | 7 | 6 | 5 | 4 | 3 | 2 | 1 | Nice |
| Agreeable | 8 | 7 | 6 | 5 | 4 | 3 | 2 | 1 | Disagreeable |
| Insincere | 8 | 7 | 6 | 5 | 4 | 3 | 2 | 1 | Sincere |
| Unkind | 8 | 7 | 6 | 5 | 4 | 3 | 2 | 1 | Kind |

**Source:** Fiedler, F. E., & Chemers, M. M. *Improving Leadership Effectiveness: The Leader Match Concept,* 2nd Edition (New York: John Wiley and Sons, 1984). Available http://depts.washington.edu/psych/faculty/fiedler.html, Online Acrobat CV, 23 March 2002. Reprinted by permission of authors.

Complete the LPC yourself. Did you describe your LPC as pleasant, friendly, supportive, interesting, cheerful, and sincere? Or did you describe the person as unpleasant, unfriendly, hostile, boring, gloomy, and insincere? People who describe their LPC in a positive way (scoring 64 and above) have *relationship-oriented* leadership styles. After all, if they can still be positive about their least preferred coworker, they must be people-oriented. By contrast, people who describe their LPC in a negative way (scoring 57 or below) have *task-oriented* leadership styles. Given a choice, they'll focus first on getting the job done and second on making sure everyone gets along. Finally, a third group with moderate scores (from 58 to 63) are more flexible in their leadership style and can be somewhat relationship-oriented or somewhat task-oriented.

### 3.2 Situational Favorableness

**situational favorableness**
the degree to which a particular situation either permits or denies a leader the chance to influence the behavior of group members

**leader-member relations**
the degree to which followers respect, trust, and like their leaders

**task structure**
the degree to which the requirements of a subordinate's tasks are clearly specified

**position power**
the degree to which leaders are able to hire, fire, reward, and punish workers

Fiedler assumes that leaders will be more effective when their leadership styles are matched to the proper situation. More specifically, Fiedler defines **situational favorableness** as the degree to which a particular situation either permits or denies a leader the chance to influence the behavior of group members.[26] In highly favorable situations, leaders find that their actions influence followers. However, in highly unfavorable situations, leaders have little or no success influencing the people they are trying to lead.

Three situational factors determine the favorability of a situation: leader-member relations, task structure, and position power. **Leader-member relations**, which is the most important situational factor, is how well followers respect, trust, and like their leaders. When leader-member relations are good, followers trust the leader and there is a friendly work atmosphere. **Task structure** is the degree to which the requirements of a subordinate's tasks are clearly specified. With highly structured tasks, employees have clear job responsibilities, goals, and procedures. **Position power** is the degree to which leaders are able to hire, fire, reward, and punish workers. The more influence leaders have over hiring, firing, rewards, and punishments, the greater their power.

Exhibit 17.7 shows how leader-member relations, task structure, and position power can be combined into eight situations that differ in their favorability to leaders. In general, Situation I, on the left side of Exhibit 17.7, is the most favorable leader situation. Followers like and trust their leaders and know what to do because their tasks are highly structured. Also, the leader has the formal power to influence workers through hiring, firing, rewarding, and punishing them. Therefore, in Situation I, it's relatively easy for a leader to influence followers. By contrast, Situation VIII, on the right side of Exhibit 17.7, is the least favorable situation for leaders. Followers don't like or trust their leaders. Plus, followers are not sure what they're supposed to be doing, given that their tasks or jobs are highly unstructured. Finally, leaders find it difficult to influence followers since they don't have the ability to hire, fire, reward, or punish the people who work for them. In short, it's very difficult to influence followers given the conditions found in Situation VIII.

### EXHIBIT 17.7

SITUATIONAL FAVORABLENESS

| Leader-Member Relations | Good | Good | Good | Good | Poor | Poor | Poor | Poor |
|---|---|---|---|---|---|---|---|---|
| Task Structure | High | High | Low | Low | High | High | Low | Low |
| Position Power | Strong | Weak | Strong | Weak | Strong | Weak | Strong | Weak |
| Situation | I | II | III | IV | V | VI | VII | VIII |

| **Favorable** | | **Moderately Favorable** | | **Unfavorable** |

### 3.3 Matching Leadership Styles to Situations

After studying thousands of leaders and followers in hundreds of different situations, Fiedler found that the performance of relationship- and task-oriented leaders followed the pattern displayed in Exhibit 17.8.

Relationship-oriented leaders with high LPC scores were better leaders (i.e., their groups performed more effectively) under moderately favorable situations. In moderately favorable situations, the leader may be liked somewhat, tasks may be somewhat structured, and the leader may have some position power. In this situation, a relationship-oriented leader improves leader-member relations, which is the most important of the three situational factors. In turn, morale and performance improve. By contrast, as shown in Exhibit 17.8, task-oriented leaders with low LPC scores were better leaders in highly favorable and unfavorable situations. Task-oriented leaders do well in favorable situations where leaders are liked, tasks are structured, and the leader has the power to hire, fire, reward, and punish. In these favorable situations, task-oriented leaders effectively step on the gas of a highly tuned car that's in perfect running condition. Their focus on performance sets the goal for the group, which then charges forward to meet it. But task-oriented leaders also do well in unfavorable situations in which leaders are disliked, tasks are unstructured, and the leader doesn't have the power to hire, fire, reward, and punish. In these unfavorable situations, the task-oriented leader sets goals, which focus attention on performance, and clarifies what needs to be done, thus overcoming low task structure. This is enough to jump-start performance, even if workers don't like or trust the leader. Finally, though not shown in Exhibit 17.8, people with moderate LPC scores, who can be somewhat relationship-oriented or somewhat task-oriented, tend to do fairly well in all situations because they can adapt their behavior. Typically, though, they don't perform quite as well as relationship-oriented or task-oriented leaders whose leadership styles are well-matched to the situation.

Recall, however, that Fiedler assumes that leaders are incapable of changing their leadership styles. Accordingly, the key to making Fiedler's contingency theory practical in the workplace is to accurately measure and match leaders to situations or to teach leaders how to change situational favorableness by changing leader-member relations, task structure, or position power. While matching or placing leaders in appropriate situations works particularly well, practicing managers have had little luck with "re-engineering situations" to fit their leadership styles. The primary problem, as you've no doubt realized, is the complexity of the theory. In a study designed to teach leaders how to re-engineer their situations to fit their leadership styles, Fiedler found that most of the leaders simply did not understand what they were supposed to do to change their leadership situations. Furthermore, if they didn't like their LPC profile (perhaps they felt they were

---

EXHIBIT 17.8

MATCHING LEADERSHIP STYLES TO SITUATIONS

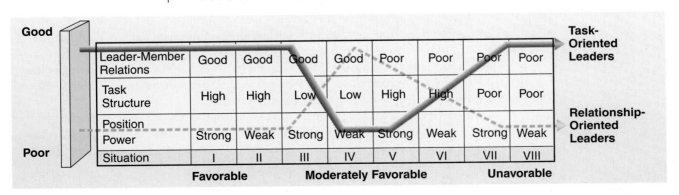

| | | | | | | | | |
|---|---|---|---|---|---|---|---|---|
| Leader-Member Relations | Good | Good | Good | Good | Poor | Poor | Poor | Poor |
| Task Structure | High | High | Low | Low | High | High | Poor | Poor |
| Position Power | Strong | Weak | Strong | Weak | Strong | Weak | Strong | Weak |
| Situation | I | II | III | IV | V | VI | VII | VIII |

Good — Poor (vertical axis)

Task-Oriented Leaders

Relationship-Oriented Leaders

**Favorable**          **Moderately Favorable**          **Unavorable**

more relationship-oriented than their scores indicated), they arbitrarily changed it to better suit their view of themselves. Of course, the theory won't work as well if leaders are attempting to change situational factors to fit their perceived leadership style and not their real leadership style.[27]

### Review 3
#### Putting Leaders in the Right Situation: Fiedler's Contingency Theory

Fiedler's theory assumes that leaders are effective when their work groups perform well, that leaders are unable to change their leadership styles, that leadership styles must be matched to the proper situation, and that favorable situations permit leaders to influence group members. According to the Least Preferred Coworker (LPC) scale, there are two basic leader styles. People who describe their LPC in a positive way have relationship-oriented leadership styles. By contrast, people who describe their LPC in a negative way have task-oriented leadership styles. Situational favorableness occurs when leaders can influence followers and is determined by leader-member relations, task structure, and position power. In general, relationship-oriented leaders with high LPC scores are better leaders under moderately favorable situations, while task-oriented leaders with low LPC scores are better leaders in highly favorable and unfavorable situations. Since Fiedler assumes that leaders are incapable of changing their leadership styles, the key is to accurately measure and match leaders to situations or to teach leaders how to change situational factors. While matching or placing leaders in appropriate situations works well, "re-engineering situations" to fit leadership styles doesn't because of the complexity of the model, which people find difficult to understand.

## 4. Adapting Leader Behavior: Path-Goal Theory

**path-goal theory**
leadership theory that states that leaders can increase subordinate satisfaction and performance by clarifying and clearing the paths to goals and by increasing the number and kinds of rewards available for goal attainment

Just as its name suggests, **path-goal theory** states that leaders can increase subordinate satisfaction and performance by clarifying and clearing the paths to goals and by increasing the number and kinds of rewards available for goal attainment. Said another way, leaders need to clarify how followers can achieve organizational goals, take care of problems that prevent followers from achieving goals, and then find more and varied rewards to motivate followers who achieve those goals.[28]

However, leaders must meet two conditions in order for path clarification, path clearing, and rewards to increase followers' motivation and effort. First, leader behavior must be an immediate or future source of satisfaction for followers. Therefore, the things you do as a leader must please your followers today or lead to future activities or rewards that will satisfy them in the future. For example, Susie Burkhart, a product manager for J.M. Smucker Company, doesn't return the calls of recruitment headhunters who are trying to lure her away to higher-paying jobs. She doesn't want to leave Smuckers because she's optimistic about her future with the company. In the last seven years, she's earned an MBA at company expense and has been promoted three times. Furthermore, she says, "I'm growing in this position," and, "The fact that people come to me for answers and decisions and I don't have to go to my superior is very empowering."[29]

Second, while providing the coaching, guidance, support, and rewards necessary for effective work performance, leader behaviors must complement and not duplicate the characteristics of followers' work environments. Thus, leader behaviors must offer something unique and valuable to followers beyond what they're already experiencing as they do their jobs or beyond that which they can already do for themselves. Exhibit 17.9 summarizes these basic assumptions of path-goal theory.

In contrast to Fiedler's contingency theory, path-goal theory assumes that leaders can change and adapt their leadership styles. Exhibit 17.10 illustrates this process, showing that leaders change and adapt their leadership styles contingent on the subordinate or the environment in which that subordinate works.

EXHIBIT 17.9

BASIC ASSUMPTIONS OF PATH-GOAL THEORY

**TO INCREASE SUBORDINATE SATISFACTION AND PERFORMANCE, LEADERS NEED TO**

- clarify paths to goals.
- clear paths to goals by solving problems and removing roadblocks.
- increase the number and kinds of rewards available for goal attainment.
- do things that satisfy followers today or will lead to future rewards or satisfaction.
- offer followers something unique and valuable beyond what they're experiencing or can already do for themselves.

**Source:** R. J. House & T. R. Mitchell, "Path-Goal Theory of Leadership," *Journal of Contemporary Business* 3 (1974): 81–97.

EXHIBIT 17.10

PATH-GOAL THEORY

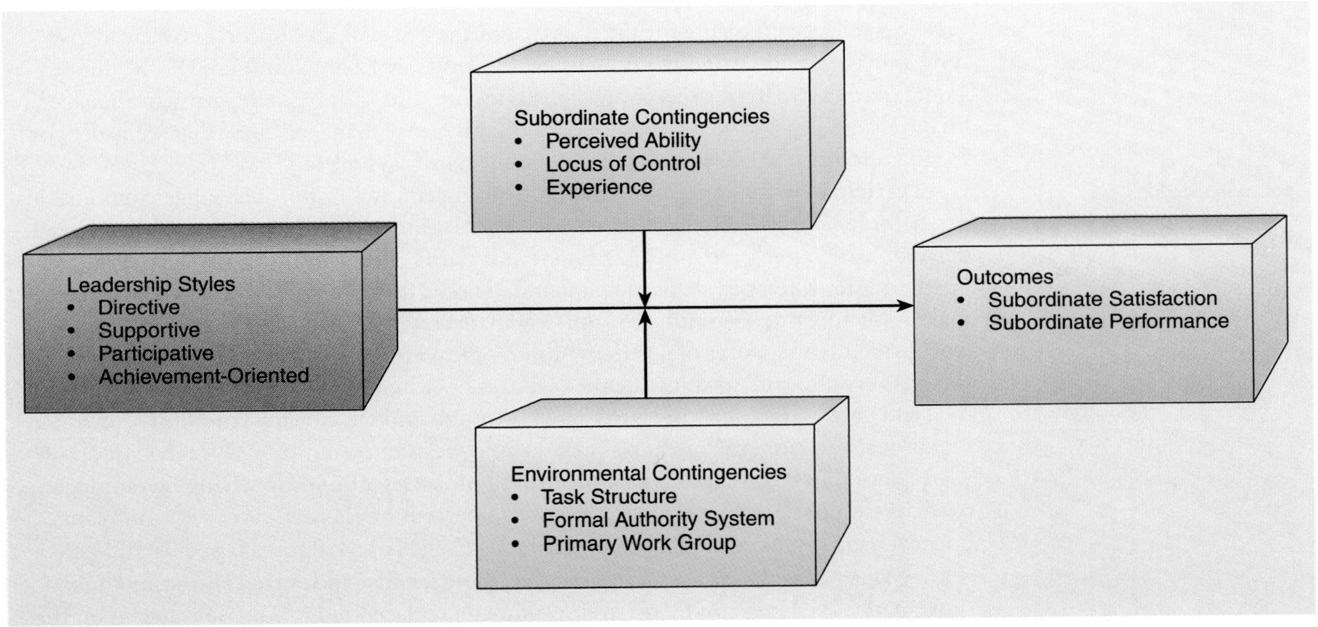

663

*Let's learn more about path-goal theory by examining* **4.1** *the four kinds of leadership styles that leaders use,* **4.2** *the environmental and subordinate contingency factors that determine when different leader styles are effective, and* **4.3** *the outcomes of path-goal theory in improving employee satisfaction and performance.*

### 4.1 Leadership Styles

**directive leadership**
leadership style in which the leader lets employees know precisely what is expected of them, gives them specific guidelines for performing tasks, schedules work, sets standards of performance, and makes sure that people follow standard rules and regulations

According to path-goal theory, illustrated in Exhibit 17.10, the four leadership styles are directive, supportive, participative, and achievement-oriented.[30] **Directive leadership** involves letting employees know precisely what is expected of them, giving them specific guidelines for performing tasks, scheduling work, setting standards of performance, and making sure that people follow standard rules and regulations. T.J. Rodgers, the CEO of Cypress Semiconductor, has developed computer software that actually stops work on computer chips if something goes wrong. It's a tremendous help in quality control. The same program, however, is also used to keep track of who meets and follows company rules and regulations. For instance, when one of Cypress's vice presidents didn't turn in his annual employee evaluations on time, the system put a stop on his paycheck. When he asked Rodgers where his paycheck was, Rodgers told him that he wouldn't get it until the evaluations were done. To no one's surprise, the vice president turned them in the very next day. However, when Rodgers was late with some of his own work, the system stopped his paycheck, too. In fact, he had to sell some Cypress stock until he caught up with his work and his paycheck was released.[31]

**Supportive** leadership involves being friendly and approachable to employees, showing concern for them and their welfare, treating them as equals, and creating a friendly climate. Supportive leadership is very similar to considerate leader behavior. Supportive leadership often results in employee job satisfaction and satisfaction with leaders. This leadership style may also result in improved performance when it increases employee confidence, lowers employee job stress, or improves relations and trust between employees and leaders.[32] For example, husband and wife Shane and Allison Alexander both work for Wal-Mart in Madisonville, Kentucky. Over the years, the Wal-Mart managers in their store have shown concern for them in a number of important ways. Said Allison, "Shane was there for a little over a year when I started. When I became pregnant, we moved in together and had only one car. Had I worked anywhere else, I would have had no hours or no job. Wal-Mart worked with us. They scheduled me for the days and Shane for the nights, and they gave us an hour in between to give him time to get home and me time to get back. If I was a few minutes late, they understood, because we lived so far away." Furthermore, she said, "As a department manager, Shane always has Saturdays and Sundays off. Since my manager knew that we never got to see each other, they started giving me some Saturdays off too."[33]

**Participative** leadership involves consulting employees for their suggestions and input before making decisions. Participation in decision making should help followers understand which goals are most important and clarify the paths to accomplishing them. Furthermore, when people participate in decisions, they become more committed to making them work. Aeroquip Group, headquartered in Maumee, Ohio, is a leading worldwide manufacturer of a variety of fluid-conveying and connecting products, that is, the metal connectors, fittings, adapters, and rubber hoses that facilitate the flow of liquids and gases. Aeroquip's products must be tough enough to withstand dust, corrosion, vibrations, and extreme operating pressure and weather conditions. Over the last few years, Aeroquip has turned its manufacturing processes around by relying on employee participation in decision making. Ninety-five percent of plant workers serve on plant improvement teams, and plant manager Don Waggener's goal for this year is 100 percent. Waggener said, "We reconfigured the whole facility, and we're continuing the improvements."[34] For example, when the company replaced old production machines, the workers who run the old machines tried out various machines and let plant engineers know which machines were easiest to operate. Employee input like this has helped Aeroquip reduce the time it takes to finish parts from eight days to 24 hours. In addition, employees who come up with good ideas are rewarded with company jackets and $25 gift certificates. Said Waggener, "We recognize it's very important to let people know we appreciate their ideas."[35]

**Achievement-oriented** leadership means setting challenging goals, having high expectations of employees, and displaying confidence that employees will assume responsibility and put forth extraordinary effort. Former U.S. Army general Norman Schwarzkopf believes that leaders generally don't ask enough of their people. Early in his career, Schwarzkopf was placed in charge of helicopter maintenance at a military base, something that he knew little about. Since readiness is always a key factor in military operations, he asked what percentage of the helicopter fleet was available for flight operations on any given day. The answer was "roughly 75 percent." Schwarzkopf recalls telling workers, "I don't know anything about helicopter maintenance, but I'm establishing a new standard—85 percent." Within a short time, 85 percent of the helicopter fleet was available for daily flight operations. The moral, according to the gen-

**supportive leadership**
leadership style in which the leader is friendly and approachable to employees, shows concern for them and their welfare, treats them as equals, and creates a friendly climate

**participative leadership**
leadership style in which the leader consults employees for their suggestions and input before making decisions

**achievement-oriented leadership**
leadership style in which the leader sets challenging goals, has high expectations of employees, and displays confidence that employees will assume responsibility and put forth extraordinary effort

664

eral, is that employees will usually not perform above your expectations, so it's important to expect a lot.[36]

### 4.2 Subordinate and Environmental Contingencies

As shown in Exhibit 17.10, path-goal theory specifies that leader behaviors should be fitted to subordinate characteristics. The theory identifies three kinds of subordinate contingencies: perceived ability, experience, and locus of control. *Perceived ability* is simply how much ability subordinates believe they have for doing their jobs well. Subordinates who perceive that they have a great deal of ability will be dissatisfied with directive leader behaviors. Experienced employees are likely to react in a similar way. Since they already know how to do their jobs (or perceive that they do), they don't need or want close supervision. By contrast, subordinates with little experience or little perceived ability will welcome directive leadership.

*Locus of control* is a personality measure that indicates the extent to which people believe that they have control over what happens to them in life. *Internals* believe that what happens to them, good or bad, is largely a result of their choices and actions. *Externals*, on the other hand, believe that what happens to them is caused by external forces outside of their control. Accordingly, externals are much more comfortable with a directive leadership style, while internals greatly prefer a participative leadership style, because they like to have a say in what goes on at work.

Path-goal theory specifies that leader behaviors should complement rather than duplicate the characteristics of followers' work environments. There are three kinds of environmental contingencies: task structure, the formal authority system, and the primary work group. As in Fiedler's contingency theory, *task structure* is the degree to which the requirements of a subordinate's tasks are clearly specified. When task structure is low and tasks are unclear, directive leadership should be used, because it complements the work environment. However, when task structure is high and tasks are clear, directive leadership duplicates what task structure provides and is not needed. Alternatively, when tasks are stressful, frustrating, or dissatisfying, leaders should respond with supportive leadership.

The *formal authority system* is an organization's set of procedures, rules, and policies. When the formal authority system is unclear, directive leadership complements the situation by reducing uncertainty and increasing clarity. But when the formal authority system is clear, directive leadership is redundant and should not be used.

*Primary work group* refers to the amount of work-oriented participation or emotional support that is provided by an employee's immediate work group. Participative leadership should be used when tasks are complex and there is little existing work-oriented participation in the primary work group. Likewise, when performing complex tasks, leaders should use participative leadership. When tasks are stressful, frustrating, or repetitive, supportive leadership is called for.

Finally, since keeping track of all of these subordinate and environmental contingencies can get a bit confusing, Exhibit 17.11 provides a summary of when directive, supportive, participative, or achievement-oriented leadership styles should be used.

### 4.3 Outcomes

Does following path-goal theory improve subordinate satisfaction and performance? Preliminary evidence suggests that it does.[37] In particular, people who work for supportive leaders are much more satisfied with their jobs and their bosses. Likewise, people who work for directive leaders are more satisfied with their jobs and bosses (but not quite as much as when their bosses are supportive), and perform their jobs better, too. Does adapting one's leadership style to subordinate and environmental characteristics improve subordinate satisfaction and performance? At this point, because of the difficulty of completely testing this complex theory, it's too early to tell.[38] However, since the data clearly show that it makes sense for leaders to be both supportive *and* directive, it also makes

EXHIBIT 17.11

**PATH-GOAL THEORY: WHEN TO USE DIRECTIVE, SUPPORTIVE, PARTICIPATIVE, OR ACHIEVEMENT-ORIENTED LEADERSHIP**

**DIRECTIVE LEADERSHIP**
- Unstructured tasks
- Inexperienced workers
- Workers with low perceived ability
- Workers with external locus of control
- Unclear formal authority system

**SUPPORTIVE LEADERSHIP**
- Structured, simple, repetitive tasks
- Stressful, frustrating tasks
- When workers lack confidence
- Clear formal authority system

**PARTICIPATIVE LEADERSHIP**
- Experienced workers
- Workers with high perceived ability
- Workers with internal locus of control
- Workers not satisfied with rewards
- Complex tasks

**ACHIEVEMENT-ORIENTED LEADERSHIP**
- Unchallenging tasks

sense that leaders could improve subordinate satisfaction and performance by adding participative and achievement-oriented leadership styles to their capabilities as leaders.

### Review 4
#### Adapting Leader Behavior: Path-Goal Theory

Path-goal theory states that leaders can increase subordinate satisfaction and performance by clarifying and clearing the paths to goals and by increasing the number and kinds of rewards available for goal attainment. However, for this to work, leader behavior must be an immediate or future source of satisfaction for followers and must complement and not duplicate the characteristics of followers' work environments. In contrast to Fiedler's contingency theory, path-goal theory assumes that leaders can and do change and adapt their leadership styles (directive, supportive, participative, and achievement-oriented), depending on their subordinate (experience, perceived ability, internal or external) or the environment in which that subordinate works (task structure, formal authority system, or primary work group).

## 5. Adapting Leader Behavior: Normative Decision Theory

For years, your company has insisted on formal business attire for men and women. However, you want to make a change to casual wear. Do you make the decision yourself and announce it, or do you consult your employees before making a decision?

Your sales divisions are organized geographically into West Coast, East Coast, Midwest, and Southwest regions. The Southwest region has seen exponential growth in the last five years and its sales representatives and managers make double the income of people in other regions. Out of fairness and out of concern that your current staff won't be able to keep up with the growth, you're going to cut the Southwest region in half, add staff, and effectively reduce the earnings of its sales representatives and managers. Do you make the decision yourself, announce it, and then live with the backlash? Do you consult all of your regional managers before making this decision? Or do you take your concerns straight to the people in the Southwest region to let them know what your concerns are?

Many people believe that making tough decisions is at the heart of leadership. However, experienced leaders will tell you that deciding how to make decisions is just as important. The **normative decision theory** (also known as the *Vroom-Yetton-Jago Model*)

**normative decision theory**
theory that suggests how leaders can determine an appropriate amount of employee participation when making decisions

helps leaders decide how much employee participation (from none to letting employees make the entire decision) should be used when making decisions.[39]

*Let's learn more about normative decision theory by investigating 5.1 decision styles and 5.2 decision quality and acceptance.*

### 5.1 Decision Styles

While nearly all of the other leadership theories in this chapter have specified leadership styles, that is, the way a leader generally behaves toward followers, the normative decision theory instead specifies five different decision styles or ways of making decisions. (See Chapter 6 for a more complete review of decision making in organizations.) As shown in Exhibit 17.12, those styles vary from *autocratic decisions* (AI or AII) on the left, in which leaders make the decisions by themselves, to consultative decisions (CI or CII), in which leaders share problems with subordinates but still make the decisions themselves, to *group decisions* (GII) on the right, in which leaders share the problems with subordinates and then have the group make the decisions. For example, GE Aircraft Engines, in Durham, North Carolina, uses this approach when making decisions. According to *Fast Company* magazine, "At GE/Durham, every decision is either an "A" decision, a "B" decision, or a "C" decision. An "A" decision is one that the plant manager makes herself, without consulting anyone."[40] Plant manager Paula Sims said, "I don't make very many of those, and when I do make one, everyone at the plant knows it. I make maybe 10 or 12 a year."[41] "B" decisions are also made by the plant manager, but with input from the people affected. "C" decisions—which make up the most common type—are made by consensus, by the people directly involved, with plenty of discussion. With "C" decisions, the view of the plant manager doesn't necessarily carry more weight than the views of those affected."[42]

---

**EXHIBIT 17.12**

DECISION STYLES AND LEVELS OF EMPLOYEE PARTICIPATION

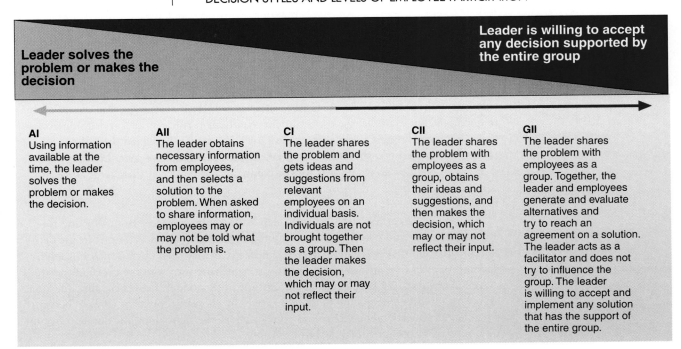

| AI | AII | CI | CII | GII |
|---|---|---|---|---|
| Using information available at the time, the leader solves the problem or makes the decision. | The leader obtains necessary information from employees, and then selects a solution to the problem. When asked to share information, employees may or may not be told what the problem is. | The leader shares the problem and gets ideas and suggestions from relevant employees on an individual basis. Individuals are not brought together as a group. Then the leader makes the decision, which may or may not reflect their input. | The leader shares the problem with employees as a group, obtains their ideas and suggestions, and then makes the decision, which may or may not reflect their input. | The leader shares the problem with employees as a group. Together, the leader and employees generate and evaluate alternatives and try to reach an agreement on a solution. The leader acts as a facilitator and does not try to influence the group. The leader is willing to accept and implement any solution that has the support of the entire group. |

**Source:** Adapted from V.H. Vroom & P. W. Yetton, *Leadership and Decision Making* (Pittsburgh: University of Pittsburgh Press, 1973), 13.

## EXHIBIT 17.13

### NORMATIVE THEORY DECISION RULES

#### DECISION RULES TO INCREASE DECISION QUALITY

**Quality Rule.** If the quality of the decision is important, then don't use an autocratic decision style.

**Leader Information Rule.** If the quality of the decision is important, and if the leader doesn't have enough information to make the decision on his or her own, then don't use an autocratic decision style.

**Subordinate Information Rule.** If the quality of the decision is important, and if the subordinates don't have enough information to make the decision themselves, then don't use a group decision style.

**Goal Congruence Rule.** If the quality of the decision is important, and subordinates' goals are different from the organization's goals, then don't use a group decision style.

**Problem Structure Rule.** If the quality of the decision is important, the leader doesn't have enough information to make the decision on his or her own, and the problem is unstructured, then don't use an autocratic decision style.

#### DECISION RULES TO INCREASE DECISION ACCEPTANCE

**Commitment Probability Rule.** If having subordinates accept and commit to the decision is important, then don't use an autocratic decision style.

**Subordinate Conflict Rule.** If having subordinates accept the decision is important and critical to successful implementation and subordinates are likely to disagree or end up in conflict over the decision, then don't use an autocratic or consultative decision style.

**Commitment Requirement Rule.** If having subordinates accept the decision is absolutely required for successful implementation and subordinates share the organization's goals, then don't use an autocratic or consultative style.

**Source:** Adapted from V.H. Vroom, "Leadership," in *Handbook of Industrial and Organizational Psychology*, ed. M.D. Dunnette (Chicago: Rand McNally, 1976). V.H. Vroom & A.G. Jago, *The New Leadership: Managing Participation in Organizations* (Englewood Cliffs, NJ: Prentice Hall, 1988).

### 5.2 Decision Quality and Acceptance

According to the normative decision theory, using the right degree of employee participation improves the quality of decisions and the extent to which employees accept and are committed to decisions. Exhibit 17.13 lists the decision rules that normative decision theory uses to increase decision quality and employee acceptance and commitment. The quality, leader information, subordinate information, goal congruence, and problem structure rules are used to increase decision quality. For example, the leader information rule states that if a leader doesn't have enough information to make a decision on his or her own, then the leader should not use an autocratic decision style.

The commitment probability, subordinate conflict, and commitment requirement rules shown in Exhibit 17.13 are used to increase employee acceptance and commitment to decisions. For example, the commitment requirement rule says that if decision acceptance and commitment are important, and the subordinates being led share the organization's goals, then you shouldn't use an autocratic or consultative style. In other words, if followers want to do what's best for the company and you need their acceptance and commitment to make a decision work, then use a group decision style and let them make the decision.

As you can see, these decision rules help leaders improve decision quality and follower acceptance and commitment by eliminating decision styles that don't fit the decision or situation they're facing. Normative decision theory then operationalizes these decision rules in the form of yes/no questions, which are shown in the decision tree displayed in Exhibit 17.14. You start at the left side of the model, answer the first question, "How important is the quality of this decision?" by choosing "high" or "low." Then answer the next question and so forth as you branch to the right along the decision tree until you get to a recommended decision style.

EXHIBIT 17.14

NORMATIVE DECISION THEORY TREE FOR DETERMINING THE LEVEL OF PARTICIPATION IN DECISION MAKING

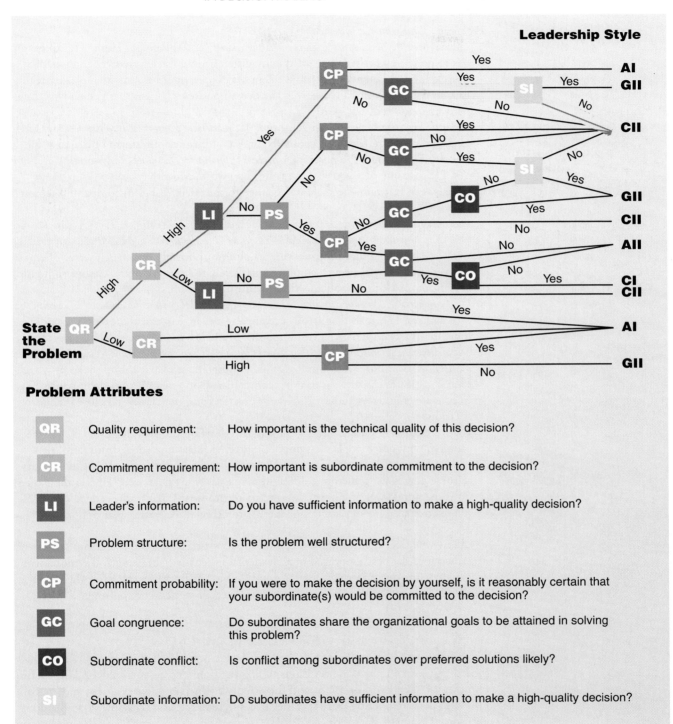

## Problem Attributes

**QR** — Quality requirement: How important is the technical quality of this decision?

**CR** — Commitment requirement: How important is subordinate commitment to the decision?

**LI** — Leader's information: Do you have sufficient information to make a high-quality decision?

**PS** — Problem structure: Is the problem well structured?

**CP** — Commitment probability: If you were to make the decision by yourself, is it reasonably certain that your subordinate(s) would be committed to the decision?

**GC** — Goal congruence: Do subordinates share the organizational goals to be attained in solving this problem?

**CO** — Subordinate conflict: Is conflict among subordinates over preferred solutions likely?

**SI** — Subordinate information: Do subordinates have sufficient information to make a high-quality decision?

Source: V.H. Vroom & A.G. Jago, *The New Leadership: Managing Participation in Organizations* (Englewood Cliffs, NJ: Prentice Hall, 1988).

669

Let's use the model by returning to the problem of whether to change from a formal business attire policy to a casual wear policy. The decision sounds simple, but working through the decision tree—as shown by the discussion below and by the yellow line in Exhibit 17.14—indicates that it is more complex than you'd think.

### Problem: Change to Casual Wear?

1. *Quality requirement: How important is the quality of this decision?* High. This question has to do with whether there are quality differences in the alternatives and whether those quality differences matter. While most people would assume that quality really isn't an issue here, it really is, given the overall positive changes that generally accompany changes to casual wear.

2. *Commitment requirement: How important is subordinate commitment to the decision?* High. Changes in culture, like dress codes, require subordinate commitment or else they fail.

3. *Leader's information: Do you have sufficient information to make a high-quality decision?* Yes. Let's assume that you've done your homework. Much has been written about casual wear, from how to make the change to the effects it has in companies (almost all positive).

4. *Commitment probability: If you were to make the decision by yourself, is it reasonably certain that your subordinate(s) would be committed to the decision?* No. Studies of casual wear (see item 3, leader information) are almost uniformly positive in terms of employees' reactions. However, employees are likely to be angry if you change something as personal as clothing policies without consulting them.

5. *Goal congruence: Do subordinates share the organizational goals to be attained in solving this problem?* Yes. The goals that usually accompany a change to casual dress policies are a more informal culture, better communication, and less money spent on business attire.

6. *Subordinate information: Do subordinates have sufficient information to make a high-quality decision?* No. Most employees know little about casual wear policies or what even constitutes casual wear in most companies. Consequently, most companies have to educate employees about casual wear practices and policies even before making a decision.

7. *CII is the answer:* With a CII, or consultative decision process, the leader shares the problem with employees as a group, obtains their ideas and suggestions, and then makes the decision, which may or may not reflect their input. So, given the answers to these questions (remember, different managers won't necessarily answer these questions the same way), the normative theory recommends that leaders consult with their subordinates first before deciding whether to change to a casual wear policy.

How well does the normative decision theory work? A leading leadership scholar has described it as the best supported of all leadership theories.[43] In general, the more managers violate the decision rules discussed in Exhibit 17.13, the less effective their decisions are, especially with respect to subordinate acceptance and commitment.[44]

## Review 5
### Adapting Leader Behavior: Normative Decision Theory

The normative decision theory helps leaders decide how much employee participation should be used when making decisions. Using the right degree of employee participation improves the quality of decisions and the extent to which employees accept and are committed to decisions. The theory specifies five different decision styles or ways of making decisions: autocratic decisions (AI or AII), consultative decisions (CI or CII), and group decisions (GII). The theory improves decision quality via the quality, leader information, subordinate information, goal congruence, and unstructured problem decision rules. The theory improves employee commitment and acceptance via the commitment probability, subordinate conflict, and commitment requirement decision rules. These decision rules help leaders improve decision quality and follower acceptance and commitment by eliminating decision styles that don't fit the decision or situation they're facing. Normative decision theory then operationalizes these decision rules in the form of yes/no questions, which were shown in the decision tree displayed in Exhibit 17.14.

# Strategic Leadership

Thus far, you have read about three major leadership ideas: traits, behaviors, and situational theories. Leader *traits* are relatively stable characteristics, such as abilities or psychological motives. Traits capture who effective leaders are. Leader *behaviors* are the actions leaders take to influence others to achieve group or organizational goals. Behaviors capture what effective leaders do (i.e., initiate structure and consideration). And *situational theories* indicate that the effectiveness of a leadership style, the way a leader generally behaves toward followers, depends on the situation. Situational theories capture what leaders need to do or not do in particular situations or circumstances. This final part of the chapter introduces a fourth major leadership idea—strategic leadership—and its components: visionary, charismatic, and transformational leadership.

**strategic leadership**
the ability to anticipate, envision, maintain flexibility, think strategically, and work with others to initiate changes that will create a positive future for an organization

**Strategic leadership** is the ability to anticipate, envision, maintain flexibility, think strategically, and work with others to initiate changes that will create a positive future for an organization.[45] For example, General Electric's former CEO, Jack Welch, was one of the most successful CEOs ever, having increased GE's stock market value from $12 billion when he took over in 1981 to more than $350 billion when he retired in August 2001.[46] From the start, Welch imparted strategic leadership by making it clear that every GE business (there are more than a dozen) needed to be "#1 or #2 in its industry." For two decades, he reinforced GE's strategic leadership by holding half-day "classes" with more than 15,000 GE managers and executives at GE's executive center in Crotonville, New York. Every week, Welch used surprise visits to GE plants and offices to maintain connections with GE's lower- and middle-level managers. Brian Nailor, a GE marketing manager, said, "We were pebbles in an ocean, but he knew about us."[47]

Thus, strategic leadership captures how leaders inspire their followers to change and to give extraordinary effort to accomplish organizational goals.

*After reading this next section, you should be able to:*
*6. explain how visionary leadership (i.e., charismatic and transformational leadership) helps leaders achieve strategic leadership.*

# 6. Visionary Leadership

In Chapter 4, we defined *vision* as a statement of a company's purpose or reason for existing. Similarly, **visionary leadership** creates a positive image of the future that motivates organizational members and provides direction for future planning and goal setting.[48]

**visionary leadership**
leadership that creates a positive image of the future that motivates organizational members and provides direction for future planning and goal setting

*Two kinds of visionary leadership are 6.1 charismatic leadership and 6.2 transformational leadership.*

## 6.1 Charismatic Leadership

*Charisma* is a Greek word meaning "gift from God." The Greeks saw people with charisma as divinely inspired and capable of incredible accomplishments. German sociologist Max Weber viewed charisma as a special bond between leaders and followers.[49] Weber wrote that the special qualities of charismatic leaders enable them to strongly influence followers. Weber also noted that charismatic leaders tend to emerge in times of crisis and that the radical solutions they propose enhance the admiration that followers feel for them. Indeed, charismatic leaders tend to have incredible influence over their

### Develop Your Charisma

It's often assumed that charisma is an unchangeable trait. However, several simple steps can develop your charisma:

1. Use symbols, metaphors, and stories to refine complex ideas into simple, powerful messages.
2. Embrace risk. Charismatics long to accomplish what hasn't been done before.
3. Defy the status quo. Fight convention. Question why things are done the way they are.
4. Step into others' shoes. Be empathetic and see things from the perspective of customers and employees.
5. Poke, prod, and challenge others to think and act differently and quickly.

Follow these steps, and you'll be more charismatic and develop a stronger relationship with your followers.

**Source:** P. Sellers, "What Exactly Is Charisma?" *Fortune*, 15 January 1996, 68. W. Parker, "Developing Your Charisma," *Work Star* Net. [Online] Available http://workstar.net/library/charisma.htm, 24 March 2002.

**charismatic leadership**
the behavioral tendencies and personal characteristics of leaders that create an exceptionally strong relationship between them and their followers

British billionaire adventurer Richard Branson dons a Virgin Cola costume and sprays the soft drink during a promotion in Tokyo. Branson's charismatic leadership has catapulted his business undertakings into the limelight and brought great success to his companies.

followers, who become zealously inspired by and attracted to their leaders. From this perspective, charismatic leaders are often seen as bigger-than-life or uniquely special.

Charismatic leaders have strong, confident, dynamic personalities that attract followers and enable them to create strong bonds between themselves and their followers. Followers trust charismatic leaders, are loyal to them, and are inspired to work toward the accomplishment of the leader's vision. Because of these qualities, followers become devoted to charismatic leaders and may go to extraordinary lengths to please them. Therefore, we can define **charismatic leadership** as the behavioral tendencies and personal characteristics of leaders that create an exceptionally strong relationship between them and their followers. Charismatic leaders also

- articulate a clear vision for the future that is based on strongly held values or morals,
- model those values by acting in a way consistent with the vision,
- communicate high performance expectations to followers, and
- display confidence in followers' abilities to achieve the vision.[50]

As mentioned above, followers trust charismatic leaders, are loyal to them, and are inspired to work toward the accomplishment of the leader's vision. But as you learned in Chapter 1, this was not the case when Jeff Weitzen became Gateway Computers' new CEO, replacing founder Ted Waitt, who then became the company's chairman. Unlike the popular Waitt, Weitzen had little interaction with Gateway's managers and employees. One employee said, "He didn't walk

AP/WIDE WORLD PHOTOS

# BeenThereDoneThat

## Richard Branson: Charisma without Hot Air

Richard Branson CEO and founder of the Virgin Group, which owns Virgin Atlantic Airways, Virgin Cola, and Virgin Mega stores, as well as hotels, video game and book publishers, and radio and television production companies is one of the most charismatic business leaders of our time. Besides his highly publicized attempts at flying a hot-air balloon around the world, Branson is known for his sense of humor, his openness to ideas, and the large amount of freedom that he grants to the people who run various parts of the Virgin "empire." In this interview with Manfred Kets de Vries, he discusses his views on business and leadership.

**Q:** What do you see as Virgin's key success factors? What makes your company different from others?

**A:** I'm absolutely certain that it's a question of the kind of people you have and the way you motivate them. I'm sure that's what makes any company successful. If you can motivate your people, use their creative potential, you can get through bad times and you can enjoy the good times together. If you fail to motivate your people, your company is doomed. . . . If your employees are happy, smiling, and enjoying their work, they will perform well. Consequently, the customers will enjoy their experience with your company. If your employees are sad, miserable, and not having a good time, the customers will be equally miserable.

**Q:** Could you say something about the way you design your organization, its architecture?

**A:** Well, our record company [now divested], I suppose, would have been the best example. My philosophy was always that if there were 50 people in a building, I would go there and ask to see the deputy managing director, the deputy sales manager, and the deputy marketing manager. I would say: "You are now the managing director, the sales manager, the marketing manager, or the press officer of a new company." And I would put them into a new building. Then again, when that company got to a certain size, say 50 people, I would do the same thing again. So we actually set up about 25 or 30 small record companies. Cumulatively, they became the biggest independent record company in the world.

**Q:** What can you say about your reward systems? You once said that you were in the business of making millionaires.

**A:** Yes, I suppose that we have made maybe 15 or 20 multimillionaires through this structure. We like to reward our key performers for their creative contribution.

**Q:** When you look at creative, high-performing organizations, they seem to have a number of characteristics in common. What do you think they are?

**A:** Obviously, speed is something that we are better at than most other companies. We don't have formal board meetings, committees, and so forth. If someone has an idea, they can pick up the phone and talk to me. I can vote "done, let's do it." Or better still, they can just go ahead and do it. They know that they are not going to get a mouthful from me if they make a mistake. Rules and regulations are not our forte. Analyzing things to death is not our kind of thing. We very rarely sit back and analyze what we do.

**Q:** Some people argue that the way you run your company is almost like a venture capital firm. Basically, anybody with a crazy idea gets a hearing.

**A:** I hope that "crazy idea" part is not too true. But to an extent, the statement is valid. . . . It's a fair comment.

**Q:** What do you see as your weaknesses? Do you have any characteristics that get in the way of your work?

**A:** I suspect not being able to say no. Hopefully, I am getting better at it now. But there are so many wonderful ideas. I do love new projects; I love new ideas. We are in a position where almost anybody and everybody who has got an idea likes to bring it to us. There aren't many companies like us, who have got, in a sense, a certain amount of entrepreneurial flair, companies that seem accessible to the public. Therefore, in any one day we receive hundreds of requests of all sorts. And some of them are very good ones.

My weaknesses really go back to the fact that I have spread myself too thin. In a purely business sense, I suspect that if I just wanted to maximize profits, I should have stayed more focused on one area and really concentrated on that one area. That's the conventional way, and I'm sure that's what most business schools teach. Perhaps it's right. But it wouldn't have been half as much fun.

I must admit that I feel very much alive when I set out to achieve something. On reflection, it's really more the fight than the actual achieving. I love people and I just love new creative challenges. Some people ask, why keep battling on when you can take it easy? My reason, basically, is that I'm very fortunate to be in the position I am. I've learned a great deal and I've had great fun doing so. I'm in a unique position of being able to do almost anything I like and achieve almost anything I wish. I don't want to waste the position that I find myself in. I know that at age 80 or 90, I would kick myself if I just frittered away this second half of my life. I really do believe that fighting competition is exciting. And it's good for business. I think that Virgin can get in there and it can compete with the biggest and improve them—and hopefully survive alongside them, have fun, and pay the bills at the same time. Basically, I admire anyone who takes on either the establishment or something like a mountain and succeeds or fails.

I sometimes wake up at night and lie there and think, "Is it all a dream?" Because it has been pretty good to date. It just seems almost too much for one man in one lifetime. So, if I am to reflect, I have been very fortunate to have so many wonderful experiences. Every day is fascinating. Every day, I am learning something new.

**Q:** When you leave Virgin, what kind of enduring mark do you want to leave behind? How do you want to be remembered?

**A:** I think that it would be nice if Virgin can be remembered as a company that challenged the established way of doing things, and that built up a number of companies that were world leaders in their own fields. That doesn't necessarily

mean being the biggest companies, but the best in that particular field. I also would like that the staff of Virgin would have very happy memories of the time that they spent working here.

**Source:** M. Kets de Vries, "Charisma in Action: The Transformational Abilities of Virgin's Richard Branson and ABB's Percy Barnevik [includes interview with Virgin Group's CEO and ABB's chairman]," *Organizational Dynamics* 26, no. 3 (1 January 1998).

the halls." Brad Beavers, a Gateway assembly line worker, said, "That other guy [Weitzen] didn't come around much."[51] So when Weitzen introduced controversial changes without consulting employees, attitudes toward him and his new management team quickly soured.

By contrast, when Ted Waitt returned as CEO, replacing Weitzen, hundreds of Gateway employees welcomed him back to the company's central factory and headquarters with banners and posters declaring, "WELCOME BACK, TED," and "TED IS COMING." When Waitt entered the building, the music of Smash Mouth's "All Star" blasted through the speakers, and one of the plant supervisors yelled, "Ted is in the house!" Another worker shouted, "He's our hero." When Waitt approached the microphone, the crowd hushed to hear him say, "It's good to be home." One of the first questions from the crowd was, "Does this mean we get to drink beer in the office again?" Waitt laughingly responded, "No! No beer in the office before five." The difference between Weitzen and Waitt was clear, charisma. Gateway's workers were devoted to Waitt and were willing to go to extraordinary lengths to please him.[52]

Does charismatic leadership work? Studies indicate that it often does. In general, the followers of charismatic leaders are more committed and satisfied, are better performers, are more likely to trust their leaders, and simply work harder.[53] Indeed, within three months of Ted Waitt's return to Gateway Computers, the close rate on sales increased 20 percent and customer satisfaction rose by 9 percent to 76 percent, jumping Gateway to one point above the industry average. Financial analyst Charlie Wolf, who specializes in the PC industry, said of Waitt, "His employees love him and when employees love their CEO, they work harder."

However, the risks associated with charismatic leadership are at least as large as its benefits, particularly if ego-driven leaders take advantage of fanatical followers.

In general, there are two kinds of charismatic leaders, ethical charismatics and unethical charismatics.[54] **Ethical charismatics** provide developmental opportunities for followers, are open to positive and negative feedback, recognize others' contributions, share information, and have moral standards that emphasize the larger interests of the group, organization, or society. Ethical charismatics produce stronger commitment, higher satisfaction, more effort, better performance, and greater trust.

By contrast, unethical charismatics pose a tremendous risk for companies. Followers can be just as supportive and committed to unethical charismatics as they are to ethical charismatics. However, **unethical charismatics** control and manipulate followers, do what is best for themselves instead of their organizations, only want to hear positive feedback, only share information that is beneficial to themselves, and have moral standards that put their interests before everyone else's. John Thompson, a management consultant, said, "Often what begins as a mission becomes an obsession. Leaders can cut corners on values and become driven by self-interest. Then they may abuse anyone who makes a mistake."[55]

For example, a former bank CEO, who we will call "William," was probably an unethical charismatic. His workers followed and feared him, never knowing when he would

**674**

**ethical charismatics**
charismatic leaders that provide developmental opportunities for followers, are open to positive and negative feedback, recognize others' contributions, share information, and have moral standards that emphasize the larger interests of the group, organization, or society

**unethical charismatics**
charismatic leaders that control and manipulate followers, do what is best for themselves instead of their organizations, only want to hear positive feedback, only share information that is beneficial to themselves, and have moral standards that put their interests before everyone else's

EXHIBIT 17.15

## ETHICAL AND UNETHICAL CHARISMATICS

| CHARISMATIC LEADER BEHAVIORS | ETHICAL CHARISMATICS | UNETHICAL CHARISMATICS |
| --- | --- | --- |
| Exercising power | Power is used to serve others. | Power is used to dominate or manipulate others for personal gain. |
| Creating the vision | Followers help develop the vision. | Vision comes solely from leader and serves his/her personal agenda. |
| Communicating with followers | Two-way communication: Seek out viewpoints on critical issues. | One-way communication: Not open to input and suggestions from others. |
| Accepting feedback | Open to feedback. Willing to learn from criticism. | Inflated ego thrives on attention and admiration of yes-men. Avoid or punish candid feedback. |
| Stimulating followers intellectually | Want followers to think and question status quo as well as leader's views. | Don't want followers to think. Want uncritical, unquestioning acceptance of leader's ideas. |
| Developing followers | Focus on developing people with whom they interact. Express confidence in them and share recognition with others. | Insensitive and unresponsive to followers' needs and aspirations. |
| Living by moral standards | Follow self-guided principles that may go against popular opinion. Have three virtues: courage, a sense of fairness or justice, and integrity. | Follow standards only if they satisfy immediate self-interests. Manipulate impressions so that others think they are "doing the right thing." Use communication skills to manipulate others to support their personal agenda. |

**Source:** J.M. Howell & B.J. Avolio, "The Ethics of Charismatic Leadership: Submission or Liberation?" *Academy of Management Executive* 6, no. 2 (1992): 43–54.

"attack" those around him. At times, he was such a tyrant that he became known as WWW, "Whatever William Wants." His top managers were terrified of him, especially during monthly meetings when he would fire questions at a randomly chosen "victim." For instance, a bank officer at the meeting might say, "Deposits are up 10 percent, and we're really pleased because it's the second month in a row," and then William would say "Why are you pleased? Do you think 10 percent is enough? Why do you jump to conclusions? Are we running a bank where 10 percent is enough?" One of the bank managers commented that "Once William was riled up, people would end up *yessing* him to death."[56]

Exhibit 17.15 shows the stark differences between ethical and unethical charismatics on several leader behaviors: exercising power, creating the vision, communicating with followers, accepting feedback, stimulating followers intellectually, developing followers, and living by moral standards. For example, in terms of creating a vision, ethical charismatics include followers' concerns and wishes by having them participate in the development of the company vision. By contrast, unethical charismatics develop a vision by themselves solely to meet their personal agendas. One unethical charismatic said, "The key thing is that it is my idea; and I am going to win with it at all costs."[57]

So, what can companies do to reduce the risks associated with unethical charismatics?[58] To start, they need a clearly written code of conduct that is fairly and consistently enforced for all managers. Next, companies should recruit, select, and promote managers with high ethical standards. Also, companies need to train leaders how to value, seek, and use diverse points of view. Leaders and subordinates also need training regarding ethical leader behaviors so abuses can be recognized and corrected. Finally, companies should celebrate and reward people who exhibit ethical behaviors, especially ethical leader behaviors.[59]

**transformational leadership**
leadership that generates awareness and acceptance of a group's purpose and mission and gets employees to see beyond their own needs and self-interest for the good of the group

While charismatic leaders are able to articulate a clear vision, model values consistent with that vision, communicate high performance expectations, and establish very strong relationships between themselves and their followers, **transformational leadership** goes further by generating awareness and acceptance of a group's purpose and mission and by getting employees to see beyond their own needs and self-interest for the good of the group.[60] Transformational leaders, like charismatic leaders, are visionary. However, transformational leaders transform their organizations by getting their followers to accomplish more than they intended and even more than they thought possible. Transformational leaders are able to make their followers feel as if they are a vital part of the organization and can help them see how their jobs fit with the organization's vision. By linking individual and organizational interests, transformational leaders encourage followers to make sacrifices for the organization, because they know that they will prosper when the organization prospers. As shown in Exhibit 17.16, there are four components of transformational leadership: charismatic leadership or idealized influence, inspirational motivation, intellectual stimulation, and individualized consideration.[61]

*Charismatic leadership or idealized influence* means that transformational leaders act as role models for their followers. Because transformational leaders put others' needs ahead of their own and share risks with followers, they are admired, respected, and trusted, and followers want to emulate them. Thus, in contrast to purely charismatic leaders (especially unethical charismatics), transformational leaders can be counted on to do the right thing and maintain high standards for ethical and personal conduct. For example, GE's former CEO, Jack Welch, acted as a role model for his employees (three vice presidents and the heads of GE's 12 businesses) by setting and monitoring specific performance targets for each of them. Each of these top managers also received a detailed, handwritten, two-page performance evaluation from Welch each year. Said Welch, "I did the evaluations on Sunday nights in my library at home. It gave me a chance to reflect on each business." Modeling their behavior after Welch, these top managers did the same with their direct reports. Thomas E. Dunham of GE's Medical Systems said, "Welch preached it from the top, and people saw it at the bottom."[62] Accordingly, Welch served as a role model for all of GE's managers.

*Inspirational motivation* means that transformational leaders motivate and inspire followers by providing meaning and challenge to their work. By clearly communicating expectations and demonstrating commitment to goals, transformational leaders help followers envision future states, such as the organizational vision. In turn, this leads to greater enthusiasm and optimism about the future. For GE's Jack Welch, inspirational

**EXHIBIT 17.16**

COMPONENTS OF TRANSFORMATIONAL LEADERSHIP

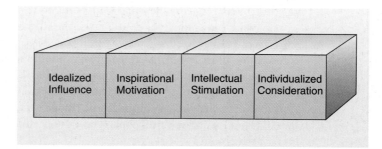

**Be a Good Follower**

David Ogilvy, founder of Olgilvy & Mather, told this story about the importance of being a good follower. He wrote:

On the night before a major battle, the first Duke of Marlborough was reconnoitering the terrain. He and his staff were on horseback. Marlborough dropped his glove. Cadogan, his chief of staff, dismounted, picked up the glove and handed it to Marlborough . . . Later that evening, Marlborough issued his final order: "Cadogan, put a battery of guns where I dropped my glove." "I have already done so," replied Cadogan. He had read Marlborough's mind, and anticipated his order. Cadogan was the kind of follower who makes leadership easy.

**Source:** D. Ogilvy, "Leadership," in *The Book of Business Wisdom*, ed. P. Krass (New York: Wiley, 1997).

motivation was rooted in his belief that everyone at GE could make a difference. Said Welch, "The idea flow from the human spirit is absolutely unlimited. All you have to do is tap into that well. I don't like to use the word efficiency. It's creativity. It's a belief that every person counts."[63] Furthermore, Welch reinforced his beliefs by spreading organizational rewards to all levels. Stock options, which used to be reserved for top managers, were given to 27,000 GE employees. Of those, more than 1,200 (800 below senior management) had options worth more than $1 million. And Welch loved spreading those rewards around. Welch said, "It meant that everyone was getting the rewards, not just a few of us. That's a big deal. We changed their game and their lives. They got their kids' tuition or a second house. That's a real kick."

*Intellectual stimulation* means that transformational leaders encourage followers to be creative and innovative, to question assumptions, and to look at problems and situations in new ways, even if they are different from the leader's ideas. For example, at General Electric's Corporate Executive Council sessions, where GE's top 30 managers meet before the end of each financial quarter, Welch pressed top managers by insisting on candid, unfiltered discussions and opinions from everyone. His executives described these sessions as "food fights" and "free-for-alls." The intent was not to bruise egos or shame poor performers, but to realistically face up to problems that needed solving. Welch also brought managers and employees from GE's 12 businesses together each January in Boca Raton, Florida, to communicate ideas and successes, so that best practices were shared across all parts of GE. The point, again, was to look for good solutions wherever they could be found.

*Individualized consideration* means that transformational leaders pay special attention to followers' individual needs by creating learning opportunities, accepting and tolerating individual differences, encouraging two-way communication and being a good listener. One of the ways in which Jack Welch showed individualized consideration was through the personal, spontaneous, handwritten notes that he sent to people throughout GE. When William Woodburn, who manages GE's industrial diamonds business, turned down a promotion because he didn't want to uproot his teenage daughter, Welch wrote to him, saying, "Bill, we like you for a lot of reasons—one of them is that you are a very special person. You proved it again this morning. Good for you and your lucky family. Make Diamonds a great business and keep your priorities straight." Woodburn responded that this gesture "showed me he cared about me not as a manager but as a person," and "that meant a lot."[64]

Finally, a distinction needs to be drawn between transformational leadership and transactional leadership. While transformational leaders use visionary and inspirational appeals to influence followers, **transactional leadership** is based on an exchange process, in which followers are rewarded for good performance and punished for poor performance. When leaders administer rewards fairly and offer followers the rewards that they want, followers will often reciprocate with effort. However, transactional leaders often overrely on discipline or threats to bring performance up to standards. While this may work in the short run, it's much less effective in the long run. Also, as discussed in Chapters 13 and 16, many leaders and organizations have difficulty successfully linking pay practices to individual performance. The result is that studies consistently show that transformational leadership is much more effective on average than transactional leadership. In the United States, Canada, Japan, and India, and at all organizational levels, from first-level supervisors to upper-level executives, followers view transformational leaders as much better leaders and are much more satisfied when working for them. Furthermore, companies with transformational leaders have significantly better financial performance.[65]

**transactional leadership**
leadership based on an exchange process, in which followers are rewarded for good performance and punished for poor performance

677

Strategic leadership requires visionary, charismatic, and transformational leadership. Visionary leadership creates a positive image of the future that motivates organizational members and provides direction for future planning and goal setting. Charismatic leaders have strong, confident, dynamic personalities that attract followers, enable them to create strong bonds, and inspire followers to accomplish the leader's vision. Followers of ethical charismatic leaders work harder, are more committed and satisfied, are better performers, are more likely to trust their leaders. Followers can be just as supportive and committed to unethical charismatics, but these leaders can pose a tremendous risk for companies. Unethical charismatics control and manipulate followers and do what is best for themselves instead of their organizations. To reduce the risks associated with unethical charismatics, companies need to enforce a clearly written code of conduct; recruit, select, and promote managers with high ethical standards; train leaders how to value, seek, and use diverse points of view; teach everyone in the company to recognize unethical leader behaviors; and celebrate and reward people who exhibit ethical behaviors. Transformational leadership goes beyond charismatic leadership by generating awareness and acceptance of a group's purpose and mission and by getting employees to see beyond their own needs and self-interest for the good of the group. The four components of transformational leadership are charisma or idealized influence, inspirational motivation, intellectual stimulation, and individualized consideration.

## What Really Happened?

At the beginning of the chapter, you read how 83 of the 170 people who worked for Sandler O'Neill, a small financial firm located on the 104th floor of World Trade Center Tower Two, died when the towers collapsed after terrorist attacks on September 11, 2001. Jimmy Dunne, the manager portrayed in this case, had taken a day off and was on the golf course when he learned about the disaster. Right after he got to the clubhouse to watch the news on TV, the towers collapsed, taking the lives of his friends and partners, Chris Quackenbush and Herman Sandler, and leaving him in charge of the company. Read the answers to the opening case to see what really happened and to learn how Jimmy Dunne met this extraordinary leadership challenge.

**How many people didn't get out? We're getting panicked calls from family members who haven't yet talked to their loved ones. What do we do if they didn't get out of the building? How will we take care of their families?**

Leaders generally use two key behaviors to achieve group and organizational goals, consideration and initiating structure, the latter of which will be discussed in the answer to the next question. Consideration is the extent to which leaders are friendly, approachable, supportive, and show concern for employees. Consideration primarily affects subordinates' job satisfaction. Specific leader consideration behaviors include listening to employees' problems and concerns, consulting with employees before making decisions, and treating employees as equals. Consideration is also very similar to the idea of supportive leadership in path-goal theory. Consideration and supportive leadership can lead to improved performance when it increases employee confidence, lowers employee job stress, or improves relations and trust between employees and leaders.

For Jimmy Dunne and the surviving employees of Sandler O'Neill, there was never any question that the company would take care of the families of the coworkers who were killed on September 11. The company immediately

hired grief counselors for them, organized a center to help them go about the grisly task of recovering remains, and established a charity fund to which people could contribute to benefit the families. Many companies affected by the tragedy took similar steps. But Dunne and Sandler O'Neill felt they should do more. Within two weeks of the tragedy, the company sent each deceased employee's family a check paying their salary through the end of the year. It also extended their health benefits for the next five years. Plus, Dunne told the families that it would also pay them the sales commissions and year-end bonuses that their loved ones would have collected had they lived. In the end, the company paid families more than 30 percent of its capital.

Why did Dunne and Sandler O'Neill extend so much consideration to deceased coworkers' families? Said Dunne, "Fifteen years from now, my son will meet the son or daughter of one of our people who died that day, and I will be judged on what that kid tells my son about what Sandler O'Neill did for his family."

**And with our offices gone, how do we keep the business running? We surely can't take care of families if we don't get back in business.**

As mentioned above, leaders use two key behaviors, consideration and initiating structure, to achieve group and organizational goals. Initiating structure is the degree to which a leader structures the roles of followers by setting goals, giving directions, setting deadlines, and assigning tasks. A leader's ability to initiate structure primarily affects subordinates' job performance.

With its primary offices completely destroyed, most of its computerized and paper records vaporized, and with almost half of its workforce dead, Sandler O'Neill's surviving managers and workers faced a tremendous challenge just keeping the company going. But the moment that Jimmy Dunne walked into the company's small office on 48th street, he declared that the company would not only survive, but would find a way to thrive. Said one employee, "He made us feel like, 'I'll show you the path through the trees.'" That first night, Dunne worked till 3 A.M., went home to shower, hug his wife, look in on his sleeping children, and was back at the office in a suit by 5 A.M. to begin rebuilding the company.

Because its survival was at stake, Dunne directed everyone to do everything they could, to call in every favor, to make sure that the company would complete all the major bond issues it was scheduled to complete before September 11. However, with its offices and files completely destroyed, how could they get started, especially in a financial business as complex as theirs? Their first break came in the form of the photographic memory of an office assistant. After answering the company phones for years, she knew the names and phone numbers of key clients from memory. This allowed people to begin working the phones and continue business. The next big break came from competitors, who gave Sandler O'Neill small slices of their business without

asking anything in return. For instance, the benevolence of J.P. Morgan resulted in a $23,000 fee. Numerous other competitors were just as generous. And with the company's survival at risk, Dunne encouraged people to put their pride aside and take any such offers. The third major break came from the large number of layoffs that were occurring on Wall Street at that time. After a year of recession, financial firms laid off thousands of employees. Dunne told a friend at another company, "If there's someone good getting cut, let me know. But only if they're good. I can't waste time on duds." By November, the company had hired bond traders, investment bankers, and researchers, two dozen new employees in all, and its recovery was well under way.

**No one has heard from Chris Quackenbush and Herman Sandler, your best friend and your mentor. If they didn't get out, that means you're in charge. Do you have what it takes to be in charge? You've always played the tough guy. But that's not what's needed now. Can you change to provide the right kind of leadership? You just don't know.**

Every company seems to have a "good cop, bad cop" combination in its leadership team. Prior to September 11, Herman Sandler was the "good cop" who encouraged people and showed patience when they made mistakes. By contrast, Jimmy Dunne was the "bad cop" who delivered bad news, confronted people when they made expensive mistakes, and fired people when it was time for them to go. Dunne once screamed at a trader, "The next time you do something smart, monkeys'll fly out of my a**."

But as the lone remaining member of the leadership team, Jimmy Dunne quickly realized that he couldn't play the "bad cop" any more. Hoping to acquire Herman Sandler's patience and overt friendliness, he began saying, "I need to be more like Herman now." Hoping to acquire Chris Quackenbush's negotiation skills and ability to remain calm, he began saying, "I need

to be more like Chris now." However, leadership researchers disagree on whether leaders have the ability to adapt or change their leadership styles. Fiedler's contingency theory assumes that leadership styles are consistent and difficult to change. Therefore, leaders must be placed in or "matched" to a situation that fits their leadership style. By contrast, path-goal theory, and normative decision theory, assume that leaders are capable of adapting and adjusting their leadership styles to fit the demands of different situations.

Was Jimmy Dunne able to change and adapt his leadership style? In part, yes, and, in part, no. Dunne became more patient and supportive because of the tender emotional state of his employees and his extraordinary commitment to providing for deceased employees' families. However, he remained true to himself by maintaining a strong focus on helping the business survive. For example, less than a week after the attacks, he issued this statement: "For the past several days, Sandler O'Neill employees, families, friends, clients, and competitors have joined together in an amazing way to do everything possible to locate our missing colleagues and to share all new information with their families. At the same time, we have also rallied our team to ensure that our business not only survives, but prospers. The best way we can honor our people is not to let terrorism stand in the way of Sandler O'Neill moving forward."

In the end, Jimmy Dunne did a remarkable job of leading Sandler O'Neill's dedicated managers and employees. Just two months after losing their main office, most of the management team, and half of its work force, the company was again earning a profit. By the end of the year, less than four months after the disaster, the company ended up having a better financial year than the year before, allowing it to pay even larger bonuses and sales commissions to the families of its deceased workers.

**Sources:** K. Brooker, "Starting Over," *Fortune*, 21 January 2002, 50. A. Geller, "Firms Decimated in Attacks Work to Rebuild Their Ranks with Alumni: Widespread Layoffs Help by Providing a Supply of High-Quality Applicants," *St. Louis Post Dispatch* (Associated Press), 24 October 2001, C1. "Company Information: Our Approach," *Sandler O'Neill & Partners, L.P.*, [Online] Available http://www.sandleroneill.com/sandler/asp/control.asp?RequestingFrame=MAIN&RequestedAction=Approach, 25 March 2002. "Family Support," *Sandler O'Neill & Partners, L.P.* [Online] Available http://sandleroneillfamily.com/, 25 March 2002. "Sandler O'Neill Announces Company Open for Business," *Sandler O'Neill & Partners, L.P.* [Online] Available http://sandleroneillfamily.com/press_releases/press091701.htm, 25 March 2002. R. Smith, "Six Months After: At Sandler, A Client Sees Enormous Strain, Tries to Lend a Hand," *The Wall Street Journal*, 8 March 2002, C11.

## Key Terms

achievement-oriented leadership *(664)*

charismatic leadership *(672)*

consideration *(655)*

contingency theory *(658)*

directive leadership *(663)*

ethical charismatics *(674)*

initiating structure *(655)*

leader-member relations *(660)*

leadership *(646)*

leadership neutralizers *(651)*

leadership style *(657)*

leadership substitutes *(651)*

normative decision theory *(666)*

participative leadership *(664)*

path-goal theory *(662)*

position power *(660)*

situational favorableness *(660)*

strategic leadership *(671)*

supportive leadership *(664)*

task structure *(660)*

traits *(652)*

trait theory *(652)*

transactional leadership *(677)*

transformational leadership *(676)*

unethical charismatics *(674)*

visionary leadership *(671)*

## What Would You Do-II

### Sustaining Leadership at Synopsys?

You are the founder and CEO of Synopsys, a $784 million leader in the design and testing of complex integrated circuit (IC) chips. In your company's 15-year history, you have watched it grow from a small, struggling, start-up, to the multi-million dollar company that it is today. It wasn't an easy task, and the company still suffers occasional setbacks, but over time, the company has developed a strong reputation among computer chip manufacturers and, in the process, has amassed a current staff of 3,100 people with operations in 79 locations throughout the world. Your firm's competitive advantage lies in assisting chip manufacturers in their design and testing of IC chips and circuits. Through computer modeling and simulation, your firm helps companies design, test, modify, and re-test complex circuits before a prototype is ever constructed. This service is vital to the chip-making industry since the testing and verification stage can consume 50 to 75 percent of the total design time. Therefore, the sooner chip manufacturers learn that their circuit designs will work, the more profit they will earn, especially if they can eliminate a majority of the "bugs" before production actually begins.

Over the years, your firm's overall success has been due in a large part to its people. In recent years, Synopsys has acquired several small companies, helping to improve the broad array of products and services that your firm provides. However, because of the competitive pressures facing your industry, recruiting and retaining qualified people is a constant battle. Competitors and other firms in the computer industry are always breathing down your neck trying to lure away your talent, and with them, take away your core competencies. Additionally, as the firm continues to grow and the field becomes more competitive, it becomes harder and harder to bring in outsiders to fill higher-level positions. In order to survive in today's competitive environment, a firm needs several layers of experienced managers to facilitate growth and innovation.

With competitive poaching of talent, the leadership problem your firm is experiencing is simply that your pool of leaders is dwindling. Unfortunately, experienced, qualified leaders cannot be hired off of the street overnight: It takes time, money, and effort to find them and develop them. Employees are not always ready for leadership, and even capable employees may not be willing to assume leadership roles. You've got to get them beyond their own self-interests to see the bigger picture and focus on the overall goals of the company.

It is your belief that, over the years, you have developed a transformational leadership style and culture within the firm. As the firm continues to grow, however, you see that it is becoming more and more difficult to sustain this type of an environment. But if Synopsys is to stay at the top of its industry, you're going to have to figure out a way. Perhaps you need to design a formal process or program to develop leaders within the organization. But how do you decide who to develop? You're the CEO, so should you pick the people yourself? Or should you consult your top managers? Maybe you should just rely on employees to express interest.

**If you were the CEO of Synopsys, what would you do to sustain the transformational leadership style that is the hallmark of your firm?**

**Sources:** Synopsys Web site: http://www.synopsys.com. V. Rice, "Catch a Rising Star," *Electronic Business*, August 2001.

## Management Decisions

### Subbing for Leaders

Six months ago when you accepted the job as the president of a small marketing agency, you knew that it would be a tough task. You had no idea, however, that it would be nearly impossible. While interviewing, you conducted some basic research and found that even though the company was profitable, it had a bad reputation of not playing fair in the advertising industry. Many people that you talked to voiced their concerns about the firm, saying that its people were sneaky, backstabbing individuals who would stop at nothing to make a buck. Despite their concerns, you accepted the position, assuming that their perceptions were somewhat biased.

Unfortunately, soon after your arrival, you began to realize that many people's perceptions might not have been far off base. Initially, George, your assistant and the vice president of the company, seemed like a good guy—a little different, possibly even abrasive, but otherwise an okay person. At first his personality didn't pose a problem. Then you began to hear conversations about George's reliance on punishment and manipulation to ensure that the marketing sales force increased their sales revenue each quarter. In fact, the more you listened, the more you heard, and the uneasier you became.

As you began to watch George more closely, you realized that he was definitely an ends-versus-the-means person. His main focus was on increasing advertising dollars for the firm (and eventually for himself), regardless of the tactics used. You also began to notice that during important meetings discussing current customers' marketing strategies, George always did a majority of the talking. Anyone who attempted to interject ideas inconsistent with George's was immediately cut off and publicly scolded. In fact, this morning as you walked past one such meeting, you overheard John, a junior-level marketing agent, propose a new strategy for an important customer. George replied to John in front of the group, saying, "Now you folks see why John is only a junior-level agent after working over 12 years with this firm. Does anyone else have any stupid comments to offer, or can we move on with our meeting?"

As you stood outside of the conference room, you realized that something must be done to change the culture, perception, and success of this firm. Clearly things can't continue as is, but George is a valuable employee despite his shortcomings. Maybe you should have a talk with him about what you expect from leaders. Resolving the problem may mean better matching George's leadership style to another work group within the company. Is that even feasible? You really need to change the culture inside the firm and the perception of the firm from outside. If not, the very existence of the firm will be on the line.

#### Questions

1. What should your expectation be of George as a leader? Is he meeting this expectation?
2. What type of leadership style is George exhibiting? Do you move George out of the leadership role, or do you coach him to change? If you coach him, what leadership style do you try to cultivate in him?
3. Which leadership substitutes could you develop to insulate your company from leadership gaps, such as the one described above?

## Management Decisions

### Learning the Ropes

When you left your position as head of Warner Bros. movie and television studio to take on the challenging job as CEO of Yahoo!, you really didn't expect such a culture shock, not to mention so many company troubles. You knew that Yahoo! was in trouble, with stock prices falling to the double digits, off highs of $273. And your inaugural effort in front of Wall Street analysts did not go well. Despite hours of careful preparation, you were pounded for sticking to closely to your script and not thinking fast enough on your feet. How ironic that Hollywood's executive darling was a behind-the-scenes kind of guy and not comfortable in such a glaring public eye!

Approximately 210 million users log on to Yahoo! properties each month, 87 million have registered personal information with the company, and 37 million use Yahoo! as their home page. That's the good news. Other good news is that you are one of the last three major portals standing, along with MSN and AOL; the rest—Excite, Go, Snap, and Lycos—are on the dot.com ash heap. As the firm has grown, however, so, too, has its organizational structure, which has become unwieldy. With 44 business units, it's hard to keep track of everyone's responsibilities. Restructuring will most certainly be unavoidable.

To top it all off, analysts are calling Yahoo! the growth story that has stopped growing (i.e., beware of dog). The main problems Yahoo! is facing are tied to the collapse of the Internet bubble and the company's reliance on advertising income as a sole revenue stream. In fact, 80 percent of your income comes from Internet advertisers. When money was flowing freely, the sales force at Yahoo! became arrogant, mistreating even important customers. In fact, arrogance became the hallmark of Yahoo!'s reputation, alienating current clients and driving away potential clients. And since Yahoo! doesn't have any proprietary content of its own (like AOL's access to all of its partner Time Warner's media assets), it couldn't afford to lose any of its revenue base. What the company could charge for—its various services—it was giving away for free to users. Yahoo! even decided against a merger with eBay when the going was good!

Now the going's gone. Revenues are off 35 percent, the company lost $84 million in the first nine months of the year, and you may need to lay off up to 12 percent of your work force. And with most other major portals closing up shop, you face stiff competition from MSN and AOL. It's hard not to be discouraged. Growth has stalled because of a lack of vision about the future. Long-term plans created during dot-com fever, when venture capital flowed freely and Yahoo! was Wall Street's darling, are insufficient for the sustained success of the business now. In fact, if pursued to their end, they may destroy the company. So the company must change not only its organizational architecture, but Yahoo! must also create an entirely new business strategy (i.e., reducing reliance on advertising revenue and generating fee-based income).

When you took the position of CEO, you thought enough of your abilities as a leader that you bought one million shares of Yahoo! at $17.62 a share. You're down $6.5 million to date. But you're not disheartened. You really think you can lead this company away from the dot com graveyard.

## Questions

1. As the leader of Yahoo!, what would be your four top priorities?
2. Which leadership theories or ideas seem most relevant to you in this situation?
3. Using the leadership theories or ideas you think most relevant, what actions would you take to begin to address the priorities you identified in question 1?

**Sources:** M. Gunther "The Cheering Fades for Yahoo: Terry Semel Aims to Make It a Great Company. But So Far, The Numbers Don't Add Up," *Fortune,* 12 November 2001, 151; N. Wingfield, "Yahoo Unveils Proposed Restructuring, Reducing Ad Reliance, Cutting 400 Jobs," *The Wall Street Journal,* 16 November 2001, http://wsj.com; B. Stone, "Learning the Ropes: For Two Decades, Terry Semel Had the Best Parking Spot in Hollywood. But to Fix Yahoo, The Ex-Mogul Is Going to Need a Lot More Than His Golden Rolodex," *Newsweek,* 30 July 2001, 38.

## Develop Your Managerial Potential

### Leadership Revisited

You can learn a lot about leadership traits, behaviors, and styles by reading books. But until you're actually in charge, you won't be able to test those ideas for yourself. Likewise, you can learn a tremendous amount about leadership by studying and observing the people who lead you. Until you are actually in the position of leading, however, you won't know if their leadership practices and styles will work for you. In short, when learning about leadership, there is no substitute for leadership experience.

Fortunately, many people are leaders, even if they don't have the title. Many people have younger brothers or sisters, friends, or family members that look up to them and follow their lead. Many employees are respected for their wisdom, knowledge, and ability to solve difficult problems, even though they are not the formal supervisor. By looking back, you may be able to think of a time when you assumed the role as a leader. It may have been in a former job, at a former school, or possibly when you were the member of an extracurricular club, fraternity, sorority, or social organization. In remembering that leadership experience, try to determine what type of a leader you were. Think about ways that you helped solve problems, ways that you worked to inspire and motivate those around you. Were you a leader or more of a manager? Did you consistently apply the same leadership style with all people and all situations or were you able to change leadership styles based on a specific problem or situation? Did your leadership style work? Was it accepted by those around you? What was the context of the situation or job? Were the individuals self-motivated, self-directed, or did you have to provide direction and assistance every step of the way? As you think back on this particular time and experience, consider using the Internet resources listed below to deepen your understanding of your own leadership style and potential. Then answer the questions that follow.

### Internet Resources

You can learn more about your personal leadership style by visiting some or all of the Web sites listed below:

**http://www.nsba.org/sbot/toolkit/LeadSA.html**
A good Web site illustrating qualities of effective leaders.

**http://www.trans-act.com/forms/leadership.htm**
A quick quiz to determine your individual propensity to lead.

**http://www.emode.com/emode/tests/leader.jsp**
A 17-question quiz that ranks your ability to lead.

**http://www.stevesullivan.com/l2.php3**
A 10-question test that determines your knowledge about leadership and provides review material to increase your awareness regarding leadership theories and applications.

To learn more about leadership and to see current articles discussing leadership theories / techniques, visit some or all of the following Web sites listed below:

**http://www.nwlink.com/~donclark/leader/leader.html**
Big Dog's Leadership page provides a basic background on leadership designed for new supervisors and managers.

**http://www.articles911.com**
The leadership category contains free articles on leadership development, improvement, practices, and assessment styles.

**http://www.personal-development.com/articles.htm**
A Web site containing many free articles aimed at developing an individual's leadership style, time management techniques, increasing self esteem, overcoming public speaking anxiety, and much more.

**Questions**

After reviewing some of the informative Web sites listed above, use your knowledge of leadership, your personal leadership style, and information gleaned from previous experiences to answer the following questions:

1. Describe a situation in which you became a leader or assumed a leadership role.
2. What surprises did you discover when assuming this role?
3. Was there anything about being a leader that you initially feared, but was in reality, much easier than you expected?
4. What was the most difficult thing about being a leader?
5. After reading this chapter on leadership, what information could you use that would make you a better leader today than you were back then?

## Study Tip

Your professor and TA are the most valuable resources in your course. If you have questions on the fundamental concepts of leadership, go to office hours. Report back to your study partner or group. For this chapter, you have an Xtra! CNN clip with a case and solutions on your CD. It's about GE's CEO succession planning from Jack Welch to Jeff Immelt. Watch the clip, read the case, and work the questions.

CHAPTER

# 18

# Managing Communication

## What Would You Do?

**Headquarters of Mutuals.com, Dallas, Texas.** When you started in the investment business, you worked for a traditional stock brokerage service where you became the top-selling broker. The only problem was that when you made money, it was at the expense of your clients. The sales commission that you earned each time that your clients purchased stocks, bonds, or other financial securities encouraged you to encourage them to trade too often or buy investments they didn't need. So, despite being the top broker in the firm, you quickly concluded that while sales commissions were great for your earnings, they were costing your clients lots of money and causing them to make bad financial decisions.

So you decided to start your own company, Mutuals.com. Unlike most financial and investment companies, Mutuals.com does not charge commissions of any kind. Instead, it offers flat-fee services. Consistent with the company's vision to "always put client needs ahead of our own," customers pay one fee and have access to unbiased advice (since commissions aren't paid, the only incentive advisors have is to choose investments that are best for the client), hundreds of thousands of pages of research and data, and direct access to 11,000 different mutual funds, all sold on a no-load, no-commission basis.

Starting a company is never easy, but Mutuals.com got off to a great start. Because of your success as a stockbroker, you were able to leverage your contacts and quickly raise $14 million in seed money. Plus, during the company's first six years in business, sales rose an average of 113 percent per year! Things should be great—but they aren't. Despite fantastic sales growth and plenty of on-hand cash, the company has lost money each year. Spending is wildly out of control. For example, somebody came up with the idea to use TV commercials to advertise the firm. Before you knew it, the firm had spent $400,000 to create a commercial and buy commercial time. It seemed like a great idea, but the commercials have brought in almost no new business. No matter how much you plead, salaries, travel, and other expenses just keep growing faster than your fast-growing revenues.

Costs aren't the only problem, though. Rapid growth means that the company isn't as small as it used to be. New employees are being hired almost as fast as you can find them. So, unlike when the company was just starting, you don't know the employees as well as you used to. In fact, you are beginning to sense that employees aren't as comfortable with you as they were before. Furthermore, surprise problems are coming across your desk. In the past, people were comfortable coming to you with problems. And they'd come to you early enough that the

problems were still small and manageable. These days, with employees and managers reluctant to let you know what's going on, the problems that come across your desk are much bigger and much more difficult to fix. Plus, to make things worse, one of your favorite employees is leaving the company. When you asked him why, he said that work wasn't fun anymore, that growth had changed the company, and that you don't seem to care about employees like you used to when the company was just starting.

Well, if Mutuals.com is ever going to be successful, things are going to have to change. But how can you get employees to tell you what's wrong? How can you send the message that you personally care about employees' thoughts and feelings? How can you communicate the message that everyone has to find ways to control costs, and do it in a way that doesn't build resentment?

**Sources:** E. Barker, "Cheap Executive Officer," *Inc.* [Online] Available http://www.inc.com/incmagazine/articles/24053.html, 1 April 2002. L. Buchanan, "Collecting Information about Individuals and Transforming It into Tailored Offerings Is the Stuff of One-To-One Marketing. Now Companies Are Taking That Concept and Focusing It on Their Own Employees," *Inc.*, 1 October 2001, 82. N. Martin, "Writing a New Chapter: An Author Tries to Make the Leap from Investment Theorist to Adviser," *Barron's*, 6 November 2000, 28. P. Rivera, "Financial Adviser Enjoys Firm's Emphasis on Goals of the Client," *Dallas Morning News*, 27 May 2001, 10L. S. Frank, "Playing the Net," *The Wall Street Journal*, 27 August 2000.

Like the CEO of Mutuals.com, it's estimated that managers spend over 80 percent of their day communicating with others.[1] Indeed, much of the basic management process—making things happen; meeting the competition; organizing people, projects, and processes; and leading—cannot be performed without effective communication. If this weren't reason enough to study communication, consider that effective oral communication, such as listening, following instructions, conversing, and giving feedback, is the most important skill for college graduates who are entering the work force.[2] Furthermore, across all industries, poor communication skills is the single most important reason that people do not advance in their careers.[3] Finally, communication is especially important for top managers. Mark DeMichele, president of Arizona Public Service Company, said, "Communication is the key to success. CEOs can have good ideas, a vision, and a plan. But they also have to be able to communicate those plans to people who work for them."[4]

This chapter begins by examining the role of perception in communication and how perception can make it difficult for managers to achieve effective communication. Next, you'll read about the communication process and the various kinds of communication found in most organizations. In the last half of the chapter, the focus is on improving communication in organizations. You'll learn about the significant barriers to effective one-on-one communication and organization-wide communication. But, more importantly, you'll learn ways to overcome those barriers, too.

# What Is Communication?

Five years ago, at Citibank offices throughout Malaysia, employee turnover was 27 percent per year, higher than the industry average, and staff morale and customer loyalty were both below 50 percent. Today, however, turnover is almost nonexistent. Furthermore, employee morale, which has surged to 80 percent, and customer loyalty, which tops 89 percent, are higher in Malaysia than in any other Citibank offices in the emerging markets of Asia, Latin America, and Africa. What accounts for this dramatic difference? Lunch. Or what management calls "pulse lunches," in which the top managers in each Citibank market take employees' "pulses" by listening to their concerns at lunch and then addressing them soon after. For example, as a result of these "pulse lunches," Citibank Malaysia now has employees formally appraise their boss's performance and gives time off to employees after they've worked especially long hours on important projects. And, to encourage more feedback and prove that management is listening, the top managers who host pulse lunches typically send out post-lunch newsletters that summarize employee concerns without naming names.[5]

**communication**
the process of transmitting information from one person or place to another

**Communication** is the process of transmitting information from one person or place to another. Citibank's "pulse lunches," which the company now uses in 102 different countries, communicate issues and problems directly from employees to top managers. Success, however, was not immediate. At first, Citibank's Malaysian employees were suspicious, wondering if their comments would be kept confidential or if management would punish people for being critical or speaking out. Mohd Rahmat, who attended one of the first lunches, said, "No one could believe that the [local] CEO wanted to come and talk to employees." Today, though, perceptions have changed because Citibank managers have worked hard to address employees' problems.[6]

*After reading the next two sections, you should be able to*
1. *explain the role that perception plays in communication and communication problems.*
2. *describe the communication process and the various kinds of communication in organizations.*

## 1. Perception and Communication Problems

One study shows that when *employees* were asked whether their supervisor gives recognition for good work, 13 percent said their supervisor gives a pat on the back, while 14

686

# BeenThereDoneThat

## How Men and Women Communicate at Work

**Deborah Tannen, author and socio-linguist, believes that men tend to view conversations as "negotiations" in which they try to achieve status and power and maintain independence. In contrast, women view conversations as a way to connect with people, to find commonality and build networks of connection and intimacy. In this interview with Richard Koonce, Tannen discusses the different ways that men and women communicate in the workplace.**

**Q:** How much do you think current communication problems in the workplace are related to gender?

**A:** Gender cross-cuts everything else. You could say that all workplace problems are about power differentials. You tell one of your staff what to do and he or she doesn't do it. Or you think your boss makes unreasonable demands. All of those things are filtered through gender. The way you expect a male boss to talk is different from how you expect a female boss to talk. You might not realize that if your boss were the other sex and talking to you in the same way, you would have a different reaction.

**Q:** You also say that no one conversational style is best and that men and women can learn important things from each other's styles.

**A:** To say that one conversational style is better than another is like saying Spanish is better than French. In most organizations, a style, usually a predominantly male one, was established as the norm before women arrived in great numbers and positions of authority. Women weren't there when the rules were set so, in that sense, women's and men's styles aren't considered equally valid.

**Q:** Given that male imprint on many corporate cultures, should women adopt male styles of communication if they want to get ahead?

**A:** There is no one right way to communicate. Women bring many styles to the workplace that are effective, sometimes more effective than the norm. They tend to make people feel included, ask for their input, and give praise—things that all people seem to like. You don't find men complaining that their bosses praise them too much. There are women who adopt typically male styles, and that works great. They're happy that way. Other women find that if they adopt male styles, they get negative responses. So, they don't feel comfortable doing that. And there are women who say, "I stick with my style and do a good job. The people I work with learn that's me." What matters is the specific situation—what a woman feels comfortable doing and how people around her react.

**Q:** How do you counsel men who want to be more effective at managing women?

**A:** If you're managing people, it's important to remember that not everyone has the same style. What's right for one person may not be right for other people. I recall someone whom I interviewed and observed, who thought he had the right style at work. Once a day, every day, he checked in with everyone who worked for him. Some people, generally men, thought that was too much. They felt that he was looking over their shoulders and didn't trust them to do a good job. They asked, "Why are you always coming in here to check on me?" For other staff members, generally women, it wasn't enough. They said, "You're not interested. You don't spend any time. Why should I be interested if you're not?" And for some people, his style was just right.

So, developing awareness that people have different styles is important. Try to raise your own sensitivity to the kind of responses you get so that you can gauge: This seems to be working well with this person, I'm okay. Or, this person isn't reacting well; what can I do differently? In some cases, you need to meta-communicate—in other words, talk to people about what you're doing.

**Q:** Are there differences in managing men and women that managers should be aware of?

**A:** There are things women have to watch out for in managing men and things men have to watch out for in managing women. When I was doing research for 9-5, I found that women expect more feedback from male bosses than they sometimes get. So, it's important for male bosses to tell women staff members when they're doing a good job and praise them if things are going well. In comparison, a lot of men told me that the best thing to do is hire good people and get out of their way. But not every man or woman is going to fit into these profiles.

**Q:** So, don't take a cookie-cutter approach to managing people based on gender?

**A:** Right. Treating all women the same is just as bad as treating women as men. You need to see individual differences in people. Women who manage men, however, probably do want to be aware that many men are sensitive to being told what to do by women. Women managers have to find a way to deal with that. Some women find a way to tell people what to do without actually giving orders.

**Source:** R. Koonce, "Language, Sex, and Power: Women and Men in the Workplace," *Training & Development* 51 (1997): 34–39.

percent said their supervisor gives sincere and thorough praise. But when the *supervisors* of these employees were asked if they give recognition for good work, 82 percent said they gave pats on the back, while 80 percent said that they give sincere and thorough praise.[7] Given that these managers and employees worked closely together, how could they have had such different perceptions of something as simple as praise?

*Let's learn more about perception and communication problems by examining the 1.1 basic perception process, 1.2 perception problems, how we 1.3 perceive others and 1.4 ourselves, and how all of these factors make it difficult for managers to achieve effective communication.*

### 1.1 Basic Perception Process

**perception**
the process by which individuals attend to, organize, interpret, and retain information from their environments

As shown in Exhibit 18.1, **perception** is the process by which individuals attend to, organize, interpret, and retain information from their environments. And since communication is the process of transmitting information from one person or place to another, perception is obviously a key part of communication. However, perception can be a key obstacle to communication, as well.

As people perform their jobs, they are exposed to a wide variety of informational stimuli, such as emails, direct conversations with the boss or coworkers, rumors heard over lunch, stories about the company in the press, or a video broadcast of a speech from the CEO to all employees. However, exposure to an informational stimulus is no guarantee that an individual will pay attention or attend to that stimulus. People experience stimuli through their own **perceptual filters**—the personality-, psychology-, or experience-based differences that influence them to ignore or pay attention to particular stimuli. Because of filtering, people exposed to the same information will often disagree about what they saw or heard. For example, every major stadium in the National Football League has a huge TV monitor on which fans can watch replays. As the slow motion videotape is replayed on the stadium monitor, you can often hear cheers *and* boos, as fans of both teams perceive the same replay in completely different ways. This happens

**perceptual filters**
the personality-, psychology-, or experience-based differences that influence people to ignore or pay attention to particular stimuli

*EXHIBIT 18.1*

BASIC PERCEPTION PROCESS

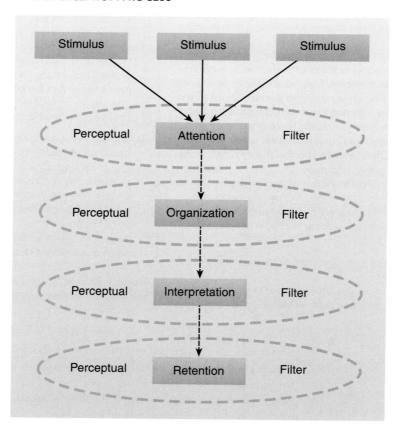

because sports fans' perceptual filters predispose them to attend to stimuli that support their team and not their opponents.

And the same perceptual filters that affect whether we believe our favorite teams were "robbed" by the referees also affect communication, that is, the transmitting of information from one person or place to another. As shown in Exhibit 18.1, perceptual filters affect each part of the *perception process*: attention, organization, interpretation, and retention.

*Attention* is the process of noticing or becoming aware of particular stimuli. Because of perceptual filters, we attend to some stimuli and not others. *Organization* is the process of incorporating new information (from the stimuli that you notice) into your existing knowledge. Because of perceptual filters, we are more likely to incorporate new knowledge that is consistent with what we already know or believe. *Interpretation* is the process of attaching meaning to new knowledge. Because of perceptual filters, our preferences and beliefs strongly influence the meaning we attach to new information (e.g., "This must mean that top management supports our project."). Finally, *retention* is the process of remembering interpreted information. In other words, retention is what we recall and commit to memory after we have perceived something. Of course, perceptual filters also affect retention, that is, what we're likely to remember in the end.

For instance, imagine that you missed the first 10 minutes of a TV show and that you turned on your TV to a scene in which two people were talking to each other in a living room. As they talked, they walked around the room and picked up and then put down various items, some of which were valuable, such as a ring, a watch, and a credit card, and some of which appeared to be drug-related, such as a water pipe for smoking marijuana. In fact, this situation was depicted on videotape in a well-known study that manipulated people's perceptual filters.[8] One third of the study participants were told that these people were there to rob the apartment. Another third of the participants were told that police were on their way to conduct a drug raid and that the people in the apartment were getting rid of incriminating evidence. The remaining third of study participants were told that these people were simply waiting for a friend to show up.

After watching the video, participants were asked to list all of the objects from the video that they could remember. Not surprisingly, the different perceptual filters (theft, drug raid, and waiting for a friend) affected what the study participants attended to, how they organized the information, how they interpreted the information, and ultimately what objects they remembered from the video. People who thought a theft was in process were more likely to remember the valuable objects in the video. Those who thought a drug raid was imminent were more likely to remember drug-related objects. There was no discernable pattern to the items remembered by those who thought that the people in the video were simply waiting for a friend.

In short, because of perception and perceptual filters, people are likely to pay attention to different things, organize and interpret what they pay attention to differently, and finally, remember things differently. Consequently, even when people are exposed to the same communications (e.g., organizational memos, discussions with managers, customers, etc.), they can end up with very different perceptions and understandings. This is why communication can be so difficult and frustrating for managers. Let's review some of the communication problems created by perception and perceptual filters.

### 1.2 Perception Problems

Perception creates communication problems for organizations, because people exposed to the same communication and information can end up with completely different ideas and understandings. Two of the most common perception problems in organizations are selective perception and closure.

At work, we are constantly bombarded with sensory stimuli—the phone ringing, people talking in the background, the sounds of our computers dinging as new email arrives, people calling our names, and so forth. As limited processors of information, we

**selective perception**
the tendency to notice and accept objects and information consistent with our values, beliefs, and expectations, while ignoring or screening out or not accepting inconsistent information

cannot possibly notice, receive, and interpret all of this information. As a result, we attend to and accept some stimuli but screen out and reject others. However, this isn't a random process. **Selective perception** is the tendency to notice and accept objects and information consistent with our values, beliefs, and expectations, while ignoring or screening out inconsistent information.

For example, United Airlines sometimes shows a video of swimming fish as its passengers board its planes. Bob Williams, United's manager of in-flight entertainment, said, "We picked the fish because some psychological research says it's soothing." However, because of selective perception, passengers haven't viewed it that way. Kyle MacLean, who regularly flies United, said, "The first time I saw it, I thought it was really odd. And the more you fly, the more irritating it gets." Furthermore, passengers hated the "soothing" music, too. Frequent United customer John Goldwater said that on one flight, "There must have been 20 people coming back up the aisle asking them to turn it off. At first, the flight attendants were reluctant, but when it became obvious that the flight was going to be delayed, they turned it off."[9]

**closure**
tendency to fill in gaps of missing information by assuming that what we don't know is consistent with what we already know

Once we have initial information about a person, event, or process, **closure** is the tendency to fill in the gaps where information is missing, that is, to assume that what we don't know is consistent with what we already know. If employees are told that budgets must be cut by 10 percent, they may automatically assume that 10 percent of employees will lose their jobs, too, even if that isn't the case. Not surprisingly, when closure occurs, people sometimes "fill in the gaps" with inaccurate information, and this can create problems for organizations.

For example, J.B. Hunt is one of the largest trucking firms in the nation. Historically, the company has been perceived as one that only hires inexperienced drivers because of its driving school (to teach people how to drive semi-trucks), because it limits its drivers to a top speed of 59 MPH (to increase gas mileage and reduce accidents), and because its drivers drive underpowered, "cab-over" trucks (where the truck has a flat front, like a bus). Truck driver Carl Jackson said, "On the CB, you would hear all kinds of jokes about J.B. Hunt drivers. These guys don't want to work for someone who is the brunt of so many jokes. It's a little dumb, but I believe that is the problem of recruiting drivers." He also said, "If they would snaz up the trucks, they would be able to overcome the stigma associated with driving for them." And while the company disputes this, it recognized that this negative perception was widespread among experienced truckers, and that it was preventing the company from hiring all of the truck drivers it needed. So, to dispel these perceptions, it closed its truck driving school to discourage brand new truck drivers from applying and then raised driver pay by 33 percent to attract experienced truck drivers.[10]

### 1.3 Perceptions of Others

**attribution theory**
theory that states that we all have a basic need to understand and explain the causes of other people's behavior

**Attribution theory** says that we all have a basic need to understand and explain the causes of other people's behavior.[11] In other words, we need to know why people do what they do. And, according to attribution theory, we use two general reasons or attributions to explain people's behavior: an *internal attribution*, in which behavior is thought to be voluntary or under the control of the individual, and an *external attribution*, in which behavior is thought to be involuntary and outside of the control of the individual.

**defensive bias**
the tendency for people to perceive themselves as personally and situationally similar to someone who is having difficulty or trouble

For example, have you ever seen anyone changing a flat tire on the side of the road and thought to yourself, "What rotten luck—somebody's having a bad day"? If you did, you perceived the person through an external attribution known as the defensive bias. The **defensive bias** is the tendency for people to perceive themselves as personally and situationally similar to someone who is having difficulty or trouble.[12] And, when we identify with the person in a situation, we tend to use external attributions (i.e., the situation) to explain the person's behavior. For instance, since flat tires are fairly common, it's easy to perceive ourselves in that same situation and put the blame on external causes, such as running over a nail.

Now, let's assume a different situation, this time in the workplace:

> A utility company worker puts a ladder on a utility pole and then climbs up to do his work. As he's doing his work, he falls from the ladder and seriously injures himself.[13]

Answer this question: Who or what caused the accident? If you thought, "It's not the worker's fault. Anybody could fall from a tall ladder," then you're still operating from a defensive bias in which you see yourself as personally and situationally similar to someone who is having difficulty or trouble. In other words, you made an external attribution by attributing the accident to an external cause, meaning the situation.

However, most accident investigations end up blaming the worker (i.e., an internal attribution) and not the situation (i.e., an external attribution). Typically, 60 to 80 percent of workplace accidents each year are blamed on "operator error," that is, the employees themselves. However, more complete investigations usually show that workers are really only responsible for 30 percent to 40 percent of all workplace accidents.[14] Why would accident investigators be so quick to blame workers? Because they are committing the **fundamental attribution error**, which is the tendency to ignore external causes of behavior and to attribute other people's actions to internal causes.[15] In other words, when investigators examine the possible causes of an accident, they're much more likely to assume that the accident is a function of the person and not the situation.

Which attribution, the defensive bias or the fundamental attribution error, are workers likely to make when something goes wrong? In general, as shown in Exhibit 18.2, workers are more likely to perceive events and explain behavior from a defensive bias. Because they do the work themselves, and because they see themselves as similar to others who make mistakes, have accidents, or are otherwise held responsible for things that go wrong at work, workers are likely to attribute problems to external causes, such as failed machinery, poor support, or inadequate training. By contrast, because they are typically observers (who don't do the work themselves), and because they see themselves

**fundamental attribution error**
the tendency to ignore external causes of behavior and to attribute other people's actions to internal causes

EXHIBIT 18.2

DEFENSIVE BIAS AND FUNDAMENTAL ATTRIBUTION ERROR

The Boss
That new employee isn't very good. I may have to get rid of him if his sales don't improve.

Fundamental Attribution Error—
the tendency to ignore external causes of behavior and to attribute other people's actions to internal causes

The Employee
That's the third sale I've lost this week because we don't have inventory!

Defensive Bias—
the tendency for people to perceive themselves as personally and situationally similar to someone who is having difficulty or trouble

The Co-worker
How can they expect us to make sales if they don't have hot-selling inventory in stock? We can't sell what's not there.

Defensive Bias—
the tendency for people to perceive themselves as personally and situationally similar to someone who is having difficulty or trouble

as situationally and personally different from workers, managers tend to commit the fundamental attribution error and blame mistakes, accidents, and other things that go wrong on workers (i.e., an internal attribution).

Consequently, in most workplaces, when things go wrong, the natural response is one in which workers and managers can be expected to take completely opposite views. Therefore, together, the defensive bias, which is typically used by workers, and the fundamental attribution error, which is typically made by managers, represent a significant challenge to effective communication and understanding in organizations.

### 1.4 Self-Perception

A manager at Exxon Corporation decided that he wanted to find a way to help his poor-performing employees improve their performance. So he sat down with each one of them and, in a positive, nonconfrontational way, explained that "I'm here to help you improve." Most of his employees took his offer in the spirit it was meant and accepted his help. However, one employee burst into tears, because no one had ever told her that her performance needed improvement. In fact, her hour-long outburst was so emotional that her manager decided that he would never "criticize" her again.[16]

The **self-serving bias** is the tendency to overestimate our value by attributing successes to ourselves (internal causes) and attributing failures to others or the environment (external causes).[17] As the example with the upset Exxon employee illustrates, the self-serving bias can make it especially difficult for managers to talk to employees about performance problems. In general, people have a need to maintain a positive self-image. This need is so strong that when people seek feedback at work, they typically want verification of their worth (rather than information about performance deficiencies) or assurance that mistakes or problems haven't been their fault.[18] And when managerial communication threatens people's positive self-image, they can become defensive and emotional. In turn, they quit listening, and communication becomes ineffective. In the second half of the chapter, which focuses on improving communication, we'll explain ways in which managers can minimize this self-serving bias and improve effective one-on-one communication with employees.

**self-serving bias**
the tendency to over-estimate our value by attributing successes to ourselves (internal causes) and attributing failures to others or the environment (external causes)

## Review 1
### Perception and Communication Problems

Perception is the process by which people attend to, organize, interpret, and retain information from their environments. However, perception is not a straightforward process. Because of perceptual filters, such as selective perception and closure, people exposed to the same information stimuli often end up with very different perceptions and understandings. Perception-based differences can also lead to differences in the attributions (internal or external) that managers and workers make when explaining workplace behavior. In general, workers are more likely to explain behavior from a defensive bias, in which they attribute problems to external causes (i.e., the situation). Managers, on the other hand, tend to commit the fundamental attribution error, attributing problems to internal causes (i.e., the worker associated with a mistake or error). Consequently, when things go wrong, it's common for managers to blame workers and for workers to blame the situation or context in which they do their jobs. Finally, this problem is compounded by a self-serving bias that leads people to attribute successes to internal causes and failures to external causes. So when workers receive negative feedback from managers, they can become defensive and emotional and not hear what their managers have to say. In short, perceptions and attributions represent a significant challenge to effective communication and understanding in organizations.

## 2. Kinds of Communication

In Oviedo, Florida, the city stopped construction of a 24-unit apartment complex when workers accidentally cut down 10 trees. The trees to be kept were marked with ribbons. However, the work crew misunderstood and thought that the ribbons meant the trees

Although ensuring that children traveling alone get to their destination is a service common to all airlines, communication breakdowns occur more often than one would think. Rachel Kurtz, pictured here, was lost in United Airlines system. When her father went to the Lansing, Michigan, airport to greet her, another Rachel got off the plane. When she finally arrived home, the 12-year-old Rachel Kurtz had been flying for 12 hours.

AP/WIDE WORLD PHOTO

*should* be cut down. David Materna, president of the apartment complex, said, "Obviously, the errors were made in our chain of command," and that they were caused by "a very unfortunate misunderstanding and miscommunication" between his supervisors and his employees.[19]

When her nine- and 12-year-old sons flew by themselves from Los Angeles to Minnesota to attend summer camp, Tiiu Lukk paid an additional $25 per ticket so that American Airlines' staff members would help the boys get to their connecting flight in Dallas and to the camp bus after arriving in Minnesota. However, when she called the camp to confirm their arrival, her sons hadn't arrived. Over the next six hours, no one at American Airlines knew where her sons were. The boys turned up at the Minnesota airport after missing a connecting flight in Dallas (and after the company failed to keep track of them as promised).

In an incident even more troublesome, America West Airlines placed an 11-year-old girl on a connecting flight headed in the wrong direction. It took 12 more hours of flying for the airline to get her to her original destination at 7 A.M. the next day. America West called the "communication breakdown" an "inexcusable mistake."[20]

In all three of these situations, the communication process between senders and receivers broke down at some point. The trees were accidentally cut down because of a misunderstanding about the meaning of the ribbons tied around them. Children flying by themselves missed their connecting flights or were put on the wrong flight because information in the booking reservations system was incorrect or not relayed to the appropriate people. Miscommunication is possible with every kind of communication.

*Let's learn more about the different kinds of communication by examining 2.1 the communication process, 2.2 formal communication channels, 2.3 informal communication channels, 2.4 coaching and counseling or one-on-one communication, and 2.5 nonverbal communication.*

## 2.1 The Communication Process

Earlier in the chapter, we defined *communication* as the process of transmitting information from one person or place to another. Exhibit 18.3 displays a model of the communication

693

EXHIBIT 18.3

## THE INTERPERSONAL COMMUNICATION PROCESS

**Sender**      **Feedback to Sender**      **Receiver**

Message to be Conveyed

Encode Message

Transmit Message

Noise

Message that was Understood

Decode Message

Receive Message

**Communication Channel**

process and its major components: the sender (message to be conveyed, encoding the message, transmitting the message), the receiver (received message, decoded message, and the message that was understood), and noise, which interferes with the communication process.

The communication process begins when a sender thinks of a message he or she wants to convey to another person. This could be what the sender wants someone else to know ("The meeting has been changed to 3:00 P.M."), to do ("Make sure to include last quarter's financial information in the proposal."), or to not do ("Sorry, the budget is tight. You'll have to fly coach rather than business class."). The next step is to encode the message. **Encoding** means putting a message into a written, verbal, or symbolic form that can be recognized and understood by the receiver. The sender then transmits the message via *communication channels*, such as the telephone or face-to-face communication, which allows the sender to receive immediate feedback; or email (text messages and file attachments), fax, beepers, voice mail, memos, and letters, in which senders must wait for receivers to respond.

If the message is received—and because of technical difficulties (e.g., fax down, dead battery on the mobile phone, inability to read email attachments) or people-based transmission problems (e.g., forgetting to pass on the message), messages often aren't—the next step is for the receiver to decode the message. **Decoding** is the process by which the receiver translates the written, verbal, or symbolic form of the message into an understood message. However, the message, as understood by the receiver, isn't always the same message that was intended by the sender. Because of different experiences or perceptual filters, receivers may attach a completely different meaning to a message than was intended.

The last step of the communication process occurs when the receiver gives the sender feedback. **Feedback to sender** is a return message to the sender that indicates the receiver's understanding of the message (of what the receiver was supposed to know, to do, or to not do). Feedback makes senders aware of possible miscommunications and enables them to continue communicating until the receiver understands the intended message.

Unfortunately, feedback doesn't always occur in the communication process. Complacency and overconfidence about the ease and simplicity of communication can lead senders and receivers to simply assume that they share a common understanding of the message and to not use feedback to improve the effectiveness of their communication. This is a serious mistake, especially since messages and feedback are always transmitted

**encoding**
putting a message into a written, verbal, or symbolic form that can be recognized and understood by the receiver

**694**

**decoding**
the process by which the receiver translates the written, verbal, or symbolic form of a message into an understood message

**feedback to sender**
in the communication process, a return message to the sender that indicates the receiver's understanding of the message

**noise**
anything that interferes with the transmission of the intended message

with and against a background of noise. **Noise** is anything that interferes with the transmission of the intended message. Noise can occur if

1. the sender isn't sure about what message to communicate.
2. the message is not clearly encoded.
3. the wrong communication channel is chosen.
4. the message is not received or decoded properly.
5. the receiver doesn't have the experience or time to understand the message.

When managers wrongly assume that communication is easy, they reduce communication to something called the "conduit metaphor."[21] Strictly speaking, conduit is a pipe or tube that protects electrical wire. The **conduit metaphor** refers to the mistaken assumption that senders can pipe their intended messages directly into the heads of receivers with perfect clarity and without noise or perceptual filters interfering with the receivers' understanding of the message. However, this just isn't possible. Even if managers could telepathically direct their thoughts straight into receivers' heads, there would still be misunderstandings and communication problems because, depending on how they're used, words and symbols typically have multiple meanings. For example, Exhibit 18.4 shows several meanings of an extremely common word, "fine." Depending on how you use it, "fine" can mean a penalty, a good job, that something is delicate, small, pure, flimsy, or that something is okay.

**conduit metaphor**
the mistaken assumption that senders can pipe their intended messages directly into the heads of receivers with perfect clarity and without noise or perceptual filters interfering with the receivers' understanding of the message

In summary, the conduit metaphor causes problems in communication by making managers too complacent and confident in their ability to easily and accurately transfer messages to receivers. Managers who want to be effective communicators need to carefully choose words and symbols that will help receivers derive the intended meaning of a message. Furthermore, they need to be aware of all steps of the communication process, beginning with the sender (message to be conveyed, encoding the message, transmitting the message) and ending with the receiver (received message, decoded message, understanding the message, and using feedback to communicate what was understood).

### 2.2 Formal Communication Channels

**formal communication channel**
the system of official channels that carry organizationally approved messages and information

The **formal communication channel** is the system of official channels that carry organizationally approved messages and information. Organizational objectives, rules, policies, procedures, instructions, commands, and requests for information are all transmitted via the formal communication system or "channel." There are three formal communication channels: downward communication, upward communication, and horizontal communication.[22]

**downward communication**
communication that flows from higher to lower levels in an organization

**Downward communication** flows from higher to lower levels in an organization. Downward communication is used to issue orders down the organizational hierarchy, to

---

| EXHIBIT 18.4 | |
|---|---|
| | MEANINGS OF THE WORD "FINE" |

1. If you exceed the 55 mph speed limit, you may have to pay a fine (meaning a penalty).
2. During the playoffs, Shaquille O'Neal turned in a fine performance (meaning excellent).
3. The machine has to run at a slow speed, because the tolerance is extremely fine (meaning tight).
4. It is difficult to put this puzzle together, since many of the pieces are so fine (meaning small).
5. Recently, experiments have been conducted on manufacturing certain drugs in space. It is hoped that these drugs, as compared to those manufactured on Earth, will be extremely fine (meaning pure).
6. Be careful when you handle that antique book. Its pages are extremely fine (meaning flimsy).
7. That's fine with me (meaning okay).

give organizational members job-related information, to give managers and workers performance reviews from upper managers, and to clarify organizational objectives and goals.[23] When an economic downturn quickly produced a significant drop in sales at Agilent, a technology company, CEO Ned Barnholt pulled together his top managers. Together, they decided that their first strategy would be to freeze hiring, cut expenses, and cut temporary workers. Then, through emails, the twice-weekly company newsletter, and a speech played over the public-address system at all Agilent facilities, Barnholt explained why the cuts were necessary, how the cuts would help the company, and then encouraged the troops to cut costs any way they could. Agilent managers reinforced the message at "coffee talks," the regular brainstorming meetings that they hold with their employees. Employees responded by using Web sites to house data electronically (to avoid printing costs), by staying with friends and family when on company travel (to avoid hotel charges), and by bringing bags of potato chips to company recruiting events (to avoid costly catering charges). Within months, thanks to effective downward communicating travel expenses dropped by 50 percent, whereas purchases of personal computers had dropped by 70 percent.[24]

**upward communication**
communication that flows from lower to higher levels in an organization

**Upward communication** flows from lower levels to higher levels in an organization. Upward communication is used to give higher-level managers feedback about operations, issues, and problems; to help higher-level managers assess organizational performance and effectiveness; to encourage lower-level managers and employees to participate in organizational decision making; and to give those at lower levels the chance to share their concerns with higher-level authorities. For example, after several billion dollars in losses, Delta Airlines chairman Ronald W. Allen announced a strategic goal of "Leadership 7.5." This goal was concerned with getting Delta's costs down from 9.26 cents per seat-mile (the cost of flying one passenger one mile) to 7.5 cents per seat-mile. Eventually, this cost-cutting strategy returned Delta to profitability. However, in an interview, when he was asked whether his cost-cutting program had upset and angered long-time Delta employees (many of whom had been laid off to cut costs), he responded, "But so be it." Delta's pilots, flight attendants, and mechanics responded angrily by sporting "So Be It" buttons to let Delta's board members, all of whom regularly flew the airline, know that they resented his cavalier attitude. In fact, Delta's board became so worried about the anger that its employees had toward Allen that they forced him into early retirement at the age of 55.[25]

**horizontal communication**
communication that flows among managers and workers who are at the same organizational level

696

**Horizontal communication** flows among managers and workers who are at the same organizational level. For instance, horizontal communication occurs when the day shift supervisor comes in at 7:30 A.M. for a half-hour discussion with the midnight shift supervisor who leaves at 8:00 A.M., or when the regional marketing director meets with the regional accounting director to discuss costs and plans for a new marketing campaign. Horizontal communication helps facilitate coordination and cooperation between different parts of a company and allows coworkers to share relevant information. It also helps people at the same level resolve conflicts and solve problems without involving high levels of management. At Oracle Software, Ray Lane implemented a program called "Vision and Values" that structured company rules regarding interpersonal communication. Because the company had grown to more than 20,000 employees, it had to stop employees from taking problems straight to founder and CEO Larry Ellison. This worked well while the company was small, but produced bottlenecks and slow decisions now that it was large. So, according to "Vision and Values," horizontal communication became the first step in problem solving. In fact, employees were not allowed to elevate problems and issues to higher levels unless they communicated first with managers and workers at their organizational level.[26]

In general, what can managers do to improve formal communication? First, decrease reliance on downward communication. Second, increase chances for upward communication by increasing personal contact with lower-level managers and workers. Third, like at Oracle software, encourage much greater use of horizontal communication. Finally, be aware of the problems associated with downward, upward, and horizontal communication, some of which are listed in Exhibit 18.5.

EXHIBIT 18.5

COMMON PROBLEMS WITH DOWNWARD, UPWARD, AND
HORIZONTAL COMMUNICATION

## COMMON PROBLEMS WITH DOWNWARD COMMUNICATION

- Overusing downward communication by sending too many messages
- Issuing contradictory messages
- Hurriedly communicating vague, unclear messages
- Issuing messages that indicate management's low regard for lower-level workers

## COMMON PROBLEMS WITH UPWARD COMMUNICATION

- The risk involved with telling upper management about problems (i.e., fear of retribution)
- Managers reacting angrily and defensively when workers report problems
- Not enough opportunities or channels for lower-level workers to contact upper levels of management

## COMMON PROBLEMS WITH HORIZONTAL COMMUNICATION

- Management discouraging or punishing horizontal communication, viewing it as small talk
- Managers and workers are not given the time or opportunity for horizontal communization
- Not enough opportunities or channels for lower-level workers to engage in horizontal communication

**Source:** G.L. Kreps, *Organizational Communication: Theory and Practice* (New York: Longman, 1990).

## 2.3 Informal Communication Channels

**informal communication channel ("grapevine")**
the transmission of messages from employee to employee outside of formal communication channels

The **informal communication channel**, sometimes called the "**grapevine**," is the transmission of messages from employee to employee outside of formal communication channels. The grapevine arises out of curiosity, that is, the need to know what is going on in an organization and how it might affect you or others. And to satisfy this curiosity, employees need a consistent supply of relevant, accurate, in-depth information about "who is doing what and what changes are occurring within the organization."[27]

For example, at the University of Texas Medical Branch (part of the UT system) any of the 13,000 employees wanting to know the truth about rumors working their way through the campus grapevine can log on to the school's Web site and click on "Rumors or Trumors." Campus administrators comment on each posted rumor and rate them using the "kernel of truth" system. As shown in Exhibit 18.6, one kernel of corn indicates a little bit of truth. Two kernels indicate that a good part of the rumor is true, but not entirely true. Three kernels indicate that the rumor is accurate. Wildly inaccurate rumors, such as the one in Exhibit 18.6 about new ID tags being able to track employees' location, are rated with a spaceship, indicating that they're too far out to be believed. Reaction thus far has been positive. Lecturer Sheryl Prather said, "It looks sincere. I've found that everything thus far has been pretty factual. It at least shows that somebody's listening to some of the talk that goes on around here and [is] putting it down on the computer where we can all see it."[28]

Grapevines arise out of informal communication networks, such as the gossip or cluster chains shown in Exhibit 18.7. In the *gossip chain*, one "highly connected" individual shares information with many other managers and workers. By contrast, in the *cluster chain*, numerous people simply tell a few of their friends. The result in both cases is that information flows freely and quickly through the organization. Some believe that grapevines are a waste of employees' time, that they promote gossip and rumors that fuel political speculation, and that they are sources of highly unreliable, inaccurate information. Yet studies clearly show that grapevines are highly accurate sources of information for a number of reasons.[29] First, because grapevines typically carry "juicy" information that is interesting and timely, information spreads rapidly. Second, since information is typically spread by face-to-face conversation, senders can seek feedback to make sure

EXHIBIT 18.6

## "RUMORS OR TRUMORS" AT THE UNIVERSITY OF TEXAS MEDICAL BRANCH

Rumor: I heard that the new "smart" ID badges will store all kinds of my private information, and worse, they can be used to track where I am at UTMB. True?

Rating: 🛸

**TRUTH-O-METER**

🛸 = Want to buy some swampland?

= A "kernel" of truth

= Maybe, but...

= The whole truth

Response: No, the cards will not contain anything but the most basic information, much as ID cards do today. No personal data, no employment history, no critical financial info or medical records. The cards will primarily verify identity (your photo and name help do that) and access, the same way magnetic strips and keys do now. In the future, they will also enable a user, at his/her discretion, to use them as a debit card for campus purchases, like a pre-paid phone card, and will help manage access to computer resources.

The cards can't track your location. The proximity readers are designed with a narrow sensitivity field (you wouldn't want doors unexpectedly unlocking because someone with access is walking in a nearby hallway). However, the system does register when you are in or out of a restricted area. This is no different than is currently the case with the magnetic key cards, and is an important aspect of maintaining security in sensitive research, clinical, and business areas.

**Source:** "UTMB's Rumors or Trumors," *The University of Texas Medical Branch.* [Online] Available http://www.utmb.edu/rumor/rumors.htm, 30 March 2002.

EXHIBIT 18.7

## GRAPEVINE COMMUNICATION NETWORKS

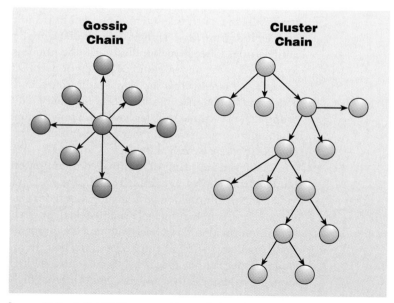

**Gossip Chain**

**Cluster Chain**

**Source:** K. Davis & J.W. Newstrom, *Human Behavior at Work: Organizational Behavior,* 8th ed. (New York: McGraw-Hill, 1989).

they understand the message that is being communicated. This reduces misunderstandings and increases accuracy. Third, since most of the information in a company moves along the grapevine, as opposed to formal communication channels, people can usually verify the accuracy of information by "checking it out" with others.

What can managers do to "manage" organizational grapevines? The very worst thing managers can do is withhold information or try to punish those who share information with others. The grapevine abhors a vacuum, and in the absence of information from company management, rumors and anxiety will flourish. For example, at GE's locomotive business in Erie, Pennsylvania, employees "are walking on pins and needles because they don't know if they're going to be the next one to get a layoff notice," said Joe Ambrose of the local United Electrical Workers union.[30] As a result of anxiety about the impending layoffs, more people than normal have sought help for alcohol and stress-related problems. Likewise, when the software services company he was working for announced it was considering layoffs, employee Tim Weidman said, "People tried to get work done, but they were posting their résumés and checking Monster.com every day. Everyone had their résumés on the street."[31]

A better strategy is to embrace the grapevine to keep employees informed about possible changes and strategies. Management consultant Arnold Brown said managers should "identify the key people in your company's grapevine and, instead of punishing them, feed them information. When a company issues a press release it knows what newspapers to contact, so why not know your internal media?"[32]

Finally, in addition to using the grapevine to communicate with others, managers should not overlook the grapevine as a tremendous source of valuable information and feedback. In fact, information flowing through organizational grapevines is estimated to be 75 to 95 percent accurate.[33] For this reason, managers should gather their courage and be willing to read the anonymous comments that angry, frustrated employees now post on Internet "gripe sites" like walmart-sucks.com, untied.com (about United Airlines), stainedapron.com (for griping restaurant workers), or vault.com, where employees post gripes about hundreds of different companies. Bob Rosner, who runs a gripe site called workingwounded.com, suggests managers look for themes rather than responding to any particular message. Mark Oldman, cofounder of vault.com, said, "Most companies are delighted that we provide a forum to talk candidly for better or worse about a company. It [vault.com] basically just digitizes what already happens offline at the water cooler."[34] Exhibit 18.8 lists other strategies that today's managers can use in dealing with gripe sites, the newest form of the traditional organizational grapevine.

### 2.4 Coaching and Counseling: One-on-One Communication

The Wyatt Company surveyed 531 U.S. companies undergoing major changes and restructuring. CEOs were asked, "If you could go back and change one thing, what would

---

EXHIBIT 18.8

ORGANIZATIONAL GRAPEVINES: DEALING WITH INTERNET GRIPE SITES

1. Correct misinformation. Put an end to false rumors and set the record straight. Don't be defensive.
2. Don't take angry comments personally.
3. Give your name and contact number to show employees that you're concerned and that they can contact you directly.
4. Hold a town meeting to discuss the issues raised on the gripe site.
5. Set up anonymous internal discussion forums on the company server. Then encourage employees to gripe anonymously on the company intranet, rather than on the Web.

---

**Source:** J. Simons, "Stop Moaning about Gripe Sites and Log On," *Fortune*, 2 April 2001, 181.

## Fire on the Mountain: Vail Hit by Eco-Terrorists

Insulated from the hustle of urban life by snow-capped mountains, Vail Mountain, Colorado, was a generally quiet resort frequented by the wealthy and the see-and-be-seen crowd. The sprawling layout of the resort was a testament to its success—until a small band of environmentalists calling itself the Earth Liberation Front (ELF) set fire to the mountain. Seven fires spread along the mile-long ridge that overlooks the resort town below. A restaurant, ski patrol building, and picnic shelter were demolished, and several ski lifts were also damaged.

The target of the attacks was Vail Resorts, the corporation that owns and runs much of the ski town: eight hotels, 82 restaurants, and many other businesses in and around Vail. At issue was the development of Category III, a new phase of the resort planned for 885 acres of mountain forest, and its impact on the lynx habitat (or lack thereof). ELF has been the source of several eco-terrorist attacks, many involving arson, and this small group of extreme environmentalists, looking for some media attention, was quick to claim responsibility for the Vail arson.

With a large portion of the resort affected by the ELF attack, Vail Resorts had a potential communication nightmare on its hands. But rather than try to deal with the problem among a few key managers, Vail executives met with employees every day to ensure that everyone had good (and consistent) information. By passing on information that it had, the company minimized any negative impact the grapevine and rumor mill might have had. Its willingness to share information may also be at the heart of the community reaction to the arson attacks. Before the fires, there was a festering rift growing between community members and the corporation, which they saw as controlling too much of the economy of the town of Vail and surrounding areas. Rather than fracture the town further, however, the ELF attack united the town and galvanized the sense of community that had previously been waning. Even the staunchest of critics, who runs a cookware store, said that the fires were "an attack on everybody and on the lifeblood of all in the valley." Few, if any, were sympathetic to the motivations of the ELF environmentalists.

Could this have happened if Vail Resorts hadn't been so willing to share the information that it had and that it was gathering about the attacks and their effect on resort operations? Maybe, but there is no doubt that sharing the information not only dowsed any ill-will that the fires could have fueled, but also rebuilt the company's reputation among the townspeople. Employees at Vail Resorts wouldn't expect anything less from a company that prides itself on communication: At Vail, the ski instructors use wireless LAN technology to improve communications with skiers taking lessons and the instructors who give them. That kind of commitment to communication is something that won't go up in smoke.

1. *Although Vail Resorts successfully emerged from the arson attacks and their aftermath, the company is and was not without communication challenges. What are they? How can they be surmounted?*

**Sources:** M. Hamblen, "Skiers on Slopes Access LAN," *Computerworld*, 16 November 1998, 51, Info-Trac Article A53131809. "Fire on the Mountain," *Time*, 2 November 1998, 77, Info-Trac Article A53220527. "Powder Burn: Arson, Money, And Mystery on Vail Mountain," *E*, May 2001, 60, Info-Trac Article A74628730.

it be." The answer? "The way we communicated with our employees." CEOs stated that instead of flashy videos, printed materials, or formal meetings, they would make greater use of one-to-one communication, especially with employees' immediate supervisors instead of with higher-level executives that employees didn't know.[35]

There are two kinds of one-on-one communication: coaching and counseling. **Coaching** is communicating with someone for the direct purpose of improving the person's on-the-job performance or behavior.[36] Managers tend to make two mistakes when coaching employees. First, they wait much too long before talking to them about the problem. Management professor Ray Hilgert said, "A manager must respond as soon as possible after an incident of poor performance. Don't bury your head. . . . When employees are told nothing, they assume everything is okay."[37] Second, when managers finally work up the courage to confront the employee, they get angry. Michael Markovitz, CEO of Argosy Education Group, said, "Managers are angry, and they yell and criticize the employee. That almost never works. It's demeaning to the employee, and the positive message gets lost. You feel mad because an employee isn't doing his or her job? Go to the gym or walk around the block—exercise is a great cure for anger. Your anger is understandable, but you still must not abuse your em-

**coaching**
communicating with someone for the direct purpose of improving the person's on-the-job performance or behavior

EXHIBIT 18.9

## SERVICES PROVIDED BY EMPLOYEE ASSISTANCE PROGRAMS (EAPS)

- Counseling—Stress, depression, relationships, substance abuse, and more.
- Child Care—Pregnancy, adoption, daycare, nutrition, fertility, and more.
- Senior Care—Health and nutrition, care options, Alzheimer's, and more.
- Legal Services—Wills, leases, estate plans, adoptions, and more.
- Health Lifestyles—Referrals and discounts on chiropractic care, acupuncture, massage therapy, vitamins, and more.
- Pet Care—Pet-sitting resources, obedience training, veterinarians, and more.
- Financial Information—Retirement planning, debt consolidation, budgeting, and more.

**Sources:** "You Can Do It. We Can Help," *CIGNA Behavioral Health.* [Online] Available http://www.hr.tcu.edu/eappages/core/html/default.html#, 30 March 2002.

**counseling**
communicating with someone about non-job-related issues that may be affecting or interfering with the person's performance

ployees."[38] In Section 3.3, you'll learn a number of specific steps for effective one-on-one communication and coaching.

By contrast, **counseling** is communicating with someone about non-job-related issues that may be affecting or interfering with the person's performance. For example, after a top-performing employee was repeatedly late and absent from work, he was asked if he had some personal problems that he needed to discuss. It turned out that he had gone through a divorce and that his teenage son, who was in trouble for truancy and stealing, was now his sole responsibility. Marina London, who counseled this manager, said, "It's very common that the personal problem is coming from somewhere else, that someone is dragging . . . [the employee] down."[39]

Today, when workers are worried, stressed, and distracted by non-job-related issues that interfere with their job performance, most managers have the option of referring them to an *employee assistance program,* or EAP. EAPs are typically free when provided as part of company benefit packages. EAPs provide referrals to organizations and professionals that help employees and their family members address personal issues. EAPs can provide immediate counseling and support in emergencies or times of crisis. Exhibit 18.9 lists the standard services provided by EAPs.

### 2.5 Nonverbal Communication

When people talk, they send verbal and nonverbal messages. Verbal messages are sent and received through the words we speak. "That was a great presentation." By contrast, nonverbal messages are sent through body language, facial expressions, or tone of voice. For instance, hearing "THAT was a GREAT presentation!" is very different from hearing "ahem [clearing throat], that was, ahem, ahem, a great presentation."

**nonverbal communication**
any communication that doesn't involve words

More specifically, **nonverbal communication** is any communication that doesn't involve words. Nonverbal communication and messages almost always accompany verbal communication and may support and reinforce the verbal message or contradict it. The importance of nonverbal communication is well established. Researchers have estimated that as much as 93 percent of any message is transmitted nonverbally, with 55 percent coming from body language and facial expressions and 38 percent coming from tone and pitch of voice.[40] And since many nonverbal cues are unintentional, receivers often consider nonverbal communication to be a more accurate representation of what senders are really thinking and feeling. If you have ever asked someone out on a date and have been told "yes," but realized that the real answer was "no," then you understand the importance of paying attention to nonverbal communication.

**kinesics**
movements of the body and face

Kinesics and paralanguage are two kinds of nonverbal communication.[41] **Kinesics** are movements of the body and face.[42] These movements include arm and hand gestures, facial expressions, eye contact, folding arms, crossing legs, and leaning toward or away

## Study *Your* Nonverbal Behavior

As much as 93 percent of any message is transmitted nonverbally. While we're often good students of others' nonverbal behavior, we're often woefully ignorant of our own. To gain some insight into your nonverbal behavior, have someone videotape you when you are speaking, preferably in two or three different situations. Then, study this tape and analyze your speaking style and your nonverbal messages and mannerisms. Look for anything that might distract a receiver from the content of your message. Also, assess whether your nonverbal messages support or contradict your verbal messages. If you see something you don't like, change it. You'll become a more effective communicator.

**paralanguage**
the pitch, rate, tone, volume, and speaking pattern (i.e., use of silences, pauses, or hesitations) of one's voice

from another person. For example, people tend to avoid eye contact when they are embarrassed or unsure of the message they are sending. Crossed arms and/or legs usually indicate defensiveness or that the person is not receptive to the message or the sender. Also, people tend to smile frequently when they are seeking someone's approval. Lawyers frequently use body language and facial movements to communicate nonverbal messages to jurors. Attorney and trial consultant Lisa Blue said, "If you want to show that the cross-examination of your witness was ridiculous or boring, you could start looking at your watch." While suing Dow Chemical, attorney Thomas Pirtle would express his disbelief by shaking his head "no," or show his disgust by waving his arms while Dow's attorneys addressed the jury. However, because of its power to sway jurors' opinions, some judges have begun tightly regulating attorneys' nonverbal behavior. U.S. district judge Samuel Kent said, "Facial gestures, nods of the head, audible sighs, anything along those lines is strictly prohibited."[43]

**Paralanguage** includes the pitch, rate, tone, volume, and speaking pattern (i.e., use of silences, pauses, or hesitations) of one's voice. For example, when people are unsure what to say, they tend to decrease their communication effectiveness by speaking softly. By contrast, when people are nervous, they tend to talk faster and louder. These characteristics have a tremendous influence on whether listeners are receptive to what speakers are saying. Again, lawyers have long used the power of their voices to influence jurors. For instance, tobacco company lawyers complained about the dramatic way in which plaintiffs' attorney Stanley Rosenblatt would dramatically read secret company documents aloud to jurors. Rosenblatt, who would vary his voice from a slow whisper to a fast, loud voice that filled the entire courtroom, said that opposing attorneys always complained that "I should read in a very flat monotone."[44]

In short, since nonverbal communication is so informative, especially when it contradicts verbal communication, managers need to learn how to monitor and control their nonverbal behavior.

### Review **2**
### Kinds of Communication

Organizational communication depends on the communication process, formal and informal communication channels, one-on-one communication, and nonverbal communication. The major components of the communication process are the sender, the receiver, noise, and feedback. The conduit metaphor refers to the mistaken assumption that senders can pipe their intended messages directly into receivers' heads with perfect clarity. However, with noise, perceptual filters, and little feedback, this just isn't possible. Formal communication channels, such as downward, upward, and horizontal communication, carry organizationally approved messages and information. By contrast, the informal communication channel, called the "grapevine," arises out of curiosity and is carried out through gossip or cluster chains. Managers should use the grapevine to keep employees informed and to obtain better, clearer information for themselves. There are two kinds of one-on-one communication. Coaching is used to improve on-the-job performance while counseling is used to communicte about non-job related issues affecting job performance. Nonverbal communication, such as kinesics and paralanguage, account for as much as 93 percent of a message's content and understanding. Since nonverbal communication is so informative, managers need to learn how to monitor and control their nonverbal behavior.

# How to Improve Communication

An employee comes in late every day, takes long lunches, and leaves early. His coworkers resent his tardiness and having to do his share of the work. Another employee makes as many as 10 personal phone calls a day on company time. Another employee has seen her job performance drop significantly in the last three months. How do you communicate with these employees to begin solving these problems? On the other hand, if you supervise a division of 50, 100, or even 1,000 people, how can you communicate effectively with everyone in that division? Moreover, how can top managers communicate effectively with everyone in the company when employees work in different offices, states, countries, and time zones? Turning that around, how can managers make themselves accessible so that they can hear what employees feel and think throughout the organization?

When it comes to improving communication, managers face two primary tasks, managing one-on-one communication and managing organization-wide communication.

*After reading the next two sections, you should be able to*
*3. explain how managers can manage effective one-on-one communication.*
*4. describe how managers can manage effective organization-wide communication.*

## 3. Managing One-on-One Communication

In Chapter 1, you learned that, on average, first-line managers spend 57 percent of their time with people, middle managers spend 63 percent of their time directly with people, and top managers spend as much as 78 percent of their time dealing with people.[45] These numbers make it clear that managers spend a great deal of time in one-on-one communication with others.

*Learn more about managing one-on-one communication by reading how to 3.1 choose the right communication medium, 3.2 be a good listener, 3.3 give effective feedback, and 3.4 improve cross-cultural communication.*

### 3.1 Choosing the Right Communication Medium

**communication medium**
the method used to deliver an oral or written message

Sometimes messages are poorly communicated simply because they are delivered using the wrong **communication medium**, which is the method used to deliver a message. For example, the wrong communication medium is being used when an employee returns from lunch, picks up the note left on her office chair, and learns she has been fired. Or, the wrong communication medium is being used when an employee pops into your office every 10 minutes with a simple request. (An e-mail would be better.)

There are two general kinds of communication media: oral and written communication. *Oral communication* includes face-to-face and group meetings through telephone calls, videoconferencing, or any other way, in which spoken messages are sent and received. Studies show that managers generally prefer oral communication over written, because it provides the opportunity to ask questions about parts of the message that they don't understand. Oral communication is also a rich communication medium, because it allows managers to receive and assess the nonverbal communication that accompanies spoken messages (i.e., body language, facial expressions, or the voice characteristics associated with paralanguage). Furthermore, you don't need a personal computer and an Internet connection to conduct oral communication. Simply schedule an appointment, track someone down in the hall, or catch someone on the phone. In fact, management consultant Tom Durel worries that with voice mail and email, managers are not as willing to engage in meaningful face-to-face, oral communication as they once were. He said, "Why is it that the first thing people do in the morning is turn on their computer and send email to a colleague in the office next door? What's wrong with getting up, walking over there, and actually *talking* to that person?"[46] However, oral communication should not be used for all communication. In general, when messages are simple, such as a quick request or presentation of straightforward information, memos or email are often the better communication medium.

*Written communication* includes letters, email, and memos. While most managers like and use oral communication, they are generally less receptive to using written communication. They may avoid written communication for a number of reasons, such as poor writing skills, poor typing skills, or not knowing (or refusing to learn) how to use Internet or corporate email systems. However, written communication is well suited for delivering

Memos often create misperceptions and send unintended messages. Yet they are sometimes necessary to create a record of decisions or responsibilities. To write good memos: (1) Don't use accusatory or autocratic language, such as "I am appalled by your decision" or "I don't like your attitude." (2) Avoid absolutes, such as "never," "cannot," and "must not." (3) Keep them short and to the point—use bullets points for structure. (4) Never write anything in a memo that you don't want everyone else to see. (5) Always consider whether a phone call or personal conversation would be more effective than a memo.

**Source:** R. Davidhizar and S. Erdel, "Send Me a Memo on It, Or Better Yet, Don't," *Health Care Supervisor* 15 (1997): 42–47. J. Gannon, "Clear Writing Leads to Better Business," *Star-Ledger (Pittsburgh Post-Gazette)*, 30 April 2002. 52.

straightforward messages and information. Furthermore, with email access available at the office, at home, and on the road (by laptop computer or Web-based email), managers can use email to stay in touch from anywhere at almost any time. And, since email and other written communications don't have to be sent and received simultaneously, messages can be sent and stored for reading at any time. This allows managers to send and receive many more messages using email than using oral communication, which requires people to get together in person or by phone or videoconference. But, said management consultant Tom Durel, "Don't assume that you did your part just because you sent out a bunch of memos. If you really want to communicate, you need to take the time to get real-time feedback."[47]

While written communication is well suited for delivering straightforward messages and information, it is not well suited to complex, ambiguous, or emotionally laden topics, which are better delivered through oral communication. Neal Patterson, CEO of Cerner Corporation, a health care software development company, learned this lesson when he made the mistake of sending a particularly angry and emotional email to 400 company managers whom he chastised for not doing their jobs. Patterson wrote:

> We are getting less than 40 hours of work from a large number of our KC-based EMPLOYEES. . . . The parking lot is sparsely used at 8 AM, likewise at 5 PM. As managers—you either do not know what your EMPLOYEES are doing or YOU do not CARE. You have created expectations on the work effort which allowed this to happen inside Cerner, creating a very unhealthy environment. In either case, you have a problem and you will fix it or I will replace you.
>
> NEVER in my career have I allowed a team which worked for me to think they had a 40-hour job. I have allowed YOU to create a culture which is permitting this. NO LONGER.[48]

Patterson also wrote, "We passed a Stock Purchase Program, allowing for the EMPLOYEE to purchase Cerner stock at a 15 percent discount, at Friday's BOD [board of directors] meeting. Hell will freeze over before this CEO implements ANOTHER EMPLOYEE benefit in this Culture."[49] He concluded the email by saying, "I will hold you accountable. You have allowed this to get to this state. You have two weeks. Tick, tock."[50]

Reaction to the message was so strong that, in just over a week, the email had been leaked throughout the entire company. And then someone, nobody knows who, posted the email on a Yahoo.com discussion board about Cerner. As word spread about the negative email, Cerner's stock price dropped from $44 to $31 per share in just three days. By the end of the week, Patterson issued another email, but this one offered an apology. Not surprisingly, that email began, "Please treat this memo with the utmost confidentiality. It is for internal dissemination only. Do not copy or email to anyone else."[51]

### 3.2 Listening

Are you a good listener? You probably think so. But, in fact, most people, including managers, are terrible listeners, retaining only about 25 percent of what they hear.[52] You qualify as a poor listener if you frequently interrupt others, jump to conclusions about what people will say before they've said it, hurry the speaker to finish his or her point, are a passive listener (not actively working at your listening), and simply don't pay attention to what people are saying.[53] On this last point, attentiveness, college students were periodically asked to record their thoughts during a psychology course. On average, 20 percent of the students were paying attention (only 12 percent were actively working at being good listeners), 20 percent were thinking about sex, 20 percent were thinking about things they had done before, and the remaining 40 percent thought about a number of things (worries, religion, lunch, daydreaming, etc.), none of which were related to class.[54]

**Listen Up!**

To be a better listener: (1) Listen to more than the first few words or phrases of each sentence. (2) Let the speaker complete the message before forming a conclusion. (3) Listen for intent as well as content. (4) Nonverbally encourage the speaker (with body language, eye contact, and facial expression). (5) Don't analyze or evaluate a message until you are sure it is complete. (6) Focus on what the person is saying, verbally and nonverbally. (7) Check your understanding by asking questions, paraphrasing, and summarizing. (8) Listen for what is *not* said.

**Sources:** R. Cousins, "Active Listening Is More Than Just Hearing," *Supervision*, September 2000, 14.

**hearing**
the act or process of perceiving sounds

**listening**
making a conscious effort to hear

**active listening**
assuming half the responsibility for successful communication by actively giving the speaker nonjudgmental feedback that shows you've accurately heard what he or she said

**empathetic listening**
understanding the speaker's perspective and personal frame of reference and giving feedback that conveys that understanding to the speaker

How important is it to be a good listener? In general, about 45 percent of the total time you spend communicating with others is spent listening. Furthermore, listening is important for managerial success, particularly as you move up in the organization. John Chambers, CEO of Cisco Systems, said, "A large part of communication skills, which people forget, is [listening]. . . . Your ability to listen as the company gets bigger also becomes more of a challenge, because you can't walk around and touch like you used to. You've got to learn how to do that in groups."[55] In fact, managers with better listening skills are rated as better managers by their employees and are much more likely to be promoted.[56]

So, what can you do to improve your listening ability? First, understand the difference between hearing and listening. According to the *Webster's New World Dictionary*, **hearing** is the "act or process of perceiving sounds," whereas **listening** is "making a conscious effort to hear." In other words, we react to sounds, such as bottles breaking or music being played too loud, because hearing is an involuntary physiological process. By contrast, listening is a voluntary behavior. So if you want to be a good listener, you have to choose to be a good listener. Typically, that means choosing to be an active, empathetic listener.[57]

**Active listening** means assuming half the responsibility for successful communication by actively giving the speaker nonjudgmental feedback that shows you've accurately heard what he or she said. Active listeners make it clear from their behavior that they are listening carefully to what the speaker has to say. Active listeners put the speaker at ease, maintain eye contact, and show the speaker that they are attentively listening by nodding and making short statements.

Several specific strategies can help you be a better active listener. First, *clarify responses* by asking the speaker to explain confusing or ambiguous statements. Second, when there are natural breaks in the speaker's delivery, use this time to paraphrase or summarize what has been said. *Paraphrasing* is restating what has been said in your own words. *Summarizing* is reviewing the speaker's main points or emotions. Paraphrasing and summarizing give the speaker the chance to correct the message if the active listener has attached the wrong meaning to it. Paraphrasing and summarizing also show the speaker that the active listener is interested in the speaker's message. Exhibit 18.10 lists specific statements that listeners can use to clarify responses, paraphrase, or summarize what has been said.

Active listeners also avoid evaluating the message or being critical until the message is complete. They recognize that their only responsibility during the transmission of a message is to receive it accurately and derive the intended meaning from it. Evaluation and criticism can take place after the message is accurately received. Finally, active listeners also recognize that a large portion of any message is transmitted nonverbally and thus pay very careful attention to the nonverbal cues transmitted by the speaker.

**Empathetic listening** means understanding the speaker's perspective and personal frame of reference and giving feedback that conveys that understanding to the speaker. Empathetic listening goes beyond active listening, because it depends on our ability to set aside our own attitudes or relationships to be able to see and understand things through someone else's eyes. Empathetic listening is just as important as active listening, especially for managers, because it helps build rapport and trust with others.

The key to being a more empathetic listener is to show your desire to understand and to reflect people's feelings. You can *show your desire to understand* by listening, that is, asking people to talk about what's most important to them and then by giving them sufficient time to talk before responding or interrupting. Management consultant Neil Grammer said, "One of the best sales meetings I've ever had taught me a valuable lesson about the importance of listening. The meeting was with an investment bank's managing director. The appointment lasted 30 minutes—28 of those minutes were spent by the director telling me everything about his business and personnel. I told him nothing more about my company and its services than I had in our initial phone conversation. As the meeting

705

EXHIBIT 18.10

CLARIFYING, PARAPHRASING, AND SUMMARIZING RESPONSES FOR ACTIVE LISTENERS

## CLARIFYING RESPONSES

- Could you explain that again?
- I don't understand what you mean.
- I'm confused. Would you run through that again?
- I'm not sure how . . . .

## PARAPHRASING RESPONSES

- What you're really saying is . . . .
- If I understand you correctly . . . .
- So your perspective is that . . . .
- In other words . . .
- Tell me if I'm wrong, but what you're saying is . . . .

## SUMMARIZING RESPONSES

- Let me summarize . . . .
- Okay, your main concerns are . . . .
- Thus far, you've discussed . . . .
- To recap what you've said . . . .

**Source:** E. Atwater, *I Hear You*, revised ed. (New York: Walker, 1992).

concluded, he enthusiastically shook my hand and proclaimed how much he was looking forward to working with me—someone who understood his business."[58]

*Reflecting feelings* is also an important part of empathetic listening, because it demonstrates that you understand the speaker's emotions. But unlike active listening, in which you would restate or summarize the informational content of what had been said, the focus is on the affective part of the message. As an empathetic listener, you can use the following statements to reflect the speaker's emotions:

- So, right now you're feeling . . .
- You seem as if you're . . .
- Do you feel a bit . . . ?
- I could be wrong, but I'm sensing that you're feeling . . .

In the end, says management consultant Terry Pearce, empathetic listening can be boiled down to these three steps. First, wait 10 seconds before you answer or respond. It will seem an eternity, but doing so prevents you from interrupting others and rushing your response. Second, to be sure you understand what the speaker wants, ask questions to clarify the speaker's intent. Third, only then should you respond with feelings and then facts (notice that facts *follow* feelings).[59]

### 3.3 Giving Feedback

In Chapter 14, you learned that performance appraisal feedback (i.e., judging) should be separated from developmental feedback (i.e., coaching).[60] At this point, we now focus on the steps needed to communicate feedback one-on-one to employees.

To start, managers need to recognize that feedback can be constructive or destructive. **Destructive feedback** is disapproving without any intention of being helpful and almost always causes a negative or defensive reaction in the recipient. In fact, one study found that 98 percent of employees responded to destructive feedback from their bosses with either verbal aggression (two-thirds) or physical aggression (one-third).[61] Surprisingly, some managers don't realize that they're giving people destructive feedback. One employee said, "A

**destructive feedback**
feedback that disapproves without any intention of being helpful and almost always causes a negative or defensive reaction in the recipient

project that my team was working on had a number of delays, and one of them involved something that I was responsible for. The pressure was on, and we were all putting in long hours to catch up. But in the middle of that, my boss called me into his office, and with the door wide open, he started yelling about the delay, about how much it was costing, and about how it was making him look bad. Anyone in that whole corner of the building could easily hear. It was so ridiculous. I was doing everything I could, and yet he lost his temper and acted as if I was doing something to personally offend him."[62]

**constructive feedback**
feedback intended to be helpful, corrective, and/or encouraging

By contrast, **constructive feedback** is intended to be helpful, corrective, and/or encouraging. It is aimed at correcting performance deficiencies and motivating employees. When providing constructive feedback, Jenet Noriega Schwind, vice president and chief people officer of Zantaz.com, an e-business archiving company, will tell employees, "What I'm going to tell you may be upsetting to you—but it's important to your success." She said, "When you are telling people things they don't necessarily want to hear, you have to deliver your message in a way that gets their attention and acceptance."[63] However, even when they want to give constructive rather than destructive feedback, managers still get nervous about discussing problems with employees. Why? Because, according to Steve Kerr, the former vice president of leadership development at GE, "From the time we're taught to talk, we're taught to lie—and it's called courtesy."[64] Furthermore, most of us assume that "leaders aren't supposed to be negative, but only constructive and positive."

In order for feedback to be constructive rather than destructive, it must be immediate, focused on specific behaviors, and problem oriented. Because the mistake or incident can be recalled more accurately and discussed in detail by the manager and the worker, *immediate feedback* is much more effective than delayed feedback. For example, if a worker is rude to a customer and the customer immediately reports the incident to management, and the manager, in turn, immediately discusses the issue with the employee, there should be little disagreement over what was said or done. By contrast, if the manager waits several weeks to discuss the incident, it's unlikely that either the manager or the worker will be able to accurately remember the specifics of what occurred. When that happens, it's usually too late to have a meaningful conversation.

*Specific feedback* focuses on particular acts or incidents that are clearly under the control of the employee. For instance, instead of telling an employee that he or she is "always late for work," it's much more constructive to say, "In the last three weeks, you have been 30 minutes late on four occasions and more than an hour late on two others." Furthermore, specific feedback isn't very helpful unless employees have control over the problems that the feedback addresses. Indeed, giving negative feedback about behaviors beyond someone's control is likely to be seen as unfair. Similarly, giving positive feedback about behaviors beyond someone's control may be viewed as insincere.

Last, *problem-oriented feedback* focuses on the problems or incidents associated with the poor performance rather than on the worker or the worker's personality. Giving feedback does not give managers the right to personally attack workers. While managers may be frustrated by a worker's poor performance, the point of problem-oriented feedback is to draw attention to the problem in a nonjudgmental way, so that the employee has enough information to correct it. So, rather than telling people that they're "idiots," focus on the problem. For instance, a shipping clerk at A&S Restaurant had a bad case of body odor. Rather than telling him "You stink" or "You're doing a lousy job because you stink," the manager explained the specific ways in which his body odor was "getting in the way of doing his job." Because the manager's feedback was specific and problem oriented and didn't attack or blame the employee, the employee didn't get defensive and took steps to take care of his body odor.[65]

### 3.4 Improving Cross-Cultural Communication

**cross-cultural communication**
transmitting information from a person in one country or culture to a person from another country or culture

As you know by now, effective communication is very difficult to accomplish. However, **cross-cultural communication**, which involves transmitting information from a person in one country or culture to a person from another country or culture, is much more difficult. For example, when a French company bought a U.S. company, it found that the American

EXHIBIT 18.11

A COMPARISON OF FRENCH AND AMERICAN VIEWS OF WORK

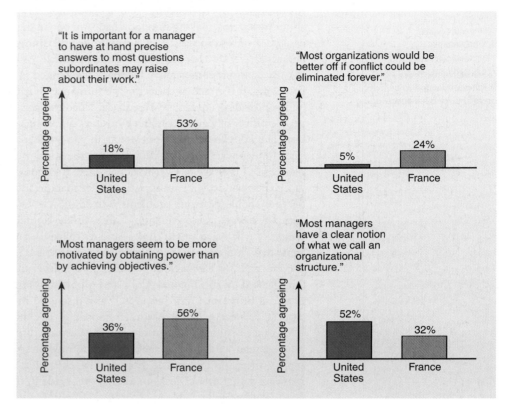

**Source:** From N.J. Adler, *From Boston to Beijing: Managing with a World View* (Cincinnati, Ohio: South-Western, 2002), based on A. Laurent, "The Cultural Diversity of Western Conceptions of Management," in *International Studies of Management and Organization*, vol. 13, no. 1–2 (Spring–Summer 1983), 75–96.

managers would not implement the new strategy that it recommended. As tensions grew worse, the American managers challenged their new French boss's strategy and explained why they hadn't followed it. By contrast, the French, who now owned the American company, simply couldn't understand why the American managers, who now worked for them, didn't just do as they were told.[66] Indeed, Exhibit 18.11, which shows the rather different views that French and American workers have about work, gives us some insight into the difficulty of cross-cultural communication in this circumstance. Overall, the French are much more likely to believe that managers need to have precise answers to subordinates' questions (53 percent versus 18 percent), that organizations would be better off without conflict (24 percent versus 5 percent), and that managers are more motivated by power than achieving objectives (56 percent versus 36 percent).[67] With such different views on these simple topics, no wonder there were communication difficulties.

There are a number of things you can do to increase your chances for successful cross-cultural communication: familiarize yourself with a culture's general work norms; determine whether a culture is emotionally affective or neutral; develop respect for other cultures; and understand how address terms and attitudes toward time (polychronic versus monochronic time, and appointment, schedule, discussion, and acquaintance time) differ from culture to culture.

In Chapter 8, you learned that expatriates who receive predeparture language and cross-cultural training make faster adjustments to foreign cultures and perform better on their international assignments.[68] Therefore, *familiarizing yourself with a culture's general work norms*, that is, the shared values, beliefs, and perceptions toward work and how it should be done, is the first step for successful cross-cultural communication. (See Chap-

When Mercedes built a manufacturing plant in Vance, Alabama, the company went to great lengths to familiarize itself with American (and Alabaman) cultural and work norms. Management successfully blended elements of German and American cultures at the Vance facility. The result: After only one year in operation, employees at the plant produced the 50,000th M-Class all-activity vehicle.

AP/WIDE WORLD PHOTOS

ter 8 for a more complete discussion of international cultures.) Fortunately, books such as *Kiss, Bow, or Shake Hands: How to Do Business in 60 Countries* (by Terri Morrison, Wayne Conaway, George Borden, and Hans Koehler), *Do's and Taboos Around the World* (by Roger E. Axtell), and *Dun & Bradstreet's Guide to Doing Business Around the World* (by Terri Morrison, Wayne Conaway, and Joseph Douress), and Web sites such as Businessculture.com and Executiveplanet.com provide a wealth of information about countries, their cultures, and their work and communication norms.

Mercedes wisely took the time to familiarize itself with U.S. culture and work norms when it built a manufacturing plant in Vance, Alabama. The management team, consisting primarily of Germans and Americans, spent six months deciding how Mercedes would blend German and American management philosophies and work practices. The biggest disagreements were over image and decorum. Consistent with its hierarchical work norms, the Germans preferred private offices along narrow hallways, whereas the Americans, who are generally more egalitarian, preferred open offices in which people of all ranks could easily find and talk to each other. Likewise, the German managers preferred formal business attire because it emphasized status differences (i.e., hierarchy), whereas the Americans pushed for casual wear, such as dress slacks with polo shirts and sweaters bearing the Mercedes logo. Because the plant is in Alabama, the team eventually opted for the open office and casual dress.[69]

*Determining whether a culture is emotionally affective or neutral* is also important to cross-cultural communication. In **affective cultures**, people are much more likely to display emotions and feelings when communicating, whereas in **neutral cultures** they do not.[70] For example, while Italians are prone to strong bursts of emotion (positive and negative), Chinese don't show strong emotions because doing so is thought to disrupt harmony and lead to conflict. Likewise, while a smiling American is displaying happiness, a smiling Japanese may be trying to hide another emotion or avoid answering a question.[71] The mistake most managers make is misunderstanding the differences between affective and neutral cultures. People from neutral cultures aren't by definition cold and unfeeling. They just don't show their emotions in the same way or intensity as people from affective cultures. The key is to recognize the differences and then make sure your judgments are not based on the lack or presence of emotional reactions. Exhibit 18.12 provides a more detailed explanation of the differences between affective and neutral cultures.

**affective cultures**
cultures in which people display emotions and feelings when communicating

**neutral cultures**
cultures in which people do not display emotions and feelings when communicating

EXHIBIT 18.12

AFFECTIVE AND NEUTRAL CULTURES

| IN AFFECTIVE CULTURES, PEOPLE | IN NEUTRAL CULTURES, PEOPLE |
|---|---|
| 1. reveal thoughts and feelings through verbal and nonverbal communication. | 1. don't reveal what they are thinking or feeling. |
| 2. express and show feelings of tension. | 2. hide tension and only show it accidentally in face or posture. |
| 3. let their emotions flow easily, intensely, and without inhibition. | 3. suppress emotions, leading to occasional "explosions." |
| 4. admire heated, animated, and intense expression of emotion. | 4. admire remaining cool, calm, and relaxed. |
| 5. are used to touching, gesturing, and showing strong facial expressions of emotions (all are common). | 5. consider physical contact, such as touching, gesturing, and strong facial expressions, taboo. |
| 6. make statements with emotion. | 6. often make statements in an unexpressive manner. |

Source: F. Trompenaars, *Riding the Waves of Culture: Understanding Diversity in Global Business* (London: Economist Books, 1994).

*Respecting other cultures* is also an important part of improving cross-cultural communication. However, because we use our own cultures as the standard of comparison, it's very easy to make the common mistake of assuming that "different" means "inferior."[72] Take this example:

> A Swiss executive waits more than an hour past the appointed time for his Spanish colleague to arrive and to sign a major supply contract. In his impatience he concludes that the Spaniard must be lazy and totally unconcerned about business.[73]

According to Professor Nancy J. Adler,

> The Swiss executive has misevaluated his colleague by negatively comparing the colleague's behavior to his own culture's standard for business punctuality. Implicitly, he has labeled his own culture's behavior as good ("The Swiss arrive on time, especially for important meetings, and that is good.") and the other culture's behavior as bad ("The Spanish do not arrive on time and that is bad.").[74]

According to Adler, "Evaluating others' behavior rarely helps in trying to understand, communicate with, or conduct business with people from another culture."[75] The key, she said, is taking a step back and realizing that you don't know or understand everything that is going on and that your assumptions and interpretations of others' behavior and motives may be wrong. So, instead of judging or evaluating your international business colleagues, observe what they do. Also, delay your judgments until you have more experience with them and their culture. Lastly, treat any judgments or conclusions you do make as guesses, and then double-check those judgments or conclusions with others.[76] The more patient you are in forming opinions and drawing conclusions, the better you'll be at cross-cultural communication.

Next, you can improve cross-cultural communication by *knowing the address terms* that different cultures use to address each other in the workplace.[77] **Address terms** are the cultural norms that establish whether you address businesspeople by their first names, family names, or titles. When meeting for the first time, Americans and Australians tend to be informal and address each other by first names, even nicknames. However, such immediate informality is not accepted in many cultures. For instance, an American manager working in one of his company's British subsidiaries introduced himself as "Chuck" to his

**address terms**
cultural norms that establish whether you should address businesspeople by their first names, family names, or titles

710

British employees and coworkers. However, even after six months on the job, his British counterparts still referred to him as Charles. And the more he insisted they call him "Chuck," the more they seemed to dig in their heels and call him "Charles."[78] So, to decrease defensiveness, know your address terms before addressing your international business counterparts.

*Understanding different cultural attitudes toward time* is another major consideration for effective cross-cultural communication.. Cultures tend to be either monochronic or polychronic in their orientation toward time.[79] In **monochronic cultures,** people tend to do one thing at a time and view time as linear, meaning that time is the passage of sequential events. There's a saying that goes like this, "There are three stages in people's lives: when they believe in Santa Claus, when they don't believe in Santa Claus, and when they are Santa Claus." The progression from childhood, to young adulthood, to parenthood (when they are Santa Claus) represents a linear view of time. Schedules are important in monochronic cultures because you schedule time to get a particular thing done. Professor Frons Trompenaars, noted researcher on international cultures and business, gives these examples of a monochronic culture:

> In London I once saw a long queue of people waiting for a bus when it started pouring ran. They all stood stolidly, getting soaked even though cover was close by, lest they lose their sequential order. They preferred to do things right rather than do the right thing. In the Netherlands, you could be the queen, but if you are in a butcher's shop with number 46 and you step up for service when number 12 is called, you are still in deep trouble. Nor does it matter if you have an emergency; order is order.[80]

By contrast, in **polychronic cultures**, people tend to do more than one thing at a time and view time as circular, meaning that time is a combination of the past, present, and future. Consider the following example from a polychronic culture:

> In the Bahamas, bus service is managed similarly to many taxi systems. Drivers own their own buses and collect passenger fares for their income. There is no set schedule nor set time when buses will run or arrive at a particular location. Everything depends on the driver.
>
> Bus drivers in the Bahamas are present-oriented; what they feel like doing on a particular day at a particular hour dictates what they will actually do. If the bus driver feels hungry, for example, the driver will go home to eat lunch without waiting for a preset lunch hour. Drivers see no need to repeat yesterday's actions today, nor to set tomorrow's schedule according to the needs and patterns of yesterday.[81]

As you can easily imagine, business people from monochronic cultures are driven to distraction by the perceived laxness of polychronic cultures, while people from polychronic cultures chafe under what they perceive as strict regimentation in monochronic cultures. Conflicts between these two views of times occur rather easily. Let's go back to Trompenaars butcher shop for an example:

> At my local butcher shop in Amsterdam, the butcher calls a number, unwraps, cuts, rewraps each item the customer wants, and then calls the next number. Once I ventured a suggestion, "While you have the salami out, cut a pound for me, too." Customers and staff went into shock. The system may be inefficient, but they were not about to let some wise guy change it.

Researchers Edward and Mildred Hall summed up the conflicts between these different views of time by saying, "It is impossible to know how many millions of dollars have been lost in international business because monochronic and polychronic people do not

---

**monochronic cultures**
cultures in which people tend to do one thing at a time and view time as linear

**polychronic cultures**
cultures in which people tend to do more than one thing at a time and view time as circular

EXHIBIT 18.13

## MONOCHRONIC VERSUS POLYCHRONIC CULTURES

**PEOPLE IN MONOCHRONIC CULTURES**

- Do one thing at a time
- Concentrate on the job
- Take time commitments seriously (deadlines, schedules)
- Are committed to the job
- Adhere religiously to plans
- Are concerned about not disturbing others (privacy is to be respected)
- Show respect for private property (rarely lend or borrow things)
- Emphasize promptness
- Are accustomed to short-term relationships

**PEOPLE IN POLYCHRONIC CULTURES**

- Do many things at once
- Are highly distractible and subject to interruptions
- Achieve time commitments, but only if possible
- Are committed to people
- Change plans easily and often
- Are more concerned with relationships (family, friends, business associates) than with privacy
- Frequently borrow and lend things
- Vary their promptness by the relationship
- Tend to build lifetime relationships

**Source:** E.T. Hall & M.R. Hall, *Understanding Cultural Differences* (Yarmouth, Maine: Intercultural Press, 1990).

understand each other or even realize that two such different time systems exist."[82] Exhibit 18.13 provides a more detailed explanation of the differences between monochronic and polychronic cultures.

Differences in monochronic and polychronic time show up in four important temporal concepts that affect cross-cultural communication: appointment time, schedule time, discussion time, and acquaintance time.[83] **Appointment time** is concerned with how punctual you must be when showing up for scheduled appointments or meetings. In the United States, any amount beyond five minutes late is considered "late." However, Swedes don't even allow five minutes, expecting others to arrive by their appointment time. By contrast, in Latin countries, people can arrive 20 to 30 minutes after a scheduled appointment and still not be considered late.

**Schedule time** is the time by which scheduled projects or jobs should actually be completed. In the United States and other Anglo cultures, a premium is placed on completing things on time. By contrast, more relaxed attitudes toward schedule time can be found throughout Asia and Latin America.

**Discussion time** concerns how much time should be spent in discussion with others. In the United States, we carefully manage discussion time to avoid "wasting" time on nonbusiness topics. In Brazil, though, because of the emphasis on building relationships, as much as two hours of general discussion on nonbusiness topics can be required before moving on to business issues.

Finally, **acquaintance time** is how much time you must spend getting to know someone before the person is prepared to do business with you. Again, in the United States, people quickly get down to business and are willing to strike a deal on the same day if the terms are good and initial impressions are positive. In the Middle East, however, it may take two or three weeks of meetings before reaching this comfort level. The French also have a different attitude toward acquaintance time. Polly Platt, author of *French or Foe*, a book that explains French culture and people for travelers and businesspeople, says, "Know that things are going to take longer and don't resent it. Realize that the time system is different. Time is not a quantity for them. We save time, we spend time, we waste time; all this comes from money. The French don't. They pass time. It's a totally different concept."[84]

### Review 3
#### Managing One-on-One Communication

One-on-one communication can be managed by choosing the right communication medium, being a good listener, giving effective feedback, and understanding cross-cultural communication. Managers generally prefer oral communication, because it provides the

**appointment time**
cultural norm for how punctual you must be when showing up for scheduled appointments or meetings

**schedule time**
cultural norm for the time by which scheduled projects or jobs should actually be completed

**discussion time**
cultural norm for how much time should be spent in discussion with others

**acquaintance time**
cultural norm for how much time you must spend getting to know someone before the person is prepared to do business with you

712

opportunity to ask questions and assess nonverbal communication. Oral communication is best suited to complex, ambiguous, or emotionally laden topics. Written communication is best suited for delivering straightforward messages and information. Listening is important for managerial success, but most people are terrible listeners. To improve your listening skills, choose to be an active listener (clarify responses, paraphrase, and summarize) and an empathetic listener (show your desire to understand, reflect feelings). Feedback can be constructive or destructive. To be constructive, feedback must be immediate, focused on specific behaviors, and problem oriented. Finally, to increase chances for successful cross-cultural communication, determine whether a culture is emotionally affective or neutral, familiarize yourself with a culture's general work norms, develop respect for other cultures, and understand how address terms and attitudes toward time (polychronic versus monochronic time, and appointment, schedule, discussion, and acquaintance time) differ from culture to culture.

## 4. Managing Organization-Wide Communication

While managing one-on-one communication is important, managers must also know how to effectively communicate to a larger number of people throughout an organization. For instance, Barry Salzman, president of DoubleClick International, the Internet advertising firm, spends 75 percent of his time traveling to 14 international offices. And every Monday, no matter where he is, he conducts a conference call with DoubleClick managers in Canada, Europe, and Asia. Says Salzman, "We try to maintain voice contact. We lose that with computers and email."[85] While this is an effective method of managing a small group of geographically dispersed people, managers can't hold a conference call with everyone in the company. Thus, managers need additional methods for organization-wide communication. For example, John Chambers, CEO of Cisco Systems, said, "It isn't [just] one-on-one communication any more; it's how do you get your message across? My average presentation today, probably half of them are in front of 500 people or more."[86] Effective leaders, however, don't just communicate to others, they also make themselves accessible, so they can hear what employees throughout their organizations are feeling and thinking.

*Learn more about organization-wide communication by reading the following sections about 4.1 improving transmission by getting the message out and 4.2 improving reception by finding ways to hear what others feel and think.*

John Chambers, CEO of Cisco, is a regular keynote speaker at Comdex, the technology trade show held annually in Las Vegas, Nevada. At Comdex 2001, Chambers waded into the audience during his keynote address. It is during events like these that Chambers can communicate his company's vision and performance to employees, customers, analysts, and other industry leaders.

© REUTERS NEW MEDIA INC./CORBIS

**The Dangers of Corporate Email**

Email is fast and convenient, but has serious pitfalls. It can be easily saved, duplicated, forwarded, and printed. The original sender has no control over who sees it. And while senders delete email on their machines, most likely other copies can be found on the company's mail server or backup tapes, which most companies run every night. Email also allows disgruntled employees to easily send out sensitive or fraudulent information to competitors or outsiders. Finally, many employees use easily guessed passwords or don't log off their computers, making it easy for an outsider to email while posing as a member of your company.

**Source:** M. Coles, "Warning Note over E-Mail Legal Danger: Firms Face Big Damages for Careless Chat," *Sunday Mail*, 20 August 2000, 41.

---

*4.1 Improving Transmission: Getting the Message Out*

Several methods of electronic communication—email, online discussion forums, televised/videotaped speeches and conferences, corporate talk shows, and broadcast voice mail—now make it easier for managers to communicate with people throughout the organization and "get the message out."

Although we normally think of *email*, the transmission of messages via computers, as a means of one-on-one communication, it also plays an important role in organization-wide communication. With the click of a button, managers can send email to everyone in the company via email distribution lists. Many CEOs now use this capability regularly to keep employees up-to-date on changes and developments in the company. For example, when Sprint, the telecommunications company, was struggling during an economic recession, CEO Bill Esrey emailed his managers and employees this message, "It will not be an easy road. While there are some signs of renewed economic health on the horizon, the extent of the recovery is far from certain. It is important that each of you understands the strategies and initiatives that we have in place. The key to our success will come from our ability to operate and execute as One Sprint [a new product/marketing offer]. It differentiates us from our competitors. They don't have the key assets in wireline and wireless that we possess. By eliminating redundancies found across the corporation, collaborating on sales and marketing to provide a One Sprint face to the customer, and linking our back office operations to support our One Sprint objectives, we can achieve our goals and hit the targets we set."[87]

Also, many CEOs and top executives make their email addresses public and encourage employees to contact them directly. For example, on the Hewlett-Packard Web site, HP managers and employees can use a Web page (**http://www.hp.com/hpinfo/execteam/email/fiorina/**) called "email carly" to email CEO Carly Fiorina with their thoughts and suggestions.

Another way to electronically promote organization-wide communication is through discussion forums. **Online discussion forums**, which are the in-house equivalent of Internet newsgroups, are Web- or software-based discussion tools that are available across the company to permit employees to easily ask questions and share knowledge with each other. The point is to share expertise and not duplicate solutions already "discovered" by others in the company. Furthermore, because online discussion forums remain online, they provide an historical database for people who are dealing with particular problems for the first time.

Online discussion forums are typically organized by topic. For example, at Ernst & Young, a major accounting and management-consulting corporation, consultants who have questions about multinational tax analysis can simply log on to the E & Y tax forum (or dozens of other forums, too). They can either post new questions and get help from others who respond with answers, or read previously posted questions and answers to see if the information they need has already been discussed. If either of those options fails, they can at least come away with the names of people in the organization that they can contact for help.[88] British Petroleum Amoco has taken this a step further by creating "Connect," which is essentially a company Yellow Pages where more than 12,000 managers and workers have entered their contact information and listed their expertise to make it easier for others to find expert help for their problems.[89]

Exhibit 18.14 lists the steps companies need to take to establish successful online discussion forums. First, pinpoint your company's top intellectual assets with a knowledge audit; then spread that knowledge throughout the organization. Second, create an online directory detailing the expertise of individual workers and make it available to all employees. Third, set up discussion groups on the intranet so that managers and workers can collaborate on problem solving. Finally, reward information sharing by making the online sharing of knowledge a key part of performance ratings.

**online discussion forums**
the in-house equivalent of Internet newsgroups; Web- or software-based discussion tools available across the company to permit employees to easily ask questions and share knowledge with each other

714

EXHIBIT 18.14

ESTABLISHING ONLINE DISCUSSION FORUMS

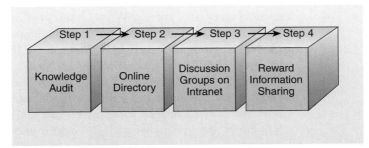

**Source:** Based on G. McWilliams & M. Stepanek, "Knowledge Management: Taming the Info Monster," *Business Week*, 22 June 1998, 170.

**televised/videotaped speeches and meetings**
speeches and meetings originally made to a smaller audience that are either simultaneously broadcast to other locations in the company or videotaped for subsequent distribution and viewing

**corporate talk shows**
televised company meetings that allow remote audiences (employees) to pose questions to the show's host and guests

Televised/videotaped speeches and meetings are a third electronic method of organization-wide communication. **Televised/videotaped speeches and meetings** are simply speeches and meetings originally made to a smaller audience that are either simultaneously broadcast to other locations in the company or videotaped for subsequent distribution and viewing. For example, when Nationwide Insurance changed its logo and marketing strategy, it rented 33 movie theaters around the country, so that its employees could watch a live 90-minute satellite broadcast from company headquarters in Columbus, Ohio. Thanks to the live satellite broadcast, CEO Dimon McFersen and other top managers were able to explain to every Nationwide employee why those changes were being made. Said McFersen, "Companies that don't change, don't survive."[90]

Corporate talk shows are a variant on televised/videotaped speeches and meetings. But instead of simply watching a televised/videotaped speech or meeting, **corporate talk shows** allow remote audience members, all of whom are typically workers or managers, to pose questions to the show's host and guests. For example, once a month, Emma Carasco, vice president of marketing and communication, and Dan Hunt, president of Caribbean and Latin American operations, host the Virtual Leadership Academy, which is a corporate talk show for Nortel Networks. A typical broadcast is seen live by 2,000 employees in 46 countries, who call in with questions about Nortel and its competitors. Why a corporate talk show? Carrasco said, "We're always looking for ways to break down barriers in the company, and people are comfortable with the talk-show format. People watch talk shows in every country in the region, and they've learned that it's okay to say what's on their mind. In fact, it's expected."[91]

In Chapter 5, you learned that *voice messaging,* or "voice mail," is a telephone answering system that records audio messages. Eighty-nine percent of respondents believe that voice messaging is critical to business communication, 78 percent believe that it improves productivity, and 58 percent would rather leave a message on a voice messaging system than with a receptionist.[92]

Former Coke CEO Doug Ivester was a dedicated user of voice mail and used it every night to leave messages for Coke's senior managers in Europe, Asia, the United States, and Latin America to listen to when they come in each morning. Said Ivester, "Neville's [Head of Coke's European Offices] in Europe this morning, but I've already left him five voice mails. I've dealt with Spain, Italy, France, and a personnel issue in Eastern Europe. And I didn't even need to talk to him once."[93] However, most people are unfamiliar with the ability to *broadcast voice mail* by sending a recorded message to everyone in the company. Broadcast voice mail gives top managers a quick, convenient way to address their work forces via oral communication. The companywide, broadcast voice mails of Phil Laskawy, chairman of the consulting and accounting firm Ernst & Young, were so well known and well liked, that among E&Y employees, they came to be known as "Travels with Phil." No matter where he was traveling on business for the company—and he traveled all over

715

the world—Phil would begin his voice mails, most of which lasted five to 10 minutes, with a weather report, a couple of bad jokes, an update on the New York Yankees baseball team (which he followed), and then the core part of his message.[94]

### 4.2 Improving Reception: Hearing What Others Feel and Think

When people think of "organization-wide" communication, they think of the CEO and top managers getting their message out to people in the company. However, organization-wide communication also means finding ways to hear what people throughout the organization are feeling and thinking. Surprisingly, most employees and managers are reluctant to share their thoughts and feelings with top managers. Surveys indicate that only 29 percent of first-level managers felt that their companies encouraged employees to express their opinions openly. Another study in 22 companies found that 70 percent of the people surveyed were afraid to speak up about problems they knew existed at work. Withholding information about organizational problems or issues is called **organizational silence**. Organizational silence occurs when employees believe that telling management about problems won't make a difference, or that they'll be punished for sharing such information.[95] Fortunately, though, company hotlines, survey feedback, frequent informal meetings, and surprise visits are ways of overcoming organizational silence.

**Company hotlines** are phone numbers that anyone in the company can anonymously call to leave information for upper management. Some companies hire outside firms to run their hotlines to maintain the complete anonymity of callers. For example, Pillsbury's hotline, which is run by InTouch Corporation, doesn't even reveal callers' gender. Toyota's employee handbook says, "Don't spend time worrying about something. Speak up!" The Toyota hotline is anonymous and available 24 hours a day, seven days a week. Every message is reviewed and fully investigated by Toyota's top human resources manager. Moreover, if the questions or statements left on the hotline would be of interest to others in the company, they are then posted on company bulletin boards (without sacrificing callers' anonymity).[96]

**Survey feedback** is information collected by survey from organization members that is then compiled, disseminated, and used to develop action plans for improvement. Many organizations make use of survey feedback by surveying their managers and employees several times a year. FedEx, for example, runs its own Survey Feedback Action program. The survey, which is administered online and is completely anonymous, includes sections for employees to evaluate their managers and the overall environment at FedEx, including benefits, incentives, working conditions, and so forth. After the surveys are completed, the results are compiled, fed back, and made public to each FedEx work group. Each group then uses the results to decide where changes and improvements need to be made and to develop specific action plans to address those problems. The final step is to look for improvements in subsequent employee surveys to see if those plans worked.[97]

Frequent, *informal meetings* between top managers and lower-level employees are one of the best ways for top managers to hear what others feel and think. Many people assume that top managers are at the center of everything that goes on in organizations. However, top managers commonly feel isolated from most of the managers and employees in their companies. Consequently, more and more top managers are scheduling frequent, informal meetings with people throughout their companies. CEO John Chambers described how this works at Cisco Systems, "The birthday breakfasts are probably the most valuable sessions I do with employees. Once a month, anybody who has a birthday in that month can come and quiz [me] for about an hour and a half, and anything is fair game. We deliberately asked directors and VPs not to participate so that people who I don't get a chance normally to listen to can participate. And every single time I learn two or three things that either I need to do differently, or things that I thought were working one way weren't."[98]

Have you ever been around a supervisor who finds out that upper management is going to be paying a visit? First, there's shock. Next, there's anxiety. And then there's panic, as

---

**organizational silence**
when employees withhold information about organizational problems or issues

**company hotlines**
phone numbers that anyone in the company can anonymously call to leave information for upper management

**survey feedback**
information collected by surveys from organizational members that is then compiled, disseminated, and used to develop action plans for improvement

everyone is told to drop what they're doing to polish, shine, and spruce up the workplace, so it looks perfect for top management's visit. Of course, when visits are conducted under these conditions, top managers don't get a realistic look at what's going on in the company. Consequently, one of the ways to get an accurate picture is to pay *surprise visits* to various parts of the organization. However, surprise visits should not be surprise inspections, which is what Volkswagen's CEO Ferdinand Piech uses them for. Piech likes to keep his people nervous by making surprise visits to VW's technical center or its huge Wolfsburg factory.[99] *Business Week* magazine described his approach this way: "In an era when team-building and employee empowerment are in vogue, Piech prefers fear as a motivator."[100]

Instead, surprise visits should be used as an opportunity to increase the chance for meaningful upward communication from those who normally don't get a chance to work with upper management. Such surprise visits are part of the culture at Enterprise Rent-a-Car. Fred Sorino, who manages an Enterprise office in Eatontown, New Jersey, said, "Once I was working at a branch in Cranbury, New Jersey, and a corporate vice president and a regional president showed up for a surprise visit. I was outside washing cars in 20-degree weather, and we were very busy. These two executives offered to help me clean the cars. I felt so awkward that I said I didn't need help, but they did it anyway." Enterprise's CEO Andy Taylor tells a similar story, saying, "We were visiting an office in Berkeley and it was mobbed, so I started cleaning cars. As it was happening, I wondered if it was a good use of my time, but the effect on morale was tremendous."[101]

### Review 4
### Managing Organization-Wide Communication

Managers need methods for organization-wide communication and for making themselves accessible, so they can hear what employees throughout their organizations are feeling and thinking. Email, online discussion forums, televised/videotaped speeches and conferences, corporate talk shows, and broadcast voice mail make it much easier for managers to improve message transmission and "get the message out." By contrast, anonymous company hotlines, survey feedback, frequent informal meetings, and surprise visits help managers avoid organizational silence and improve reception by hearing what others in the organization feel and think.

## What Really Happened?

At the beginning of the chapter, you read about the start-up of Mutuals. com, a new financial company that charges flat fees instead of commissions for its services. Despite spectacular sales growth, the company had yet to earn a profit. Expenses were out-of-control, employees were reluctant to bring problems and issues to management's attention, and many in the company felt that management didn't care about employees any more. Read the answers to the opening case to see what really happened and to learn how the managers at Mutuals.com met this communication challenge.

**Well, if Mutuals.com is ever going to be successful, things are going to have to change. But how can you get employees to tell you what's wrong?**

When people think of communication, they think of the CEO and top managers getting their message out to people in the company. However, communication also means finding ways to hear what people throughout the organization are feeling and thinking. Surprisingly, most employees and managers are reluctant to share their thoughts and feelings with top managers. Surveys indicate that only 29 percent of first-level managers felt that their companies encouraged employees to express their opinions openly. Another study in 22 companies found that 70 percent of the people surveyed were afraid to speak up about problems they knew existed at work. Withholding information about organizational problems or issues is called organizational silence. Organizational silence occurs when employees believe that telling management about

problems won't make a difference, or that they'll be punished for sharing such information.

This was precisely the situation at Mutuals.com. Employees had begun to doubt whether it was worthwhile to bring problems and issues to the attention of top management any more. To solve this problem, CEO Rick Sapio started a new program called "Hassles." Sapio said, "If something takes up more than two minutes of your day, and it's not part of your ordinary job, then that's a hassle." More specifically, the point of the "Hassles" program is to get rid of the daily annoyances that make Mutuals.com's employees less productive. Employees who encounter problems or frustrations can send an email to an internal email folder labeled "hassles." For example, one emailed hassle read, "When we get a [sales] lead, why can't it be automatically added to the database without my having to retype it?" Another said, "Why do I need to fill out a form to request a vacation day?" And another said, "I have to constantly walk to the printer, and it's too far away from my desk." Each hassle, and about 100 come in per month, is supposed to be addressed by company management within a week. Chief financial officer Stefanie Nall, who is in charge of fixing the hassles, said, "The goal is 100 percent, but some of these are very substantial problems that require, for example, rewriting the software for our database. Within a month we probably get 75 percent solved."

### How can you send the message that you personally care about employees' thoughts and feelings?

Perhaps the best way to prove to employees that you care about their thoughts and feelings is to show them that you're listening. Active listening means assuming half the responsibility for successful communication by actively giving the speaker nonjudgmental feedback that shows you have accurately heard what he or she said. Active listeners make it clear from this behavior that they are listening carefully to the speaker. Active listeners put the speaker at ease, maintain eye contact, and show the speaker that they are attentively listening by nodding and making short statements.

The Hassles program described above has done a great job of encouraging employees to tell management what's wrong. However, some employees found it to be too impersonal. And that was the problem. As the company grew, Mutuals.com and its management had become too impersonal. To address this problem, CEO Rick Sapio now makes time every week for face-to-face discussions with anyone in the company. Every Friday morning, he sends an email that typically says that he'll be in the "back conference room from 11 A.M. to noon." During that hour, Sapio does one thing. He listens to employees' problems and concerns.

Sapio said, "You can tell people your door is open all you want, and they'll still think, 'No, he's the CEO. He's too busy.' But if you're sitting with nothing in front of you in a room with no more than a table, the message is 'I'm not busy. I am waiting here to talk to you.' And people come."

### How can you communicate the message that everyone has to find ways to control costs and do it in a way that doesn't build resentment?

Constructive feedback is intended to be helpful, corrective, and/or encouraging. It is aimed at correcting performance deficiencies and motivating employees. In order for feedback to be constructive rather than destructive, it must be immediate, focused on specific behaviors, and problem oriented. Because the mistake or incident can be recalled more accurately and discussed in detail by the manager and the worker, immediate feedback is much more effective than delayed feedback. Specific feedback focuses on particular acts or incidents that are clearly under the employee's control. Finally, problem-oriented feedback focuses on the problems or incidents associated with the poor performance rather than on the worker or the worker's personality.

Mutuals.com began giving managers and employees constructive feedback about costs and excess spending when it began "closing its books every day." Without going into a detailed explanation of accounting, this means that all financial transactions are entered into the "books" the day they occur and that Mutuals.com now has daily, real-time figures on the company's revenues and expenses. By contrast, most companies close their books only once or twice a year.

After making sure the company had immediate feedback on expenses and revenues, the next step was to get specific about spending. CEO Rick Sapio does this by meeting with his top managers every day at 4:37 P.M., right after the New York Stock Exchange closes. Each person at the meeting has full responsibility for one revenue item and one expense item. Said Sapio, "Every line item on our financial statement has a name next to it. So if travel's out of whack, I'll say, 'Ernie, give us a report on how we can lower travel next week.'" Those daily meetings then lead to weekly meetings, in which Sapio reviews and discusses detailed income statements (profits and losses) and balance sheets (assets and liabilities) with all employees. At one of those weekly meetings, an employee mentioned that transaction charges for trades (a cost to the firm) were rising just as fast as revenues. As a result, Sapio followed up by negotiating with the company's trading firm for a 25 percent cut in transaction charges.

The last step in providing constructive feedback about costs was to focus on the problems or incidents associated with excess spending rather than on the worker or the worker's personality. So the company implemented a policy in which employees would have to pay for unapproved expenses with their own money. When company president Eric McDonald spent $300 over his budget for an in-house employee dinner, it came out of his pocket. When CEO Sapio paid a consultant $6,000 to coach him on his leadership skills, he forgot to get the management team's approval before spending the money. He figured they would approve the expenditure after the fact. They didn't. Sapio paid the $6,000 himself.

**Sources:** E. Barker, "Cheap Executive Officer," *Inc.* [Online] Available http://www.inc.com/incmagazine/articles/24053.html, 1 April 2002. L. Buchanan, "Collecting Information about Individuals and Transforming It into Tailored Offerings Is the Stuff of One-To-One Marketing. Now Companies Are Taking That Concept and Focusing It on Their Own Employees," *Inc.*, 1 October 2001, 82. N. Martin, "Writing a New Chapter: An Author Tries to Make the Leap from Investment Theorist to Adviser," *Barron's*, 6 November 2000, 28. P. Rivera, "Financial Adviser Enjoys Firm's Emphasis on Goals of the Client," *Dallas Morning News*, 27 May 2001, 10L. S. Frank, "Playing the Net," *The Wall Street Journal*, 27 August 2000, 3.

acquaintance time *(712)*
active listening *(705)*
address terms *(710)*
affective cultures *(709)*
appointment time *(712)*
attribution theory *(690)*
closure *(690)*
coaching *(700)*
communication *(686)*
communication medium *(703)*
company hotlines *(716)*
conduit metaphor *(695)*
constructive feedback *(707)*
corporate talk shows *(715)*
counseling *(710)*
cross-cultural communication *(707)*
decoding *(694)*

defensive bias *(690)*
destructive feedback *(706)*
discussion time *(712)*
downward communication *(695)*
empathetic listening *(705)*
encoding *(694)*
feedback to sender *(694)*
formal communication channel *(695)*
fundamental attribution error *(691)*
hearing *(705)*
horizontal communication *(696)*
informal communication channel
("grapevine") *(697)*
kinesics *(701)*
listening *(705)*
monochronic cultures *(711)*
neutral cultures *(709)*

noise *(695)*
nonverbal communication *(701)*
online discussion forums *(714)*
organizational silence *(716)*
paralanguage *(702)*
perception *(688)*
perceptual filters *(688)*
polychronic cultures *(711)*
schedule time *(712)*
selective perception *(690)*
self-serving bias *(692)*
survey feedback *(716)*
televised/videotaped speeches and
meetings *(715)*
upward communication *(696)*

## What Would You Do-II

### Improve Communication? How About Start Communicating?

As the Chief Information Officer (CIO) at Intel, you spend a large amount of time thinking about technology and researching technological changes. You laugh when you think of how you used to be your parent's television remote control, having to change the channel or volume manually. Now, in your own home, it seems that if the remote control is missing or inoperable, watching television becomes more of a chore and less entertaining. Although email has been around only a few years, it seems that, like remote controls, everyone is addicted to it and cannot live without it. Perhaps this is why you and your staff receive so many desperate phone calls when glitches or routine maintenance cause the email servers to be taken offline. In fact, just yesterday, your staff had to take the main email server down to install a new patch that would serve to filter out a new string of spam messages (unsolicited email messages marketing products or services). Although this repair took less than one hour, you and your department received over 100 phone calls questioning when the email server would become operational again.

At Intel, the number of email messages sent and received seems to multiply every year. Worldwide, Intel averages around 3 million email messages a day, with some people averaging at least 300 messages in a 24-hour period. Given this amount of traffic, it is a miracle that the IT system works as well as it does. After all, you just read an article in *The Wall Street Journal* about how AOL Time Warner chose to use its consumer-based email system (AOL) for its business email server and is paying a very high price for what should have been a cheap solution to email. Important messages are routinely lost in the AOL system. Large attachments typical to the publishing industry (the Time Warner arm) are causing the AOL server to crash on a regular basis. As a result, AOL executives are abandoning the notion of corporate pride in using their own products—they just want a system that works!

Thankfully, your system runs well over 350 days a year. But technological efficiency is not the only issue: Efficient use of email is also an issue. In looking at your own in-box, you can see many instances where the use of email could have been improved or eliminated. For example, excluding all of the unsolicited, non-company-related emails you receive on a daily basis, your in-box is still clogged with numerous company-related emails that do not pertain to you or your department. Additionally, many of the emails you receive do not contain headings in the subject box, thereby requiring you to open and read the message to see if it is relevant. And once you do open the message, more often than you'd like, you find incomplete sentences, poor grammar, incoherent thoughts, or even a complete lack of purpose or action statement.

At recent executive meetings, you have spurred discussions focusing on the current use of email at Intel and you have been instrumental in forming a committee to brainstorm ways to improve the productivity of email messages and to eliminate sending and receiving non-company-related email messages within the organization. The same committee has also been charged with developing specific standards or guidelines to follow when communicating within the organization via email.

Out of this committee came a study developed to determine the amount of time spent on email on an average work day. The results of this study revealed that the average Intel employee spends approximately two-and-a-half hours a day reading, responding, sending, and deleting email messages. For white-collar positions, this can amount to a loss of productivity equal to approximately 6 percent of a worker's salary on an annual basis. In addition to the loss of productivity, the increasing quantity and size of email messages eats away at valuable bandwidth, thereby increasing the potential for system overload and server downtime. To further complicate matters, you read an article in a recent trade magazine which predicted that, due to

719

changes in Internet-based marketing, unsolicited emails and overall email volume is expected to rise by 45 percent in coming years.

You can't just throw out your email system and make people go back to FedEx, faxes, and phone calls (although some divisions of AOL Time Warner did just that). The first committee meeting is imminent. What will you suggest in the way of specific guidelines to reduce the amount of email being sent on a daily basis? You will also need to pinpoint how to improve the quality of the email that remains.

**If you were the CIO of Intel, what would you do to improve email communication within your firm?**

**Source:** A. Poe, "Don't Touch That 'Send' Button!," *HR Magazine*, July 2001, 74–80. M. Rudick and L. O'Flahavan, "Email for Good, Not Evil," *Training & Development*, May 20001, 113. A. Overholt, "Intel's Got (Too Much) Mail," *Fast Company*, March 2001, 56, available online at http://www.fastcompany.com, "Dangerous and Unproductive Email Costs UK Business," *Information Systems Auditor*, December 2001, 7. M. Rose and M. Peers, "AOL's Latest Internal Woe: 'You've Got Mail—Oops, No You Don't,'" *The Wall Street Journal*, 22 March 2002, B1, B5.

## Management Decisions

### Selling in Latin America

As you glance at the calendar on your desk, you realize that you only have two weeks left to prepare for your first international assignment. Since your recent promotion to the position of regional sales manager of the Southeast region for a mid-sized, multinational, telecommunications firm, you have spent the majority of your time working out of the home office in Atlanta, Georgia. What time you did spend traveling was spent visiting customers and offices in and around the Southeast region. Your new job entails describing your firm's products and services; explaining the benefits, price, and terms; and, once the customer agrees, closing the sale by signing a formal contract containing the necessary information.

During last month's regional managers' meeting, your boss informed you that because of your ability to speak Spanish fluently and your recent success in the Southeastern region of the United States, you would soon assume part of the Latin American region and would be responsible for meeting and dealing with customers in Mexico and parts of South America, in addition to your Southeastern region duties. Although you are excited at the prospect of traveling abroad, you are also a little nervous because, other than a week-long, school-sponsored trip to Ciudad Juarez, Mexico, you have never ventured out of the United States before.

The company's travel office has helped relieve some of your anxiety by performing a majority of the paperwork involved, preparing your passport, making your travel arrangements, and putting you in touch with the former regional manager for Latin America. Even though she has been a tremendous asset by telling you which hotel chains and restaurants are "decent" and

which are not, showing you how to avoid some of the customs inspection problems, and giving you an updated potential-customer database, she hasn't provided much information regarding the local culture of the area or your prospective customers' expectations. As a continent, Latin America is less developed in the area of telecommunications than the United States, so you are excited about the sales potential of the area. However, you also have some concerns.

One major area of concern is the myriad of cultural differences between the United States and Latin America. You believe that one of the reasons that you were so successful in the Southeastern region is because you really knew and understood your customers and their needs. Given the fact that you will be making cold calls, requesting appointments, making presentations to individuals and groups, and attempting to close on contractual agreements involving thousands of dollars, you feel your concerns are legitimate.

### Questions

1. As the manager in question, what could you do to help put an end to your uneasiness?
2. Although you speak Spanish, you know that language is not the only element of cross-cultural fluency. What issues will you be confronting with regards to cross-cultural communication in your new Latin American position? What can you do to overcome the obstacles to cross-cultural communication?

**Sources:** D. Benton, *Applied Human Relations*, 5th Edition (Prentice Hall, 1995), 533–544. G. Hofstede, "Organizational Dynamic," *AMACOM*, Summer 1980, 375–394.

## Management Decisions

### Reading the Signals

You are beaming with confidence as you walk down the hall to your supervisor's office. In just a few hours, you are presenting the company's new advertising campaign and strategy to the board of directors. At this meeting, the board will decide to either adopt the entire proposal or subcontract all of the marketing activities to an outside firm. Therefore, it is imperative to you and your staff that this presentation be a success. John, your supervisor, delegated the marketing campaign to you be-

cause of your educational background and previous work experience in the marketing field. The proposed ad campaign is the culmination of six months work and countless hours spent by you and your staff devising the future direction of advertising and marketing for the company. As a result, you are thoroughly pleased with what you believe is a true work of art.

As you approach John's office, you notice that he is busily typing away at his computer. John has an open-door policy and always encourages his staff to approach him with any situation, big or small. You knock lightly and John glances up to acknowledge your arrival. You inform him that you wanted to brief him on your upcoming presentation to the board. You also ask if now is a bad time and suggest that you can come back when it is more convenient. John responds that now is as good a time as any as he turns back toward his computer screen. Seeing that he is busy, you give John a quick run down of the proposal and your intended presentation. You leave many of the specifics out since John has either seen or participated in a majority of the advertising plans and is aware of the strategy's direction and overall theme.

As you launch into a discussion of your presentation with him, you notice that he is nodding in agreement with the information being given; however, he has not stopped typing, nor has he looked up at you since you walked into his office. Feeling that your discussion is purely one-sided, you close by asking if there is anything else that you should consider or include in your presentation that would make it more appealing or understandable to the group. John looks up from his computer and replies, "No, it sounds good to me. I can't think of anything else." He then turns back toward his computer and resumes typing.

When you leave John's office, you realize that your level of confidence is not as strong as it was just a few moments ago. In fact, you are now beginning to doubt that the board will accept your proposal at all. Throughout John's career, he has made many presentations to the board and seems to know exactly what they want to hear. In order to increase the effectiveness of your presentation, you were really counting on John's experience and input to help you make a perfect delivery. You glance at your watch realizing that you only have two hours until your big debut.

**Questions**
1. What would you do in this situation: Would you go back and ask John bluntly to listen to your presentation and provide his expert advice, or would you deliver the presentation like you had previously planned? Why?
2. What could the manager in question have done differently in this situation?

**Sources:** J. Cole, "Spotting Communication Problems," *Getting Results— For the Hands-On Manager*, May 1997, 8. A. Warfield, "Do You Speak Body Language?" *Training and Development*, April 2001, 60–61.

## Develop Your Managerial Potential

### I Don't Agree, But I'm Listening

Being a good listener is a critical part of effective communication. Without it, you're unlikely to be a good manager. Therefore, the purpose of this assignment is to help you develop your listening skills. And, there's no better way to do that than to talk to someone whose views are quite different from yours.

In the best of situations, being a good listener is difficult. Because of perceptual filters, distractions, or daydreams, you retain only about 25 percent of what you hear. However, it can be almost impossible to be a good listener when you're talking to someone who has very different views and opinions. When you talk to people with different views, it's easy to interrupt, jump to conclusions about what they'll say, and hurry them to finish their points (which you don't want to listen to anyway), so you can "correct" their thinking with your opinions.

To complete this assignment, you'll have to find someone who has different views or opinions on some topic (handgun control, abortion, capital punishment, and euthanasia are just some of the topics on which you can always find someone with a different viewpoint). Once you've found someone, conduct a 10-minute listening session, following this simple rule: Before stating your opinion, you must first accurately reflect or paraphrase the statement that your listening partner just made (be

sure to reread Section 3.2 on listening). So, if your listening partner said, "Women shouldn't have to ask anyone for permission for what they do to their bodies. If they decide they want an abortion, they should go ahead and have it," you would have to accurately paraphrase that statement in your own words before being allowed to make your point or disagree with your partner's. If you don't paraphrase it correctly, your listening partner will tell you. If you or your partner have difficulty accurately paraphrasing a statement, then ask the other person to repeat the statement, and try again. Also, don't parrot the response by repeating it word for word. Good listening isn't mimicry. It's capturing the essence of what others have said in your own words. And, before your listening partner responds, he or she, too, has to accurately paraphrase what you say. Continue this listening-based discussion for 10 minutes.

**Questions**
1. Was this different from the way in which you normally discuss contentious topics with other people? Why or why not?
2. Was it difficult to reflect or paraphrase your listening partner's perspectives? Explain and give an example.
3. What led to more effective listening for you, active listening techniques or empathetic listening techniques? Explain.

## Study Tip

Studying for comprehensive exams doesn't have to be a chore. Form a study group. Photocopy the *Management* 2e glossary and cut it into strips, one term per strip. Put all strips into a large bowl. Divide into teams and draw out one strip at a time. Quiz the opposing team and then read the correct answer. You

can do the same with the chapter outlines at the beginning of each chapter. You can tabulate points, but you'll all win!

For this chapter, you have two Xtra! CNN clips with cases and solutions on your CD. Watch and learn about the skills-oriented topics of love at work and business etiquette.

## Chapter 1

1. "Driving Innovation: The Automobile Repair Process, Accenture Helps Daimler-Chrysler Dealers Automate Customer Data Collection," Accenture, http://www. accenture.com/xdoc/en/industries/products/automotive/chrysler.pdf, 3 June 2001.

2. L. Lavelle, "Industry Outlook 2001: Professional Services," *Business Week*, 1 January 2001, 134.

3. J.A. Byrne, "The Craze for Consultants," *Business Week*, 25 July 1994, 60–66.

4. T. Peters, "The Leadership Alliance" (Pat Carrigan excerpt), *In Search of Excellence* (Northbrook, IL: Video Arts, distributor, 1985), videocassette.

5. C. Terhune, "Retail Giant Aims to Spur Sales with Less-Cluttered Stores, Increased Customer Service," *The Wall Street Journal*, 8 March 2001, B1.

6. *Ibid.*

7. R. Stagner, "Corporate Decision Making," *Journal of Applied Psychology* 53 (1969): 1–13.

8. D.W. Bray, R.J. Campbell, & D.L. Grant, *Formative Years in Business: A Long-Term AT&T Study of Managerial Lives* (New York: Wiley, 1993).

9. B. Dumaine, "The New Non-Manager Managers," *Fortune*, 22 February 1993, 80–84.

10. *Ibid.*

11. K. Brooker, "I Built This Company, I Can Save It," *Fortune*, 30 April 2001, 94.

12. J. Simons, "Has Palm Lost Its Grip?" *Fortune*, 28 May 2001, 105.

13. J. Creswell, "Would You Give This Man Your Company?" *Fortune*, 28 May 2001, 127.

14. *Ibid.*

15. Staff Reporter, "Entrepreneur Mary Kay Ash: Unflagging Faith Lifted Her to Top of Cosmetics World," *Investor's Business Daily*," 5 May 1998, A1.

16. A. Farnham, "Mary Kay's Lessons in Leadership," *Fortune*, 20 September 1993, 68–77.

17. G. Colvin. "The Changing Art of Becoming Unbeatable" *Fortune*, 24 November 1997, 299–300.

18. K. Brooker, "The Chairman of the Board Looks Back," *Fortune*, 28 May 2001, 63. K. Labich, "Is Herb Kelleher America's Best CEO?" *Fortune*, 2 May 1994, 44–52.

19. H.S. Jonas, III, R.E. Fry, & S. Srivastva, "The Office of the CEO: Understanding the Executive Experience," *Academy of Management Executive* 4 (1990): 36–47.

20. J.S. Lublin & M. Murray, "CEOs Leave Faster Than Ever Before as Boards, Investors Lose Patience," *The Wall Street Journal Interactive*, 27 October, 2000.

21. K. Labich, "Is Herb Kelleher America's Best CEO?" *Fortune*, 2 May 1994, 44–52.

22. H.S. Jonas, III, R.E. Fry, & S. Srivastva, "The Office of the CEO: Understanding the Executive Experience," *Academy of Management Executive* 4 (1990): 36–47.

23. M. Murray, "As Huge Firms Keep Growing, CEOs Struggle to Keep Pace," *The Wall Street Journal*, 8 February 2001, A1.

24. *Ibid.*

25. B. Saporito, "David Glass Won't Crack under Fire," *Fortune*, 3 February 1991, 75–80.

26. *Ibid.*

27. *Ibid.*

28. D. Milbank, "'New-Collar' Work: Telephone Sales Reps Do Unrewarding Jobs that Few Can Abide," *The Wall Street Journal*, 9 September 1993, A1.

29. *Ibid.*

30. B.M. Bass, *Stogdill's Handbook of Leadership* (New York: Free Press, 1981).

31. J. Vrba, "The 'Grass Roots' Training of a Young Administrator," *Nursing Homes*, 1 April 1995.

32. S. Tully, "What Team Leaders Need to Know," *Fortune*, 20 February 1995.

33. *Ibid.*

34. K. Hultman, "The 10 Commandments of Team Leadership," *Training & Development*, 1 February 1998, 12–13.

35. S. Tully, "What Team Leaders Need to Know," *Fortune*, 20 February 1995.

36. N. Steckler & N. Fondas, "Building Team Leader Effectiveness: A Diagnostic Tool," *Organizational Dynamics*, Winter 1995, 20–34.

37. J.S. Case, "What the Experts Forgot to Mention," *Inc.*, 1 September 1993, 66.

38. S. Tully, "What Team Leaders Need to Know," *Fortune*, 20 February 1995.

39. H. Mintzberg, *The Nature of Managerial Work* (New York: Harper & Row, 1973).

40. C.P. Hales, "What Do Managers Do? A Critical Review of the Evidence," *Journal of Management Studies* 23, no. 1 (1986): 88–115.

41. J. Huey, "The World's Best Brand," *Fortune*, 31 May 1993, 44.

42. M. Boyd, "Motivating on a Dime," *Sales & Marketing Management*, 1 March 1995.

43. B. Einhorn & M. Kripalani, "India 3.0: Bangalore Wants to Move Beyond Simple Code," *Business Week*, 26 February 2001, 16.

44. C. Hymowitz, "How Some CEOs Get the Energy to Work Those Endless Days," *The Wall Street Journal*," 3 March 2001, B1.

45. D. Hauss, "Technology Gives Early Warning of News Breaks," *Public Relations Journal*, 1 May 1995.

46. M. Murray, "As Huge Firms Keep Growing, CEOs Struggle to Keep Pace," *The Wall Street Journal*, 8 February 2001, A1.

47. K. Hutchison, "Sears Sets Initiatives to Boost Bottom Line," *Retailing Today*, 21 May 2001, 1.

48. "Nortel Operating Chief Resigns; Firm Steps Up Search for CEO," *Dow Jones Business News*, 11 May 2001.

49. J. Flaherty, "Bosses Make Cost Consultants out of Blue-Collar Workers," *New York Times*, 18 April 2001.

50. M. Rose, "Cost Cuts, Other Shocks Lift Profits but Sap Morale at *Reader's Digest*," *The Wall Street Journal*, 18 April 2000.

51. S. Ascarelli & J. R. Hagerty, "British Telecom to Split Up in Broad Renewal—Moving to Cut Huge Debt, BT Will Try to Raise $8.38 Billion in Offering," *The Wall Street Journal*, 11 May 2001, A11.

52. D.W. Linden, "You Want Somebody to Like You, Get a Dog." *Forbes*, 28 August 1995, 44–46.

53. K. Capell, C. Tromben, W. Echikson, & W. Zellner, "Renegade Ryanair: Can CEO Michael O'Leary Capture the Continent?" *Business Week*, 14 May 2001.

54. L.A. Hill, *Becoming a Manager: Mastery of a New Identity* (Boston, MA: Harvard Business School Press, 1992).

55. R.L. Katz, "Skills of an Effective Administrator," *Harvard Business Review,* September-October 1974, 90–102.

56. B. Schlender, "The Beast is Back," *Fortune,* 11 June 2001, 75.

57. C.A. Bartlett & S. Ghoshal, "Changing the Role of Top Management: Beyond Systems to People," *Harvard Business Review,* May-June 1995, 132–142.

58. F.L. Schmidt & J.E. Hunter, "Development of a Causal Model of Process Determining Job Performance," *Current Directions in Psychological Science* 1 (1992): 89–92.

59. J.B. Miner, "Sentence Completion Measures in Personnel Research: The Development and Validation of the Miner Sentence Completion Scales," in *Personality Assessment in Organizations,* eds. H.J. Bernardin & D.A. Bownas (New York: Praeger, 1986), 147–146.

60. M.W. McCall, Jr. & M.M. Lombardo, "What Makes a Top Executive?" *Psychology Today,* February 1983, 26–31. E. van Velsor & J. Brittain, "Why Executives Derail: Perspectives across Time and Cultures," *Academy of Management Executive,* November 1995, 62–72.

61. M.W. McCall, Jr. & M.M. Lombardo, "What Makes a Top Executive?" *Psychology Today,* February 1983, 26–31.

62. S.N. Chakravarty, "The Best-Laid Plans . . .," *Forbes,* 3 January 1994, 44–45.

63. T.E. Ricks, "The New Brass Get in Touch with Their 'Inner Jerks,'" *The Wall Street Journal Interactive Edition,* 19 January 1998.

64. A.K. Naj, "Corporate Therapy: The Latest Addition to Executive Suite Is Psychologist's Couch," *The Wall Street Journal,* 29 August 1994, A1.

65. S. Stecklow, "Chief Prerequisite for College President's Job: Stamina," *The Wall Street Journal,* 1 December 1994, B1.

66. J. Pfeffer, "Producing Sustainable Competitive Advantage through the Effective Management of People," *Academy of Management Executive* 9 (1995): 55–72.

67. *Ibid.*

68. J. Pfeffer, *The Human Equation: Building Profits by Putting People First* (Boston, MA: Harvard Business School Press, 1996). J. Pfeffer, *Competitive Advantage through People: Unleashing the Power of the Work Force* (Boston, MA: Harvard Business School Press, 1994).

69. M.A. Huselid, "The Impact of Human Resource Management Practices on Turnover, Productivity, and Corporate Financial Performance," *Academy of Management Journal* 38 (1995): 635–672.

70. D. McDonald & A. Smith, "A Proven Connection: Performance Management and Business Results," *Compensation & Benefits Review* 27, no. 6 (1 January 1995): 59.

71. B. Schneider & D.E. Bowen, "Employee and Customer Perceptions of Service in Banks: Replication and Extension," *Journal of Applied Psychology* 70 (1985): 423–33. B. Schneider, J.J. Parkington, & V.M. Buxton, "Employee and Customer Perceptions of Service in Banks," *Administrative Science Quarterly* 25 (1980): 252–67.

### Chapter 2

1. E. Beck, "Germany Orders Wal-Mart, Rivals to Increase Prices in Their Stores: Antitrust Office Says Wal-Mart, Two Others Sold Food Below Cost," *The Wall Street Journal Europe,* 11 September 2000.

2. J. Apperson, "Liquor Retailer Protests Md. Law Store Says Banning Bulk-Discount Buys Is Antitrust Violation," *The Baltimore Sun,* 3 July 2000, 1A.

3. P. Sinton, "No Wine Across the Line / Vintners Confront States' Shipping Laws," *The San Francisco Chronicle,* 29 January 2001, B1.

4. Tedeschi, "Acquisitions Have Made eVineyard the Top Online Wine Seller, But It Still Must Show That the Concept Can Succeed," *The New York Times,* 7 May 2001, 9.

5. S. Ginsberg, "CEO's Aggressive, No-Nonsense Style Leads EA to Victory," *San Francisco Business Times,* 26 September 1997. R. Manning, "Countdown to Christmas: Titans Tout Their Newest Video-Gaming Systems in L.A.," *The Courier-Journal* (Louisville, KY), 26 May 2001, 10S.

6. E. Romanelli & M.L. Tushman, "Organizational Transformation as Punctuated Equilibrium: An Empirical Test," *Academy of Management Journal* 37 (1994): 1141–1166.

7. H. Banks, "A Sixties Industry in a Nineties Economy," *Forbes,* 9 May 1994, 107–112.

8. L. Cowan, "Cheap Fuel Should Carry Many Airlines to More Record Profits for 1st Quarter," *The Wall Street Journal,* 4 April 1998, B17A.

9. G. Morgenson, "Denial in Battle Creek," *Forbes,* 7 October 1996, 44–46.

10. J.B. White & J.S. Lublin, "Some Concerns Try to Rebuild Loyalty among Employees," *The Wall Street Journal Interactive Edition,* 27 September 1996.

11. K.A. Dolan, "Help Wanted: Urgent!" *Forbes,* 7 October 1996, 18–20.

12. M. Leibovich, "A Rain God Confronts a Harsh Climate; CEO's Optimism Tested by Downturn," *The Washington Post,* 6 April 2001, A01.

13. M. Conlin, M. Mandel, M. Ardnt, & W. Zeller, "Suddenly, It's the Big Freeze: As the Economy Cools, the Hiring Door Slams Shut on Job Seekers," *Business Week,* 16 April 2001, 38.

14. *Ibid.*

15. B. Powell & C. Kano, "Monster Problems: Japan Is Getting Pretty Scary. So Is the U.S. in for a Fright?" *Fortune,* 2 April 2001, 82.

16. R. Norton, "Where Is This Economy Really Heading?" *Fortune,* 7 August 1995, 54–56.

17. Los Angeles Times, "Encarta vs. Britannica," *Newsday,* 14 March 2001, C10.

18. D. Carpenter, "Struggling Britannica Reunites Online Unit with Parent," *Chicago Sun-Times (A.P.),* 17 May 2001.

19. J. Fletcher, "Extreme Nesting," *The Wall Street Journal,* 7 January 2000, W1.

20. R. Sharpe, "Nannies on Speed Dial: There Is Growing Army of Domestic Help Out There, And More and More Families Are Picking Up the Phone," *Business Week,* 18 September, 2000, 108.

21. *Ibid.*

22. D. Frum, "Speed Brake," *Forbes,* 11 October 1993, 162.

23. "The Family and Medical Leave Act of 1993," *U.S. Department of Labor.* [Online] Available http://www.dol.gov/dol/esa/public/regs/compliance/whd/whdfs28.htm, 18 June 2001.

24. A. Caffrey, "Bay State's Enforcement of 'Rideshare' Draws Fire," *The Wall Street Journal,* 18 March 1998, NE1.

25. R.J. Bies & T.R. Tyler, "The Litigation Mentality in Organizations: A Test of Alternative Psychological Explanations," *Organization Science* 4 (1993): 352–366.

26. D. Jones, "Fired Workers Fight Back . . . and Win: Laws, Juries Shift Protection to Terminated Employees," *USA Today,* 2 April 1998, B1.

27. S. Gardner, G. Gomes, & J. Morgan, "Wrongful Termination and the Expanding Public Policy Exception: Implications and Advice," *SAM Advanced Management Journal* 65 (2000): 38.

28. D. Jones, "Fired Workers Fight Back . . . and Win: Laws, Juries Shift Protection to Terminated Employees," *USA Today,* 2 April 1998, B1.

29. J. Semas, "Companies Want to Recall Defective Product Liability Laws," *San Francisco Business Times,* 18 August 1995.

30. *Ibid.*

31. S. Hill, "30 Small-Business Trends You Should Act on Now!" *Fortune,* 2 April 2001, 148.

32. "Investor Relations: Frequently Asked Questions," *D.R. Horton.* [Online] Available, http://199.230.26.95/dhi/faq.shtml, 18 June 2001.

33. S. Hill, "30 Small-Business Trends You Should Act on Now!" *Fortune,* 2 April 2001, 148.

34. D. Smart & C. Martin, "Manufacturer Responsiveness to Consumer Correspondence: An Empirical Investigation of Consumer Perceptions," *Journal of Consumer Affairs* 26 (1992): 104.

35. H. Appelman, "I Scream, You Scream: Consumers Vent Over the Net," *The New York Times,* 4 March 2001.

36. "What's New in Cotton," *Lifestyle Monitor, Cotton Incorporated.* [Online] Available http://www.cottoninc.com/lifemon2a.htm, 4 October 1996.

37. "Forever in Blue Jeans," *Lifestyle Monitor, Cotton Incorporated.* [Online] Available http://www.cottoninc.com/wwd/homepage.cfm?PAGE=2677, 22 February 2001.

38. S.G. Maycumber, "Cotton Inc.'s Lifestyle Monitor Puts Together a Year's Data; Price Looms Large in Apparel Purchases," *Daily News Record,* 4 January 1996, 11.

39. S.A. Zahra & S.S. Chaples, "Blind Spots in Competitive Analysis," *Academy of Management Executive* 7 (1993): 7–28.

40. Bianco & P. Moore, "Downfall: The Inside Story of the Management Fiasco at Xerox," *Business Week,* 5 March 2001, 82.

41. J.M. Moran, "Getting Closer Together—Videophones Don't Deliver TV Quality Sound, Visuals, But They're Improving," *The Seattle Times,* 15 March 1998.

42. F. McCarthy, "The Shape of Phones To Come: Report: Telecommunications: Starting as a Hobbyist Movement Five Years Ago, 'Voice over Internet Protocol' Is Quietly Remaking the Telephone System Worldwide," *The Economist,* 23 March 2001, available online.

43. J. Fowler, "Long-Distance Calls Via Internet Shakeup Global Industry," *Associated Press Newswires,* 6 March 2001.

44. T. Shurley, "Internet Phone System Could Revolutionize Long Distance," *Springfield Business Journal,* 29 May 1995.

45. K.G. Provan, "Embeddedness, Interdependence, and Opportunism in Organizational Supplier-Buyer Networks," *Journal of Management* 19 (1993): 841–856.

46. N. Gaouette, "Israel's Diamond Dealers Tremble: Diamond Colossus Debeers Today Launches Fundamental Changes to $56 Billion Retail Market," *Christian Science Monitor,* 1 June 2001, available online.

47. F. Shalom, "Clothing Firms Fight Wal-Mart Price Rollbacks," *Montreal Gazette,* 6 July 1995, available online.

48. C. Duff, "Big Stores' Outlandish Demands Alienate Small Suppliers," *The Wall Street Journal,* 27 October 1995, B1.

49. D. Birch, "Staying On Good Terms," *Supply Management,* 12 April 2001, 36.

50. K. Stringer, "People Who Need People: The Relationship Between Buyer and Supplier Can't Be Handled Entirely Online; A Case in Point: Nancy Naatz," *The Wall Street Journal,* 21 May 2001, R14.

51. B.K. Pilling, L.A. Crosby, & D.W. Jackson, "Relational Bonds in Industrial Exchange: An Experimental Test of the Transaction Cost Economic Framework," *Journal of Business Research* 30 (1994): 237–251.

52. W. Tucker, "Over-Regulation and the Black Market," *Consumers' Research Magazine* 74 (1 October 1991): 32.

53. S. Kazman, "Large Vehicles Are the Solution, Not the Problem," *The Wall Street Journal,* 12 March 1998, A18.

54. R. Spencer, "Final Standards Issued on Care at Nation's Nursing Homes," *Los Angeles Times,* 11 November 1994, D-2.

55. B. Menninger & D. Margolies, "Business Groans under Weight of Regulations," *Puget Sound Business Journal,* 3 March 1995, 16.

56. "Sports Stars Team Up to Defeat Tobacco Use and Secondhand Smoke," *PR Newswire,* 22 May 2001.

57. B. Sizemore, "Peta: Lean and Mean Norfolk-Based Group's Zeal Pushes the Envelope Too Far for Some," *The Virginian-Pilot,* 3 December 2000, A1.

58. "Ecopledge.com Names New Targets; Corporations Asked to Improve Environmental Practices," *U-Wire,* 19 April 2001.

59. "Technology Weighs Heavily on Minds of Hoteliers," *Hotel & Motel Management,* 6 November 1995.

60. L. Holson, "In California, Blackouts Spur a Search for Home Remedies," *The New York Times,* 31 May 2001, 1.

61. D.F. Jennings & J.R. Lumpkin, "Insights Between Environmental Scanning Activities and Porter's Generic Strategies: An Empirical Analysis," *Journal of Management* 4 (1992): 791–803.

62. B. Ettore, "Managing Competitive Intelligence," *Management Review,* October 1995, 15–19.

63. S.E. Jackson & J.E. Dutton, "Discerning Threats and Opportunities," *Administrative Science Quarterly* 33 (1988): 370–387.

64. J.B. Thomas, S.M. Clark, & D.A. Gioia, "Strategic Sensemaking and Organizational Performance: Linkages among Scanning, Interpretation, Action, and Outcomes," *Academy of Management Journal* 36 (1993): 239–270.

65. R. Daft, J. Sormunen, & D. Parks, "Chief Executive Scanning, Environmental Characteristics, and Company Performance: An Empirical Study," *Strategic Management Journal* 9 (1988): 123–139. D. Miller & P.H. Friesen, "Strategy-Making and Environment: The Third Link," *Strategic Management Journal* 4 (1983): 221–235.

66. S. Kraft, "Tradition under Siege Supermarkets? Sacre Bleu! A Shopping Revolution Imperils French Merchants," *Los Angeles Times,* 5 May 1996, D10.

67. S. Branch & E. Beck, "For Unilever, It's Sweetness and Light—Company Buys Ben & Jerry's, Famed Ice-Cream Maker, And Slim-Fast on Same Day," *The Wall Street Journal,* 13 April 2000, B1.

68. C. Fishman, "Sanity Inc.: SAS Institute Inc. Is the Most Important Software Company You've Never Heard Of. It's Also the Sanest Company in America—A Place Where Employees Can Eat Lunch with Their Kids, Everyone Gets Unlimited Sick Days, And the Gate Clangs Shut at 6 P.M.," *Fast Company,* 1 January 1999, 84.

69. Salter. "Insanity Inc.: Trilogy Software Inc. Is One of the Fastest-Growing Software Companies Around. It's Also One of the Craziest Companies Around—A Place Where New Employees Cram All Day, Work All Night, And Take a Break by Hopping on a Plane to Play Roulette in Vegas," *Fast Company,* 1 January 1999, 100.

70. C. Fishman, "Sanity Inc.: SAS Institute Inc. Is the Most Important Software Company You've Never Heard Of. It's Also the Sanest Company in America—A Place Where Employees Can Eat Lunch with Their Kids, Everyone Gets Unlimited Sick Days, And the Gate Clangs Shut at 6 P.M.," *Fast Company,* 1 January 1999, 84.

71. C. Salter. "Insanity Inc.: Trilogy Software Inc. Is One of the Fastest-Growing Software Companies Around. It's Also One

of the Craziest Companies Around—A Place Where New Employees Cram All Day, Work All Night, And Take a Break by Hopping on a Plane to Play Roulette in Vegas," *Fast Company*, 1 January 1999, 100.

72. P. Elmer-DeWitt, "Mine, All Mine; Bill Gates Wants a Piece of Everybody's Action. But Can He Get It?" *Time*, 5 June 1995.

73. D.M. Boje, "The Storytelling Organization: A Study of Story Performance in an Office-Supply Firm," *Administrative Science Quarterly* 36 (1991): 106–126.

74. S. Walton & J. Huey, *Sam Walton: Made in America.* (New York: Doubleday, 1992).

75. D. Rushe, "Wal-martians," *Sunday Times—London*, 10 June 2001, 5.

76. L. McCauley, "How May I Help You?: Unit of One," *Fast Company*, 1 March 2000, 93.

77. D.R. Denison & A.K. Mishra, "Toward a Theory of Organizational Culture and Effectiveness," *Organization Science* 6 (1995): 204–223.

78. C. Fishman, "Sanity Inc.: SAS Institute Inc. Is the Most Important Software Company You've Never Heard Of. It's Also the Sanest Company In America—A Place Where Employees Can Eat Lunch with Their Kids, Everyone Gets Unlimited Sick Days, And the Gate Clangs Shut at 6 P.M.," *Fast Company*, 1 January 1999, 84.

79. "Company Profile," F.H. Faulding & Company. [Online] Available http://www.faulding.com.au/home/comp_profile/mission/mission.html, 21 June 2001.

80. S. Yearout, G. Miles, & R. Koonce, "Multi-Level Visioning," *Training & Development*, 1 March 2001, 31.

81. T. Brown, "A Vision from Scratch," *Across the Board*, 1 May 2001, 77.

82. P.E. Bierly, III. & J.C. Spender, "Culture and High Reliability Organizations: The Case of the Nuclear Submarine," *Journal of Management* 21 (1995): 639–656.

83. E. Schein, *Organizational Culture and Leadership*, 2nd ed. (San Francisco: Jossey-Bass, 1992).

84. L. Hays, "Gerstner Is Struggling as He Tries to Change Ingrained IBM Culture," *The Wall Street Journal*, 13 May 1994, A1.

85. S. Albert & D.A. Whetten, "Organizational Identity," *Research in Organizational Behavior* 7 (1985): 263–295. C.M. Fiol, "Managing Culture as a Competitive Resource: An Identity-Based View of Sustainable Competitive Advantage,"

*Journal of Management* 17 (1991): 191–211.

86. J. Huey (with G. Bethune and H. Kelleher), "Outlaw Flyboy CEOs: Two Texas Mavericks Rant about the Wreckage of the U.S. Aviation Industry—And Reveal How They've Managed to Keep Their Companies above the Miserable Average," *Fortune*, 13 November 2000, 237.

87. R. Heaster, "A Shift in Direction: Yellow Corp. Seeks Return to Strength with New Leader," *Kansas City Star*, 24 July 1996, B1.

88. C. Daniels, "Does This Man Need a Shrink? Companies Are Using Psychological Testing to Screen Candidates for Top Jobs. But Should a Shrink Determine Your Professional Future?" *Fortune*, 5 February 2001, 205.

89. *Ibid.*

90. S. Chakravarty, "Hit 'Em Hardest with the Mostest. (Southwest Airlines' Management)," *Forbes*, 16 September 1991, 48.

91. K. Godsey, "Slow Climb to New Heights; Combine Strict Discipline with Goofy Antics and Make Billions," *Success*, 1 October 1996, 20.

## Chapter 3

1. A. Losciale, "Survey Finds More Than 75% of Workers Say They Have Seen Unethical Conduct," *The Salt Lake Tribune*, 27 May 2000, C2.

2. C. Smith, "The Ethical Workplace," *Association Management* 52 (2000): 70–73.

3. E. Petry, A. Mujica, & D. Vickery, "Sources and Consequences of Workplace Pressure: Increasing the Risk of Unethical and Illegal Business Practices," *Business & Society Review* 99 (1998): 25–30.

4. M. Jackson (Associated Press), "Workplace Cheating Rampant, Half of Employees Surveyed Admit They Take Unethical Actions," *Peoria Journal Star*, 5 April 1997.

5. A. Losciale, "Survey Finds More Than 75% of Workers Say They Have Seen Unethical Conduct," *The Salt Lake Tribune*, 27 May 2000, C2.

6. C. Smith, "The Ethical Workplace," *Association Management* 52 (2000): 70–73.

7. S. Stamberg, "Aaron Feuerstein, Owner of Malden Mills, Explains the Reasoning behind His Employee Policies in the Aftermath of a Devastating Fire," *NPR: Morning Edition*, 20 March 2001.

8. M. Maremont, "Blind Ambition: How the Pursuit of Results Got Out of Hand at Bausch & Lomb," *Business Week*, 23 October 1995.

9. M. Bordwin, "Don't Ask Employees to Do Your Dirty Work," *Management Review*, 1 October 1995.

10. G. Simpson & S. Thurm, "Web of Interests: At Cisco, Executives Accumulate Stakes in Clients, Suppliers—Firm Says This Is Legitimate but Has Revised Policy; FBI Probes One Deal—A 'Disguised Compensation'?" *The Wall Street Journal*, 3 October 2000, A1.

11. M. Maremont, "Blind Ambition: How the Pursuit of Results Got Out of Hand at Bausch & Lomb," *Business Week*, 23 October 1995.

12. E. Nelson, "Bausch & Lomb Will Disburse up to $68 Million to Settle Suit," *The Wall Street Journal Interactive Edition*, 2 August 1996.

13. K. Gibson, "Excuses, Excuses: Moral Slippage in the Workplace," *Business Horizons* 43 no. 6 (2000): 65. S.L. Robinson & R.J. Bennett, "A Typology of Deviant Workplace Behaviors: A Multidimensional Scaling Study," *Academy of Management Journal* 38 (1995): 555–572.

14. *Ibid.*

15. L. Peek & B. Webster, "Sabotage Feared over Airliners' Cut Wires," *The Times of London*, 9 June 2001, 14.

16. S. Gaudin, "Computer Sabotage Case Back in Court," *Network World Fusion*, 19 April 2001, 12.

17. L. Lorek, "Sticky Fingers," *Interactive Week from ZDWire*, 27 March 2001.

18. M. France & M. Arndt, "After the Shooting Stops: When Employees Are Murdered on the Job, The Trauma Can Last for Years. How Companies Cope," *Business Week*, 12 March 2001, 98.

19. J. Merchant & J. Lundell, "Workplace Violence: A Report to the Nation." *The University of Iowa Injury Prevention Center.* [Online] Available http://www.pmeh.uiowa.edu/iprc/NATION.PDF, 24 June 2001.

20. M.P. Coco, Jr., "The New War Zone: The Workplace," *SAM Advanced Management Journal* 63, no. 1 (1998): 15. M.G. Harvey & R.A. Cosier, "Homicides in the Workplace: Crisis or False Alarm?" *Business Horizons* 38, no. 10 (1995): 11.

21. D. Palmer & A. Zakhem, "Bridging the Gap Between Theory and Practice: Using the 1991 Federal Sentencing Guidelines as a Paradigm for Ethics Training," *Journal of Business Ethics* 29 no. ½ (2001): 77–84.

22. D.R. Dalton, M.B. Metzger, & J.W. Hill, "The 'New' U.S. Sentencing Commission Guidelines: A Wake-Up Call for

726

Corporate America," *Academy of Management Executive* 8 (1994): 7–16.

23. B. Ettore, "Crime and Punishment: A Hard Look at White-Collar Crime," *Management Review* 83 (1994): 10–16.

24. F. Robinson & C.C. Pauze, "What Is a Board's Liability for Not Adopting a Compliance Program?" *Healthcare Financial Management* 51, no. 9 (1997): 64.

25. *Ibid.*

26. B. Schwartz, "The Nuts and Bolts of an Effective Compliance Program," *HR Focus* 74 no. 8 (1997): 13(2).

27. L.A. Hays, "A Matter of Time: Widow Sues IBM over Death Benefits," *The Wall Street Journal*, 6 July 1995.

28. T.M. Jones, "Ethical Decision Making by Individuals in Organizations: An Issue-Contingent Model," *Academy of Management Review* 16 (1991): 366–395.

29. B. Mook, "Group Gets Tough on 'Software Piracy,'" *Denver Business Journal*, 6 March 1998, 19A.

30. L. Kohlberg, "Stage and Sequence: The Cognitive-Developmental Approach to Socialization," in *Handbook of Socialization Theory and Research*, ed. D.A. Goslin (Chicago: Rand McNally, 1969). L. Trevino, "Moral Reasoning and Business Ethics: Implications for Research, Education, and Management," *Journal of Business Ethics* 11 (1992): 445–459.

31. L.T. Hosmer, "Trust: The Connecting Link Between Organizational Theory and Philosophical Ethics," *Academy of Management Review* 20 (1995): 379–403.

32. R.K. Bennett, "How Honest Are We?" *Reader's Digest*, December 1995, 49–55.

33. L. Callaway, "On the Wallet Watch—Honesty's Not Big Apple's Policy," *New York Post*, 31 July 2000, 41.

34. A. Golab, "Results of Honesty Test: Mostly 'Finders, Keepers'," *Chicago Sun-Times*, 12 March 1999, 3.

35. M.R. Cunningham, D.T. Wong, & A.P. Barbee, "Self-Presentation Dynamics on Overt Integrity Tests: Experimental Studies of the Reid Report," *Journal of Applied Psychology* 79 (1994): 643–658.

36. H.J. Bernardin, "Validity of an Honest Test in Predicting Theft among Convenience Store Employees," *Academy of Management Journal* 36 (1993): 1097–1108.

37. J.M. Collins & F.L. Schmidt, "Personality, Integrity, and White Collar Crime: A Construct Validity Study," *Personnel Psychology* (1993): 295–311.

38. W.C. Borman, M.A. Hanson, & J.W. Hedge, "Personnel Selection," *Annual Review of Psychology* 48 (1997).

39. P.E. Murphy, "Corporate Ethics Statements: Current Status and Future Prospects," *Journal of Business Ethics* 14 (1995): 727–740.

40. "Living the Commitments: Bribes and Kickbacks," Nortel Networks. [Online] Available http://www.nortelnetworks.com/corporate/community/ethics/living7.html#3, 24 June 2001.

41. "Living the Commitments: Gifts and Entertainment," Nortel Networks. [Online] Available http://www.nortelnetworks.com/corporate/community/ethics/living7.html#2, 24 June 2001.

42. S.J. Harrington, "What Corporate America Is Teaching about Ethics," *Academy of Management Executive* 5 (1991): 21–30.

43. L.A. Berger, "Train All Employees to Solve Ethical Dilemmas," *Best's Review—Life-Health Insurance Edition* 95 (1995): 70–80.

44. M. McCarthy, "How One Firm Tracks Ethics Electronically," *The Wall Street Journal*, 21 October 1999, B1.

45. R. McGarver, "Doing the Right Thing," *Training* 30 (1993): 35–38.

46. L. Trevino, G. Weaver, D. Gibson, & B. Toffler, "Managing Ethics and Legal Compliance: What Works and What Hurts," *California Management Review* 41 no. 2 (1999): 131–151.

47. "Business Ethics Training: Teaching Right from Wrong," *The Salt Lake Tribune*, 11 June 2000, E5.

48. L. Trevino, G. Weaver, D. Gibson, & B. Toffler, "Managing Ethics and Legal Compliance: What Works and What Hurts," *California Management Review* 41 no. 2 (1999): 131–151.

49. B. Ettore, "Crime and Punishment: A Hard Look at White-Collar Crime," *Management Review* 83 (1994): 10–16.

50. M. Schwartz, "Business Ethics: Time to Blow the Whistle?" *Globe and Mail*, 5 March 1998, B2.

51. M. Jacobs, "The Legal Option: Employees Dreamed of Getting Rich from Stock Options; Now They're Heading to Court to Make Sure Those Dreams Come True," *The Wall Street Journal*, 12 April 2001, R9.

52. M.P. Miceli & J.P Near, "Whistleblowing: Reaping the Benefits," *Academy of Management Executive* 8 (1994): 65–72.

53. "Police/Fire Report," *Sacramento Bee,* 18 January 1996, N2.

54. H.R. Bower, *Social Responsibilities of the Businessman* (New York: Harper & Row, 1953).

55. B. Carton, "Animal Instincts: Gillette Faces Wrath of Children in Testing on Rats and Rabbits," *The Wall Street Journal*, 5 September 1995.

56. "Ban Animal Testing," The Body Shop. [Online] Available http://www.bodyshop.com/usa/aboutus/animal.html, 24 June 2001.

57. "Best Investments: Total Return to Shareholders (10 Years)," *Fortune 500*. [Online] Available, http://www.fortune.com/indexw.jhtml?list_frag=list_f5_co_bestinvest_10.jhtml&channel=list.jhtml, 24 June 2001.

58. "How Much of a Difference Will the Rate Make?" *The Motley Fool*. [Online] Available http://www.calcbuilder.com/cgi-bin/calcs/SAV8.cgi/themotleyfool, 24 June, 2001.

59. J. Chipman, "U.S. Boy Scouts Pay Price for Anti-Gay Policy: High-Profile Corporations Cut Ties, Withdraw Donations," *National Post*, 29 December 2000, A16.

60. S.L. Wartick & P.L. Cochran, "The Evolution of the Corporate Social Performance Model," *Academy of Management Review* 10 (1985): 758–769.

61. T. Donaldson & L.E. Preston, "The Stakeholder Theory of the Corporation: Concepts, Evidence, and Implications," *Academy of Management Review* 20 (1995): 65–91.

62. M.B.E. Clarkson, "A Stakeholder Framework for Analyzing and Evaluating Corporate Social Performance," *Academy of Management Review* 20 (1995): 92–117.

63. P. Sherer, "Deals & Deal Makers: Of Burgers and Bonds: DLJ Draws Fire as Deal Sours—AmeriServe Offering Didn't Alert Investors of Burger King Gripes," *The Wall Street Journal*, 11 May 2000, C1.

64. J. Carlton, "Home Builders Centex and Kaufman Agree Not to Buy Endangered Wood," *The Wall Street Journal*, 31 March 2000, A4.

65. L.E. Preston, "Stakeholder Management and Corporate Performance," *Journal of Behavioral Economics* 19 (1990): 361–375.

66. E.W. Orts, "Beyond Shareholders: Interpreting Corporate Constituency Statutes," *The George Washington Law Review* 61 (1992): 14–135.

67. A.B. Carroll, "A Three-Dimensional Conceptual Model of Corporate Performance," *Academy of Management Review* 4 (1979): 497–505.

68. Ibid.

69. J. Lublin & M. Murrary, "CEOs Leave Faster Than Ever Before as Boards, Investors Lose Patience," *The Wall Street Journal Interactive*, 27 October 2000.

70. C. Bowman, "Success of Capital Area's War on Smog Challenged," *Sacramento Bee*, 7 February 1998, A1.

71. B. Robertson, "Bakery Aromas Create Smog in Sacramento, Calif., EPA Says," *Sacramento Bee*, 22 February 2000.

72. A. Gerlin, "A Matter of Degree: How a Jury Decided That a Coffee Spill Is Worth $2.9 Million," *The Wall Street Journal*, 1 September 1994, A1.

73. L. Wozniak, "Spilled Coffee Burns Customer, Who Sues," *St. Petersburg Times*, 19 May 1995, 1E.

74. M. Jackson (Associated Press), "Sales Promotions Tied to Charity Deserve Scrutiny," *Peoria Journal Star*, 30 December 1997, B2.

75. "Common Questions: How Does This Work?" *The Hunger Site*. [Online] Available http://www.thehungersite.com/cgi-bin/WebObjects/CTDSites.woa/261/wo/NK7000Cr800Br700rB/4.0.29.1.3.0.1.0.19.0.CustomContentLinkDisplayComponent.0.0, 24 June 2001.

76. T. Bryant, "Judge Rejects New Trial in Case of Woman Paralyzed in Suzuki Samurai Accident," *St. Louis Post-Dispatch*, 2 February 1998, C4. "Inclined to Roll, Suzuki Samurai Car Gets Unfavorable Rating Because of Tipping Tendency," *Time*, 13 June 1988, 51.

77. S. Power & N. Shirouzu, "Bridgestone Position Angers Lawmakers—Firm Balks at Wider Recall of Tires, Setting Stage for House Showdown," *The Wall Street Journal*, 5 September 2000, A3.

78. R. Silverman & K. Dunham, "Tire Recall: The Road Gets Rough—Consultants Split on Bridgestone's Crisis Management," *The Wall Street Journal*, 11 August 2000, A6.

79. K. Kranhold & E. White, "The Perils and Potential Rewards of Crisis Managing for Firestone," *The Wall Street Journal*, 8 September 2000, B1.

80. N. Templin, "Nissan Recalls and Destroys Some Minivans," *The Wall Street Journal*, 9 December 1993, B1.

81. P. Romeo, "McDonald's Battles Critics with $160M Recycling Plan," *Nation's Restaurant News*, 30 April 1990, 18–19. S. Shundich, "Green in Green: Beyond the Three Rs: There's a Whole New Set of Expectations When Food Service Operations Talk about Profiting from Environmental Initiatives," *Restaurants & Institutions*, 15 September 1995.

82. A. McWilliams & D. Siegel, "Corporate Social Responsibility: A Theory of the Firm Perspective," *Academy of Management Review* 26 no.1 (2001): 117–127.

83. H. Haines, "Noah Joins Ranks of Socially Responsible Funds," *Dow Jones News Service*, 13 October 1995.

84. M.B. Meznar, D. Nigh, & C.Y. Kwok, "Effect of Announcements of Withdrawal from South Africa on Stockholder Wealth," *Academy of Management Journal* 37 (1994): 1633–1648.

85. J. Seglin, "The Right Thing: When Good Ethics Aren't Good Business," *The New York Times*, 18 March 2001, available online.

86. T. Singer, "Can Business Still Save the World?" *Inc.*, 1 April 2001, 58.

87. D. Kadlec & B. Van Voorst, "The New World of Giving: Companies Are Doing More Good, and Demanding More Back," *Time*, 5 May 1997, 62.

88. P. Carlin, "Will Rapid Growth Stunt Corporate Do-Gooders?" *Business and Society Review*, Spring 1995, 36–43.

89. B. Finley, "Critics of Starbucks: Gifts Don't Amount to a Hill of Beans," *Denver Post*, 17 April 1998, A23. M. Scott, "An Interview with Howard Schultz, CEO of Starbucks Coffee," *Business Ethics Magazine*, November/December 1995.

90. M. Alexander, "Charity Begins at the Coffee Cup," *Sunday Star-Times*, 17 June 2001, E4.

## Chapter 4

1. N. Shirouzu, J. White, & T. Zaun, "U-Turn: A Revival at Nissan Shows There's Hope for Ailing Japan Inc.—Carlos Ghosn Is Overhauling Culture by Challenging Suppliers and Assumptions—Bringing Back the 'Z' Car," *The Wall Street Journal*, 16 November 2000, A1.

2. E.A. Locke & G.P. Latham, *A Theory of Goal Setting & Task Performance* (Englewood Cliffs, NJ: Prentice Hall, 1990).

3. M.E. Tubbs, "Goal-Setting: A Meta-Analytic Examination of the Empirical Evidence," *Journal of Applied Psychology* 71 (1986): 474–83.

4. D. Gordon, B. Begun, & F. Conway, "The Dominator: The World's Greatest Golfer Seems to Get Better and Better. How Does He Do It?" *Newsweek*, 18 June 2001, 42.

5. J. Bavelas & E.S. Lee, "Effect of Goal Level on Performance: A Trade-Off of Quantity and Quality," *Canadian Journal of Psychology* 32 (1978): 219–240.

6. A. Farnham, "Mary Kay's Lessons in Leadership," *Fortune*, 20 September 1993. "Company Information: Products and Sales," *Mary Kay Cosmetics*. [Online] Available, http://www.marykay.com/Home/Community/Headquarters/Company/Products.asp, 29 June 2001.

7. D. Greising, P. Dwyer, & W. Zeller, "A Destination, But No Flight Plan," *Business Week*, 16 May 1994, 74–75.

8. M. Henterly, "Delta Will Move Cargo into Separate Division," *Cincinnati Enquirer*, 8 November 1995.

9. C.C. Miller, "Strategic Planning and Firm Performance: A Synthesis of More Than Two Decades of Research," *Academy of Management Performance* 37 (1994): 1649–1665.

10. H. Mintzberg, "Rethinking Strategic Planning," Part I: Pitfalls and Fallacies, *Long Range Planning* 27 (1994): 12–21; Part II: New Roles for Planners: 22–30. H. Mintzberg, "The Pitfalls of Strategic Planning," *California Management Review* 36 (1993): 32–47.

11. B. Martinez, "Making Amends: Aetna Tries to Improve Bedside Manner in Bid to Help Bottom Line—Insurer's New CEO Relaxes Rules That Had Alienated Physicians and Patients—Reining In 'Mother, May I?'" *The Wall Street Journal Interactive*, 23 February 2001, A1.

12. K. Pope, "International: Runaway Growth at Phone Giant Nokia Humbles Newcomer after Early Success," *The Wall Street Journal*, 12 March 1996.

13. K. Capell, W. Echikson, & P. Elstrom, "Surprise! Nokia Doesn't Walk on Water: Its About-Face on Growth Will Hurt Credibility," *Business Week*, 25 June 2001, 30.

14. H. Mintzberg, "The Pitfalls of Strategic Planning," *California Management Review* 36 (1993): 32–47.

15. P. Tam, "Will Quantity Hurt Pixar's Quality?—Computer-Animation Studio Bets It Can Boost Output to One Feature a Year," *The Wall Street Journal*, 15 February 2001, B1.

16. E.A. Locke & G.P. Latham, *A Theory of Goal Setting & Task Performance* (Englewood Cliffs, NJ: Prentice Hall, 1990).

17. A. King, B. Oliver, B. Sloop, & K. Vaverek, *Planning and Goal Setting for Improved Performance, Participant's Guide* (Cincinnati, OH: Thomson Executive Press, 1995).

18. E.A. Locke & G.P. Latham, *A Theory of Goal Setting & Task Performance* (Englewood Cliffs, NJ: Prentice Hall, 1990).

19. J.R. Hollenbeck, C.R. Williams, & H.J. Klein, "An Empirical Examination of the Antecedents of Commitment to Difficult Goals," *Journal of Applied Psychology* 74 (1989): 18–23.

20. G. Lucier & S. Seshadri, "GE Takes Six Sigma Beyond the Bottom Line," *Strategic Finance* 82 no. 11 (2001): 40–46.

21. S. Creedy, "USAir Flies New Route to Financial Survival," *Pittsburgh Post-Gazette*, 7 January 1996.

22. *Ibid.*

23. A. Bandura & D.H. Schunk, "Cultivating Competence, Self-Efficacy, and Intrinsic Interest through Proximal Self-Motivation," *Journal of Personality and Social Psychology* 41 (1981): 586–598.

24. E. Walker, "CEO of Office Depot Works to Help Firm Reach Goals," *The Miami Herald*, 12 May 2001, 1C.

25. E.A. Locke & G.P. Latham, *A Theory of Goal Setting & Task Performance.* (Englewood Cliffs, NJ: Prentice Hall, 1990).

26. L. McCauley, "Relaunch!: Unit of One," *Fast Company*, 1 July 2000, 97.

27. E.H. Bowman & D. Hurry, "Strategy through the Option Lens: An Integrated View of Resource Investments and the Incremental-Choice Process," *Academy of Management Review* 18 (1993): 760–782.

28. D. Takahashi, "Deals & Deal Makers: Intel Rolls Dice on Tech Upstarts—And Hits Jackpot," *The Wall Street Journal*, 8 February 2000, C1.

29. N.A. Wishart, J.J. Elam, & D. Robey, "Redrawing the Portrait of a Learning Organization: Inside Knight-Ridder, Inc.," *Academy of Management Executive* 10 (1996): 7–20.

30. *Ibid.*

31. J. Samuelson, "The Geeky Garbageman," *Forbes*, 8 April 1996.

32. J.C. Collins & J.I. Porras, "Organizational Vision and Visionary Organizations," *California Management Review*, Fall 1991, 30–52.

33. *Ibid.*

34. *Ibid.*

35. *Ibid.*

36. W. George, "Building a Mission-Driven, Values-Centered Organization," Speech given at the Premier CEO's Conference in Aspen Colorado 17 September 1998. [Online] Available http://www.medtronic.com/newsroom/mgmtspeech_sept17.html, 1 July 2001.

37. *Ibid.*

38. J.C. Collins & J.I. Porras, "Organizational Vision and Visionary Organizations," *California Management Review*, Fall 1991, 30–52.

39. N. Shirouzu, J. White, & T. Zaun, "U-Turn: A Revival at Nissan Shows There's Hope for Ailing Japan Inc.—Carlos Ghosn Is Overhauling Culture by Challenging Suppliers and Assumptions—Bringing Back the 'Z' Car," *The Wall Street Journal*, 16 November 2000, A1.

40. J.A. Pearce & F. David, "Corporate Mission Statements: The Bottom Line," *Academy of Management Executive* 1 (1987): 109–116.

41. S. Kraft, "Disney Magic Is Finally Starting to Work at French Theme Park," *Los Angeles Times*, 4 February 1996, Business p. 1.

42. P. Prada, "Euro Disney's Net Income Climbs 64%," *The Wall Street Journal*, 17 November 2000, A17. P. Prada, "Ja, Ja, Americana's Fabulosa—In Europe, Theme Parks Draw Crowds with Thrill Rides, Burgers and Bugs Bunny," *The Wall Street Journal*, 21 June 2001, B1.

43. L. Iococca, with W. Novak, *Iococca* (New York: Bantom, 1984).

44. E. Marlow & R. Schilhavy, "Expectation Issues in Management by Objectives Programs," *Industrial Management* 33, no. 4 (1991): 29.

45. "WebMBO Teams with Deloitte & Touche to Deliver Innovative Web-Based 'Management-By-Objectives and Performance Management' Solutions," *PRNewswire*, 19 June 2001.

46. C. Coleman, "BankOne Clips WingspanBank, Folding Online Unit into Parent," *The Interactive Wall Street Journal*, 29 June 2001, http://interactive.wsj.com/archive/retrieve.cgi?id=SB993742031496871086.djm.

47. D. Morse, "A Policy Change at Gap Will Test Brotherly Ties," *The Wall Street Journal*, 11 April 2001, B1.

48. L. Aron, "Cutting Corporate Travel Costs," *Across the Board* 37 no. 3 (2000): 28–31.

49. M. Podmolik, "The Shortest Distance: Online Reservations Change Rules for Travelers, Agents," *Crain's Chicago Business*, 7 February 2000, SR1.

50. N. Humphrey, "References a Tricky Issue for Both Sides," *Nashville Business Journal* 11 (8 May 1995): 1A.

51. M. Seminerio, "Nielsen: Penthouse Web Site Popular with PC Companies," *PC Week Online*, 2 April 1996.

52. M. Savage, "Keeping Watch—It's Not 1984, But Tools for Monitoring Employee Web Activity Are Catching On, Solution Providers Say," *Computer Reseller News*, 2 October 2000, 32.

53. *Ibid.*

54. S. Sherman, "Stretch Goals: The Dark Side of Asking for Miracles," *Fortune*, 13 November 1995, 231.

55. *Ibid.*

56. C. O'Dell, "Out-of-the-Box Benchmarking," *Management Review* 83 (1 January 1994): 63.

57. R. Vartabedian, "Chrysler Board Cuts Bonuses of Top Execs, Cites Lag in Quality," *Los Angeles Times*, 29 March 1996, D-1.

58. B. Wysocki, Jr., "Power Grid: Soft Landing or Hard? Firm Tests Strategy on 3 Views of Future—Most Likely, Duke Energy Decides, Is a Growth Era of 'Flawed Competition'—Retailing Gas on the Internet," *The Wall Street Journal*, 7 July 2000, A1.

59. G. Robbins, "Scenario Planning," *Public Management*, 1 March 1995, 4.

60. P.J. Schoemaker, "Scenario Planning: A Tool for Strategic Thinking," *Sloan Management Review* 36 (1995): 25.

61. M. Stepanke, "How Fast Is Net Fast? On the Internet, Companies Have to Be Ready to Change Goals or Strategy Virtually Overnight," *Business Week*, 1 November 1999, EB52.

62. F. Keenan, "Opening the Spigot: Faucet Maker Moen Uses the Web to Streamline Design. Rivals Are Eating Dust," *Business Week*, 4 June 2001, EB16.

63. S.C. Wheelwright & K.B. Clark, "Creating Project Plans to Focus Product Development," *Harvard Business Review*, March-April 1992, 70.

64. D. Dimancescu & K. Dwenger, "Smoothing the Product Development Plan," *Management Review* 85, no. 6 (1996): 36.

65. S.L. Brown, "Product Development: Past Research, Present Findings, and Future Directions," *Academy of Management Review* 20 (1995): 343–378.

66. L. Ohr," Delivering Taste and Convenience," *Prepared Foods*, February 2001, 28.

67. *Ibid.*

68. J. Martin, "Ignore Your Customer," *Fortune*, 1 May 1995, 121.

69. M. Iansiti, "Shooting the Rapids: Managing Product Development in Turbulent Environments," *California Management Review* 38 (1995): 36–58.

70. F. Warner, "Lear Won't Take a Back Seat: For Decades, Lear Corp. Made Car Seats. Today, with the Help of Virtual Reality and Other Digital Technologies, Lear Makes a Whole Lot More—And Makes It a Whole Lot Faster. Along the Way, The Company Learned How to Get Real about What Technology Can and Cannot Do," *Fast Company*, 1 June 2000, 178.

71. *Ibid.*

## Chapter 5

1. R. Lenzner, "The Reluctant Entrepreneur," *Forbes*, 11 September 1995, 162–166.

729

2. M. Rich, "Dear CEO: Are You Tracking Your Cubicles?" *The Wall Street Journal,* 19 April 2001, B8.

3. *Ibid.*

4. J. Laing, "Get Wired: Why Cable Will Beat the Bells in the Race to Wire Your Home," *Barrons,* 20 August 2001, 23.

5. *Ibid.*

6. R.D. Buzzell & B.T. Gale, *The PIMS Principles: Linking Strategy to Performance* (New York: Free Press, 1987); M. Lambkin, "Order of Entry and Performance in New Markets," *Strategic Management Journal* 9 (1988): 127–40.

7. N. Deogun, "Banks Introduce New ATMs That Deliver Host of Services," *The Wall Street Journal Interactive Edition,* 5 June 1996.

8. G.L. Urban, T. Carter, S. Gaskin, & Z. Mucha, "Market Share Rewards to Pioneering Brands: An Empirical Analysis and Strategic Implications," *Management Science* 32 (1986): 645–659.

9. G. Hamel, "Smart Mover, Dumb Mover: Think the First Mover Advantage Is a Myth? You're Wrong: Most Pioneering Dot Coms Failed Not Because They Were First but Because They Were Dumb," *Fortune,* 3 September 2001, 191.

10. E. Nelson, "Retailing: Why Wal-Mart Sings, 'Yes, We Have Bananas!'" *The Wall Street Journal,* 6 October 1998, B1.

11. U. Tosi, "Commercial Aircraft Are Fast Becoming Flying Computer Systems: Their Downlinked Bitstreams Can Be Critical to High Profits and Happy Landings," *Forbes ASAP,* 4 December 1995, 100–102.

12. *Ibid.*

13. *Ibid.*

14. *Ibid.*

15. J. Novack, "The Data Miners," *Forbes,* 12 February 1996.

16. M. Halper, "Setting Up Is Hard to Do: Data Warehouses Do Not Grow on Trees," *Forbes ASAP,* 8 April 1996, 50–51.

17. J. Novack, "The Data Miners," *Forbes,* 12 February 1996.

18. N. Hutheesing, "Get the Bugs Out," *Forbes,* 8 April 1996.

19. T. Mack & T. Ewing, "In the Real World, Meanwhile . . . ." *Forbes,* 18 December 1995, 284.

20. Steven D. Lubar, *Infoculture* (Boston: Houghton Mifflin, 1993).

21. L. Finnegan, "WinWedge 32 May Be Too Good; Easy-To-Use Software Collects Data So Well It's Overloading Federal Systems," *Government Computer News* 15 (15 April 1996): 35.

22. Steven D. Lubar, *Infoculture* (Boston: Houghton Mifflin, 1993).

23. N. Rubenking, "Hidden Messages," *PC Magazine,* 22 May 2001, 86.

24. "Data Mining: Advanced Scout*," IBM Research Web Site.* [Online] Available http://www.research.ibm.com/xw-scout, 31 December 1995.

25. "Data Mining: Advanced Scout*," IBM Research Web Site.* [Online] Available http://www.research.ibm.com/xw-scout, 31 December 1995.

26. N. Rubenking, "Hidden Messages," *PC Magazine,* 22 May 2001, 86.

27. F.J. Derfler, Jr., "Secure Your Network," *PC Magazine,* 27 June 2000, 183–200.

28. "Virus Attack: Protect your PC," *Cnet.com Web Site.* [Online] Available http://home.cnet.com/software/ 0-3746.html, 1 October 2000.

29. N. Wingfield, "A Stolen Laptop Spells Trouble for Qualcomm Chief Jacobs," *The Wall Street Journal Interactive Edition,* September 19, 2000.

30. A. Laplante, "Invitation to Customers: Come into Our Database," *Forbes ASAP,* 28 August 1995, 124–130.

31. C. Ey, "E-Mail Saves Companies Time, Money and Effort," *Dallas Business Journal,* 17 Nov 1995, C13–14.

32. M.A. Verespej, "The E-Mail Monster: Can One Manager Handle 250 E-Mail Messages a Day, Plus 15 Voicemails an Hour?" *Industry Week,* 19 June 1995, 52–53.

33. M. Campanelli & N. Friedman, "Welcome to Voice Mail Hell: The New Technology Has Become a Barrier Between Salespeople and Customers. Here's How Smart Sellers Are Breaking Through," *Sales & Marketing Management* 147 (May 1995): 98–101.

34. "The Joys of Voice Mail," *Inc.,* November 1995, 102.

35. *Ibid.*

36. T. Andrews, "E-Mail Empowers, Voice-Mail Enslaves," *PC Week,* 10 April 1995, E11.

37. P. Hise, "Life after Voice-Mail Hell. Winguth, Donahue and Co., Los Altos, CA Executive Search Firm, Brings Back Human Receptionist Due to Customer Dissatisfaction with Voice Mail Service," *Inc.,* August 1994, 101.

38. C. O'Malley, "Document Conferencing," *Computer Shopper Online.* [Online] Available www.zdnet.com/cshopper/content/ 9604/feature3/sub1.html, 23 June 1996. Originally published in the April 1996 issue of *Computer Shopper.*

39. J. Young, "The Transcontinental Blackboard," *Forbes,* 23 October 1995, 322–323.

40. J. van den Hoven, "Executive Support Systems & Decision Making," *Journal of Systems Management* 47, no. 8 (March-April 1996): 48.

41. M. Stevenson, "He Sees All He Knows All," *Canadian Business* 67, no. 5 (Spring 1994): 30.

42. A. O'Donnell, "Get Smart: Insurance Companies Know How to Collect Data. The Challenge is Doing Something Meaningful, Something Intelligent, With It. In the End, Only the Smart Will Survive," *Insurance & Technology,* 1 April 2001, 30.

43. "Intranet," Webopedia [online], http://www.webopedia.com/TERM/i/ intranet.html, available 26 August 2001.

44. R.C. Kennedy, "Intranets in Action," *PC/Computing,* June 1996, 150.

45. B. Richards, "Intranet Offers Rewards for Firms Big and Small," *The Wall Street Journal Interactive Edition,* 17 June 1996.

46. J. Barlow, "Intranet Replaces Office Grapevine," *Houston Chronicle,* 7 May 2000, Business 1.

47. S. Hamm, D. Welch, W. Zellner, F. Keenan, & P. Engardio, "Down but Hardly out: Downturn Be Damned. Companies Are Still Anxious to Expand Online Because the Net Is a Way to Boost Sales and Shrink Costs," *Business Week,* 26 March 2001, 126.

48. J. Barlow, "Intranet Replaces Office Grapevine," *Houston Chronicle,* 7 May 2000, Business 1.

49. V.S. Pasher, "Employee Benefits Info within a Few Clicks," *National Underwriter Life & Health—Financial Services Edition,* 14 April 1997, S4.

50. R. Ayre, "Intranet How-To: Setting Up Shop," *PC Magazine,* 23 April 1996, 151–158. F.J. Derfler, "The Intranet Platform: A Universal Client?" *PC Magazine,* 23 April 1996, 105–113.

51. R.C. Kennedy, "Intranets in Action," *PC/Computing,* June 1996, 150.

52. D. Zimmerman, "Report on EDI Tracks Labor Savings," *Supermarket News,* 16 January 1995, S2.

53. A. Kessler, "Fire Your Purchasing Managers," *Forbes ASAP,* 10 October 1994, 33.

54. D. Tobey, "Paperless Purchasing," *Hotel & Motel Management* 2, no. 3 (6 November 1995): 104.

55. "Extranet," Webopedia [online], http:// www.webopedia.com/TERM/E/extranet. html, available 26 August 2001.

56. S. Hamm, D. Welch, W. Zellner, F. Keenan, & P. Engardio,"Down but Hardly out Downturn Be Damned. Companies Are Still Anxious to Expand

Online Because the Net Is a Way to Boost Sales and Shrink Costs, " *Business Week*, 26 March 2001, 126.

57. M. McDonald, "SWA: Ticket Less Travel Saved Us Millions in Agent Pay," *Travel Weekly* 2 (20 November 1995): 1.

58. L. Walker, "Plugged In for Maximum Efficiency; Undaunted by Dot-Com Flameout, Companies Move to Streamline Operations by Harnessing the Web," *Washington Post*, 20 June 2001, G1.

59. S. Hamm, D. Welch, W. Zellner, F. Keenan, & P. Engardio, "Down but Hardly out Downturn Be Damned. Companies Are Still Anxious to Expand Online Because the Net Is a Way to Boost Sales and Shrink Costs," *Business Week*, 26 March 2001, 126.

60. K.C. Laudon & J.P. Laudon, *Management Information Systems: Organization and Technology* (Upper Saddle River, NJ: Prentice-Hall, 1996).

61. T. Chea, "Apache Shareholders Approve Sale of Assets," *Washington Post*, 14 June 2001, E5.

62. S. Oliver, "What Are My Chances, Doc?" *Forbes*, 31 July 1995, 136–137.

63. M. France, "Smart Contracts," *Forbes ASAP* 2 (29 August 1994): 117.

## Chapter 6

1. L.A. Hill, *Becoming a Manager: Mastery of a New Identity* (Boston: Harvard Business School Press, 1992).

2. K.R. MacCrimmon, R.N. Taylor, & E.A. Locke, "Decision Making and Problem Solving" in *Handbook of Industrial and Organizational Psychology*, ed. M.D. Dunnette (Chicago: Rand McNally, 1976), 1397–1453.

3. N. Wingfield, "Amazon Gives Upbeat Earnings Outlook, Plans to Start Selling PCs at Its E-store," *The Wall Street Journal*, 6 June 2001, B2.

4. K.R. MacCrimmon, R.N. Taylor, & E.A. Locke, "Decision Making and Problem Solving" in *Handbook of Industrial and Organizational Psychology*, ed. M.D. Dunnette (Chicago: Rand McNally, 1976), 1397–1453.

5. G. Kress, "The Role of Interpretation in the Decision Process," *Industrial Management* 37 (1995): 10–14.

6. D. Milbrank, "We Feel Your Pain, Congress Is Saying, With Real Empathy," *The Wall Street Journal*, 1 April 1996.

7. S. Hansell, "Listen Up! It's Time for a Profit," *New York Times*, 20 May 2001, 1.

8. J. Delaney, "Buying Guide: Desktops," *PC Magazine*, 20 June 2001. [Online] Available http://www.pcmag.com/

article/0,2997,s%253D1564%2526a%253D5587,00.asp, 4 July 2001.

9. J. Koblenz, "How a Car Earns a Best Buy," *Consumers Digest*, 1 January 1993, 54.

10. P. Djang, "Selecting Personal Computers," *Journal of Research on Computing in Education*, 25 (1993): 327.

11. K. Galloway, "America's Best Insurance Cities," *Best's Review/Property-Casualty Insurance Edition*, 1 November 1994, 38.

12. J.G. March, *A Primer on Decision Making: How Decisions Happen* (New York: Free Press, 1994).

13. R. Johnson, "Surviving a Slowdown—Strategies for the Storm: How Some Managers Are Hoping to Weather the Economic Slump," *The Wall Street Journal*, 14 May 2001, R6.

14. J. Orbell, "Hamlet and the Psychology of Rational Choice under Uncertainty," *Rationality and Society* 5 (1993): 127–140.

15. J. Nocera, "Bill Gross Blew Through $800 Million in 8 Months (and he's got nothing to show for it). Why Is He Still Smiling?," *Fortune*, 5 March 2001, 70.

16. M.H. Bazerman, *Judgment in Managerial Decision Making* (New York: John Wiley & Sons, 1994).

17. B. Silverman, "Unconventional Wisdom: Twelve Remarkable Innovators Tell How Intuition Can Revolutionize Decision Making," *Sales & Marketing Management* 146 (1994): 106–107.

18. P.J. Hoffman, P. Slovic, & L.G. Rorer, "An Analysis-of-Variance Model for Assessment of Configural Cue Utilization in Clinical Judgment," *Psychological Bulletin* 69 (1968): 338–349.

19. L. Gutierrez & J. Fussell, "In a Culture of Mistrust, Fear Is Part of Parenting. Statistics Are Reassuring, But Parents Remain Wary," *The Kansas City Star*, 25 March 2001, A1.

20. K.C. Cole, "Brain's Use of Shortcuts Can Be a Route to Bias," *Los Angeles Times*, 1 May 1995, A1.

21. P.J. Schoemaker & J.E. Russo, "A Pyramid of Decision Approaches," *California Management Review*, Fall 1993, 9–33.

22. I. Graham, I. Stiell, A. Laupacis, L. McAuley, M. Howell, M. Clancy, P. Durieux, N. Simon, J. Emparanza, J. Aginaga, Jr., A. O'Connor, & G. Wells. "Awareness and Use of the Ottawa Ankle and Knee Rules in 5 Countries: Can Publication Alone Be Enough to Change Practice?" *Annals of Emergency Medicine* 37 no. 3 (2001): 259–66.

23. R. Koselka, "The New Mantra: MVT," *Forbes*, 11 March 1996, 114–118.

24. G. Bell, "'I Want My MVT' Drive Marketing Results with Multivariable Testing

Techniques." *Direct Marketing*, 60 no. 8 (December 1997): 34(3).

25. R. Koselka, "The New Mantra: MVT," *Forbes*, 11 March 1996, 114–118.

26. G. Bell, "'I Want My MVT' Drive Marketing Results with Multivariable Testing Techniques." *Direct Marketing*, 60 no. 8 (December 1997): 34(3).

27. *Ibid.*

28. W. Mossberg, "In Time for Elections: Software to Help You Make Up Your Mind," *The Wall Street Journal*, 8 February 1996.

29. K. Yakai, "To Do or Not To Do: Two Business-Oriented Decision Makers," *PC Magazine*, 23 January 1996.

30. B.M. Staw. "Knee-Deep in the Big Muddy: A Study of Escalating Commitment to a Chosen Course of Action," *Organizational Behavior and Human Performance*, 16 (1976): 27–44.

31. A. Curry, "The First Couldn't Last," *U.S. News & World Report*, 8 January 2001, 37. J. McCormick, "You Snooze, You Lose," *Newsweek*, 21 July 1997, 50.

32. J. Ross & B.M. Staw, "Organizational Escalation and Exit: Lessons from the Shoreham Nuclear Power Plant," *Academy of Management Journal*, 36 (1993): 701–732.

33. J. McCormick, "You Snooze, You Lose," *Newsweek*, 21 July 1997, 50.

34. D. Ghosh, "De-Escalation Strategies: Some Experimental Evidence," *Behavioral Research in Accounting* 9 (1997): 88–112.

35. *Ibid.*

36. "New LILCO Chief Brings Blast of Aggressiveness to Floundering Utility," *The Wall Street Journal*, 28 April 1984, 1.

37. J. Ross & B.M. Staw, "Organizational Escalation and Exit: Lessons from the Shoreham Nuclear Power Plant," *Academy of Management Journal*, 36 (1993): 701–732.

38. *Ibid.*

39. J. Angwin, "Can These Dot-Coms Be Saved?—Profit Eludes Priceline as Expansion Takes Its Toll," *The Wall Street Journal*, 25 January 2001, B1.

40. Press Releases, "WebHouse Club Announces 90-Day Wind-Down of Name-Your-Price Grocery and Gasoline Internet Service," Priceline.com [Online], October 5, 2000, http://www.corporate-ir.net/ireye/ir_site.zhtml?ticker=pcln&script=410&layout=-6&item_id=121342.

41. B. Dumaine, "The Trouble with Teams," *Fortune*, 5 September 1994, 86–92.

42. G. Zachary, "The Rage for Global Teams," *Technology Review* 101, no. 4 (July–August 1998): 33.

43. L. Pelled, K. Eisenhardt, & K. Xin, "Exploring the Black Box: An Analysis of Work Group Diversity, Conflict, and Performance," *Administrative Science Quarterly* 44, no. 1 (March 1, 1999): 1.

44. T. Gutner, "Do Top Women Execs = Stronger IPOs? A Study Finds That the More of Them a Startup Has, The Better It Does," *Business Week*, 5 February 2001, 122.

45. "How to Form Hiring Teams," *Personnel Journal* 73, no. 3 (August 1994): S14.

46. I.L. Janis, *Groupthink* (Boston: Houghton Mifflin, 1983).

47. C.P. Neck & C.C. Manz, "From Groupthink to Teamthink: Toward the Creation of Constructive Thought Patterns in Self-Managing Work Teams," *Human Relations* 47 (1994): 929–952.

48. G. Moorhead, R. Ference, & C.P. Neck, "Group Decision Fiascoes Continue: Space Shuttle Challenger and a Revised Framework," *Human Relations* 44 (1991): 539–550.

49. C. Dressler, "Keeping Minutes While You Waste Hours," *Los Angeles Times*, 14 January 1996, D-18.

50. A. Mason, W.A. Hochwarter, K.R. Thompson, "Conflict: An Important Dimension in Successful Management Teams," *Organizational Dynamics* 24 (1995): 20.

51. C. Olofson, "So Many Decisions, So Little Time: What's Your Problem?" *Fast Company*, 1 October 1999, 62.

52. *Ibid.*

53. R. Cosier & C.R. Schwenk, "Agreement and Thinking Alike: Ingredients for Poor Decisions," *Academy of Management Executive* 4 (1990): 69–74.

54. *Ibid.*

55. K. Jenn & E. Mannix, "The Dynamic Nature of Conflict: A Longitudinal Study of Intragroup Conflict and Group Performance," *Academy of Management Journal* 44 no. 2 (2001): 238–251. R.L. Priem, D.A. Harrison, & N.K. Muir, "Structured Conflict and Consensus Outcomes in Group Decision Making," *Journal of Management* 21 (1995): 691–710.

56. A. Van De Ven & A.L. Delbecq, "Nominal Versus Interacting Group Processes for Committee Decision Making Effectiveness," *Academy of Management Journal* 14 (1971): 203–212.

57. A.R. Dennis & J.S. Valicich, "Group, Sub-Group, and Nominal Group Idea Generation: New Rules for a New Media?" *Journal of Management* 20 (1994): 723–736.

58. S.G. Robelberg, J.L. Barnes-Farrell, & C.A. Lowe, "The Stepladder Technique: An Alternative Group Structure Facilitating Effective Group Decision Making," *Journal of Applied Psychology* 77 (1992): 730–737.
S.G. Rogelberg, & M.S. O'Connor, "Extending the Stepladder Technique: An Examination of the Self-Paced Stepladder Groups," *Group Dynamics: Theory, Research, and Practice* 2 (1998): 82–91.

59. R.B. Gallupe, W.H. Cooper, M.L. Grise, & L.M. Bastianutti, "Blocking Electronic Brainstorms," *Journal of Applied Psychology* 79 (1994): 77–86.

60. R.B. Gallupe & W.H. Cooper, "Brainstorming Electronically," *Sloan Management Review*, Fall 1993, 27–36.

61. *Ibid.*

62. G. Kay, "Effective Meetings through Electronic Brainstorming," *Management Quarterly* 35 (1995): 15.

63. A. LaPlante, "90s Style Brainstorming," *Forbes ASAP*, 25 October 1993, 44.

## Chapter 7

1. R. Leifer & P.K. Mills, "An Information Processing Approach for Deciding upon Control Strategies and Reducing Control Loss in Emerging Organizations," *Journal of Management* 22 (1996): 113–137.

2. "Say Baa-Baa to Bad Driving," *London Times*, 28 July 1996.

3. L. Lee, "Sick of Scams from Shoppers, Retailers Look to Cut Returns," *The Wall Street Journal Interactive Edition*, 18 November 1996.

4. J. Ordonez, "How Burger King Got Burned in Quest to Make the Perfect Fry—After Huge Product Launch, The Crispy Starch Stick Pulls in Only Limp Sales—Next Up: A New, New Spud," *The Wall Street Journal*, 16 January 2001, A1.

5. J. Martin & J.E. Davis, "Are You as Good as You Think You Are? There's Only One Way to Know for Sure," *Fortune*, 30 September 1996, 142.

6. P. Scott, "Selling Civility: Secret Shoppers," *The Wall Street Journal*, 29 June 2001, W17.

7. J.Y. Luchars & T.R. Hinkin, "The Service-Quality Audit: A Hotel Case Study," *Cornell Hotel & Restaurant Administration Quarterly* 37, no. 1 (1996): 34.

8. Wiener, N. *Cybernetics; Or Control and Communication in the Animal and the Machine*. New York: Wiley, 1948.

9. C. Deutsch, "And to Penny-Pinching Wizardry," *New York Times*, 6 May 2001, 1.

10. H. Koontz & R.W. Bradspies, "Managing through Feedforward Control: A Future-Directed View," *Business Horizons*, June 1972, 25–36.

11. D. Clark, "Marketing, Performance Earn Windows NT Place in the Sun," *The Wall Street Journal Interactive Edition*, 29 July 1996.

12. R. Leifer & P.K. Mills, "An Information Processing Approach for Deciding upon Control Strategies and Reducing Control Loss in Emerging Organizations," *Journal of Management* 22 (1996): 113–137.

13. C. Binkley, "Mississippi Gamble: Finest Casino That Could Be Built Was the Goal," *The Wall Street Journal*, 2 February 2000, A1.

14. S.G. Green & M.A. Welsh, "Cybernetics and Dependence: Reframing the Control Concept," *Academy of Management Review* 13 (1988): 287–301.

15. T. Eblen, "Airlines Must Try to Fill All Seats, Charge the Highest Possible Fare," *Knight-Ridder/Tribune Business News*, 23 June 1996.

16. E. Allday, "Will Pool Business Evaporate?" *The Wall Street Journal Interactive Edition*, 7 August 1996.

17. J. Stossel, "Protect Us from Legal Vultures," *The Wall Street Journal*, 2 January 1996.

18. S. Joyce, "Tort Wars: Curb Frivolous Lawsuits, Unjust Awards," *San Diego Union-Tribune*. 19 November 1995.

19. S. Roan, "C-Sections on Rise as View of Risks Changes," *Los Angeles Times*, 29 January 2001, A1.

20. M. Brannigan & E. de Lisser, "Ground Control: Cost Cutting at Delta Raises the Stock Price but Lowers the Service," *The Wall Street Journal*, 20 June 1996, A1.

21. L. Miller, "Business Fliers Make Use of On-Line Travel Services," *The Wall Street Journal Interactive Edition*, 2 August 1996.

22. Institute of Management & Administration, "Companies Look to Technology to Rein In Rising T&E Costs," *Managing Accounting Systems & Technology*, 1 June 2001.

23. "E-Commerce II: Travel, E-business Flying High," *Toronto Globe & Mail*, 15 June 1999, C2.

24. L. Ward, "Compaq Changes Direction: Computer Giant Shifting to Services," *Dallas Morning News*, 26 June 2001, 1D.

25. S. Carey, "Frustrated Firms Buy Planes to Streamline Travel Plans," *The Wall Street Journal Interactive Edition*, 11 October 1996.

26. P. Davis, "Outrageous Perks: Coffee Breaks Are Becoming Coffee Escapes," *The Wall Street Journal Interactive Edition*, 8 August 1996.

27. S. Shellenbarger, "Is the Awful Behavior of Some Bad Bosses Rooted in Their

Past?" *The Wall Street Journal*, 17 May 2000, B1.

28. S. Shellenbarger, "Workers, Emboldened by Tight Job Market, Take On Their Bosses," *The Wall Street Journal*, 17 May 2000, B1.

29. M. Weber, *The Protestant Ethic and the Spirit of Capitalism* (New York: Scribner's, 1958).

30. L. Criner, "Politicians Come and Go, Bureaucracies Stay and Grow," *Washington Times*, 11 March 1996, 33.

31. A.C. Greenberg, "Memos from the Chairman," *Fortune*, 29 April 1996, 173–175.

32. Y. Ono, "The Long Knives: A Restaurant Chain in Japan Chops Up the Social Contract—Workers and Managers Alike Fall Under Brutal System of Perform or Perish—How Mr. Ohta Lost His Bonus," *The Wall Street Journal*, 17 January 2001, A1.

33. L. Lavelle & F.J. Jespersen, "While the CEO Gravy Train May Be Slowing Down, It Hasn't Jumped the Rails. In 2000, Despite Weakening Returns, U.S. Company Chieftains Bagged on Average a Princely $13.1 Million," *Business Week*, 16 April 2001, 76.

34. S. Williford, "Nordstrom Sets the Standard for Customer Service," *Memphis Business Journal*, 1 July 1996, 21.

35. R. T. Pascale, "Nordstrom: Respond to Unreasonable Customer Requests!" *Planning Review* 2 (May-June 1994): 17.

36. *Ibid.*

37. *Ibid.*

38. J.R. Barker, "Tightening the Iron Cage: Concertive Control in Self-Managing Teams," *Administrative Science Quarterly* 38 (1993): 408–437.

39. *Ibid.*

40. *Ibid.*

41. *Ibid.*

42. *Ibid.*

43. C. Manz & H. Sims, "Leading Workers to Lead Themselves: The External Leadership of Self-Managed Work Teams," *Administrative Science Quarterly* 32 (1987): 106–128.

44. J. Slocum & H.A. Sims, "Typology for Integrating Technology, Organization and Job Design," *Human Relations* 33 (1980): 193–212.

45. C.C. Manz & H.P. Sims, Jr., "Self-Management as a Substitute for Leadership: A Social Learning Perspective," *Academy of Management Review* 5 (1980): 361–367.

46. S. Levy, "Strip Mining the Corporate Life," *Newsweek*, 12 August 1996, 54–55.

47. J. Lublin, "More Big Companies End Perks; Critics Say Cutbacks Sap Morale," *The Wall Street Journal*, 4 January 2001, B1.

48. B. McWilliams, "The Measure of Success," *Across the Board*, 1 February 1996, 16.

49. R.S. Kaplan & D.P. Norton, "Using the Balanced Scorecard as a Strategic Management System," *Harvard Business Review*, January-February 1996, 75–85. R.S. Kaplan & D.P. Norton, "The Balanced Scorecard: Measures that Drive Performance," *Harvard Business Review*, January-February 1992, 71–79.

50. *Ibid.*

51. S.L. Fawcett, "Fear of Accounts: Improving Managers' Competence and Confidence through Simulation Exercises," *Journal of European Industrial Training*, February 1996, 17.

52. J. Cole, "New Boeing CFO's Assignment: Signal a Turnaround Quickly," *The Wall Street Journal*, 26 January 1999, B1.

53. M.H. Stocks & A. Harrell, "The Impact of an Increase in Accounting Information Level on the Judgment Quality of Individuals and Groups," *Accounting, Organizations and Society*, October-November 1995, 685–700.

54. B. Morris, "Roberto Goizueta and Jack Welch: The Wealth Builders," *Fortune*, 11 December 1995, 80–94.

55. G. Colvin, "America's Best & Worst Wealth Creators: The Real Champions Aren't Always Who You Think. Here's an Eye-Opening Look at Which Companies Produce and Destroy the Most Money for Investors—Plus a New Tool for Spotting Future Winners," *Fortune*, 18 December 2000, 207.

56. B. Morris, "A Conversation with Roberto Goizueta and Jack Welch," *Fortune*, 11 December 1995, 96–102.

57. B. Morris, "Roberto Goizueta and Jack Welch: The Wealth Builders," *Fortune*, 11 December 1995, 80–94.

58. S. Tully, "The Real Key to Creating Wealth," *Fortune*, 20 September 1993, 38–50.

59. "Handling Complaints," Office of Consumer and Business Affairs. [Online] Available http://www.ocba.sa.gov.au/ba_complaints.htm, 2 September 2001. F.F. Reichheld, "Learning from Customer Defections," *Harvard Business Review*, March-April 1996, 56–69.

60. P. Hepworth, "Connecting Customer Loyalty to the Bottom Line," *Canadian Business Review*, 1 January 1994, 40.

61. F.F. Reichheld, "Learning from Customer Defections," *Harvard Business Review*, March-April 1996, 56–69.

62. C.B. Furlong, "12 Rules for Customer Retention," *Bank Marketing* 5 (January 1993): 14.

63. P. Hepworth, "Connecting Customer Loyalty to the Bottom Line," *Canadian Business Review*, 1 January 1994, 40.

64. F. F. Reichheld, "Lead for Loyalty," *Harvard Business Review* 79 (July August 2001): 76.

65. T.K. Gilliam, "Closing the Customer Retention Gap," *Bank Marketing* 3 (December 1994): 51.

66. A. Orr, "After the Order . . . . (Customer Retention Strategies)," *Target Marketing* 3 (July 1996): 20.

67. C.A. Reeves & D.A. Bednar, "Defining Quality: Alternatives and Implications," *Academy of Management Review* 19 (1994): 419–445.

68. "Readers' Choice Poll 1997: International Airline Rankings," *Conde Nast Traveler*. [Online] Available http://travel.epicurious.com/travel/g_cnt/05_poll97/air/inter_intro.html, 26 June 1998.

69. "Singapore Airlines presents Our Awards & Accolades," *Singapore Airlines Web Site*. [Online] Available http://www.singaporeair.com/saa/app/saa?hidHeaderAction=onHeaderMenuClick&hidTopicArea=Awards$Accolades, 3 September 2001.

70. "Airline Way Above Rest in Rankings," *South China Morning Post*, 9 August 1996. Available through *The Wall Street Journal Interactive*.

71. "SIA Unveils the New US$100 Million SpaceBed—The Biggest Business Class Bed in the Sky," *Singapore Airlines Web Site*. [Online] Available javascript: linksToLinkInMenu('NewsViewer','Text/english/PressReleases/NR_1501.html'), 17 August 2001.

72. D.R. May & B.L. Flannery, "Cutting Waste with Employee Involvement Teams," *Business Horizons*, September-October 1995, 28–38.

73. D. Bendall, "Dishwashers (includes related article on proper maintenance of dishwashers)," *Restaurant Hospitality*, 1 February 1998, 89.

74. I. Amato, "Green Chemistry Proves It Pays: Companies Find New Ways to Show That Preventing Pollution Makes More Sense Than Cleaning Up Afterward," *Fortune*, 24 July 2000, 270.

75. M.A. Verespej, "Trash to Cash: The Bottom Line, The Environment, And Companies Can Profit from Waste Reduction," *Industry Week*, 5 December 1995, 53–55.

76. I. Amato, "Green Chemistry Proves It Pays: Companies Find New Ways to Show That Preventing Pollution Makes

More Sense Than Cleaning Up Afterward," *Fortune* 24 July 2000, 270.

77. A. Gynn, "Sears, WMI Continue Recycling Program," *Waste News*, 5 March 2001, 2.

78. T. Minahan, "Manufacturers Take Aim at End of the Supply Chain," *Purchasing*, 23 April 1998, 111. T. Moran, "Life-Cycle Managers Show Real Vehicle Costs," *Automotive News Europe*, 25 May 1997, 8.

79. J. Sprovieri, "Environmental Management Affects Manufacturing Bottom Line," *Assembly*, 1 July 2001, 24.

80. J. Sabatini, "The Color of Money," *Automotive Manufacturing & Production*, 1 June 2000, 74.

81. J. Szekely & G. Trapaga, "From Villain to Hero (Materials Industry's Waste Recovery Efforts)," *Technology Review*, 1 January 1995, 30.

82. M. Keller, "Many in Dark about Disposal of Fluorescents," *Minneapolis-St. Paul City Business*, 14 January 1994, 11.

83. B. Rose, "Where Old Computers Go: While Too Many Are Dumped Illegally, Sr Center Salvages Thousands," *Press Democrat*, 18 June 2001, D1.

84. H. Norr, "Recycling the HP Way: PC-Maker's Program Blocks Toxic Effects of Discarded Computers," *San Francisco Chronicle*, 21 May 2001, B1.

85. C.A. Reeves & D.A. Bednar, "Defining Quality: Alternatives and Implications," *Academy of Management Review* 19 (1994): 419–445.

## Chapter 8

1. A. Bernstein, & E. Malkin, "Backlash," *Business Week,* 24 April 2000, 38. J. Calmes, "American Opinion (A Special Report): Despite Buoyant Economic Times Americans Don't Buy Free Trade," *The Wall Street Journal,* 10 December 1998, A10. *USA Today,* 25 February 1992. *Lou Harris Survey,* March 1990; March 1992.

2. *Ibid.*

3. J. Calmes, "American Opinion (A Special Report): Despite Buoyant Economic Times Americans Don't Buy Free Trade," *The Wall Street Journal,* 10 December 1998, A10.

4. "Recent Media Mergers," *Chicago Sun-Times,* 8 September 1999, 63. P. Colford, "1998: A Very Big Deal: Mergers Make Giants and Shrink Competition," *Newsday,* 23 December 1998.

5. "Global Foreign Direct Investment to Exceed $1 Trillion, UNCTAD Predicts," *United Nations Conference On Trade And Development.* [Online] Available http://www.unctad.org/en/docs/pr2856.en.pdf, 8 September 2001. International Accounts Data, Bureau of Economic Analysis. [Online] Available www.bea.doc.gov/bea/di1.htm, 8 September 2001.

6. "Global Foreign Direct Investment to Exceed $1 Trillion, UNCTAD Predicts," *United Nations Conference On Trade And Development.* [Online] Available http://www.unctad.org/en/docs/pr2856.en.pdf, 8 September 2001.

7. "Chapter 7: Industry, Technology, and the Global Marketplace—U.S. Technology in the Marketplace," *Science and Engineering Indicators 2000.* [Online] Available http://www.nsf.gov/sbe/srs/seind00/access/c7/c7s1.htm#c7s1l2, 8 September 2001.

8. *Ibid.*

9. "Fact Sheet: U.N. Regular Budget Scale of Assessment," *United States Mission To The United Nations.* [Online] Available http://www.un.int/usa/fact6.htm, 8 September 2001.

10. B. Crossette, "Europeans Reject U.S. Bid to Lower U.N. Dues," *New York Times*, 3 October 2000, 12. P. Tooher, "Hello, Euro: Currency Opens New Era for Continent," *Arizona Republic*, 3 January 1999, E14.

11. "What Is the G20?" G8 Information Centre. [Online] Available http://www.g7.utoronto.ca/g7/g20/g20whatisit.html, 9 September 2001.

12. "Country Fact Sheet: United States, Number of Parent Corporations and Foreign Affiliates, Latest Available Year." *World Investment Report 2000: Cross-border Mergers* and Acquisitions and Development. [Online] http://www.unctad.org/en/pub/ps4wir00fs.en.htm, 8 September 2001.

13. K. Granzin, "Motivational Influences on 'Buy Domestic' Purchasing: Marketing Management Implications from a Study of Two Nations," *Journal of International Marketing* 9 (2001): 73–96.

14. G. Knight, "Consumer Preferences for Foreign and Domestic Products," *Journal of Consumer Marketing* 16 no. 2 (1998): 151–162.

15. J. White, G. White, & N. Shirouzu, "Passing Era: Soon, The Big Three Won't Be, As Foreigners Make Inroads in U.S.—Toyota Draws Near Chrysler as Investments Pay Off; Dealers Shift Loyalties—'A Life-Threatening Disease'," *The Wall Street Journal*, 13 August 2001, A1.

16. "Japan: Annual Fresh Deciduous Fruit Report," *U.S. Department of Agriculture Reports*, 17 September 1997. Available at USDA.gov.

17. B. Thevenot, "Clawing for Survival, Louisiana's Crab Processors Are Being Pinched by Low Prices and Foreign Competition," *New Orleans Times-Picayune*, 6 October 1999, A1.

18. L. Grant, "More U.S. Diamond Buyers Turn to Canada: Gem Seekers Want to Avoid Stones at Center of Conflicts," *USA Today*, 17 July 2001, B2.

19. D. Luhnow, "Crossover Success: How NAFTA Helped Wal-Mart Reshape the Mexican Market—Lower Tariffs, Retail Muscle Translate into Big Sales; Middlemen Are Squeezed—'Like Shopping in the U.S.,'" *The Wall Street Journal*, 31 August 2001, A1.

20. J. Urquhart, "Canada Seeks to Protect Its Magazines from Losing Ad Revenue to Foreigners," *The Wall Street Journal*, 30 September 1998, B12.

21. M. Kanabayashi, "Japan Hits China with Agricultural Curbs," *The Wall Street Journal*, 11 April 2001, A15.

22. World Trade Organization, "The Agreements: Anti-Dumping, Subsidies, Safeguards, Contingencies, etc. [Online] Available www.wto.org/about/agmnts7.htm#subsidies, 24 January 1999.

23. Associated Press, "U.S. Takes Aim at Chinese Beetle in Trade Battle," *The Plain Dealer*, 12 September 1998, 2c.

24. D. Michaels, "U.S. Questions U.K.'s Big Loans to British Aerospace for Airbus Jet," *The Wall Street Journal*, 14 March 2000, A27.

25. J. Bovard, "The Customs Service's Fickle Philosophers," *The Wall Street Journal*, 7 July 1991, A10.

26. A. Tanzer, "Here's One Asian Industry That Isn't Declining: Software Piracy. It Is Costing American Companies Billions of Dollars in Lost Revenues," *Forbes*, 7 September 1998, 162.

27. "Directorate General for Enlargement: Introduction—EU Enlargement—A Historic Opportunity," *Europa—The European Union Online.* [Online] Available http://europa.eu.int/comm/enlargement/intro/index.htm#An%20unprecedented%20enlargement, 9 September 2001.

28. *Ibid.*

29. P. Behr, "NAFTAmath: A Texas-Sized Surge in Trade; Six Months after Treaty's Enactment, Booming Sales to Mexico Overshadow U.S. Job Losses," *Washington Post*, 21 August 1994, H1.

30. G. Smith & E. Malkin, "Mexico's Makeover," *Business Week*, 21 December 1998, 28. D. Blount, "Canada Favors Life after NAFTA," *Denver Post*, 22 November 1998, A10.

31. R. Zoellick, "With NAFTA, Everyone Wins: Lower-Income Americans Have Especially Benefited From NAFTA," *Los Angeles Times*, 31 July 2000, B13.

32. G. Smith, E. Malkin, J. Wheatley, P. Magnusson, & M. Arndt, "Betting on Free Trade: George Bush Wants to Turn North and South America into the World's Biggest Single Market. Is It for Real or Just a Dream?" *Business Week*, 23 April 2001 32.

33. Declaration of Principles, Summit of the Americas, "Free Trade Area of the Americas." [Online] Available www.ftaa-alca. org/EnglishVersion/miami_e.htm, 27 January 1999.

34. G. Smith, E. Malkin, J. Wheatley, P. Magnusson, & M. Arndt, "Betting on Free Trade: George Bush Wants to Turn North and South America into the World's Biggest Single Market. Is It for Real or Just a Dream?" *Business Week*, 23 April 2001 32.

35. "ASEAN Free Trade Area (Afta): An Update," *Association of Southeast Nations*. [Online] Available http://www.aseansec. org/view.asp?file=/general/publication/ afta-upd.htm, 10 September 2001.

36. "Member Economies' Websites," *Asia-Pacific Economic Cooperation*. [Online] Available http://www.apecsec.org. sg/member/memb_websites.html, 10 September 2001.

37. "Big Mac Currencies," *Economist*, 21 April 2001, 74.

38. "Competitiveness Indicators," *The World Bank Group*. [Available] http://wbln0018. worldbank.org/psd/compete.nsf/ d3fe1ba1940f13908525650d0053554f/ c2b07f0ad3cc44d68525650d00536564? OpenDocument, 12 September 2001.

39. M. Vachris & J. Thomas, "International Price Comparisons Based on Purchasing Power Parity." *Monthly Labor Review* 122 no. 10 (1999): 3–12. [Online] Available http://stats.bls.gov/opub/mlr/1999/10/ art1full.pdf, 12 September 2001.

40. "Japanese Trade Barriers Cost Consumers," *The Associated Press,* 14 December 1994. "Japan's Protection Racket: How Much Do Barriers to Imports Cost Japanese Consumers?" *The Economist*, 7 January 1995, 58. M. Williams, P. Dvorak, P. Landers, & M. Kanabayashi, "Japan Must Finish Stalled Reforms, Many Say, Or Risk Losing Its Might," *The Wall Street Journal Interactive*, 16 March 2001.

41. E. Thornton, "Revolution in Japanese Retailing," *Fortune* 3 (7 February 1994): 143.

42. P. Dwyler, P. Engardio, Z. Schiller, & S. Reed, "Tearing Up Today's Organization Chart," *Business Week*, 18 November 1994, 80–83.

43. B. McKay, "New Formula: To Fix Coca-Cola, Daft Sets Out to Get Relationships Right—He Woos European Officials and Lets Managers Adapt Tactics to Their Markets—Lessons from Old Masters," *The Wall Street Journal*, 23 June 2000, A1.

44. A. Sundaram & J.S. Black, "The Environment and Internal-Organization of Multinational Enterprises," *Academy of Management Review* 17 (1992): 729–757.

45. H.S. James, Jr., & M. Weidenbaum, *When Businesses Cross International Borders: Strategic Alliances and Their Alternatives* (Westport, CT: Praeger Publishers, 1993).

46. R. Badam, "India Hooked on 'Millionaire' Show," *Associated Press*, 4 September 2000.

47. *Ibid.*

48. "LNG Imports Needed to Meet Growing US Gas Supply Deficit," *Oil & Gas Journal*, 2 October 2001, 28.

49. "Frequently Asked Questions about Acquiring a McDonald's Franchise," McDonald's. [Online] Available http://www. mcdonalds.com/corporate/franchise/faq/ index.html, 14 September 2001.

50. A.E. Serwer, "Trouble in Franchise Nation," *Fortune*, 6 March 1995, 115.

51. "Business Performance: Moving Forward," *Tricon Worldwide*. Available http://www.triconw.com/bus_perf/ default.htm, 14 September 2001.

52. D. Hemlock, "World Wise: Strategies That Work around the Corner Don't Always Work in Locales Abroad, Office Depot's Chief Executive Says," *South Florida Sun*, 18 December 2000, 16.

53. *Ibid.*

54. "Company Profile," Fuji Xerox. [Online] Available http://www.fujixerox.co.jp/ eng/company/profile.html, 14 September 2001.

55. L. Hill, "Benchmark MRO expertise," *Air Transport World* 38 no. 8 (2001): 51–52.

56. "Company Profile," SasolChevron. [Online] Available http://www.sasolchevron. com/index2.html, 15 September 2001.

57. D.P. Hamilton, "Fuji Xerox Is a Rarity in World Business: A Joint Venture That Works," *The Wall Street Journal*, 26 September 1996, R19. E. Terazono & C. Lorenz, "Fuji Xerox Marriage Successful: Growing Pains with Parent Easing," *The Financial Post*, 24 September 1994, 55.

58. T. Weber, "Bringing Concert in Tune: Joint Venture Suffers under Operational, Institutional Problems," *Telephony*, 18 June 2001, 46.

59. B.R. Schlender, "How Toshiba Makes Alliances Work," *Fortune*, 4 October 1993, 116–120.

60. D. Sparks, "Partners," *Business Week*, 25 October 1999, 106. B.A. Walters, S. Peters, & G.G. Dess, "Strategic Alliances and Joint Ventures: Making Them Work," *Business Horizons*, July-August 1994, 5–10.

61. W. Beaver, "Volkswagen's American Assembly Plant: Fahrvernugen Was Not Enough," *Business Horizons*, 11 November 1992, 19.

62. *Ibid.*

63. M.W. Hordes, J.A. Clancy, & J. Baddaley, "A Primer for Global Start-Ups." *Academy of Management Executive*, May 1995, 7–11.

64. B.M. Oviatt & P.P. McDougall, "Toward a Theory of International New Ventures," *Journal of International Business Studies*, Spring 1994, 45–64.

65. B.M. Oviatt, P.P. McDougall, "Global Start-Ups: Entrepreneurs on a Worldwide Stage," *Academy of Management Executive*, May 1995, 30–44.

66. B. Powell, R. Tomlinson, E. Nee, J. Fox, C. Murphy, D. Stipp, J. Schlosser, A. Taylor III, J. Guyon, A. Serwer, J. Rohwer, B. O'Reilly, D. Roth, & P. Sellers, "Next-Generation Global Leaders, 25 Rising Stars: What Will the World Look Like a Decade or Two from Now? Who Knows? But These Young Business Leaders Surely Will Have Helped Shape It," *Fortune*, 14 May 2001, 140.

67. J. Huey, "The World's Best Brand," *Fortune*, 31 May 1993, 44.

68. R. Jacob, "The Big Rise: Middle Classes Explode around the Globe, Bringing New Markets and New Prosperity," *Fortune*, 30 May 1994, 74.

69. "Operations Review: Selected Market Results," *The Coca-Cola Company 2000 Annual Report*. [Online] Available http:// annualreport2000.coca-cola.com/ operations/selected.html, 15 September 2001.R. Tomkins, "Coca-Cola Strives to Rival Tap Water: Despite 48% of Global Market, Coke Chafes at Fact It Supplies only 3% of Every Human's Required Daily Liquid Intake," *Financial Post*, 30 October 1997, 77. J. Huey, "The World's Best Brand," *Fortune*, 31 May 1993, 44.

70. P. Prada, "Ja, Ja, Americana's Fabulosa— In Europe, Theme Parks Draw Crowds with Thrill Rides, Burgers and Bugs Bunny," *The Wall Street Journal*, 21 June 2001, B1.

71. "Fact Sheet, Call Center Solutions: How Call Centers Can Work for You," *The Netherlands Foreign Investment Agency*.

[Online] Available http://www.nfia.com/html/solution/fact.html, 15 September 2001.

72. J. Oetzel, R. Bettis, & M. Zenner, "How Risky Are They?" *Journal of Word Business* 36 no. 2 (Summer 2001): 128–145.

73. K.D. Miller, "A Framework for Integrated Risk Management in International Business," *Journal of International Business Studies*, 2nd Quarter 1992, 311.

74. M. Forney, "Foreigners Must Disclose Internet Secrets to China Soon—Encryption Rules for Firms Threaten Growth of the Web," *The Wall Street Journal*, 25 January 2000, A10.

75. "Country Data: Available Data," *The PRS Group*. [Online] Available http://www.prsgroup.com/countrydata/availabledata.html, 16 September 2001.

76. G. Anping, "Old Contract Laws Need Repair to Fit into New Reality," *China Daily*, 7 May 1994, 4–1.

77. F. Bleakley, "High School Seniors Mind Their Business and Even Profit by It: Teens Learn by Their Goofs in Import-Export World; Racy Towels Go Too Far," *The Wall Street Journal*, 20 June 1995, A1.

78. P. Waldman, "Your Lingerie in Iran, Even If It's for Sale: Censors Decide Many Topics Are Unmentionable in Ads," *The Wall Street Journal*, 21 June 1995, A1.

79. G. Hofstede, "The Cultural Relativity of the Quality of Life Concept," *Academy of Management Review* 9 (1984): 389–398. G. Hofstede, "The Cultural Relativity of Organizational Practices and Theories," *Journal of International Business Studies*, Fall 1983, 75–89. G. Hofstede, "The Interaction Between National and Organizational Value Systems," *Journal of Management Studies*, July 1985, 347–357.

80. R. Hodgetts, "A Conversation with Geert Hofstede," *Organizational Dynamics*, Spring 1993, 53–61.

81. M. Janssens, J.M. Brett, F.J. Smith, "Confirmatory Cross-Cultural Research: Testing the Viability of a Corporation-Wide Safety Policy," *Academy of Management Journal* 38 (1995): 364–382.

82. R.G. Linowes, "The Japanese Manager's Traumatic Entry into the United States: Understanding the American-Japanese Cultural Divide," *Academy of Management Executive* 7 (1993): 21–40.

83. J.S. Black, M. Mendenhall, & G. Oddou, "Toward a Comprehensive Model of International Adjustment: An Integration of Multiple Theoretical Perspectives," *Academy of Management Journal* 16 (1991): 291–317. R.L. Tung, "American Expatri-

ates Abroad: From Neophytes to Cosmopolitans," *Columbia Journal of World Business*, 22 June 1998, 125.

84. L. Copeland & L. Griggs, *Going International* (New York: Random House, 1985).

85. R.A. Swaak, "Expatriate Failures: Too Many, Too Much Cost, Too Little Planning," *Compensation and Benefits Review* 27, no. 6 (21 November 1995): 47.

86. J.S. Black & M. Mendenhall, "Cross-Cultural Training Effectiveness: A Review and Theoretical Framework for Future Research," *Academy of Management Review* 15 (1990): 113–136.

87. R.L. Thornton & M.K. Thornton, "Personnel Problems in 'Carry the Flag' Missions in Foreign Assignments," *Business Horizons*, 1 January 1995, 59.

88. W. Arthur, Jr., & W. Bennett, Jr., "The International Assignee: The Relative Importance of Factors Perceived to Contribute to Success," *Personnel Psychology* 48 (1995): 99–114.

89. R. Donkin, "Recruitment: Overseas Gravy Train May Be Running Out of Steam—Preparing Expatriate Packages Is Challenging the Expertise of Human Resource Management," *The Financial Times*, 30 November 1994, 10.

90. J. Lublin, "Your Career Matters: To Smooth a Transfer Abroad, A New Focus on Kids," *The Wall Street Journal*, 26 January 1999, B1.

## Chapter 9

1. "Stock Charting for AOL Time Warner, Inc." *The Wall Street Journal*. [Online] Available http://interactive.wsj.com/mds/mds.cgi?route=BOEH&template=company-research&profile-name=Portfolio1&profile-version=3.0&profile-type=Portfolio&profile-format-action=include&profile-read-action=skip-read&profile-write-action=skip-write&p-sym=aol&p-type=usstock&p-name=&section=stock-charting&profile-end=Portfolio&p-headline=wsjie&the-symbol=aol&osymb=US-aol&time=2yr&freq=1mo&wtype=64&compidx=aaaaa%7E0&comp=&ma=1&maval=200&uf=0&sid=438962&symb=US-aol&lf=1&lf2=0&lf3=0&x=61&y=6, 23 September 2001.

2. A. "Making the Web Pay in Small Ways; Local Internet Providers Thrive in Shadows of Giants Cha," *Washington Post*, 22 February 2000, A1.

3. J. Barney, "Firm Resources and Sustained Competitive Advantage," *Journal of*

*Management* 17 (1991): 99–120. J. Barney, "Looking Inside for Competitive Advantage," *Academy of Management Executive* 9 (1995): 49–61.

4. G. Keizer, "The Best and Worst ISPs: We Survey 2000 PCWorld.com Visitors, Conduct Performance Tests, and Compare Features," *PC World*. [Online] Available http://www.pcworld.com/resource/printable/article/0,aid,18624,00.asp, 23 September 2001.

5. *Ibid.*

6. J. Sandberg & J.P. Miller, "CompuServe Posts Big Quarterly Loss—On-line Pioneer to Retreat from Consumer Market and End Family Service," *The Wall Street Journal*, 22 November 1996.

7. M. Lake, M. Wood, & G. Keizer, "Access Internet: CNET Reviews 5 Major ISPs," *Cnet*. [Online] Available http://www.cnet.com/internet/0-3762-8-4951560-1.html?tag=st.is.3762-8-4951560-4.MORE.3762-8-4951560-1, 6 March 2001.

8. P. Boyle, "Editor's Choice: America Online," *PC Magazine*, 11 June 1996.

9. A. "Making the Web Pay in Small Ways; Local Internet Providers Thrive in Shadows of Giants Cha," *Washington Post*, 22 February 2000, A1.

10. G. Keizer, "The Best and Worst ISPs: We Survey 2000 PCWorld.com Visitors, Conduct Performance Tests, and Compare Features," *PC World*. [Online] Available http://www.pcworld.com/resource/printable/article/0,aid,18624,00.asp, 23 September 2001.

11. S. Hart & C. Banbury, "How Strategy-Making Processes Can Make a Difference," *Strategic Management Journal* 15 (1994): 251–269.

12. R.A. Burgelman, "Fading Memories: A Process Theory of Strategic Business Exit in Dynamic Environments," *Administrative Science Quarterly* 39 (1994): 24–56. R.A. Burgelman & A.S. Grove, "Strategic Dissonance," *California Management Review* 38 (1996): 8–28.

13. L. Guerrero, "Dishes Gain on Cable TV: Cost, Features Nudge Viewers to Satellites," *Chicago Sun-Times*, 9 January 2001, 12.

14. D. Foust, D. Rocks, & M. Kripalani, "Doug Daft Isn't Sugarcoating Things: He's Already Shaking Up Coke. But Can He Bring Back the Fizz?" *Business Week*, 7 February 2000, 36.

15. A. Fiegenbaum, S. Hart, & D. Schendel, "Strategic Reference Point Theory," *Strategic Management Journal* 17 (1996): 219–235.

736

16. L. Johannes, & J. Lublin, "Kodak Hires Web Guru to Develop Its Digital Plans—Can Silicon Valley's Ted Lewis Help 'Big Yellow' Bring Its Future into Sharper Focus?" *The Wall Street Journal*, 9 October 2000, B1.

17. B. Howard, M. Muchmore, & B. Gottesman, "14th Annual Reader's Survey: Service & Reliability, Desktops," *PC Magazine*, August 2001, 115.

18. D.J. Collis, "Research Note: How Valuable Are Organizational Capabilities?" *Strategic Management Journal* 15 (1994): 143–152.

19. K. Freiberg & J. Freiberg, *Nuts! Southwest Airlines' Crazy Recipe for Business and Personal Success* (Austin, TX: Bard Press, 1996).

20. A. Fiegenbaum & H. Thomas, "Strategic Groups as Reference Groups: Theory, Modeling and Empirical Examination of Industry and Competitive Strategy," *Strategic Management Journal* 16 (1995): 461–476.

21. "On the Map: Company Profile," *Gannett Company*. [Online] Available http://www.gannett.com/map/gan007.htm, 24 September 2001.

22. "Tribune at a Glance: Publishing," *Tribune Company*. [Online] Available http://www.tribune.com/report2000/tc2000ar02_3.html, 24 September 2001. "Knight Ridder Newspapers," *Knight Ridder*. [Online] Available http://www.kri.com/papers/index.html, 24 September 2001.

23. R.K. Reger & A.S. Huff, "Strategic Groups: A Cognitive Perspective," *Strategic Management Journal* 14 (1993): 103–124.

24. "The New York Times Company: Our Businesses," *The New York Times Company*. [Online] Available http://www.nytco.com/company/busi.html, 24 September 2001.

25. "The Company, The Corporate Profile," *Dow Jones*. [Online] Available http://www.dowjones.com/corp/index_aboutdow.htm, 24 September 2001.

26. Gannett Web Site, "Company History." [Online] Available www.gannett.com/map/history.htm, 24 September 2001.

27. W.B. Werther, Jr. & J.L. Kerr, "The Shifting Sands of Competitive Advantage," *Business Horizons*, May-June 1995, 11–17.

28. *Ibid.*

29. J. Samuelson, "Tough Guy Billionaire," *Forbes*, 24 February 1997, 64–66.

30. "Menards Vs. Home Depot," WCCO Channel 4000. [Online] Available http://www.channel4000.com/news/dimension/news-dimension-19991117-205633.html, 25 September 2001.

31. *Ibid.*

32. H. Rudnitsky, "What Business Are We In?" *Forbes*, 10 March 1997, 68–70.

33. M. Williams, "Intel, Chastened by Missteps, Alters Strategy to Concentrate on Chips—Folding Some Services Ventures and Cutting Costs, It Keeps Budget Big for Core Product," 16 March 2001, B1.

34. M. Lubatkin, "Value-Creating Mergers: Fact or Folklore?" *Academy of Management Executive* 2 (1988): 295–302. M. Lubatkin & S. Chatterjee, "Extending Modern Portfolio Theory into the Domain of Corporate Diversification: Does It Apply?" *Academy of Management Journal* 37 (1994): 109–136. M.H. Lubatkin & P.J. Lane, "Psst . . . The Merger Mavens Still Have It Wrong!" *Academy of Management Executive* 10 (1996): 21–39.

35. J. Baglole, "War of the Doughnuts—Krispy Kreme, Tim Horton's of Canada to Square Off in Each Other's Territory," *The Wall Street Journal*, 23 August 2001, B1.

36. K. Brooker, "Plugging the Leaks at P&G: A First-Year Report Card for CEO Durk Jager," *Fortune*, 21 February 2000, 44.

37. J.A. Pearce, II, "Selecting Among Alternative Grand Strategies," *California Management Review*, Spring 1982, 23–31.

38. R. Sidel & A. Raghavan, "Quarterly Stock Market Review—Where Did All the Mergers Go? Slowdown in Deals May Persist—Talks Increased, Deals Didn't; Experts Have Few Hopes for a Rebound," *The Wall Street Journal*, 2 Monday 2001, C14.

39. S. Chandler, "Walgreen's Adding 500 Stores, Posts Record Profit," *Chicago Tribune*, 3 January 2001, 2.

40. T. Zaun, "For Subaru, Imitation Is the Most Irksome Form of Flattery—Popularity in the U.S. of Crossover Vehicles Leads to Competition," *The Wall Street Journal*, 31 January 2001, A18.

41. J.A. Pearce, II, "Retrenchment Remains the Foundation of Business Turnaround" *Strategic Management Journal* 15 (1994): 407–417.

42. S. McCartney, S. Carey, & G. Hitt, "Mayday Call: U.S. Airline Industry Faces Cash Crunch, Pleads for a Bailout—Major Carriers Cut Capacity By 20% as They Struggle to Replenish Liquidity—'No Posturing Going on Here'," *The Wall Street Journal*, 17 September 2001, A1.

43. Q. Hardy, "Strained Relations: A Software Star Sees Its 'Family' Culture Turn Dysfunctional—PeopleSoft Made Its Work a Cause, But a Slump Is Shaking the Faithful—The Sting from Red Pepper," *The Wall Street Journal*, 5 May 1999, A1.

44. E. Lee, "Changes at PeopleSoft Pump Up Company's Bottom Line, " *Knight-Ridder Tribune*, 6 May 2001.

45. K. Dolan, "Compassion Pays," *Forbes*, 24 February 1997, 86–90.

46. M. Trottman, "Now Available on Start-Up Airlines: Leather Seats, Wine, Satellite TV," *The Wall Street Journal*, 25 October 2000, B1.

47. R. Winslow & B. Martinez, "Efforts to Switch Patients to Generic Prozac Advance—Pharmacy-Benefit Managers Launch Aggressive Bids to Lower Drug Costs," *The Wall Street Journal*, 20 August 2001, A3.

48. M. Williams, "Intel Cuts Some Chip Prices as Sales Flag," *The Wall Street Journal*, 17 July 2001, B6.

49. "What You Need to Know," AAA Carolinas. [Online] Available http://www.aaacarolinas.com/carbuyer/needtoknow.html, 29 September 2001.

50. R.B. Lieber, "Turns Out This Critter Can Fly," *Fortune*, 27 November 1995, 110–112.

51. S. Beatty, "Pay TV: Unconventional HBO Finds Its Own Success Is a Hard Act to Follow—As the Cable Network Seeks to Keep Its Hip Cachet, The Costs Get Enormous—Tom Hanks' Second D-Day," *The Wall Street Journal*, 29 September 2000, A1.

52. M. Conlin, "Love Those Logs," *Forbes*, 10 August 1998, 89–90.

53. R.E. Miles & C.C. Snow, *Organizational Strategy, Structure, and Process* (New York: McGraw Hill, 1978). S. Zahra & J.A. Pearce, "Research Evidence on the Miles-Snow Typology," *Journal of Management* 16 (1990): 751–768. W.L. James & K.J. Hatten, "Further Evidence on the Validity of the Self Typing Paragraph Approach: Miles and Snow Strategic Archetypes in Banking," *Strategic Management Journal* 16 (1995): 161–168.

54. L. Egan, "The Little Latin Airline That Could: LanChile Is Diversifying Aggressively into Cargo, Linking Up with Global Partners, And Gaining Altitude Fast," *Business Week*, 2 July 2001, 30.

55. "U.S. Innovation Stories," *3M*. [Online] Available http://www.3m.com/frontindex_us.jhtml, 30 September 2001.

56. E. Ramstad, "Using a Personal Approach, Many Tiny PC Firms Thrive," *The Wall Street Journal Interactive Edition*, 8 January 1997.

57. R. Ho, "Do You Want to Dance? Head to the Bowling Alley," *The Wall Street Journal Interactive Edition*, 24 January 1997.

58. R. Gibson & C.Y. Coleman, "How Burger King Emerged as a Threat to McDonald's," *The Wall Street Journal Interactive Edition*, 27 February 1997.

59. *Ibid.*

60. M. Chen, "Competitor Analysis and Interfirm Rivalry: Toward a Theoretical Integration," *Academy of Management Review* 21 (1996): 100–134. J.C. Baum & H.J. Korn, "Competitive Dynamics of Interfirm Rivalry," *Academy of Management Journal* 39 (1996): 255–291.

61. *Ibid.*

62. M. Stopa, "Wendy's New-Fashioned Growth: Buy Hardee's," *Crain's Detroit Business*, 21 October 1996.

63. L. Lavelle, "The Chickens Come Home to Roost, And Boston Market Is Prepared to Expand," *The Record*, 6 October 1996.

64. N. Shirouzu, "Though Japan Nears Saturation, Burger King Turns Up the Heat," *The Wall Street Journal Interactive Edition*, 31 January 1997.

65. M. Trottman, "Now Available on Start-Up Airlines: Leather Seats, Wine, Satellite TV," *The Wall Street Journal*, 25 October 2000, B1.

66. M. Trottman, "Legend Air Ends Operations after Love Field Battle," *The Wall Street Journal* 6 March 2001, A4.

67. J.C. Baum & H.J. Korn, "Competitive Dynamics of Interfirm Rivalry," *Academy of Management Journal* 39 (1996): 255–291.

68. L. Stones, "3Com Restructures, Pulls Out of High-End Markets," *Business Day*, 23 March 2000, 21.

69. J.G. Auerbach, "CVS Chain Grows Rapidly as Smaller Rivals Cry Foul," *The Wall Street Journal Interactive Edition*, 24 February 1997.

70. R. Hotten, "Fords 20% Cut Ignites Price War: Up to 3,000 Off in New Battle of the Showrooms," *Sunday Mail*, 1 October 2000, 1.

71. B. Antoncic & R. D. Hisrich, "Intrapreneurship: Construct Refinement and Cross-Cultural Validation," *Journal of Business Venturing* 16 (2001): 495–527.

72. P. Lenzner & B. Upbin, "Monsanto v. Malthus," *Forbes*, 10 March 1997, 58–64.

73. G.T. Lumpkin & G.G. Dess, "Clarifying the Entrepreneurial Orientation Construct and Linking It to Performance," *Academy of Management Review* 21 (1996): 135–172.

74. R.B. Lieber, "Beating the Odds," *Fortune*, 31 March 1997, 82–90.

75. D. Miller & P. Friesen, "Archetypes of Strategy Formulation," *Management Science* 24 (1978): 921–933.

76. D. Machan, "Ziti for Dogs," *Forbes*, 24 February 1997, 95–95.

77. N. Venkatraman, "Strategic Orientation of Business Enterprises: The Construct, Dimensionality, and Measurement," *Management Science* 35 (1989): 942–962.

78. Z. Moukheiber, "Cybercops," *Forbes*, 10 March 1997, 170–172.

79. P. Newcomb, "Peanut Butter and Pearl Jam," *Forbes*, 10 February 1997, 152.

## Chapter 10

1. T.M. Amabile, R. Conti, H. Coon, J. Lazenby, & M. Herron, "Assessing the Work Environment for Creativity," *Academy of Management Journal* 39 (1996): 1154–1184.

2. *Ibid.*

3. A.H. Van de Ven & M.S. Poole, "Explaining Development and Change in Organizations" *Academy of Management Review* 20 (1995): 510–540.

4. G. Naik & T. Kamm, "Bold Stroke: Olivetti Reinvents Itself Once More, This Time as a Telecom Giant—Chief Colannino's Brash Move on Telecom Italia Portends New Greatness, If It Works—'The Italians Love to Talk'," *The Wall Street Journal*, 22 February 1999, A1.

5. J. Krasner, "Blimp Management 101: Find a Crew with a Firm Grasp of the Bottom Line," *The Wall Street Journal*, 25 October 2000, NE4.

6. T.M. Amabile, R. Conti, H. Coon, J. Lazenby, & M. Herron, "Assessing the Work Environment for Creativity," *Academy of Management Journal* 39 (1996): 1154–1184.

7. P. Anderson & M.L. Tushman, "Managing through Cycles of Technological Change," *Research/Technology Management*, May/June 1991, 26–31.

8. R.N. Foster, *Innovation: The Attacker' Advantage* (New York: Summit, 1986).

9. iComp Index 2.0. Intel Corporation Web Site. [Online] Available http://www. intel.com/procs/performance/icomp/ index.htm, 5 December 1997.

10. J. Burke, *The Day the Universe Changed* (Boston: Little, Brown, and Company, 1985).

11. R.N. Foster, *Innovation: The Attacker' Advantage* (New York: Summit, 1986).

12. M.L. Tushman, P.C. Anderson, & C. O'Reilly, "Technology Cycles, Innovation Streams, and Ambidextrous Organizations: Organization Renewal through Innovation Streams and Strategic Change," in *Managing Strategic Innovation and Change*, eds. M.L. Tushman & P. Anderson (1997), 3–23.

13. G. Cowley & A. Underwood, "Surgeon, Drop That Scalpel," *Newsweek Special Issue: The Power of Invention*, Winter 1997–1998, 77–78.

14. "Pony Express," *Encyclopædia Britannica Online*. [Online] Available http://www. eb.com:180/bol/topic?eu=62367&sctn=1, 6 March 1999.

15. J.R. Aldern, "The Victorian Internet: The Remarkable Story of the Telegraph and the Nineteenth Century's On-Line Pioneers (Review)," *Smithsonian*, 1 January 1999.

16. E. Schlossberg, *Interactive Excellence: Defining and Developing New Standards for the Twenty-First Century* (New York: Ballatine, 1998).

17. W. Abernathy & J. Utterback, "Patterns of Industrial Innovation," *Technology Review* 2 (1978): 40–47.

18. H. Bolande, "Satellite Industry Looks to Web Access for Credibility in Telecommunications," *The Wall Street Journal*, 8 December 2000, B6.

19. M. Forney, ". . . As Beijing Pushes Its Own Technology," *The Wall Street Journal*, 5 June 2000, A27.

20. T.M. Amabile, R. Conti, H. Coon, J. Lazenby, & M. Herron, "Assessing the Work Environment for Creativity," *Academy of Management Journal* 39 (1996): 1154–1184.

21. *Ibid.*

22. M. Csikszentmihalyi, *Flow: The Psychology of Optimal Experience* (New York: Harper & Row, 1990).

23. B. Dumaine, "Closing the Innovation Gap," *Fortune*, 2 December 1991, 56.

24. *Ibid.*

25. J. Pereira, "The 'Big' Idea: Itz Toys Flipped When 2 Kids Invented a New Game—Justin and Matthew, 11 and 12, Are Standouts; Linsay, Age 9, Is Scoring with Rapunzel," *The Wall Street Journal*, 12 February 2001, A1.

26. K.M. Eisenhardt, "Accelerating Adaptive Processes: Product Innovation in the Global Computer Industry," *Administrative Science Quarterly* 40 (1995): 84–110.

27. *Ibid.*

28. R. Gibson, "Starbucks Plans to Test a Paper Cup that Insulates Hands from Hot Coffee," *The Interactive Wall Street Journal*, 22 February 1999. S. Kravetz, "These People Search for a Cup that Suits

the Coffee It Holds," *The Wall Street Journal*, 24 March 1998, A1.

29. R. Winslow, "Atomic Speed: Utility Cuts Red Tape, Builds Nuclear Plant Almost on Schedule," *The Wall Street Journal Interactive*, 22 February 1984.

30. A. Taylor, III., "Kellogg Cranks Up Its Idea Machine: To Grow, The Company Needs New Products. But Will Fiber-Enriched Potato Chips Be a Hit?" *Fortune*, 5 July 1999, 181.

31. L. Kraar, "25 Who Help the U.S. Win: Innovators Everywhere Are Generating Ideas to Make America a Stronger Competitor. They Range from a Boss Who Demands the Impossible to a Mathematician with a Mop," *Fortune*, 22 March 1991.

32. *Ibid.*

33. M.W. Lawless & P.C. Anderson, "Generational Technological Change: Effects of Innovation and Local Rivalry on Performance," *Academy of Management Journal* 39 (1996): 1185–1217.

34. S. Anderson & M. Uzumeri, "Managing Product Families: The Case of the Sony Walkman," *Research Policy* 24 (1995): 761–782.

35. "Solutions Through Partnerships," *Appliance*, 1 September 1996.

36. P. Ponticel, "Integrated Product Process Development," *Automotive Engineering*, 1 October 1996.

37. A. Taylor, III & J. Kahn, "How Toyota Defies Gravity: Its Secret Is Its Legendary Production System," *Fortune*, 8 December 1997, 100.

38. J. O'Brien, "Accelerating the Process from Big Idea to Burning Rubber Foot on the Gas: High-Speed Approach to Car Production," *Birmingham Post*, 4 April 2001, 21.

39. N. Wingfield, "Can These Dot-Coms Be Saved?—Cash Supply Shrinks While Webvan Losses Continue," *The Wall Street Journal*, 25 January 2001, B1.

40. P. Strebel, "Choosing the Right Change Path," *California Management Review*, Winter 1994, 29–51.

41. K. Lewin, *Field Theory in Social Science: Selected Theoretical Papers* (New York: Harper & Brothers, 1951).

42. I. Gashurov, "Can Anyone Fix the United Way? The FORTUNE 500's Favorite Charitable Organization Needs a Managerial Face-Lift. It Recently Bounced the Woman Who Tried to Do Just That," *Fortune*, 27 November 2000, 170.

43. B. Upbin, "Bit Paramedics," *Forbes*, 3 November 1997, 154–156.

44. J. Schofield, "Intel Chips in with Improvements," *Computer Weekly*, 26 November 1998, 61.

45. G.P. Zachary, "High Tech Is Forming a Role as an Indicator," *The Wall Street Journal Interactive*, 30 September 1996.

46. H. Stout, "Crunch Time: After Its Biggest Client Abruptly Disappears, A Start-Up Scrambles," *The Wall Street Journal*, 5 April 2000, B1.

47. W. Weitzel & E. Jonsson, "Reversing the Downward Spiral: Lessons from W.T. Grant and Sears Roebuck," *Academy of Management Executive* 5 (1991): 7–22.

48. *Ibid.*

49. T. Agins, L. Bird, & L. Jereski, "Overdoing It: A Thirst for Glitter and a Pliant Partner Got Barney's in a Bind," *The Wall Street Journal Interactive*, 19 January 1996.

50. "The Rise and Fall of the House of Barneys: A Family Tale of Chutzpah, Glory, and Greed (Review)," *Publishers Weekly*, 22 February 1999, 73.

51. *Ibid.*

52. D. Moin, V.M. Young, & A. Friedman, "Dickson Pool Sees Barney's IPO," *Women's Wear Daily*, 5 August 1997. Available online.

53. L. Bird, "Barney's to Close Original Store and Three Others," *The Asian Wall Street Journal Interactive*, 19 June 1997.

54. D. Moin, "Barney's New Owners Plan to Retain Company, Grow Business: Strategy Calls for Boosting Sales, Increasing Cash Flow This Year," *Daily News Record*, 15 February 1999. Available online.

55. B. Herzog, "Lessons in Enterprise—Trouble in the Tower—Atwaters General Manager Stephan Earnhart Learns the Importance of Considering," *Portland Oregonian*, 1 October 2000, E1.

56. K. Lewin, *Field Theory in Social Science: Selected Theoretical Papers* (New York: Harper & Brothers, 1951).

57. *Ibid.*

58. A.B. Fisher, "Making Change Stick," *Fortune*, 17 April 1995, 121.

59. J.P. Kotter & L.A. Schlesinger, "Choosing Strategies for Change," *Harvard Business Review*, March-April 1979, 106–114.

60. M. Johne, "The Human Factor: Integrating People and Cultures after a Merger," *CMA Management*, 1 April 2000, 30.

61. *Ibid.*

62. J. Sweatman, "Propaganda . . . It Simply Won't Work." *Corporate Trends*. [Online] Available http://www.corporatetrends.com.au/sweat1.html, 21 October 2001.

63. T. Petzinger, Jr., "Bovis Team Helps Builders Construct a Solid Foundation." *The Wall Street Journal Interactive Edition*, 21 March 1997.

64. T. Petzinger, Jr., "Forget Empowerment, This Job Requires Constant Brainpower," *The Wall Street Journal Interactive Edition*, 17 October 1997.

65. R.H. Schaffer & H.A. Thomson, J.D, "Successful Change Programs Begin with Results," *Harvard Business Review on Change* (Boston: Harvard Business School Publishing, 1998), 189–213.

66. T. Petzinger, Jr., "Forget Empowerment, This Job Requires Constant Brainpower," *The Wall Street Journal Interactive Edition*, 17 October 1997.

67. R.N. Ashkenas & T.D. Jick, "From Dialogue to Action in GE WorkOut: Developmental Learning in a Change Process," in *Research in Organizational Change and Development*, Vol. 6, eds. W.A. Pasmore & R.W. Woodman (Greenwhich, CT: JAI Press, 1992) 267–287.

68. T. Stewart, "GE Keeps Those Ideas Coming," *Fortune*, 12 August 1991, 40.

69. J.D. Duck, "Managing Change: The Art of Balancing," *Harvard Business Review on Change* (Boston: Harvard Business School Publishing, 1998), 55–81.

70. J. Markoff, "Microsoft Relies Again on an Inner Circle," *New York Times*. [Online] Available http://www.nytimes.com, 25 March 2001.

71. W.J. Rothwell, R. Sullivan, & G.M. McLean, *Practicing Organizational Development: A Guide for Consultants* (San Diego, CA: Pfeiffer & Company, 1995).

72. N. Shirouzu, "Gadget Inspector: Why Toyota Wins Such High Marks on Quality Surveys—Hajime Oba Is a Key Coach as Japanese Auto Maker Steps Up U.S. Production—Striving to Reach Heijunka," *The Wall Street Journal*, 15 March 2001, A1.

73. *Ibid.*

74. W.J. Rothwell, R. Sullivan, & G.M. McLean, *Practicing Organizational Development: A Guide for Consultants* (San Diego, CA: Pfeiffer & Company, 1995).

75. R.N. Ashkenas & T.D. Jick, "From Dialogue to Action in GE WorkOut: Developmental Learning in a Change Process," in *Research in Organizational Change and Development*, Vol. 6, eds. W.A. Pasmore & R.W. Woodman (Greenwhich, CT: JAI Press, 1992), 267–287.

76. J. Ford & L.W. Ford, "The Role of Conversations in Producing Intentional Change in Organizations," *Academy of Management Review* 20 (1995): 541–570.

77. A. King, B. Oliver, B. Sloop, & K. Vaverek, *Planning and Goal Setting for Improved Performance, Participant's Guide*

739

(Cincinnati, OH: Thomson Executive Press, 1995).

78. K. Freiberg & J. Freiberg, *Nuts! Southwest Airlines' Crazy Recipe for Business and Personal Success* (Austin, TX: Bard Press, 1996).

79. J.P. Kotter, "Leading Change: Why Transformation Efforts Fail," *Harvard Business Review* 73, no. 2 (March-April 1995): 59.

80. W. Zellner, "The Right Place, The Right Time: CEO Bethune Has Continental Climbing," *Business Week*, 27 May 1996, 74.

81. G. Bailey, "Manager's Journal: Fear Is Nothing to Be Afraid Of," *The Wall Street Journal Interactive Edition*, 27 January 1997.

82. M. Hammer & S. A. Stanton, "The Pioneering Consultants Who Touched Off the Reengineering Movement Are Urging a New Imperative: Getting Top Managers to Stop and Reassess Where Their Companies Are Headed," *Fortune*, 24 November 1997, 291–296.

83. G. Bethune, "From Worst to First: Continental Airlines Has Achieved One of the Most Dramatic Business Turnarounds of the Nineties," *Fortune*, 25 May 1998, 185–190.

84. M. Brelis, "I've Got the Trust for CEO Bethune, The Key to Continental's Turnaround Is an Empowered Work Force, Not Slash-And-Burn," *Boston Globe*, 3 June 2001, E1.

85. G. Bethune, "From Worst to First: Continental Airlines Has Achieved One of the Most Dramatic Business Turnarounds of the Nineties," *Fortune*, 25 May 1998, 185–190.

86. *Ibid.*

87. M. Brelis, "I've Got the Trust for CEO Bethune, The Key to Continental's Turnaround Is an Empowered Work Force, Not Slash-And-Burn," *Boston Globe*, 3 June 2001, E1.

88. *Ibid.*

89. *Ibid.*

### Chapter 11

1. B. Schlender, "Microsoft: The Beast Is Back," *Fortune*, 11 June 2001, 75.

2. M. Hammer & J. Champy, *Reengineering the Corporation : A Manifesto for Business Revolution* (New York: Harper & Row, Publishers, 1993).

3. Marketing & Media, "Borders Will Reorganize Its Structure to Focus on Product Categories," *The Wall Street Journal*, 29 January 2001, B9.

4. J. G. March & H.A. Simon, *Organizations* (New York: John Wiley & Sons, 1958).

5. "Outline of Principal Operations," *Sony Corporation*. [Online] Available http://www.sony.com/SCA/outline.html, 4 November 2001.

6. "Business Segments," *Bayer Group*. [Online] Available http://www.bayer.com/en/unternehmen/arbeitsgebiete/index.html, 4 November 2001.

7. GE Annual Report. [Online] Available http://www.ge.com/annual00/financial/images/GEannual00_financials.pdf, 3 November 2001.

8. "American Express Company Annual Report 2000," *American Express*. [Online] Available http://www.onlineproxy.com/amex/2001/ar.html, 4 November 2001.

9. "Products," *Coca-Cola Enterprises*. [Online] Available http://www.cokecce.com/srclib/nav/process_nav.asp?strBody=company/products.htm, 4 November 2001.

10. L.R. Burns, "Adoption and Abandonment of Matrix Management Programs: Effects of Organizational Characteristics and Interorganizational Networks," *Academy of Management Journal* 36 (1993): 106–138.

11. E. Beck, "Familiar Cry to Unilever: Split It Up! Anglo-Dutch Firm Is Set to Streamline, but Some Want More," *The Wall Street Journal*, 4 August 2000, A7.

12. "Business Groups," *Unilever*. [Online] Available http://www.unilever.com/co/ut_bg.html, 4 November 2001.

13. H. Fayol, *General and Industrial Management*, translated by Constance Storrs (London: Pitman Publishing, 1949).

14. M. Weber, *The Theory of Social and Economic Organization*, translated and edited by A.M. Henderson & T. Parsons (New York: The Free Press, 1947).

15. H. Fayol, *General and Industrial Management*, translated by Constance Storrs (London: Pitman Publishing, 1949).

16. S. Bistayi, "Delegate—or Not?" *Forbes*, 21 April 1997, 20–21.

17. L. Goldman, "Brinker International: Red-Hot Chili's Food Distributors: Casual Dining—Table Service and a Modest $10-to-$25 Tab—Will Be the Hot Sector, Even in a Slowing Economy," *Forbes*, 8 January 2001, 134.

18. J. Rutledge, "Management by Belly Button," *Forbes*, 4 November 1996, 64.

19. E.E. Lawler, S.A. Mohrman, and G.E. Ledford, *Creating High Performance Organizations: Practices and Results of Employee Involvement and Quality Management in Fortune 1000 Companies* (San Francisco: Jossey-Bass, 1995).

20. E. Esterson, "Inner Beauties (Use of Internets by Small Businesses)," *Inc.*, 17 November 1998, 78.

21. C. Quintanilla, "Food: Come and Get It! Drive-Throughs Upgrade Services," *The Wall Street Journal Interactive*, 5 May 1994.

22. R.W. Griffin, *Task Design* (Glenview, IL: Scott, Foresman, 1982).

23. F. Herzberg, *Work and the Nature of Man* (Cleveland, OH: World Press, 1966).

24. A. Markels, "Team Approach: A Power Producer Is Intent on Giving Power to Its People—Groups of AES Employees Do Complex Tasks Ranging from Hiring to Investing—Making Sure Work Is 'Fun,'" *The Wall Street Journal*, 3 July 1995, A1.

25. *Ibid.*

26. J.R. Hackman & G.R. Oldham, *Work Redesign* (Reading, MA: Addison-Wesley, 1980).

27. T. Burns & G.M. Stalker, *The Management of Innovation* (London: Tavistock, 1961).

28. M. Hammer & J. Champy, *Reengineering the Corporation: A Manifesto for Business Revolution* (New York: HarperBusiness, 1993).

29. *Ibid.*

30. J.D. Thompson, *Organizations in Action* (New York: McGraw-Hill, 1967).

31. J.B. White, "'Next Big Thing': Re-Engineering Gurus Take Steps to Remodel Their Stalling Vehicles," *The Wall Street Journal Interactive Edition*, 26 November 1996.

32. *Ibid.*

33. G.M. Spreitzer, "Individual Empowerment in the Workplace: Dimensions, Measurement, and Validation," *Academy of Management Journal* 38 (1995): 1442–1465.

34. M. Schrage, "I Know What You Mean. And I Can't Do Anything about It," *Fortune*, 2 April 2001, 186.

35. K.W. Thomas & B.A. Velthouse, "Cognitive Elements of Empowerment," *Academy of Management Review* 15 (1990): 666–681.

36. C. Terhune, "CSX Unit Breaks Tradition to Overhaul Safety Rules," *The Wall Street Journal*, 7 April 1999, F1.

37. D.A. Morand, "The Role of Behavioral Formality and Informality in the Enactment of Bureaucratic Versus Organic Organizations," *Academy of Management Journal* 20 (1995): 831–872.

740

38. L. Munoz, "The Suit Is Back—Or Is It?; As Dot-Coms Die, So Should Business Casual. But the Numbers Don't Lie," *Fortune*, 25 June 2001, 202. F. Swoboda, "Casual Dress Becomes the Rule," *The Las Vegas Review-Journal*, 3 March 1996.

39. K. McCullough, "Analysis: More Companies Allowing Employees to Dress Down, Which Makes Productivity Go Up," *The Money Club*, 26 March 1996.

40. *Ibid.*

41. "Designing the Ever-Changing Workplace," *Architectural Record*, September 1995, 32–37.

42. K.A. Edelman, "Take Down the Walls!" *Across the Board* 34 (1 March 1997).

43. F. Andrews, "Book Value: Learning to Celebrate Water-Cooler Gossip," *The New York Times*, February 25, 2001, L6.

44. M. Rich, "Shut Up so We Can Do Our Jobs!—Fed Up Workers Try to Muffle Chitchat, Conference Calls and Other Open-Office Din," *The Wall Street Journal*, 29 August 2001, B1.

45. L. Gallagher, "At Work: Get Out of My Face: Open Offices Were Hailed as the Answer to Hierarchical, Rigid Organizations. Employees Would Rather Have Privacy," *Forbes*, 18 October 1999, 105.

46. K.A. Edelman, "Take Down the Walls!" *Across the Board* 34 (1 March 1997).

47. M. Rich, "Shut Up so We Can Do Our Jobs!—Fed Up Workers Try to Muffle Chitchat, Conference Calls and Other Open-Office Din," *The Wall Street Journal*, 29 August 2001, B1.

48. *Ibid.*

49. K.A. Edelman, "Take Down the Walls!" *Across the Board* 34 (1 March 1997).

50. A. Camuffo, P. Romano, & A. Vinelli, "Back to the Future: Bennetton Transforms Its Global Network," *Sloan Management Review* 46 (2001): 46–52.

51. G.G. Dess, A.M.A. Rasheed, K.J. McLaughlin, & R.L. Priem, "The New Corporate Architecture," *Academy of Management Executive* 9 (1995): 7–18.

52. B. Einhorn, "Laptop King: In a Year That's Decimated High Tech, Taiwan's Unstoppable Quanta Is Posting Double-Digit Sales Growth," *Business Week*, 11 May 2001, 48.

53. *Ibid.*

54. *Ibid.*

55. *Ibid.*

56. E. Kasper-Fuehrer & N. Ashkanasy, "Communicating Trustworthiness and Building Trust in Interorganizational Virtual Organizations," *Journal of Management* 27 (2000): 235–254.

57. J.H. Sheridan, "The Agile Web: A Model for the Future?" *Industry Week*, 4 March 1996, 31.

58. *Ibid.*

59. C.C. Snow, R.E. Miles, & H. J. Coleman, Jr., "Managing 21st Century Network Organizations," *Organizational Dynamics*, Winter 1992, 5–20.

60. J.H. Sheridan, "The Agile Web: A Model for the Future?" *Industry Week*, 4 March 1996, 31.

61. D. Ulrich & S. Kerr, "Creating the Boundaryless Organization: The Radical Reconstruction of Organization Capabilities," *Planning Review*, September-October 1995, 41–45.

62. R. Ashkenas, D. Ulrich, T. Jick, & S. Kerr, *The Boundaryless Organization: Breaking the Chains of Organizational Structure* (San Francisco: Jossey-Bass, 1995).

63. D. Ulrich & S. Kerr, "Creating the Boundaryless Organization: The Radical Reconstruction of Organization Capabilities," *Planning Review*, September-October 1995, 41–45.

64. G.G. Dess, A.M.A. Rasheed, K.J. McLaughlin, & R.L. Priem, "The New Corporate Architecture," *Academy of Management Executive* 9 (1995): 7–18.

## Chapter 12

1. J.H. Boyett & J.T. Boyett, *Beyond Workforce 2000* (New York: Dutton, 1995).

2. *Ibid.*

3. R. Stodghill, "The Coming Job Bottleneck," *Business Week*, 24 March 1997, 183–185.

4. K. Wallsten, "Diversity Pays Off in Big Sales for Toyota Dealership," *Workforce*, September 1998, 91–92.

5. R.S. Johnson, "The 50 Best Companies for Asians, Blacks, & Hispanics: Talent Comes in All Colors," *Fortune*, 3 August 1999, 94.

6. R.S. Johnson, "The 50 Best Companies for Asians, Blacks, & Hispanics: Talent Comes in All Colors," *Fortune*, 3 August 1999, 94. F. Esposito, S. Garman, J. Hickman, N. Watson, & A. Wheat, "America's 50 Best Companies for Minorities," *Fortune*, 9 July 2001, 122.

7. Equal Employment Opportunity Commission, "Affirmative Action Appropriate under Title VII of the Civil Rights Act of 1964, As Amended. Chapter XIV—Equal Employment Opportunity Commission, Part 1608." [Online] Available http://frwebgate.access.gpo. gov/cgi-bin/get-cfr.cgi?TITLE=29&PART=1608&SECTION=1&TYPE=TEXT, 3 April 1999.

8. J.H. Birnbaum, "Fannie Mae: Spinning Idealism into Gold by Building a Diverse Work Force and Lending to More Minority Homebuyers," *Fortune*, 3 August 1998, 101.

9. Equal Employment Opportunity Commission, "Federal Laws Prohibiting Job Discrimination: Questions and Answers." [Online] Available http://www.eeoc.gov/facts/qanda.html, 4 April 1999.

10. A.P. Carnevale & S.C. Stone, *The American Mosaic: An In-Depth Report on the Future of Diversity at Work* (New York: McGraw-Hill, 1995).

11. T. Roosevelt, "From Affirmative Action to Affirming Diversity," *Harvard Business Review* 68, no. 2 (1990): 107–117.

12. R. Morin & S. Warden, "Americans Vent Anger at Affirmative Action," *Washington Post*, 25 March 1995, A1.

13. A.M. Konrad & F. Linnehan, "Formalized HRM Structures: Coordinating Equal Employment Opportunity or Concealing Organizational Practices?" *Academy of Management Journal* 38, no. 3 (1995): 787–820.

14. *Hopwood v. State of Tex.*, 78 F.3d 932, 64 USLW 2591, 107 Ed. Law Rep. 552 (5th Cir.[Tex.], 18 Mar 1996) (NO. 94-50569, 94-50664).

15. J. Madore, "Losing Historical Advantages: White Males Say They're Hurt, Too," *Newsday*, 9 April 2000, A45.

16. *Ibid.*

17. M.E. Heilman, C.J. Block, & P. Stathatos, "The Affirmative Action Stigma of Incompetence: Effects of Performance Information Ambiguity," *Academy of Management Journal* 40, no. 3 (1997): 603–625.

18. K.C. Cole, "Jury Out on Whether Affirmative Action Beneficiaries Face Stigma: Research Studies Arrive at Conflicting Conclusions," *The Los Angeles Times*, 1 May 1995, 18.

19. G. Robinson & K. Dechant, "Building a Business Case for Diversity," *Academy of Management Executive* 11, no. 3 (1997): 21–31.

20. *Ibid.*

21. *Ibid.*

22. "Judge Approves Settlement of Coca-Cola Bias Lawsuit," *The Wall Street Journal*, 30 May 2001, B7.

23. A. Reifenberg, "Texaco Settlement in Racial-Bias Case Endorsed by Judge,"

*The Wall Street Journal*, 26 March 1997, B15.

24. R.R. Schmitt, "State Farm Pays $157 Million in Sex Discrimination Case," *The Wall Street Journal Europe*, 30 April 1992, 15.

25. B. Egelko, "Home Depot Bias Suit Settled for $87 Million," *The Sacramento Bee* (Associated Press), 21 September 1997, A3.

26. J. Muller, "Ford, The High Cost of Harassment: Despite a $17.5 Million Settlement, A Judge Opens the Way for a Potentially More Damaging Class Action," *Business Week*, 15 November 1999, 94.

27. P. Wright & S.P. Ferris, "Competitiveness through Management of Diversity: Effects on Stock Price Valuation," *Academy of Management Journal* 38 (1995): 272–85.

28. *Ibid.*

29. R.B. Lieber & L. Urresta, "Pacific Enterprises Keeping Talent: After Being Encouraged to Explore Jobs Elsewhere, Most Employees Stay Put," *Fortune*, 3 August 1998, 96.

30. W. He & F. Hobbs, "Minority Purchasing Power: 2000 to 2045," *Minority Business Development Agency, U.S. Department of Commerce*, September 2000.

31. *Ibid.*

32. J. Kahn, "Diversity Trumps the Downturn: Hiring and Promoting Minorities Isn't Optional Anymore—It's Essential—And There's Nothing Like an Economic Crunch to Prove It," *Fortune*, 9 July 2001, 114.

33. L. Himelstein & S.A. Forest, "How Much Progress Have Women Made in Corporate America?" *Business Week*, 17 February 1997, 64.

34. L.E. Wynter, "Business & Race: Advocates Try to Tie Diversity to Profit," *The Wall Street Journal*, 7 February 1996, B1.

35. W.W. Watson, K. Kumar, L.K. Michaelsen, "Cultural Diversity's Impact on Interaction Process and Performance: Comparing Homogeneous and Diverse Task Groups," *Academy of Management Journal* 36 (1993): 590–602. K.A. Jehn, G.B. Northcraft, & M.A. Neale, "Why Differences Make a Difference: A Field Study of Diversity, Conflict, and Performance in Workgroups," *Administrative Science Quarterly* 44 (1999): 741–763.

36. F. Rice, "How to Make Diversity Pay," *Fortune*, 8 August 1994, 78.

37. J. Kahn, "Diversity Trumps the Downturn: Hiring and Promoting Minorities Isn't Optional Anymore—It's Essential—

And There's Nothing Like an Economic Crunch to Prove It," *Fortune*, 9 July 2001, 114.

38. K. Kelly, "Diversity Rules: It's No Easy Task for a Business Owner to Keep the Melting Pot from Boiling Over," *Business Week*, 1 September 1997, ENT22.

39. M.R. Carrell & E.E. Mann, "Defining Workplace Diversity Programs and Practices in Organizations," *The Labor Law Journal* 44 (1993): 743–764.

40. D.A. Harrison, K.H. Price, & M.P. Bell, "Beyond Relational Demography: Time and the Effects of Surface- and Deep-Level Diversity on Work Group Cohesion," *Academy of Management Journal* 41 (1998): 96–107.

41. *Ibid.*

42. *Ibid.*

43. N. Munk, "Finished at Forty: In The New Economy, the Skills that Come with Age Count for Less and Less. Suddenly, 40 Is Starting to Look and Feel Old," *Fortune*, 1 February 1999, 50.

44. S.E. Sullivan & E.A. Duplaga, "Recruiting and Retaining Older Workers for the Millenium," *Business Horizons* 40 (12 November 1997): 65.

45. N. Munk, "Finished at Forty: In the New Economy, the Skills that Come with Age Count for Less and Less. Suddenly, 40 Is Starting to Look and Feel Old," *Fortune*, 1 February 1999, 50.

46. S.R. Rhodes, "Age-Related Differences in Work Attitudes and Behavior," *Psychological Bulletin* 92 (1983): 328–367.

47. A. Fisher, "Wanted: Aging Baby-Boomers," *Fortune*, 30 September 1996, 204.

48. G.M. McEvoy & W.F. Cascio, "Cumulative Evidence of the Relationship Between Employee Age and Job Performance," *Journal of Applied Psychology* 74 (1989): 11–17.

49. S.E. Sullivan & E.A. Duplaga, "Recruiting and Retaining Older Workers for the Millenium," *Business Horizons* 40 (12 November 1997): 65.

50. B.L. Hassell & P.L. Perrewe, "An Examination of Beliefs about Older Workers: Do Stereotypes Still Exist?" *Journal of Organizational Behavior* 16 (1995): 457–468.

51. A. Hunt, "American Opinion (A Special Report)—Women, Politics and the Marketplace—Major Progress, Inequities Cross 3 Generations: Grandmother, Mother, Daughter Reveal a Tempered Optimism Amid 'Universally Held Views,'" *The Wall Street Journal*, 22 June 2000, A9.

52. "The Glass Ceiling in 2000: Where Are Women Now? Labor Day Fact Sheet," *Catalyst*. [Online] Available http://www.catalystwomen.org/press/factsheets/factslabor00.html, 26 January 2001.

53. "Infobrief: Women CEOs," Catalyst. [Online] http://www.catalystwomen.org/press/infobriefs/infobrief2.html, 26 November 2001.

54. B.R. Ragins, B. Townsend, & M. Mattis, "Gender Gap in the Executive Suite: CEOs and Female Executives Report on Breaking the Glass Ceiling," *Academy of Management Executive* 12 (1998): 28–42.

55. P. Dwyer, M. Johnston, & K.L. Miller, "Europe's Corporate Women: Their Progress into Boardrooms and Executive Suites Is Glacial. What's the Likelihood of Change?" *Business Week*, 15 April 1996, 40.

56. J.R. Hollenbeck, D.R. Ilgen, C. Ostroff, & J.B. Vancouver, "Sex Differences in Occupational Choice, Pay, and Worth: A Supply-Side Approach to Understanding the Male-Female Wage Gap," *Personnel Psychology* 40 (1987): 715–744.

57. L. Bernier, "Out of the Typing Pool into Career Limbo in 1985, These Women Vowed to Smash the Glass Ceiling, Few Did," *Business Week*, 15 April 1996, 43.

58. Korn-Ferry International, 1993.

59. Department of Industry, Labor and Human Relations, *Report of the Governor's Task Force on the Glass Ceiling Commission* (Madison, WI: State of Wisconsin, 1993).

60. E.H. Buttner & D.P. Moore, "Women's Organizational Exodus to Entrepreneurship: Self-Reported Motivations and Correlates with Success," *Journal of Small Business Management* 35 (1997): 33–46.

61. S. Hamm, "Why Are Women So Invisible?" *Business Week*, 25 August 1997, 136.

62. B.R. Ragins, B. Townsend, & M. Mattis, "Gender Gap in the Executive Suite: CEOs and Female Executives Report on Breaking the Glass Ceiling," *Academy of Management Executive* 12 (1998): 28–42.

63. B. Morris, "If Women Ran the World, It Would Look a Lot Like Avon: In a Beauty Contest Unlike Any Other, Four of the Six Candidates for the Next CEO Are Women," *Fortune*, 21 July 1997, 74.

64. T.B. Foley, "Discrimination Lawsuits Are a Small-Business Nightmare: A Guide to Minimizing the Potential

742

Damage," *The Wall Street Journal*, 28 September 1998, 15.

65. D.A. Thomas & S. Wetlaufer, "A Question of Color: A Debate on Race in the U.S. Workplace," *Harvard Business Review* 75 (September/October 1997): 118–132.

66. G.N. Powell, & A.D. Butterfield, "Effect of Race on Promotions to Top Management in a Federal Department," *Academy of Management Journal* 40 (1997): 112–128.

67. D.A. Neal & W.R. Johnson, "The Role of Premarket Factors in Black-White Wage Differences," *Journal of Political Economy* 104, no. 5 (1996): 869–895.

68. M. Fix, G.C. Galster, & R.J. Struyk, "An Overview of Auditing for Discrimination," in *Clear and Convincing Evidence: Measurement of Discrimination in America*, eds. Michael Fix and Raymond Struyk (Washington, DC: The Urban Institute Press, 1993), 1–68.

69. M. Bendick, Jr., C.W. Jackson, & V.A. Reinoso, "Measuring Employment Discrimination through Controlled Experiments," in *African-Americans and Post-Industrial Labor Markets*, ed. James B. Stewart (New Brunswick: Transaction Publishers, 1997), 77–100.

70. P.B. Riach & J. Rich, "Measuring Discrimination by Direct Experimental Methods: Seeking Gunsmoke," *Journal of PostKeynesian Economics* 14, no. 2 (Winter 1991–1992): 143–50.

71. A.P. Brief, R.T. Buttram, R.M. Reizenstein, & S.D. Pugh, "Beyond Good Intentions: The Next Steps toward Racial Equality in the American Workplace," *Academy of Management Executive* 11 (1997): 59–72.

72. L.E. Wynter, "Business & Race: Federal Agencies, Spurred On by Nonprofit Groups, Are Increasingly Embracing the Use of Undercover Investigators to Identify Discrimination in the Marketplace," *The Wall Street Journal*, 1 July 1998, B1.

73. Equal Employment Opportunity Commission, "Charge Statistics: FY 1992 through FY 1998." [Online] Available http://www.eeoc.gov/stats/charges.html, 17 April 1999.

74. S.J. Well, "When the Bias Is in the Hiring," *Journal Record* (Oklahoma City), 26 March 1998, 1.

75. U.S. Department of Justice, "The Americans with Disabilities Act: Questions and Answers." [Online] Available http://www.usdoj.gov/crt/ada/ada.html, 27 November 2001.

76. U.S. Bureau of the Census, "Census Brief: Disabilities Affect One-Fifth of All Americans." [Online] Available http://www.census.gov/prod/3/97pubs/cenbr975.pdf, 19 April 1999.

77. F. Bowe, "Adults with Disabilities: A Portrait," *President's Committee on Employment of People with Disabilities* (Washington, DC: GPO, 1992). D. Braddock & L. Bachelder, *The Glass Ceiling and Persons with Disabilities*, Glass Ceiling Commission, U.S. Department of Labor (Washington, DC: GPO, 1994).

78. Louis Harris and Associates, Inc., *Public Attitudes toward People with Disabilities* (Washington DC: National Organization on Disability, 1991). Louis Harris and Associates, Inc., *The ICD Survey II: Employing Disabled Americans* (New York: Author, 1987).

79. R. Greenwood & V.A. Johnson, "Employer Perspectives on Workers with Disabilities," *Journal of Rehabilitation* 53 (1987): 37–45.

80. S. Livingston, "A Closer Look: Americans With Disabilities Act—A Question of Access, Job Barriers Remain on Landmark Law's 10th," *The Cleveland Plain Dealer*, 23 July 2000, 1H.

81. *Ibid.*

82. F. Schwadel, "Sears Sets Model for Compliance with Disabilities Act, Study Says," *The Wall Street Journal*, 4 March 1996, B5.

83. D.L. Stone & A.A. Colella, "Model of Factors Affecting the Treatment of Disabled Individuals in Organizations," *Academy of Management Review* 2 (1996): 352–401.

84. R.D. Ashmore & F.K. Del Boca, "Conceptual Approaches to Stereotypes and Stereotyping, in *Cognitive Processes in Stereotyping and Intergroup Behavior*, ed. D.L. Hamilton (Hillsdale, NJ: Erlbaum, 1981), 1–35.

85. D. Braddock & L. Bachelder, *The Glass Ceiling and Persons with Disabilities*, Glass Ceiling Commission, U.S. Department of Labor (Washington, DC: GPO, 1994).

86. "Study on the Financing of Assistive Technology Devices and Services for Individuals with Disabilities: A Report to the President and the Congress of the United States," *National Council on Disability*. [Online] Available http://www.ncd.gov/newsroom/publications/assistive.html, 28 November 2001.

87. *Ibid.*

88. R.B. Cattell, "Personality Pinned Down," *Psychology Today* 7 (1973): 40–46. C.S. Carver & M.F. Scheier, *Perspectives on Personality* (Boston: Allyn & Bacon, 1992).

89. B. O'Reilly & K.A. Kelly, "Does Your Fund Manager Play the Piano? How about Bridge? And How Does He Feel about Baseball? The Surprising Personality Traits of the People Who Manage America's Money," *Fortune*, 29 December 1997, 139.

90. J.M. Digman, "Personality Structure: Emergence of the Five-Factor Model," *Annual Review of Psychology* 41 (1990): 417–440. M.P. Barrick & M.K. Mount, "The Big Five Personality Dimensions and Job Performance: A Meta-Analysis," *Personnel Psychology* 44 (1991): 1–26.

91. C. Wolff, "Peabody Enhances Employee Relations," *Lodging Hospitality*, October 1996, 9.

92. J. Blonsick, "Other Views—My Word: Trust Your Airline Pilot," *Orlando Sentinel*, 28 November 1999, G3.

93. P. LaBarre, "Lighten Up! Blurring the Line Between Fun and Work Not Only Humanizes Organizations but Strengthens the Bottom Line," *Industry Week* 2 (5 February 1996): 53.

94. "Southwest Air's Leader Takes 'Radical' Approach," *Tucson Citizen*, 22 October 1993, B1.

95. S. Caudron, "Hire for Attitude: It's Who They Are that Counts," *Workforce*, August 1997, 20–26.

96. O. Behling, "Employee Selection: Will Intelligence and Conscientiousness Do the Job?" *Academy of Management Executive* 12 (1998): 77–86.

97. J.M. Collins & F.L. Schmidt, "Personality, Integrity, and White Collar Crime: A Construct Validity Study," *Personnel Psychology* 46 (1993): 295–311.

98. M.R. Barrick & M.K. Mount, "The Big Five Personality Dimensions and Job Performance: A Meta-Analysis," *Personnel Psychology* 44 (1991): 1–26.

99. M.K. Mount & M.R. Barrick, "Five Reasons Why the 'Big Five' Article Has Been Frequently Cited," *Personnel Psychology* 4 (1998): 849–857.

100. *Ibid.*

101. J.A. Lopez, "Talking Desks: Personality Types Revealed in State Workstations," *Arizona Republic*, 7 January 1996, Section D, 1.

102. T.W. Adorno, E. Frenkel-Brunswik, D.J. Levinson, & R.N. Stanford, *The Authoritarian Personality* (New York: Harper & Row, 1950).

743

103. D. Takahashi, "Cypress Semiconductor Rides the Industry Upswing—But Chip Maker's Tough Boss Isn't Celebrating Despite Record Demand," *The Wall Street Journal*, 13 December 1999, B1.

104. R.G. Vleeming, "Machiavellianism: A Preliminary Review," *Psychological Reports* 53 (1979): 295–310.

105. F.L. Geis & T.H. Moon, "Machiavellianism and Deception," *Journal of Personality and Social Psychology* 41 (1981): 766–775.

106. R. Christie & R.L. Geis, *Studies in Machiavellianism* (New York: Academic Press, 1970), 312.

107. E. de Lisser, "Breakaway (A Special Report): Upfront, Survivor Hatch as Mentor," *The Wall Street Journal*, 25 September 2000, J4.

108. B. Vancheri, "Off the Island, Into The Fire: Richard Hatch Talks about How He Plays the Game," *Pittsburgh Post-Gazette*, 26 August 2000, B16.

109. K.D. Grimsley, "Warriors in the Workplace: As Readers' Dispatches Attest, The Enemy Is Often the Next Cubicle," *Washington Post*, 25 January 1998, H1.

110. L.H. Primavera & M. Higgins, "Non-Verbal Rigidity and Its Relationship to Dogmatism and Machiavellianism," *Perceptual and Motor Skills* 36 (1973): 356–358. T.J. Prociuk & L.J. Breen, "Machiavellianism and Locus of Control," *Journal of Social Psychology* 98 (1976): 141–142. G.W. Russell, "Machiavellianism, Locus of Control, Aggression, Performance and Precautionary Behavior in Ice Hockey," *Human Relations* 27 (1974): 825–837.

111. K.A. Matthews, "Psychological Perspectives on the Type A Behavior Pattern," *Psychological Bulletin* 91 (1982): 293–323.

112. M. Friedman & R.H. Rosenman, *Type A Behavior and Your Heart* (New York: Fawcett Crest, 1974).

113. J.G. Auerbach, "A Will to Win: An EMC Salesman Who Never Eases Up Helps Data Firm—Even on a Rare Vacation, John Chatwin Pursues Storage-System—Athletes' Competitive Edge," *The Wall Street Journal*, 8 July 1998, A1.

114. M. Lee & R. Kanungo, *Management of Work and Personal Life* (New York: Praeger, 1984).

115. J. Schaubroeck, D.C. Ganster, & B.E. Kemmerer, "Job Complexity, 'Type A' Behavior, and Cardiovascular Disorders," *Academy of Management Journal* 37 (1994): 37.

116. J. Useem & L. Munoz, "A Manager for All Seasons," *Fortune*, 30 April 2001, 66.

117. M.T. Matteson & J.M. Ivancevich, "The Coronary-Prone Behavior Pattern: A Review and Appraisal," *Social Science and Medicine* 14 (1980): 337–351.

118. J.E. Bishop, "Health: Hostility, Distrust May Put Type A's at Coronary Risk," *The Wall Street Journal Interactive*, 17 January 1989.

119. M. Snyder, "The Self-Monitoring of Expressive Behavior," *Journal of Personality and Social Psychology* 30 (1974): 526–537.

120. M. Snyder, "Self-Monitoring Processes," in *Advances in Experimental Social Psychology* 12, ed. L. Berkowitz (New York: Academic Press, 1979), 85–128.

121. D.F. Caldwell & C.A. O'Reilly, "Boundary Spanning and Individual Performance: The Impact of Self-Monitoring," *Journal of Applied Psychology* 67 (1982): 123–127. S.J. Zaccaro, R.J. Foti, & D.A. Kenny, "Self-Monitoring and Trait-Based Variance in Leadership: An Investigation of Leader Flexibility across Multiple Group Situations," *Journal of Applied Psychology* 76 (1991): 308–315. R.A. Baron, "Personality and Organizational Conflict: Effects of the Type A Behavior Pattern and Self-Monitoring," *Organizational Behavior and Human Decision Process* 44 (1989): 281–296.

122. M. Kilduff & D.V. Day, "Do Chameleons Get Ahead? The Effects of Self-Monitoring on Managerial Careers," *Academy of Management Journal* 37 (1994): 1047–1060.

123. A.H. Church, "Managerial Self-Awareness in High-Performing Individuals in Organizations," *Journal of Applied Psychology* 82 (1997): 281–292.

124. D.F. Caldwell & C.A. O'Reilly, III, "Boundary Spanning and Individual Performance: The Impact of Self-Monitoring," *Journal of Applied Psychology* 67 (1982): 123–127. M. Kilduff & D.V. Day, "Do Chameleons Get Ahead? The Effects of Self-Monitoring on Managerial Careers," *Academy of Management Journal* 37 (1994): 1047–1060. H.S. Friedman & T. Miller-Herringer, "Nonverbal Display of Emotion in Public and Private: Self-Monitoring, Personality and Expressive Cues," *Journal of Personality and Social Psychology* 62 (1991): 766–775.

125. J.B. Rotter, "Generalized Expectancies for Internal versus External Control of Reinforcement," *Psychological Monographs* 80 (1966): Whole No. 609. J.B. Rotter, "Some Problems and Misconceptions Related to the Construct of Internal versus External Control of Reinforcement," *Journal of Consulting and Clinical Psychology* 43 (1975): 56–67.

126. P. Sellers, "So You Fail. Now Bounce Back!" *Fortune*, 1 May 1995, 48.

127. T.M. Burton, "Visionary's Reward: Combine 'Simple Ideas' and Some Failures; Result: James Sweeney Bought Back His Old Company Cheap; Never Give Up, He Says—Father's Lesson: Take Risks," *The Wall Street Journal*, 3 February 1995, A1.

128. P.E. Spector, "Behavior in Organizations as a Function of Employee's Locus of Control," *Psychological Bulletin* 91 (1982): 482–497.

129. R.S. Lazarus, *Emotion and Adaptation* (New York: Oxford University Press, 1991).

130. "The Secrets of Happiness," *Psychology Today* 25 (July 1992): 38.

131. B.M. Staw, N.E. Bell, and J.A. Clausen, "The Dispositional Approach to Job Attitudes: A Lifetime Longitudinal Test," *Administrative Science Quarterly* 31 (1986): 56–77.

132. "Success Story," *Dallas Morning News*, 12 August 2001, 10L.

133. A.M. Isen & R.A. Baron, "Positive Affect and Organizational Behavior," in *Research in Organizational Behavior* 12, eds. B.M. Staw & L.L. Cummings (Greenwich, CT: JAI Press, 1990). J.M. George & A.P. Brief, "Feeling Good–Doing Good: A Conceptual Analysis of the Mood at Work—Organizational Spontaneity Relationships," *Psychological Bulletin* 112 (1992): 310–329. R.D. Iverson & P.J. Erwin, "Predicting Occupational Injury: The Role of Affectivity," *Journal of Occupational and Organizational Psychology* 70 (1997): 113–128. D.P. Skarlicki, R. Folger, & P. Tesluk, "Personality as a Moderator in the Relationship Between Fairness and Retaliation," *Academy of Management Journal* 42 (1999): 100–108.

134. P. Totterdell, S. Kellett, K. Teuchmann, & R.B. Briner, "Evidence of Mood Linkage in Work Groups," *Journal of Personality and Social Psychology* 74 (1998): 1503–1515.

135. M.E.P. Seligman & S. Schulman, "Explanatory Style as a Predictor of Productivity and Quitting among Life Insur-

ance Sales Agents," *Journal of Personality and Social Psychology* 50 (1986): 832–838.

136. T.D. Schellhardt, "In a Tight Factory Schedule, Where Does Religion Fit In?" *The Wall Street Journal Interactive Edition*, 4 March 1999.

137. Staff, "The Diverse Work Force," *Inc.*, January 1993, 33.

138. D.A. Thomas & R.J. Ely, "Making Differences Matter: A New Paradigm for Managing Diversity," *Harvard Business Review* 74 (September/October 1996): 79–90.

139. D.A. Thomas & S. Wetlaufer, "A Question of Color: A Debate on Race in the U.S. Workplace," *Harvard Business Review* 75 (September/October 1997): 118–132.

140. D.A. Thomas & R.J. Ely, "Making Differences Matter: A New Paradigm for Managing Diversity," *Harvard Business Review* 74 (September/October 1996): 79–90.

141. J. Kahn, "Diversity Trumps the Downturn," *Fortune*, 9 July 2001, 114.

142. G. Bylinsky & A. Moore, "Women Move Up in Manufacturing," *Fortune*, 15 May 2000, 372.

143. J.R. Norton & R.E. Fox, *The Change Equation: Capitalizing on Diversity for Effective Organizational Change* (Washington, DC: American Psychological Association, 1997).

144. *Ibid.*

145. D.A. Thomas & R.J. Ely, "Making Differences Matter: A New Paradigm for Managing Diversity," *Harvard Business Review* 74 (September/October 1996): 79–90.

146. R.R. Thomas, Jr., *Beyond Race and Gender: Unleashing the Power of Your Total Workforce by Managing Diversity* (New York: AMACOM, 1991).

147. *Ibid.*

148. T. Cox, Jr., "The Multicultural Organization," *Academy of Management Executive* 5 (1991): 34–47.

149. S. Lubove, "Damned If You Do, Damned If You Don't: Preference Programs Are on the Defensive in the Public Sector, But Plaintiffs' Attorneys and Bureaucrats Keep Diversity Inc. Thriving in Corporate America," *Forbes*, 15 December 1997, 122.

150. L.S. Gottfredson, "Dilemmas in Developing Diversity Programs," in *Diversity in the Workplace*, eds. S.E. Jackson and Associates (New York: Guildford Press, 1992).

151. K. Kelly, "Diversity Rules: It's No Easy Task for a Business Owner to Keep the Melting Pot from Boiling Over," *Business Week*, 1 September 1997, 22.

152. R.B. Lieber & L. Urresta, "Pacific Enterprises Keeping Talent: After Being Encouraged to Explore Jobs Elsewhere, Most Employees Stay Put," *Fortune*, 3 August 1998, 96.

153. A. Markels, "Management: How One Hotel Manages Staff's Diversity," *The Wall Street Journal*, 20 November 1996, B1.

154. L.E. Wynter, "Business & Race: Allstate Rates Managers on Handling Diversity," *The Wall Street Journal*, 1 October 1997, B1.

155. H. Rosin, "Texaco Takes the Diversity Tiger by the Tail: In a Holy Crusade against Racism, The Oil Giant Is Bombarding Employees with Orwellian Admonishments to 'Respect the Individual,'" *Toronto Globe & Mail*, 14 February 1998, D4.

156. A.P. Carnevale & S.C. Stone, *The American Mosaic* (New York: McGraw-Hill, 1995).

157. D. Fenn, "Diversity: More than Just Affirmative Action," *Inc.*, July 1995, 93.

158. J.R. Joplin & C.S. Daus, "Challenges of Leading a Diverse Workforce," *Academy of Management Executive* 11 (1997): 32–47.

159. T. Parker-Pope, "P&G Makes Strong Pitch to Keep Its Women Employees," *The Asian Wall Street Journal*, 15 September 1998, 12.

160. F. Rice, "How to Make Diversity Pay," *Fortune*, 8 August 1994, 78.

## Chapter 13

1. B. Dumaine, "The Trouble with Teams," *Fortune*, 5 September 1994, 86–92.

2. J.R. Katzenback & D.K. Smith, *The Wisdom of Teams* (Boston: Harvard Business School Press, 1993).

3. S.G. Cohen & D.E. Bailey, "What Makes Teams Work: Group Effectiveness Research from the Shop Floor to the Executive Suite," *Journal of Management* 23, no. 3 (1997): 239–290.

4. W. Zellner, "Team Player: No More 'Same-Ol'-Same-Ol'," *Business Week*, 17 October 1994, 95.

5. S.E. Gross, *Compensation for Teams* (New York: American Management Association, 1995). B.L. Kirkman & B. Rosen, "Beyond Self-Management: Antecedents and Consequences of Team

Empowerment," *Academy of Management Journal* 42 (1999): 58–74. G. Stock & T.M. Hout, *Competing Against Time* (New York: Free Press, 1990). S.C. Wheelwright & K.B. Clark, *Revolutionizing New Product Development* (New York: Free Press, 1992).

6. R.S. Wellins, W.C. Byham, & G.R. Dixon, *Inside Teams* (San Francisco: Jossey-Bass Publishers, 1994).

7. D. Kiley, "Crafty Basket Makers Cut Downtime, Waste. So Far, Changes Saving $3 Million a Year," *USA Today*, 10 May 2001, B3.

8. R.D. Banker, J.M. Field, R.G. Schroeder, & K.K. Sinha, "Impact of Work Teams on Manufacturing Performance: A Longitudinal Field Study," *Academy of Management Journal* 39 (1996): 867–890.

9. C. Enz & J. Siguaw, "Best Practices in Human Resources," *Cornell Hotel & Restaurant Administration Quarterly* 41 (February 2000), 48.

10. C. Fishman, "Whole Foods Is All Teams," *Fast Company*, April 1996, 103.

11. "Beating the Joneses (Learning What the Competition Is Doing)," *Industry Week* 1 (7 December 1998): 27.

12. G. Stalk & T.M. Hout, *Competing against Time: How Time-Based Competition Is Reshaping Global Markets* (New York: The Free Press, 1990).

13. H.K Bowen, K.B. Clark, C.A. Holloway, & S.C. Wheelwright, *The Perpetual Enterprise Machine* (New York: Oxford Press, 1994).

14. C. Dahle, "Xtreme Teams," *Fast Company*, 1 November 1999, 310.

15. *Ibid.*

16. J.L. Cordery, W.S. Mueller, & L.M. Smith, "Attitudinal and Behavioral Effects of Autonomous Group Working: A Longitudinal Field Study," *Academy of Management Journal* 34 (1991): 464–476. T.D. Wall, N.J. Kemp, P.R. Jackson, & C.W. Clegg, "Outcomes of Autonomous Workgroups: A Longterm Field Experiment," *Academy of Management Journal* 29 (1986): 280–304.

17. M. Vanac, "Working the Line: U.S. Businesses Retool Modes of Production and Ratchet Up Morale," *Plain Dealer*, 2 September 2001, H1.

18. *Ibid.*

19. *Ibid.*

20. "Declaration of Interdependence," Whole Foods Market. [Online] Available http://www.wholefoodsmarket.

com/company/declaration.html, 15 January 2002.

21. "Whole Foods Had Fresh Approach," *Work & Family Newsbrief,* January 2001, 4.

22. R.S. Wellins, W.C. Byham, & G.R. Dixon, *Inside Teams* (San Francisco: Jossey-Bass Publishers, 1994).

23. J. Hoerr, "The Payoff from Teamwork: The Gains in Quality Are Substantial—So Why Isn't It Spreading Faster?" *Business Week,* 10 July 1989, 56.

24. T. Aeppel, "Missing the Boss: Not All Workers Find Idea of Empowerment As Neat As It Sounds—Some Hate Fixing Machines, Apologizing for Errors, Disciplining Teammates—Rah-Rah Types Do the Best," *The Wall Street Journal,* 8 September 1997, A1.

25. J. George, "Extrinsic and Intrinsic Origins of Perceived Social Loafing in Organizations," *Academy of Management Journal* 35 (1992): 191–202.

26. T.T. Baldwin, M.D. Bedell, & J.L. Johnson, "The Social Fabric of a Team-Based M.B.A. Program: Network Effects on Student Satisfaction and Performance," *Academy of Management Journal* 40 (1997): 1369–1397.

27. P.W. Mulvey, J.F. Veiga, & P.M. Elsass, "When Teammates Raise a White Flag," *Academy of Management Executive* 10, no. 1 (1996): 40–49.

28. *Ibid.*

29. J. Hoerr, "The Payoff from Teamwork: The Gains in Quality Are Substantial—So Why Isn't It Spreading Faster?" *Business Week,* 10 July 1989, 56.

30. National Labor Relations Board, *Fact Sheet on the National Labor Relations Board.* [Online] Available http://www.nlrb.gov/facts.html, 15 January 2002.

31. K. Hein, "Is Teamwork against the Law?" *Incentive* 170, no. 8 (August 1996): 7.

32. G. Burkins, "Senate Debates Right to Set Up Worker Teams," *The Wall Street Journal,* 10 July 1996, B1.

33. C. Joinson, "Teams at Work," *HRMagazine,* 1 May 1999, 30.

34. R. Wageman, "Critical Success Factors for Creating Superb Self-Managing Teams," *Organizational Dynamics* 26, no. 1 (1997): 49–61.

35. A. Taylor, III., "Can the Germans Rescue Chrysler?" *Fortune,* 30 April 2001, 106.

36. M.A. Cusumano, "How Microsoft Makes Large Teams Work Like Small Teams," *Sloan Management Review* 39, no 1 (Fall 1997): 9–20.

37. R.T. King, Jr., "Jeans Therapy: Levi's Factory Workers Are Assigned to Teams, And Morale Takes a Hit—Infighting Rises, Productivity Falls as Employees Miss the Piecework System— 'It's Not the Same Company,'" *The Wall Street Journal,* 20 May 1998, A1.

38. *Ibid.*

39. M. Curtius, "There Is No 'I' in 'Team'—And Maybe No Point, Either: The Trend Continues but Doesn't Always Succeed. Finding the Proper Structure, Motivating Employees and Getting Managers out of the Way Can Sometimes Help," *Los Angeles Times,* 24 February 1997, D25.

40. R.T. King, Jr., "Jeans Therapy: Levi's Factory Workers Are Assigned to Teams, and Morale Takes a Hit—Infighting Rises, Productivity Falls as Employees Miss the Piecework System—'It's Not the Same Company,'" *The Wall Street Journal,* 20 May 1998, A1.

41. B.L. Kirkman & B. Rosen, "Beyond Self-Management: Antecedents and Consequences of Team Empowerment," *Academy of Management Journal* 42 (1999): 58–74.

42. M. Curtius, "There Is No 'I' in 'Team'—And Maybe No Point, Either: The Trend Continues but Doesn't Always Succeed. Finding the Proper Structure, Motivating Employees and Getting Managers out of the Way Can Sometimes Help," *Los Angeles Times,* 24 February 1997, D25.

43. G. Harris, "The Cure: With Big Drugs Dying, Merck Didn't Merge—It Found New Ones," *The Wall Street Journal,* 10 January 2001, A1.

44. G. Bylinsky, "Heroes of U.S. Manufacturing," *Fortune,* 19 March 2001, 177.

45. B.L. Kirkman & B. Rosen, "Beyond Self-Management: Antecedents and Consequences of Team Empowerment," *Academy of Management Journal* 42 (1999): 58–74.

46. K. Kelly, "Managing Workers Is Tough Enough in Theory. When Human Nature Enters the Picture, It's Worse," *Business Week,* 21 October 1996, 32.

47. S. Easton & G. Porter, "Selecting the Right Team Structure to Work in Your Organization," in *Handbook of Best Practices for Teams,* Volume 1, ed. G.M. Parker (Amherst, MA: Irwin, 1996).

48. C. Caggiano, "Worker, Rule Thyself," *Inc.,* February 1999, 89–90.

49. D. Stafford, "Hotel Lets Its Workers 'Own' Their Duties: Ritz-Carlton, Kansas City, Tries a Program That Emphasizes Teamwork, Self-Direction," *The Kansas City Star,* 6 February 1996, D1.

50. Knight-Ridder, "Electrician Gets with the Team at Ford Plant," *Chicago Tribune,* 7 April 1996, 8.

51. M. Maynard, "Saturn Workers May Dump Unique Contract," *USA Today,* 17 February 1998, 03B.

52. R.J. Recardo, D. Wade, C.A. Mention, & J. Jolly, *Teams* (Houston: Gulf Publishing Company, 1996).

53. D.R. Denison, S.L. Hart, & J.A. Kahn, "From Chimneys to Cross-Functional Teams: Developing and Validating a Diagnostic Model," *Academy of Management Journal* 39, no. 4 (1996): 1005–1023.

54. C. Parnell, "Teamwork: Not a New Idea, But It's Transforming the Workplace" (Transcript), *Vital Speeches,* 1 November 1996, 46.

55. A.M. Townsend, S.M. DeMarie, & A.R. Hendrickson, "Virtual Teams: Technology and the Workplace of the Future," *Academy of Management Executive* 13, no. 3 (1998): 17–29.

56. A.M. Townsend, S.M. DeMarie, & A.R. Henfrickson, "Are You Ready for Virtual Teams?" *HRMagazine* 41, no.9 (1996): 122–126.

57. Selah School District Web Site, "The Boeing 777." [Online] Available http://www.selah.wednet.edu, 9 September 1998.

58. R.S. Wellins, W.C. Byham, & G.R. Dixon, *Inside Teams* (San Francisco: Josey-Bass Publishers, 1994).

59. A.M. Townsend, S.M. DeMarie, & A.R. Hendrickson, "Virtual Teams: Technology and the Workplace of the Future," *Academy of Management Executive* 13, no. 3 (1998): 17–29.

60. W.F. Cascio, "Managing a Virtual Workplace," *Academy of Management Executive* 14 (2000): 81–90.

61. R. Katz, "The Effects of Group Longevity on Project Communication and Performance," *Administrative Science Quarterly* 27 (1982): 245–282.

62. C. Kleiman, "Virtual Teams Make Loyalty More Realistic," *Chicago Tribune,* 23 January 2001, Business 1.

63. D. Mankin, S.G. Cohen, & T.K. Bikson, *Teams and Technology: Fulfilling the Promise of the New Organization* (Boston: Harvard Business School Press, 1996).

64. S. Carey, "USAir 'Peon' Team Pilots Start-Up of Low-Fare Airline," *The Wall Street Journal,* 24 March 1998, B1.

65. K. Lovelace, D. Shapiro, & L. Weingart. "Maximizing Cross-Functional New Product Teams' Innovativeness and Constraint Adherence: A Conflict Communications Perspective," *Academy of Management Journal* 44 (2001): 779–793.

66. G. Anthes, "Think Globally, Act Locally: Running Global IT Operations Effectively Often Means Creating Standard Systems and Processes That Have to Be Tweaked to Meet Local Requirements," *Computer World*, 28 May 2001, 36.

67. L. Holpp & H.P. Phillips, "When Is a Team Its Own Worst Enemy?" *Training*, 1 September 1995, 71.

68. S. Asche, "Opinions and Social Pressure," *Scientific America* 193 (1995): 31–35.

69. Nucor Homepage, "The Nucor Story." [Online] Available http://www.nucor.com/story.htm, 10 May 1999.

70. S.G. Cohen, G.E. Ledford, & G.M. Spreitzer, "A Predictive Model of Self-Managing Work Team Effectiveness," *Human Relations* 49, no. 5 (1996): 643–676.

71. T. Petzinger, Jr., "How Lynn Mercer Manages a Factory That Manages Itself," *The Wall Street Journal*, 7 March 1997, B1.

72. K. Bettenhausen & J.K. Murnighan, "The Emergence of Norms in Competitive Decision-Making Groups," *Administrative Science Quarterly* 30 (1985): 350–372.

73. M.E. Shaw, *Group Dynamics* (New York: McGraw Hill, 1981).

74. J.R. Katzenback & D.K. Smith, *The Wisdom of Teams* (Boston: Harvard Business School Press, 1993).

75. S.E. Jackson, "The Consequences of Diversity in Multidisciplinary Work Teams," in *Handbook of Work Group Psychology*, ed. Michael A. West (Chichester, UK: Wiley, 1996).

76. A.M. Isen & R.A. Baron, "Positive Affect as a Factor in Organizational Behavior," in *Research in Organizational Behavior* 13, eds. L.L. Cummings & B.M. Staw (Greenwich, CT: JAI Press, 1991), 1–53.

77. C.R. Evans & K.L. Dion, "Group Cohesion and Performance: A Meta Analysis," *Small Group Research* 22, no. 2 (1991): 175–186.

78. R. Stankiewicsz, "The Effectiveness of Research Groups in Six Countries," in *Scientific Productivity*, ed. F.M. Andrews (Cambridge: Cambridge University Press, 1979), 191–221.

79. F. Rees, *Teamwork from Start to Finish* (San Francisco: Josey-Bass, 1997).

80. S.M. Gully, D.S. Devine, & D.J. Whitney, "A Meta-Analysis of Cohesion and Performance: Effects of Level of Analysis and Task Interdependence," *Small Group Research* 26, no. 4 (1995): 497–520.

81. E. Matson, "Four Rules for Fast Teams," *Fast Company*, August 1996, 87.

82. F. Tschan & M.V. Cranach, "Group Task Structure, Processes and Outcomes," in *Handbook of Work Group Psychology*, ed. Michael A. West (Chichester, UK: Wiley, 1996).

83. D.E. Yeatts & C. Hyten, *High Performance Self Managed Teams* (Thousand Oaks, CA: Sage Publications, 1998).

84. *Ibid.*

85. D.S. Kezsbom, "Re-Opening Pandora's Box: Sources of Project Team Conflict in the '90s," *Industrial Engineering* 24, no. 5 (1992): 54–59.

86. A.C. Amason, W.A. Hochwarter, K.R. Thompson, "Conflict: An Important Dimension in Successful Management Teams," *Organizational Dynamics* 24 (1995): 20.

87. A.C. Amason, "Distinguishing the Effects of Functional and Dysfunctional Conflict on Strategic Decision Making: Resolving a Paradox for Top Management Teams," *Academy of Management Journal* 39, no. 1 (1996): 123–148.

88. K.M. Eisenhardt, J.L. Kahwajy, & L.J. Bourgeois, "How Management Teams Can Have a Good Fight," *Harvard Business Review* 75, no. 4 (July/August 1997): 77–85.

89. *Ibid.*

90. C. Nemeth & Owens, "Making Work Groups More Effective: The Value of Minority Dissent," in *Handbook of Work Group Psychology*, ed. Michael A. West (Chichester, UK: Wiley, 1996).

91. J.M. Levin & R.L. Moreland, "Progress in Small Group Research," *Annual Review of Psychology* 9 (1990): 72–78. S.E. Jackson, "Team Composition in Organizational Settings: Issues in Managing a Diverse Work Force," in *Group Processes and Productivity*, eds. S. Worchel, W. Wood, & J. Simpson (Beverly Hills, CA: Sage, 1992).

92. K.M. Eisenhardt, J.L. Kahwajy, & L.J. Bourgeois, III, "How Management Teams Can Have a Good Fight," *Harvard Business Review* 75, no. 4 (July/August 1997): 77–87.

93. *Ibid.*

94. B.W. Tuckman, "Development Sequence in Small Groups," *Psychological Bulletin* 63, no. 6 (1965): 384–399.

95. S.E. Gross, *Compensation for Teams* (New York: American Management Association, 1995).

96. J.F. McGrew, J.G. Bilotta, & J.M. Deeney, "Software Team Formation and Decay: Extending the Standard Model for Small Groups," *Small Group Research* 30, no. 2 (1999): 209–234.

97. *Ibid.*

98. J. Case, "What the Experts Forgot to Mention: Management Teams Create New Difficulties, But Succeed for Xel Communication," *Inc.*, 1 September 1993, 66.

99. J.R. Hackman, "The Psychology of Self-Management in Organizations," in *Psychology and Work: Productivity, Change, and Employment*, eds. M.S. Pallak, & R. Perloff (Washington DC: American Psychological Association, 85–136).

100. A. O Leary-Kelly, J.J. Martocchio, D.D. Frink, "A Review of the Influence of Group Goals on Group Performance," *Academy of Management Journal* 37, no. 5 (1994): 1285–1301.

101. Nucor Homepage, "The Nucor Story." [Online] Available http://www.nucor.com/story.htm, 10 May 1999.

102. A. Zander, "The Origins and Consequences of Group Goals," in *Retrospections on Social Psychology*, ed. L. Festinger (New York: Oxford University Press, 1980), 205–235.

103. M. Erez & A. Somech, "Is Group Productivity Loss the Rule or the Exception? Effects of Culture and Group-Based Motivation," *Academy of Management Journal* 39, no. 6 (1996): 1513–1537.

104. S. Sherman, "Stretch Goals: The Dark Side of Asking for Miracles," *Fortune*, 13 November 1995.

105. D. Armstrong, "IBM Finds Method to Make Faster Chips," *The Wall Street Journal*, 8 June 2001, B5.

106. K.R. Thompson, W.A. Hochwarter, & N.J. Mathys, "Stretch Targets: What Makes Them Effective?" *Academy of Management Executive* 11, no. 3 (1997): 48–60.

107. S. Tully, "Why to Go for Stretch Targets," *Fortune*, 14 November 1994, 145.

108. S. Sherman, "Stretch Goals: The Dark Side of Asking for Miracles," *Fortune*, 13 November 1995.

109. S. Shellenbarger, "Are Saner Workloads the Unexpected Key to More

Productivity?" *The Wall Street Journal*, 10 March 1999, B1.

110. G. Mazurkiewicz, "Let Your Techs Manage Themselves," *Air Conditioning, Heating & Refrigeration News*, 25 December 2000, 10.

111. B. Dumaine, "The Trouble with Teams," *Fortune*, 5 September 1994, 86–92.

112. G.A. Neuman, S.H. Wagner, N.D. Christiansen, "The Relationship Between Work-Team Personality Composition and the Job Performance of Teams," *Group & Organization Management* 24, no. 1 (1999): 28–45.

113. M.A. Campion, G.J. Medsker, & A.C. Higgs, "Relations Between Work Group Characteristics and Effectiveness: Implications for Designing Effective Work Groups," *Personnel Psychology* 46, no. 4 (1993): 823–850.

114. B.L. Kirkman & D.L. Shapiro, "The Impact of Cultural Values on Employee Resistance to Teams: Toward a Model of Globalized Self-Managing Work Team Effectiveness," *Academy of Management Review* 22, no. 3 (1997): 730–757.

115. M.A. Campion, G.J. Medsker, & A.C. Higgs, "Relations Between Work Group Characteristics and Effectiveness: Implications for Designing Effective Work Groups," *Personnel Psychology* 46, no. 4 (1993): 823–850.

116. S. Caudron, "Team Staffing Requires New HR Role," *Personnel Journal* 73, no. 5 (1994): 88.

117. T.R. Tudor, R.R. Trumble, & J.J. Diaz, "Work-Teams: Why Do They Often Fail?" *S.A.M. Advanced Management Journal* 61, no. 4 (Autumn 1996): 31.

118. D. Zoia, "GM Manufacturing: Brand Spanking New," *Ward's Auto World*, March 2000, page numbers unavailable online.

119. M.A. Verespej, "Super Sack," *Industry Week*, 16 October 1995, 53.

120. R.S. Wellins, W.C. Byham, & G.R. Dixon, *Inside Teams* (San Francisco: Jossey-Bass Publishers, 1994).

121. C. Joinson, "Teams at Work," *HRMagazine*, 1 May 1999, 30.

122. *Ibid.*

123. R.S. Wellins, W.C. Byham, & G.R. Dixon, *Inside Teams* (San Francisco: Jossey-Bass Publishers, 1994).

124. S. Caudron, "Tie Individual Pay to Team Success," *Personnel Journal* 73, no. 10 (October 1994): 40.

125. *Ibid.*

126. S.E. Gross, *Compensation for Teams* (New York: American Management Association, 1995).

127. R.S. Wellins, W.C. Byham, & G.R. Dixon, *Inside Teams* (San Francisco: Jossey-Bass Publishers, 1994).

128. J.R. Schuster & P.K. Zingheim, *The New Pay: Linking Employee and Organizational Performance* (New York: Lexington Books, 1992).

129. R.E. Yates, "Molding a New Future for Manufacturer, Keys Are Planning, People—and Plastics," *Chicago Tribune*, 2 January 1994.

130. S.G. Cohen & D.E. Bailey, "What Makes Teams Work: Group Effectiveness Research from the Shop Floor to the Executive Suite," *Journal of Management* 23, no. 3 (1997): 239–290.

131. R. Allen & R. Kilmann, "Aligning Reward Practices in Support of Total Quality Management," *Business Horizons* 44 (May 2001): 77–85.

132. J.H. Sheridan, "'Yes' to Team Incentives," *Industry Week*, 4 March 1996, 63.

## Chapter 14

1. M. Barrier, "Hiring the Right People," *Nation's Business* 84, no. 6 (June 1996): 18.

2. G. Zachary, "Shortage of Nurses Hits Hardest Where They Are Needed the Most," *The Wall Street Journal*, 24 January 2001, A1.

3. B. Schneider & N. Schmitt, *Staffing Organizations*, 2nd ed. (Glenview, IL: Scott, Foresman and Company, 1986).

4. M. Jones, "Four Trends to Reckon with," *HR Focus* 73 (1996): 22–24.

5. C. Joinson, "Moving at the Speed of Dell," *HRMagazine* 44, no. 4 (1 April 1999): 50.

6. D.M. Atwater, "Workforce Forecasting," *Human Resource Planning* 18, no. 4 (1995): 50.

7. K. Chen, "Some Companies Treat Slump as Chance to Build Staff They'll Need to Grow," *The Wall Street Journal*, 10 April 2001, B1.

8. J. Eig, "Do Part-Time Workers Hold Key to When the Recession Breaks?" *The Wall Street Journal*, 3 January 2002, A1.

9. D.M. Atwater, "Workforce Forecasting," *Human Resource Planning* 18, no. 4 (1995): 50. D. Ward, "Workforce Demand Forecasting Techniques," *Human Resource Planning* 19, no. 1 (1996): 54.

10. C. Joinson, "Moving at the Speed of Dell," *HRMagazine* 44, no. 4 (1 April 1999): 50.

11. *Ibid.*

12. A.J. Walker, "The Analytical Element Is Important to an HRIS," *Personnel Administrator* 28 (1983): 33–35, 85.

13. "eTenet—General Information—About Us," *Tenet*. [Online] Available http://www.etenet.com/GeneralInfo/aboutus.asp, 26 January 2002.

14. M.A. Cross, "Software Becomes a Strategic Tool for Human Resources Departments," *Health Data Management*, 19 July 1997.

15. L. Asinof, "Click & Shift: Workers Control Their Benefits On-Line," *The Wall Street Journal*, 21 November 1997, C1.

16. *Ibid.*

17. T. Jolls, "Technology Continues to Redefine HR's Role," *Personnel Journal* 76, no. 7 (July 1997): 46.

18. *Ibid.*

19. "Qwiz Online," *Quiz*. [Online] Available http://www.qwiz.com/default.cfm?action=online, 26 January 2002.

20. S. Bing, "The Feds Make a Pass at Hooters," *Fortune*, 15 January 1996, 82.

21. C. Roush & J. Cummings, "Hooters Wins EEOC Skirmish in Sexual Bias Battle," *Atlanta Constitution*, 2 May 1996, F1. J. Malone & C. Roush, "Restaurant Chain Goes to Battle," *Atlanta Constitution*, 16 November 1995, Section F, p. 3. D. Cardinal, "Hooters Girls on Endangered Species List," *Business Record (Des Moines, Iowa)*, 11 December 1995, 19. K.D. Grimsley, "Hooters Plays Hardball with the EEOC," *Washington Post*, 12 December 1995, Section H, p. 1. Anonymous, "EEOC's Politically Correct Crusade against Hooters a Wasted Effort," *Nation's Restaurant News*, 4 December 1995, 19. S. Keating, "Feds Press Equal-Opportunity Ogling: Hooters Says EEOC Effort to Force Male Waiters Is Absurd," *Denver Post*, 16 November 1995, Section C, p. 1. J. Hayes, "Hooters Comes Out against EEOC Sex-Bias Suit," *Nation's Restaurant News*, 27 November 1995, 3.

22. Associated Press, "Hooters Settles Suit, Won't Hire Waiters," *Denver Post*, 1 October 1997, A11.

23. P.S. Greenlaw & J.P. Kohl, "Employer 'Business' and 'Job' Defenses in Civil Rights Actions," *Public Personnel Management* 23, no. 4 (1994): 573.

24. Associated Press, "Hooters Settles Suit, Won't Hire Waiters," *Denver Post*, 1 October 1997, A11.

25. N. Shirouzu, "Nine Ford Workers File Bias Suit Saying Ratings Curb Older Staff," *The Wall Street Journal*, 15 February 2001. "Ford Reaches Tentative Settlement in Suits," *The Wall Street Journal*, 19 December 2001, B12.

26. J.L. Ledvinka, *Federal Regulation of Personnel and Human Resource Management* (Boston: Kent Publishing Company, 1982), 137–198.

27. E. Emery, "U.S. Fines Steel Mill $487,000: OSHA Inspection Finds 107 Safety Violations In Plant," *Denver Post*, 23 August 2000, C1.

28. P.S. Greenlaw & J.P. Kohl, "Employer 'Business' and 'Job' Defenses in Civil Rights Actions," *Public Personnel Management* 23, no. 4 (1994): 573.

29. "Judge Approves Settlement Of Coca-Cola Bias Lawsuit," *The Wall Street Journal*, 30 May 2001, B7.

30. "Rent-A-Center Settles Gender-Bias Lawsuit, Will Pay $12.3 Million," *The Wall Street Journal*, 2 November 2001, no page number available.

31. W. Peirce, C.A. Smolinski, & B. Rosen, "Why Sexual Harassment Complaints Fall on Deaf Ears," *Academy of Management Executive* 12, no. 3 (1998): 41–54.

32. A. Levin, "Prudential Hit with 10 Discrimination Suits," *National Underwriter* 103, no. 4 (1999): 2.

33. W. Peirce, C.A. Smolinski, & B. Rosen, "Why Sexual Harassment Complaints Fall on Deaf Ears," *Academy of Management Executive* 12, no. 3 (1998): 41–54.

34. *Ibid.*

35. U.S. Equal Employment Opportunity Commission, "Facts about Sexual Harassment." [Online] Available http://www.eeoc.gov/facts/fs-sex.html, 23 May 1999.

36. W. Peirce, C.A. Smolinski, & B. Rosen, "Why Sexual Harassment Complaints Fall on Deaf Ears," *Academy of Management Executive* 12, no. 3 (1998): 41–54.

37. *Ibid.*

38. E. Larson, "The Economic Costs of Sexual Harassment," *Liberty Haven*. [Available] Online http://www.libertyhaven.com/personalfreedomissues/consensualcrimesorsexualissues/ecosexual.html, 27 January 2002.

39. K. Dunham & G. Ip, "Slow Economy Takes Unusually Heavy Toll on White-Collar Jobs," *The Wall Street Journal*, 5 November 2001, A1.

40. R. Buckman, "Help Wanted: Wall Street Hiring Now," *The Wall Street Journal*, 14 April 1999, C1.

41. C. Hymowitz, "Shrewd New Tactics Help Two Companies Snare the Top Talent," *The Wall Street Journal*, 29 February 2000, B1. P. Nakache, "Cisco's Recruiting Edge—Find 'Em, Lure 'Em, Keep 'Em Happy: Devising New Ways to Steal Top Talent from Competitors Has Given This Silicon Valley Standout

an Important Advantage," *Fortune*, 29 September 1997, 275.

42. R.D. Gatewood & H.S. Field, *Human Resource Selection* (Fort Worth, TX: Dryden Press, 1998).

43. *Ibid.*

44. *Griggs v. Duke Co.*, 401 US 424, 436 (1971). *Albemarle Paper Co. v. Moody*, 422 US 405 (1975).

45. P.R. Chowdhury, "Human Resources: Beyond Downsizing, Growing the TCM Manager," *Business Today*, 7 January 1999, 172.

46. "Fujisawa Launches 'Jobs Challenge' Policy," *Market Letter*, 17 September 2001, no page number available.

47. J.A. Breaugh, *Recruitment: Science and Practice* (Boston: PWS-Kent, 1992).

48. "Fujisawa Launches 'Jobs Challenge' Policy," *Market Letter*, 17 September 2001, no page number available.

49. P.R. Chowdhury, "Human Resources: Beyond Downsizing, Growing the TCM Manager," *Business Today*, 7 January 1999, 172.

50. J. Breaugh & M. Starke, "Research on Employee Recruitment: So Many Studies, So Many Remaining Questions" *Journal of Management* 26 (2000): 405–434.

51. P. Nakache, "Cisco's Recruiting Edge—Find 'Em, Lure 'Em, Keep 'Em Happy: Devising New Ways to Steal Top Talent from Competitors Has Given This Silicon Valley Standout an Important Advantage," *Fortune*, 29 September 1997, 275.

52. S. Gale, "Internet Recruiting: Better, Cheaper, Faster," *Personnel Journal*, 1 December 2000, 74.

53. J. King, "Who's in the Online Pool?" *Computerworld*, 10 February 1997, 24. L.J.S. Vohra, "Online Recruiting Fills Positions," *Denver Business Journal*, 9 August 1996, 27A.

54. D. Fenn, "Hiring: Searching for the Chosen Few," *Inc.*, March 1996, 96.

55. C. Camden & B. Wallace, "Job Application Forms: A Hazardous Employment Practice," *Personnel Administrator* 28 (1983): 31–32.

56. J.S. Pouliot, "Topics to Avoid with Applicants," *Nation's Business* 80, no. 7 (1992): 57.

57. J. Kennedy, "Europeans Expect Different Type of Résumé," *Chicago Sun-Times*, 3 June 1999, 73.

58. R.D. Broussard & D.E. Brannen, "Credential Distortions: Personnel Practitioners Give Their Views," *Personnel Administrator* 31 (1986): 129–146. K.A. Edelman, "Fiction 101: Résumé

Writing," *Across the Board*, February 1997, 62.

59. M. Mandell, "The High Cost of Hiring Fakers," *World Trade* 11, no. 3 (1998): 56.

60. S. Adler, "Verifying a Job Candidate's Background: The State of Practice in a Vital Human Resources Activity," *Review of Business* 15, no. 2 (1993/1994): 3–8.

61. T. Thiesen, "Prisoners of the Past: Workers with Criminal Records Have Tough Time," *Orlando Sentinel*, 3 October 2001, G1.

62. M.P. Cronin, "This Is a Test," *Inc.*, August 1993, 64–69.

63. S. Marshall, "Spot Inflated Résumés with Simple Sleuthing," *The Asian Wall Street Journal*, 7 April 2000, P3.

64. J. Hunter, "Cognitive Ability, Cognitive Aptitudes, Job Knowledge, and Job Performance," *Journal of Vocational Behavior* 29 (1986): 340–362.

65. E.E. Cureton, "Comment," in Edwin R. Henry, *Research Conference on the Use of Autobiographical Data as Psychological Predictors* (Greensboro, NC: The Richardson Foundation, 1965), 13.

66. J.R. Glennon, L.E. Albright, & W.A. Owens, *A Catalog of Life History Items* (Greensboro, NC: The Richardson Foundation, 1966).

67. R.D. Gatewood & H.S. Field, *Human Resource Selection* (Fort Worth, TX: Dryden Press, 1998).

68. J.M. Digman, "Personality Structure: Emergence of the Five-Factor Model," *Annual Review of Psychology* 41 (1990): 417–440. M.R. Barrick & M.K. Mount, "The Big Five Personality Dimensions and Job Performance: A Meta-Analysis," *Personnel Psychology* 44 (1991): 1–26.

69. D. Fenn, "Hiring: Employee Auditions," *Inc.*, June 1996, 116.

70. M.S. Taylor & J.A. Sniezek, "The College Recruitment Interview: Topical Content and Applicant Reactions," *Journal of Occupational Psychology* 57 (1984): 157–168.

71. M.A. Campion, D.K. Palmer, & J.E. Campion, "A Review of Structure in the Selection Interview," *Personnel Psychology* 50, no. 3 (1997): 655–702.

72. D. Stafford, "Workers Train, Companies Gain: Harmon Industries, Sprint, Others Make a Big Commitment," *Kansas City Star*, 16 February 1999, D1.

73. *Ibid.*

74. S. Livingston, T.W. Gerdel, M. Hill, B. Yerak, C. Melvin, & B. Lubinger,

749

"Ohio's Strongest Companies All Agree That Training Is Vital to Their Success," *Plain Dealer*, 21 May 1997, 30S.

75. T.D. Schellhardt, "Management: Behind the Scenes at One CEO's Performance Review," *The Wall Street Journal*, 27 April 1998, B1.

76. *Ibid.*

77. J. Tyler, & E. Biggs, "Practical Governance: CEO Performance Appraisal," *Trustee* 54 no. 5 (2001): 18–21.

78. T. Dixon Murray, "Setting Standards: Work Keys Is a Relatively New Process Used to Pre-Screen Job Applicants, Evaluate Training Needs and Determine Raises," *Plain Dealer*, 18 October 1998, 1H.

79. L. Kroll, "At Work: Good Morning, HAL: Aetna Jumped over a Lot of Hurdles When It Cut Back Face-to-Face Training in Favor of Cyberclasses. Was It Worth It?" *Forbes*, 8 March 1999, 118.

80. T. Weber, "The New Dress Code for Corporate Training: Slippers and Pajamas?" *The Wall Street Journal*, 31 January 2001, B1.

81. D.L. Kirkpatrick, "Four Steps to Measuring Training Effectiveness," *Personnel Administrator* 28 (1983): 19–25.

82. U. Gupta, "TV Seminars and CD-ROMs Train Workers," *The Wall Street Journal*, 3 January 1996, B1.

83. J. Stack, "The Curse of the Annual Performance Review," *Inc.*, 1 March 1997, 39.

84. D. Murphy, "Are Performance Appraisals Worse Than a Waste of Time? Book Derides Unintended Consequences," *San Francisco Chronicle*, 9 September 2001, W1.

85. J. Yankovic, "Are the Reviews In?" *Pittsburgh Business Times* 16 (28 October 1996): 7.

86. T.D. Schellhardt, "Annual Agony: It's Time to Evaluate Your Work, And All Involved Are Groaning— Employees Dislike Reviews, Even If Favorable; Bosses Wonder How to Do Them, Some Prefer Frequent Talks," *The Wall Street Journal*, 19 November 1996, A1.

87. U.J. Wiersma & G.P. Latham, "The Practicality of Behavioral Observation Scales, Behavioral Expectation Scales, and Trait Scales," *Personnel Psychology* 39 (1986): 619–628. U.J. Wiersma, P.T. Van Den Berg, & G.P. Latham, "Dutch Reactions to Behavioral Observation, Behavioral Expectation, and Trait Scales," *Group & Organization Management* 20 (1995): 297–309.

88. D.J. Woehr & A.I. Huffcutt, "Rater Training for Performance Appraisal: A Quantitative Review," *Journal of Occupational and Organizational Psychology* 67, no. 3 (1994): 189–205.

89. J. Stack, "The Curse of the Annual Performance Review," *Inc.*, 1 March 1997, 39.

90. B. O'Reilly, "360-Degree Feedback Can Change Your Life," *Fortune*, 17 October 1994, 93.

91. C. Hymowitz, "Do '360' Job Reviews by Colleagues Promote Honesty or Insults?" *The Wall Street Journal*, 12 December 2000, B1.

92. D.A. Waldman, L.E. Atwater, & D. Antonioni, "Has 360 Feedback Gone Amok?" *Academy of Management Executive* 12, no. 2 (1998): 86–94.

93. H.H. Meyer, "A Solution to the Performance Appraisal Feedback Enigma," *Academy of Management Executive* 5, no. 1 (1991): 68–76.

94. T.D. Schellhardt, "Annual Agony: It's Time to Evaluate Your Work, And All Involved Are Groaning—Employees Dislike Reviews, Even If Favorable; Bosses Wonder How to Do Them, Some Prefer Frequent Talks," *The Wall Street Journal*, 19 November 1996, A1.

95. G.C. Thornton, "Psychometric Properties of Self-Appraisals of Job Performance," *Personnel Psychology* 33 (1980): 263–271.

96. H.H. Meyer, "A Solution to the Performance Appraisal Feedback Enigma," *Academy of Management Executive* 5, no. 1 (1991): 68–76.

97. T. Aeppel, "Toyota Plant Roils the Hiring Hierarchy of an Indiana Town," *The Wall Street Journal*, 6 April 1999, A1.

98. G.T. Milkovich & J.M. Newman, *Compensation,* 4th ed. (Homewood. IL: Irwin,1993).

99. S. Shellenbarger, "Tight Labor Market Is Putting Squeeze on Quality Day Care," *The Wall Street Journal*, 21 October 1998, B1.

100. M.L. Williams & G.F. Dreher, "Compensation System Attributes and Applicant Pool Characteristics," *Academy of Management Journal* 35, no. 3 (1992): 571–595.

101. M. Rich, "To Serve and Defect: Governments Struggle to Keep Key Jobs Filled," *The Wall Street Journal*, 16 September 1998, S1.

102. Business Brief, "Profit-Sharing Checks Hit Record for Hourly Workers," *The Wall Street Journal Interactive*, 28 January 2000.

103. M. Bloom, "The Performance Effects of Pay Dispersion on Individuals and Organizations," *Academy of Management Journal* 42, no. 1 (1999): 25–40.

104. J. Reingold & R. Grover, "Executive Pay: The Numbers Are Staggering, But So Is the Performance of American Business. So How Closely Are They Linked?" *Business Week*, 19 April 1999, 72. J. Reingold & F. Jespersen, "Executive Pay: It Continues to Explode—And Options Alone Are Creating Paper Billionaires," *Business Week*, 17 April 2000, 100. L. Lavelle, & F. Jespersen, "Executive Pay: While the CEO Gravy Train May Be Slowing, It Hasn't Jumped the Rails," *Business Week*, 16 April 2001, 76.

105. W. Grossman & R.E. Hoskisson, "CEO Pay at the Crossroads of Wall Street and Main: Toward the Strategic Design of Executive Compensation," *Academy of Management Executive* 12, no. 1 (1998): 43–57.

106. M. Bloom, "The Performance Effects of Pay Dispersion on Individuals and Organizations," *Academy of Management Journal* 42, no. 1 (1999): 25–40.

107. J.S. Rosenbloom, "The Environment of Employee Benefit Plans," in *The Handbook of Employee Benefits,* ed. J.S. Rosenbloom (Chicago: Irwin, 1996), 3–13.

108. "Employer Costs for Employee Compensation in the Northeast Region," *Bureau of Labor Statistics.* [Available] Online http://www.bls.gov/ro2/ececne. htm, 30 January 2002.

109. A.E. Barber, R.B. Dunham, & R.A. Formisano, "The Impact of Flexible Benefits on Employee Satisfaction: A Field Study," *Personnel Psychology* 45 (1992): 55–75. B. Heshizer, "The Impact of Flexible Benefits on Job Satisfaction and Turnover Intentions," *Benefits Quarterly* 4 (1994): 84–90. D.M. Cable & T.A. Judge, "Pay Preferences and Job Search Decisions: A Person-Organization Fit Perspective," *Personnel Psychology* 47 (1994): 317–348.

110. B.T. Beam & J.J. McFadden, *Employee Benefits* (Chicago: Dearborn Financial Publishing, 1996).

111. J.A. Tannenbaum, "Small Companies Find New Way to Retain Employees—Payroll-Deduction Plans Springing Up to Pay for Things Like Car Insurance," *The Wall Street Journal*, 12 January 1999, B3.

112. J. Lublin, "Left Out of a Meeting? Parking Space Taken? Worry About Your Job," *The Wall Street Journal*, 3 April 2001, B1.

113. K. Labich & E.M. Davies, "How to Fire People and Still Sleep at Night. Shedding Employees Is Something Almost Every Manager Dreads. But If You Don't Think Hard about the Process, You and Your Company Could Be Headed Straight for a World of Woes," *Fortune*, 10 June 1996, 64.

114. *Ibid.*

115. P. Michal-Johnson, *Saying Good-Bye: A Manager's Guide to Employee Dismissal* (Glenview, IL: Scott, Foresman and Company, 1985).

116. M. Bordwin, "Employment Law: Beware of Time Bombs and Shark-Infested Waters," *HR Focus*, 1 April 1995, 19.

117. T. Bland, "Fire at Will, Repent at Leisure," *Security Management* 44 (May 2000), 64.

118. J.R. Morris, W.F. Cascio, & C.E. Young, "Downsizing after All These Years: Questions and Answers about Who Did It, How Many Did It, And Who Benefited from It," *Organizational Dynamics* 27, no. 3 (1999): 78–87.

119. "Los Angeles Times. Layoffs Rise as Firms Find It's Profitable; 523,000 Are Fired as of Oct., 200,000 More Than in 1997; Pink Slips in Golden Times; Study Shows Strategy May Ultimately Lower Earnings, Stock Prices," *Baltimore Sun*, 30 November 1998, 5C.

120. J.R. Morris, W.F. Cascio, & C.E. Young, "Downsizing after All These Years: Questions and Answers about Who Did It, How Many Did It, And Who Benefited from It," *Organizational Dynamics* 27, no. 3 (1999): 78–87.

121. K.E. Mishra, G.M. Spreitzer, & A.K. Mishra, "Preserving Employee Morale during Downsizing," *Sloan Management Review* 39, no. 2 (1998): 83–95.

122. J.E.D. Scott, "Smith Tries to Soothe the Pain of Closing Its Plant," *Memphis Business Journal*, 29 July 1996, 11.

123. J. Ackerman, "Helping Layoff Survivors Cope: Companies Strive to Keep Morale High," *Boston Globe*, 30 December 2001, H1.

124. *Ibid.*

125. *Ibid.*

126. D. Ferrari, "Designing and Evaluating Early Retirement Programs: The State of Wyoming Experience," *Government Finance Review* 15, no. 1 (1999): 29–31.

127. R. Mullins, "Early Retirement Programs Can End Up Being Costly," *Business Journal-Milwaukee*, 20 January 1996, Section 1, p. 25.

128. D.R. Dalton, W.D. Todor, & D.M. Krackhardt, "Turnover Overstated: The Functional Taxonomy," *Academy of Management Review* 7 (1982): 117–123.

129. J.R. Hollenbeck & C.R. Williams, "Turnover Functionality versus Turnover Frequency: A Note on Work Attitudes and Organizational Effectiveness," *Journal of Applied Psychology* 71 (1986): 606–611.

130. C.R. Williams, "Reward Contingency, Unemployment, And Functional Turnover," *Human Resource Management Review*, in-press.

## Chapter 15

1. D. Michaels, "Inspired by U.S.'s Southwest, Ryanair's Discount Fares Reshape European Travel," *The Wall Street Journal Interactive*, 6 September 2000.

2. J. Ordonez, "Fast-Food Lanes Are Getting Even Faster," *The Wall Street Journal*, 18 May 2000, A1.

3. "Economy," *The Wall Street Journal*, 12 May 1999, A2.

4. W.M. Cox & R. Alm, *The Myths of Rich & Poor* (New York: Basic Books, 1999). R.L. Bartley, "The Seven Fat Years," *The Wall Street Journal Interactive*, 30 April 1992. S. Nasar & L. Smith, "Do We Live as Well as We Used To?" *Fortune*, 14 September 1987, 34.

5. "Philanthropy in the American Economy," *Council of Economic Advisers*. [Online] Available http://clinton4.nara.gov/media/pdf/philanthropy.pdf, 19 February 2002.

6. "Auto Affordability Stabilized in Third Quarter," *Comerica*. [Online] http://www.comerica.com/cma/cda/main/0,1555,2_A_576,00.html, 19 February 2002.

7. S. Carney, "U.S. Auto Productivity Improving," *Detroit News*. [Online] Available http://detnews.com/2001/autos/0106/15/b01-236332.htm, 15 June 2001.

8. J.B. White, "Wide Gap Exists between GM, Rivals in Labor Productivity," *The Wall Street Journal*, 16 July 1998, A4.

9. Bureau of Labor Statistics, "Multifactor Productivity: Frequently Asked Questions." [Online] Available http://stats.bls.gov/mprfaq.htm, 7 March 1998.

10. J. Dodge, "Dell's Internet-Based Plant Keeps Production Efficient," *The Wall Street Journal Interactive Edition*, 26 September 2000.

11. J. Pletz, "Dell Computer's Basic Building Blocks: Famous Model for Computers Translates Well to Construction," *Austin American-Statesman*, 10 April 2000, D1.

12. J. Teresko, "The Value of Velocity," *Industry Week*, 1 October 2001, 43.

13. American Society for Quality, "ASQ Glossary of Terms Search." [Online] Available http://www.asq.org/info/glossary/definition.html#q, 24 February 2002.

14. R.E. Markland, S.K. Vickery, & R.A. Davis, "Managing Quality" (Chapter 7), *Operations Management: Concepts in Manufacturing and Services* (Cincinnati, OH: South-Western College Publishing, 1998).

15. "DLT 8000," *Quantum Corporation*. [Online] Available http://www.quantum.com/Products/Tape+and+Drives/DLT+8000/Default.htm, 24 February 2002.

16. D. Sherman, "Engineering for Insurance," *Automotive Industries* 181 (Feb. 2001): 55.

17. J.H. Sheridan, "At a Glance: Physio-Control Corp." *Industry Week*, 21 October 1996, 46.

18. L.L. Berry & A. Parasuraman, *Marketing Services* (New York: Free Press, 1991).

19. P. Judge, "When a Customer Believes in You . . . They'll Stick with You Almost No Matter What," *Fast Company* 47 (June 2001): 138.

20. *Ibid.*

21. *Ibid.*

22. *Ibid.*

23. American Society for Quality, "ANSI ASC Z–1 Committee on Quality Assurance Answers the Most Frequently Asked Questions about the ISO 9000 (ANSI/ASQ Q9000) Series." [Online] Available http://www.asq.org/standcert/iso.html, 29 March 1998.

24. R. Henkoff, "The Not New Seal of Quality (ISO 9000 Standard of Quality Management)," *Fortune*, 28 June 1993, 116.

25. *Ibid.*

26. P. Sebastian, "Business Bulletin: A Special Background Report on Trends in Industry and Finance," *The Wall Street Journal*, 14 November 1996, A1.

27. "Frequently Asked Questions and Answers about the Malcolm Baldrige National Quality Award," *National Institute for Standards and Technology*. [Online] Available http://www.nist.gov/public_affairs/factsheet/baldfaqs.htm 25 February 2002.

28. "Fees for the 2002 Award Cycle," *Baldrige National Quality Program 2002.* [Online] Available http://www.quality.nist.gov/Fees.htm, 25 February 2002.

29. "Frequently Asked Questions and Answers about the Malcolm Baldrige National Quality Award," *National Institute for Standards and Technology.* [Online] Available http://www.nist.gov/public_affairs/factsheet/baldfaqs.htm 25 February 2002.

30. J. Main, "How to Win the Baldrige Award," *Fortune,* 23 April 1990, 101.

31. "Criteria for Performance Excellence," *Baldrige National Quality Program 2002.* [Online] Available http://www.quality.nist.gov/PDF_files/2002_Business_Criteria.pdf, 25 February 2002.

32. *Ibid.*

33. *Ibid.*

34. " 'Baldrige Index' Consistently Outperforms the S&P 500," *National Institute for Standards and Technology.* [Online] Available http://www.nist.gov/public_affairs/releases/S&P500.htm, 25 February 2002.

35. J.W. Dean, Jr. & J. Evans, *Total Quality: Management, Organization, and Strategy* (St. Paul, MN: West Publishing Co., 1994).

36. J.W. Dean, Jr & D.E. Bowen, "Management Theory and Total Quality: Improving Research and Practice through Theory Development," *Academy of Management Review* 19 (1994): 392–418.

37. C. Hall, "La Madeleine CEO Leads Turnaround: Bakery Chain Begins Recovery from Years of Infighting, Lack of Control," *Dallas Morning News,* 6 August 2000, 1H.

38. S. Thurm, "At Fast-Moving Cisco, CEO Says: Put Customers First, View Rivals as 'Good Guys,'" *The Wall Street Journal,* 1 June 2000, B1.

39. G. Baum, "The Dynamic 100 Cisco's CEO John Chambers: If You Can't Beat 'Em, Buy 'Em," *Forbes ASAP,* 23 February 1998.

40. G. Bylinsky, "Heroes of U.S. Manufacturing," *Fortune,* 19 March 2001, 178B.

41. R. Levering, M. Moskowitz, L. Munoz, & P. Hjelt, "The 100 Best Companies to Work for," *Fortune,* 4 February 2002, 72.

42. R. Hallowell, L.A. Schlesinger, & J. Zornitsky, "Internal Service Quality, Customer and Job Satisfaction: Linkages and Implications for Management," *Human Resource Planning* 19 (1996): 20–31. J.L. Heskett, T.O. Jones, G.W. Loveman, W.E. Sasser, Jr., & L.A. Schlesinger,

"Putting the Service-Profit Chain to Work," *Harvard Business Review,* March-April 1994, 164–174.

43. J. Huey, G. Bethune, & H. Kelleher, "Two Texas Mavericks Rant about the Wreckage of the U.S. Aviation Industry—And Reveal How They've Managed to Keep Their Companies above the Miserable Average," *Fortune,* 13 November 2000, 237.

44. Company Profile, "CVS Gears 'Service-Profit Chain' to the Customer," *Chain Drug Review,* 11 December 2000, 44.

45. *Ibid.*

46. K.L. Freiberg & J.A. Freiberg, *NUTS! Southwest Airlines' Crazy Recipe for Business and Personal Success* (Austin, TX: Bard Press, 1996), 289.

47. G. Brewer, "The Ultimate Guide to Winning Customers: The Customer Stops Here," *Sales & Marketing Management* 150 (March 1998): 30.

48. *Ibid.*

49. T. Levitt, "Production-Line Approach to Service," *Harvard Business Review,* September-October 1972, 41–52. T. Levitt, "Industrialization of Service," *Harvard Business Review,* September-October 1976, 63–74.

50. L.L. Berry & A. Parasuraman, "Listening to the Customer—The Concept of a Service-Quality Information System," *Sloan Management Review* 38, no. 3 (Spring 1997): 65. C.W.L. Hart, J.L. Heskett, & W.E. Sasser, Jr., "The Profitable Art of Service Recovery," *Harvard Business Review,* July-August 1990, 148–156.

51. M. Adams, "When Something Is Wrong, Those Who Care Make It Right: Give Employees the Power to Help Customers, Experts," *USA Today,* 12 September 2000, 11E.

52. D.E. Bowen & E.E. Lawler, III, "The Empowerment of Service Workers: What, Why, How, and When," *Sloan Management Review* 33 (Spring 1992): 31–39. D.E. Bowen & E.E. Lawler, III, "Empowering Service Employees," *Sloan Management Review* 36 (Summer 1995): 73–84.

53. D.E. Bowen & E.E. Lawler, III, "The Empowerment of Service Workers: What, Why, How, and When," *Sloan Management Review* 33 (Spring 1992): 31–39.

54. D. Machalaba, "Amtrak Boss Struggles to Get Train Service on Track in the U.S.," *The Wall Street Journal,* 16 January 2001, A1.

55. S. Berne, "Five Fabulous Food Plants," *Prepared Foods,* 1 June 1996, 80.

56. "TCBY Timeline," *TCBY.* [Online]] Available http://www.tcby.com/smoothie/

about/newtimeline.html, 28 February 2002.

57. G. McWilliams, "How Dell Fine Tunes Its PC Pricing to Gain Edge in a Slow Market: Working with Suppliers, It Quickly Passes Changes in Costs to Customers, Three Prices for One Product," *The Wall Street Journal,* 8 June 2001, A1.

58. J. Leib, "Wilkerson's Breath of Fresh Air: Pneumatics Firm Re-Engineers Its Production Ways," *Denver Post,* 9 June 1997, E1.

59. G.V. Frazier & M.T. Spiggs, "Achieving Competitive Advantage through Group Technology," *Business Horizons* 39 (1996): 83–88.

60. "The Top 100 Beverage Companies: The List," *Beverage Industry,* July 2001, 30.

61. E. Gruber, "Cutting Time," *Modern Machine Shop,* March 2001, 102.

62. Bruce, "Heil 'Automated Job Shop' Produces Custom Trailers on Assembly Lines," *Trailer/Body Builders,* 30 December 1998. Available on line at trailer-bodybuilders.com

63. "Attack Submarines—SSN," *United States Navy Fact File.* [Online] Available http://www.chinfo.navy.mil/navpalib/factfile/ships/ship-ssn.html, 1 March 2002.

64. "Heinz to Temporarily Suspend 400 Jobs at Pittsburgh Plant," *Eurofood,* 1 November 1995, 15.

65. E. Eldridge, "Signs Indicate Auto Industry Needs Tune-up: Automakers Cut Production as Inventory Swells," *USA Today,* 26 February 2001, 7B.

66. K. Tran, "Microsoft, Nintendo Report Sales Are Robust for Xbox," *The Wall Street Journal,* 21 November 2001, B11.

67. C. Marshall, "Linerboard: Market Recovery Will Continue; Price Hikes Predicted for 1998," *Pulp & Paper,* 1 January 1998, 13.

68. D. Drickhamer, "Reality Check," *Industry Week,* November 2001, 29.

69. D. Drickhamer, "Zeroing In on World-Class," *Industry Week,* November 2001, 36.

70. F. Zappa, "The End of Paperwork? Electronic Commerce Promises to Save Billions of Dollars and Millions of Hours," *Nation's Restaurant News,* 3 November 1997, S10.

71. J.R. Henry, "Minimized Setup Will Make Your Packaging Line S.M.I.L.E.," *Packaging Technology & Engineering,* 1 February 1998, 24.

72. J. Donoghue, "The Future Is Now," *Air Transport World,* 1 April 2001, 78.

73. W. Zinn & P. Liu, "Consumer Response to Retail Stockouts," *Journal of Business Logistics* 22 (2001): 49.

74. F. Brookman, "Managing Inventory (EDI)," *Women's Wear,* 19 September 1997, 20.

75. E. Powell, Jr., & F. Sahin, "Economic Production Lot Sizing with Periodic Costs and Overtime," *Decision Sciences* 32 (2001): 423–452.

76. T. Minahan, "JIT: A Process with Many Faces," *Purchasing,* 4 September 1997, 42.

77. "Fully Automated System Achieves True JIT," *Modern Materials Handling,* 1 April 1998, DPI22.

78. N. Shirouzu, "Why Toyota Wins Such High Marks on Quality Surveys," *The Wall Street Journal,* 15 March 2001, A1.

79. *Ibid.*

80. C. Crowell, "Seeing the Big Picture through Software (Manufacturing Resource Planning Computer Programs)," *American Metal Market,* 22 July 1997, 12.

## Chapter 16

1. J.P. Campbell & R.D. Pritchard, "Motivation Theory in Industrial and Organizational Psychology," *Handbook of Industrial and Organizational Psychology,* ed. M.D. Dunnette (Chicago: Rand McNally, 1976).

2. P. Thomas, "Waitress Makes the Difference in Bringing Deaf to Pittsburgh," *The Wall Street Journal Interactive Edition,* 2 March 1999.

3. ESPN, "Winter Olympics, Bobsled, Past Results." [Online] Available http://espn.go.com/olympics98/bobsled/almanac.html, 9 June 1999.

4. Team Jamaica.com, "Jamaica Bobsleigh History." [Online] Available http://www.bobsledcity.org/Jamaicabobsleigh/services.htm, 9 June 1999.

5. N. Mangi, "It's Payback Time: Freedom, Perks, And Parties Aren't Enough Anymore. What Top People Want Now from Small Employers Is a Raise—A Big One," *Business Week,* 9 October 2000, F24.

6. *Ibid.*

7. K.A. Dolan, "When Money Isn't Enough," *Forbes,* 18 November 1996, 164–170.

8. E.A. Locke, "The Nature and Causes of Job Satisfaction," *Handbook of Industrial and Organizational Psychology,* ed. M.D. Dunnette (Chicago: Rand McNally, 1976).

9. A.H. Maslow, "A Theory of Human Motivation," *Psychological Review* 50 (1943): 370–396.

10. C.P. Alderfer, *Existence, Relatedness, and Growth: Human Needs in Organizational Settings* (New York: Free Press, 1972).

11. D.C. McClelland, "Toward a Theory of Motive Acquisition," *American Psychologist* 20 (1965): 321–333. D.C. McClelland & D.H. Burnham, "Power is the Great Motivator," *Harvard Business Review* 54, no. 2 (1976): 100–110.

12. J.H. Turner, "Entrepreneurial Environments and the Emergence of Achievement Motivation in Adolescent Males," *Sociometry* 33 (1970): 147–165.

13. L.W. Porter, E.E. Lawler, III, & J.R. Hackman, *Behavior in Organizations* (New York: McGraw-Hill, 1975).

14. M.A. Wahba & L.B. Birdwell, "Maslow Reconsidered: A Review of Research on the Need Hierarchy Theory," *Organizational Behavior and Human Performance* 15 (1976): 212–240. J. Rauschenberger, N. Schmitt, & J.E. Hunter, "A Test of the Need Hierarchy Concept by a Markov Model of Change in Need Strength," *Administrative Science Quarterly* 25 (1980): 654–670.

15. E.E. Lawler, III & L.W. Porter, "The Effect of Performance on Job Satisfaction," *Industrial Relations* 7 (1967): 20–28.

16. L.W. Porter, E.E. Lawler, III, & J.R. Hackman, *Behavior in Organizations* (New York: McGraw-Hill, 1975).

17. P. Carbonara & A. Schulz, "What Are You Worth?" *Fortune,* 12 June 2000, 264.

18. L.W. Porter, E.E. Lawler, III, & J.R. Hackman, *Behavior in Organizations* (New York: McGraw-Hill, 1975).

19. D. Spurgeon, "Fast-Food Industry Pitches 'Burger-Flipping' as Career," *The Wall Street Journal,* 29 May 2001, B1.

20. *Ibid.*

21. C. Caggiano, "What Do Workers Want?" *Inc.,* November 1992, 101–104. "National Study of the Changing Workforce," *Families and Work Institute.* [Online] Available http://www.familiesandwork.org/nationalstudy.html, 16 March 2002.

22. L. Buchanan, Managing One-to-One," *Inc.,* 1 October 2001, 82.

23. *Ibid.*

24. Aon Consulting, "America@Work: A Focus on Benefits and Compensation. [Online] Available http://www.aon.com/pdf/america/awork2.pdf, 12 June 1999.

25. J. Laabs, "Satisfy Them with More Than Money," *Personnel Journal* 77, no. 11 (1998): 40.

26. Aon Consulting, "America@Work: A Focus on Benefits and Compensation." [Online] Available http://www.aon.com/pdf/america/awork2.pdf, 12 June 1999.

27. D. Fairlamb, "The Euro, Round 2: Will the Advent of Notes and Coins Help or Hurt Growth?" *Business Week,* 2 July 2001, 44.

28. D. Woodruff, "Salary Spread in Euroland May Force Firms to Compete More for Top Workers," *The Wall Street Journal,* 20 January 1999, B9. C. Adams, "Trade Unions Cheer Extra Tool for Pay Negotiations," *Financial Times,* 14 December 2001, page numbers unavailable online.

29. *Ibid.*

30. S. Stecklow, "Fast Finns' Fines Fit Their Finances—Traffic Penalties Are Assessed According to Driver Income," *The Wall Street Journal,* 2 January 2001, A1.

31. J. Reingold & R. Grover, "Executive Pay: The Numbers Are Staggering, But So Is the Performance of American Business. So How Closely Are They Linked?" *Business Week,* 19 April 1999, 72. J. Reingold & F. Jespersen, "Executive Pay: It Continues to Explode—And Options Alone Are Creating Paper Billionaires," *Business Week,* 17 April 2000, 100. L. Lavelle, & F. Jespersen, "Executive Pay: While the CEO Gravy Train May Be Slowing, It Hasn't Jumped the Rails," *Business Week,* 16 April 2001, 76.

32. C.T. Kulik & M.L. Ambrose, "Personal and Situational Determinants of Referent Choice," *Academy of Management Review* 17 (1992): 212–237.

33. C. DeNavas-Walt, R. Cleveland, & M. Roemer, "Money Income in the United States," *U.S. Census Bureau.* [Online] Available http://www.census.gov/prod/2001pubs/p60-213.pdf, 17 April 2002.

34. J.S. Adams, "Toward an Understanding of Inequity," *Journal of Abnormal Social Psychology* 67 (1963): 422–436.

35. J. Greenberg, "Employee Theft as a Reaction to Underpayment Inequity: The Hidden Costs of Pay Cuts," *Journal of Applied Psychology* 75 (1990): 561–568.

36. R.A. Cosier & D.R. Dalton, "Equity Theory and Time: A Reformulation," *Academy of Management Review* 8 (1983): 311–319. M.R. Carrell & J.E. Dittrich, "Equity Theory: The Recent Literature, Methodological Considerations, And New Directions," *Academy of Management Review* 3 (1978): 202–209.

37. J.D. Opdyke, "Alaska Air, Union Soften Tough Talk in Bargaining," *The Wall Street Journal,* 2 June 1999, NW1.

38. J. Bendich, "When Is a Temp Not a Temp?" *Trial Magazine,* 1 October 2001, 42.

39. G.P. Zachary, "Some Companies Claim Workers Are Exempt or Raise Output Goals," *The Wall Street Journal Interactive Edition,* 24 June 1996.

753

40. J. Pollack, "Exemption under the Fair Labor Standards Act: The Cost of Misclassifying Employees," *Cornell Hotel & Restaurant Administration Quarterly* 42 (2001): 16.

41. K. Aquino, R.W. Griffeth, D.G. Allen, & P.W. Hom, "Integrating Justice Constructs into the Turnover Process: A Test of a Referent Cognitions Model," *Academy of Management Journal* 40, no. 5 (1997): 1208–1227.

42. D. Roth, "As Corporate Fears Turn from Hacks to Attacks, Securitas Is Suddenly Finding Its Guards in Demand," *Fortune*, 10 December 2001, 216.

43. S. Barr, "While the SEC Watches the Markets, The Job Market Is Draining the SEC," *Washington Post*, 10 March 2002, C3.

44. S. De Bruxelles, "Computer Firm Pays Out £17m to Keep Its Staff," *The Times*. [Online] Available http://www.thetimes.co.uk/news/pages/tim/99/06/12/timnwsnws01033, 12 June 1999.

45. C. Fishman, "Sanity, Inc.," *Fast Company*, January 1999, 85–96.

46. R. Folger & M.A. Konovsky, "Effects of Procedural and Distributive Justice on Reactions to Pay Raise Decisions," *Academy of Management Journal* 32 (1989): 115–130. M.A. Konovsky, "Understanding Procedural Justice and Its Impact on Business Organizations," *Journal of Management* 26 (2000): 489–512.

47. E. Barret-Howard & T.R. Tyler, "Procedural Justice as a Criterion in Allocation Decisions," *Journal of Personality and Social Psychology* 50 (1986): 296–305. R. Folger & M.A. Konovsky, "Effect of Procedural and Distributive Justice on Reactions to Pay Raise Decisions," *Academy of Management Journal* 32 (1989): 115–130.

48. R. Folger & J. Greenberg, "Procedural Justice: An Interpretive Analysis of Personnel Systems," in *Research in Personnel and Human Resources Management*, Volume 3, eds. K. Rowland & G. Ferris (Greenwich, CT: JAI Press, 1985). R. Folger, D. Rosenfield, J. Grove, & L. Corkran, "Effects of 'Voice' and Peer Opinions on Responses to Inequity," *Journal of Personality and Social Psychology* 37 (1979): 2253–2261. E.A. Lind & T.R. Tyler, *The Social Psychology of Procedural Justice* (New York: Plenum Press, 1988). M.A. Konovsky, "Understanding Procedural Justice and Its Impact on Business Organizations," *Journal of Management* 26 (2000): 489–512.

49. K.A. Dolan, "When Money Isn't Enough," *Forbes*, 18 November 1996, 164–170.

50. V.H. Vroom, *Work and Motivation* (New York: John Wiley & Sons, 1964). L.W. Porter & E.E. Lawler, III, *Managerial Attitudes and Performance* (Homewood, IL: Dorsey Press & Richard D. Irwin, 1968).

51. N. Wood, "Caribou Coffee," *Incentive* 17 (January 1997): 28–29.

52. L. Buchanan, "Managing One-to-One," *Inc.*, 1 October 2001, 82.

53. *Ibid.*

54. P.V. LeBlanc & P.W. Mulvey, "How American Workers See the Rewards of Work," *Compensation & Benefits Review* 30 (February 1998): 24–28.

55. S. Scholl, "Allstate Pay for Performance Methodology Rewards Excellence," *ACANEWS* 41, no. 8 (1998): 24.

56. K.W. Thomas & B.A. Velthouse, "Cognitive Elements of Empowerment," *Academy of Management Review* 15 (1990): 666–681.

57. D. Sheff, "Richard Branson: The Interview," *Forbes ASAP*, 24 February 1997, 95–102.

58. D. Milbank, "Workplace: Companies Turn to Peer Pressure to Cut Injuries as Psychologists Join the Battle," *The Wall Street Journal*, 29 March 1991, B1.

59. E.L. Thorndike, *Animal Intelligence* (New York: MacMillan, 1911).

60. D. Milbank, "Workplace: Companies Turn to Peer Pressure to Cut Injuries as Psychologists Join the Battle," *The Wall Street Journal*, 29 March 1991, B1.

61. B.F. Skinner, *Science and Human Behavior* (New York: MacMillan, 1954). B.F. Skinner, *Beyond Freedom and Dignity* (New York: Bantam Books, 1971). B.F. Skinner, *A Matter of Consequences* (New York: New York University Press, 1984).

62. A.M. Dickinson & A.D. Poling, "Schedules of Monetary Reinforcement in Organizational Behavior Management: Latham and Huber Revisited," *Journal of Organizational Behavior Management* 16, no. 1 (1992): 71–91.

63. B. Boydston, "Frequent-Flier Miles: Worker Entitlement or Company Asset? Corporations Find Tracking Award Difficult," *Star Tribune*, 29 March 1999, 5D.

64. R. Ho, "Attending to Attendance," *The Wall Street Journal Interactive*, 7 December 1998.

65. D. Grote, "Manager's Journal: Discipline without Punishment," *The Wall Street Journal*, 23 May 1994, A14.

66. L. Lavelle & F. Jespersen, "While the CEO Gravy Train May Be Slowing Down, It Hasn't Jumped the Rails," *Business Week*, 16 April 2001, 76.

67. G.A. Yukl, G.P. Latham, & E.D. Pursell, "The Effectiveness of Performance Incentives under Continuous and Variable Ratio Schedules of Reinforcement," *Personnel Psychology* 29 (1976): 221–231.

68. E. Pedalino & V.U. Gamboa, "Behavior Modification and Absenteeism: Intervention in One Industrial Setting," *Journal of Applied Psychology* 59 (1974): 694–698.

69. J.B. Miner, *Theories of Organizational Behavior* (Hinsdale, IL: Dryden, 1980).

70. A.M. Dickinson & A.D. Poling, "Schedules of Monetary Reinforcement in Organizational Behavior Management: Latham and Huber Revisited," *Journal of Organizational Behavior Management* 16, no. 1, (1992): 71–91.

71. F. Luthans & A.D. Stajkovic, "Reinforce for Performance: The Need to Go beyond Pay and Even Rewards," *Academy of Management Executive* 13, no. 2 (1999): 49–57.

72. J. Glater, "Management: Seasoning Compensation Helps TV Operation Improve Morale," *New York Times*. [Online] Available http://query.nytimes.com/search/abstract?res=F60717F93A5F0C748CDDAA0894D9404482, 7 March 2001.

73. K.D. Butterfield, L.K. Trevino, & G.A. Ball, "Punishment from the Manager's Perspective: A Grounded Investigation and Inductive Model," *Academy of Management Journal* 39 (1996): 1479–1512.

74. R.D. Arvey & J.M. Ivancevich, "Punishment in Organizations: A Review, Propositions, and Research Suggestions," *Academy of Management Review* 5 (1980): 123–132.

75. R.D. Arvey, G.A. Davis, & S.M. Nelson, "Use of Discipline in an Organization: A Field Study," *Journal of Applied Psychology* 69 (1984): 448–460. M.E. Schnake, "Vicarious Punishment in a Work Setting," *Journal of Applied Psychology* 71 (1986): 343–345.

76. G.A. Yukl & G.P. Latham, "Consequences of Reinforcement Schedules and Incentive Magnitudes for Employee Performance: Problems Encountered in a Field Setting," *Journal of Applied Psychology* 60 (1975): 294–298.

77. R. Maynard, "Harboring No Illusions about How to Grow," *Nation's Business* 85 (1 February 1997): 10.

78. E.A. Locke & G.P. Latham, *Goal Setting: A Motivational Technique That Works* (Englewood Cliffs, NJ: Prentice-Hall,

1984). E.A. Locke & G.P. Latham, *A Theory of Goal Setting and Task Performance* (Englewood Cliffs, NJ: Prentice-Hall, 1990).

79. T. Petzinger, Jr., "Competent Workers and a Complex Leader Keep Big Oil in Check," *The Wall Street Journal,* 4 December 1998, B1.

80. G.P. Latham & E.A. Locke, "Goal Setting—A Motivational Technique That Works," *Organizational Dynamics* 8, no. 2 (1979): 68.

81. *Ibid.*

82. Z. Zhiwei, J.A. Wallin, & R.A. Reber, "Safety Improvements: An Application of Behaviour Modification Techniques," *Journal of Applied Management Studies* 15 (2000): 135–140.

## Chapter 17

1. C. Hymowitz, "In the Lead: How Cynthia Danaher Learned to Stop Sharing and Start Leading," *The Wall Street Journal,* 16 March 1999, B1.

2. G. Colvin, "The Changing Art of Becoming Unbeatable," *Fortune,* 24 November 1997, 299–300.

3. W. Bennis, "Why Leaders Can't Lead," *Training & Development Journal* 43, no. 4 (1989).

4. "Autodesk Reports Fourth Quarter Results: Company Exceeds Pro Forma Earnings Per Share Expectations by Ten Cents," *Autodesk.* [Online] Available http://investors.autodesk.com/ireye/ir_site.zhtml?ticker=ADSK&script=410&layout=9&item_id=261616, 22 March 2002.
C. Hymowitz, "In the Lead: Some Managers Are More Than Bosses—They're Leaders, Too." *The Wall Street Journal,* 8 December 1998, B1.

5. A. Zaleznik, "Managers and Leaders: Are They Different?" *Harvard Business Review* 55 (1977): 76–78. A. Zaleznik, "The Leadership Gap," *The Washington Quarterly* 6 (1983): 32–39.

6. K. Freiberg & J. Freiberg, *Nuts! Southwest Airlines' Crazy Recipe for Business and Personal Success* (Austin, TX: Bard Press, 1996).

7. R. Rogoski, "Agent of Change," *Triangle Business Journal,* 21 May 1999, 21.

8. W. Bennis, "Why Leaders Can't Lead," *Training & Development Journal* 43, no. 4 (1989).

9. J. Cole, "Lockheed CEO Faces Criticism for Secrecy, Setbacks—Unmet Cost Targets, Failed Rocket Launches Bedevil Defense Contractor," *The Wall Street Journal,* 17 June 1999, B4.

10. J.P. Howell, D.E. Bowen, P.W. Dorfman, S. Kerr, & P.M. Podsakoff, "Substitutes for Leadership: Effective Alternatives to Ineffective Leadership," *Organizational Dynamics,* 22 June 1990, 20. S. Kerr & J.M. Jermier, "Substitutes for Leadership: Their Meaning and Measurement," *Organizational Behavior and Human Performance* 22 (1978): 375–403.

11. T.A. Stewart, A. Harrington, & M.G. Solovar, "America's Most Admired Companies: Why Leadership Matters," *Fortune,* 2 March 1998, 70.

12. R.J. House & R.M Aditya, "The Social Scientific Study Of Leadership: Quo Vadis?" *Journal of Management* 23 (1997): 409–473. S.A. Kirkpatrick & E.A. Locke, "Leadership: Do Traits Matter?" *Academy of Management Executive* 5, no. 2 (1991): 48–60.

13. *Ibid.*

14. T.A. Stewart, A. Harrington, & M.G. Solovar, "America's Most Admired Companies: Why Leadership Matters," *Fortune,* 2 March 1998, 70.

15. J.J. Gabarro, *The Dynamics of Taking Charge* (Boston: Harvard Business School Press, 1987).

16. J. Carlton, "Thinking Different: At Apple, A Fiery Jobs Often Makes Headway and Sometimes a Mess—He Knows How to Market but Clashes with Cloners and Belittles His Foes—Skewered on the Gil-O-Meter," *The Wall Street Journal,* 14 April 1998, A1.

17. S.A. Kirkpatrick & E.A. Locke, "Leadership: Do Traits Matter?" *Academy of Management Executive* 5, no. 2 (1991): 48–60.

18. E.A. Fleishman, "The Description of Supervisory Behavior," *Personnel Psychology* 37 (1953): 1–6. L.R. Katz, *New Patterns of Management* (New York: McGraw-Hill, 1961).

19. R. Charan & G. Colvin, "Why CEOs Fail," *Fortune,* 21 June 1999, 69–78.

20. J. White & N. Shirouzu, "A Stalled Revolution Puts a Ford in the Driver's Seat," *The Wall Street Journal,* 31 October 2001, A1.

21. P. Weissenberg & M.H. Kavanagh, "The Independence of Initiating Structure and Consideration: A Review of the Evidence," *Personnel Psychology* 25 (1972): 119–130.

22. R.J. House & T.R. Mitchell, "Path-Goal Theory of Leadership," *Journal of Contemporary Business* 3 (1974): 81–97. F.E. Fiedler, "A Contingency Model of Leadership Effectiveness," in ed. L. Berkowitz, *Advances in Experimental Social Psychol-* ogy (New York: Academic Press, 1964). V.H. Vroom & P.W. Yetton, *Leadership and Decision Making* (Pittsburgh: University of Pittsburgh Press, 1973). P. Hersey & K.H. Blanchard, *The Management of Organizational Behavior,* 4th ed. (Englewood Cliffs, NJ: Prentice-Hall, 1984). S. Kerr & J.M. Jermier, "Substitutes for Leadership: Their Meaning and Measurement," *Organizational Behavior and Human Performance* 22 (1978): 375–403.

23. F.E. Fiedler & M.M. Chemers, *Leadership and Effective Management* (Glenview, IL: Scott, Foresman, 1974). Fiedler, F. E., & Chemers, M. M., *Improving Leadership Effectiveness: The Leader Match Concept,* 2nd Edition (New York: John Wiley and Sons, 1984).

24. J. Carlton, "Thinking Different: At Apple, A Fiery Jobs Often Makes Headway and Sometimes a Mess—He Knows How to Market but Clashes with Cloners and Belittles His Foes—Skewered on the Gil-O-Meter," *The Wall Street Journal,* 14 April 1998, A1.

25. Fiedler, F. E., & Chemers, M. M., *Improving Leadership Effectiveness: The Leader Match Concept,* 2nd Edition (New York: John Wiley and Sons, 1984).

26. F.E. Fiedler, "The Effects of Leadership Training and Experience: A Contingency Model Interpretation," *Administrative Science Quarterly* 17, no. 4 (1972): 455. F.E. Fiedler, *A Theory of Leadership Effectiveness* (New York: McGraw-Hill, 1967).

27. L.S. Csoka & F.W. Fiedler, "The Effect of Military Leadership Training: A Test of the Contingency Model," *Organizational Behavior and Human Performance* 8 (1972): 395–407.

28. R.J. House & T.R. Mitchell, "Path-Goal Theory of Leadership," *Journal of Contemporary Business* 3 (1974): 81–97.

29. S. Branch, M. Borden, T. Maroney, & N. Tarpley, "The 100 Best Companies to Work for in America," *Fortune,* 11 January 1999, 118.

30. R.J. House & T.R. Mitchell, "Path-Goal Theory of Leadership," *Journal of Contemporary Business* 3 (1974): 81–97.

31. "Corporate America's Toughest Bosses," *Fortune,* 18 October 1993, 38.

32. B.M. Fisher & J.E. Edwards, "Consideration and Initiating Structure and Their Relationships with Leader Effectiveness: A Meta-Analysis," *Proceedings of the Academy of Management,* August 1988, 201–205.

33. M. Gimein, "Wal-Mart's Founder Made a Pact with Employees: He Would Be

Fair to Them, And They Would Work Hard for Him. It Was a Good Deal, But Can It Survive in the 24-Hour Service Economy?" *Fortune*, 18 March 2002, 120.

34. G. Bylinsky, "America's Elite Factories: Whether It's Trucks, Circuit Breakers, Or Critical Aircraft Parts, No Plant Turns Them Out with Less Waste Motion or Leaner Inventories Than These Paragons of Productivity," *Fortune*, 14 August 2000, 232.

35. *Ibid.*

36. G. Gendron, "Schwarzkopf on Leadership," *Inc.*, January 1992, 11.

37. J.C. Wofford & L.Z. Liska, "Path-Goal Theories of Leadership: A Meta-Analysis," *Journal of Management* 19 (1993): 857–876.

38. R.J. House & R.M Aditya, "The Social Scientific Study of Leadership: Quo Vadis?" *Journal of Management* 23 (1997): 409–473.

39. V.H. Vroom & A.G. Jago, *The New Theory of Leadership: Managing Participation in Organizations* (Englewood Cliffs, NJ: Prentice Hall, 1988).

40. C. Fishman, "How Teamwork Took Flight: This Team Built a Commercial Engine—And Self-Managing GE Plant—From Scratch," *Fast Company*, 1 October 1999, 188.

41. *Ibid.*

42. *Ibid.*

43. G.A. Yukl, *Leadership in Organizations*, 3rd ed. (Englewood Cliffs, NJ: Prentice-Hall, 1995).

44. B.M. Bass, *Bass & Stogdill's Handbook of Leadership: Theory, Research, and Managerial Applications* (New York: The Free Press, 1990).

45. R.D. Ireland & M.A. Hitt, "Achieving and Maintaining Strategic Competitiveness in the 21st Century: The Role of Strategic Leadership," *Academy of Management Executive* 13, no. 1 (1999): 43–57.

46. J. Useem & N. Watosn, "It's All Yours, Jeff. Now What? General Electric's Jeffrey Immelt Inherits the Best-Managed, Best-Regarded Company in America. Which Is Exactly Why His Job Looks Impossible," *Fortune*, 17 September 2001, 64.

47. J.A. Byrne, "A Close-Up Look at How America's #1 Manager Runs GE," *Business Week*, 8 June 1998, 90.

48. P. Thoms & D.B. Greenberger, "Training Business Leaders to Create Positive Organizational Visions of the Future: Is It Successful?" *Academy of Management*

*Journal* [Best Papers & Proceedings], 1995, 212–216.

49. M. Weber, *The Theory of Social and Economic Organizations*, trans. R.A. Henderson & T. Parsons (New York: Free Press, 1947).

50. D.A. Waldman & F.J. Yammarino, "CEO Charismatic Leadership: Levels-of-Management and Levels-of-Analysis Effects," *Academy of Management Review* 24, no. 2 (1999): 266–285.

51. K. Brooker, "I Built This Company, I Can Save It," *Fortune*, 30 April 2001, 94.

52. *Ibid.*

53. K.B. Lowe, K.G. Kroeck, & N. Sivasubramaniam, "Effectiveness Correlates of Transformational and Transactional Leadership: A Meta-Analytic Review of the MLQ Literature," *Leadership Quarterly* 7 (1996): 385–425.

54. J.M. Howell & B.J. Avolio, "The Ethics of Charismatic Leadership: Submission or Liberation?" *Academy of Management Executive* 6, no. 2 (1992): 43–54.

55. P. Sellers, "What Exactly Is Charisma?" *Fortune*, 15 January 1996, 68.

56. J.A. Byrne, W.C. Symonds, & J.F. Siler, "CEO Disease—Egotism Can Breed Corporate Disaster—And the Malady Is Spreading," *Business Week*, 1 April 1991, 52.

57. J.M. Howell & B.J. Avolio, "The Ethics of Charismatic Leadership: Submission or Liberation?" *Academy of Management Executive* 6, no. 2 (1992): 43–54.

58. *Ibid.*

59. J.M. Burns, *Leadership* (New York: Harper & Row, 1978). B.M. Bass, "From Transactional to Transformational Leadership: Learning to Share the Vision," *Organizational Dynamics* 18 (1990): 19–36.

60. B.M. Bass, "From Transactional to Transformational Leadership: Learning to Share the Vision," *Organizational Dynamics* 18 (1990): 19–36.

61. B.M. Bass, *A New Paradigm of Leadership: An Inquiry into Transformational Leadership* (Alexandra, VA: U.S. Army Research Institute for the Behavioral and Social Sciences, 1996).

62. J.A. Byrne, "A Close-Up Look at How America's #1 Manager Runs GE," *Business Week*, 8 June 1998, 90.

63. *Ibid.*

64. *Ibid.*

65. B.M. Bass, "From Transactional to Transformational Leadership: Learning to Share the Vision," *Organizational Dynamics* 18 (1990): 19–36.

## Chapter 18

1. E.E. Lawler, III, L.W. Porter, & A. Tannenbaum, "Manager's Attitudes toward Interaction Episodes," *Journal of Applied Psychology* 52 (1968): 423–439. H. Mintzberg, *The Nature of Managerial Work* (New York: Harper & Row, Publishers, 1973).

2. J.D. Maes, T.G. Weldy, & M.L. Icenogle, "A Managerial Perspective: Oral Communication Competency Is Most Important for Business Students in the Workplace," *Journal of Business Communication* 34 (1997): 67–80.

3. R. Lepsinger & A.D. Lucia, *The Art and Science of 360 Degree Feedback* (San Francisco: Pfeiffer, 1997).

4. I.M. Botero, "Good Communication Skills Needed Today," *The Business Journal: Serving Phoenix and the Valley of the Sun*, 21 October 1996.

5. S. Luh, "'Pulse Lunches at Asian Citibanks Feed Workers' Morale, Lower Job Turnover," *The Wall Street Journal*, 22 May 2001, B11.

6. *Ibid.*

7. E.E. Jones & K.E. Davis, "From Acts to Dispositions: The Attribution Process in Person Perception," in *Advances in Experimental and Social Psychology*, Volume 2, ed. L. Berkowitz (New York: Academic Press, 1965), 219–266. R.G. Lord & J.E. Smith, "Theoretical, Information-Processing, and Situational Factors Affecting Attribution Theory Models of Organizational Behavior," *Academy of Management Review* 8 (1983): 50–60.

8. J. Zadney & H.B. Gerard, "Attributed Intentions and Informational Selectivity," *Journal of Experimental Social Psychology* 10 (1974): 34–52.

9. J. Costello, "The Latest Entry in Growing List of Travel Irritations: Flying Fish," *The Wall Street Journal Interactive*, 22 June 1999.

10. L. Cowan, "J.B. Hunt's Drive to Improve Its Image among Truckers May Be Paying Off," *The Wall Street Journal Interactive*, 20 February 1998.

11. H.H. Kelly, *Attribution in Social Interaction* (Morristown, NJ: General Learning Press, 1971).

12. J.M. Burger, "Motivational Biases in the Attribution of Responsibility for an Accident: A Meta-Analysis of the Defensive-Attribution Hypothesis," *Psychological Bulletin* 90 (1981): 496–512.

13. D.A. Hofmann & A. Stetzer, "The Role of Safety Climate and Communication

in Accident Interpretation: Implications for Learning from Negative Events," *Academy of Management Journal* 41, No. 6 (1998): 644–657.

14. C. Perrow, *Normal Accidents: Living with High-Risk Technologies* (New York: Basic Books, 1984).

15. A.G. Miller & T. Lawson, "The Effect of an Informational Opinion on the Fundamental Attribution Error," *Journal of Personality and Social Psychology* 47 (1989): 873–896. J.M. Burger, "Changes in Attribution Errors over Time: The Ephemeral Fundamental Attribution Error," *Social Cognition* 9 (1991): 182–193.

16. E. Bernstein, "The Stagnant, Uncriticized Employee—But Those Open to Feedback Seen as Approachable, Primed for Success," *San Antonio Express-News*, 20 February 1997, 1F.

17. F. Heider, *The Psychology of Interpersonal Relations* (New York: Wiley, 1958). D.T. Miller & M. Ross, "Self-Serving Biases in Attribution of Causality: Fact or Fiction?" *Psychological Bulletin* 82 (1975): 213–225.

18. J.R. Larson, Jr., "The Dynamic Interplay between Employees' Feedback-Seeking Strategies and Supervisors' Delivery of Performance Feedback," *Academy of Management Review* 14, No. 3 (1989): 408–422.

19. J. Edwards, "Oviedo Builders Cut Down Conservation Trees: The Owner of the Under-Construction Oviedo Grove Apartments Admitted There Was Miscommunication with Workers," *Orlando Sentinel*, 12 January 1999, D1.

20. A. Pascual, "Thumb-Sucker at 37,000 Feet, Airlines Are Paying Closer Heed to Kids Who Fly Alone," *Business Week* 3 September 2001, 92.

21. M. Reddy, "The Conduit Metaphor—A Case of Frame Conflict in Our Language about Our Language," in *Metaphor and Thought*, ed. A. Ortony (Cambridge, England: Cambridge University Press, 1979), 284–324.

22. G.L. Kreps, *Organizational Communication: Theory and Practice* (New York: Longman, 1990).

23. *Ibid.*

24. D. Roth, "How to Cut Pay, Lay Off 8,000 People, And Still Have Workers Who Love You," *Fortune*, 4 February 2002, 62.

25. M. Brannigan & J.B. White, "'So Be It': Why Delta Air Lines Decided It Was Time for CEO to Take Off—Issue Was Morale, Not Profit, As a Once-Split Board Came to a Consensus," *The Wall Street Journal*, 30 May 1997, A1.

26. J. Martin & A. Kover, "Meet Six Hot Young Managers Who Have What It Takes to Lead in the 21st Century," *Fortune*, 26 June 1996, 76.

27. G.L. Kreps, *Organizational Communication: Theory and Practice* (New York: Longman, 1990).

28. K. Moran, "Web Used to Answer Rumors: UT Medical Staff Gets Truth Quickly," *Houston Chronicle*, 18 April 1999, 35.

29. W. Davis & J.R. O'Connor, "Serial Transmission of Information: A Study of the Grapevine," *Journal of Applied Communication Research* 5 (1977): 61–72.

30. M. Murray, "Waiting for the Ax to Fall—Stress Mounts as More Firms Announce Large Layoffs, But Don't Say Who or When," *The Wall Street Journal*, 13 March 2001, B1.

31. K. Furore, "Companies That Have Downsized Battle to Keep Morale High Among Remaining Workers," *Chicago Tribune*, 17 March 2002, 5.

32. C. Hymowitz, "Managing: Spread the Word, Gossip is Good," *The Wall Street Journal Interactive*, 4 October 1988.

33. W. Davis & J.R. O'Connor, "Serial Transmission of Information: A Study of the Grapevine," *Journal of Applied Communication Research* 5 (1977): 61–72. C. Hymowitz, "Managing: Spread the Word, Gossip is Good," *The Wall Street Journal Interactive*, 4 October 1988.

34. K. McDonald, "Out of Site, Still in Mind—Website Protests Morgan Stanley Ban," *New York Post*, 12 May 1999, 46.

35. W.C. Redding, *Communication within the Organization: An Interpretive View of Theory and Research* (New York: Industrial Communication Council, 1972).

36. D.T. Hall, K.L. Otazo, & G.P. Hollenbeck, "Behind Closed Doors: What Really Happens in Executive Coaching," *Organizational Dynamics* 27, No. 3 (1999): 39–53.

37. R. McGarvey, "Lords of Discipline," *Entrepreneur Magazine*, 1 January 2000, no page number available.

38. *Ibid.*

39. Anonymous, "Surviving a Work-Life Crisis: Troubles at Home Can Make It Hard for Workers to Do Their Best Job," *Buffalo News*, 24 August 1999, D1.

40. A. Mehrabian, "Communication without Words," *Psychology Today* 3 (1968): 53. A. Mehrabian, *Silent Messages* (Belmont, CA: Wadsworth, 1971). R. Harrison, *Beyond Words: An Introduction to Nonverbal Communication* (1974). A. Mehrabian, *Non-Verbal Communication* (Chicago, IL: Aldine, 1972).

41. M.L. Knapp, *Nonverbal Communication in Human Interaction*, 2nd ed. (New York: Holt, Reinhart & Winston, 1978).

42. H.M. Rosenfeld, "Instrumental Affiliative Functions of Facial and Gestural Expressions," *Journal of Personality and Social Psychology* 24 (1966): 65–72. P. Ekman, "Differential Communication of Affect by Head and Body Cues," *Journal of Personality and Social Psychology* 2 (1965): 726–735. A. Mehrabian, "Significance of Posture and Position in the Communication of Attitude and Status Relationships," *Psychological Bulletin* 71 (1969): 359–372.

43. R.B. Schmitt, "Judges Try Curbing Lawyers' Body-Language Antics," *The Wall Street Journal*, 9 September 1997, B1.

44. *Ibid.*

45. C.A. Bartlett & S. Ghoshal, "Changing the Role of Top Management: Beyond Systems to People," *Harvard Business Review*, May-June 1995, 132–142.

46. P. Roberts, "Homestyle Talkshows," *Fast Company*, October 1999, 162.

47. *Ibid.*

48. E. Wong, "A Stinging Office Memo Boomerangs; Chief Executive Is Criticized after Upbraiding Workers by E-Mail," *New York Times*, 5 April 2001, C1.

49. *Ibid.*

50. *Ibid.*

51. *Ibid.*

52. R.G. Nichols, "Do We Know How to Listen? Practical Helps in a Modern Age," in *Communication Concepts and Processes*, ed. J. DeVitor (Englewood Cliffs, NJ: Prentice-Hall, 1971). P.V. Lewis, *Organizational Communication: The Essence of Effective Management* (Columbus, OH: Grid Publishing Company, 1975).

53. E. Atwater, *I Hear You*, revised ed. (New York: Walker, 1992).

54. R. Adler & N. Towne, *Looking Out/Looking In* (San Francisco: Rinehart Press, 1975).

55. S. Thurm, "At Fast-Moving Cisco, CEO Says: Put Customers First, View

Rivals As 'Good Guys,'" *The Wall Street Journal*, 1 June 2000, B1.

56. B.D. Seyber, R.N. Bostrom, & J.H. Seibert, "Listening, Communication Abilities, and Success at Work," *Journal of Business Communication* 26 (1989): 293–303.

57. E. Atwater, *I Hear You*, revised ed. (New York: Walker, 1992).

58. N. Grammer, "The Art—and Importance—of Listening," *Toronto Globe & Mail*, 25 June 1999, B11.

59. P. Sellers, A. Diba, & E. Florian, "Get Over Yourself—Your Ego Is out of Control. You're Screwing Up Your Career," *Fortune*, 30 April 2001, 76.

60. H.H. Meyer, "A Solution to the Performance Appraisal Feedback Enigma," *Academy of Management Executive* 5, No. 1 (1991): 68–76.

61. T.D. Schellhardt, "Annual Agony: It's Time to Evaluate Your Work, And All Involved Are Groaning—Employees Dislike Reviews, Even if Favorable; Bosses Wonder How to Do Them—Some Prefer Frequent Talks," *The Wall Street Journal*, 19 November 1996, A1.

62. "Beware of Bad Boss," Graduating Engineer Online. [Online] Available http://www.graduatingengineer.com/articles/feature/10-01-01a.html, 31 March 2002.

63. C. Hymowitz, "How to Tell Employees All the Things They Don't Want to Hear," *The Wall Street Journal*, 22 August 2000, B1.

64. *Ibid.*

65. L. Reibstein, "What to Do When an Employee Is Talented and a Pain in the Neck," *The Wall Street Journal Interactive*, 8 August 1986.

66. G. Gitelson, J. Bing, & L. Laroche, "How The Cultural Trap Deepens In Cross-Border Deals," *Dealmakers*, 1 December 2001, no page numbers available.

67. From N.J. Adler, *From Boston to Beijing: Managing with a World View* (Cincinnati, Ohio: South-Western, 2002), based on A. Laurent, "The Cultural Diversity of Western Conceptions of Management," in *International Studies of Management and Organization*, vol. 13, no. 1–2 (Spring-Summer 1983), 75–96.

68. J.S. Black & M. Mendenhall, "Cross-Cultural Training Effectiveness: A Review and Theoretical Framework for Future Research," *Academy of Management Review* 15 (1990): 113–136.

69. D.A. Blackmon, "A Factory in Alabama Is the Merger in Microcosm," *The Wall Street Journal*, 8 May 1998, B1.

70. F. Trompenaars, *Riding the Waves of Culture: Understanding Diversity in Global Business* (London: Economist Books, 1994).

71. N. Forster, "Expatriates and the Impact of Cross-Cultural Training," *Human Resource Management* 10 (2000): 63–78.

72. N.J. Adler, *From Boston to Beijing: Managing with a World View* (Cincinnati, Ohio: South-Western, 2002).

73. *Ibid.*

74. *Ibid.*

75. *Ibid.*

76. *Ibid.*

77. R. Mead, *Cross-Cultural Management* (New York: Wiley, 1990).

78. *Ibid.*

79. Edward T. Hall, *The Dance of Life* (New York: Double-day, 1983).

80. F. Trompenaars, *Riding the Waves of Culture: Understanding Diversity in Global Business* (London: Economist Books, 1994).

81. N.J. Adler, *From Boston to Beijing: Managing with a World View* (Cincinnati, Ohio: South-Western, 2002).

82. E.T. Hall & M.R. Hall, *Understanding Cultural Differences* (Yarmouth, Maine: Intercultural Press, 1990).

83. E.T. Hall & W.F. Whyte, "Intercultural Communication: A Guide to Men of Action," *Human Organization* 19, No. 1 (1961): 5–12.

84. N. Libman, "French Tip: Just Walk the Walk and Talk the Talk, But Not Too Loud," *Chicago Tribune Online*, 17 March 1996.

85. H. Lancaster, "Global Managers Need Boundless Sensitivity, Rugged Constitutions," *The Wall Street Journal*, 13 October 1998, B1.

86. S. Thurm, "At Fast-Moving Cisco, CEO Says: Put Customers First, View Rivals As 'Good Guys,'" *The Wall Street Journal*, 1 June 2000, B1.

87. "Archive: Letter to Sprint employees from CEO Bill Esrey (2/6/02)," *Dotcomscoop.com*. [Online] Available http://www.dotcomscoop.com/article.php?sid=201, 2 April 2002.

88. "Ernst & Young Online: Collaborate," *Ernst & Young*. [Online] Available http://www.ey.com/global/gcr.nsf/US/Collaborate_-_EY_Online_-_Ernst_&_Young_LLP, 2 April 2002.

89. T.A. Stewart, "Telling Tales at BP Amoco: Knowledge Management at Work," *Fortune*, 7 June 1999, 220.

90. "Fortune 500 Company Steals Screen Time & Spotlight from Star Wars," *PR Newswire*, 20 May 1999.

91. C. Olofson, "Global Reach, Virtual Leadership," *Fact Company*. [Online] Available http://www.fastcompany.com/online/27/minm.html, 2 April 2002.

92. M. Campanelli & N. Friedman, "Welcome to Voice Mail Hell: The New Technology Has Become a Barrier between Salespeople and Customers. Here's How Smart Sellers Are Breaking Through," *Sales & Marketing Management* 147 (May 1995): 98–101.

93. N. Deogun, "Advice to Coke People from Their New Boss: Don't Get Too Cocky—Goizueta's Successor Puts His Stamp on the Firm in a Lot of Small Ways—Soda for the Buffett Crowd," *The Wall Street Journal*, 9 March 1998, A1.

94. E. Florian & W. Henderson, "Class of '01: Ellen Florian Spotlights Four Retirees—Their Legacies, Their Plans, And What They've Learned That Can Help You Work Better," *Fortune*, 13 August 2001, 185.

95. E.W. Morrison, "Organizational Silence: A Barrier to Change and Development in a Pluralistic World," *Academy of Management Review* 25 (2000): 706–725.

96. Toyota Motor Manufacturing, USA, *Team Member Handbook*, February 1988, 52–53. G. Dessler, "How to Earn Your Employees' Commitment," *Academy of Management Review* 13, No. 2 (1999): 58–67.

97. K. Mi, "Fedex Delivers Red-Carpet Express Service: Company Celebrates," *Korea Herald Financial Times*, 28 August 2001, no page number available.

98. S. Thurm, "At Fast-Moving Cisco, CEO Says: Put Customers First, View Rivals as 'Good Guys,'" *The Wall Street Journal*, 1 June 2000, B1.

99. D. Woodruff & K. Naughton, "Hard-Driving Boss: Ferdinand Piech Is Determined to Make Volkswagen into a Global Force," *Business Week*, 5 October 1998, 82.

100. *Ibid.*

101. B. O'Reilly, "Forget Hertz and Avis: Enterprise's Quiet Invasion of Small-Town America—Along with Quirky Hiring Practices and a Generous Supply of Doughnuts—Has Made It the Nation's Biggest Rental Car," *Fortune*, 28 October 1996, 125.

**360-degree feedback**
a performance appraisal process in which feedback is obtained from the boss, subordinates, peers and coworkers, and the employees themselves

**a-type conflict (affective conflict)**
disagreement that focuses on individual- or personally-oriented issues

**absolute comparisons**
a process in which each criterion is compared to a standard or ranked on its own merits

**accommodative strategy**
a social responsiveness strategy in which a company chooses to accept responsibility for a problem and to do all that society expects to solve that problem

**achievement-oriented leadership**
leadership style in which the leader sets challenging goals, has high expectations of employees, and displays confidence that employees will assume responsibility and put forth extraordinary effort

**acquaintance time**
cultural norm for how much time you must spend getting to know someone before the person is prepared to do business with you

**acquisition**
purchase of a company by another company

**acquisition cost**
the cost of obtaining data that you don't have

**action plan**
the specific steps, people, and resources needed to accomplish a goal

**active listening**
assuming half the responsibility for successful communica-tion by actively giving the speaker nonjudgmental feedback that shows you've accurately heard what he or she said

**address terms**
cultural norms that establish whether you should address businesspeople by their first names, family names, or titles

**adverse impact**
unintentional discrimination in which there is a substantially different rate of selection in hiring, promotion, or other employment decisions that works to the disadvantage of members of a particular race, sex, age, ethnicity, or protected group

**advocacy groups**
groups of concerned citizens who band together to try to influence the business practices of specific industries, businesses, and professions

**affective cultures**
cultures in which people display emotions and feelings when communicating

**affectivity**
the stable tendency to experience positive or negative moods and to react to things in a generally positive or negative way

**affirmative action**
purposeful steps taken by an organization to create employment opportunities for minorities and women

**age discrimination**
treating people differently (e.g., in hiring and firing, promotion, and compensation decisions) because of their age

**aggregate product plans**
plans developed to manage and monitor all new products in development at any one time

**agreeableness**
the degree to which someone is cooperative, polite, flexible, forgiving, good-natured, tolerant, and trusting

**analyzers**
an adaptive strategy that seeks to minimize risk and maximize profits by following or imitating the proven successes of prospectors

**anchoring and adjustment bias**
unrecognized tendency of decision makers to use an initial value or experience as a basis of comparison throughout the decision process

**application sharing**
communications system that allows two or more people in different locations to make changes in a document by sharing control of the software application running on one computer

**appointment time**
cultural norm for how punctual you must be when showing up for scheduled appointments or meetings

**Asia-Pacific Economic Cooperation (APEC)**
regional trade agreement between Australia, Canada, Chile, the People's Republic of China, Hong Kong, Japan, Korea, Mexico, New Zealand, Papua New Guinea, Peru, Russia, the United States, and all the members of ASEAN, except Cambodia, Laos, and Myanmar

**assemble-to-order operation**
manufacturing operation that divides manufacturing processes into separate parts or modules that are combined to create semi-customized products

**assessment centers**
a series of managerial simulations, graded by trained observers, that are used to determine applicants' capability for managerial work

**Association of South East Nations (ASEAN)**
regional trade agreement between Brunei Darussalam, Cambodia, Indonesia, Laos, Malaysia, Myanmar, the Philippines, Singapore, Thailand, and Vietnam

**association or affinity patterns**
when two or more database elements tend to occur together in a significant way

**attack**
a competitive move designed to reduce a rival's market share or profits

**attribution theory**
theory that states that we all have a basic need to understand and explain the causes of other people's behavior

**authoritarianism**
the extent to which an individual believes that there should be power and status differences within organizations

**authority**
the right to give commands, take action, and make decisions to achieve organizational objectives

**autonomous work groups**
groups that operate without managers and are completely responsible for controlling work group processes, outputs, and behavior

**autonomy**
the degree to which a job gives workers the discretion, freedom, and independence to decide how and when to accomplish the job

759

**availability bias**

unrecognized tendency of decision makers to give preference to recent information, vivid images that evoke emotions, and specific acts and behaviors that they personally observed

**average aggregate inventory**

average overall inventory during a particular time period

**awareness training**

training that is designed to raise employees' awareness of diversity issues and to challenge the underlying assumptions or stereotypes they may have about others

**BCG matrix**

A portfolio strategy, developed by the Boston Consulting Group, that managers use to categorize the corporation's businesses by growth rate and relative market share, helping them decide how to invest corporate funds

**background checks**

procedures used to verify the truthfulness and accuracy of information that applicants provide about themselves and to uncover negative, job-related background information not provided by applicants

**balanced scorecard**

measurement of organizational performance in four equally important areas: finances, customers, internal operations, and innovation and learning

**bar code**

a visual pattern that represents numerical data by varying the thickness and pattern of vertical bars

**bargaining power of buyers**

a measure of the influence that customers have on a firm's prices

**batch production**

manufacturing operation that produces goods in large batches in standard lot sizes

**behavior control**

regulation of the behaviors and actions that workers perform on the job

**behavioral addition**

the process of having managers and employees perform new behaviors that are central to and symbolic of the new organizational culture that a company wants to create

**behavioral formality**

workplace atmosphere characterized by routine and regimen, specific rules about how to behave, and interpersonal detachment

**behavioral informality**

workplace atmosphere characterized by spontaneity, casualness, and interpersonal familiarity

**behavioral observation scales (BOS)**

rating scales that indicate the frequency with which workers perform specific behaviors that are representative of the job dimensions critical to successful job performance

**behavioral substitution**

the process of having managers and employees perform new behaviors central to the "new" organizational culture in place of behaviors that were central to the "old" organizational culture

**balance sheets**

accounting sheets that provide a snapshot of a company's financial position at a particular time

**bargaining power of suppliers**

a measure of the influence that suppliers of parts, materials, and services to firms in an industry have on the prices of these inputs

**benchmarking**

the process of identifying outstanding practices, processes, and standards in other companies and adapting them to your company

**biographical data (biodata)**

extensive surveys that ask applicants questions about their personal backgrounds and life experiences

**bona fide occupational qualification (BFOQ)**

an exception in employment law that permits gender, age, religion, and so forth, to be used when making employment decisions, but only if they are "reasonably necessary to the normal operation of that particular business." BFOQs are strictly monitored by the Equal Employment Opportunity Commission.

**boundaryless organization**

a speedy, responsive, and flexible organization in which vertical, horizontal, external, and geographic boundaries are removed or minimized

**bounded rationality**

decision-making process restricted in the real world by limited resources, incomplete and imperfect information, and managers' limited decision-making capabilities

**brainstorming**

a decision-making method in which group members build on each others' ideas to generate as many alternative solutions as possible

**budgeting**

quantitative planning through which managers decide how to allocate available money to best accomplish company goals

**budgets**

qualitative plans through which managers decide how to allocate available money to best accomplish company goals

**bureaucratic control**

use of hierarchical authority to influence employee behavior by rewarding or punishing employees for compliance or noncompliance with organizational policies, rules, and procedures

**bureaucratic immunity**

the ability to make changes without first getting approval from managers or other parts of an organization

**business confidence indices**

indices that show managers' level of confidence about future business growth

**buyer dependence**

degree to which a supplier relies on a buyer because of the importance of that buyer to the supplier and the difficulty of selling its products to other buyers

**c-type conflict (cognitive conflict)**

disagreement that focuses on problem- and issue-related differences of opinion

**cafeteria benefit plans (flexible benefit plans)**

plans that allow employees to choose which benefits they receive, up to a certain dollar value

**cash cow**

a company with a large share of a slow-growing market

**cash flow analysis**

type of analysis that predicts how changes in a business will affect its ability to take in more cash than it pays out

**centralization of authority**

the location of most authority at the upper levels of the organization

**chain of command**

the vertical line of authority that clarifies who reports to whom throughout the organization

**change agent**

the person formally in charge of guiding a change effort

**change forces**

forces that produce differences in the form, quality, or condition of an organization over time

**change intervention**

the process used to get workers and managers to change their behavior and work practices

**character of the rivalry**

a measure of the intensity of competitive behavior between companies in an industry

**charismatic leadership**

the behavioral tendencies and personal characteristics of leaders that create an exceptionally strong relationship between them and their followers

**closure**
tendency to fill in gaps of missing information by assuming that what we don't know is consistent with what we already know

**coaching**
communicating with someone for the direct purpose of improving the person's on-the-job performance or behavior

**coercion**
using formal power and authority to force others to change

**cognitive ability tests**
tests that measure the extent to which applicants have abilities in perceptual speed, verbal comprehension, numerical aptitude, general reasoning, and spatial aptitude

**cognitive maps**
graphic depictions of how managers believe environmental factors relate to possible organizational actions

**cohesiveness**
the extent to which team members are attracted to a team and motivated to remain in it

**commission**
a compensation system in which employees earn a percentage of each sale they make

**common-enemy mission**
company goal of defeating a corporate rival

**communication**
the process of transmitting information from one person or place to another

**communication cost**
the cost of transmitting information from one place to another

**communication medium**
the method used to deliver an oral or written message

**company hotlines**
phone numbers that anyone in the company can anonymously call to leave information for upper management

**company vision**
a company's purpose or reason for existing

**compensation**
the financial and nonfinancial rewards that organizations give employees in exchange for their work

**competitive advantage**
providing greater value for customers than competitors can

**competitive analysis**
a process for monitoring competitors that involves identifying competitors, anticipating their moves, and determining their strengths and weaknesses

**competitive inertia**
a reluctance to change strategies or competitive practices that have been successful in the past

**competitors**
companies in the same industry that sell similar products or services to customers

**complex environment**
an environment with many environmental factors

**complex matrix**
a form of matrix departmentalization in which project and functional managers report to matrix managers, who help them sort out conflicts and problems

**component parts inventories**
the basic parts used in manufacturing that are fabricated from raw materials

**compression approach to innovation**
an approach to innovation that assumes that incremental innovation can be planned using a series of steps, and that compressing those steps can speed innovation

**concentration of effect**
the total harm or benefit that an act produces on the average person

**conceptual skill**
the ability to see the organization as a whole, how the different parts affect each other, and how the company fits into or is affected by its environment

**concertive control**
regulation of workers' behavior and decisions through work group values and beliefs

**concurrent control**
a mechanism for gathering information about performance deficiencies as they occur, eliminating or shortening the delay between performance and feedback

**conditions of certainty**
conditions in which decision makers have complete information and knowledge of all possible outcomes

**conditions of risk**
conditions in which decision makers face a very real possibility of making the wrong decision

**conditions of satisfaction**
a statement of the specific, measurable, and observable conditions that must be met in order for change to be successful

**conditions of uncertainty**
conditions in which decision makers don't know the odds of winning or losing

**conduit metaphor**
the mistaken assumption that senders can pipe their intended messages directly into the heads of receivers with perfect clarity and without noise or perceptual filters interfering with the receivers' understanding of the message

**conferencing system**
communications system that lets two or more users in different locations see and talk to each other as if they were in the same room

**conscientiousness**
the degree to which someone is organized, hardworking, responsible, persevering, thorough, and achievement-oriented

**consideration**
the extent to which a leader is friendly, approachable, supportive, and shows concern for employees

**consistent organizational cultures**
when a company actively defines and teaches organizational values, beliefs, and attitudes

**constructive feedback**
feedback intended to be helpful, corrective, and/or encouraging

**contingency theory**
leadership theory that states that in order to maximize work group performance, leaders must be matched to the situation that best fits their leadership style

**continuous change**
change that occurs when change forces are strong and resistance forces are weak

**continuous-flow production**
manufacturing operation that produces goods in a continuous, rather than a discrete, rate

**continuous improvement**
an organization's ongoing commitment to constantly assess and improve the processes and procedures used to create products and services

**continuous reinforcement schedule**
schedule that requires a consequence to be administered following every instance of a behavior

**control**
a regulatory process of establishing standards to achieve organizational goals, comparing actual performance against the standards, and taking corrective action, when necessary

**control loss**
situation in which behavior and work procedures do not conform to standards

**controlling**
monitoring progress toward goal achievement and taking corrective action when needed

**conventional level of moral development**
second level of moral development in which people

make decisions that conform to societal expectations

**conversations for closure**
conversations that end the change process by indicating that the work is done and the change process is complete

**conversations for performance**
conversations about action plans, in which managers and workers make specific requests and promise specific results

**conversations for understanding**
conversations that generate a deeper understanding of why change is needed, what problems have been occurring, and what might be done to solve those problems

**cooperative contract**
an agreement in which a foreign business owner pays a company a fee for the right to conduct that business in his or her country

**core capabilities**
the internal decision-making routines, problem-solving processes, and organizational cultures that determine how efficiently inputs can be turned into outputs

**core firms**
the central companies in a strategic group

**corporate talk shows**
televised company meetings that allow remote audiences (employees) to pose questions to the show's host and guests

**corporate-level strategy**
the overall organizational strategy that addresses the question "What business or businesses are we in or should we be in?"

**cost leadership**
the positioning strategy of producing a product or service of acceptable quality at consistently lower production costs than competitors can, so that the firm can offer the product or service at the lowest price in the industry

**counseling**
communicating with someone about non-job-related

issues that may be affecting or interfering with the person's performance

**country of manufacture**
country where product is made and assembled

**country of origin**
the home country for a company, where its headquarters is located

**creative work environments**
workplace cultures in which workers perceive that new ideas are welcomed, valued, and encouraged

**creativity**
the production of novel and useful ideas

**cross-cultural communication**
transmitting information from a person in one country or culture to a person from another country or culture

**cross-functional team**
team composed of employees from different functional areas of the organization

**cross training**
training team members how to do all or most of the jobs performed by the other team members

**customer defections**
performance assessment in which companies identify which customers are leaving and measure the rate at which they are leaving

**customer departmentalization**
organizing work and workers into separate units responsible for particular kinds of customers

**customer focus**
an organizational goal to concentrate on meeting customers' needs at all levels of the organization

**customer satisfaction**
an organizational goal to provide products or services that meet or exceed customers' expectations

**customs classification**
a classification assigned by government officials that affects the size of the tariff and consideration of import quotas

**cybernetic**
the process of steering or keeping on course

**cybernetic feasibility**
the extent to which it is possible to implement each step in the control process

**data clusters**
when three or more database elements occur together (i.e., cluster) in a significant way

**data encryption**
transforms data into complex, scrambled digital codes that can only be unencrypted by authorized users who possess unique decryption keys

**data mining**
the process of discovering unknown patterns and relationships in large amounts of data

**data warehouse**
stores huge amounts of data that have been prepared for data mining analysis by being cleaned of errors and redundancy

**decentralization**
the location of a significant amount of authority in the lower levels of the organization

**decision criteria**
the standards used to guide judgments and decisions

**decision making**
the process of choosing a solution from available alternatives

**decision rule**
set of criteria that alternative solutions must meet to be acceptable to the decision maker

**decision support system (DSS)**
an information system that helps managers to understand specific kinds of problems and potential solutions and to analyze the impact of different decision options using "what if" scenarios

**decoding**
the process by which the receiver translates the written, verbal, or symbolic form of a message into an understood message

**deep-level diversity**
differences communicated through verbal and nonverbal behaviors, such as personality and attitudes, that are learned only through extended interaction with others

**defenders**
an adaptive strategy aimed at defending strategic positions by seeking moderate, steady growth and by offering a limited range of high-quality products and services to a well-defined set of customers

**defensive bias**
the tendency for people to perceive themselves as personally and situationally similar to someone who is having difficulty or trouble

**defensive strategy**
a social responsiveness strategy in which a company chooses to admit responsibility for a problem but do the least required to meet societal expectations

**de-forming**
a reversal of the forming stage, in which team members position themselves to control pieces of the team, avoid each other, and isolate themselves from team leaders

**degree of dependence**
the extent to which a company needs a particular resource to accomplish its goals

**delegation of authority**
the assignment of direct authority and responsibility to a subordinate to complete tasks for which the manager is normally responsible

**Delphi technique**
a decision-making method in which a panel of experts responds to questions and to each other until reaching agreement on an issue

**de-norming**
a reversal of the norming stage, in which team performance begins to decline as the size, scope, goal, or members of the team change

**departmentalization**
subdividing work and workers into separate organizational units responsible for completing particular tasks

**dependent demand systems**
inventory system in which the level of inventory depends on the number of finished units to be produced

**design competition**
competition between old and new technologies to establish a new technological standard or dominant design

**design iteration**
a cycle of repetition in which a company tests a prototype of a new product or service, improves on that design, and then builds and tests the improved prototype

**desktop videoconferencing**
communications system that allows two or more people in different locations to use video cameras and computer monitors to see and hear each other and share documents

**de-storming**
a reversal of the storming phase, in which the team's comfort level decreases, team cohesion weakens, and angry emotions and conflict may flare

**destructive feedback**
feedback that disapproves without any intention of being helpful and almost always causes a negative or defensive reaction in the recipient

**devil's advocacy**
a decision-making method in which an individual or a subgroup is assigned the role of a critic

**dialectical inquiry**
a decision-making method in which decision makers state the assumptions of a proposed solution (a thesis) and generate a solution that is the opposite (antithesis) of that solution

**dictionary rule**
decision rule that requires decision makers to rank criteria in order of importance and then test alternative solutions

against those criteria in rank order, so that alternatives that meet the most important criterion must then meet the second most important criterion, and so on

**differentiation**
the positioning strategy of providing a product or service that is sufficiently different from competitors' offerings such that customers are willing to pay a premium price for it

**direct competition**
the rivalry between two companies that offer similar products and services, acknowledge each other as rivals, and act and react to each other's strategic actions

**direct foreign investment**
a method of investment in which a company builds a new business or buys an existing business in a foreign county

**directive leadership**
leadership style in which the leader lets employees know precisely what is expected of them, gives them specific guidelines for performing tasks, schedules work, sets standards of performance, and makes sure that people follow standard rules and regulations

**disability**
a mental or physical impairment that substantially limits one or more major life activities

**disability discrimination**
treating people differently because of their disabilities

**discontinuous change**
sudden change that occurs when change and resistance forces are strong and resistance forces can no longer hold back the change forces

**discretionary responsibilities**
the expectation that a company will voluntarily serve a social role beyond its economic, legal, and ethical responsibilities

**discussion time**
cultural norm for how much time should be spent in discussion with others

**disparate treatment**
intentional discrimination that occurs when people are purposely not given the same hiring, promotion, or membership opportunities because of their race, sex, age, ethnic group, national origin, or religious beliefs

**disposition**
the tendency to respond to situations and events in a predetermined manner

**disseminator role**
the informational role managers play when they share information with others in their departments or companies

**distal goals**
long-term or primary goals

**distinctive competence**
what a company can make, do, or perform better than its competitors

**distributive justice**
the perceived degree to which outcomes and rewards are fairly distributed or allocated

**disturbance handler role**
the decisional role managers play when they respond to severe problems that demand immediate action

**diversification**
a strategy for reducing risk by buying a variety of items (stocks or, in the case of a corporation, types of businesses), so that the failure of one stock or one business does not doom the entire portfolio

**diversity**
a variety of demographic, cultural, and personal differences among an organization's employees and the customers

**diversity audits**
formal assessments that measure employee and management attitudes, investigate the extent to which people are advantaged or disadvantaged with respect to hiring and promotions, and review companies' diversity-related policies and procedures

**diversity pairing**
mentoring program in which people of different cultural

backgrounds, genders, or races/ethnicities are paired together to get to know each other and change stereotypical beliefs and attitudes

**dog**
a company with a small share of a slow-growing market

**document conferencing**
communications system that allows two or more people in different locations to simultaneously view and make comments about a document

**dominant design**
a new technological design or process that becomes the accepted market standard

**downsizing**
the planned elimination of jobs in a company

**downward communication**
communication that flows from higher to lower levels in an organization

**dynamic environment**
environment in which the rate of change is fast

**dysfunctional turnover**
loss of high-performing employees who voluntarily choose to leave a company

**early retirement incentive programs (ERIPs)**
programs that offer financial benefits to employees to encourage them to retire early

763

**economic order quantity (EOQ)**
a system of formulas that minimizes ordering and holding costs and helps determine how much and how often inventory should be ordered

**economic responsibility**
the expectation that a company will make a profit by producing a valued product or service

**economic value added (EVA)**
the amount by which company profits (revenues, minus expenses, minus taxes) exceed the cost of capital in a given year

**efficiency**
getting work done with minimum of effort, expense, or waste

**effectiveness**

accomplishing tasks that help fulfill organizational objectives

**electronic brainstorming**

a decision-making method in which group members use computers to build on each others' ideas and generate many alternative solutions

**electronic data interchange (EDI)**

the direct electronic transmission of purchase and ordering information from one company's computer system to another company's computer system

**electronic scanner**

an electronic device that converts printed text and pictures into digital images

**emotional stability**

the degree to which someone is angry, depressed, anxious, emotional, insecure, and excitable

**empathetic listening**

understanding the speaker's perspective and personal frame of reference and giving feedback that conveys that understanding to the speaker

**employee involvement team**

team that provides advice or makes suggestions to management concerning specific issues

**employee separation**

the voluntary or involuntary loss of an employee

**employee stock ownership plans (ESOPs)**

a compensation system that awards employees shares of company stock in addition to their regular compensation

**employee turnover**

loss of employees who voluntarily choose to leave the company

**employment benefits**

a method of rewarding employees that includes virtually any kind of compensation other than wages or salaries

**employment references**

sources such as previous employers or co-workers who can provide job-related information about job candidates

**empowering workers**

permanently passing decision-making authority and responsibility from managers to workers by giving them the information and resources they need to make and carry out good decisions

**empowerment**

feelings of intrinsic motivation, in which workers perceive their work to have impact and meaning, and perceive themselves to be competent and capable of self-determination

**encoding**

putting a message into a written, verbal, or symbolic form that can be recognized and understood by the receiver

**entrepreneur role**

the decisional role managers play when they adapt themselves, their subordinates, and their units to incremental change

**entrepreneurial orientation**

the set of processes, practices, and decision-making activities that lead to new entry, characterized by five dimensions: autonomy, innovativeness, risk-taking, proactiveness, and competitive aggressiveness

**entrepreneurship**

the process of entering new or established markets with new goods or services

**environmental change**

the rate at which a company's general and specific environments change

**environmental complexity**

the number of external factors in the environment that affect organizations

**environmental munificence**

degree to which an organization's external environment has an abundance or scarcity of critical organizational resources

**environmental scanning**

searching the environment for important events or issues that might affect an organization

**equity theory**

theory that states that people will be motivated when they perceive that they are being treated fairly

**era of ferment**

phase of a technology cycle characterized by technological substitution and design competition

**escalation of commitment**

the tendency for a person who has already made a decision to more strongly support that original decision despite negative information that clearly indicates it was wrong

**ethical behavior**

behavior that conforms to a society's accepted principles of right and wrong

**ethical charismatics**

charismatic leaders that provide developmental opportunities for followers, are open to positive and negative feedback, recognize others' contributions, share information, and have moral standards that emphasize the larger interests of the group, organization, or society

**ethical intensity**

the degree of concern people have about an ethical issue

**ethical responsibility**

the expectation that a company will not violate accepted principles of right and wrong when conducting its business

**ethics**

the set of moral principles or values that defines right and wrong for a person or group

**evaluation apprehension**

fear of what others will think of your ideas

**executive information system (EIS)**

data processing system that uses internal and external data sources to provide the information needed to monitor and analyze organizational performance

**expatriate**

someone who lives and works outside his or her native country

**expectancy**

the perceived relationship between effort and performance

**expectancy theory**

theory that states that people will be motivated to the extent to which they believe that their efforts will lead to good performance, that good performance will be rewarded, and that they will be offered attractive rewards

**experiential approach to innovation**

an approach to innovation that assumes a highly uncertain environment, and uses intuition, flexible options, and hands-on experience to reduce uncertainty and accelerate learning and understanding

**expert system**

information system that contains the specialized knowledge and decision rules used by experts and experienced decision makers, so that nonexperts can draw on this knowledge base to make decisions

**exporting**

selling domestically produced products to customers in foreign countries

**external environments**

all events outside a company that have the potential to influence or affect it

**external locus of control**

the belief that what happens to you is largely the result of factors beyond your control

**external recruiting**

the process of developing a pool of qualified job applicants from outside the company

**extinction**

reinforcement in which a positive consequence is no longer allowed to follow a previously reinforced behavior, thus weakening the behavior

**extranet**

allows companies to exchange information and conduct transactions with outsiders by providing them direct, Web-based access to authorized parts of a company's intranet or information system

**extraversion**
the degree to which someone is active, assertive, gregarious, sociable, talkative, and energized by others

**extrinsic reward**
a reward that is tangible, visible to others, and given to employees contingent on the performance of specific tasks or behaviors

**feedback**
the amount of information the job provides to workers about their work performance

**feedback control**
a mechanism for gathering information about performance deficiencies after they occur

**feedback to sender**
in the communication process, a return message to the sender that indicates the receiver's understanding of the message

**feedforward control**
a mechanism for monitoring performance inputs rather than outputs to prevent or minimize performance deficiencies before they occur

**figurehead role**
the interpersonal role managers play when they perform ceremonial duties

**financial ratios**
calculations typically used to track a business's liquidity (cash), efficiency, and profitability over time compared to other businesses in its industry

**finished goods inventories**
the final outputs of manufacturing operations

**firewall**
hardware or software device that sits between the computers in an internal organizational network and outside networks, such as the Internet

**firm-level strategy**
corporate strategy that addresses the question "How should we compete against a particular firm?"

**first-line managers**
managers who train and supervise performance of non-managerial employees and who are directly responsible for producing the company's products or services

**first-mover advantage**
the strategic advantage that companies earn by being the first to use new information technology to substantially lower costs or to make a product or service different from competitors

**fixed interval reinforcement schedule**
intermittent schedule in which consequences follow a behavior only after a fixed time has elapsed

**fixed ratio reinforcement schedule**
intermittent schedule in which consequences are delivered following a specific number of behaviors

**flow**
a psychological state of effortlessness, in which you become completely absorbed in what you're doing and time seems to pass quickly

**focus strategy**
the positioning strategy of using cost leadership or differentiation to produce a specialized product or service for a limited, specially targeted group of customers in a particular geographic region or market segment

**formal communication channel**
the system of official channels that carry organizationally approved messages and information

**forming**
the first stage of team development in which team members meet each other, form initial impressions, and begin to establish team norms

**four-fifths (or 80 percent) rule**
a rule of thumb used by the courts and the EEOC to determine whether there is evidence of disparate impact. A

violation of this rule occurs when the selection rate for a protected group is less than 80 percent or four-fifths of the selection rate for a non-protected group.

**franchise**
a collection of networked firms in which the manufacturer or marketer of a product or service, the franchisor, licenses the entire business to another person or organization, the franchisee

**Free Trade Area of the Americas (FTAA)**
regional trade agreement that, when signed, will create a regional trading zone encompassing 36 countries in North and South America

**freeware**
computer software that is free to whoever wants it

**functional departmentalization**
organizing work and workers into separate units responsible for particular business functions or areas of expertise

**functional turnover**
loss of poor-performing employees who voluntarily choose to leave a company

**fundamental attribution error**
the tendency to ignore external causes of behavior and to attribute other people's actions to internal causes

**gainsharing**
compensation system in which companies share the financial value of performance gains, such as productivity, cost savings, or quality, with their workers

**gender discrimination**
treating people differently because of their gender

**General Agreement on Tariffs and Trade (GATT)**
worldwide trade agreement that reduces and eliminates tariffs, limits government subsidies, and protects intellectual property

**General Electric Workout**
a three-day meeting in which managers and employees

from different levels and parts of an organization quickly generate and act on solutions to specific business problems

**general environment**
the economic, technological, sociocultural, and political trends that indirectly affect all organizations

**generational change**
change based on incremental improvements to a dominant technological design such that the improved technology is fully backward compatible with the older technology

**geographic departmentalization**
organizing work and workers into separate units responsible for doing business in particular geographical areas

**glass ceiling**
the invisible barrier that prevents women and minorities from advancing to the top jobs in organizations

**global business**
the buying and selling of goods and services by people from different countries

**global new ventures**
new companies with sales, employees, and financing in different countries that are founded with an active global strategy

**goal**
a target, objective, or result that someone tries to accomplish

**goal acceptance**
the extent to which people consciously understand and agree to goals

**goal commitment**
the determination to achieve a goal

**goal difficulty**
the extent to which a goal is hard or challenging to accomplish

**goal-setting theory**
theory that states that people will be motivated to the extent to which they accept specific, challenging goals and receive feedback that indicates

their progress toward goal achievement

**goal specificity**
the extent to which goals are detailed, exact, and unambiguous

**government import standard**
specified to protect the health and safety of citizens

**grand strategy**
a broad corporate-level strategic plan used to achieve strategic goals and guide the strategic alterna-tives that managers of individual businesses or subunits may use

**groupthink**
a barrier to good decision making caused by pressure within the group for members to agree with each other

**growth strategy**
strategy that focuses on increasing profits, revenues, market share, or the number of places in which the company does business

**hearing**
the act or process of perceiving sounds

**holding cost**
the cost of keeping inventory until it is used or sold, including storage, insurance, taxes, obsolescence, and opportunity costs

**horizontal communication**
communication that flows among managers and workers who are at the same organizational level

**hostile work environment**
form of sexual harassment in which unwelcome and demeaning sexually related behavior creates an intimidating and offensive work environment

**human resource information systems (HRIS)**
computerized systems for gathering, analyzing, storing, and disseminating information related to the HRM process

**human resource management**
the process of finding, developing, and keeping the right

people to form a qualified work force

**human resource planning (HRP)**
using an organization's goals and strategy to forecast the organization's human resource needs in terms of attracting, developing, and keeping a qualified work force

**human skill**
the ability to work well with others

**ISO 9000**
a series of five international standards, from ISO 9000 to ISO 9004, for achieving consistency in quality management and quality assurance in companies throughout the world

**imperfectly imitable resource**
a resource that is impossible or extremely costly or difficult for other firms to duplicate

**income statements**
types of statements, also called "profit and loss statements," that show what has happened to an organization's income, expenses, and net profit over a period of time

**incremental change**
the phase of a technology cycle in which companies innovate by lowering costs and improving the functioning and performance of the dominant technological design

**independent demand system**
inventory system in which the level of one kind of inventory does not depend on another

**individualism-collectivism**
the degree to which a person believes that people should be self-sufficient and that loyalty to one's self is more important than loyalty to team or company

**industry regulation**
regulations and rules that govern the business practices and procedures of specific industries, businesses, and professions

**industry-level strategy**
corporate strategy that addresses the question "How should we compete in this industry?"

**informal communication channel ("grapevine")**
the transmission of messages from employee to employee outside of formal communication channels

**information**
useful data that can influence peoples' choices and behavior

**information overload**
situation in which decision makers have too much information to attend to

**initiating structure**
the degree to which a leader structures the roles of followers by setting goals, giving directions, setting deadlines, and assigning tasks

**initiative conversations**
conversations that start the change process by discussing what should or needs to be done to bring about change

**innovation streams**
patterns of innovation over time that can create sustainable competitive advantage

**inputs**
in equity theory, the contributions employees make to the organization

**instrumentality**
the perceived relationship between performance and rewards

**intermittent reinforcement schedule**
schedule in which consequences are delivered after a specified or average time has elapsed or after a specified or average number of behaviors has occurred

**internal environment**
the events and trends inside an organization that affect management, employees, and organizational culture

**internal locus of control**
the belief that what happens to you is largely the result of your own actions

**internal motivation**
motivation that comes from the job itself rather than from outside rewards

**internal recruiting**
the process of developing a pool of qualified job applicants from people who already work in the company

**internal-transformation mission**
company goal of remaining competitive by making dramatic changes in the company

**Internet**
a global network of networks that allows users to send and retrieve data from anywhere in the world

**interorganizational process**
a collection of activities that take place among companies to transform inputs into outputs that customers value

**interpersonal skills**
skills, such as listening, communicating, questioning, and providing feedback, that enable people to have effective working relationships with others

**interviews**
selection tool in which company representatives ask job applicants job-related questions to determine whether they are qualified for the job

**intranets**
private company networks that allow employees to easily access, share, and publish information using Internet software

**intraorganizational process**
the collection of activities that take place within an organization to transform inputs into outputs that customers value

**intrapreneurship**
entrepreneurship within an existing organization

**intrinsic reward**
a natural reward associated with performing a task or activity for its own sake

**inventory**
the amount and number of raw materials, parts, and fin-

ished products that a company has in its possession

**inventory turnover**
the number of times per year that a company sells or "turns over" its average inventory

**job analysis**
a purposeful, systematic process for collecting information on the important work-related aspects of a job

**job characteristics model (JCM)**
an approach to job redesign that seeks to formulate jobs in ways that motivate workers and lead to positive work outcomes

**job description**
a written description of the basic tasks, duties, and responsibilities required of an employee holding a particular job

**job design**
the number, kind, and variety of tasks that individual workers perform in doing their jobs

**job enlargement**
increasing the number of different tasks that a worker performs within one particular job

**job enrichment**
increasing the number of tasks in a particular job and giving workers the authority and control to make meaningful decisions about their work

**job evaluation**
a process that determines the worth of each job in a company by evaluating the market value of the knowledge, skills, and requirements needed to perform it

**job rotation**
periodically moving workers from one specialized job to another to give them more variety and the opportunity to use different skills

**job shops**
manufacturing operations that handle custom orders or small batch jobs

**job specialization**
a job composed of a small part of a larger task or process

**job specifications**
a written summary of the qualifications needed to successfully perform a particular job

**joint venture**
a strategic alliance in which two existing companies collaborate to form a third, independent company

**just-in-time (JIT) inventory system**
inventory system in which component parts arrive from suppliers just as they are needed at each stage of production

**kanban**
a ticket-based system that indicates when to reorder inventory

**kinesics**
movements of the body and face

**knowledge**
the understanding that one gains from information

**leader role**
the interpersonal role managers play when they motivate and encourage workers to accomplish organizational objectives

**leader-member relations**
the degree to which followers respect, trust, and like their leaders

**leadership**
the process of influencing others to achieve group or organizational goals

**leadership neutralizers**
subordinate, task, or organizational characteristics that can interfere with a leader's actions or make it impossible for a leader to influence followers' performance

**leadership style**
the way a leader generally behaves toward followers

**leadership substitutes**
subordinate, task, or organizational characteristics that make leaders redundant or unnecessary

**leading**
inspiring and motivating workers to work hard to achieve organizational goals

**learning-based planning**
learning better ways of achieving goals by continually testing, changing, and improving plans and strategies

**legal responsibility**
the expectation that a company will obey society's laws and regulations

**liaison role**
the interpersonal role managers play when they deal with people outside their units

**licensing**
agreement in which a domestic company, the licensor, receives royalty payments for allowing another company, the licensee, to produce its product, sell its service, or use its brand name in a specified foreign market

**line authority**
the right to command immediate subordinates in the chain of command

**line function**
an activity that contributes directly to creating or selling the company's products

**line-flow production**
manufacturing processes that are pre-established, occur in a serial or linear manner, and are dedicated to making one type of product

**listening**
making a conscious effort to hear

**locus of control**
the degree to which individuals believe that their actions can influence what happens to them

**Maastricht Treaty of Europe**
regional trade agreement between most European countries

**Machiavellianism**
the extent to which individuals believe that virtually any type of behavior is acceptable in trying to satisfy their needs or meet their goals

**magnitude of consequences**
the total harm or benefit derived from an ethical decision

**make-to-order operation**
manufacturing operation that does not start processing or assembling products until a customer order is received

**make-to-stock operation**
manufacturing operation that orders parts and assembles standardized products before receiving customer orders

**management**
getting work done through others

**management by objectives (MBO)**
a four-step process in which managers and employees discuss and select goals, develop tactical plans, and meet regularly to review progress toward goal accomplishment

**manufacturing flexibility**
degree to which manufacturing operations can easily and quickly change the number, kind, and characteristics of products they produce

**market commonality**
the degree to which two companies have overlapping products, services, or customers in multiple markets

**materials requirement planning (MRP)**
a production and inventory system that determines the production schedule, production batch sizes, and inventory needed to complete final products

**matrix departmentalization**
a hybrid organizational structure in which two or more forms of departmentalization, most often product and functional, are used together

**maximizing**
choosing the best alternative

**mechanistic organization**
organization characterized by specialized jobs and responsibilities, precisely defined, unchanging roles, and a rigid chain of command based on

centralized authority and vertical communication

**media advocacy**
an advocacy group tactic of framing issues as public issues, exposing questionable, exploitative, or unethical practices, and forcing media coverage by buying media time or creating controversy that is likely to receive extensive news coverage

**meta-analysis**
a study of studies, a statistical approach that provides the best scientific estimate of how well management theories and practices work

**middle managers**
managers responsible for setting objectives consistent with top management's goals, and planning and implementing subunit strategies for achieving these objectives

**milestones**
formal project review points used to assess progress and performance

**minimum threshold rule**
decision rule that requires alternative solutions to meet all of the established minimum decision criteria

**mission**
statement of a company's overall goal that unifies company-wide efforts toward its vision, stretches and challenges the organization, and possesses a finish line and a time-frame

**modular organization**
an organization that outsources noncore business activities to outside companies, suppliers, specialists, or consultants

**monitor role**
the informational role managers play when they scan their environment for information

**monochronic cultures**
cultures in which people tend to do one thing at a time and view time as linear

**mood linkage**
a phenomenon in which one worker's negative affectivity

and bad moods can spread to others

**Moore's law**
prediction that every 18 months, the cost of computing will drop by 50 percent as computer-processing power doubles

**motivation**
the set of forces that initiates, directs, and makes people persist in their efforts to accomplish a goal

**motivation to manage**
an assessment of how enthusiastic employees are about managing the work of others

**multifactor productivity**
an overall measure of performance that indicates how much labor, capital, materials, and energy it takes to produce an output

**multifunctional teams**
work teams composed of people from different departments

**multinational corporation**
corporation that owns businesses in two or more countries

**multivariable testing**
a systematic approach of experimentation used to analyze and evaluate potential solutions

**national culture**
the set of shared values and beliefs that affects the perceptions, decisions, and behavior of the people from a particular country

**needs**
the physical or psychological requirements that must be met to ensure survival and well being

**needs assessment**
the process of identifying and prioritizing the learning needs of employees

**negative affectivity**
personality trait in which individuals tend to notice and focus on the negative aspects of themselves and their environments

**negative frame**
couching a problem in terms of a loss, thus influencing decision makers toward becoming risk-seeking

**negative reinforcement**
reinforcement that strengthens behavior by withholding an unpleasant consequence when employees perform a specific behavior

**negotiator role**
the decisional role managers play when they negotiate schedules, projects, goals, outcomes, resources, and employee raises

**neutral cultures**
cultures in which people do not display emotions and feelings when communicating

**noise**
anything that interferes with the transmission of the intended message

**nominal group technique**
a decision-making method that begins and ends by having group members quietly write down and evaluate ideas to be shared with the group

**nonsubstitutable resource**
a resource, without equivalent substitutes or replacements, that produces value or competitive advantage

**nontariff barriers**
nontax methods of increasing the cost or reducing the volume of imported goods

**nonverbal communication**
any communication that doesn't involve words

**normative control**
regulation of workers' behavior and decisions through widely shared organizational values and beliefs

**normative decision theory**
theory that suggests how leaders can determine an appropriate amount of employee participation when making decisions

**norming**
the third stage of team development, in which team members begin to settle into their roles, group cohesion grows,

and positive team norms develop

**norms**
informally agreed-upon standards that regulate team behavior

**North American Free Trade Agreement (NAFTA)**
regional trade agreement between the United States, Canada, and Mexico

**objective control**
use of observable measures of worker behavior or outputs to assess performance and influence behavior

**objective performance measures**
measures of job performance that are easily and directly counted or quantified

**online discussion forums**
the in-house equivalent of Internet newsgroups; Web- or software-based discussion tools available across the company to permit employees to easily ask questions and share knowledge with each other

**open office systems**
offices in which the physical barriers that separate workers have been removed in order to increase communication and interaction

**openness to experience**
the degree to which someone is curious, broad-minded, and open to new ideas, things, and experiences; is spontaneous; and has a high tolerance for ambiguity

**operational plans**
day-to-day plans, developed and implemented by lower-level managers, for producing or delivering the organization's products and services over a 30-day to 6-month period

**operations management**
managing the daily production of goods and services

**opportunistic behavior**
transaction in which one party in the relationship benefits at the expense of the other

**optical character recognition**
software to convert digitized documents into ASCII text

(American Standard Code for Information Interchange) that can be searched, read, and edited by word processing and other kinds of software

**options-based planning**
maintaining planning flexibility by making small, simultaneous investments in many alternative plans

**ordering cost**
the costs associated with ordering inventory, including the cost of data entry, phone calls, obtaining bids, correcting mistakes, and determining when and how much inventory to order

**organic organization**
organization characterized by broadly defined jobs and responsibility, loosely defined, frequently changing roles, and decentralized authority and horizontal communication based on task knowledge

**organizational change**
a difference in the form, quality, or condition of an organization over time

**organizational culture**
the values, beliefs, and attitudes shared by organizational members

**organization decline**
a large decrease in organizational performance that occurs when companies don't anticipate, recognize, neutralize, or adapt to the internal or external pressures that threaten their survival

**organizational development**
a philosophy and collection of planned change interventions designed to improve an organization's long-term health and performance

**organizational dialogue**
the process by which people in an organization learn to talk effectively and constructively with each other

**organizational heroes**
people celebrated for their qualities and achievements within an organization

**organizational innovation**
the successful implementation of creative ideas in organizations

**organizational plurality**
a work environment where (1) each member is empowered to contribute in a way that maximizes the benefits to the organization, customers, and themselves, and (2) the individuality of each member is respected by not segmenting or polarizing people on the basis of their membership in a particular group

**organizational process**
the collection of activities that transforms inputs into outputs that customers value

**organizational silence**
when employees withhold information about organizational problems or issues

**organizational stories**
stories told by organizational members to make sense of organizational events and changes and to emphasize culturally consistent assumptions, decisions, and actions

**organizational structure**
the vertical and horizontal configuration of departments, authority, and jobs within a company

**organizing**
deciding where decisions will be made, who will do what jobs and tasks, who will work for whom

**outcome/input (O/I) ratio**
in equity theory, an employee's perception of the comparison between the rewards received from an organization and the employee's contributions to that organization

**outcomes**
in equity theory, the rewards employees receive for their contributions to the organization

**outplacement services**
employment-counseling services offered to employees who are losing their jobs because of downsizing

**output control**
regulation of worker results or outputs through rewards and incentives

**overreward**
when you are getting more outcomes relative to your inputs than the referent to whom you compare yourself

**overt integrity test**
written test that estimates employee honesty by directly asking job applicants what they think or feel about theft or about punishment of unethical behaviors

**paralanguage**
the pitch, rate, tone, volume, and speaking pattern (i.e., use of silences, pauses, or hesitations) of one's voice

**partial productivity**
a measure of performance that indicates how much of a particular kind of input it takes to produce an output

**participative leadership**
leadership style in which the leader consults employees for their suggestions and input before making decisions

**path-goal theory**
leadership theory that states that leaders can increase subordinate satisfaction and performance by clarifying and clearing the paths to goals and by increasing the number and kinds of rewards available for goal attainment

**perception**
the process by which individuals attend to, organize, interpret, and retain information from their environments

**perceptual filters**
the personality-, psychology-, or experience-based differences that influence people to ignore or pay attention to particular stimuli

**performance appraisal**
the process of assessing how well employees are doing their jobs

**performance feedback**
information about the quality or quantity of past performance that indicates

whether progress is being made toward the accomplishment of a goal

**performing**
the fourth and final stage of team development, in which performance improves because the team has matured into an effective, fully functioning team

**personal aggression**
hostile or aggressive behavior toward others

**personality**
the relatively stable set of behaviors, attitudes, and emotions displayed over time that makes people different from each other

**personality-based integrity test**
written test that indirectly estimates employee honesty by measuring psychological traits, such as dependability and conscientiousness

**personality tests**
tests that measure the extent to which applicants possess different kinds of job-related personality dimensions

**piecework**
a compensation system in which employees are paid a set rate for each item they produce

**planning (management functions)**
determining organizational goals and a means for achieving them

**planning**
choosing a goal and developing a strategy to achieve that goal

**policy**
standing plan that indicates the general course of action that should be taken in response to a particular event or situation

**policy uncertainty**
the risk associated with changes in laws and government policies that directly affect the way foreign companies conduct business

**political deviance**
using one's influence to harm others in the company

769

**political uncertainty**
the risk of major changes in political regimes that can result from war, revolution, death of political leaders, social unrest, or other influential events

**polychronic cultures**
cultures in which people tend to do more than one thing at a time and view times as circular

**pooled interdependence**
work completed by having each job or department independently contribute to the whole

**portfolio strategy**
corporate-level strategy that minimizes risk by diversifying investment among various businesses or product lines

**position power**
the degree to which leaders are able to hire, fire, reward, and punish workers

**positive affectivity**
personality trait in which individuals tend to notice and focus on the positive aspects of themselves and their environments

**positive frame**
couching a problem in terms of a gain, thus influencing decision makers toward becoming risk-averse

**positive reinforcement**
reinforcement that strengthens behavior by following behaviors with desirable consequences

**postconventional level of moral development**
third level of moral development in which people make decisions based on internalized principles

**preconventional level of moral development**
first level of moral development in which people make decisions based on selfish reasons

**predictive patterns**
help identify database elements that are different

**primary stakeholder**
any group on which an organization relies for its long-term survival

**principle of distributive justice**
ethical principle that holds that you should never take any action that harms the least among us: the poor, the uneducated, the unemployed

**principle of government requirements**
ethical principle that holds that you should never take any action that violates the law, for the law represents the minimal moral standard

**principle of individual rights**
ethical principle that holds that you should never take any action that infringes on others' agreed-upon rights

**principle of long-term self-interest**
ethical principle that holds that you should never take any action that is not in your or your organization's long-term self-interest

**principle of personal virtue**
ethical principle that holds that you should never do anything that is not honest, open, and truthful, and which you would not be glad to see reported in the newspapers or on TV

**principle of religious injunctions**
ethical principle that holds that you should never take any action that is not kind and that does not build a sense of community

**principle of utilitarian benefits**
ethical principle that holds that you should never take any action that does not result in greater good for society

**private spaces**
spaces used by and open to just one employee

**proactive strategy**
a social responsiveness strategy in which a company anticipates responsibility for a problem before it occurs and would do more than society expects to address the problem

**probability of effect**
the chance that something will happen and then harm others

**problem**
a gap between a desired state and an existing state

**procedural justice**
the perceived fairness of the process used to make reward allocation decisions

**procedure**
standing plan that indicates the specific steps that should be taken in response to a particular event

**processing cost**
the cost of turning raw data into usable information

**processing information**
transforming raw data into meaningful information

**product boycott**
an advocacy group tactic of protesting a company's actions by convincing consumers not to purchase its product or service

**product departmentalization**
organizing work and workers into separate units responsible for producing particular products or services

**product prototype**
a full-scale, working model of a final product that is being tested for design, function, and reliability

**production blocking**
a disadvantage of face-to-face brainstorming in which a group member must wait to share an idea because another member is presenting an idea

**production deviance**
unethical behavior that hurts the quality and quantity of work produced

**productivity**
a measure of performance that indicates how many inputs it takes to produce or create an output

**profit sharing**
a compensation system in which a percentage of company profits is paid to employees in addition to their regular compensation

**project team**
team created to complete specific, one-time projects or tasks within a limited time

**project manufacturing**
manufacturing operations designed to produce large, expensive, specialized products

**property deviance**
unethical behavior aimed at the organization's property

**prospectors**
an adaptive strategy that seeks fast growth by searching for new market opportunities, encouraging risk-taking, and being the first to bring innovative new products to market

**protecting information**
the process of insuring that data are reliably and consistently retrievable in a usable format for authorized users, but no one else

**protectionism**
a government's use of trade barriers to shield domestic companies and their workers from foreign competition

**proximal goals**
short-term goals or subgoals

**proximity of effect**
the social, psychological, cultural, or physical distance between a decision maker and those affected by his or her decisions

**public communications**
an advocacy group tactic that relies on voluntary participation by the news media and the advertising industry to get an advocacy group's message out

**punctuated equilibrium theory**
theory that holds that companies go through long, simple periods of stability (equilibrium), followed by short periods of dynamic, fundamental change (revolution), and ending with a return to stability (new equilibrium)

**punishment**
reinforcement that weakens behavior by following behaviors with undesirable consequences

**purchasing power**
a comparison of the relative cost of a standard set of goods and services in different countries

**quality**
a product or service free of deficiencies, or the characteristics of a product or service that satisfy customer needs

**quasi-control**
reducing dependence or restructuring dependence when control is necessary but not possible

**question mark**
a company with a small share of a fast-growing market

**quid pro quo sexual harassment**
form of sexual harassment in which employment outcomes, such as hiring, promotion, or simply keeping one's job, depend on whether an individual submits to sexual harassment

**quota**
limit on the number or volume of imported products

**racial and ethnic discrimination**
treating people differently because of their race or ethnicity

**rare resource**
a resource that is not controlled or possessed by many competing firms

**rater training**
training performance appraisal raters in how to avoid rating errors and increase rating accuracy

**rational decision making**
a systematic process of defining problems, evaluating alternatives, and choosing optimal solutions

**raw data**
facts and figures

**raw material inventories**
the basic inputs in a manufacturing process

**reactive strategy**
a social responsiveness strategy in which a company chooses to do less than society expects

**reactors**
an adaptive strategy of not following a consistent strategy, but instead reacting to changes in the external environment after they occur

**reciprocal interdependence**
work completed by different jobs or groups working together in a back-and-forth manner

**recovery**
the strategic actions taken after retrenchment to return to a growth strategy

**recruiting**
the process of developing a pool of qualified job applicants

**reducing dependence**
abandoning or changing organizational goals to reduce dependence on critical resources

**reengineering**
fundamental rethinking and radical redesign of business processes to achieve dramatic improvements in critical measures of performance, such as cost, quality, service, and speed

**referent**
in equity theory, others with whom people compare themselves to determine if they have been treated fairly

**refreezing**
supporting and reinforcing the new changes so they "stick"

**regional trading zones**
areas in which tariff and non-tariff barriers on trade between countries are reduced or eliminated

**regulation costs**
the costs associated with implementing or maintaining control

**reinforcement**
the process of changing behavior by changing the consequences that follow behavior

**reinforcement contingencies**
cause-and-effect relationships between the performance of specific behaviors and specific consequences

**reinforcement theory**
theory that states that behavior is a function of its consequences, that behaviors followed by positive consequences will occur more frequently, and that behaviors followed by negative consequences, or not followed by positive consequences, will occur less frequently

**related diversification**
creating or acquiring companies that share similar products, manufacturing, marketing, technology, or cultures

**relationship behavior**
mutually beneficial, long-term exchanges between buyers and suppliers

**relative comparisons**
a process in which each decision criterion is compared directly to every other criterion

**representative bias**
unrecognized tendency of decision makers to judge the likelihood of an event's occurrence based on its similarity to previous events

**resistance forces**
forces that support the existing state of conditions in organizations

**resistance to change**
opposition to change resulting from self-interest, misunderstanding and distrust, or a general intolerance for change

**resource allocator role**
the decisional role managers play when they decide who gets what resources

**resource flow**
the extent to which companies have access to critical resources

**resource similarity**
the extent to which a competitor has similar amounts and kinds of resources

**resources**
the assets, capabilities, processes, information, and knowledge that an organization uses to improve its effectiveness and efficiency, to create and sustain competitive advantage, and to fulfill a need or solve a problem

**response**
a competitive countermove, prompted by a rival's attack, to defend or improve a company's market share or profit

**restructuring dependence**
exchanging dependence on one critical resource for dependence on another

**results-driven change**
change created quickly by focusing on the measurement and improvement of results

**retrenchment strategy**
strategy that focuses on turning around very poor company performance by shrinking the size or scope of the business

**retrieval cost**
the cost of accessing already-stored and processed information

**risk propensity**
a person's tendency to take or avoid risks

**role-model mission**
company goal of imitating the characteristics and practices of a successful company

**rules and regulations**
standing plans that describe how a particular action should be performed, or what must happen or not happen in response to a particular event

**S.M.A.R.T. goals**
goals that are specific, measurable, attainable, realistic, and timely

**satisficing**
choosing a "good enough" alternative

**scenario planning**
the process of developing plans to deal with several possible future events and trends that might affect the business

**schedule of reinforcement**
rules that specify which behaviors will be reinforced, which consequences will follow those behaviors, and the schedule by which those consequences will be delivered

**schedule time**
cultural norm for the time by which scheduled projects or jobs should actually be completed

**S-curve pattern of innovation**
a pattern of technological innovation characterized by slow initial progress, then rapid progress, and then again by slow progress as a technology matures and reaches its limits

**secondary firms**
the firms in a strategic group that follow related, but somewhat different, strategies than do the core firms

**secondary stakeholder**
any group that can influence or be influenced by the company and can affect public perceptions about its socially responsible behavior

**selection**
the process of gathering information about job applicants to decide who should be offered a job

**selective perception**
the tendency to notice and accept objects and information consistent with our values, beliefs, and expectations, while ignoring or screening out or not accepting inconsistent information

**self-control (self-management)**
control system in which managers and workers control their own behavior by setting their own goals, monitoring their own progress, and rewarding themselves for goal achievement

**self-designing team**
team that has the characteristics of self-managing teams but that also controls team design, work tasks, and team membership

**self-limiting behavior**
behavior in which team members choose to limit their involvement in a team's work

**self-managing team**
team that manages and controls all of the major tasks of producing a product or service

**self-monitoring**
the ability to adjust one's behavior to different situations and environments

**self-serving bias**
the tendency to over-estimate our value by attributing successes to ourselves (internal causes) and attributing failures to others or the environment (external causes)

**semi-autonomous work group**
group that has the authority to make decisions and solve problems related to the major tasks of producing a product or service

**sequence patterns**
when two or more database elements occur together in a significant pattern, but one of the elements precedes the other

**sequential interdependence**
work completed in succession, with one group or job's outputs becoming the inputs for the next group or job

**service recovery**
restoring customer satisfaction to strongly dissatisfied customers

**setup cost**
the costs of downtime and lost efficiency that occur when changing or adjusting a machine to produce a different kind of inventory

**sexual harassment**
form of discrimination in which unwelcome sexual advances, requests for sexual favors, or other verbal or physical conduct of a sexual nature occur while performing one's job

**shadow-strategy task force**
a committee within the company that analyzes the company's own weaknesses to determine how competitors could exploit them for competitive advantage

**shared spaces**
spaces used by and open to all employees

**shareholder model**
view of social responsibility which holds that an organization's overriding goal should be profit maximization for the benefit of shareholders

**shareware**
computer software that you can try before you buy, but if you keep it beyond the trial period, usually 30 days, you must buy it

**shrinkage**
employee theft of company merchandise

**simple environment**
an environment with few environmental factors

**simple matrix**
a form of matrix departmentalization in which project and functional managers negotiate conflicts and resources

**single-use plans**
plans that cover unique, one-time-only events

**situational (SWOT) analysis**
an assessment of the strengths and weaknesses in an organization's internal environment and the opportunities and threats in its external environment

**situational favorableness**
the degree to which a particular situation either permits or denies a leader the chance to influence the behavior of group members

**skills-based diversity training**
training that teaches employees the practical skills they need for managing a diverse work force, such as flexibility and adaptability, negotiation, problem solving, and conflict resolution

**skill-based pay**
compensation system that pays employees for learning additional skills or knowledge

**skill variety**
the number of different activities performed in a job

**social consensus**
agreement on whether behavior is bad or good

**social integration**
the degree to which group members are psychologically attracted to working with each other to accomplish a common objective

**social loafing**
behavior in which team members withhold their efforts and fail to perform their share of the work

**social responsibility**
a business's obligation to pursue policies, make decisions, and take actions that benefit society

**social responsiveness**
the strategy chosen by a company to respond to stakeholders' economic, legal, ethical, or discretionary expectations concerning social responsibility

**specific ability. tests (aptitude tests)**
tests that measure the extent to which an applicant possesses the particular kind of ability needed to do a job well

**specific environment**
the customers, competitors, suppliers, industry regulations, and advocacy groups that are unique to an industry and that directly affect how a company does business

**spokesperson role**
the informational role managers play when they share information with people outside their departments or companies

**sporadic change**
change that occurs in random patterns or for accidental reasons

**stability strategy**
strategy that focuses on improving the way in which the company sells the same products or services to the same customers

**stable environment**
environment in which the rate of change is slow

**staff authority**
the right to advise, but not command, others who are not subordinates in the chain of command

**staff function**
an activity that does not contribute directly to creating or selling the company's products, but instead supports line activities

**stakeholder model**
theory of corporate responsibility which holds that management's most important responsibility, long-term survival, is achieved by satisfying the interests of multiple corporate stakeholders

**stakeholders**
persons or groups with a "stake" or legitimate interest in a company's actions

**standardization**
solving problems by consistently applying the same rules, procedures, and processes

**standards**
a basis of comparison when measuring the extent to which various kinds of organizational performance are satisfactory or unsatisfactory

**standing plans**
plans used repeatedly to handle frequently recurring events

**star**
a company with a large share of a fast-growing market

**stepladder technique**
when group members are added to a group discussion one at a time (i.e., like a stepladder), the existing group members first take the time to listen to each new member's thoughts, ideas, and recommendations, and then the group, in turn, shares the ideas and suggestions that it had already considered, discusses the new and old ideas, and then makes a decision

**stereotypes**
negative, false, overgeneralized beliefs about people in particular categories

**stock options**
a compensation system that gives employees the right to purchase shares of stock at a set price, even if the value of the stock increases above that price

**stockout**
situation in which a company runs out of finished product

**stockout costs**
the costs incurred when a company runs out of a product, including transaction costs to replace inventory and the loss of customers' goodwill

**storage cost**
the cost of physically or electronically archiving information for later use and retrieval

**storming**
the second stage of development, characterized by conflict and disagreement, in which team members disagree over what the team should do and how it should do it

**strategic alliance**
agreement in which companies combine key resources, costs, risk, technology, and people

**strategic dissonance**
a discrepancy between upper management's intended strategy and the strategy actually implemented by lower levels of management

**strategic group**
a group of companies within an industry that top managers choose to compare, evaluate, and benchmark strategic threats and opportunities

**strategic leadership**
the ability to anticipate, envision, maintain flexibility, think strategically, and work with others to initiate changes that will create a positive future for an organization

**strategic plans**
overall company plans that clarify how the company will serve customers and position itself against competitors over the next two to five years

**strategic reference points**
the strategic targets managers use to measure whether a firm has developed the core competencies it needs to achieve a sustainable competitive advantage

**stretch goals**
extremely ambitious goals that, initially, employees don't know how to accomplish

**structural accommodation**
the ability to change organizational structures, policies, and practices in order to meet stretch goals

**structured interviews**
interviews in which all applicants are asked the same set of standardized questions, usually including situational, behavioral, background, and job-knowledge questions

**subjective performance measures**
measures of job performance that require someone to judge or assess a worker's performance

**suboptimization**
performance improvement in one part of an organization but only at the expense of decreased performance in another part

**subsidies**
government loans, grants, and tax deferments given to domestic companies to protect them from foreign competition

**supervised data mining**
user tells the data mining software to look and test for specific patterns and relationships in a data set

**supplier dependence**
degree to which a company relies on a supplier because of the importance of the supplier's product to the company and the difficulty of finding other sources of that product

**suppliers**
companies that provide material, human, financial, and informational resources to other companies

**supportive leadership**
leadership style in which the leader is friendly and approachable to employees, shows concern for them and their welfare, treats them as equals, and creates a friendly climate

**surface-level diversity**
differences such as age, gender, race/ethnicity, and physical disabilities that are observable, typically unchangeable, and easy to measure

**survey feedback**
information collected by surveys from organizational members that is then compiled, disseminated, and used to develop action plans for improvement

**sustainable competitive advantage**
a competitive advantage that other companies have tried

unsuccessfully to duplicate and have, for the moment, stopped trying to duplicate

**tactical plans**
plans created and implemented by middle managers that specify how the company will use resources, budgets, and people over the next six months to two years to accomplish specific goals within its mission

**targeting**
mission stated as a clear, specific company goal

**tariff**
a direct tax on imported goods

**task identity**
the degree to which a job requires, from beginning to end, the completion of a whole and identifiable piece of work

**task interdependence**
the extent to which collective action is required to complete an entire piece of work

**task significance**
the degree to which a job is perceived to have a substantial impact on others inside or outside the organization

**task structure**
the degree to which the requirements of a subordinate's tasks are clearly specified

**team diversity**
the variances or differences in ability, experience, personality, or any other factor on a team

**team leaders**
managers responsible for facilitating team activities toward goal accomplishment

**team level**
the average level of ability, experience, personality, or any other factor on a team

**teamwork**
collaboration between managers and nonmanagers, across business functions, and between companies, customers, and suppliers

**technical skills**
the ability to apply the specialized procedures,

techniques, and knowledge required to get the job done

**technological discontinuity**
scientific advance or unique combination of existing technologies that creates a significant breakthrough in performance or function

**technological substitution**
purchase of new technologies to replace older ones

**technology**
knowledge, tools, and techniques used to transform input into output

**technology cycle**
cycle that begins with the "birth" of a new technology and ends when that technology reaches its limits and is replaced by a newer, substantially better technology

**televised/videotaped speeches and meetings**
speeches and meetings originally made to a smaller audience that are either simultaneously broadcast to other locations in the company or videotaped for subsequent distribution and viewing

**temporal immediacy**
the time between an act and the consequences the act produces

**testing**
systematic comparison of different product designs or design iterations

**threat of new entrants**
a measure of the degree to which barriers to entry make it easy or difficult for new companies to get started in an industry

**threat of substitute products or services**
a measure of the ease with which customers can find substitutes for an industry's products or services

**top managers**
executives responsible for the overall direction of the organization

**total quality management (TQM)**
an integrated, principle-based, organization-wide strategy for improving product and service quality

**trade barriers**
government-imposed regulations that increase the cost and restrict the number of imported goods

**traditional work group**
group composed of two or more people who work together to achieve a shared goal

**training**
developing the skills, experience, and knowledge employees need to perform their jobs or improve their performance

**trait rating scales**
a rating scale that indicates the extent to which a worker possesses particular traits or characteristics

**trait theory**
leadership theory that holds that effective leaders possess a similar set of traits or characteristics

**traits**
relatively stable characteristics, such as abilities, psychological motives, or consistent patterns of behavior

**transactional leadership**
leadership based on an exchange process, in which followers are rewarded for good performance and punished for poor performance

**transformational leadership**
leadership that generates awareness and acceptance of a group's purpose and mission and gets employees to see beyond their own needs and self-interest for the good of the group

**transient firms**
the firms in a strategic group whose strategies are changing from one strategic position to another

**transition management team (TMT)**
a team of 8 to 12 people whose full-time job is to completely manage and coordinate a company's change process

**Type A personality**
a person who tries to complete as many tasks as possible in the shortest possible time and is hard driving, competitive, impatient, perfectionistic, angry, and unable to relax

**Type A/B personality dimension**
the extent to which people tend toward impatience, hurriedness, competitiveness, and hostility

**Type B personality**
a person who is relaxed, easygoing, and able to engage in leisure activities without worrying about work

**uncertainty**
extent to which managers can understand or predict which environmental changes and trends will affect their businesses

**underreward**
when the referent you compare yourself to is getting more outcomes relative to their inputs than you are

**unethical charismatics**
charismatic leaders that control and manipulate followers, do what is best for themselves instead of their organizations, only want to hear positive feedback, only share information that is beneficial to themselves, and have moral standards that put their interests before everyone else's

**unfreezing**
getting the people affected by change to believe that change is needed

**unity of command**
a management principle that workers should report to just one boss

**unrelated diversification**
creating or acquiring companies in completely unrelated businesses

**unsupervised data mining**
user simply tells the data mining software to uncover whatever patterns and relationships it can find in a data set

**upward communication**
communication that flows from lower to higher levels in an organization

**valence**
the attractiveness or desirability of a reward or outcome

**validation**
the process of determining how well a selection test or procedure predicts future job performance. The better or more accurate the prediction of future job performance, the more valid a test is said to be.

**valuable resource**
a resource that allows companies to improve efficiency and effectiveness

**value**
customer perception that the product quality is excellent for the price offered

**variable interval reinforcement schedule**
intermittent schedule in which the time between a behavior and the following consequences varies around a specified average

**variable ratio reinforcement schedule**
intermittent schedule in which consequences are delivered following a different number of behaviors, sometimes more and sometimes less, that vary around a specified average number of behaviors

**variation**
a deviation in the form, condition, or appearance of a product from the quality standard for that product

**virtual organization**
an organization that is part of a network in which many companies share skills, costs, capabilities, markets, and customers to collectively solve customer problems or provide specific products or services

**virtual private network**
encrypts Internet data at both ends of the transmission process

**virtual team**
team composed of geographically and/or organizationally

dispersed coworkers who use telecommunication and information technologies to accomplish an organizational task

**virus**
a program or piece of code that attaches itself to other programs on your computer and can trigger anything from a harmless flashing message to the reformatting of your hard drive to the system-wide network shutdown

**visible artifacts**
visible signs of an organization's culture, such as the office design and layout, company dress code, and company benefits and perks, like stock options, personal parking spaces, or the private company dining room

**vision**
inspirational statement of an organization's enduring purpose

**visionary leadership**
leadership that creates a positive image of the future that motivates organizational members and provides direction for future planning and goal setting

**voluntary export restraints**
voluntarily imposed limits on the number or volume of products exported to a particular country

**whistleblowing**
reporting others' ethics violations to management or legal authorities

**wholly owned affiliates**
foreign offices, facilities, and manufacturing plants that are 100 percent owned by the parent company

**work force forecasting**
the process of predicting the number and kind of workers with specific skills and abilities that an organization will need in the future

**work sample tests**
tests that require applicants to perform tasks that are actually done on the job

**work team**
a small number of people with complementary skills who hold themselves mutually accountable for pursuing a common purpose, achieving performance goals, and improving interdependent work processes

**workplace deviance**
unethical behavior that violates organizational norms about right and wrong

**work-in-process inventories**
partially finished goods consisting of assembled component parts

**world gross national product**
the value of all the goods and services produced annually worldwide

**wrongful discharge**
a legal doctrine that requires employers to have a job-related reason to terminate employees

775

O'Neill, Paul, 421, 457
Ontrack Data International, 366
Oracle Software, 91, 230, 696
Orr, Dominic, 208
Otto, Don, 229

Pacific Enterprises, 441, 464
Palm, Inc., 10
Palmer, Bill, 484
Paragon Medical, 599
Park, Alice, 3
Parker, Jim, 224
Parker, Peter, 358
Parnell, Charles, 486
Passarella, Kathy, 62
Patterson, David, 547
Patterson, Neal, 704
Peabody Hotel, 453–454
Pearce, Terry, 706
Penney, James Cash, 87
People for the Ethical Treatment
    of Animals (PETA), 54–55,
    75, 92, 106–107
PeopleSoft, 327
PepsiCo, 503
Pericles, 117
Peterson, Chuck, 165
Peto, Richard, 6
Pet Pasta Products, 338
Pfeffer, Jeffrey, 30–31, 482
Pharmacia & Upjohn, 401–402
Phelps, Sherry, 454
Philbin, Regis, 277
Piccadilly Cafeteria, 450
Piech, Ferdinand, 717
Pierce, Charles, 205
Pillsbury, 716
Pinette, John, 421
Pinto, Ian, 528
Pirtle, Thomas, 702
Pitman, Robert, 197
Pixar Animation Studios, 118
Platt, Polly, 712
Plitt Company, 614
Polaroid, 479
Popper, Karl, 359
Porter, Michael, 328, 330
Pottruck, David S., 525
Power, Patrick, 288
PPG Industries, 356
Prather, Sheryl, 697
Pratt & Whitney, 281
Pressman, Bob, 368
Pressman, Gene, 368
Price, Steve, 516
Priceline.com, 205
Primarion, 124
Pritchard, Marc, 594
Procter & Gamble, 323, 345,
    384–385, 391–392, 422,
    428, 465, 474

Prodigy, 306
Prudential Insurance, 156
Prudential Relocation Management, 295
Prusak, Laurence, 61
Puckett, John, 495
Pulwer, Mitch, 138
Putnam, Howard, 648

Quackenbush, Chris, 645–646,
    678–679
Quanta Computer, 424
Quantum Corporation, 569
Questrom, Allen, 403
Quinlan, Michael R., 280–281
Quinn, Dick, 517
Quinn, Tim, 231

Radford, Toby, 263
Raffio, Tom, 500
Rahmat, Mohd, 686
Raiffa, Howard, 190
Raike, Jeff, 355
Random House, 265
Rawitsch, Jim, 282
Raymer, Carol, 232
Raymundo, Tony, 515
Reader's Digest, 20
Red Cross, 101
Red Hat Software, 124
Red Lobster, 333
Reese, John, 518
Regal Cinemas, 221–222,
    255–257
Regent Square Tavern, 606–607
Rent-A-Center, 521
Reynolds, Beverly, 478
Reynolds, Travis, 28
Ribbens, Jack, 571
Richman, Robin, 230
Ricks, David, 276, 293
Rigby, Michael, 339
Rise, Mark, 640
Rite Aid, 158
Ritz-Carlton, 484
R.J. Reynolds, 172
Rocky Mountain Steel Mills, 521
Roddick, Anita, 96–97
Rodgers, T.J., 456, 663–664
Rogan Corporation, 502
Rollnick, William, 99
Rolls-Royce, 249
Rosenblatt, Stanley, 702
Rosenbluth, Hal, 454
Rosenbluth International, 454
Rosner, Bob, 699
Rossotti, Charles, 229
Roth, John, 19
Rowe, John, 116
Royal Insurance, 60
Royko, Mike, 77

R.R. Donnelly & Sons, 157
Rudder, Eric, 374
Rudenstine, Neil, 26
Russo, David, 58, 62
Russo, Thomas, 91
Rutledge, John, 407
Ryan, Nancy, 422
Ryanair, 21, 564, 599
Ryder, Thomas, 20
Rytsola, Jaako, 616

Salmi, Bob, 160
Salzman, Barry, 713
Samsung Corporation, 319
Sandler, Herman, 645–646,
    678–679
Sandler O'Neill & Partners,
    645–646, 678–679
Sapio, Rick, 717–718
Sara Lee, 140
SAS, 58–59, 62, 622
Sasol, 281
SasolChevron, 281
Saturn, 486, 570–571
Savage, Randy, 478
Savastano, Paul, 151
SBC Communications, 442
Schaefer, Barbara, 515
Schaefer, Jim, 635
Schlage Lock Company, 127
Schlossberg, Edwin, 353
Schneider, Steve, 373
Schrader, Bob, 484
Schrage, Michael, 418
Schulz, Howard, 64–65, 287
Schwartz, Tom, 231
Schwarzkopf, Norman, 664
Schwind, Jenet Noriega, 707
Scott, Lee, 61
Scott, William, 615
Scott Paper, 20–21
Sears, Brian, 90
Sears Roebuck, 19, 52, 97, 451
Selby, James, 370
Shames, Barry, 131–132
Shames Construction, 131–132
Shartzer, Sandi, 484
Shell Oil, 215
Shim, Jae K., 132, 244
Shoney's, 437
Shoreham Nuclear Power Plant,
    204–205
Shultz, Ed, 104
Siegel, Joel G., 132, 244
Silicon Graphics Incorporated,
    140–141
Sims, Paula, 505–506, 667
Singapore International Airlines,
    250
Singer, Joseph, 104
Sinnreich, Arem, 325

Smith, Anne Shen, 441
Smith, Fred, 23
Smith & Wesson, 102, 104
SNECMA, 281
Sneed, Mark, 268
Sollar, Charles, 570
Solutia, 137–138
Sony, 265, 363–364, 395, 591
Sorino, Fred, 717
Southwest Airlines, 11, 12, 37,
    67, 312, 380–381, 454, 580,
    582, 646–647, 648, 652
Spielberg, Steven, 330
Spinmaster, 360
Sportime International, 360
Springfield Remanufacturing
    Company, 5
Sprint, 539, 714
Stahle, Phyllis, 582
Stalker, G.M., 415
Starbucks Coffee, 64–65,
    104–105, 287, 360
State Farm Insurance, 441
Staw, Barry, 204
Steelcase, 422
Steele, Rob, 465
Stevenson, Mark, 391, 428
Stinson, Burke, 421
Strum, David, 613
Student Advantage, 225
Stybel, Laurence, 553
Suburu, 324
Sumitomo Corporation, 276
Summit Polymers, 5
Sun Microsystems, 421
Sunrise Assisted Living, 328
Super Sack, 501
Suzuki Corporation, 100
Svoboda, Jeff, 138
Sweeney, James, 459
Swenson, Winn, 76
Syufy, Raymond, 256

Taco Bell, 249
Tallahassee Furniture Co., 532
Tannen, Deborah, 687
Taylor, Andy, 717
Taylor, Frederick W., 185, 233,
    629
Technical Materials, 525
Technology Professionals Corporation, 613
Tenet Healthcare Corp., 516
Texaco, 440, 441, 465
Texas Industries, 524
Thixomat, 614
Thomas, Dave, 463
Thompson, John, 674
Thompson, Rachel, 435
Thompson, Richard, 338
Thompson, Robin, 435

Fiedler's contingency theory. *See* Contingency theory
Field simulation, 293
Figurehead role, 16
Filters
 email, 195
 perceptual, 688
Final assembly, 589
Financial ratios, 241–243
Finished goods inventories, 589
Firewalls, 162–163
Firm-level strategies, 333–339
 direct competition, 333–337
 entrepreneurship and intrapreneurship, 337–339
First-line managers, 13, 14–15
 role of, in planning, 130–133
First-mover advantage, 152
Fixed interval reinforcement schedule, 631
Fixed ratio reinforcement schedules, 631
Flexibility
 manufacturing, 586–588
 planning, 123–125
Flexible benefit plans, 551
Flow, 357
Focus strategy, 330
Forecasting, work force, 515–516
Foreign investment, direct, 265–267
Formal authority system, 665
Formal communication channels, 695–697
Forming stage of team development, 494
Four-fifths (80 percent) rule, 521–522

Frame
 negative, 196
 positive, 196
Franchise, 279
Franchisee, 279
Franchiser, 279
Freedom, 359
Free Trade Area of the Americas (FTAA), 273–274
Freeware, 170
FTAA (Free Trade Area of the Americas), 273–274
Functional departmentalization, 395–396
Functional turnover, 555
Fundamental attribution error, 691

Gainsharing, 502
GATT (General Agreement on Tariffs and Trade), 271–272
GE Business Screen, 322

Gender differences in communication, 687
Gender discrimination, 446–449
General Agreement on Tariffs and Trade (GATT), 271–272
General Electric Workout, 373–374
General environment, 43–49
 economy, 44–46
 political/legal component of, 48–49
 sociocultural component of, 46–48
 technological component of, 46
Generational change, 363
Geographic departmentalization, 399, 401
Glass ceiling, 446
Global business, 264
 climate for, 283–289
 consistency or adaptation, 276–277
 cooperative contracts, 278–279
 cultural differences, 289–292
 customers, 275
 dual-career issues, 295
 exporting, 277–278
 forms of, 277–283
 franchising, 279
 impact of, 264–269
 joint venture, 279, 281–282
 language and cross-cultural training, 293–294
 licensing, 278
 location, 285–286
 markets, 283–285
 new ventures, 282–283
 political risk, 286–289
 preparing for international assignment, 292–296
 strategic alliances, 279, 281–282
 trade agreements, 271–275
 trade barriers, 269–271, 275
 wholly owned affiliates, 282
Global consistency, 276
Global new ventures, 282–283
Goal acceptance, 635
Goal commitment, 120
Goal difficulty, 635
Goals, 634
 developing commitment to, 120
 distal, 121
 proximal, 121
 setting, 119–120
 S.M.A.R.T., 119, 378
 stretch, 134, 135, 497

team, 496–498
 tracking progress toward, 121–122
Goal-setting theory, 634–638
 components of, 635
 motivating with, 635–637
Goal specificity, 635
Gossip chain, 697–698
Government import standards, 270
Government requirements, principle of, 86
Grand strategies, 323–327
Grapevine, 697–699
Graphic rating scales, 544
*Griggs v. Duke Power Co.*, 527–528
Gross national product, world, 266
Group decision making
 advantages and pitfalls of, 206–208
 brainstorming, 212
 Delphi technique, 209–211
 devil's advocacy, 209, 210
 dialectical inquiry, 209, 210
 electronic brainstorming, 212–214
 groupthink, 207
 nominal group technique, 209
 stepladder technique, 211–212
 structured conflict, 208–209
Group decisions, 667
Groups
 strategic, 312–313
 work. *See* Teams; Work groups
Groupthink, 207, 480
Growth needs, 610
Growth strategy, 324

Hackers, 164
Halo error, 543
Harassment, sexual, 522–524
Hard drives, 160
 crashes of, 161
Hawthorne studies, 499
Headline News
 Alan Greenspan, 45
 communication, 700
 Disney's Go.com, 325
 employment perks, 614
 health benefits for transsexuals, 199
 information security and layoffs, 165
 innovation, 355
 IRS, 229
 leadership, 649
 lemon cars, 571
 mentoring for diversity, 466
 Nike and worker rights, 103

restructuring at JCPenney, 403
 sexual harassment, 524
 Starbucks' global expansion, 287
 teamwork, 503
 violence in workplace, 18
Hearing, 705
Heroes, organizational, 61
Hierarchical pay structures, 549, 551
Higher-order needs, 610
History, organizational, 60
Holding cost, 594
Honesty, 654
Horizontal communication, 696–697
Hostile work environment, 522
Hot desks, 422
Hotlines, company, 716
HRIS, 516–518
Human relations, 233
Human resource information systems (HRISs), 516–518
Human resource management (HRM), 512
 compensation, 547–552
 determining needs, 512–525
 developing qualified workers, 538–547
 employee separations, 552–556
 employment legislation, 518–525
 finding qualified workers, 525–538
 first department of, 514
 keeping qualified workers, 547–556
 performance appraisal, 543–547
 planning, 514–518
 process, 513
 recruiting, 526–530
 selection, 530–538
 training, 539–543
Human skill, 23

iComp index, 349
Idealized influence, 676
Imperfectly imitable resource, 306
Import standards, government, 270
Inaction stage of organization decline, 368
In-basket exercise, 535
Income statements, 241–242
Incremental change, 354
 managing innovation during, 362–365
Independent demand systems, 597